Strategic Human Resource Management

Strategic Human Resource Management

William P. Anthony
Pamela L. Perrewe
K. Michele Kacmar

Florida State University

The Dryden Press
Harcourt Brace Jovanovich College Publishers

Fort Worth   Philadelphia   San Diego   New York   Orlando   Austin   San Antonio
Toronto   Montreal   London   Sydney   Tokyo

Editor in Chief	Robert A. Pawlik
Acquisitions Editor	Robert Gemin
Developmental Editor	Michele Tomiak
Project Editor	Cheryl Hauser
Production Manager	Marilyn Williams
Senior Book Designer	John Ritland
Cover Illustrator	Rebecca Ruegger

Address for Editorial Correspondence
The Dryden Press, 301 Commerce Street, Suite 3700, Fort Worth, TX 76102

Address for Orders
The Dryden Press, 6277 Sea Harbor Drive, Orlando, FL 32887
1-800-782-4479, or 1-800-433-0001 (in Florida)

ISBN: 0-03-096543-8

Library of Congress Catalog Number: 92-073431

Printed in the United States of America

3 4 5 6 7 8 9 0 1 2 036 9 8 7 6 5 4 3 2 1

The Dryden Press
Harcourt Brace Jovanovich

Photo credits appear on pages 775–777, which constitute a continuation of the copyright page.

To Roz, Cathie, and Sarah
Frank, Erin, Jenny, Stephen, and Matthew
Chuck

The Dryden Press Series in Management

PREFACE

· · · · · · · · ·

Few of you who read this textbook will actually become personnel managers in organizations. But most of you will become human resource managers because at some point in your career, you will have a group of people whom you will manage. Some of you will be in a position to influence human resource policy significantly in your organization even if you are not in your firm's personnel or human resource department. Of course, no matter where you are in the organization, you will be affected by your organization's human resource policy, simply because you are a member of that organization.

The bulk of this textbook examines the formulation and implementation of human resource policy at the *strategic* level. In other words, we are most concerned with the major aspects of how an organization deals with its people—how it acquires them, utilizes them, rewards them, and separates them. We are concerned with the interplay of the personnel or human resource department and line managers as strategic decisions are made and implemented on human resource acquisition and use in organizations. We are also concerned with how strategic human resource decisions interplay with the overall strategic decisions an organization makes.

The book examines typical functions in personnel, such as recruitment, selection, training, rewarding (wage and salary analysis), and so on, but it does so from a strategic perspective. Specifically, it explores how these functions integrate with the overall strategy of the firm in order for the firm to become more effective and efficient—in short, more competitive.

Features

The textbook relies heavily on actual case examples of human resource strategies and practices of organizations. Not only are these examples used liberally

in each chapter, each chapter also begins and ends with an actual case of an organization's strategies. The last part of the textbook is devoted to a compendium of comprehensive cases showing how specific companies integrate their human resource strategy with their overall corporate strategy. The cases are a unique feature and integral to this textbook. They make the study of strategy come alive.

Part of the method of strategic analysis is case problem solving. The cases used throughout and at the end of the book have the most value when you try to analyze the situation and suggest courses of action. By applying the concepts discussed in the textbook through case analysis, you will see their relevance in actual organizational situations.

The cases that are used throughout this book ask you to identify present and potential problems and issues and to formulate strategies for their resolution. This requires that you take a problem/issue solving approach to *apply* material in this text. The cases revolve around real organizations you will most likely recognize. They have real human resource problems and challenges. You will need to be both reactive and proactive in examining these cases. Some companies are included that have readily apparent current human resource problems needing immediate sollutions. We included other companies because their cases demonstrate good examples of typical human resource policy: They may have a few readily apparent human resource problems at the moment, but problems could be developing on the horizon.

The cases at the end of each chapter are relatively short and are followed by a few questions to guide you in analyzing the cases, using the material covered in the chapter. In reviewing these cases, you will see very few really right or wrong answers to the questions. Be concerned with examining both the overall strategies as well as the human resource strategies involved in each case. Try to determine how well each type of strategy is working and whether the human resource strategy seems to be meshing well with both overall strategy and other functional strategies. Ask yourself what you could do if you were in a position to change things. The cases at the end of the book are comprehensive and require you to integrate the material covered throughout the text in order to analyze them successfully.

The textbook contains several examples in each chapter of primary issues currently confronting human resource strategists. Focus boxes provide insight into the ways companies and their human resource departments deal with international concerns, ethical concerns, and management of today's culturally diverse work force. HR Challenges boxes offer insight into the ways different organizations deal with the challenges presented to them on a day-to-day basis.

Another special feature of the book is its management applications. For example, in order to highlight how any manager, human resource or otherwise, can have an impact on the practices of the human resource function, the end of the chapter summaries are provided in the form of management guidelines. These guidelines summarize the key ideas presented in the chapter, but they are restated in the form of guidelines or admonitions for management action.

Plan of the Book

The textbook is organized into six parts as shown in Exhibit P.1. Part One examines the concept of organization strategy and how it relates to an organization's human resources. We begin in Chapter 1 by examining the strategic approach to human resource management. An overview of the strategic approach, a historical perspective of human resource management, and a discussion of how these two concepts can be integrated are provided. Chapter 2 examines the global and external environments of the organization and their impact on corporate and human resource strategy.

The formulation of a corporate strategy is the subject of Chapter 3. The strategy formulation process is discussed, along with an examination of specific types of corporate strategies. Chapter 4 looks at decision making and information systems as they relate to human resources. We emphasize decision processes as they affect human resources and on

tracking human resource data and issues in organizations.

Part Two focuses on the ways organizations acquire and place people. Legal issues such as equal employment, sexual harassment, and managing a diverse work force are covered in Chapter 5. Chapter 6 focuses on the human resource planning and staffing function. It deals with planning for the appropriate number and type of employees needed by the organization. Chapter 7 discusses job analysis in light of determining job requirements. Chapter 8 emphasizes job design and redesign. Chapter 9 then examines how to obtain these employees through strategic recruiting and selection methods.

Next we move to Part Three, Strategies for Maximizing Human Resource Productivity. Assuming that the employees have been hired and placed, we are now interested in maximizing their productivity. First, Chapter 10 looks at socialization and training and development methods. Then, we look at ways of getting employees involved and motivated in Chapter 11. Providing fair and equitable monetary and other rewards that encourage desired performance is the subject of Chapter 12. Chapter 13 ends this part with a look at how performance appraisal can be used to develop employees and make them more productive.

In Part Four we examine ways of maintaining human resources in the organization. We begin in Chapter 14 by discussing various benefit programs available today for organizations. Chapter 15 looks at health, safety, and stress in today's organizations. Ethics, employee rights, and employer responsibilities are the subjects of Chapter 16. Dealing with troubled employees, a major issue today for many organizations, is a major focus of this chapter.

Part Five examines strategies for dealing with unions. First, we examine the changing nature of unions in Chapter 17. Chapter 18 then outlines various strategies for bargaining with unions.

In Part Six, the last textual part of the book, Chapter 19 focuses on strategies for restructuring or retrenching organizations. Particular emphasis is placed on layoff and termination strategies.

The book concludes with Part Seven, a series of comprehensive cases that explain a variety of strategic human resource issues of actual organizations. The emphasis is on applying the ideas learned throughout the book in examining real-world organizational issues.

Organizational Strategy and Human Resource Management

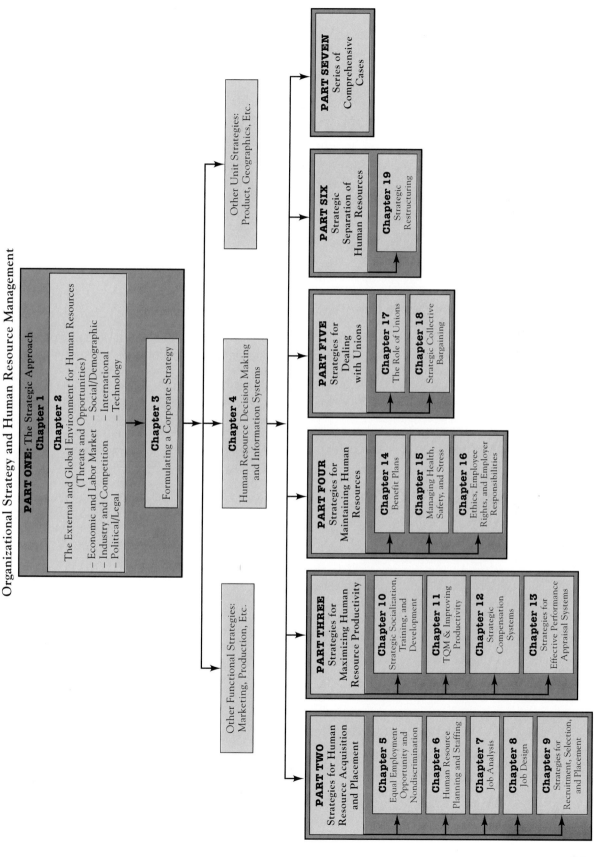

PART ONE: The Strategic Approach
Chapter 1

Chapter 2
The External and Global Environment for Human Resources
(Threats and Opportunities)
– Economic and Labor Market   – Social/Demographic
– Industry and Competition   – International
– Political/Legal   – Technology

Chapter 3
Formulating a Corporate Strategy

Chapter 4
Human Resource Decision Making
and Information Systems

Other Functional Strategies:
Marketing, Production, Etc.

Other Unit Strategies:
Product, Geographics, Etc.

PART TWO
Strategies for Human Resource Acquisition and Placement

Chapter 5
Equal Employment Opportunity and Nondiscrimination

Chapter 6
Human Resource Planning and Staffing

Chapter 7
Job Analysis

Chapter 8
Job Design

Chapter 9
Strategies for Recruitment, Selection, and Placement

PART THREE
Strategies for Maximizing Human Resource Productivity

Chapter 10
Strategic Socialization, Training, and Development

Chapter 11
TQM & Improving Productivity

Chapter 12
Strategic Compensation Systems

Chapter 13
Strategies for Effective Performance Appraisal Systems

PART FOUR
Strategies for Maintaining Human Resources

Chapter 14
Benefit Plans

Chapter 15
Managing Health, Safety, and Stress

Chapter 16
Ethics, Employee Rights, and Employer Responsibilities

PART FIVE
Strategies for Dealing with Unions

Chapter 17
The Role of Unions

Chapter 18
Strategic Collective Bargaining

PART SIX
Strategic Separation of Human Resources

Chapter 19
Strategic Restructuring

PART SEVEN
Series of Comprehensive Cases

Support Materials

Strategic Human Resource Management has available a variety of materials to aid both the student and the instructor.

- The *Study Guide* provides a review of each chapter's material and contains assignments to help students recall objective chapter material and hone their analytical abilities in applying the concepts presented in the chapter.

- *Video Cases* offer glimpses into real-world organizations and their human resource strategies and policies.

- The *Instructor's Manual and Test Bank* contains, for each chapter, learning goals, a detailed lecture outline, answers to end-of-chapter review questions, and answers to end-of-chapter case analysis questions. Also included are a set of experiential exercises for further student practice, and summaries of end of book cases with additional information not supplied in the cases. The test bank, available in either printed or computerized form, contains approximately fifty multiple-choice, fifteen true/false, five short-essay, and one minicase for each chapter.

- A set of *transparency acetates* of key illustrations from the text is available to complement lectures.

Acknowledgments

Many people helped us with this textbook. Don Daake wrote and researched the initial drafts of Chapters 17 and 18. Charles Fornaciari did the same for Chapters 16 and 19. Barbara Hassell did the initial drafts of Chapter 12. In addition, we would like to thank Mark Dawkins, Tom DeLaughter, Denise Rotondo Fernandez, Wayne Hochwarter, Mark Imhof, Karen Morton, Peter Stanwick, Marilyn Thompson, and Neal Thomson for their assistance in library research, case writing, and revisions of various chapters.

The following people assisted with typing various portions of the manuscript: Cathie Anthony, Sarah Anthony, Mitzi Hennessey, Diane Ice, Kelly Shrode, and Laura Waltke.

We are especially grateful to the professors who reviewed the manuscript throughout its various stages: Brendan D. Bannister, Northeastern University; Nathan Bennett, Louisiana State University; David E. Bowen, Arizona State University West; Gerald E. Calvasina, University of North Carolina—Charlotte; Stephen J. Carroll, University of Maryland, College Park; Jeffrey G. Covin, Georgia Institute of Technology; Joseph H. Culver, University of Texas at Austin; Dan R. Dalton, Indiana University; Thomas G. Gutteridge, Southern Illinois University at Carbondale; Ken Jennings, University of North Florida; Thomas H. Jerdee, University of North Carolina at Chapel Hill; Robert C. Liden, University of Illinois at Chicago; Michael T. Quinn, California State University, Long Beach; Marcus Hart Sandver, Ohio State University; Sid Siegel, Drexel University; Scott A. Snell, Pennsylvania State University; David Tansik, University of Arizona; and Mark A. Wesolowski, Miami University.

Our thanks go to our editor, Butch Gemin; our developmental editor, Michele Tomiak; and others who helped in the process. Even though we have been aided greatly by this help, any errors of commission or omission rest with us.

WPA
PLP
KMK
Tallahassee, Florida

CONTENTS

• • • • • • • • •

Chapter 8
Job Design　**240**

Chapter 9
*Strategies for Recruitment, Selection, and
Placement*　**268**

PART THREE

Strategies for Maximizing Human Resource Productivity   303

Chapter 10
Strategic Socialization, Training, and Development   304

Chapter 11
Total Quality Management and Improving Productivity   348

PART FIVE
....

Strategies for Dealing with Unions   579

Strategic Human Resource Management

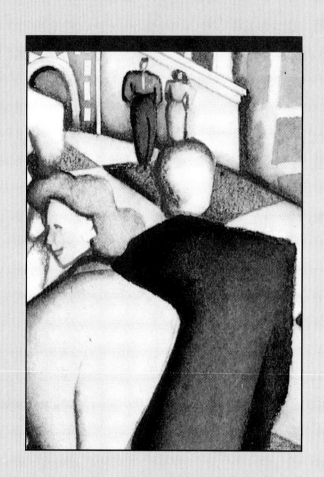

PART ONE

The Strategic Approach

3

1

The Strategic Approach to Human Resource Management

The environment within which an organization operates is dynamic. External and internal forces are constantly changing the rules of the game, and the organization must amend or adopt new strategies to remain competitive. A change in strategy will determine the direction of each function within the organization, including the human resource management function. This chapter examines the definition of strategy and the history of human resource management, and it begins to lay the foundation for how these two concepts interrelate with each other.

• • • • • • • • •

CHAPTER OBJECTIVES

As a result of studying this chapter, you should be able to

1. Define the concept of strategy and explain the basics of the strategy formulation process.

2. Distinguish the strategic approach to human resources from the traditional functional approach.

3. Explain the relationship of decision making to the strategy formulation process.

4. Explain the environment-organization link and the strategic approach.

5. Explain the relationship of human resource strategy with overall organizational strategy and functional strategy.

6. Understand the history and evolution of the field of human resources.

CASE: GM Shrinks[1]

On April 22, 1988, General Motors Corporation announced a strategic retreat that significantly shrank the largest industrial company in the world for the first time in its 80-year history. GM placed itself on a corporate crash diet in an effort to shed both factories and workers to stop its falling net income. It repeated this announcement on December 18, 1991, when it reported plans to close 21 of its plants and eliminate 74,000 jobs in four years, 9,000 of which will be white collar.

GM once claimed almost 50 percent of the U.S. auto market. By 1990 that share had fallen to below 35 percent (see Exhibit 1.1), largely due to the increased sales of imports, Fords, and Chryslers. In order to match its sales, car production capacity will be reduced. Unlike the past, in which plant closings and employee layoffs were a regular part of the business cycle, these changes are not temporary. Rather they represent a major downsizing that will result in a considerable restructuring of the firm.

The downsizing or retrenchment began in 1988 and will continue through 1995. During this period, nearly every Japanese automaker is expected to open a new full-scale plant in the United States. While GM eventually hopes to regain its market share, the move indicates that the company anticipates an overcapacity in the North American car market, at least in the foreseeable future. This anticipation may have led to GM's scale back levels in the fourth quarter of 1991. They estimated production levels of 718,000 cars and 380,000 trucks but only produced 673,633 cars and 317,592 trucks. Although GM's former chairman, Roger Smith, had previously maintained that the carmaker's market-share drop was temporary, the move suggested that GM shared the belief Ford Motor Company held in 1981 when it went through a similar retrenchment.

By 1992, it is expected that the company will be operating close to 100 percent of its capacity with all plants running two shifts a day, five days a week. The company has not been at that level since spring 1984. In the 1985–88 period, GM varied its strategy from producing all the cars it could to running several plants below capacity for periods of time. In between, the company offered deep discounting with low financing and cash-back offers to clear its oversupply of cars.

Many have blamed Roger Smith for the lack of vision that resulted in the lagging GM market share and inconsistent production strategy. They believe GM should have taken steps to downsize years ago when it became apparent that imports would maintain a strong, permanent share of the market instead of continually denying their existence. Some even argue

| EXHIBIT 1.1 | GM's Share: Annual Unit Sales as a Percentage of U.S. New Car Market |

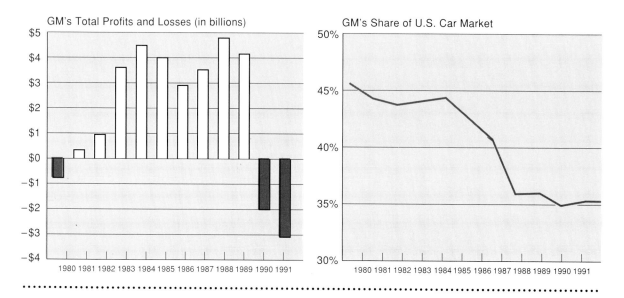

that the proposed cuts are not enough to make GM fully cost competitive in the global industry.

The possibility of closing plants is a very sensitive subject for employees and the United Auto Workers (UAW), especially since the fall 1987 labor agreement was sold to its members based on increased job security. The head of the UAW GM department believed the strategy was a "loser."

GM followed a similar entrenchment strategy in Europe during the mid-1980s. This resulted in a profit of $1.88 billion in 1987 over a loss of $568 million in 1986 in European operations. It is hoped that the retrenchment will produce a similar badly needed financial reversal in North America. In 1991, GM lost $1 million an hour, 24 hours a day, for 52 weeks, or $1,500 on each of the 3.5 million cars and trucks it produced in 1991.

By gearing its capacity to the low end of the business cycle, GM is following a similar retrenchment strategy instituted earlier by Ford. Ever since Ford permanently reduced capacity in 1981, it now must run plants overtime, add third shifts, or increase production efficiencies in order to meet increased demand.

Human Resource Changes

Even with GM's revised cost-cutting plan, General Motors Corporation has contributed (jointly with the UAW) $805 million to educate, train, and retrain its working and laid-off employees. As of January 1989, GM's total commitment, including what the individual plants have allocated to this enthusiastic program, comes to over 1.3 billion since 1984.

This is a new way of doing business for GM. In the past the managers competed fiercely with each other, concentrating on their individual departments while ignoring the difficulties other blue-collar workers and departments might be having. But this is all changing. With the realization that personnel, not technology, is its most important commodity with regard to the bottom line, the company is working hard to replace its old image with one of teamwork and unity. GM is striving for a winning team spirit in hopes that this will lead to better productivity, an improved competitive position in the marketplace, and, eventually, higher profits, more jobs, and job security. Consequently, through its employees GM hopes ultimately to recapture what it once owned—50 percent of the market share.

Saturn

One of GM's brightest hopes for recapturing its market share is its newest division. GM's estimated $3.5 billion start-up of Saturn in Spring Hill, Tennessee, has a specific competitive goal: to build better cars than the Japanese. Saturn is taking aim at the imports and plans to sell over 80 percent of its cars to customers who had intended to buy an import. Because less than 5 percent of the car-buying market knows what Saturn is all about, Saturn officials say that generating awareness will be the first objective in early advertising; they plan to do this by focusing on the people behind the car. Most of Saturn's workforce, 20 percent of which is composed of women, was recruited and screened from UAW locals in 38 states and has given up future options to ever work at another GM division. The workers have a shop-floor average salary of $34,000, with 20 percent of that dependent on company profits, productivity, and car quality. On the other hand, each worker is eligible for a bonus for beating targeted production goals.

[handwritten margin note: Strategic Decision →]

Saturn is breaking ground in four new areas: (1) as a partnership between management and UAW; (2) through its franchise agreements with dealers giving them rights to establish multiple outlets over larger than average territories; (3) as an integrated manufacturing complex; and (4) through its emphasis on teamwork, internally with Saturn's employees and externally with Saturn's suppliers.

Saturn opened up in the top markets for import sales across the country with 250,000 cars a year in 1991 and hopes to produce 360,000 a year by the end of 1995.

Developing Accountability in the Worker

GM hopes to help employees acquire the new skills, knowledge, and abilities needed for product improvement through education, training, and retraining programs. Approximately 5 percent of laid-off workers (2,500) have been retrained and placed in new jobs with other companies as of January 1989. Almost all currently employed workers went through some type of program at their local GM plant. GM is making this possible by allowing employees to attend classes on a regular basis during company time. However, in order for GM to survive its second major downsizing attempt, Chairman Robert Stempel will need to instill accountability in all of his workers. While he may not like it, he may have tell even his favorite workers that their futures at GM are dependent on measurable results.

• • • • • • • • •

In this case, GM has selected the strategy of retrenchment. This strategy will cause some major impacts on its human resource practices, such as an increase in the number of workers transferred to other GM plants, a slower rate of hiring, a reduction in overtime pay, and a larger number of workers being laid off or terminated. While these changes may seem adverse for current employees, if a retrenchment strategy was not undertaken by GM at this point, more dire consequences, such as possible bankruptcy, could occur. Adopting this strategy now, should allow GM to strengthen its competitive position more quickly.

STRATEGIC CHOICES

When managers, like those at GM, are faced with deciding which corporate strategy they should embark upon, several decisions must be made. The following is only a partial list of some of the strategic choices managers face.

1. Routinely managers must evaluate where they are. They must decide if they should remain with the strategy they have selected and implemented or if they need a new strategy.
2. To make this decision, managers must know exactly what has and hasn't changed since the current strategic approach was implemented. For example, has the economy changed dramatically in any way that may influence whether or not the selected strategy will continue to be effective?
3. If any changes are suggested, it is important that managers understand the ripple effects these changes may have on other functions? For example, if a growth strategy is selected, will the human resources unit be able to provide the qualified personnel needed to develop this strategy?
4. Finally, managers should try to evaluate the current approach and what any changes to this approach might have on what their competitors do? For example, if GM offers a low financing rate, is Chrysler or Ford in a position to offer an even lower rate, thereby making GM's offer unattractive?

THE STRATEGIC APPROACH

Chances are you have encountered, or soon will encounter, the strategic approach in your course of studies. It is used in marketing, finance, and information systems courses and serves as the heart of the capstone course in most business programs: the policy course. However, it has not been widely used as an approach to human resource/personnel management.

Even though you will not likely become a personnel manager in a firm, you will very likely manage human resources if the position you take gives you some authority over other employees. Even if this does not happen, you will be affected by the human resource decisions made in your firm.

Strategy Defined

A strategy is a way of doing something. It is a game plan for action. It usually includes the formulation of a **goal** and a set of **action plans** for accomplishment. It implies consideration of the **competitive forces** at work in managing an organization and the impact of the **outside environment** on organization actions.

While managers have probably managed strategically for many years, the strategic approach is relatively new to management literature. The concept of strategy has its roots in military literature, particularly that developed by the Chinese strategist Sun Tzu.[2] However, Alfred Chandler's work, *Strategy and Structure*, as well as the development of management by objectives (MBO), set the stage for the present day popularity of the strategic focus in business and management books.[3]

Management by objectives (MBO) has been popular in business writings since the mid-1950s when it first was used by Peter Drucker in his classic *The Practice of Management.*[4] MBO essentially involves three steps: setting a mission or purpose, setting goals or objectives, and determining action plans for goals or objectives.

The strategic focus accepts these three basic ideas of MBO but goes beyond them by giving explicit recognition to both the outside and competitive environments. The actions and reactions of competition are the heart of the modern approach to strategy. Two popular works of Michael Porter no doubt have enhanced this competitive focus.[5] These two books examine how strategy can be used to obtain competitive advantage and have been widely read and referred to by people in both academic institutions and businesses.

For our purpose we define **strategy** as *the formulation of organizational missions, goals and objectives, as well as action plans for achievement, that explicitly recognize the competition and the impact of outside environmental forces.*

Before we can clearly see how strategy formulation impacts the human resource function of an organization, we must first understand what human resources in an organization is all about. The following section provides a brief history of the field of human resources and the popular functional approach to human resource management.

AN OVERVIEW OF HUMAN RESOURCE MANAGEMENT[6]

The Craft System

People who worked during the 1600s to 1700s were guided by a craft system. Under this system, the production of goods and services was generated by small groups of workers in relatively small workplaces, usually in a home. The work was customized and supervised by a master craftsman. Each master craftsman had several apprentices and journeymen who actually performed the work. When the craftsman retired, the most senior journeyman would normally replace him or her. There was no confusion about career paths and no disputes over wages. This type of system held for over 200 years.

As demand for products increased, the craft system could not keep up. Craftsmen had to hire more and more journeymen and apprentices, and the small workplace became more like a small factory. At the same time, machines were being introduced that could be used to help produce high-quality products much faster than could experienced craftsmen. These changes helped usher in the Industrial Revolution.

Scientific Management

In the early 1900s, many changes occurred in the workplace. Machines and factory methods were introduced that increased production. However, with this increased production came several problems. Since the machines required several people to operate, the number of workers increased dramatically. This forced managers to develop rules, regulations, and procedures in order to control the workers. Some of the regulations required an increase in job specialization, which led to boring, monotonous jobs. Specialization also allowed managers the ability to replace quickly and economically any worker who demanded too much or caused a problem. One of the most significant developments that arose during this time was a process called scientific management.

The premise of scientific management is that there is one best way to do a job. This one best way will be the cheapest, fastest, and most efficient way to perform the task. While the process may not be the safest or the most humane, it will allow the company to make the most profit. Frederick Taylor, the father of scientific management, spent his career collecting data and analyzing the specific motions required to perform various jobs. He would then break the job into specific tasks and refine the motions needed to complete the task until it could be refined no more. He would then select, train, and closely monitor workers who performed the tasks. Those workers who were successful (that is, those who followed the orders of management exactly and by doing so significantly increased their production) earned a great deal of money. Those who were not successful were terminated.

While scientific management did prove to be an effective management tool that increased the productivity of workers, it was criticized for treating the worker like a tool and not like a person. To compensate for this tendency to depersonalize the work environment, welfare secretaries were hired. People in these positions oversaw programs for the welfare of the employees, such as the installation of libraries and recreational facilities, financial assistance programs, or medical and health programs. The welfare programs were the forerunner of modern day benefit packages and the welfare secretary position was the forerunner of the current-day human resource manager.

Human Relations

The next significant step in the development of human resources occurred in the late 1920s and early 1930s: the Hawthorne studies. Elton Mayo and Fritz Roethlisberger were asked by Western Electric to determine what could be done to increase the productivity of workers at the Hawthorne Works plant in Chicago. While the researchers were specifically examining the effect lighting had on productivity, their results really had nothing to do with the lighting level. What they concluded was that the human interaction and attention paid to the workers by the researchers caused their productivity to increase. This finding was the first one to indicate that the social factors in a work environment could have a significant effect on the productivity of workers.

Fueled by the findings of the Hawthorne studies, further research on social factors and how individuals respond to them was undertaken. Results from these studies indicated that the needs of employees must be understood and acted upon by management in order for a worker to be satisfied and productive. Communication between the worker and his or her superior was stressed as was the need for a more participative workplace atmosphere. More often than not, however, these tactics did little to increase a worker's productivity. The idea that a happy worker is a productive worker failed to be proven, and many of the concepts were abandoned. It is interesting to note that the focus of the human relations era is now the backbone of more recent employee involvement programs that have been found to increase the productivity of workers and increase the profits of companies that adopt them.

Behavioral Science

Expanding on the human relations school of thought of including academic findings from various other disciplines such as psychology, political science, sociology, and biology, the behavioral science era was born. Behavioral science focuses more on the total organization and less on the individual. It examines how the workplace affects the individual worker and how the individual worker affects the workplace. Some feel that the modern day fields of organization behavior (OB), the study of employee behavior in the organization; organizational development (OD), the process of changing employee and organizational attitudes and beliefs; and human resource management (HRM) grew out of the behavioral science era.

Human Resource Functions

Through the years, the welfare secretaries' jobs became larger and larger. As laws were passed that restricted the rights of employers and employees, the welfare secretaries were required to stay informed and determine what impact those laws would have on the organization. The employees in these positions also were required to keep files about employees, maintain payroll systems, and counsel employees. As more and more jobs were delegated to the welfare secretaries, offshoots began to form. One group of welfare secretaries would take responsibility for payroll duties, setting wages, and determining raises. A second group focused on hiring and training workers, while yet another would concentrate on working with the union to negotiate an acceptable contract. Each of these offshoots eventually became a function of the human resources unit.

Current day human resource units are responsible for a variety of activities including employment and recruiting, training and development, compensation, benefits, employee services, employee relations, personnel records, health and safety, and company grounds.[7] A recent addition to this list is human resource planning and strategy formulation and implementation. We examine how this is accomplished in the following section.

....

THE STRATEGIC APPROACH TO HUMAN RESOURCE MANAGEMENT

The strategic approach to human resource management applies the concept of strategy to managing a firm's human resources. This approach has six key elements as shown in Exhibit 1.2. Let's look at each of these.

Recognition of the Impact of the Outside Environment

The outside environment presents a set of **opportunities** and **threats** to the organization in the form of laws, economic conditions, social and demographic changes, domestic and international political forces, technology, and so on. Strategic human resource strategy explicitly recognizes the threats and opportunities in each area and attempts to capitalize on the opportunities while minimizing or deflecting the effect of threats.

Recognition of the Impact of Competition and the Dynamics of the Labor Market

Employers compete for employees just as they do for customers. The forces of competition in attracting, rewarding, and using employees has a major affect on corporate human resource strategy. Forces play out in both local, regional, and national labor markets. The joint GM-Toyota venture, New United Motors Inc. (NUMI), through its construction of a plant in Fremont, California, had a major effect on and was very much affected by the local labor market in its area. Labor market dynamics of wage rates, unemployment rates, working conditions, benefit levels, minimum wage legislation, and competitor reputation all have an impact on and are affected by strategic human resource decisions.

Long-Range Focus

A strategic focus tends to set the long-range direction of a company's human resource style and basic approach. Strategy can be changed but it is not always easy. It depends on the inertia, flexibility, and management philosophy of the firm. The intent, however, is to develop a consistent strategy to guide the firm into its future. Sometimes the word **vision** is used to capture this idea.

Choice and Decision-Making Focus

Strategy implies choosing among alternatives. It implies making major decisions about human resources—decisions that commit the organization's resources toward a particular direction. For example, when Ford established its management-labor worker participation program in the mid-1980s, it did so because of a major decision to increase employee involvement. Of course, the fact that Nissan, Toyota, and other Japanese automakers had successfully used such programs for years probably served as part of the impetus to follow suit. Ford's strategy of employee involvement, based upon its "Quality is Job 1" campaign, was adopted because of a perceived need to resolve issues or prevent new ones from forming—specifically, to improve product quality.

··

| EXHIBIT 1.2 | Characteristics of a Strategic Approach to Human Resource Management |

HUMAN RESOURCE STRATEGY

- Explicitly recognizes the impact of the outside environment
- Explicitly recognizes the competition and the dynamics of the labor market
- Has a long-range focus (3–5 years)
- Focuses on the issue of choice and decision making
- Considers all personnel, not just hourly or operational employees
- Is integrated with overall corporate strategy and functional strategies

··

In other words, strategy has a problem-solving or problem-preventing focus. Strategy concentrates on the question, "What should the organization do and why?" This action orientation requires that decisions be made and carried out.

Consideration of All Personnel

A strategic approach to human resources is concerned with *all* of the firm's employees, not just its hourly or operational personnel. Traditionally, human resource management focuses on hourly employees, with most clerical exempt employees also thrown in. However, as the province of human resource management has broadened, the focus today, at least from a strategic perspective, is on all employees—from top-level management to unskilled operative workers. Consequently, we are just as much concerned with executive pay and benefit plans as we are of hourly wages. We are just as interested in top management's wage and benefit package at Chrysler as we are that of hourly union members in the plant. We want to examine management development and training as well as hourly skill training programs.

Integration with Corporate Strategy

The particular human resource strategy adopted by a firm should be integrated with the firm's corporate strategy. In other words corporate strategy should drive human resource strategy. Tom Kelley, the 1989 chairman of the American Society of Personnel Administrators' Board of Directors (now the Society of Human Resource Management), remarked that human resource managers "are involved in the strategic planning of global issues, rather than the day-to-day personnel transactions of the previous personnel administrators . . . [and] along with that strategic planning process, it is imperative that the Human Resource Professional establish goals and objectives that support the corporate goals."[8]

If corporate strategy is to grow and dominate a market, such as Apple Computer's strategy in the early 1980s, then human resource strategy would have to focus on the rapid acquisition and placement of employees. If retrenchment is the strategy, as was shown in the GM case at the beginning of the chapter, then no or low hiring plus layoff and termination of employees is the strategy. Exhibit 1.3 summarizes some key overall strategies and the associated human resource applications that demonstrate this concept.

··

EXHIBIT 1.3	Examples of Organizational Strategies and Associated Human Resource Strategies

CORPORATE STRATEGY	EXAMPLE	HUMAN RESOURCE STRATEGIES
Retrenchment (cost reduction)	GM	Layoffs, Wage Reduction, Productivity Increases, Job Redesign, Renegotiated Labor Agreements
Growth	Intel	Aggressive Recruiting and Hiring, Rapidly Rising Wages, Job Creation, Expanding Training and Development
Renewal	Chrysler	Managed Turnover, Selective Layoff, Organizational Development, Transfer/Replacement Productivity Increases, Employee Involvement
Niche Focus	Kentucky Fried Chicken	Specialized Job Creation, Elimination of Other Jobs, Specialized Training and Development
Acquisition	GE	Selective Layoffs, Transfers/Placement, Job Combinations, Orientation and Training, Managing Cultural Transitions

··

Differences from Typical Functional Approach to Personnel

The strategic management approach to human resources and the typical functional approach differ in many ways. As Leonard Schlesinger states, human resource management needs to get out of the "people business" and into the business of people.[9] In other words, human resource managers and other human resource professionals need to be full players on the management team.

Exhibit 1.4 enumerates the major differences between the strategic human resource approach and the traditional personnel management approach along six dimensions: planning, authority, scope, decision making, integration, and coordination. Basically, *the strategic human resource approach is involved in strategic planning and decision making and coordinates all human resource functions for all employees.* The approach vests more authority in the chief human resource officer in the organization. It also views the human resource function as an *integral part* of all corporate functions: marketing, production, finance, legal, and so on. The strategic human resource approach accepts the vice-president of human resources as an integral part of the management team. Exhibit 1.5 (on page 16) shows a typical organization chart that includes human resources in the top level of management and, by doing so, provides the human resource vice-presidents with the same authority as the other functional vice-presidents.

| EXHIBIT 1.4 | Difference between Strategic Human Resource Approach and Traditional Personnel Approach | |

DIMENSIONS	STRATEGIC HUMAN RESOURCE APPROACH	TRADITIONAL PERSONNEL MANAGEMENT APPROACH
Planning and Strategy Formulation	Involved in formulating overall organizational strategic plan and aligning human resource functions with company strategy	Involved in operational planning only
Authority	High status and authority for top personnel officer—e.g. vice-president for Human Resources	Medium status and authority—e.g. personnel director
Scope	Concerned with all managers and employees	Concerned primarily with hourly, operational, and clerical employees
Decision Making	Involved in making strategic decisions	Makes operational decisions only
Integration	Fully integrated with other organizational functions: marketing, finance, legal, production	Moderate to small integration with other organizational functions
Coordination	Coordinates all human resource activities; e.g. training, recruitment, staffing, EEO, etc.	Does not coordinate all human resource functions

In order for the vice-president of human resources to have any significant impact on the corporation, he or she must be able to do several things. First, he or she must know when to delegate responsibility and when to remain involved. If a project warrants the top person's input, then the vice-president should remain involved. If it does not, then the project should be delegated to a knowledgeable subordinate who is instructed to keep the vice-president informed. Second, the vice-president must have the respect of his or her peers because it is through these people that things will get done. Keeping the relationships well oiled will help to make the wheels turn when necessary. In order to make sensible policy decision, a vice-president must have a good idea of how employees at all levels in the organization think. If a policy decision will be unpopular with the majority of the workers, it will not be a good policy. However, there is no way to know the popularity of a policy without knowing how others think and feel. Finally, a vice-president must have a good rapport with the chief executive officer (CEO). To build this needed rapport, the vice-president should get immersed in the business, understand the financial ramifications of the human resource policies, and try to be objective when dealing with the CEO. By practicing these fundamentals the vice-president of human resources can have a significant impact on the organization.[10]

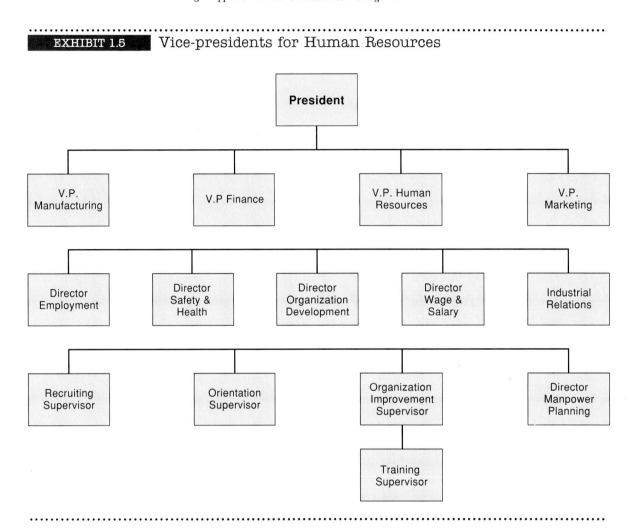

EXHIBIT 1.5 Vice-presidents for Human Resources

All Managers Are Human Resource Managers

The strategic human resource management approach views all managers as human resource managers. Human resource management issues are not simply the province of the human resources unit. Rather, all managers must take responsibility for efficient and effective utilization of their subordinates. By the same token, human resource managers, because they are in a *staff* position, must view their role as essentially supportive of *operating (line)* managers. That is, they should see their role as advising, helping, and providing expert guidance to line managers on human resource issues. In essence, human resource professionals should view the people whom they advise as customers and themselves as service representatives.[11]

As environmental changes confront organizations with increasingly more complex people issues, they can, in turn, affect the bottom line—profits or survival of the organization. Keeping abreast of these issues requires a broader understanding of human resource management and an increased time commitment for the line manager away from the particular business function. The human resource department, therefore, is a watchful eye that frees up the line managers across the organization

Managing Resistance of Line Managers

Because the role of a human resource professional falls under the title of staff, not line, human resource managers have no true authority over line managers. Instead, they act as a guidance counselor for line managers by offering suggestions and ideas when problems arise. Sometimes the advice they offer is accepted and used and other times it is not. When it is not and the problem escalates, the line managers can become resentful. Likewise, if the advice is accepted and implemented and it does not work, problems can occur. However problems occur, human resource managers need to find ways to resolve these difficulties.

It is often suggested that stopping the problems before they occur is the easiest way to handle them. To do this, human resource managers need to follow several simple guidelines. First, human resource managers must be very knowledgeable about the business. They need to understand the products, the markets, and the finances of the organization as well. If they are truly tapped into the organization, then the ideas they offer will reflect an understanding of all aspects of the organization and how the changes will impact each area.

Human resource managers must also maintain a client perspective to be effective, and they must always remember that they are in the service business. Good human resource managers ask "clients" for honest appraisals of their work. They always monitor the outcomes of the suggestions they have made and make additional suggestions for changes if warranted. In short, they offer a "guarantee" with their services.

To succeed, human resource managers must have people on staff who support their efforts. Changes cannot be made without a willingness on the part of others to give new ideas a try. It is a good idea for human resource managers to enlist the help of others as soon as possible. Also, it is imperative that the majority of human resource managers' support comes from above them. Human resource managers should be sure that the senior management is visibly supportive of their efforts.

SOURCE: Adapted from Richard Korn, "Managing Line Resistance," *Personnel Administrator*, July 1989, pp. 98–100.

by helping with the people-related business issues and working with the line managers to respond to the issues.[12] While this relationship can lead to staff-line conflict, such conflict is not necessarily all bad if it results in full discussion of key human resource issues and better role clarification of the parties involved.

ENVIRONMENT-ORGANIZATION LINK AND THE STRATEGIC APPROACH

As we have indicated, the strategic approach explicitly recognizes the impact of the outside environment on both the firm and the formulation of human resource strategy. Exhibit 1.6 shows this link. Chapter 2 discusses the outside environment and its impact in more depth. However, at this point we are interested in the impact on strategy formulation from a broad conceptual view.

The outside environment presents a set of *opportunities* and *threats* to the firm. In formulating strategy the firm seeks to take advantage of the opportunities while minimizing or deflecting the threats. What might be a threat to one firm can be an opportunity to another. The oil shocks of the 1970s threatened oil-fired electrical utilities but provided a great opportunity for coal producers and shippers.

Environmental Scanning

The firm learns of its environment through a **scanning** process. This refers to the gathering of information about environmental issues on a regular basis and

· ·

| **EXHIBIT 1.6** | The Environment-Organization Link |

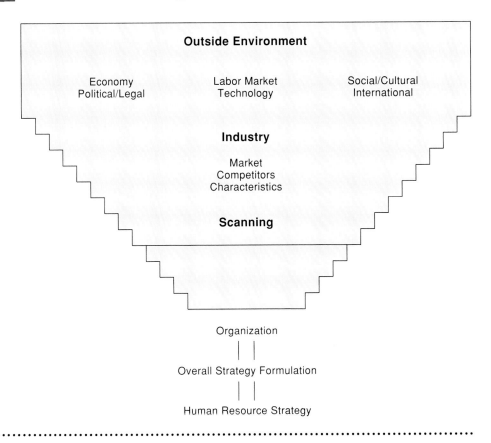

· ·

interpreting them in light of the organization's business. Scanning is the first step to strategic planning and strategy formulation. A scan and forecast is developed that serves the basis for the plan.

Competitive and market analysis is also important to strategy formulation. When the steel industry finally decided to restructure during the severe recession of the 1980s, they chose this strategy largely because of the severe competition from Japanese and German steel makers. Japan and Germany had rebuilt their steel-making facilities (largely with U.S. dollars) after World War II. This technology was more efficient than that in place in the United States. Consequently, during the early 1980s U.S. steel plants were closed in Pennsylvania, West Virginia, and other industrial areas. Many people lost good-paying jobs and have been unable to find work paying a comparable wage. People who travel the Monongahela and Eastern Ohio River Valleys still see rusted hulks of former steel plants sitting idle. Much steel-making capacity has been lost to foreign producers.

A firm tries to achieve a **sustainable competitive advantage** by analyzing competition.[13] This advantage is a long-term **distinctive competence** that sets one company apart from the competition. It answers the question, "Why would someone buy our service or product over someone else's?" This advantage can be based on any number of factors: price, cost, service, quality, image, reliability, convenience, safety,

KFC Finds Success Where Others Have Failed—In China

After 18 months of tough negotiations, Kentucky Fried Chicken opened its first restaurant in Beijing, China. While KFC has dubbed its venture an instant success and touts daily sales of nearly $3,000 a day, other fast-food competitors are not so sure the success will continue. Research findings of both Burger King and McDonalds' indicate that the vital ingredients for fast-food success—high quality supplies, a disciplined labor force, and receptive consumers—may not be available in China.

Daniel Ng, managing director of McDonald's Restaurants in Hong Kong, said that he has been talking with Chinese authorities about the possibility of entering the Far East fast-food market for the past ten years. He concedes that, while being the first to break into a new marketplace is good, he would rather be sure that it is done right, even if it means being last.

Officials at Burger King hold a similar attitude. Their preliminary research study conducted two years prior to the KFC opening indicated that a full-blown feasibility study was ill advised at this point in time. The main problems they foresaw were the difficulty of procuring supplies and the uncertainty that there would be enough interested customers to ensure a strong return on their investment.

Pizza Hut, which is owned by Pillsbury, the same parent company as KFC, is the only other fast-food franchise that has expressed an interest in doing business in China. However, their plans will surely rest on whether or not KFC really did find the key to success in Beijing.

SOURCE: Adapted from Brian Caplan, "Kentucky Hatches Its Chickens in Beijing," *Asian Business,* February 1988, p. 17.

or any combination of the above. Mercedes-Benz has a sustainable competitive advantage in reliability and image over many other automobiles.

The market also brings on **industry structure.** The industry structure involves a number of factors: growth rates, concentration ratio (the number of firms that have a large percentage of the market), substitute products or services in related industries, technology, change, and so on.

A key aspect in industry analysis is determining **critical success factors** or **keys to success.** These are what it takes to be successful in that industry. For example, to be successful in fast foods a firm must have convenient locations, quick service, a consistent standard of product quality, store cleanliness, mass advertising, high volume, and low margins. McDonald's, Wendy's, Kentucky Fried Chicken, Burger King, Hardees, and other chains are successful because they have largely acquired these characteristics.

Success factors for other industries would be different. For example for department stores, success factors are magnet mall locations, wide variety or choice of merchandise, good service, good- to high-quality merchandise, and a liberal customer return policy, among others. The point is that a firm must know the critical success factors of its industry and formulate a strategy that allows it to meet these factors.

The human resource strategy is based on overall corporate strategy and needs to be consistent with it. A department store emphasizing friendly, competent service to customers would have to hire, train, and reward employees so that such services were efficiently and effectively provided.

Finally, **technology** has a major impact on strategy formulation and on human resource strategy in particular. The technology available in the environment plus that actually adopted by an organization, has a profound effect on job design decisions which, in turn, affects many other human resource decisions such as pay, training, work assignment, leadership, and so on. Think of the technology employed

HR CHALLENGES •

Human Resources at America's Most Admired Companies

Every year *Fortune* magazine asks experts in various fields to rate businesses to determine which are most admired. The categories on which they are judged are quality of management, quality of products or services, innovativeness, long-term investment values, financial soundness, and the ability to attract, develop and keep talented people.

For the past six years, Merck, a pharmaceutical giant, has won the top honors. Interestingly enough, much of the success of the firm can be traced back to the human resource functions. For example, promotions and salaries for senior managers at Merck are based on how many people that person recruited and trained. Merck emphasizes the basic human resource functions of finding the best person, getting that person into the right job, and providing him or her with the skills and tools needed to succeed. These functions are just as important to the company as are the functions of the researchers who develop new chemicals for the firm to sell.

Merck works hard to preserve its reputation. The CEO, Roy Vagelos, visits six to eight college campuses each year. During these visits he talks with both the

medical schools and the business schools about new drugs and the wonderful opportunities available at Merck. These talks do not go unnoticed. Over the past several years, Merck has been able to lure top scientific talent away from the faculties of Harvard, MIT, and Yale. Once hired, these researchers are provided with plenty of reasons to stay at Merck. Research and development money is made available to Merck's scientists in large amounts. In 1991, approximately 12 percent of sales (about $1 billion) was funneled back into the labs. In return for this treatment, the researchers are asked to keep the marketable drugs coming. And they do.

Merck has found that its key to being number one is in the way it recruits, trains, develops, and supports its human resources. If it can keep its employees happy, it can maintain its reputation. If it can maintain its reputation, it will continue to be rated the number one corporation in America.

SOURCE: Adapted from Kate Ballen, "America's Most Admired Companies," *Fortune*, February 10, 1992, pp. 40–72; and Susan Caminiti, "The Payoff from a Good Reputation," *Fortune*, February 10, 1992, pp. 73–77.

by an automobile manufacturer on the assembly line. The configuration of machines, movement, and technical expertise caused by the kind of technology employed creates a set of constraints within which human resource decisions must be made. To change these constraints, the technology must be changed. For example, robotic technology is being substituted for people using hand tools in a repetitive manner.

INTEGRATING HUMAN RESOURCE STRATEGY WITH CORPORATE AND FUNCTIONAL STRATEGIES

GM's corporate strategy of retrenchment that we examined in the case at the beginning of this chapter will drive human resource, marketing, operations (production) finance, and other functional policies. GM appears to be resigning itself to a 35 percent market share, at least in the foreseeable future, because it is permanently closing 11 plants instead of using temporary layoffs, the traditional way of dealing with sales falloffs in the auto industry. It is also relying heavily on Saturn. Thus, GM's overall corporate retrenchment strategy will have profound effects on its functional strategies, including its human resource strategy. Exhibit 1.7 shows how the Saturn project has been used to link corporate strategies to business strategies to the human resource strategies.

EXHIBIT 1.7 Example of Corporate to Business to Human Resource Management Strategies

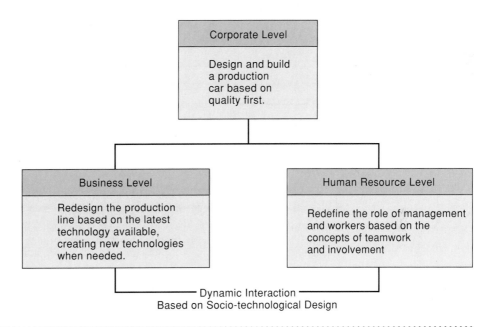

General Motors Saturn Project

Corporate Level

Design and build a production car based on quality first.

Business Level

Redesign the production line based on the latest technology available, creating new technologies when needed.

Human Resource Level

Redefine the role of management and workers based on the concepts of teamwork and involvement

Dynamic Interaction
Based on Socio-technological Design

Corporate Strategy Drives Functional Strategies

As seen in Exhibit 1.8, corporate strategy should drive functional strategy. In other words, a firm determines its overall strategy and then sets functional strategy to carry it out. For example, GM's retrenchment strategy will cause downsizing in human resource management, consolidation in production and operations, cutbacks or at least very moderate growth in marketing (including advertising expenditures), restructuring and consolidation in finance, restructuring of engineering, and so on. The major functions of GM will be affected in a substantial way by the retrenchment strategy.

Also note in Exhibit 1.8 that functional strategy can impact corporate strategy in that a firm must consider existing functional strategy when setting corporate strategy. For example, the existing human resource strategy and capabilities will be a major factor to consider in formulating corporate strategy.

Also, various functional strategies must be integrated with one another. It would be inconsistent for GM to adopt a high-growth human resource strategy while scaling back production and operations. Nor would high investment in new plant and equipment be an appropriate financial strategy for retrenchment. Marketing strategy must be focused at an anticipated 35 percent market share instead of the 50 percent to which GM has traditionally been accustomed.

EXHIBIT 1.8 · Corporate Strategy Drives Functional Strategies

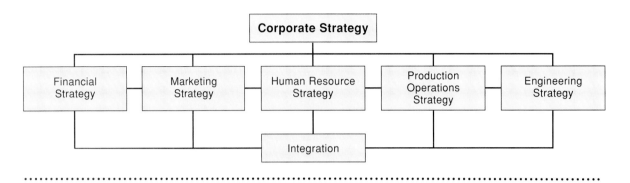

The implication for human resource managers is that they must be acutely aware of overall corporate strategy and how human resource strategy dovetails with it. Moreover, they need to be aware of functional strategies and attempt to integrate human resource strategy with them. This awareness argues for participation in the strategy formulation process at both the corporate and functional levels as has been discussed previously in this chapter.

A summary model of organizational strategy and its relationship to human resource strategies is presented in Exhibit 1.9. Notice the substrategies that make up overall human resource strategy. Substrategies are developed for prehiring and hiring, motivation, retraining and retention, and separating human resources. Exhibit 1.9 shows the substrategies for each of these areas.

STRATEGY FORMULATION, DECISION MAKING, AND PROBLEM SOLVING

The strategy formulation process is not a neat and clean process. It advances in fits and starts and is subject to much revision and ad hoc interpretation. It approximates the "garbage can theory" of decision making in that there is much post hoc attribution or explanation of why certain actions were carried out.[14] Sometimes action drives strategy rather than the reverse. Decision makers then justify a particular course of action by looking for a strategy that supports it.

Thus, strategic formulation is a *dynamic* process.[15] It is evolutionary in nature and is subject to change as outside environmental conditions, competition, or internal conditions change. This flexibility in strategy formulation and implementation is essential to the process. Since strategy formulation deals with the future (for example, what we will do in the future, how, and why) and since no one can predict the future with certainty, the process must be kept flexible. The firm must be able to respond to changes as they occur—*in spite of* the plans.

The ability of a large corporation such as Ford Motor Company to completely change and refocus strategy in the early 1980s to the "Quality is Job 1" campaign shows how Ford was able to meet new threats in both domestic (Chrysler) and

EXHIBIT 1.9   Organizational Human Resource Strategy

foreign competition as well as the unexpected fuel price shocks of the late 1970s and early 1980s.

This ability to redirect strategy formulation is sometimes called **logical incrementalism**.[16] This concept refers to the additional measured change or reaction to a particular event. Actions appear to be taken in a step-by-step fashion without the appearance of an overall plan. For example, a particular environmental pressure (such as a new unexpected law) or a competitive threat (such as an unanticipated price cut) could cause a firm to take a calculated course of action that was not originally planned as part of the strategy. A series of these actions might make it appear that the strategy is simply one of **reaction** rather than **proaction**, that is, the company is reacting to the latest threat. In other words, "the squeaky wheel gets the grease."

While the reactive label might be appropriate if every course of action a firm undertook was in response to a threat, it certainly would not be appropriate if the firm followed a well-formulated strategy but was able to modify it as conditions changed. In this case, the firm would be proactive—establishing plans and strategy ahead of time—but flexible. Yet the line between flexibility in strategy and a reactive mode sometimes can be a thin one.

Another way to view this phenomenon is to make a distinction between **intended strategy** and **realized strategy.** The intended strategy is the strategy that is formulated during the planning period. The realized strategy is that which the organization actually follows. Often the realized strategy is different from the intended strategy because unanticipated forces affect the planned strategy.

···

EXHIBIT 1.10   Strategy and Decision Making

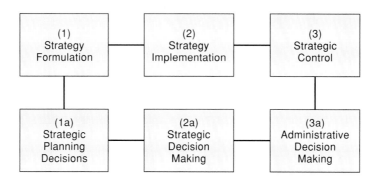

···

Decision Making and Choice

Strategies give rise to decisions, as is shown in Exhibit 1.10. **Strategy formulation** occurs during **strategic planning.** During this stage the organization establishes its identity (mission), and decides where it wants to go (goals and objectives) and how it wants to get there (action plans).

Strategy formulation decisions lead to **strategy implementation decisions.** Decisions must be made about how the strategies are to be implemented. When McDonald's decided to expand its menu and hours of operation by opening for breakfast, a whole series of strategic implementation decisions had to be made about menu items, specific hours of operation, hiring and training of employees, whether the breakfast would be optional or required of franchises, and so on. Strategic decisions are made on how to implement the strategies formulated in the first step.

Finally **strategic control** must be exercised. During this stage decisions are made to ensure that what actually happens is what the company wants to happen. Once McDonald's made all the decisions required to offer a breakfast, then the company had to determine which menu items would meet McDonald's food quality tests and could be prepared in a convenient manner with fast-food operations. Certainly, adjustments and corrective actions had to be made, since things seldom work out exactly as planned.

Thus strategic control decisions give rise to **administrative decision making.** Administrative decisions are the day-to-day decisions that are made with the following factors in mind:

Gathering information about performance

Adjusting behaviors and/or strategies

Taking other forms of *corrective action* such as discipline or counseling

Theoretically, decisions in each area should reinforce one another. Strategic formulation decisions should drive strategy implementation and strategy control. Sometimes the reverse happens—strategy control drives strategy formulation. A firm adopts a different strategy because it was unable to make controlling decisions to implement the existing strategy.

For example, for decades colleges and universities followed a strategy designed to protect female students. This strategy was referred to as *in loco parentis* (in place

HR CHALLENGES ●

What a CEO Wants from an HR Executive

In a recent survey, 23 CEOs were asked, "What is it that you want from an HR executive?" Their responses varied. However, some of the common adjectives used to describe the ideal HR executive included proactive, innovative, visionary, aggressive, initiating, and supportive. More specific descriptions were given by several of the CEOs interviewed.

For example, Herbert M. Baum, president of Campbell Soup Company's North American Division, is seeking a human resource executive who will fit in with his "Dead Poets Society" group. As the name borrowed from the movie implies, Baum is looking for a human resource executive who can be inspired by the unorthodox or flamboyant. Each month the society meets for dinner. The chairperson for the monthly meeting of the society is rotated throughout all of the members. Whoever is selected to chair that month pays for dinner and sets the agenda. By the end of the two- to three-hour dinner, many opportunities are identified and many problems have been solved. In order for the human resource executive to be a vital component in the society, Baum expects him or her to know the business. Not only should he or she know the business of human resources, but the business of Campbell's Soup.

Philip Hunter, CEO of Hunter Associates Laboratory in Reston, Virginia, wants a human resource executive who can keep his human resources on track, whatever track Hunter chooses. To do this, he expects the human resource manager to understand all aspects of the human resource field. He wants someone who can hire, train, develop, and do so legally. He wants someone who can help him refocus his organization into a total quality-management company. He knows that the key to success in his business is having quality people on staff and a line of more quality people waiting outside to take the place of the people inside. To achieve these goals, Hunter knows he needs a professional human resource executive at his side.

SOURCE: Adapted from Stephanie Overman, "What Does the CEO Want?" *HRMagazine*, October 1991, pp. 41–43.

of the parents). It was usually achieved through a series of policies and rules restricting student visitations, hours, and other living and social arrangements. However, universities moved away from this strategy in the early 1970s, largely because they were unable to continue to exercise that type of control over students. Newfound student freedoms and power were advocated through free speech, demonstrations, and office takeovers on campuses. The universities soon relinquished control over women's hours, dorm visitations, and other "parental" rules. The lack of control caused a change in strategy rather than the other way around. A similar example occurred in 1989 when the Chinese government changed its views on democracy as a result of the violent student demonstrations that the government was unable to control at that time.

Strategy and Policy

The concepts of strategy and policy are sometimes confused. Strategy is the overall game plan that the organization attempts to implement. Policy provides broad guidelines to action. Policy establishes the parameters or rules under which the game is to be played. For example, the universities' basic strategy under *in loco parentis* was to protect the students, especially females. Various policies on living arrangements were adopted to achieve this strategy. The armor base goal behind the strategy was to preserve and protect the morals and safety of students.

Problem Solving

The university situation of the early 1970s demonstrates that many strategies are formed as a result of a problem. In other words, strategy formulation often occurs

....

| EXHIBIT 1.11 | Reactive and Proactive Strategy Formulation |

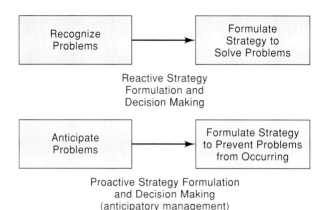

....

because there is a problem to be solved. This is a *reactive* approach to strategy formulation and decision making. When a *proactive* approach is taken, strategies are formed in *anticipation* of problems. This is sometimes called **anticipatory decision making** (see Exhibit 1.11). Human resource managers are able to attend national conferences or legislative hearings that concern their respective industries. They can then report back to their chief executive officers and tell them about rising issues or legislation currently in process and assess how their organization needs to respond. The result is a proactive strategy.[17] Proactive strategy formulation, while the recommended style, is often difficult to achieve. Despite good forecasting efforts, it is not always possible to anticipate problems.

● ● ● ● ● ● ● ● ●

MANAGEMENT GUIDELINES

Based on the material covered in this chapter, we can provide the following management guidelines.

1. Corporate strategy should be determined first, then human resource strategy should be developed. The human resource strategy that is developed should be consistent with the corporate strategy.

2. Human resource strategy should be consistent with other functional strategies, such as finance, marketing, and engineering.

3. The strategy formulation process should remain flexible and readily adaptable to change.

4. Human resource managers, particularly those at the top of the organization, should be involved in the strategy formulation process.

5. Human resource strategy should consider all human resources in the organization, not just hourly or operative employees.

6. The outside environment and competition should be explicitly considered in formulating both overall organizations and human resource strategy.

....
QUESTIONS FOR REVIEW

1. What is meant by the term strategy?

2. What is meant by a strategic approach to human resources?

3. How does the strategic approach to human resources differ from the functional approach?

4. What role does the outside environment and competition have in formulating organizational strategy?

5. Why should human resource strategy be consistent with both organizational strategy and functional strategy?

6. What role does problem solving and decision making play in strategy formulation?

7. How has the field of human resources changed over the past 200 years? Why?

CASE: Volkswagen Turnaround[18]

The Volkswagen Beetle was one of the most popular forms of transportation for college students in the 1960s and early 1970s. It was a sign of the counterculture. Even Ham Jordan, President Jimmy Carter's key aid, drove a Beetle throughout the Carter years in Washington, D.C. The microbus was the van of choice of the flower children. VW commercials often provided more entertainment than the television shows they sponsored. No one thought the Beetle would ever die—but it did.

Now the Volkswagen AG itself is in deep trouble. Although still the leading selling automobile in Europe with almost 15 percent of the market in 1987, Fiat (14.3 percent), Peugeot (12 percent) and even Ford (12 percent) are gaining on them. What happened? In a word—Audi. While the Audi is not completely responsible, it did have a major impact on many of Volkswagen's problems.

Sales Fall

As Exhibit 1.12 shows, the peak of VW sales occurred in 1970 at almost 600,000 units. By 1989 sales had fallen dramatically to just over 128,000 units.

In 1968, VW of America accounted for 39 percent of the parent company's business. By 1987 this had fallen to 8.5 percent. Audi sales in the United States dropped from 74,241 in 1985 to 21,225 in 1989. This drop was caused by quality problems especially the sudden acceleration issue of the Audi 5000 model, which Audi had not been able

to counteract effectively. Consumers simply did not wish to buy what they saw to be a dangerous and unsafe car.

Restructure

In order to revive its business in the world auto market, VW plans to take five major actions. First, it closed its assembly plant in Westmoreland, Pennsylvania. This was its greatest symbolic defeat since the plant was touted as the key to U.S. market growth when it opened in the 1970s. However, the Rabbit and Golf models produced at the plant never caught on with the American public.

Second, the company sold its unprofitable Triumph-Adler office equipment in order to raise cash and better focus on the automobile market. Third, VW plans to turn around operations in Spain and South America through cost cutting and productivity improvements.

Fourth, the company continued to offer extensive rebates during 1988 (of up to $4,000 per car on the Audi 5000) to clean out unsold inventory of all models, and it lowered its U.S. prices as much as 15 percent in 1989. Finally, the firm introduced several new models. During 1988, modestly changed versions of the 5000 model rolled out in two styles—the 100 and 200. Later in the fall a racier V8 version called the 300 would arrive to counteract the image of the 5000. VW expects to introduce a six-cylinder version of the five-cylinder 100 and is planning a fuel-efficient, convertible, all-aluminum sedan in 1993. These efforts are aimed at increasing sales from 45,000 to 50,000 by the mid-1990s.

In addition, the firm plans to expand and redesign the convertible Cabriolet model with new color schemes and features to attract affluent women buyers. In mid-1989 VW brought out the Corrado to compete against Mazda's RX-7 and the less-expensive Porsche AG models. The Passat was unveiled in 1990 at $14,770 to compete in the mid-size market, thus becoming the company's first mid-size debut. Finally, a $100,000 super luxury car is also planned.

Fahrvergnugen

Literally translated, Fahrvergnugen means the "pleasure of driving." VW has coupled their restructuring with this new but traditionally humorous campaign aimed at generating a bit of curiosity to hold consumers' attention long enough to notice VW's new strides, namely that they make more than just the Beetle. Management has decided that the company's competitive advantage is the way people feel when they drive a VW, and the new slogan mirrors the view. It is hoped that the new campaign will get consumers to inquire about Fahrvergnugen in the dealerships instead of just asking about the price or rebate, thereby giving the salesperson a chance to deal with value as a selling point.

EXHIBIT 1.12 VW's Fading Glory: U.S. Sales for Volkswagen of America, Including Audi Sales after 1971 (in thousands)

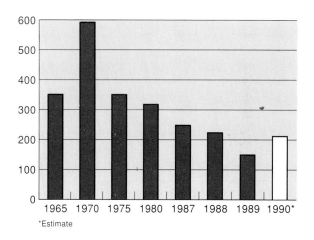

*Estimate

This restructuring and development of new models should save this essentially healthy automobile company. Although it is doing extremely well in Europe, the company believes it must succeed in the United States to remain a viable world-class auto company. These changes will have major and dramatic impact on the firm's human resources. People have lost their jobs in Westmoreland. Other dealerships will close. But new people will be hired as new products are developed and new dealerships will be added as the firm revives. In the long run, the firm will benefit, even though drastic action must be taken in the short run.

QUESTIONS

1. What role did a failed marketing and product development strategy have in VW's demise?

2. Do you think the planned restructuring and new product development will turn the company around? What will have to happen for these strategies to work?

3. How will the new strategies affect the firm's human resource strategy? Should any protections be provided for the employees at the Westmoreland plant who lost their jobs? If so, what ones?

4. At the time of this writing, Congress was considering a trade bill which would require companies to give advanced notification to communities before they closed a plant. Do you think such a bill is warranted? Why or why not?

5. What ethical responsibilities does the company have to each of these groups?

a. Employees

b. Stockholders

c. Dealers

6. Both the GM and VW cases have similarities in that restructuring and retrenchment is being undertaken to achieve renewal. However, the two cases also differ. In what ways do the two situations differ? Do you agree that retrenchment and restructuring are required by each company to achieve renewal? Is the retrenchment strategy *always* required in order to achieve renewal? Explain your answer.

ADDITIONAL READINGS

Anthony, William P. *Practical Strategic Planning: A Guide and Manual for Line Managers.* Westport, CT: Quorum Books, 1985.

Devanna, Mary Anne, Charles Fombrun, Noel Tichy, and E. Kirby Warren. "Strategic Planning and Human Resource Management." *Human Resource Management* 21, Spring 1982, pp. 11+.

Dolliver, Mark. "Volkswagen's Latest: Point Gets Lost in the Translation." *Adweek's Marketing Week.* February 12, 1990, p. 63.

Fossum, John A., and Donald F. Parker. "Building State-of-the-Art Human Resource Strategies." *Human Resource Management* 22, Spring/Summer 1983, pp. 97+.

Gwynne, S. C. "The Right Stuff." *Time.* October 29, 1990, pp. 74–84.

Hax, Arnoldo C. "A New Competitive Weapon: The Human Resource Strategy." *Training and Development Journal* 39, no. 5, May 1985, pp. 76–82.

Kelley, Tom. 1989 chairman of the American Society of Personnel Administrators' Board of Directors (now the Society of Human Resource Management), in an interview by John T. Adams III, "Strategic Partnerships in HRM." *Personnel Administrator.* January 1989, pp. 76–82.

Kravitz, Dennis. *The Human Resources Revolution.* 1988, San Francisco, CA: Jossey-Bass.

Linkow, Peter. "Human Resource Development at the Roots of Corporate Strategy." *Training and Development Journal* 39, no. 5, May 1985, pp. 85–87.

McLellan, R., and G. Kelly. "Business Policy Formulation: Understanding the Process." *Journal of General Management* 6, no. 1, Autumn 1980, pp. 38–47.

Mahoney, Thomas A., and John R. Deckop. "Evolution of Concept and Practice in Personnel Administration/Human Resource Management." *Journal of Management* 12, no. 2, Summer 1986, pp. 223–241.

Miller, Edwin, L., Schan Beechler, Bhal Bhatt, and Roghi Nath. "The Relationship Between the Global Strategic Planning Process and the Human Resource Management Function." *Human Resource Planning* 9, no. 1, 1986, pp. 9–23.

Ohmae, Kenichi. *The Mind of the Strategist.* New York: Penguin Books, 1983.

Peters, Thomas J., and Robert H. Waterman. *In Search of Excellence: Lessons from America's Best-Run Companies.* New York: Harper and Row, 1982.

Porter, Michael E. *Competitive Strategy: Techniques for Analyzing Industries and Competitors.* New York: The Free Press, 1980.

Quinn, James Brian, Henry Mintzberg, and Robert M. James. *The Strategy Process.* Englewood Cliffs, NJ: Prentice Hall, 1988.

Schmid, Hillel. "Managing the Environment: Strategies for Executives in Human Services Organizations." *Human Systems Management* 6, 1986, pp. 307–315.

Serafin, Raymond. "VW Pronounces Ad Shift." *Advertising Age.* February 5, 1990, p. 16.

Stertz, Bradley A. "Volkswagen Tries for a Little Mystique." *Wall Street Journal.* February 7, 1990, p. B6.

Thompson, Arthur A., Jr., and A. J. Strickland III. *Strategic Formulation and Implementation: The Tasks of the General Manager.* 3rd ed. Plano, TX: Business Publications, Inc., 1986.

Thompson, Arthur A., Jr., and A. J. Strickland III. *Strategic Management: Concepts and Cases.* 4th ed. Plano, TX: Business Publications, Inc., 1987.

Thompson, Arthur A., Jr., A. J. Strickland III, and William E. Fulmer. *Readings in Strategic Management.* 2nd ed. Plano, TX: Business Publications, Inc., 1987.

Walker, James W., and Gregory Moorehead. "CEOs: What They Want from HRM." *Personnel Administration.* December 1987, pp. 50–59.

Woodruff, David. "Audi Finally Gets Some Traction." *Business Week.* October 15, 1990, pp. 78–79.

....
NOTES

1. Adapted from S. C. Gwynne, "The Right Stuff," *Time,* October 29, 1990, pp. 74–84; Jacob M. Schlesinger, "GM to Reduce Company to Match Its Sales: Move to Shrink Itself Is First for Auto Maker," *Wall Street Journal,* April 25, 1988, p. 2; Paul Ingrassia, "And Now for the General Motors Story," *Wall Street Journal,* May 9, 1988, p. 9; Jacob M. Schlesinger and Joseph B. White, "The New Model GM Will Be More Compact but More Profitable," *Wall Street Journal,* June 6, 1988, pp. 1, 14; Jacob M. Schlesinger and Paul Ingrassia, "GM Woos Employees by Listening to Them, Talking of its 'Team,'" *Wall Street Journal,* January 12, 1989, pp. 1 and A6; speech by Allan Smith, executive vice-president of General Motors, "The People Factor in Competitiveness," presented at the University Club of Chicago, Illinois, December 6, 1988; A. Taylor, "Can GM Remodel Itself?" *Fortune,* January 13, 1992, pp. 26–34; and Neal Templin and Bradley Stertz, "Automakers Abandon Hope for a Spring Recovery,"

Wall Street Journal, January 27, 1992, p. B4; Jack Falvey, "Fix General Motors Now," *Wall Street Journal,* February 3, 1992, p. A12; Frank Swoboda and Warren Brown, "GM's Wrenching Task," *Tallahassee Democrat,* March 8, 1992, pp. E1+; Alex Taylor, "Can GM Remodel Itself?" *Fortune,* January 13, 1992, pp. 26–34; Joseph White and Bradley Stertz, "GM's Debt is Downgraded by Moody's; Big Three Chiefs Warn Japan on Trade Gap," *Wall Street Journal,* January 8, 1992, p. A2; Joseph White, "Stempel Says GM Turnaround Will Take Time," *Wall Street Journal,* March 11, 1992, pp. A3+.

2. See Lionel Giles, ed. and trans., *Sun Tzu on the Art of War.* (London: Luzae, 1910).

3. Alfred O. Chandler, Jr., *Strategy and Structure* (Cambridge, MA: MIT Press, 1962).

4. Peter Drucker, *The Practice of Management* (New York: Harper & Row, 1955).

5. Michael Porter, *Competitive Strategy* (New York: The Free Press, 1980), and Michael Porter, *Competitive Advantage* (New York: The Free Press, 1985).

6. This section is based on the following sources: W. F. Cascio, *Managing Human Resources* (New York: McGraw Hill, 1992); M. R. Carrell, F. E. Kuzmits, and N. F. Elbert *Personnel/Human Resource Management* (New York: Macmillian, 1992); W. B. Werther, and K. Davis, *Human Resources and Personnel Management* (New York: McGraw Hill, 1989); and A. W. Sherman, and G. W. Bohlander, *Managing Human Resources* (Cincinnati: South-Western, 1992).

7. "Bulletin to Management," *SHRM-BNA Survey* No. 56, Washington, DC: Bureau of National Affairs, Sept. 26, 1991, pp. 2–3.

8. Tom Kelley, 1989 chairman of the American Society of Personnel Administrators' Board of Directors (now the Society of Human Resource Management) in an interview by John T. Adams, III, "Strategic Partnerships in HRM," *Personnel Administrator,* January 1989, pp. 76–82.

9. Leonard A. Schlesinger, "The Normative Underpinnings of Human Resource Strategy," *Human Resource Management* 22, Spring/Summer 1983, pp. 83–96.

10. Robert Berra, "What It Takes to Succeed at the Top," *HRMagazine,* October 1991, pp. 34–37.

11. Peter Rosik, "Building a Customer-Oriented Department," *HRMagazine,* October 1991, pp. 64–66.

12. Randall S. Schuler, "Repositioning the Human Resource Function: Transformation or Demise?" *The Executive* 4, no. 3, August 1990, pp. 49–60.

13. Porter, *Competitive Advantage.* This concept is very similar to the concept of "differential advantage" used in marketing or "economic or comparative advantage" used in economics.

14. Michael D. Cohen, James C. March, and Johan P. Olsen, "A Garbage Can Model of Organizational Choice," *Administrative Science Quarterly* 17, no. 1, March 1972, pp. 1–25.

15. Arthur A. Thompson, Jr., and A. J. Strickland III, *Strategic Management,* 4th ed. (Plano, TX: Business Publications Inc., 1987), Ch. 1.

16. James Brian Quinn, *Strategies for Change: Logical Incrementalism* (Homewood, IL: Richard D. Irwin, 1980).

17. Tom Kelley, 1989 chairman of the American Society of Personnel Administrators' Board of Directors (now the Society of Human Resource Management), in an interview by John T. Adams III, "Strategic Partnerships in HRM," *Personnel Administrator,* January 1989, pp. 76–82.

18. Bradley A. Stertz and Thomas F. O'Boyle, "Volkswagen Aims to Halt Skid in U.S.: The Beetle Dream Is Now an Audi Nightmare," *Wall Street Journal,* May 6, 1988, p. 6; Thomas F. O'Boyle, "War of Attrition for Europe's Auto Market Intensifying," *Wall Street Journal,* May 17, 1988, p. 34; Terrance Roth, "Volkswagen Is Planning Cost Reductions of $754.7 Million to Aid Competition," *Wall Street Journal,* May 31, 1988, p. 20; David Woodruff, "Audi Finally Gets Some Traction," *Business Week,* October 15, 1990, pp. 78–79; Mark Dolliver, "Volkswagen Latest: Point Gets Lost in the Translation," *Adweek's Marketing Week,* February 12, 1990, p. 63; Bradley A. Stertz, "Volkswagen Tries for a Little Mystique," *Wall Street Journal,* February 7, 1990, p. B6; and Raymond Serafin, "VW Pronounces Ad Shift," *Advertising Age,* February 5, 1990, p. 16.

2

The External and Global Environment for Human Resources

The environment within which an organization operates is constantly changing, and the success of the organization lies in its ability to adopt or amend strategies to compensate or take advantage of the changes. In this chapter we break down the environment into areas of concern for human resource management with emphasis primarily on a broad and global view. We examine the components of the environment, how an organization learns of these components, and the basic strategies the organization can take in dealing with the environment, with particular emphasis on the resultant human resource strategies.

• • • • • • • • •
CHAPTER OBJECTIVES

After reading this chapter, you should be able to

1. Describe the components of an organization's external and global environments.

2. Explain how an organization knows or learns of these environments.

3. Describe how these environments impact the firm.

4. Describe the various basic positions an organization can establish with its environment.

Ma Bell Learns to Compete[1]

In late 1983, a federal antitrust suit forced American Telephone and Telegraph Company to divest itself of three-fourths of its $150 billion in assets. The trend toward competition, which had been developing in trucking, airlines, and other industries since the late 1970s, hit the communications industry, and AT&T in particular, full force. New rules to the ball game were being written. The breakup led to greater flexibility in the regulation of AT&T proper. No longer would monopoly power and government regulation provide a safe harbor for AT&T. The environment was being radically restructured. In other words, times were changing.

Meeting this drastic change in the environment has been a major challenge for AT&T. As a regulated utility, costs not efficiency drove its profits. Higher costs just expanded the base in which its regulated rate of return was calculated. This automatically boosted earnings. Competition changed all this. First, AT&T had to spin off its regional phone companies—the so-called baby bells—which now operate independently. In fact, AT&T now competes with the seven regional companies in short long-distance services. The company also lost its monopoly in the long-distance market as satellite technology opened this market to a host of competitive long-distance companies: Microtel, U.S. Sprint, and MCI, among others. In addition, resellers have emerged who buy long-distance time on AT&T lines at wholesale prices then resell it to customers. No longer could AT&T count on an assured income stream from long-distance and regional telephone services. It had to aggressively compete in the marketplace.

Competitive Strategy

Essentially, AT&T adopted a three-pronged competitive strategy: cut costs, develop new products, and aggressively market. Costs were cut by eliminating 27,000 jobs plus another 48,000 through layoffs and retirements. This amounted to approximately 20 percent of the workforce. Some work was shifted overseas. For example, residential phones are now made in Singapore. The number of models in AT&T's phone line was cut from 54 to 12. Domestic plants were automated. Sales personnel at its retail telephone stores were put on a commission bases. In short, the company adopted many of the same cost-cutting tactics used by nonregulated companies during the restructuring of the early 1980s.

New products were developed, especially computers suited to AT&T's particular needs. After all, the company believed that its Private Branch

Exchange (PBX) and switching systems were, in fact, computers. The company worked with Olivetti to develop new personal computers. In 1990, AT&T struck a deal with NEC Corporation in which some of AT&T's computer-aided design technology was traded for some of NEC's advanced logic chips. AT&T also formed a joint venture with Mitsubishi to make and market Mitsubishi Electric's memory chips in exchange for access to the technology that goes into designing the chip and the right to sell the semiconductor. Business office systems that had ties to telecommunications were also developed. The company adopted a strategy of information management that tried to link telecommunications with office computing.

AT&T also adopted an aggressive marketing campaign. The company hired Cliff Robertson as a television spokesperson. It began to develop creative advertisements for television, radio, and newspapers, and it even adopted telecommunications personal-selling strategies by calling various households to persuade them to select AT&T when asked to choose their long-distance carrier. A 600-member sales force was created just to sell computers, especially the new minicomputer and the powerful new personal computer. In fact, the move paid off as AT&T edged out IBM, NCR, and Digital Equipment for an order of 1,600 Unix-based personal computers at McDonald's.

In addition to the establishment of the 600-member sales force, it created many other new sales and marketing positions. The employees used to staff these posts were not hired from outside the firm but were transferred from other departments. This was only a small part of AT&T's innovative restructuring plan. While seeking to increase productivity, the company retrained many of its employees to work in sales and marketing positions. The downside of this large retraining project is that because many of these jobs required voluntary transfers on the part of the employees, employees who did not take the newly created posts were reassigned or terminated. Even though the firm did not force resignations, it did try to reduce nonrevenue-producing staff positions and to streamline overhead costs.

However frugal AT&T has become, they are continuing their generous pension, insurance, health care plans, and others benefits. As of July 1989, they were still providing a noncontributory-defined pension benefit plan covering substantially all management and nonmanagement employees. Nonmanagement employee benefits are based on a nonpay-related plan while the benefits for management employees are based on a career-average pay plan.

Like current employees, AT&T's retirees are also being cared for. The company's provided benefit plan includes health care and life insurance. In 1986 the company paid the annual insurance premiums, which amounted to $227 each, for approximately 87,000 retired employees.

As CEO James Olson stated, "No matter how correct our strategy is, our future rests with the men and women of AT&T who must make this strategy work."

Morale

All of this change has had an adverse effect on many employees who had grown up in the traditional AT&T culture. Under regulation, loyalty, commitment, and longevity was rewarded in a sort of "cradle to grave" management philosophy. The company took care of its employees as long as they went along. Innovation, challenge, and new ideas were not rewarded.

Therefore, this change has been particularly difficult for long-time employees brought up in the old system. Many could not adjust and have taken early retirement, quit, or transferred to the baby bells. Others have been fired. Some have managed to stay on the job by biding their time until early retirement.

Fortunately, AT&T has been considered one of the most innovative companies in labor relations. Early in the restructuring period, top company managers met with leaders of the company's two unions every few months for so-called common interest forums. Financial figures and improvements in products and services were discussed. In 1985, this process almost collapsed. However, by 1987 it had been revived. Progress has been made in improving the layoff process through crisis counseling, retraining, and transfer. While labor relations have not completely healed, they are improving, as is employee morale.

● ● ● ● ● ● ● ● ●

The AT&T case demonstrates the dramatic effect a change in a firm's external environment can have on its overall and human resource strategies. Deregulation changed the rules dramatically, virtually overnight. Employees and managers hired and schooled in one set of rules had to learn an entirely new set. Whereas loyalty and stability were once the primary employee attributes rewarded, innovation and change became the new desirable attributes. Reward systems had to change, socialization and training processes were modified, and performance appraisal now emphasized newly determined employee actions. The uncertainty caused by these changes hurt morale and further affected the company's deteriorating relationship with the unions. Yet, as the case indicates, AT&T is making a sound comeback. It is competing aggressively in both its old markets of long-distance service and telecommunications equipment and in its new market of computer technology.

STRATEGIC CHOICES

An organization makes strategic decisions in dealing with its environment. These decisions serve to link the organization with its environment and to establish the basic direction of the organization, as is shown in Exhibit 2.1. A firm can establish several basic strategic postures with the environment. Four, which follow the Miles and Snow topology,[2] are outlined below.

1. An organization can adopt a defender strategy. **Defenders** focus on a narrow line of products and strongly defend their position in the market

EXHIBIT 2.1   Strategic Decisions Link the Organization with the Environment

against anyone—competitors, government, and so on. Traditional cigarette companies prior to diversification, such as Liggett and Myers, used this strategy.

2. A second choice would be to become a prospector. **Prospectors** always are looking for new market opportunities and aggressively seek to develop both new products and new markets. IBM fits this strategy well, as does the new AT&T.

3. A firm can adopt an analyzer posture. **Analyzers** have a split personality. They have one product in a stable market and one in a changing market. In the stable market they operate routinely; in the rapidly changing market they closely watch their competitors and then adapt as best they can. The Schering-Plough Corporation uses this strategy. Known for producing mostly "me too" drugs (copies of drugs already on the market), the company has one stable product, the antibiotic Garamycin, that has been the mainstay of its prescription drug line. As the company watched its competitors advance in the biotech field, it embarked on a crash program to develop the drug Interferon.

4. Finally, firms can become reactors. A **reactor** company sees major changes in its environment but has difficulty changing quickly enough to meet these changes. Bethlehem Steel and other major steel companies have this strategy primarily because of fixed capital investment, size, and a high wage structure. Changing fast enough to meet foreign competition in steel is a continuing challenge for domestic steel companies.

Adopting any of these strategic profiles will impact human resources. Defenders would want aggressively trained specialists in the industry in order to produce and market their narrow line of products. Prospectors would want aggressive entrepreneurial types of people who are willing to take risks to develop new products and markets. Analyzers would value both stability and innovation in employees depending on which unit the employee worked. Finally, reactors would want employees who were less resistant to change and able to help the organization move along its chosen path.

Now that we have examined the basic strategic choices an organization makes in dealing with the environment, we can now examine the environmental components that impact overall strategy and human resource strategy formulation.

....

| EXHIBIT 2.2 | External Environment Sectors or Components |

EXTERNAL ENVIRONMENT

....

....
COMPONENTS OF THE EXTERNAL ENVIRONMENT

For our purposes, the external environment has seven sectors, as is shown in Exhibit 2.2. We are particularly interested in the trends that occur in each sector so that environmental change can be anticipated.

Economy

The economy sets the general level of business. While the government gathers many statistical measures of the economy, the three we are most interested in are the gross national product, inflation, and real disposable income. While other measures are also important (for example, leading indicators, lagging indicators, and so on), we focus on the three named above because they provide good basic descriptions of overall economic activity.

Gross National Product

Gross national product (GNP) is a total measure of all goods and services produced in a country for a period of time, usually one quarter or one year. It gives a broad measure of overall economic performance. Exhibit 2.3 shows the U.S. GNP for 1982 through 1991. Even though GNP has had its ups and downs during periods of

··

| **EXHIBIT 2.3** | GNP Growth in the United States |

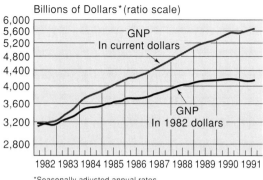

Billions of Dollars*(ratio scale)

*Seasonally adjusted annual rates

··

prosperity and recession, it has grown from $3,200 billion to $4,800 billion over the last eight years.

Inflation

Inflation measures the increase in the price of products and services. While there are various ways to measure inflation, for example, the GNP deflator, the producer price index, and the wholesale price index, the most popular measure of inflation is the consumer price index (CPI). Exhibit 2.4 shows the CPI for the 1983–1991 period. The index increased from about 98 to about 138. Note that there were some very rapid price increases surrounding the very stable prices during 1985 through 1987.

Real Disposable Income

This is a measure of after-tax income adjusted for inflation. It is a broad measure of the amount of money the citizens of a society have to purchase goods and services. Exhibit 2.5 (on page 39) shows how real disposable income increased from 1982 to 1991. Per capita disposable income in current dollars increased from about $9,500 per year in 1982 to just over $16,000 in 1990.

Labor Market

The labor market is a very important factor in determining human resource strategy. The labor market is the configuration of individuals working or available for employment in a particular geographic region—either a nation, region, state, or local area. Four key measures of the labor market will be examined: unemployment rate, education levels, occupation levels, and the age and sex mix.

Unemployment Rate

The unemployment rate measures the number or percent of people looking for work but unable to find it. It does not measure people not working and *not* looking for

---

EXHIBIT 2.4   CPI in the United States

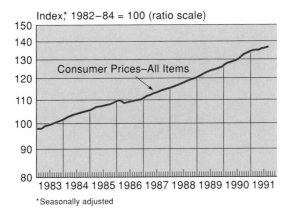

Index,* 1982–84 = 100 (ratio scale)

Consumer Prices–All Items

1983 1984 1985 1986 1987 1988 1989 1990 1991

*Seasonally adjusted

---

work as being unemployed (homemakers, retirees, and students, for example). These people are simply considered as being "out of the labor force."[3]

As Exhibit 2.6 (on page 40) shows, during the second half of the 1980s, the unemployment rate varied from a high of about 7.2 percent to a low of less than 5 percent in 1988. Note also in Exhibit 2.6 that the rate for African-Americans has been about twice that of white people and that of teenagers three times as high as the general rule. Of course, during periods of low unemployment it is often difficult to attract employees.[4]

Education Levels

The education level of the U.S. labor force is shown in Exhibit 2.7 (on page 41). Notice that workers with college degrees earn about twice that of those with a high-school education.

Occupational Levels

The U.S. labor force has become more white collar and professional and less blue collar and laborer, as is shown in Exhibit 2.8 (on page 42). Notice also the growth increase in employment in the service industries and the decline in manufacturing, mining, and farming shown in Exhibit 2.9 (on page 43). With respect to specific occupations, throughout the 1990s it is expected that the largest single job percentage climb will be for paralegals. With respect to an occupational field, health care will grow the most, followed by entry-level computer and customer service jobs.[5]

Labor Force 2000: What Will It Look Like?

The baby boomer generation—those people born between 1946 and 1964—produced millions of new participants in the work force. This large and comparatively homogenous group of workers made business employment decisions less complex. Now, the baby boomers are reaching middle age, and businesses must adapt to the changes in the work force to remain competitive in the 1990s and beyond.

FOCUS ON DIVERSITY •

Help for Teenage Unemployment

Alex Perez lives on New York City's lower east side. Because he is unemployed, he looks for work, but only sometimes. Most of the time he "hangs out" with some of the more than 100,000 teenagers like himself. Alex is unskilled and does not have a high school diploma. These two factors make both him and potential employers unsure of what he can do.

Alex is not alone. Only one in five teenagers in New York has a job or is looking for one. Other metropolitan areas face a similar situation. In Philadelphia, Chicago, and Detroit, fewer than 40 percent of the teenagers are in the labor force. These numbers are even higher for African-American and Hispanic youths.

Reasons for this problem are many. Some say that as an increasing number of laid-off white-collar workers enter the work force, the skill requirements grow. Others suggest that the types of industry that are prevalent in these areas of the country are not conducive to part-time jobs. Discrimination also has been cited as a cause of high teenage unemployment.

Whatever the reason, solutions must be found. In New York, youth counselors are working with teenagers to help them understand the job search process and to motivate them to continue to look. Sometimes these interventions work. For example, Asalmah Muhammad, an 18-year-old from Brooklyn, found a job with Mitsui through the Summer Jobs Program. The first time she had ever seen a Japanese person was during her interview. She admits that without the program she would have never even thought of applying at Mitsui.

SOURCE: Adapted from Paul Duke, Jr., "Urban Teen-Agers, Who Often Live Isolated from the World of Work, Shun the Job Market," *Wall Street Journal*, August 14, 1991, p. A10.

One of the greatest challenges that businesses face is the fact that the baby boomers are not having children of their own, or are postponing having children until their late 30s and early 40s. As a result, many businesses will have trouble filling entry-level positions due to the declining number of new workers. However, demographers have an eye on California. It seems that California is a proven bellwether of national legislative change, and this may translate into population changes as well. If this is true, there could be a rise in the number of births. Currently, one of every six births in the United States occurs in California. While the state still faces a shortage of people in the 15 to 24-year-old range, it appears that there will be an ample supply of workers in 20 years.[6]

This problem is made worse due to the fact that jobs are demanding more technical skills. The time when a worker could survive with a high school diploma is rapidly coming to an end. More and more businesses are requiring that their employees have writing, mathematical, computer, and other advanced skills to be able to work in today's more complex business environment.[7] Businesses are already having a difficult time filling technical positions (such as computer technicians), skilled/craftsman positions (such as mechanics and carpenters), and even basic unskilled labor positions.[8] This problem is made even worse by the fact that an increasing number of students are dropping out of school each year. The high school graduation rate for the United States is about 71 percent. The lowest level is found in the Southeast where only 67 percent of the high school students receive degrees.[9] Businesses are now in the position of having to pay higher wages for a smaller work pool, and investing additional money in job training programs.

The aging of the baby boomers has created another problem. The work force that was once predominantly white, male, and middle class is becoming more diversified. The 1960s and 1970s saw the entry of women into the workplace. Many of them are waiting until they reach their 30s and 40s before they have their first children.[10] For the first time, businesses must cope with maternity leaves, flexible work schedules, and even single mothers. The labor force participation rate for women

| EXHIBIT 2.5 | Real Disposable Income in the United States |

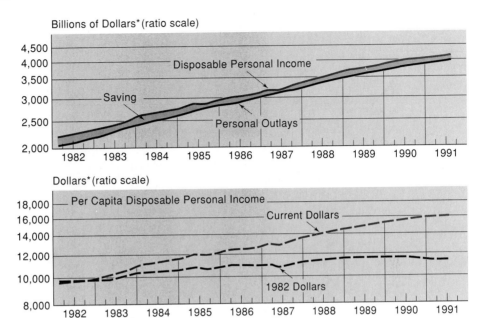

Billions of Dollars*(ratio scale)

Dollars*(ratio scale)

*Seasonally adjusted annual rates

with children under 3 rose to 54.5 percent in the fourth quarter of 1991.[11] The 1980s began the great wave of minority entries into the work force. This trend, which is expected to last well into the twenty-first century, also presents difficulties for businesses. Only 15 percent of the new employees in the work force through the year 2000 will be white males. The rest will be women, African-Americans, Hispanics, Asians, and other ethnic groups.[12] *Nation's Business* describes the problem this way:

> Little by little, senior executives and management experts across America are recognizing that these vast demographic shifts demand a new way of running things—an approach often called "managing diversity." This means recognizing that diversity is already a fact of life, learning to understand "culturally different" workers and creating an environment in which they will flourish.[13]

Another impact on cultural diversity in the workplace is the increasing number of foreigners settling in the United States. In October of 1991, a new law went into effect that raised the number of legal immigrants entering the United States annually to 700,000. Not only do these new Americans make the workplace more culturally diverse, they also tend to lower the education level. Approximately 36 percent of the male immigrants in 1988 lacked a high school education, more than double the rate for American males.[14]

These changing demographic patterns all affect the way firms operate. Old methods and traditions are rapidly becoming obsolete. Business managers must be aware of and adapt to these trends if they wish to succeed in the coming years.

EXHIBIT 2.6   Unemployment Rates in the United States, 1985–1990

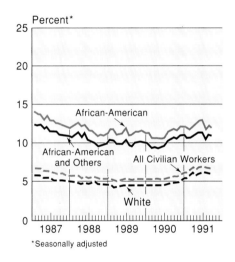

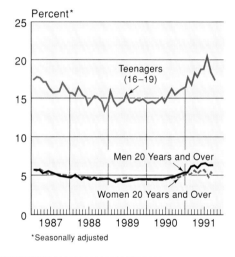

Age and Sex

As Exhibit 2.10 (on page 44) shows the labor force is more female and older than in the past. Almost 60 percent of women are now in the labor force compared to 80 percent of men. Male rates are declining while female rates are increasing. In the 35-to-44-year age group of women the participation rate is over 70 percent. Exhibit 2.10 shows the projected age and sex composition of the labor force in 1995.

Technology

The next environmental sector we examine is technology. Technology has a major influence on the formulation of overall and human resource strategy. Technology is the art and science of the production and distribution of goods and services.[15] It has

EXHIBIT 2.7   Education Levels of the U.S. Labor Force

Year	Civilian Labor Force (000)	Less Than 4 Years of High School	4 Years of High School Only	1 to 3 Years of College	4 Years or More of College
1970	61765	36.1% 22297	38.1% 23532	11.8% 7288	14.1% 8709
1975	67774	27.5% 18638	39.7% 26906	14.4% 9759	18.3% 12403
1980	78010	20.6% 16070	39.8% 31048	17.6% 13730	22.0% 17162
1985	88424	15.9% 14059	40.2% 35546	19.0% 16801	24.9% 22018
1988	94870	14.7% 13946	39.9% 37853	19.7% 18689	25.7% 24382

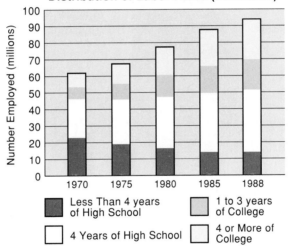

Distribution of Labor Force (Education)

Legend:
- Less Than 4 years of High School
- 4 Years of High School
- 1 to 3 years of College
- 4 or More of College

a substantial impact on the design of jobs in an organization—a critical human resource issue.

The most significant technological advance over the last twenty-five years affecting employment has been the revolution in information handling brought on by the computer, including the personal computer. The computer has allowed much quicker access to and processing of information and has upgraded job requirements for most clerical and staff assistant jobs. In *In the Age of the Smart Machine*, Shoshana Zuboff argues that the effects of the computer have yet to be felt since work itself will change completely as information becomes more readily available right at the work station.[16] Computers have also spawned robotics, the use of computer-controlled machines, in such diverse areas as welding in auto assembly and forming in steel production. For example, robotic welders and other automated computer-controlled processes reduced the labor force by one-half, from over 1,400 people to about 700 employees, at the Chicago Heights Ford stamping plant over the

....

EXHIBIT 2.8   Employment by Occupational Group

Employment by Major Occupational Groups
1986 Data (000 Omitted)

Managers and Administrative Workers	Professional and Technical Workers	Sales Workers	Clerical and Administrative Support	Agriculture, Forestry, Fishing, etc. Workers	Production, Materials, Maintenance	Service Workers
6665 7.20%	15930 17.22%	10574 11.43%	17136 18.52%	525 0.57%	27461 29.68%	14240 15.39%

Percentage Distribution of Employed
By Major Occupational Category

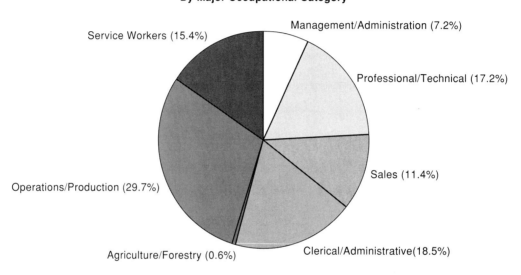

....

1981–1988 period. Robotics has led to the development of **artificial intelligence**—the use of computers to simulate the knowledge and thinking patterns of experts.

Other significant technological advances include superconductivity, genetic engineering, fiberoptics, and microelectronics. **Superconductivity** refers to transmitting electricity at almost zero resistance. This will revolutionize electrical transmission from power lines to electrical circuitry in computers. **Genetic engineering** refers to artificially changing the DNA molecule in genes to change biological characteristics. **Fiberoptics** allows the transmission of data, voice, pictures, or other types of information along a beam (laser) light. Finally, **microelectronics** will result in even smaller computers, new artificial organs, and many other developments in electronics where space is a limitation.

Technology is changing rapidly, and monitoring as well as predicting this change is a strategic challenge for all organizations. Developing new products that are not obsolete before they hit the market requires systematic attention to this sector of the external environment.

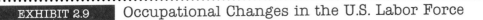

EXHIBIT 2.9   Occupational Changes in the U.S. Labor Force

Employees in Goods Producing Industries
1950–1988 (000 omitted)

Legend: Mining, Construction, Durable Goods, Nondurable Goods

Employees in Three Major Sectors
1950–1988 (000 omitted)

Legend:
— ▲ — Service Producing Employees
— ■ — Goods Producing Employees
— ♦ — Government Employees

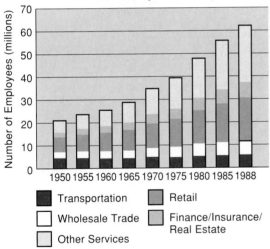

Number of Employees
in Service Producing Industries
1950–1988 (000 omitted)

Legend: Transportation, Wholesale Trade, Other Services, Retail, Finance/Insurance/Real Estate

Employment Trends (by industry) Selected Years (1950–1988)	1950	1955	1960	1965	1970	1975	1980	1985	1988
Goods Producing									
Mining	901	792	712	632	623	752	1027	927	721
Construction	2364	2839	2926	3232	3588	3525	4346	4673	5125
Durable Goods	8094	9541	9459	10405	11208	10688	12187	11490	11437
Nondurable Goods	7147	7341	7337	7656	8158	7635	8098	7770	7967
Total Goods Producing	18506	20513	20434	21925	23577	22600	25658	24860	25250
Service Producing									
Transportation	4034	4141	4004	4036	4515	4542	5146	5238	5548
Wholesale Trade	2635	2926	3143	3466	3993	4415	5275	5717	6029
Retail Trade	6751	7610	8248	9250	11047	12645	15035	17356	19110
Finance/Ins./RE	1888	2298	2629	2977	3645	4165	5160	5955	6676
Other Services	5357	6240	7378	9036	11548	13892	17890	22000	25600
Total Service Producing	20665	23215	25402	28765	34748	39659	48506	56266	62963
Government	6026	6914	8353	10074	12554	14686	16241	16394	17372

Legal/Political

Probably no other sector of the external environment has had a greater impact on human resource management than the changes in the legal environment over the past sixty years. Legislation has been passed covering virtually every aspect of the employment relationship from hiring to firing. Exhibit 2.11 (on page 45) lists the significant court cases and Exhibit 2.12 (on pages 46 ad 47) provides a summary of

EXHIBIT 2.10 Age, Sex, and Race of the Labor Force Projected to 1995 and Beyond

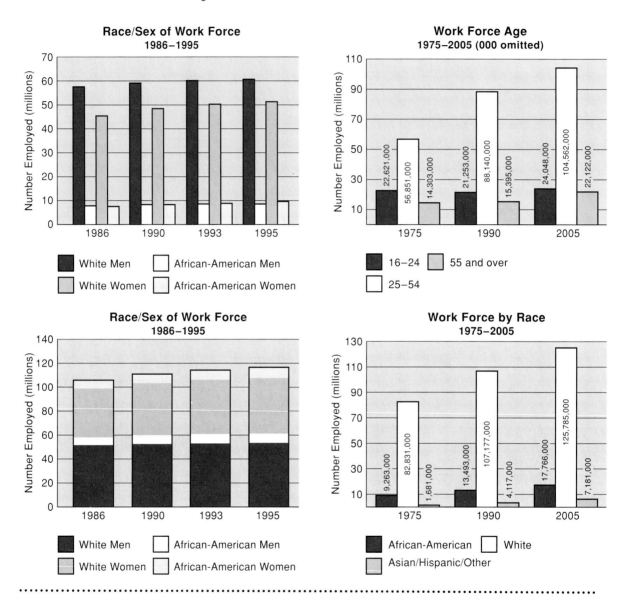

the legislation for this sixty year period. However, we do not discuss these laws in this chapter. Rather, we will deal with each law and significant court case as we review key issues in human resource management in the following chapters.

The legal environment provides a complex web of rules that very much constrains and specifies what can legally be done in human resource management. These

EXHIBIT 2.11	Major Court Cases Related to Human Resources

CASE	YEAR
Griggs v. *Duke Power* Strengthened 1964 Civil Rights Act by requiring companies to prove that selection procedures do not discriminate.	1971
Albemarle Paper v. *Moody* "Tests" must be valid predictors of performance; burden of proof falls on employer.	1975
Washington v. *Davis* Tests are not illegal, even if they cause "adverse" impact, as long as they are job related.	1976
Kaiser Aluminum v. *Weber* "Reverse discrimination" (favoring blacks over whites) in affirmative action is *not* illegal, at least when a company and union voluntarily agreed to an affirmative action plan for training.	1979
Texas Department of Community Affairs v. *Burdine* Burden of proof in sex discrimination rests first with employee that application was made then rejected, then with employer to prove nondiscrimination.	1981
Ford Motor Company v. *EEOC* Employer may cut off liability for back pay in discrimination penalty if job reinstatement is offered.	1982
Arizona Governing Committee v. *Norris* Deferred compensation can discriminate against women if they receive lower monthly benefits, despite equal contributions. Gender cannot be used to predict longevity.	1983
Memphis Fire Fighters, Local v. *Stotts* A bona fide seniority system takes precedence over affirmative action in a layoff.	1984
Wards Care v. *Atonio* Substantially weakened disparate impact standard of *Griggs* v. *Duke Power*. Plaintiff must shoulder the burden of *disproving* an employer's assertion that a practice adopted and administered by the employer itself is a legitimate one. Cannot just cite statistics to "prove" discrimination.	1989
Martin v. *Wilks* White men could challenge a court-approved affirmative action plan.	1989
Patterson v. *McClean* Plaintiff cannot sue under the 1866 Civil Rights Act for discrimination in employment.	1989

laws developed because of abuses in the labor market: child labor, sexual harassment, lack of protection against injury or layoff for old age and disability, and systematic discrimination of groups, resulting in extreme poverty. We sometimes forget the abuses that spawned the plethora of laws related to employment and human resources summarized in Exhibit 2.12.

··

| EXHIBIT 2.12 | Major Laws Related to Human Resources |

ACT	YEAR

EQUAL EMPLOYMENT OPPORTUNITY

Title VII, Civil Rights Act — 1964
Prohibits discrimination in employment on basis of race, religion, color, sex, or national origin.

Executive Orders 11246 and 11375 — 1965/1967
Requires federal contractors and subcontractors to eliminate employment discrimination and prior discrimination through affirmative action.

Age Discrimination in Employment Act (as amended) — 1967/1978
Prohibits discrimination against persons ages 40–70, and restricts mandatory retirement requirements, except where age is a "bona fide occupational qualification."

Executive Order 11478 — 1969
Prohibits discrimination in the Postal Service and in the various government agencies on the basis of race, color, religion, sex, national origin, handicap, or age.

Pregnancy Discrimination Act — 1978
Prohibits discrimination against women affected by pregnancy, childbirth, or related medical conditions. Requires that they be treated as all other employees for employment-related purposes, including benefits.

Equal Pay Act — 1963
Requires equal pay for men and women performing substantially the same work.

Vocational Rehabilitation Act, Rehabilitation Act of 1974 — 1973/1974
Prohibits employers with federal contracts over $2,500 from discriminating against handicapped individuals.

Vietnam Veterans Readjustment Act — 1974
Prohibits discrimination against Vietnam-era veterans by federal contractors and the U.S. government and requires affirmative action.

Americans with Disabilities Act — 1990
Makes it illegal to discriminate against individuals with disabilities in employment, public accommodation, public services, transportation, and telecommunications.

Civil Rights Act — 1991
Focuses on establishing an employer's responsibility for justifying hiring practices that seem to adversely affect people because of their race, color, religion, sex, or national origin.

WAGE AND HOUR

Fair Labor Standards Act — 1936
Sets minimum wage and overtime payment regulations.

Walsh-Healey Act — 1936
Sets pay at prevailing wage for federal supply contracts over $10,000.

Davis-Bacon Act — 1931
Sets pay at prevailing wage for federal construction projects over $2,000.

··

EXHIBIT 2.12 continued

ACT	YEAR

HEALTH AND BENEFITS

Occupational Safety and Health Act (OSHA) — 1970
Establishes comprehensive safety and health guidelines.

Early Retirement Income Security Act (ERISA) — 1974
Regulates pension funds to ensure that employees actually get money when
they retire.

Social Security Act — 1935
Establishes old age and survivors' insurance and retirement income.
Establishes unemployment insurance system.

Workers Compensation Laws — Early 1900s
Provides compensation for job related injuries.

PROTECTION

Federal Privacy Act — 1974
Provides protection for federal employee records and other information.

Consumer Credit Protection Act — 1968
Limits and restricts the amount of wages that can be garnished.

TRAINING

Job Training Partnership Act — 1983
Establishes a system of federal funding for training programs with business
(superceded MTDA and CETA).

LABOR LAW

Wagner Act (National Labor Relations Act) — 1935
Essentially legalized unions.

Taft-Hartley (Labor-Management Relations Act) — 1947
Specified illegal actions of unions; enhanced power of employers.

Landrum-Griffin (Labor-Management Reporting and Disclosure Act) — 1959
Provided protections for union members; restricted union actions toward
members.

IMMIGRATION

Immigration Reform and Control Act — 1986
Makes hiring of illegal immigrants illegal; imposes major record-keeping
requirements to document employees.

Because of the complexity of the law and the frequency of changing interpretations due to court cases and administrative rule making, wise managers rely on legal advice from an attorney when questions arise. In this textbook we cover the basics that most managers should be familiar with, but our intent is not to train managers to be attorneys in employment law.

The political aspect of this sector refers to the political processes and mood of the nation, which has ebbed and flowed from conservative to liberal throughout its history. In recent history, the relatively liberal years of Kennedy/Johnson in the 1960s were followed by the conservative years of Nixon, Ford, and Reagan in the 1970s, 1980s, and 1990s. Even the Carter administration is viewed as somewhat conservative.

Under the more conservative political climate, especially under Reagan in the 1980s, the enforcement of antitrust laws were not as stringent as they were previously. Hence, the 1980s saw many takeovers and mergers—a favorite corporate strategy of that decade. Perhaps 1990s will see a less conservative climate and a tightening of antitrust enforcement.

Political trends are closely related to social and demographic trends in that politics is largely shaped by the character and mood of the people of a society. This is the next sector we will examine.

Social/Demographic

This sector of the environment refers to social and demographic characteristics that make up a society. It includes its cultural values, norms, and institutions as well as its physical characteristics of age, sex, and geographic breakdowns. Life-style issues are also part of this issue.

In general, the U.S. population is becoming older and more urban. The most significant population trend of this century has been the baby boom generation born after World War II. As this group ages, the median age of the population will age and life-styles will change. In 1970, the median age was 28.0. By 1990 it was 32.8 and it is projected to be 37.3 by 2030.

Exhibit 2.13 shows the projected growth of the top twenty major population areas from 1987 to 2005. The most rapidly growing areas are in the Sunbelt from California through Texas to Florida. Exhibit 2.14 shows the 20 metropolitan areas with the most rapid growth from 1980 to 1987 and their expected down turn from 1987 to 2010.

Total U.S. population is expected to increase to 260,000,000 by 1995 from 239,000,000 in 1985. Overall population growth and regional migration has an overall impact on strategy formulation. Labor force composition is driven by population characteristics: age and geographic distribution, growth, and so on. These factors very much affect corporate and human resource strategy.

For example, many companies have moved operations and headquarters to the Sunbelt. A growing labor force, low sentiment for unions, space, lower taxes, better climate, and lower wage rates all have been factors in this movement. The movement feeds on itself. As companies move so do people. Many families left the rust bowl sections in the upper midwest and Northeast to find jobs in California, Texas, Florida, Arizona, North Carolina, and other Sunbelt states. However, this trend may be changing.[17]

| EXHIBIT 2.13 | Projected Growth for Top 20 Metropolitan Areas by Total Increase |

	POPULATION*		CHANGE 1987–2005	PERCENTAGE POINT CHANGE
	1987	2005		
Los Angeles–Long Beach, CA	8,225.1	10,230.3	2,005.3	24.4%
Anaheim–Santa Ana, CA	2,255.5	4,141.0	1,885.5	83.6
Dallas, TX	2,397.7	3,827.2	1,429.4	59.6
Atlanta, GA	2,556.0	3,848.6	1,292.6	50.6
Oakland, CA	1,994.3	3,101.1	1,106.8	55.5
Tampa–St. Petersburg–Clearwater, FL	1,960.4	3,036.4	1,076.0	54.9
Phoenix, AZ	1,864.5	2,839.2	974.6	52.3
San Jose, CA	1,454.4	2,351.4	897.0	61.7
Denver, CO	1,693.9	2,529.5	835.5	49.3
Sacramento, CA	1,317.5	2,149.9	832.4	63.2
Washington, D.C.–MD–VA	3,541.0	4,367.6	826.6	23.3
San Diego, CA	2,196.5	3,011.9	815.4	37.1
Orlando, FL	919.1	1,712.4	793.3	86.3
Fort Lauderdale–Hollywood–Pompano Beach, FL	1,185.3	1,948.7	763.4	64.4
Nassau–Suffolk, NY	2,703.6	3,416.1	712.6	26.4
San Francisco, CA	1,587.4	2,254.1	666.7	42.0
Houston, TX	3,316.7	3,974.8	658.2	19.8
Minneapolis–St. Paul, MN–WI	2,307.7	2,922.1	614.4	26.6
West Palm Beach–Boca Raton–Delray Beach, FL	786.7	1,377.2	590.4	75.0
Riverside–San Bernardino, CA	2,017.6	2,592.2	574.5	28.5

* In thousands

Competition

The strategies and practices of competitors have a major impact on strategy formulation. If a company discovers that its competitor pays higher wages for similar jobs, that company must decide to match or exceed those wage rates if it expects to attract and retain a productive work force.

Other strategies of competitors can set the overall level of business of a particular firm. For example, even though Apple Computer has experienced tremendous growth since its founding, it faced major competition when IBM entered the personal computer market in the mid-1980s. IBM is a formidable competitor and initially had an adverse effect on Apple. Apple hired John Scully from Pepsico as its CEO to design a new corporate and marketing strategy and has rebounded nicely.

Its stock rose from $18 a share to over $44 by 1988 *after* a two for one split.

FOCUS ON DIVERSITY ●

The Midwest on the Rise Again

Watch out "Coasties" and "Southerners," the "Mid-westerners" are on the rise. In the 1980s, people left the Midwest and headed for either the coasts or the south. What they left behind, they thought, was the "Rust Belt," outdated factories and shrinking rural communities. But now, when the coasts and the south are reporting declines in financial-services, computer and defense spending, and real estate values, the Midwest is moving forward. While most of its success can be attributed to its diversified manufacturing base, which has begun to expand due to a surge in exports, all areas look good. In fact, even the farmers look for a good year.

A quick comparison of statistics will help to prove the point. While retail sales on the coasts were down, they were up in the Midwest. Unemployment on the coasts was up while it fell in the Midwest. The price of single-family housing sank on both coasts in 1990; in the Midwest, defined as the 13-state region from Ohio

to Nebraska, it rose 4 percent. However, even with the rise in house prices in the Midwest, they are still extremely affordable. For example, the median house price in Peoria, Illinois, during the first quarter of 1991 was $48,400, which is about $7,000 less than a 1991 Cadillac Allante.

These positive statistics are wooing back Midwesterners who left during the 1980s. The chamber of commerce in Omaha, Nebraska, reported a record number of inquiries about moving to the area. The unemployment rate of 2.9 percent probably fueled the inquiries. But Indiana and Wisconsin have also seen an increase in the number of people returning after short stays on the coasts. Most of the returning cite Midwestern values and living pace as the reason for their return. Whatever the reason, the Midwest is on the rise again.

SOURCE: Adapted from Robert Rose and Alex Kotlowitz, "Midwest's Revenge: Once the 'Rust Belt,' Heartland Fares Better than Coastal States," *Wall Street Journal,* July 30, 1991, p. A1+

Competitive factors have always been a major force in strategy formulation, but they took on renewed importance during the early 1980s when the United States experienced its worst recession since the depression of the 1930s. Michael Porter's book, *Competitive Strategy,* set the tune for the new competitiveness.[18] He presents a model for analyzing the competitive environment, which is shown in Exhibit 2.15. Note that this model considers all relevant aspects of competition from specific competitive actions to substitute products. Essentially, Porter's model indicates that there are four major factors that determine the competitive arena for an individual firm. These are (1) the potential new entrants into the marketplace, (2) the firm's customers, (3) the actions of various suppliers, and (4) the availability of substitutes for the firm's products. Each of these forces interacts with the others in a dynamic fashion to establish a certain level and type of competition.

For example, the competitive arena of the auto industry is much different than that for the restaurant industry because each of the four major forces at work are so different. Compared with the restaurant industry, the auto industry has few substitute products, few potential new entrants, a rather limited set of suppliers, and customers who make infrequent purchases.

We will revisit the issue of competition in Chapter 3, Formulating a Corporate Strategy, since it has such profound effects on a company. We will also explain how overall corporate strategy formulation affects human resource strategy in Chapter 3. However, at this time we can summarize the competitive arena by noting two major trends. First, competition has become global in many markets, especially consumer electronics and computers, steel, and automobiles. No longer can U.S. firms ignore the strong competition that comes from other countries, especially Germany, Japan, Taiwan, and Korea. Second, U.S. firms experienced a major acquisition binge during the 1980s as we have previously indicated. This series of acquisitions and mergers involved both foreign firms and domestic firms and has served to consolidate the

| EXHIBIT 2.14 | The Top 20 Metropolitan Areas Where Rapid Growth from 1980 to 1987 Is Expected to Lead to Negative Growth from 1987 to 2010 |

		ANNUAL POPULATION GROWTH 1970–87	ANNUAL POPULATION GROWTH 1987–2010	PERCENTAGE POINT CHANGE
1	Naples, FL	7.24	2.78	−4.46
2	Fort Collins–Loveland, CO	4.05	0.70	−3.35
3	Fort Myers–Cape Coral, FL	6.11	2.81	−3.30
4	Brownsville–Harlingen, TX	3.71	0.46	−3.25
5	Reno, NV	3.83	0.73	−3.10
6	Ocala, FL	5.71	2.63	−3.08
7	Fort Pierce, FL	6.00	2.97	−3.03
8	McAllen–Edinburg–Mission, TX	4.34	1.54	−2.80
9	Daytona Beach, FL	3.98	1.35	−2.63
10	Las Vegas, NV	4.65	2.03	−2.62
11	Olympia, WA	4.02	1.41	−2.61
12	Sarasota, FL	4.41	1.84	−2.57
13	Boise City, ID	3.26	0.77	−2.49
14	Bremerton, WA	3.22	0.83	−2.39
15	Richland–Kennewick–Pasco, WA	2.81	0.51	−2.30
16	Brazoria, TX	3.21	0.96	−2.25
17	Vancouver, WA	3.04	0.82	−2.22
18	Boulder–Longmont, CO	2.89	0.71	−2.18
19	West Palm Beach–Boca Raton–Delray Beach, FL	4.85	2.70	−2.15
20	Lakeland–Winter Haven, FL	3.08	0.94	−2.14

power of many into the hands of a few in many domestic industry sectors. The strategy of acquisition and takeover has been a consistent one during the 1890s and has caused firms to design both offensive and defensive competitive takeover strategies. In particular the *hostile* takeover has been troublesome for many firms. We will examine this in the next chapter also.

Market (Customer/Clients)

The last major sector of the environment that affects strategy formulation is the market. There is no question that the market and industry characteristics drive much of the corporate strategy. This environmental sector is closely related to competition since competitive forces interplay within specific markets. But the sector goes beyond competition. For example, the market itself presents a set of challenges for a firm. The firm must answer these questions, among others:

EXHIBIT 2.15   Porter's Forces of Competition Model

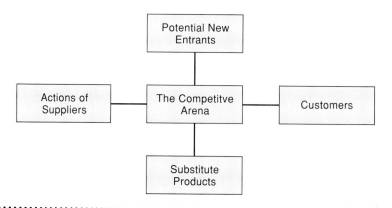

1. Who exactly is the customer?
2. Do we have several distinct customer groups?
3. How shall we define our market(s)?
4. What industry and market characteristics must we be aware of?
5. How is our market and customer changing?
6. What does it take to be successful in our market(s)?
7. What wage and employment patterns exist in our market(s)?

Developing accurate answers to these questions is critical for successful strategy formulation. Again we examine this issue in more depth in Chapter 3.

So we see that these seven environmental sectors present much information for the organization—almost too much information to be handled in an efficient way. How does an organization get a grip on this formidable environment? How does it *know* this environment? How does it decide what it needs to know and what it can safely ignore? In short, how can an organization manage the information presented to it by the environment? These issues are addressed in the Knowing the Environment section, later in this chapter.

GLOBAL BUSINESS ENVIRONMENT

The global business environment has changed dramatically since the end of World War II in 1945. The United States became the world's economic superpower as a result of the war. The war destroyed the economies of Great Britain, France, Italy, Germany, and Japan, and these nations had to rely on U.S. aid to rebuild. However, these nations began to reassert their industrial might and challenged the United States' economic supremacy during the 1970s. Traditional U.S. products, such as electronics, steel, automobiles, and heavy machinery, all faced stiff foreign competition. The 1980s produced more competition with the rise of newly industrialized countries, such as South Korea, Singapore, and Taiwan.[19] The decade ended with a partial move toward a market-based economy by many former communist nations, like the Soviet Union and Poland.

EXHIBIT 2.16	The Ten Largest Public Companies in the World by Market Value as of June 30, 1991 (in millions of U.S. dollars)

RANK 1991	RANK 1990	NAME	COUNTRY	VALUE	PERCENTAGE CHANGE FROM 1989
1	1	Nippon Telephone and Telegraph	Japan	$96,749	23
2	6	Exxon	U.S.	$72,656	68
3	3	Royal Dutch/Shell Group	Neth./UK	$69,296	−9
4	4	General Electric	U.S.	$64,611	9
5	5	Industrial Bank of Japan	Japan	$60,110	1
6	13	Philip Morris	U.S.	$58,815	20
7	2	International Business Machines	U.S.	$55,614	N/A
8	8	Fuji Bank	Japan	$53,822	−15
9	12	Mitsubishi Bank	Japan	$53,039	−23
10	10	Dai-Ichi Kangyo Bank	Japan	$51,890	−27

Some of the most sweeping changes have occurred and continue to occur in the new Commonwealth of Independent States. Maps become out of date overnight as yet another republic announces its freedom. As these new republics acquire their independence, they are beginning to realize that they will not be able to become economically stable on their own. Foreign investment and joint ventures have already begun. AT&T sold a digital switching system directly to the Armenian government, bypassing Moscow for the first time, and Chevron and Amoco are both attempting to gain access to the huge Tenghiz oil field. Some firms are waiting until Russia and the republics establish an effective credit and banking infrastructure at the republic level so that the ruble, which cannot be converted into dollars, regains some value. It is important that these firms do not wait too long, because the window of opportunity may be smaller than first imagined.[20]

The changes that occurred over the past few years have resulted in a more complex global business environment and vastly expanded markets. Not only are foreign firms building plants and doing business in the United States, but U.S. firms are operating overseas as well. For example, American computer giant IBM earned over $4 billion in profits on overseas revenues of $34.4 billion in 1988. This represented 58 percent of the company's total revenues and 75 percent of its profits for the year.[21] General Motors, Ford, Chrysler, Xerox, Texaco, and Mobil all have international subsidiaries big enough to be included in the list of the 500 largest corporations outside of the United States.[22] *Fortune* magazine now provides a ranking of the top 500 global firms as well as its Fortune 500 list. Clearly, organizations now compete in a global economy.[23]

The U.S. gross domestic product (GDP), which measures the total value of all goods and services produced in a country in a year, was $4.8 billion in 1988. In comparison, the GDP of the European Common Market nations[24] was $4.7 billion, while Japan's GDP was $2.8 billion.[25] Japan has even surpassed the United States in the market value of its firms. As shown in Exhibit 2.16, the ten largest industrial firms in the world in terms of market value in 1991 included five Japanese firms, four U.S. firms, and one European firm.[26] The United States is no longer the only market in the world.

The 1890s proved the importance of the international sector, which will be more significant in the 1990s and beyond as the world economy develops further. This expansion of the international sector presents new *opportunities* for firms, but it also presents new *threats*. As a result, each firm must consider many issues when deciding whether to operate in the global business environment.

Causes of More Global Business

Why do firms choose to operate overseas? One of the most common reasons is the ability to *reduce costs*. By locating plants abroad, firms can be closer to their supply of raw materials. This step eliminates the need for expensive transportation, insurance, and administration costs. The availability of inexpensive labor also reduces costs. Labor costs in the United States are affected by more than minimum wage and overtime laws and labor contracts. Taxes, such as social security, unemployment, and worker's compensation, and employee perquisites all add to labor costs. In contrast, many nations do not have or enforce wage laws, and labor unions and perquisites are often weak or nonexistent. As a result, firms can significantly reduce their labor costs by establishing plants overseas. Finally, costs can be reduced by building semifinished goods abroad. By producing most of an item abroad, especially labor-intensive products, firms can drive costs below domestic costs. To prosper, global firms must invest wherever opportunity is the greatest, whether that means the United States, Mexico, South Korea, or Japan.[27]

 Firms will choose to locate abroad due to *less government regulation* in other countries. Two of the most common factors are pollution controls and safety requirements placed on firms. Plant emission controls, OSHA requirements, waste disposal, and many other pollution and safety laws increase the costs of doing business in the United States. These requirements may not exist or are waived in other countries, especially in those that are trying to attract new businesses.

Locating abroad can enable firms to be closer to their product markets. This cuts transportation costs and helps firms to learn the unique characteristics of each market.

The international sector can provide access to growth opportunities that are not available at home. Several U.S. banks and stockbrokerages operate subsidiaries in Tokyo, Japan, to be near the world's largest securities market, which is nearly three times bigger than the New York Stock Exchange. So far the results are mixed. American competitors such as Chase, Citicorp, and Security Pacific have all lost money. On the other hand, Salomon Brothers, Morgan Stanley, and Goldman Sachs earned a combined pretax income of over $74 million in the first half of 1989. As John Wadsworth of Morgan Stanley's Tokyo office states, "The opportunities here are huge."[28]

Firms also locate facilities abroad to take advantage of labor force quantity and quality. It is not difficult to find areas where the people want to work and where the local government wants foreign firms to be there to put its people to work. While the labor quantity may be abundant, there can be problems with quality. Some nations, such as South Korea, have an educated and skilled workforce. In other nations some workers, such as farmers migrating to the cities, often lack the basic skills needed for jobs in factories.[29]

Many firms will locate facilities overseas to *avoid or reduce trade and tariff barrier problems*. Japanese automobile manufacturers have been abiding by a self-imposed export quota to the United States since the mid-1980s to avoid potential tariff prob-

FOCUS ON INTERNATIONAL ISSUES •

The Exportation of Clerical Jobs

In a small Irish town of 3,000, where unemployment averages nearly 20 percent, Cigna Corporation, an insurance company from Connecticut, has hired 120 young Irish workers to process medical claims flown in daily from the United States. The pay for these workers averages about $11,000 a year. Across town, at Mc-Graw-Hill Data Services–Ireland, 40 women working full-time and a dozen part-time workers maintain the worldwide circulation files for McGraw-Hill, Inc., magazines by a direct link to McGraw-Hill's mainframe computers in Highstown, New Jersey.

These two examples are just that: examples of a trend. American businesses are moving "back office" jobs overseas where the wages are cheaper, people speak English, and the state of the art telecommunications facilities allow instantaneous links to American companys' host computers. The most popular locations for these back offices are Barbados, Jamaica, the Philippines, Singapore, and Ireland. The jobs in these offices can range from simple accounting, medical transcriptions, and telemarketing, to technical support for high-technology products.

But don't blame it all on American companies. Many have been lured to Ireland. To increase it's attractiveness to foreign companies, Ireland took many steps. The country invested $3.5 billion to upgrade its telecommunications network with both satellite technology and fiber-optic cables. They have supplied tax breaks, employment grants, training grants, construction grants, and have promised a 10 percent tax rate until the year 2010.

Once there, the businesses find qualified employees and very little turnover. With an over 20 percent unemployment rate, people hold on to jobs with all their might. With virtually no turnover, there is increased pressure on management to select high-quality employees the first time. Also, because the employees value their jobs, accuracy is extremely high. The only drawback on the personnel side is that workers want to leave when the work day is over and overtime is not an option.

SOURCE: Adapted from Bernard Wysocki, Jr., "Overseas Calling: American Firms Send Office Work Abroad to Use Cheap Labor," *Wall Street Journal*, August 14, 1991, p. A1+.

---

lems with the American government. But, this quota does not apply to Japanese cars built in the United States. As a result, more and more Toyotas, Hondas, Mazdas, and Nissans are being built in Georgetown, Kentucky; Marysville, Ohio; Flat Rock, Michigan; and Smyrna, Tennessee.[30] In the first half of 1989, Japanese firms built almost 15 percent of the cars made in the United States, compared to less than 8 percent in 1980.[31]

Improved transportation and communication systems, at least with developed countries, have helped increase the number of firms doing business abroad. Markets that were physically inaccessible 20 or 30 years ago are now open as new technologies like satellites, computers, facsimile machines, container shipping, and air freight are adopted. Inducements provided by countries to encourage companies to relocate or start an operation overseas have also led to increased international business. Nations are willing to provide these inducements, often in the form of tax breaks or cheap loans for new plants, in order to get the jobs and foreign exchange created by new business activity.[32]

Important Global Business Arenas

Pacific Rim

In their book, *Megatrends 2000,* John Naisbitt and Patricia Aburdene devote an entire chapter to "The Rise of the Pacific Rim." Leveraging both massive labor pools and technology-driven economies, the countries of the **Pacific Rim** are experiencing the fastest period of economic expansion in history. They are growing at a rate that is five times the growth rate during the Industrial Revolution.[33] The current economy-building phase of the Pacific Rim development is being led by Japan. Japan is injecting money and developmental decision making into the area and is trying to coordinate the emerging economies. In its view, Japan's Ministry of International Trade and Industry (MITI) sees that "Indonesia will pay special attention to textiles, forest products, and plastics. . . . Thailand will focus on furniture, toys, and die cast molds . . . and Malaysia will concentrate on sneakers, copiers, and television picture tubes."[34]

The vast majority of the Pacific Rim's human resources are unskilled and semi-skilled workers. These workers are being trained and used in factory settings at a fraction of the cost the rest of the world would demand. Malaysia's director of the Industrial Development Authority explained that in Malaysia over 200,000 young people are leaving school each year, which means that to break even and keep at or below the current unemployment rate of 7.9 percent, at least 200,000 new jobs need to be created each year.[35]

The Pacific Rim is an emerging area for new investment and development. The validity of some analysts' perception of the Pacific Rim as being the world's next economic empire, however, is debatable when compared to what lies beyond 1992 for the European Community.

European Community (EC)

The year 1992 marks the largest deregulation of any demographic entity ever. The removal of most of Europe's internal trade barriers will be a great step forward for the economies of Europe, aligning them to effectively compete with Japan and the United States. Organizations will be better able to react to changes in consumer needs and desires, the result being more competition and more choices for the consumer. Although there still remains powerful resistance from the big industries in Europe, including automobiles, agriculture, and airlines, the vision has been set since 1986 and there is no turning back.[36]

Already, investors have flocked to the region to get an edge on the future. Some have moved because their competition has; others have moved because of fears of a Protectionist Atmosphere following 1992 aimed at protecting the Community from foreign dumping.[37] Unlike the Pacific Rim, the European Community's industrial base is more established as is its consumer base. This means that *both industrial* and *consumer* industries have more choices for profit in the EC than currently exists in the Pacific Rim.

Analyst have worried that a slowed growth rate, 2.75 percent for 1990, could affect job development and increase the already 9 percent unemployment rate. The slowdown has been blamed primarily on a recessionary economy. Europe, however, has experienced a tremendous drop in unemployment which was at 9 percent in 1990, down from 11.5 percent in 1985.[38]

The transition of the EC into a unified economy will mean that firms will be forced to compete in an open market without internal barriers. For human resource management, this means organizations will begin to rely more heavily on recruiting people with specific skills, like a knowledge of the politics and tax and labor laws of newly targeted countries, and the bi- or trilingual professionals needed to anchor the ventures.

FOCUS ON DIVERSITY •

Twin Cities across the Border

Some people are confused by all the talk about free-trade agreements with Mexico. These people live on the border towns between Mexico and the United States. The people who live in towns such as Laredo, Texas, and Nuevo Laredo, Mexico, view their towns as twin cities, much like Minneapolis and St. Paul. Nearly everyone living in Laredo is related to someone living in Nuevo Laredo. Over 95 percent of the people living in "Los Dos Laredos" are of Hispanic origin.

However, the connection between the two cities is based on more than just blood. The years of cross-border shopping has changed the face of Laredo. It is geared to the Mexican consumer. So closely are the two communities tied that in 1982 when the peso was devalued, 800 stores in Laredo went bust. Many merchants in Laredo live and die by the dollar-peso exchange rate.

What makes "Los Dos Laredos" and other border towns different from other American towns? Plenty. On average, residents of border towns are younger, poorer, and more likely to come from a large family than other Americans. The average age for women in border towns is 28 while the national average is 34 and men in border towns average 25 years of age while nationwide the average is 31. Border-town residents rank low in disposable income in the United States. Laredo residents had an average income of $13,800 in 1988 as compared to $27,000 in Dallas. Finally, about 10 percent of border town families have 6 members or more. The national average for family size is 2.6.

Laredo and other border towns do not view these differences as a problem. Instead, the stores view it as a marketing segment. Local grocery stores, instead of stocking rack after rack of microwavable dinners, offer family-size boxes of detergent and 50-pound sacks of rice. Another difference between other Americans and border town residents that affects marketing is a strong brand loyalty. This loyalty is fueled by the deep family orientation held by border town residents. People will graduate from college and take a pay cut in order to move home.

SOURCE: Adapted from Blayne Cutler, "Welcome to Borderland," *American Demographics*, February 1991, pp. 44–57.

Mexico

Boasting low labor costs and a large population, Mexico is also fertile ground for investment. Trade between the United States and Mexico was around $50 billion a year in 1990, up from $29.7 billion in 1986, and a free-trade agreement is making rounds in Washington that could spell out increased foreign investment in Mexico.[39] An almost immediate impact of a trade agreement would be the stabilization of Mexico's high inflation—the very factor most foreign investors are wary of.

Other environmental concerns in Mexico include its dilapidated infrastructure. Mexico has already begun reconstruction on some of its infrastructure, swapping debt for equity with foreign investors who then help in the rebuilding. The phone company, which was government owned and notorious for poor service, has been privatized and has begun to be modernized. The mail service has been given a new life with the entrance of Federal Express. Road construction has also been turned over to private industry. The new roads are toll roads, which are run by the construction company until the costs for building the roads and a reasonable profit are collected. After that, they will be turned over to the government.[40]

Mexico's president, Carlos Salinas de Gortari, has come a long way in allowing stronger employment of Mexico's human resources by attracting outside investors. Since the mid-1980s, he has privatized more than three-quarters of Mexico's state-owned companies, and the revenue from these sales, which is estimated at $4 billion, will go toward reducing the national debt. He has sent some prominent business and labor leaders to jail for corrupt practices and started a campaign against tax evasion.[41] *Maquiladoras*, U.S. owned assembly plants, which are host to nearly half a million Mexican workers at the border of Mexico and the United States, are growing at roughly 15 percent per year.[42] This is evidence of foreign (U.S.) investors taking advantage of Mexico's cheap labor. Mexico's economic volatility, however, still remains to be tamed and for those organizations willing to take the risks associated with Mexico's current environment, the long term consequences of lowered labor costs are attractive.

Ways Global Business Operations Differ from Domestic

Global business differs from domestic operations in several ways. Culture is often a key issue in these differences. Each nation has its own custom-value orientations, and problems can easily develop in the global environment. Selecting a manager for an overseas assignment is becoming increasingly difficult. High failure rates from poorly matched past assignments have increased costs. Thus, selecting an expatriate is an important human resource function in today's global businesses.[43] Further, some managers view an international assignment as a career risk. If the post to which you are assigned is cut or does not work out, you may lose your job.[44] The humorous problems Michael Keaton's character faced as an American union leader working in a Japanese-managed automobile factory in the movie *Gung-Ho* highlights the real differences that often exist between two cultures. The Japanese custom of strong worker loyalties to their companies contrast sharply with the hostile labor-management relationship exemplified by the "Big Three" American automobile manufacturers and the United Auto Workers union.[45] However, things are changing. The younger Japanese generation, those aged 20 to 39 years, seem to want different things than their parents. They are no longer willing to put their employers' needs and desires ahead of their own. They want two-day weekends and diversions unlike those enjoyed by their parents. Some Japanese firms have realized that their employees are different than they used to be and that the company must change to meet the needs of the younger generation. For example, NEC put together a task force of 100 young employees to draft a new corporate vision for the twenty-first century.[46]

The political environment also differs from nation to nation, and this creates both opportunities and risks for international business. The events in China in 1989 highlight the political risks of doing business abroad. Many U.S. firms started doing business in China as part of the government's drive to build its economy. American products manufactured in China include trucks, chemicals, processed foods, appliances, and apparel. But, the student protest in Tiananmen Square and the Chinese government's reaction has forced foreign firms to reexamine their presence in the country.[47] More recently, China's lack of respect for U.S. copyrights and patents led to heated debates and nearly an all-out trade war between the two countries. However, just before the U.S. deadline, an agreement was reached. China promised to outlaw theft of software and agreed to protect patents of agricultural chemicals and pharmaceuticals. In return, Washington decided to lighten its view of trading with China.[48]

Some of the misunderstandings that occur between the United States and China may be traced back to the management style in China. China's managers tend to be squeezed into low power positions. This position forces them to develop warm relationship with workers by offering favors and loosening operating rules. Because they have such a relationship, they can use shame on their employees and request direct help from employees' family. China's managers also rely upon *guanxi*, which means business occurs through the back door. The acceptance and reliance on these types of practices help explain the problems the United States had over patent rights and software pirating.[49]

Businesses must also face other political risks. The Iranian revolution of Ayatollah Khomeini not only caused the overthrow of the Shah of Iran, but resulted in the nationalization of U.S. business assets. Khomeini made the United States a scapegoat for many of Iran's problems, and his solutions included the nationalization of assets, the taking of American hostages, and the economic isolation of Iran from the Western world.[50]

Issues like bribery also take on international significance. In the United States, bribing a public official is illegal. In many nations, however, bribery is an expected part of doing business with the government. The problem becomes worse when clashes occur. It is still a violation of U.S. law for an American firm to commit bribery, even if the recipient of the bribe is the member of a foreign government. How does a firm compete abroad if it isn't allowed to play by the rules of the host nation?

The global legal environment also differs from the domestic environment. Many firms operate with mix of expatriate managers and local employees. Laws about responsibility for corporate actions are often more severe in other countries than in the United States. In Venezuela, top executives can be imprisoned without bail if their firms are accused of violating Venezuelan law. Venezuelan officials issued over 45 arrest warrants in 1989 to executives of firms suspected of being involved in a foreign exchange scandal. As a result, many foreign managers have fled the country to avoid prosecution for acts that would have been the responsibility of lower level employees in the United States.[51]

The infrastructure of each nation also varies considerably. Road, telephone, water, sewage, and other systems may range from modern to nonexistent. All these systems affect the ability of a firm to operate in the global environment. If an operation requires massive amounts of power, like a steel plant, then the region must be able to supply power to the plant or it must have adequate roads for transporting fuel to the plant. If the local government is unwilling or unable to provide these services, the firm must measure the worth of building the necessary systems itself.

Business practices also differ in the global environment. What's acceptable in France may not be acceptable in Honduras. These differences may be as small as the standard hours of business or as large as what makes a contract. In many nations a handshake may be as binding as a legal contract in the eyes of a local businessperson. At best, a failure to realize these differences will cause hard feelings. At worst, it may wind up costing a firm a lot of money.

Whatever differences exist, if the firm is organized and managed correctly, it will be able to face any global problem. The following six principles can be used to make a firm's strategy come alive and prosper in a global economy.

1. Build a fluid, dynamic organization so that it is relatively easy to respond to changes and opportunities as they arise. This means both people and structure must be adaptable.
2. Create mechanisms to respond to revolutionary change instead of routine change.
3. Keep specialization to a minimum and stress interchangeability.
4. Draft the best players, regardless of their expertise. If you hire the best players, they can learn whatever you need and will be instrumental in helping to achieve number 3 above.

5. Develop from within, but stimulate from outside. Because you are hiring the best players, there is no reason to fill positions from outside. However, it is also suggested that new ideas be infused into the organization by hiring consultants or temporary workers.
6. Encourage everyone to take full responsibility for everything. Encourage managers to develop their workers' talents. Encourage workers to make decisions and follow through.[52]

Financial and Currency Problems

Even though there are many advantages to operating overseas, firms must consider several potential financial and currency problems. Since most local transactions overseas are conducted in the currency of the host country, firms must deal with *converting the foreign currency back into the home money.* In nations where transactions are conducted in pounds, yen, deutschemarks, francs, or dollars, conversion is not a problem. However, even when firms deal in these currencies, they may still face exchange rate risks. These risks include changing prices for each currency against other currencies and the frequency of trading for each currency on the financial markets. A profit made abroad may become a loss at home because of exchange rate problems.

Another problem facing firms is a *lack of hard currency,* or currency freely convertible to another currency. For example, the currencies of many communist nations are not officially convertible to U.S. dollars. As a result, firms doing business in many communist nations must either purchase products in that country or find a firm that is willing to trade dollars for the nation's currency.

Rapid inflation is another financial risk. Many nations, especially those that are classified as lesser developed countries (LDCs), can experience inflation rates ranging from 100 percent to 1,000 percent or more annually. This instability in prices ruins the country's currency value and makes it difficult for foreign firms to operate there. Thus a business is faced with the question of ignoring a potentially lucrative market or taking a risk in an unstable economy.

Black markets present another problem for firms doing business abroad. Many domestic products do not have the same international copyright and patent protection that they have at home. As a result, many foreign firms will copy the product and sell it at a substantially lower price. This is particularly true for the computer software industry. Black market copies of software programs such as the Lotus 1-2-3 spreadsheet sell for $40 to $50 in Hong Kong's computer stores.[53] Does a firm simply not choose to compete abroad to avoid these problems? Or, does it risk piracy for the sake of new markets? If it chooses to compete, how does it counteract these problems?

Firms may also experience *pay issue problems* abroad.[54] For example, should a firm pay a construction foreman based in Saudi Arabia the local rate or the rate for the job in the United States? If the firm pays the U.S. rate, what happens when the foreman leaves the job? Does the firm fill the position with a local at the local wage rate, and risk an "Ugly American" label, or does it pay the American rate, thus creating a pay gap in the community?

Finally, firms face *currency control and accounting problems.* Many nations require that a certain percentage of a firm's revenues from that country remains within the country. Also, accounting laws on topics ranging from capital depreciation to tax payments vary drastically from nation to nation. This further complicates a firm's business since it must obey the accounting laws of both its home and host country.

EXHIBIT 2.17	The Ten Largest Banks in the World Based on Assets

(in millions of U.S. dollars)

RANK		NAME	NATION	ASSETS*	PERCENTAGE CHANGE FROM 1989
1990	1989				
1	1	Dai-Ichi Kangyo Bank	Japan	$470,299	24
2	2	Mitsui Taiyo Kobe Bank	Japan	$438,673	18
3	3	Sumitomo Bank	Japan	$428,690	17
4	4	Fuji Bank	Japan	$422,456	19
5	5	Mitsubishi Bank	Japan	$419,747	22
6	6	Sanwa Bank	Japan	$412,503	21
7	8	Credit Agricole	France	$305,299	11
8	7	Industrial Bank of Japan	Japan	$299,160	15
9	9	Banque Nationale de Paris	France	$291,962	11
10	12	Credit Lyonnais	France	$287,418	20

*In millions of U.S. dollars

For example, under U.S. law American banks must issue quarterly financial reports, maintain fairly high reserve levels, and receive no tax benefits for bad debt provisions. Many foreign banks (and even foreign branches operating in the United States) are not subject to these requirements. This has helped to increase the cost of capital for American banks and has led to the retreat of American banks from the world market and an increased presence of foreign banks in the United States. Japanese banks now control 25 percent of the bank market in California, and the 260 foreign banks operating the United States controlled 21 percent of the U.S. market in 1989.[55] In fact, Japan has become so dominant in banking that it now has the seven of the ten largest banks in the world as shown in Exhibit 2.17. Much of this success can be attributed to laws and accounting rules being more favorable to banks in Japan than in other nations.

KNOWING THE ENVIRONMENT

For most organizations, the environment is an ambiguous mass of information. Of course not everything in the external environment is of equal importance for the organization. Information in some sectors deserves closer monitoring than information in other sectors. How does an organization decide this issue? To answer, we examine three closely related concepts: (1) the *enacted environment*, (2) the *domain* and *domain consensus*, and (3) the *task environment*.

Enacted Environment

Karl Weick explains that an organization does not and cannot conceivably know everything there is to know in the external environment.[56] Rather, the organization *creates* its own environment out of the external environment. This is called *enactment*. Enactment means the organization creates a relevant environment for itself by aggressively scoping, narrowing, and scanning the external environment. In effect, the organization creates the environment to which it reacts; it does not react to the entire environment. The difference between creating the environment and reacting to it is a fine but important difference. In effect, the top managers in the organization state, "this is our environment, given what we are trying to accomplish. We will be concerned with these aspects and will ignore, at least temporarily, other aspects of the environment." Organizations then give meaning to the environment based on what they determine to be important for their proper functioning.

An enacted environment implies a *proactive* approach in dealing with the environment. The organization takes an active and aggressive role in actually defining its environment. On the other hand, a *reactive* approach implies that the organization is not aggressive, but merely reacts to its environment. It does not define its environment, but instead allows important factors in the environment define the environment for the organization. It reacts to the crisis of the moment.

Unfortunately, an organization may so narrowly define its environment through the enactment process that it neglects to consider important forces that may affect it. For example, very few organizations monitored the Oil Producing Exporting Countries (OPEC) in the early 1970s and were caught completely off guard by the oil embargo and rapid energy price rise of 1973 and 1974. From that point on, of course, OPEC actions were monitored.

GM and other domestic auto manufacturers initially believed overseas competition from Nissan, Toyota, Mitsubishi, Mazda, and other Japanese auto manufacturers would not be a formidable force on a long-term basis and only casually monitored these competitor actions. They were more concerned with monitoring the actions of each other. On the other hand, Japanese automakers were intent upon studying the American automakers. In order to get a closer look, many Japanese automakers entered into joint ventures with domestic automakers. Eventually, the American automakers realized that they were teaching the Japanese in a few short years what it took them years to learn.[57]

Of course, the 1970s and 1980s clearly established the competitive staying power and force of these Japanese auto manufacturers. Many other automobile manufacturers are trying to imitate their production techniques in the hopes of imitating their success. Tom LaSorda, president of Adam Opel AG, is building a new car plant in Eisenach, Germany. His goal is to have people think they have entered a Toyota plant and not an Opel plant. He acknowledges that the concepts and processes that he is implementing are foreign to his work force. However, he feels that this is the way of the future. He adds that his project simply reflects the increasing globalization of the auto industry. After all, he is a Canadian, working for a German subsidiary of a U.S. carmaker implementing Japanese systems.[58]

Domain and Domain Consensus

The domain is that part of the environment the organization *stakes out* for itself. The organization formally states that a certain part of the environment will be its *territory*: both literally and figuratively. the domain consists of the (1) range of products offered, (2) population served, and (3) services rendered.[59] The organization focuses its efforts on these three areas while giving less attention to the other areas.

Domain consensus forms when those who have a vested interest in the organization agree to its domain. Those with a vested interest are sometimes called its **stakeholders.** For example, stakeholders of UAL, Inc. (formerly Allegis), the parent company of United Airlines, include top management, stockholders, employees, customers, suppliers, and lenders. When these groups reach a general consensus as to what UAL's domain is, then domain consensus forms. Consensus sometimes is difficult to form, such as in the electric utility industry in the 1980s when investors, management, and communities could not agree on the use of nuclear generation. At best, consensus forms on a relative basis and is subject to wide shifts over time.

When domain consensus does not form, conflicts can arise as to which parts of the external environment should be monitored. This conflict causes confusion and backbiting when the company is blindsided by an unexpected occurrence from a poorly monitored sector. The Steelworkers Union faulted management at U.S. Steel for not closely monitoring and anticipating the foreign steel invasion of the 1970s. The argument is that management at U.S. Steel had become lax in aggressively anticipating the foreign threat, thus causing the demise of the big steel maker in that industry.[60]

Task Environment

A third concept related to knowing the environment is called the **task environment.** This significant portion of the domain has the greatest impact on an organization's goals because it includes all groups that can influence the organization. For example, the task environment for AT&T in the introductory case of this chapter would include the associated industries of satellite transmission, electronic switching, fiber optics, and computers. AT&T would need to monitor the technology, action of competitors, and consumer behavior in these markets and set goals appropriately. It would also monitor governmental regulations and developments in related industries (for example, network broadcasting, cable television, and so on).

Environmental Scanning

Environmental scanning is the process of examining the external environment to determine trends and projections of factors that will affect the organization.[61] It is closely related to the strategic planning process and serves as the forecast on which the plan is built. Assumptions about the future are derived from the plan.

The scan focuses primarily as the organization's enacted environment. The task environment is scanned the most; elements outside of the task environment are not ignored, but they receive less attention. Scanning is done to prevent information overload for decision makers. Scanning should focus on providing relevant information for planning and decision making.

The primary environmental areas that should be scanned for human resource management planning and decision making are the labor market, legal environment, and technology. This does not mean that other elements, such as the international environment, should be ignored; but it does mean that the three sectors identified tend to have a major impact on human resource decisions. Of course if a firm has overseas operations, these three environmental sectors in other countries of operation need to be examined.

Exhibit 2.18 summarizes these concepts of domain, domain consensus, task environment, and enactment. Notice that the enactment and scanning process result in a narrowing or focusing of the external environment.

EXHIBIT 2.18   Organizations Enact and Limit the Environment

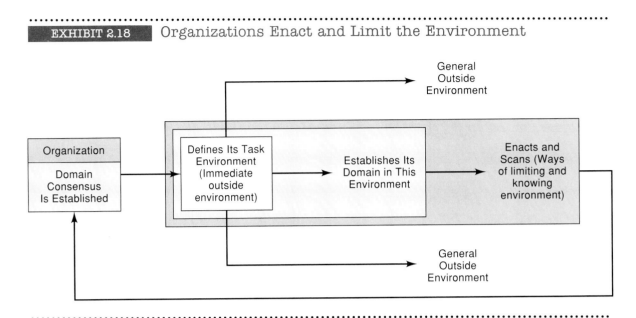

Human Resources' Role in Environmental Scanning

Human resources is in the best position of any unit in the organization to scan the environment for human resources and labor market issues. As Exhibit 2.18 shows, human resources obtains environmental information and feeds it to key decision makers. In fact, human resources may play a major role in making the decision as explained above. Human resources also has the responsibility of obtaining internal organizational information for consideration by strategic decision makers.

Notice that the human resource unit plays a **boundary spanning** role in that it helps to link the organization to its environment through scanning the environment. We will expand on this linking role when we discuss recruiting and selection as well as termination, retirement, and layoff—other linking processes—in later chapters.

Environmental Summary

We can see that the environment presents a multitude of important but ambiguous information to a firm. Yet for effective strategy formulation, a firm must monitor the relevant portions of each environment sector: the economy, the labor market, technology, the social and demographics market, competitors, and the legal/political sectors. Organizations do this through a process of enactment that involves scoping and scanning tactics to reduce the relevant parts of the environment to manageable proportions. In doing this, the organization attempts to establish the set of environmental threats and opportunities presented to it by the environment.

In the next chapter, we see how the organization uses these environmental threats to formulate basic organization and resultant human resource strategies.

• • • • • • • • •

MANAGEMENT GUIDELINES

The information presented in this chapter can be used to generate several guidelines relevant to managers. These guidelines are presented below.

1. The external and global environments are very important for an organization and must be monitored.

2. Organizations monitor the environment through a process of enactment and scoping to make the available information manageable.

3. The international, labor market, and technological sectors of the environment will have profound effects on human resource management during the 1990s.

4. Organizations use this information to formulate overall and basic human resource strategies.

5. Organizations have several choices in designing a basic posture with regard to the environment, from prospector to reactor.

6. The basic strategy chosen by an organization has profound *impact* on the resultant human resource strategy.

7. Anticipating environmental trends requires a proactive management approach in strategy formulation.

QUESTIONS FOR REVIEW

1. Why should an organization be interested in its external environment?

2. What are the basic sectors of the external environment?

3. What are the key aspects of each environmental sector?

4. What profound changes are likely to occur in the labor market sector and how will this affect human resource management issues?

5. How is the global environment changing?

6. What changes are occurring in the technology environment and what are the implications for human resource management?

7. How does an organization scope or limit its external environment for monitoring purposes?

8. What are the basic choices of an organization as to the basic posture it takes with its external environment?

9. Discuss the environmental changes faced by AT&T as described in the case at the beginning of this chapter and explain how these changes have affected basic AT&T strategy?

10. How have the above changes affected the human resource strategy of AT&T?

11. Can a large company such as AT&T ever really completely know its environment? Would it be easier for a smaller company, such as a locally owned restaurant in your community, to know its environment? Discuss your answers.

12. If you were hired as an entry-level manager in a company such as AT&T, of what relevance would the external environment have to you in your job?

13. Many have written that the external environment changes very rapidly often in unpredictable ways. Do you agree? Why or why not? Assuming that the environment does change in unpredictable ways, what relevance does this have for both (1) attempting to take a proactive approach and (2) strategy formulation?

14. What perils exist for an organization that narrowly defines its external environment? How can these perils be avoided?

CASE: Lorenzo and Texas Air [62]

Frank Lorenzo battled to keep his airline safely in the air and financially viable. Lorenzo faced intense competition on most route systems and severe problems with Eastern's strong unions and poor image. Texas Air typified the upheaval and change that can occur in a firm as it battles to meet new challenges.

The now defunct Texas Air formed as a result of Frank Lorenzo taking a fairly small airline, Texas International, to the big time through a series of aggressive mergers and acquisitions during the mid-1980s. Lorenzo acquired Continental, Peoples Express, Eastern, and Jet Capital Corporation (a holding company) as a result of a deregulated environment for air transport. Fares and routes were deregulated and thrown open to competition. The result was drastic cuts in air fares, increases in air passenger traffic and routes, intense competition among carriers, and the creation of many new airlines. In addition, large airlines have attempted to get larger in the marketplace in order to have the power to acquire terminal gates, agreements with travel agents, and stronger promotion. Aggressive promotion techniques, such as frequent flyer programs, have proliferated throughout the industry.

Effect on Human Resources

These environmental changes have had a profound effect on human resource management in the industry. The key to survival has been to cut costs, and human resource costs were primary targets for cutting. Unions were busted where possible. For example, in 1983 Lorenzo placed Continental, his flagship carrier at the time, into bankruptcy, thus abrogating union contracts. He also adopted a two-tier wage system where employees hired after a specified date were paid significantly less on a job than those already holding the job. Flexibility also was a key watch word. Flexible assignment of employees to jobs, which was pioneered by Peoples Express, was adopted wholeheartedly by Texas Air. Baggage handlers collected tickets and vice versa, for example. Lorenzo was not as successful, however, with Eastern Air. Safety, image, and labor problems plagued the carrier until its death.

Finally, Texas Air, like all airlines, tried to increase the productivity of its human resources by attempting to get more work and more hours of work out of each employee at little increase, if any, in salary. Pilots and flight attendants flew dangerously close to or even exceeded maximum federal flight time standards. Maintenance employees rushed jobs and cut corners to save time, raising questions of safety.

A New Ball Game

Deregulation and the resultant intense competition completely changed the legal and competitive environment for air carriers. This provided a tremendous opportunity for aggressive companies such as Texas Air. It also caused massive changes in the way human resources are treated in the industry. Delta and Piedmont, carriers with no unions, adjusted easily. Texas Air, with unions at Continental and Eastern, had a more difficult time. Established work patterns and employment relationships change slowly. Oftentimes the environment changes faster than a firm's ability to change human resource policy and practice. Sometimes it takes an aggressive CEO such as Lorenzo to be a catalyst for changes in human resource strategy, even though such changes are likely to cause uncertainty and bitterness among some employees.

QUESTIONS

1. What parts of the external environment changed the most for Texas Air? How did they change?

2. Lorenzo had a reputation at Texas Air for being ruthless with employees in order to cut costs. When is such harsh treatment justified? Do you feel it was justified in the Texas Air case, given the change in the external environment for air transport? Discuss your answer.

3. How would you judge whether Texas Air's new human resource policies under deregulation were effective? What criteria would you use and why?

4. Do you agree that it takes an aggressive CEO such as Lorenzo to bring about real change in a firm's human resource policy or could this be done by the firm's human resource unit? Explain.

· · · · · · · · · · · · · ·
ADDITIONAL READINGS

Bacas, Harry. "Desperately Seeking Workers." *Nation's Business.* February 1988, pp. 16–17, 20–23.

Bacon, Kenneth H. "Population and Power Preparing for Change." *Wall Street Journal.* June 6, 1988, pp. 1, 5.

Badaracco, Joseph. *The Knowledge Link.* Cambridge, MA: Harvard Business School Press, 1991.

Baker, Stephen. "Now Mexico Looks Like a Fiesta for Investors." *Business Week.* August 28, 1989, pp. 42–43.

Bernstein, Aaron. "America's Income Gap: The Closer You Look, the Worse It Gets." *Business Week.* April 17, 1989, pp. 78–79.

Bogue, Marcus C., and Elwood S. Buffa. *Corporate Strategic Analysis.* New York: Free Press, 1986.

Borrus, Amy, Dinah Lee, Victoria English, and Blanca Riemer. "Who's the Biggest of Them All?" *Business Week.* July 17, 1989, pp. 139–177.

Borrus, Amy, and John Carey. "An Open Door the U.S. Isn't Using." *Business Week.* May 15, 1989. pp. 59–62.

Boyett, Joseph, and Harry Conn. *Workplace 2000: The Revolution Reshaping American Business.* New York: Penguin, 1991.

Bradshaw, Thorton F., Daniel F. Burton, Jr., Richard N. Cooper, and Robert D. Hormats. *America's New Competitors.* New York: Harper & Row, 1989.

Brauchli, Marcus W. "Trading in Tokyo." *Wall Street Journal.* August 16, 1989, pp. A1-6, A8-1.

Carlson, Rose, and Eugene Carlson. "Made in Michigan." *Wall Street Journal.* August 11, 1988, pp. 1-6, 17-1.

Carson, Carol S. "GNP: An Overview of Source Data and Estimating Methods." *Survey of Current Business* 67 (1987), pp. 103–126.

Carter, Susan, John Rossanto, Frank J. Comes, and John Templeman. "Why the Ayatollah Is Whipping Up a New Wave of Fanaticism." *Business Week.* March 6, 1989, p. 47.

Coates, Joseph, Jennifer Jarratt, and John Mahaffie. *Future Work.* San Francisco: Jossey-Bass Publishers, 1990.

Cooper, James C., and Kathleen Madigan. "As the Expansion Faces Bigger Bills." *Business Week.* April 24, 1989, p. 21.

Daft, Richard L., Juhani Sormunen, and Don Parks. "Chief Executive Scanning, Environmental Characteristics and Company Performance: An Empirical Study." *Strategic Management Journal.* March/April 1988, pp. 123–140.

de Cordoba, Jose. "Wanted in Caracas." *Wall Street Journal.* August 24, 1989, pp. A1-1, A6-1.

Dess, Gregory G., and Donald W. Beard, "Dimensions of Organizational Task Environments." *Administrative Science Quarterly* 29 (1984), pp. 52–73.

Dowling, Peter, and Randall Schuler. *International Dimensions of Human Resource Management.* Boston: PWS Kent, 1990.

Dreyfuss, Joel. "Reinventing IBM." *Fortune.* August 21, 1989, p. 38.

Dwyer, Paula, Laura Jereski, Zachary Schiller, and Dinah Lee. "The Raging Battle over 'Intellectual Property.'" *Business Week.* May 22, 1989, p. 88.

Egelhoff, William G. *Organizing the Multinational Enterprise.* New York: Harper & Row, 1989.

Ellig, Bruce R. "Employee Resource Planning and Issues of the 1980's." *Personnel* 63, no. 2. February 1986, pp. 24–30.

Fahey, Liam, and William R. King. "Environmental Scanning for Corporate Planning." *Business Horizons.* August 1977, p. 63.

Fernandez, John. *Managing a Diverse Workforce.* New York: Lexington Books, 1991.

Finney, Martha I. "The ASPA Labor Shortage Survey." *Personnel Administrator.* February 1989, pp. 35–42.

Frumkin, Norman. *Tracking America's Economy.* Armonk, NY: M. E. Sharpe, 1988.

Fuller, Graham. *The Democracy Trap: Perils of the Post-Cold War World.* Novato, CA: Dutton, 1991.

Fullerton, H. N., Jr. "Labor Force Projections: 1986–2000." *Monthly Labor Review* 110 (1987), pp. 19–29.

Fyock, Catherine. *America's Work Force Is Coming of Age.* New York: Lexington Books, 1990.

Gamota, George, and Wendy Frieman. *Gaining Ground.* New York: Harper & Row, 1989.

Glasgall, William, Dori Jones Yang, Dinah Lee, Joe Weber, and Amy Borrus. "Has Beijing Burned Its Bridges with Business?" *Business Week.* June 19, 1989, pp. 32–33.

Gleckman, Howard. "Mike Dukakis Has His Own Industrial Policy—But Will It Work?" *Business Week.* March 28, 1988, p. 37.

Goldenberg, Susan. *Hands Across the Ocean: Managing Joint Ventures with a Spotlight on China and Japan.* Novato, CA: Dutton, 1988.

Gross, Neil. "IBM Clones a Strategy from the Clonemakers." *Business Week.* August 21, 1989, p. 42.

Guenther, Robert, and Michael R. Sesit, "U.S. Banks Are Losing Business to Japanese at Home and Abroad." *Wall Street Journal.* October 12, 1989, p. A12.

Harrison, Roger, "Strategies for a New Age." *Human Resource Management* 22. Fall 1983, pp. 209+.

Hawkins, Chuck. "Is Paul Stern Tough Enough to Toughen Up Northern Telecom?" *Business Week.* August 14, 1989, pp. 84–85.

Health, Robert L., and Associates. *Strategic Issues Management: How Organizations Influence and Respond to Public Interests and Policies.* San Francisco: Jossey-Bass, 1988.

Holloway, Thomas M., and Richard W. Peach. "Demographics for the 1990's," *Mortgage Banking.* March 1988, pp. 60–72.

Jamieson, David, and O'Mara, Julie. *Managing Workforce 2000.* San Francisco; Jossey-Bass, 1991.

Johnson, Chalmers, Laura D'Andrea Tyson, and John Zysman, eds. *Politics and Productivity.* Cambridge, MA: Ballinger, 1989.

Kelly, Rita Mae. *The Gendered Economy.* Newbury Park, CA: Sage, 1991.

Koberg, Christine S., "Resource Scarcity, Environmental Uncertainty, and Adaptive Organizational Behavior." *Academy of Management Journal* 30, no. 4. December 1987, pp. 798–812.

Knouse, Stephen, Paul Rosenfeld, and Amy Culbertson. *Hispanics and Work.* Newbury Park, CA: Sage, 1992.

Kraar, Louis. "Japan's Gung-Ho U.S. Car Plants." *Fortune.* January 30, 1989, pp. 98–108.

Kraar, Louis. "Korea, Tomorrow's Powerhouse." *Fortune.* August 15, 1988, pp. 75–81.

Kuhn, Susan E., and David J. Morrow. "The Fortune International 500 Directory." *Fortune.* July 31, 1989, pp. 291–318.

Langley, Monica. "America First." *Wall Street Journal.* May 16, 1988, pp. A1-6, A8-1.

Lee, James R., and David Walters. *International Trade in Construction, Design and Engineering Services.* New York: Harper & Row, 1989.

Licht, Walter. "How the Workplace Has Changed in 75 Years." *Monthly Labor Review.* February 1988, pp. 19–25.

Lindroth, Joan. "How to Beat the Coming Labor Shortage." *Personnel Journal* 61:4. April 1982, pp. 268–272.

Maidment, Fred. "American Economy Suffers from Lack of Educated and Trained Work Force." *The Atlanta Journal and Constitution.* December 28, 1987, p. 9.

Main, Jeremy. "Business Schools Get a Global Vision." *Fortune.* July 17, 1989, pp. 78–86.

Maremont, Mark. "British Telecom Is Getting Less British All the Time." *Business Week.* August 14, 1989, p. 62.

Mendenhall, Mark, and Gary Oddou. *Readings and Cases in International Human Resource Management.* Boston: PWS Kent, 1990.

Mercer, David. *Managing the External Environment.* Newbury Park, CA: Sage, 1992.

Moffett, Matt. "Back in Business." *Wall Street Journal.* July 26, 1989, pp. A1-1, A8-4.

Naisbitt, John, and Patricia Aburdene. *Megatrends 2000: Ten New Directions for the 1990's.* New York: Morrow, 1990.

Nakarmi, Laxmi, Larry Armstrong, and William J. Holstein, "Korea." *Business Week.* September 5, 1988, pp. 44–50.

Negandhi, Anant, and Arun Savara. *International Strategic Management.* New York: Lexington Books, 1989.

Nelton, Sharon. "Meet Your New Work Force." *Nation's Business.* July 1988, pp. 14–21.

Noyelle, Thierry J., and Anna B. Dutka. *International Trade in Business Services.* New York: Harper & Row, 1989.

Ohmae, Kenichi. *Triad Power: The Coming Shape of Global Competition.* New York: Free Press, 1985.

Orlorne, George S. "Human Resource Strategies for the 80's." *Training* 22, no. 1. January 1985, pp. 47–50.

Osterman, Paul. *Employment Futures.* New York: Oxford University Press, 1988.

Porter, Michael. *The Competitive Advantage of Nations.* New York: Free Press, 1990.

Prescott, John E., "Environments as Moderators of the Relationship between Strategy & Performance." *Academy of Management Journal* 29, no. 2. June 1986, p. 329.

Punnett, Betty J., and David Ricks. *International Business.* Boston: PWS-Kent, 1992.

Redman, Christopher. "Charging Ahead." *Time.* September 18, 1989, pp. 40–45.

Reed, Stanley. "When the Dust Settles, Iran May Be Facing West." *Business Week.* June 19, 1989, p. 50.

Schiller, Zachary, Ted Holden, and Mark Maremont. "P&G Goes Global by Acting Like a Local." *Business Week.* August 28, 1989, p. 58.

Schmid, Hillel, "Managing the Environment: Strategies for Executives in Human Service Organizations." *Human Systems Management* 6 (1986), pp. 307–315.

Sekaran, Uma, and Frederick Leong. *Womanpower.* Newbury Park, CA: Sage, 1991.

Singleton, Loy A. *Global Impact.* New York: Harper & Row, 1989.

Solis, Dianna. "For Many Employers, Immigration Law Is Still Puzzling and a Burden to Follow," *Wall Street Journal.* June 27, 1988, p. 15.

Solomon, Charlene Marmer, "The Corporate Response to Work-Force Diversity." *Personnel Journal.* August 1989.

Steers, Richard M., Yoo Keum Shin, and Gerardo Ungson. *The Chaebol.* New York: Harper & Row, 1989.

Tatsuno, Sheridan M. *Created in Japan.* New York: Harper & Row, 1989.

Thiederman, Sondra. *Bridging Cultural Barriers for Corporate Success.* New York: Lexington Books, 1990.

Treece, James B., and John Hoerr. "Shaking Up Detroit." *Business Week.* August 14, 1989, pp. 74–80.

Wessel, David. "Census Bureau Study Finds Shift in Fertility Patterns." *Wall Street Journal.* June 26, 1989, p. B1-4.

Winter, Ralph E. "Costs Increase as Labor Supply Dries Up." *Wall Street Journal.* March 10, 1989, p. A2-2.

Woodruff, David. "Detroit's Big Worry for the 1990's: The Greenhouse Effect." *Business Week.* September 4, 1989, pp. 103–107.

Worthy, Ford S. "The Perils of Getting Tough on Korea." *Fortune.* June 5, 1989, pp. 263–268.

Yang, Dori Jones, Dinah Lee, William J. Holstein, and Maria Shao. "China: The Great Leap Backward." *Business Week.* June 19, 1989, pp. 28–32.

· · · · · · · · · · · · · · · ·
NOTES

1. *AT&T 1986 Annual Report,* February 7, 1987, pp. 3, 23, 24; John Keller, Geoff Lewis, Todd Mason, Russell Mitchell, and Thane Peterson, "AT&T—The Making of a Comeback," *Business Week,* January 18, 1988, pp. 56–62; Jeffery A. Tannenbaum, "AT&T to Cut Hiring, Change Jobs of Workers," *Wall Street Journal,* July 22, 1989, p. 3; "AT&T to Transfer up to 1,500 of Staff to Sales Organization," *Wall Street Journal,* July 25, 1989, p. 9; and Bernard Wysocki, Jr., "Cross-Border Alliances Become Favorite Way to Crack New Markets," *Wall Street Journal,* March 26, 1990, p. A1+.

2. Raymond E. Miles and Charles C. Snow, *Organization Strategy, Structure, and Process* (New York: McGraw-Hill, 1978), pp. 29–30.

3. There is some evidence that the unemployment rate actually undercounts unemployment because of the discouraged worker hypothesis. Some people who actually want to work may have given up looking. These people are not counted as unemployed.

4. It should be noted that during the Great Depression of the 1930s the unemployment rate reached 25 percent on several occasions.

5. Albert Karr, "Health Care Jobs," *Wall Street Journal,* June 19, 1990, p. A1.

6. "California," *HRMagazine,* April 1991, p. 41.

7. "Investing in GEMS: Global Employees, Mobile and Skilled," *HRMagazine,* January 1991, p. 37.

8. Martha I. Finney. "The ASPA Labor Shortage Survey," *Personnel Administrator,* February 1989, pp. 36–42.

9. Martha Brannigan, "Work Force Skills Lag in the Southeast, Despite Reforms," *Wall Street Journal,* February 18, 1992, p. A1.

10. David Wessel, "Census Bureau Study Finds Shift in Fertility Patterns," *Wall Street Journal,* June 26, 1989, p. B1.

11. Sue Schellenbarger, "Women with Children Increase in Work Force," *Wall Street Journal,* February 12, 1992, p. B1.

12. Sharon Nelton, "Meet Your New Work Force," *Nation's Business.* July 1988, pp. 14–21.

13. Ibid., pp. 14–15.

14. "More Skilled Workers Coming to the U.S.," *Fortune,* September 9, 1991, p. 14.

15. B. J. Hodge and William P. Anthony, *Organization Theory* 3rd ed. (Boston: Allyn and Bacon, 1988), p. 428.

16. Shoshana Zuboff, *In the Age of the Smart Machine: The Future of Work and Power* (New York: Basic, 1988).

17. Robert Rose and Alex Kotolowitz, "Midwest's Revenge: Once the 'Rust Belt,' Heartland Fares Better than Coastal States," *Wall Street Journal,* July 30, 1991, p. A1+.

18. Michael Porter, *Competitive Strategy: Techniques for Analyzing Industries and Competitors* (New York: Free Press, 1980).

19. Ford S. Worthy. "The Perils of Getting Tough on Korea," *Fortune,* June 5, 1989, pp. 263–268.

20. Paul Hofheinz, "Let's Do Business," *Fortune,* September 23, 1991, pp. 62–68.

21. Joel Dreyfuss, "Reinventing IBM," *Fortune,* August 21, 1989, p. 38.

22. Susan E. Kuhn and David J. Morrow, "The Fortune International 500 Directory," *Fortune,* July 31, 1989, pp. 291–318.

23. Nicholas Fasciano, "The Fortune Global 500," *Fortune,* July 29, 1991, pp. 237–280.

24. The European Common Market consists of Belgium, Britain, Denmark, France, Greece, Ireland, Italy, Luxembourg, the Netherlands, Portugal, Spain, and West Germany.

25. Christopher Redman, "Charging Ahead," *Time,* September 18, 1989, p. 40.

26. "The World's 100 Largest Public Companies," *Wall Street Journal,* September 20, 1991, p. R8.

27. Emily Thornton, Thomas Martin, and Cindy Kano, "What Now for the U.S. and Japan," *Fortune,* February 10, 1992, pp. 80–95.

28. Marcus W. Brauchli, "Trading in Tokyo," *Wall Street Journal,* August 16, 1989, p. A1;6.

29. Louis Kraar, "Korea, Tomorrow's Powerhouse," *Fortune,* August 15, 1988, pp. 75–81; and Laxmi Nakarmi, Larry Armstrong, and William J. Holstein, "Korea," *Business Week,* September 5, 1988, pp. 44–50.

30. Thomas O'Boyle, "New Neighbor: To Georgetown, KY, Toyota Plant Seems a Blessing and a Curse," *Wall Street Journal,* November 26, 1991, p. A1+.

31. James B. Treece and John Hoerr, "Shaking Up Detroit," *Business Week,* August 14, 1989, pp. 74–80.

32. Ford Worthy, "Getting on in the Ground Floor," *Fortune,* Pacific Rim, 1990, pp. 63–67.

33. John Naisbitt and Patricia Aburdene, *Megatrends 2000: Ten New Directions for the 1990's* (New York: Morrow, 1990).

34. Bernard Wysocki, Jr., "In Asia, the Japanese Hope to 'Coordinate' What Nations Produce," *Wall Street Journal.* August 20, 1990, p. A1.

35. Ibid.

36. Shawn Tully, "Europe Hits the Brakes on 1992," *Fortune,* December 17, 1990, pp. 133–140.

37. Heinz Weihrich, "Europe 1992: What the Future May Hold," *Academy of Management Executive* 4, 1990, pp. 7–18.

38. Shawn Tully, "Europe Hits the Brakes on 1992," *Fortune.* December 17, 1990, pp. 133–140.

39. Stephen Baker, David Woodruff, and Bill Javetski, "Along the Border, Free Trade Is Becoming a Fact of Life," *Business Week,* June 18, 1990, pp. 41–42; and "North American Free Trade Agreement," *HRMagazine,* December 1991, pp. 85–86.

40. Nancy Perry, "What's Powering Mexico's Success?" *Fortune,* February 10, 1992, pp. 109–115.

41. Ibid.

42. Stephen Baker, David Woodruff, Bill Javetski, "Along the Border, Free Trade Is Becoming a Fact of Life," *Business Week,* June 18, 1990, pp. 41–42.

43. Gilbert Fuchsberg, "The Costs of Overseas Assignments Climb, Firms Select Expatriates More Carefully," *Wall Street Journal,* January 9, 1992, p. B1+.

44. "Risky Opportunity," *HRMagazine,* June 1990, p. 26.

45. Louis Kraar, "Japan's Gung-Ho U.S. Car Plants," *Fortune,* January 30, 1989, pp. 98–108; and Joseph White, Gregory Patterson, and Paul Ingrassia, "American Auto Makers Need Overhaul to Match the Japanese," *Wall Street Journal,* January 10, 1992, pp. A1, A4.

46. Emily Thronton, "50 Fateful Years From Enemy to Friend to _____?" *Fortune,* December 16, 1991, pp. 126–134.

47. Dori Jones Yang, Dinah Lee, William J. Holstein, and Maria Shao, "China: The Great Leap Backward," *Business Week,* June 19, 1989, pp. 28–32; and William Glasgall, Dori Jones Yang, Dinah Lee, Joe Weber, and Amy Borrus, "Has Beijing Burned Its Bridges with Business?" *Business Week,* June 19, 1989, pp. 32–33.

48. Pete Engardio and Laurence Zuckerman, "Yankee Traders Breathe a Sigh of Relief," *Business Week,* February 3, 1992, pp. 39–42.

49. James Wall, "Managers in the People's Republic of China," *The Academy of Management Executive* 4, 1990, pp. 19–32.

50. Susan Carter, John Rossanto, Frank J. Comes, and John Templeman, "Why the Ayatollah Is Whipping Up a New Wave of Fanaticism," *Business Week,* March 6, 1989, p. 47; and Stanley Reed, "When the Dust Settles, Iran May Be Facing West," *Business Week,* June 19, 1989, p. 50.

51. Jose de Cordoba, "Wanted in Caracas," *Wall Street Journal,* August 24, 1989, p. A1-1.

52. John Dupuy, "Learning to Manage World-Class Strategy," *Management Review,* October 1991, pp. 40–44.

53. Paul Dwyer, Laura Jereski, Zachary Schiller, and Dinah Lee, "The Raging Battle over 'Intellectual Property'," *Business Week,* May 22, 1989, p. 88.

54. Calvin Reynolds, "Are You Ready to Make IHR a Global Function?" HRNews, February, 1992, pp. C1–C3.

55. Robert Guenther and Michael R. Sesit, "U.S. Banks Are Losing Business to Japanese at Home and Abroad," *Wall Street Journal,* October 12, 1989, pp. A1, A12.

56. Karl Weick, *The Social Psychology of Organizing* (Reading, MA: Addison-Wesley, 1969).

57. Brian Dumaine, "The Best Management Books of 1991," *Fortune,* January 27, 1992, pp. 113–114.

58. Timothy Aeppel, "Opel Designs Car Plant on Japanese Lines," *Wall Street Journal,* January 21, 1992, p. A16.

59. Sol Levine and Paul E. White, "Exchange as a Conceptual Framework for the Study of Interorganizational Relationships," *Administrative Science Quarterly* 5, March 1961, pp. 583–701.

60. Stephen S. Cohen and John Zysman, *Manufacturing Matters: The Myth of the Post Industrial Economy* (New York: Basic Books, 1987).

61. Liam Fahey and William R. King, "Environmental Scanning for Corporate Planning," *Business Horizons,* August 1977, p. 63.

62. Paulette Thomas and Thomas Petzinger, Jr., "Frank Holds Steady His Course for Texas Air," *Wall Street Journal,* May 12, 1988, p. 6; Paulette Thomas and Laurie McGinley, "U.S. Extends Investigation of Texas Air to Allow Employees to Log Complaints," *Wall Street Journal,* June 2, 1988, p. 4; Laurie McGinley and Paulette Thomas, "U.S. Finds Eastern, Continental Air Safe, but Cautions Labor Conflict Poses Risks," *Wall Street Journal,* June 3, 1988, p. 3; and Laurie McGinley, "At La Guardia Airport, Passenger Surge Causes Delays and Congestion," *Wall Street Journal,* June 1, 1988, pp. 1, 18.

3 Formulating a Corporate Strategy

When a company makes decisions about such issues as the market in which it will compete, how it can ensure continued growth over the next several years, and ways in which it can better utilize its human resources, it is formulating corporate strategy. To formulate strategies, managers try to find a way for their organizations to best fit into the environment in which they function. To do this, they must understand the current environment as well as predict any changes that may occur to that environment, all the while being sure that they understand their customers' needs and desires. Obviously, formulating corporate strategy is a difficult and time-consuming process. This chapter explains how managers go about this process and the direct impact this process has on the firm's human resources.

• • • • • • • • •
CHAPTER OBJECTIVES

After studying this chapter, you should be able to

1. Describe the strategy formulation process.
2. List and define at least ten generic strategies.
3. Differentiate between line of business and corporate strategies.
4. Explain the role of the personnel/human resources department in strategy formulation.
5. Explain the contingency or situational approach to strategy formulation.

Sweet on NutraSweet[1]

Robert Shapiro, the chairman and chief executive officer of NutraSweet Company, sees himself as a man with a mission: to promote the company's aspartame artificial sweetener. Shapiro's enthusiasm underlies an impressive personal record. The one-time law professor and government lawyer joined G. D. Searle & Company, then NutraSweet's parent, in 1979. A few years later, he helped devise the evolutionary marketing strategies that made NutraSweet widely known as a brand name, rather than just an ingredient. In only four years, he transformed the fledgling sweetener division into a giant, with $711 million in sales in 1986.

But now, Shapiro's brainchild is stumbling into adolescence and faces the daunting problems of a maturing business. The decisions he makes are likely to shape the company for years to come.

Growth in demand for NutraSweet is slowing. After four years of uninterrupted sales growth, NutraSweet's sales tumbled in 1988. The company, a unit of St. Louis–based Monsanto Company since Monsanto's 1985 acquisition of Searle, is scrambling to develop new products and improve customer relationships in the face of likely new competition.

Goodbye Saccharin

The tremors follow years of spectacular success. More than 78 million Americans over 18 years of age use low-calorie foods and beverages. NutraSweet has already replaced saccharin in most diet soft drinks and has found its way into products ranging from Jell-O to laxatives. Now the company is trying to build markets with a new tactic: getting consumers to view aspartame as an alternative to sugar.

But while NutraSweet initially spurred huge rebounds in powdered soft-drink sales, that market has weakened recently. NutraSweet insiders believe that the slack in growth reflects inventory adjustments by customers and say that overall consumer demand for NutraSweet products—particularly regular diet soft drinks—continues to grow. However, "the enormous growth curves" of the first few years "have to slow down," Shapiro concedes.

Meanwhile, new competition awaits. Hoechst Celanese AG, a West German multinational corporation, produces Sunette. Pfizer Inc. and Johnson & Johnson's McNeil Specialty Products have both filed petitions with the FDA. Like Sunette, Pfizer's alitame and McNeil's sucralose are heat stable, which is a major advantage for cooking and baking uses. NutraSweet has lost patent protection in Canada, its second-largest market; in

Europe, where NutraSweet already faces generic competition, the product's price plunged nearly 50 percent between 1985 and 1987. Although Nutra-Sweet's U.S. patent doesn't expire until 1992, two pharmaceutical companies have already asked federal regulators to approve rival noncaloric sweeteners. NutraSweet also is scrambling to repair relationships with many customers who had been angered in the product's early growth by the company's unusually aggressive pricing policies and hardball sales tactics.

Strategic Thinking

Shapiro has proved himself to be a strategic thinker who was willing to take risks. He championed the "branded ingredient" strategy that became the cornerstone of NutraSweet's success. Rather than market the ingredient quietly to food and beverage makers, NutraSweet executives gave it a name and a logo, and advertised directly to consumers while persuading customers to feature NutraSweet on containers and in ads. The NutraSweet logo appears on more than 1,200 products. The tactic has paid off. The U.S. Department of Agriculture figures show that the per capita consumption of aspartame in 1987 was 1.12 ounces, which is equivalent to 14 pounds of sugar.

Such a strategy had been used with products like Teflon and Scotch-guard, but it was a first for the food industry. "Any conventional marketing company wouldn't have done it—they would have been scared," says Mr. Miller of Ogilvy & Mather. "Bob thankfully wasn't steeped in that consumer-marketing background."

Shapiro also devised a radical pricing strategy that charged different U.S. customers different amounts depending on the value NutraSweet added to their product. But that hardball approach angered customers, particular soft-drink makers who were used to dealing with more pliant suppliers.

"They had a monopoly and they really overplayed it," says a top executive at one soft-drink company. "To me, if you have a monopoly, you should be the nicest guy on the block."

Shapiro concedes NutraSweet "did a lousy job," but says the company has been working hard to repair its image recently by hiring several sales and trade relations employees from the soft-drink industry and teaming up with customers on cooperative promotionals.

Meanwhile, the company is trying to build markets with a new tactic: positioning aspartame as an alternative to sugar in products that have never been marketed in a sugar-free form. Federal regulators recently approved the use of NutraSweet in fruit drinks, and Shapiro talks of replacing even orange juice with an aspartame variety. Yogurt, a top seller in Europe, is next. The company also hopes to expand its European business, which remains relatively small despite such products as NutraSweet herring and cole slaw.

Mr. Shapiro says low production costs and a strong brand name will carry NutraSweet through its patent expirations. But NutraSweet scientists are already searching for the "son of aspartame."

Human Resource Impact

Finally, Shapiro also must adapt his entrepreneurial style to a company that now has about 1,200 employees. NutraSweet had no sales or personnel manuals and practically no written policies. "When we hire people from a large company, there's a bit of a culture shock," says Nick Rosa, vice-president of sales.

The small company had managed its human resources on an informal basis. Job descriptions were outdated or nonexistent. Personnel promotion policies were rather haphazard. All of this had to be corrected to reflect the rapid employment growth experienced by the company due to the tremendous success of NutraSweet. Shapiro was able to use his expertise in designing a more formalized and systematic personnel system.

The company undertook a number of actions. First a personnel manual was written that spelled out the company's hiring procedures, wage and salary plan, sick leave, holiday policy, and related issues. Next the firm conducted a job analysis, which resulted in a set of updated job descriptions for each job and a job hierarchy for pay purposes. The job specifications or skill, experience, and knowledge requirements that resulted form this job analysis led to improvements in training and development programs and promotion policy.

A director of human resources was appointed whose job it was to coordinate and manage the personnel and human resource function. While line managers were left with most of the real authority in personnel and human resource matters, they were assisted by a professional staff with specialized knowledge in personnel and human resource issues.

● ● ● ● ● ● ● ●

This case shows the effect an overall corporate strategy formulation can have on human resource strategy. As the small firm became large because of a highly successful new product, the rather informal, unsystematic personnel policies and strategies had to be made more systematic and formal to handle a larger workforce.

STRATEGIC CHOICES

Besides quick growth, managers must contend with several other strategic choices. Some of the more important questions that must be addressed when formulating a corporate strategy are outlined below.

1. What strategy will the company adopt to maintain its lead in the marketplace?

2. How can the company ensure continued sales growth and maintenance of its employee work force in order to avoid retrenchment, layoff, and termination?
3. How can it adapt to its ever changing environment?
4. How can it collect the information it needs to understand and influence its environment?
5. Should the firm change operating environments? If so, to which one? Why?

THE STRATEGY FORMULATION PROCESS

Organizations devise and adopt strategies to compete and survive. Oftentimes particular strategies are not clearly articulated, but rather can be inferred from the organization's actions. When this is the case, it is possible for the strategies to fail because all of the parties involved do not understand the strategy. Further, misunderstanding can lead to noncompliance which helps the strategy fail.[2] Sometimes they are clearly articulated, but organization actions are not consistent with the strategy. Nevertheless, a strategy exists when there is a pattern, either articulated or suggested through action. Without a pattern there would be no strategy.[3]

The strategy formulation process is not neat and clean, nor should it be. Even though it should be systematic, strategy must remain *flexible*. This requirement for flexibility contributes to the messy appearance of the strategy formation process—revisions are made as conditions change; new ideas are incorporated; and ineffective actions are discontinued.

One example of flexibility in strategy formulation was Pillsbury's changes with Burger King management and its promotional campaign in June 1988. At that time, Burger King's advertisements focused on the theme, "We do it like you'd do it." However, this approach was not working as evidenced by falling sales. New leadership was selected and a new strategy was adopted. Even though the 1986–1987 strategy was carefully formulated, it was changed because Pillsbury's management did not feel it was working as it should. This flexibility and change, while necessary, can be confusing when trying to determine exactly what an organization's strategy happens to be.

A second factor that makes the strategy formulation process difficult to understand is *secrecy*. Many firms, particularly those in highly competitive markets, do not want to make their strategy public because they do not want competition to use it to their advantage. For example, NutraSweet's strategy described at the beginning of this chapter is no doubt more complex than that related by the articles on which the case was based.

Yet, even though it is often difficult to determine the precise strategy of a firm, a strategy exists, no matter how ill-formed or ambiguous it might be.

Strategic Planning

The basis of strategy formulation is usually the strategic planning process. *Strategic planning is the systematic determination of strategic goals and the strategies to obtain them.* Many organizations formulate strategy through a series of **strategic planning retreats**—usually off-site meetings of key executives where plans are made and strategies formulated. For example, Clay Electric Cooperative in Florida holds an annual strategic planning retreat each summer in Jacksonville Beach, Florida. At this

EXHIBIT 3.1	The Strategic Planning Process

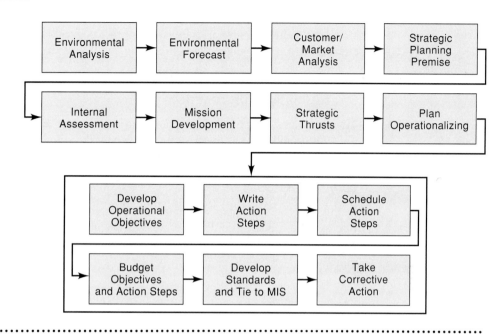

retreat, the previous year's strategic plan, strategies, and goals are reviewed and new ones are set for the coming year and beyond.

Strategic plans are generally *long term (3–5 years or more) plans* that involve major decisions and the commitment of large amounts of organizational resources to key goals. While there are several models of strategic planning, they usually involve a series of analytical steps, such as those presented in Exhibit 3.1. Note that the model begins with broad consideration of environmental factors and ends with specific operational steps. We will briefly examine each step in the process.[4]

Environmental Analysis

The first step in developing a strategic plan is to examine the outside environment surrounding the organization. The idea is to do a point-in-time analysis of significant aspects of the outside environment as they affect the organization, as was discussed in Chapter 2.

Environmental Forecast

This step is concerned with predicting how the environment is changing. Trends are explored and new issues of impact are identified. Implications for the future of the organization are explored. We also discussed this step in Chapter 2.

Customer/Market Analysis

Establishing a sharper understanding of why the organization exists (such as to serve a market) is the next step in the planning process. Emphasis is placed on analyzing how the market is changing and developing a profile of the customer of tomorrow.

Strategic Planning Premises

These premises reflect key assumptions made about the future. They are based on the forecast and serve as the basis for developing the strategic plan.

Internal Assessment

In this step, we attempt to determine the strengths and weaknesses of the organization as it now exists in order to establish a planning base. The internal assessment and environmental analysis serve as the basis for the SWOT (strengths, weaknesses, opportunities, threats).

Mission Development

This step in the planning process outlines the role and mission of the organization in view of the environment it faces and the resources it has or can reasonably expect to obtain. The mission provides the ultimate rationale for the organization's existence and gives the organization identity.

Strategic Thrusts

These are the three or four major strategies or key goals on which the organization plans to focus its efforts in the next 3–5 years. They reflect the mission and forecast.

Plan Operationalizing

The way to implement the strategic plan, from the development of operational objectives through the process of taking corrective action, is reflected here. Even though we present the strategic planning process in this step-by-step process, in reality it is not this simple. Even though it is best to proceed in the order suggested here, most organizations will revisit previous steps as they move through the process. This is a good policy check, and it emphasizes the need to make the planning process flexible.

A summary model of this process appears in Exhibit 3.2. Note the impact that the environment, competition, and strengths and weaknesses have on the strategy formulation process. When formulating strategy, organizations should try to capitalize on their strengths while taking advantage of environmental opportunities in order to beat their competition. Strategy also is formulated to protect the organization from environmental threats and to overcome internal weaknesses. For example, NutraSweet is attempting to beat the threat of new competition by strengthening customer brand loyalty to the NutraSweet brand—an inherent strength of the company.

EXHIBIT 3.2 Key Factors in Strategy Formulation

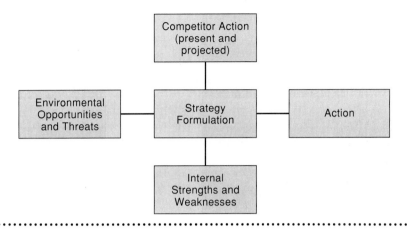

Future Orientation

Strategy formulation is an attempt to anchor the organization at some position in the future. This future orientation is a key concept to strategy formulation. Decisions made today to formulate strategy are done so as to place the organization at a particular position at a particular point in time. What every organization attempts to do is to create a desirable future for itself.

For example, in Chapter 1, when Volkswagen decided to change Audi's position in the market, it created a desirable future for the company by making decisions specifying new products and other actions that would turn the company around over a four-year period.

Strategy is goal oriented and goals exist in the future. In strategy formulation, organizations learn from the past—they learn from their mistakes—but they cannot change the past. "We should have done this" or "We should have done that" have relevance only in so far as they specify what the company should do now.

Evolutionary Process

The strategy formulation process is evolutionary in nature. It evolves over time as conditions change. Sometimes this process is more revolutionary than evolutionary. When Lee Iaccoca became the CEO of Chrysler, strategy changed quickly and abruptly. When an organization faces an immediate danger or crisis, quick change in strategy is needed. Even though such rapid change in strategy does occur, organizational inertia works against it.

Inertia is the tendency of an organization to stay on its present course or in its present form. The stronger the inertia, the less likely change will occur. Organizational inertia serves to anchor the organization and is the principle reason why strategy formulation is evolutionary rather that revolutionary most of the time.

Factors that enhance inertia include organization culture, tradition, competitive forces, size, and the ability to standardize routines. However, sometimes inertia can be overcome by sudden changes or disturbances. For example, the space shuttle

Challenger disaster forced Morton-Thoikol, the boosters contractor, as well as NASA, to undertake major changes in management and operational procedures in order to prevent such a disaster from occurring again.

Philosophical and Ethical Dimensions

Strategy is heavily laden with the personal philosophies and codes of ethics of key decision makers in an organization. Of course this is clearly seen in family-run organizations, even large ones such as Ford Motor Company in the 1920s. Henry Ford *was* Ford Motor and his philosophy and ethical values dominated the company.

Yet, even in larger organizations where the power is diffused, the philosophy and values of decision makers shape the strategy. For years, General Motors has been known as a company that widely distributes decision authority for strategy formulation among members of its executive committee. The personal values and ethics of individuals on this committee come to play in decisions involving product safety, design, fuel economy, dealer relations, customer warranties, labor costs, and so on. For example, in the initial discussion about the installation of passive restraint systems in autos (air bags), some believed that such installation was sound from a moral standpoint, even though the official position of GM was not to install such systems on all makes and models automatically. This position contrasted with that of Chrysler, which printed a personal pledge from Lee Iacocca in the *Wall Street Journal* advertisements to have such systems installed in every car and truck Chrysler makes. Such a competitive action may have caused GM to change its position on the issues.

Stakeholder Analysis

Another major influence on the formulation of strategy are *stakeholders.* Stakeholders are groups of people who have a major interest or claim on the operations or output of the organization.[5] They are also referred to as **constituent** groups. While the specific stakeholder groups for a particular organization are unique to that organization, Exhibit 3.3. shows a general model of the stakeholder group concept while Exhibit 3.4 shows the stakeholder groups for a human resources unit.

Notice that some of an organization's stakeholders are actual members of the organization: employees, managers and boards of directors (except for outside board members). However, notice the range of outside groups that can affect the formulation of an organization's strategy—all the way from unions to suppliers, distributors, and government regulatory agencies. Each of these groups lay claim on part of the organization's output. Employees want more wages and job security; stockholders want more dividends and higher stock prices; customers want quality products and services at the lowest possible price.

Obviously, an organization cannot possibly satisfy all of these groups completely. Therefore, it bargains, negotiates, and **compromises.** No group receives maximum returns on their claims from the organization; rather the organization tries to at least minimally satisfy each group.

Of course the claims of some groups sometimes become stronger than others. Eastern Airlines' unions push strongly for a wage increase. Ford's dealers argue for better financing terms. A public interest group demonstrates against GM's involvement in South Africa. A corporate raider tries to buy enough stock to take control of a company. With each of these situations, the organization must decide what its

···

| EXHIBIT 3.3 | Example Stakeholder Groups of an Organization |

basic position will be, and how this position will affect the organization now and in the future.

Theory of Countervailing Power

As groups make claims on organizational resources and outputs, they compete against each other. In this competitive arena, each group attempts to enhance its power position relative to other groups. It often does this by combining with other groups with similar interests. Galbraith explained this several years ago in his theory of countervailing power.[6]

This theory states that as certain organizations, groups, or institutions become powerful in the environment, other organizations will coalesce to build a competing power base to, in effect, try to countervail the power of the first group. This serves to reduce the relative power differential between the initially powerful organization or group and the coalesced organizations or group. Exhibit 3.5 depicts this theory.

This theory can be used to explain various activities. For example, it has been used to explain the formation of industrial unions to enhance the power of the

EXHIBIT 3.4 Example Stakeholder Groups of the Human Resource Subunit

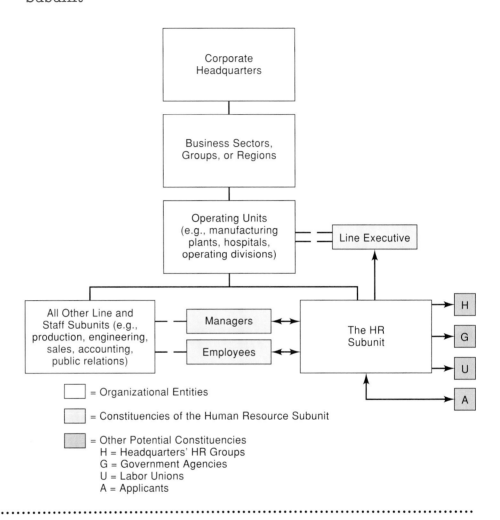

individual employee when dealing with large and powerful employers. Major retail chains, such as Sears, formed so that the chain would have more buying power than individual stores in dealing with major manufacturers. True-Value Hardware stores are an affiliation of locally owned stores that formed into a unit to deal with manufacturers of hardware goods.

This theory has a major bearing on policy formulation. Organizations may subordinate their own interests in order to form a grouping to enhance their power, as can be seen in the heavy involvement of organizations through associations for lobbying, advertising, and public relations. Associations such as the Iron and Steel Institute, American Dairy Council, American Bankers Association, and American Medical Association are but a few of the many associations that have become more powerful and vocal as they attempt to influence both legislation and public opinion on behalf of their members.

●●●

█ EXHIBIT 3.5 █   The Theory of Countervailing Power

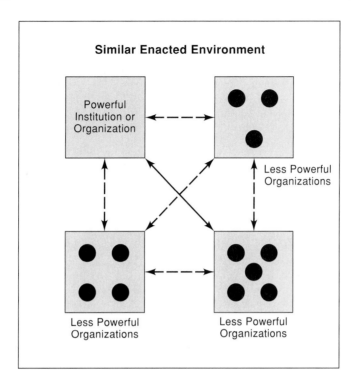

●●●

Thus, the distribution of power in society and the resultant action of individual organizations in response to this distribution has a major influence on the strategy formulation process in an individual organization.

Social Forces

The final outside influence on policy formulation is made up of the *social forces* at work in the society in which the organization exists. Social forces are the trends in the economy, politics, and culture of a society. These ebb and flow with time. The liberalism of the Kennedy and Johnson administrations gave way to the conservatism of the Reagan administration as the political mood of the country shifted.

Sometimes these shifts are dramatic, as occurred with both the civil rights movement in the United States and the cultural revolution in the Peoples Republic of China in the 1960s and the Khomeini revolution in Iran in the late 1970s. Other times they are less dramatic but just as powerful, such as the increasing labor force participation of women in career-oriented jobs during the 1960s, 1970s, and 1980s in the United States.

The point is that these underlying societal forces affect heavily strategy formulation in individual organizations. Of course, this is recognized by many organizations in the strategy formulation process. For example, when performing an environmental scan, strategists attempt to discern and forecast these trends and to position their organization to capitalize on them. This is why John Naisbitt's book

Megatrends

1. The U.S. economy has shifted from an industrial society to an information society. Over the past 30 years, employment has shifted from blue-collar to white-collar or information workers. Almost five times as many workers are employed in producing or processing information as are employed in manufacturing.
2. High technology will result in high-touch (desire for human interaction) reactions. Technological advances cannot be forced on an unwilling population. Human interaction will still be necessary and acceptance of high technology will depend on its provision for interpersonal relations.
3. The U.S. economy is moving from a national economy to a global economy. The United States is no longer self-sufficient and cannot isolate itself from the rest of the world.
4. Corporate managers are moving from short-term to long-term concerns in their thinking and actions. Far-sighted competitors, such as Japan, gained at the expense of the United States' short-term perspective.
5. Business and government are moving from centralization to decentralization. Our complex society means states and local governments will move toward political power and small firms will make the technological advances rather than large conglomerates.
6. There has been a return to self-reliance from dependence on outside institutions. People no longer want to depend on the government, the union, the corporation, or the school system.
7. A movement from representative democracy to participatory democracy is developing. People want to be part of the decisions that affect them.
8. A change from hierarchical to networking structures is occurring. Information is power and the computer provides access to information.
9. The centers of power have made a geographic shift from North to South. Population, jobs, and government power are moving from northern states to the southern and western states.
10. People are demanding variety in their choices rather than a single option. The individual, not the family, is the nation's building block.

SOURCE: John Naisbett, *Megatrends: Ten New Directions Transforming Our Lives* (New York: Warner, 1982).

Megatrends was such a top seller for so long in the early 1980s—so many decision makers are hungry for information that expands on and predicts these trends.[7] Of course not everyone agrees with these trends and some have been severely criticized.[8]

TYPES OF STRATEGIES

While it is impossible to list completely all of the strategies available to an organization, it is possible to identify a core set of **generic strategies.** These are distinctly identifiable, basic strategies that an organization may choose to follow. The appropriateness of each strategy for a particular organization is situational in that it depends on the environment, market, social forces, mission, and internal strengths and weaknesses faced by a particular organization. Moreover, the selection of the strategy will have a profound impact on human resource strategy. In fact, as we have indicated and will discuss further in this chapter, human resource strategy should also affect the formation of corporate strategy.

Two primary levels of generic strategy are discussed: corporate or organization-wide strategies and business or industry-level strategies. It is important to note that in a single-product company operating in one line of business or industry, there is virtually no difference between corporate-wide and business-level strategies. Exhibit

....

| EXHIBIT 3.6 | Generic Corporate- and Business-Level Strategies |

I. Generic Corporate-Level Strategies
   A. Growth strategies
      1. Concentration
         a. Market development
         b. Product development
         c. Horizontal integration
      2. Vertical integration
         a. Backward integration
         b. Forward integration
      3. Diversification
         a. Concentric
         b. Conglomerate
      4. Implementation of growth strategy
         a. Internal growth
         b. Acquisition
         c. Merger
         d. Joint venture

   B. Stability strategy
      1. Neutral
      2. Harvest (milk the investment)
   C. Defensive strategies
      1. Turnaround
      2. Divestiture
      3. Liquidation
      4. Bankruptcy
      5. Captive
   D. Combination strategies
II. Generic Business-Level Strategies
   A. Overall cost leadership
   B. Product/service differentiation
   C. Market segment focus
   D. Preemptive strategies

....

3.6 summarizes the types of strategies found at each level. We will briefly examine each one.

Generic Corporate-Level Strategies

These strategies are adopted and followed by the organization as a whole. They fall into four main categories: (1) growth, (2) stability, (3) defensive, and (4) combination.

Growth Strategies

Most organizations wish to grow. As a matter of fact, a study by William Glueck of 358 *Fortune* companies indicated that 54.2 percent pursue this strategy.[9] A **concentration growth strategy** means that the organization plans to focus its growth on a single product or a group of closely related products, as is the situation with Coors Breweries, which has a very narrow line of brewery products compared to the vast number of different products from Anheuser-Busch.

A growth strategy can be pursued in three ways. First, the existing market can be developed by expanding market share or moving into new geographic regions. Second, the product can be slightly changed or developed. Perhaps a new or closely aligned product can be added (such as the introduction of Coors Light to the Coors line). Third, a concentration growth strategy can be achieved through horizontal integration. Here, another product in the same business is added, usually through buying an organization, as when Dr. Pepper bought Canada Dry in 1982.

The James River Corporation, a Virginia paper goods manufacturer, is aggressively pursuing a growth strategy using the methods discussed above. First, the company is attempting to expand its market share by pushing its product in the northeastern states. Second, it is developing a host of new paper products, such as coated paper plates, that it hopes will win a large share of the $500 million-per-year paper plate market. Third, through the process of horizontal integration, it has purchased other paper goods companies, such as Connecticut's Dixie Northern.[10]

Vertical integration is another way to achieve growth. Here, the organization can either acquire its suppliers (backward integration) or acquire its distributors (forward integration); some organizations do both. Miller Brewing has purchased its own aluminum can manufacturing facilities in addition to acquiring some of its distribution channels.

The third way growth can occur is through **diversification.** Diversification occurs when an organization moves into products or services that are clearly different from its current businesses. Diversification has two forms. **Concentric diversification** occurs when related but clearly differentiated products or services are developed or obtained. Coca-Cola's purchase of Minute Maid is an excellent example. **Conglomerate diversification** occurs when the firm diversifies into an area totally unrelated to the product or service. Bic's development of the disposable safety razor resulted in a product totally unrelated to its pen business.

The **implementation of growth strategies** can be accomplished through four basic methods: internal growth, acquisition, merger, and joint venture. **Internal growth** occurs when current market share with current products is expanded (for example, GM sells more Chevrolets relative to competitive brands). An **acquisition** occurs when one company buys another and absorbs it but keeps its own name; a **merger** occurs when two companies join to form a new company and adopt a new name. A **joint venture** occurs when two or more companies work together for a specific project, such as oil exploration and drilling; they pool their resources and take a risk for a specific endeavor.

Stability Strategies

As opposed to growth strategies, stability strategies attempt to maintain the status quo. The two basic stability strategies are neutral and harvest. **Neutral strategies** are do-nothing approaches. The organization just keeps doing what it always has done without a growth goal in mind. A **harvest strategy,** sometimes called "milk-the-investment" strategy, represents an end-game strategy identified by Kathryn Harrigan in *Strategies for a Declining Business.*[11] The idea is to retrieve the value of earlier investments because the firm intends to sell its assets and get out of the business.

Defensive Strategies

A third set of corporate-level strategies involves actions taken to reverse a negative situation or overcome a crisis or problem. These are often called **retrenchment** strategies. An organization can adopt five basic defensive strategies. **Turnaround** strategies are designed to reverse a negative trend, such as falling profits or increasing costs. Layoffs, cutting wages, reducing expense accounts, and cutting advertising are all forms of turnaround strategies. LTV Steel, for example, postponed paying $180 million in pension fund contributions in order to cut costs.[12] Later, the company declared bankruptcy and could not pay bonuses to employees who had taken early retirement.

A second type of defensive strategy is **divestiture.** This occurs when an organization sells or divests itself of a business or part of a business, as ITT did with many of its operations during the mid-1980s. In a **liquidation,** the organization is either sold or dissolved. DeLorean Motor Company, which was dissolved several years ago, and Walter E. Heller Corporation, a financial investment company that was sold to Fuji Bank of Japan in 1984, are good examples of liquidations.

Since the Bankruptcy Reform Act of 1978, **bankruptcy** is now being used as a defensive strategy. Chapter 11 (in Title 11 of the United States Code), which involves a reorganization, is the device most used to rehabilitate corporate debtors who are having financial difficulties; it can be a way to escape a heavy debt load, contracted high wages, or even legal claims. Continental Airlines used Chapter 11 to negate its labor contracts with its unions, while Manville Corporation used this method to avoid high legal costs caused by asbestos claims.

The final defensive strategy is to become a **captive** of another organization. This situation occurs when an organization allows another organization to manage it in return for promising to buy a certain amount of the captive's products or services. This strategy often occurs between a small- to medium-sized supplier and a major manufacturer or retailer.

Combination Strategies

The last major set of corporate-level strategies occurs when an organization simultaneously uses different strategies for different units. Next to growth strategies, this strategy is the most common one. Large diversified corporations, for example, are using the combination strategy when they acquire new companies while selling others. They carve out market segments and develop new products, and they acquire suppliers and distributors, and so on. General Motors' recent actions, which involved dropping and adding models while acquiring Hughes Aircraft and EDS, are a good example of using a combination strategy.

Generic Business-Level Strategies

Business-level strategies are strategies employed by an organization for one of its particular product or service lines. This type of plan tends to be less generic than corporate-level strategies because it must be tailored to fit the unique circumstances of each organization. However, four basic strategy types are often used to classify business-level strategies: (1) overall cost leadership, (2) product/service differentiation, (3) market segment focus, and (4) preemptive strategies.

Overall Cost Leadership

This strategy allows an organization to cut its prices by producing the product or service cheaper than the competition does. An organization achieves this strategy through extensive experience, cheap labor, size (economics of scale), reduced overhead, or more efficient technology. By providing cheaper goods and services, an organization can either sell at a lower price than its competition, garner a larger share of the market, or maintain its price and achieve a higher profit margin.

Product/Service Differentiation

An organization uses this strategy to create a perception in the market of the uniqueness of its product or service. A **brand image,** such as Bud Light beer or Polo sportswear, a **quality image,** such as Mercedes or Rolls Royce, or **customer service,** such as IBM offers, are but three ways to achieve this differentiation. Differentiation relies on convincing customers that the product or service is so unique that the customer should buy it.

Market Segment Focus

This strategy attempts to carve out a part of the market and focus organizational efforts on serving it. The market segment focus may be done on the basis of a demographic factor, such as age, income, family size, or geographic region. The idea is to achieve a competitive advantage within a narrowly focused market segment rather than to appeal to a broad market. A high-fashion men's clothing store and Porsche automobiles are examples of a market segmentation strategy.

Preemptive Strategies

These strategies are undertaken to disrupt the normal state of affairs in an industry or product line. This strategy essentially rewrites the rules of the game to compete in the industry. Such preemptive strategies may occur because of new product developments, as happened when Xerox became the first company in the office copier market, or they may occur with market segmentation in an unsegmented market, as happened when Miller Brewing developed the first low-calorie beer, Miller Lite. This type of strategy also could be based on costs, as was the case when Peoples Express Airlines was built around the concept of low price and discount air fares.

In each of these cases, the organization came up with an innovative product or tactic that caught the competition off guard. Hence, the competition had to scramble to remain viable.

Two Key Strategies for Human Resource Management

Two gross generic categories of strategy seem to have had the greatest impact on human resource management in recent years. A review of the literature by Cynthia Fisher classified strategies into these two categories:[13]

1. Growth–prospector–high-tech entrepreneurial strategies
2. Mature–defender–cost efficiency strategies

Firms in the growth mode will require creative, innovative, and risk-taking behavior from employees. Mature–defender firms will need just the opposite kind of behavior—repetitive, predictable and carefully specified behavior. Human resource management systems under each mode will be substantially different in terms of function. Human resource management units in growth firms typically recruit at all levels from the external labor market in order to obtain enough employees at all skill levels to meet growth needs. They tend to appraise people based on results rather than process or traits. They also tend to look to the long term for success and usually do not pursue innovative efforts that fail. Performance incentives serve as the basis for compensation; where bonuses, profit sharing and stock options are common, base salaries will be modest.[14]

Mature–defender–cost competitors will do the opposite in personnel actions.[15] They tend to recruit primarily at the entry level and promote from within. They emphasize doing things the right way in appraisal and focus on quantifiable short-term results. Compensation is based on hierarchical wage structures determined by job evaluation. Length of service, loyalty, and other traits are rewarded rather than

HR CHALLENGES ●

Examples of the Two Key Strategies for HRM

Growth–Prospector–High-Tech Entrepreneurial Strategy

Apple Computer began in a California garage in 1975. Its employment grew very rapidly from 2,000 in 1980 to 6,700 in 1989. Creativity was the key ingredient desired in employees. Employees were recruited at all levels in the company. Hours and dress were very flexible. In the early years, the style of management reflected the creative entrepreneurial whims of its youthful founders: brilliant college dropouts Steve Wozniak, 23, and Steve Jobs, 19. Their freewheeling style led to an organization described as "camp run amok." In March of 1977, Apple introduced its Apple II aimed primarily at the home and school markets.

Along with growth and success came the realization that the business market was a potential source of additional expansion. As sales in the company grew, employees, opportunities, and new problems were presented to the "entrepreneurial" staff. The Apple II was rushed to the market in 1980 without adequate quality control, and the product failed miserably. The reintroduction of the Apple III in 1981 unfortunately coincided with IBM's entry into the market with the PC. Apple did score a success with the IIe in 1983, but the Lisa model met with considerable market resistance because of its price. It became clear that Apple needed to retain its creative spirit, but at the same time react to the turbulent market environment. In the summer of 1981 Apple began an intensive search for a new CEO. In April 1983, John Scully from Pepsi-Cola was hired as CEO. Scully brought a new sense of professionalism, marketing expertise, and organizational skills. The more formalized structure led to conflicts and disagreements with the founders. In January of 1985 Wozniak removed himself as a major decision maker. In April, 1985, the Apple board of directors removed Steve Jobs from his Macintosh position.

Scully's human resource management challenge was to retain Apple's innovative spirit, but in a more business-like atmosphere that could support an ever growing market. He has recently reorganized Apple into four internal operating divisions: Apple Products, Apple USA, Apple Europe, and Apple Pacific. According to Scully, one of the primary reasons for the company's reorganization is the preservation of the employees' independent spirit, innovation, and passion to build great products. The human resource management decision to reorganize into the four divisions distributed leadership of the company. This flatter organizational structure allows Apple to react more quickly to technological and market changes.

Mature–Defender–Cost Efficiency Strategy

More often than not, firms that have adopted this strategy have been around for some time. A good example is the Campbell Soup Company. In the fall of 1989 Campbell closed four U.S. plants, consolidated operations overseas, and eliminated about 2,800 jobs. Its original plant in Camden, New Jersey, was among those closed. During 1989 its plants ran at only about 60 percent of its capacity. These closings were in addition to several plants closed in 1988. Workers affected by the closings were given at least six-months notice and severance benefits.

The company president and CEO indicated that the restructuring and plant consolidations were part of "an ongoing effort to slim down" and become a more efficient global competitor.

The company also retrofitted many of its older plants with new technology and is studying prototype plans for a major technological breakthrough involving sophisticated computer applications. The firm acknowledged that the restructuring will cause a massive change in job design structure and skills needed. Training programs will need to be redesigned.

SOURCE: Charles W. L. Hill and Gareth R. Jones; *Strategic Management*, 2nd ed. (Boston: Houghton Mifflin, 1992), pp. 87–89; 176–179.

performance. Financial incentives may be present but tend to be available only to few select employee groups.

●
ROLE OF THE MARKET AND COMPETITION IN STRATEGY FORMULATION

Probably no other factor has had such a major influence on strategy formulation and human resource strategy during the 1980s as has *competitive analysis*. Even though we have already briefly discussed this in Chapters 1 and 2, it is useful to review it at this point to see its impact on strategy formulation.

The essential action that an organization attempts to achieve with respect to its competitors is to achieve a **sustainable competitive advantage (SCA).**[16] Although this idea has been around for a long time, it took on new meaning and urgency in the 1980s as American corporations attempted to become more competitive in a global economy.

Basically a sustainable competitive advantage is a differential advantage a particular organization can achieve over its competition. It may be low cost, such as the inexpensive Hyundai in the automotive market; it may by brand loyalty, such as that enjoyed by Coke; or it may be complete customer satisfaction, such as that offered by Sears. In fact, it could be just about anything an organization can come up with to differentiate itself from its competition: speed, friendliness, reliability, image or prestige, convenience, and so on. What matters is that the organization can establish in the customer's mind that such a differential advantage exists and that the organization can sustain this advantage over time.

Competitive Analysis[17]

In performing a competitive analysis, the market, industry, competition, and the organization itself are examined. To do this, several additional levels of analysis must occur. An illustration of some of the concerns is presented in Exhibit 3.7.

These are not easy questions to answer to be sure, but they must be answered in order to establish and maintain a sustainable competitive advantage. This advantage may be a package of product/service attributes as opposed to any one attribute. People buy BMW's for prestige, reliability, and resale value. People shop at Sears not only because of its goal of complete customer satisfaction, but also because of location, convenience, and product selection.

Cost-Cutting Competitive Strategy

As we previously stated, the mature–cost-defender–efficiency strategy was common during the 1980s when many organizations attempted to become more competitive by cutting costs. This strategy had a significant effect on human resources in individual organizations that adopted it in at least three major ways: wages or their rate of increase was slowed significantly; a significant number of employees were cut or the rate of growth was slowed, especially for higher paid and staff employees; and production was shifted to lower-wage labor markets, such as the southern United States or developing countries. Sometimes these actions were taken at the initiative of the company; sometimes they occurred as a result of a takeover or merger. Regardless, when an organization adopts a more competitive strategy that emphasizes cost cutting, the decision has a profound impact on human resource strategies in all phases of human resource activity: hiring, placement, pay, layoff, outplacement, retraining, retirement, and so on. The effects and implications of this cost-cutting strategy on human resources are so significant that they will be explored throughout this book.

The popularity of cost-cutting strategies reflects the attempt of corporations to reach a more competitive level on a global basis. Competing with imports produced by foreign manufacturers in lower-wage countries required U.S. corporations to find ways to cut costs to remain competitive. Human resource costs, of course, were not the only ones attacked. Just-in-time inventory reflects efforts to shift the carrying

....

| **EXHIBIT 3.7** | Some Issues to Consider for a Competitive Analysis |

MARKET

1. What is the market? Who now purchases the product/service and why?
2. What is the potential market? Who *could* purchase the product?
3. How fast is the market growing?
4. Can product/service usage be increased or has saturation been achieved?

INDUSTRY

1. Within what industry does the market exist? How narrowly should the industry be defined (e.g., transportation industry vs. railroad industry; oil industry vs. energy industry)?
2. What barriers to entry and exit exist in the industry?
3. Who dominates the industry and why?
4. What substitute products exist for industry products?
5. What is the growth stage of the industry (e.g., emerging, rapid, mature, declining)?
6. What are the critical success factors to be successful in the industry?

COMPETITION

1. Who are the major competitors? What are their descriptive profiles (e.g., size, location, product features, etc.)?
2. What does each competitor do well? What does each do poorly?
3. What gaps exist in the market? What service or product features not now being provided could be provided?
4. Can this service or product be provided profitably? How do we know this?

INTERNAL ORGANIZATION

1. What are our strengths and weaknesses?
2. What are our unique attributes relative to the competition?
3. How can we capitalize on these attributes?
4. Do we have or can we obtain additional resources to capitalize on these attributes or to develop new ones?
5. Can we be profitable relying on these attributes?
6. How can we sustain this differential over time? How is present competition likely to change? How is new competition likely to change?
7. Can we convince the customer that we do indeed have something better to offer? How many do we have to convince to remain profitable (e.g., what must be our market share)?

....

costs of inventories to suppliers. Tax and other inducements bargained for from states reflect corporate efforts to reduce relocation and new plant construction costs. This concern with cost cutting pervades and will likely continue to pervade human resource and other strategies throughout the 1990s as global competition becomes even more intense.

Customer Perspective

In addition to understanding the industrial and market forces at work in formulating a sustainable competitive advantage, it is very important to look at the firm's product or service from the eyes of the customer.[18] What the firm believes to be its competitive advantage does not matter if it varies from what the customer wants. Henry Ford was initially successful by competing on the basis of price. He was known to declare that the customer could have any color Ford he or she wanted, as long as it was black. This strategy worked until customers wanted style and color. GM quickly became dominant in the market by offering these attributes as a competitive advantage while Ford stuck to price.

Understanding the customer and what the customer expects and looks for in the product is at the heart of determining a sustainable competitive advantage. This calls for customer and consumer research and the incorporation of these findings into new product/service development as well as into the firm's advertising and promotional campaign. The sustainable competitive advantage must be communicated to the customer and amplified in his or her mind if it is to be successful. It does IBM no good to convince a customer that its new OS/2 operating system for its PC is better, thus justifying its price, if PC customers would rather pay a lower price for an IBM clone without OS/2.

In the next section, we see further the role that human resource strategy plays in helping companies to achieve a sustainable competitive advantage as it formulates and achieves its overall strategy.

ROLE OF HUMAN RESOURCES IN STRATEGY FORMULATION

Up to now, we have argued that overall corporate strategy should drive functional, including human resource, strategies. That is, a company should first decide what it needs to do as a whole to achieve a strategic competitive advantage and then formulate specific strategies for each functional area—marketing, finance, operations/productions, human resources—to carry it out. We have stated that in formulating overall strategy, the company should consider various aspects of each functional strategy. It needs to assess how well it is performing in each functional area.

Thus, in reality, the formulation of corporate strategy is really **interactive** with the formulation of functional strategy. In other words, by considering its capabilities in each functional area, the company is actually using its existing functional strategy and capabilities to help shape its future corporate strategy.

This interactive effect is an important notion, particularly with respect to human resource strategy. Lengnick-Hall and Lengnick-Hall argue in "Strategic Human Resource Management" that, "Reciprocal interdependence between a firm's business strategy and its human resources strategy underlies the proposed approach to the strategic management of human resources."[19] Their conceptual diagram, shown in Exhibit 3.8, depicts this reciprocal interdependence. Notice that the formation of corporate competitive advantage not only influences, but is influenced by, human resource strategy. Certainly economic conditions, industry structure, the labor market, and other factors depicted in the exhibit must be considered. But these are considered in light of the interactive effect of competitive strategy and human resource strategy.

We will see this happening in the Super-Lube example. From its very beginning, a major ingredient in forming Super-Lube's overall corporate strategy was a human resource strategy that stressed competent and courteous employees. This, plus a limited geographic focus, has enabled Super-Lube to achieve success in the highly competitive quick-lube market.

HR CHALLENGES •

Super-Lube's Sustainable Competitive Advantage

Super-Lube 10 Minute Oil Change is a Tallahassee, Florida, based corporation involved in the quick oil change business. This market is relatively new and offers drive-in drive-out convenience in oil changes and lubrication. Over one hundred separate firms operate in this market with Jiffy-Lube being the largest. With 21 stations, Super-Lube ranked number five in the market nationally in 1988.

Quick-Lube Industry

The quick-lube industry began in the late 1970s in the upper Midwest. Its primary offering is convenience, since the customer does not have to leave the car for a long period of time for servicing. The primary services provided are oil changes and lubrications, although some companies also provide free tire fills, tune-ups, and brake checks.

The quick-lube industry has grown rapidly because of the demise of full-service gas stations and the rise of self-service brought on by the oil crisis. The social trend toward greater convenience also has been a major reason for the success of the industry. It is estimated that one-third of the oil change business is now handled by quick-lube type stations, one-third by garages, service stations, and auto dealers, and one-third by do-it-yourselfers. Analysts believe the quick-lube sector will grow rapidly to perhaps two-thirds of the market by 1995.

Super-Lube

The strategy of Super-Lube can be explained as follows: to be absolutely the best fast oil change facility in the market areas served *and* to gain a position of clear market dominance therein. Strategic priorities follow:

1. Complete customer satisfaction through friendly, competent, and courteous service.

2. Highest consistent standards of performance.
3. High level of employee job satisfaction and opportunity for advancement.
4. Comparatively high return to stockholders within a three-year period.

Since its founding in 1983, the company has emphasized fast, competent, courteous service as their key trademark. They pride themselves on clean, attractive stations that will make both male and female customers feel comfortable.

Human resources have always played a key role in overall corporate strategy. Bright, helpful, courteous people are hired at substantially above minimum wage. Employees are thoroughly trained in the Super-Lube way—both from technical and customer relations standpoints. Within six months, employees are placed on a merit bonus system that supplements their pay.

The company projects growth to 22 stations by 1991. All stations and land are company owned; none are franchised. Total sales were well over $2 million in 1988 with net operating revenue about $125,000.

Company founder and president, John Lewis, attributes the bulk of the company's success to the outstanding employees it has been able to attract and hold. The company has a very good reputation in the entire industry with respect to employee competence and courtesy.

Super-Lube shows how a firm was able to use its human resources to help it achieve a strategic competitive advantage in the marketplace. The overall corporate strategy of dominance in a limited number of markets was achieved by being the first in these markets and then using well-trained, polite employees to obtain and keep customer loyalty.

SOURCE: Adapted from "Special Stockholders' Meeting Report," Super-Lube 10-Minute Oil Change (Tallahassee, FL, 1988), p. 1.

Other examples exist. Ford's "Quality Is Job 1" strategy would have had little chance of success had the company not explicitly considered both present and future human resource capability and strategy when formulating its quality strategy. 3M's strategy of innovation heavily depends on programs for innovation instituted with employees. Without innovative employees, the program would not work. The same is true of Florida Power and Light's (FP&L) Quality Improvement Program. The heart of this program rests with employee Quality Improvement Groups. FP&L has spent much money and effort in forming, guiding, and training these groups during the 1980s.

EXHIBIT 3.8   Reciprocal Interdependence of Corporate Strategy and Human Resource Strategy

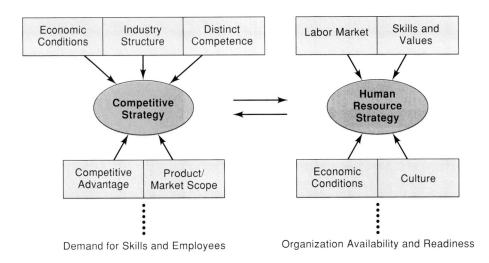

Demand for Skills and Employees   Organization Availability and Readiness

A New Role for Human Resources

So we see that human resources plays a different and expanded role under the strategic human resource approach. No longer is human resource strategy simply personnel management strategy with operative employees driven by overall corporate strategy. In short, no longer is personnel management simply left out of the strategic competitive arena. As Michael Porter has argued in *Competitive Advantage*, human resource management can help a firm achieve a competitive advantage.[20] By involving human resource considerations when overall strategy is formulated, human resources can help achieve a strategic advantage. We saw this in the Super-Lube case and we see it with other firms that have fully integrated human resource considerations in strategy formulation.

Unfortunately, however, in the 1980s, many companies that focused on human resource strategy issues when forming corporate strategy looked at the issue simply from a cost-cutting perspective. As we suggested earlier in this chapter, the cost-cutting strategy was a predominant one in human resource strategy formulation during the 1980s. We saw this strategy manifested in the policies of Ford, GM, and U.S. Steel—in short, almost all major older U.S. firms have tried to reduce labor costs in order to be more competitive.

Because of this cost-cutting strategy many employees have lost jobs, taken early retirement, or suffered wage cuts. While such actions are often necessary, organizations do not always provide needed transition assistance. Employee assistance, such as severance pay, outplacement (that is, helping a person find a new job), and retraining could cushion the effect of cost-cutting strategies on labor.

Line versus Staff Conflict

Human resource managers have long suffered from the line versus staff conflict situation that tends to arise in so many organizations. We will review this issue and see how this conflict affects the new strategic role for human resources.

First, it is important to remember that all managers are human resource managers. That is, all managers have subordinates that they rely on to carry out work. For example, in the NutraSweet case at the beginning of the chapter, the company was operating under Robert Shapiro's entrepreneurial style. Line managers made all of the personnel decisions.

Second, the functions of hiring, training, placing, paying, and otherwise dealing with the work force must be done by somebody in the organization. If a human resource unit does not exist, then line managers must perform all of these actions themselves.

Third, human resource units are set up as specialized departments to help line managers in their role as human resource managers. In other words, human resource units help line managers carry out the human resource functions of hiring, paying, and so on. As the NutraSweet company grew, many of these personnel functions were transferred from line managers to the human resource staff.

Fourth, in some organizations human resource units are given wide latitude to do some of the hiring, benefit determination, training, and so on. In these organizations, the human resource unit may be criticized for "taking on too much" or "taking too much authority away from line managers."

Fifth, in many organizations human resource units serve as police units. They enforce the myriad of laws in human resources that a company must abide by: wage and hour, social security, discrimination, benefits, safety and health, and so on. They also are often given the job of enforcing company human resource policy. This results in personnel telling line managers what they can and cannot do according to the law or corporate policy. At NutraSweet, Shapiro's introduction of a policy manual involved more than just the writing of policy; the policies had to be enforced. This responsibility falls on both the line and staff managers. This division of responsibility can sometimes cause line-staff conflict because goals and objectives can differ between departments.

Finally, because human resource units do not have primary authority to produce or market a product or service, and line managers do, line managers often view human resource people as "out of touch" with the real world. Line managers have production and sales quotas and deadlines that must be met. They see themselves "on the firing line," or "in the trenches." To them human resources has none of these deadlines and pressures. Instead, they often see human resource specialists as people who throw roadblocks or hindrances in their way—as people who have the luxury of sitting back in their offices dreaming up new rules and regulations to thwart efficient operations.

This raises the issue of the *credibility* of the human resource unit. Unfortunately in some organizations, employees in human resource units are often viewed as people who could not cut it in a line position. While this problem is not as serious as it once was because the human resource function has become more professionalized, it can be a problem in some organizations and must be dealt with.

All of these factors cause line-staff conflict and believability issues. This conflict and credibility gap can be so serious as to prevent human resources from playing a strong role in strategy formulation. Therefore, conflict must be reduced and credibility enhanced if the human resources function is to be fully involved in strategy formulation. What can be done? Let us examine some courses of action.[21]

Enhancing Credibility and Reducing Staff-Line Conflict

As Exhibit 3.9 points out, a company can take a number of actions to reduce line-staff conflict and enhance the credibility of the human resource unit. First, it should ensure that people who staff the human resource unit are competent, trained, and experienced in the various human resource functions.

Second, the human resource unit's role should be clearly spelled out in corporate policy vis-à-vis line manager roles. "Who has responsibility of what and when" needs to be determined, put in writing, and shared among line managers and the human resource unit. Both line managers and human resource professionals should play a role in this responsibility determination.

Third, human resource people should view their role as support to line not vice versa. The human resource unit exists to help line managers do a better job as human resource managers. Even though human resources must enforce human resource laws and policies, they essentially exist to help line managers and to keep them out of trouble.

Fourth, human resources and line managers should work together in formulating human resource policies, programs, and actions. For example, at Clay Electric Co-operative in Florida, even though the human resource unit was given the primary responsibility to come up with a new performance appraisal system, it did so by working with line managers every step of the way. At each step the work of the human resource unit was "bounced off" of the line managers in group sessions, and their suggestions were incorporated into modified versions of the system.

Fifth, human resource people should practice "managing by wandering around" as Peters and Austin call it in *A Passion for Excellence*.[22] In other words, human resource people should get out of their offices and out to where the work is done—the factory, office, mine, or field. Human resource isolation from line work can be a serious cause of low credibility and staff-line conflict. In fact, because of this many companies, including Proctor & Gamble, IBM, and GE, do not place people in human resource positions until they have had line experience and training.

Sixth, line managers need to understand the important and significant role that human resources play in today's environment. The human resource unit takes many burdensome chores away from line managers, which actually makes their jobs much easier. Line managers sometime forget this fact.

Line-staff conflict can seldom be completely eliminated. All of these actions should serve to enhance the human resource unit's credibility and reduce line-staff conflict thereby opening the door for greater participation of human resource professionals in the strategy formulation process.

CONTINGENCY OR SITUATIONAL APPROACH TO STRATEGY

Before we close this chapter, one additional consideration must be reviewed: the **situational** nature of strategy formulation. Basically, this idea states that what might be good for one firm may not be good for another. The formulation of a proper strategy for a particular firm is **firm specific.** Thus, the strategy is **contingent** upon

....

EXHIBIT 3.9 ## Some Ways to Enhance the Human Resource Unit's Credibility and Reduce Line-Staff Conflict

1. Hire only competent and experienced people for the personnel unit.
2. Clearly spell out personnel unit responsibilities in relation to line management responsibilities.
3. Have personnel staff members view their roles as supportive to line staff members.
4. Have personnel and line staff members work together in forming personnel policies.
5. Ensure that personnel staff members have firsthand contact and experience with line operations.
6. Ensure that managers remember the important role personnel plays in reducing burdensome tasks.

....

specific aspects of the firm. The proper strategy is determined by the unique internal characteristics of the firm and the specific environmental opportunities and threats faced by it. This is true of firms even in the same industry—what is right for Ford may not be right for GM and vice versa.

However, the situational or contingency approach does not mean that firms should ignore what other firms are doing. In fact, in the case of their competitors, firms need to consider explicitly the strategies of the competition in formulating their own strategy. A firm can examine its competition, see what they are doing, and make judgments as to whether its situation is similar enough to allow it to use a similar or modified version of the strategy.

Sometimes strategies roll like waves across the business landscape. In cases like these, a particular strategy catches on with a lot of firms. As pointed out several places in this book, merger and acquisition and cost-cutting were very popular strategies in the 1980s. In the area of human resources, two popular strategies have been labor cost cutting and human resource involvement. Even though its tempting to jump uncritically on the bandwagon with wholesale adoption of a popular strategy, each firm should carefully examine the strategy and its own situation to determine if it is, in fact, right for it.

To a large extent, this decision depends on two key factors: (1) how well a firm monitors what goes on around it and (2) and firm's philosophy with respect to strategy innovation. We examined the first factor when we discussed scanning and knowing the environment in Chapter 2. We will now address strategy innovation.

Philosophy of Innovation and Strategy

Companies that wish to be "firstest with the mostest," Peter Drucker's term in "Entrepreneurial Strategies," design their own strategies that fit their own circumstances.[23] They do not follow or copy others. They are risk takers and want to be the first ones out with the new strategy, new product, new feature, or new service. They want to be first to enter a new market. For them strategy formulation is completely situational because there is no one to copy. Apple Computer is an example of a firm with this strategy.

At the other extreme are the followers. Seldom do they develop a new strategy. They have a low tolerance for risk. They want to go with the tried and true. They closely watch others, see what works, and adopt it in their own firm. For them

....

| EXHIBIT 3.10 | Factors That Determine a Firm's Point on the Strategy Innovation Continuum |

THE DYNAMICS OF THE MARKET AND COMPETITION

The more dynamic the market, the more likely innovation is rewarded.

THE AMOUNT AND EXTENT OF GOVERNMENT REGULATION

The more government regulation is exerted, the less likely innovation is rewarded.

THE PERSONAL PHILOSOPHY OF TOP MANAGEMENT

The more conservative the philosophy, the less likely innovation will occur.

PREVIOUS EXPERIENCE WITH INNOVATION

This works both ways. On the one hand, previous positive experience with innovation will foster more innovation. On the other hand, some firms who have successfully innovated in the past tend to stick with these innovations beyond their usefulness in the market. Consider, for example, GM's over-reliance on standard styling and car components across division lines. Initially successful in the early 1980s, this policy became dysfunctional in the late 1980s as Chevrolet, Pontiac, Buick, Oldsmobile and Cadillac became less differentiated in the customer's mind.

THE COST OF INNOVATION

When costs of innovation are high, there is less likelihood of significant innovation. Witness the reluctance of U.S. steel producers to adopt the new technology used by Japanese and German steel producers.

AGE OF THE FIRM

Often times it is a new company that comes up with the new product, not an existing company in the industry. Apple invented the PC, not IBM. Xerox invented electrostatic copying, not mimeograph machine makers. The quick-lube market was developed by new firms, not the existing oil companies, gas station dealers, or auto dealers.

....

strategy formulation is less situational than it is with the innovators, although they often adjust an existing strategy to fit their own circumstances. Makers of IBM compatible personal computer, such as Standard Computer, follow this strategy.

The strategy innovators have the opportunity to experience huge successes as a result of hitting the market first, as did Apple with the Apple II. But they also can experience failure as did Peoples Express with cut-rate pricing and "jack-of-all-trades" job assignment for employees. (Peoples Express filed for bankruptcy and was absorbed by Texas Air in the mid-1980s.) The particular point along the strategy innovation continuum for any given firm depends on a number of factors, which are presented in Exhibit 3.10.

All of these factors affect the degree of innovation in strategy formulation. Regardless of position along the innovation continuum, strategy will need to be situational for it to be successful. It will likely be more situational with more innovative firms, however, than it will be with less innovative ones. The less innovative ones will borrow successful existing strategy and use it as best they can.

• • • • • • • • •

MANAGEMENT GUIDELINES

We can summarize the key points of this chapter with the following guidelines:

1. Strategy formulation is not a neat and clean process. It moves in "fits and starts" with much backtracking and revision. It is evolutionary in nature more often than it is revolutionary.

2. Strategy and the process of formulating it must be kept flexible and adaptable.

3. Much strategy formulation occurs in the strategic planning process especially in the environmental scan and internal assessment.

4. Firms often adopt a set of generic strategies.

5. The market and especially competition play a very important role in the formation of strategy and the firm's sustainable competitive advantage.

6. Even though corporate strategy should drive functional strategy, human resource units play an interactive role with respect to overall corporate strategy formulation.

7. For human resources to maximize its role in strategy formulation, it must reduce the line-staff conflict and credibility gap that may exist between it and line managers.

8. All strategy is situational. The proper strategy for a particular firm depends on the unique situation faced by that firm. What works for one firm may not work for another.

QUESTIONS FOR REVIEW

1. Describe the strategy formulation process and the role strategic planning plays in the process. Specifically, explain the role of the environmental scan and the internal assessment (SWOT).

2. Why should strategy be flexible and adaptive in nature?

3. List and explain six key generic strategies.

4. Distinguish between line of business and corporate strategies and give examples of each.

5. What role does the market and competition play in strategy formulation? Specifically, what is a sustainable competitive advantage and why is this idea important?

6. What are the ways a firm can obtain or achieve a sustainable competitive advantage?

7. We have stated that corporate strategy should drive functional and human resource strategy. We also have stated that the formation of corporate and human resource strategy is interactive in nature. Do you see an apparent contradiction in these two statements? Explain your answer.

8. What is the line-staff conflict and credibility gap that often exists between the human resource unit and line managers? What causes this conflict?

9. How can line staff conflict and the credibility gap between line managers and the human resource unit be reduced? Why must it be reduced?

10. What do we mean when we say that strategy formation is situational or contingent in nature? Why is this important to understand?

11. What role does a firm's posture on innovation play in strategy formulation?

CASE: BankAmerica Formulates New Strategy[24]

The bank that invented bank charge cards is back. BankAmerica Corporation reported that its net income rose 114 percent for the first half of 1989 to $579 million dollars or $2.88 a share. After suffering a $1.8-billion loss from 1985 through 1987, BankAmerica expected to post a record net income of over $1 billion in 1989. The earnings reflected broad-based gradual improvement from huge losses taken from 1985 to 1987.

A major thrust into the retail market has led the surge in profits. In recent months the growth of late-night banking, Saturday and Sunday banking, 24-hour-a-day dial-a-banker, and sweepstakes has provided vigorous growth opportunities. This "combat" banking, as it is called by BankAmerica's CEO, Richard Rosenberg, has played a significant role in the biggest bank turnaround in U.S. history.

Just a few years ago BankAmerica was on the rocks, yet record profits are now expected after three years of record losses. A billion dollars in bad loans evaporated in a year. The stock, long shunned by investors increased five fold from a low in 1987 of $6.87 to a high of $36.12 in September of 1989. And all of this was orchestrated by defectors from a rival bank and an executive who, many say, initially caused the mess.

A strange thing is happening at BankAmerica Corporation: It is recovering. For three years running, BankAmerica chalked up more loan losses than any other American bank, living or dead. Along the way to disaster, it alienated employees, customers, investors, and regulators with predictions of imminent recovery that were persistently proved wrong.

Founder of Bank Charge Cards Suffers Heavy Losses

How could such a large, successful bank have taken such a sharp turn for the worse? How could a bank which stressed innovation in policy have ended up on the rocks? BankAmerica introduced the United States to the BankAmericard during the mid-1960s. This highly successful all-purpose charge card soon became the industry standard. Mastercharge soon followed. Eventually BankAmericard became Visa and it is still the most popular charge card in the country. Yet its basic strategic policy failed. Huge uncollectible debts, mostly to third-world countries, became a drag on earnings and operations. Bank and charge card competition heated up. The bank's market share shrank from 51 percent in 1983 to 34 percent in 1987. Loan losses increased from $907 million in 1984 to $1,419 million in 1986. Net earnings went from a positive $346 million in 1984 to a loss of $955 million in 1987. The company's stock price fell from about $18 a share in 1984 to about $7 a share in 1987. The previous aggressive "go-go" strategy had gone sour. A new strategy was needed.

Turnaround Strategy

In 1988, BankAmerica reported its first profit since 1984. But the gains came at the cost of sweeping, painful moves that permanently changed the bank. These days, the company almost flaunts spartan attitudes and firings; until 1986, it took pride in never laying off anyone. One of the first actions taken was to freeze salaries of many employees and set up an incentive system to compensate managers on the basis of productivity. A former branch manager describes what happened to one of his friends, also a bank manager, who was demoted to a simple loan officer. "He had some bad quarters and whammo, they dunked him." Morale further slumped because the turnaround was led by former officers of BankAmerica's archrival, Wells Fargo and Company, an unsentimental crowd that signed on for various reasons and shows no compunction about purging old-timers.

Most observers doubted that BankAmerica would ever again be a global power. Since 1983, in an incredible vanishing act, it dropped $27 billion in assets (to $94.3 billion), gutted much of a once-expansive foreign network, and retreated to its home turf in California. However, in 1991, BankAmerica took a giant step toward becoming the nation's most powerful bank. This step was an agreement to acquire Security Pacific Corporation. This was an extremely big step, and an extremely large merger. Adding Security to BankAmerica results in yearly core earnings prior to taxes of about $4.75 billion, compared to Citicorp's 1990 core earnings of about $3.5 billion.

Clausen Takes Over, Again

In 1986, BankAmerica looked as if it might not have a future at all. On September 16, 1986, rumors that it would fail roared out of Europe, depressing the dollar and scaring away some corporate deposits. The bank didn't collapse, but the five-year reign of Samuel H. Armacost as its chief executive did. A month later, the board summoned back his predecessor, Tom Clausen, who had recently retired as the World Bank's president. The step was extraordinary: Clausen had led BankAmerica's plunge into international lending and other risky ventures that helped cause the huge loan losses that unseated Armacost. Clausen is quoted as saying, "When I came back people said 'My God, they've brought that fool Clausen back who caused all these problems in the first place . . . The board must be crazy.' Well we've come a fur piece. Maybe I'm not as dumb as people thought."

The two chief executives could hardly differ more. "Sam was perhaps a little too benevolent to make the tough decisions," Alfred Grove, a senior energy lending officer, says in vast understatement. "Tom has never been an indecisive guy."

Clausen is all business, coldly analytical and demanding, someone better at recalling abstruse financial ratios that his own home phone number, which he keeps written down at his desk. Admirers say he brought stability and discipline, exactly what the then-teetering giant needed. He fired two executive vice-presidents for bungling a computer project. To plug press leaks, he abolished a management forum that Armacost had viewed as an exercise in corporate democracy.

By April 1988, when Clausen took his first week off, his fast pace had scared off his first administrative assistant and run others ragged. However, he seemed to have done the job. When he stepped down from his office at BankAmerica, the firm's 1989 net income topped $1 billion. His replacement, Richard Rosenberg, was a Wells Fargo veteran who joined BankAmerica in 1985.

Wells Fargo Executives

Rosenberg and the other former Wells Fargo executives who dominate the managing committee as well as other key posts are a tough bunch. Wells Fargo has become the most profitable big bank in the West with a ruthless operating style, a sharp contrast with BankAmerica's history of paternalism.

Take BankAmerica's executive vice-president and branch chief, Thomas Peterson. His predecessor inspired the troops with rainbow lapel pins. Peterson phoned one senior aide and introduced himself in this manner: "This is Tom Peterson. Why the hell are you opening a branch in Santa Cruz? Meet me in Santa Cruz tomorrow morning at 7:30."

The influx from Wells Fargo has upset some once-senior BankAmerica officials who either left or slipped into reduced roles. An employee-morale survey showed a rise among the rank and file but a decline among middle managers. One of the old-timers relates, "We've viewed Wells Fargo as the evil empire forever." Some employees are starting to call it the bank Wells of America. But given BankAmerica's recent track record, "you don't necessarily want stability," says Allen Sanborn, a longtime executive vice-president. "The reality is, these guys know how to make a buck. I view them as positive and needed."

Human Resource Changes

Together, the new team toughened up the place. Some 5,000 jobs were cut in 1988 on top of the 27,000 that were cut since 1983 reducing total worldwide employment in the company to 54,700. The bank used to give "redeployed" workers a month to find other jobs internally. Now, with the pickings so slim, they get just two weeks. Those remaining are treated more like renewable commodities than coddled "boys and girls," as A. P. Giannini, the bank's founder, had called them.

"I come from a place that was very, very efficient," Peterson says, "and we're going to do the same thing here." The branch network has been trimmed. Its 62 area management groups have been cut to 31. The four regional managers who formerly had a staff of 40 now have 10 each.

In the 850 branches, the corporate crown jewels, most managers' base salaries were frozen and all future increases were linked to performance. Most teller jobs were changed to part-time, slashing hours and benefits. Customers are also feeling a squeeze. A Marin County branch, for instance, has stopped cashing foreign currencies for dollars for free. "We had a tendency to give things away," Peterson says. "We can't do that anymore."

Future Challenges

BankAmerica officials hope that, like the earlier problems, the improving finances will feed on themselves. The company is counting on a stronger credit rating to allow it to become more than a minor leaguer in pitching lucrative interest-rate and currency swaps. Money to promote a flagging global corporate computer service is becoming available. So is support for a beefed-up team of deal makers to broker mergers among California companies.

Finally, the bank must repair its sagging employee relations. Morale and job security are low, especially among middle managers but also among customer-contact people such as tellers. The bank has difficulty attracting top-flight talent at middle manager and lower levels. Its concern with needed cost cutting, especially in human resource costs, have caused once strong employee relations built through paternalism to crumble.

QUESTIONS

1. Characterize the new strategy adopted by Bank-America. Why did it adopt this strategy?

2. What have been the effects of this strategy on human resource strategy?

3. What are the ethical and moral dimensions of the human resource strategy adopted?

4. Did the bank have any alternatives in basic corporate strategy, or was the strategy adopted its only choice?

5. What specific human resource strategy would you now suggest for the bank? How would you make this strategy work? Can they afford it?

6. Would you take an entry-level management job with BankAmerica? Why or why not?

....
ADDITIONAL READINGS

Allio, R. J. *The Practical Strategist.* New York: Harper & Row, 1988.

Baird, L., I. Meshoulam, G. DeGive. "Meshing Human Resources Planning with Strategic Business Planning: A Model Approach." *Personnel* 60(5) (1983), pp. 14–25.

Buller, P. F., and N. K. Napier. "Strategy and Human Resource Management Integration in Fast Growth versus Other Mid-sized Firms." Paper presented at the 1990 Academy of Management Meeting. San Francisco, 1990.

Carroll, G. R., and D. Vogel. *Organizational Approaches to Strategy.* New York: Harper & Row, 1988.

Cheek, L. M. "Cost Effectiveness Comes from the Personnel Function." *Harvard Business Review* 51(3) (1973), pp. 96–105.

Child, J. "Organization Structure, Environment, and Performance: The Role of Strategic Choice." *Sociology* 6 (1972), pp. 2–22.

Cooper, A. C., and D. Schendel. "Strategic Responses to Technological Threats." *Business Horizons* 19(1) (1976), pp. 1–9.

DeSanto, J. F. "Work Force Planning and Corporate Strategy." *Personnel Administrator* 28(10) (1983), pp. 33–42.

Deutch, A. "How Employee Retention Strategies Can Aid Productivity." *Journal of Business Strategy* 2(4) (1982), pp. 106–109.

Dimick, D. E., and V. V. Murray. "Correlates of Substantive Policy Decisions in Organizations: The Case of Human Resource Management." *Academy of Management Journal* 21 (1978), pp. 611–623.

Dyer, L. "Bringing Human Resources into the Strategy Formulation Process." *Human Resource Management* 22(3) (1983), pp. 257–271.

Dyer, L. "Strategic Human Resources Management and Planning." In K. M. Rowland and G. R. Ferris, Eds. *Research in Personnel and Human Resources Management,* Greenwich, CT: JAI Press, 1985, pp. 1–30.

Dyer, L. "Studying Human Resource Strategy: An Approach and an Agenda." *Industrial Relations* 23(2) (1984), pp. 156–169.

Evans, Alastair J. "Britain and the United States: A Comparison of Human Resource Strategies." *Personnel Journal* 61:9. September 1982, pp. 656–662.

Finkelstein, S. and D. Hambrick. "Top-Management Team Tenure and Organizational Outcomes: The Moderating Role of Managerial Discretion." *Administrative Science Quarterly* 35 (1990), pp. 484–503.

Flamholtz, E. "A Model for Human Resource Valuation: A Stochastic Process with Service Rewards." *Accounting Review* 46(2) (1971), pp. 253–267.

Fombrun, C. "Environmental Trends Create New Pressures on Human Resources." *Journal of Business Strategy* 3(1) (1982), pp. 61–69.

Foltz, Roy. "Senior Management Views the Human Resource Function." *Personnel Administrator* 27:9, September 1984, pp. 37–50.

Frantzreb, R. B., L. T. Landau, and D. P. Lundberg. "The Valuation of Human Resources." *Business Horizons* 20(3) (1977), pp. 73–80.

Galbraith, J. R., and R. J. Kazanjian. *Strategy Implementation: Structure, System and Process.* 2nd ed. St. Paul: West, 1986.

Galosy, J. R. "Meshing Human Resources Planning with Strategic Business Planning: One Company's Experience." *Personnel* 60(5) (1983), pp. 26–35.

Gilbert, D. R., Jr., E. Hartman, J. J. Muriel, and R. E. Freeman. *A Logic for Strategy.* New York: Harper & Row, 1988.

Green, Robert, and Russel, G. Roberts. "Strategic Integration of Compensation and Benefits." *Personnel Administrator* 28:5 (May 1983), pp. 79–83.

Guth, W., and I. MacMillian. "Strategy Implementation versus Middle Management Self-Interest." *Strategic Management Journal* 7 (1986), pp. 313–327.

Harvey, L. J. "Effective Planning for Human Resource Development." *Personnel Administrator* 28(10) (1983), pp. 45–52.

Hayes, R. H., and S. C. Wheelwright. "The Dynamics of Process-Product Life Cycles." *Harvard Business Review* 57(2) (1979), pp. 127–136.

Hofer, C. W., and D. Schendel. *Strategy Formulation: Analytical Concepts.* St. Paul: West, 1978.

Hrebiniak, L. G. and W. F. Joyce. *Implementing Strategy.* New York: Macmillan, 1984.

Kerr, J., and E. Jackofsky. "Aligning Managers to Strategies: Management Development versus Selection." *Academy of Management Review* 10 (1989), pp. 157–170.

Krackhardt, D. "Assessing the Political Landscape: Structure, Cognition, and Power in Organizations." *Administrative Science Quarterly* 35 (1990), pp. 342–369.

Lawrence, P. *Executive Summary—The History of Resource Management in America.* Human Resource Management Future Conference, Harvard Business School, May 9–11, 1984.

Lengnick-Hall, C., and M. Lengnick-Hall. "Strategic Human Resource Management: A Review of the Literature and a Proposed Typology." *Academy of Management Review* 13 (1988), pp. 454–470.

Lengnick-Hall, C. A., and R. R. McDaniel, Jr. "Scanning Policies, Structure and Adaptability in Human Service Systems." *American Business Review* 2(1) (1984), pp. 12–23.

Lenz, R. T. "Determinants of Organizational Performance: An Interdisciplinary Review." *Strategic Management Journal* 2(2) (1981), pp. 131–154.

Leontiades, M. "Choosing the Right Manager to Fit the Strategy." *Journal of Business Strategy* 2(2) (1982), pp. 58–69.

Lieberman, M., L. Lau, and M. Williams. "Firm-Level Productivity and Management Influence: A Comparison of U.S. and Japanese Automobile Producers." *Management Science* 36 (1990), pp. 1193–1215.

Lindblom, C. "The Science of Muddling Through." *Public Administration Review* 19 (1959), pp. 79–88.

Lindroth, J. "How to Beat the Coming Labor Shortage." *Personnel Journal* 61(4) (1982), pp. 268–272.

MacMillan, I. C., and P. E. Jones. *Strategy Formulation: Power and Politics.* 2nd ed. St. Paul: West, 1986.

MacMillan, I. C., and R. S. Schuler. "Gaining a Competitive Edge through Human Resources." *Personnel* 62(4) (1985), pp. 24–29.

Maier, H. "Innovation, Efficiency, and the Quantitative and Qualitative Demand for Human Resources." *Technological Forecasting and Social Change* 21 (1982), pp. 15–31.

Miles, R., C. C. Snow, A. D. Meyer, and H. J. Coleman, Jr. "Organization Strategy, Structure, and Process." *Academy of Management Review* 3 (1978), pp. 546–662.

Mintzberg, H. "Strategy Formation: Schools of Thought," In *Perspectives on Strategic Management,* edited by J. Fredrickson, New York: Harper & Row, 1990, pp. 105–235.

Olian, J. D., and S. L. Rynes. "Organizational Staffing: Integrating Practice with Strategy." *Industrial Relations* 23(2) (1984), pp. 170–183.

Perry, L. T. "Least-cost Alternatives to Layoffs in Declining Industries." *Organizational Dynamics* 14(4) (1986), pp. 48–61.

Pitts, R. A., and C. C. Snow. *Strategies for Competitive Success.* New York: Wiley, 1986.

Porter, M. E. *Competitive Strategy.* New York: Free Press, 1980.

Porter, M. E. *Competitive Advantage.* New York: Free Press, 1985.

Reed, R., and R. DeFillippi. "Causal Ambiguity, Barriers to Imitation, and Sustainable Competitive Advantage." *Academy of Management Review,* 15 (1990), pp. 88–102.

Rumelt, R. P. *Strategy, Structure and Economic Performance in Large American Industrial Corporations.* Boston: Harvard Graduate School of Business Administration, 1974.

Schuler, R. S., and I. C. MacMillan. "Gaining Competitive Advantage through Human Resource Management Practices." *Human Resource Management,* 23(3) (1984), pp. 241–256.

Schuler, R. S., and S. E. Jackson. "Linking Competitive Strategies with Human Resource Management Practices." *Academy of Management Executive* 1 (1987), pp. 207–219.

Schultheiss, E. E. *Optimizing The Organization.* New York: Harper & Row, 1988.

Scott, B. R. *Stages of Corporate Development–Part 1* (Case No. 9-371-294). Boston: Intercollegiate Case Clearinghouse, 1971.

Smith, E. C. "Strategic Business Planning and Human Resources: Part I. *Personnel Journal* 61(8) (1982a), pp. 606–610.

Smith, E. C. "Strategic Business Planning and Human Resources: Part II." *Personnel Journal* 61(9) (1982b), pp. 680–682.

"Strategic Planning: Hedging Future Shock." *Personnel Administrator,* December 1987, pp. 73–80.

Stumpf, S. A., and N. M. Hanrahan. "Designing Organizational Career Management Practices to Fit the Strategic Management Objectives." In R. S. Schuler and S. A. Youngblood, eds., *Readings in Personnel and Human Resource Management.* 2nd ed., St. Paul: West, 1984, pp. 326–348.

Sweet, J. "How Manpower Development Can Support Your Strategic Plan." *Journal of Business Strategy* 3(1) (1982), pp. 77–81.

Szilagyi, A., and D. Schweiger. "Matching Managers to Strategies: A Review and Suggested Framework." *Academy of Management Review* 9 (1984), pp. 626–637.

Tichy, N. M., C. J. Fombrun, and M. A. Devanna. "Strategic Human Resource Management." *Sloan Management Review* 23(2) (1982), pp. 47–61.

Tsui, A. S., "A Multiple-Constituency Model of Effectiveness: An Empirical Examination at the Human Resource Subunit Level." *Administrative Science Quarterly* 35 (1990), pp. 458–483.

Wagel, W. H., and H. Z. Levine. "Surveying the Past. Planning the Future." *Personnel.* June 1989, pp. 25–44.

Walton, R. E. *From Control to Commitment: Transforming Work Force Management in the United States.* Harvard Business School's 75th Anniversary Colloquium on Technology and Productivity, 1984.

Wils, T., and L. Dyer. *Relating Business Strategy to Human Resource Strategy: Some Preliminary Evidence.* Paper presented at the meeting of the Academy of Management. Boston, August 1984.

NOTES

1. Wendy L. Hall, "At NutraSweet, Shapiro Has a Mission," *Wall Street Journal,* May 7, 1987, p. 36; and Donna Tapellini, "Competitors Are Beginning to Circle NutraSweet's Territory," *Adweek's Marketing Week* December 5, 1988, p. 38.

2. Selwyn Feinstein, "Best Laid Plans," *Wall Street Journal,* May 1, 1990, p. A1.

3. R. E. Miles, C. C. Snow, A. D. Meyer, and H. J. Coleman, Jr., "Organizational Strategy, Structure, and Process," *Academy of Management Review* 3 1978, pp. 546–662.

4. For more detail, see William P. Anthony, *Practical Strategic Planning: A Guide for Line Managers* (Westport, CT: Greenwood Press, 1985), Chs. 1 and 2.

5. R. E. Freeman, *Strategic Management: A Stakeholder Approach* (Boston: Pitman, 1984).

6. John Kenneth Galbraith, *The New Industrial State* (Boston: Houghton Mifflin, 1967).

7. John Naisbett, *Megatrends: Ten New Directions for Transforming Our Lives* (New York: Warner, 1982).

8. Emily Yoffe, "Naisbett's Clip Joint: The Selling of Content Analysis and Megatrends," *Harpers,* September 1983, pp. 16 +.

9. William F. Glueck, *Business Policy and Strategic Management,* 3rd ed. (New York: McGraw-Hill, 1980), p. 290.

10. Kimberly Carpenter and John P. Tarpey, "A Southern Paper Maker's Yankee Campaign," *Business Week,* October 14, 1985, pp. 77–82.

11. Kathryn R. Harrigan, *Strategies for Declining Business* (Lexington, MA: D. C. Heath, 1980).

12. William C. Symands, "It's Every Man for Himself in the Steel Business," *Business Week,* June 3, 1985, p. 76.

13. Cynthia D. Fisher, "Current and Recurrent Challenges in HRM," *Journal of Management* 15, no. 2, June 1989, pp. 157–180.

14. Ibid., p. 158.

15. Ibid., p. 159.

16. Michael Porter, *Competitive Advantage* (New York: Free Press,.1985), pp. 11, 515; and Kevin P. Coyne, "Sustainable Competitive Advantage— What It Is, What It Isn't," *Business Horizons,* January–February 1986, pp. 54–56.

17. This section is based on M. E. Porter, *Competitive Strategy* (New York: Free Press, 1980); and M. E. Porter, *Competitive Advantage* (New York: Free Press, 1985).

18. Kevin Coyne, *Sustainable Competitive Advantage,* p. 55.

19. Cynthia A. Lengnick-Hall and Mark L. Lengnick-Hall, "Strategic Human Resources Management: A Review of the Literature and a Proposed Typology," *Academy of Management Review* 13, no. 3, July 1988, pp. 466–467.

20. Michael Porter, *Competitive Advantage.*

21. See also James A. McCambridge and Vicki S. Kaman, "Programs That Strengthen Relations," *HRMagazine,* May 1992, pp. 75–78.

22. Tom Peters and Nancy Austin, *A Passion for Excellence* (New York: Random House, 1985), p. 11.

23. Peter Drucker, "Entrepreneurial Strategies," in *Innovation and Entrepreneurship* (New York: Harper & Row, 1985).

24. Richard B. Schmitt, "BankAmerica Regains a Lot of Lost Ground but Not Earlier Clout," *Wall Street Journal,* July 18, 1988, pp. 1, 6; G. Christian Hill, "BankAmerica Reports 2nd-Quarter Net of $162 Million After Year-Ago Loss," *Wall Street Journal,* July 22, 1988, p. 3; Charles McCoy, "Combat Banking—A Slashing Pursuit of Retail Trade Brings BankAmerica Back," *Wall Street Journal,* October 2, 1989, pp. A1, A8; Charles McCoy and Ralph King, Jr., "Add Security Pacific to BankAmerica: The Result Is Clout," *Wall Street Journal,* August 13, 1991, p. A1 +; and Joan Hamilton, "There Were No Heroes at BankAmerica," *Business Week,* August 27, 1990, p. 12.

4

Human Resource Decision Making and Information Systems

One important feature that distinguishes a strategic approach to human resource management is its focus on big decisions that have to be made about human resources. These decisions involve hiring, training, termination, and so on. This chapter explores various ways decisions are made and the role that human resource units play in the decision process.

Good information is critical to making good decisions. Computers have enabled human resource managers to gather, store, and analyze much more information in a more systematic fashion when making critical human resource decisions. The introductory case that follows, describing Mrs. Fields and the use of computers in human resource decision making, shows just how valuable computers can be.

● ● ● ● ● ● ● ● ●
CHAPTER OBJECTIVES

After reading and studying this chapter, you should be able to

1. Explain the strategic decision process and relate it to human resource decisions.

2. Distinguish between rational and "garbage can" processes of decision making.

3. Explain how human resource decisions can be costed.

4. Explain the ethical dimensions of human resource decisions.

5. Explain how human resource information systems aid the human resource decision process.

CASE: How a Computer Keeps Mrs. Fields from Losing Her Cookies[1]

Computers have made the workplace more efficient. Even in the "low-tech" cookie business, operations can be programmed to smooth the production flow as well as schedule personnel. Mrs. Fields Cookies is a good example of how to utilize technology in human resource management.

The real Mrs. Fields is Debra Fields, who started the company with her husband Randy, a former systems programmer for IBM. Together they have built a corporation that includes their original company and others, such as La Petitie Boulangerie and Retail Operations Intelligence (ROI) Systems. The ROI division sells its expertise to other companies.

From its beginning in 1977, the couple's enterprise has grown substantially. Success in their own business and competition from other businesses led them into other markets and other industries.

The company's strategy was typical of the trends of the 1980s. Increased competition from other cookie companies and from substitutes, such as specialty confectionery companies, caused problems. In 1988, problems from the "combination stores" concept hurt business. Analysts said that the company had made strategic mistakes. The Fields hoped to recoup through diversification and globalization. By 1990, the company was selected by NutraSweet's Desserve Foods Division for a joint marketing effort, the first time NutraSweet had made such a move with another company.

How a Cookie Company Can Use Computers

Paul Quinn heads up ROI, Mrs. Fields' management information systems. He directs the efforts of Mrs. Fields' diversified divisions and markets the systems to over 600 other locations.

One of the features of the ROI system is that it has several components, called modules, which handle most of the day-to-day operations in human resource management. Among the modules already up and running are the daily production planner, and components that focus on interviewing, labor schedules, and skill testing. One benefit of a computerized human resource information system is that it standardized routine tasks, such as interviewing prospective employees. A further benefit is that it can then customize the standard employment questionnaire to fit the individual responses of the applicant.

For example, suppose Jane Dough is looking for a part time job at Mrs. Fields Cookies to help pay expenses while she is in school. She would be instructed to sit at a computer terminal and answer the series of questions that appear on the screen. The questions take about 15 minutes to answer. Some are true/false, others are multiple choice. So far, this could be done with a printed form. However, the computer is programmed to ask additional questions based on Jane's answers. If she says she is interested in temporary work, the computer asks how long she would plan to stay with the company. The follow-up question is similar to one that a store manager might ask in conducting an interview. But, not all store managers are able to keep current with legislation affecting employment recruiting practices. The computerized system is updated to make certain that only legal language is used in the interviewing process. The computer package also is programmed to catch discrepancies, such as overlapping dates in previous employment.

After Jane has finished answering the questions the computer tabulates a score on her responses based on minimum qualifications the company has set. This score provides information to help the manager decide whether or not to hire Jane. However, although the computer program is a part of the human resource information system, it is not there to replace the human resource decision making system. That job is still handled by people.

Suppose Jane is hired and after working for a couple of months in the baking operations wants to work at the front counter because that position pays more. She must pass the skills test before being considered for the change. The skill training module works like the interviewing module. It asks questions about tasks and gives correct responses and a final score so that Jane can get instant feedback on her skill level. A "help text" explains why an answer was right or wrong, and the test then becomes a tutor. If Jane doesn't pass, she can retake the test immediately or get further training before trying again. Jane isn't the only one who benefits from this system. The human resource staff at the company's headquarters feed her responses into a data base. If several sources show the same problem then the program is checked for wording errors. If there is no problem there, then the human resource staff looks at the training techniques, materials, or work force skill levels for problems. Again, this system is designed to provide information to the people who are responsible for the company's human resources.

More Uses for Computers

In addition to hiring and training, the human resource information system (HRIS) is used by Mrs. Fields Cookies to schedule personnel for production. Information is fed into the computer on a number of employees, their preferred or available hours, and anticipated traffic in the store. Even breaks are programmed so that each outlet operates at peak efficiency. The system then schedules personnel on an hourly basis. If Jane calls in sick, the labor scheduler module quickly formulates an alternate schedule and alerts the manager.

• • • • • • • • •

While Mrs. Fields is a leader in HRIS management, it is not alone. Over 2,000 human resource information systems were in operation at the beginning of the 1990s, with more systems coming on line, according to Dianne and Peter Kirrane, consultants who specialize in expert systems. Older systems using paper forms can make timely information virtually impossible. Today, companies like Arthur Andersen specialize in designing systems to provide the human resource manager with vital information in seconds.

Despite intense competition, Mrs. Fields has kept her cookie business healthy. Part of the credit goes to the human resource information system used by the company to speed the flow of information from the source to where it is needed throughout the corporation.

STRATEGIC CHOICES

Managers must make a number of strategic choices regarding human resource decision making and information systems. Some of the most important ones are outlined below:

1. Managers must decide which decision making approach is appropriate.
2. Managers must determine how closely human resource practices should be linked to strategic decisions.
3. Managers should understand the impact of employee involvement in decision making and carefully determine which employees, if any, to include in the process.
4. Management must determine how to calculate the cost effectiveness of a firm's human resources function.
5. Managers must decide if the company would benefit from a computerized human resource information system. If the answer is yes, then the management must determine who should have access to the system, what information should be stored, and how to keep the information safe.

THE STRATEGIC DECISION PROCESS

The essence of strategy formulation is decision making. What should the company do and why? How does it decide what to do? What role do the firm's human resources play in these strategic decisions? These are difficult questions, but they are the essence of a strategic approach. Strategy emphasizes planned and sometimes unplanned action and recognizes that an organization must choose from a set of alternative courses of action, from the very specific to the broad. For example:

- Should a certain person be hired?
- Should an employee be fired?
- What shall we pay our employees?
- What new products and markets should we be developing?
- How much do we want to grow?

······················

| EXHIBIT 4.1 | Evolution of Decision-Making Theories |

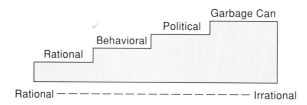

Rational —————————————— Irrational

······················

- How shall we finance growth?
- Do we need to lay off employees to cut costs?

The list of questions goes on and on. All of the cases in this book emphasize the importance of making these important choices.

In making decisions, organizations try to reduce uncertainty. They wish to gather enough information to feel fairly confident that they are making the right decision. They certainly do not want to leave out any important considerations. Reducing uncertainty reduces risk. How does an organization decide how much information it needs for human resource decision making? How does the organization obtain and use the information? How does an organization decide what to do? What is the strategic decision process? How are human resource decisions intertwined with strategic decisions?

We begin to examine these questions by reviewing the evolution of the decision-making process as outlined in Exhibit 4.1. The decision-making theories presented are introduced in order of rationality. The first theory, the rational perspective, relies completely on rationality, while the last theory discussed, the garbage can theory, relies little on rationality. It is also interesting to note that this is also the order in which serious research attention was paid to each theory.

Rational Theory of Decision Making[2]

Much writing and research emphasizes a rational approach to decision making, in which decision makers carefully examine and weigh each factor in a decision and choose a course of action that maximizes benefits to the firm while minimizing costs. In business, profitability is often the benefit to be maximized, although the desire to maximize shareholder wealth is becoming more common.

Regardless, the rational decision-making process is usually similar to that shown in Exhibit 4.2. Note that this is a rational process of gathering, analyzing, and evaluating pertinent information and then choosing the "best" course of action.

Behavioral and Political Theories

In the rational model, there is little room for gut feeling or intuition. There is little room for emotion. The rational process emphasizes those factors that can be quantified. This theory relies heavily on numbers and on "number-crunchers," people who do the analysis.

Certainly such systematic, quantified rational analysis is very important in decision making, but many decision makers do not follow this model precisely. A fair

· ·

EXHIBIT 4.2   The Rational or Scientific Problem-Solving and Decision-Making Process

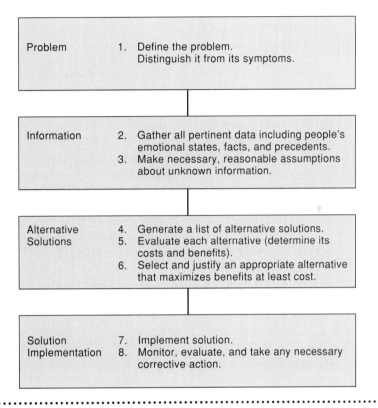

| Problem | 1. Define the problem. Distinguish it from its symptoms. |

| Information | 2. Gather all pertinent data including people's emotional states, facts, and precedents. 3. Make necessary, reasonable assumptions about unknown information. |

| Alternative Solutions | 4. Generate a list of alternative solutions. 5. Evaluate each alternative (determine its costs and benefits). 6. Select and justify an appropriate alternative that maximizes benefits at least cost. |

| Solution Implementation | 7. Implement solution. 8. Monitor, evaluate, and take any necessary corrective action. |

· ·

amount of evidence suggests that managers use intuition, gut feeling, and other so-called nonrational techniques in making decisions.[3] Furthermore, some of the most important decisions we make in our personal lives are not made in a rational, analytical manner that emphasizes quantification of costs and benefits. Consider the decision to choose a job. Certainly we weigh the salary, benefits, and other quantitative factors involved. But we also weigh many intangibles, such as the personal style of company interviewers and the atmosphere or culture of the firm. The firm also weighs intangibles in selecting an employee. For example, NCR weighs such nonquantitative factors as "judgment, adaptability, and professional poise."[4] These decisions are made partially for emotional, not truly rational, reasons.

Is there room for emotionalism in business decision making? Perhaps, but it is often referred to as "qualitative," as opposed to quantitative, decision making. In other words, recognition is made that not all important factors in a decision can be quantified, but this should not disqualify them from consideration.

Also recognized under the qualitative theory of decision making is the fact that firms do not always maximize, rather firms satisfice. Herbert Simon argues that firms try to make decisions that are, in essence, compromises. The results of the decision *reasonably* satisfy stockholders, employees, managers, government regulations, and other stakeholders and constituent groups, but may not *completely* satisfy any one group.[5]

Firms satisfice instead of maximize when making decisions for two primary reasons. First, there is simply too much information to know and process in order to make a maximizing decision. In spite of the computer, obtaining 100 percent of the available information is too difficult. The assumption made by economists that full and perfect knowledge is possible is in reality unrealistic. Thus managers operate under "bounded rationality."

Second, owners or stockholders, while important stakeholders, are not the only stakeholders. Profit maximization primarily benefits owners. These interests in reality must be balanced against the interests of others such as customers, employees, the government, and society as a whole, as we discussed in Chapter 2. Making decisions based on only quantifiable variables in order to maximize profit or benefit for owners is an incomplete view of decision making, according to qualitative decision theorists.

Another concept that the qualitative decision theorists believe in that the quantitative camp does not is **cognitive dissonance.** Cognitive dissonance occurs when a decision maker, after reflecting back on the decision, begins to question whether or not he or she made the right decision. Quantitative decision scholars would argue that this second guessing would not happen because the one best decision was made. However, all of us have felt some apprehension with a decision we have made in the past, especially if the decision was important. Real estate agents firmly believe in cognitive dissonance; however, they refer to it as "buyer's remorse." One of the most difficult tasks a real estate agent must perform is dealing with a client's cognitive dissonance."[6]

Garbage Can Model of Decision Making

An area of qualitative decision making that has received much discussion is the garbage can model. It is important to review it in more depth to see how it relates to strategic decision making.[7]

The garbage can model of decision making is based on the *reconstructive interpretation of historical events.* Past events are given new meaning in light of present outcomes. For example, were you ever disappointed when you did not get asked to a special dance or party? You may have said, "Oh well, it doesn't matter. I really didn't want to go anyway. I would have probably had to talk to Judy and she's such a bore. I'm glad I have time to stay home and catch up on my homework." However, if after the big dance or party, you found out that the band was terrible, they ran out of food, and people generally had a miserable time, you may have gloated and said or thought, "See how smart I am. I chose not to go to the party. I made the right decision."

After the event, once the decision has been made and played out, facts are sorted through, and only those that justify the decisions are chosen and carefully interpreted to reinforce the course of action. **Attributions** or meanings are given to these facts to reinforce your view of the decision. You sort through the garbage can of events that led up to the decision and focus on only those pieces that can be used to justify your decision. This is called **retrospective reconstruction** of historical data, and all of us do this to some extent.

The garbage can model is sometimes used in human resource decisions in organizations. When people are employed for certain tasks, or let go from them, sometimes the garbage can model is used to justify the actions of those who did the hiring or firing. For example, suppose Judy (the bore from the party) also had been the one

....

| EXHIBIT 4.3 | Characteristics of the Rational and Qualitative Models of Decision Making |

RATIONAL MODEL	QUALITATIVE MODEL
Clear definition of problem	Problems are often unclear
Extensive gathering of needed information	Incomplete information for decisions
	Intangible factors often important
Factors judged using cost-benefit analysis	Emotional, intuitive or "gut" decision making
Quantitative or "number crunching" based-decisions	
Organization benefit maximization/cost minimization decisions	Satisficing, or compromise decisions due to incomplete information and demands of stakeholders
Careful analysis and monitoring of decision	Use of retrospective reconstruction to justify decisions

....

in charge of a committee responsible for putting on the dance. She probably spent the rest of the weekend sorting through her garbage can of attributions for the responses she would need when she had to face her friends on Monday. By then she will have rewritten history to prove beyond any shadow of a doubt that (1) it was inevitable that the dance was a disaster and (2) it wasn't her fault. But, don't be too hard on Judy; remember that we all have a tendency to rationalize.

One of your authors purchased a GM diesel in 1981. In retrospect, it was not a good decision since the car had many repair needs and was virtually worthless after five years. However, when kidded about this purchase, the owner invested in all types of retrospective reconstruction to convince others that it was the right choice. All of the advantages of a diesel were reiterated (but none of the disadvantages). Plus, since about 50 percent of GM Oldsmobiles sold in 1981 were diesels, in numbers there was strength—the author was not the only one who supposedly made a mistake. Even today, some people still swear by (not at) their GM diesel.

Evidence suggests that decision makers in organizations use retrospective reconstruction to justify poor decisions, such as the GM diesel purchase, as well as good decisions.[8] Many times decision makers will make the right decision, but for the wrong reason. They then must go back and reinterpret information differently to justify the decision.

The garbage can model and other qualitative decision theories are more complex than the rational model, but they may more accurately reflect the actual decision process. They certainly raise the issue of how people interpret and use information in making decisions, which, once understood, helps to explain the role that human resources plays in strategic decision making. Exhibit 4.3 summarizes the characteristics of the rational and qualitative models of decision making.

Attribution Theory

Inherent in assigning meaning to information, events, and behavior is **attribution theory.** *People assign meaning based on the specific attributions or associations they make.*

This meaning may or may not be the intended meaning. We develop cause-effect relationships and meaning sets based again on schemas and cognitive maps that have been developed over time based on our experience. The problem arise when we make attributions that are nonexistent or unintended.

For example, suppose your boss comes over to your workplace to chat. You interpret this behavior to mean that she is checking up on you. However, in reality, she really just wanted to be friendly. The attribution you made to the behavior is entirely different from her intentions.

What makes this situation even more problematic is the difficulty in determining a person's true attribution made with respect to a particular behavior because attributions are often not verbalized. Even direct questioning may not reveal a person's true attribution—instead a **socially desirable** or acceptable answer may be given. For example, if a person is prejudiced against women supervisors and works for a woman supervisor, he may, in reality, attribute a good decision made by the supervisor to luck rather than skill. When asked, of course, he may reply skill rather than luck because skill is a more socially desirable answer.

Thus, in the decision-making process determining the attributions people make of events, behaviors, and situations is important in order to understand the reasoning process behind their decisions.

Tacit Knowledge or Intuition

The final issue we need to examine in decision making is the role that intuition or tacit knowledge plays in the process. *Tacit knowledge or intuition is abstracted personal knowledge that cannot be brought directly into active awareness.*[9] There is evidence that decision makers rely on tacit knowledge or intuition in making decisions, yet it is not easy to bring this knowledge into direct consciousness.[10] Tacit knowledge becomes imbedded in a person's subconscious and is used without conscious thought.

So when a manager is asked why a decision was made in a particular way and responds, "Oh I don't know, I just had a gut feeling," he is expressing reliance on tacit knowledge or intuition without being able to explain consciously why it works.

Yet understanding what specific tacit knowledge is at work in a particular decision is helpful in order to better understand how and why a particular decision is made as it was. For example, such understanding may help to reduce bias in selection decisions. Or it may further illuminate why some decision makers always seem to make the right promotion decision, even when its not clear from "objective" facts. Gioia and Ford recommend self-communication processes, including introspection and affective reflection, in order to better understand one's store of tacit knowledge.[11] One way this can be done is to write out scripts that one believes describe a decision process. For example, a manager could write a script that describes the process she goes through in making a hiring decision. Or, using **verbal protocol analysis,** one could tape record the verbal replication of the thoughts of a decision maker as he or she goes through the process of making a particular decision, as Isenberg has done.[12]

INTEGRATING HUMAN RESOURCES IN STRATEGIC DECISIONS

People in organizations make decisions. Even in automatic decisions, such as an automatic cutoff in a launch sequence for a space rocket, someone programmed a computer to shut down the firing sequence if certain data were present or not present. Automatic or programmed decisions are ultimately people-driven, even though in some cases tracing back the sequence to the place where human involvement occurred can be complex.

In this section we examine the human resource impact of decisions from four perspectives. First, we look at the issue of the substitutability of capital for labor. Second, we look at the impact of strategic decisions on human resources in general in the organization. Third, we examine the political forces at work in human resources. Finally, we examine the role of the human resources unit in strategic decision making.

Capital versus Labor

From a strategic and economic perspective, the underlying decision an organization must make regarding its human resources is its capital/labor ratio. Each organization must decide to what extent it will substitute capital for labor and vice versa. In other words, an organization must decide to what extent it will fill its jobs by substituting machines for people.

Since the Industrial Revolution, organizations have substituted capital for labor by using machine power to replace human power. Generally, this has led to higher levels of productivity and lower per unit costs of production. The back hoe replaced the ditch digger; the automatic glass blowing machine replaced hand blowers; the high-speed printing press replaced the hand press, and so on. Mass production—changeable parts and specialized machines performing the same function over and over again to produce huge quantities—has allowed for tremendous increases in productivity.

Today the same capital and labor decision is being made in factories, offices, and mines around the country, only today it involves substituting smart machines—the computer—for other machines and labor.[13] Personal computers replace electric typewriters and calculators in offices; automated management and control systems replace people-controlled machines in paper and steel plants; robots replace welders on automobile assembly lines; automated answering devices answer telephones and guide people to the right extension; automatic teller machines replace tellers at banks; optical scanners read prices off grocery items instead of clerks ringing in the price—the list goes on and on.

Organizations invest in these smart machines because, in general, they do the job cheaper and more efficiently than people. But these changes do not come without both monetary and human costs. Some people who are laid off may never get a job again. Those that do find work may find work at much lower paying jobs. Other people enter retraining programs to learn new skills in order to operate the smart machines. Still others must move and relocate to cities in parts of the country offering suitable employment. Finally, others may become alienated and like the hippies of the 1960s, either drop out of society or buy a bed and breakfast in Vermont as a form of rebellion against technology.

This technological change brings dislocations, which are the costs of substituting capital for labor. These costs are largely borne by society as a whole rather than by industrial firms, so they are often not considered by the firm when making a technological decision to automate a job or process. In fact, some firms often have no choice. In order to remain competitive from a cost basis in worldwide markets they *must* automate and they do. We saw this during the 1980s with steel, rubber, autos, and a host of other major industries, and we will likely continue to see it as other industries including financial services, insurance, and even housing become globalized.

The extensive job design consequences of substituting capital for labor by incorporating more technology into jobs is fully explored in the next chapter.

Strategic Decision Impact on People in the Organization

In our discussion above it is obvious that automating jobs has a significant impact on human resources. However, many important or strategic decisions are often considered non–human resource decisions. In other words, restructuring a loan package from lenders is usually considered only a financial decision. A decision to develop a new product is usually looked at from research and development, marketing, engineering, design, and production perspectives. A decision to change a company name or logo is usually a public relations decision.

Yet all of these decisions have a human resource dimension. First, people make the decision. People who make strategic decisions in an organization constitute what is called the **dominant coalition.**[14] The dominant coalition almost always includes top management, but it also often includes people with technical expertise in an area under consideration. More and more frequently, top level human resource managers are included in the dominant coalition.[15] For example, a computer and information systems specialist in the organization may have a significant role to play in making a decision to purchase a new information management system. The same is true of a design engineer in new product development.

So the composition of the dominant coalition may change depending on the strategic decision under consideration. The extent to which people further down in the organization have input to membership in the dominant coalition is a major factor in determining the extent of **participation** in the decision process. In general, many organizations have tried to involve their managers and employees more in the decision process and thereby increase their input. However, this involvement is usually in routine or operating decisions rather than strategic decisions. The theory behind employee involvement is that by giving lower-level managers and employees more of a role to play in decisions they will have a higher commitment to the decision output.

Japanese auto companies exemplify this policy through their **quality circles,** which are groups of employees who meet to recommend ways to improve production and quality. The Motorola Participative Management Program and Florida Power and Light's Quality Improvement Program (which won Japan's prestigious Deming Award in 1989) are patterned after the Japanese participative model.

Involving people throughout the organization in decisions provides an opportunity to consider the human resource impact of the decision. People who eventually have to carry out the strategic decision made by the dominant coalition may be in the best position to provide input and advice on what must be done to make the decision work.

For example, a plant closing decision that would involve transfer, retraining, and severance rights for employees certainly would involve the union, if one were present. If no union were present, employees still might be involved through transition committees. Steel companies have used this technique, even to the extent of allowing the employees to buy the plant, as was done with Wierton Steel in West Virginia.

···

| EXHIBIT 4.4 | Examples of Strategic Decisions That Have Major and Minor Impacts on Human Resources |

EXAMPLES OF STRATEGIC DECISIONS THAT TEND TO HAVE
A DIRECT HUMAN RESOURCE IMPACT

Plant Location	Job Design/Redesign
Plant Closing	Production Technology
Wage Cutting	Supervisory Style
Restructuring	Organization Culture Changes
Collective Bargaining	Market Expansion/Retrenchment
Automation	

EXAMPLES OF STRATEGIC DECISIONS THAT TEND TO HAVE
INDIRECT HUMAN RESOURCE IMPACT

Loan/Portfolio Restructuring	Public Relations Campaign
Stock Issuance	Changes in Accounting Methods
Logo/Name Change	
Product Feature Change	

···

So, obtaining input down through the organization through participative management and involvement techniques is a popular way to expose the human resource implications of strategic decisions. Of course, this is best done with decisions that very much affect human resources compared to those that do not. Exhibit 4.4 lists samples of decisions that tend to have a direct impact on human resources and those that have little or no direct effect.

Political Influences in Human Resource Management

The strategic perspective of human resource management looks at the long term implications of human resource decisions and integrates the human resource strategy with the organization's overall strategy. In keeping with the discussion on the dominant coalition, the members in the organization influence the human resource information system. They influence not only who will be hired and promoted, but also the criteria used in hiring and job evaluation decisions. Not all behavior is political, but it is political when it attempts to manage or control the meanings, norms, and behavior of employees in an organization.

"Political influence, like any other behavior in organizations, does not operate in a vacuum. The stipulation that people answer for their actions clearly can exercise substantial impact on their behavior in such situations, including political influence behavior."[16]

Managers may hire employees based on political influence. Although, at the time, they may say that the person hired "fit" better in the organization, the definition of "fit" may be a political one based on who the managers think they can influence or control. If they hire enough employees who fit their mold, then they can create a powerful political base in the organization.

··

EXHIBIT 4.5 Continuum of Staff Involvement for Personnel Unit in Strategic Decisions Affecting Human Resources

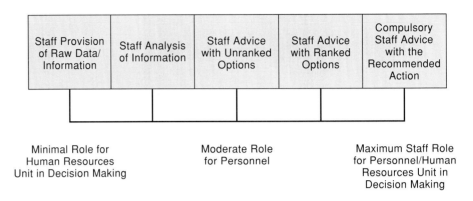

··

Role of the Human Resource Unit in Strategic Decisions

When a strategic decision has a major impact on human resources, such as those at the top of Exhibit 4.4, the human resource unit should have a major role to play in the decision. Human resource professionals are in the best position to advise and otherwise influence the decision process. However to become true business partners, human resource managers must focus their attention on issues that are of concern to the company's chief executive.[17]

Traditionally, the human resource unit has *not* been part of the dominant co-alition. Largely this is because of the staff or advisory role human resources plays. However, even though the role of human resources is still largely advisory, the *level* of human resource units has been elevated as explained in Chapter 2. Today companies have vice-presidents of human resources both at the corporate and divisional level. This enhances their membership in the dominant coalition. Yet because human resources is essentially staff in nature, the models of influence on decisions tend to fall along the continuum of staff involvement in decision making. Exhibit 4.5 summarizes this continuum and we discuss them below.

Levels of Staff Involvement in Decisions

The organization's human resource unit can have anywhere from a minimal role to play in strategic decisions to a maximum role. At the far left of the continuum the human resource unit simply provides raw data and information to the dominant coalition. For example, if a company were considering closing a plant, the human resource unit would simply provide the decision makers with information on the number of people affected, severance costs, early retirement costs, and so on, with no analysis.

In the next position to the right, the human resource unit would analyze the data. Graphs and trends might be developed. Interpretive paragraphs would be written and implications would be spelled out regarding the plant closing.

In the middle position, the staff role of human resources is carried a step further. Here specific recommendations as to what the company should do with respect to the human resource issues raised in the closing would be developed but would be unranked. In other words, human resources would simply lay out the options with the associated costs and benefits of each option, but the decision makers would choose the option. In the plant closing example, human resources might detail the costs and benefits of retraining, transfer, outplacement, early retirement, layoff, and severance programs.

In the fourth position to the right, human resources ranks the options as to what they would recommend and why. Finally, in the fifth option the rank order is provided plus an admonition is made—no decision could be made without first hearing and considering the options recommended by human resources. The principle of **compulsory staff advice** forces line decision makers to at least consider staff advice before making the decision, even if they decide not to take it. This gives human resources its strongest staff authority in influencing strategic decisions.

Of course, remember that we are discussing strategic decisions that have a major human resource impact. In those decisions that are strictly human resource decisions—such as decisions on how to best administer a pay plan or how to set up a human resource division—human resources exercises **line authority** over those employed in the unit. The vice-president of human resources (or whatever the head human resource person is called) has line authority to manage the unit.

Possible Line Authority in Strategic Decisions

Taking the plant closing example a step further, suppose the human resource unit were given not just a staff role to play in making a plant closing decision but a line role. In other words, the human resource unit would share in the line authority for the plant closing decision. The human resource vice-president's "vote" would carry as much weight as the manufacturing vice-president's vote. Here, the authority of the human resource unit is no longer staff but has become line. This is rare in strategic decision making, but does happen occasionally. However, with increasing authority and responsibility being given to the human resource unit, direct line authority over strategic decisions will likely become more common.

HUMAN RESOURCE COSTING

Making human resource decisions because "it's the right thing to do," or because it will "make employees happy" are increasingly less acceptable reasons to justify policy. Today, organizations want to know how human resource policy affects the bottom line. Some of the more common costing measures include HRMex or the human resource department's expenses as a percent of company operating expense. This figure was approximately 0.9 percent in 1990. Another costing measure is COMPex or the current compensation costs as a percent of the company's operating expenses. This value averaged 30 percent in 1990.[18]

Human resource managers are increasingly being asked to justify decisions and programs on a cost-benefit basis. They are being held accountable in a financial sense for policy and procedure. They are being asked time and time again, "Are our programs and policies worth it? Are our decisions producing the desired results?"

No doubt cost competitive factors and restructuring efforts have exacerbated this demand for accountability. But so has human resource's traditional defense of their programs, which has emphasized less tangible benefits such as good morale and job satisfaction. Line managers today want to know how these benefits contribute to the bottom line.

Human Resource Accounting

When asked to name their most important resource, many managers will respond "our people." When asked to put a value on their human resources, most managers say they cannot or that their people are invaluable. Yet valuing human resources has been a subject of inquiry since the late 1960s. The R. G. Barry Corporation of Columbus, Ohio, made the first major attempt to put a value on their human resources.[19] This model uses **historical costs** (actual expenses for recruiting, training, development, and so on) to determine the firm's investments in its employees and thus the **asset value** for the employee. This is a traditional way for accountants to value any resource, such as a building.[20] The asset value of the human resource staff can also be computed by calculating the human resource expenditure per employee. This calculation includes the cost of all human resource activities and staff divided by the number of employees covered by human resource services. In 1988, the average per capita expenditure per employee was $629. This value rose to $654 in 1989 and to $730 in 1990.[21]

Besides asset value, replacement costs, present value of future earnings, and value to the organization have been used to place a value on a firm's human resources. However, a major limitation to all of these approaches is that they focus on **inputs** and **outputs.** In other words, they do not relate a firm's investment in people with the output the people produce.[22]

Newer approaches attempt to put a dollar value on the **behavioral outcomes** produced by working in an organization. Costs are determined for such behaviors as absenteeism, turnover, and poor job performance. This method measures the **economic consequences** of employee behavior, not the value of the individual.

Costing Employee Behaviors

The costing approach appears to be more useful today compared to the human resource accounting approach.[23] Financial quantification of a set of common behavior and performance outcomes use standard cost accounting procedures applied to employee behavior. To do this, cost elements associated with each behavior must be identified and their separate and independent dollar values computed.

For example, look at costing labor turnover. High turnover can be a very expensive proposition for any organization. To compute turnover costs, dollar figures must be attached to **separation costs, replacement costs** (including recruiting and hiring), and **training** and **orientation costs.** In addition, there is an **opportunity cost** of having the job unfilled for a period of time or filled with a less than fully trained person. The opportunity cost is the foregone productivity because the job was not filled or because it was filled with a new, less well-trained employee.

Fast Food Example

A firm may put up with high turnover if it feels that the costs of curing the problem are greater than turnover costs themselves. Look at a typical fast-food operation such as McDonald's, for example. Suppose a McDonald's franchise experiences a 100 percent annual average turnover rate, about the national average for fast-food stores. In calculating the costs of this turnover, the costs of people leaving (separation), hiring, training, and foregone productivity would be compared with the costs of reducing the turnover. Assume for a moment that the costs of reducing turnover to say 25 percent involve the following:

1. Increasing wages by $1 per hour.
2. Implementing career tracks and promotion routes for all employees.
3. Increasing the benefits package.
4. Allowing employees a more flexible work schedule.

Also assume that when calculating the above costs the franchise determines that the above costs far outweigh the turnover costs. In this case the franchises may put up with 100 percent turnover as the less costly alternative.

Of course in estimating the costs of the four steps above, errors may be made since costs are estimated or projected, *not* actual. Also, it may be possible to reduce turnover by doing only step one or steps one and two. In other words, an **incremental approach** could be used to see if a step affects the turnover rate. This would be less costly than attempting all four steps at once.

Utility Theory

Through trial-and-error experience, a firm may develop fairly accurate costs of various behaviors. It may be possible to provide a pretty accurate estimate of resultant benefits. Yet since choices are involved, the decision should be to select the option that provides the maximum payment or *utility*. The study of this area of decision making is called **utility theory.**[24] Utility theory provides a framework for making decisions that requires decision makers to state goals clearly, specify outcomes of the decision options, and attach differing values or utilities to each outcome. Probabilities for the outcome of each decision also can be specified. This information is used to construct a payoff table or matrix.

Returning to the McDonald's franchise turnover example, we can see how utility theory might work. The object is to cut turnover. Four possible steps were identified. If we assign a dollar value to the effect of each alternative—the amount it will save in turnover—plus the probability that it will occur, we then have the following payoff matrix:

	EFFECT		PAYOUT PROBA-BILITY		(COSTS SAVED)
Payoff, Option 1 (Raise Wages):	$5,000	×	.60	=	$3,000
Payoff, Option 2 (Career Tracks):	3,000	×	.20	=	600
Payoff, Option 3 (Benefits Package):	2,000	×	.10	=	200
Payoff, Option 4 (Flexible Hours):	1,500	×	.10	=	150

Clearly, in the above example, we will get our highest probably payout by raising wages (Option 1). The effect of this option is that we will reduce turnover costs by $3,000 ($5,000 estimated cost reduction × .60 probability of occurrence).

The final step would be to compare the cost of this option to the cost of the other options to compute a cost/benefit ratio for each. This can be computed as shown on the following page:

OPTION	ANNUAL COST	ANNUAL PAYOUT (BENEFIT)	COST/BENEFIT RATIO
1	$10,000	$3,000	.30
2	5,000	600	.12
3	4,000	200	.05
4	3,000	150	.05

Using the above hypothetical figures, Option 1 would be chosen: it costs the most ($10,000), but has the highest payout relative to cost giving it the highest cost/benefit ratio of .30.

Of course this example is hypothetical. Actual figures of a problem of this type would differ because of individual firm circumstances. Furthermore, probabilities, even though based on experience and judgment, are still somewhat subjective. Nevertheless, this affords a much more rigorous analysis of decision options than typical seat-of-the-pants decision making that so often characterizes human resource decisions.

From a strategic standpoint, human resource costing and utility analysis offer much opportunity for the human resource professional. Far more sophisticated models using predictors, criterion cutoffs, and sophisticated mathematical notation are available in the literature. These models, coupled with computer manipulation and software packages, make it possible for even the most minimally skilled novice to incorporate quantitative cost analysis in human resource decisions. The emphasis on controlling human resource costs will likely spur more reliance on these quantitative techniques throughout the 1990s; however, they are unlikely to completely replace qualitative decision making discussed at the beginning of the chapter. Judgment will always play a role in human resource decision making.

Now we will examine human resource information systems as a way to track key information about human resources. Making good human resource decisions implies that we have a solid information set on which to base our decisions. We cannot cost human resource decisions if we do not have a cost data base available.

HUMAN RESOURCE INFORMATION SYSTEMS

The basis for good human resource decisions is good human resource information. Human resource information should be provided to both human resources and line managers in such a way that it facilitates decision making. This concept is known as a **decision-support system (DSS).** A decision support system places information for decision making literally at the fingertips of decision makers. Using personal computers or terminals, human resources and line managers can call up information as needed for recruiting, promoting, paying, or developing decisions.

A **human resource information system (HRIS)** is made up of numerous elements. Each element must function properly if the system is going to benefit the organization. Basically, a **system** is a set of activities that takes *inputs* (an application for employment in the finance department, for example), *transforms* them into useful items (a hiring approval from the personnel department), and then *outputs* the new items to where they can be used (sends the approval to the finance department). Most systems also have some form of *control* mechanism (the finance department sends back a completed new employee report) that enables supervisors to manage the operation of the system.[25]

HR CHALLENGES •••

An HRIS for New York City

In order to become more efficient, New York City's Department of Personnel installed an automated on-line HRIS system called PRISE (Personnel Reporting and Information System for Employees). The department is responsible for providing numerous services to the city's 60 agencies and more than 200,000 employees. These services include auditing and controlling each agency's personnel activities, such as hiring, transferring, and promoting. Before the installation of PRISE in late 1984, most of the city's personnel system was based on a traditional manual system of cards and folders. The city often experienced backlogs of 15 days or more under the old system, and it was almost impossible to tell exactly where a transaction was in the

system. As a result, it was almost impossible to locate the file or to determine where any delays in processing had occurred.

The new system not only eliminated these problems, but provided other advantages as well. Backup files and records are now automatically generated and personnel employees spend more time solving problems and providing assistance as opposed to filling out forms. PRISE has helped the New York City's Department of Personnel reduce errors, eliminate backlogs, and provide more useful answers to inquiries for managers.

SOURCE: Adapted from Stephen Rosenberg, "Flexibility in Installing Large Scale HRIS: New York City's Experience," *Personnel Administrator*, December 1985, pp. 39–46.

The combination of inputs, transformation, outputs, and feedback is the basis of any system as shown in Exhibit 4.6. Systems may be found on a departmental level, a plant level, or even an organization level. In short, a system is any activity that involves inputs, transformations, outputs, and feedbacks, and one system may be a subsystem—or a part of—another system. The HRIS is usually a part of the organization's larger management information system (MIS), which would include accounting, production, and marketing functions, to name just a few. The HRIS' special function is to gather, collect, and help analyze the data necessary for the human resources department to do its jobs properly.

What distinguishes a manual system from an HRIS is the use of computers or **information technology**. A big advantage of an information technology-based HRIS is that it can provide many more DSS functions than a manually based system. For the rest of the chapter we will assume that an HRIS represents a computer-based system unless otherwise noted. With this in mind, we will examine the components of an HRIS in more depth.

Inputs

The inputs of an HRIS resemble that of a manual based system. Employee information, company policies and procedures, and other personnel-related information must be entered into the system in order to be used. This information is usually entered from documents (such as an application form on an insurance report) into a computer terminal or a personal computer connected to a mainframe computer. Information can be typed in, digitally read—or scanned—from documents, loaded into the system from other computers, or retrieved from other machines connected to the computer (for example, the time clock is linked to the computer).

A computerized HRIS is superior to manual systems in many respects. Since much of the information is automatically entered into the system, errors are less likely to occur. Also, the HRIS' ability to connect to other computers exposes it to data that would otherwise be too difficult or costly to obtain. For example, the U.S. government and several private organizations maintain databases—or lists of

---

EXHIBIT 4.6   An HRIS Model

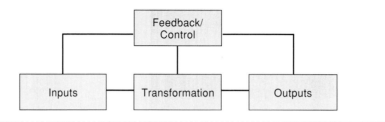

---

information on certain topics—that can be accessed by computers. If the human resource manager of a New York-based firm realized that its Georgia plant would be needing a new, entry-level chemical engineer within six months, he or she could connect into a database that would report the number of persons graduating from college with a bachelor's degree in chemical engineering in the Southeast during the past year, and their average starting salaries. Another advantage of an automated HRIS is backlog reduction. A well-designed HRIS will allow for more efficient input operation than a manual system could provide.

Transformations

This portion of the system is most closely associated with the actual computer. It also usually includes the software, or the written instructions that tell the computer what to do, how to do it, and when to do it. Computers and software for human resource information systems, range from simple and inexpensive to complex and expensive. Many small firms can establish a functional HRIS to meet their needs with a personal computer and standard database and spreadsheet programs. Large multinational firms may need to use a mainframe computer running sophisticated custom-designed programs to meet their needs. Whichever route taken (or possibly something in between), each firm has an HRIS.

During the transformation stage, the input information is changed into something more useful to the organization. In information systems the computer and the software usually perform the transformation (input hours worked by an employee transformed into a calculation of gross pay, taxes, other deductions, and net pay, for example). We highlight this stage by continuing with the example of the New York firm needing a chemical engineer in Georgia. The manager's database inquiry may have provided the following information:

> Number of chemical engineering graduates last year: 1,216
>
> Number of graduates in the Southeast: 432
>
> Number of chemical engineering graduates hired: 1,114
>
> Number of graduates hired in the Southeast: 516
>
> Average annual starting salary of chemical engineering graduates: $32,400
>
> Average annual starting salary in the Southeast: $34,800

At this point the information does not have any meaning for the manager. It is just a set of numbers that may or may not be significant for the firm. But, suppose that the following information was in the computer concerning the new position:

Minimum budgeted annual salary: $22,000

Maximum budgeted annual salary: $28,000

The system would compare the salary information against the budgeted funds and be ready to produce a report on the situation. The report would indicate that the demand for chemical engineers in the Southeast is high and that the average annual starting salary is higher than the firm is currently willing to pay. This comparison of information constitutes the transformation process of the example. Of course transformations can take many forms, whether it is the generation of a report, the calculation of a paycheck, or another function. Essentially then, the transformation process changes the input into a new form that is more usable to the organization.

Again, the HRIS has several advantages over the manual system. The first advantage is speed and efficiency. The comparison of the database report to the budget may have taken days or weeks to perform with several employee hours involved in looking up and comparing the data. Another advantage is that many operations could be performed that would not have been—or could not have been—done in the past. The enormous power of a computer system may allow for activities such as a weekly comparison of absenteeism rates and worker productivity that would have been too expensive in the past.

Outputs

The next step is the actual use of the newly processed material. In the above example, the output would be the production of the report on the chemical engineer for the human resource manager, or the printing of the paycheck for the employee. These are new items whose distinct use has been created by the transformation. The information technology used in the output stage is varied. It may involve material produced by printers, terminal screens, or any number of other devices. A well-designed HRIS will begin to show its worth as a DSS during this stage. The report on the potential problem in hiring a new chemical engineer for the Georgia plant alerts the manager to the fact that action must be taken or a decision made under the current guidelines. It should be noted that a decision support system does not make the decision for the manager, but provides high-quality information necessary to make a good decision. For information to be of high-quality, it must meet the following five criteria:

1. *Accurate.* The information must correctly reflect what it reports. A 100 percent accuracy rate is not always needed; for example, less accuracy is needed when measuring employee age trends than in reporting EEO compliance.
2. *Significant and relevant.* The information provided must be usable and usable information must be available in a timely manner.
3. *Comprehensive.* Information should provide a complete picture of the problem and possibly offer alternative solutions.
4. *Readable and visual impact.* Information must be easily understandable; it should not be in lists or tables when it can be in graphs and charts.
5. *Consistency of format.* The same information should not come in several different varieties when one standard is possible.[26]

These elements, if present, will help to ensure the usefulness of a firm's HRIS. But the question remains, what do firms typically use their HRIS for? The next section on feedback will examine this issue.

Feedback

Feedback represents the managerial control element of a system. The feedback element helps to ensure that the outputs are the ones that the system seeks to achieve. Most human resource information systems report information on numerous human resources activities. The following brief list gives some of the more common HRIS functions and what is typically included within each function:

Wages and Salaries: company pay structure, planned raises, and wage histories

Benefits: company benefit packages, data on benefits used/accumulated

EEO compliance: information on minority hiring, recruitment, and advancement

Labor relations: labor contract data, grievance information, and worker seniority lists

Training and development: information on various training programs, employees who have received training, and planned training and development activities

Health and safety: information on company accidents and the individuals involved, costs of accidents, and other data required by government and insurance reports

Management succession/career planning: information on skills, specialties, accomplishments, and possible promotions

HR planning: projections of future needs

Staffing: includes job assignments and possibly employee specialties

HR data management: includes basic employee information such as wages, social security numbers, and job titles

Monitoring and reporting HR policy: a DSS component, helps organizations compare actual HR performance to desired HR performance

General organizational data: includes organization structure, management levels, and special functions information

Demographics: information about worker availability, education, ages

External databases: information on other companies or economic trends[27]

This list is not comprehensive. Some firms' human resource information systems will have all this information and more. Other firms will only need part of this list to meet their needs. Now that we know what an HRIS is and what it does, we will examine how it can be used as a tool for corporate strategy.

Tying an HRIS to Corporate Strategy

When used properly, an HRIS can be a valuable tool for strategic planning and implementation. HRIS information should help decision makers better understand how human resource management can be a valuable competitive tool. It can be used to monitor morale, efficiency, and labor costs. It can be used to plan for the future human resource needs of the firm or to anticipate changes in the competitive environment. Its use is only limited by the extent to which the organization uses it to make strategic human resource decisions. Many firms are beginning to realize the value of using human resources to gain a **strategic advantage**—or a unique skill or competence that other firms do not have. This trend is likely to continue into the 1990s and beyond as firms attempt to cope with the challenges that lie ahead.

Chevron Strategically Uses Its HRIS

Chevron Corporation has an HRIS called CHRIS (Chevron Human Resource Information System). While this system organizes and monitors the every day human resources at Chevron, it also is used to do much more. CHRIS aids Chevron in strategic (long-range), operational (short-term), and tactical (immediate) decisions.

Chevron, the fourth largest integrated oil company in the world, employs 51,000 employees in 13 major operating companies in 58 countries. Chevron's merger with Gulf Oil in 1984 left it in a position of not being able to effectively and efficiently manage its extensive human resources, so it developed CHRIS to cope. CHRIS helps Chevron's human resource staff serve corporate human resources and human resource departments in all 13 companies and at all levels within the

companies. Chevron lists the following strategic imperatives for CHRIS:

- Establish and maintain a proactive business stance.
- Integrate Chevron business objectives with human resources functions and systems.
- Identify solutions to meet internal demands.
- Provide a greater degree of functional integration through the consolidation of similar human resource activities.
- Identify incentives and constraints to change.
- Increase computer literacy.

SOURCE: Adapted from Jay F. Straight, Jr., "Introducing CHRIS: Chevron's Human Resources Information System," *Personnel Administrator*, May 1987, pp. 24–28.

Types of HRISs

As mentioned earlier, an HRIS can be as small as a single personal computer or as large as one or more mainframe computers connected to each other. Depending on the firm's structure and philosophy of management concerning centralization of resources and decisions, an HRIS can be configured in one of several different ways. The most typical types of HRIS configurations are concentrated, distributed, and independent, or a hybrid combination of the first three.[28] Their features are summarized in Exhibit 4.7.

A *concentrated* HRIS places all control and accountability in one centralized location. This placement gives management the greatest degree of control over the system and reduces costs, but limits the flexibility of persons who need to use or access the system's information.

A *distributed* HRIS features both a central facility and multiple other sites connected to the facility and/or each other. This feature still allows for a great deal of management control over the operation and design of the system while providing some flexibility for its users.

Next, an *independent* system features multiple systems that may or may not be connected to each other. This system provides the greatest amount of flexibility to individual users who can design systems to fit their specific needs. Management control is often minimal, and this can result in increased costs due to different users "reinventing the wheel," or creating a new system function that may already exist somewhere else in the organization.

A final HRIS design configuration is the *hybrid* approach. Many firms have found it useful to have certain elements of their HRIS centralized while allowing other functions to be left to the discretion of individual users. In certain circumstances hybrid systems can be designed to provide the right mix of centralization-control and decentralization-autonomy within an organization, but the drawbacks to hybrid systems are that they tend to be very expensive since many different functions must be supported.

EXHIBIT 4.7 Features of Various HRIS Design Configurations

CONCENTRATED

Centralized Computer Facility
Strong Management Control
Reduced Costs
Limited User Flexibility and Access

DISTRIBUTED

Central Facility with Other Sites Connected
Strong Management Control
Increased User Flexibility and Access

INDEPENDENT

Multiple Systems
Minimal Management Control
High User Access and Flexibility
High Costs and Redundancy of Functions

HYBRID

A Mix of System Designs
Allows for Centralization of Certain Functions and Decentralization of Others
Level of Management Control Varies
Flexibility Levels Vary
Higher Costs Than Other Configurations

Once an organization has decided on the capabilities and configuration of its HRIS, it needs to ensure that its users actually know how to use and do use the system. This is the subject of the next section.

Making an HRIS Work

Ensuring that an HRIS works for an organization involves two key issues: (1) training users and (2) tying strategies and decisions.

Just as it is the role of a human resource department to provide training to members of an organization in certain areas, the department also must make sure that its employees and other users are properly trained in the use of the HRIS. Training often includes introducing users to new terms and familiarizing them with the capabilities of the system. Commercial systems developers often provide training to organizations. If the system is developed in-house, then the training function may fall to the department that created the system.

The second step in making an HRIS work is tying strategies and decisions. Even if users know how to use the system, it will not serve the organization if they cannot perceive any benefits from its use. As a result, a firm should make sure that the system serves necessary functions and provides information that will aid decision makers in achieving organization goals and strategies. If management feels that the HRIS is not being used effectively, an HRIS audit can be conducted. This entails examining company-specific reasons for having an HRIS, for gathering the data included, for the procedures used to access the data, for the reports it provides, and many other functional characteristics. Misuse, underuse, and potential uses all are uncovered.[29]

Privacy and the HRIS

The final issue we will discuss concerning human resource information systems relates to the privacy of the information it contains. A prime reason an organization would install an HRIS is to make it easier to find information. This ease of accessing information also has a downside: it is easier for unauthorized individuals to obtain private information (both company and personnel information) or for system users to accidentally disclose private information. Some laws exist that provide penalties for illegally obtaining certain kinds of employee information, but this doesn't always stop it from happening. An employee whose employer has accidentally divulged her performance appraisal history (when only her salary history was supposed to be released) to a bank loan division will not be any less upset if it was an accident. Organizations should make every attempt to provide safeguards against revealing private information—whether illegally or accidentally obtained. Protections such as system passwords, restricting access to confidential information on a need-to-know basis, and physically locking up files at the end of each day is just the first step in protecting the organization's reputation, its competitive position, and its legal liability.[30] Other issues that need to be considered include carefully defining and limiting user authorization, verifying that a user is actually the person authorized to use the system, encoding the data if it is transmitted and also when it is stored, and audit trails which provide a clear picture of who accessed what and when. By incorporating some or all of these ideas, the HRIS system should be secure.[31]

Summary of Human Resource Information Systems

In summary, it can be seen that a human resource information system serves a number of functions within an organization. An HRIS can help to reduce errors, increase efficiency, and reduce costs for an organization. As a decision support system, it can provide valuable information to decision makers and alert them to potential future problems or opportunities. The HRIS can be used as a strategic tool to help firms better plan and prepare for the future and reduce costs. The HRIS' configuration also will reflect the organization's attitude about how human resource decisions are made, whether it is distributed, centralized, or independent. Of course, for an HRIS to be effective, users must be properly trained how to use it and it must be used by those whom it is intended to serve. Finally, a computer-based HRIS raises concerns about the privacy of information that it contains. Proper care must be taken to restrict access to the system to those individuals who have a legitimate need for its information.

The HRIS' collection of information and the need to maintain its privacy brings about another issue—ethics. The next section discusses the role of ethics in human resource decision making.

························· ························· ························· ·····

| EXHIBIT 4.8 | Ethical Considerations |

Duties of HR Departments

- Training old and new employees on ethical policies
- Liaison between management and labor on ethical interpretations
- Creating, updating, monitoring, enforcing ethical policies

Ethical Systems

Ethics and Laws

Situational Ethics

Ethics and Employee Rights and Responsibilities

Ethics and Employee Discipline

Ethics and the Employee's Right to Privacy

ETHICS AND HUMAN RESOURCE DECISION MAKING

Human resource managers have a unique role in organizations. Unlike other managers whose concerns may range from monitoring product quality to finding the most favorable interest rate on a capital loan, the main responsibility of a human resource manager is the organization's employees. Human resource managers must try to protect the different needs of the organization and its employees, and their role not only implies power, but responsibility as well.

The human resource department often receives the task of creating, updating, monitoring, and enforcing an organization's ethics policy. It provides training to both old and new employees on the organization's ethical policies and often serves as the liaison between management and labor on interpretations of the code. As a result, most human resource managers are viewed as the ethical watchdog in the organization as far as people go.[32]

This section will discuss the unique role of individuals in organizations and the ethical considerations that arise as a result. The effect of the Judeo-Christian ethic in American firms will then be compared to the ethical systems of other cultures and the clashes that they may occur. Next, the relationship between ethics and laws will be examined, leading to a discussion of situational ethics and the effects of employee rights and responsibilities on ethics. The section concludes with an examination of ethics and discipline on and off the job and the question of ethics and the employee's right to privacy. Exhibit 4.8 lists the topics covered in this section.

People Are a Different Type of Resource

Unlike machines, buildings, equipment, or capital, people are a unique resource that require special attention from management. A manager cannot work a human being for twenty-four consecutive hours like he or she could with a machine just because the company has an important deadline to meet. And unlike a machine, a manager cannot just replace an employee because a new and improved version is available. People have emotions and feelings and their behavior is a reflection of how they are being treated. If a manager treats an employee poorly, then the employee is likely to adjust his or her performance accordingly. The concept of human dignity holds serious implications for managers who fail to recognize its impact. Many of the trends discussed earlier put great pressures on companies to perform well, but they also have significant ethical implications. Solutions to problems are often elusive and costly. What seems to be an inexpensive short-run solution to a problem may have serious implications for an organization farther down the road. Daniel Sherrick, associate general counsel of the United Auto Workers Union, reports that one company was severely hurt by its refusal to keep its employees informed on the progress of negotiations to sell off an operating unit. Rumors about potential layoffs and firings hurt morale and strained relations between management and the workers. Even when the sale was completed and employees learned that no changes would take place, the harm was irreversible. Sherrick states:

> By the time we got the news, though, the membership was so disheartened, so distrustful and so cynical that they never completely recovered. They had lived with months of uncertainty, months of the company's refusal to provide information and months of knowing that tremendous change was in the works and might threaten their jobs. Most of the locals [local union plants] asked that I personally visit their plant to explain in person the provisions of the sales agreement to the local union leadership. When I went, I saw a group of people totally demoralized by uncertainty and powerlessness, and hostile to management—both the former management and the future management. Unlike many situations the news I brought was good. . . . Even so, the employees were bitter and it will take the new owners years to generate the kind of trust and mutual respect that had existed in the plant between management and labor prior to the transition.[33]

It is clear that many management decisions will have ethical components that relate to the unique needs of employees. Failure to consider the impact of these decisions with respect to the employees could have long-run implications more severe than anticipated.

The Judeo-Christian Ethic Drives Managers in the United States

Another part of the ethics problems emerging today as a result of the previously discussed trends is the intermingling and clashing of cultures as business becomes more international in scope. Most managers in the United States have a clear idea of what is and what is not ethical behavior because they have lived their entire lives under the country's dominant Judeo-Christian work ethic. Unethical concepts like bribery, sexual harassment, and conflict of interest are well established, and in many instances have the force of law behind them. Many of these distinctions lose their clarity in the international arena, however. For example, is it considered ethical for a salesperson to pay for a client's dinner in Korea? Or does the breaking of a verbal contract in Pakistan have the same implications that it does in the United States? Many differences in cultural norms are immediately evident—the eye-for-an-eye philosophy of punishment in many Islamic nations and the traditional, seen-but-not-heard role of women in Japan—but determining the ethics of each individual nation or culture is difficult. Many of today's ethical problems arise as a result of the clash of ethical codes between countries. In short, what is accepted practice here may be unethical or illegal abroad.

Relation of Ethics to Law

In many instances there is also a fine line between ethics and the law because laws are often codified ethics. This may provide additional pressure when one enters a new environment, because one may have to determine where do ethics end and the laws begin. Laws relating to ethics may often be vague or ill defined. As a result, problems often arise as one attempts to determine what is really meant by the law. The letter of the law may allow for employee monitoring, but the spirit of the law may be otherwise. How does one determine what is the right course of action? A failure to take advantage of a loosely defined law may mean lost business and profits, whereas taking advantage of the loophole may mean nothing more than vague grumbling such as "their way of doing business could be improved." On the other hand, if it is the spirit of the law that is followed, then a violation of law may be extremely costly. This situation becomes more complicated when the relationship between the letter of the law and the spirit of the law is not quite settled. Organizations that bet on the outcomes of affirmative action guidelines, maternity-leave rules, and other employee related issues often face the very expensive possibility of losing once the issue is resolved in the legal system.

Situational Ethics

Another problem arises with situational ethics. Often, one may be in a position of being able to accomplish a goal for the "greater good" of the organization or society if short-run ethical considerations are ignored. Does one forego the short-run problems for the sake of the long-term benefit? At what point does the greater good outweigh ethical behavior? At what point does ethical behavior outweigh the greater good? The advent of electronic communications technology serves to highlight these problems. Many firms monitor employee phone communications to prevent unauthorized personal calls or to set and monitor performance standards. Other electronic technologies are now available that allow organizations to monitor almost any form of employee communication. When do the needs of an organization to meet its goals exceed the needs of its employees? For instance, should a company monitor the electronic mail messages of employees it suspects are divulging company secrets to competitors? What happens if the company does monitor the messages and then discovers that someone else was the culprit? Or what happens if the company monitors the messages and discovers the employee has accepted another job two months from now? Should the company begin looking for a replacement immediately even though it has not been formally notified that the employee is going to quit? Should the company fire the employee so it does not have to pay the employee's month of accrued vacation time? Should the company do nothing, even though it knows of a perfect replacement worker who may take the job if it is offered right now? Situations involving ethical decisions are difficult, and there is no correct textbook answer on how to resolve them.

Managers are often faced with a similar ethical problem of trying to determine the "right thing" to do in making a decision. The trend toward downsizing may make it necessary to lay off 300 of a company's most skilled and dedicated workers to save costs, but should it be done the week before Christmas? If the manager doesn't lay off the workers at Christmas, she may not be able to meet the payroll at the end of January for the remaining workers. Here the manager is faced with two conflicting courses of action that will result in harm either way. Both decisions have unknown ethical implications. Managers are often placed in the situation of having to make the distinction between ethical and nonethical actions without knowing what the consequences will be.

Ethical dimensions also may affect the very manner in which a company does business. For example, it may be easier to lower quality-control standards to save costs than it is to completely redesign a product to meet the threat of international competition, but do customers have the right to know that what they're buying today may not be as safe as what they bought yesterday? Is it ethical *not* to tell customers that quality standards have been lowered? Another example of ethical considerations can be found in the increasingly competitive drug industry. New drugs may take years and millions of dollars to develop, and once they are developed, it make take several more years before the drug is approved for sale by a regulatory agency. It may seem reasonable that a company should be able to charge high prices to recoup its investment, especially when it owns the patent for the drug, but what if the drug is insulin—a necessity of life for diabetics—or a treatment for AIDS? When Burroughs Wellcome Company introduced the AIDS fighting drug AZT in 1987, its price for a year's prescription was over $10,000—far higher than any but the most wealthy patients could afford. Industry sources believe that Burroughs Wellcome is earning a 70 percent to 80 percent profit margin on AZT, which is standard for new drugs. The company has since cut prices on the drug—it now costs about $8,000 a year—but federal funding for patients is limited in the United States. Peter Staley, a member of the AIDS Coalition to Unleash Power, states "there's a difference between a $500 drug sold at 80 percent margins and an $8,000 drug sold at 80 percent margins. We have a drug that could slow a worldwide epidemic, and its being sold only to the people and the countries that can afford it. Africa isn't getting AZT."[34] DDC, another AIDS combating drug, is being pirated by underground labs and sold on the black market. This undercuts potential sales by the drug's patent owner, Hoffman-La Roche, Inc., which invested millions of dollars in its development.[35]

The costs of ethical lapses in organization decision making also are becoming quite expensive. American Express recently agreed to donate $8 million to banker Edward J. Safra's favorite charities as a result of a rumor campaign it started about his business practices. GTE won a $110 million verdict against the Home Shopping Network when the network tried to place the blame for its poor customer service on its GTE phone system.[36] Many companies seek to avoid these problems by instituting and enforcing strict ethical standards, such as that of Deluxe Check Printers in Exhibit 4.9, and often it is the responsibility of the human resource department to draft, monitor, and enforce these standards.

Ethics and Employee Rights and Responsibilities

Ethics do not only apply to managers. Employees at all levels of the organization must deal with ethical issues. Many workers are faced with decisions, such as reporting work-rule violations of fellow workers, and the decision as to when to report and not to report can be difficult. Often, an employee who does decide to report a fellow employee's violation will contact an immediate superior, or possibly the human resource department if the infraction occurs in another department besides the employee's own. For example, should an employee report a fellow worker's tardiness if a coworker was thirty minutes late to work and the boss did not notice it? Should the employee be reported if it was the third time in the past month he was late? How about the third time in the last week? Or, what if the employee was late, but he knows that if the boss asks that he will be able to cover up the fact with a simple

··

EXHIBIT 4.9 Deluxe Check Printing Company Code of Business Conduct

OUR BUSINESS CONDUCT

Our overriding goal is integrity—integrity in our products and in our business conduct. Every Deluxe employee is expected to conduct business in a way that is socially responsible. No act of impropriety advances the interests of the Company.

Our policy is to obey the law—in letter and spirit.

We seek no special favors or considerations from suppliers, customers, competitors, or government.

We avoid relationships or arrangements with competitors that would limit the vigor and competition in our markets.

We are straightforward and aboveboard in all of our relationships.

- We convey true claims for our products.
- We endeavor to deliver quality products.
- We encourage fair comparisons of our products and services.
- We purchase on the basis of what is in our best interest by seeking maximum value for each dollar spent.

We seek long-lasting relationships with all whose activities touch upon our own.

We comply with all generally accepted accounting rules and controls.

We make no corporate payments to government officials or candidates for public office.

We do not give gifts of other than nominal value or accept gifts of other than nominal value from those with whom we do business.

We seek to conserve the resources and protect the quality of the environment in areas where we operate.

··

lie? There are often ethical situations regarding the use of company property. Is it stealing if an employee takes home a company calculator worth six dollars and does not return it if she is working on a project for the company at home? How about if the calculator is worth fifty dollars? Many employees view the ability to use the company mailroom, make long-distance personal phone calls, or occasionally take supplies for their own use as job perquisites, but is it ethical? Some companies will tolerate these actions to an extent, but at what point does it become unethical behavior, and at what point does is become stealing? Employees receive certain rights at work, but in turn they are given certain responsibilities for these rights. These rights and responsibilities often go beyond what is written in the company's policy and procedure manuals, and it is often difficult to determine what the most ethical course of action is—or what constitutes an ethical action—as a result. The role of the human resource department should be to clarify these issues and provide appropriate training within the company so that confusion is minimized. We will discuss this issue in more detail in Chapter 9.

Ethics and Discipline On and Off the Job

Another area of concern is the relationship between company ethical guidelines and discipline policies with on-and-off-the-job freedoms. On-the-job ethical problems may be easy to prove and deal with, but off-the-job violations present a number of problems. For example, can a company discipline an employee who had a six-pack of beer after he left work on Friday night? Probably not. How about if the employee had a six-pack an hour before he showed up to work on Monday morning? Many ethical violations occurring off-the-job, such as drug and alcohol use, have on-the-job implications, but proving them may be difficult. Organizations are increasingly being given the right by the legal system to deal with these situations, and the human resource department is often given the responsibility by the organization of being investigator, judge, and jury. The difficulty arises in making sure that individuals receive due process and fair treatment. In unionized organizations rules for dealing with these considerations are often formalized in contracts, but in many other organizations the process may be extremely informal, and mistakes can be dangerous. Whenever possible, an organization should have a clear set of rules outlining what constitutes a violation of company policies, what the penalty is for each violation, and the process for determining whether or not a violation has occurred. Companies that enforce policies in an inconsistent or arbitrary manner are likely to meet with high costs as they defend their actions in court.

Ethics and the Employee's Right to Privacy

In the last section we discussed the problems of maintaining privacy of HRIS information. In addition to the problems of maintaining the privacy and secrecy of HRIS information, there are several ethical implications as well. Human resource managers constantly receive requests for information about employees, jobs, and other important company data. Often these requests are legitimate, but at what point does the need to know outweigh the need for privacy? For example, should the human resource manager release individual personnel evaluations from the accounting department to the finance department, which is considering an overhaul of its evaluation structure? Should the human resource manager allow the release of information concerning employee wages in the Boston plant to the production line manager at the new Tacoma plant? As we mentioned earlier, the human resource department has a great deal of private information about its employees, and decisions regarding the distribution of this information should be made with the utmost care.

Summary of Ethics and Human Resource Decision Making

Numerous ethical considerations relate to human resource decision making. Many decisions involve ethical components that may be more serious than the immediate situation at hand due to their impact on the organization's personnel. Other decisions are difficult because their ethical implications are not always clear. It is often hard to know the ethical norms outside of one's own culture, or to understand the relationship between ethics and the law. Other situations may involve ethical trade-offs. The human resource department plays a central role in the ethical considerations of its organization. Its close ties to the organization's employees often places it in the position of being the organization's ethical watchdog. This role not only includes instituting policies and monitoring compliance, but also serving as investigator and judge as well. In turn, the human resource department must deal with the ethical considerations of properly using and protecting the employee information it maintains.

HUMAN RESOURCE AUDIT

Because of the ever-increasing demand for high productivity in order to compete in today's marketplace, the human resource department needs to justify its usefulness to the organization. **Personnel research** is one of the primary means by which the human resource department assesses itself. Personnel research involves the evaluation of the department's effectiveness in serving the organization's personnel needs. It helps the organization analyze what, if any, changes and improvements need to be made in its personnel practices and policies.[37] One of the key tools for conducting personnel research is the **personnel audit.**

The personnel audit is used to collect data to help the organization determine how well its human resource functions are performing. Personnel audits collect information using a number of methods. These methods can include employee observation, surveys, questionnaires, review of HRIS data, or a combination of these methods. The audit's main function is to help decision makers understand what is happening with various personnel activities, such as recruitment, hiring, separation, and training.

Why Do an Audit?

Personnel research often begins due to management perceptions that certain programs or activities are not performing as planned. A personnel audit may indicate that a specific program does not meet its goals and needs further research before it can be revised. Of course, the audit may indicate that the program or activity is adequate and that no further action needs to be taken. In either case, the personnel audit is the investigation into an area of concern to the organization's decision makers.[38]

Another reason to conduct an audit is that it often produces results that were not anticipated. For example, an audit of employee turnover during the past year may indicate that turnover is within acceptable limits. But, the audit also may indicate that the firm's reward and compensation system is beginning to contribute to increased turnover.

Ways of Doing the Audit

How does an organization conduct a personnel audit? One method is to do the audit with in-house staff, but this may perpetuate many of the errors and misconceptions of the past. Another method is to hire a third-party human resource consultant, but the consultant may miss some of the subtleties of the organization's system, or the consultant may come into the organization with a preconceived set of solutions. Many firms use their lawyers to advise them on the legality of their programs, but lawyers often lack the basic training needed to evaluate the efficiency and effectiveness of the entire program. Each method has its advantages and disadvantages, and it is up to the firm to determine beforehand what it seeks to achieve with its audit.[39] This will help determine which method, or combination of methods, is best for the firm's purposes.

Using the Information to Emphasize Human Resource Operations

As mentioned previously, several methods can be used to collect the data, including observations, surveys, questionnaires, and data reviews. These techniques are used

| EXHIBIT 4.10 | Personnel Audit Measurements and Their Organization's Underlying Indicators |

RATE	PERSONNEL FUNCTIONS TO EXAMPLE
Turnover Rate	Salary and benefits package
• Quit rate	Supervisory products
• Termination rate	Job design
• Layoff rate	Retirement plan
• Retention rate	
• Retirement rate	
• Length of service rate	
Job Attendance Rate	Exit interviews
• Absence rate	Discipline
• Tardiness rate	Convenience of lunchroom and rest room
	Sick-pay policy
Overtime Rate	Employee planning and scheduling
	Shortage of staff
	Selection and training process
Position Vacancy Rate	Recruitment and selection process
	Salary and benefit package
	Company image in community
Error/Scrap Rate	Recruitment selection and placement
	Training and development
	Job satisfaction
Training Development Rate	Recruitment and selection
	Training and development
Grievance Rate	Supervisory practices
	Job dissatisfaction

to gather information and compare it to some expected or predicted outcome. For example, the audits can compare rates or ratios like turnover, attendance, or training and development against past firm or industry levels of performance. Surveys can be used to measure morale and job satisfaction or wages and salaries.[40] All of these factors serve as broad measures of the success of underlying personnel and organizational functions. For example, poor attendance and tardiness rates may indicate poor morale, an overly permissive sick-pay policy, lack of line supervisor discipline, or maybe just a poorly laid out plant that prevents employees from returning from breaks on time. Exhibit 4.10 provides additional examples. The technique used will depend on the information sought. Surveys are an excellent way to measure effects on large groups, while interviews and observations can be used for a more comprehensive analysis of smaller groups. Information from the HRIS may be valuable in itself, or it may be used to compare against information from outside sources or internal research.

HR CHALLENGES •

Exactly How Do Businesses Evaluate Their HR Departments?

A recent study by researchers at the University of Iowa indicated that approximately one-third of the businesses in their survey seldom or never conduct evaluations of their human resource departments. Another one-third said that they conduct human resource reviews at least annually, while the final one-third fell somewhere in the middle.

The two most frequently cited reasons for not evaluating the human resource function were difficulty in conducting a scientific evaluation and difficulty in quantifying human resource's return on investment.

However, this did not seem to stop the one-third of the respondents who frequently evaluate their human resource departments. When asked what type of evaluation is performed, they indicated a more judgmental and qualitative process is used rather than a quantitative

or scientific one. Further, when asked who performs the evaluation, the majority of the respondents indicated that the human resource function evaluates itself.

The results of this study indicate that human resource departments are clearly not being evaluated properly. Further, the true value of the human resource function to the organization is not being made clear. Even in organizations in which evaluations are performed, the informally gathered information by the people in the department will not hold much weight. Before human resource departments can be judged on their merit, procedures must exist for determining how well they perform.

SOURCE: Adapted from Margaret Cashman and James McElroy, "Evaluating the HR Function," *HRMagazine*, January 1991, pp. 70–73.

However the information is gathered, the main purpose of the personnel audit is to evaluate the effectiveness of the organization's human resource function, and the information should reflect this. It should show both the department's strengths and weaknesses and provide management with a clear picture of the department's role in the organization. The audit also should allow management to evaluate the human resource department's broader role in helping the organization meet its strategic goals and objectives.

FUTURISM AND DECISIONS

Scenario Projection

The final role of the personnel unit in strategic decision making is to help project the consequences of decisions as they might affect human resources. This role involves an "if-then" type of analysis. For example, when the United States federal government decided to switch from the traditional civil service system to one embodying the Senior Executive Service (SES), human resource professionals were involved in projecting possible scenarios.

The SES is an exempt category of highly paid senior professionals in federal government service. The reason the SES was established was to give agency managers more flexibility in appointing and rewarding top-level agency personnel. It also emphasized a high-level development program for SES potential managers that would incorporate both on- and off-the-job learning experiences.[41]

Decisions that established the SES were made in order to correct perceived inadequacies in the civil service system. A more flexible system that did not guarantee tenure of top-level administrators and one that provided bonuses for top performance was viewed as being more effective. Human resource professionals believed that the system used by business for top management also would work in government. However, because of the political nature of government agencies, this may not be the case. At any rate, the resulting scenario of making the SES change was aimed at achieving results similar to that in the private sector.

Intended and Unintended Consequences

It appears that the SES has accomplished its intended goals, but like most major changes there have been both intended and unintended consequences of the decision. Every decision carries with it potential downside losses and negative impacts. Many of these can be anticipated just as benefits of the decision can be anticipated. However, decisions also bring *unanticipated consequences*—both positive and negative. Since they are unanticipated they have not been forecasted prior to the decision. What can human resource managers do to deal with this situation?

First, since people are complex individuals, decisions that affect them tend to be complex and often create unexpected responses. Human beings are not machines that always react in a certain programmed way to a particular action or decision. Thus, decision makers need to take into account the variability of individual response when making decisions affecting human resources. Human resource managers have a responsibility to point out this variability and help line managers anticipate variable responses. This also calls for flexibility in decisions and policy formulation. There will be exceptions and policy decisions must allow for them.

Second, scenario projection of decision outcomes using both quantitative and qualitative techniques can help to surface unintended consequences. In particular, **mental imagery** can be used to project decision outcomes by allowing decision makers to use projective imagery to mentally role-play a decision.[42]

For example, suppose a firm was considering changing its pay system by adopting a pay for performance policy. Under this system, people would be paid a group bonus if they exceeded predetermined goals. By using projective imagery a group of managers could try to determine the consequences of this action by experiencing the following mental imagery script under the guidance of a facilitator.

> Assume that you are about to announce our new bonus pay system to your employees. Imagine that you are meeting with them in your conference room. See their faces. You announce and explain the new bonus system. You listen to their reactions. What questions are they asking? What do you say in response? Do you see them as being happy or unhappy? Do you see some individual employees being much more happy or much less happy compared to the rest? What do you see the employees doing or saying after they leave the room?

Mental imagery using a script such as the one above helps people to experience a decision vicariously prior to it being made. Human resource professionals have a responsibility to help line managers better pinpoint decision consequences, and imagery can help.[43]

• • • • • • • • •

MANAGEMENT GUIDELINES

The final test of any decision is does it work? In other words, did the decision bring about the intended results? To this end, here are some management guidelines that should be observed in decision making:

1. The essence in formulating strategy is making decisions.

2. Both qualitative and quantitative techniques for making decisions should be used.

3. Retrospective reconstruction plays an important role in helping managers understand and justify decisions.

4. Individual scripts, schemas, and cognitive maps provide the basis for assimilating and interpreting information.

5. Relying on tacit knowledge or intuition can enhance the decision process if used with rational decision methods.

6. The better and more accurately that managers make sense of what goes on around them both in and outside of the organization the better their decisions will be.

7. When a strategic decision has a major impact on human resources, the human resource unit should have a major role to play in the decision.

8. Human resources should be the major unit used to scan the environment for human resource and labor market issues.

9. Human resources should project both intended and unintended consequences of decisions as they might affect human resources.

10. Human resource information systems can significantly increase the organization's ability to achieve its strategic goals.

11. Many decisions have significant ethical considerations. Human resources should make the companies ethical policies clear and fair.

QUESTIONS FOR REVIEW

1. What does decision making have to do with policy formulation?

2. Contrast the rational approach to decision making with the qualitative approach.

3. What is the garbage can model of decision making?

4. What are schemas, scripts, and cognitive maps and what do they have to do with decision making?

5. What is cognitive dissonance? Describe a time when you suffered from cognitive dissonance.

6. What is mental imagery and how can it be used to enhance the understanding of new information in decision making?

7. What is attribution theory and how does it relate to decision making?

8. What role does tacit knowledge or intuition have in decision making?

9. What is the role of the human resource unit in strategic decisions?

10. What are the levels of staff involvement for the human resource unit in decision making?

11. Should human resources exercise more line authority in strategic decision making? Why or why not?

12. How can the human resource unit help to project both intended and unintended consequences of decisions?

13. What is the main purpose of a human resource information system? Name some of the typical HRIS functions.

14. What are the elements of a human resource information system? What are the typical configurations of a human resource information system?

15. What are the characteristics of high-quality human resource information?

16. What role does the human resource department play in organizational ethics?

17. Describe the human resource audit and its goals.

CASE: Delta Soars[43]

Annual budgets don't exist at Delta Air Lines, Inc. Who needs them when Chairman Ronald Allen personally reviews every nonrecurring expenditure greater than $1,000?

Such old-fashioned policies have served Delta well. The company played it safe through the era of breakneck expansion that swept the industry, cautiously plodding while other airlines sped ahead. Now, a decade after the onslaught of airline deregulation, the nation's third-largest airline in terms of capacity has emerged as the strongest carrier in a battle-scarred industry, poised to profit from the weaknesses of its competitors.

While Texas Air and Pan Am went deeply into hock to expand, Delta remains the least-leveraged airline in the industry. When United battled its pilots and Eastern warred with its machinists, Delta maintained the most loyal work force in the skies. Its profit margins are the industry's fattest and its stock was the industry's highest flier in 1988.

Now, Delta is finally shedding some of the stodginess that sheltered it through the tumult of deregulation. Roughly $1.4 billion in new aircraft are coming in, and hundreds of additional flights, including a number overseas, are being planned.

"We've gained momentum as we've grown, and now we're like a freight train coming down the track," says W. Whitley Hawkins, senior vice-president of marketing.

Lagged on Reservation System

For all the company's newfound boldness, one long-term worry gnaws at Delta—a major one. As a result of waiting too long to get into the business, the company's computerized reservation system today has a meager 4 percent to 5 percent share of the travel agent market, leaving United, American, Texas Air, and TWA to enjoy most of the marketing benefits and fee income provided by these systems.

To push its system, Delta is offering travel agents an array of back-office software systems and a whiz-bang feature that stores video images of cruise ships, rental cars, and other travel products on a hard disk. But the company admits it is stuck playing a catch-up game. "We should have been in there sooner," says Allen.

Thankfully for investors—and unhappily for competitors—Delta wasn't so complacent when it came to routes. Its $860-million purchase of Western Airlines in 1986 filled a huge hole in the northwest corner of Delta's route map, expanding the cities served by Delta to 156 from 106 and enlarging its fleet to 386 from 245. With a year of advance planning, the merger aroused little of the employee discontent that was visible in Northwest's purchase of Republic, for instance, and few of the gut-wrenching operational problems that occurred after Continental's acquisition of Peoples Express.

"This was unequivocally the most successful merger since deregulation," says Timothy Pettee, airline analyst at Bear, Stearns and Company.

Today, Delta internally projects an expansion at its hub in Cincinnati to 200 flights a day by 1992 from the current 129. Dallas-Fort Worth is slated for 300 flights a day by 1993, up from 207. The company's main hub in Atlanta won't grow much beyond its current 400 flights a day, although the recent growth there has included service to Shannon and Dublin, Ireland.

Won Disney Title

Long a laggard in marketing, Delta is linking some of its expansion to long-term promotions. For instance, by pledging a $1 million annual fee and $10 million toward a new amusement park attraction, Delta grabbed Eastern's title as the official airline of DisneyWorld.

Company officials lovingly refer to the Disney character as their "golden mouse," and will only smile when asked about the profitability of the tie-in. But, as a result of it, Delta increased daily service at Orlando, Florida, in 1989 to 80 flights from 65 in 1988. New service between Orlando and Frankfurt, West Germany, may give Delta the springboard from which to launch local service in Europe, which major U.S. airlines covet as a growth market.

Delta's expansion plans will help make its aircraft fleet—already the youngest and most fuel-efficient in the nation—all the more so. To expand its number of long-range aircraft for service to South Korea, Taiwan, and other foreign destinations, the company has supplemented its Lockheed L-1011 wide-bodies with late-model Airbus Industries A-340s, Boeing 747-400s or McDonnell-Douglas MD-11s.

The company retired in 1988—much earlier than most airlines—the last of its DC-8 and DC-10 aircraft, clearing the way for about three dozen ultramodern 757-200s and MD-88s in 1989.

The company also plans to retire many of the older 727 and 737 aircraft it acquired in the Western acquisition, partly to standardize fleet maintenance but also in an effort to serve the most populous cities with bigger aircraft. Delta officials are convinced that airport overcrowding will eventually cause federal regulators to restrict landings. Thus, on service from Western's old Salt Lake City hub to New York, Delta now flies 757s, which hold 187 passengers, instead of 737s, which carry 128.

Delta can easily finance this growth because of its huge profits. The Western acquisition spread fixed costs over more aircraft seats. And Delta's revenue in 1987 totaled 12.7 cents per passenger per mile, nearly 15 percent above the industry average. Analysts expect record earnings for its fiscal year ended June 30 of about $500 million, nearly double the $263.7 million of the year earlier.

Pro People

In a service business, morale and productivity are the most important assets, and by nearly all accounts, both are high at Delta. Flight attendants are considered especially critical links; indeed, Chairman Allen and other top managers recently sat through a day-long presentation on such prosaic matters as the optimum number of meal carts to maintain aboard Delta's new 757s. During the 1988 Democratic National Convention, for which Delta was the official airline, some 900 unpaid employee volunteers worked at parties and hospitality suites.

Delta keeps employees happy—and, more particularly, unions off the property—by maintaining among the highest pay scales in the industry. American Airlines currently is fighting to preserve its so-called B scales—the lower wage rates established for newly hired people. Delta, by contrast, voluntarily eliminated the last of its two-tier wage scales in 1988.

"We aren't anti-union," says Allen, who came up through the ranks of personnel himself. "We're pro-people."

Its well-paid employees were so loyal to the company that during the 1982 recession they chipped in and bought Delta a plane for its fleet. Delta's family-like conservative culture has served it well. Tradition runs so deep at Delta, the company still holds its annual stockholder meeting in Monroe, Louisiana, where it began operations as a cropduster in 1924. Skeptics wonder how much this conservative culture will inhibit future change.

QUESTIONS

1. What strategic decisions has Delta made that have enabled the firm to meet the challenges of deregulation?

2. What role does employee loyalty play in Delta's success?

3. Will Delta's conservative pro-family philosophy with respect to its people hinder its ability to handle change in the future? Explain your answer.

4. Explain Delta's overall strategy and its human resource strategy. Do you see conflict or harmony between the two strategies?

5. What strategic decisions is Delta likely to face in the future? How should it prepare for these decisions?

················
ADDITIONAL READINGS

Abelson, Robert F. "Psychological Status of the Script Concept." *American Psychologist.* July 1981, Target, pp. 715–729.

Anderson, Kirk J. "Putting the 'I' in HRIS." *Personnel.* September 1988, pp. 12–24.

Angle, Harold L., Charles C. Manz, and Andrew H. Van de Ven. "Integrating Human Resource Management and Corporate Strategy: A Preview of the 3M Story." *Human Resource Management* 24, no. 1. Spring 1985, pp. 51–68.

Anthony, William P., E. Nick Maddox, and Walter J. Wheatley, Jr. *Envisionary Management: A Guide for Human Resource Professionals.* Westport, CT: Quorum Books, 1988.

Anthony, William P. and Jane C. Wager. "Executive Management Development Program in the U.S. Department of the Navy." In Halil Copur, ed. *HRMOB Proceedings* 1, Philadelphia: The Association of Human Resources Management and Organization Behavior, 1987, pp. 50–54.

Argyris, Chris. "Organizational Learning and Management Information Systems." *Data Base* (1982), pp. 3–11.

"Automate the Entire Employment Function." *HRMagazine.* June 1991, pp. 36–38.

Axelrod, R., ed. *Structure of Decision: The Cognitive Maps of Political Elites.* Princeton, N.J.: Princeton University Press, 1976.

Bateman, T., and C. Zeithaml. "The Psychological Context of Strategic Decisions: A Model and Convergent Experimental Findings." *Strategic Management Journal* (1989), vol. 10, pp. 59–74.

Bensu, Janet. "Use Your Data Base in New Ways." *HRMagazine.* March 1990, pp. 33–34.

Berger, P., and T. Luckmann. *The Social Construction of Reality.* New York: Doubleday, 1967.

Bolman, L. G., and T. E. Deal. *Reframing Organizations.* San Francisco: Jossey-Bass, 1991.

Bourgeois, L. J. "Performance and Consensus." *Strategic Management Journal* 1 (1980), pp. 227–248.

Briscoe, Dennis R., Robert F. O'Neil, and Ellen Cook. "Strategic Human Resources Decision-Making: An Economic Lesson. *Human Resource Management* 21, Summer/Fall 1982, pp. 2 +.

Brummet, R. L., E. Flamhol, and W. Pyle. "Human Resource Accounting—A Challenge for Accountants." *Accounting Review* 43 (1968), pp. 217–224.

Burton, Richard M., "Variety in Strategic Planning: An Alternative to the Problem Solving Approach." *Columbia Journal of World Business* 19, no. 4. Winter 1984, pp. 92–98.

Butler, J. E., G. R. Ferris and N. K. Napier. *Strategy and Human Resources Management.* Cincinnati: South-Western, 1991.

Cascio, Wayne F. *Costing Human Resources: The Financial Impact of Behavior in Organizations.* 2nd ed. Boston: PWS-Kent, 1987.

Chaganti, R. "Strategic Orientation and Characteristics of Upper Management." *Strategic Management Journal* 8 (1987), pp. 393–401.

Chase, Marilyn. "Burroughs Wellcome Reaps Profits, Outrage from its AIDS Drug." *Wall Street Journal.* September 15, 1989, pp. A1, A5.

Chase, Marilyn. "Popular AIDS Treatment Is Illicit Copy of Hoffman-La Roche's New Drug DDC." *Wall Street Journal.* July 16, 1991, p. B1.

Cohen, Michael D., James C. March, and Johan P. Olsen. "A Garbage Can Model of Organizational Choice." *Administrative Source Quarterly* 17, no. 1. March 1972, pp. 1–25.

Cohen, Y. and J. Pfeffer. "Organizational Hiring Standards," *Administrative Science Quarterly,* No. 31 (1986), pp. 1–24.

"Compensation and the Computer." *HRMagazine.* March 1991, pp. 24–26.

Cyert, R. N., and J. G. March. *A Behavioral Theory of the Firm.* Englewood Cliffs, NJ: Prentice-Hall, 1963, pp. 27–32.

Dalton, D., and I. Kesner. "Organizational Performance as an Antecedent of Inside/Outside Chief Executive Succession: An Empirical Assessment." *Academy of Management Journal* 28 (1985), pp. 749–762.

Delaney, Chester. "Integrated Powerhouse." *HRMagazine.* March 1990, pp. 30–32.

Diers, Cynthia D. "Make the HRIS More Effective." *Personnel Journal*. May 1990, pp. 92–94.

Dunnington, Judith I. "Successful HRIS Implementation Planning." *Personnel Journal*. February 1990, pp. 78–84.

Dyer, Lee. "Bringing Human Resources into the Strategy Formulation Process." *Human Resource Management* 22, Fall 1983, pp. 257+.

Edwards, Gary, and Kirk Bennett. "Ethics and HR: Standards in Practice." *Personnel Administrator*. December 1987, pp. 62–66.

Ferris, Gerald R., and Timothy A. Judge. "Personnel/Human Resources Management: A Political Influence Perspective." *Journal of Management* 17, no. 2 (1991), pp. 447–488.

Fisher, Cynthia D. "Current and Recurrent Challenges in Human Resource Management."
Journal of Management 15, no. 2, June 1989, pp. 157–180.

Fischer, Robert L. "HRIS Quality Depends on Teamwork." *Personnel Journal*. April 1991, pp. 47–51.

Fredrickson, J. "Effects of Decision Motive and Organizational Performance Level on Strategic Decision Processes." *Academy of Management Journal* 28 (1985), pp. 821–843.

Fredrickson, J. *Perspectives on Strategic Management*. New York: HarperBusiness, 1990.

Fredrickson, J. "The Strategic Decision Process and Organizational Structure." *Academy of Management Review*, 11 (1986), pp. 280–297.

Geyelin, Milo. "Corporate Mudslinging Gets Expensive." *Wall Street Journal*. August 4, 1989, p. B1.

Gioia, Dennis A., and Cameron M. Ford. "Tactic Knowledge, Self-Communication, and Organizational Sensemaking." In L. Thayer, ed. *Organization→Communication: Emerging Perspectives III*. New York: Ablex, 1992 (in press).

Gold, David. *Strategic Management of Human Knowledge, Skills, and Abilities: Workforce Decision Making in Post-Industrial Era*. San Francisco: Jossey-Bass, 1991.

Gupta, A. "Contingency Linkages Between Strategy and General Manager Characteristics: A Conceptual Examination." *Academy of Management Review*, 9 (1984), pp. 399–413.

Hedberg, B., and Sten Jonsson. "Designing Semi-confusing Information Systems for Changing Organizations." *Data Base* (1982), Target, pp. 12–25.

Henson, Row. "Computer Databases Built for HR." *HRMagazine*. April 1991, pp. 59–61.

Hofer, Charles W., and Dan Schendel. *Strategy Formulation: Analytical Concepts*. St. Paul: West, 1978.

Hogarth, Robin M. *Judgement and Choice: The Psychology of Decision*. 2nd ed. New York: John Wiley and Sons, 1987.

"The HRIS and HR Applications Software." *HRMagazine*. November 1990, pp. 28–32.

Isenberg, Dan. "Thinking and Managing: A Verbal Protocol Analysis of Managerial Problem Solving." *Academy of Management Journal* 29, no. 4, December 1986, pp. 775–788.

Isenberg, Daniel J. "The Structure and Process of Understanding: Implication for Managerial Action." In H. P. Sims and D. A. Gioia. *The Thinking Organization: Dynamics of Organizational Social Cognition*. San Francisco: Jossey-Bass, 1986.

Jenkins, Michael L., and Gayle Lloyd. "How Corporate Philosophy and Strategy Shape the Use of HR Information Systems." *Personnel*. May 1985.

Knapp, Jeffrey. "Trends in HR Management Systems." *Personnel*. April 1990, pp. 56–61.

LaVan, Helen, Nicholas J. Mathys, and Wayne Hochwarter. "Insecurity in Numbers." *Computers in Personnel*. Spring 1989, pp. 51–53.

Lehren, Jeff. "Competing for a Position in the Business World." Unpublished Handout, NCR Corporation, Orlando, Florida,

n.d. Lehren is in charge of college recruiting for NCR Corporation for the Florida Region.

Lindblom C. "The Science of Muddling Through," *Public Administration Review* 19 (1959), pp. 79–88.

Linneman, Robert E., and Harold E. Klein. "Using Scenarios in Strategic Decision Making." *Business Horizons* 28, no. 1, January–February·1985, pp. 64–74.

McElroy, John. "The HRIS as an Agent of Change." *Personnel Journal*. May 1991, pp. 105–111.

McGregor, Eugene B., Jr., and John Daly. "The Strategic Implications of Automation in Public Sector Human Resource Management." *Review of Public Personnel Administration*. Fall 1989, pp. 29–47.

MacInnis, D. J., and L. L. Price. "The Role of Imagery in Information Processing: Review and Extensions." *Journal of Consumer Research* 13 (1987), pp. 473–491.

Marceluk, Robert D. "Accountability and Control of Human Resource Information." *Personnel Administrator*. July 1985, pp. 24–26.

Mathis, Robert L. and John H. Jackson. *Personnel/Human Resource Management*. 5th ed. St. Paul, MN: West 1988, p. 599.

Meyer, Gary. "Hard-working Micros Aid Managers." *HRMagazine*. August 1990, pp. 54–60.

Minneman, William A. "A Home Buyer's Guide to HRIS." *HRMagazine*. June 1990, pp. 79–84.

Montazemi, A. R., and D. W. Carrath. "The Use of Cognitive Mapping for Information Requirements Analysis." *MIS Quarterly*. March 1986, Target, pp. 45–55.

Myers-Goodman, Joan. "Auditing the Data in the HRIS." *Personnel*. August 1990, pp. 10–13.

Nazario, Sonia. "Boom and Despair." *Wall Street Journal*. September 22, 1989, pp. R26–R27.

O'Connell, Sandra E. "Now That It's Time to Choose an HRIS." *Personnel Administrator*. November 1989, p. 2428.

Oliva, Terrance A., Diana L. Day, and Wayne S. DeSarbo. "Selecting Competitive Tactics: Try a Strategy Map." *Sloan Management Review*. Spring 1987, pp. 5–14.

Ouchi, W. G. "The Relationship between Organizational Structure and Organizational Control." *Administrative Science Quarterly*, no. 22 (1977), pp. 95–113.

Pae, Peter. "Kodak to Again Restructure Operations." *Wall Street Journal*. August 18, 1989, p. B2.

Pasqualetto, Joe, and Abha Kuman. "Hooking Up an HRIS." *Personnel*. July 1990, pp. 4–6.

Perrow, Charles. *Complex Organizations*. 3rd ed. New York: Random House, 1986.

Perry, Stephen. "An HRIS for the '90's." *Personnel Journal*. August 1990, pp. 75–78.

Pfeffer, J. "A Political Perspective on Careers: Interests, Networks, and Environments." In M. G. Arthur, D. T. Hall, and B. S. Lawrence, eds. *Handbook of Career Theory*. New York: Cambridge University Press, 1989, pp. 380–396.

Pflaum, Marvin B. "Optimal Interface with an HRIS." *Personnel Journal*. May 1990, pp. 78–84.

Polanyi, M. *Personal Knowledge*. Chicago: University of Chicago Press, 1958.

Polanyi, M. *The Tacit Dimension*. Garden City, NJ: Doubleday, 1966.

Prahalad, C. K. "Developing Strategic Capability: An Agenda for Top Management." *Human Resource Management* 22, Fall 1983, pp. 237+.

Quinn, J. B., "Strategic Goals: Process and Politics." *Sloan Management Review*, Vol. 19(1) (1977), pp. 21–37.

Richardson, Alan. "Mental Practice: A Review and Discussion Parts I & II." *The Research Quarterly* Vol. 38, nos. 1 and 2 (1967), pp. 95–107 and pp. 263–273.

Romaprasad, A., and E. Pam. "A Computerized Interactive Technique for Mapping Influence Diagrams (MIND)." *Strategic Management Journal,* 6 (1985), pp. 377–392.

Rosenbaum, J. E. "Organization Career Systems and Employee Misperceptions." In M. G. Arthur, D. T. Hall, and B. S. Lawrence, eds. *Handbook of Career Theory.* New York: Cambridge University Press, 1989, pp. 617–632.

Rosenberg, Stephen. "Flexibility in Installing Large Scale HRIS: New York City's Experience." *Personnel Administrator.* December 1985, pp. 39–46.

Rowan, Roy. *The Intuitive Manager.* Boston: Little, Brown, 1986.

Russ, G. S. "Shaping Reality through Organizational Communications: Symbolic Interpretations of Stakeholder Management." Unpublished doctoral dissertation, Texas A&M University, 1990.

Schon, D. A. *The Reflective Practitioner.* New York: Basic Books, 1983.

Schweiger, D., W. Sandberg, and J. Ragan. "Group Approaches for Improving Strategic Decision Making: A Comparative Analysis of Dialectical Inquiry, Devil's Advocacy, and Consensus." *Academy of Management Journal* 29 (1986), pp. 51–71.

Schwenk, C. "Cognitive Simplification Processes in Strategic Decision-Making." *Strategic Management Journal,* 5 (1984), pp. 111–128.

Seagal, Jonathan A., and Mary A. Quinn. "How to Audit Your HR Programs." *Personnel Administrator.* May 1989, pp. 67–70.

Sherrick, Daniel W. "Corporate Restructuring: Perspective of Organized Labor." In The Center for Business Ethics at Bentley College, ed. *The Ethics of Organizational Transformation: Mergers, Takeovers, and Corporate Restructuring.* October 15 and 16, 1987, pp. 8–9.

Shrivastava, P., and J. Grant. "Empirically Derived Models of Strategic Decision-Making Processes." *Strategic Management Journal* 6 (1985), pp. 97–113.

Sims, Hank P., Jr., Dennis A. Gioia, and Associates. *The Thinking Organization: Dynamics of Organizational Cognition.* San Francisco: Jossey-Bass, 1986.

Spirig, John E. "HRIS Topics: CBT—Computer-Based Training—Hold Key Benefits for a Changing User Community." *Employment Relations Today.* Winter 1990–1991, pp. 325–328.

Stagner, R. "Corporate Decision Making: An Empirical Study." *Journal of Applied Psychology,* 53 (1969), pp. 1–13.

Stair, Ralph, and Barry Render. *Quantitative Analysis for Management.* Boston: Allyn and Bacon, 1985.

Straight, Jay F., Jr. "Introducing CHRIS: Chevron's Human Resources Information System." *Personnel Administrator.* May 1987, pp. 24–28.

Szilagyi, A., and D. Schweiger. "Matching Managers to Strategies: A Review and Suggested Framework." *Academy of Management Review* 9 (1984), pp. 626–637.

Tannenbaum, Scott I. "Human Resource Information Systems: User Group Implications." *Journal of Systems Management.* January 1990, pp. 27–32.

Taylor, G. Stephen, and J. Stephen Davis. "Individual Privacy and Computer-Based Human Resource Information Systems." *Journal of Business Ethics.* July 1989, pp. 569–576.

Treece, James B., and John Hoerr. "Shaking Up Detroit." *Business Week.* August 14, 1989, pp. 74–80.

Ungson, G. R., D. N. Braunstein, and P. D. Hall. "Managerial Information Processing: A Research Reveiw." *Administrative Science Quarterly* 26 (1981), Target, pp. 116–134.

Wack, Pierre, "Scenarios: Shooting the Rapids." *Haravard Business Review* 64, no. 6. November–December 1985, pp. 139–150.

Ward, Miriam, and Liza Han. "Personnel Computing: Find New Users for an Old HRIS." *Personnel Journal.* October 1990, pp. 108–116.

"Who's in Charge of HR Information?" *HRMagazine.* August 1990, pp. 30–34.

Woodruff, R. C., Jr. "Human Resource Accounting." *Canadian Chartered Accountant* 97 (1970), pp. 156–161.

Yate, Martin. *Keeping the Best.* Boston, MA: Bob Adams, 1991.

Zmud, Robert W. *Information Systems in Organizations.* Glenview, IL: Scott-Foresman, 1983.

Zuboff, Shoshanna. *In the Age of the Smart Machine.* New York: Basic Books, 1988.

· · · · · · · · · · · · · · · · ·
NOTES

1. Steven P. Galante, "Fresh-Cookie Stores Feel Bite as Snack-Food Market Shifts," *Wall Street Journal,* February 24, 1986, p. 37; Buck Brown, "How the Cookie Crumbled at Mrs. Fields: Company Seeks to Revive Itself by Diversifying," *Wall Street Journal,* January 26, 1989, p. B1; "Mrs. Fields Inc.," *Wall Street Journal,* February 15, 1989, p. B10; Dianne E. Kirrane and Peter R. Kirrane, "Managing by Expert Systems," *HR Magazine,* March 1990, pp. 37–39; and Richard Koenig, "NutraSweet Allies with Mrs. Fields for Diet Food Line," *Wall Street Journal,* September 19, 1990, p. B6.

2. Any basic decision sciences text expands upon this approach. For example, see Ralph Stair and Barry Render, *Quantitative Analysis for Management* (Boston: Allyn and Bacon, 1985).

3. See, for example, Daniel J. Isenberg, "The Structure and Process of Understanding: Implication for Managerial Action," in H. P. Sims and D. A. Gioia, eds., *The Thinking Organization: Dynamics of Organizational Social Cognition* (San Francisco: Jossey Bass, 1986); Roy Rowan, *The Intuitive Manager* (Boston: Little, Brown, 1986); and Amanda Bennett, "We've Got a Hunch Intuition Is 'In'," *Wall Street Journal,* October 4, 1990, p. B1.

4. Jeff Lehren, "Competing for a Position in the Business World," Unpublished Handout, NCR Corporation, Orlando, Florida, n.d. Lehren is in charge of college recruiting for NCR Corporation for the Florida Region.

5. Herbert A. Simon, *Administrative Behavior,* 2nd ed. (New York: Macmillan, 1957), pp. xxv–xxvi.

6. L. Festinger, *Theory of Cognitive Dissonance* (Stanford, CA: Stanford University Press, 1957).

7. Much of this discussion is based on work by Michael D. Cohen, James C. March, and Johan P. Olsen, "A Garbage Can Model of Organizational Choice," *Administrative Source Quarterly* 17, no. 1, March 1972, pp. 1–25, and by Charles Perrow, *Complex Organizations,* 3rd ed. (New York: Random House, 1986).

8. R. Axelrod, ed., *Structure of Decision: The Cognitive Maps of Political Elites* (Princeton, NJ: Princeton University Press, 1976).

9. M. Polanyi, *The Tacit Dimension* (Garden City, NJ: Doubleday 1966); and M. Polanyi, *Personal Knowledge* (Chicago: University of Chicago Press, 1958).

10. D. A. Schon, *The Reflective Practitioner* (New York: Basic Books, 1983).

11. Dennis A. Gioia and Cameron M. Ford, "Organizational Sensemaking, Tacit Knowledge and Communication with Self," in L. Thayer, ed., *Organization Communication: Emerging Perspectives III* (Norwood, NJ: Ablex Publishing, 1992 [in press]).

12. Dan Isenberg, "Thinking and Managing: A Verbal Protocol Analysis of Managerial Problem Solving," *Academy of Management Journal* 29, no. 4, December 1986, pp. 775–788.

13. Shoshana Zuboff, *In the Age of the Smart Machine* (New York: Basic Books, 1988).

14. R. N. Cyert and J. G. March, *A Behavioral Theory of the Firm* (Englewood Cliffs, NJ: Prentice-Hall 1963), pp. 27–32.

15. Linda Thornburg, "HR Gears Down to Increase Flexibility," *HRMagazine,* December 1991, pp. 72–74.

16. Gerald R. Ferris and Timothy A. Judge, "Personnel/Human Resources Management: A Political Influence Perspective," *Journal of Management* 17, no. 2, 1991, p. 450.

17. Y. K. Shetty and Paul Buller, "Regaining Competitiveness Requires HR Solutions," *Personnel*, July 1990, pp. 8–12.

18. "New Human Resources Benchmarks," *Saratoga Institute Report*, Saratoga, CA, 1991, p. 1.

19. R. C. Woodruff, Jr., "Human Resource Accounting," *Canadian Chartered Accountant* 97, 1970, pp. 156–161.

20. R. L. Brummet, E. Flamhol, and W. Pyle, "Human Resource Accounting—A Challenge for Accountants," *Accounting Review* 43, 1968, pp. 217–224.

21. "The Personnel/Human Resources Department: 1989–1990," *SHRM-BNA Survey #54*, June 28, 1990, p. 10, Washington, DC: Bureau of National Affairs.

22. Wayne F. Cascio, *Costing Human Resources: The Financial Impact of Behavior in Organizations*, 2nd ed. (Boston: PWS-Kent, 1987, p. 5.

23. Ibid., p. 6.

24. Ibid., pp. 147–170.

25. Robert W. Zmud, *Information Systems in Organizations* (Glenview, IL: Scott-Foresman, 1983), pp. 65–67.

26. Kirk J. Anderson, "Putting the 'I' in HRIS," *Personnel*, September 1988, pp. 12–24.

27. Michael L. Jenkins and Gayle Lloyd, "How Corporate Philosophy and Strategy Shape the Use of HR Information Systems," *Personnel*, May 1985, p. 29; and Alfred J. Walker, "New Technologies in Human Resource Planning," *Human Resource Planning*, November 4, 1986, pp. 149–151.

28. Robert D. Marceluk, "Accountability and Control of Human Resource Information," *Personnel Administrator*, July 1985, pp. 24–26.

29. Joanne Wisniewski, "The Needs-Based HRIS Audit," *HRMagazine*, September 1991, pp. 61–64.

30. Helen LaVan, Nicholas J. Mathys, and Wayne Hochwarter, "Insecurity in Numbers," *Computers in Personnel*, Spring 1989, pp. 51–53.

31. Lynn Adams, "Securing Your HRIS in a Microcomputer Environment," *HRMagazine*, February 1992, pp. 56–61.

32. Gary Edwards and Kirk Bennett, "Ethics and HR: Standards in Practice," *Personnel Administrator*, December 1987, pp. 62–66.

33. Daniel W. Sherrick, "Corporate Restructuring: Perspectives of Organized Labor," in The Center for Business Ethics at Bentley College ed., *The Ethics of Organizational Transformation: Mergers, Takeovers and Corporate Restructuring*, October 15 and 16, 1987, p. 8.

34. Marilyn Chase, "Burroughs Wellcome Reaps Profits, Outrage from its AIDS Drug," *Wall Street Journal*, September 15, 1989, p. A5.

35. Chase, Marilyn, "Popular AIDS Treatment Is Illicit Copy of Hoffman-La Roche's Drug DDC," *Wall Street Journal*, July 16, 1991, p. B1.

36. Milo Geyelin, "Corporate Mudslinging Gets Expensive," *Wall Street Journal*, August 4, 1989, p. B1.

37. Robert L. Mathis and John H. Jackson, *Personnel/Human Resource Management*, 5th ed. (St. Paul, MN: West, 1988), p. 599.

38. Jonathan A. Seagal and Mary A. Quinn, "How to Audit Your HR Programs," *Personnel Administrator*, May 1989, pp. 67–70.

39. Ibid., p. 67.

40. Ibid., pp. 992–1003.

41. William P. Anthony and Jane C. Wager, "Executive Management Development Program in the U.S. Department of the Navy," in Halil Copur, ed., *HRMOB Proceedings*, vol. 1 (Philadelphia: The Association of Human Resources Management and Organization Behavior, 1987), pp. 50–54.

42. Alan Richardson, "Mental Practice: A Review and Discussion Parts I and II," *The Research Quarterly* 38, nos. 1 and 2, 1967, pp. 95–107 and pp. 263–273.

43. William P. Anthony, E. Nick Maddox, and Walter J. Wheatley, Jr., *Envisionary Management: A Guide for Human Resource Professionals* (Westport, CT: Quorum Books, 1988).

44. Paulette Thomas, "Playing It Safe Has Made Delta a Winner," *Wall Street Journal*, July 25, 1988, p. 4; and Scott Tiar, "Why the Folks at Delta Are Walking on Air," *Business Week*, August 1, 1988, pp. 92–93.

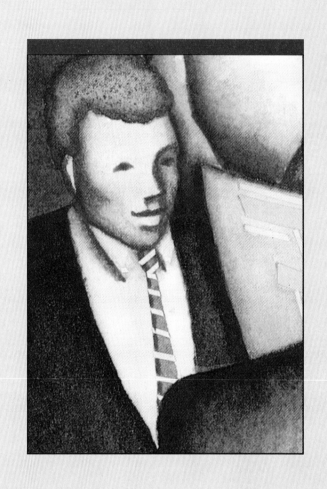

• • • • • • • • •

5 Equal Employment Opportunity and Nondiscrimination

This chapter examines the role of equal employment opportunities and nondiscrimination. Specific laws prohibiting employment discrimination based on sex, race, national origin, age, religion, disabilities and health-related issues (including AIDS), and status as a Vietnam veteran will be covered. Affirmative action programs, the issue of "equal pay for equal work," the Equal Pay Act will be covered as well as the controversial topic of comparable worth.

• • • • • • • • •
CHAPTER OBJECTIVES

As a result of studying this chapter, you should be able to

1. Discuss the strategic choices available to firms regarding equal employment opportunities.

2. Understand the meaning of Title VII of the Civil Rights Act, Bona Fide Occupational Qualifications (BFOQs), and discrimination in employment decisions.

3. Describe the regulations that prohibit employment discrimination because of sex, race, national origin, age, religion, handicaps and health-related issues (including AIDS), or status as a Vietnam veteran.

4. Discuss recent Equal Employment Opportunity (EEO) case law.

5. Describe the components for strengthening or establishing affirmative action programs.

6. Discuss the Equal Pay Act of 1963 as well as some of the controversies surrounding comparable worth.

7. Discuss strategic EEO guidelines for managers.

CASE: Accounting Firm Held Accountable under Title VII[1]

In May 1989, the Supreme Court ruled that Price Waterhouse, one of the "Big 8" accounting firms, violated Title VII of the 1964 Civil Rights Act. Ann B. Hopkins, a senior manager at Price Waterhouse, was nominated for partnership in the firm in August 1982, and a decision was made by the partners in early 1983 to deny her a partnership. Hopkins was the only woman among 88 candidates being considered, and she had brought $34 to $44 million worth of business to the firm, more than any other candidate. When Hopkins was not renominated for partnership in 1984, she left the firm and filed suit, charging that sexual stereotyping was the reason she had been rejected.

Too Aggressive

At the time Hopkins was denied partnership in the firm, the Price Waterhouse evaluations described her as "macho, harsh, and aggressive," speculating that she "may have overcompensated for being a woman." A male supporter in the firm advised her to "walk more femininely, talk more femininely, dress more femininely, wear makeup, have her hair styled, and wear jewelry."

All of the comments in the evaluations made by the Price Waterhouse Partners dealt with Hopkins' "interpersonal skills," and her aggressive behavior was derided as "unladylike." Hopkins believed she was denied promotion because her superiors believed she acted too much like a man.

Burden of Proof

Price Waterhouse attorneys argued that sexual stereotypes were not unlawful unless they were a decisive factor in partnership determinations. They argued that Hopkins' poor interpersonal skills constituted a nondiscriminatory reason for the denial of partnership. Price Waterhouse further contended that Hopkins bore the burden of refuting its explanation by proving that the business reasons were not the "true reasons" for the decision and that her sex was the motivating factor.

Hopkins' attorneys argued that the use of sex-based stereotypes violated Title VII and that women should not have to prove that discriminatory action was the sole reason for the employment decision. In this case, the

Supreme Court was called upon to decide whether or not "stereotyping" was the basis for the denial of partnership status and if this constituted unlawful discrimination.

The Supreme Court Ruling

The Supreme Court ruled that when there is direct evidence of both lawful and unlawful motives for an employment action, the burden is on the employer to establish that the discriminatory reasons were not determinative and that it would have made the same decision based on the purely nondiscriminatory factors. Supreme Court Justice William Brennan stated, "we are beyond the day when an employer could evaluate employees by assuming or insisting that they matched the stereotype associated with their group." He further stated, "an employer who objects to aggressiveness in women but whose positions require this trait places women in an intolerable and impermissible Catch-22; out of a job if they behave aggressively and out of a job if they don't. Title VII lifts women out of the bind."

On May 14, 1990, Price Waterhouse was ordered to make Hopkins a partner as of 1983 and award her back pay and full seniority. Based upon the earnings of Hopkins, the back pay award was approximately $250,000. Price Waterhouse was also responsible for the cost of Hopkin's attorney and all court costs.

The Court's ruling in *Price Waterhouse* v. *Hopkins* is significant for at least two reasons. First, it recognizes "sexual stereotyping" as a discriminatory element in evaluations. Second, it shifts the burden of proof to the employer when direct evidence suggests that sex played a substantial role in a challenged decision.

The basic premise of unlawful discrimination is that an employer should not be able to make employment decisions, such as promoting, hiring, discharging, compensating, training, and so on, based on the applicant's or employee's age, race, sex, national origin, or religion. The term "protected group" is used to describe the people who are protected under the particular discrimination law. While it is commonly believed that only minorities and females, for example, are protected groups and white males are not, the term "protected group" can include whites and males in certain circumstances.

• • • • • • • • •

The concept of equal opportunity is an ideal basic to the free enterprise system. The positive growth of any economy results from nurturing and using the ability of all persons to their fullest extent. Merit, not irrelevant factors such race, sex, or religion, is the most important consideration in our society. Under a meritorious system, the best performers and competitors should be rewarded.

This concept means that all persons have an equal opportunity to demonstrate their merit. Unfortunately, a substantial number of employers have discriminated against certain classes of individuals based on characteristics such as gender or race.

As a result, the government passed laws to end discrimination that prevented members of society from having an equal chance at available employment and the training and experience necessary to pursue all employment opportunities.

STRATEGIC CHOICES

An organization has a number of important strategic choices to make regarding equal employment opportunities (EEO). These choices are outlined below:

1. The organization can choose to be proactive or reactive in its strategy toward equal employment opportunities.
2. The organization can choose the breadth of its focus.
3. The organization can decide on the depth of its EEO plan.
4. The organization can choose the *degree of tie* between its EEO plan and the overall strategic plan of the firm.
5. The organization can decide on the degree of *formality* in its approach to EEO.

Strategic Choices for EEO

Proactive or Reactive

An organization can decide to plan carefully and anticipate any potential discriminatory practices. This means examining new *and* existing employment policies to ensure equal opportunities. In addition, proactive organizations can develop equal opportunity programs, including affirmative action programs, to ensure that any discriminatory practices are eliminated. Affirmative action programs will be discussed later in this chapter. Some organizations, however, are more reactive to EEO and minimally satisfy only those regulations required by law and demanded by the courts.

Breadth

An organization can choose a narrow focus by meeting EEO regulations in hiring and promotion decisions only. However, organizations can choose a broader scope by ensuring equal opportunities in areas such as training, rewarding, and so on. Although organizations are required by law to ensure fair and equal treatment in all areas of employment, many organizations fall short of this requirement.

Depth

The organization can choose to have an EEO plan that mostly involves only a few employees (for example, the heads of the human resource department) in its management and enforcement. On the other hand, it can involve all organizational personnel in an effort to promote *commitment* to nondiscriminatory practices throughout the organization.

Tie with Strategy

The organization's EEO policies can be tied loosely, if at all, to the firm's overall strategic plan. Conversely, the EEO policies can be fully integrated with the strategic plan of the organization. Integration of the firm's EEO policies and its overall strategic plan can best occur by fully integrating the two through strategic human resource planning, as discussed in Chapter 6.

Formality

Finally, the organization can choose to have a rather informal plan that depends upon the knowledge of its managers or personnel staff regarding EEO regulations. On the other hand, the organization can have a formalized plan that is clearly spelled out in writing and policy and backed up by supporting documentation and data.

EMPLOYMENT DISCRIMINATION[2]

What Is Discrimination?

Discrimination in employment decisions is usually manifested in one of three ways: (1) disparate treatment, (2) disparate or adverse impact, and (3) present effects of past discrimination.[3]

Disparate Treatment

A manager who intentionally treats an applicant or employee differently because of race, color, religion, national origin, sex, or age is guilty of **disparate treatment**. One example of disparate treatment is rejecting Oriental applicants because of the concern that one or more might be an illegal alien. Another way disparate treatment can occur is through the application of a rule against applicants or employees of a protected group. For example, an organizational rule that allows men to marry but prohibits women from marrying treats women differently from men and violates Title VII. Finally, disparate treatment can arise from sexual, racial, religious, or national-origin harassment. For example, managers violate the law if they make sexual advances or demands as a condition for employment or promotion.

Adverse Impact

Seemingly neutral qualifications for employment or promotions have been found to have adverse impact on some minority groups. It has been found that some job qualifications thought to be necessary for effective performance in organizations are not actually needed, and have an adverse impact on members of minority groups, women, or older workers. For example, requirements of minimum height or weight can have adverse impact on women, as well as on some ethnic groups. Some employment tests tend to eliminate certain minority groups disproportionately, yet have a questionable relationship to job performance.

The Equal Employment Opportunity Commission (EEOC) has developed a general rule to determine adverse impact. It is called the *Four-Fifths Rule.* The rule states that if the ratio of minority hires to minority applicants is less than four-fifths (80 percent) of the ratio of majority hires to majority applicants, a prima facie case of discrimination exists.

....

EXHIBIT 5.1 ## Example of an Insurance Company's Employment Philosophy and Policy

1. We have an obligation to our policyholders to determine realistically our needs for employees and to select the best qualified available personnel to handle their insurance business.
2. We shall hire, promote, compensate, and provide terms, conditions, and privileges of employment solely on the basis of the companies' personnel requirements and each individual's qualifications.
3. In fulfilling our obligations we will not practice, tolerate, or condone discrimination because of race, color, religion, sex, national origin, age, or handicap.
4. We shall comply at all times with the letter and the spirit of all national, state, and local laws pertaining to employment.
5. Just as we will not discriminate against prospective employees because of race, color, religion, sex, national origin, age, or handicap, we will not terminate any competent person to make room for another on the basis of any of these reasons.

....

Past Discrimination

The third way employers have been guilty of discrimination is by perpetuating the effects of past discriminatory policies. For example, a policy of hiring persons who are referred by current employees before hiring other applicants may appear to be a nondiscriminatory policy. However, if the work force is white because of discrimination in the past, the use of an employee referral policy in hiring may tend to perpetuate the white work force because new recruits might come primarily from the white community.

Seniority systems have been challenged because of their perpetuation of past discrimination practices. However, if a seniority system was not developed out of an intent to discriminate, it is not unlawful, even though it may result in restrictions of employment opportunities. For example, if women were not hired into an organization until recently, a seniority system that based promotion on seniority would have an unequal impact on female employees. The seniority system in this case would be considered nondiscriminatory (if it were developed without the intent of being discriminatory) because it applies equally to all groups.

Title VII of the Civil Rights Act

Title VII of the Civil Rights Act of 1964 prohibits discrimination against any individual based on race, color, religion, sex, or national origin in any employment condition (for example, training or hiring). Title VII was amended in 1972, which strengthened enforcement and expanded coverage to include government employees, educational institutions, and private employers of more than 15 persons. Title VII was amended again in 1978, which made it illegal to discriminate because of pregnancy, childbirth, or related conditions. The Civil Rights Act of 1991 was enacted partially in response to a series of U.S. Supreme Court decisions on civil rights in 1989. The new act overturned portions of eight Supreme Court decisions. The Civil Rights Act of 1991 will be discussed in more detail later in the chapter. Exhibit 5.1 illustrates a company's employment philosophy and policy regarding discrimination.

Bona Fide Occupational Qualifications (BFOQ)

Discrimination on the basis of race, religion, sex, or national origin is permissible when any of these factors are considered to be bona fide occupational qualifications. This means that any of these factors are considered to be reasonably necessary for the operation of a particular business. For example, a director can specify and hire a male (or female) in a play for a male (or female) role. Preferences of the employer or clients are irrelevant and do not constitute BFOQs. It is important to remember that the burden of proof lies with the employer to demonstrate BFOQs.

TYPES OF DISCRIMINATION

Sex Discrimination

Title VII of the Civil Rights Act of 1964 prohibits discrimination because of the gender of a person. This law has been amended to include pregnancy discrimination and sexual harassment. This section will cover all three areas.

Discrimination

When the sex of an employee or job applicant is one of the factors upon which an employment decision is based, the decision is most likely unlawful. The law has two exceptions: bona fide occupational qualifications (BFOQs) and business necessity. The BFOQ exception has been discussed. Essentially, this means that in some rare instances an individual's sex may be reasonably necessary to carry out a particular job function. Business necessity is also a defense to a charge of discrimination. This means that factors such as safety or efficiency of operation are at risk. Arguing that a female or male "image" is desired is *not* sufficient to justify a business necessity for sex discrimination. Similarly, reasons such as "women are too moody to handle this job" would not justify discrimination.

The use of height or weight requirements may be challenged and found to be discriminatory if the requirements eliminate a significantly greater number of women than men. Other types of sex discrimination include refusing employment to a woman based on the assumption that parenthood might result in a female employee being absent more than a male employee. Sex stereotyping can also result in unlawful sex discrimination. For example, if a male manager evaluates the performance of a female subordinate more critically because she demonstrates stereotypically masculine characteristics (for example, assertiveness), he would be guilty of sex discrimination. The opening case to this chapter provides another example. The Supreme Court ruled that the use of sex-based stereotypes for employment decisions violated Title VII.

Interestingly, homosexuals are not covered under Title VII. Although some states and local governments prohibit discrimination against homosexuals, it is not prohibited by federal EEO laws. As of 1990, only Wisconsin and Massachusetts had outlawed discrimination on the basis of sexual orientation in public accommodation, housing, credit, and employment.

| EXHIBIT 5.2 | Sample of Guidelines to Prevent Sexual Harassment |

1. Develop a written policy prohibiting sexual harassment.
2. Inform managers and employees of the policy.
3. Inform managers and employees of the appropriate action to take if they are harassed.
4. *Promptly* investigate any complaints.
5. Take appropriate action against the offender.

Sexual Harassment

Sexual harassment is also a violation of Title VII of the Civil Rights Act. The highly publicized hearings regarding sexual harassment charges made by the law professor, Anita Hill, against the then Supreme Court nominee Clarence Thomas, made the issue of sexual harassment more salient.[4] Essentially, sexual harassment means unwelcome verbal or physical conduct from others of a sexual nature. There are two types of sexual harassment: *quid pro quo* and environmental.[5] *Quid pro quo* occurs when unwelcome sexual advances or requests for sexual favors are made explicitly or implicitly as a condition for employment. For example, if a manager tells a job applicant that, in terms of hiring, "it would be beneficial for you to go out on a date with me," this would constitute *quid pro quo* sexual harassment. The environmental type of sexual harassment involves unwelcome conduct that interferes with the employee's job performance or creates an offensive working environment. Every employee has the right to work in a work environment free of discriminatory intimidation or insult. Photographs and posters of nude women in the workplace and verbal or written obscenities are examples of what can be defined as a sexually hostile environment. Recently, a number of female employees of Stroh's Brewery in St. Paul, Minnesota, claimed they had been sexually harassed. What is unique is that the women charged that Stroh's advertising campaigns contributed to the alleged workplace harassment. The suit asked Stroh to stop using women as sexual objects and specifically asked that the series of television advertisements featuring the Swedish Bikini Team be discontinued. Although Stroh agreed to discontinue the advertisements, the company denied allegations of sexual harassment and argued against the connection between the advertisements and workplace behavior.[6]

An employer should take all necessary steps to prevent sexual harassment in the workplace. Some guidelines to prevent harassment include developing a written policy prohibiting sexual harassment, informing managers and employees of the policy, informing managers and employees of appropriate action to take if they are harassed, promptly investigating any complaints, and taking appropriate action against the offender (see Exhibit 5.2). Even if the employer has a policy against sexual harassment, the employer can still be held liable for the actions of managers, employees, and even customers and vendors if the employer *knew* or *should have known* about the occurrence and failed to take appropriate action. The best defense against sexual harassment claims is to have a well-designed grievance procedure and to encourage employees to speak up.[7] Exhibit 5.3 illustrates an example of a company policy on sexual harassment. A policy statement should be consistent with the firm's grievance procedure, specific and objective.[8] A man or a woman can be the victim of harassment or the harasser. The victim does not have to be of the opposite sex from the harasser.

···

| EXHIBIT 5.3 | Example of a Company Policy on Sexual Harassment*

1. Sexual harassment is a violation of the corporation's EEO policy. Abuse of anyone through sexist slurs or other objectionable conduct, is offensive behavior.
2. Management must ensure that a credible program exists for handling sexual harassment problems. If complaints are filed, they should receive prompt consideration without fear of negative consequences.
3. When a supervisor is made aware of an allegation of sexual harassment, the following guidelines should be considered:
   a. Obtain information about the allegation through discussion with the complainant. Ask for and document facts about what was said, what was done, when and where it occurred, and what the complainant believes was the inappropriate behavior. In addition, find out if any other individuals observed the incident, or similar incidents, to the complainant's knowledge. This is an *initial* step. In no case will the supervisor handle the complaint process alone.
   b. If the complaint is from an hourly employee, a request for union representation at any point must be handled as described in the labor agreement.
   c. The immediate supervisor or the department head and the personnel department must be notified *immediately*. When a complaint is raised by, or concerns an hourly employee, the local labor relations representative is to be advised. Where a complaint is raised by or concerns a salaried employee, the personnel director is to be advised.
4. The personnel department will conduct a complete investigation of the complaint for hourly and salaried employees. The investigation is to be handled in a professional and confidential manner.

*Policy example is based on General Motor's Corporate policy on sexual harassment.

···

Pregnancy Discrimination

Under the Pregnancy Discrimination Act of 1978, a female employee or job applicant may not be treated differently from a male because of the female's pregnancy or capacity to become pregnant. Essentially, a woman is protected against being fired or refused a promotion or job because she is pregnant or has had an abortion. As long as they can still work, pregnant employees cannot be forced to quit or go on leave. Some states have variations of a parental leave law which enable both parents to take time off from work to care for their newborn child. However, only a few states require the employer to guarantee the same job to the employee upon returning.

Special problems arise when an organization manufactures or uses products or processes that may be harmful to female reproductivity or the unborn child. Interestingly, a policy that excludes women from the workplace because of reproductive or fetal hazards may violate Title VII, even if they can be justified by scientific evidence.

Race Discrimination and Harassment

Race discrimination means that employment decisions are based on an employee's race or color. Charges of race discrimination remain the most common type of EEO complaint. Under Title VII, employers have a responsibility to maintain a bias-free work environment and correct any discriminatory situations. Similar to sexual ha-

Immigration Act Compliance

With the continuing influx of immigrants into the United States work force, the need for proper identification and work authorization forms has become a primary concern to American businesses. Headlines alert the public to the problems of not only hiring illegal aliens, but discriminating against immigrants as well. In 1986, the Immigration Reform and Control Act was established to clarify the hiring process of immigrants and curb employment discrimination by providing clear, concrete guidelines for employers to follow in the hiring process.

It is important that employers be aware of the dynamics of the act and remember it when hiring immigrants. Employment decisions should *not* be based upon national origin, citizenship status, foreign appearance, name, or accent, but rather on an employee's qualifications. Any decision based upon the above attributes may be construed as discriminatory, resulting in a host of legal headaches.

According to the act, employers are required to complete an I-9 verification form within three business days of the hire. This necessitates the documentation of not only the employee's identity, but work authorization as well. Shown below is a selection of documents that can establish both identity and work authorization.

The employer should be careful not to ask for "more" or "better" proof from one group of individuals and not another as this, too, may be viewed as discriminatory.

The following documents establish identity and work authorization:

1. U.S. Passport
2. Certificate of U.S. Citizenship
3. U.S. Citizen ID Card
4. Certificate of Naturalization
5. Alien Registration Card with photograph
6. Unexpired foreign passport with attached employment authorization
7. Temporary Resident Card with attached employment authorization

Finally, employers should *never* knowingly hire illegal aliens. The legal ramifications of this type of employment practice are serious and far outweigh any perceived benefits. By using these guidelines to comply with the Immigration Act's requirements, the employer will ease the hiring process and reduce any threat of discrimination.

SOURCE: Contributed by Donald Levine, Esq., Levine & Ginsburg Ltd., Chicago, IL.

rassment, it is unlawful to engage in racial harassment. Racial harassment includes racial and ethnic slurs or jokes directed at minority employees or made in the presence of minority employees. In addition, it is unlawful to address minority employees by their first name if nonminority employees are addressed by titles such as "Mr." or "Ms." The failure of a nonminority employee to train a minority employee properly is also considered a form of racial harassment.

Almost any factor can be used to determine if minorities have been treated differently from nonminority employees. For example, comparing performance ratings, average salaries, records of termination and employee training opportunities are all ways in which minority groups are compared with nonminority groups. Thus, it is important for managers to maintain accurate records of all employment decisions.

National Origin Discrimination and Harassment

The national origin aspect of the employment discrimination discussion affects members of all national groups and groups of persons of common ancestry or heritage. National origin discrimination differs from race or color discrimination because other factors besides skin color or obvious race identification may be the basis for discrimination. For example, an employee's or job applicant's Cajun accent or manner of speaking cannot be made part of the employment decision. Similar to race

HR CHALLENGES ●

Double Damages for Age Discrimination

In *Brown* v. *M&M Mars* (1989), the U.S. Court of Appeals for the 7th Circuit ruled that to award double back pay damages under the federal Age Discrimination and Employment Act (ADEA) a plaintiff does not need to prove that the employer's conduct was "outrageous," only that the employer knew or demonstrated reckless disregard for the discrimination laws regarding older workers. Brown had been a supervisor since 1978 and was discharged in 1983 for not handling a production

problem properly. Rejecting the company's position that the discharge was based upon performance, the jury found that age was a determining factor. The 7th Circuit confirmed that the company's articulated reasons for discharging Brown were a cover-up and that there was sufficient circumstantial evidence to support the jury's award of double damages.

SOURCE: *Resource: Legal Report,* Society for Human Resource Management, October 1989, p. 15.

discrimination and harassment, the employer is responsible for the conduct of its employees regarding ethnic slurs and other harassing comments or actions.

A related issue deals with the influx of immigrants entering the United States. Employers must be concerned about hiring illegal aliens; however, they must be careful not to discriminate against immigrants. The 1986 Immigration Reform and Control Act was established to provide guidelines for employers to follow in the hiring process.

Age Discrimination and Harassment

The Age Discrimination in Employment Act (ADEA) of 1967 protects employees 40 years of age and older from discrimination based on their age. In general, an employer cannot force an employee to retire after turning 70. In addition, an employer, generally, cannot refuse to hire or promote an individual because he or she is 70 or older. Unlike Title VII, ADEA allows victims of age discrimination or harassment to have their case heard before a jury. In the fall of 1990, President George Bush signed into law the Older Workers Benefit Protection Act. This law was enacted to include employee-benefit programs under the coverage of the ADEA.[9]

Similar to sex discrimination and sexual harassment, an employer has a duty under the law to maintain a work environment free from age discrimination and harassment. A preference for employees who will remain on the job for a long time might be considered unlawful if it causes the exclusion of older workers. An employer must demonstrate a bona fide occupational qualification if challenged on eliminating individuals from certain positions because of age.

Subjective hiring or promotion decisions should be examined carefully. For example, qualities such as "energetic" might be viewed as not applying to older workers. In addition, cost-cutting is not a legitimate reason for firing older workers and replacing them with younger and equally qualified employees merely because the older employee earns more money, although this is often done through early retirement programs. For example, an employer may make an exceptionally good offer to a group of older employees to encourage retirement. This is legal as long as it is made to all employees over a specific age in an occupational class and if no one is compelled to retire. Finally, some organizations have been requiring their employees to sign "waivers" that forfeit the employee's right to file an age discrimination claim. According to a 1989 survey by the U.S. General Accounting Office, approximately 25 to 30 percent of major corporations required their employees to waive their rights

Sixtysomething

Much of America is mentally trapped in stereotyping people over 60 years old as being worn out, having slower minds, and longing for retirement. Despite the fact that federal laws are against mandatory retirement, our culture seems to push employees toward leaving organizations early. In 1950, about half of all men at the age of 65 were still working; today, only 15 percent still work and the median retirement age has dropped to 61. A recent survey by the American Association of Retired Persons (AARP) shows that as many as 40 percent of retired people would prefer to return to the work force.

America is facing an era of labor shortages. With the number of 18- to 44-year-olds expected to drop by 1.6 million over the next decade, the country will need its older workers as never before. Progressive corporations are already moving in these directions. One third of the reservations staff at Days Inn are considered "older workers." McDonald's actively recruits older employees, offering them flexible working hours and training them in a "McMasters" program. Sears, Roebuck,

and Co. has expanded its part-time staff, relying primarily on older workers. Finally, Polaroid (among other companies) offers "retirement rehearsals," allowing its employees to try out a short-term leave before retirement; if the change is too dramatic and the employee is unhappy, the job is still there.

Public leaders are needed to help spread the trend of utilizing older workers. Warren Buffett has built an investment empire by paying close attention to both his companies and employees. When asked about leaving a woman in charge of one of his companies after her 94th birthday, he said, "She is clearly gathering speed and may well reach her full potential in another five or ten years. Therefore, I've persuaded the Board to scrap our mandatory-retirement-at-100 policy . . . My God, good managers are so scarce I can't afford the luxury of letting them go just because they've added a year to their age."

SOURCE: Adapted from David R. Gergen, "Sixtysomething," *U.S. News & World Report*, April 16, 1990.

to file a claim of age discrimination in order to participate in the organization's early retirement incentive program. The practice of having employees sign unsupervised waivers has come under fire and recent legislation has been introduced to restrict the use of age discrimination waivers.[10]

Religious Discrimination

Title VII of the Civil Rights Act prohibits employment discrimination on the basis of religion, including all aspects of religious practice and beliefs. Discrimination occurs when an employee is forced to choose between giving up an employment opportunity or a fundamental belief or practice. The most common problem occurs when an employee asks the manager to accommodate a religious need and there is a scheduling conflict that must be resolved (for example, conflict might arise if management asks a Seventh Day Adventist to work on Saturdays). Some training techniques have also been found to be unlawfully discriminating against certain religions (such as yoga or meditation).

When religious conflicts arise, the employer must make every effort to reasonably accommodate the employee. Reasonable accommodations include the use of voluntary substitutes, flexible work scheduling, transfers to other departments, or changes in job assignments or training methods. Agnostics and atheists are also protected from religious discrimination. For example, an atheist cannot be forced to attend meetings that include prayer. Employers who can demonstrate that they are unable to reasonably accommodate an employee's or job applicant's religious practice or beliefs without undue hardship on the company are not engaging in religious discrimination.

FOCUS ON CULTURAL DIVERSITY •

Using Peyote: Religious Discrimination?

Discriminating against a job applicant because he uses peyote, a mescaline hallucinogen derived from a cactus, as part of his religion was determined a violation of Title VII of the Civil Rights Act. In *Toledo* v. *Nobel-Sysco, Inc.* (1989), the plaintiff applied for a truck driving job with Nobel, a restaurant supply business. The job required driving on mountain roads and working on weekends. When the plaintiff applied for the job he was told that he was qualified, provided he had not used drugs during the last two years (a policy specified in Nobel's employment advertisements). The plaintiff informed the company that he had used peyote twice in the past six months as part of his religion with the Native American Church. The Native American Church believes that peyote heals and helps its practitioners communicate with God. When he was rejected, the plaintiff filed a claim alleging religious discrimination. Although peyote is legal for use in religious services, the company was concerned with liability should the driver have an accident. Experts agreed that an individual should not drive a truck for at least 24 hours after using peyote.

During the hearings, Nobel offered the following to the plaintiff: reinstatement with $500 in back pay, a limit of two peyote ceremonies per year, a requirement that he give one week's notice prior to taking part in a ceremony, and permission to take time off after each ceremony. The plaintiff refused all offers.

The Tenth Circuit reversed an earlier trial court's decision and ruled that a settlement made during the course of an administrative proceeding is *not* a reasonable attempt to accommodate. Since Nobel had made no attempt to accommodate the plaintiff until a discrimination charge was filed, the plaintiff had no obligation to cooperate with the employer. The court found that Nobel would not experience undue hardship in accommodating the plaintiff.

SOURCE: Adapted from *HR News*, Society for Human Resource Management, February 1990, p. A9; and *The Florida Law Weekly*, *Federal*, vol. 4, no. 12, April 20, 1990, pp. S254–S255.

Handicap Discrimination

The Rehabilitation Act of 1973 requires all federal contractors not to discriminate against and to take affirmative action to employ job applicants or employees with physical or mental handicaps.[11] The Acquired Immune Deficiency Syndrome (AIDS) is now classified as a form of handicap, thus, this disease is covered under the Rehabilitation Act. Although most handicaps are readily detectable, some are not. The law covers both types. In addition, the law covers cases in which an employee does not have a handicap, but is perceived as having one. Managers should not assume that a particular employee is not capable of performing certain types of jobs. Instead, the manager should allow the employee to make the decision if he or she can perform a specific job. Although the Rehabilitation Act applies only to companies with a federal government contract or subcontract, many states have laws that cover handicapped workers.

Handicapped individuals are protected under law if they are handicapped but are qualified and able to perform the job. Employers are required to make *reasonable accommodations* for handicapped employees. Often, accommodation involves no more than common sense and does not need to be expensive to be effective. Wheelchair users need space for their chairs entering and leaving as well as in work areas. Local building codes state the amount of space required. Wheelchair ramps, wider doorways, and accessible restrooms are all necessary to accommodate handicapped workers in wheelchairs. Specially designed workstations in which desks or worktables can be raised and lowered mechanically can help the handicapped worker to feel more comfortable and perform effectively.

A variety of devices are available for telephones to amplify hearing and speech for hearing impaired employees. Individuals with severe hearing loss can use more elaborate telecommunication devices. Individuals with vision impairments can be accommodated in various ways. For example, raising lettering or Braille symbols on signs and elevator buttons can be extremely helpful. Agencies dealing with specific disabilities, such as State Commissions for the Blind and Visually-Impaired, and state and local rehabilitation facilities are good sources for assistance in providing successful accommodations.

The law does not extend to alcohol or drug abusers.[12] However, it is recommended that a company encourage any employee with an alcohol or drug abuse problem to seek professional help (such as through an Employee Assistance Program) prior to any disciplinary measures or discharge. In addition, the law does not extend to employees who have currently contagious diseases or infections and who, because of this disease, would be a direct health or safety threat to others. AIDS cases do not fall under this category because research has shown that AIDS cannot be transmitted through casual contact. Employers should not wait until they are confronted with an AIDS case before developing a comprehensive AIDS policy. Policies and educational programs need to be implemented before a crisis situation occurs. Medical evidence showing that AIDS cannot be contracted through casual contact will not appear genuine to employees if the evidence is presented to them *after* a co-worker is known to have AIDS.

Americans with Disabilities Act

The Americans with Disabilities Act (ADA) of 1990 prohibits discrimination against individuals with disabilities. Under the ADA, the term disability is defined as it is in Title V of the Rehabilitation Act of 1973; however, the ADA is *not* limited to federal grantees or contractors.[13] The ADA has been described as "revolutionary" because of the scope of protection it provides to individuals with disabilities. The ultimate goal is the integration of persons with disabilities into all segments of society.[14]

The ADA is made up of five sections.[15] Title I (employment) makes it illegal to discriminate against a qualified individual with a disability and imposes an obligation for employers to make reasonable accommodations for the disabled. From July 26, 1992, until July 26, 1994, employers with 25 or more employees are covered by the ADA. After July 26, 1994, employers with 15 or more employees will be covered. The ADA covers physical and mental impairments such as visual, speech, and hearing impairments, cerebral palsy, epilepsy, multiple sclerosis, AIDS, cancer, heart disease, mental retardation, and emotional illness.[16] The ADA prohibits most preemployment health questions. Although an illegal user of drugs is not protected under the ADA, a rehabilitated drug user or someone who is participating in a supervised rehabilitation program is protected.

Title II (public service) makes it illegal for state or local governments to discriminate against qualified disabled persons in the provision of public services and includes requirements regarding the accessibility of public transportation for individuals with disabilities. Title III of the ADA (public accommodation) makes it illegal for public accommodations (such as restaurants, retail stores, or places of recreation) to discriminate against individuals with disabilities in the provision of goods, benefits, services, facilities, privileges, advantages, or accommodations. In addition, Title III requires existing public accommodation to be made accessible. Titles II and III took effect on January 26, 1992.

HR CHALLENGES ●●●

Rx for AIDS in the Workplace

The prescription for dealing with Acquired Immune Deficiency Syndrome (AIDS) in the workplace continues to be education. Through the efforts of government agencies, employers, and local groups, most members of the population now realize that AIDS cannot be spread by the casual contact that is encountered in the workplace. The incidence of AIDS among health care professionals dealing with AIDS patients has remained remarkably low. In fact, many people have not yet had to deal with a coworker, a family member, or a friend who has tested HIV positive and progressed through the disease process.

This situation will surely change during the 1990s. Even the conservative estimate of the Centers for Disease Control (which calculated that 800,000 to 1.3 million Americans were infected with the AIDS virus in 1990) indicates that it is likely that employees in large organizations will know one or more persons infected with the AIDS virus. The need for the dissemination of accurate information about all aspects of AIDS will thus be critically important in the years to come. Assistance programs will be dealing with more and more employees infected with the AIDS virus. Education will be the method by which human resource managers deal with the guilt, anger, fear, and concern of employees.

The courts have consistently ruled the AIDS sufferers are covered by existing handicap laws; therefore discrimination against employees testing for AIDS is illegal. It is imperative for employers to ensure that these employees' rights are maintained and that the confidentiality is a requirement.

The following guidelines developed by the Citizens' Commission on AIDS for New York City should form the basis for the development of policies that deal with AIDS in the workplace. Similar guidelines have been developed by other cities including Boston, San Francisco, Chicago, Philadelphia, and Miami.

- Employees with AIDS or HIV infection are entitled to the same rights and opportunities as people with other serious or life-threatening illnesses.
- Employment policies must comply with laws and regulations.
- Employment policies should be based on scientific and epidemiological evidence that people with AIDS or HIV infection do not pose a risk of transmission of the virus to coworkers through ordinary contact.
- The highest levels of management and union leadership should unequivocally endorse nondiscriminatory employment policies and educational programs about AIDS.
- Employers and unions should communicate their support of these policies to workers in simple, clear, and unambiguous terms.
- Employers should provide employees with sensitive, accurate, and up-to-date education about risk reduction in their personal lives.
- Employers have a duty to protect the confidentiality of employees' medical information.
- To prevent work disruption and the rejection by coworkers of an employee with AIDS or HIV infection, employers and unions should undertake education for all employees before such an incident occurs and as needed thereafter.
- Employers should not require HIV screening as part of general preemployment or workplace physical examination.
- In those occupational settings where there may be a potential risk of exposure to HIV, employers should provide training and equipment for infection control procedures.

SOURCE: Adapted from J. Wieser, S. Fuller, M. Shriver, and D. Oelhafen, "Rx for AIDS in the Workplace," *Human Resource Management Today*, Spring/Summer, 1990.

Title IV of the ADA (telecommunications) requires all common carriers in interstate communication to ensure that telecommunications systems are available to individuals with hearing and speech impairments and to provide reasonable technological accommodations. Title IV is effective July 26, 1993. Title V (miscellaneous) is a more general "catch all" provision that relates ADA to other laws. Among the provisions, retaliation against individuals who exercise their rights under the act is made illegal. The effective date of this section is determined by the analogous sections in Title I through IV.

EQUAL EMPLOYMENT OPPORTUNITY COMMISSION

The Equal Employment Opportunity Commission (EEOC) enforces compliance with Title VII, the Equal Pay Act (discussed later in the chapter), the Pregnancy Discrimination Act, the Age Discrimination Act, the Rehabilitation Act, and the Americans with Disabilities Act. The EEOC has the authority to process, investigate, and conciliate grievances alleging discrimination. Conciliation is the process of trying to reach an out-of-court settlement.

Any charge filed against an organization must be made within 180 days of the discriminatory act. Where there is a state or local agency with the authority to handle discrimination, the charging party must file the complaint with the agency. This individual has 30 days after the state or local ruling to file with the federal EEOC if dissatisfied with the decision. The EEOC then conducts an investigation to determine if reasonable cause exists that discrimination occurred. The charging party is interviewed and counselled on EEOC procedures. If reasonable cause is believed to exist, the EEOC attempts to conciliate the dispute. If reasonable cause is not found, the case is dismissed.

After a charge is filed, the employer is notified within ten days and a fact finding conference is held subsequently. The charging party and the employer present evidence to an EEOC specialist (conciliator). The EEOC specialist tries to work out a satisfactory settlement with both sides. If the EEOC is unable to conciliate the charge, it will be considered by EEOC attorneys for a possible lawsuit to be filed in federal district court. However, if the EEOC decides not to file a lawsuit, a "right to sue letter" will be issued permitting the charging party to take the case to court. (Exhibit 5.4 presents the EEOC complaint processing system).

AFFIRMATIVE ACTION[17]

Similarities exist between the legal concepts of "discrimination" and "affirmative action"; however, there are important differences. Equal Employment Opportunity laws are designed to rid the workplace of current and future discriminatory acts. **Affirmative action** is designed to remedy past discrimination by requiring employers to hire and promote minorities and females based on the number of *qualified* minorities and females in the recruiting vicinity.

Who Is Required to Develop Affirmative Action Programs?

According to the Executive Orders 11246, 11375, and 11478, federal contractors and subcontractors are required to develop, implement, and maintain a written affirmative action program (AAP). Specifically, companies with at least 50 employees and a $50,000 contract or subcontract with the federal government (or with another company doing business with the federal government) are usually compelled to develop, implement, and maintain a written AAP on an annual basis. If a company does not meet the criteria above, it is not required to comply. For example, a company with 5,000 people and a $5,000 contract with the federal government is not required to comply with AAP regulations. However, companies found guilty of discrimination may be required to have an AAP.

EXHIBIT 5.4 EEOC Complaint Processing System

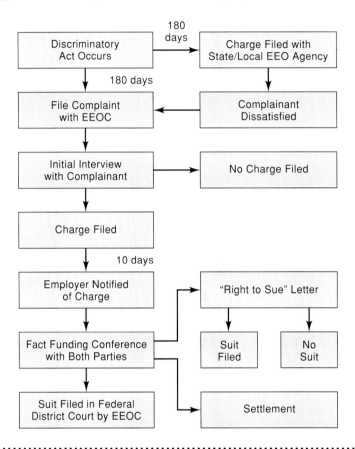

Court decisions have made a distinction between *voluntary* and *required* AAP. Many employers have developed an affirmative action program on a volunteer basis. If an AAP is voluntary, the employer is not required to adhere to the goals of the plan. However, if a plan is required, an employer has been ordered by the court to have an AAP and is obligated to adhere to the goals of the plan.

How Affirmative Action Operates

According to Seligman in "How Equal Opportunity Turned into Employment Quotas,"[18] affirmative action operates on four levels. The first level is *pure nondiscrimination* and embodies a willingness to treat all races and both sexes the same in employment decisions. Many critics find the approach insensitive to the deleterious effects of past discrimination because this level of affirmative action may not increase minority and female employment in nonstereotyped positions significantly.

The second level of affirmative action hires and/or promotes employees entirely based on merit. However, this level includes a concerted effort to expand the number of minority and female applicants and employees (such as minority-focused recruiting efforts).

The third and fourth levels of affirmative action programs use *preferential hiring* and the use of *quota systems*, respectively. Preferential hiring means that the company systematically favors minorities and females in hiring and promotion decisions. The quota system includes preferential hiring and goes further by advocating a specific number of minorities and females that should be hired and/or promoted in the organization.

Reverse Discrimination

Critics of preferential hiring and the use of quota systems have argued that this can lead to reverse discrimination against white males. *Reverse discrimination* occurs when an equally or more qualified nonminority, usually a white male, is not hired or promoted in favor of a racial or sexual minority group member. For example, in *City of Richmond* v. *Croson Company* (1989), the Supreme Court addressed the problem of reverse discrimination. The Richmond City Council adopted the Minority Business Utilization Plan, which required prime contractors (to whom the city awards construction contracts) to set-aside 30 percent of the dollar amount of the contract for minority business enterprises. The Court held that the minority contractor set-aside requirement denied equal protection because it discriminated on the basis of race. Essentially, the Supreme Court recognized that preferential treatment for "protected classes" can have a discriminatory effect against other groups, who may be in the majority of the population.[19]

It is important that employers realize that nothing about affirmative action requires companies to recruit, hire, or promote employees not qualified to do the job under question. Affirmative action means that employers should make every effort to place minorities and females into jobs in which minorities and females are underutilized.

Establishing Affirmative Action Programs

Many employers face penalties for violation of equal employment opportunity and affirmative action regulations. The development of a comprehensive affirmative action program is an important step in avoiding expensive litigation. Elements of an effective program, shown in Exhibit 5.5, include underutilization and availability analyses, the examination of current job specifications and descriptions, the development of goals and timetables, effective recruiting, and the development of a comprehensive inventory of existing employee skills. Each of these is described below.

Underutilization and Availability Analyses

An underutilization analysis examines the number of protected group members (for example, minorities) employed and the types of jobs they hold in an organization. An availability analysis examines the number of protected group members who are available to work in the relevant labor market. The firm should determine where minorities and women are clustered, excluded, or underutilized based on reasonable expectations from the labor market. An availability analysis can be developed with data from a state labor department or the U.S. Census Bureau. The availability analysis is the basis for determining whether underutilization is occurring within a company.

....

| EXHIBIT 5.5 | Components of an Effective Affirmative Action Program |

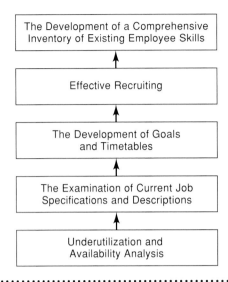

....

Examination of Job Specifications and Descriptions

Employers should examine the current job specifications and descriptions in their company to ensure precision. The firm should establish prescribed qualifications and wage scales based on the actual job to ensure that barriers to minorities and women are not present. Irrelevant qualifications or qualifications that exceed the requirements of the job have been the cause of many law suits.

Development of Goals and Timetables

Employers should correct underutilization of minorities and women by establishing measurable and realistic hiring and promoting goals. In addition, employers should develop realistic timetables by which these goals are to be actualized. The firm's goals should remedy exclusion and/or underutilization of protected groups in specified jobs.

Effective Recruitment

Employers can actively recruit minorities and women to fill positions that have been found to exclude or underutilize minorities and women. Systematic record keeping should describe the flow of minorities and women seeking employment and promotions. Job application forms should not contain information about race or sex.

Inventory of Current Employee Skills

A comprehensive skills inventory of current employees can help to establish a baseline for training and development programs. Employers can learn the skill level of the firm's employees, which is important for identifying qualified employees to fill higher-level positions. In addition, employers can use this information to create training and development programs for all employees, including minorities and women. General Motors, for example, has spent millions of dollars in order to provide a variety of educational programs for minorities and women.

....
RECENT EEO CASE LAW

In 1989, the Supreme Court set new limits in the area of civil rights by reexamining laws against job discrimination. The significance of the Supreme Court's decisions on civil rights is best understood when compared with earlier decisions in fair employment legislation. In one of the landmark employment cases, *Griggs* v. *Duke Power Company,* the Court ruled in 1971 that companies must be able to prove that their selection procedures do not discriminate unfairly. In essence, the *Griggs* v. *Duke Power Company* case involved promotion and transfer policies requiring employees to have a high school diploma and to obtain satisfactory scores on two aptitude test. One of these tests, the Wonderlic Intelligence Test, failed African-Americans at a higher rate than whites. In addition, fewer African-Americans had high school diplomas than whites. The aptitude test and the high school diploma were not judged to be job-related. The Court held that when plaintiffs demonstrate that otherwise neutral employment practices disproportionately and adversely affect minorities and women, they have demonstrated that a Title VII violation exists. In order to avoid this violation, employers had to demonstrate that (1) the plaintiff's statistics were wrong or (2) the practices at issue were dictated by business necessity.

According to civil rights activists, the Court (1) put limits on the abilities of individuals to bring employment discrimination suits *(Wards Cove* v. *Atonio),* (2) allowed challenges to affirmative action programs that had been in effect for years *(Martin* v. *Wilks* and *AT&T* v. *Lorance),* and (3) decided that federal governmental laws do not cover racial harassment in the workplace *(Patterson* v. *McLean).* According to civil rights leader, Ralph G. Neas, overturning the decision was the number one legislative priority of the civil rights community during 1990 (see Exhibit 5.6).[20]

The Civil Rights Act of 1991 was, for the most part, in response to the U.S. Supreme Court decisions in 1989. The new civil rights law makes it easier for certain workers to sue their employers over alleged job discrimination. The law creates new, but limited, rights for women and the disabled to collect money damages that already are available to racial minorities. In addition, the act provides for compensatory and punitive damages for victims of intentional discrimination and jury trials may be requested. Further, the new law applies to on-the-job problems as well as hiring issues.[21] Exhibit 5.7 summarizes the major provisions of the 1991 Civil Rights Act. Interestingly, one very important unsettled issue is whether the legislation is "retroactive" and thus applies to conduct that occurred prior to November 1991

....

EXHIBIT 5.6   Summary of EEO Case Law

SUPREME COURT CASES	IMPLICATIONS
Wards Cost v. Atonio	Limits the ability of employees to bring employment discrimination suits by shifting the burden of proof to the employee.
Martin v. Wilks	Allows reverse discrimination challenges to affirmative action programs that have been in effect for years.
AT&T v. Lorance	Limits the ability of employees to challenge seniority plans that unfairly discriminate by deciding that charges must be filed when the plan is adopted, not later.
Patterson v. McLean Credit Union	Narrows the view of Section 1981 by deciding that racial harassment in the workplace is not covered.
City of Richmond v. Croson Company *	Considers preferential treatment for protected classes to have a discriminatory effect against other groups; reverse discrimination.

* *City of Richmond* v. *Croson Company* was discussed earlier.

....

when it was enacted. If the act is determined to be retroactive, those who have actions pending may be entitled to seek the act's expanded remedies, such as compensatory and punitive damages and a jury trial.[22]

....

LEGAL ISSUES IN COMPENSATION

The Equal Pay Act of 1963

The Equal Pay Act requires that men and women who work for the same organization be paid the same for work that is equal in skill (such as experience or training), effort (mental or physical effort), responsibility (the degree of accountability), and working conditions (the physical surroundings and hazards).[23] This act was passed as an amendment to an earlier compensation law called the Fair Labor Standards Act of 1938. Essentially, the Fair Labor Standards Act applies to employees engaged in interstate commerce.[24] The Equal Pay Act also forbids wage discrimination on the basis of sex, but extends coverage to employees in executive, administrative, professional, and outside sales force categories, as well as employees in most state and local governments, hospitals, and schools. Pay discrimination against minorities and women is also covered under Title VII.

Pay differentials between equal jobs can be justified, however, when they are based on a seniority system, a merit system, a system based on measuring earnings by quality or quantity of production, or any factor other than sex. Under the Equal

EXHIBIT 5.7   Major Provisions of the 1991 Civil Rights Act

- *Damages and Jury Trials:* Provides for compensatory and punitive damages for victims of intentional discrimination suing under Title VII, the ADA, or federal employment sections of the Rehabilitation Act. The combined amount of compensatory and punitive damages depends upon the size of the employer, with caps ranging from $50,000 to $300,000. Jury trials may be requested by any party seeking compensatory or punitive damages.

- *"Race Norming" of Employment Tests:* Prohibits adjustments in test scores, use of different cutoff scores, or other amendments to employment-related tests based upon race, color, religion, sex, or national origin.

- *Expanded Coverage under Section 1981:* Amends interpretation of language in Supreme Court decision in *Patterson* v. *McLean*, regarding the right "to make and enforce contracts." Prior to this decision, Section 1981 was applied to race discrimination in all aspects of the employment contract, that is, hiring, duration of employment, and contract termination. After the *Patterson* decision, Section 1981 applied to hiring only. The Civil Rights Act of 1991 restores the pre-*Patterson* interpretation specifying that the term "make and enforce" contracts includes all benefits, privileges, terms, and conditions of the employment relationship. This is significant since there are no caps on awards for compensatory and punitive damages under Section 1981.

- *Mixed Motive Cases:* Reverses *Price Waterhouse* v. *Tompkins*, in which the Supreme Court held that an employer could avoid liability for discrimination by showing that it would have made the same employment decision in the absence of discrimination. Under the new act, this rule is changed by providing that an illegal employment practice has occurred if discrimination was a motivating factor, even though other factors also motivated the employment decision. In such cases, plaintiffs may recover declaratory and injunctive relief, attorneys fees, and costs.

- *Disparate Impact:* Reverses the Supreme Court decision of *Wards Cove* v. *Antonio*, which stated that plaintiffs injured by disparate impact discrimination had to prove that the challenged practices were not significantly related to legitimate business objectives. Under the 1991 act, an employer must demonstrate that a challenged practice is job-related and consistent with "business necessity" after the plaintiff has shown that the employment practice caused a disparate impact. Once the employer had met its burden, the plaintiff must prove that an alternative practice exists having less of a disparate impact and that the employer refused to adopt it. If the employer can prove that its employment practice does not cause disparate impact, it is not required to show the practice is required by business necessity.

- *Extraterritorial Employment:* Defines "employee" in both Title VII and the ADA to include U.S. citizens employed abroad and provides exemptions for otherwise unlawful employment actions if compliance violates laws of the foreign country where the employee works. Additionally, the 1991 act creates a presumption that violations of Title VII by foreign corporations controlled by an American employer are violations by the American employer itself.

- *Glass Ceiling:* The Glass Ceiling Commission was established to study barriers to advancement of minorities and women in the work force and to recommend means of overcoming those barriers. Also establishes National Award for diversity and excellence in executive management.

Pay Act, employers must correct any pay inequities by raising the pay of lower-paid employees, not by lowering the pay of higher paid employees.

Comparable Worth

Comparable worth means that jobs requiring comparable knowledge, skills, and abilities should be paid similar amounts. Comparable worth and the Equal Pay Act (EPA) differ in that EPA requires equal pay for male and female employees who do work that is substantially equal. Comparable worth would mean employers would be required to provide equal pay for work of *equal value*. For example, a 1980 court case examined if nurses (a predominantly female job) should be paid the same as tree trimmers (a predominantly male job).[25]

The issue of comparable worth was developed primarily as an answer to the persistent wage gap between men and women employees. On average, women's earnings are approximately 60 percent of men's earnings. Comparable worth advocates that employees who work on "comparable" jobs (even though the actual job duties may differ) should be paid equally. Rather than comparing jobs based on job duties, proponents of comparable worth advocate comparing jobs based on four factors: (1) knowledge and skill level, (2) effort, (3) responsibility, and (4) working conditions.

The most publicized comparable worth case occurred in the state of Washington. The state was sued by the American Federation of State, County, and Municipal Employees (AFSCME). The union alleged that women who worked for the state of Washington were experiencing pay discrimination. The state's job evaluation plan placed many of the jobs traditionally held by women at a higher level but the wage rates were less than jobs traditionally held by men. Although the discrimination charges were upheld in U.S. District Court, the U.S. Supreme Court ultimately ruled against the women claiming comparable worth. However, following the decision, the state of Washington and the AFSCME reached a settlement in which the state paid $41.4 million on pay equity adjustments from April 1986 through June 1987 to employees such as nurses, library technicians, and clerk typists. Supplemental pay increases will bring the total to $482 million by 1992.[26]

One of the biggest problems facing comparable worth advocates is the cost of replacing the supply-and-demand market with a government-run job evaluation system. Closing the earnings gap between men and women has been estimated as costing $320 billion a year.[27] In addition, some have argued that a more effective solution would be to encourage women to enter nontraditional occupations and provide them with equal access to education, training, and employment, rather than raise the price of labor for specific jobs.[28]

....

CURRENT STRATEGIC ISSUES IN EQUAL EMPLOYMENT OPPORTUNITY

The Glass Ceiling

The term *glass ceiling* refers to the often subtle attitudes and prejudices that create barriers that block women and minorities from climbing the corporate ladder[29] or, in some cases, even moving laterally.[30] Glass ceilings have recently begun to receive a great deal of attention because of the Department of Labor's investigation into

EXHIBIT 5.8	Top Ten Positions Occupied by Women Have You Really "Come a Long Way, Baby"?		

RANK	1990	1940	1890
1	Secretary	Servant	Servant
2	Cashier	Stenographer, secretary	Agricultural laborer
3	Bookkeeper	Teacher	Dressmaker
4	Registered nurse	Clerical worker	Teacher
5	Nursing aide, orderly	Sales worker	Farmer, planter
6	Elementary school teacher	Factory worker (apparel)	Laundress
7	Waitress	Bookkeeper, accountant, cashier	Seamstress
8	Sales worker	Waitress	Cotton-mill operative
9	Child-care worker	Housekeeper	Housekeeper, steward
10	Cook	Nurse	Clerk, cashier

these invisible barriers. After reviewing a study done in September 1990 by researchers at the University of California, Los Angeles, in conjunction with Korn/Ferry International, the Department of Labor announced plans to begin investigating and removing glass ceilings in large government contractors.

The U.C.L.A./Korn/Ferry study revealed that women and minorities hold less than five percent of the senior management positions among the Fortune 500 companies surveyed.[31] This represents an increase of only two percent in the last ten years for women and minority representation in executive positions.[32] Given that women and minorities comprise over 50 percent of the work force, these facts have sparked the attention of officials at the Department of Labor.[33] As can be seen in Exhibit 5.8, the leading occupations for women have not really changed much over the last 100 years.

In a study that tracked the career paths of male and female MBAs, evidence for glass-ceiling effects was discovered. Over the time of the study, females received on average the same number of promotions as men; however, they experienced lower salary increases, fewer managerial promotions, and lower hierarchical levels as compared to men of similar background and experience.[34]

Pursuant to the discovery of glass-ceiling effects, investigations were begun to find out why women and minorities cannot penetrate the invisible barriers, other than as a result of overt and covert discrimination. An 18-month study by the Department of Labor in 1990–1991 reveals that, in many cases, women and minorities were not given critical training early on that would have made promotions possible. In addition, women and minorities were often passed over for the higher visibility projects that would have allowed them to prove themselves. Finally, white males were found to mentor and help other white males. Given that very few top management positions are occupied by women and minorities, less mentoring seems to be occurring with the groups who need it the most.[35] Mentoring has been found to be related to organizational advancement.[36] Mentors provide critical training, share inside information, lend social support, and serve as a buffer between the organization and the mentored employee. Women who have been mentored have been found to advance more rapidly than those without mentors.[37] However, women are less likely to develop a mentoring relationship than men.[38] Since mentoring appears to be a factor in organizational success, encouraging it may help to crack glass-ceiling barriers.

Managers should be aware of the possible glass ceiling within their organization. The following guidelines can help to encourage women and minority promotions into higher level positions.

1. Formal Training. If promotions depend on critical and specialized skills, it is important that training opportunities are offered to all employees.
2. Networking. Encourage women and minorities to communicate and exchange information and ideas about the job (that is, to engage in networking). In addition, managers can bridge various "networks," including white male networks, by arranging for representatives from different networks to meet and discuss job-related issues. Of course, it is also important to discourage white males from networking in private clubs where women and minorities are officially excluded.
3. Mentoring. Mentoring refers to an informal relationship between top managers and newer, lower level employees that helps the newer employees to gain status and get promoted. Mentors often achieve these results by explaining the corporate culture, providing strategic advice, suggesting career moves, and supporting these employees for promotion. As mentioned earlier, the Department of Labor found that some white male managers tend to mentor other white males. One way to overcome this tendency is to create a more formalized mentoring program and pair top managers with women and minorities.
4. Diversity Training. Top managers may need to have some diversity training in order to understand gender and cultural differences. For example, diversity training programs have shown why women make decisions differently than men. This will be discussed in more detail in the next section.

Breaking the subtle barriers of the glass ceiling will require the efforts of human resource professionals.[39] The human resource professional should not only make sure that discrimination does not exist, but also make sure companies make a good faith effort to allow women and minorities to advance. Continuing to maintain glass ceilings will not go unnoticed for long, and the cost of "fixing" their ill effects may be a major cost to organizations in the future.

Managing Workplace Diversity

Today's work force is becoming increasingly diverse. Although affirmative action has done much to open doors for women, minorities, and older employees, the retention and advancement of a diverse work force will require dramatic changes in corporate culture and human resource policies.[40] For example, the concept of treating everyone equally is now being replaced by emphasizing individualism. The corporate culture will have to consider the ethnic, cultural, educational, and gender differences that now represent today's work force. New human resource policies will have to reflect the unique needs of individuals rather than focusing on only one "mold" for all employees.[41]

The goal of diversity management is not to treat employees inequitably, but to provide a package of career opportunities tailored to individual needs. Organizations must recognize and appreciate employee differences if employees are to contribute their full potential. In addition, the shortage of skilled employees, coupled with an excess of skill-intensive jobs will require organizations to respond to employee needs.[42]

Not only must organizations recognize and appreciate employee differences, they must learn to utilize the differences in an optimal manner. For example, many women have stronger intuitive and people skills than men do. Allowing women to utilize these skills, as opposed to forcing them to adopt the "male command-and-control" style, will turn this difference into a positive attribute.[43]

Further evidence for gender differences has come from the medical profession. Men have been found to have fewer fibers connecting the verbal and emotional areas of the brain. This may be an explanation, in part, for why men have more difficulty in expressing emotion than women. In contrast, men have a superior ability to understand abstract relationships, which may predispose them to disciplines such as mathematics and engineering.[44] Overall, valuing diversity may not only result in increased employee satisfaction, but may lead to unique competitive advantages by tapping special skills.

Human resource management programs can also support work force diversity by offering flexible work schedules and job redesigns. For example, arranging for employees to work at home can accommodate parents with young children, those with elder care responsibilities, disabled workers, and older employees. Career tracking, mentoring, and development programs need to be implemented to open new opportunities to many groups of employees who have not traditionally been able to reach upper management levels.[45] Managing diversity means enabling all members of a work force to perform to their potential professionally.

• • • • • • • • •

MANAGEMENT GUIDELINES

Title VII suits based on alleged violations of the law prohibiting discrimination in employment and executive orders requiring affirmative action have been litigated for three decades. Penalties for EEO violations not only include monetary sanctions for organizations, but public embarrassment and the possible loss of consumer loyalty. Thus, it is imperative that organizations develop and implement a comprehensive plan to ensure equity in employment decisions. Components of an effective affirmative action program are discussed earlier in the chapter. The following strategic guidelines will help to ensure the success of affirmative action programs and equal employment opportunity policies.[46]

1. All levels of management, including top management, should be committed to the entire program. If employees perceive a lack of commitment from management, they may become less willing to try to make the program work and suspect of management's motives for implementing EEO policies or AAPs.

2. Every employee should understand fully the organization's policy on equal employment. Managers and employees need to be aware of both their obligations and their rights.

3. The organization should appoint an equal employment opportunity officer with the following responsibilities:

a. The handling of all contracts with and approvals of information submitted to government agencies.

b. The coordination of the organization's EEO programs.

c. The interpretation of EEO laws, regulations, statutes, and executive orders with the assistance of the organization's legal counsel.

d. The dissemination of information to all employees regarding the organization's EEO policies and guidelines.

4. Top management, including EEO officers, should ensure that the organization recruits, selects, trains, transfers, promotes, lays off, and compensates employees on the basis of ability and other meritorious qualifications without discrimination because of sex, race, color, religion, age, national origin, or ancestry.

5. Top management should ensure that the organization does not discriminate any qualified job-applicant or employee because of a mental or physical handicap or status as a disabled or Vietnam-era veteran.

6. Managers should act to *remedy any deficiencies* in its equal employment opportunity and affirmative action programs. This includes evaluating the utilization of minorities, females, physically or mentally handicapped individuals, and disabled or Vietnam-era veterans.

7. Managers should consider *establishing results-oriented goals* and timetables to eliminate the underutilization of minorities and females throughout the organization. If quotas or goals are used, this does not mean that the organization should hire unqualified applicants or promote unqualified employees. Quotas and goals should be developed subject to the availability of qualified minority and female applicants.

Managers should be careful *not to limit, segregate, or classify employees* in any way that would tend to deprive them of employment opportunities or adversely affect any employee's status because of sex, race, color, religion, national origin, or ancestry.

9. Managers should ensure that the organization *does not use sexual or racial stereotyping* in any oral or written description of an applicant or employee. In addition, managers must eliminate any sexism or racism, whether conscious or otherwise, in any evaluation process.

····················
QUESTIONS FOR REVIEW

1. What are the important strategic choices managers should make regarding equal employment opportunities?

2. Discuss Title VII of the Civil Rights Act. What does this act prohibit? Be specific.

3. What is a bona fide occupational qualification (BFOQ)? Give an example of a BFOQ.

4. The chapter covered three ways to demonstrate discrimination in employment decisions. What are those?

5. What is the difference between sex discrimination and sexual harassment?

6. What is the difference between race discrimination and national origin discrimination?

7. Has recent EEO case law affected civil rights? If so, how?

8. What is the difference between equal employment opportunity laws and affirmative action?

9. What is reverse discrimination? Think of an example.

10. What are the components of an effective affirmative action program?

11. What is the difference between the Equal Pay Act and comparable worth?

12. Do you believe implementing comparable worth laws and guidelines would have a positive or negative impact on the work force? Do you believe comparable worth is realistic?

 State Farm Target of Second Bias Suit [47]

The State Farm group is one of the most prominent multiple line insurance operations in the United States. In 1988, the property-casualty members of the group recorded $20.2 billion of net premium writings and ran as the leading group in the writing of property-casualty insurance. However, during the last ten years, State Farm has become the target of two bias suits, one instituted in 1979 in the state of California, the other instituted in 1989 in Texas.

In June 1989 in Houston, Texas, seven women filed a $100-million discrimination suit in federal court against State Farm Mutual Automobile Insurance Company and three affiliates, charging that the company's hiring practices discriminated against women and minorities. The lawsuit, which seeks class-action status, claims that State Farm discriminated against Texas women, blacks, and persons of Spanish descent in hiring agents, claims adjusters, and underwriters. The plaintiffs in the case charge that these positions, paying from $75,000 to $95,000 annually, were reserved for white males. "This is a very lucrative job and one that historically was passed on by nepotism and cronyism in what is described as a 'good old boys' network," said Guy Saperstein, a lawyer from Oakland, California, who also brought a California suit.

State Farm representatives felt the company could defend its operations in Texas and released statistics indicating that the company had a work force in the state of 2,337 employees, of whom 1,540 were women and 929 minorities (132 of the minority employees were female). State Farm representatives also state that among the 61 trainee agent appointments made in Texas over the past two years, 40 were women or minorities, and that the company has as large a representation of females and minorities in Texas as any other company operating there.

This is the second bias case State Farm has had to face in recent years. In February 1988, the company lost a nine-year-old sex discrimination case in California that could end up costing State Farm over $300 million. The California suit, filed in 1979 in the U.S. District Court in

San Francisco, was brought by three women, charging that State Farm discriminated against women when recruiting and hiring new agents. Under the terms of this settlement, each of the plaintiffs, or their estates, will receive $1.2 million, and the company will fill 50 percent of its new agency positions in California for the next ten years with women. Other California women who applied for positions with State Farm from 1974 to 1987 were also entitled to compensation under the terms of the agreement, which affects both life and property-casualty agents. The women who qualify for settlement funds could be paid between $15,575 and $420,822 plus interest, depending on the length of time since they applied for jobs as agents. To alert possible claimants, State Farm will advertise and issue letters to former job applicants.

Bruce Callis, State Farm vice-president, said a woman would have to show not only that she applied for the agent job but also that she would have gotten the job based on the requirement at the time. In California, agents must pass the state insurance test, so women claiming damages against State Farm from 1979 on must demonstrate that they have passed, or can pass, he said.

Since 1979, State Farm has been using an industrywide aptitude test that all recruits must pass, he added. Women who claim they were discriminated against from 1979 on must pass that test also, Callis said.

The California suit was recently settled by State Farm with a sum believed to be the largest ever paid for violations of the Civil Rights Act of 1984. State Farm agreed to pay $157 million to 814 women participating in the settlement. Each woman will receive approximately $193,000. As a result of the suit, State Farm's hiring efforts have improved substantially.

QUESTIONS

1. Discuss the various types of discrimination charges facing State Farm.

2. Is the fact that State Farm has "as large a representation of females and minorities in Texas as any other company" a good defense?

3. What impact might the 1989 EEO case law have on this or a similar discrimination case?

⋯⋯⋯⋯ ADDITIONAL READINGS

Albert, Rory Judd, and Neal S. Schelberg. "Benefit Plans Redefined under ADEA." *Pension World* 25, iss. 10 (1989), pp. 45–48.

Banta, William, F. *AIDS in the Workplace: Legal Questions and Practical Answers.* Lexington, MA: Lexington Books, 1988.

Cohen, Murray E., and Cynthia Fryer Cohen. "Comparable Worth and Compensation: Complexities and Controversies in the

United States." *Equal Opportunities International* (UK) 6, iss. 2 (1987), pp. 7–10.

Creighton, Helen. "Age Discrimination." *Nursing Management* 20, iss. 2 (1989), pp. 21–22.

Dennis, Helen. *Fourteen Steps in Managing an Aging Workforce.* Lexington, MA: Lexington Books, 1988.

Gaines, Sally. "State Farm Settles Sex Bias Case." *Chicago Tribune.* January 20, 1988, p. 1.

Hale, Noreen. *The Older Worker: Effective Strategies for Management and Human Resource Development.* San Francisco: Jossey-Base Publishers, 1990.

Israel, David, and Stephen Beiser. "Immune from the ADEA." *Personnel Administrator* 34, iss. 11 (1989), p. 102.

Jolly, James P., and James G. Frierson. "Playing It Safe." *Personnel Administrator* 34, iss. 6 (1989), pp. 44–50.

Knowles, Robert G. "Women Sue State Farm Over Status." *National Underwriter (Life/Health/Financial Services)* 93, no. 27. July 3, 1989, p. 1.

LaVan, Helen, Marsha Katz, Maura S. Malloy, and Peter Stonebraker. "Comparable Worth: A Comparison of Litigated Cases in the Public and Private Sectors." *Public Personnel Management* 16, iss. 3 (1987), pp. 281–293.

Lewis, Chad T. "Assessing the Validity of Job Evaluation." *Public Personnel Management* 18, iss. 1 (1989), pp. 45–53.

Mamorsky, Jeffrey D. "Supreme Court Permits Age-Based Benefit Distinctions in Plans." *Journal of Compensation & Benefits* 5, iss. 3 (1989), pp. 175–177.

Matusewitch, Eric. "Retirement: An Executive Decision?" *Personnel Journal* 68, iss. 7 (1989), pp. 86–89.

Miceli, Marcia P., John Blackburn and Stephen Mangum. "Employers' Pay Practices and Potential Responses to 'Comparable Worth' Litigation: An Identification of Research Issues." *Journal of Business Ethics* (Netherlands) 7, iss. 5 (1988), pp. 347–358.

Mulcahy, Colleen. "State Farm Settles Major Sex Bias Case." *National Underwriter (Life/Health/Financial Services)* 92, no. 5. February 1, 1988, p. 6.

Powell, Gary N. "Male/Female Work Roles—What Kind of Future?" *Personnel* 66, iss. 7 (1989), pp. 47–50.

Schroeder, Patricia, and Constance Horner. "Comparable Worth: A Wrong Turn; Point-Counterpoint." *Bureaucrat* 16, iss. 4 (1987/1988), PP. 4–9.

Shearer, Robert A. "Paramour Claims Under Title VII: Liability for Co-Worker/Employer Sexual Relationships." *Employee Relations Law Journal* 15, iss. 1 (1989), pp. 57–66.

Stacy, Donald R. "Avoid Double Dipping without Incurring an ADEA Violation." *Compensation & Benefits Review* 21, iss. 6 (1989), pp. 48–57.

"State Farm Faces a $100 Million Bias Suit." *The New York Times* June 24, 1989, p. 24.

"State Farm Is Cited in Texas Suit Charging Hiring Discrimination." *Wall Street Journal.* June 23, 1989, p. B12.

Susser, Peter A., and David H. Jett. "In a Recently Published Notice, the EEOC Has Set Forth Its View of Sexual Harassment After Vinson." *Employment Relations Today* 16, iss. 1 (1989), pp. 81–87.

Turner, Ronald. *The Past and Future of Affirmative Action: A Guide and Analysis for Human Resource Professionals and Corporate Counsel.* Westport, CT: Quorum Books, 1990.

·················
NOTES

1. Ginger C. Reed, "Employers' New Burden of Proof in Discrimination Cases," *Employment Relations Today* 16, no. 2, Summer 1989, pp. 111–

113; Andrea Sachs, "A Slap at Sex Stereotypes," *Time,* May 15, 1989, p. 66; Deborah L. Jacobs, "Smile When You Say That, Partner," *MS,* January to February 1989, p. 137; "Court Rules on 'Sex Stereotyping,'" *Monthly Labor Review* 112, July 1989, p. 45; "Myth America in the Workplace," *U.S. News & World Report,* May 15, 1989, p. 14; "High Court Rules in PW Bias Case," *Journal of Accountancy* 168, no. 1, July 1989, p. 16; D. Israel and P. Sweeney, "Supreme Court Allows Relief for Female Plaintiff," *HRNews Legal Report,* August 1990.

2. The discrimination discussion that follows is based on the *Equal Employment Opportunity Manual for Managers and Supervisors.* A publication of the American Society for Personnel Administration and Commerce Clearing House, Inc. (1989).

3. D. P. Twomey, *A Concise Guide to Employment Law* (Cincinnati; South-Western, 1986).

4. For discussions of the hearings, see *Time,* October 21, 1991; and *U.S. News and World Report,* October 21, 1991.

5. J. A. Segal, "The Sexlessness of Harassment," *HRMagazine,* August 1991, pp. 71–73.

6. C. Kleiman, "Sexual Harassment Suit Claims Ads Affect Workplace Behavior," *Tallahassee Democrat,* March 1992, p. 24D.

7. S. J. Garvin, "Employer Liability for Sexual Harassment," *HRMagazine,* June 1991, pp. 101–108.

8. M. Lengnick-Hall, "Checking Out Sexual Harassment Claims," *HRMagazine,* March 1992, pp. 77–81.

9. D. Israel and G. McConnell, "New Law Protects Older Workers," *HRMagazine,* March 1991, pp. 77–79.

10. *Resource: Legal Report,* Society for Human Resource Management, October 1989, p. 7.

11. E. J. Conry, G. R. Ferrera, and K. H. Fox, *The Legal Environment of Business,* 2nd ed., (Boston: Allen and Bacon, 1990).

12. Ibid.

13. P. A. Morrissey, "How Is Disability Defined?" *HRNews,* January 1991, p. 6.

14. R. Pimentel and M. Lotito, "Shining Light on ADA," *HRMagazine,* February 1992, pp. 47–49.

15. The following section is based on D. Gold and B. Unger, "ADA Prohibits Most Preemployment Health Questions," *HRNews,* March 1992, p. A5; and W. F. Casio and J. W. Walker, *HRM Update,* (New York: McGraw-Hill, 1992.

16. S. R. Meisinger, "The Americans with Disabilities Act: Begin Preparing Now," *HR Legal Report,* Winter 1991, pp. 1–12.

17. This discussion was based largely upon the *Equal Employment Opportunity Manual.*

18. D. Seligman, "How Equal Opportunity Turned into Employment Quotas," *Fortune,* March 1973, p. 162.

19. Conry et al., *The Legal Environment of Business.*

20. Tim Smart, "This Civil Rights Bill May Fly—If It Stays Light Enough," *Business Week,* February 5, 1990, p. 35.

21. P. M. Barrett, "Some Specifics about the New Law," *Wall Street Journal,* November 4, 1991, p. B1.

22. B. Murphy, W. Barlow, and D. Hatch, "Retroactivity of the Civil Rights Act of 1991 Unsettled," *Personnel Journal,* March 1992, p. 24; and C. Naidoff, "Understanding the Civil Rights Act of 1991," *Management Review,* April 1992, pp. 58–59.

23. U.S. Department of Labor, Equal Pay for Equal Work Under the Fair Labor Standards Act (Washington, DC: Interpretative Bulletin, August 31, 1971).

24. *Employment Relations under the Fair Labor Standards Act* (Washington, DC: U.S. Department of Labor, Employment Standards Administration, Wage and Hour Division, revised May 1980, reprinted August 1985).

25. *Lemons v. City and County of Denver 1980,* 620 F. 2d, 228.

26. *AFSCME v. State of Washington,* 770 F.2d 1401 (Ninth Circuit, 1985) as adapted from Reichenberg, "Pay Equity in Review," pp. 220–221.

27. "Twenty Questions on Comparable Worth, The Equal Employment Advisory Council, 1984." Reprinted in *Personnel Administrator* 30, April 1985, p. 65.

28. Julie M. Buchanan, "Comparable Worth: Where Is It Headed?" *Human Resources: Journal of the International Association for Personnel Women 2*, Summer 1985, p. 12.

29. S. B. Garland, "Throwing Stones at the 'Glass Ceiling,' " *Business Week*, August 19, 1991, p. 29.

30. J. Lopez, "Study Says Women Fare Glass Walls as Well as Ceiling," *Wall Street Journal*, March 3, 1992, p. B1.

31. C. M. Dominguez, "A Crack in the Glass Ceiling," *HRMagazine*, December 1990, pp. 65–66.

32. Ibid.

33. Garland, "Throwing Stones at the 'Glass Ceiling.' "

34. T. H. Cox and C. V. Harquail, "Career Paths and Career Success in the Early Career Stages of Male and Female MBAs," *Journal of Vocational Behavior* 39(1), 1991, pp. 54–75.

35. Garland, "Throwing Stones at the 'Glass Ceiling.' "

36. K. E. Kram, "Phases of the Mentor Relationship," *Academy of Management Journal* 26(4), 1983, pp. 608–625.

37. B. R. Ragins, "Barriers to Mentoring: The Female Manager's Dilemma," *Human Relations* 42(1), 1989, pp. 1–22.

38. Ibid.

39. Overman, "HR Urged to Strike Blow against Glass Ceiling," *HRNews* 10, September 1991, pp. 1, 3.

40. B. Rosen and K. Lovelace, "Piecing Together the Diversity Puzzle," *HRMagazine*, June 1991, pp. 71–84.

41. L. Baytos "Launching Successful Diversity Initiatives," *HRMagazine*, March 1992, pp. 91–97.

42. D. Herbst and G. Skarr, "How a Small Company Can Celebrate Diversity," *HRNews*, April 1991, p. 12.

43. A. Saltzman, "Trouble at the Top," *U.S. News and World Report*, June 17, 1991, pp. 40–48.

44. Ibid.

45. Rosen and Lovelace, "Piecing Together the Diversity Puzzle."

46. The management guidelines were based largely on the work of Walter Manley, Esq., unpublished manuscript (1989) and on the content of the chapter.

47. Robert G. Knowles, "Women Sue State Farm Over Status," *National Underwriter (Life/Health/Financial Services)* 93, no. 27, July 3, 1989, p. 1; Colleen Mulcahy, "State Farm Settles Major Sex Bias Case," *National Underwriter (Life/Health/Financial Services)* 92, no. 5, February 1, 1988, p. 6; "State Farm Faces a $100 Million Bias Suit," *New York Times*, June 24, 1989, p. 24; "State Farm Is Cited in Texas Suit Charging Hiring Discrimination," *Wall Street Journal*, p. B12; Sally Gaines, *Tribune*, January 20, 1988; Jonathan Lansner, "State Farm Settles Sex-Bias Case," *Orange County Register*, Santa Ana, California, January 20, 1988; Richard B. Schmitt, "State Farm's $157 Million Settlement Caps Discrimination Suit by 814 Women," *Wall Street Journal*, April 29, 1992, p. A3.

6 Strategic Human Resource Planning and Staffing

Human resource planning and staffing is a vital link between strategic planning and human resource management. Human resource planning is the process of making decisions in hiring and staffing for the organization. Planning and staffing involve job design, recruiting, screening, compensation, training, promotion, and work policies. In this chapter, we present factors found within the organization and throughout its environment that influence human resource planning. We also offer guidelines for managing and analyzing human resource planning requirements.

• • • • • • • • •
CHAPTER OBJECTIVES

As a result of studying this chapter, you should be able to

1. Define strategic human resource planning.
2. Explain the critical link between strategic management and strategic human resource planning.
3. Identify and explain the external and internal factors that affect a human resource plan.
4. Identify and explain the steps in constructing a human resource plan.
5. Explain the relationship of strategic human resource planning to the staffing function.

CASE: Is NCNB Spreading Itself Too Thin?[1]

North Carolina National Bank Corp.(NCNB), North Carolina banking's biggest winner, is betting the bank on becoming one of the nation's biggest financial institutions. In 1988, it began acquiring First RepublicBank of Dallas, one of Texas's biggest banking losers.

Nearly all of the quagmired Texas holding company's banking operations were taken over by NCNB in a bailout, largely financed by the Federal Deposit Insurance Corporation (FDIC) with standby assistance from H. Ross Perot, the Texas billionaire.

NCNB, based in Charlotte, North Carolina, thus becomes the newest out-of-stater to seize a share of the spoils of the devastated Texas banking industry. Three other recapitalized Texas banking concerns—Chemical Banking Corp.'s Texas Commerce Bancshares, First Interstate Bancorp's Texas operation, and A. Rovert Abboud's First City Bancorp of Texas—have been aggressively jockeying for the state's commercial and consumer banking business.

NCNB Beginnings

NCNB brings to the fray a scrappy self-confidence and a disdain toward skeptics who think the company is going too far, too fast. "People have been skeptical about us since we were a $400-million bank," said Francis "Buddy" Kemp, NCNB's former president, now chairman of the Texas banking operation for NCNB. Since 1960, when NCNB was formed with $400 million in assets, its assets have grown to $116 billion, making it the third largest bank holding concern in the country.

NCNB got where it is today through a very aggressive growth strategy. It was a product of several mergers of small banks in the late 1950s and started out way behind Wachovia Corp. of Winston-Salem, the old money prestige bank in North Carolina. NCNB ran hard, took more chances, lent to more small businesses, bought such nonbank subsidiaries as factoring and consumer finance companies, and opportunistically exploited any openings it could find. In 1981, for instance, it found a loophole that enabled it to buy banks in Florida and then did so ahead of out-of-state rivals. It is now the second largest banking concern in that state.

NCNB's Chairman Hugh McColl embodies NCNB's unusually strong institutional personality by driving the aggressive acquisition program. But, the board of directors is no rubber stamp. McColl's leadership has led the bank's growth strategy on one of the fastest tracks in modern times. An ex-marine, he has run in marathons and once used a grenade as a paper-weight. McColl's style has not been one designed to win friends. He once told a potential target bank's chairman who was reluctant to negotiate a merger that he was "about to launch my missiles." McColl concedes, "There are people who don't like me that have never met me. There are people who have met me that don't like me, too. I'm quite able to offend both ways."

Human Resource Issues

To revive First RepublicBank, McColl sent in the troops: some 250 of NCNB's best and brightest officers, led onto the banking beachhead by five of NCNB's top ten executives. They included Kemp, who at the time was NCNB's president, to become chairman of the Texas bank; Timothy P. Hartman, the company's chief financial officer, who became the vice-chairman and chief financial officer in Texas; Ralph M. Carestio, Jr., head of NCNB's real estate lending; and Kenneth D. Lewis, head of NCNB's Florida operations.

As some see it, NCNB's structure and style are well suited to the task. Though the company's planning and controls are highly centralized, its field personnel are given much operating authority. It is also one of the biggest college recruiters in banking, stocking its field operations with MBAs and other freshly minted graduates who are trained to make decisions and be aggressive. "NCNB is clearly geared up to be able to move out and hit the ground running," says Henry J. Coffey, Jr., an analyst at J. C. Bradford & Co., Nashville.

NCNB also has experience with managing turnarounds. It built its Florida operation by acquiring small, subpar banks, whipping them into shape, and making them grow. The Florida banks contributed about half of NCNB's profit prior to its merger with C & S Sovran bank in 1991. But, in the process, NCNB also developed a reputation for being heavy-handed about doing things the NCNB way, driving away many managers and customers.

That is one major reason the bank has had trouble finding willing merger partners in the Southeast. NCNB's reputation was also a hazard in Texas, where the acquired bank was already in tumult. Prior to the acquisition by NCNB, First RepublicBank had been under the control of the FDIC after being in the throes of integrating RepublicBank Corp. and Interfirst Corp. (the two holding companies that merged to form First RepublicBank Corp.).

Too Much to Handle?

The scale of the Texas undertaking was well beyond anything NCNB had ever tried. Its Florida operation prior to the First RepublicBank takeover had been acquired and nurtured over a five-year period and had about $10 billion in assets. The "clean" part of the Texas bank that NCNB acquired had about $20 billion in assets. Fellow bankers wondered not only whether NCNB could get a handle on Texas, but also whether it would lose its grip in its major markets in North Carolina and Florida, where business prospects were much less dicey. The North Carolina banks had been run by the well-regarded Kemp, and the Florida banks would also need a new leader with Lewis's exit. Bank analysts agreed with many bankers. Said one of them, "This has the potential to range from a disaster to a bonanza."

Following the Texas takeover, NCNB continued to acquire other operations and, in 1989, moved in on one of its most lucrative targets ever, C&S Bank of Florida. C&S was a profitable institution with a solid reputation. It was able to fend off initial attempts. In 1991, following bitter on-again, off-again negotiations, the two giants agreed to join. Bennet Brown, chairman of C&S, had recently merged his conservative institution with Sovran to form C&S/Sovran. C&S found itself weaker after discovering that Sovran's portfolio of real estate loans was worse than expected.

Brown is a stark contrast to the feisty McColl and is more concerned with pursuing a "conservative and cautious" approach. He speaks quietly about the welfare of protecting stockholders and customers. "We have never stressed bigness or power," he says. "We're just going to deliver financial services and make a good profit at it."

Brown says he is concerned about his employees, too. The NCNB-C&S/Sovran merger is estimated by analysts to eliminate some 9,000 jobs. Using the same strategy as he did in Texas, McColl plans to "airlift" 150 of his employees to C&S/Sovran's offices in the Washington area to begin charging away at C&S/Sovran's real estate loan problems. McColl has set a goal of saving $350 million in costs within three years.

After its merger with C&S/Sovran is complete, NCNB will change its name to NationsBank. The new organization will have McColl as its president and chief executive officer. Brown will become chairman of the combined institution. NationsBank will become the third largest banking concern in the United States after Citicorp and Chemical Banking Corp. and will be the largest banking concern in five states (see Exhibit 6.1). Whether the combined cultures can merge successfully and whether the strategy of rapid growth will succeed are two major issues that must be addressed through human resource planning and staffing.

• • • • • • • • •

S trategic human resource planning is the key link between a firm's strategic plan and its overall human resource management function as shown in Exhibit 6.2. The strategic human resource plan is a projection as to how the firm plans to acquire and utilize its human resources. It affects and is affected by the firm's overall strategic plan, and it serves as the basis for overall human resource management.

Now we begin to look at how organizations fill the jobs. How do they decide how many people they need? How do they determine the skill/ability mix of these

EXHIBIT 6.1　Ranking among Banks That a Combined NCNB-C&S/Sovran Will Have in Selected Southern States

STATE	RANK
South Carolina	1
Georgia	1
North Carolina	1
Virginia	1
Texas	1
Florida	2
Tennessee	3
Maryland	3
Washington, D.C.	5

people? What should be the mix of hiring from the outside versus promoting from within? How are vacancies estimated?

NCNB had to answer all these questions, plus more. Imagine how complex this must be for a rapidly growing firm of more than 27,000 employees. How would you determine proper employment levels?

STRATEGIC CHOICES

The key choices in strategic human resource planning can and must be made along several key dimensions. These dimensions reflect the degree to which an organization engages in planning per se. Each dimension represents a choice a firm makes when committing to any type of planning activity. First, the organization can choose to be *proactive* or *reactive* in human resource planning. That is, it can decide to carefully anticipate needs and systematically plan to fill them far in advance, or it can simply react to needs as they arise. Of course careful planning to fill human resource needs better helps to ensure that the organization obtains the right number of employees with the proper skills and abilities at the time they are needed.

The second decision the organization makes determines its *breadth*. Essentially, the organization can choose a narrow focus by planning in only one or two human resource areas, such as recruitment or selection, or it can choose a broad focus by planning in all human resource areas including training, rewarding, and so on. This continuum is depicted in Exhibit 6.3.

The third choice involves the *formality* of the plan. The organization can choose to have a rather informal plan that is mostly in the heads of its managers and personnel staff, or it can have a *formalized* plan that is clearly spelled out in writing backed up by supporting documentation and data. A survey conduced by the Hay Group Consultants of 2,100 organizations found that only 21 percent of the organizations surveyed had formal human resource plans in 1988. It was rudimentary in only 30 percent of these firms.[2]

The fourth choice involves the *degree of tie* the human resource plan has with the strategic plan. The plan can be *loosely tied*, if at all, to the firm's strategic plan, or it can be *fully integrated* with the strategic plan. As we have indicated, integration

EXHIBIT 6.2 Strategic Human Resource Planning Serves as the Key Link between the Overall Strategic Plan and Human Resource Management

of the strategic plan and strategic human resource management can best occur by fully integrating the two through strategic human resource planning.

Finally, the fifth choice in the human resource plan involves *flexibility*—the ability of the plan to anticipate and deal with contingencies. As we have indicated, organizations do not like high levels of uncertainty. They reduce this uncertainty by planning, which includes forecasting and predicting possible future conditions and events. Human resource planning can contain many contingencies, which reflect differing scenarios and thereby assure that the plan is flexible and adaptable, or it can be fairly set and geared to one scenario, thereby requiring much time and effort to obtain change—assuming it can be changed at all.

Exhibit 6.4 summarizes these five major choices faced by the organizations in strategic human resource planning. An organization will often tend to be to the left or to the right on all continua rather than to the left on some and to the right on others, although there are exceptions. A firm could be at one end of the extreme on some plan characteristics and at the other end on other characteristics. Contrast, for example, the human resource planning done by Apple Computers during the first two years of its existence with that done under CEO John Scully. Apple's rapid growth in a short period of time occurred haphazardly with little real human resource planning. Under Scully, formalized flexible plans were developed and fully integrated with the company's overall strategic plan; yet these were often reactive because of the firm's growth cycles in the mid-1980s.[3]

Organizational Growth Cycles and Planning

The stage of an organization's growth can have an important effect on the human resource planning adopted by the organization.[4] Small organizations just starting out in the **embryonic stage** often do little human resource planning. What planning that is done is often informal and reactive in nature. (Professors often receive calls from small organizations in their communities with job openings. When asked, "When do you need the person?" the reply often is, "Yesterday!") Many young firms do not recruit for replacements until *after* the positions become vacant. Little real anticipative recruiting and hiring is done.

As the organization enters the second stage, **rapid growth,** the need for planning becomes more apparent. Human resource forecasting becomes a necessary addition. Internal development of people also begins to receive attention in order to keep up with growth.

A **mature firm** experiences less flexibility and variability. Growth has slowed and the organization tends to become set in its ways. The work force ages as few younger people are hired. Planning becomes more formalized and less flexible and

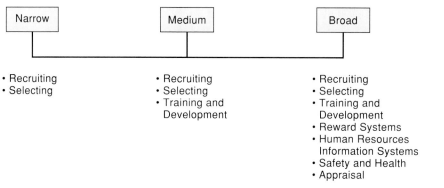

EXHIBIT 6.3 The Breadth of Focus in Human Resource Planning Can Be Narrow or Broad

Narrow	Medium	Broad
• Recruiting • Selecting	• Recruiting • Selecting • Training and Development	• Recruiting • Selecting • Training and Development • Reward Systems • Human Resources Information Systems • Safety and Health • Appraisal

innovative. Concerns with retirement, mid-career plateauing, and possible retrenchment dominate planning.

Finally, in the aging or **declining stage,** human resource planning takes a different focus. Planning is done for layoff, retrenchment, and retirement, and since decisions are often made after serious financial and sales shocks are experienced by the organization, planning is often reactive in nature. In some cyclical industries such as autos, however, layoffs can be and are planned well in advance. Only if the organization attempts *renewal* and renaissance (rebirth) will strategic human resource planning focus on growth again.

In the next section, we examine the overall framework and nature of human resource planning.

THE NATURE OF HUMAN RESOURCE PLANNING

Human resource planning is the process of making decisions regarding the acquisition and utilization of human resources. As such, it is part of the strategic decision-making process outlined in Chapter 3. In particular, the human resource plan focuses on an analysis of the organization's objectives and the plan for acquiring resources to meet those objectives. The organization's objectives and the resource acquisition process are analyzed in terms of the role that human resources plays in achieving organizational goals.

Human resource planning is the sum total of the plan formulated for the recruiting, screening, compensation, training, job structure, promotion, and work rules of an organization's human resources. It is a process designed to translate the corporate plans and objectives into future quantitative and qualitative employment requirements, together with plans to fulfill those requirements over both the shorter and longer terms, through human resource utilization, human resource development, employment and recruiting, and information systems.[5]

This definition emphasizes structuring plans to carry out what are considered to be the traditional personnel management functions of hiring, training, compensation, and promotion. Thus, even though the primary focus of human resource planning is on obtaining people to fill jobs, human resource planning is a pervasive

EXHIBIT 6.4 Continual Strategic Choices in Human Resource Planning

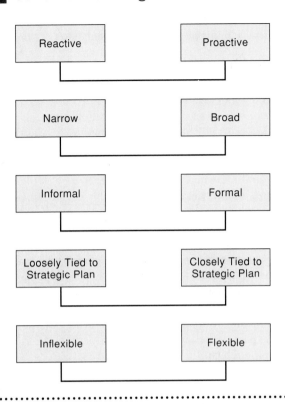

function in that it involves planning for the operation of other areas of human resource management as well.

Economic Forces

Human resource planning is influenced by national employment and economic policy planning. National economic policy planning has set the stage for national policy in training and education and the level of economic activity through monetary and fiscal policy. Congress and various federal agencies, such as the Department of Labor, particularly the Employment and Training Administration, and certain agencies within the Department of Health and Human Services and the Department of Education, play a major role. Laws are passed to encourage certain types of training or the hiring of certain groups. For example, the Jobs Training Partnership Act encourages private sector hiring of disadvantaged groups.

Economic and human resource policy at the national level changes as the priorities of a particular Congress or administration change. For example, under Presidents Kennedy and Johnson a great deal of effort and funds were spent to develop plans to deal with specific employment problems. Those administrations established programs for remedial education and skill training, mobility benefits, equal employment opportunity, and labor market information system. Most of these programs in this period were directed at improving the employment relationship of minorities and disadvantaged groups in keeping with the philosophy of the New Frontier of the Kennedy administration and the Great Society of the Johnson administration.

However, during the Nixon and Ford administrations, human resource priorities changed. These administrations increased emphasis on improving the employment situation of veterans and in improving the already existing federal offices, such as the federal-state divisions of employment, to help all levels of employment. The emphasis on programs for the disadvantaged and minorities was reduced.

The Nixon administration also decentralized the national human resource planning effort by establishing regional offices throughout the nation and, through the revenue sharing program, by asking each state to handle the employment planning function for the state. The responsibility for national human resource planning has shifted from a centralized federal government in Washington to decentralized regional offices and individual state governments.

The Carter administration continued this decentralized approach to human resource planning but sought to increase the scope and funding of programs for the disadvantaged and minorities. The Reagan and Bush administrations reduced the emphasis on the federal government's role in human resource planning and provided incentives for private industry to take over more of the planning and training function. Reagan also instituted the "block grant" concept for the states as opposed to previous grants by category for human resource utilization. This plan gave states more flexibility in using human resource funds. Under this plan, money is allocated to state and local governments as a block or whole, not by program or funding category. This allows the states to allocate funds to priority programs with a minimum of federal red tape.[6]

National economic and human resource policy plays a major underlying role in a firm's human resource planning. For example when federal programs were established to improve the employment opportunities for the unskilled, disadvantaged, and unemployed, all individual organizations were asked to commit extra efforts for recruiting, training, and employing these individuals.

Often federal programs will stimulate an organization to increase human resource planning efforts. Federal laws and court interpretations of those laws dealing with equal employment opportunity and affirmative action often make it necessary for many organizations to review their human resource planning process. The thrust of affirmative action planning involves the development of an organizational plan to recruit, train, and employ more members of minorities and women than are presently employed by the organization. As organizations review the number of employees presently employed in various positions and develop plans to replace these employees to ensure that minorities are being recruited, they usually end up making a comprehensive review of their total human resource planning system.

The Labor Market

We reviewed some aspects of the changing labor market in Chapter 2, but we return to this factor because of its importance in human resource planning. To a great extent, organizations view the labor market as a pool of skills and abilities that will be tapped as the need arises. For most job requirements, employees with appropriate skills and abilities are readily available. From time to time, organizations will experience shortages of people with certain skills or find that the wage level is so high that they cannot "afford" to hire the type of people that are needed to fill the available jobs. For example, for many years employers faced a shortage of people with computer expertise. The relationship between the organization's job require-ments and the available pool of skills and abilities is typically viewed by managers as a sequential process whereby the organization first establishes the best job struc-ture in terms of job content and task assignments, determines each job's worth in the production process (job evaluation), and then proceeds to hire and develop human resources that match these requirements. Often things do not work out so smoothly for a firm because the labor market is not perfect and it is constantly changing. Shortages and surpluses of skill areas develop and workers are laid off permanently as plants close. Auto workers must move from Detroit to Ohio, Ten-nessee, Kentucky, and California if they want to continue working in the auto industry.

Economists typically indicate four main determinants of labor supply:

1. The size, age, sex, and educational composition of the population.
2. The demand for goods and services in the economy.
3. The nature of production technology.
4. The labor force participation rates (people working or looking for work) of major subgroups (for example, women).

Skill Changes and Personnel Shortages

These changes have led to many skill shortages as well as areas of oversupply. When the human resource educational/skill mix differs significantly from the skills required by employers, personnel shortages develop. Employers have jobs open, but cannot find people with the skills needed. Many people who want jobs are not hired because they do not have the skills demanded. This mismatch between job skill requirements and the skills of the labor force has plagued the U.S. economy during the 1970s and 1980s and can have serious negative impact on the economy of a society. For ex-ample, employment rates in traditional industries such as steel, auto, and rubber, have fallen off, as demand and technology in these areas change; yet severe person-nel shortages are occurring in such high-tech areas as computers, information pro-cessing, and genetic engineering. In many cases, rust-belt jobs in traditional industries in the Midwest have moved to Sunbelt jobs in information systems and services.

This human resource dislocation in part drives inflation, since employers bid up the wage rate for the few qualified workers in the high-demand fields. The wage rates of computer-trained auto mechanics, for example, soared in the late 1980s. At the same time, relative wage rates tumbled in the old-line industries. The federal government has reacted to this situation by encouraging employers to improve the computer-related skills of employees by developing training programs. These pro-grams are embodied in the Jobs Training Partnership Act, a joint federal-private business action that provides the skills necessary for many entry level jobs in high-tech industries and various federally funded vocational and technical education pro-grams at two-year technical schools.

Because of the increased educational attainment level of workers, the types of skills needed by employers in the 1990s will likely be much more sophisticated than they were in the 1970s and 1980s. For example, various new engineering, computer, and medical technical jobs require much higher skills than previously required. Even the automotive mechanic of the 1990s will be more highly skilled than his or her counterpart in the 1980s because of the more sophisticated design of automobile computers, engines, and related systems and because of the tremendous variety in automotive models within a given manufacturer's line.

Thus, any human resource plan must assess the human resource educational/skill level of the labor market from which it draws, predict future changes in this mix, assess the effect of federal human resource programs, and then plan recruiting, training, and job design systems that take maximum advantage of the forecasted educational/skill mix. Human resource management units perform a boundary spanning or scanning role when assessing labor market characteristics, as was explained in Chapter 2. Recognizing that the labor market and federal legislation and activities related to it have a major impact on any company's individual human resource plan, now we look at a model or procedure for constructing a human resource plan.

MODEL FOR HUMAN RESOURCE PLANNING

Exhibit 6.5 shows an overall model or procedure for constructing a human resource plan. We will examine each step in the process.

Determine Growth/Retrenchment Objectives

Notice the impact that outside factors in the environment, as well as market opportunities and the personal values of strategic managers, have in formulating an organization's growth objectives. Growth/retrenchment objectives drive the human resource plan. If an organization decides to scale back, retrench, or restructure, people will be let go. We saw this so much in the 1980s. Eastern Airlines, Ford, General Motors, Beatrice, and AT&T among others all went through major retrenchments. Even very successful companies, such as IBM and Harcourt Brace Jovanovich, experienced periods of retrenchment in the late 1980s.

If a company grows rapidly with little retrenchment, such as Apple, American Express, or NCNB did in the 1980s, employment will expand. Growth objectives are a key part of an organization's overall strategic plan. Almost all strategic plans deal with the size the company wishes to be in the future. For example, under Jack Welch, General Electric has decided it wants to be either number one or two in every industry it enters or it will either not enter it or will exit if already in it.[7] This is a key facet of GE's strategic plan. Managed growth is a popular catch word today because companies also can grow too fast. Two excellent examples are People Express and Air Florida. Both companies grew faster than their internal operations could handle and both died. There are costs to growth.

Growth/retrenchment objectives may be expressed in terms of sales, market share, asset size, return on investment, development of new products and services or selling off product lines, and development of new markets or abandonment of markets.

Human resource departments need to align the strategic human resource plan with the firm's growth/retrenchment strategy. A growth-oriented strategy will need to be supported by a human resource strategy of aggressive recruiting, hiring, and training. Many of the high-tech companies, such as Apple, NeXT, and Microsoft, were ill-prepared for their rapid growth and either could not find qualified personnel or had to pay premium prices to fulfill their needs. Since it is not always clear how fast a company might grow, the top executive team needs to be prepared with a set of contingency plans that allow a reasonable range of options.

....

| EXHIBIT 6.5 | A Model for Constructing a Human Resource Plan

```
            ┌─────────────────────────────────┐
            │  Personal Values and Norms of   │
            │  Strategic Managers and Internal│
            │  Organization Political Environment│
            └─────────────────────────────────┘
                           │
                           ▼
┌──────────────────┐   ┌─────────────────────────┐   ┌──────────────────┐
│ Social Economic  │──▶│ Determine Organizational │◀──│ Perceived Market │
│ Legal Political  │   │ Growth/Retrenchment      │   │ Opportunities    │
│ Environment      │   │ Objectives               │   │                  │
└──────────────────┘   └─────────────────────────┘   └──────────────────┘
                           │
                           ▼
                   ┌─────────────────────────┐
                   │ Determine Human         │
                   │ Resource Objectives     │
                   └─────────────────────────┘
                           │
                           ▼
┌──────────────────┐   ┌─────────────────────────┐   ┌──────────────────┐
│ Changes in       │──▶│ Examine the Job         │◀──│ Changes in       │
│ Technology       │   │ Structure and Design    │   │ Aspiration and   │
│                  │   │                         │   │ Skill Level      │
└──────────────────┘   └─────────────────────────┘   └──────────────────┘
                           │
                           ▼
                   ┌─────────────────────────┐
                   │ Examine the Future Skill│
                   │ Requirements by         │
                   │ Occupation or Job       │
                   │ Category                │
                   └─────────────────────────┘
                           │
                           ▼
                   ┌─────────────────────────┐
                   │ Estimate Human Resource │
                   │ Shortage or Surplus for │
                   │ Each Occupational       │
                   │ Category                │
                   └─────────────────────────┘
                           │
                           ▼
                   ┌─────────────────────────┐
                   │ Establish Specific      │
                   │ Objectives, Plans, and  │
                   │ Policies for Recruiting,│
                   │ Selection, Placement,   │
                   │ Training, Compensation, │
                   │ Promotions, Layoffs,    │
                   │ Terminations            │
                   └─────────────────────────┘
```

....

In contrast to the fast-growing firms are those facing retrenchment and declining markets. Here, human resource planning must deal with hard and unpleasant issues. The firm may want to act in a guarded way so as not to alert suppliers, customers, and employees of an impending cutback. It is important, though, that the strategic plan address these issues to minimize damage and make the best of a difficult situation. During the mid-1980s, companies in the farm equipment business, such as Deere and Company, faced massive layoffs. Deere and Company was more successful than most in maintaining its public image and critical human resources by proactive planning and executing the cutbacks in a humane and thoughtful way. By 1988–1989 the company had returned to high levels of profitability with a trimmed but efficient work force.

Divestitures and mergers provide a challenge for the human resource department. Merging two or more firms may involve cutbacks or at least reassignment.

EXHIBIT 6.6 Firm Strategy–Human Resource Strategy Relationship

Firm Strategy		Human Resource Strategy
Growth/Expansion	◄ — ►	Aggressive Hiring, Training, Promotions
Retrenchment	◄ — ►	Layoffs, Terminations, Early Retirement
Diversification	◄ — ►	New Corporate Staff Configuration, Promotions, Training, Hiring
Mergers, Acquistions	◄ — ►	Corporate Acculturation, Hiring or Laying Off
Divestitures	◄ — ►	Staff Reconfiguration, Layoffs, Reassignments
Differentiation	◄ — ►	Decentralized Hiring and Training
Low Cost Producer	◄ — ►	Cost Reduction, Wage Cuts, Efficiency Improvements
Luxury/High Quality	◄ — ►	Hiring Highly Skilled Personnel, Training, Special Compensation Plans

Conflicting corporate cultures need to be meshed and this needs to be part of the strategic plan.

Divestiture involves issues such as staff reconfiguration, reassignments, and layoffs. Union contracts and other labor agreements may need to be considered. Careful negotiations and agreements with the acquiring company need to be planned for and executed.

A product differentiation or divisionalization will require a decentralized approach in human resource issues. Hiring, recruiting, and training can often better be handled at the local level. Companywide standards, though, may be set at the corporate level.

A company may decide to fill a particular niche based on cost/price segmentation. A low-cost producer would require a human resource strategy that involved wage cuts, efficiency improvements, and perhaps staff reductions. At times companies are forced into this position by a competitor. Iowa Beef Processors, through its tough, some would say antiunion posture, forced other traditional high labor/cost producers, such as Hormel, to attempt wage cuts at its operations. The result was a bitter strike.

On the other hand, a company may choose to pursue a luxury, high quality niche. Special training, recruitment of highly skilled personnel, and a unique compensation plan will be of particular importance. Exhibit 6.6 summarizes the Firm Strategy–Human Resource Strategy connection.

These objectives are usually expressed in terms of a time frame or **planning horizon**—the length of time over which the objectives and the plan for accomplishing them will occur.

The planning horizon for growth in many organizations seldom exceeds fifteen years and is often expressed in terms of short-range, intermediate-range, and long-range periods. General Electric is widely known for preparing long-range forecasts for products needed in the next century. Auto companies, such as Ford, General Motors, and Chrysler also emphasize long-range objectives. As a rule of thumb, short-range is defined as a horizon of one year or less, intermediate-range as two to four years, and long-range as five to fifteen years. Often the long-range objectives are quite general, and the intermediate and short-range objectives are much more specific. This specificity is especially true of short-range or **operational** objectives.

Retrenchment objectives typically have a shorter time frame—often one year or less—since cutbacks cannot necessarily be easily predicted and often come unexpectedly. However, as we saw in the GM case in Chapter 1, the company has been planning for several years to permanently downsize its auto operations to a 33 percent market share.

Human resource professionals often play a role in helping to form growth/retrenchment objectives if the firm has adopted a strategic human resource approach, as we explained in Chapters 1 through 3. They can provide advice on how internal staffing needs will likely change as well as the likely availability of people with necessary skills.

Determine Human Resource Objectives

Once the organization's objectives are specified, communicated, and understood by all affected, then the personnel or human resource unit should *specify its objectives with regard to human resource utilization in the organization.* In developing these objectives, specific policies need to be formulated to address the following questions:

1. Shall we attempt to fill positions from within or by hiring individuals from the labor market?
2. Can we meet our commitments to affirmative action and equal employment opportunity?
3. How do our training and development objectives interface with our human resource planning objectives?
4. What union constraints do we face in human resource planning, and what policies should we develop to effectively handle these constraints?
5. What is our policy toward providing everyone in the organization with a meaningful, challenging job (job enrichment)? Will we continue to have some boring, routine jobs or should we eliminate them?
6. Can some positions and jobs be eliminated so that we can become more competitive?[8]
7. To what extent can we automate production and operations, and what shall we do about those displaced?
8. How do we ensure that we have a continuously adaptive and flexible work force?

These are not easy questions to answer, but they go to the heart of human resource planning. Imagine a large company such as Federal Express or IBM facing these questions. With far flung growing domestic and international operations,

| EXHIBIT 6.7 | Example Human Resource Objectives |

1. To develop and implement a pay for performance system by January 1, 1993 (large bank).
2. To achieve the staffing plans for the 1992–1994 period (information services company).
3. To reduce employment levels in current manufacturing operations by 10 percent per year from 1991–1993 (plastics manufacturer).
4. To implement a career development plan for all employees by July 1, 1992 (state agency).
5. To ensure that all supervisors receive sixty hours of classroom training prior to appointment of supervision by July 1, 1993 (utility).
6. To establish a computerized human resource skills inventory of all employees by April 1, 1991 (credit union).
7. To reduce employee turnover by 33 percent by January 1, 1992 (convenience store chain).
8. To develop and implement an aggressive program to hire older employees by September 1, 1994 (fast-food chain).
9. To achieve a 60/40 inside/outside mix for promotion during the next three years (large restaurant chain).

developing an overall human resource plan that systematically answers these questions is essential for managed growth.

Exhibit 6.7 shows some actual human resource objectives for various organizations. Notice the variety of specific human resource areas addressed: promotion, staffing, training and development, career development, employment levels, pay, and so on. A large firm with a well-developed human resource plan, such as Campbell's or American Express, would have a large number of human resource objectives spelled out at the corporate level and each division would have a list of its own subobjectives. These would continue down to the unit level as shown in Exhibit 6.8. Taking the objectives to this level is what makes them operational as shown in Exhibit 6.8. If the objectives are never taken to that level of specificity, they will never be achieved. Translating the objective to the unit level in the trenches is required for implementation.

Notice also that human resource objectives should be integrated with other functional area objectives. For example, training and development objectives should be geared toward and integrated with production, sales and skill needs. Staffing needs should be coordinated with forecasted growth in sales and so on. This kind of integration is not always easy to achieve but is necessary. Having human resources play the role of full partner in the strategic planning process will help to ensure better integration among functional areas.

Examine Job Design and Structure

In Chapter 8 we will examine the design of jobs. This is an important step in strategic human resource management. It is also an important step in human resource planning. Companies should not take the particular configuration of jobs that exist at a particular point in time as unchangeable; in fact, during the 1980s many

EXHIBIT 6.8   Integration of Human Resource Objectives

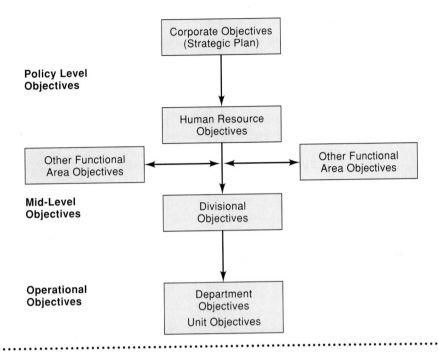

changes in job design and structure occurred. Think of how much the robotic welding process used in auto assembly differs from the hand welding of earlier times.

Computer-assisted design/computer assisted manufacturing (CAD/CAM), an infant industry, is already having a major effect on employment in some industries. For example, computer assisted design can greatly increase the work output of designers, such as design engineers in the auto industry, leading to a reduced work force with a very high increase in productivity for the remaining designers. Estimates show that CAD/CAM can improve productivity in an operation by 300 percent.[9]

The same effects can be experienced in the manufacturing end of the operation. Computer assisted manufacturing can greatly increase output per employee while reducing the need for employees. **Robotics**—the use of computer assisted machines to weld, cut, and so on—is an essential part of CAM, and we are likely to see a greater usage of robots in many disagreeable and dirty jobs and in jobs that require very close tolerances.

We have only begun to feel the effects of CAD/CAM. Sales for the CAD/CAM industry were about $700 million in 1981 and grew to $4 billion by 1986. CAD/CAM can be used in any organization to design, draft, and print out specifications of products. CAD/CAM can also use this information to generate instructions for the numerical control equipment needed to make these products. Some of the companies now using CAD/CAM include the main Prat & Whitney jet engine plant of United Technologies, International Harvester Company, Merck & Company, General Motors, Nissan Motors, and Koltanbar Engineering.

This very significant technological change will have a major impact on human resource plans developed by companies where CAD/CAM can be used. Most human resource planning is of an incremental nature from year to year. But CAD/CAM is likely to cause major changes in the human resource plan. Not only will fewer engineers, designers, and factory operators be needed in these companies, but the skill requirements for those hired will likely be changed. For example, people who can work with, as well as repair and maintain CAD/CAM, will be needed.

Therefore, examining jobs in light of new technological change will likely result in a reconfiguration of jobs in the organization. This will greatly impact staffing, training, hiring, and other aspects of the overall human resource plan.

A second major factor to be examined in this step are the aspirations and skill levels of employees. This issue deals with the motivation levels, work ethic, expectations, and job skills employees bring to a job. For years, the trend has been that employees want jobs that are challenging, responsible, and that provide opportunities for advancement and involvement—jobs which require higher skills. Company efforts at involvement and participation through various programs such as **quality circles, quality improvement programs** or **participative management programs** rest on the fundamental belief that employees want an enriched job experience that involves their minds as well as their hands. Motorola, Florida Power and Light, Ford, and Nissan are all companies that have heavily invested in programs of this nature, as we have pointed out elsewhere in this book. The changing nature of employee aspirations, expectations, and skills will cause companies to redefine and restructure jobs to some extent to reflect these changes.

The final issue to discuss in terms of technology and human resource planning is the shortages of trained personnel for engineering, computer, and other high-tech related occupations. Our analysis in Chapter 2 shows that, from a macro perspective, a tremendous growth in employment openings in these occupations is forecasted. These data also show the projected shortage of people to fill these occupations. From an employer's micro perspective, this means that it will be increasingly more difficult for organizations to attract and keep people with engineering, computer, and high-tech skills.

Another disturbing phenomenon related to this issue is the "eating your own seed corn" dilemma. Personnel shortages in engineering and computer occupations have caused many firms to hire university faculty members from engineering and computer information programs at salaries greatly in excess of the university salary. This, of course, leads to further shortages in the production of college-educated engineers and computer information specialists for the future.

Estimate Future Skill Requirements by Occupation or Job Category

Once the new job structure and design is determined, the next step is to examine the skills required in each job category. As noted above, job structure changes due to technology or other reasons will cause skill changes. Computers in cars require different skills for mechanics. Robot welders in auto assembly changed the skill mix in auto factories. Word processors and personal computers changed the skill requirements for secretaries. For example, one convenience store chain restructured district manager jobs by changing information analysis and reporting requirements and requiring that computers with modems be used.

Occupational skills change over time. Therefore, it is important at this stage that an organization have a complete, current listing of all occupational categories in the organization with explanatory job descriptions that specify the duties, skills, and qualifications required for each job. Such a **skills bank** should be computerized and easily accessed for promotion and training purposes. Estimations of how these skills will change need to be built into the human resource plan.

For example, during the late 1980s, a large wholesaler in the auto industry in the southeastern United States made a decision that each manager and clerical employee would have a personal computer on their desks for their use. This necessitated a massive training program to ensure that all clerical and managerial employees were computer literate so that the PCs would actually be used. The training need was forecasted well before the computers were ordered so that a training program could be established and funded, ready to be implemented once the computers were ordered. Key people were sent to off-site training programs so that they could train other employees once the computers arrived.

Forecasting future skill needs and preparing to fill those needs today is a critical feature of the strategic approach to human resource planning.

Estimate Human Resource Shortages or Surpluses for Each Occupational Category

This takes us to the fifth step in the human resource planning model. The human resource shortage or surplus should be estimated for each occupational and job category. Decisions should be made about what to do to deal with estimated surpluses or shortages in view of the organization's human resource utilization objectives. Exhibit 6.9 presents a procedure that is useful in estimating a given surplus or shortage for a particular occupation or job category. Note that this procedure ties in consideration of human resource objectives in filling jobs from within via internal promotions and organizational growth objectives.

If a surplus is predicted for an occupational category, the human resource plan needs to consider if these individuals will be discharged, temporarily laid off, transferred, or provided with a cash bonus for quitting, severance pay, or given early retirement. These decisions will probably be determined by the organization's overall human resource objectives for training and development.

If a shortage is predicted, then the organization must hire from the outside labor market if it expects to fill the resulting job vacancies. This decision may cause the organization to review its human resource objectives with regard to hiring from the outside market vis-à-vis other objectives. For example, if the organization finds that it has to pay a higher than expected wage to attract new people, it may decide to make do with fewer people and either schedule more overtime or subcontract out some of the work. In fact, many organizations do this at least on a temporary basis. Computer and software companies commonly used this practice in the mid-1980s. Of course, most construction contractors do this as a matter of course, as do most state departments of transportation for road maintenance and construction. Subcontracting and the use of overtime is especially desirable if the shortage is reviewed as temporary (six months or less).

Transition Matrix (Markov Analysis)

The changes or movements of human resources within an organization are called the "flows" of employees. One method of mathematically determining and depicting the flows of people in an organization is through use of Markov Analysis using a "transition matrix."[10] A simple example will help explain how this works. Assume

··

| **EXHIBIT 6.9** | A Procedure for Estimating Human Resource Shortage or Surplus for a Job or Occupational Category |

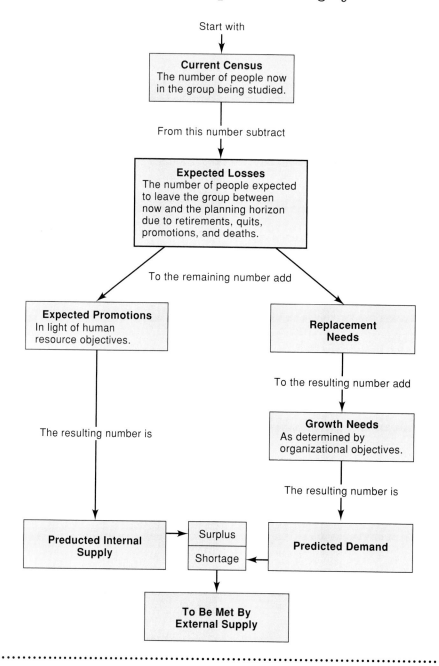

an organization had 100 Clerk Is and 50 Clerk IIs in 1992. As of 1994, only 80 percent of the original 100 Clerk Is may have remained in that position, and only 60 percent of the original 50 Clerk IIs may still be employed by the organization as Clerk IIs. The transition matrix on the following page shows this flow:

1992	1994	
	CLERK I	CLERK II
CLERK I	80% (s)	
CLERK II		60% (s)

(s) = stayed

Suppose that the following conditions actually existed as of 1994. Ten of the Clerk Is were promoted to Clerk II, ten of the Clerk Is left the organization, 15 of the Clerk IIs left the organization, and five were demoted to Clerk I. This flow analysis would appear as follows:

1992	1994			
	CLERK I	CLERK II	LEFT ORGANIZATION	TOTAL
CLERK I	80% stayed	10% promoted	10%	100%
CLERK II	10% demoted	60% stayed	30%	100%

This information could then be integrated into the human resource plan to chart a trend. These percentages are then used as indicators of the probability of transition in each category to project future supply movement. The staffing level in each category at the beginning of a planning period is multiplied by the transition probabilities within each category. Then the columns are summed to yield the future labor supply within job categories.

The analysis is somewhat complex and appears to be used mostly at larger firms. Weyerhaeuser, Eaton, and Corning have reported using it with mixed results.[11] Clearly more research and refinement is needed. However, we are likely to see more widespread use as computer software is refined to make it easier to use.

Computer Simulation

Computer simulation of future staffing needs and levels is becoming more common as Lotus 1-2-3 type software becomes available. Disney World uses a computer model to predict employment levels by job category at the theme park. This model is especially useful where seasonal factors affect employment.

Since forecasting contains an inherent amount of uncertainty, this technique and others are limited in their usefulness and application by the reliability and validity of the input data. The identification of key variables believed to affect future trends is very important. But selection of these key variables is not enough to ensure success. They must be measured accurately. The data must also be received in a timely fashion because old data are not as useful as new data. Organizations generally rely on past educational and job experience to predict future performance.

However, establishing valid criteria for this type of forecasting is difficult to do, much more difficult than using historical data or future requirements as a means of setting overall organizational objectives.[12] For example, if an organization wished to determine how many workers would be needed in a specific department in five years, a computer model (a representation of reality) might be utilized. Critical variables would have to be selected. These may include anticipated technological changes, outside labor force changes, required skills, absenteeism and turnover rates, past growth rates within the department, and so on. The model would then give the organization an estimated number of workers.

Not only could the firm obtain a single estimate, but it could also obtain, through manipulation or modification of the variables, estimates under varying situations and conditions. For example, Disney develops and runs various alternative future scenarios. How many employees would be needed if the quit rate doubled in certain jobs? How many would be needed if visitor growth rate to the park fell by 25 percent? Forecasting varying scenarios and using the model to manipulate various data under each scenario, makes computer simulation an extremely useful tool in human resource planning.

Linear Programming

Another technique to plan and forecast changes in employment by job level is linear programming. Linear programming, a method used to determine the optimal way of allocating scarce resources among competing demands, has been used by Lilien and Rao to describe the movements of people through the organization.[13] It is a quantitative method of analysis technique used for maximizing an objective function, expressed in the form of a mathematical equation (for example, MAX $z = \$10x + \$30y$), subject to some particular set of constraints, also expressed in mathematical notation (for example, $4x + 6y < 12$; $8x + 4y < 16$). There are several ways to solve linear programming problems, ranging from a graphic method for less complicated problems to computer utilization for more detailed or complex problems.

Linear programming has proven beneficial in areas such as aggregate planning, distribution, product mix decisions, and scheduling. Parsons used a combination of a matrix and demand analysis in allocating manpower.[14] Drandell worked along similar lines using exponential smoothing and regression analysis.[15] The U.S. Office of Personnel Management has used each of these in its manpower planning operations in the federal government.[16] Imagine the difficulty of planning to fill job vacancies and job growth in an organization as large as the U.S. government! Much of this work is decentralized in each agency, but centralized coordination and planning assistance is provided by the Office of Personnel Management. With over two million employees, human resource planning would be impossible in the federal government without these sophisticated models.

Delphi Techniques

Another technique used in planning and forecasting and recently used in human resource planning is the Delphi technique.[17] In the Delphi technique, a panel of experts is used to arrive at a consensus opinion about growth and scenarios. These experts come from numerous related fields, and they fill out a detailed questionnaire concerning the issue to be addressed. They also supply their own personal opinions on the issue. Later these experts receive a summary of the responses. If their opinion differs from the summary, they are asked to reconsider their original viewpoint. If they still hold the same opinion thereafter, they are asked to give an explanation for their stance. This process is repeated, usually three or four times, until a consensus prediction is reached. One important aspect of the Delphi technique lies in its anonymity. This helps to avoid "groupthink" and reduce conflict among the panel members.

Delphi processes can be used to derive overall trends in changing job demands. For example, the Florida Association of Independent Insurance Agents used the process to speculate changing job demands and characteristics in the offices of independent insurance agents. The Delphi technique developed scenarios of highly automated insurance offices using computers and word processors to handle record keeping, billing, and claims payments. These scenarios were "played out" to forecast changing needs in terms of skills and numbers of office employees, including the agent.

Summary of Forecasting Surpluses/Shortages and Changing Skill Needs

All of these techniques must be clearly integrated with the needs of line managers, who help supply the necessary data and help make decisions. Plans must be monitored and evaluated to ensure that they are meeting objectives. If necessary, plans must be redesigned as input data or forecasts change. Human resource planning is a dynamic process rather than a static event. In this regard, the human resource plan responds to changes in the organization's goals and its environment, as well as internal desires of work levels and line manager desires.

Establish Specific Objectives for Human Resource Functions

The final step in human resource planning is to establish specific objectives for each human resource function. Specific objectives should be established for everything from recruiting to terminating.

The overall human resource plan should drive the specific operational objectives established for each human resource function as shown in Exhibit 6.10. These then determine specific operational policies, programs, and activities developed to meet objectives. Both specific functional objectives and operating programs are integrated with the overall human resource plan by means of a feedback loop. If realistic objectives and program activities cannot be set or met under the human resource plan, then the plan should be modified. As seen in Exhibit 6.10, the entire resource plan is integrated with the organization's overall strategic plan.

Tie the Human Resource Plan to a Human Resource Information System

Tying the human resource plan to a human resource information system (HRIS) will better help the formulation and implementation of the plan. Even though we discussed human resource information systems in Chapter 4, we briefly review the concept here as it relates to human resource planning.

To be useful for planning, a HRIS should take on the dimensions of a decision support system. That is, it should be an on-line, easily accessible system of information available to human resource decision makers and planners. This ensures quick access of relevant information by people who need it. It also helps to ensure that the plan will be a living document—an organic/environmental plan—that can change. Human resource plans must be kept flexible to deal with environmental uncertainty and turbulence caused by rapidly changing international, technological, competitive, and economic conditions. Consider, for example, the NCNB case at the beginning of the chapter. The volatility of the Texas economy depends on the price of petroleum. The price of petroleum is heavily affected by conditions in the Middle

··

EXHIBIT 6.10 Specific Operational Objectives

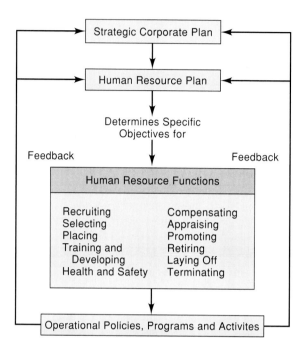

··

East. NCNB's human resource plan will need to be very responsive to changing conditions. Planning for NCNB will need to be coordinated but decentralized and integrated through a good HRIS. Managers will need to have flexible hiring plans that can change quickly as the need for bank employees at various levels changes. Plans for training will need to be dynamic. Promotion plans will need to be flexible. Even though NCNB is planning for rapid growth in the Texas market, contingency plans should be in place for layoffs, terminations, and early retirements in case the economy of Texas suffers further reversals.

A good HRIS with a strong decision support system will help any organization to keep its human resource plan viable, flexible, and meaningful.

Consider Local Area Impact

The final issue affecting human resource planning decisions by organizations is the fact that the law in many states now requires companies to notify local governments of major employment decisons. At the national level, the WARN Act makes it mandatory that a company that is considering closing a plant provide advance notice to all concerned units where the plant is located.[18] The law requires that this advanced notification must occur 90 days before closing. The idea behind this advance notification is to give employees and local government units time to plan for the dislocations that will result from the closing. For example, social welfare services, unemployment compensation, and employment counseling and placement organiza-

HR CHALLENGES •

Union Oil Company

The Union Oil Company is one organization that has attempted to integrate human resource planning and human resource information systems into its strategic corporate planning process. Union Oil has found that human resource planning is joining financial and operations planning as an essetial element of its long-term planning efforts. The questions raised with regard to human resource planning were many, but out of its efforts, Union Oil has developed five programs.

The first program is an extensive **data bank**. The company found that the employee information on file was insufficient, and the company needed more than just a typical skills inventory. The emphasis is placed on fact versus what the employees say about themselves in addition to information on skills, career interests, and nonjob-related activities. All the employee information is easily retrievable from the data bank for use by management. Each year, employees correct and update their profiles. Not only does this enable Union Oil to fulfill government requirements that information be correct, but it also keeps management informed about other employee-relations matters, such as equal employment opportunities, labor relations, and employee benefit plans.

The second program is a mathematical **simulations model** of the changing organization. Union Oil believes this enables the company to keep current and helps to identify potential problems. The organization's work force is broken down by age, function, geographic distribution, status, and skills categories. The model also considers the flow of employees into and out of the organization and takes into account both operational relationships and the aging process. Using assumptions applicable to each category, the model predicts what the organization and all its components will be like during the next five years. When compared to actual results, the model's trend predictions have been accurate within ±5 percent. To aid in seeing how policy changes will affect the company, a satellite model allows executives to study these outcomes and obtain the estimated cost of such changes.

A third program resulting from the human resource plan are its forecasts for company **recruiting**. The simulation model provides estimated attrition rates. These are combined with the company's human resource needs, which relate output-per-employee trends to the company's long-term operating goals. Corporate needs are determined by comparing the ratio of trends to those in operations.

The fourth program is a plan for **succession**. Unit heads, on an annual basis, are provided with forecasts that predict the number of openings to occur in the next five years. This report compares 20 percent of the previous year's prediction with the number of openings that actually occurred. It also lists each member of the particular unit who will reach the average retirement age of 62 within the forecast period. This program has proven accurate enough to be credible. These forecasts become the basis for succession planning. A planning group then utilizes the forecasts to focus its attention on a particular position that has been selected to plan for successors.

The final program allows Union Oil to **relate output to goals**. This model, using multiple regression analysis, helps to determine the mix and weighting of statistical and economic data employed. The major force, however, is the relationship between output-per-employee trends and overall operating goals. In 1972, this model predicted a 15 percent decline in the number of marketing employees. In actuality, the oil crisis and other events increased the reduction to 25 percent. A 1975 update forecasted a further decline of 15 percent by 1979.

Union Oil does not claim that the model is infallible; the company recognizes its defects. With subjectivity and intuition playing an important role in human resource planning, many managers have raised questions about the degree of quantification in the planning process. But experience with the system has helped even these managers to recognize that the simulation is a tool, not a final product. One limitation that has been recognized is that the model has extreme difficulty placing a dollar value on an employee's service to the organization. In these instances, using a scenario or the Delphi technique have proven more successful.

SOURCE: Adapted from William E. Bright, "How One Company Manages Its Human Resources," *Harvard Business Review*. January–February, 1976, pp. 81–93.

tions are all affected by a major plant closing in an area. Local and state governments were actively involved in recruiting new industry during the 1980s. It follows, then, that they believe they have a stake or substantial interest in the decisions made by local industry. We are more likely to see more effort in this area as the federal law takes full effect.

• • • • • • • • •

MANAGEMENT GUIDELINES

So we see that human resource planning is an important and fundamental aspect to strategic human resource management. Such planning helps to establish a *proactive* approach to human resource management and it helps to integrate human resources with corporate-level strategic planning. Furthermore, it helps to ensure that specific objectives, programs, policies, and activities of each human resource function are fully integrated.

While human resource planning is not easy—especially in larger organizations—the use of computer models and other mathematical techniques help to make it a more manageable process. The following management guidelines should be observed during the human resource planning process.

1. The human resource plan should be fully integrated with the overall organizational strategic plan, especially the firm's growth objectives.

2. Outside influences of economic conditions, technology, the labor market, and so on should be given adequate consideration when developing the human resource plan.

3. Changes in job design should be explicitly recognized in the plan; the plan should not assume that the structure of jobs in the future will be the same as today.

4. The plan should explicitly realize that staffing levels should be based on increasing productivity in order for the firm to remain cost competitive. Just because a job becomes vacant does not mean that it should automatically be filled. Perhaps it should be eliminated or combined with another job.

5. Estimating future shortages or surpluses by job or skill category should use computer techniques and quantitative models as appropriate in order to better manage the process.

6. The specific operational objectives of each functional area in personnel should be integrated with the overall human resource plan.

7. Specific personnel programs, policies, and activities should be integrated with the specific functional objectives.

8. The human resource plan should involve heavy amounts of line management input at all points in the process.

9. The human resource plan should be kept flexible and adaptable so it can change as conditions change.

QUESTIONS FOR REVIEW

1. What is a strategic human resource plan? Why is it important?

2. What impact do outside forces have on the strategic human resource plan (for example, labor market, technology, economic conditions, and so on)?

3. Why should the human resource plan be integrated with the overall organizational strategic plan? How can this integration be achieved?

4. Outline an overall model or procedure for developing a strategic human resource plan.

5. List and define some quantitative techniques for estimating a surplus or shortage in a job category or occupation.

6. Why is it important to use the computer and quantitative techniques in human resource planning?

7. How can specific human resource functional objectives be linked with the human resource plan? Why is this linkage important?

8. Why should specific human resource programs, policies, and activities be linked with human resource objectives?

9. Why should a human resource plan be kept flexible?

10. Why should line managers be involved in helping to formulate a human resource plan?

CASE: Polaroid—Hard Landing[19]

The day after Thanksgiving in 1948, a new camera went on sale at a Boston department store. Worried it wouldn't sell well, nervous officials of the small company that made it cut the price to $89.75 from $95 at the last minute. They thought the 56 cameras they had produced might be gone by Christmas. The cameras sold out that day.

After struggling more than a decade, Polaroid Corp.—run by a young scientist named Edwin H. Land—had a big winner. Its instant camera developed photos on the spot, in 60 seconds. It was a technological marvel, and it captivated America.

As Polaroid's laboratories made one breakthrough after another in the 1950s and 1960s, the company grew rapidly. By the early 1970s, its stock was one of the highest highfliers, selling at more than 100 times annual earnings. Polaroid was more than just another success story, it was an icon to American ingenuity. Land exhorted his em-

ployees, "Do not undertake a program unless the goal is manifestly important and achievement is nearly impossible."

The Downhill Slide

But in the late 1970s, things started to go wrong. Polaroid's market matured. Its visionary founder lost his vision. Newer, better gadgets captured the public's fancy. In 1988 the company became a takeover target. Shamrock Holdings Inc., a television and radio concern owned by the Roy E. Disney family, tried to buy Polaroid for $2.28 billion.

Polaroid's history is, in some ways, the latest twist in the decline of American industry. But unlike the auto and steel producers, Polaroid isn't an old-line manufacturer. It is one of the earliest postwar high-tech pioneers, a nonunion company lauded for enlightened employee relations. Yet, its heady growth has given way to hard times for similar reasons. In becoming big, the company became bureaucratic. The Japanese have emerged as industry innovators—in Polaroid's case, indirectly, with 35mm and video cameras. Instead of adding jobs, Polaroid is cutting them.

Missing Creative Spark

Worse yet, the company has lost its creative spark. "Polaroid hasn't had a breakthrough product for years," says Peter Wensberg, a former Polaroid executive. Despite lavish spending on research, efforts to diversify have largely flopped. "The problem for so many big companies is that they don't have an encore," says Thomas V. DiBacco, a professor of business history at American University. "No company can stay very long in a staid position. A lot of firms several decades old, what do they do after they achieve success? It's one of the biggest dilemmas, trying to find the next stage."

Some other companies have had trouble finding the next stage. Avon Products Inc.'s sales have languished because its door-to-door sales strategy faltered as so many women began to work outside of the home, and Nike Inc. stubbed its toe when smaller competitors managed to sell athletic shoes as fashion items.

Future Hopes

"Polaroid has been very myopic," comments Alex Henderson, an analyst at Prudential-Bache Securities. He says Polaroid's executives have failed to commercialize the good technology in its laboratories. "They limited their definition of what markets they're in. . . . It's the 'not-invented-here' syndrome," he adds. He suggest that Polaroid's imaging technology might be valuable in developing products for the computer publishing and medical-diagnostics markets, but only if the company enters joint ventures with companies offering expertise in those areas.

Exactly what Land thinks of all this is not known. He has cut all ties with the company since retiring in 1982, and he doesn't give interviews. But for him, Polaroid has always been far more than a business. In response to a question at an annual meeting he once said, "The bottom line? The bottom line is in Heaven!"

Polaroid was Land's life mission. By all accounts a genius, he quit Harvard University in 1932, one semester before graduating, to start a research lab. By aligning microscopic crystals in a specifc pattern, he earlier had developed the first synthetic polarizing material, which sharply reduced glare when light passed through it. That feat had long eluded scientists.

Initially, this discovery was a technology in search of a product. Land tried to peddle it for car headlights, but auto makers rejected it. It was used, mundanely, for sunglasses and desk lamps. Though business was lousy, a steady stream of discoveries came out of Polaroid's labs. Some critics believed that the company, in its early days, resembled a research project run by a group of graduate students.

During World War II, Polaroid survived on military work and during that period came inspiration. While he was taking photos in 1943, Land's three-year-old daughter asked why she couldn't see them right away.

Perfect Timing

The instant camera took several years to develop and, ironically, didn't use Mr. Land's polarizing invention but rather other technologies from Polaroid's labs. But it was the right product at the right time. Americans were just becoming addicted to instant gratification. The baby boom had begun, and proud parents wanted to photograph their growing families. So what if instant cameras and film cost more? Postwar America was increasingly affluent.

Under Land, a savvy showman, Polaroid embraced live television to sell cameras. Entertainers such as Steve Allen took photos in front of the audience. "The essence of TV is dramatization. We had viewers holding their breath. Would it work? Every now and then, it didn't, but that was OK," says Joseph Daly, an executive at DDB Needham Worldwide ad agency, which had the Polaroid account for 30 years. "Never was a product more suited for TV."

It was a period of intense excitement. Many Polaroid employees worked six days a week—and loved every minute. "It wouldn't be unusual to work around the clock a few days in a row. Nobody got too tired because it was exciting. We'd sleep on a lab table or office desk or on the floor," recalls Richard Young, a former executive who joined the company in the early 1950s as assistant research director. Polaroid hands held Land in awe, and for good reason—his 533 patents are second only to Thomas Edison's 1,093.

Polaroid sold its one millionth camera in 1956 and went public the next year. In 1960, sales hit $99.4 million; in 1970 they hit $444 million.

Crowning Achievement

In 1972 came Land's crowning achievement: the pocket-sized SX-70 camera. He was featured on the covers of Life magazine ("A genius and his magic camera") and Time ("Here comes those great new cameras"). His Polaroid stock was valued at more than $700 million.

The SX-70 scored a great sales success, but Polaroid's stock plummeted because the huge expense of developing the camera held down profit growth. Adding to the pressure, Kodak ended Polaroids' monopoly by entering the instant-camera market in 1976. Polaroid promptly sued, charging patent infringement, but the case would not be decided in its favor until 1985.

Then came Land's greatest flop: Polavision instant movies, which were introduced in 1977. The camera cost too much at $700, didn't have sound, and took only 2-½ minutes of film at a time. Land had the right idea but the wrong technology. The Japanese had something better: video recorders, whose hours-long tapes could be reused and played back on a TV set.

Even worse, another Japanese product—klutz-proof 35mm cameras—took America by storm in the late 1970s and early 1980s. One-hour photo shops made instant cameras moot. From a high of $9.4 million in 1978, Polaroid's instant-camera sales plunged to $3.5 million in 1985. Also during those years, the company profits fared just as badly, skidding from a record $118.4 million on sales of $1.38 billion to $36.9 million on sales of $1.30 billion.

Ignoring the Outside World

Polaroid's management was too inbred to notice that the world was changing, critics say. "Here's a company that had a field to itself for a long, long time. Many executives spent their entire careers on internal problems and technology. Some didn't consider it important to take a close look at the outside world," says Murray Swindell, a former marketing executive and one of many officials who departed in frustration in the early 1980s.

In 1982, at age 73, Land himself left Polaroid, partly because the Polavision flop had forced him to share power and partly to pursue basic research on how the brain sees color. Land's successors—William J. McCune, Jr., now 73, who was named chief executive in 1980 and is now chairman, and I. MacAllister Booth, 56, who became chief executive in 1986—have spent their careers at Polaroid.

The company now finds itself in a strategic bind with no easy way out. Some analysts and former executives think that the company should try to diversify, while others think that it should stick close to home.

But the major problem remains: Instant photography has lost its magic, despite the introduction of an improved, third-generation camera, Spectra, in 1986. Camera sales picked up a bit, but last year they declined again because 35mm cameras are improving even more.

The 35mms "have automatic everything: auto focus, auto load, auto rewind, auto zoom," says Jack Crunkleton, the general manager of Camera Shop, Inc., an Eastern chain. "Affluent people still count on 35mm for better-quality pictures. It will be hard for Polaroid to get back to the growth days."

Diversification

Polaroid has decided, belatedly, to enter the convention-film market. "There's a lot of value in the Polaroid name," Swindell says. "There are any number of products we could have marketed . . . . But we couldn't get Land's attention. He preferred to stick to instant photography." The move into a market that Mr. Land steadfastly avoided symbolizes the company's shift away from his notion that instant photography is the only photography worth pursuing.

Polaroid itself argues that instant photography isn't just a quaint gimmick of the past, and it is working on a next-generation system that combines electronics with the use of heat to develop film. The technology could be used to make photographic prints of images stored electronically and initially viewed on computer or TV screens. "Instant imaging will become the dominant form [of photography], surpassing conventional film. . . . We do not want to be just 'that other form of imaging'; we want to be No. 1," a spokesperson says.

Employment Cuts

But that won't be easy. "Japanese expertise in the imaging area will really put a lot of pressure on a company like Polaroid," says Young, the former executive.

In 1988, Polaroid, under pressure from Shamrock's takeover proposal, announced more job cuts—employment dropped 12,500 from a high of nearly 21,000 in 1978—and set up an employee stock-ownership plan holding 14 percent of its stock. Interestingly, in the midst of down-sizing, Polaroid was rated one of the best 100 companies to work for.

More than its forays into new technology, Polaroid's best defense against Shamrock may be its legal victory in the Kodak case. Polaroid is awaiting a trial on the damages, and its shareholders might hesitate to sell their stock too soon. The company is seeking $5.7 billion: analysts estimate it will eventually get $1 billion to $2 billion.

"That would give them a lot of flexibility to make acquisitions, spend more on research and development and put more into advertising," says Brenda Lee Landry, an analyst at Morgan Stanley & Company.

QUESTIONS

1. What has been Polaroid's overall growth strategy? How has this affected its human resource planning and strategy?

2. Whose fault is it when employment falls as it has at Polaroid from 21,000 to 12,500? What responsibility, if any, do operative employees have?

3. Why would employees work virtually around the clock as they did in the early days of Polaroid?

4. Compare and contrast the human resource plan Polaroid had in the 1950s, 1960s, and 1970s with its plan for the 1980s. How do cutbacks and retrenchment change a human resource plan? Could these cuts have been avoided given Land's basic strategy and dominance in the firm? If so, how?

5. What other companies do you know of that failed to mature to other growth stages with new products after the initial product played out? What causes this to happen?

· · · · · · · · · · · · · · · · · ·
ADDITIONAL READINGS

Anthony, William P. "Get to Know Your Employees: The Human Resource Information System." *Personnel Journal.* April 1977, pp. 179–183.

Baker, C. Richard. "Personnel and Organization Structures Factors in Planning." *Managerial Planning.* May–June 1977, pp. 26–28.

Bartholomew, David J., and Andrew F. Forbes. *Statistical Techniques for Manpower Planning* (New York: Wiley, 1979).

Branch, P., and E. Mansfield. "Firm's Forecasts of Engineering Employment." *Management Science* 28, February 1982, pp. 156–160.

Burack, E. H. "Corporate Business and Human Resource Planning Practices: Strategic Issues and Concerns." *Organization Dynamics* 15. Summer 1986, pp. 73–87.

Burack, E. H. "Human Resource Planning and Labor Market Information—Need for Change, Now." *Public Personnel Management* 7. September 1978, pp. 279–286.

Burack, E. H. *Planning for Human Resources.* Lake Forest, IL: Brace-Park Press, 1989.

Burack, E. H., and N. J. Mathys. *Human Resource Planning.* 2nd ed. Lake Forest, IL: Brace-Park Press, 1987.

Burack, Elmer. *Creative Human Resource Planning and Applications.* Englewood Cliffs, NJ: Prentice-Hall, 1988.

Butensky, C. F., and O. Harari. "Models vs. Reality. An Analysis of Twelve Human Resource Planning Systems." *Human Resource Planning* 6, no. 1 (1983), pp. 11–25.

Cascio, W., ed. *Human Resource Planning, Employment and Placement.* Washington D.C.: The Bureau of National Affairs, 1989.

Clark, Harry L., and Dona R. Thurston. *Planning Your Staffing Needs: A Handbook for Personnel Workers.* U.S. Civil Service Commission. Bureau of Policies and Standards (order through Superintendent of Documents). Washington D.C.: U.S. Government Printing Office, 1977, p. 360.

Courtney, R. S "A Human Resource Plan That Helps Management and Employees Prepare for the Future." *Personnel* 63, no. 5. May 1986, pp. 32–40.

Deckhard, N. S., and K. W. Lessey. "A Model for Understanding Management Manpower: Forecasting and Planning." *Personnel Journal* 54 (1975), pp. 169–173+.

Dill, W. R., D. P. Gavar, and W. C. Weber. "Models and Modeling for Manpower Planning." *Management Science* 13 (1966), pp. B142–B167.

Drandell, M. "A Composite Forecasting Methodology for Manpower Planning Using Objective and Subjective Criteria." *Academy of Management Journal* 18 (1975), pp. 510–519.

Gatewood, R. D., and B. W. Rockmore. "Combining Organizational Manpower and Career Development Needs: An Operational Human Resource Planning Model." *Human Resource Planning* 9, no. 3 (1986), pp. 81–96.

Gehrman, D. B. "Objective Based Human Resource Planning." *Personnel Journal* 60. December 1981, pp. 942–946.

Greer, Charles R., and Daniel Armstrong. "Human Resource Forecasting and Planning: A State of the Art Investigation." *Human Resource Planning* 3, no. 2. April 1980, pp. 67–78.

Henderson, J. C., et al. "Integrated Approach for Manpower Planning in the Service Sector." *Omega* 10, no. 1 (1982), pp. 61–73.

Hill, A. W. "Strategic Human Resource Planning: How to Succeed." *Management Review* 75. November 1986, pp. 79–80.

Hollmann, R. W. "Strategic Planning." *Personnel Administrator.* March 1989, pp. 97–100.

Hopkins, D. S. P. "Models for Affirmative Action Planning and Evaluation." *Management Science* 26. October 1980, pp. 994–1006.

Kanter, Rosabeth M. "Frontiers for Strategic Human Resource Planning and Management." *Human Resource Management* 22. Spring/Summer 1983, pp. 9–21.

Kerr, Clark, and Paul D. Staudohan, eds. *Economics of Labor in Industrial Society.* San Francisco: Jossey-Bass, 1986.

Klein, E. "Determinants of Manpower Utilization and Availability." *International Labour Review* 122. March–April 1983, pp. 183–195.

McAvoy R., and D. M. Hubsch. "Manpower Planning and Corporate Objectives: Two Points of View." *Management Review* 70. August 1981, pp. 55–59.

Manzini, A. O., and J. D. Gridley. "Human Resource Planning for Mergers and Acquisitions: Preparing for the 'People Issues' That Can Prevent Merger Synergies." *Human Resource Planning* 9, no. 2 (1986), pp. 51–57.

Miller, E. L., S. Beechler, B. Bhatt, and R. Nath. "The Relationship between the Global Strategic Planning Process and the Human Resource Management Function." *Human Resource Planning* 9, no. 2 (1986), pp. 9–29.

Mirengoff, Wm. *CETA, Accomplishments, Problems, Solutions: A Report by the Bureau of Social Science Research, Inc.* Kalamazoo, MI: W. E. Upjohn Institute for Employment Research, 1982.

Morlock, J. "Impact and Implications of Changing Federal Manpower Policy on the Administration and Implementation of Social Manpower Programs." *Labor Law Journal* 32. August 1981, pp. 514–518.

Morrison, M. H. "The Aging of the US Population: Human Resource Implications." *Monthly Labor Review* 106. May 1983, pp. 13–19.

Muczyk, J. P. "Comprehensive Manpower Planning." *Mangerial Planning* 30. November/December 1981, pp. 36–41.

Niehaus, Richard. *Computer-Assisted Human Resources Planning.* New York: Wiley, 1979.

Niehaus, R. J., ed. *Strategic Human Resource Planning Applications.* The Philadelphia Conference proceedings. 1987.

Nkomo, S. M. "Human Resource Planning and Organizational Performance: On Exploratory Analysis." *Strategic Management Journal* 8 (1987), pp. 387–392.

Nkomo, S. M. "The Theory and Practice of HR Planning: The Gap Still Remains." *Personnel Administrator* 31. August 1986, pp. 71–84.

Rothwell, W. J., and Kazanas, H. C. *Strategic Human Resources Planning and Management.* Englewood Cliffs, NJ: Prentice-Hall, 1989.

Rush, I. C. "Strategic Planning for Human Resources." *Business Quarterly* 46. Summer 1981, pp. 40–43.

Russ, C. F., Jr. "Manpower Planning Systems." *Personnel Journal* 61. January 1982, pp. 40–45.

Scarborough, N., and T. W. Zimmerer. "Human Resources Forecasting: Why and Where to Begin." *Personnel Administration* 27. May 1982, pp. 55–61.

Smith, W. J., and F. A. Zeller. "Impact of Federal Manpower Policy and Programs on the Employment and Earnings Experiences of Special Problem Groups of the Unemployed: A Critical Historical Overview." *Labor Law Journal* 32. August 1981, pp. 518–528.

Strauss, J. S., and E. H. Burack. "The Human Resource Planning Professional: A Challenge in Change." *Human Resource Planning* 6, no. 1 (1983), pp. 1–9.

Subramaniam, S. "Engineering Manpower Planning in an Airline." *Long Range Planning.* August 1977, pp. 56–60.

Sylvia, Robert A. "TOSS: An Aerospace System That's GO for Manpower Planning." *Personnel.* January–February 1977, pp. 56–64.

Thomsen, D. J. "Keeping Track of Managers in a Large Corporation." *Personnel* 53. November 1976, pp. 23–30.

Ulrich, David. "Human Resources Planning As a Competitive Edge." *Human Resource Planning* 9, no. 2 (1986), pp. 41–50.

Valliant, Richard, and George Milkovich. "Comparison of Semi-Markov and Markov Models in a Personnel Forecasting Application." *Decision Sciences.* April 1977, pp. 465–477.

Zanakis, S. H., and M. W. Maret. "Markovian Goal Programming Approach to Aggregate Manpower Planning." *Journal of the Operational Research Society* 32. January 1981, pp. 55–63.

NOTES

1. John Helyar, "Hard-Charging NCNB Seizes a Large Share of Banking in Texas," *Wall Street Journal,* August 1, 1988, pp. 1, 7; Lenard M. Apcar, "First RepublicBank Bailout May Damage Capital-Raising Efforts by Other Banks," *Wall Street Journal,* August 1, 1988, p. 3; Rick Christie and Martha Brannigan, "Head On Clash: Expansionist Banker Faces Traditionalist in C & S Takeover Try," *Wall Street Journal,* April 20, 1989, pp. 1, 6; Martha Brannigan, "NCNB, C & S/Sovran Agree to a $4.26 Billion Merger," *Wall Street Journal,* July 22, 1991, pp. 3, 10; and Martha Brannigan, "NCNB-C & S Merger Will Stir Up South: Regional Powerhouse May Force Rivals to Merge," *Wall Street Journal,* July 23, 1991, p. 2.

2. Albert Karr, "Labor Letter," *Wall Street Journal,* May 17, 1988, p. 1.

3. Brenton R. Schlender, "Shedding His Shyness, John Scully Promotes Apple—and Himself," *Wall Street Journal,* August 18, 1988, pp. 1, 8.

4. Eddie Smith, "Strategic Business Planning and Human Resources: Part I," *Personnel Journal* 61, no. 8, August 1982, pp. 606–610.

5. Elmer H. Burach, "Corporate Business and Human Resources Planning Practices: Strategic Issues and Concerns," *Organization Dynamics* 15, Summer 1986, pp. 73–87.

6. Richard P. Nathan, "Clearing Up the Confusion over Block Grants," *Wall Street Journal,* November 3, 1981, p. 3.

7. Russell Mitchell and Judith Dobrzynski, "Jack Welch: How Good a Manager?" *Business Week*, December 14, 1987, pp. 92–103.

8. Thomas M. Hunt and George Stalk, "Working Better and Faster with Fewer People," *Wall Street Journal*, May 15, 1987, p. 14.

9. Robert J. Koyma, "Low Cost CAD/CAM Units: Major Growth Area?" *Management Information Systems Weekly*, June 3, 1981, p. 4.

10. K. M. Rowland and M. G. Sovereign, "Markov Chain Analysis of Internal Manpower Supply," *Industrial Relations* 9, 1969, pp. 88–89.

11. P. F. Buller and W. R. Maki, "A Case History of a Manpower Planning Model," *Human Resource Planning* 4, 1981, pp. 129–138; and J. A. Hooper and R. F. Catalanello, "R. F. Markov Analysis Applied to Forecasting Technical Personnel," *Human Resource Planning* 4, 1981, pp. 41–45.

12. William P. Anthony, "Get You Know Your Employee—The Human Resource Information System," *Personnel Journal*, April 1977, pp. 179–183, 202.

13. Gorg L. Lilian and Ambar G. Rao, "A Model for Manpower Management," *Management Science* 21, no. 12, 1975, pp. 1447–1457.

14. James A. Parsons, "Manpower Allocation to Meet Cyclic Requirements," *Journal Systems Management* 27, no. 6, 1976, pp. 26–27.

15. Milton Drandell, "A Composite Forecasting Methodology for Manpower Planning Utilizing Objective and Subjective Criteria," *Academy of Management Journal* 18(3), 1975, pp. 510–519.

16. G. A. Keenay, R. W. Morgan, and K. H. Ray, "An Analytical Model for Company Manpower Planning," *Operational Research Quarterly* 28(4) ii, 1977, pp. 983–995.

17. Andre L. Nelberq, Andrew H. Van de Ven, and David H. Gustafson, *Group Techniques for Program Planning: A Guide to Nominal Group and Delphi Processes* (Glenview, IL: Scott-Foresman, 1975).

18. David Israel and Stephen P. Beiser, "Plant Closings and Layoffs Follow Special Rules," *HRMagazine*, July 1991, p. 71.

19. Lawrence Ingrossio, "How Polaroid Went from Highest Flier to Takeover Target," *Wall Street Journal*, August 12, 1988, pp. 1, 16; Lawrence Ingrossio, "Kodak's Motion Denied by Judge in Polaroid Case," *Wall Street Journal*, August 12, 1988, p. 16; Ronald Grover, "Maybe I'll Raid You—And Maybe I Won't," *Business Week*, September 5, 1988, p. 25; and K. H. Hammonds, "Why Polaroid Must Remake Itself Instantly," *Business Week*, September 19, 1988, pp. 66–72.

7

Job Analysis

Job analysis is one of the most important functions of a human resource manager. Performance appraisal, job design, personnel selection, employee training, and career development and planning are among the many activities that depend upon the information gathered in the job analysis.[1] The process of systematically collecting information about jobs, for any of those purposes, is referred to as a **job analysis**. A job analysis results in two important documents: the **job description** (which describes the activities of a job) and the **job specification** (which describes the qualifications required to perform the job). The job analysis will be discussed in detail later in the chapter.

• • • • • • • • •
CHAPTER OBJECTIVES

As a result of studying this chapter, you should be able to

1. Discuss the strategic choices regarding job analysis that are available to organizations.

2. Define job analysis and discuss its relationship to job descriptions and job specifications.

3. Discuss the various uses and types of job analysis information.

4. Describe how managers or personnel specialists collect the data for a job analysis.

5. Discuss the relationship between organizational strategy, the subsequent emphasis on certain human resource activities, and the job analysis methods appropriate for specific human resource activities.

6. Describe the steps involved in a typical job analysis.

CASE: People Express[2]

From its inception in 1981, People Express and its CEO, Donald C. Burr, have gone against the traditional policies on how to run an airline. Using the 1978 airline deregulation as his opportunity to create a new type of airline, Burr had, by the end of 1985, built People Express into the fifth largest passenger carrier in the United States with revenue of $978 million and over 3,800 employees.

However, by the summer of 1986, the man who Harvard Business school chose as the case study of a 1980s-style entrepreneur faced some difficult decisions. In 1985, People Express recorded a loss of $27.5 million and had lost 205 pilots (18 percent of People's total), 419 flight attendants (15 percent of its total), and 4 managing officers. By 1986, People Express was acquired by Texas International and ceased to exist as a separate airline. Yet its unique approach to assigning jobs within the company provides many examples for study.

Job Assignments and Descriptions

Using words such as "worker participation" and "responsibility-sharing," Burr's strategy was to avoid hiring "organization" men and women in his company. In fact, personality tests were used to weed out potential employees who would not fit in with People's philosophy. Although his "humanistic" approach seemed to be a fresh idea, it was, in fact, based on Douglas McGregor's *The Human Side of Enterprise*, which was published over a quarter of a century ago.

The employees at People were divided into three types of managers: customer service managers (flight attendants), flight managers (pilots) and maintenance managers. All three types of managers were supervised by managing officers.

In addition to their primary responsibilities, each employee was responsible to do work in support functions. Employees would be rotated into such areas as recruiting, training, marketing, and accounting. This job rotation was perceived as a way to not only reduce the amount of overhead cost, but also to teach the employees about every aspect of the operation. "Everybody is a teacher and a learner," said team manager Jim Miller, referring to the 3,800-strong work force. "Training is a very, very big part of People Express. We're in the business of training leaders, so we have no training budget—whatever it takes is what we'll spend."

This "cross-utilization," as Burr called it, resulted in pilots working as schedule drafters, cargo specialists, or even inventory managers. Even though the government restricts the flying time allowed for pilots to be in the air to 30 hours per week, it was not unusual for the pilots to work up to 70 hours a week when these support functions were included.

People's managing officers were also included in the rotation of responsibilities. "It's good to see what our people and our customers have to put up with out there," said Jack Browning, who left his role as a managing officer once a week to check in customers.

People Express contracted out such work as aircraft maintenance, baggage handling, and telephone reservations so that the professional staff were separated from what Burr called a "blue-collar value system . . . prone to unionization."

People claimed that although job rotation has high initial costs, the company would benefit enormously in the long run. "It makes our people more well rounded," said Miller. "They'll make more intelligent decisions, certainly more than specialists will." By having the flight attendants work behind the scenes, the attendants realized how all the different functions of the company operated. "One of the beautiful things about job rotation is that when our flight attendants fly all day long and the company does not make any money, they know why. They want customers on board."

People also believed that it was beneficial to have the pilots work in other areas after their 30 hours of flying time had been accumulated. "Our pilots know how to save fuel—thank God, they know what that means." Miller continued. "They know what we're paying for fuel, too. They're the ones who go out there and buy it." The pilots also had the responsibility in their support duties to direct where and when the aircrafts were being sent into service.

Job Specifications

Although they perceived job rotation as a way of cutting costs and increasing awareness of different aspects of the organization, People also acknowledged the drawbacks. "There are some costs with job rotation from people making mistakes because they haven't done the function before, but these costs are minute. And they're minute because we keep things simple. It's one of our corporate precepts: Keep things simple and understandable," stated Robbie Benson, the human resource general manager.

People's philosophy was to try and make the work procedures as easy as possible to learn so that managers could rotate from department to department without disrupting the operation. The trainers were fellow managers within the department who readily shared their experience. By making each position as easy to learn as any other, People discouraged employees from building protective boxes around their positions. Miller stated, "[Employees] build stuff into their jobs that you couldn't understand if you wanted to. Instead, we make things simple. We want anybody to be able to go in and basically do a function." Miller went on to state that People encouraged employees to move "outside" their individual boxes. "If you go out of the box, your hand (in other organizations) gets slapped . . . It's a crazy way to run anything. If you help people learn about all sides of the business, they're going to be much happier and they're going to perform better."

Compensation

Burr believed that there were huge benefits for employees to be not only workers but shareholders. "Salaries," Burr stated, "are costs and expenses. Dividends and high stock prices are the rewards of ownership." By the end of 1985, People's full-time managers collectively owned approximately a third of the airline. It was a requirement of employment that every employee must buy (at a 70 percent discount) and own at least 100 shares of stock. People's strategy was to offer the employees a generous profit-sharing program in order to compensate for the below-average wage rates.

Not only did the profit-sharing philosophy increase paychecks (up to 27 percent of the employee's salary), but it also reduced People's expenses. While the industry average of wages compared to revenue is 35 percent, at People's, it was only 20 percent.

Although this mixture of compensation was initially accepted without question, there were rumblings within the ranks. Pilots who were willing to take any job back when People started in the early 1980s, were more vocal about their complaints once the industry started to recover in 1985.

On the basis of People's organization chart, pilots were considered to be at the same level as flight attendants. Pilots were also quick to highlight that they were paid far less for much more work. While pilots from other airlines earn from $90,000 to $170,000, People's pilots are paid from $22,000 to $70,00 less than that.

But, this compensation and status "inequity" did not only apply to the pilots. Burr had seen some senior managers leave because, as Burr stated, they did not believe in People's philosophy. "Some needed the standard perks. They said, 'How can you tell me that I should have the same salary as Joe Chief Pilot?' "

Summary

When Donald Burr left his job as president of Texas International Airline in 1980, he believed that he could put together an airline that would "develop a better way for people to work together." Whether it was shown by a pilot buying fuel or a managing officer checking in passengers, People's philosophy had been to make every employee not only an expert on the company, but also a part owner.

However, the airline that Harvard Professor D. Quinn Mills called "the most comprehensive and self-conscious effort to fit a business to the capabilities and attitudes of today's work force" would fall on hard times. By the end of 1986, People was crippled due to over expansion, increased competition, a failed acquisition of Frontier Airline, and continuous money problems that resulted in a bunkruptcy filing. After only five years of operations, People was successfully taken over by Texas Air, which was lead by Donald Burr's former boss, Frank Lorenzo.

• • • • • • • • •

STRATEGIC CHOICES

An organization must make numerous choices with regard to job analysis. Four of the most basic strategic choices are described below:

1. The extent of *employee involvement* in job analysis.
2. The *level of detail* of the analysis.
3. *When and how often* an organization conducts the job analysis.
4. *Past-oriented versus future-oriented* job analysis.

Extent of Employee Involvement in the Job Analysis Process

The job analysis process involves collecting information about specific jobs (or all jobs) in an organization. It is a systematic examination of the duties, responsibilities, skills, and knowledge required to perform the job. Although information should only be collected about the job and not the person holding the job, the job incumbent is often consulted. It is important to remember that in a job analysis it is the job that is analyzed and not the employee. However, employees are often asked to supply vital information about the contents of the job, given their familiarity with it.

The extent of employee involvement is an important strategic decision. If employees are too involved in the process, the information may be biased because many employees may "inflate" the duties and responsibilities their jobs require in order to make the job appear more important than it is. On the other hand, if employees are not involved or only minimally involved, they become suspicious about the motive behind the job analysis and feel their jobs are being threatened. A lack of involvement from employees may also lead to incomplete and inaccurate information. The extent to which employees are involved depends upon the needs of both the organization and the employees.

The job analysis needs of the organization include the need to have accurate information. However, the organization may also be concerned about employees' reactions to having their jobs analyzed. To prevent employee dissatisfaction, uncertainty, and anxiety, organizations should communicate the reasons for conducting the job analysis and keep employees informed about the job analysis process (for example, who is responsible for collecting the information, the timetable for completion, and who to contact if employees have questions or concerns). Merely communicating with employees may not be sufficient involvement, however. Obtaining information about the jobs directly from employees by means of interviewing or questionnaires increases their level of involvement and may be one of the best ways to obtain accurate and current information.

Employee Involvement through Committees

To increase employee involvement even further, some organizations have formed committees of elected employees from various departments to ensure the job analysis information is correct. For example, at a southern steel mill, both management and employees selected representatives to be on a job analysis committee. The committee met regularly to discuss the progress of the project. These interdepartmental committees also serve as a check and balance system by discussing each job being analyzed and verifying that no job has "inflated" duties or responsibilities.

Although the use of committees may be time consuming, they provide an excellent way to involve employees in a process that is often viewed as threatening and stressful. By involving employees, the organization can reduce stress and, at the same time, collect accurate information. Managers must decide whether the benefits gained from employee involvement outweigh the costs of additional time incurred. In addition, managers should not automatically assume all employees want to be involved. Some employees may prefer not to take on more responsibility by serving as a committee member. These decisions must be made based on both organizational and employee needs.

The Level of Detail

Job analysis information can vary from being very detailed, as in time and motion studies, to very broad, as in analyzing the job based on general duties. The level of analysis affects the nature of the data collected. The level of analysis can be thought of as a hierarchy ranging from employee attributes and specific task behaviors to occupational groupings and job families (see Exhibit 7.1). For example, **employee attributes** (such as mathematical aptitude) and specific **task behaviors** (such as using a calculator to multiply employees' hourly wage by the number of hours worked) can be combined to create a **task** (such as calculating employee wages). Specific tasks can be grouped into different **positions** (such as bookkeeper) within an organization. A position constitutes different individuals performing the same group of tasks in a particular organization. When these positions are combined, a **job** is created (for example, bookkeeper in organization A versus bookkeeper in organization B). Jobs similar across several firms are considered to belong to an **occupation** (such as bookkeeper, accounting clerk, or budget analyst). Finally, similar occupations can be grouped into a **job family** (such as computing and account-recording jobs). The decision to conduct a very detailed versus nondetailed job analysis depends upon at least two factors: (1) the type of job being analyzed, and (2) the primary purpose for conducting the job analysis.

The type of job being analyzed will affect the level of detail in a job analysis. For example, analyzing the number of movements an employee makes and the frequency of job-related movements would be more relevant for a crane operator's job than a personnel manager's job. It would probably be more informative to analyze a personnel manager's job by describing the various duties and responsibilities the job requires. A crane operator, on the other hand, is required to make specific movements to perform the job. In general, it is more plausible to apply a more detailed job analysis to a blue-collar job than a white-collar job. However, this is not to suggest that blue-collar jobs should be analyzed in more detail than white-collar jobs, only that it may be easier and more relevant to do so.

EXHIBIT 7.1 Level of Detail in Job Analysis Information

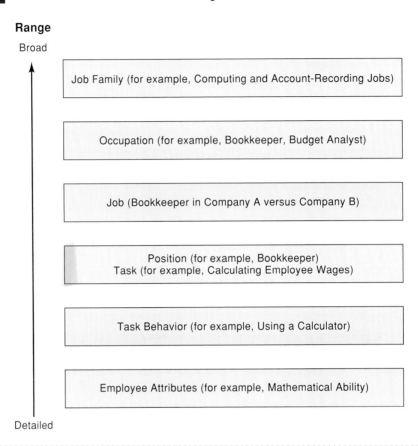

Range

Broad

Job Family (for example, Computing and Account-Recording Jobs)

Occupation (for example, Bookkeeper, Budget Analyst)

Job (Bookkeeper in Company A versus Company B)

Position (for example, Bookkeeper)
Task (for example, Calculating Employee Wages)

Task Behavior (for example, Using a Calculator)

Employee Attributes (for example, Mathematical Ability)

Detailed

When deciding upon the level of detail in a job analysis, a manager must also consider the purpose for conducting the job analysis. For example, if the primary purpose for analyzing the job is for a mass input for intensive training programs or input to use in determining how much the job is worth, the level of detail may be great. However, if the job analysis is being done to add clarification to the roles and responsibilities of job holders, a less detailed job analysis may be warranted. Obviously, the time involved and cost constraints are also considered by managers when determining the level of detail desired for the job analysis. Finally, the level of detail is influenced by whether the firm intends to redesign the job. If jobs are to be consolidated (combining jobs), broad duties need to be considered. If jobs are to be added or differentiated, more task detail is needed.

When and How Often to Conduct a Job Analysis

Another strategic decision is when to conduct a job analysis. Today many organizations conduct a job analysis as part of the restructuring effort (Chapter 6 reviewed restructuring in more depth). Jobs are analyzed in order to see which ones can be cut by combining them with others.

If an organization has never conducted a formal job analysis, one is probably warranted. Job analysis should be conducted (1) if new jobs are created or eliminated, (2) if jobs are changed due to new equipment or computerization, or (3) if employees and manages feel one is needed. When new jobs are added, for example, when a company begins to expand, these new jobs should be analyzed. In addition, any old jobs that may be affected by creating new ones should be examined and considered for elimination or combination.

Often, an organization will update equipment or purchase state-of-the-art computer systems that change some of the duties and responsibilities of certain jobs. If any major change takes place in the organization, jobs affected by these changes should be analyzed.

Finally, employees or managers may feel it is time to conduct a job analysis on certain jobs because perceived inequities exist. For example, employees might believe their job is more difficult and requires more skills than other similarly paid jobs. If a number of employees are concerned about possible inequities, managers may decide to conduct a formal job analysis to resolve these feelings. If the organization has experienced no major changes and employees and managers have not perceived a need for a job analysis, then updating the old job analysis information every two to three years is usually sufficient.

Past- versus Future-Oriented Job Analysis

If an organization is changing rapidly due to rapid growth or technological change, a more future-oriented approach to job analysis may be desired. Traditional job analysis information describes how the job has been done in the past and how it is being done currently. If desired, managers can reorient traditional job analysis approaches to have a future-oriented perspective by predicting changes in the job industry during a specified time period reaching six months to two years. Decisions are made as to how the job will probably be done or the way it should be done in the future. This will allow firms to begin hiring and training people for these jobs prior to the actual change. For example, personal computers began to replace electric typewriters, thus, changing the character of many secretarial jobs. Many firms anticipated these changes and began retraining secretaries prior to changing over to personal computers.

Although it is not possible to clearly identify how future changes will affect jobs, these changes can often be anticipated. In *Strategic Human Resource Development*, Rothwell and Kazanas argue that future changes can be simulated by (1) identifying *what* trends (such as environmental or organizational) may affect jobs, (2) identifying *how* these trends may affect jobs, and (3) setting up conditions like those expected or desired—complete with new machines or work methods—and observing employees performing under these simulated conditions.[3]

JOB ANALYSIS

Personnel managers, and managers in general, traditionally have been concerned with the analysis of jobs. The job analysis process results in two very important documents: the job description and the job specification. **Job descriptions** describe the duties, responsibilities, working conditions, and activities of a particular job. **Job specifications** describe employee qualifications, such as experience, knowledge, skills,

··

████ **EXHIBIT 7.2** ████ Traditional Uses of Job Analysis Information		
	PROGRAMS FOR SALARY RATED	PROGRAMS FOR HOURLY RATED
Job Evaluation	98%	95%
Recruiting and Placing	95	92
Conducting Labor and Personnel Relations	83	79
Utilizing Personnel	72	67
Training	61	63

··

or abilities, that are required to perform the job. Although the reasons for conducting a job analysis are numerous, the establishment of wage rates and recruiting and placement needs usually compel management to undertake a systematic program of job analysis. Exhibit 7.2 describes the *traditional ways* in which job analysis programs have been used for both salary and hourly rated jobs.

Job Evaluation

The information gathered during a job analysis is mostly used as input for the organization's job evaluation system. The job evaluation determines the worth of a particular job to the organization. This information is primarily used to determine the pay for the job. Thus, employees should be paid more for working on more difficult jobs. Job analysis information is instrumental in determining which jobs contain more difficult tasks, duties, and responsibilities. This is discussed further in Chapter 12 on compensation systems.

Recruitment, Selection, and Placement

A good job analysis should provide information useful in planning for recruitment, selection, and placement. Managers will be better able to plan for the staffing of their organizations if they have an understanding of the skills needed and the types of jobs that will most likely open up in the future. Further, selecting an individual for a job requires a thorough understanding of the type of work to be done and the qualifications necessary to perform the work. Selecting individuals to fill positions is only effective if there is a clear and accurate understanding of what the job entails. Job analysis information is also useful for detecting unnecessary job requirements. For example, a manager for a manufacturing plant may be able to hold recruiting and salary costs down if the job analysis reveals that it is not necessary for first-line supervisors to have a college degree. Finally, placing employees into jobs by means of promotions and transfers is made easier if the details of what the job entails are known and the qualifications necessary to do the job are well understood.

Labor and Personnel Relations

Information generated from the job analysis can help both labor and management understand what should be expected from each job incumbent and how much employees should be compensated for performing a particular job. Obviously, the information generated from the job analysis is most beneficial if it is clearly communicated

HR CHALLENGES . . . .

Strategic Steps in Job Evaluation

Although job evaluations are designed to measure the worth of a job, the data collection procedures for a job evaluation are all too often open to subjectivity and manipulation. Whether intentional or unintentional, an evaluator's failure to assess the worth of a job accurately can result in lower ratings and pay for employees. Management commitment to honesty in the job evaluation and job analysis process is imperative. Management can help ensure that equitable and honest job evaluations are performed by (1) assigning more than one job analyst or evaluator to each job, and (2) providing more than one method of job analysis. In addition, double-checking job evaluations for accuracy and increasing employee participation in the rating of jobs can also help to decrease the possibility of deceptive practices.

SOURCE: Adapted from G. E. Kaupins, "Lies, Damn Lies, and Job Evaluations," *Personnel* 66, 1989, pp. 62–65.

to both employees and management. This communication can help alleviate perceived inequities among employees. For example, many employees would like to know why their jobs do not pay as well as other jobs. Much of the controversy about comparable worth has revolved around this issue. Comparable worth will be discussed in more detail in Chapter 12.

Utilizing Personnel

All managers would like to utilize their employees optimally. However, performance appraisals often reveal that many employees are not performing even adequately. Job analysis information can help both employees and managers pinpoint the root of the problem. By comparing what the employee is *supposed* to be doing with what the employee is *actually* doing, supervisors can determine if the employee is performing adequately and, if not, what areas need improvement. Sharing this information with the employee can be enlightening for both parties. Employees may not have realized what was expected of them and what their work role entailed. Thus, job analysis information can help clear up any uncertainties employees might have regarding their work performance and work role.

Training and Development

Job analysis information can also be useful for training and development needs. By clearly depicting what the job entails and what qualifications are necessary to do the job, managers should be able to discover any qualification deficiencies. Most deficiencies are probably best remedied by training or retraining employees. In addition to identifying training needs, job analysis information is helpful in career development. Specifically, managers will be able to tell employees what *will be* expected if the employee desires a transfer or promotion. This information can help employees prepare for career advancement

. . . .

JOB ANALYSIS DATA COLLECTION

The process of collecting information about jobs for any of the purposes outlined in Exhibit 7.2 is referred to as a **job analysis.** Exhibit 7.3 illustrates the types of infor-

| EXHIBIT 7.3 | Types of Job Analysis Information |

WORK ACTIVITIES

- Job-oriented activities (description of the work activities performed, expressed in "job" terms, usually indicating what is accomplished, such as galvanizing, weaving, cleaning, and so on; sometimes such activity descriptions also indicate how, why, and when a worker performs an activity; usually the activities are those involving active human participation, but in certain approaches they may characterize machine or system functions)
- Work activities/processes
- Procedures used
- Activity records (such as films)
- Personal accountability/responsibility

WORKER-ORIENTED ACTIVITIES

- Human behaviors (behaviors performed in work, such as sensing, decision making, performing physical actions, or communicating)
- Elemental motions (such as those used in methods analysis)
- Personal job demands (human expenditures involved in work, such as energy expenditure)

MACHINES, TOOLS, EQUIPMENT AND WORK AIDS USED

JOB-RELATED TANGIBLES AND INTANGIBLES

- Materials processed
- Products made
- Knowledge dealt with or applied (such as law or chemistry)
- Services rendered (such as laundering or repairing)

WORK PERFORMANCE

- Work measurement (that is, time taken)
- Work standards
- Error analysis
- Other aspects

JOB CONTEXT

- Physical working conditions
- Work schedule
- Organized context
- Social context
- Incentives (financial and nonfinancial)

PERSONAL REQUIREMENTS

- Job-related knowledge skills (such as education, training, or work experience required)
- Personal attributes (such as aptitudes, physical characteristics, personality, interests required)

Popular Analysis Data Collection Methods

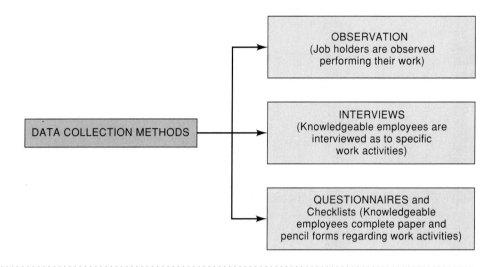

mation usually collected. This information typically becomes the basis for the job description and the job specification.

Job information is collected in several ways depending upon the purposes to be served by the organization. Typically, the organization chart is reviewed to identify the jobs to be included in the analysis. Often a restructuring, downsizing, merger, or rapid growth will initiate this review. A job may be selected because it has undergone undocumented changes in job content. In these situations the request for analysis of a job may originate with the employee, union, supervisor, or manager. Often new job demands have not been reflected in changes in compensation. Employee salaries are based, in part, upon the nature of the work. As new job demands arise and as the work changes, compensation appropriate to the job may also have to change. The employee or the manager may request a job analysis to determine the appropriate compensation, but they may also be interested in formally documenting changes in recruitment, placement, and training for a particular job.

A number of methods have been used to collect job analysis information. Managers should consider using a number of different methods of data collection because it is unlikely that any one method will provide all the necessary information needed for a job analysis. Three of the most popular forms of data collection include (1) observation of tasks and behaviors with the job holders, (2) interviews, and (3) questionnaires and checklists. These are summarized in Exhibit 7.4 and are discussed in the following sections.

Observation

Job holders are observed performing their work. Observation may be continuous or intermittent based on work sampling (observing only a sampling of tasks performed). For many jobs, observation may be of limited usefulness because the job does not consist of physically active tasks. For example, observing a bookkeeper reviewing reports or filling out forms may not lead to very valuable information about the job. Thus, observation is most useful when the job is composed of physically active tasks, such as those performed by an assembler on an automobile production line or a receptionist handling phone calls and visitors. However, even with more active jobs, observation does not always reveal vital information, such as the importance or difficulty of the tasks. Given the limitations of using observation as the only data collection method for job analysis, it is helpful to incorporate additional methods for obtaining job analysis information. Observation is most helpful to managers or job analysts as a means to gain a general familiarity with the job.

Interviewing

Employees knowledgeable about a particular job (for example, job holders, supervisors, or individuals who have worked on the job before) are interviewed as to the specific work activities that comprise the job. Usually a structured interview form is used to record information. Exhibit 7.5 shows a sample of a structured interview form used to collect data.

Interviewing can be a rather time consuming and, thus, costly method of data collection. For example, if a company has 25 jobs and two people are interviewed for each job for 30 minutes, the time involved in the interview process alone is a minimum of 25 hours. Managerial and professional jobs are more complicated and may require between one and two hours of interviewing. Given the time-consuming nature of interviews, managers and job analysts might prefer to use the interview as a means to answer specific queries generated from observations and questionnaires.

Questionnaires and Checklists

The use of questionnaires and checklists is most efficient when a number of widely dispersed employees are to be questioned about their jobs. The questionnaire allows for a relatively quick and inexpensive way to collect information about the job. At least one employee knowledgeable about the job should complete the questionnaire. If possible, it is often desirable to have two or even three people complete the questionnaire for purposes of verification. Additional data collection is often necessary if some questions need clarifying or some information is missing. Follow-up observations and interviews are not uncommon if a questionnaire or checklist is chosen as the primary means for collecting job analysis information. Exhibit 7.6 shows an example of part of a structured questionnaire/checklist.

Questionnaires and checklists provide the employee with a simplified method for providing important information. The difficulty arises in constructing a structured questionnaire. It must be extremely detailed and comprehensive so that valuable information is not missed. Obviously, management must decide whether the benefits of a simplified method of data collection outweigh the costs of its construction. Strategically, managers would most likely favor methods of data collection that do not require a lot of work up front if the content of jobs changes frequently. However, another option might be to adopt an existing structured questionnaire. Three of the most notable structured questionnaires are the Position Analysis Questionnaire (PAQ), the Management Position Description Questionnaire (MPDQ), and the Functional Job Analysis (FJA). These will be discussed in the following section.

....

EXHIBIT 7.5 Job Analysis Structured Interview Form

Name_____ Age_____

Date_____ Length of Time with Company_____

Present Job Title and Grade_____

	Section or	Supervisor's
Dept._____	Group_____	Name_____

_____

1. Purpose of Job: _____

_____

_____

_____

_____

2. Describe major duties of your job:_____

_____

_____

_____

_____

3. Other, less important job duties:_____

_____

_____

_____

_____

	Continually	Frequently	Occasionally
4. Machines or equipment used:			
_____	_____	_____	_____
_____	_____	_____	_____
_____	_____	_____	_____

....

....

| **EXHIBIT 7.6** | Structured Questionnaire/Checklist |

How much previous similar or related work experience is <u>necessary for a person starting this job?</u>

____None   ____1 to 3 years   ____More than 10 years
____Less than 3 months   ____3 to 5 years
____3 months to 1 year   ____5 to 10 years

How long should it take an employee with the <u>necessary</u> education and previous experience (as shown above) to become generally familiar with details and to do this job reasonably well?

____2 weeks or less   ____3 to 6 months   ____1 to 2 years
____2 weeks to 1 month   ____6 months   ____more than 2 years
____1 month to 3 months

What amount of supervision does this job ordinarily require? Check one.

____Frequent, all but minor variations are referred to supervisor.

____Several times daily, to report or to get advice and/or assignments. Follow established methods and procedures; refer exceptions.

____Occasional, since most duties are repetitive and related, with standard instructions and procedures as guides. Unusual problems are referred, frequently with suggestions for correction.

____Limited supervision. The nature of the work is such that it is performed to a large extent on own responsibility after assignment, with some choice of method. Occasionally develop own methods.

____Broad objectives are outlined. Work is judged primarily on overall results with much choice of method. Frequently develop methods to achieve desired results.

....

....
A TYPOLOGY OF JOB ANALYSIS METHODS

According to Patrick Wright and Kenneth Wexley in "How to Choose the Kind of Job Analysis You Really Need," job analysis methods can be placed into a typology depending upon the kind of information they yield.[4] Job analysis methods can focus on uncovering the things a worker does on the job (descriptions) or they can focus on describing the qualifications of a worker performing the job (specifications). In addition, job analysis methods can differ in the degree of uniformity of the information collected. Methods like the Position Analysis Questionnaire and the Functional Job Analysis use standardized formats. Methods like the critical incident

EXHIBIT 7.6 continued

____Little or no direct supervision. Have wide choice in selection, development, and coordination of methods within broad framework of general policies.

PHYSICAL DEMANDS
____Applicable
____Not Applicable

Lifting:
____10 lbs. max.   ____100 lbs. max.
____20 lbs. max.   ____Over 100 lbs.
____50 lbs. max

Mobility:
____Standing   ____Kneeling   ____Walking
____Crouching   ____Sitting   ____Crawling
____Stooping   ____Climbing   ____Reaching

WORK HAZARDS
____Applicable
____Not Applicable
____Mechanical   ____Electrical   ____Chemical
____Fire   ____Radiation   ____Explosives
____Height   ____Atmospheric   ____Responsibility for
                                             safety or self
____Accident Hazards   ____Responsibility for
                                             safety of others

PERSONAL DEMANDS/STRESS
____Applicable
____Not Applicable
____Overtime   ____Heat   ____Dirt   ____Outside
                                                          Weather
____Shift Work   ____Stress   ____Noise   ____Monotony
____Split Shift   ____Repetitious   ____Fumes   ____Water
                       Operations

technique and the job-element method, however, require job analysts to develop the procedure "from scratch." Although these methods are less standardized, they have the advantage of yielding more detailed position-specific information.

A typology of job analysis methods, according to the kind of information they yield, is presented in Exhibit 7.7. Job analysis methods can yield standardized and/or position-specific information regarding the worker and/or the job. **Standardized job analysis methods** mean that the information obtained is uniform and there is a standard against which jobs can be compared. Standardization indicates the extent to which a method yields data/information in the form of norms so that jobs analyzed in different settings can be compared. Many human resource managers, however,

EXHIBIT 7.7 Typology of Job Analysis Methods

POSITION-SPECIFIC INFORMATION

Job Element
Domain Sampling Approach
Threshold Traits Analysis
   (TCA Component)
	Critical Incident Technique
	Task Inventory-CODAP
	Domain Sampling Approach
	Functional Job Analysis
	Threshold Traits Ananlysis
	   (DATA Component)

———— WORKER-ORIENTED ————   ———— JOB-ORIENTED ————

Ability Requirements Scales
Position Analysis Questionnaire*
Management Position
   Description Questionnaire*
Threshold Traits Analysis
   (SJA Component)
Functional Job Analysis
	Functional Job Analysis
	Position Analysis Questionnaire*
	Management Position
	   Description Questionnaire*
	Threshold Traits Analysis
	   (DATA Component)

STANDARDIZED INFORMATION

*Standardized information about the worker can come from
a database analysis of individual PAQs and MPDQs.

need to analyze jobs that are comprised of tasks considered unique to their organization. In those instances, the human resource manager would want to use a position-specific job analysis method. **Position-specific methods** yield information specific to a job within a particular organization (that is, a position).

Job analysis methods can also be compared on a worker- versus job-oriented basis. **Worker-oriented job analysis methods** yield information regarding workers' activities on the job. Specifically, these methods identify actual worker behaviors necessary to perform the job. **Job-oriented job analysis methods** yield information about the actual tasks that comprise the job. The following section briefly describes nine of the most commonly used job analysis procedures.[5]

METHODS OF JOB ANALYSIS

The **critical incident technique** uses job holders, supervisors, or other "experts" to describe job-related behaviors critical to successful performance. This approach focuses on the things a worker does (incidents) that distinguish that person as an effective or ineffective employee. In order to be considered *critical*, an incident must occur in a situation in which the intent of the act seems clear to the observer and where its consequences leave little doubt about the effects. The data collection process results in a mass of incidents descriptive of effective and ineffective job behaviors in critical situations. In addition, they describe behaviors that reflect outstanding versus poor performance on the job. These incident descriptions are examined and put into job dimension categories that characterize particular facets of job performance. This procedure provides position-specific information about the job.

....

| EXHIBIT 7.8 | Job-Element Method

Rater's Name and Grade_____

Job Rated: Title and Grade_____

Element	Barely acceptable workers 2 All have 1 Some have 0 Almost none have	To pick out superior worker 2 Very important 1 Valuable 0 Does not differentiate	Trouble likely if not considered 2 Much trouble 1 Some trouble 0 Safe to ignore	Practicality demanding this element 2 All openings 1 Some openings 0 Almost no openings
Ability to add 2-digit numbers	2	0	2	2
Can cook hamburgers	0	1	1	0
Can scrub floors	1	1	1	2
Etc.				

....

Another method that produces position-specific information is the **job-element method**. However, this procedure yields worker-oriented information rather than job-oriented information. The Civil Service has used the job element approach to identify the worker characteristics associated with effective performance. People familiar with the job identify the knowledge, skills, abilities, and personal traits (job elements) needed to perform the job. As can be see in Exhibit 7.8, each of these job elements are rated on four scales: barely acceptable (number of employees who have this element), superior (number of superior employees who have this element), trouble likely (probability of trouble occurring if an employee does not have the element), and practical (practicality of expecting to find people with the element). The job element approach helps the human resource manager decide whether the element is a characteristic workers must have before beginning the job or whether it is an element likely to require training. This method yields position-specific information about the worker.

The **ability requirements scales** focus on worker characteristics rather than job characteristics. Unlike the job-element method, however, the scales in this technique yield standardized information. Tasks are described, contrasted, and compared in terms of the abilities that a given task requires of the performer. These abilities are relatively enduring traits of the employee performing the task. An assumption is made that each task requires specific abilities for effective performance. Tasks requiring similar abilities are placed in the same category.

Abilities are listed under perceptual-motor, physical performance, and cognitive domains. Behaviorally anchored scales define the abilities to be rated. Specifically, a set of behaviorally anchored scales measure how much each of 37 abilities is needed to perform the job. For example, the ability, *verbal comprehension*, has behavioral anchors that range from "understanding a comic book" to "understanding in its entirety a mortgage contract for a new home." Thus, this technique gives standardized information about the worker.

··

| **EXHIBIT 7.9** | Position Analysis Questionnaire (PAQ) |

ORGANIZATION OF THE PAQ

The job elements in the PAQ are organized in six divisions as follows (examples of two job elements from each division are included):

1. *Information input.* (Where and how does the worker get the information he uses in performing his job?)

   Examples: Use of written materials
   Near-visual differentiation

2. *Mental processes.* (What reasoning, decision-making, planning, and information-processing activities are involved in performing the job?)

   Examples: Level of reasoning in problem solving
   Coding/decoding

3. *Work output.* (What physical activities does the worker perform and what tools or devices does he use?)

   Examples: Use of keyboard devices
   Assembling/disassembling

4. Relationships with other persons. (What relationships with other people are required in performing the job?)

   Examples: Instructing
   Contacts with public, customers

5. *Job context.* (In what physical or social contexts is the work performed?)

   Examples: High temperature
   Interpersonal conflict situations

6. *Other job characteristics.* (What activities, conditions, or characteristics other than those described above are relevant to the job?)

··

The **Task Inventory–CODAP** is a structured job analysis questionnaire consisting of a list of tasks relevant to some occupational area. This method uses job "experts" (individuals familiar with the content of the jobs) to create a list of tasks and then rate each task according to the relative amount of time spent on it. Because the list of tasks involved in the performance of a job is likely to differ across jobs, task inventories must be developed separately for each occupational area. These ratings are entered into a computer (CODAP is a computer program that summarizes job analysis ratings), analyzed, and converted into job dimensions. This method guarantees position-specific information about the job. The air force has used task inventories successfully for years to monitor the changes that occur in jobs as a result of technological or personal changes.

The **Position Analysis Questionnaire (PAQ)** contains 194 job elements. The job analyst/human resource manager rates a specific job on the 194 descriptors by judging the degree to which an element (or descriptor) is present. These elements are grouped into six general categories.[6] Exhibit 7.9 describes the categories and gives examples of rating scales used to collect information and rate jobs. The PAQ

EXHIBIT 7.9 continued

RATING SCALES USED WITH THE PAQ

There is provision for rating each job on each job element. Six types of rating scales are used, as follows:

LETTER IDENTIFICATION	TYPE OF RATING SCALE
U	Extent of Use
I	Importance to the job
T	Amount of Time
P	Possibility of Occurrence
A	Applicability
S	Special Code (used in the case of a few specific job elements)

A specific rating scale is designated to be used with each job element, in particular the scale considered most appropriate to the content of the element. All but the "A" (Applicability) scale are 6-point scales, with "0" (which is coded as "N") being used for "Does not apply," as illustrated below:

RATING	IMPORTANCE TO THE JOB
N	Does not apply
1	Very minor (importance)
2	Low
3	Average
4	High
5	Extreme

has been thoroughly researched and enables a statistical comparison of the dimensions of jobs in an organization. Responses to the PAQ can be sent to PAQ Services in Logan, Utah, for scoring. This analysis provides an estimate of worker attributes predictive of success in a particular job. In addition, this analysis provides a comparison of a specific job with other job classifications. Although the PAQ is an extremely practical job analysis method, the use of the PAQ is not as widespread as one might believe because reading skills are necessary to use it.

A similar procedure has been developed to describe managerial jobs. The **Management Position Description Questionnaire (MPDQ)** developed the thirteen factors shown in Exhibit 7.10 that may be used to describe managerial jobs. These factors resulted from a 208-item questionnaire completed by 434 managers. The PAQ and the MPDQ yield standardized information about the worker and the job.

Functional job analysis (FJA) is a method in which the functions of a job can be examined in relation to three classifications: data, people, and things. Within each of these classifications are degrees or levels with corresponding numbers (see Exhibit 7.11 on page 226). The lower the number, the more the job is involved

....

| **EXHIBIT 7.10** | Management Position Description Questionnaire (MPDQ) Factors |

1. *Product, Marketing, and Financial Strategy Planning:* This factor indicates long-range thinking and planning. The concerns of the incumbent are broad and oriented toward the future of the company. They may include such areas as long-range business potential, objectives of the organization, solvency of the company, what business activities the company should engage in, and the evaluation of new ideas.

2. *Coordination of Other Organization Units and Personnel:* The incumbent coordinates the efforts of others over whom he or she exercises no direct control, handles conflicts or disagreements when necessary, and works in an environment where he or she must cut across existing organizational boundaries.

3. *Internal Business Control:* The incumbent exercises business controls; that is, reviews and controls the allocation of manpower and other resources. Activities and concerns are in the areas of assignments of supervisory responsibility, expense control, cost reduction, setting performance goals, preparation and review of budgets, protection of the company's monies and properties, and employee relations practices.

4. *Products and Services Responsibility:* Activities and concerns of the incumbent in technical areas related to products, services, and their marketability. Specifically included are the planning, scheduling, and monitoring of products and services delivery along with keeping track of their quality and costs. The incumbent is concerned with promises of delivery that are difficult to meet, anticipates new or changed demands for the products and services and closely maintains the progress of specific projects.

5. *Public and Customer Relations:* A general responsibility for the reputation of the company's products and services. The incumbent is concerned with promoting the company's products and services, the goodwill of the company in the community, and general public relations. The position involves first-hand contact with the customer, frequent contact and negotiation with representatives from other organizations, and understanding the needs of customers.

6. *Advanced Consulting:* The incumbent is asked to apply technical expertise to special problems, issues, questions, or policies. The incumbent should have an understanding

....

with that particular function. These numbers and levels can be compared to the job elements reported in the *Dictionary of Occupation Titles* (DOT), which is a standardized data source describing a wide range of jobs. For example, in Exhibit 7.12, a typical personnel manager's job is described. The numbers next to the job title (166.117-018) are important if you want to utilize the information in the DOT. The first three numbers (166) represent the occupational code, title, and industry, respectively. The next three numbers (117) represent the degree to which a typical personnel manager is involved with data, people, and things, respectively. The final three numbers indicate the alphabetical order of job titles within the same occupational grouping that have the same involvement over data, people, and things. The DOT job descriptions are endorsed by the federal government.

Managers can adapt the standardized job descriptions from the DOT to the specific jobs within the firm. The DOT is particularly useful when a large number of jobs need to be analyzed. Rather than "starting from scratch," managers can use the DOT as a guide. The DOT may also prove invaluable to managers who are not personnel specialists. In summary, the functional job analysis, and its use of the

EXHIBIT 7.10 continued

of advanced principles, theories, and concepts in more than one required field. He or she is often asked to apply highly advanced techniques and methods to address issues and questions, which very few people in the company can do.

7. *Autonomy of Action:* The incumbent has a considerable amount of discretion in the handling of a job, engages in activities that are not closely supervised or controlled, and makes decisions that are often not subject to review. The incumbent may have to handle unique problems, know how to ask key questions even on subject matters with which he or she is not intimately familiar, and engage in free-wheeling or unstructured thinking to deal with problems that are themselves abstract or unstructured.

8. *Approval of Financial Commitments:* The incumbent has the authority to approve large financial commitments and obligate the company. The incumbent may make final and, for the most part, irreversible decisions, negotiate with representatives from other organizations, and make many important decisions on almost a daily basis.

9. *Staff Service:* The incumbent renders various staff services to supervisors. Such activities can include fact gathering, data acquisition and compilation, and record keeping.

10. *Supervision:* The incumbent plans, organizes, and controls the work of others. The activities are such that they require face-to-face contact with subordinates on almost a daily basis. The concerns covered by this factor revolve around getting work done efficiently through the effective utilization of people.

11. *Complexity and Stress:* The incumbent has to operate under pressure. This may include activities of handling information under time pressure to meet deadlines, frequently taking risks, and interfering with personal or family life.

12. *Advanced Financial Responsibility:* Activities and responsibilities concerned with the preservation of assets, making investment decisions, and other large-scale financial decisions that affect the company's performance.

13. *Broad Personnel Responsibility:* The incumbent has broad responsibility for the management of human resources and the policies affecting them.

DOT, is an invaluable source of information. This job analysis method yields position-specific information about the job and standardized information about the worker and the job.

The **domain sampling approach** requires individuals familiar with the job to be analyzed (job experts) to make up a list of tasks that constitute each job. For each task, they decide on the knowledge, skills, and abilities (KSAs) necessary for effective performance. **Knowledge** is defined as the degree to which a job holder is required to know specific technical material. **Skill** is defined as adequate performance on tasks requiring the use of tools, equipment, and machinery. Finally, **abilities** refer to the physical and mental capacities needed to perform tasks not requiring the use of tools, equipment, or machinery. Each of these KSAs is rated for importance and relative amount of time spent using it while performing the job. The domain sampling approach yields position-specific information about the worker and the job.

The final job analysis method is the **threshold traits analysis**. This approach was designed to provide normative data on the worker attributes required for successful job performance across all types of jobs. In this method, a job inventory

....

| **EXHIBIT 7.11** | Dictionary of Occupational Titles Classifications |

DATA (4TH DIGIT)	PEOPLE (5TH DIGIT)	THINGS (6TH DIGIT)
0 Synthesizing	0 Mentoring	0 Setting Up
1 Coordinating	1 Negotiating	1 Precision Working
2 Analyzing	2 Instructing	2 Operating-Controlling
3 Compiling	3 Supervising	3 Driving-Operating
4 Computing	4 Diverting	4 Manipulating
5 Copying	5 Persuading	5 Tending
6 Comparing	6 Speaking-Signaling	6 Feeding-Offbearing
	7 Serving	7 Handling
	8 Taking Instructions-Helping	

....

questionnaire listing the tasks and demands of the job is administered to a representative group of job experts or job holders. Each questionnaire statement is assigned to a specific job function (tasks and demands) and, as can be seen in Exhibit 7.13, each function is linked with a specific trait. This technique furnishes standardized and position-specific information about the worker and the job. The threshold traits analysis has three components. First, demand and task analysis (DATA component) uses job experts or job holders to develop a list of job tasks and the conditions under which they are performed. These tasks are then rated and grouped under 21 standardized job dimensions. Second, job experts or job holders determine the level of each of 33 standardized job traits (SJT component) needed to reach acceptable performance on the job. The trait level refers to the relative intensity or complexity of the trait and can be either common or unique depending on its frequency of occurrence in the labor pool. For example, in the motivational domain, the trait *control-dependability* consists of three levels of intensity: Level 0—disposition to perform in closely supervised situations; Level 1—disposition to perform without direct supervision; and Level 2—disposition to perform without direction or follow-up. The number of levels vary depending upon the trait. Finally, technical competence analysis (TCA component) further examines the job to reveal any other knowledge or skills necessary for successful performance.

These job analysis methods are all viable alternatives for the human resource manager. Unfortunately, many methods are chosen simply because the human resource manager is familiar with it. Only a few researchers have discussed job analysis as an activity that can enhance the strategy of an organization. Given that job analysis provides managers with clear descriptions and specifications about jobs, it is possible to determine which jobs are the most critical for a particular organizational strategy or objective. For example, if management decides to downsize an organization, the information provided by the job analysis should prove invaluable once a company decides which jobs to retain, change, or eliminate. Similarly, an organization with a growth strategy can use this information to decide on areas that are in need of expansion or development.[7] The following section examines which job analysis methods are best for various human resource activities and how strategy affects which human resource activities will be emphasized.

██ EXHIBIT 7.12 ██   Sample Job Title and Description from *Dictionary of Occupational Titles*

166.117-018 MANAGER, PERSONNEL. (profess. & kin.)

Plans and carries out policies relating to all phases of personnel activity. Recruits, interviews, and selects employees to fill vacant positions. Plans and conducts new employee orientation to foster positive attitude toward company goals. Keeps record of insurance coverage, pension plan, and personnel transactions, such as hires, promotions, transfers, and terminations. Investigates accidents and prepares reports for insurance carrier. Conducts wage survey within labor market to determine competitive wage rate. Prepares budget of personnel operations. Meets with shop stewards and supervisors to resolve grievances. Writes separation notices for employees separating with cause and conducts exit interviews to determine reasons behind separations. Prepares reports and recommends procedures to reduce absenteeism and turnover. Contracts with outside suppliers to provide employee services, such as canteen, transportation, or relocation service. May keep records of hired employee characteristics for governmental reporting purposes. May negotiate collective bargaining agreement with BUSINESS REPRESENTATION LABOR UNION (profess. & kin.)

···

ORGANIZATION STRATEGY, HUMAN RESOURCE ACTIVITIES, AND JOB ANALYSIS METHODS

Organizational strategy can have a direct impact on many human resource activities, such as the selection process, job evaluations, and performance appraisals. These human resource activities require specific job analysis methods. The relationship between an organization's strategy, human resource activities, and job analysis methods can be critical for human resource managers.

As discussed in Chapter 2, Miles and Snow developed a strategy typology of organizations. *Defenders* have narrow and relatively stable product-market domains, *prospectors* continually search for product and market opportunities, and *analyzers* operate in two types of product-market domains—one relatively stable and the other changing. These strategies affect the emphasis and the nature of many human resource activities. We will examine five specific human resource activities; the selection process, performance appraisals, job evaluations, career planning, and human resource planning. The purpose of discussing other human resource issues in the job analysis chapter is twofold. First, the following discussion is designed to integrate strategy with some of the major *uses* of job analysis. Second, the discussion should enable the reader to better understand many of the complexities and interrelationships between a job analysis and traditional human resource activities. The following discussion is based primarily on the work by Miles and Snow and by Wright and Wexley.[8]

Selection

Selection tests can be categorized as either achievement tests or aptitude tests. Achievement tests demonstrate whether an applicant can perform the job at the

··

EXHIBIT 7.13 List of Threshold Trait Analysis (TTA) Job Functions, Corresponding Traits, and Abbreviated Trait Definitions

Threshold Traits Analysis

Area	Job Functions	Trait	Description—Can
Physical	Physical Exertion	1. Strength	Lift, pull or push physical objects
		2. Stamina	Expend physical energy for long periods
	Bodily Activity	3. Agility	React quickly; has dexterity, coordination
	Sensory Inputs	4. Vision	See details and color of objects
		5. Hearing	Recognize sound, tone and pitch
Mental	Vigilance and Attention	6. Perception	Observe and differentiate details
		7. Concentration	Attend to details amid distractions
		8. Memory	Retain and recall ideas
	Information Processing	9. Comprehension	Understand spoken and written ideas
		10. Problem-solving	Reason and analyze abstract information
		11. Creativity	Produce new ideas and products
Learned	Quantitative Computation	12. Numerical Computation	Solve arithmetic and numerical problems
	Communications	13. Oral Expression	Speak clearly and effectively
		14. Written Expression	Write clearly and effectively
	Action Selection and Projection	15. Planning	Project a course of action
		16. Decision-making	Choose a course of action
	Application of Information and Skill	17. Craft knowledge	Apply specialized information
		18. Craft Skills	Perform a complex set of activities
Motivational	Unprogrammed	19. Adaptability–Change	Adjust to interruptions and changes
	Cycled	20. Adaptability–Repetition	Adjust to repetitive activities
	Stressful — Working	21. Adaptability–Pressure	Adjust to critical and demanding work
	Secluded — Conditions	22. Adaptability–Isolation	Work alone or with little personal contact
	Unpleasant	23. Adaptability–Discomfort	Work in hot, cold, noisy work places
	Dangerous	24. Adaptability–Hazards	Work in dangerous situations
	Absence of Direct Supervision	25. Control–Dependability	Work with minimum of supervision
	Presence of Difficulties	26. Control–Perseverance	Stick to a task until completed
	Unstructured Conditions	27. Control–Initiative	Act on own, take charge when needed
	Access to Valuables	28. Control–Integrity	Observe regular ethical and moral codes
	Limited Mobility	29. Control–Aspirations	Limit desire for promotion
Social	Interpersonal Contact	30. Personal Appearance	Meet appropriate standards of dress
		31. Tolerance	Deal with people in tense situations
		32. Influence	Get people to cooperate
		33. Cooperation	Work as a member of the team

···

time of testing. This often involves applicants performing samples of work using actual job tasks. In order to develop reliable and valid work sample tests, specific information about the job is needed. Thus, the best job analysis methods would be domain sampling, critical incident technique, or task inventory-CODAP. Aptitude tests, on the other hand, attempt to measure an applicant's potential or ability to learn. Information about the actual job may not be as relevant as information about the worker. Thus, information needed to develop an aptitude test may be obtained with the Position Analysis Questionnaire, the Management Position Description Questionnaire, functional job analysis, job-element method, ability requirement scales, or domain sampling.

The strategy adopted by an organization can affect whether an achievement test or an aptitude test is utilized for selection purposes. If an organization adopts a

....

| EXHIBIT 7.14 | The Relationship between Organizational Strategy and Types of Selection Tests |

Organizational Strategy	Preferred Selection Test
Defender (building human resources) ⟶ Aptitude	
Prospector (aquiring human resources) ⟶ Achievement	
Analyzer (allocating human resources) ⟶ Aptitude	

....

defender strategy, its emphasis is on building human resources. Little recruiting is done above the entry level and training programs are usually formal and extensive. Since the focus is on skill building, aptitude tests may be preferred. Aptitude tests can be used to identify employees who have the potential to learn from training. However, an organization with a defender strategy may want to use an achievement test to determine if an applicant has the initial skills needed for selection or promotion.

An organization with a prospector strategy emphasizes acquiring human resources. Rather than "making" qualified employees through training, the focus is on "buying" already qualified personnel. Recruiting is sophisticated, and training is usually informal and limited. Since the focus is on skill identification and acquisition, achievement tests would most likely be preferred.

Finally, an organization with an analyzer strategy emphasizes allocating human resources. Training programs are usually formal and extensive. Since the focus is on skill building, identifying applicants' potential to learn is important. Thus, aptitude tests would be the preferred method of selection. Exhibit 7.14 summarizes the relationship between a firm's organizational strategy and its preferred selection test.

Performance Appraisal

Performance appraisal techniques measure employee traits, behaviors, or results. The trait approach (rating employees on traits such as temperament) has been criticized due to its subjectivity and because many trait appraisals have not been developed with the use of a thorough job analysis. However, the trait approach can be a useful measure if done correctly. Since trait approaches require position-specific information about the worker, either the job-element method or the threshold traits analysis would be a good choice.

Behaviorally oriented appraisal systems (such as Behaviorally Anchored Rating Scales) measure employees' actually job-oriented behaviors. Results-oriented appraisals measure the outcomes or the products generated by employees. Management-by-Objectives is often the basis for results-oriented appraisals. Since both types of appraisal systems require position-specific information about the work, the critical incident technique and the task inventory-CODAP are often viewed as the best choices.

The strategy of an organization can affect the choice of performance appraisal systems. Organizations with a defender or analyzer strategy use process-oriented procedures when examining performance. Process-oriented procedures are based on

··

| EXHIBIT 7.15 | The Relationship between Organizational Strategy and Performance Appraisal Systems |

Organizational Strategy	Performance Appraisal System
Defender (identification of training needs) ——▶	Behaviorally Oriented System
Prospector (identification of staffing needs) ——▶	Results-Oriented System
Analyzer (identification of training needs) ——▶	Behaviorally Oriented System

··

critical incidents or production targets. These organizations emphasize the identification of training needs. Thus, a behaviorally oriented appraisal system would most likely be preferred by organizations with these strategies.

Organizations with a prospector strategy use results-oriented procedures (such as profit targets). These organizations focus on the identification of staffing needs. Since the concern is with the ultimate result, results-oriented systems are often the logical choice. Exhibit 7.15 summarizes the relationship between organizational strategy and the preferred performance appraisal system.

Job Evaluation

Job evaluation is concerned with comparing different jobs across work-related factors (that is, skill, effort, responsibility, and working conditions) to determine the relative (dollar) worth of, and placement in, a hierarchy for each job. Given that the focus is on comparing jobs, standardized job analysis methods are usually recommended. In addition, since information on both the worker and the job is needed, techniques like the Position Analysis Questionnaire, the Management Position Description Questionnaire, functional job analysis, and threshold traits analysis are most effective for this purpose.

The strategy of an organization can affect the importance of conducting a job evaluation. An organization with a prospector strategy focuses on acquiring or "buying" human resources. Since the concern is with attracting qualified employees, competitive salaries are extremely important. Thus, organizations with a prospector strategy would, most likely, be interested in conducting frequent job evaluations to ensure both internal equity (fair salaries within the company) and external equity (fair salaries between companies).

Organizations with a defender strategy focus on building human resources from the entry level. Since recruiting above the entry level is not a priority, job evaluations may not be viewed as a major concern. However, if turnover in the organization is high (often due to low pay), a complete job evaluation may be needed.

Organizations with an analyzer strategy focus on allocating human resources but are still concerned with some higher level recruiting. Similar to prospectors, organizations with an analyzer strategy would want to have job evaluations conducted; however, the emphasis probably would not be as strong. Exhibit 7.16 summarizes

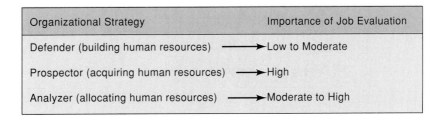

EXHIBIT 7.16 The Relationship between Organizational Strategy and the Importance of Conducting a Job Evaluation

Organizational Strategy	Importance of Job Evaluation
Defender (building human resources)	⟶ Low to Moderate
Prospector (acquiring human resources)	⟶ High
Analyzer (allocating human resources)	⟶ Moderate to High

the importance of conducting frequent job evaluations according to the strategy of the organization.

Career Planning

Career planning involves identifying and comparing employees' current abilities with those required for a specific job. Strategies are devised to develop any skills or abilities employees lack. Since standardized information about the worker is needed, the ability requirements scales, the Position Analysis Questionnaire, the Management Position Description Questionnaire, threshold traits analysis, and functional job analysis are all viable options.

Career planning is most likely to be salient in organizations that have a defender strategy or an analyzer strategy. Defenders and analyzers focus on formal and extensive training and skill building, thus, career planning is emphasized. Since prospectors are more likely to "buy" needed personnel through sophisticated recruiting techniques, career planning is less of a concern. However, attracting qualified personnel may require some career planning activities. Most individuals are not interested in working for organizations that offer little or no career advancement opportunities. Exhibit 7.17 summarizes the importance of career planning according to the strategy of the organization.

Human Resource Planning

Human resource planning calls for an analysis of personnel needs in a dynamic environment and the development of activities that aid an organization's adaptation to change. These activities can include any of the aforementioned personnel functions. Since the analytic phase requires standardized information about the worker and the job, and the developmental phase requires position-specific information about the worker and the job, the threshold traits analysis is the recommended job analysis method. This method will allow for both standardized and position-specific information about the worker and the job.

Human resource planning should be a concern for all organizations, regardless of their specific strategy. However, prospectors (and, to a lesser extent, analyzers) are in changing markets; thus, human resource planning may be critical for survival. Since defenders have more predictable markets, these organizations may be less

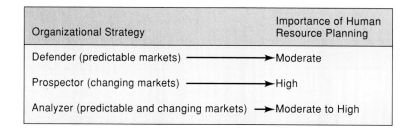

EXHIBIT 7.17 The Relationship between Organizational Strategy and the Importance of Career Planning

Organizational Strategy	Importance of Career Planning
Defender (formal and extensive training) ⟶	High
Prospector (sophisticated recruiting) ⟶	Moderate
Analyzer (formal and extensive training) ⟶	High

EXHIBIT 7.18 The Relationship between Organizational Strategy and Human Resource Planning

Organizational Strategy	Importance of Human Resource Planning
Defender (predictable markets) ⟶	Moderate
Prospector (changing markets) ⟶	High
Analyzer (predictable and changing markets) ⟶	Moderate to High

concerned with extensive human resource planning. Exhibit 7.18 summarizes the importance of human resource planning according to the strategy of the organization.

In summary, the strategy of an organization can have a direct impact on many human resource activities. These activities, as Wright and Wexley argue, should be considered when choosing a job analysis method. However, regardless of the specific method chosen, certain guidelines should be followed for an effective job analysis. The following section outlines the general steps involved when conducting a job analysis.

CONDUCTING A JOB ANALYSIS

The process of conducting a job analysis involves a number of steps. Although firms may differ in the exact job analysis procedure, the following steps should serve as a guide. Exhibit 7.19 summarizes these steps and each step is discussed in the following sections.

Step 1—Determine the Purpose for Conducting a Job Analysis

The first decision human resource managers typically make is the purpose for conducting a job analysis. Has the company been experiencing rapid growth or downsizing and, thus, found the need to add to, delete from, or change the current job

··

EXHIBIT 7.19 Steps in Conducting a Job Analysis

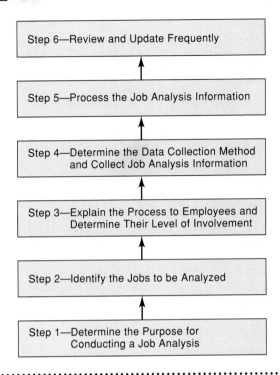

in any way? Has a merger taken place? Are employee salaries equitable? The purpose for conducting a job analysis should be explicit and tied to the overall strategy of the firm in order to increase the likelihood of a successful job analysis program.

Step 2—Identify Jobs to Be Analyzed

The second task mangers typically undertake is deciding which jobs need to be analyzed. If a formal job analysis has never been performed, then this task is easy—analyze *all* of the jobs. If, however, the organization has undergone changes that have affected only certain jobs or new jobs have been added, then managers must pinpoint the exact jobs to be analyzed.

Step 3—Explain the Process to Employees and Determine Their Level of Involvement

The purpose of conducting a job analysis should not be kept from the employees and managers. They should be informed of who will be conducting the analysis, why the job analysis is needed, who to contact if they have questions or concerns, the schedule or timetable of events, and their role in the job analysis. Too often, employees are uncertain about these issues and begin to feel their jobs are being threatened. To reduce any anxiety employees may be experiencing, communication is of the

. . . .

EXHIBIT 7.20 Job Description

Department: Executive   *Job title:* Executive
            President's   Secretary
            Office

Reports to: President

Major Function: Responsible for providing administrative and secretarial assistance to the President, Company officials and Board members.

Primary Duties and Responsibilities:

1. Performs typing, filing, answers telephone, composes routine letters, operates office equipment, prepares reports, and provides other office and administrative assistance.
2. Reviews and distributes incoming mail for the president, maintains his calendar of appointments, and arranges mutually agreeable meeting times and dates.
3. Prepares board report for distribution to the board members and company management, arranges and coordinates travel schedules for board members, and arranges for off-site meetings.
4. Acts as liaison between company officials, board members, customer executives, and state and federal government officials when the president is out of town.
5. Administers special airline fare discount program and coordinates travel advances/reports for staff and plans president's trips.
6. Performs other duties as assigned.

. . . .

utmost importance. If anxieties and uncertainties exist among employees, accurate job analysis information will be difficult to obtain. Another means of reducing anxiety and adding validity to the process is to form a committee (elected by the employees) to represent various jobs and serve as a verification check that the job analysis information gathered is accurate. These elected committee members can also help answer questions and concerns employees may have.

Step 4—Determine the Data Collection Method and Collect Job Analysis Information

The fourth step consists of actually collecting the job analysis information. Managers must decide which method or combination of methods will be used and how to collect the information. Once this has been determined and the job analysis information is in the process of collection, managers must make sure the information is complete. If additional information is required for purposes of clarification, it is best to go back immediately and gather it while the job analysis issues are still salient to employees.

Step 5—Process the Job Analysis Information

Once the job analysis information has been collected, it is important to place it into a form that will be useful to managers and personnel departments. As previously mentioned, the job analysis information is used to create both job descriptions and job specifications. Job descriptions, as can be seen in Exhibit 7.20, describe the

....

EXHIBIT 7.21   Job Specifications

Department: Executive   *Job title:* Executive
               President's   Secretary
               Office
Reports to: President

───

Required Knowledge, Skills, and Abilities:

1. Knowledge of office routines and procedures.
2. Knowledge of the executive secretarial field.
3. Skill in the operation of computerized office equipment.
4. Skill in typing, filing, answering the telephone, and composing routine letters and reports.
5. Ability to act as a liaison between company officials, board members, customer executives, and state and federal government officials when president is out of town.
6. Ability to plan and prioritize work.

....

duties required to do the job. The description from the job duties can vary from very broad and general guidelines to very specific and precise statements. The level of detail depends upon the organizational needs. Although longer job descriptions provide additional information, the marginal value of such additional information may not warrant the extra effort and expense.

Job specifications describe the qualifications required to do the job and can be seen in Exhibit 7.21. The personal qualifications an employee must possess in order to perform the duties and responsibilities depicted in the job description are contained in the job specifications. Typically, the job specifications detail the knowledge, skills and abilities relevant to a job including education, experience, specialized training, personal traits, and manual dexterity. At times, an organization may also include the physical demands the job places upon an employee. The physical demands of a job might include the amount of walking, standing, reaching, or lifting that is required of the employee. In addition, the condition of the physical work environment and the hazards employees may encounter may also be included among the physical demands of a job.

The importance of job specifications is derived from a number of sources. First, certain jobs have qualifications required by the law. For example, airline pilots, attorneys, and medical doctors all need to be licensed. Another type of job specification is based more on professional tradition. For example, university professors must usually hold a Ph.D or equivalent degree if they are going to be in a tenure-track position. Whether having a Ph.D or its equivalent is important for teaching and research is still debatable and has not been empirically verified beyond question. Finally, job specifications might involve establishing certain standards or criteria that are deemed to be necessary for successful performance. This approach, however, depends primarily upon the judgment of the employer.

For example, secretarial and clerical workers may be required to demonstrate typing speeds in excess of 100 to 120 words per minute. Management positions may only be available to those applicants with at least three to five years experience in a similar position. It is important to remember, however, that these job specifications

HR CHALLENGES ●

Job Specifications for a Typical Entry Level Human Resource Management Position

What are the most important skills an individual should have for an entry level human resource management position? Thomas Bergmann and M. John Close examined this and other related issues when they sampled 300 of the largest firms in the United States. A total of 142 questionnaires were returned and usable. The results of their survey indicated that (1) employers usually recruit for human resource management positions within rather than outside the organization, (2)

employers prefer business administration graduates to social science graduates, respectively, and (3) employers *are* interested in new college graduates with the appropriate coursework even if they have little or no experience.

SOURCE: Adapted from T. S. Bergmann, and M. J. Close, "Preparing for Entry Level Human Resource Management Positions," *Personnel Administrator*, April 1984, pp. 95–99.

must be directly linked to the job description. Specifically, job specifications must be job relevant.

Step 6—Review and Update Frequently

The final step is actually an ongoing phenomenon. Given that organizations are dynamic, jobs seldom go unchanged for very long. Managers and personnel specialists need to review job descriptions and specifications frequently. The job analysis process can be time consuming and costly. Thus, it is to the organization's advantage to update information on all jobs rather than repeating the entire process in a few years. If no major changes have occurred within the organization, then a complete review of all jobs should be performed every three years.[9] Obviously, more frequent reviews are necessary if organizational changes occur.

● ● ● ● ● ● ● ● ●

MANAGEMENT GUIDELINES

The following strategic guidelines should be examined when deciding whether to conduct a job analysis.

1. The reasons for conducting a job analysis should be clearly specified (such as establishing wage rates or recruiting) to help ensure that all relevant information is examined.

2. The primary purpose for conducting a job analysis should serve as input for the types of information collected (for example, work activities, machines and tools used, or job context).

3. The purpose for the job analysis, the types of information required, time and cost constraints, the extent of employee involvement, and the level of detail desired should be specified before choosing one or more of the available methods of data collection.

4. The strategy of an organization can influence which human resource activities will be emphasized. In turn, certain human resource activities (such as selection or performance appraisal) may require different job analysis methods.

5. Managers should follow or include the following steps when conducting a job analysis:

a. Determine the purpose for the job analysis.

b. Identify the jobs to be analyzed.

c. Explain the process to employees and involve them.

d. Collect job analysis information.

e. Process the job analysis information.

f. Review and update frequently.

6. The job analysis should be designed such that job descriptions and job specifications can be derived easily.

7. Managers should communicate all relevant information to employees concerning the job analysis to prevent unnecessary uncertainty and anxiety.

8. If major organizational changes have taken place, managers should consider conducting a job analysis.

9. If major organizational changes are anticipated, managers should consider conducting a more future-oriented job analysis.

QUESTIONS FOR REVIEW

1. Why should managers conduct a job analysis? What purpose does it serve?

2. What are the advantages and disadvantages to using each of the described data collection methods?

3. Describe the steps in the job analysis process.

4. Discuss the pros and cons of involving employees in the job analysis process.

5. What is a future-oriented job analysis? When would you want to use it?

6. What are job descriptions and job specifications? What is their relationship to the job analysis?

7. How often should a job analysis be conducted?

8. Discuss the various methods of job analysis.

9. Under what conditions should each of these job analysis methods be used?

CASE: Britiah Shipbuilders [10]

The mid-1970s to the mid-1980s had been a very turbulent time for British Shipbuilders. British Shipbuilders and its subsidiaries are principally engaged in the design, development, production, and sale of merchant ships and the development and production of slow speed diesel marine engines. Within those ten years, this English firm went from a stable nationalized organization, to a corporation that had its most profitable sector (warships) privatized, its markets continuously threatened by international competition, and an ongoing threat by the British government to withdraw its subsidies to the mammoth shipbuilder.

Due to these environmental factors, British Shipbuilders had to implement a drastic shift in its strategy in order to survive. Instead of competing on price alone, it focused its strategy on finding specific market niches where high technology products were required and the lowest bid did not always win the contract. This revised strategy forced the complete restructuring of the organization. The most visible impact this restructuring had on British Shipbuilders was in the shrinkage in its number of employees.

Employment

Employment had gone from 86,000 in 1977 to under 7,000 just ten years later. This severe consolidation of the organization created a magnitude of problems, one of which was the reduction in employee morale.

The two sectors remaining after the privatization faced low morale from both the workers and the managers. A major effect of this low morale was the increasingly more difficult job of trying to recruit and retrain both skilled managers and technical staff.

Strategy

By reevaluating its overall strategy, British Shipbuilders shifted the development of the managers from a focus on technical skills to a focus on overall managerial skills. The company realized that a broader development of the manager would lead to an easier identification and implementation of future technological advantages that had become mandatory in order for British Shipbuilders to survive.

The mandate that the company faced was to identify what traits were needed for each job and which manager would be able to meet those requirements. In order to solve this problem, British Shipbuilders used an expert system software that contained knowledge pertaining to personnel and could sort, manipulate and generate logical decisions based on a preset base of expertise.

The Expert System

The job of the personnel department was to supply the data for the expert system. The end result of this process was to match the job requirements with the employees. The information supplied by the personnel department included job analysis, evaluation and grading, organizational design, selection and recruitment methods, performance appraisal, and psychological assessment. The personnel department found that the hardest data to identify was information related to job dimensions and personal attributes.

Personnel started the process by identifying over 200 job dimensions that represented separate activities. Analysis of these dimensions resulted in consolidating the number by isolating dimensions that were clearly discrete and did not overlap each other. For each dimension, different levels were used to identify separate ideas (a range from very low to exceptional). From over 200 dimensions, personnel had reduced the number down to 70 with four to six levels.

The second step was to identify all the possible attributes that the employees could possess. From a list of over 100, the choices were narrowed down to 50 with five or six descriptive levels. The attributes were then grouped into five classes. The two dominant classes were management skills and personal qualities. Management skills included such attributes as organizing ability, ability to delegate, motivating, ability to control, decisiveness, and business acumen. Personal qualities were identified as appearance, drive or ambition, acceptance of change, social skills, creativity, diligence, and reasoning ability.

Once this data was inputed on the computer, the expert system software would link the job dimensions and the attribute levels. The underlying goal of using the expert system was to identify the organizational needs for a functional or job basis, which would then match the employees with those needs and then start selecting, training, and developing the employees so that the match between the employee and the job was right.

Implementing the System

The implementation of the expert system was based on a two-step process. The first phase was to analyze generic job types in senior management positions in the functional areas such as marketing, personnel, production, and finance. The second step was to measure the attributes of both the present and potential managers with the job specifications set by the personnel department. The ranking of the employee's attributes to the job specification can vary in degree from irrelevant to mandatory. In order to assess each manager's attributes, British Shipbuilders used interviews, application forms, performance appraisals, potential assessments, and psychometrics.

The British Shipbuilders case presents a situation in which an expert system was primarily implemented to match people with jobs and to find quality employees as quickly as possible. However, the shift in the job evaluation process yielded additional benefits for the company.

By inputing all the essential components of all generic jobs in a computerized system, the firm now has an invaluable data pool that can help it to determine not only the selection and training of the employees, but also employee development and career planning. This data base can be updated continuously as employees move around the organization. Implementing the expert system forced the firm to reevaluate not only the job descriptions within the organization, but also the capabilities of the employees and how they are matched with their present jobs and any potential future jobs.

Another positive side effect is the procedure itself. Even though it may be perceived to be very rigid and impersonal, British Shipbuilders has found that the process has encouraged more interaction between the superiors, the subordinates, and the career counselors.

QUESTIONS

1. Do you think developing an expert system (as described in the British Shipbuilders case) is a cost effective human resource activity? Why or why not?

2. Do you believe it is feasible to identify all or most of the possible attributes that an employee could possess?

3. Do you believe it is feasible to identify all or most of the possible job dimensions that represent every organizational activity?

4. Is the strategy of matching employee attributes with job dimensions an effective one for most organizations?

ADDITIONAL READINGS

Ash, R. A., and S. L. Edgell. "A Note on the Readability of the Position Analysis Questionnaire (PAQ)." *Journal of Applied Psychology* 60 (1975), pp. 765–766.

Cain, P. S., and B. F. Green. "Reliabilities of Selected Ratings Available from the *Dictionary of Occupational Titles.*" *Journal of Applied Psychology* 68 (1983), pp. 155–165.

Conley, P. R., and P. R. Sackett. "Effects of Using High- versus Low-Performing Job Incumbents as Sources of Job-Analysis Information." *Journal of Applied Psychology* 72 (1987), pp. 434–437.

DiNisi, A. S., E. T. Cornelius III, and A. G. Blencoe. "Further Investigation of Common Knowledge Effects on Job Analysis Ratings." *Journal of Applied Psychology* 72 (1987), pp. 262–268.

Dowell, B. E., and K. N. Wexley. "Development of a Work Behavior Taxonomy for First-Line Supervisors." *Journal of Applied Psychology* 63 (1978), pp. 563–572.

Friedman, L., and R. J. Harvey. "Can Raters with Reduced Job Descriptive Information Provide Accurate Position Analysis Questionnaire (PAQ) Ratings?" *Personnel Psychology* 39 (1986), pp. 779–789.

Gael, Sidney. *Job Analysis: A Guide to Assessing Work Activities.* (San Francisco, CA: Jossey-Bass, 1983).

Harvey, Robert J., Lee Friedman, Milton D. Hakel, and Edwin T. Cornelius III. "Dimensionality of the Job Element Inventory, A Simplified Worker-Oriented Job Analysis Questionnaire." *Journal of Applied Psychology* 73, no. 4 (1988), pp. 639–646.

Harvey, Robert J., and Susana R. Lozada-Larsen. "Influence of Amount of Job Descriptive Information on Job Analysis Rating Accuracy." *Journal of Applied Psychology* 73, no. 3 (1988), pp. 457–461.

Hunt, Allen H., and Timothy L. Hunt. *Human Resource Implications of Robotics.* (Kalamazoo, MI: W. E. Upjohn Institute for Employment Research, 1982).

Levine, E. L., R. A. Ash, and N. Bennett. "Exploratory Comparative Study of Four Job Analysis Methods." *Journal of Applied Psychology* 65 (1980), pp. 524–535.

Levine, E. L., R. A. Ash, H. Hall, and F. Sistrunk. "Evaluation of Job Analysis Methods by Experienced Job Analysts." *Academy of Management Journal* 26, no. 2 (1983), pp. 339–348.

McCormick, E. J., P. R. Jeanneret, and R. C. Mecham. "A Study of Job Characteristics and Job Dimensions as Based on the Position Analysis Questionnaire (PAQ)." *Journal of Applied Psychology* 56 (1982), pp. 347–368.

McGregor, Douglas. *Human Side of Enterprise.* (New York: McGraw-Hill, 1960).

Miller, A. R., D. J. Treiman, P. S. Cain, and P. A. Roos, eds. *Work, Jobs, and Occupations: A Critical Review of the Dictionary of Occupational Titles.* (Washington, DC: National Academy Press, 1980).

Mullins, Wayman C., and Wilson W. Kimbrough. "Group Composition as a Determinant of Job Analysis Outcomes." *Journal of Applied Psychology* 73, no. 4 (1988), pp. 657–664.

Tornow, W. W., and P. R. Pinto. "The Development of a Managerial Taxonomy: A System for Describing, Classifying, and Evaluating Executive Positions." *Journal of Applied Psychology* 61 (1976), pp. 410–418.

NOTES

1. Patrick M. Wright and Kenneth N. Wexley, "How to Choose the Kind of Job Analysis You Really Need," *Personnel,* 62, May 1985, pp. 51–55.

2. John Byrne, "Up, Up and Away?" *Business Week,* November 25, 1985, pp. 80–89; Reggi Ann Dubin, "Growing Pains at People Express," *Business Week,* January 28, 1985, pp. 90–91; and Geraldine Spruell, "Will Competition Knock the People out of People Express?" *Training and Development Journal,* May 1986, pp. 50–53.

3. William J. Rothwell and N. C. Kazanas, *Strategic Human Resource Development* (Englewood Cliffs, NJ: Prentice-Hall, 1989), p. 140.

4. Wright and Wexley, "How to Choose the Kind of Job Analysis You Really Need."

5. For a more in-depth discussion, the reader is encouraged to consult Benjamin Schneider and Neal Schmitt, *Staffing Organizations* (Glenview, IL: Scott, Foresman, 1986); and Edwin A. Fleishman and Marilyn K. Quaintance, *Taxonomies of Human Performance* (Orlando, FL: Academic Press, 1984).

6. Ernest J. McCormick, *Job Analysis: Methods and Applications* (New York: AMACOM, 1979), pp. 144–145.

7. J. E. Butler, G. R. Ferris, and N. K. Napier, *Strategy and Human Resources Management* (Cincinnati, OH: South-Western, 1991).

8. R. Miles and C. Snow, "Designing Strategic Human Resources System," *Organizational Dynamics* 13, Summer 1984, pp. 36–52; and Wright and Wexley, "How to Choose."

9. Robert L. Mathis and John H. Jackson, *Personnel/Human Resource Management* (St. Paul: West, 1985), p. 177.

10. Hugh Green, "Matching People to Jobs: An Expert System Approach," *Personnel Management,* September 1987, pp. 42–45.

8 *Job Design*

How a job is designed has a tremendous impact on the effectiveness of the organization and the quality of work life for employees. Given the importance of job design, it should be tied directly to the strategies and goals of the organization.

Job design can be thought of as a blueprint of tasks required to accomplish a job successfully. Job design and redesign techniques have become more complex due to the downsizing that has plagued many organizations. Essentially, fewer challenging jobs are available and employees are sometimes placed in jobs for which they are clearly overqualified.[1]

● ● ● ● ● ● ● ● ●
CHAPTER OBJECTIVES

As a result of studying this chapter, you should be able to

1. Discuss the various environmental, organizational, and behavioral factors that need to be considered in job design.
2. Discuss early approaches to job design.
3. Describe the various individual and group design options.
4. Describe how the job characteristics model can aid managers in job design or redesign.
5. Discuss the sociotechnical model and the characteristics of autonomous work groups.
6. Discuss the relationship between organizational strategy and job design.
7. List and describe the steps involved in the strategic framework for job redesign.

CASE: Fearful Skies and the Bored X-ray Operators[2]

As Americans make plans to fly abroad, many find themselves concerned about terrorism. The airplane explosion over Lockerbie, Scotland, left them with reason for concern. Who can forget how terrorists planted a bomb aboard Pan Am Flight 103 in December 1988, killing 270 people?

In May 1989, the fear of terrorism struck again. One of Iran's most powerful leaders, Hashemi Rafsanjani, suggested that Americans, French and British be murdered—five for every Palestinian killed by Israelis. "It is not hard to kill Americans or Frenchmen," Rafsanjani said, adding that hijacking planes for hostages was another possibility.

The United States government is trying to respond to these dangerous threats. Because bombs can be hidden and disguised in ordinary items such as radios and laptop computers so that X rays cannot spot them, the Transportation Department is considering a total ban on such items. However, the fact remains that there are few defenses against sophisticated terrorists. Worse, even those procedures that exist can collapse through human failings, when airport workers are overloaded and overwhelmed by hoards of impatient passengers and mountains of luggage.

The Lockerbie case is sobering. Investigators think a passenger who boarded in Frankfurt and transferred at London for the flight to New York unwittingly checked a bag with a radio concealing the bomb. "We saw the disciplined London and Frankfurt airports as something of an obstacle for terrorists," says Mike Ackerman, a partner in a Miami security consulting firm. But terrorists not only got a bomb on, "they made it look easy."

X-ray Limitations

All X-ray machines depend on interpretations by operators, some of whom may be ill trained or poorly motivated. The Transportation Department task force reports that training of U.S. X-ray screeners was described as "perfunctory."

To avoid paying high airline wages and flight benefits, U.S. carriers generally hire outside security firms to perform screening. The firms, which often get hired by submitting the lowest bid, pay screeners poorly, sometimes only slightly above the minimum wage. Two contractors interviewed by the task force said fast-food chains were their chief competitors for staff. "The restaurants occasionally paid more . . . , and even if pay were the same, had the advantage because they provide meals as well," the task force said.

Perhaps the biggest problem is the nature of the job itself. "Anyone standing in front of a monitor watching suitcase after suitcase go by is bound over time to become tired and inattentive," the task force stated. At peak periods, it added, screeners are confronted with "long lines of anxious passengers, putting the screening crew under extreme pressure" to rush bags through.

In Europe, government employees usually screen passengers, with American carriers often performing a second screening. But the same problems afflict screeners overseas, of course.

Since the Lockerbie disaster, the U.S. Department of Transportation has ordered American carriers to intensify security procedures on all bags checked in Europe and the Middle East. Federal regulation requires that bags be searched or X-rayed and all must be matched to a passenger on board. But even today, bags checked on most carriers at most airports around the world are neither searched nor X-rayed. They are put, unexamined, on airplanes.

Pan Am has since charged the Federal Aviation Administration with approving security procedures in Frankfurt that the airline later found were in violation of federal regulations. Pan Am did not match each bag checked with a passenger on board; it simply relied on the X-ray screeners to identify bombs in unmatched bags. Terrorists have countered by using unwitting bomb carriers.

For example, an Irish woman passed through London Heathrow security—which was equipped with an X-ray machine—with a suitcase that was packed with a bomb prepared by her Arab boyfriend. The timer was concealed in a calculator and the bomb was in the bottom of the suitcase. Fortunately, El Al security personnel at the gate discovered the bomb just before the woman boarded.

• • • • • • • • •

One of the major problems is with the way an X-ray machine operator's job is designed. The work is so repetitive, no wonder the workers become bored, tired, and inattentive. Given the potential disastrous effects of an inattentive X-ray machine operator, airlines might consider evaluating the current job design. Redesigning the work of airline X-ray personnel to be more interesting and motivating could save a lot of lives.

STRATEGIC CHOICES

The decision to initially design or later redesign jobs in an organization should not be made hastily. Managers must consider a number of factors before deciding upon a job redesign effort. Any job redesign program should be carefully examined and consistent with the overall strategy of the organization. Environmental, organizational, and behavioral factors should be considered before designing jobs for the first time or redesigning jobs because of a needed change.

Environmental Factors

Political System

All organizations are affected by the political systems in their environment. Organizations must comply with international, national, state, and local laws, regulations, and ordinances if they want to survive. Managers need to be aware of a plethora of laws because virtually every aspect of their organizational operations is affected by legal considerations. In the United States, there are numerous laws covering wages, hiring practices, benefits, drug testing, and safety standards. These laws can have a direct or indirect impact on the design of the job. For example, safety regulations may directly affect the design of certain jobs. Consider a factory worker who walks between dangerous machinery or moving belts because this is the most efficient path to obtain his needed supplies. The Occupational Safety and Health Act (OSHA) would most likely prohibit such behavior. The organization would need to redesign this job to avoid employee injuries and a fine from OSHA. If a number of jobs required employees to walk through dangerous areas, the organization might need to consider a total redesign effort.

Organizational managers must also consider the political systems in other countries. Organizations in the United States are affected by problems such as the grain shortages in the Soviet Union and international terrorism. The opening case to this chapter demonstrates how the jobs of airline X-ray operators may be redesigned to better detect terrorist bombs. It is vital that managers consider their political and economic environments in order to design or redesign jobs within the organization.

Social Expectations

The acceptability of a job's design is partially due to societal expectations. For example, uneducated immigrants flocked to America in the early days of the automobile industry. They were willing to accept low-paying jobs that were routine, physically difficult, and demanding of long work days. Often these immigrants were willing to accept this type of job because they had left countries where work was unavailable. Today, however, employees are better educated and expect a higher quality of work life from their jobs. Failure to meet these expectations can lead to low motivation, dissatisfaction, lower performance, and higher absenteeism and turnover. Culture, the work ethic, and religion all help to shape societal expectations.

Organizational Factors

Automation

One important decision managers have to make when designing jobs initially or when considering job redesign is whether they want to automate the job and, if so, to what degree. Job redesign through automation has been undertaken by many companies, including companies in the automobile and steel industries, in order to cut labor costs. Reducing labor costs has helped many organizations to achieve or remain competitive in world markets. For example, as a strategic choice, the firm must decide how much it wants to substitute capital for labor through automation, robotics, and other highly technical innovations. A company can reduce per unit labor costs by automating more, thus reducing the number of employees. For example, McDonald's is trying out a grill that cooks hamburgers on both sides at once. This new device could eliminate the hamburger flipper. PepsiCo has developed a beverage dispenser that fills cups by computer.[3] General Motors introduced robotics on the assembly line, changing many of the jobs while making others obsolete.

Automation can open up more interesting and challenging jobs for employees in the organization by automating the more repetitive and routine jobs. Automation (for example, word processors or laser printers) has given secretaries more time for new and higher-level duties. Firms are training secretaries as managerial assistants and paraprofessionals. Thus, secretarial skills are broadening, partially due to automation. At Quanex Corporation in Houston, many secretaries take on marketing or personnel responsibilities.[4] However, automation should not be seen as a panacea for job enrichment. Automation often leads to more routine jobs, a decrease in social interaction, displacement, or even the elimination of jobs.[5] Continually performing repetitive and routine jobs, although efficient, can lead to employee boredom, fatigue, tardiness, absenteeism, performance decrements, and ultimately lower productivity. This issue will be explored in greater detail later in the chapter.

Technology

Many managers want to have state-of-the-art equipment in their organization. Often keeping up with the latest developments in the technical field can help keep a company on the "cutting edge." For managers who master the newest in office technologies, the payoff can be more power and greater control.[6] Just as often, however, investing in expensive equipment can serve to be a waste of resources. Investing in a new computer system, for example, may not be cost effective. Not only should the cost of the equipment be a concern, but managers must consider the costs of any additional training needed to teach employees the new system, any loss of productivity due to training or computer down time during implementation, and how jobs will be affected. For example, some very specific workplace effects attributable to computerization have been identified from the research.[7] The implementation of a computer-aided design system has been found to increase and change communication patterns on the job, increase skill requirements, and increase the formalization of work methods. Interestingly, computer-aided designs have not affected job displacement or wages significantly.

If managers fail to understand and prepare for the revolutionary capabilities of high-technology computer systems, new technology can become as much an expense and inconvenience as a benefit.[8] If the new system changes a number of jobs, additional considerations need to be made. First, are the employees skilled enough to work their newly designed job? Do they want to take on additional (or fewer) responsibilities? Will the time and effort required for training and learning be cost effective? How well can the organization respond to new incentives if jobs are substantially changed?[9] Finally, are the employees committed to the job redesign change and willing to try and make it work? A recent longitudinal study examined the adjustment of unskilled workers transferring from traditional assembly lines to computer-automated batch production. Results suggest that actual changes to jobs increased employee stress, and decreased job satisfaction, organizational commitment, and the perceived quality of work life.[10]

An essential ingredient for a successful job redesign effort is employee training. Ingersoll-Rand, for example, developed a special program designed to help employees cope with plant modernization.[11] Ingersoll-Rand in Athens, Pennsylvania, is the primary manufacturing location for the company's power tool division. Parts of the plant were over 100 years old. In order to remain competitive, Ingersoll-Rand needed to modernize its machinery. Employees had been operating conventional machine tools (such as cranks, dials, and buttons), however, as a result of the job redesign effort, employees were expected to operate numerically controlled machinery. They had to perform computer setups, interact with this new technology, and integrate these skills with their regular work teams. Essentially, production methods went from the traditional assembly line system to cellular manufacturing. The training program was conducted by Penn State University's Institute for Research in Training and Development. The training took place on two levels: basic skills (reading, writing, and arithmetic) and floor skills (the daily skills needed to operate the computerized equipment). The results have exceeded expectations. The training program helped Ingersoll-Rand profit from plant modernization, since computerization has kept costs down and products priced competitively. Just as important, the employee response to the program was extremely favorable: 99 percent of the eligible employees volunteered to participate. In addition, many of these employees have gone beyond the training program and are continuing their education in the classroom. Managers should carefully analyze all aspects of any job redesign program to give it the best chance for success.

Cross-Functional Integration

Cross-functional integration is the act of combining jobs into one. Recently, a number of organizations have begun cross-functional integration in order to cut labor costs and raise productivity. Service firms have been particularly interested in this strategy because of today's tight labor market and tomorrow's expected labor shortage in the service industry. For example, Manor Care, which operates the Sleep Inn hotel chain, is designing its hotels with the flair of an industrial engineer. By simplifying jobs and carefully examining the time it takes to complete these jobs, Manor Care is able to combine jobs and keep its staff size down.[12] A typical 100-bed Sleep Inn will employ only 12 full-time employees, 13 percent fewer than the average no-frills hotel. To simplify housekeeping, the nightstands are bolted to the walls so that workers do not need to vacuum around the legs. The closet has no doors to open and shut. The shower is round to prevent dirt from collecting in the corners. These labor-saving ideas give housekeepers more time to do additional tasks, such as working with room service or even at the front desk.

The hotel's security system helps the owners keep track of the time it takes a housekeeper to clean a room. The employee inserts a card that tells the front-desk computer where the housekeeper is located, when he or she entered the room, and when the housekeeper finished cleaning and exited the room. This same computer can bar a guest's access to the room after checkout time and automatically turns off the heat or air-conditioning. Thus, by simplifying jobs, combining jobs, and utilizing technology, Manor Care is able to cut its labor force and raise wages while remaining competitive.

Behavioral Factors

Labor Pool Skill Mix

Before attempting a job design or redesign program, managers should decide whether their employees' skills will match or "fit" the new jobs. Sometimes additional training is all that is necessary. However, on occasion, employees will not have the abilities or education to perform the newly designed jobs. This can lead to dissatisfaction, frustration, and poor performance. If the job design or redesign effort simplifies the work too much, employees may become bored, apathetic, unchallenged, and dissatisfied. These individual factors could lead to poor performance and lower productivity even if the job has been designed to be more efficient.

Fitting Employee Needs versus Technology

Designing or redesigning jobs can be made to fit the employees, the existing technology, or a combination of both. Managers must decide which direction they believe is most appropriate for their organization. Designing jobs for people involves an important examination of the wants, needs, and desires of employees. For example, jobs can be designed to increase the meaningfulness of the work for employees', satisfaction, and motivation. The job characteristics model, which addresses the issue, will be discussed later in this chapter. Designing jobs to fit the technology is often a primary concern. For example, organizations that have large amounts of money invested into machinery and equipment (such as the General Motors assembly line) must keep these capital investments in mind if job redesign is considered. Another approach is to consider both the technology and needs of the people simultaneously. This approach is called sociotechnical systems. Basically, it involves forming autonomous work groups that recognize the importance of integrating the social system with the technical system. This approach will be explored further later in the chapter. Before examining new approaches to job redesign, early job design efforts will be discussed.

Early Job Design Efforts

Scientific Management

Frederick Taylor, the father of "scientific management," focused on the efficiency of operations after the turn of the century. Taylor's scientific management principles and general management philosophy emphasized the following components:

1. Specialization (narrow range of tasks per job)
2. Clear and specific job descriptions
3. Systematic scheduling of work and rest breaks
4. Close supervision

Utilizing the scientific management approach, industrial engineers and job analysts focused on specialization in designing jobs so that they would not exceed the abilities of the workers. As a result, most jobs were mechanistic and reduced to extremely simple and repetitive tasks. These tasks lent themselves to time and motion studies and piece rate reward systems. Although efficient, scientific management overlooked the human element when designing the job. Many workers became bored, tired, and dissatisfied with their repetitive jobs. In effect, the personal goals of the

HR CHALLENGES •

Early Job Specialization and Mechanization in the United States

As the United States began to evolve into a more industrialized nation, many organizations began to increase in size and complexity. In order to manage this complexity, organizations began to specialize by breaking the components of the job down into smaller segments and adopting scientific management principles.

The use of specialization and mechanization (the use of machines to perform work) also made it easier to manage the influx of immigrant workers. Many of the immigrant workers had poor communications skills in terms of the English language and they performed best on jobs that were designed to be performed in a more simple and repetitive manner. This emphasis on specialization led to the development of many highly automated assembly lines and, consequently, created many repetitive and boring jobs.

Finally, labor unions in the United States had an influence on the specialization and mechanization of jobs. By pursuing a high-wage strategy for employees, unions provided employers with incentives to change technology and redesign jobs in order to use less labor (which was costly) and more machinery. Specialization

and mechanization were also consistent with union concerns about job control. Job control unionism involves highly formalized contracts and grievance procedures to handle disputes during the term of the contracts. This system can only work if jobs are unambiguously defined and changes in job definitions and work assignments are sharply delineated. If this is not the case, it is impossible to attach specific wages and employment rights to specific jobs. Given that industrial engineers had been following scientific management practices and guidelines (for example, breaking the work down into discrete, well-defined jobs and attaching wages to specific jobs through time-motion studies and job evaluation), unions found much of their work was already done for them.

SOURCES: Adapted from T. Kochan, H. Katz, and R. McKersie, *The Transformation of American Industrial Relations,* (New York: Basic Books, 1986); R. Freeman and J. Medoff, *What Do Unions Do?,* (New York: Basic Books, 1984); and P. Taft, "Organized Labor and Technical Change: A Backward Look," in G. Somers, E. Cushman, and N. Weignberg, eds., *Adjusting to Technological Change,* (New York: Harper & Row, 1963).

---

employee (growth and challenge) were sacrificed for the goals of the organization (productivity).

Human Relations

In the early 1930s, managers became aware of the need to emphasize employee morale and cooperation. Treating employees as "human beings" as opposed to machines and acknowledging their needs was the emphasis of the human relations movement. Historically, three critical factors gave impetus to this new approach to management: the Great Depression, the labor movement, and the Hawthorne studies.[13] The depression was due to a number of factors including a piling up of business inventories and consumer resistance to rising prices. After the stock market crash, management realized that production was not the only important organizational factor. Marketing, finance, and personnel also needed to be emphasized. Unemployment, a weakening of confidence, and a general discontent made human problems more salient to managers. Human relations became a more significant issue.

The passage of the Wagner Act in 1935 gave employees the right to organize and unionize. The organized labor movement helped make managers aware of the employee concerns. Typical areas of employee concern included fair wages, decent working conditions, and reasonable hours. Although many organizations initially resisted labor interference, organized labor was now legal and management (some more willingly than others) began to work with employees to resolve grievances and emphasize employee relations.

....

EXHIBIT 8.1 Various Individual and Group Job Design Approaches

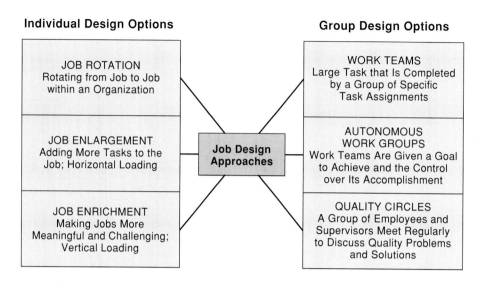

Individual Design Options   **Group Design Options**

JOB ROTATION
Rotating from Job to Job
within an Organization

JOB ENLARGEMENT
Adding More Tasks to the
Job; Horizontal Loading

JOB ENRICHMENT
Making Jobs More
Meaningful and Challenging;
Vertical Loading

Job Design Approaches

WORK TEAMS
Large Task that Is Completed
by a Group of Specific
Task Assignments

AUTONOMOUS
WORK GROUPS
Work Teams Are Given a Goal
to Achieve and the Control
over Its Accomplishment

QUALITY CIRCLES
A Group of Employees and
Supervisors Meet Regularly
to Discuss Quality Problems
and Solutions

Options in job design

The final contributing factor to the human relations movement was a series of studies conducted at the Hawthorne Works of the Western Electric Company outside Chicago. Conducted under the direction of Harvard professor Elton Mayo, the Hawthorne studies demonstrated the importance of group influences in affecting individual behavior and performance. These studies concluded that group norms and standards had a more significant impact on worker output than did money. Together, the Great Depression, the labor movement, and the Hawthorne studies gave impetus to a new organizational emphasis—the human factor. Today, managers are interested in determining how to design jobs to better motivate their employees.

The importance of job design can be seen in the results of a study that surveyed over 56,000 people. Individuals were asked to rate the most important factor in a job. Interesting work was rated as the most important factor in a job over security, pay, advancement opportunities, pleasant coworkers, or a considerate boss. Thus, it appears that the job itself can provide a significant source of motivation for employees.[14]

Job Redesign Approaches

As shown in Exhibit 8.1, a variety of individual and group job design options are available for managers. Job rotation, job enlargement, and job enrichment are among the approaches concerned with designing or redesigning individual tasks. Approaches for designing or redesigning jobs or groups include forming work teams, autonomous work groups, and quality circles.

Job Rotation

Job rotation does not change the actual job content. Employees are rotated from one job to another after a specified period of time. This technique was used by People Express in the opening case in the previous chapter. Job rotation often increases the number of employee skills and duties and can add flexibility to the organization. For example, organizations that emphasize specialization and trained employees on only one task do not have the flexibility to substitute employees on jobs if someone is absent or abruptly quits. However, training every employee to be a "jack of all trades" is not always advantageous to the organization, as illustrated in the People Express case.

Job Enlargement

Job enlargement increases the number of tasks an individual performs, thereby increasing the diversity of a job. Adding more tasks to the job (horizontally loading) increases variety for the worker. Job enlargement's major shortcoming is that many workers do not perceive enlargement as adding variety, but as simply giving them more work to do. Thus, job enlargement can add variety to highly specialized jobs; however, it does little to add meaning and significance to the job.

Job Enrichment

Job enrichment increases the depth of a job by expanding the job vertically. Managers must add meaningfulness to the job and allow workers more control over their work if the job is going to be perceived as enriched. In addition, the job should provide feedback to workers regarding their performance. The following list illustrates how Travelers Insurance enriched the jobs of its key-punch operators: [15]

1. The random assignment of work was changed so that each operator was responsible for specific accounts.
2. The task of key-punching was expanded to include some planning and control functions.
3. The operators were given direct contact with clients. If a problem arose, the client dealt with the operator—not a supervisor.
4. The operators were given the control to plan their schedule, prioritize their work, and correct their own coding errors.
5. Weekly computer printouts of errors were sent to the operator rather than the supervisor.

Travelers Insurance found the results of its enrichment program to be outstanding. The changes saved Travelers an estimated $90,000 a year. The quantity and quality of performance increased, errors and absenteeism were reduced, and worker attitudes seemed to improve.

Work Teams

To create a work team, a group of workers is given a large task to complete and the team members are responsible for deciding on specific task assignments, solving production problems, and continually improving work activities. The members of the work team can rotate the tasks among members or assign specific tasks to members. The group has a supervisor who oversees the entire operation. [16] The supervisor must concentrate on coaching and training while keeping the team's focus in line with the goals of the entire organization. [17] Construction builders often use work teams to complete a house, for example. The goal of a work team is to implement job enlargement at the group level. A recent study suggests that the success of work teams is primarily due to the workers' awareness of time constraints and deadlines.[18] The case at the end of the chapter shows how much General Motors is now using work teams in production.

A newer concept, team selling, has become popular with a number of large corporations. For example, General Electric Company has teamed over 50 salespeople from nine different businesses to sell equipment to be used on the General Motors Saturn car project. Hewlett-Packard Company and Apple Computer Incorporated have switched to a team-based approach. These particular teams generally consist of a leader, who serves as a source of information and strategist, and a team of workers, which can include specialists from every part of the company. Although a team approach is an efficient way to meet the needs of large, competitive firms, it requires a fundamental redesign of the entire organization. Thus, it is not surprising that a survey of 476 large companies by the U.S. General Accounting Office showed that while 27 percent were using work teams, these teams usually involved fewer than one-fifth of the employees.[19]

Implementing work teams can present problems for the organization. Supervisors and managers often feel that the use of work teams dilutes their power and authority. Further, if the number of team members is too large (over 15), smaller interest groups tend to develop.[20] In order for more teams to be successful, management must consider these problems and monitor the transition process carefully. By keeping the groups small in number and providing clear, explicit roles for the supervisor, the organization can ensure that the opportunity for team success is high.

Autonomous Work Groups

Forming autonomous work groups recognizes the importance of integrating the social system with the technical system. This is a socio-technical approach to job design. In essence, an autonomous work group is responsible for achieving a goal and is given a considerable amount of control over work assignments, rest breaks, prioritizing, inspection procedures, and so on. Some autonomous work groups even have the freedom to select their members. Autonomous work groups can be thought of as implementing job enrichment (vertical loading) at the group level. The most widely publicized use of autonomous work groups occurred at the Volvo automobile plant in Sweden. Volvo's top management reported lower turnover, absenteeism, and production costs, and a higher quality of work life for their employees.[21]

Recently, Monsanto Chemical Company has made some dramatic changes at its fibers plant in Greenwood, South Carolina. Monsanto has instituted its own version of autonomous work groups. The employees in the work groups divide the work and make key decisions themselves. One of the workers said that he knew 20 years ago that he could direct his own job, but nobody wanted to hear what he had to say. This has now changed. Workers are getting involved in decision making and quality control. Using autonomous work groups has enabled Monsanto to get by with fewer supervisors, which has, subsequently, left more money for employee training. Quality has improved and productivity has increased 47 percent in the last four years. This program is not without problems, however. By focusing on quality and productivity, employees have become less safety-conscious and injuries have increased. In addition, fewer management positions have caused promotions to be scarce. Nonetheless, the autonomous work group approach will remain. As Jack W. Treece, Greenwood's personnel chief, argues, "Once you give people freedom, you can't take it back."[22]

Quality Circles

The concept of a quality circle primarily focuses on maintaining and enhancing the quality of a product. However, quality circles have been used as management development devices. Management development systems (including quality circles) in the leading Japanese firms have produced executives and managers who are commonly thought to be among the best in the world.[23] Although originally developed in the United States, Japan has used quality circles more extensively. Recently, however, quality circles have become increasingly popular in the United States. Typically, quality circles include a group of seven to ten employees and supervisors who meet at regular intervals (usually once a week) to discuss quality-control problems and solutions. The quality circle is a management-employee group effort designed to find and solve production and coordination problems. The Lockheed Missile and Space Company is one of the first American organizations to implement and study the effects of an extensive quality circle program. Results of their program are reported to have saved the company six dollars for every one dollar it spent on the process. In addition, defects in manufacturing declined by two-thirds and job satisfaction among quality circle members increased.[24] The potential for improving individual performance and organizational effectiveness has given impetus to the respect and support that quality circles now receive from many management and union members.[25]

In order to achieve the potential benefits from a quality circle, management must be committed to the concept and provide good training to the members. Employees must not be allowed to use the meeting time to explore problems with working conditions, environmental issues, or salary and benefit systems. Instead, the focus must be on work-process problems and concerns.[26] In fact, many of the problems found in trying to implement Japan's popular quality circles here in the United States are due to misconceptions about their true intent and purpose.[27] However, if the proper focus is attained, quality circles could produce tremendous benefits for almost any U.S. company.

Strategic Guidelines for Job Design

Two of the most comprehensive frameworks for job design are the job characteristics model and the sociotechnical model. The job characteristics model proposes specific characteristics of jobs that can lead to important psychological states. In turn, these psychological states lead to a number of positive personal and work outcomes.[28] The sociotechnical model is concerned with the interaction between the technological system and the social system in an organization. These approaches are discussed below.

The Job Characteristics Model

As shown in Exhibit 8.2, the job characteristics model recognizes that individuals may perceive and respond to the same stimuli differently. Thus, its designers, Hackman and Oldham, proposed that the relationship between core job characteristics and the psychological states is moderated by an individual's growth need strength. Similarly, the relationship between the psychological states and the personal and work outcome is moderated by growth need strength. *Growth need strength is the need to learn, grow, and be challenged.* This means that if employees perceive their jobs as

....

EXHIBIT 8.2 Hackman-Oldham's Job Characteristics Model

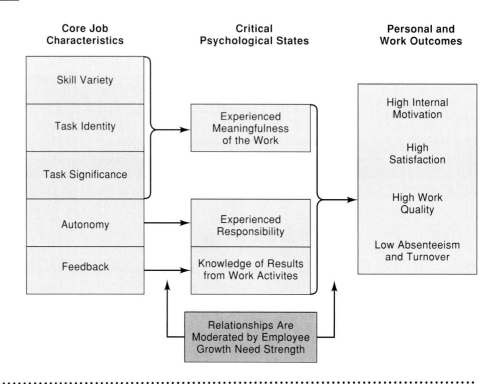

....

being high on the core job characteristics and they have a high growth need strength these employees are more likely to experience the psychological state. If employees perceive the psychological states from their work and they have high growth need strength, they are more likely to experience the personal and work outcomes. In essence, this model works best for employees with a need to learn, grow, and be challenged (high growth need strength).

The five core job characteristics are defined in the following terms:

1. *Task identity*—seeing a whole piece of work. The employees can complete a task from beginning to end with an identifiable outcome.
2. *Task significance*—importance of the job: The characteristic is determined by the impact the employee's work has on others within or outside the organization.
3. *Skill variety*—the degree to which employees are able to do a number of different tasks using many different skills, abilities, and talents determines the skill variety.
4. *Autonomy*—the degree to which employees have control over their work. This refers to the amount of discretion and independence employees have regarding such things as scheduling, prioritizing, and determining procedures for task completion.
5. *Feedback*—the degree to which the job offers information to employees regarding performance and work outcomes.

The three psychological states are defined in the following terms:

1. *Experienced meaningfulness*—the degree to which employees perceive the work as being meaningful, valuable, and worthwhile.
2. *Responsibility*—the degree to which employees feel accountable and responsible for the outcomes of their work.
3. *Knowledge of results*—the degree to which employees know and understand how well they are performing on the job.

Although the five job characteristics are widely accepted, recent evidence suggests that an expanded set of job characteristics among other modifications may be more predictive of employee attitudes and behaviors.[29] Further, the characteristics of the job should be matched with the abilities and needs of jobholders.[30]

Job Diagnostic Survey

Hackman and Oldham developed a questionnaire for testing the job characteristics model called the Job Diagnostic Survey.[31] The survey contains measures of the core job characteristics, critical psychological states, personal and work outcomes, and growth need strength. Research results indicate that the job diagnostic survey can discriminate between different jobs.

Strategies for Managers

The job characteristics model offers managers strategic guidelines for increasing core job dimensions in the workplace. As depicted in Exhibit 8.3, each strategic guideline affects one or more of the job characteristics.

A recent application of the job characteristics model offers some evidence that this approach can be useful to improve both employee satisfaction and performance.[32] Sales jobs in a large department store were redesigned in the following manner:

1. Skill variety. Salespeople were asked to try to think of and use different selling approaches, new merchandising displays and new record keeping methods.
2. Task identity. Salespeople were asked to keep a personal record of daily sales in dollars, keep a daily record of the number of sales/customers, and determine a display area that would be theirs and keep it orderly and finished looking.
3. Task significance. Salespeople were reoriented to the store objectives, reminded of the importance of their display areas to selling, and told that, to the customers, the salespeople are "the store."
4. Autonomy. Salespeople were encouraged to develop and use their own unique sales approaches, select their own breaks, and make suggestions for improvement in any phase of policy or operations.
5. Feedback. Salespeople were encouraged to keep personal records of their performance, observe and help each other with selling techniques, and invite supervisor and customer reactions to merchandise, service, and so forth.

The salespeoples' effective performance behaviors (conversing with customers, handling returns, and showing merchandise, for example) increased while ineffective

···

| **EXHIBIT 8.3** | Effect of Strategic Guidelines on Job Characteristics |

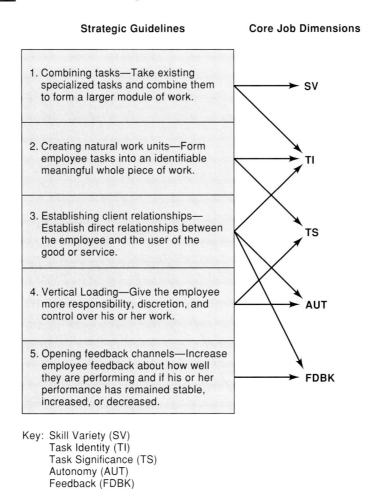

Key: Skill Variety (SV)
      Task Identity (TI)
      Task Significance (TS)
      Autonomy (AUT)
      Feedback (FDBK)

···

performance behaviors (such as socializing with coworkers or leaving their work stations without legitimate reason) decreased. Satisfaction also increased for this group of salespeople. Another group of salespeople who did not receive the intervention (the control group) showed no change in performance. This is one of the most recent examples of how job redesign can be used as a strategic intervention for both employee and organizational benefits.

The Sociotechnical Model

The sociotechnical approach to job design was started in the 1950s by the Tavistock Institute in London. One of the first studies conducted by this research team examined the effects of implementing an efficient long-wall method (assembly line) in a coal mine on productivity.[33] The intervention failed because management did not consider the problems associated with removing the coal miners from their small

FOCUS ON INTERNATIONAL ISSUES ••••••••••••••••••••••••••

Volvo

When Pehr Gyllenhammer became the head of Volvo in Sweden, he inherited serious turnover and absenteeism problems. Convinced that the employees wanted more meaningful work, he decided to use the sociotechnical model to redesign the job. Traditionally automobile assembly plants had used an assembly line to manufacture automobiles. Gyllenhammer arranged the technological process to reflect more natural modules of work and formed autonomous work groups to give employees more control over their work and to increase the meaningfulness of their work.

The Volvo assembly plant in Kalmar was totally redesigned in 1974. The autonomous work groups performed work according to general and natural modules, such as modules for the electrical system, brake system, interior, and steering and controls. Employees within these work modules had control over scheduling their work, breaks, inspecting their work, and even electing their own group leader.

The Volvo plants in Uddevalla, Sweden, are also mass-producing the Volvo without using assembly lines. However, Uddevalla goes much further than Kalmar. There are six assembly plants with eight teams each. The teams manage themselves by handling scheduling, quality control, hiring, and other duties usually performed by supervisors. Each team works in one area and assembles four cars every shift. Since workers are trained to handle all assembly jobs, they work an average of three hours before repeating the same task. Thus, Uddevalla is able to avoid the classic problem associated with assembly lines: boredom, inattention,

poor quality, and high absenteeism. Morale seems high at Uddevalla.

It wasn't an effectiveness problem or a lack of problems that prompted Volvo to design its plants using a radically different approach. The country's highly educated, well-trained labor force does not like to work in factories and many Swedish manufacturers are having trouble attracting and retaining employees. Volvo's conventional assembly-line plants suffer absenteeism rates of 20 percent and almost one-third of its employees turn over annually. Absenteeism at Uddevalla is only 8 percent, although at Kalmar, absenteeism is at 17 percent. If the autonomous work groups increase efficiency over the long run, American automobile manufacturers may consider designing plants with this concept in mind.

The reported results from Volvo, thus far, have been favorable. Since the sociotechnical intervention, Volvo reports reduced turnover and an overall increase in the quality of work life. Caution must be taken, however, because the effects of this sociotechnical job redesign effort have never been systematically or empirically examined. The reports from Volvo are largely based on perceptions and anecdotal evidence. Although one should remain skeptical, Volvo's management team believes their job redesign effort has, for the most part, been successful.

SOURCE: Adapted from J. Kapstein, "Volvo's Radical New Plant: 'The Death of the Assembly Line'?" *Business Week*, August 28, 1989, pp. 92–93; and B. Jonsson and A. Lank, "Volvo: A Report on the Workshop on Production Technology and Quality of Working Life," *Human Resources Management*, Winter 1985, p. 463.

autonomous work groups. The work environment includes both technical and social aspects. These two systems are interrelated and influence each other. The sociotechnical model proposes a fit among the needs of individuals, groups, and technological processes for effective organizational goal attainment. This approach gave impetus to autonomous work groups, which provide employees with control over the design and management of their work. Volvo and General Foods provide two widely publicized company examples using a sociotechnical approach.

Managing Autonomous Work Groups

Autonomous work groups need a manager, but not a manager that attempts to plan, organize, or control the group. These activities are the responsibilities of the members of the work group. Managers of autonomous work groups should carefully monitor any organizational changes that might affect the work group and serve as a liaison between the work group and top management. Unfortunately, most managers do not

HR CHALLENGES •

General Foods

The General Foods pet food plant in Topeka, Kansas, was designed around the concept of autonomous work groups. Each work group consisted of 7 to 14 members including a group leader. Every group was responsible for deciding members' work tasks, selecting new members, and developing and training new members. Another innovative feature in the Topeka plant was the idea of pay for knowledge. Employees were compensated for each additional job they learned. This not only encouraged employees to learn more jobs, but it added flexibility to the organization by ensuring that more than one person could perform each job. The plant was designed to facilitate informal gatherings for better coordination and social interaction by removing unnecessary status symbols such as plush offices or preferential parking spaces. In addition the company decentralized decision making down to the operating employees rather than keeping it centralized with top management. Decentralization was thought to be motivating and necessary if employees were actually going to be working in autonomous work groups.

The Topeka plant began to show some fairly impressive improvements. Fixed overhead was 33 percent lower than comparable plants, quality rejects were reduced by 92 percent, employee morale was good, the plant's safety record was excellent, and turnover and absenteeism were low. Although General Foods no longer owns the plant, many of these positive characteristics remain. However, top management has attempted to take control of the operations, which has caused numerous problems. Managers are sometimes insecure about letting employees have a lot of control over their own work and work-related decisions because they fear a loss of power. Managing autonomous work groups requires different skills than managing traditional work groups.

SOURCE: Adapted from B. Saporito, "The Revolt Against Working Smarter," *Fortune*, July 21, 1986, pp. 58–64; and R. E. Walton, "The Topeka Story: Teaching an Old Dog New Tricks," *The Wharton Magazine*, Spring 1978, pp. 38–46.

have the training or skills to act in an advisory, consultative, or liaison role. Thus, it is imperative that all managers of autonomous work groups receive the appropriate training required to monitor the broader organizational events. In addition, these managers need to be given the power to help develop effective work teams that are consistent with the overall goals of the organization.[34]

Organizational Strategy and Its Relationship with Job Design

An organization's job design should be consistent with the overall strategy of the organization. Beginning in the early 1970s, Raymond Miles and Charles Snow examined the competitive strategies of several hundred companies in more than a dozen different industries.[35] Over time, they realized that all of the competitive approaches revolved around a few fundamental business strategies. As discussed in Chapter 1, they observed the defender strategy (narrow and relatively stable product-market domains), the prospector strategy (continual searches for product and market opportunities and experiments with responses to environmental trends), and the analyzer strategy (operating in two types of product-market domains—one relatively stable and the other changing). Miles and Snow found that successful firms displayed a consistent strategy supported by complementary organizational structures, designs, and management processes. Those firms in which the strategy was poorly aligned with the structure, design, or process of the organization were termed reactors and performed less well than the other three types.[36]

FOCUS ON INTERNATIONAL ISSUES •

Texas Instruments Bets Its Marbles on Chips

During a recent strategy meeting at Texas Instruments (TI), it was decided that TI should return to making computer chips. According to Jerry R. Junkins, chairman of TI, the projected demand for chips during the 1990s should generate a semiconductor market worth approximately $1 billion. TI is the only U.S. chipmaker that did not abandon this market under the pressure of the Japanese in the early and mid-1980s. Many of the semiconductor industry experts admire TI's new strategy and expect the company to make a strong comeback. However, Junkins is planning TI's future on a volatile and dynamic random access memory business. During the 1990s, the progress of TI will be interesting to watch.

SOURCE: Adapted from J. Bartimo, "TI Bets Most of Its Marbles on Chips," *Business Week*, Jan. 29, 1990, pp. 73–74.

Organizations operating under a defender strategy have a limited, stable product line with predictable markets. This type of strategy is consistent with high volume and low cost production. Thus, the jobs should be designed with an emphasis on efficiency and process engineering (such as assembly lines). The goal of this type of design is to achieve economies of scale.

Organizations operating under a prospector strategy have a broad, changing product line with changing markets. This type of strategy focuses on being first on the market. The jobs should be designed to emphasize effectiveness and product design. There should be a low degree of routinization and mechanization (such as can be seen at Hewlett-Packard). The goal of this type of design is flexibility.

Building flexibility into an organization is not often an easy and inexpensive task. At this writing, for example, Ford Motor Company is starting up a new flexible manufacturing plant to build innovative modular engines for the 1990s.[37] They are taking a billion-dollar gamble on their modular engine concept. American automobile manufacturers typically design individual factories to build a single engine type. The factories produced the same basic engine for decades. This seemed to work fine when the American automotive industry could count on steady sales and stable markets. However, changing government fuel-economy regulations, intense competition from the Japanese, and changes in consumer tastes have forced many automobile manufacturers to reevaluate their mechanistic factories. Ford's new plant will have flexible manufacturing equipment, and the modular design will allow for the production of more than a dozen engine sizes and configurations on one line. In addition, this new plant design will allow inexpensive, rapid shifts to smaller, lighter engines. Ford and its competitors are a long way from knowing if this concept will be a success. However, most believe that carmakers will need modular design and flexible manufacturing to remain competitive in a changing and more volatile industry.

Finally, organizations operating under an analyzer strategy have both a stable and a changing product line with predictable and changing markets. The focus is on being second on the market. Although the organization is concerned with high volume and low cost, there is some emphasis on prototypical designs. The analyzer strategy uses a dual technological core—one with a stable and a flexible component. Thus, this strategy lies somewhere between the defender and prospector extremes. The jobs are designed to emphasize process engineering and product or brand management. Texas Instruments is a company that uses an analyzer strategy.[38] Texas Instruments (TI) believes that it can compete in product development by emphasizing uniqueness. In addition, this firm can compete with efficient mass producers. TI

....

| EXHIBIT 8.4 | The Growing Importance of Flexible Work Schedules

Availability of flexible scheduling
according to a survey of 259 companies

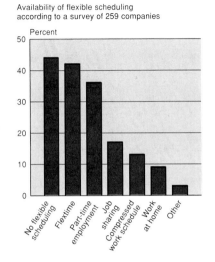

When asked what is highly important for recruitment
now and what will grow in the early 1990s, human
resource executives at 216 large companies
cited the following incentives in these percentages:

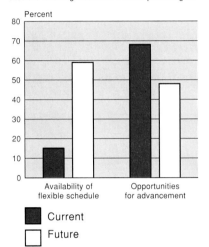

....

prides itself on its ability to shift the organization's structure, design, and management process to match the phases of its product life cycles. Recently, TI has gone back to making computer chips.

Work Flexibility: A Current Strategic Issue in Job Design

The 1980s has been called the decade of career obsessions.[39] However, in the 1990s, men and women are trying to create a better balance between work and family. In 1989, Felice Schwartz wrote a controversial article in *Harvard Business Review* on women managers and their conflict between career and family. She suggested that businesses needed to adapt to this conflict by introducing flextime, job sharing, and other personnel policies that would add flexibility to work schedules.[40]

The controversy stems from her conclusion and recommendation that corporate officials treat women in managerial positions according to whether they are on a "career track" or a "career/family track" also called the "mommy track." Critics have been concerned that this could provide companies with a rationale for discrimination against women who have or plan to have children. In other words, the fear is that career tracks would be equated with "fast" tracks and mommy tracks would be equated with "slow" or "dead-end" tracks.[41] Regardless of problems associated with career tracking, organizations are being pressed by employees and society in general to offer more flexible work schedule options for *both* men and women. In a recent survey, 56 percent of the organizations reported offering some type of flexible scheduling (see Exhibit 8.4).

As can be seen in Exhibit 8.4, **flextime**, which gives employees some decision latitude as to when they begin and end their work day, and **part-time employment** are the most popular options for introducing flexibility into the job. **Job sharing**, in which an employee shares his or her job with another employee, **compressed work schedules**, in which employees put in their 40 hours in less than a full five-day work week (for example, working ten hours for four days), and **working at home** are less popular options, but will most likely become more common due to the importance of flexibility in the work place.

Telecommuting is a more recent trend in which employees can work from their home or another location of their choice and communicate through the use of computers, express mail, facsimiles, and improved telephone networks. For example, Charles Lazarus, the chief executive of Toys 'R' Us, has a computerized office in his vacation house on Long Island and is considering putting one in his home in the Bahamas.[42] His system ties into his company's sophisticated computer system, allowing him to track the sales of all of the company's 20,000 products in any part of the world.

Although women (especially baby boomers in their thirties and forties) seem to be leading the push for more flexibility in their work schedule, men are also interested in flexible scheduling. In fact, in a recent survey by Robert Half International, an executive recruiting firm, it was reported that more than half of the 500 men polled said they would be willing to cut their salaries as much as 25 percent to have more family or personal time and about 45 percent said they would likely decline a promotion if it meant spending less time with their families.[43]

Whether managers choose to redesign (or design) a small portion of the organization, a new plant, or the entire firm, a well-integrated job design plan is crucial. The following section will discuss the steps involved in implementation.

Strategic Framework for Implementation

Recognizing the need for job redesign and understanding its underlying processes are only part of an overall job redesign effort. Ricky Griffin has developed an integrative strategic implementation framework.[44] As summarized in Exhibit 8.5, nine steps are outlined for a successful strategic job redesign program.

Recognizing the Need for Change

The first step in strategic job redesign is the recognition that a change is needed. A number of factors in the workplace typically serve as indicators that a change is needed. Employee complaints about their job and a subsequent decline in motivation and performance is often the first sign that the design of the job is in need of improvement. If managers want to retain and attract good employees, a well-designed, motivating job is imperative.

Another factor that could lead to strategic job redesign is the technology available to an organization. New computer advancements such as NeXT developed by Stephen Jobs[45] for more efficient production processes often necessitates new work methods. If companies want to stay competitive, they may make a strategic decision to acquire state of the art equipment. New equipment or methods often create the need to redesign some jobs.

Selection of the Intervention

After determining that a change is needed, managers must decide upon the appropriate intervention. Job redesign is only one of the many options available to the

---

A Strategic Framework for Implementing Job Redesign in Organizations

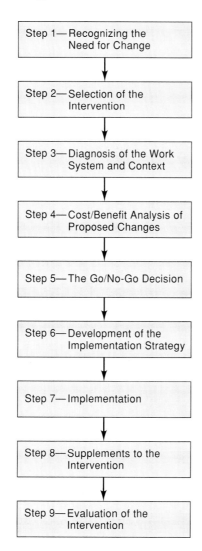

Step 1—Recognizing the
Need for Change

Step 2—Selection of the
Intervention

Step 3—Diagnosis of the Work
System and Context

Step 4—Cost/Benefit Analysis of
Proposed Changes

Step 5—The Go/No-Go Decision

Step 6—Development of the
Implementation Strategy

Step 7—Implementation

Step 8—Supplements to the
Intervention

Step 9—Evaluation of the
Intervention

---

human resource manager. For example, a manager recognizes a drop in employee motivation and performance. This could be the result of numerous factors—such as poor communication, leadership or training—not necessarily a poor job design. If, however, employees complain of boring, unchallenging work, job redesign may be the most logical intervention. This step requires managerial experience, intuition, and tacit knowledge in order to choose the appropriate intervention strategy.

Diagnosis of the Work System and Context

An in-depth diagnosis of the work system and context is important after management decides to implement a job redesign program. Human resource managers need to ensure that any job redesign effort is consistent with the existing work system. In *Task Design,* Ricky Griffin described six areas that need to be examined when diagnosing the work system and context:[46]

1. Diagnosis of existing jobs. For example, evaluate using methods such as job analyses and the job diagnostic survey.
2. Diagnosis of the existing work force. For example, compare the current performance, motivation, and satisfaction of employees with the desired level of performance, motivation, and satisfaction.
3. Diagnosis of technology. For example, technology may be a constraint due to expensive equipment and heavy machinery.
4. Diagnosis of organization design. Categorize the organization as being either mechanistic or organic. Determine the organization culture—is it accepting of change?
5. Diagnosis of leader behavior. The cooperation of the supervisor is crucial in order to reinforce a job redesign effort.
6. Diagnosis of group and social processes. The degree of group cohesiveness is crucial if the job redesign effort includes the development of autonomous work groups.

Cost/Benefit Analysis of Proposed Changes

The possible costs of a job redesign intervention must be balanced against potential benefits. Cost to an organization might include new machinery, downtime during the transition, and possible wage increases due to increased employee responsibility and task performance. Benefits from the job redesign effort include an increase in worker motivation, satisfaction, commitment to the organization, performance, and a decrease in absenteeism, turnover, tardiness, errors, and grievances. The goals of a job redesign intervention should be realistic and the benefits should outweigh any costs incurred.

The Go/No-Go Decision

After conducting a cost/benefit analysis, managers should make a decision to "go with" a job redesign intervention or consider other alternatives. It is important for managers to consider both short-term and long-term consequences and determine how this meshes with the overall strategy of the organization. Even after a systematic cost/benefit analysis, managers often feel they do not have all of the information to make the correct decision. Managers must rely on both quantitative information as well as their expertise and intuition.

Development of the Implementation Strategy

Strategy considerations for implementation include (1) who will plan the job redesign intervention, (2) what actual job changes will have to be made, (3) who will be affected by these changes, and (4) when will the intervention take place. These strategic issues should be systematically developed prior to initiating any changes. Some researchers advocate a participative approach using employees, supervisors, and consultants to plan the job redesign intervention.[47] Others, however, advocate participation in some situations and a top-down approach in other situations.[48] The decision for participation will depend upon the degree to which employees have important information, the degree to which employees need to accept the change, and the degree to which employees desire to add their input to the plan.

Decisions also have to be made regarding the jobs to be changed, who would be affected by the change, and whether the intervention will be individual-based or group-based. For example, group-based interventions (such as autonomous work groups) should only be used if there is an obvious benefit over individual-based interventions, due to their added complexity.[49] Finally, the planning group must determine the time frame for implementation. Considerations include how long it will take to purchase new equipment, install the equipment, and train the employees on the new equipment.

Implementation

The actual intervention seldom occurs without unforeseen problems. The best protection against implementation difficulties is to carefully diagnose the work situation, develop a specific strategy, and follow a detailed plan based on the previous steps.

Supplements to the Intervention

Supplemental changes are often necessary, particularly regarding contextual factors in the organization. For example, changes in the structure of the organization, workflow patterns, or reward system may be necessary due to the job redesign intervention. For example, if autonomous work groups are formed, the organization cannot continue to pay workers based on individual achievement. Group performance as opposed to individual performance will have to be the basis for evaluation. Thus, the organizational reward system should reinforce the job redesign intervention.

Evaluation of the Intervention

The final step determines if the job redesign intervention was effective. If managers want to see the impact of a change, employee perceptions, performance, and other work related outcomes need to be measured prior to actual intervention. After the intervention, improvements can be measured by comparing the outcomes after the intervention with the outcomes prior to the intervention. Unfortunately, this step is often not included as part of an organizational job redesign effort, possibly due to additional time and cost constraints. Managers should thoroughly examine the effects of any intervention and evaluate the cost and benefits incurred. This information is invaluable as input for future strategic decisions in the workplace.

• • • • • • • • •

MANAGEMENT GUIDELINES

Deciding how to design a job or implement a job redesign program is an important decision for managers. The management guidelines that follow should be considered before making these types of decisions.

1. Human resource managers need to carefully monitor the *interaction* between employees and jobs in their organizations to ensure that a productive relationship is achieved and maintained.

2. Job design or redesign should be undertaken only after careful consideration is given to environmental, organizational, cost, and behavioral factors.

3. After job redesign, managers need to conduct a job analysis in order to update job descriptions, specifications, and evaluations (see Chapters 7 and 12).

4. The reward system in the organization should reflect the new roles and responsibilities caused by job design or redesign.

5. The employees' growth need strength and their desire for job redesign should be given at least as much weight as costs and technical aspects of efficiency before developing and implementing a job design or redesign program.

6. A strategic framework for job redesign should be used as a guide by managers throughout the entire job design or redesign program to ensure a systematic and consistent approach.

QUESTIONS FOR REVIEW

1. Discuss the strategic choices managers should make before considering redesigning jobs.

2. What were some of the problems associated with scientific management?

3. Discuss the various individual and group job design options.

4. Discuss the job characteristics model. Explain how growth need strength affects the model.

5. How can a manager increase the core job dimensions for his or her employees? What strategies are available?

6. Discuss the strategic framework for implementing job redesign. Explain the importance of intervention evaluation.

7. Should a job redesign be undertaken if it will improve efficiency even if the employees do not want it? Explain your answer.

8. Discuss the fundamental premises of the sociotechnical model. What are some advantages to using autonomous work groups?

9. Can employees be trained to work in autonomous work groups if they are unwilling or incapable of doing so? Explain your answer.

10. In what ways could the X-ray jobs discussed in this chapter's opening case be redesigned? How could this be accomplished?

 CASE: We've Got to Make It[50]

I'm on my way to work on the assembly line in Lansing, Michigan, at General Motors' newest plant, the only one that makes Buick Reattas, priced at $25,000 apiece. It's called a craft center now. Its predecessor, "the old forge plant," was slated for closing—before labor and management struck a deal: Management yielded some say to give labor more responsibility for quality, and labor gave up or combined some jobs to save others. I want to see how—and if—labor/management teams really work.

In good times, there were 2,000 workers at the old factory. By 1984, there were 700. General Motors no longer needed the axles made there; the plant was obsolete. Last December, the first Reatta rolled off the line. Now, 675 men and women work there at a base pay of $14.49 an hour. They are full of hope for the Reatta's success—and for their own survival.

But survival requires change. "It's a lot more difficult working *together*," says one worker. "When labor and management used to fight, hell, that was easy. You'd take a position and hold it—win or lose. Now it's compromising all the way through to solve problems."

Bob Thompson, 45, the plant manager, maintains that labor/management teamwork can succeed. Once a month, he puts in a day building cars with union members. "I found that when I put on coveralls and went to work on the floor, some management people didn't even recognize me as a human being," says Thompson. "That really hurt me. It made me think about how the hourly workers must feel about that."

Thompson told his managers to get to know the crafts-men, as the workers are now called, and to listen to them. "Thompson's not afraid of hard work," says one craftsman. "I'd like to see the rest of them management turkeys come down here and work for a day. Half of them probably would quit."

When I had asked Thompson for a chance to work on the assembly line, he said I could, if the union agreed. Then he added, "Just remember you have to build the same high-quality cars that we do." I kept hearing the word "quality" over and over.

I went next to shop committee chairman, Stan Pewoski, with the same request. Pewoski, 42, has been a union officer for 17 years. I told him that I had worked as an auto mechanic, sold car parts, edited a car magazine, and that I write about cars for a living. He told me, "Okay, so long as you don't screw up. Quality is the thing."

"We want to succeed," he says. "When a plant closes, you lose more than jobs. You lose your families, your homes, your style of living. And what other work would we find out there?"

I also asked for—and got—free access to the plant. I can explore on my own.

It's a whisker before seven on a warm morning in Lansing. I'm given a vinyl cover to keep the belt buckle on my jeans from scratching the paint on the new Reattas.

Stan turns me over to his brother, Larry Pewoski, a craftsman in the final-assembly section. "Watch me build a car, then you build one," says Larry. He's 39, with 20 years experience.

In front of us is the shell of a car, parked on four stanchions. The body has been welded, sanded, and painted. Now, teams of workers will add more than 2,000 compo-nents, including the engine, transmission, and interior, before a Reatta is driven away.

This team approach differs vastly from the assembly line Henry Ford made famous. Under the old process, still used by many factors, every 50 seconds, hour after hour, workers attach the same one or two pieces to a constantly moving line of cars. Miss a piece? Too late. The resultant problem—if detected by an inspector—will be fixed in a special repair area. That's a big if.

"You sort of plan to fail when you put 30 people in a row with one-way nut drivers," says Bernie Ballesteros, a manager in the trim-and-chassis area. "Say that a screw goes crooked—ZZZT! Well, the gun's got no reverse. What's the guy gonna do—take it out with his teeth?"

Here, most aspects of the old assembly line are gone. Each car sits for 28 minutes as teams install a variety of pieces. The variety reduces boredom. The worker's per-sonal involvement in producing top quality humanizes the process. Ideally, errors are corrected on the spot and costs are cut, since inspectors are no longer needed.

Promptly at 7 A.M., Larry opens the car's right door, held shut by tape (no latch yet). Onto the car's floor he puts pieces of carpet padding, a harness made of dozens of multicolored wires, and a box of screws.

Larry's bearded partner, Rod Zimmerman, 37, wearing a black "Harley Davidson" T-shirt that matches the color of the car, loads in the gas pedal and the parking brake. He places a paper towel over the greasy brake to keep himself and the car clean—his own neat trick.

Soon, Larry carries another harness and some cables to the car. He slips the wires through the firewall as Zim-merman routes them down the door sill. Larry pushes the gear-shifter cable and a vacuum line into the firewall. Zimmerman then fastens them. Many other painstaking processes follow.

At 7:27, Larry punches his code number through the car's identification sheet. He's inspecting the car they've just finished. No short cuts. No wasted motion. No man-agers in sight.

An "Automatic Guided Vehicle" comes into our bay. It's a self-propelled platform that moves a car to each work station. The team's coordinator, Darwin Maas, 49, walks beside it. "Careful—that one there is crazy," Maas says, pointing to the AGV. A still-new computer program isn't perfected yet and sometimes the AGV's lose their way. The AGV positions itself under the car, lifts it off the stanchions and backs out.

Maas had worked for 22 years at the axle plant. Here, he directs the work, eyes the quality and represents the team at meetings with supervisors.

Another AGV delivers another car. Now it's my turn. The wiring harnesses are heavy. Grab one wrong, and it becomes a squirming octopus. I fumble with black screws and squint in search of black holes in the black car.

This is no place for amateurs. Lose your concentration, and you can cut your fingers on unfinished edges. Make a mistake, and you jeopardize the reputation of the entire team. It's myth that anyone can build a car. Even with coaching and a lot of sweat—physical fitness is a must—I can't finish in the expected 28 minutes. They work harder to recover the time I lose.

At 11:30, the team gets a half-hour for lunch, which today turns into a celebration. The results of the first quality audit are in, showing the initial Reattas to be among the best cars produced by GM. Copies of the excellent rating sheets are taped up in the work stations.

Along a hallway near the assembly area hang color pictures of the cars that pulled jobs to Japan—Toyotas, Mazdas, and Nissans—along with their excellent quality ratings.

Later, Maas spots a gap in the undercoating inside a fender. He registers a complaint and soon a worker from the body shop, from which the car came, is fixing the undercoating. "It just takes one vehicle to give you a bad reputation," Maas says. "I'll tell you what: If this plant shuts down, it's going to be because of management, not because of union workers."

Most of the workers were hired right out of high school. There are husbands and wives in this plant, brothers and sisters, parents and their offspring. But what happens to high-school grads now? "Let's not kid each other," Stan Pewoski says. "It's going to be a long, long time before we get to new hires, with all the plant closings. My son, Jon, is 22, married, and making auto parts in a nonunion shop in Grand Rapids for about $8 an hour. I've got a daughter, Cindy, who's 20 and working as a cook for about $5 an hour."

This break in the old ways heightens the workers' suspicion of outsiders. For example, some of the managers are on loan from Cadillac in Detroit, only 86 miles—and another world—away. These managers are there to help during the plant's start-up. "If they screw up this plant, *they'll* go somewhere else," one worker tells me. "But where can *we* go?"

He's got a point—145,000 hourly workers have vanished from GM payroll nationwide. GM also has eliminated 40,000 white-collar jobs.

After one day on the line, I spend two days wandering on my own, trying to cover all 650,000 square feet of the plant's floor space. Word spreads that Frank Sinatra, Jr., has ordered a dark gunmetal model. "He's got a lot of rich friends—maybe they'll all buy new Reattas," says one worker.

I go to a quality control meeting. Every day, five completed cars are picked at random and scrutinized for defects by about 60 labor and management people in an auditorium built just for this purpose. Thompson comes over. "See that ding in the fender?" he asks me, pointing to a car. I have to shift position several times before finding the dent. "Will a customer ever see that?" he asks. "I don't know—but why take the chance?" The ding will be fixed.

As a car writer, the problems seem minor to me: a grille protrudes slightly; one trunk is hard to close; a brake pedal squeaks. Thompson asks about the redesigned speaker grille. It's a design problem, not an assembly problem, all agree. We're told a new design already has been ordered.

I take a hard look at the Reatta, calculating its chances. The paint is superb. The design turns heads. Fewer than 5,500 will be made this year but every one has a buyer.

At the end of my final day, I watch trucks being loaded with finished cars. I think of Al Martin, 49, and Connie May, 51, who seal the windshield openings. I think of Don Wollenberg, 38, and Steve Nettleton, 37, who install the wiper motor and hood latch. And I think of all the workers whose names I don't know. Assembly quality is only one element of success. But it's an important element, and I'm convinced these cars have been built right. And even though the $25,000 Reatta holds but two people, there are 675 jobs riding on every car.

Although the Reatta was a high quality car, GM's Buick division canceled the car after the 1991 model. Sales on the Reatta were too slow to justify its continuation. In addition, the marketing efforts were inadequate to stimulate widespread interest in this high priced, two-seater car. Interestingly, the Reatta plant is now being used to produce electric cars, expected on the market in the near future.

QUESTIONS

1. Why do some workers argue that working together with management is more difficult than fighting with management?

2. How did job redesign help to keep the plant alive?

3. Explain how the General Motors Reatta plant uses the team approach.

4. Do you believe the team approach would work for other car manufacturers? Why or why not?

5. How has the team approach used by the General Motors Reatta plant affected the quality of the cars produced?

....
ADDITIONAL READINGS

Adler, S., R. B. Skov, and N. J. Salvemini. "Job Characteristics and Job Satisfaction: When Cause Becomes Consequence." *Organizational Behavior and Human Decision Processes* 35 (1985) pp. 266–278.

Campion, Michael A. "Interdisciplinary Approaches to Job Design: A Constructive Replication with Extensions." *Journal of Applied Psychology* 73, no. 3 (1988), pp. 467–481.

Cummings, T. "Self-regulating Work Groups: A Sociotechnical Synthesis." *Academy of Management Review* 3 (1978), pp. 625–634.

Dunham, R. B., J. L. Pierce, and M. B. Casteneda. "Alternative Work Schedules: Two Field Quasi-Experiments." *Personnel Psychology* 40 (1987), pp. 215–242.

Fein, M. "Job Enrichment: A Reevaluation." *Sloan Management Review*, Winter 1974, pp. 69–88.

Fried, Y. and G. R. Ferris. "The Validity of the Job Characteristics Model: A Review and Meta-Analysis." *Personnel Psychology* 40 (1987), pp. 287–322.

Gerhart, B. "How Important Are Dispositional Factors as Determinants of Job Satisfaction? Implications for Job Design and Other Personnel Programs." *Journal of Applied Psychology* 72 (1987), pp. 366–373.

Gerstein, Marc S. *The Technology Connection: Strategy and Change in the Information Age.* Reading, MA: Addison-Wesley OD Series, 1987.

Graen, G. B., T. A. Scandura, and M. R. Graen. "A Field Experimental Test of the Moderating Effects of Growth Need

Strength on Productivity." *Journal of Applied Psychology* 71 (1986), pp. 484–491.

Griffin, R. W. "Objective and Social Sources of Information in Task Redesign: A Field Experiment." *Administrative Science Quarterly* 28 (1983), pp. 194–200.

Griffin, Ricky W., Thomas S. Bateman, and Sandy J. Wayne. "Objective and Social Factors as Determinants of Task Perceptions and Responses: An Integrated Perspective and Empirical Investigation." *Academy of Management Journal* 30 (1987), pp. 501–523.

Hackman, J. R. and G. R. Oldham. *Work Redesign.* Reading, MA: Addison-Wesley, 1980.

Idaszak, J. R. and F. Drasgow. "A Revision of the Job Diagnostic Survey: Elimination of a Measurement Artifact." *Journal of Applied Psychology* 72 (1987), pp. 69–74.

Idaszak, Jacqueline R., William P. Bottom, and Fritz Drasgow. "A Test of the Measurement Equivalence of the Revised Job Diagnostic Survey: Past Problems and Current Solutions." *Journal of Applied Psychology* 73, no. 4 (1988), pp. 647–656.

Kulik, Carol T., Greg R. Oldham, and Paul H. Langner. "Measurement of Job Characteristics: Comparison of the Original and the Revised Job Diagnostic Survey." *Journal of Applied Psychology* 73, no. 3 (1988), pp. 462–466.

Loher, B. T., R. A. Noe, N. L. Moeller, and M. P. Fitzgerald. "A Meta-Analysis of the Relation of Job Characteristics to Job Satisfaction." *Journal of Applied Psychology* 70 (1985), pp. 280–289.

Majchrzak, Ann. *The Human Side of Factory Automation: Managerial and Human Resource Strategies for Making Automation Succeed.* San Francisco: Jossey-Bass, 1988.

Nemetz, P. and L. Fry. "Flexible Manufacturing Organizations: Implications for Strategy Formulation and Organization Design." *Academy of Management Review* 13 (1988), pp. 627–638.

Olmsted, B. and S. Smith. *Creating a Flexible Workplace: How to Select and Manage Alternative Work Options.* New York: AMACOM Books, 1989.

O'Reilly, C., G. Parlette, and J. Bloom. "Perceptual Measures of Task Characteristics: The Biasing Effects of Differing Frames of References and Job Attitudes." *Academy of Management Journal* 33 (1980), pp. 118–131.

Roberts, K. and W. Glick. "The Job Characteristics Approach to Task Design: A Critical Review." *Journal of Applied Psychology* 66 (1982), pp. 193–217.

Taylor, F. W. *The Principles of Scientific Management.* New York: Harper & Row, 1911.

Unstot, D. D., C. H. Bell, and T. R. Mitchell. "Effects of Job Enrichment and Task Goals on Satisfaction and Productivity Implications for Job Design." *Journal of Applied Psychology* 61 (1976), pp. 379–394.

Van der Zwann, A. H. "The Sociotechnical Systems Approach: A Critical Evaluation." *International Journal of Production Research* 13 (1975), pp. 149–163.

Wall, T. D., N. J. Kemp, P. R. Jackson, and C. W. Clegg. "Outcomes of Autonomous Workgroups: A Long-Term Field Experiment." *Academy of Management Journal* 29 (1986), pp. 280–304.

Zuboff, S. *The Age of the Smart Machine.* New York: Basic Books, 1988.

···············
NOTES

1. R. D. Middlemist and M. A. Hitt, *Organizational Behavior: Managerial Strategies for Performance* (St. Paul, MN: West, 1988), p. 171.

2. William M. Carley, "Fearful Skies: Airline Security Offers Only Weak Protection Against Bombs on Jets," *Wall Street Journal*, May 10, 1989, pp. 1, 12; "Pan Am Employees Allege FAA Approved Use of Faulty Security Measures in Europe," *Aviation Week & Space Technology* 312, no. 5, April 9, 1990, p. 63.

3. A. Murray, "Jobs Don't Guarantee a Sound Economy," *Wall Street Journal*, October 24, 1988, p. 1.

4. A. Karr, "Secretaries Seek More Authority, with Some Success," *Wall Street Journal*, August 22, 1989, p. 1.

5. O. Shenkar, "Robotics: A Challenge for Occupational Psychology," *Journal of Occupational Psychology*, March 1988, pp. 103–112.

6. J. Dreyfuss, "Catching the Computer Wave," *Fortune*, September 1988, pp. 78–82.

7. A. Majchrzak, T. Chang, W. Barfield, R. Eberts, and G. Salvendy, *Human Aspects of Computer-Aided Design* (Philadelphia: Taylor & Francis, 1987), pp. 160–196.

8. R. Hayes and R. Jaikumar, "Manufacturing's Crisis: New Technologies, Obsolete Organizations," *Harvard Business Review*, September–October, 1988, pp. 77–85.

9. P. Collins, J. Hage, and F. Hull, "Organizational and Technological Predictors of Change in Automaticity," *Academy of Management Journal*, September 1988, pp. 512–543.

10. A. Majcmrzak and J. Cotton, "A Longitudinal Study of Adjustment to Technological Change: From Mass to Computer-Automated Batch Production," *Journal of Occupational Psychology*, March 1988, pp. 43–66.

11. J. Sheedy, "Retooling Your Workers Along with Your Machines," *Wall Street Journal*, July 31, 1989, p. A10.

12. D. Wessel, "Working Smart: With Labor Scarce, Service Firms Strive to Raise Productivity," *Wall Street Journal*, June 1, 1989, pp. A1, A12.

13. Fred Luthans, *Organizational Behavior*, 6th ed. (New York: McGraw-Hill, 1992), pp. 23–25.

14. Clifford E. Jergensen, "Job Preferences (What Makes a Job Good or Bad?)," *Journal of Applied Psychology*, June 1978, pp. 267–276.

15. J. Richard Hackman, Greg R. Oldham, R. Janson, and K. Purdy, "A New Strategy for Job Enrichment," *California Management Review*, Summer 1975, pp. 57–71.

16. B. Dutton, "A Case for Work Teams," *Manufacturing Systems*, July 1991, pp. 9(7), p. 58.

17. Ibid.

18. C. J. Gersick, "Time and Transition in Work Teams: Toward a New Model of Group Development," *Academy of Management Journal*, March 1988, pp. 9–41.

19. E. Ehrlich, J. Hoerr, M. Mondel, D. Castellion, A. Fins, and T. Mason, "The Password Is 'Flexible'," *Business Week*, September 25, 1989, pp. 152–154.

20. G. S. Odiorne, "The New Breed of Supervisor: Leaders in Self-Managed Work Teams," *Supervision* 52(8), pp. 14–17.

21. Luthans, *Organizational Behavior.*

22. J. Ellis, "Monsanto Is Teaching Old Workers New Tricks," *Business Week*, August 21, 1989, p. 67.

23. M. Wakabayashi, G. Graen, M. Graen, and M. Graen, "Japanese Management Progress: Mobility into Middle Management," *Journal of Applied Psychology*, May 1988, pp. 217–227.

24. R. L. Cole, "Made in Japan—Quality Control Circles," *Across the Board* 16, 1979, pp. 72–78.

25. T. Tang, P. Tollison, and H. Whiteside, "The Effect of Quality Circle Initiation on Motivation to Attend Quality Circle Meetings and on Task Performance," *Personnel Psychology*, Winter 1987, pp. 799–814; and A. Whatley and W. Hoffman, "Quality Circles Earn Union Respect," *Personnel Journal*, December 1987, pp. 89–93.

26. P. F. Koons, "Getting Comfortable with TQM," *Bureaucrat* 20(2), Summer 1991, pp. 35–38.

27. S. Watanabe, "The Japanese Quality Control Circle: Why It Works," *International Labor Review* 130(1), 1991, pp. 57–80.

28. J. Richard Hackman and Greg R. Oldham, "Motivation through the Design of Work; Test of a Theory," *Organizational Behavior and Human Performance* 16, 1976, pp. 250–279.

29. S. J. Zaccaro and E. F. Stone, "Incremental Validity of an Empirically Based Measure of Job Characteristics," *Journal of Applied Psychology,* May 1988, pp. 245–252; Y. Fried and G. Ferris, "The Validity of the Job Characteristics Model: A Review and Meta-Analysis," *Personnel Psychology,* Summer 1987, pp. 287–322.

30. C. T. Kulik, G. R. Oldham, and J. R. Hackman, "Work Design as an Approach to Person-Environment Fit," *Journal of Vocational Behavior,* December 1988, pp. 278–296.

31. J. Richard Hackman and Greg R. Oldham, "Development of the Job Diagnostic Survey," *Journal of Applied Psychology* 60, 1976, pp. 159–170.

32. Fred Luthans, Barbara Kemmerer, Robert Paul, and Lew Taylor, "The Impact of a Job Redesign Intervention on Sales-persons' Observed Performance Behaviors," *Group and Organization Studies,* March 1987, pp. 55–72.

33. E. Trist and K. Banforth, "Social and Psychological Consequences of the Long-Wall Method of Coal-Getting," *Human Relations,* February 1951, pp. 3–38.

34. J. R. Hackman and G. R. Oldham, *Work Redesign* (Reading, MA: Addison-Wesley, 1980); C. Manz and H. Sims, "Leading Workers to Lead Themselves: The External Leadership of Self-Managing Work Teams," *Administrative Science Quarterly,* March 1987, pp. 106–129.

35. R. Miles, C. Snow, A. Meyer, and H. Coleman, Jr., "Organizational Strategy, Structure, and Process," *Academy of Management Review,* July 1978, pp. 546–562.

36. Ibid. R. Miles and C. Snow, "Designing Strategic Human Resources Systems," *Organizational Dynamics* 13, Summer 1984, pp. 36–52.

37. D. Woodruff, "A Dozen Motor Factors—Under One Roof," *Business Week,* November 20, 1989, pp. 92–93.

38. Miles and Snow, "Designing Strategic Human Resources Systems."

39. C. Trost and C. Hymowitz, "Careers Start Giving In to Family Needs," *Wall Street Journal,* June 18, 1990, pp. B1, B5.

40. C. Trost, "How One Bank Is Handling a 'Two Track' Career Plan," *Wall Street Journal,* March 3, 1989, pp. B1, B8.

41. Women and Work, *Employment Relations Bulletin* 7, no. 8, April 1989.

42. L. Castro, "Managers Declare Independence to Run Businesses from Their Personal Utopias," *Wall Street Journal,* September 3, 1991, pp. B1, B4.

43. Ibid.

44. Ricky W. Griffin, *Task Design: An Integrative Approach* (Glenview, IL: The Scott Foresman Series in Management and Organizations, 1982), pp. 207–227.

45. "Steve Jobs Comes Back," *Newsweek,* October 1988, pp. 46–51.

46. Griffin, *Task Design.*

47. Raymond J. Aldag and Arthur P. Brief, *Task Design and Employee Motivation* (Chicago, IL: Scott, Foresman, 1979).

48. Hackman and Oldham, *Work Redesign.*

49. Ibid.

50. Ken Zino, "We've Got to Make It," *Parade Magazine,* September 4, 1988, pp. 22–25; J. Mitchell, "GM to Discontinue the Buick Reatta, Citing Slow Sales," *Wall Street Journal,* March 5, 1991, pp. A4, A5; and "Reatta Plant to Produce Electric Cars," *Washington Post,* March 5, 1991, vol. 114, p. P8.

9

Strategies for Recruitment, Selection, and Placement

Recruiting and selecting the right employees have always been a challenge for managers. Current economic and demographic factors of the labor force will undoubtedly increase the challenges managers face. During the next decade the overall growth in the work force will slow down as fewer young people enter the work force and the employees already working begin to grow older. Approximately 83 percent of new entrants into the labor force will be minorities, immigrants, and women.[1] The diversity among workers will call for new strategies and approaches to recruitment and selection. In addition, jobs will require increasingly skilled workers. This chapter examines recruiting and selection strategies for the 1990s.

• • • • • • • • •
CHAPTER OBJECTIVES

After studying this chapter, you should be able to

1. Discuss the recruiting methods available to organizations.
2. Understand the selection process organizations use to choose employees.
3. Explain strategies for effective recruitment and selection.
4. Discuss how an organization's strategy can affect its recruitment and selection process.
5. Explain how an organization should select staff to support implementation of its strategy.

CASE: Xerox Manages Worker Diversity[2]

With the rapidly shifting demographic makeup of the work force, U.S. corporations are facing an ever increasing diversity of workers. By the year 2000, only 32 percent of the workers entering the labor force will be white nonHispanics, a drop from 44 percent of the work force in 1986. The biggest growth will be seen in the number of women entering the work force (51 percent), followed by Hispanics, the fastest growing minority, which will have a 15% growth rate. Blacks will account for 13 percent of all new entering employees, while Asian and other minorities are expected to account for 6 percent of all new workers by the end of the century.

Encouraging and Promoting Minorities

The Xerox corporation has acknowledged the shifting makeup of its work force and believes that the proper management of worker diversity will become a necessity in the future. David Kearns, CEO of Xerox, states that "We have to manage diversity right now and much more so in the future. American business will not be able to survive if we do not have a large diverse work force because those are the demographics." Kearns goes on to state, "If you fail to include women and minorities, you've restricted yourself from a major part of the labor pool, which economically doesn't make sense. Beyond that, one of the major advantages you get out of having women and minorities in business is that they bring in a whole new set of ideas. Right now, American business needs new ideas and thought if we're going to compete on a worldwide basis."

Xerox has supported its beliefs by encouraging and promoting minorities into fast-track management positions. While the average percent of minorities in managerial positions across U.S. firms was 9 percent in 1989 (based on the Equal Employment Opportunity Commission), 16 percent of Xerox managers are minorities. Xerox also exceeded the industry average of 12 percent by filling 18 percent of its professional positions with minorities.

Training Is Key to Success

Simply recruiting and hiring a diverse work force does not guarantee success. The key to Xerox's success comes from the implementation of training programs that foster support and cooperation among minorities. "You can't just hire large numbers of women and minorities and think it'll work," Kearns cautions. "You need a process to identify the right experiences people will need to move ahead. You need to have training programs for your managers that talk about managing diversity. What are the issues of managing minorities and women, because there are things that are different."

Xerox began to encourage the development and management of diversity during the 1970s when the managers of Xerox's affirmative action program looked at the careers of ten top executives to determine which key position helped them the most in their careers. The result of the study showed that the pivotal position for success was the first-level sales manager. The managers of the affirmative action program also discovered that all 500 first-level sales manager positions were held by white employees.

Encouraging Affirmative Action

Xerox started to encourage affirmative action by basing 20 percent of a manager's performance review on the manager's success with human resource management, which included affirmative action. The performance program has been met with some resistance from white managers. As Theodore Payne, Xerox's affirmative action manager, states, "There are some . . . who just could not adjust."

To avoid upsetting the informal structures already established, Xerox did not try to dismantle the white male "old boy" network within Xerox; instead, the company encouraged the growth of networking. The minority caucuses met on their own to develop advancement strategies. A major change sought and won by the caucuses was to allow the posting of "stepping stone" job openings, which was a major breakthrough since a number of major U.S. corporations still refuse to implement this policy.

By selecting the best people from all minority groups, Xerox believes that it is better prepared than most other U.S. firms to compete in an ever increasing global market. As a top marketing executive at Xerox states, "We'd like to be able to stand up and say that we've done that [beaten international competition] as a multicultural company . . . I think that will serve as a beacon for the rest of American industry."

● ● ● ● ● ● ● ● ●

STRATEGIC CHOICES

Managers have a number of choices to make regarding their recruiting and selection strategies. These strategies are outlined below:

1. An organization can make a strategic choice to *focus recruiting efforts on minorities and women.*
2. Organizations can choose to *"make" or "buy" their employees* (that is, hire less skilled workers or hire skilled workers and professionals).

3. Organizations make strategic decisions regarding the *budget allocated* for recruiting and selecting employees.
4. An organization can make a strategic choice to explore *untapped labor sources.*
5. Organizations make strategic decisions regarding the *technological sophistication* of their recruiting and selection devices.
6. An organization can choose the extent to which *internal versus external recruiting methods* are used, (that is, recruiting within the organization or outside the organization).

Recruiting Efforts Focused on Minorities and Women

The changing demographics of the work force will undoubtedly affect recruiting and selection efforts in the current decade. Organizations can choose to recruit minorities and women actively or maintain the status quo. Managers are acknowledging that a different set of incentives will be needed to hire and train future employees. Women will represent the largest percentage of new workers. Given that many of these women will have caretaker responsibilities for their children or elderly relatives, flexible work schedules, job sharing, child-care facilities and/or support will be crucial to them. Many employers are already implementing programs designed to attract and retain women. Recently, an agreement with the National Treasury Employees Union (NTEU) has made it possible for the Internal Revenue Service to offer affordable, on-site child care at eight IRS offices. According to Greg Denier, the NTEU director of research, employee response has been "overwhelmingly favorable."[3]

Minorities and immigrants are also getting more attention from company recruiters. Traditionally, these groups have not received the level of education and training necessary to enter technical fields. Mentoring programs and internships allow employers to sponsor students through college with the possibility of hiring them. In addition, employers are providing training to minority and immigrant workers to develop an educated work force that will remain on the job. Aetna Life & Casualty offers courses on basic writing skills and job-specific training. Thus far, 40 of the 41 recruits are still working at Aetna.[4]

Make or Buy Decision

Organizations can make a strategic decision to hire less skilled labor and invest in training and educational programs, or they can recruit and hire skilled labor and professionals. Essentially, this is the "make" (hire less skilled workers) or "buy" (hire skilled workers and professionals) decision. Managers who recruit only skilled labor and professionals can expect to pay considerably more for these employees.

The advantage to hiring skilled labor and professionals is that they possess the necessary skills to begin working immediately and little training is required. However, the amount of money it might take to attract skilled labor and professionals may outweigh the benefits. In addition, many organizations may prefer to conduct their own training programs to ensure some measure of standardization. For example, IBM has an elaborate training program designed to promote not only skill acquisition but socialization and commitment to the organization.

HR CHALLENGES •••

From Welfare to Work Force

Many Americans erroneously assume that welfare recipients simply do not want to work. We can open any newspaper to the classified advertisement section and locate numerous ads placed by companies searching for workers. It would seem that anyone on welfare wanting a job should simply answer some of those countless ads. If this were the case, however, the American Works Company, located in Hartford, Connecticut, and New York City, would be out of business.

American Works has been extremely successful tapping into a labor force typically ignored by the business world. By exclusively recruiting and training welfare recipients for entry-level positions, American Works gets people off of welfare and into the workplace, saves the taxpayers money, and provides hiring employers with a valuable tax credit. If the social benefits of helping welfare recipients find jobs were included, American Work's profits would be even greater.

The crucial element in the American Works' approach to finding jobs for those on welfare who want to work is its focus on assimilating the worker into the system. American Works teaches basic interviewing and job skills, as well as proper English. It also acts as mediator between the applicant and employer during a four-month trial period while the employee is adjusting to the new job. Roughly 70 percent of the employees trained by American Works are retained by the companies and almost 90 percent stay in the job past the first year. Overall, companies are pleased with their new employees, stating that compared to other applicants, they are better prepared to accept responsibility, more motivated, and ready to work.

SOURCE: Adapted from *HRMagazine,* "From Welfare to Work Force," July 1991, pp. 36–38.

Budget

In 1988, a survey of 4,000 U.S. companies conducted by the Professional Employment Research Council (PERC) revealed that only 35 percent of the companies responding measured the cost of hiring an employee. In 1989, that figure fell to 33 percent.[5] If most firms do not attempt to determine their hiring costs, they are not in a position to control these costs rationally. Organizations can make a strategic decision to control hiring costs only after determining the approximate cost-per-hire. Information on employee recruitment, selection, orientation, and start-up (such as training) costs is imperative if managers choose to develop and manage cost-effective programs. The costs associated with employee replacement in organizations should also be figured into the cost-per-hire.

Organizations with very low turnover and growth may be less concerned about cost-effective hiring due to the infrequency of hiring. However, organizations that experience high turnover would be very concerned about controlling these hiring costs.

Finally, managers must consider geographical factors when budgeting for recruiting and selection. Some areas may have a severe shortage of workers, an intense competition for qualified applicants, or a high cost of living that necessitates more extensive recruiting methods, more incentives (such as benefits), and a higher salary to attract qualified workers.

Untapped Labor Sources

Organizations can make a strategic decision to tap into less traditional labor pools. Three labor sources that have been getting the attention of recruiters recently are the handicapped, the homeless, and welfare recipients. Handicapped workers, also

HR CHALLENGES ●

Keeping the Competitive Edge

James McElwain is vice-president for personnel resources and education for NCR and the winner of the 1989 American Society of Personnel Administrators Award of Professional Excellence for Human Resource Management. McElwain argues that "NCR is in a highly competitive industry. We need to keep a competitive edge and I believe that people differences give us that competitive edge. Having top people and productive people working for NCR is an advantage . . . We have to seek a competitive advantage in the people we hire."

One of the programs at NCR, called project 6K, is designed to improve the way that NCR hires new employees. The goal is to use standardized procedures to recruit the best college students for entry-level positions. Project 6K has a numerical system for colleges

and universities. Schools are given a rating between one (the highest rating) and four (the lowest rating). In the number one category, students with a grade point average of 3.2 or higher would be selected. At a school ranked in the number four category, only students with grade point averages of 3.4 or higher would be considered. McElwain is quick to point out that even schools rated number four are still very good schools.

The jobs available at NCR are generally entry-level positions. As jobs become open, NCR promotes from within. McElwain emphasizes that NCR's Project 6K strategy is to hire the very best entry-level employee, retain them, and promote from within.

SOURCE: Adapted from B. Leonard, "High-Winning Game Plan," *Personnel Administrator*, September 1989, pp. 58–62.

called "physically challenged" workers, have not been pursued seriously as potential hires by many organizations. However, the fact that 68 percent of handicapped persons are employable and *want* to work, coupled with the labor shortage, has made recruiters aware of this valuable employee resource.[6] Although special accommodations are often needed (see Chapter 5 on equal employment opportunity), handicapped workers offer organizations a plethora of knowledge, skills, and abilities.

Another labor source that has been left untapped is the homeless. Although still in experimental stages, Days Inns successfully placed numerous homeless people into jobs. Homeless workers are offered a hotel room for a small fee, along with wages. Days Inns hopes to fill more vacant positions and offer homeless individuals a new beginning.[7] Finally, targeting recruiting efforts toward welfare recipients may be beneficial for the organization as well as society in general (see the boxed article titled "From Welfare to Work Force").

Technological Sophistication

Organizations make strategic decisions regarding the methods used in recruiting and hiring. Often these decisions are influenced by the available technology. The infiltration of computers has made it possible for employers to scan national and international applicant qualifications. Although impersonal, computers have given employers and job applicants a wider scope of options in the initial screening stage. For example, NCR, the multinational computer company that employs 64,000 people, utilizes advanced computer technology to recruit from only the best colleges and universities.[8] NCR's recruiting methods are described in the boxed article titled "Keeping the Competitive Edge."

Job applicants have begun sending videotapes of themselves to companies (and colleges) in hope of gaining access. Videotaping enables the job applicant to contact a number of organizations without the time and expense of travel. Managers are able to conduct an initial screening of applicants based on the videotapes. Some organizations have developed their own videotapes as a recruiting device.

Finally, the newest method of recruiting, "telerecruiting," has become increasingly popular. Telerecruiting allows the screening process to be done by telephone. Large organizations have begun to form telerecruiting departments, which screen job applicants and put their resume information on a computer.[9] This procedure has enabled managers to interview and hire new employees more quickly. Employers who do not have the staff or budget to develop a telerecruiting department can get assistance from outside services that do the telerecruiting for them.

Internal versus External Recruiting Methods

Internal recruiting methods include posting position openings and distributing memos within the organization. This method of recruiting looks to internal sources to fill positions and encourages promotions from within. External recruiting methods include advertising position openings in newspapers and magazines and looking to external sources to fill positions. Whether managers choose internal or external methods depends upon the degree to which the organization's strategy encourages promotions and transfers from within the organization. Recruiting from within can lead to job satisfaction and motivation if employees see new career opportunities available. In addition, filling positions with existing employees ensures, to a large extent, that these employees are socialized as to the organization's culture or "personality." However, external recruiting helps to bring new ideas and approaches to the organization. In the university system, faculty positions are almost always filled by using external recruiting methods and sources. In academia, new ideas and approaches are encouraged, thus Ph.D students rarely become part of the faculty at the same school where they received their degree.

....

RECRUITING METHODS

Most job openings are filled with people from within the organization and entry-level positions are the most likely to be filled by external sources.[10] Methods of internal recruiting include job posting, skills inventories, job bidding, and referrals. Methods of external recruiting include school and college recruiting, advertising, employment agencies, and executive search firms. The advantages and disadvantages of internal versus external recruitment are depicted in Exhibit 9.1. Each of these methods will be discussed in the following section.

Internal Recruiting

Job Posting

Many positions can be filled by posting the job opening on bulletin boards or announcing the opening in the company newsletter. A job posting procedure enables employees to strive for a better position within the company. Notices of position openings should include all important information about the job (for example, brief job description, the education or training required, the salary, and whether it is full- or part-time). Although posting jobs can be an efficient method of recruiting, a number of problems have also been associated with it. For example, job posting can

....

| EXHIBIT 9.1 | Internal versus External Recruitment: Advantages and Disadvantages |

INTERNAL RECRUITMENT

Advantages
1. Employees familiar with the organization.
2. Lower recruiting and training costs.
3. Increases the morale and motivation of employees.
4. Probability of success due to better assessment of abilities and skills.

Disadvantages
1. Political infighting for promotions.
2. Inbreeding
3. Morale problem for those not promoted.

EXTERNAL RECRUITMENT

Advantages
1. New ideas and approaches.
2. "Clean slate" regarding company-specific experiences from which to build.
3. Level of knowledge and skill not available in current organization.

Disadvantages
1. Employee may not "fit" with the organization.
2. Lowered morale and commitment of employees.
3. Adjustment takes longer.

....

lead to conflict if an employee perceives he is more qualified for the job than his chosen peer. In addition, competing for jobs can put a supervisor in a very stressful situation. A supervisor might have to decide among three very qualified employees—all of whom would do a good job.

Skills Inventories

Another internal recruiting method is use of skills inventories. Essentially, a skills inventory includes a list of employee names, their education, training, present position, work experience, relevant job skills and abilities, and other qualifications. The organization can search through the company skill inventory in order to identify potential candidates for the position opening.

Job Bidding

When a union is present, the labor-management agreement typically establishes job-bidding procedures. These procedures typically specify that all jobs covered by the agreement must be filled by qualified applicants from within the bargaining unit. Those interested in the vacancy "bid" for the job by applying, if they are qualified. The position is filled by the individual with the highest seniority from among the qualified applicants. In some cases, applicants take competitive examinations and the position is filled by the highest scoring applicant. In either case, only those currently employed are permitted to apply. This has the effect, especially among blue-collar and other unionized jobs, of filling only entry level positions from external sources.

Referrals

An excellent source of information is the current employee who may know someone who would be qualified and interested in the open position. This source of information is very low cost, yet can yield a number of good prospects. Employees usually have a clear understanding of what the job entails and what type of person would "fit" with the organization. However, managers should be aware that when the organization does not have a representative number of minorities, referrals have been considered a violation of Title VII of the Civil Rights Act.[11]

External Recruiting

School and College Recruiting

Recruiting at high schools or vocational schools is often the strategic approach adopted by organizations with position openings at the entry level or in internal training programs. Recruiting at the college level serves as a major source for acquiring managerial, professional, and technical skills.[12] College recruiting can be expensive, so human resource managers should be certain that a college degree is needed for successful performance in the position openings. In general, professionals (such as engineers and human resource managers) are recruited nationally while more technical or lower level jobs are recruited regionally or locally.

Large organizations (such as IBM) often have recruiters all over the country (and sometimes outside of the country) searching for qualified candidates. Smaller organizations usually recruit locally or regionally. One of the most important decisions human resource managers must make is from which schools and colleges they should recruit. Many organizations make a strategic decision to recruit from certain schools or colleges exclusively. The rationale for limiting the number (besides time and money) includes recruiting from only prestigious schools to enhance the reputation of the organization and recruiting from schools from which the organization makes financial donations.

Advertising

Advertising job openings in newspapers, magazines, newsletters, and other media sources (such as radio) is a relatively inexpensive recruiting mechanism. The *Wall Street Journal*, for example, has a large section devoted to managerial and professional openings. Advertising is also useful for filling open positions quickly. However, advertising is not usually targeted at a specific audience, thus, the organization may receive numerous responses from unqualified or marginally qualified candidates. For example, McDonald's has recently included an abbreviated application blank on every paper placemat. These placemats are given to customers when they pick up their food order. McDonald's views every customer as a potential employee! The cost of screening candidates may preclude the use of media sources for most jobs other than entry level. The effectiveness of media advertising for position openings should be examined periodically. Evaluating the success or failure of recruiting efforts by counting the number of qualified candidates is *not* a recommended method. For example, it is far more expensive and time consuming to screen 100 applicants and find 5 qualified candidates than to screen 15 applicants and find 5 qualified candidates.[13] Evaluating recruiting efforts will be examined later in this chapter.

Public Employment Agencies

All states provide employment services to job seekers and employers. An effort has been undertaken in recent years to improve the image and the services provided by the public employment service. Traditionally, employers and job seekers believed that the public employment system was only useful for filling blue-collar, unskilled jobs. In part, this resulted from the association the public employment system has with the payment of unemployment compensation. Another problem with the service has been its preoccupation with filling placement goals or quotas at the expense of effective screening of candidates for jobs. Individuals without proper qualifications were sometimes sent to particular jobs simply because the service was attempting to meet its referral and placement quotas. However, the service has been used successfully by employers even though this utilization has been focused on unskilled or low-skilled jobs.

Private Employment Agencies

Private employment agencies vary considerably in size and effectiveness for good sources of employees and must be chosen carefully by employers and job seekers alike. For a fee, these agencies will conduct the preliminary applicant screening for the organization. Agencies usually charge the job seeker a fee if he is hired by an employer through the agency. The employer may agree to pay all, part, or none of this fee. Regardless, the fee is usually based upon some multiple of the employee's salary. Unfortunately, some agencies are more concerned with placing employees quickly than in effecting a good match between the employee and the organization. Human resource managers can reduce problems if they supply the employment agency with a detailed description of the position to be filled. Relevant information about the job should include a job title, job description, the education level needed, special training or skills required, and pay ranges.

Executive Search Firms

Some employment agencies focus their efforts on seeking quality management-level employees. An executive search is characterized by aggressive action on the part of consultants and management who actively pursue the optimal candidate. The search is directed toward identifying those whose careers are on track with their current employers and those who are not actually looking for another job, but who would be interested in considering another opportunity. Recently, some companies have decided to not limit this type of recruiting activity to executives. Recruiting for any position within the organization can be done by sending out "scouts" to look for good employees who are not necessarily looking for another job.[14]

While most recruiting activities focus on selecting from those who apply, search activities focus on selecting from among candidates who have to be found. Since search activities are often directed at candidates from companies with competitive products or services, the industry backgrounds of those identified are usually closely related to the industry of the organization conducting the search.[15]

Retaining Employees

One of the primary roles of a recruiting effort is to attract a number of qualified applicants; however, retaining those employees selected is also an important issue.

Too often a recruiter attempts to "sell" the organization to the candidate and subsequently inflates the positive characteristics of the organization while minimizing any negative features. This is often termed the "flypaper" approach, which assumes that if an organization can attract people, these new employees will "stick" with the organization.

Realistic Job Previews

Many human resource managers, as well as organizational researchers, believe that if recruiters portray a more accurate and balanced picture of the organization that more of the candidates hired will remain with the organization (even though fewer may actually accept the job offer).[16] This is due primarily to meeting new employees' expectations. If a new employee has unrealistic expectations about the organization, any unmet expectations could lead to a disgruntled worker. The process of giving recruits a more accurate picture of the job and the organization, including the negative aspects, is called a realistic job preview.

Some studies have demonstrated that realistic job previews (RJP) can reduce turnover, lower expectations about the job, and increase job satisfaction and organizational commitment because of the following explanations:[17]

1. RJPs may provide a "vaccination" of expectations against the negative aspects of organizational life by lowering the expectations of new hires.
2. RJPs may facilitate effective matching between applicants and the job and organization by giving more accurate information.
3. RJPs may increase commitment because the choice to join the organization was made without external pressure or coercion.

RJPs have been found to be most effective for organizations experiencing a high level of turnover or for entry-level jobs in which the job applicant may not have an accurate perception of (a) what the job entails or (b) the expectations of the organization.[18] Due to the problems of slightly-reduced acceptance rates, RJPs are most feasible when there is an abundance of applicants for a position.

Career Development

College graduates entering the work force for the first time or "first careerists" are clear about their expectations and are less willing to adapt their values and work styles to accommodate their employers. Given the shrinking labor force and the fact that 19 out of 20 college graduates who enter the labor force over the 1986–2000 period are expected to find college level jobs, the labor conditions are on the side of the college graduate.[19] In general, first careerists want coaching, training, rewards, and quick promotions. Information gathered from in-depth interviews with college graduates and representatives of 20 major corporations revealed a clear pattern of desires and expectations.[20] The following factors entice the first careerist to stay with the job and the company:

1. Immediate involvement in the essential work of the firm.
2. The ability to apply their newly learned knowledge and skills.
3. The opportunity to understand the big picture of the firm.
4. Rapid career development.
5. Rapid salary advancement.
6. The opportunity to learn new skills.

Companies are responding to these needs by offering a variety of programs for new employees. For example, Allied-Signal, Inc., has implemented a new orientation program designed to give new employees an opportunity to learn about how the organization works and what its values are. In addition, many companies are implementing sophisticated programs for first careerists that include career planning, management training, and mentoring.

One factor that should be considered prior to selection is the "fit" between the individual career objectives and the career path that can realistically be offered by the firm. Career plateauing, which refers to the point in a career where future hierarchical movement is unlikely,[21] has become a real problem in organizations today. Downsizing and delaying have severely restricted the potential for vertical movement in many managerial career paths.

Career plateauing can lead to, among other things, poor performance, job dissatisfaction, or the individual leaving the organization.[22] It is in the employer's best interest to either select those employees whose personal career goals match viable career paths within the company or to inform the employees up front, during the RJP about the alternate methods the organization might use to foster continued growth in the employee. Such methods include present job (in-place) development, cross-functional rotational moves, specialization within a function (or discipline or specialty), and lateral moves within a specific geographic location.[23]

Recruiting and the Legal Environment

Recruiting and hiring employees must be done within the legal environment of the organization. To avoid problems in the early stages of the hiring process, preemployment application forms should not ask questions that could later be used to unfairly discriminate against a candidate. Specifically, job applicants and screening interviews should never include questions referring to the candidate's gender, religion, or race. Employers need to obtain a certain amount of information from the job candidate but, as can be seen in Exhibit 9.2, there is a correct and an incorrect way of seeking these questions.

Affirmative action principles should also be observed in the recruiting process. For example, it is recommended that minorities be used in the recruiting process and minority leaders contacted for possible employment candidates. Using the phrase "an equal opportunity employer" is important but this alone is not enough to fulfill the goals of affirmative action. Since affirmative action plans include goals for increasing the number of minorities and women holding certain jobs, the organization's recruiting efforts should be directed toward meeting these goals. Many organizations make an effort to recruit from predominately female and/or black colleges. For example, the Xerox case in this chapter demonstrates how making a strategic decision to recruit, hire, and train minorities can help the affirmative action goals of the corporation while achieving success from a diverse work force. Affirmative action is discussed in more detail in Chapter 5.

Evaluating Recruiting Methods

Given the importance of recruiting to the organization, the methods used in recruiting should be evaluated periodically to warrant continued use. One of the most important reasons to evaluate recruiting methods is to determine the costs versus the benefits of various methods. When recruiting methods do not attract enough

....

| EXHIBIT 9.2 | Choosing the Right Questions

NATIONAL ORIGIN

Unacceptable:

> Are you a U.S. citizen?
>
> State your birthplace and the birthplace of your spouse (or relatives).

Acceptable:

> Are you lawfully employable full-time in the United States by citizenship or by obtaining the proper authorization?
>
> What languages do you speak, read, and write fluently? (Ask only if job-related.)

AGE

Unacceptable:

> How old are you?
>
> State your date of birth.

Acceptable:

> Are you over the age of 18?

MARITAL AND FAMILY STATUS

Unacceptable:

> Are you married?
>
> How many children do you have?
>
> List your child-care arrangements.

Acceptable:

> Will you be able and willing to travel as required by the job?
>
> Are you willing to relocate if necessary?

ORGANIZATIONS

Unacceptable:

> Please list all clubs or social organizations to which you belong.

Acceptable:

> List any professional, trade groups, or organizations that you consider relevant to your job.

....

applicants, many organizations respond by raising starting salaries. Although some job applicants may be enticed by money, this may not be the most cost-effective method of recruiting. Further, employees within the organization may perceive inequity if new employees are brought in at a similar or even higher salary.

Recruiting costs include factors such as the cost of advertising, the salaries and travel expenses of recruiters, travel expenses of potential job applicants, and

EXHIBIT 9.2 continued

PHYSICAL CONDITION

Unacceptable:

Do you have any handicaps or disabilities?

Complete the following medical history.

Have you had any recent or past illnesses or operations? If yes, please list the type and date of the illness.

When was your last physical exam?

Have you ever filled a claim for workers' compensation?

Acceptable:

Do you have any disabilities that could limit your ability to perform the job for which you applied?

Are there any jobs or types of jobs for which you should not be considered because of a disability or health condition?

ARREST/CONVICTION RECORD

Unacceptable:

Have you ever been arrested?

Acceptable:

Have you ever been convicted of a crime? (It is recommended to only ask about a specific crime or crimes that may be reasonably related to performing the job in question.)

MILITARY (appropriate only if job-related)

Unacceptable:

Have you served in the U.S. Armed Forces? If so, what type of discharge did you receive?

Acceptable:

In what branch of the U.S. Armed Forces did you serve?

What type of education or training did you receive in the military?

recruiting agency fees. These costs will have to be weighted against factors such as the proportion of acceptances to offers. At a minimum, organizations should compare the length of time applicants from each recruiting source *stay* with the organization with the cost of *hiring* from that particular source. The effectiveness of recruiting methods will vary among organizations and even jobs within the same organization.

| EXHIBIT 9.3 | The Selection Process |

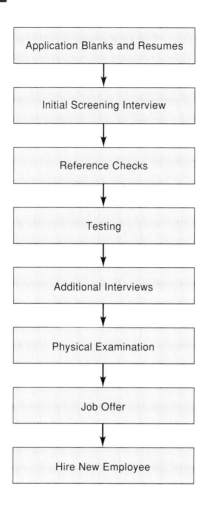

Note: Many organizations are now giving physical examinations and/or drug testing earlier in the process than is depicted in this figure.

THE SELECTION PROCESS

Selection is the process of choosing individuals who have the necessary qualifications to perform a particular job well. Organizations differ as to the complexity of their selection systems. Some organizations make a strategic decision to fill positions quickly and inexpensively by scanning over application blanks and hiring individuals based on this information alone. Other organizations, however, make a strategic decision to choose the best person possible by having an elaborate and sometimes costly selection system. These systems may require potential employees to fill out application blanks and provide information for a background check, take a number of job-relevant tests, and perform well through a series of interviews. Most organizations have more than one selection device. Exhibit 9.3 presents an overview of the selection process. Each element in this process will be discussed.

Application Blanks and Resumes

The initial screening of potential employees is usually done by examining resumes and/or having the applicant fill out an application blank. Application blanks usually include information regarding the name and address of the applicant, work history, education, training, skills, and references. Much of the information gathered on application blanks is objective so that the human resource manager can verify it. Some organizations have developed *weighted application blanks*, in which responses to questions on the application form are compared with measures of job performance (such as absenteeism, theft, or productivity). Thus, certain items are found to be more important than others in regard to performance. The important or "predictive" items are then weighted and used to help select future employees. Although weighted application blanks have been found to be predictive of future performance,[24] the time and cost of developing an effective system is often prohibitive.

Resumes are often used in place of an application blank. Job applicants develop their own resumes, which should include essentially the same information. Managers will sometimes ask for both the resume and application blank, since the resume contains only the information the applicant is willing to voluntarily share. Interestingly, studies have estimated that between 20 percent and 50 percent of the information reported in resumes is false or inflated.[25] Thus, caution must be taken if this is a primary selection device. Exhibit 9.4 illustrates an abbreviated resume.

References

Most organizations will ask an applicant for a list of references to include previous supervisors or coworkers. Since this list of references is generated by the employee, these individuals will most likely present a positive image of the applicant. Letters of recommendation are also considered a type of reference. Again, these letters are usually solicited by the applicant, so many employers do not consider these as a good selection device by themselves. Studies have found, however, that if the letter contains specific behavioral examples, the applicant is viewed more favorably.[26]

Reliability and Validity in Testing

Selection testing is a means of obtaining standardized information from potential employees. Standardization means that the test contains the same content for each applicant and is administered and scored in the same way for everyone. Using tests as a selection device is useful only when the tests are reliable and valid.

Reliability

Test reliability means that the test is consistent in its measurement. Two common types of reliability will be discussed: stability and internal consistency. Both stability and internal consistency rely on a correlation coefficient as the index for reliability. Essentially, a correlation coefficient is a numerical index that represents the degree of relationship between two variables. A correlation coefficient indicates the direction as well as the strength of a relationship. Correlations vary from -1.00 to $+1.00$. A negative correlation means that as one variable increases, the other

EXHIBIT 9.4 Sample Resume

ELIZABETH LYNN ANDERSON

ADDRESS: 4943 W. College Ave.
            Chicago, IL 60655
            (312) 893-3574

EDUCATION:

August 1990   Masters of Business Administration
                  University of Chicago
                  Chicago, IL

May 1987   Bachelor of Science in Psychology
                  Purdue University
                  West Lafayette, IN

RELEVANT WORK EXPERIENCE:

August, 1988–Present: ILLINOIS DEVELOPMENT CENTER
                        Lyons, IL
                        Student Assistant

Assisted in contract research on various projects to further the economic development of Illinois. Headed an in-depth Small Business feasibility study analyzing new business growth and site selection. Developed an annual Marketing Plan that included advertising and promotional strategies, competitive analysis, and a budget for operations.

January, 1986–August, 1988:   HARRIS CORPORATION
                              Oak Park, IL
                              Program Administrator

Responsible for tracking and reporting the schedule and budget on a multimillion dollar program. Compiled data for cost trends and variance analysis. Presented monthly program status to upper level management. Assisted in the preparation of proposals, including analysis of material and manpower requirements. Knowledge of computer programs includes Program Management System, Focus, Qwiknet, and Lotus 1-2-3.

References Available Upon Request

---

variable decreases (for example, as employee satisfaction increases, intentions to quit decrease). Conversely, a positive correlation means that both variables vary together (as employee satisfaction increases, intentions to remain with the organization increase). The strength of the relationship is determined by the magnitude of the correlation. The closer the correlation comes to 1.00 (or -1.00), the stronger the relationship. A zero correlation indicates no relationship between two variables.

A test is considered stable if the same values are obtained for a group of people when measurements of their performance are made at two different time periods. A correlation is computed between scores at time 1 and scores at time 2. Thus, an employee who takes a test today and takes the same test next week should obtain approximately the same scores. This method of determining reliability is called test-retest.

Internal consistency means that the items on a test are measuring the same trait or ability. Thus, items on the test should be correlated with each other. When using this method of reliability, a test is given to a group of people. A number is computed that represents the average correlation of each item with every other item on the test. This number is called a coefficient alpha and this number varies from 0 to 1.00. A coefficient alpha of .80 or higher means the items on the test measure the same thing. Of course, this does not tell you *what* you are measuring.

Validity

Specifically, if a test is valid, it accurately and consistently measures what it purports to measure. A test must be reliable if it is valid but the reliability of a test does not ensure validity. Thus, a test might accurately and consistently measure "something," but if human resource managers do not know what that "something" is, the test is reliable but not valid. Two types of validity will be discussed: content and criterion-related.

Content validity means that the test items are representative of behaviors to be exhibited in some performance domain. For example, suppose a human resource manager develops a typing test for selecting secretaries. If the secretarial job includes typing, computer knowledge, and shorthand, the test is not content valid because the test is not a representative sample of what abilities are needed to perform the job. The selection method must be designed to include the key aspects of the job if content validity is to be achieved. Of course, content validation can only be used when job applicants are expected to have a particular job skill or knowledge that is directly tied to job performance.

Criterion-related validity focuses on comparing the results of a particular selection device (such as the interview or a paper and pencil test) with one or more independent performance measures (criteria). The relationship between scores on a selection test and the criterion variable, such as successful job performance, indicates the degree to which the selection test is job-related. In order to determine criterion-related validity, information from the job analysis (see Chapter 7) is used to determine both the predictors (those aspects of the job deemed necessary for successful performance, such as hand-eye coordination) and criteria (such as job performance). If the selection tests (predictors) correlate with job performance (criterion), the selection tests are deemed valid. Criterion-related validity is the preferred method of test validation because of its emphasis on job relatedness.[27]

Selecting the wrong person for a job can lead to a number of problems for the employee and the organization. These negative consequences include employee and employer dissatisfaction, poor performance, and turnover. Poor selection devices are extremely costly to an organization and human resource managers should make every effort to ensure that their measures are both reliable and valid indicators of successful performance.

Types of Selection Tests

A number of selection tests have been developed to aid the human resource manager in selecting employees. The following section will cover mental ability tests, work sample tests, trainability tests, personality and interest inventories, and polygraph tests as selection devices.

Mental Ability Tests

Paper and pencil tests have been developed by psychologists and are purchased by organizations to measure mental ability and aptitude. Ability and aptitude tests examine a variety of traits, such as general intelligence, an understanding of spatial relationships, numerical skills, reasoning, and comprehension. Large organizations may even have a psychologist on staff who is responsible for selection tests.

Work Samples

Also called performance tests, work sample tests measure the ability to *do* something rather than the ability to *know* something.[28] These tests may measure motor skills or verbal skills. Motor skills include physically manipulating various job-related equipment (such as trade tests for electricians, roofers, or painters). Verbal skills include problem-solving and language skills (for example, situational role-playing may be used to determine a candidate's suitability for a supervisory position). Work sample tests should test the *important* aspects of the job. Since job applicants are actually performing a small portion of the job, these tests are difficult to "fake."

Trainability Tests

For jobs in which training is necessary due to (a) the skill level of the job applicants or (b) the changing nature of the job, trainability tests are useful. Essentially, the goal is to determine the trainability of the candidate. In the first step of the process, the trainer demonstrates how to perform a particular task. Second, the job applicant is asked to perform the task while the trainer helps to coach him or her through the process several times. Finally, the candidate is expected to perform the task independently. The trainer carefully monitors the performance recording any errors to determine the overall trainability of the job applicant.

Both work sample tests and trainability tests have been shown to have high to moderate success predicting job performance.[29] Many managers, as well as job applicants, prefer these types of tests over the cognitive ability or aptitude tests because of their face validity (that is, the tests are *perceived* to be valid measures of future work performance by applicants and managers). Essentially, job applicants are more readily able to understand why they are suited or not suited for a particular job by actually performing the job or a portion of the job.

Personality and General Interest Tests

Personality and general interest inventories are tests with no "correct" or "incorrect" answers to them. Interest tests are used to measure an individual's work and career orientations. Personality tests focus on identifying traits or typical behaviors of individuals and are used to measure a variety of traits including aggression, self-esteem, and Type A behavior. Although personality tests can be costly, they can help human resource managers determine individual characteristics not obtained from a resume, thus increasing the likelihood of finding a good "fit" between the job position and the employee. Most human resource managers and psychologists caution, how-

....

EXHIBIT 9.5   The Kolbe Conative Index: How You Do What You Do

FACT FINDER. This person evaluates, probes, and deliberates. Strong fact finders include judges, researchers, journalists, and lawyers.

FOLLOW THROUGH. This person coordinates, plans, and schedules. Particularly strong traits in a planner, designer, or programmer.

QUICK START. This person originates, experiments, and improvises. Examples include entrepreneurs, promoters, and salespeople.

IMPLEMENTOR. This person crafts, constructs, repairs, and demonstrates; might include manufacturers, builders, athletes, surgeons, or artisans.

....

ever, that personality and general tests are not usually predictive of performance on the job and should not be used as selection devices. Nevertheless, some evidence exists in support of the use of personality inventories as a selection device.[30]

A serious criticism of personality tests is their tendency to be invasive in that they seek to "uncover revealing data about a person's psyche."[31] Companies who use this type of preemployment test must therefore ensure that the information they seek and how they use this information is relevant to the job in order to stave off potential lawsuits by rejected applicants. The legal challenges to written preemployment tests, in particular personality tests, could possibly result in legislation restricting their use.[32]

Recently, a new employment test called the Kolbe Conative Index (KCI) was developed to measure what employees will or will not do. The test is based on conation, which refers to the drive or inclination to do something. For example, the test might include the following question: If I ran a business, I would (choose one) provide steady performance; make carefully thought-out decisions; develop new products and be innovative; or maintain high quality workmanship. The 36-item test categorizes individuals according to four traits (see Exhibit 9.5). The combination of scores describes the individual's "mode of operation." Mismatched modes of operation with jobs are believed to be the reason for most problems in the workplace. However, the KCI has not been tested by independent academic researchers and many critics say that its claims of detecting why most workplace problems occur are unwarranted.

Polygraphs

Commonly called lie detectors, polygraph tests measure an individual's respiration, blood pressure, and perspiration while this individual answers a series of questions. Although they are only about 70 percent accurate, prior to 1988 over 2 million polygraph tests were administered every year and 98 percent of the testing took place in private industry.[33] However, in June 1988, President Reagan approved new legislation that severely restricted the use of polygraph testing in employment. The new law disallows polygraph testing of job applicants for the purpose of preemployment screening but allows polygraph testing of those employees under reasonable suspicion of workplace theft or any other practice involving economic loss to the employer.[34] In addition, employees may not be discharged or disciplined solely on the basis of a

FOCUS ON ETHICS AND SOCIAL RESPONSIBILITY ••••••••••••••

To Tell the Truth

NEWSFLASH: American employees steal $40 billion worth of goods and services from businesses every year! Such an astounding figure was estimated by the U.S. Chamber of Commerce and works out to $7,125 a minute in thefts, which is 10 times the cost of the nation's street crime. It is no wonder that U.S. employers are grasping at any tools that might assist them in policing dishonest employees. The methods employers choose to screen applicants may be dependent upon factors outside of their control, however.

What "guns" are available to help employers screen applicants and fight the crimes committed by employees inside organizations? The 1988 Employee Polygraph Protection Act declared preemployment screening by polygraph illegal in most cases (the government can still use polygraph testing). Credit checks have proven to be unreliable predictors of integrity. Although helpful, background and reference checks are proving to be less and less valuable to employers since the applicants' former employers are less willing to provide information beyond verifying when the candidate was employed. One obvious reason that companies are hesitant about providing information about a former employee is the fear of the potential legal ramifications.

One tool employers may use to screen dishonest applicants is the paper-and-pencil assessment instrument known as an integrity or honesty test. Although honesty tests certainly have their share of critics, the American Psychological Association (APA) recently released a report stating that the preponderance of the evidence supports the idea that some of the tests can help predict which prospective employees may be undependable or steal. The question has been raised, however, whether the users of these tests even understand how to interpret what the scores mean? The APA report recommends better training for employers who use and interpret the exams and proposes that the tests not be used as a primary or sole means for assessing an applicant's qualifications. Although an earlier report released by Congress's Office of Technology Assessment raised questions about the reliability of honesty tests, the APA report may serve to reduce those concerns. At any rate, the debate about whether honesty tests should be used as a preemployment screening device is certainly not over.

SOURCES: Adapted from R. Zemke, "Do Honesty Tests Tell the Truth?" *Training*, October 1990, pp. 75–81; and G. Fuchsberg, "Prominent Psychologists Group Gives Qualified Support to Integrity Tests," *Wall Street Journal*, March 7, 1991, p. A6.

polygraph test. Interestingly, the use of integrity or honesty testing may be on the rise. Although integrity testing is seriously being considered as a means to screen potentially dishonest applicants, organizations must proceed with caution. Some tests have so little supporting research that their claims are almost fraudulent.[35]

The Interview

Most organizations, regardless of size, use interviewing as a selection method. Interestingly, interviews have been criticized for being unreliable sources of information due to perceptual and judgment errors on the part of the interviewer.[36] For example, interviewers often form a **first impression** of the job applicant based on information obtained on the application blank or the first two minutes of the interview. Initial impressions are often resistant to change, even though they are made with little objective information. Interviewers may base subsequent questions and judge the candidate's responses on these first impressions in an attempt to confirm their beliefs about the candidate.

Another type of perceptual error is called the **halo effect.** In this case, one characteristic or behavior of the job applicant (positive or negative) overrides all or most other characteristics. Thus, if an applicant comes to the interview dressed very professionally, the interviewer might unconsciously evaluate other characteristics (such as dependability or knowledge of the business field) more positively.

Contrast effects have also been found to distort interviewers' judgments about job applicants. Contrast effects occur when the interviewer evaluates a job applicant by comparing this person to previous job applicants. For example, an average applicant might be judged as excellent if prior applicants were of very poor quality. Similarly, this same person might be evaluated lower if he or she follows a high-quality applicant.

Other perceptual errors that can distort an interviewer's evaluation include stereotyping, leniency, strictness, and central tendency errors. These perceptual errors are discussed in detail in Chapter 13 on performance evaluations.

Establishing a system for conducting an interview can improve the reliability and validity of interview assessments.[37] The following guidelines should be followed when establishing a system for interviewing:

1. Determine the job requirements through a formal job analysis.
2. Focus on only those knowledge requirements, skills, abilities, and other characteristics necessary to perform the job well.
3. Develop interview questions based on the information gathered in the job analysis.
4. Conduct the interview in a relaxed setting. Try to put the job applicant at ease with giving general information about the company and asking simple questions.
5. Evaluate each candidate according to his or her relevant job knowledge, skills, and abilities.

In addition to these guidelines, human resource managers must choose which *type* of interview to conduct. Interviews can be classified into three general categories: structured, semistructured, and unstructured. The following section describes each of these categories. In addition, stress interviews will be discussed.

Structured

When conducting a structured interview, the interviewer asks questions from a prepared list and does not deviate from this list except for some follow-up questions. During the interview, the interviewer records his thoughts and reactions on a standard organizational form. When different interviewers reach the same or very similar conclusions about a given candidate, this is an example of high inter-rater reliability. Generally, structured interviews have a high inter-rater reliability and can be helpful if gathering precisely the same information from each candidate is very important. In addition, structured interviews help to ensure that all necessary information is obtained. Unfortunately, this type of interview is very restrictive, thus important and relevant information about the candidate may never be discussed. This approach can also be frustrating to job candidates who are not allowed to elaborate on or qualify their responses.

Semistructured

In a semistructured interview only the major questions are prepared in advance and recorded on a standardized form. This type of interview involves some planning on the part of the interviewer but allows for some flexibility regarding exactly what and how questions are asked. Although the inter-rater reliability of the information is not as high as with the structured interview, the information obtained may be richer and possibly more relevant. In essence, this approach to interviewing allows the interviewer to ask the key questions without imposing unnecessary restrictions on the interviewee. For example, Hershey Food uses a form of the semistructured interview called behavioral interviewing.[38] Candidates are asked what they would do to resolve a real-life work problem. They are given a work situation and asked how they would respond if actually confronted with this situation. By using semistructured behavioral interviewing, John T. Phillips, Director of Training and Development at S. C. Johnson & Son, Inc., hopes to discover if the job candidate will "fit" with the company.[39] Thus, the applicant would not be asked, "How would you reprimand an employee?" Instead, a job candidate might hear, "Give me a specific example of a time you had to reprimand an employee and tell me what action you took. In addition, what was the result of your reprimand?" Although the initial situation given to the job applicant is planned, the response and follow-up questions are of a less structured nature.

Unstructured

The unstructured interview involves little or no planning on the part of the interviewer. Due to a lack of planning, the interviews tend to vary greatly between interviewees and also between interviewers. In addition, important job-related issues may be left unexplored. Unstructured interviews have low inter-rater reliability and seldom yield valid or useful information. Thus, unstructured interviews are not recommended as a selection device.

Stress

The stress interview attempts to create anxiety in the job candidates and to put pressure on them in order to see how they perform under these conditions. The interviewer usually behaves aggressively and at times insults the candidate. Managers who have used this approach justify it by arguing that, if hired, the job candidate would be placed in a stressful position. This type of interview can help the human resource manager evaluate how a job candidate might react under stress. Of course, this type of interview often creates a negative image of the interviewer and the company, thus, the job candidate may decide to look elsewhere. Given the possibility of losing an excellent job candidate, stress interviews are not common. If a position is inherently stressful and the organization would like to ascertain the candidate's stress management skills, simply asking an applicant to recall a time when he or she dealt with a stressful situation, such as an irate customer, may be adequate. Simulating a stressful work experience is another viable technique.[40]

Physical Examination

Many organizations require a complete physical examination prior to hiring to ensure the job candidate is physically able to perform the job. For example, airline pilots are required by law to undergo an extensive physical examination. Physical examinations can also be useful for placement purposes. Individuals with lung or breathing problems may be best placed into jobs void of any smoke, dust, or fumes. In addition, a good physical examination should document any physical problems to avoid the possibility of worker compensation claims being filed against the company for a preexisting condition.

Physical examinations can also include drug and alcohol testing. Employers are reluctant to hire individuals who abuse drugs or alcohol, partially because of the higher absenteeism and turnover rates among these employees. In addition, employees do not work to their full potential and are more susceptible to accidents when they are under the influence of drugs or alcohol. Although many employees find substance abuse testing programs in violation of their privacy, local, state, and federal regulations have not provided a standard and definitive set of guidelines for testing.

Acquired Immune Deficiency Syndrome (AIDS) testing has become a very controversial topic for businesses.[41] In general, most medical specialists believe that AIDS testing in organizations is unnecessary because the disease cannot be contracted from AIDS patients under normal working conditions. Although AIDS testing is not part of a routine physical examination, some cities, such as San Francisco, have adopted city ordinances prohibiting discrimination on the basis of AIDS. Discrimination issues regarding the acquired immune deficiency syndrome are discussed in Chapter 5.

Many larger companies choose to employ an in-house physician versus going to the outside. A company physician has the advantage of knowing the physical demands and hazards for jobs and may be better able to help make knowledgeable decisions about hiring or placement. Obviously, the cost of an in-house physician may be prohibitive for many organizations.

Job Offer and Hiring

The final steps in the selection process are the job offer and hiring of the job candidate. Employers extend a job offer to the candidate describing the types of duties and responsibilities the new employee will be expected to perform. The employer usually discusses salary (although this is often established well before the actual hiring occurs), benefits, promotions, vacation time, sick leave, employee assistance programs, and other amenities of the organization. Although many of these issues were probably discussed during recruitment, it is always wise to keep important organizational policies and strategies salient to the employee. Finally, important documents are completed and signed (such as the employment contract and benefit forms), and the new employee begins his or her new job and new role as a member of the organization.

Managerial Selection Devices

Selection devices for managers can differ from nonmanagerial employee selection. In general, selection devices for managers should assess numerous skills and abilities because of the wide range of skills needed for successful performance. Assessment centers (which can last from one day to one week) were developed to tap these numerous managerial skills by collecting work sample information. Work samples can include (a) in-basket techniques, in which the job candidate must decide how to organize numerous letters and memorandums by priority and ask for more information, delegate, or make a decision regarding these letters and memorandums, (b) leaderless group discussions, in which the candidate engages in a typical simulated meeting, (c) role-playing, in which the candidate interacts with other "managers" or "subordinates," and (d) speech making. Each potential manager is assessed by several raters to increase the reliability of the hiring or promotion decision. Assessment centers have been found to be a valid means of assessing managerial potential,[42] but they are extremely costly, thus they are usually used for upper level, or top managerial positions.

Evaluating Selection Methods

Any human resource activity should be evaluated to determine the effectiveness of that activity. This is especially true for selection activities. Evaluating past selection methods can be useful in the estimation of budget costs and the determination of the most effective methods.

Research indicates that well-designed ability, work sample, and trainability tests can be valid predictors of job performance.[43] The research on employee selection devices indicates that professionally designed tests (including paper-and-pencil ability tests) can be valid predictors of performance in all settings. Further, these tests seem to be valid for both minority and majority job applicants.[44] The consequences of selecting individuals who do not perform well or who soon leave the organization is not only a waste of valuable employee time, but it is extremely costly.

Consequences of Not Hiring an Applicant

Not hiring certain individuals can also have numerous consequences. As depicted in Exhibit 9.6, both personal and societal outcomes are affected by rejecting an individual who should have been selected or by correctly rejecting an individual who should not have been selected. This model illustrates possible applicant reactions to rejection. For example, the applicant may believe he is truly lacking in important skills, thus, the applicant may respond by trying to develop skill deficiencies or seek another job not requiring that particular skill. However, the applicant may believe that the rejection was a decision error on the part of the organization and seek similar employment. These behavioral responses can lead to organizational as well as societal consequences.

....
STRATEGIES FOR EFFECTIVE RECRUITING AND SELECTION

The strategy of the organization can affect the recruiting and selection process. The following section is based on Miles and Snow's strategy typology discussed in previous chapters, namely, defenders, prospectors, and analyzers.[45] In general, organizations with different strategies should recruit different types of individuals for employment.[46]

Organizations with a defender strategy have narrow and relatively stable product-market domains. As a result of their narrow focus, these types of organizations seldom make major changes in their technology, structure, or methods of operation. They devote most of their attention to improving efficiency. Defenders emphasize "making" employees rather than "buying" highly trained or educated employees. Thus, little recruiting is done above the entry level and selection is based on weeding out undesirable or unqualified applicants. Defenders emphasize training their employees and usually have formal and extensive training programs. Thus, defenders

EXHIBIT 9.6   The Consequences of Rejecting an Applicant

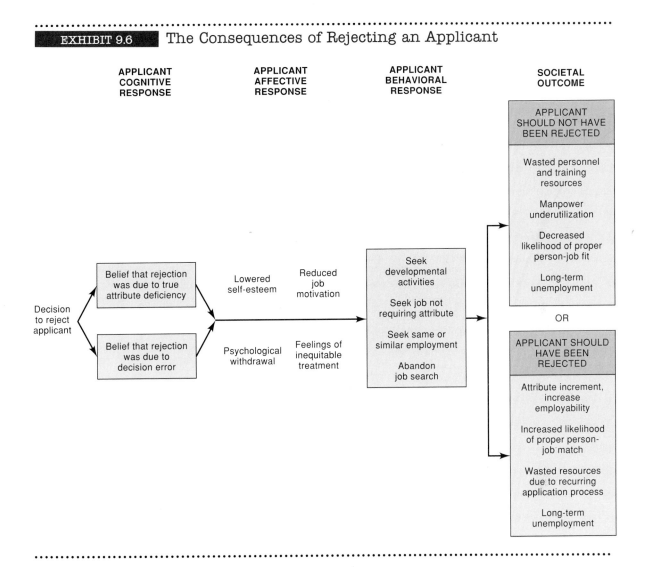

might choose to use trainability tests or to give mental ability or aptitude tests to identify those individuals most likely to learn from training. Finally, defenders will usually seek out people with backgrounds in finance or production given their narrow and stable market.[47]

Organizations with a prospector strategy search for product and market opportunities and experiment with responses to emerging environmental trends. Often, these types of organizations create change and uncertainty to which competing organizations must respond. Prospectors emphasize "buying" their employees rather than "making" employees through elaborate training programs. Recruiting methods are sophisticated at all levels of the hierarchy and efforts are focused on identifying appropriate skills and acquiring these qualified individuals. Given the emphasis on "buying" employees, training programs are limited. Thus, prospectors might prefer to use work sample tests as a selection device. Finally, because prospectors seek to exploit new product and market domains, they often look for individuals with basic marketing or engineering research skills.[48]

Organizations with an analyzer strategy operate in two types of product-market domains, one relatively stable and the other changing. In stable areas, these organizations operate routinely and efficiently. However, in their more innovative areas, managers watch the competition carefully for new ideas and quickly respond or adapt to those that appear to be the most promising. Analyzers use a mix of recruiting and selection approaches and emphasize both "make" and "buy" strategies. Training programs are usually formal and extensive, although little recruitment is done outside the organization. Analyzers might prefer to use a variety of selection devices given their emphasis on both "make" and "buy" strategies. Given that analyzers operate in mixed markets, they look for individuals with abilities in applied research, marketing, and also production.[49]

The organizational strategy not only affects the recruiting approaches and selection criteria of a firm, but also affects which attitudes and personality traits are seen as the best match or "fit" between the applicant and the organization.[50] For example, employees with a need for risk taking and a high tolerance for change and ambiguity would be well suited in an organization with a prospector strategy. Conversely, an employee with a need for structure and a low tolerance for change and ambiguity might be better suited in an organization with a defender strategy.[51]

Managers must not only be sure that the selection criteria are job-related, but they should consider if the criteria are consistent with the strategies and culture of the organization. The relationships between strategy and recruiting and between selection and training are still somewhat speculative. These relationships assume that staffing decisions are (a) consistent with one another and (b) consistent with the strategy of the firm.[52] Thus, these relationships should only be viewed as a general guide for managers.

STRATEGIC STAFFING TO SUPPORT STRATEGY IMPLEMENTATION

The focus of this chapter has so far been on identifying the key aspects of recruiting and selection that are necessary for an employer to find the right people. Although accurate and comprehensive techniques are critical to effective acquisition, they represent only part of the process that organizations must consider. Taking a broader perspective, human resource professionals recognize that proper staffing is critical to the implementation of the strategic plan of the firm. After all, employees should enhance and facilitate the firm's strategy, not complicate it.

Strategic staffing involves three groups of activities: (1) the acquisition of personnel, (2) the orientation and socialization of new employees, and (3) the movement of employees into the proper positions within the organization.[53] This section will focus on how staffing will enhance strategic implementation via the three activities mentioned above.

Acquisition of Employees

Generally speaking, the role of acquisition in strategic implementation refers to getting the right people in key places.[54] Once there, they can maximize their contribution to the organization's goals. Acquiring people with the right skill mix and characteristics for any given position is the crux of human resource management. One major trend in employee acquisition is the use of contingent personnel.

As organizations focus on cost-cutting strategies, the use of contingent personnel as opposed to permanent employees receives more consideration from top management. Contingent personnel refers to those employees hired from temporary employment agencies, leased from employee leasing companies, or obtained through independent contracting to perform specific tasks.[55] The costs of maintaining the employee on the payroll system and completing the paperwork involved to be in compliance with federal employee regulations are greatly reduced, and to some extent eliminated, if contingent personnel are utilized. Thus, the organization can realize sizeable savings in administrative human resource costs through the use of contingent personnel. Additionally, the use of contingent personnel can be increased or decreased to coincide with the changes in business conditions without severely penalizing the organization.[56] Contingent personnel may be obtained through the use of temporary employees, employee leasing, and independent contracting.

Temporary Employees

The best way to utilize temporary employees is to have them fill short-term work requirements. In the past, the work performed by temporaries was typically clerical in nature. Recently, however, managerial and technical workers have become available through temporary agencies.[57] Organizations must be careful when using a particular temporary worker for a long period of time, though, because legal complications may ensue if the temporary begins to believe that he or she shares a "community of interests" with permanent employees (affirmative action requirements, collective bargaining requirements, and so on).[58] Long-term requirements would perhaps be better served through employee leasing.

Employee Leasing

A growing approach to solving long-term contingency needs is the use of employee leasing. Firms lease employees for long-term or indefinite time periods from companies who specialize in providing workers to client firms. The leasing company maintains the ability to hire and fire employees, is responsible for paying the employees and providing benefits, and complies with all federal regulations concerning employees in the workplace.[59] Essentially, the employee-leasing company becomes the coemployer of the workers. The client firm is relieved of the administrative duties and costs associated with maintaining permanent employees. This can be a considerable savings even though firms may often pay the leasing company 126 percent to 136 percent of what that same employee's salary would be if he or she were a permanent employee.[60]

The employee-leasing area is a fairly new concept and is growing very fast. Unfortunately, the immaturity of the field coupled with the growth has lead to the existence of some lower quality employee-leasing companies. Lower quality companies can cause problems, such as not honoring employee insurance claims.[61] One way to find an honest, well-run employee-leasing company is to ask questions such as, "How long has this company been in business?" and "Is the company willing to give me information on previous clients' satisfaction and on the details of their insurance coverage and company?"[62] If a manager is careful, employee leasing is one solution to long-term contingency needs.

Independent Contractors

Hiring independent contractors is one of the oldest, most long-standing methods of filling contingent personnel requirements. Many companies, for example, currently hire independent contractors for maintenance or security work. Increasingly, though, other work requirements needing special skills or technical expertise are being filled by independent contractors.[63] As with the other methods of hiring contingent personnel, the organization saves the administrative costs while gaining specialized knowledge and expertise.

Although using contingent personnel may not be appropriate for all companies, it is an alternative that may be extremely useful and economical for companies with special needs in their work force. Depending on the extent to which contingent personnel are used to replace permanent employees, considerable cost savings can be realized, which allows funds to be spent elsewhere in the organization to help it achieve its goals and objectives.

Socialization and Orientation

The socialization and orientation of a new employee can be critical to the employee's acceptance of his or her new role and subsequent performance. Although socialization and orientation will be discussed in detail in Chapter 10, the emphasis here is on indoctrinating new employees to the strategic goals and objectives of the company at the outset. This process ensures that employee commitment will be increased and that the new employee's reasons for joining and staying with the company will be reaffirmed.[64]

Movement of Employees

The last aspect of strategic staffing involves the movement of employees into positions that best utilize their specific skills and abilities. Typically, we think of promotion as the movement in organizations that fulfills this role and achieves objectives. As hierarchical movement in the company becomes less likely due to downsizing, restructuring, or career plateauing, lateral moves and sometimes demotion become necessary movements.[65] If this process is managed properly, however, these movements can be positive and need not represent a de facto "career end."

Promotion can motivate and challenge employees, allowing them to grow intellectually while making an even greater contribution to the overall corporate goals. Unfortunately, most companies do not have an endless career tract for every employee, and for those in nonmanagerial or technical positions, the upward movement is almost nonexistent. Nevertheless, a few companies are creating technical and nonmanagerial career tracts for those who do not desire a managerial role in the company.[66] These alternative movements coincide with managerial tract movements in terms of recognition and compensation, creating incentive for employees in these areas to further their careers and continue to grow. The dual career-path choice is not for all firms, however, because it tends to be more costly than traditional movement systems.[67]

Lateral moves are increasingly being used as a way to broaden employee skills and present continued challenge. Learning a new job or a new aspect of the business is beneficial to both the employee and the company and should not be overlooked as a viable method for achieving corporate goals.[68] Especially important to firms pursuing an international expansion strategy, lateral transfers of American managers to foreign operations can be critical to the success or failure of the global expansion.[69] It is the creation of this broad perspective and the familiarity with several aspects of the firm's business that is often critical to formulating and implementing successful strategic plans.

Demotion is the final movement that must be considered in organizations. Although it is often viewed as a "dirty word," demotion is sometimes inevitable because of mergers and downsizing.[70] In the face of layoffs and cuts in the work force, many employees may gladly accept a decrease in responsibility and authority in order to stay employed. Although demotion need not always be a result of disciplinary action, this is often the case, and many organizations simply will not consider it as a career movement to enhance strategy.[71] Demotion often results in employee dissatisfaction, poor subsequent performance, and eventually, turnover.[72] All of these effects are costly to the organization, and should be minimized as much as possible.

Strategic staffing can and should be used to enhance and facilitate the strategic plan of the organization. Any implementation of an organizational goal or objective should include an analysis of the types and extent of staffing changes necessary. This allows the strategic plan to be carried out in the most efficient, timely manner.

• • • • • • • • •

MANAGEMENT GUIDELINES

Decisions regarding recruitment and selection are crucial for effective organizational performance. The following management guidelines should be helpful when making these decisions.

1. Managers should consider recruiting minorities, females, handicapped, and older workers as the work force demographics change.

2. Managers can often improve employee satisfaction and commitment and lower turnover costs by promoting from within the company when feasible.

3. Realistic job previews can provide employees with accurate expectations and, as a result, the organization may benefit from higher employee satisfaction and lower turnover.

4. Career development should usually be part of any training program for new hires.

5. Preemployment forms should be free of questions that could be perceived as discriminating.

6. Affirmative action principles, if observed in the recruiting and selection process, can help to develop a more diverse work force.

7. Measurement reliability and validity should always be a consideration in the recruiting and selection process.

8. The specific recruiting and selection methods should be consistent with the strategic thrust of the firm.

9. Recruiting and selection methods should be evaluated as to their effectiveness.

QUESTIONS FOR REVIEW

1. What types of strategic choices do managers have when deciding on recruiting and selection efforts?

2. What is the purpose of a realistic job preview?

3. What are the legal issues regarding recruiting and selection procedures?

4. What are the pros and cons of the selection tests discussed in this chapter?

5. Why should selection measures be reliable and valid? What does this mean?

6. How does the strategy of the firm affect the recruiting and selection process?

7. Why is it important to evaluate the effectiveness of recruitment and selection methods?

 CASE:

Recruiting Efforts at Apple Computer, Inc.: The Use of Advertising[73]

In 1988, Apple Computer, Inc., the California-based, Fortune 200 corporation, was chosen as the winner of the Vantage Awards in the *Personnel Journal's* annual recruitment advertising competition. The five advertisements implemented that year were polished and the words chosen were concise and rich in meaning.

The Goals of Apple Computer, Inc.

Apple's individual style and substance make each ad a winner. However, it is the overall consistency with the corporate image and product advertising that helps to make the company's recruitment ads outstanding. The multinational corporation's recruitment advertising strategies have been shaped by its growth and unifies the following three goals:

1. To create great personal computer products. The company views computers as tools that empower people and places the *individual*, not the *organization*, at the center of the computing universe.

2. To have a passion for changing the world. Apple strives to make personal computers that change the way people learn and work and makes an effort to be a catalyst for improving how people do things.

3. To build an exciting environment. Apple attempts to make working at the company a rewarding and exciting experience by providing openness, shared vision, and the freedom to learn.

Company executives say that an organization can be only as productive as its individual members. Improving the computer user's experience is at the core of everything Apple does.

Recruiting through Advertising

Apple's winning advertisements were developed by two separate agencies. Apple's recruitment ad strategy is communicated on three hierarchial levels. First, Apple's product marketing group communicates objectives to its staffing management. Then, staffing managers touch base with the recruitment advertising agencies. Finally, corporate echelons directly contact potential employees.

Recruitment ad style that is consistent with product advertising is one of the primary reasons for the success of Apple's $900-million advertising campaign. Standards are first set by the company's marketing division, which gives guidelines for the ad agencies to follow; however, they do not dictate the content of these ads. Such details as logo placement, trademark colors, typeface, and use of the company slogan are listed in a 20-page booklet that the marketing division gives to agencies that work on Apple communications.

In general, companies do not use the exact same recruitment advertising strategy. Some use a variety of strategies while others stick with one primary strategy. Many companies attempt to set their business apart from others by placing a corporate trademark on every ad. In addition, using slogans can be inspiring to potential employees. These strategies can be effective if used properly. This is exactly what Apple Computer and the ad agencies have accomplished. The firm's corporate trademark, a little apple (missing a bite) and slogan, "The power to be your best," are generally used in all ads. Other slogans that cater to specific positions in the company are well thought out and inspiring. For example, imagine working for a company that expresses these concepts and philosophies: "We're looking for artists of the mind," "Silicon, metal, plastic, heart and soul," "Find the finance person in this ad," and, of course, the familiar Apple trademark is always present. Because of the emphasis Apple has given to these slogans, it is no wonder the firm's campaign has been so successful.

Consistency is a powerful recruitment tool for Apple. The firm's corporate trademark and slogan have become familiar to computer enthusiasts worldwide. Because the Apple trademark is a strong visual element, it gives potential Apple recruits an immediate sense of recognition. Research has shown that people are more likely to read an ad with which they are reasonably familiar.

There are several methods used to attract applicants, such as college newspaper ads, fliers, and handouts. Apple executives often choose a direct-mail campaign because they believe it to be the most effective way to reach candidates. The end result is fewer advertising costs, higher returns from advertising investment, and a higher probability of targeting the potential recruits.

Apple Computer's Refined Strategy

Apple has refined its recruitment ad strategy. The firm's campaign now directs the attention of potential recruits to the company and to the opportunities available within it rather than focusing on the jobs alone. The recruitment ad format developed by the marketing division promotes consistency and saves time because the basic format of the ads are preapproved. The ad agencies and recruitment managers can focus more on developing copy that directly appeals to target recruits and less time on trying to fit each group's ad together. Although this chapter has examined the numerous recruiting methods available, Apple has chosen to focus on one popular type of recruiting strategy—advertising. Apple Computer, Inc., has found an innovative way of attracting good employees by using consistent recruitment advertising that allows for future refinement and updating.

QUESTIONS

1. Do you believe that Apple's successful advertising strategy is their only recruitment method? Why or why not?

2. This case focuses on one external recruiting strategy. What are some internal recruiting strategies that might be effective for Apple Computer?

3. Can you tell if Apple has more of a "make" or "buy" recruiting strategy from the information presented in the case?

4. How would your answer to question 3 change if you assumed that Apple Computer has a prospector strategy?

···············
ADDITIONAL READINGS

Bies, Robert J., and Debra L. Shapiro. "Voice and Justification: Their Influence on Procedural Fairness Judgements." *Academy of Management* 31. September 1988, pp. 676–685.

Buck, David N. "Staffing Internal Audit Departments in the Year 2000." *Internal Auditor* 47. April 1990, pp. 24–30.

Cosentino, Chuck, John Allen, and Richard Wellins. "Choosing the Right People." *HRMagazine* 35. March 1990, pp. 66–70.

Cowan, Robert A. "Sacred Cows—Roadblock to Professional Staffing?" *Manufacturing Systems* 8. March 1990, pp. 58–61.

Dossin, Milton N., and Nancie L. Merritt. "Sign-On Bonu$e$ Score for Recruiters." *HRMagazine* 35. March 1990, pp. 42–43.

Dreyfuss, Joel. "Get Ready for the New Work Force." *Fortune* 121. April 23, 1990, pp. 165–181.

Elliott, Brian. "Astride the Demographic Time-Bomb." *Accountancy (UK)* 105. March 1990, pp. 110, 112.

Greenbury, Linda. "What Do I Want to Do?" *Women in Management Review (UK)* 3 (1988), pp. 202–206.

Harrison, Sheila S., and Geraldine D. Jones. "Star Search: The Black Enterprise Executive Recruiter Directory." *Black Enterprise* 20. April 1990, pp. 74–82.

Herman, Roger E. "The Competitive Environment." *Security Management* 34. April 1990, pp. 107–110.

Hildenbrandt, Herbert W., and Jinuyin Liu. "Chinese Women Managers: A Comparison with Their U.S. and Asian Counterparts." *Human Resource Management* 27. Fall 1989, pp. 291–314.

Kaman, Vicki S., and Cynthia Bentson. "Roleplay Simulations for Employee Selection: Design and Implementation." *Public Personnel Management* 17. Spring 1988, pp. 1–8.

Kleinschrod, Walter A. "Temporary Help Complete Your Personnel Picture." *Today's Office* 24. January 1990, pp. 28–40.

Koch, Jennifer. "Apple Ads Target Intellect." *Personnel Journal* 69. March 1990, 107–114.

Landes, Jennifer. "GAMC Report: Agent Referrals Produce Agents." *National Underwriter* 94. March 26, 1990, pp. 3, 22.

Lee, Paula Munier. "The Employee Equation: A New System for Solving Your Business's 'People Problems.'" *Small Business Reports* 15. April 1990, pp. 61–71.

Licht, Walter. "How the Workplace Has Changed in 75 years." *Monthly Labor Review* 111. February 1988, pp. 19–25.

McQuaid, Maureen, and Daren Winkler. "Using PMTs in Handicapped Workshops." *MTM Journal of Methods-Time Measurement* 13 (1987), pp. 50–58.

Marx, Jonathon. "Organizational Recruitment as a Two-Stage Process: A Comparative Analysis of Detroit and Yokohama." *Work & Occupations* 15. August 1988, pp. 276–293.

Matte, Harry. "Cheese Plant Closing Opens New Doors." *Personnel Administrator* 33. January 1988, pp. 52–56.

Packer, Arnold. "Skills Shortage Looms: We Can Handle It." *HRMagazine* 35. April 1990, pp. 38–42.

Rhodes, David W. "Shootout in the Classroom." *Journal of Business Strategy* 11. March–April 1990, pp. 50–52.

Samorodov, Aleksandr. "Coping with the Employment Effects of Restructuring in Eastern Europe." *International Labour Review* 128 (1989), pp. 357–371.

Schnorbus, Paula. "The Confidence Game." *Marketing & Media Decisions* 23. May 1988, pp. 133–148.

Smith, Charles. "Cosmic Disturbance: Political Scandal Hits Operations of Japan's Recruit Group." *Far Eastern Economic Review (Hong Kong)* 143. March 30, 1989, pp. 44–45.

Sonnerfield, Jeffrey A., and Maury A. Peiperl. "Staffing Policy as a Strategic Response: A Typology of Career Systems." *Academy of Management Review* 13. October 1988, pp. 588–600.

Stanton, Michael. "Cooperative Education: Working towards Your Future." *Occupational Outlook Quarterly* 32. Fall, 1988, pp. 22–29.

Supposs, Dean A. "What Accident Histories Can Tell You." *Business & Health* 7. March 1989, pp. 43–44.

Sweeney, Dennis C., Dean Haller, and Frederick Sale, Jr. "Individually Controlled Career Counseling." *Training & Development Journal* 41. August 1987, pp. 58–61.

Tobias, Lester L. "Selecting for Excellence: How to Hire the Best." *Non Profit World* 8. March–April 1990, pp. 23–25.

Zhou, Songnian. "A Trace-Drive Simulation Study of Dynamic Load Balancing." *IEEE Transactions on Software Engineering* 14. September 1988, pp. 1327–1341.

···············
NOTES

1. E. Blacharczyk, "Recruiters Challenged by Economy, Shortages, Unskilled," *HR News*, February 1990, p. B1.

2. Ibid; J. Braham, "No, You Don't Manage Everyone the Same," *Industry Week*, February 6, 1989, p. 29; and L. E. Wynter and J. Solomon, "A New Push to Break the 'Glass Ceiling,'" *Wall Street Journal*, November 15, 1989, p. B1.

3. E. Blacharczyk, "Recruiters Challenged."

4. Ibid., p. B4.

5. J. Jarrell, "A Wider Vision Needed to Control Hiring Costs," *HR News*, February, 1990, p. B2.

6. E. Blacharczyk, "Recruiters Challenged," p. B4.

7. Ibid.

8. B. Leonard, "High-Winning Game Plan," *Personnel Administrator*, September 1989, pp. 58–62.

9. Ibid.

10. B. Schneider and N. Schmitt, *Staffing Organizations*, 2nd ed. (Glenview, IL: Scott, Foresman, 1986).

11. R. Mathis and J. Jackson, *Personnel/Human Resource Management*, 5th ed. (St. Paul: West, 1988).

12. A. E. Marshall, "Recruiting Alumni on College Campuses," *Personnel Journal*, April 1982, pp. 264–266.

13. C. Edwards, "Aggressive Recruitment," *Personnel Journal*, January 1986, pp. 40–48.

14. E. E. Spragins, "Hiring Without," *Inc.*, February 1992, pp. 80–87.

15. J. B. Spangenberg, "Executive Search: A Misunderstood Resource," *HRNews*, February, 1990, p. B6.

16. B. M. Meglino, A. S. DeNisi, S. A. Youngblood, and K. J. Williams, "Efforts of Realistic Job Previews: A Comparison Using an Enhancement and a Reduction Preview," *Journal of Applied Psychology*, May 1988, pp. 259–266.

17. J. P. Wanous, *Organizational Entry: Recruitment, Selection, and Socialization of Newcomers* (Reading, MA: Addison-Wesley, 1980).

18. R. Riley, B. Brown, M. Blood, and C. MaLatesta, "The Effects of Realistic Previews: A Study and Discussion of the Literature," *Personnel Psychology*, Winter 1981, pp. 823–834.

19. M. Manter and J. Benjamin, "How to Hold on to First Careerists," *Personnel Administrator*, September 1989, pp. 43–48.

20. Ibid.

21. T. P. Ference, J. A. F. Stoner, and E. K. Warren, "Managing the Career Plateau," *Academy of Management Review* 2, 1977, pp. 602–612.

22. Pricilla M. Elsass and David A. Ralston, "Individual Responses to the Stress of Career Plateauing," *Journal of Management* 15, 1989, pp. 35–47.

23. Douglas T. Hall and Judith Richter, "Career Gridlock: Baby Boomers Hit the Wall," *Academy of Management Executive* 4, 1990, pp. 7–22.

24. J. Hunter and R. Hunter, "Validity and Utility of Alternative Predictors of Job Performance," *Psychological Bulletin* 96, 1984, pp. 72–98.

25. J. Andrew, "Resume Liars Are Abundant, Experts Assert," *Wall Street Journal*, April 24, 1981, p. 25; A. Gates, "The Secret Life of Making a Good Hire," *Working Woman*, February 1992, pp. 70–72.

26. B. Wonder and K. Keleman, "Increasing the Value of Reference Information," *Personnel Administrator*, March 1984, pp. 98–103.

27. C. Fischer, L. Schoenfeldt, and J. Shaw, *Human Resource Management* (Boston: Houghton Mifflin, 1990).

28. W. Cascio, *Managing Human Resources: Productivity, Quality of Work Life, Profits* (New York: McGraw-Hill, 1989).

29. W. Cascio and N. Phillips, "Performance Testing: A Rose among Thorns?" *Personnel Psychology*, Winter 1979, pp. 751–766.

30. D. Day and S. Silverman, "Personality and Job Performance: Evidence of Incremental Validity," *Personnel Psychology*, Spring 1989, pp. 25–36; and R. Helmreich, L. Sawin, and A. Carsrud, "The Honeymoon Effect in Job Performance: Temporal Increases in the Predictive Power of Achievement Motivation," *Journal of Applied Psychology* 71, 1986, pp. 185–188.

31. K. M. Evans and R. Brown, "Reducing Recruitment Risk through Preemployment Testing," *Personnel* 65, September 1988, pp. 55–64.

32. R. Zemke, "Do Honesty Tests Tell the Truth?" *Training* 27, October 1990, pp. 75–81.

33. "Wired Up," *Time*, August 1983, p. 17.

34. S. Moss, "Polygraph Protection Act," *Personnel Today* 3, Fall 1988, p. 2.

35. E. E. Spragins, "T or F? Honesty Tests Really Work," *Inc.*, February 1992, p. 104.

36. R. Arvey, "The Employment Interview: A Summary and Review of Recent Research," *Personnel Psychology*, Summer 1982, pp. 281–322.

37. B. Felton and S. Lamb, "A Model for Systematic Selection Interviewing," *Personnel* 59, 1982, pp. 40–49.

38. A. Karr, "Creative Interviewing Takes Firmer Hold, and the Job Pinch Worsens," *Wall Street Journal*, May 8, 1990, p. A1.

39. J. Solomon, "The New Job Interview: Show Thyself," *Wall Street Journal*, December 4, 1989, p. B1.

40. C. R. Bell and D. Anderson, "Selecting Super Service People," *HRMagazine*, February 1992, pp. 52–54.

41. P. Myers and D. Myers, "AIDS: Tackling a Tough Problem through Policy," *Personnel Administrator*, April 1987, pp. 95–108.

42. B. Gaugler, D. Rosenthal, G. Thornton, and C. Bentson, "Meta-analyses of Assessment Center Validity," *Journal of Applied Psychology* 72, 1987, pp. 493–511.

43. P. Sackett and M. Wilson, "Factors Affecting the Consensus Judgement Process in Managerial Assessment Centers," *Journal of Applied Psychology* 67, 1982, pp. 10–17.

44. F. Schmidt and J. Hunter, "Employment Testing: Old Theories and New Research Findings," *American Psychologist*, October 1981, pp. 1128–1137.

45. R. Miles and C. Snow, *Organization Strategy, Structure and Process* (New York: McGraw-Hill, 1978); and R. Miles and C. Snow, "Designing Strategic Human Resources Systems," *Organizational Dynamics*, 1983, pp. 36–52.

46. J. Olian and S. Rynes, "Organizational Staffing: Integrating Practice with Strategy," *Industrial Relations*, Spring 1984, pp. 170–183.

47. Ibid.

48. Ibid.

49. Ibid.

50. G. Milkovich and W. Glueck, *Personnel—Human Resource Management: A Diagnostic Approach* (Plano, TX: Business Publications, 1985).

51. S. Rynes, H. Heneman III, and D. Schwab, "Individual Reactions to Organizational Recruiting: A Review," *Personnel Psychology*, Autumn 1980, pp. 529–542.

52. Ibid.

53. J. Butler, G. Ferris, N. Napier, *Strategy and Human Resources Management*, South-Western Series in Human Resources Management, (Cincinnati: South-Western, 1991).

54. Ibid.

55. J. Ross, "Effective Ways to Hire Contingent Personnel," *HRMagazine*, February 1991, pp. 52–54.

56. Ibid.

57. Ibid.

58. Ibid.

59. P. Keaton and J. Anderson, "Leasing Offers Benefits to Both Sides," *HRMagazine*, July 1990, pp. 53–58.

60. Ibid.

61. "Sidestepping the Potholes in Employee Leasing," *Inc.*, August 1991, pp. 84–85.

62. Ibid.

63. Ross, "Effective Ways to Hire Contingent Personnel."

64. Butler et al., *Strategy and Human Resources Management.*

65. Ibid.

66. R. Goddard, "Lateral Moves Enhance Careers," *HRMagazine*, December 1990, pp. 69–74.

67. Ibid.

68. P. Thompson and S. Hammond, "From Career Plateau to Peak Performance," *Executive Excellence* 5, 1988, pp. 14–15.

69. Butler et al., *Strategy and Human Resources Management.*

70. Ibid.

71. J. Kohl and D. Stephens, "Is Demotion a Four-Letter Word?" *Business Horizons* 33, 1990, pp. 74–76.

72. E. Roskies and C. Louis-Guerin, "Job Insecurity in Managers: Antecedents and Consequences," *Journal of Organizational Behavior* 11, 1990, pp. 345–359.

73. J. Koch, "Apple Ads Target Intellect," *Personnel Journal* 69, no. 3, 1990, pp. 107–114; and J. Berry, "Apple Strategy May Change with Boss," *Adweek Western Advertising News* 40, 1990, p. 64.

10 Strategic Socialization, Training, and Development

It is imperative that organizations socialize their employees into the culture of the organization so that they can become effective, productive members soon after entering the firm. One of the main courses of doing this is through training and development. Both formal and informal methods of orienting new employees can be used, as well as both on-the-job and off-the-job methods of training. Development is a concept that is broader than training, which is tied more closely to the skills and aptitude of the employee. To explore these topics, we include the important elements of training programs and materials used in the training and development process and indicate how they relate to the human resource strategy of the firm.

• • • • • • • • •
CHAPTER OBJECTIVES

As a result of studying this chapter, you should be able to

1. Define culture and explain its relationship to the socialization process.
2. Explain the socialization process.
3. Explain the role training and development play in socialization and in improving performance.
4. List and describe training and development methods.

CASE: GE—Corporate Confrontational Culture [1]

General Electric was one of the fastest growing companies of the 1980s. Much of this growth occurred through the acquisitions of several key companies: RCA, Montgomery Ward Credit, a Miami television station, Roper Corp., Borg-Warner Plastics, Kidder Peabody, NBC, and Employers Reinsurance. By 1988, the company's sales reached $40 billion a year. Earnings stood at $3.4 billion, with projected earnings of $5 billion by 1991. John F. Welch, Jr., chairman and CEO, is reaping the credit.

"Welch is the best CEO in the world today," says former GE executive Richard W. Miller, echoing many academics and GE executives past and present. "There is no corporation in the world with stronger management."

But others see the 52-year-old executive with the combative temper and boyish grin as a possible problem in the long term. Despite all the admiration for Mr. Welch, a minority view is forming. It pictures GE as a growing collection of disparate companies in which a domineering personality substitutes for business focus. That it has worked so far, critics say, is no shield against a day of reckoning. "The person who follows Jack Welch at GE has a big problem because GE is being run according to his style and his breadth," even Miller acknowledges.

The churning of GE has produced little more than a retooled version of a 1970s conglomerate, contends Harvard Business School professor Michael Porter. Thomas Peters, author of *In Search of Excellence*, seems to agree. Once "the most glorious technology company of the century, GE has become a hodgepodge," he said.

Puzzled Analysts

Analysts say that GE shares lagged in 1988 to 35 percent below 1987's high partly because portfolio managers found it too complex. "Who can figure out how things fall to the bottom line in financial services or what GE pays in taxes? Nobody," says Nicholas Heymann of Drexel Burnham Lambert, Inc. "People have a tendency to say, 'It can't go on. I can't understand it.'"

Other past and present executives also worry that Welch's ruthless reshuffling has battered GE's legendary corporate loyalty. "Loyalty to a company, it's nonsense," responds Welch testily. But even he concedes that small-technology companies with close-knit communications may be more a model for American management than GE.

Meanwhile, Porter says that Welch's strategy of investing only in businesses that are first or second in their markets is a 15-year-old idea that leads managers to focus on size instead of competitive advantage. It also stifles creativity, claims Peters, who adds that GE hasn't created a new business for decades.

Culture, Welch Style

Welch deals summarily, though generously, with GE employees who don't share his vision or measure up to his standards. "Some people past a certain age aren't trainable, and they do better to leave GE," says Brian H. Rowe, the head of the aircraft-engine group. As Welch's hand-picked lieutenant running medical systems, John M. Trani, puts it, "The Welch theory is those who do, get, and those who don't, go." Thus, GE's executive corps increasingly reflects Welch's own drive and personality. Divorced after 28 years of marriage, Welch is a man whose true love is business.

Talk about GE's growing size and complexity stirs a grin of boyish delight. His conversation is laced with mentions of "winning" and a "bias to action," phrases increasingly echoed in GE ranks. Ever blunt, he calls his managers "grunts" and "turkeys." He sometimes is "excitable to excess," Vice-Chairman Hood says.

Leonard Vickers, a former marketing vice-president, recalls reviewing an ad agency presentation with Welch. "I was using my indirect English to tell the agency it wasn't on target," Vickers says. "Jack just picked up the storyboard, threw it on the floor and said, 'See? We don't like it! It doesn't work!'"

Abrasive from the moment he started his career in GE's nascent plastics business in 1960, Welch manages by what he calls "constructive conflict," a hazing-by-shouting-match approach that requires managers to argue strenuously with him, even if they agree.

"You can't even say hello to Jack without it being confrontational," says Ralph D. Ketchum, the former head of GE's lighting business, whom Welch abruptly "retired" in 1986. "If you don't want to step up to Jack toe-to-toe, belly-to-belly and argue your point, he doesn't have any use for you. He's very smart, so he has an opinion about everything."

An aggressive salesman of his management ideas, Welch visits every class at the company's training center, an institution that rivals the best university business schools. New GE managers get a taped message discussing his visions and values for GE, such as ownership, candor, quality, and entrepreneurship. He has tightened control over promotions and approves career moves of GE's top 500 managers. His prime job, he says, is "resource allocator" of money and people.

His ability to excite loyalty among the troops, says James Baughman, the head of corporate management development, bears comparison with Alfred Sloan of General Motors Corp. and Thomas Watson, Sr., of IBM.

Two Guys

"I look at Jack as two guys," says Grant Tinker, the former NBC head whom Welch tried desperately to keep. "He's a good guy you can hang out with, a man's man. The same guy walks into the office, and he's like a chess player. People aren't people anymore. Apparently, he can live that way."

But can GE? Critics say the fallout from Welch's 1987 swap in GE's consumer-electronics business for the medical-equipment lines of Paris-based Thomson CRG illustrates the price GE pays for his style. Many consumer-electronics managers had come only recently from GE's healthier major-appliance business, lured by Welch's willingness to attempt a turnaround in consumer electronics. When he suddenly sold the business, they were dumbfounded. Stephen F. Holmes, who had been general manager of product design for all GE major appliances and who had transferred to consumer electronics only two months before the sale, jumped ship to GE's archrival, Whirlpool Corporation. Holmes declines to be quoted, but colleagues say that after devoting his whole career to GE, he felt betrayed.

Welch, who suggested the swap to Thomson, says it was the only way to get Thomson's medical-equipment business, which he says will be more profitable than consumer electronics. As for managers who moved their families to take jobs in consumer electronics, they "are better off," he says, because the business will do better under Thomson.

But the swap sent a message throughout GE. "A lot of people tend to feel any business is up for sale," says George Smith, a manager at GE's aerospace operations, where defense cuts have further increased insecurity. He also hears "a lot of talk about loyalty and that it doesn't hurt people to have multi-industry or multi-company experience."

Avoiding Bureaucracy

The message Welch says he is sending, however, is that by cutting management layers and delegating responsibility, "we are trying to create an atmosphere where people want to work, a nonbureaucracy where people have a chance to flourish. Now, do all of them absorb it and grab it? Not yet. That is my job."

Yet those who do "grab it" may simply be learning loyalty to Welch, some people say. "Jack's ideal manager is strong, independent, a great leader—and will agree with him," contends Jacques Robinson, a former vice-president who lost out to Miller for the top job in consumer electronics. Welch retorts, "I hope I have gut people around here."

No one knows the long-term cost—or benefit—of the Welch culture at GE. But there are signs that it may not work at NBC. News employees remain suspicious of their new parent's motives, according to a recent survey, partly because GE has made it clear that they must cut costs.

Producers complain about less indulgence for new news programming, and they worry as much about costs as about covering events.

For the moment, Welch may be able to ignore his critics. GE's management talent is deep, departed managers say, and Welch contends that stress and insecurity are greatest in businesses going through cyclical downturns anyway. Moreover, he says, GE must adopt a get-tough culture to survive in the 1990s as global competition intensifies.

Says Robert Smialek, who left medical systems for broader responsibility as group vice-president at Tracor, Inc., an instruments concern, "If you're looking for a relaxing place to work that leads gradually to retirement, you won't enjoy GE. Not everybody is happy there. But when the supply of management talent so exceeds demand, you can afford to lose people. In the future, that might not be the case. But Jack is agile enough to change his approach when the time comes."

• • • • • • • • •

The GE case shows the impact a CEO can have on establishing the culture and socialization process in a company. Jack Welch is an aggressive, combative individual who has definite ideas about how he wants GE to grow and operate, even to the extent that he visits every class at the company's training center. It seems obvious that Welch wanted to change the culture at GE by establishing it as an aggressive competitor. He wants the company to be number one or two in every industry it enters. Socializing people—getting them to conform to the new culture—is a difficult task. Yet Welch seems to have been successful, and GE sales and profits have been growing.

STRATEGIC CHOICES

An organization must make three basic choices with regard to socialization and the development of employees:

1. Does the firm want employees who conform to the organization, or does it want employees who are creative and show innovation?
2. Should the organization develop its human resources ("grow its own") or should it focus on hiring employees who are already developed ("buy its own")?
3. Should the organization find ways to improve the performance of marginal workers, or should it simply replace them?

Each of these choices is analyzed the in the following sections.

CONFORMITY VERSUS CREATIVITY AND INNOVATION

All organizations want their employees to conform to some extent to prevent an organizational anarchy. Organizations need rules, procedures, and policy in order to function as an organization. Structural hierarchy and job descriptions spell out job duties, responsibilities, authority, and reporting relationships.

So the issue is not, shall we have conformity? Rather the issue is how much conformity shall we have. Conformity reduces variation and uncertainty. Uncertainty reduces risk because it enhances predictability. But conformity comes at a price—when there is "too much" conformity, innovation and creativity are stifled. When innovation and creativity among organizational members are stifled, the organization finds it difficult to come up with new ideas, approaches, products, and creative solutions to problems.

So, the issue becomes: How can we get the conformity from organizational members that we need in order to function as an organization while, at the same time, encourage employees to develop their creativity?

Companies such as Nissan and Toyota have solved this problem through the quality circle concept to encourage creativity among employee groups. Employees meet periodically to discuss ways to improve both production and quality. 3M uses a form of "intrapreneurship" that encourages employees to actually form mini-companies within 3M to develop and market new products and ideas.[2] This is how the highly successful Post-It notes and Thinsulate were developed for 3M.

Yet not all firms want creativity from their employees. Even a highly successful company such as IBM has a very specific dress code that is strictly enforced for all customer contact employees. This outward manifestation represents IBM's thinking that most employees should basically follow a well-formulated and established policy in order for the company to be successful, although during the mid-1980s the company decentralized the policy formulation process somewhat.[3] Yet the rigid culture, which forces conformity, continues to exist at IBM.[4]

So just because a company requires conformity under a rigid culture does not mean it cannot be successful. It may obtain its creativity and innovation through structured research and development programs and other formal organizational units charged with this responsibility. Still, the amount of socialization used to exact conformity is a key strategic decision for a firm.

DEVELOPING PEOPLE VERSUS HIRING DEVELOPED PEOPLE

The second key decision regarding socialization, training, and development involves the extent to which the firm will train and develop employees versus hiring them already well trained and developed. For example, Proctor & Gamble exerts a great deal of time and effort in the comprehensive training of new employees, whereas Parker Foods, a much smaller organization based in Colorado, tries to hire people with extensive experience. The same is true of IBM compared to a smaller computer company such as Standard.

—Size is often a major factor in this decision. Larger companies often can afford to spend extensive amounts on training and developing new employees; most of the firms that offer training are large Fortune 500 companies who can afford to do so. Both IBM and Proctor & Gamble have served as training grounds for hosts of smaller firms in their respective industries. Statistically, however, this accounts for a very small percentage of companies providing training for American workers. Only five-tenths of 1 percent of all of the companies in the United States deliver 90 percent of the workplace training.[5] Some critics feel that not nearly enough money is being spent on training the American work force. Most agree that organizations should be spending at least 5 percent of their funds on training, however currently the figure is closer to 2 percent.[6] Further, some firms spend nothing on training while others concentrate the training they do provide on managers, technical employees, and professionals.[7] When training is provided, it often does not focus on what employers list as the number one deficiency of the American work force: written communication.[8]

— Frequently, a company will hire untrained and inexperienced people for two major reasons. First, they can get them for a fairly low wage rate and, secondly, they can train the employee in their preferred way of carrying out the job. Many companies hire new college graduates for these reasons while shunning more experienced and expensive employees. Another factor that influences this decision is the firm's policy to promote from within versus hiring from the outside. Firms such as GM and Polaroid have a strong promote from within policy and, therefore, tend to hire inexperienced people at entry level positions in order to provide promotion opportunities. Apple Computer, on the other hand, hires experienced people for higher level jobs primarily because of the very rapid growth the firm experienced in the 1980s. In fact, Apple hired many people from IBM, a firm known for its thorough training and orientation program. This presents a dilemma for many firms that provide thorough training—they may end up training employees who leave and eventually work for competitors. Some firms known for their sophisticated training programs, such as Electronic Data Systems (EDS), have tried to prevent this from happening by requiring new employees to sign a form indicating that they will repay EDS for their training if they take a job with a competitor during a specified number of years after completing the EDS training program.

So the organization must decide how much time, effort, and money it wishes to invest in a training and development program relative to its position on hiring well-trained and experienced employees. Of course, even those firms that hire well-trained and experienced employees will have at least a minimal training and development program to show employees "how we do it here."

IMPROVING VERSUS REPLACING POOR PERFORMANCE

— A third key strategic choice in the socialization and development of employees involves how much the firm will invest in an employee to improve subpar performance. Several key issues must be considered: the probability of improving the performance, the cost of improving performance, legal considerations, replacement costs, and top management philosophy.

When employees do not perform their jobs up to the standards expected in some companies, they are terminated. In other companies, they are coached, counseled, and trained in hopes of improving their performance. With the emphasis on drug and substance abuse rehabilitation and the legal protections prohibiting discriminatory actions (including termination) based on age, sex, race, religion, or disability, companies often seek ways to improve an employee's performance instead of terminating them. Employee Assistance Programs (EAP) have been developed to help the substance abuser or troubled employee. In addition, many employers fear that termination for poor performance could result in litigation charges of discrimination. Because of this, employers who at one time might have immediately terminated an employee (for drunkenness, for example) now may continue the person's employment, but require that the employee enter an EAP.

....

| EXHIBIT 10.1 | The Bidirectional Relationship of Organizational Strategy and Culture |

```
┌─────────────┐                      ┌─────────────┐
│  STRATEGY   │ ◄─ ─ ─ ─ ─ ─ ─► │   CULTURE   │
└─────────────┘                      └─────────────┘
```

....

Thus, today an employer must decide whether additional socialization and training can salvage marginal performers or whether a swift-termination policy is more desirable.

Strategy and Culture

An organization's strategy and its corporate culture are closely related. The relationship is bidirectional in nature, as shown in Exhibit 10.1. That is, both concepts impact one another. For the corporate strategy to be implemented the proper culture must be in place. If it is not, cultural change may be necessary. On the other hand, culture can facilitate or limit the very strategies that are even considered.

When Lee Iacoca took over Chrysler he sought to make the company a trim flexible, innovative organization. The bloated bureaucracy resisted change and new ideas. Iacoca cut thousands of jobs not only in an attempt to reduce costs but also to dramatically reverse prevailing cultural values. He was able to bring in managers who shared his vision of the organization. To some degree the new strategy necessitated a new culture and yet once a new culture was created new strategies were possible. A similar thing happened at Cray Research, Inc., when John Rollwagan, chairman of Cray, asked the CEO, Marcelo Gumucio, to step down. The bureaucracy at Cray became too much for the free-form culture it had. Rollwagan's reasoning for asking for the chairman's resignation was that the reports and procedures demanded by Gumucio were clashing with the "Cray-style" culture that Rollwagan was nurturing.[9]

The culture of a low-cost mass producer will likely be quite different than that of a specialized custom-made machine tool company. The mass production operation will value conformity, rules, and will probably have a clearly defined hierarchy of control. The machine tool company that creates one-of-a-kind products based on customer needs and specifications will favor a more team-oriented, flexible environment. Exhibit 10.2 outlines some possible strategy/culture links.

Frequently organizations that attempt to diversify encounter a strategy-culture dilemma. Large conglomerates with diverse businesses may seek only minimal cultural conformity. The conglomerate is viewed primarily as a financial umbrella and little is to be gained by attempting uniformity. The situation is frequently different, however, when two or more companies merge horizontally. Culture clashes are seen as one of the major causes of failure. When Philadelphia's Mellon Bank acquired its rival, Girard, two very different philosophies collided. Mellon insisted that the Girard organization conform. The combined merged organization suffered huge losses. An example of a successful cultural merger was the uniting of Baxter Travenol and American Hospital and Supply. Both companies were committed to creating an

FOCUS ON INTERNATIONAL ISSUES •

Blending Organizational Cultures: The French Way

In 1988, Hachette, a French magazine empire, purchased Diamandis Communications, an American publishing firm whose magazines included *Woman's Day*, *Road & Track*, and *Popular Photography* among others. While critics felt that the acquisition seemed like a good idea at the time, they later ate their words after the battle of the cultures took place.

The battle seemed to center on the chairman and chief executive of Diamandis Communications, Peter Diamandis. After the acquisition, Diamandis remained on in these roles, but he soon found that he was having trouble adjusting to how Hachette did things. Admittedly, Diamandis had trouble taking advice, even from the golf pro he hired to help with his game. This personality shortcoming may have been the source of the majority of the problems that arose.

Hachette officials tended to take away a great deal of the responsibility Diamandis had as they began making changes to his magazines and altering decisions he had made. At first the changes were confined to decisions about layouts and advertisers, but eventually Hachette dropped Diamandis' favorite magazine, *Memories*, a nostalgia magazine which Hachette felt missed the mark with French readers who did not recognize people like Ted Williams and Fred Astaire about whom the stories were written.

While more and more responsibility was taken away from Diamandis, more and more responsibility was given to the French editors. American editors were left out of the decision-making meetings creating an atmosphere of back stabbing and little trust. American managers began talking in the halls with exaggerated French accents and ignoring their French counterparts. As morale dropped, people began to leave, including Diamandis.

In September of 1990, Hachette officials asked Diamandis if he would like to leave the company at the end of his contract. He suggested that he and two of his top officials not wait but leave immediately. The next day, the phones were being answered "Hachette Magazines." All told, the payroll fell 35 percent in the two years after the merger. An entire floor at Hachette Magazine headquarters had been leased. While expansion was the main reason Hachette purchased Diamandis Communications, that plan will have to wait until the corporate culture could be reestablished and the organization became stable again.

SOURCE: Adapted from Patrick Reilly, "Egos, Culture Clash When French Firm Buys U.S. Magazines," *Wall Street Journal*, February 15, 1991, pp. A1+.

entirely new organization with a combined culture building on the strengths of both former companies.

／ Another strategy/culture issue arises when a company, in response to its environment, changes its strategy. Apple Computers stared out as a very freewheeling organization in the garage of two young entrepreneurs. In the early days Steve Jobs and Steve Wozinak encouraged this flexible, nonconformist atmosphere. As the company grew, more controls and discipline were required in order to meet new markets. When the board of directors decided that it could indeed compete with companies such as IBM and Compaq in the business market, they removed Jobs from his position in the company and replaced him with a professional business team headed by John Scully. Scully achieved the goals set forth, but the early culture was a casualty.

One of the criticisms of American "smokestack" industries is that they cannot develop and sustain new strategic positions. American steel companies are a prime example. Their cultures are so entrenched and based on a different economic reality that they seem incapable of effective strategic positions. Starbuck and Hedberg, based on their study of a large Swedish company, believed that the only way to bring about the necessary revolutionary changes is to remove top management and bring in a new team.[10]

| EXHIBIT 10.2 | Examples of Different Strategy/Culture Environments |

STRATEGY	CULTURE	TRAINING AND DEVELOPMENT EMPHASIS	EXAMPLE
Low Cost, Mass Production, Formal Hierarchy	Conformity, Rule	Strong Orientation in Company Policies and Practices	General Motors
Specialized Custom Product	Flexible Team Oriented, Creative License	Team Building, Problem Solving	Berg Pipe Company
Growth Oriented	Aggressive, Risk Taking	Assertiveness, Problem Solving	Compaq Computer
Stable, Maintenance Concious Mild Conformity	Risk Adverse, Quality	TQM and Policy Orientation	Alcoa
High-Profit, Luxury markets	Quality Conscious Elitist	TQM, Craftsmanship	Rolls Royce

Managers need to understand the dynamics of the strategy/culture connection. It is important not only in the successful formulation and implementation of strategy but also filters what type of strategy is even possible in the first place. Strategic decisions often lead to changing culture. Sometimes it may be necessary to change the culture before it is possible to undertake a certain strategy.

SOCIALIZATION AND CULTURE

Whenever anyone joins any organization, they must conform to the organizational requirements to some extent. The price of organizational membership is conformity. But the organization is also changed by each new member, sometimes ever so slightly, sometimes in a major way. Bob Adams was hired at a Chrysler plant the same day Lee Iacocca was hired as chairman. Adams had little effect on Chrysler; Iacocca had a major effect.

In *Bonds of Organization*, C. Wright Bakke calls this process of adjustment "the fusion process."[11] It is shown in Exhibit 10.3. It is also known as inducement-contribution theory.[12] This theory states that a person gives up something to join an organization (such as time, effort, or attention), but will do so if the organization returns something of greater or equal value (such as money or security). The fusion process is an important part of acculturation.

Culture and Acculturation

The culture of a group or society is a set of values (shared beliefs), history, tradition, norms, mores, and artifacts that the group holds in common.[13] Culture is the cement or glue that holds a society or group together. Generally, culture consists of those items listed in Exhibit 10.4.

EXHIBIT 10.3 Bakke's Fusion Process

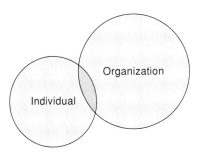

Conformity and Adaptation

Even though culture is an anthropological term, during the 1980s, the term found application to business organizations.[14] What used to be called organizational climate by authors such as Keith Davis[15] is now referred to as organizational culture to reflect the more pervasive nature of the concept.

Much of Culture Is Hidden

Even though culture is represented by art and artifacts, it is rather intangible, hidden, and not easily recognized. Some people refer to the obvious aspects of culture, such as art and artifacts, as being only the tips of the iceberg. Much of culture is hidden, as shown in Exhibit 10.5 (on page 316). It is not easy to see an organization's history or tradition. Even certain norms may be difficult to determine at least to the new organizational member or casual observer.

Culture is a powerful force in any organization. Companies such as IBM, 3M, and Apple take great pride in building and maintaining their desired culture. Not knowing or ignoring an organization's culture can be perilous for any organizational member. This is why organizations often spend much time and money instilling their culture in new employees through sometimes long and expensive orientation and training programs. An example is P&G College of Procter & Gamble. In order to imprint people as they enter the organization, Procter & Gamble sends all new hires to P&G College for three or four days during their first year.[16]

Culture Is Hard to Change

Changing a culture can be extremely difficult. Culture is usually valued by organizational members and they are slow to change any aspect of it. Sometimes it takes a major crisis to change culture. This was true of Chrysler when Lee Iacoca took over as the new CEO. One reason he was so successful in changing Chrysler's existing culture was because the situation at the time was critical. Change had to be made quickly if the firm was to survive, and he was the right person to make change happen. Changing GE's culture after Jack Welch leaves may take his successor much longer because it is perceived as working well.

··

| EXHIBIT 10.4 | Components of Culture

Values—Basic beliefs; strongly held attitudes about important ideas.

Norms—Accepted standards of behavior.

History and Tradition—The historical or traditional way of doing and thinking about things.

Mores—Customs or rituals that the society believes in and follows.

Myths—Common stories or folklore passed from one generation to another.

Art and Artifacts—Art, symbols, weapons, pottery and so on that are physical representa-
tions of the culture.

··

Culture Serves as Behavior Control

Culture helps to ensure conformity. When people "buy into a culture" they buy into
norms, rules, mores, traditions, and myths of that culture. As we saw earlier, under
the inducements-contribution theory, people will do this only if they feel that the
price of acceptance of organizational culture is worth the benefits received in the
way of money, security, job enjoyment, and so on.

Of course, few employees completely buy into an organizational culture. They
make an **accommodation** to at least get by. They may reject parts of the culture
either implicitly or explicitly. This may manifest itself in dress, refusal to take part
in certain corporate sponsored rituals (such as attending the company Christmas
party) or in other even more subtle ways, such as refusing to learn about corporate
history or tradition.

Acculturation

The process of acquiring the culture of an organization or society is known as **acculturation.** To be a member of a group, one must adopt certain group requirements.
The fusion process and exchange theory discussed above help us to understand how
and to what extent an individual will actually acquire a culture. Most organizations
have means to help people acquire their culture. Essentially this process involves
orientation and training activities.

Initially, during recruitment and selection, people who, in the eyes of the interviewers or evaluators, would have a difficult time acquiring the culture are screened
out. So to some extent the acculturation process actually starts during the hiring
and selection process. Those that are finally hired receive an orientation to the
organization—either formal or informal or both—and some training.

In the remainder of this chapter, we will focus on showing how orientation and
training relate to both culture acquisition and performance improvement. In other
words, an organization is not only interested in having a person acquire its culture,
but it also wants the person to do things right (performance) in that culture.

··

ORIENTATION

Probably nothing does more to begin the acculturation process in a specific organization than the orientation program. *Orientation is the process of welcoming new*

··

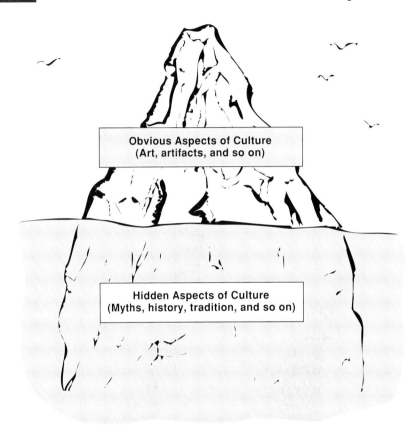

Obvious Aspects of Culture
(Art, artifacts, and so on)

Hidden Aspects of Culture
(Myths, history, tradition, and so on)

··

employees, bringing them into the organization, and familiarizing them with organization operations and culture. Orientation occurs two ways: formally and informally. The **formal orientation** is conduced by the organization. Then, **informal orientation** occurs through daily interactions with fellow employees.

Formal Orientation Programs

Has a fellow employee ever voiced something very derogatory about the organization shortly after you were hired? What a way to start off! Unfortunately, this happens too often. In this case, the *informal* orientation received has precisely the opposite effect of the formal orientation. Orientation helps to form the individual's schema and create the maps he or she will have about the organization. One reason they are so important is because, once formed, these schema are difficult to change. Often "first impressions are lasting impressions."

Too often, formal orientation programs are taken too lightly by organizations and employees alike. This is unfortunate since the new employees *will* be oriented one way or the other—either formally by the organization or informally through interactions with fellow employees. While formal orientation programs do not replace informal orientation, they at least provide the organization with the opportunity to give the employee its "best shot." If the organization does this systematically with all new employees and reinforces what is presented back on the job, then the

HR CHALLENGES

Disney's Orientation Program

One of the most successful orientation programs for American firms is the one developed by Disney. Everyone—all employees hired at all levels—attends Disney University and must pass Traditions I before going for specialized training. Traditions I is an all-day experience in which the Disney philosophy, tradition, and culture are presented.

At Disney, employees are called "cast members" and whenever they work with the public they are "on stage." Customers are called "guests." Employees are told about all functions and how they relate to the "show." They are reminded of how important their role is in making the show a success. Even ticket takers receive four eight-hour days of instruction in order for them to know locations of restrooms, when the parade starts, show schedules, and so on. In other words, they are required to know more than the ticket-taking job; they are also

expected to know other information to make the guest's stay as enjoyable as possible.

Disney emphasizes the "Disney Way" in orientation, training, and follow-up employee evaluations. Because of this emphasis the company is sometimes criticized for "brainwashing" its employees. The firm requires conformity to the Disney way and employees are given little opportunity to express creativity and innovation.

Yet when one examines the success of Disney theme parks, the wide use of part-time and student help, and the critical nature of their jobs in terms of customer contact, a rigid, highly formalized orientation and training program is probably the best. And of course, it's difficult to argue with success.

SOURCE: Adapted from Thomas J. Peters and Robert H. Waterman, Jr., *In Search of Excellence.* (New York: Harper & Row, 1982), p. 168.

informal orientation will more than likely reinforce rather than conflict with the formal orientation.

In "Where the Training Dollars Go," Chris Lee reports that 76 percent of firms with 50 or more employees have a formal orientation program.[17] Several companies have excellent orientation programs—IBM, Frito-Lay, and Dana Corporation among them. Many of these firms follow the steps outlined in Exhibit 10.6 that highlight the way to develop a strong orientation program.

While some firms have overall orientation programs designed for any and all employees, others develop specific orientation programs for one job classification or one unit. Exhibit 10.7 shows the elements of the Quaker Oats orientation program for college graduates in sales. Notice that the Quaker philosophy is an important part of the program. Also note that some sales skills (presentation skills and promotional materials) are also covered. All new sales hires are put through this three-to six-month orientation before receiving additional sales training.

Barnett Banks offers a full ten days of orientation. Topics covered include Barnett's history, current strategic plan, financial background, personnel policies, marketing and growth plans, job responsibilities, responsibilities of selected jobs, and administrative matters. After this orientation, employees receive eleven months of additional training.[18]

Employee Handbook

Often the focus of the orientation program is an orientation handbook or employee manual that covers many of these topics. Exhibit 10.8 (on page 320) shows the table of contents for a typical employee manual. A manual typically covers standards of conduct, benefits, nondiscrimination policy, and so on. While each manual is different, the table of contents in Exhibit 10.8 is typical of many employee manuals. The manual also usually contains a welcoming letter and an official receipt by the employee. The receipt is becoming more common as organizations attempt to document the fact that the employee has been informed of key issues for disciplinary

· ·

EXHIBIT 10.6 Tips for Building a Strong Orientation Program

The very first step in welcoming new employees into the organization is the orientation program. However, an ever increasing number of firms are sending a stale, stagnant message to their employees. To fix this problem, organizations need to focus on updating and revamping their orientation programs. Some suggestions for making needed changes follow.

1. Keep the paperwork portion of the orientation light the first day. Information overload can be a real turnoff for employees. Try to separate the required paperwork into two piles: those forms that must be completed the first day and those that can wait a week or two.

2. Start the orientation with an informal meeting with the new recruits immediate supervisor. The meeting should be brief, no more than 20 minutes, and it should start on time. This meeting will serve two purposes. First, the employee will see that his or her immediate supervisor is a person with whom he or she can come to with problems and concerns. Second, it shows that the firm and the supervisor stress punctuality.

3. Alternate heavy information such as benefits and insurance forms with short taped or live accounts of the organization with the CEO or other important and not so important organizational members. This helps to reassure the new employees that the organization is made up of people and not just forms and rules.

4. Provide the new employees with a glossary of terms unique to the organization. This can be done in a variety of ways. For example, two long time employees can act out a scene in which the organization's jargon is used and then allow the new employees to guess what the terms stand for. Afterwards, the same scene can be acted out by two new employees who have mastered the corporate lingo. Having employees learn the organization language up front is an easy way to help them begin to think like an organizational member. This exercise also cuts down on the feelings of being an outsider once the employee begins working.

5. Find a buddy for each new employee. The matching of employees with new recruits does not have to focus on the job to be performed. Sometimes it may be useful to match people on a personality basis rather than on a job basis. Further, this allows the new employee to build links with employees outside their immediate department further reinforcing the organizations culture of working together as an organization.

· ·

and legal reasons. That is, an employee could claim he or she had not been informed of a particular rule or policy; a signed receipt helps to avoid this situation.

It is a good idea to have an employee manual or other orientation handbook even in small organizations. This makes it absolutely clear what is expected in terms of conduct and what the employee can expect in terms of treatment and benefits. Not only can a manual serve to enhance communication with employees, but it also can serve as documentation in cases of grievances, complaints, or suits. Of course if a union is present, the union agreement should also be given to employees by either the union or the personnel department at the time of hiring.

Common Components of an Orientation

Welcoming

Orientations frequently begin with an official welcoming of the employee. In small organizations, this should be done by the CEO. In larger organizations, someone

··

| EXHIBIT 10.7 | Quaker Oats Orientation for Sales Trainees |

√ Field training with District Manager
√ Quaker's Company Philosophy
√ Presentation Skills
√ Organization Structure
√ Use of Sales Promotion Materials, Trade Allowances, and Consumer Events
√ Administrative Details

- Payroll
- Health Insurance
- Leave and Vacation Policy

- Pension Benefits
- Employee Benefits
- Forms

··

from personnel and/or the immediate supervisor should welcome the employee and make him or her feel comfortable and accepted.

Meeting the Boss and Fellow Employees

The employee should be introduced to those with whom he or she will work by either the supervisor or someone from personnel. In some cases, a peer employee or buddy might also serve as a person to introduce the new employees to his or her coworkers. These introductions are very important and should not be taken lightly. It is at this point that the employee is brought into the team. Teamwork and acceptance by the team is essential.

Completion of Paperwork

All essential paperwork should be completed during orientation so that the employee gets paid accurately and on time. Various tax and insurance forms as well as time cards, citizenship-resident documentation, and other items need to be properly completed in a timely fashion. There is nothing more aggravating for a new employee than to miss the first paycheck or to be paid improperly because the correct forms were not completed accurately. Someone in the company should be given the responsibility to be the expert on new hires. This person should ensure that all needed forms for new hires are completed promptly and accurately.

Benefit and Retirement Systems

Most employees find this subject very confusing. Therefore, in addition to giving new employees a pamphlet or employee handbook that discusses the benefit and retirement system, it should also be carefully explained to them.

Company Policies, Procedures, Rules, and Discipline

Again these items are usually compared in the handbook or labor agreement, but they should be orally explained to the employee by the supervisor or someone in personnel. There should be no misunderstandings here. A sign-off policy is a good

....

EXHIBIT 10.8 Table of Contents for Employee Manual

idea to use here so the employee cannot state that he or she was never told of an infraction.

Introduction to Job Duties and Initial Training

Of course the job duties will have been discussed during the hiring interview. However, they should be reviewed again. The job description, goals (objectives), and employee performance evaluation form and process all should be reviewed. The employee needs to know the following:

> What he or she is to do (job description).
>
> What is to be accomplished (job goals or objectives).
>
> How he or she will be evaluated (performance evaluation).

Failure to clearly point out and discuss these items at the time of hiring will likely cause many problems later. The employee needs to also be given initial training as to how the job is done at the particular company with specific follow-up training conducted later.

Follow-up

Finally, after a period of one to three months, a follow-up session should be held with the employee by either the supervisor or someone in personnel. This may tie in to the ending of the employee's probationary period. The use of such a period is a good idea to give both the employee and the employer time to assess whether a good choice has been made. Employers should not use the term *permanent employee* in the handbook once the probationary period ends. In wrongful discharge cases some courts have ruled that this *implies a contractual obligation*. It is better to state that the employee moves from probationary to "regular" status. A careful review of the employee's performance at the end of the probationary period and a review of company policies and rules will help ensure that the employee is fitting in properly.

Now we will examine how the informal orientation process operates in the organization.

Informal Orientation

Many companies go to great lengths to ensure that the initial formal and informal interviews new employees have with existing employees in day-to-day job operations reinforce what has been covered in the formal orientation program. For example, Dana Corporation, under the leadership of former Chairman Rene McPherson, emphasized a one-page statement of philosophy, which was communicated to new and existing employees over and over again. This helped to reinforce corporate philosophy with existing employees as well as new ones. This philosophy covers four key points: [19]

1. Face-to-face communication of all performance figures with all employees is critical.

2. Training and the opportunity for development should be provided to all employees.
3. Job security should be provided for all people.
4. Incentive programs based on ideas, suggestions, and hard work should be established as a reward.

A short, simple, straight-forward statement, such as the one above, consistently emphasized and communicated, can go a long way to ensure that the formal orientation strategy for acculturation is reinforced on the job. This is particularly so if the CEO exemplifies the desired culture. John Scully of Apple, Lee Iacoca of Chrysler, Jack Welch of GE, Rene McPherson when he was at Dana, and Tom Watson when at IBM, all are examples of CEOs who stressed and exemplified the culture they wanted employees to adopt. CEOs carry great symbolic power when they exemplify a strategy they desire the firm to carry out.

Reinforcement

In addition to the exemplary role played by the CEO in reinforcing a desired cultural strategy, the organization should also have systems that reinforce behavior that exemplifies the desired culture. For example, if participation and employee involvement are keystones in a desired organization's culture, then employees and managers who are engaged in participative behavior should be rewarded for it. These rewards could be in the form of salary increases or incentive pay, promotions, praise, and symbols (such as plaques or certificates) Negative sanctions could be experienced by those who do not participate in desired activities. These could include the absence of the above rewards as well as managerial and peer censure in the form of verbal and written comments. At the extreme, it might even involve termination.

The point is this: If the organization wants a particular culture to be acquired and maintained, it must develop and implement a strategy to this effect. Simply sending new employees to a one-day orientation program, while a start, will not guarantee that the acculturation process will occur as desired. The informal acculturation process (orientation) must reinforce the formal if the desired strategy is to be successful.

Let's now turn to developmental strategies that organizations use to enhance and improve the performance of their employees. We examine this under training and development strategies and programs.

TRAINING, DEVELOPMENT, AND PERFORMANCE IMPROVEMENT

John Young, president of Hewlett-Packard Company, stated in 1988 that "a person entering the work force today can expect to be retrained five times in his work-life."[20] In 1988, Hewlett-Packard Company spent $250 million, or 5 percent of company revenue to train its 87,000 workers. Even though this is the case, a survey by Wyatt Company reported in the *Wall Street Journal* finds that only 48 percent of some 5,000 workers interviewed think their companies have done a good job providing them with training. Older workers especially complained that they haven't been given adequate training to do their jobs well.[21]

The goal of training and development programs of all organizations should be to maintain or improve the performance of individuals and, in so doing, that of the organization. There may be situations where anything over a zero failure rate is intolerable. Consider the case of air transportation. The crash of United Flight 173 in Sioux City, Iowa, in July 1989 demonstrated how critical training can be. Many experts credit the "cockpit resource training" of the pilots from making the disaster even worse. Miraculously, 185 of 296 survived. Richard Hackman, a Harvard social psychology professor, studies cockpit crews. He remarks that the training is designed to create "a superb self-correcting team, so if an individual does make a mistake and screw up, the team is working well and corrects it. There is case after case where the aircraft technically was able to fly out of trouble, and the crew members individually were able to, and yet they got into trouble." During the training, the pilots learn from the mistakes of others and learn how to balance self-reliance with the ability to listen to others.[22] Thus training can indeed have a major impact.

While some training and development experiences carry with them reward connotations (such as one-week training program, all expenses paid, in Hawaii), the goal, nevertheless, should be performance enhancement.

Many organizations spend much time, effort, and money on the training and development of their employees, including managers. This is true of even some smaller organizations. In 1987, American corporations budgeted $32 billion for training for 38.8 million employees with sales people getting the most training of any group and clerical workers the least.[23] In some organizations, this system is very sophisticated and quite formalized like at Federal Express. It uses a database of 25 interactive videodiscs to train its 35,000 employees. Before a courier ever delivers a package he or she receives three weeks of training and a customer service agent receives five weeks of training before answering a call.[24] In others, it is very informal and unstructured. Whether or not the system is highly structured, a major responsibility of any organization is to *invest* in the education and development of its employees by formulating and implementing a human resource development strategy that includes programs, objectives, and procedures for development programs, on-and-off-the-job training, and other learning experiences.

For example, Barnett Banks of Florida has a banker development program that is about twelve months long and combines on-the-job with off-the-job learning and development experiences. Note in Exhibit 10.9 that a formal apprenticeship program follows the initial training and development program. All new employees hired into banking operations, the major hiring track for college graduates at Barnett, enter the program. Barnett estimates that it invests approximately $30,000 in each new hire in this program *excluding* salary. Of course, the company hopes that the investment will more than pay for itself in terms of performance.

Proctor & Gamble, IBM, and 3M are other companies noted for their extensive training and development programs, not only for initial hires, but also for present employees. Even smaller companies, such as Sunshine Junior Stores, a convenience store chain in the Southeastern United States, have implemented a comprehensive training and development program for assistant store managers, store managers, and district managers. The program consists of on-the-job, video tape, and classroom training. Model training stores are used along with in-house classroom trainers and outside consultants. One area that has recently been added to a number of management training programs is sexual harassment education. More than 90 percent of Fortune 500 companies will offer employees special training about sexual harassment by 1993, up from 58 percent in 1988.[25]

··

EXHIBIT 10.9   Barnett's Banker Development Program

The Barnett Banker Development Program is a standard program offered to college graduates regardless of affiliate placement. The core training program, which is approximately twelve months in length, combines the development of general management with comprehensive banking skills, and is divided into five phases

- Orientation (10 days)
- Banking Fundamentals
     (3 months)
- Consumer Banking (3 months)
- Residential Real Estate
     (1 month)
- Commerical Credit (4 months)

In each phase, you will receive on-the-job experience and classroom instruction. Approximately 30 percent of the training will be in the classroom, allowing you to spend 70 percent of the time on-the-job applying the skills you've learned in practical work experience.

After you complete the core program an internship placement will follow. The internship is designed to offer indepth and advanced exposure to a particular area of banking. The placement will be determined by the strategic needs of the affiliate and your aptitude. The internship areas are

- Commercial Credit
- Consumer Banking
- Residential Real Estate

Training does not end after your internship. Barnett offers technical and managerial training and development programs designed to enhance your opportunity for further advancement and growth.

···

Training and Development

Training refers to instruction provided for a current job. It has a rather narrow focus and should provide skills that will benefit the organization rather quickly. The financial benefits to the organization will usually occur quickly. **Development,** on the other hand, has a broader scope and may not be focused on either the present or future job but more on the organization's general long-term needs. The payoff is less direct and can only be measured in the long term.[26] Let's consider an example to illustrate the difference.

If an organization taught its managers to use Lotus 1-2-3 to manage their budgets, that would constitute training. If these same managers took courses in general systems theory and management information systems to help the company to develop into a more efficient, effective organization over the long term, the effort would more properly be labeled as a development activity. Both are obviously important and need emphasis.

The terms *training* and *development* refer to the total structure of on-the-job and off-the-job programs utilized by organizations in developing employee skills and knowledge necessary for proficient job performance and career advancement. **Management development** refers to the training and development programs for supervi-

Career Paths Help Keep Training and Development on Track

As the abundance of baby boomers continues to clog corporate ladders, organizations are making changes. Many firms have implemented dual-career tracks to allow more individuals to climb up the corporate ladder. Generally, one ladder is the management track and the other is a professional track. By installing two tracks, organizations hope to change the idea that moving into management is the only way to "make it to the top."

To develop these dual-career paths, one firm, British Petroleum Exploration (BPX), assigned teams to develop two truly comparable tracks in terms of responsibility, rewards, and influence for management and for individual contributors. Current paths were scrapped and the teams began developing things as they should be done, not as they were currently done. The result was a dual-career track that employees could jump between and progress up as their BPX's needs, abilities, and interests changed. Many other firms, such as ITT, IBM, and NCR, have similar programs.

The benefits of these types of programs are evident. However, there are potential costs as well. For example,

even though the ladders are designed to let employees move from one to the other, at some point this becomes impossible. This is especially true for managers who have been away from the technical aspects of the job so long that their skills are obsolete. Also, the organization's compensation costs can increase as employees begin to climb their chosen ladders. Further, organizational costs for implementing and monitoring the system can also be quite high.

However these new career plans are enacted, the human resources unit will have the major responsibility for them. Making sure that all of the human resource professionals understand the process can make the transition period and subsequent operations of the dual tracks much easier.

SOURCE: Adapted from Robert Goddard, "Lateral Moves Enhance Careers," *HRMagazine*, December 1990, pp. 69–74; James McElwain, "Succession Plans Designed to Manage Change," *HRMagazine*, February 1991, pp. 67–71; and Milan Moravec and Robert Tucker, "Transforming Organizations for Good," *HRMagazine*, October 1991, pp. 74–76.

sors and managers and often excludes programs for professionals (such as engineers, salespeople, and accountants), skilled operative employees (such as draftsmen, tool and die makers, and bookkeepers), and semiskilled and unskilled operatives (such as assembly line workers, packers, and material handlers, unless these individuals are being prepared for supervision or management).

Any meaningful training and development system must be closely integrated with other human resource strategies in the organization if it is to operate most effectively. Organizations that have effectively integrated training and development with other human resource strategies in performance appraisal, promotion, or pay advances recognize the importance of the training function. This integration also helps to ensure that development strategies help support other related personnel strategies.

Training and Development and Organizational Development

There is some confusion in the literature and among professional managers as to the meanings of training and development and organizational development. **Organizational development** (OD) is a term that has received wide attention over the past three decades. OD differs from training and development by focusing on the overall improvement of an organization—its structure, policies, procedures, objectives, and so on—not just its managers or other personnel. Often change in organizational culture is also a focus. OD is change oriented and almost always involves the use of a **change agent**—either an internal or outside consultant who *facilitates* the change effort aimed at improving the organization.

The socialization process is used throughout the tenure of an employee and the life of the organization. When Steve Jobs ran Apple, the development of the organization and that of employees was somewhat "loose," like a think tank. When John Sculley was brought in as a change agent, the process became "tight," like a military organization. This change came as the organization moved from an early phase of its life cycle to a more mature phase.

Probably the greatest criticism leveled at training and development, particularly management development, is the inability of participants in training programs to practice on the job what has been learned in the classroom seminar. For example, many management development programs stress participative leadership styles, humanistic management, and Theory Y assumptions (that is, employees are internally motivated, committed to the organization, will seek and accept responsibility, and will innovatively solve problems) about people, yet when training participants try to practice these beliefs back on the job, they often find that they are thwarted by an autocratic Theory X (that is, employees will avoid work and therefore must be controlled and monitored in order to reach organizational goals) organizational culture.[27]

This blockage of the "transfer of training" is a very serious impediment to making training effective. After all, if the organization itself needs to be changed, rather than the behavior of individuals in the organization, training activities in and of themselves may have little effect. The organization's objectives, policies, structure, procedures, methods, and philosophy should be examined so that the organizational context in which the training will be practiced is consistent with the concepts taught to the managers in training and development programs. This approach to training, therefore, calls for training to be part of an organization's overall development program. For example, EDS is currently revamping its entire culture so that the training and development management receives is consistent with how the organization functions.[28]

Of course, viewing training as part of OD is a much more complex and significant undertaking than simply sending a couple of managers off to a three-day management development program sponsored by the American Management Associations. Yet, it is precisely the organizational context in which the new training will be practiced that must be made congruent with the training and development concepts taught. Otherwise, managers and professionals will find that all the best-intentioned, high-quality training will be of little use back on the job. This is but another example of the need to integrate human resource strategies among the various human resource functions in order for them to have maximum effect.

Blockage of the Transfer of Training

Let's explore the blockage of training issue further, since it is such a key one in development. Trainers and training managers are often admonished to make training "relevant" in order for it to be used by trainees on the job. But what does this mean? Presumably, "relevant" means that the actual training relates directly to either the job held or to a job to which a person may be promoted. That is, the training deals with the specific skills and knowledge that must actually be practiced on the job. For example, supervisors must know how to solve problems on the job. So a training program on problem-solving methods and techniques for supervisors would presumably be relevant.

EXHIBIT 10.10 Factors That Encourage the Use of Training Back on the Job

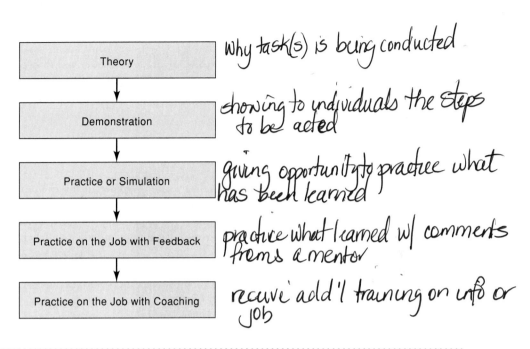

Theory — *Why task(s) is being conducted*

Demonstration — *showing to individuals the steps to be acted*

Practice or Simulation — *giving opportunity to practice what has been learned*

Practice on the Job with Feedback — *practice what learned w/ comments from a mentor*

Practice on the Job with Coaching — *receive add'l training on info or job*

Know

But making the training relevant does not always ensure the transfer of training. As we indicated earlier, culture on the job may not reinforce the training learned. The trainee may not actually understand *how* to practice the skill and knowledge back on the job even though it is relevant. For this reason, five factors that encourage the actual use of training back on the job should be observed in any program.[29] These factors work in a successive fashion; that is, the addition of each factor to the training program increases the likelihood the training will be practiced on the job. These factors are summarized in Exhibit 10.10.

Theory

People need to know the theory that underlies the training they are receiving. Discussion of the theory helps people to understand why they are being asked to perform tasks in a certain way.

For example, a training session on problem solving might include a discussion on problem-solving methods and the theory and concepts that underlie each method. If the theory is explained in such a fashion that the trainee can understand it and see its relationship to the problem-solving methods, the chances of them using the problem-solving methods on the job are enhanced. Theory explanation need not be a long and involved academic discourse. It can be kept short and to the point.

Demonstration

When a demonstration of the concepts and methods being taught occurs, the chances of the participants using the idea on the job increases. Here, the trainees are given the opportunity to actually see how the particular method or technique works. For example, if communication techniques are being taught, participants are more likely to use the techniques if they are able to observe and discuss a demonstration of the techniques during the training session. This makes the concept, theory, and technique "come alive." The participants learn through a *vicarious process.* In other words, they learn by example.

Laboratory Practice or Simulation

When participants are able to actually practice the desired technique, the transfer of learning to do the job increases. Here the participants learn by doing. They are actually given the opportunity to experience the desired method or technique in a simulated setting. This type of learning is enhanced further when feedback and critique are provided to participants by other participants and/or the instructor. They practice the expected behavior or techniques in a classroom or lab setting that they are expected to practice on the job. Of course, this is the type of training used by most computer courses.[30]

A communication training program, for example, would allow the participants to perform mock communication sessions in a role-playing situation. The class and/or instructor would provide feedback and critique the participants at the conclusion of the session.

Practice in a simulated situation allows the participants to experience the expected behavior and the feelings that accompany it. The person sees the problems involved in carrying out the expected action. When the problems are overcome and success is experienced, the trainee has an increased sense of confidence brought about by an actual, although simulated experience. Of course if failure is experienced in simulation, and the individual is not able to overcome the failure in a succeeding simulation, there is little likelihood that he or she will try the new technique back on the job.

Practice on the Job with Feedback

When the individual is given an opportunity to actually try the behavior on the job under some guidance, there is a greater likelihood that the trainee will continue to practice the behavior in his or her job environment. During and after this opportunity, the person is provided with evaluative feedback. This type of training, much like on-the-job training, is the basis for most apprenticeships.

Practice on the Job with Coaching

The best way to tie the training and job practice on the job together is to extend the period during which feedback and guidance is provided on the job while the trainee practices the desired behavior. This method differs from the one above in that job coaching continues for a considerable period of time as opposed to a one-shot trial on the job with feedback.

Of course this method requires that someone be available to coach. This could be an immediate supervisor, if he or she is trained in the desired behavior, a training consultant employed by the organization, or a **mentor** located someplace else in the organization who is responsible for guiding various subordinates. If the responsibility falls on the immediate supervisor, the role of the supervisor now changes. He or she becomes a coach or catalyst skilled in the behavior desired on the part of subordinates. The manager becomes a teacher as well as a manager.

Obviously, not all managers make good coaches or teachers, and this is a serious limitation. Training on how to coach and teach can be expensive and fruitless if various managers do not accept coaching or instruction as a legitimate part of their role. Yet, if on-the-job coaching is provided for a sustained period after the training, the training is very likely to be used on the job by the trainees.

All managers in an organization from top to supervisory should be training and development oriented. Training and development is essentially a line function. The training staff, should you have one, should assist and advise, but the major responsibility rests with line managers.

If a company wants to see young managers grow, it perhaps should not rely solely on mentoring and training courses, but it should also include a little danger. In a survey of 600 professional or managerial men and women at big companies, 60 percent defined developmental experiences as being at risk in a novel or unsupervised environment, while only 12 percent cited a relationship with a supervisor or mentor, and just 7 percent named training courses. Examples of risky involvement include asking someone to turn around a business who has never had such experience or sending a computer novice to computerize a unit.[31]

Training Responsibilities

Following the theme that training is a line function with staff assistance, we can review the major responsibilities for training and development shared by top management, personnel, the immediate supervisor, and the employee, as shown in Exhibit 10.11.

Top Management Responsibilities

The commitment of the chief executive officer and top management is critical for effective training to take place throughout the organization. Managers tend to manage as they are managed. Any developmental program that doesn't have the attention, understanding, and commitment from top management will be severely limited in terms of the basic changes it can bring about.

Top management has the responsibility to provide the general policies and procedures required to implement the training program. They need to provide administrative control to ensure that managers and employees comply with the program and give it a conscientious commitment.

Setting the proper culture for encouraging training and development rests with top management. If top management does not do this, establishing the proper climate in the organization will be very difficult.

[handwritten margin note: Establishes Culture]

EXHIBIT 10.11 Training and Development Is a Shared Responsibility

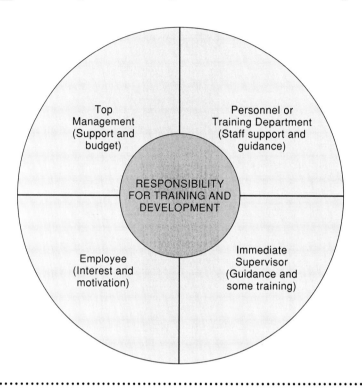

The Human Resource Department

The human resource department in the organization performs essentially a staff support function. It *assists* line management in training and development by providing expertise, resources, and sponsoring training conferences and programs.

The Immediate Supervisor

Each employee's immediate supervisor on up the organizational hierarchy has the direct responsibility for ensuring that training and development occurs. A proper example should be set. The supervisor should encourage employees to develop themselves and should provide time for this to occur.

The Employee

Even though human resource professionals and line management must facilitate and manage the training and development process, the primary responsibility for training and development lies with the individual employee. However, even though this is so, the immediate supervisor should not use this as an excuse for not doing anything

....

EXHIBIT 10.12   Steps in the Training Needs Analysis and Design

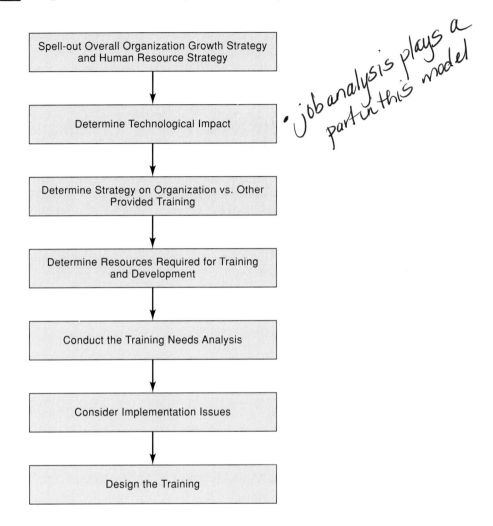

job analysis plays a part in this model

```
┌─────────────────────────────────────────┐
│ Spell-out Overall Organization Growth    │
│ Strategy and Human Resource Strategy     │
└─────────────────────────────────────────┘
                    ↓
┌─────────────────────────────────────────┐
│       Determine Technological Impact     │
└─────────────────────────────────────────┘
                    ↓
┌─────────────────────────────────────────┐
│ Determine Strategy on Organization vs.   │
│        Other Provided Training           │
└─────────────────────────────────────────┘
                    ↓
┌─────────────────────────────────────────┐
│ Determine Resources Required for         │
│        Training and Development          │
└─────────────────────────────────────────┘
                    ↓
┌─────────────────────────────────────────┐
│     Conduct the Training Needs Analysis  │
└─────────────────────────────────────────┘
                    ↓
┌─────────────────────────────────────────┐
│     Consider Implementation Issues       │
└─────────────────────────────────────────┘
                    ↓
┌─────────────────────────────────────────┐
│          Design the Training             │
└─────────────────────────────────────────┘
```

....

Has the most responsibility for training

to facilitate employee development. The immediate supervisor, indeed the whole organization, must provide the atmosphere, resources, and encouragement for self-development. Nevertheless, the employee has the responsibility for demonstrating interest in personal career development relative to the goals of the organization. Finally, each employee should encourage other employees to take advantage of development opportunities.

So we see that the responsibilities for training and development are shared among human resources, top management, the immediate supervisor, and the employee. Let's now look at how companies decide what training and development programs should be offered. The seven steps that make up the **training needs analysis** are shown in Exhibit 10.12.

Training Needs Analysis and Design

Every organization must ensure that its training and development program meets its human resource needs in terms of the skills and competencies required. It must also decide what training and development it will do itself and what it expects other organizations, such as schools, to do. Finally, it must decide what skills and competencies it wishes to instill though training once people are hired.

In order to make these evaluations, an organization should systematically determine its needs for training and development. This systematic assessment is more than a yearly or biyearly survey that asks employees what training needs they believe they have. For example, from a strategic standpoint, the assessment should be tied to the growth plan of the organization as well as the individual career plans of employees. For example, when United began flying international flights it soon realized that its employees needed a good dose of international awareness if it was going to become a global airline. Through a program entitled "Best Airline—The Global Challenge," United will eventually train 28,000 of its workers. While ground personnel learn about visas, vaccinations, and cultural differences, the flight crew are pushed to sharpen their service skills. The entire training program focuses on the "Triple A" motto: Adjust our thinking to accommodate differences and accept customers on their terms.[32] In the following sections, we discuss some of the steps involved in doing a systematic assessment of training needs in the organization.

Link the Organizational Growth and Human Resource Strategy

The first step is to tie the training and development plan to the overall organization and human resource strategy and plan. The human resource strategy should be geared to the firm's strategy on growth and expansion, as we pointed out in earlier chapters. In this way, skill needs are determined based upon occupational skill areas that are likely to grow as the firm meets its growth objectives. In assessing organizational growth, changes in product or service offerings and markets should be examined so that a determination can be made not only on the *rate* of growth, but also the *type* of growth experienced.

Determine the Technological Impact

Skill needs change as technology changes and this will affect the needed skill mix as the firm meets its growth objectives. Organizations need to avoid "training for obsolescence" by giving people skills that quickly become useless to the organization. Examinations of production process and machinery, research and development, office equipment changes, and so on would all be appropriate in designing training programs.

Determine the Strategy on Providing Training versus Other-Provided Training

How much training and development will the organization provide, and how much will be provided by other organizations? How much training and development does the organization expect employees to have prior to hiring, and how much will the organization provide while employed? Frequently, the organization expects an employee to have minimum competency in a skill area when hired and trains only to update and/or for promotion purposes. Also, the organization may expect general training and education, such as that of a college graduate, and it then provides specific orientation and training as to how "we do it." These issues should be examined when designing a training program.

While organizations may expect a minimum competence level from even the lowest level employee, these expectations may no longer be fulfilled. Recent surveys have found that as many as 92 percent of American firms report having employees who lack basic skills. Basic skills can be defined as the ability to use printed and written information to function effectively on the job, including the ability to read, write, and comprehend the English language and perform required computational skills.[33] While organizations admit that there is a problem, few plan to sharpen their employees skills through remedial training. Instead, they have decided to pursue other strategies to remain competitive such as cutting wages, exporting jobs to lower paying regions, and automating as many jobs as possible.[34]

There are some exceptions. For example, Weber Metals in Paramount, California, has a predominantly Hispanic work force. Many of its workers have a limited education and speak little English. Management, realizing that these limitations would hamper its attempts to implement a total quality management program, took steps to change it. The company began by offering on-site English, history, and government classes two to three times a week. Weber paid for books, materials, and other related expenses. Students who graduated received certificates of completion and some even received additional recognition from the Immigration and Naturalization Service. To expand the courses offered, a computerized classroom was installed. Courses in 24 different areas are offered on the computers and students can work at their own pace. An added advantage of the new computerized courses is that as the students learn a subject, they also learn how to use a computer.[35]

Olsten Corporation, a temporary services firm, also is waging war on illiteracy in the workplace. Olsten was one of six corporate sponsors of the 1988 National Literacy Honors Event. It also sponsored city- and state-wide spelling bees and hired a spokesperson to conduct seminars as part of its workplace literacy outreach.[36] Because basic literacy skills control the slope of the learning curve for all employees, literacy among employees has profound implications for product quality, customer service, efficiency, and workplace safety.[37]

In order to compete in a global economy, more organizations will need to follow the lead of firms like Weber and Olsten. This becomes even more clear when statistics are cited about the views on education in foreign countries. For example, the high-school graduation rate for Japanese workers is over 90 percent. The Singapore government requires employers to pay 1 percent of the payroll of unskilled, low-paid workers into a skills development fund, unless they pay high wages or offer a high-quality training program of their own. Finally, Korea has won the world vocational-training championship seven times. The best the United States ever placed is thirteenth.[38]

Determine the Resources Available for Training and Development

Training and development cost money and time. Facilities, materials, instructors, and other resources can be quite expensive. How much of this expense does the organization wish to absorb? Is the training and development expense a worthwhile

FOCUS ON INTERNATIONAL ISSUES •

The Costs Can Be High without the Cross-Cultural Training of Expatriates

While most employees who have been assigned to a foreign post receive training in the functional skills they will need in their new assignments, cross-cultural training may be overlooked. However, failure by an expatriate is rarely caused by a lack of functional skills; instead, they fail due to their inability to adapt to an unfamiliar culture.

Expatriate failures can be costly. It is estimated that each failure costs the company anywhere from $250,000 to $1 million. And the failures are frequent. The failure rate for expatriates in London is 18 percent, Brussels 27 percent, Tokyo 36 percent, and Saudi Arabia 68 percent. These rates can be lowered by training newly assigned expatriates in several commonly difficult areas for overseas assignments such as the two listed below.

Negotiation Styles

Negotiation styles differ from country to country. For example, Russian negotiators are conflict oriented and attempt to put their counterpart on the defensive. Italians frequently argue trivial points to excess. Asian negotiators use a consensus-oriented style that attempts to include all participants equally. Americans try to win as much as they can for their side even if it means the other side must give up something for this to happen.

On-the-Job-Communication

The American communication style used at work is not shared by other cultures. For example, in France it can take business associates over six months to feel comfortable enough to address their business associates by their first names. Also, keep-

ing more than a one-foot distance between yourself and an Arab colleague with whom you are talking is seen as impolite. But stand that close to your Spanish business associates and they would be insulted.

American customs can insult and offend non-American business associates in a host of other ways. For example, asking a French person "Where do you live" or "What do you do" would be equivalent to someone asking you "How much do you make?" Using the phrase "Let's do lunch" with a German business counterpart will motivate them to pull out their calendar and begin searching for a mutually agreeable time. Exposing the underside of your foot in the Middle East or the palm of your hand in Africa is a rude and demeaning gesture. Finally, it is nice to bring a small, wrapped gift to the home of a Japanese business associate when invited over. However, do not wrap it in white paper. This is a sign of death.

Minor slips, such as the ones listed above, will be made by many expatriates in foreign countries for the first time. That is why expatriate training in the culture of the host country is just as important, if not more so, than functional training. Various consulting firms can be used to provide specialized training. One such firm was founded by the wife of an expatriate upon their abrupt return from an assignment in Bogota that failed. Obviously, it is important for expatriates to listen to the voice of experience before they leave. Quick cultural lessons can save the high costs of yet another expatriate failure.

SOURCE: Adapted from Shari Caudron, "Training Ensures Success Overseas," *Personnel Journal,* December 1991, pp. 27–30.

investment compared to other organizational investments? All of these questions need to be addressed. It is senseless to conduct a large scale training needs analysis survey only for the organization to decide later that it really does not have much money for training and development after all. Thus, in this phase of the analysis, the organization needs to forecast an expected rate of return, so to speak, on its training and development expenses.

Such a forecasted return is not easy to accomplish. Perhaps historical training expenses and benefits can be examined and some sort of trend forecast made. Also, a comparison of competitor training expenses and benefits might be estimated, although this information might be difficult to obtain. Certainly a comparison of the costs of in-house versus contracted training and development related to anticipated benefits would be helpful. Sometimes it is possible to identify specific costs that can be saved by improving performance, such as reduced waste or scrap. Also, training can improve productivity. This is the aim of most time management programs. The point is, a firm must decide how much it can spend on training and development relative to what it hopes to accomplish.

Conduct the Training Need Analysis

At this point, the organization is in a position to analyze its training and development needs. The actual analysis can be performed using a number of techniques as follows:

1. Mailed questionnaire to employees or a sample.
2. Interviews with employees or a sample.
3. Projections by managers.
4. Review of career plans, performance appraisals, and operations reports.

[handwritten margin note: Feedback can determine needs w/i structure]

Implementation Issues

Once the gathering and analysis of the needs analysis data is completed, it must be related to strategic growth objectives, the training budget, changes in technology, and internally or externally provided training. Also, it is helpful at this point, to determine how the training needs interface with other components of the human resource system, such as hiring, human resource planning, and rewarding. It might be that some training needs can be met through changing the hiring process. For example, Centel Corporation, a large utility, has reduced its training in basic electricity principles by hiring people who have taken these courses in vocational or technical schools.

Once these determinations have been made, then the organization is in a position to determine how many of the training needs it intends to meet and how. In other words, it can begin to formulate its training plan, which specifies courses and other learning experiences, other resources, participants, and a budget. A systematic training needs analysis will help keep the training plan relevant, realistic, and useful to the organization and the individual employee.

TRAINING AND DEVELOPMENT METHODS

We have identified a set of responsibilities for top management, the immediate supervisor, personnel, and the employees in training and career development. We have also examined procedures for a training needs analysis. Now we look at how training is actually carried out in the organization. What specific types of training and development methods exist to help individuals carry out responsibilities in meeting training needs? Training methods fall into two broad categories: on-the-job training (OJT) and off-the-job training. Any comprehensive training system in an organization will utilize both types of training.

On-the-Job Training (OJT)

While people associate OJT with providing a person with the skills to do a minimum level on the job, it can and should be much more than that. Figure 13.10 shows the

EXHIBIT 10.13 On-the-Job Training Techniques

1. *Expanded responsibilities.* This is a frequently used training technique that expands the job duties, assignments, and responsibilities of an individual both horizontally and vertically in the organization. Opportunities are created for the individual in his or her present job to practice higher level and diverse skills not normally required in the present job.

2. *Job rotation.* Also called *cross training,* this involves moving individuals to various types of jobs within the organization at the same level or next immediate higher level for periods of time. This may be as short as an hour or two or as long as a year. Many organizations use this approach during the first two or three years of a person's career to familiarize him or her with broad functional operations and processes of the organization.

3. *Staff development meetings.* These are special staff meetings to discuss facets of each individual's job and to develop ideas for improving job performance. These meetings may be held away from the job in a "retreat-type" atmosphere.

4. *"Assistant to" positions.* This involves having promising employees serve as staff assistants to higher skill level jobs for a specified period of time (often one to three months) to become more familiar with the higher skilled positions in the organization.

5. *Problem-solving conferences.* These are conferences called to solve a specific problem being experienced by a group or the organization as a whole. It involves brainstorming and other creative means to come up with mutually determined solutions to basic problems.

6. *Mentoring.* This technique assigns a guide or knowledgeable person higher up in the organization to help a new employee "learn the ropes" of the organization and to provide other advice. Usually a social relationship is developed so that the employee feels she or he can go to the mentor for advice that cannot be asked of the immediate superior.

7. *Special assignments.* These are special tasks or responsibilities given to an individual for a specified period of time. The assignment may be writing up a report, investigating the feasibility for a new project, process, service, or product, preparing a newsletter, or evaluating a company policy or procedure.

8. *In-company training done by company trainers.* These programs can cover such topics as safety, new personnel procedures, new product or services, affirmative action, and technical programs.

9. *In-company training done by outside consultants.* Here recognized experts are brought to the company to conduct training on such topics as goal setting, communications, assessment techniques, safety, and other current topics of importance. They often supplement training done by company trainers.

10. *Consultant (internal or external) advisory reviews.* Experts in specialized fields meet with various managers and employee groups to investigate and help solve particular problems. The emphasis is on problem solving rather than training.

11. *Distribution of reading matter.* Often one of the most overlooked training methods, this formal program is created to circulate books, journals, selected articles, new business material, and so on to selected employees. An effective program also includes periodic scheduled meetings to discuss the material.

12. *Apprenticeship.* This refers to training provided through working under a journeyman or master in a craft. The apprentice works alongside a person skilled in the craft and is taught by that person. While this often occurs on the job, it sometimes is done in off-the-job settings. Apprenticeship programs also often include some classroom work. Craft unions frequently take advantage of apprenticeship training and, in some cases, may be responsible for the entire program. Apprenticeship programs are best known in the skilled crafts, such as masonry, electrician, bricklaying, and carpentry.

| EXHIBIT 10.14 | Off-the-Job Training and Education Opportunities

1. *Outside short courses and seminars.* These are specialized courses conducted by educational institutions, professional associations, or private consulting and training firms that last one day to one week. If managers selectively attend programs that complement their career development plan, these courses can be extremely beneficial.

2. *College or university degree and certificate programs.* More and more universities are offering evening and weekend classes that lead to a degree or certificate. Often these are in professional fields such as management, accounting, finance, or law. Many employers have a tuition refund program which will reimburse employees for all or part of the tuition and book expense.

3. *Advanced management programs at colleges and universities.* UCLA, Harvard, MIT, Ohio State, and other well-known universities offer in-residence programs of two weeks to a full year for top management. Often they cover material typically found in an MBA program, but at a very accelerated rate.

4. *Correspondence schools.* If individuals can practice rigorous self-discipline, home correspondence study can be an excellent self-development tool. However, an employee needs to ensure that the correspondence school with which he or she deals is reputable.

5. *Outside meetings and conferences.* Most managers and professionals have opportunities to attend trade and professional conferences and conventions during the year. If participants actually attend the scheduled meetings and workshops at these conferences, these can be excellent learning experiences.

types of training a comprehensive OJT program could include. The list includes a wide range of training techniques.

Off-the-Job Training

An effective training system supplements OJT with various forms of the off-the-job training. Most of this type of training is classroom training. Some of the more frequently used types of training are shown in Exhibit 10.14.

Instructional Techniques for Training and Development

The past few years have seen a virtual explosion in training techniques. These new techniques plus the tried-and-true methods give an organization a wide variety of training techniques from which to choose in building an effective program. Exhibit 10.15 summarizes these techniques.

Instructional Resources

Training and development are performed with a wide variety of resources. The most important training resource is the immediate superior of an individual in an organization. His or her on-the-job advice, counsel, and coaching are the keys to an effective program.

Many organizations also have a department of training and development within the organization. This department normally employs several internal trainers and consultants who can be used in a wide variety of programs.

EXHIBIT 10.15 Training Techniques

LECTURE-DISCUSSION

Almost all training programs, particularly outside programs, utilize this technique. Most college classes utilize this technique extensively. It has the advantage of being spontaneous and allows the participants to become involved in exploring concepts and in seeking clarification. It requires a professional training leader with broad expertise in the field and related fields under discussion. The major disadvantage is that this technique is difficult to use with large groups.

LECTURE

This method is very useful for large groups. It requires a training leader who is dynamic and who can organize and present material in an effective fashion. For best use it should be supplemented with additional types of training techniques. Eighty-two percent of firms use the lecture method.

MULTIMEDIA PRESENTATIONS

Lecture and lecture-discussion work best when a multimedia approach is used. This involves using handouts of materials (such as subject outlines, advanced reading assignments, and cases), films, slides, film strips, videotapes, audio cassettes, overhead projectors, flip charts, and the old stand-by, the chalkboard. The major disadvantage here is that sophisticated equipment can fail at the most inopportune time. Also, the multimedia approach is but one tool for management development. It can't substitute for an effective instructor. Eighty-three percent of companies report using videotapes in training.

JOB COACHING

The best on-the-job technique is coaching. This involves either the individual's immediate supervisor or a mentor (a person located elsewhere in the organization who can help the employee). The mentor acts as a guide, counselor, friend, and interested party in helping his or her subordinates perform their jobs more effectively and in developing a comprehensive career plan for each subordinate.

Private consulting and training organizations such as the American Management Associations (AMA) and the American Management Research (AMR) organization offer a wide variety of management and professional programs on an annual basis. These organizations use private consultants, personnel directors, and university professors to conduct much of their training. Most universities with programs in business conduct a wide variety of programs in management and related areas. Some outstanding universities with comprehensive programs include Michigan, Michigan State, Ohio State, Harvard, Stanford, MIT, and Northwestern. However, a university in a particular organization's immediate geographic area can usually conduct many programs at a cost substantially below that of the large major universities mentioned above. Many universities, such as Florida State University, offer training and development programs through their Small Business Development Center and the Center for Professional Development.

The federal government, through several agencies, conducts various programs and provides other training resources for organizations. For example, the U.S. Office

EXHIBIT 10.15 continued

SELF-PACED (PROGRAMMED)

Self-paced learning techniques use programmed texts and exercises to guide students through a step-by-step series of learning experiences. It is a learner-centered method of instruction and seldom, if ever, requires the services of an instructor at the time the training occurs. The technique presents subject matter to the trainees in small steps, which require them to respond and immediately inform them of appropriateness of their responses.

COMPUTER-ASSISTED INSTRUCTION

Actually this is a form of multimedia, self-paced instruction learning. Some computer-assisted techniques can be quite sophisticated and expensive. When used as a part of a total educational program, it can be quite effective.

GAMING AND ROLE-PLAYING (SIMULATION)

This technique gives participants actual practice in applying concepts in an artificial situation. An opportunity to solve a problem is provided, and the participants actually act out the solution. Gaming usually involves some element of competitiveness in which one group tries to outperform other groups. In the hands of a skillful seminar leader, this technique can be an extremely useful training tool since it gives participants actual practice before peers, yet allows them to make mistakes without having the repercussions such mistakes would have on the job.

CASE ANALYSIS

Usually combined with role-playing and/or gaming, this technique also gives participants the opportunity to solve an actual or hypothetical problem. If used without gaming or role-playing, it relies very heavily on group discussion without the participants putting themselves in the actual roles of individuals in the case. Cases are used extensively in this book.

of Personnel Management conducts programs in human resources, compensation, management by objectives, and other topic areas. The Small Business Administration provides training and advice to smaller business organizations. Various units in the U.S. Department of Labor conduct programs on safety and health, wage and hour legislation, affirmative action, labor law, and collective bargaining.

The Employment and Training Administration of the federal government provides much training assistance and funding for many entry level and low-to-medium skilled jobs through the Joint Training Partnership Act (JTPA). Often this training can be received at little or no cost to the employer.

EVALUATION OF TRAINING AND DEVELOPMENT

Assessing the effectiveness of an organization's overall training and development effort is extremely difficult. Yet, it is extremely important. Valid results of training are essential for building a credible program. The ultimate measure of training effectiveness is the health of the organization. Is the organization meeting its mission and goals? Are its employees competent? Is the work done efficiently and effectively? These are broad questions and good training is but one factor that contributes to a positive response for each question.

Assessing the effectiveness of skills training is usually easier than evaluating management and professional development training. One can observe whether a trainee can perform the necessary skills on the job. It is difficult to assess whether managers are more effective as a result of a specific training episode. This is particularly so of general management training as opposed to training in a specific area of management, such as handling grievances or meeting EEO guidelines. The more specific the management training, the easier it is to assess whether the manager who has experienced the training performs better than those who have not.

For example, one would assume that a supervisor trained in EEO law and techniques would take illegal action far fewer times than a person not properly trained in the techniques. Simply following up the EEO record of supervisors trained in the technique compared to those not trained would give us some idea of the effectiveness of EEO training.

The major difficulty with assessing the effectiveness of supervisory education and training is that the practice of supervision involves such a wide and varied set of tasks that it is difficult to measure the specific effect of any one input on the performance of these tasks. Is a good manager good because of his college experience, the job experience, rearing, specific supervisory training courses, or because he or she has good subordinates, an effective boss, and a booming economy? How do we establish specific cause-and-effect relationships? This makes evaluation of management training and education difficult. What is often done is an "affect" type of evaluation which asks program participants (trainees) to simply rate various aspects of the program, including the content, materials, and instructors, on some type of scale such as "useful to not useful." Space is also usually provided for open-ended responses.

While responses to these questions provide useful information to the planners and instructors in a program, they usually are biased by the high "affect-level" that participants usually experience at the end of the program. The evaluation usually measures feelings and opinions of the program at the very end of the program before participants have had a chance to reflect on and practice the concepts learned.

Longitudinal Cost-Benefit Analysis with Control Groups

A methodologically superior assessment technique of training effectiveness would attempt to determine all of the measurable benefits from a training program over given time periods measured at periodic intervals (such as three months, six months, and one year). These benefits would be compared to the costs of the program. Ideally, this information would then be compared with a similar group of employees who did not go through the training program. Any differences in the benefits (as measured by improving job performance) of the group who experienced the training program could be at least partially attributable to the training effort.

The following procedure can be used to make this type of evaluation:

1. Randomly assign employees of a similar occupation or level in the organization to two groups. One group of employees will receive the training, the other will not.

EXHIBIT 10.16 A Model of the Longitudinal Cost-Benefit Analysis for Training Effectiveness Using a Control Group

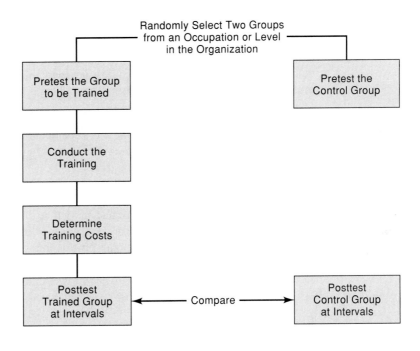

2. Conduct a pretest measure of performance and/or knowledge of both groups to determine their present level of performance and/or knowledge.
3. Conduct the training for one group.
4. Accurately assess all costs of the training effort, including instructor, media costs, facilities, and employee time away from the job.
5. Conduct a posttest measure of performance and/or knowledge of both groups at periodic intervals after the completion of training.
6. Compare the benefits of the program as measured by higher performance and more complete job knowledge with the costs of the program for the trained group.
7. Compare the posttest performance and job knowledge of the trained group with the nontrained or control group.

This procedure can be diagrammed as shown in Exhibit 10.16.

Applying the Training Effectiveness Model: An Example

Even though the cost-benefit training effectiveness model is seldom used because it is time consuming and requires denying some people training, it can be an effective way to systematically determine the results of training. This is especially so if accurate performance measures exist for the job on which dollar estimates can be made. Let's look at an example to see how this evaluation model works.

Assume you are the training director for a business organization that has a number of field salespeople. You have noticed, after receiving a selected number of periodic performance appraisals of these salespeople, that many seem to be having a problem selling a new product that your company has recently developed.

You decide that this problem is significant and that product notices and staff meetings have not helped significantly in reducing the problem. A comprehensive training program is called for. You realize that even though not all salespeople are in need of the program, many are. Using the following procedure, you set up, conduct, and evaluate the program:

1. Determine the specific training and development needs of the group by examining performance appraisals, assessment center results, conferences with supervisors, and other methods.
2. Design specific performance objectives that the training is to accomplish.
3. Identify the salespeople who need the training.
4. Assign one-half of those identified to a group that will receive the training and the other half to a control group that will not receive the training.
5. Conduct a pretest for both groups on the performance objectives the training is to cover.
6. Design the training program including topics, instructors, media, cases, exercises, handouts, and so on.
7. Conduct the training program for the group to be trained.
8. Assess the total cost of the training program including all instructional and travel costs, loss of time away from job, and so on.
9. Conduct a posttest at periodic intervals for both sales groups on specific performance measures that the training covered.
10. Compare the performance measures of the salespeople who went through the program with those who did not.
11. Compare the benefits, as measured as improvement in performance measures for the trained group, with the costs of the program.

Admittedly, most training directors do not go through such an elaborate procedure. It is costly and often it is difficult to withhold training from those who may need it. But this procedure will give an organization a much more documented basis on which to assess training effectiveness and plan future programs. Additionally, this information is very useful for presenting a case to top management on the value of training and development for the organization. Then, when the organization goes through a period of economic downturn, a strong case can be made not to drastically cut or eliminate the training budget, as so often happens.

● ● ● ● ● ● ● ● ●

MANAGEMENT GUIDELINES

Our focus in this chapter has been on viewing orientation and training as two related key issues for improving performance and productivity in the organization. While there are other ways to improve productivity, such as the adoption of new technology and methods, orientation and training is very much linked to these efforts. In other words, orientation and training of employees has a very strong role to play in using and adapting to a new technology and instituting new methods. Here are some management guidelines that can be delineated based on the information presented in this chapter.

1. An effective training program needs to be integrated with a comprehensive development program to reinforce the concepts and practices stressed in training on the job.

2. Effective training also requires a commitment to self-development from all employees, top management support, a comprehensive on-the-job training program supplemented with off-the-job training, and support from first-line supervisors.

3. The responsibilities for effective training and development are shared by the organization's top management, the human resource department, the immediate supervisor, and the employee. The greatest responsibility lies with the employee. The immediate supervisor has the next greatest responsibility in the role as coach and advisor. The human resource department assists line management in training by acting as supportive staff to line management. Top management must give wholehearted support to the process.

4. Methods for training and development involve various on-the-job techniques, and as expanded responsibilities, job rotation, "assistant to" positions and other techniques. Programs include outside short courses and seminars, college degree programs, and correspondence courses. An effective training and development program achieves a unique blend of on-the-job and off-the-job methods suitable for the individuals in the particular organization.

5. Instructional techniques have mushroomed over the past few years and include lecture, lecture-discussion, multimedia, job coaching, programmed instruction, case analysis, role playing, and gaming. Newer techniques involve computer-assisted instruction. A good program utilizes all techniques as appropriate rather than relying on any one technique at the exclusion of others.

6. It is important that an organization choose resources that best meet its needs for training and development.

7. The real success of a training and development program can be assessed ultimately on the basis of the success and health of the organization. However, assessments should be made of specific programs through some longitudinal analysis. The ideal assessment framework would involve a cost-benefit analysis of a training program compared to a control group not receiving the training.

QUESTIONS FOR REVIEW

1. How can an organization's culture impact the training efforts of an organization?

2. What is socialization? Why is it important to an organization?

3. Compare and contrast training and development.

4. List and describe four different on-the-job training methods.

5. If you were asked to design a socialization program for all employees who entered your organization, what would the program look like?

6. How often should an orientation program be updated? Why?

7. What can an organization do to determine which employees need training and what type of training they need?

8. When is it to an organization's advantage to hire employees who need training and when is it advantageous to hire employees who are already trained?

9. What factors will influence whether or not an employee who is a marginal performer gets trained or gets fired?

10. How can an organization ensure that their employees conform? Why is this beneficial? When is it a problem?

11. Describe the steps in the training need analysis process.

12. How can the organization determine if their training program is effective?

13. Compare and contrast two of the off-the-job training opportunities described in this chapter.

CASE: Development—The Ford Experience[39]

"There's nothing glamorous about trying to change an organization—it takes a strong resolution to change, and persistence," Nancy Badore, program director of the Executive Development Center of Ford Motor Company in Dearborn, Michigan, said. "You just have to walk down the road, and stick with it. We've been consciously trying to change, and to apply the lessons we've learned about change management. We've been sticking with it for about eight years now—and it's every bit as difficult every step of the way.

"We outdistanced the literature early on. We've been fortunate that we've been able to look at many different models and learn from them—and then had to rely on our own experience.

"At Ford, we've gone through three progressive stages of change during the past eight years. Toward the end of each stage, pressure within the organization mounted to create the setting for the next stage of change—and it would have been impossible to grow past each stage if the organization hadn't positively responded to this internal pressure."

Stage I: Quality Improvement/Plant Level

"During the first stage, we focused on how to create and improve quality, and we concentrated at the plant level. We worked with plant managers and union leadership, and shared information with employees about business objectives. We were learning to focus our organization on an issue—and quality was the issue.

"After two to three years, it was clear that more people needed to be included in the quality effort—above the plant level—or the progress that had been made at the plant level would be stymied, and people would become frustrated. These pressures created the second stage."

Stage II: Intermediate Level

"At the intermediate or division level, changes increased in speed. There was more education involved—much of the learning we did was derived from Japanese management techniques and 'excellent' companies. Study groups and task forces were the primary vehicles we used to introduce change at this level.

"Again it became clear that, for change to continue spreading throughout the organization, the next-highest level of management would need to be involved."

Stage III: Senior-Most Management Level

"By the time our senior-most management level became involved, we had come to realize an important lesson: that *everyone* must take responsibility for change—that a piece of a problem is in everybody, and everybody has to act and not wait for others to become perfect. At the same time, in taking responsibility for change, each individual must recognize limitations, and the need for help from higher levels of management or other parts of the company."

Executive Development

"At the senior level, one task force recognized the combination of high people skills and high quality could put us at a tremendous competitive advantage. Management began placing great emphasis on encouraging continual challenges and acquiring new skills and perspectives. With this in mind, we set out to create an executive development center. Our senior executive program has been introduced to the top 2,000 managers. The program is being institutionalized, with plans for everyone to come back for another session every couple of years, with revised content.

"Now, we are introducing a second generation of programs, centering on special topics—issues we can beat competition on." These issues include the following.

- "We are organized functionally, but we must behave globally.
- We don't have any generalists, like Proctor & Gamble. We must define what a generalist manager is here, and prepare people for a transition into that role.
- We don't have a product until a car has been assembled—and when producing a very complex product in volume, accountability is difficult to achieve."

QUESTIONS

1. What role does change play in Ford's concept of development? Do you agree with this role? Why or why not?

2. Ford instituted an integrated development program at four levels: plant, intermediate, senior, and executive. How does development at each level relate to each other level? Why is this important in a development program?

3. Critique the three challenges faced by Ford that are listed at the end of the case. Do you see other challenges for Ford besides those listed? If so, what are they?

· · · · · · · · · · · · · · · · ·
ADDITIONAL READINGS

Bard, Roy, Chez R. Bell, Leslie Stephen, and Linda Webster. *The Trainer's Professional Development Handbook*. San Francisco: Jossey-Bass, 1987.

Bernold, Thomas, and James Finkelstein, eds. *Computer Assisted Approaches to Training Foundations of Industry's Future*. New York: North-Holland, 1988.

Bresnick, David. *Managing Employment and Training Programs Making JTPA Work*. New York: Human Services Press, 1986.

Brinkeroff, Robert O. *Achieving Results from Training: How to Evaluate Human Resource Development to Strengthen Programs and Increase Impact*. San Francisco: Jossey-Bass, 1987.

Brown, Duane, Linda Brooke, and Associates. *Career Choice and Development*. San Francisco: Jossey-Bass, 1984.

Calvert, Robert, Jr. "Training America: The Numbers Add Up." *Training and Development Journal*. November 1985, pp. 35–37.

Carnivale, Anthony R. "The Learning Enterprise." *Training and Development Journal*. January 1986, pp. 18–26.

Carnivale, Anthony, Leila Gainer, and Ann Meltzer. *Workplace Basics*. San Francisco: Jossey-Bass, 1990.

Carnivale, Anthony, Leila Gainer, and Ann Meltzer. *Workplace Basics Training Manual*. San Francisco: Jossey-Bass, 1990.

Carnivale, Anthony, Leila Gainer, and Ann Schultz. *Training the Technical Work Force*. San Francisco: Jossey-Bass, 1990.

Carnivale, Anthony, Leila Gainer, and Janice Villet. *Training in America: The Organization and the Strategic Role of Training*. San Francisco: Jossey-Bass, 1990.

Casner-Lotto, Jill, and Associates. *Successful Training Strategies: Twenty-six Innovative Corporate Models*. San Francisco: Jossey-Bass, 1988.

Chalofsky, Neal E. and Carlene Reinhart, *Effective Human Resource Development*. San Francisco: Jossey-Bass, 1988.

Cook, D. R. "Improving Employee Development Programs." *Personnel Administrator* 23. July 1978, pp. 38–40.

Cothran, Tom. "Build or Buy?" *Training*. May 1987, pp. 83–85.

Dayel, Mohammed. "Taking the Mystery Out of Career Development." *Personnel* 55. March–April 1978, pp. 46–53.

Fisher, D. W. "Educational Psychology Involved in On-the-job Training." *Personnel Journal* 56. October 1977, pp. 16–19.

Fraser, R. F., et al. "System for Determining Training Needs." *Personnel Journal* 57. December 1978, pp. 682–85.

Frost, Peter, Larry Moore, Meryl Louis, Craig Lundberg, and Joanne Martin. *Organizational Culture*. Beverly Hills: Sage, 1985.

Fucini, Joseph, and Suzy Fucini. *Working for the Japanese: Inside Mazda's American Auto Plant*. New York: Free Press, 1990.

Hall, F., and M. Albrecht. "Training for EEO, What Kinds and for Whom?" *Personnel Administrator* 22. October 1977, pp. 25–28.

Harris, P. R., "Cultural Awareness Training for Human Resource Development." *Training and Development Journal* 33. March 1978, pp. 64–74.

Hastings, Robert E. "Career Development: Maximizing Options." *Personnel Administrator* 23. May 1978, pp. 58–61.

Hyman, Jeff. *Training at Work*. New York: Routledge, 1992.

Kilman, Ralph A., Mary J. Saxton, Roy Serpa, and Associates. *Gaining Control of the Corporate Culture*. San Francisco: Jossey-Bass, 1985.

Langford, H. "Need Analysis in the Training Department." *Supervisory Management* 23. August 1978, pp. 18–25.

Leach, John. "Career Management Focusing on Human Resources." *Personnel Administrator* 22. November 1977, pp. 59–66.

Lee, Chris. "Where the Training Dollars Go." *Training*. October 1987, pp. 51–65.

Miner, John B. "The OD-Management Development Conflict." *Business Horizons* 16, no. 6. December 1973, p. 35.

Mirabel, T. E. "Forecasting Future Training Costs." *Training and Development Journal* 32. July 1978, pp. 78–87.

Moore, M. L. and T. Dutton. "Training Needs Analysis: Review and Critique." *Academy of Management Review* 3. July 1978, pp. 532–545.

Morgan, Marilyn, T. Douglas, and Alison Martier. "Career Development Strategies in Industry—Where are We and Where Should We Be?" *Personnel* 56. March–April 1979, pp. 13–30.

Mumford, Alan. *Gower Handbook of Management Development*. Brookfield, VT: Gower Publishing, 1991.

Murray, Margo, and Marna Owen. *Beyond the Myths and Magic of Mentoring: How to Facilitate an Effective Mentoring Program*. San Francisco: Jossey-Bass, 1991.

Nadler, Leonard, and Garland D. Wiggs. *Managing Human Resource Development*. San Francisco: Jossey-Bass, 1986.

Nadler, Leonard, and Garland D. Wiggs. *Managing Human Resource Development: A Practical Guide*. San Francisco: Jossey-Bass, 1986.

Olson, Lawrence. "Training Trends: The Corporate View." *Training and Development Journal.* September 1986, pp. 32–35.

Oliver, Robert, *Career Unrest: A Source of Creativity.* New York: Columbia Business School, 1982.

Ott, J. Steven. *The Organizational Culture Perspective.* Chicago: Dorsey Press, 1989.

Phillips, Jack J. *Handbook of Training Evaluation and Measurement Methods.* Houston: Gulf Publishing Company, 1987.

Phillips, Jack J. *Recruiting, Training and Retraining New Employees* San Francisco: Jossey-Bass, 1987.

Prior, John. *Gower Handbook of Training and Development.* Brookfield, VT: Gower Publishing, 1991.

Quick, Thomas. *Training Managers So They Can Really Manage: Confessions of a Frustrated Trainer.* San Francisco: Jossey-Bass, 1991.

Reid, Thomas J. "The Context of Management Development." *Personnel Journal* 53, no. 4. April 1974, pp. 280–87.

Ressler, Ralph. *Career Education: The New Frontier.* Worthington, OH: C. A. Jones, 1973.

Rosow, Jerome M. and Robert Zoger. *Training—The Competitive Edge: Introducing New Technology into the Workplace.* San Francisco: Jossey-Bass, 1988.

Rothwell, William, and Dale Brandenburg. *The Workplace Literacy Primer.* Amherst, MA: HRD Press, 1990.

Saffold, Guy S., III. "Culture, Traits, Strength, and Organizational Performance: Moving Beyond 'Strong' Culture." *Academy of Management Review* 13, no. 4. October 1988, pp. 546–558.

Schein, Edgar H. *Career Dynamics: Matching Individual and Organizational Needs.* Reading, MA: Addison-Wesley, 1980.

Scott, R. K. "Management's Dilemma: To Train or Not to Train People." *Training and Development Journal* 32. February 1978, pp. 3–6.

Swanson, Richard A., and Diane B. Gradric. *Forecasting Financial Benefits of Human Resource Development.* San Francisco: Jossey-Bass, 1988.

Tabbush, V. C. "Investment in Training: A Broader Approach." *Journal of Human Resources* 12. Spring 1977, pp. 252–257.

This, L. "Results-Oriented Training Designs." *Training and Development Journal* 34. June 1980, pp. 14–22.

Timperly, Stuart R. *Personnel Planning and Occupational Choice.* London: Allen and Irwin, 1974.

Wehrenberg, S., and R. Kuhnle. "How Training through Behavior Modeling Works." *Personnel Journal* 59. July 1980, pp. 576–804.

Wellbank, Harry L., Douglas T. Hall, Marilyn A. Morgan, et al. "Planning Job Progression for Effective Career Development and Human Resources Management." *Personnel* 55. March–April 1978, pp. 54–64.

Wiggenhorn, William. "Motorola U: Training Becomes an Education." *Harvard Business Review.* July–August, 1990.

·················
NOTES

1. Janet Gyon, "GE Chairman Welch, Though Much Praised, Starts to Draw Critics," *Wall Street Journal,* August 4, 1988, pp. 1, 8; Russell Mitchell and Judith A. Dobrzynski, "Jack Welch: How Good a Manager? New Corporate Culture Has Made GE More Competitive—But at a Price," *Business Week,* December 14, 1987, pp. 92–103; Thomas Stewart, "GE Keeps Those Ideas Coming," *Fortune,* August 12, 1991, pp. 41–49; and James Hyatt and Amal Kumar Naj, "GE Is No Place for Autocrats, Welch Decrees," *Wall Street Journal,* March 3, 1992, p. B1.

2. For more explanation of this concept, see Gifford Pinchot, *Intrapreneuring* (New York: Harper & Row, 1985).

3. Randall Smith, "IBM, Once a Dictatorship, Is Now a Vast Decentralized Democracy," *Wall Street Journal,* April 7, 1986, p. 26.

4. Dennis Kneale, "Working at IBM: Intense Loyalty in a Rigid Culture," *Wall Street Journal,* April 7, 1986, p. 27.

5. Bill Leonard, "Study Links Training, Competitive Woes," *HRNews,* July 1991, pp. 1+.

6. Albert Karr, "Corporate Job Training Expands, but Is Still Inadequate," *Wall Street Journal,* June 19, 1990, p. A1.

7. Christopher Conte, "Corporate Commitment to Training Is Inadequate and Uneven, Analysts Say," *Wall Street Journal,* October 22, 1991, p. A1.

8. Joe Lamoglia, "Study: Training Doesn't Match Skills Needed," *HRNews,* October 1991, p. 3.

9. Russell Mitchell, "Can Cray Reprogram Itself for Creativity?" *Business Week,* August 20, 1990, p. 86.

10. W. Starbuck and B. Hedberg, "Saving an Organization from a Stagnating Environment," in H. Thorelli, ed., *Strategy + Structure = Performance* (Bloomington: Indiana University Press, 1977), pp. 249–258.

11. C. Wight Bakke, *Bonds of Organization* (New York: Harper & Row, 1950).

12. See Chester I. Barnard, *The Functions of the Executive* (Cambridge: Harvard University Press, 1938); and Herbert A. Simon, *Administrative Behavior,* 2nd ed. (New York: John Wiley & Sons, 1957). A related concept is "exchange theory." See Peter Blau, *Exchange and Power in Social Life* (New York: Harper & Row, 1950).

13. Edgar H. Schein, *Organizational Culture and Leadership* (San Francisco: Jossey-Bass, 1985).

14. Ibid.

15. Keith Davis, *Human Behavior at Work,* 3rd ed. (New York: McGraw-Hill, 1972).

16. Zachary Schiller, "Ready, Aim, Market: Combat Training at P&G College," *Business Week,* February 3, 1992, p. 56.

17. Chris Lee, "Where the Training Dollars Go," *Training* (October 1987), p. 64.

18. "Banker Development Program for Management Associates," *Barnett: Extra Effort Does Make the Difference* (Jacksonville, FL: Barnett Banks, 1988).

19. Peters and Waterman, *In Search of Excellence,* pp. 248–249.

20. Selwyn Feinstein, "Labor Letter: Worker Training Get High Priority at Companies," *Wall Street Journal,* November 22, 1988.

21. Ibid.

22. Judith Valente and Bridget O'Brian, "Airline Cockpits Are No Place to Solo: Crews Taught That Teamwork Improves Safety," *Wall Street Journal,* August 2, 1989.

23. Chris Lee, "Where the Training Dollars Go," *Training,* p. 51.

24. Diane Filipowski, "How Federal Express Makes Your Package Its Most Important," *Personnel Journal,* February 1992, pp. 40–46.

25. Joann Lubin, "Harassment Moves Atop Agenda in Many Executive Education Programs," *Wall Street Journal,* December 2, 1991, pp. B1+.

26. David E. Bartz, David R. Schwandt, and Larry W. Hillman, "Differences Between 'T' and 'D'," *Personnel Administrator,* June 1989, pp. 164–170.

27. Gilda Dangot-Simpkin, "How Come Nothing Changed," *HRMagazine,* November 1991, pp. 66–68.

28. "The Transformation of EDS' Culture," *Open Line* (Dallas: EDS, Spring 1990).

29. These factors and conclusions come from a paper that examined 200 studies covering the effectiveness of training by Bruce Joyce and Beverly Showers, "Training Ourselves to Teach: The Messages of Research" (Palo Alto: Stanford University, 1982).

30. Ralph Ganger, "HRIS Logs on to Strategic Training," *Personnel Journal,* August 1991, pp. 50–55.

31. Jolie Soloman, "Managing," *Wall Street Journal,* February 17, 1989, p. B1.

32. Shari Caudron, "Training Helps United Go Global," *Personnel Journal*, February 1992, pp. 103—105.

33. "Employees Lacking Basic Skills Can't Adapt to Corporate Change," *1990 SHAM/CC Survey*, June 1990, pp. 1–12.

34. John Hoerr, "Business Shares the Blame for Workers' Low Skills," *Business Week*, June 25, 1990, p. 71.

35. Sinclair Hugh, "A Business Education Partnership," *HRMagazine*, July 1991, pp. 49–52.

36. Ceel Pasternak, "Business Helps Educate," *HRMagazine*, May 1990, p. 20.

37. Richard Zalman, "The 'Basics' of In-House Skills Training," *HRMagazine*, February 1991, pp. 74–78.

38. Albert Karr, "U.S. Business Suffers from Education, Training Gaps," *Wall Street Journal*, January 7, 1992, p. A1.

39. *HR Reporter*, Bureau of National Affairs, September 1988, p. 5. Used with permission.

11 *Total Quality Management and Improving Productivity*

A main goal of any organization is to be productive. Some organizations successfully reach this goal, while others fail. Although each successful organization follows a different formula, some common productivity principles are found in all successful organizations, such as training and development, company-wide communication, and trust in employees. These and other productivity principles are examined in this chapter.

• • • • • • • • •
CHAPTER OBJECTIVES

After reading this chapter, you should be able to

1. Understand the concept of productivity.
2. Recognize ways to increase productivity.
3. Define involvement and explain the benefits of having an involved staff.
4. Be familiar with techniques available to help increase employee involvement.

CASE: Motivating Motorola[1]

In recent years American managers have taken a closer look at the effectiveness of Japanese management and have questioned why workers in the United States seem to lack motivation and why American productivity has declined. What is it about Japanese management style that motivates their workers and increases productivity? In short, corporate America continues to struggle with how to motivate workers.

Motorola—Number 1 in the United States

Motorola, one of the world's leading high-tech companies, set out to resolve the motivation problem with their workers. Rather than merely mimic Japanese management style, Motorola adopted a strategic approach that adds an American twist to the Japanese style of management. Although Motorola has embraced such Japanese tactics as driving relentlessly for market share, sharply upgrading quality, and constantly honing manufacturing processes to pare costs, they have exploited "Yankee Know-How" in areas where Japanese companies have been notoriously weak, such as in marketing and software development. "American-style" Japanese management has put Motorola in the driver's seat in telecommunications. Worldwide, Motorola is now number four and gaining.

Strategic Approach

Robert W. Galvin, the son of the founder of Motorola, and his "handpicked" CEO successor, George Fisher, have engaged in a top-to-bottom overhaul of Motorola's market share both at home and abroad. Motorola has committed itself to a more participative management style and will prepare its workers to participate *effectively* by emphasizing education and training for all employees. The company has also emphasized research and development, high quality and low cost, and interdepartmental collaboration.

Education and Training

To instill the work force with the new corporate goals, Motorola launched a massive education drive for all 105,000 employees, both workers and managers. The company spends roughly $60 million a year on educating its employees by offering courses in global competitiveness and risk-taking, for example. The courses also teach workers practical skills in statistical process control and ways of reducing product cycle times.

Training programs help workers to develop new skills and problem-solving techniques. Motorola offers executive programs to discuss real-world topics and problems that do not necessarily have clearcut answers. Such programs enable managers to more effectively deal with a changing environment. For example, Darlene Gerster, a training and development manager at Motorola, states that the company's "Manager of Managers' Program" helps employees learn the process of thinking through an idea, developing it, and championing it through the organization. Motorola's programs emphasize that managers must be willing to take certain risks in order to adapt to dynamic, changing environments.

By investing in training and development, Motorola is helping its employees to gain confidence in their ability to participate effectively in the decision-making process. Like Motorola, other leading corporations have incorporated case studies into their training and development programs that utilize their own real-life strategic and business issues. Thus, participants in the programs are gaining more practical and applicable experience from which to draw on in the future.

Research and Development

Motorola continues to correct for the myopic vision that seems to be intrinsic to other U.S. organizations. The company has distanced itself from the "short-term fix," opting instead for a more long-term focus. It has pumped $100 million into research and development to be spent over a ten-year period. Such an investment is expected to yield long-term benefits rather than short-run, immediate returns. Motorola's commitment to research and development has resulted in "miniaturized" telecommunications products that, according to John J. Egidio, president of Metromedia Paging Services, Inc., seem to have "scooped the world by a year or two." When Motorola introduced its MicroTac cellular phone and wristwatch pager to the market, for example, it basically "knocked the wind out of the sails of Japanese rival products."

High Quality and Low Cost

Fisher feels that Americans used to fall into the trap of assuming that high quality costs more. But high quality and low cost go hand in hand. His "find it and fix it" quality control philosophy has been saving Motorola approximately $250 million annually. The director of quality estimates that company-wide defects have been reduced from nearly 3,000 per million products in 1983 to less than 200 per million. Motorola's ability to improve quality efficiency while reducing costs has been nothing short of spectacular and was a major reason why the company was awarded a Malcolm Baldridge National Quality Award.

Collaboration

In an effort to create unified team spirit, Motorola is tearing down the traditional walls that isolate various departments, such as design, manufacturing, and marketing. Motorola is attempting to establish a new tradition of collaboration among disciplines. Representatives from each discipline are now encouraged to get involved in new projects from the start.

• • • • • • • •

As can be seen in the Motorola case, the company has chosen to break away from the traditional "American way" of doing business. The change in Motorola's attitude toward spending money on programs whose benefits are not immediate is a nontraditional strategic approach. For example, money spent on training and education is viewed as more of an investment than a cost. Motorola has realized that an investment in its workforce ensures the company a greater sense of enthusiasm and commitment among Motorola employees. However, there are other possible strategic choices businesses can make. Some of these choices are outlined below.

STRATEGIC CHOICES

Choosing to include employee involvement in the management of the organization as a means of increasing productivity is a strategic decision in itself. Included in this decision, however, are several other considerations.

1. Top management must decide how much faith it has in its employees. Should managers simply ask for input about how to improve the organization or should they instill in their employees the power necessary to implement these changes? Some organizations have implemented suggestion boxes or quality circles in which lower-level employees and higher-level employees meet as a group to discuss ways to increase efficiency. Suggestions made by employees are studied and, perhaps at some point in time, implemented. Any savings that may occur from the idea may be split among the workers, or a bonus is paid directly to the person who suggested the change. Other organizations have taken this a step further and actually endowed the employees who provided the suggestions with the power to implement it. The level of involvement employees are allowed in an organization is a strategic choice upper-level management must make, and it ultimately will be based on how much trust management has in their employees.

2. In order to enable a staff to be productive, the organization must provide the tools needed to perform effectively. These tools can take on a variety of forms, such as education, equipment, or information. Whatever form they take, providing these tools is expensive. Managers must make a strategic choice concerning how much the firm is willing to invest in equipping the employees.

3. Another strategic choice managers must make is whether or not the organization's culture is supportive of an involved work environment. Because it

is difficult to change or adapt an organization's culture, top management must be behind a decision of this nature. Opening up lines of communication and sharing responsibility and power with subordinates may be difficult for some managers to do. However, if the managers see their bosses openly communicating and sharing responsibilities, they may be more open to trying these techniques with their subordinates too.

PRODUCTIVITY

What Is Productivity?

In simple terms, productivity can be defined as output per hour.[2] But this is far too simple. Productivity comes in various forms. For example, some define productivity as the change in unit labor costs, or how much each item costs to produce. Others suggest that productivity is the value of production over paid hours. This ratio determines profitability as well as productivity. Whichever way productivity is defined, it is used to determine if the firm has been successful.

Recent reports comparing U.S. manufacturing productivity rates to other countries present mixed findings. Some suggest that the United States is leading the way. For example, Exhibit 11.1 compares the United States and six other countries on two productivity measures: annual change in manufacturing unit labor costs from 1985 to 1990 and manufacturer increases in output per hour from 1988 to 1989. On one chart, the United States is number one, on the other, it is dead last. Which figures are correct? They both are. But how can that be?

The numbers in Exhibit 11.1 do not tell the whole story. While it is true that the productivity growth rate has fallen over 60 percent since the 1950s and 1960s, this was an abnormal productivity period. The United States was recovering from World War II and the Great Depression and was using untapped accumulations of innovation and savings. Once recovery was complete, productivity slowed. But in comparison to previous years, it appeared to fall. In absolute terms, the productivity level of U.S. manufacturing continues to be the highest in the world.[3]

By some measures Americans have never worked harder. The percentage of Americans in the work force has risen steadily since 1948 and has risen over 75 percent for women. Sixty-five percent of married households have 2 or more people working and over 6 percent of Americans hold two jobs. Not only do we work more at work, we also work more at home. American men average 44 hours a week for pay, and an additional 14 hours of work at home. Their Japanese counterparts average 52 hours of work for pay, but only 3.5 hours at home. In total, American men work harder than Japanese men.[4]

Defining productivity in service organizations is not as easy. While output per hour could be measured by the number of customers serviced, other factors come into play. Two of the recurring factors are quality and service.[5] In practice the goal of most service organizations is to provide the fastest, most efficient, and friendliest service possible to any and all customers. In terms of productivity, this may mean that minimizing errors or eliminating reworking is stressed. Or it may mean that smiling and offering to go the extra mile for a customer is stressed. In any case, the idea is to make the service industry more productive by having better serviced customers. One major component of a productive staff is the leadership provided.

....

EXHIBIT 11.1   Manufacturer Productivity Ratings

ANNUAL PERCENTAGE CHANGE IN MANUFACTURING UNIT LABOR COSTS

COUNTRY	PERCENTAGE CHANGE
United States	− 0.1
Canada	+ 7.9
Italy	+ 14.3
Germany	+ 15.6
France	+ 11.0
Britain	+ 10.8
Japan	+ 10.3

MANUFACTURER PRODUCTIVITY INCREASES IN OUTPUT PER HO

COUNTRY	1988	1989	PERCENTAGE CHANGE
United States	2.2%	1.8%	− 4
Canada	1.6%	2.1%	+ 5
Italy	2.6%	2.7%	+ 1
Germany	4.3%	4.3%	0
France	4.7%	4.4%	− 3
Britain	5.0%	4.7%	− 3
Japan	4.4%	5.3%	+ 9

....

Leadership and Productivity

An area's productivity, or lack there of, can frequently be traced back to the leadership provided that area. In a recent study of 12 major companies, workers felt they, and the people with whom they worked, were committed to providing a quality product. The problem in doing this, they reported, arose at the management level, specifically, top management. Two-thirds of the workers surveyed indicated that quality of the work completed was not an important measure of performance in their organization. This feeling was frequently supported by top managers who verbally stressed the importance of quality workmanship, but offered incentives based only on the number of units produced.[6]

One of the first people to even discuss the idea of enhancing quality productivity through leadership was the statistician Dr. W. Edwards Deming. Although he was virtually given saint status in Japan, Deming's philosophy, which helped to rebuild Japan after World War II, was virtually ignored in the United States. However, Deming's ideas have been given a second look as U.S. firms now strive to become more productive. Deming's management philosophy is stated in the form of 14 principles. These principles are listed in Exhibit 11.2. As you read these principles, notice how closely they reflect the ideas currently being accepted and used in American firms.

One of Deming's suggestions was to change the management style that has been used in American business for decades. This is a very difficult task. In order for managers to support quality production, they must abandon many of the techniques

FOCUS ON INTERNATIONAL ISSUES ••••••••••••••••••••••

Exactly Who Is W. Edwards Deming?

William Edwards Deming was born on October 14, 1900. After growing up in Iowa and Wyoming, he obtained his first degree in electrical engineering in 1921 from the University of Wyoming. He continued his education at the University of Colorado, earning a master's degree in mathematics and Physics, and he finally received his Ph.D from Yale in mathematical physics in 1928. He began working for the United States Department of Agriculture where considerable attention was being placed on statistical experimental design. Deming enjoyed this work and wanted to continue it. To do this, he moved to London to study under the "father of statistics," Sir Ronald Fisher.

During summer jobs while in school, Deming had learned of the work of Walter Shewhart. Shewhart focused on the statistical control of processes and charting these controls. He believed that there were two variables in the output process: controlled and uncontrolled. While Shewhart focused his attention on improving production processes, Deming realized that these ideas were applicable to all aspects of business. He proved his assumption was correct by applying the concepts to the administrative processes used to prepare the 1940 census, for which he worked.

After this success, he began to teach people involved with the war effort about his 14 principles of quality management. While they listened and implemented some, they never internalized his ideas. After the war, businesses were not interested in becoming more efficient because America was the only country producing anything. There was virtually no competition.

General Douglas MacArthur asked Deming to join him on two trips to Japan to help advise the Japanese in how to reconstruct their country. The contacts he made while on these trips are what made Deming so famous in Japan. He gave the same speech to Japanese managers that he had given to American managers, but the Japanese listened and implemented his 14 principles. His teachings help Japan become what it is today.

Deming was "introduced" to America in a 1980 documentary called "If Japan Can, Why Can't We" produced by Clare Crawford-Mason. She interviewed Deming and marveled at the fact that he was living only minutes from the White House yet *no one* would listen to his remedy for the stagnation in American business. However, after her story aired, Americans began to listen. Deming traveled throughout the United States giving his seminars to American managers, and some even began to implement his ideas. Two of the most well-known converts are Nashua and Ford. Both of these companies have benefitted greatly from Deming's advice.

SOURCE: Adapted from Henry Neave, *The Deming Dimension,* (Knoxville: SPC Press, 1990).

they have used for years in favor of more open and sharing techniques. Delegating the power, prestige, and control that took managers years to build is a bitter pill to swallow, even if it is for the good of the company. However, some managers have been able to successfully mold their leadership style to promote the new quality-minded workplace. Let's examine a few of these cases.

Success Stories

Xerox Corporation, who won the prestigious Malcolm Baldridge National Quality Award that is explained in Exhibit 11.3, has found a way to remold the corporate culture to one that supports and emphasizes quality. The focus at Xerox is on the individual person. If each person who works for Xerox becomes a quality advocate and is extremely knowledgeable about the techniques used to perform his or her job, the result is a quality product. To achieve this goal, Xerox developed a "Leadership through Quality" program that focused on skills training, customer satisfaction, strong union support, and community involvement. By making each employee responsible for Xerox's success, providing the skills and tools necessary to perform the job, and

EXHIBIT 11.2 Deming's Fourteen Points for Managers

1. Create constancy of purpose toward improvement of product and service with the aim to become competitive, to stay in business, and to provide jobs.
2. Adopt a new philosophy. We are in a new economic age created by Japan. We can no longer live with commonly accepted styles of American management, nor with commonly accepted levels of delays, mistakes, or defective products.
3. Cease dependence on inspection to achieve quality. Eliminate the need for inspection on a mass basis by building quality into the product in the first place.
4. End the practice of awarding business on the basis of the price tag. Instead, minimize the total cost.
5. Improve constantly and forever the system of production and service to improve quality and productivity, and thus constantly decrease costs.
6. Institute training on the job.
7. Institute supervision. The aim of supervision should be to help people, machines, and gadgets do a better job. Supervision of management is in need of overhaul, as well as supervision of production workers.
8. Drive out fear, so that everyone may work effectively for the company.
9. Break down the barriers between departments. People in research, design, sales, and production must work as a team to foresee problems of production.
10. Eliminate slogans, exhortations, and targets for the work force that ask for zero defects and new levels of productivity. Such exhortations only create adversarial relationships. The bulk of the causes of low productivity belong to the system and thus lie beyond the power of the work force.
11. Eliminate work standards that prescribe numerical quotas for the day. Substitute aids and helpful supervision.
12. Remove the barriers that rob the hourly worker of his [or her] right to pride of workmanship. The responsibility of supervisors must be changed from sheer numbers to quality. Remove the barriers that rob people in management and engineering of their right to pride of workmanship. This means abolish the annual rating, or merit rating, and managment by objective.
13. Institute a vigorous program of education and retraining.
14. Put everyone in the company to work to accomplish the transformation.

---

reinforcing the goals, Xerox has reached it's goal of creating a total quality organization.[7]

Another successfully managed company is McDonald's. The founder, Ray Kroc, purchased the franchise rights from Dick and Mac McDonald who ran a small fast-food take-out kitchen in San Bernadino, California. He realized that the formula they used, quick, good food at reasonable prices, was worth his investment, and he knew that the brothers had no intention of expanding. Kroc, who died in 1981 at age 84, has been described as short-tempered, politically conservative, tireless, perpetually optimistic, and a fanatic for cleanliness. He motivated workers through maxims that continue to adorn bulletin boards in today's McDonald's. Some of the all-time favorites include "Free enterprise will work if you will" and "If you've got time to lean you've got time to clean."[8]

Sam Walton, or Mr. Sam as he was known by his employees, was another interesting success case. Since 1962 Walton developed his single store into a 1,300-

··

| EXHIBIT 11.3 | The Malcolm Baldridge National Quality Award |

1992 EXAMINATION ITEMS AND POINT VALUES

1992 EXAMINATION CATEGORIES/ITEMS	POINT VALUES
1.0 LEADERSHIP	90
1.1 Senior Executive Leadership	45
1.2 Management for Quality	25
1.3 Public Responsibility	20
2.0 INFORMATION AND ANALYSIS	80
2.1 Scope and Management of Quality and Performance Data and Information	15
2.2 Competitive Comparisons and Benchmarks	25
2.3 Analysis and Uses of Company-Level Data	40
3.0 STRATEGIC QUALITY PLANNING	60
3.1 Strategic Quality and Company Performance Planning Process	35
3.2 Quality and Performance Plans	25
4.0 HUMAN RESOURCE DEVELOPMENT AND MANAGEMENT	150
4.1 Human Resource Management	20
4.2 Employee Involvement	40
4.3 Employee Education and Training	40
4.4 Employee Performance and Recognition	25
4.5 Employee Well-Being and Morale	25
5.0 MANAGEMENT OF PROCESS QUALITY	140
5.1 Design and Introduction of Quality Products and Services	40
5.2 Process Management—Product and Service Production and Delivery Process	35
5.3 Process Management—Business Processes and Support Services	30
5.4 Supplier Quality	20
5.5 Quality Assessment	15
6.0 QUALITY AND OPERATIONAL RESULTS	180
6.1 Product and Service Quality Results	75
6.2 Company Operational Results	45
6.3 Business Process and Support Service Results	25
6.4 Supplier Quality Results	35
7.0 CONSUMER FOCUS AND SATISFACTION	300
7.1 Customer Relationship Management	65
7.2 Commitment to Customers	15
7.3 Customer Satisfaction Determination	35
7.4 Customer Satisfaction Results	75
7.5 Customer Satisfaction Comparison	75
7.6 Future Requirements and Expectations of Customers	35
Total Points	1000

··

store retail chain known as Wal-Mart. Even though Walton followed a savvy, innovative, and carefully mapped strategy to build his chain, this was masked by the cheerleading front that was Walton's style. He avoided putting stores in cities, and instead, focused on the heartland of America. His employees are called associates and work more like teammates than employees. Each store is in healthy competition with other Wal-Mart stores for recognition as the "best of the area." The rewards are shared by the entire store and doing so builds a more teamlike environment.[9]

Not all leaders have been successful. One example of a leader who failed was Shearson Lehman Hutton, Inc's, former CEO, Peter Cohen. Cohen's reputation in the industry prior to his taking the CEO position was one of a disciplined and thorough executive. While the securities business is known for inept management, Cohen was found to be an exception to the rule. So, what forced him to resign as CEO after just two short years? Plenty. Instead of using the managerial style that made him a good choice for the job, he changed, and in a big way. His own personal ambitions began to overshadow the company's goals, and he lost control of the company and of himself. In the weeks preceding his resignation, he gained weight, looked like he was losing sleep, and argued with everyone. After asking for, but not receiving, a confidence vote from his boss, James Robinson, chairman of American Express, he resigned.[10]

The success stories presented above have several commonalities. All of the companies discussed are in the service business, and all have CEO'S who believe in their employees. The companies are also a "nice" place to work. Management treats the employees fairly and with dignity. This type of leader can be considered a servant leader. Servant leaders share the following characteristics:

- They take people and their work very seriously.
- They listen and take their leads from the workers.
- They heal the wounds of their workers.
- They are sure of themselves, but humble.
- They are stewards for their companies.[11]

Not all CEOs behave this way. Some prefer to be tough as nails and brutal to their staff. Edwin Artzt, chairman of Procter & Gamble, is one such boss. Artzt's aim is to build a tougher, faster, more global P&G. To do this, he is stressing individual accountability, not the team approach used in recent years. He demands that managers consistently beat the competition to market with the latest detergents, face creams, and diapers. He views lightening quick reflexes as the only way to succeed in the new global marketplace and will do anything necessary to get his organization to that point.[12]

Fortune magazine selected America's toughest bosses in 1980, 1984, and again in 1989. Five of those who made the list in 1989 are presented in Exhibit 11.4 with a description of how their staffs view them and how they view themselves. Note as you read through the thoughts in Exhibit 11.4 that they are dramatically different. It is wise to remember that the way you want to be viewed may not be the way others actually view you.

The number of tough bosses may be on the rise. Hard times seem to be pushing managers back into the Stone Age of management. Many organizations are taking back the power they gave employees, closing their open doors, and stopping the communication flows. The workplace is becoming a perform or die environment. Most experts blame it on the lingering recession that is forcing managers to make

---

EXHIBIT 11.4 America's Toughest Bosses of 1989

FRANCISCO A. LORENZO, CHAIRMAN, TEXAS AIR

How others see him:　He thinks he's a great manager, but he's not. He's incredibly impulsive. He is not trusted inside or outside the organization. He is a good dealmaker.

How he sees himself:　I have to be tough, but fair. We built this company from businesses that were failing. We didn't just take over a big company and blow out the cobwebs.

HARRY E. FIGGIE, JR., CHAIRMAN, FIGGIE INTERNATIONAL

How others see him:　From horrendous to delightful, from idiotic to brilliant. Working for him was a nightmare. He is really abusive. He is the Steinbrenner of industry.

How he sees himself:　You don't build a company like this with lace on your underwear. We bought small companies with no management depth. There's no room for error.

CARL E. REICHARDT, CHAIRMAN, WELLS FARGO & COMPANY

How others see him:　Carl's bag is execution, not talk. He's blunt, and you don't want to make mistakes around him. His narrow focus may be limiting middle management, and a lot are leaving.

How he sees himself:　Good operations succeed with a minimum of foolishness and glitter. Maybe I am tough. But my 80-year-old mother will be shocked to learn of it.

RICHARD J. MAHONEY, CHAIRMAN, MONSANTO

How others see him:　He has a big ego and subordinates have to stroke him a lot. He listens, but he doesn't understand. He has little empathy with subordinates. He can't believe he's wrong.

How he sees himself:　I am demanding, not mean. Forgiveness is out of style, shoulder shrugs are out of fashion. Hit the targets on time without excuses.

JIM MANZI, CHAIRMAN, LOTUS DEVELOPMENT

How others see him:　You had better have all the answers before you go in; he doesn't suffer comments like, "I'll get back to you on that."

How he sees himself:　Real tough guys rely on positional authority. I think that's disgusting. I shy away from it. I rely on trust. And no one is penalized for thinking slowly. That would be stupid.

---

cuts in human resources. Often these painful decisions must be based on productivity, and memories tend to be short. If a manager cannot remember what you have done for him or her lately, then it may mean you walk out the door.[13]

EXHIBIT 11.5 Types of Followers

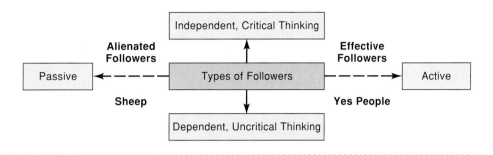

What Does It Take to Be a Good Leader?

One thing it takes to be a good leader is good followers. While all of us may not be managers in our lives, each of us will fulfill the role of follower. It seems no matter how high you climb up the corporate ladder, you always have a boss. As a boss, you can make your job easier by hiring good followers. But what exactly is a good follower? Good followers manage themselves well. They are committed to the organization, its purpose, its mission, and to others. They focus their efforts for maximum impact. Finally, they are courageous, honest, and credible.[14]

Exhibit 11.5 divides followers into four categories: sheep, yes people, alienated followers, and effective followers. Sheep are passive and uncritical. While they follow, they take no initiative and no responsibility. Avoid hiring sheep. Yes people are less passive, but have no opinions. Weak bosses like to hire yes people in order to build a strong support network for themselves. Strong bosses should avoid hiring yes people. Alienated followers have critical, analytic minds, but lack the ability to follow through on their plans. Once constructive employees, they have given up and tuned out. Managers who screen out cynical applicants usually avoid hiring alienated followers. The final category, effective followers, is where all of your employees should fall. Effective followers think for themselves and carry out their responsibilities without supervision. They are self-starters and independent problem-solvers. They are team players and have become adept at following.[15]

Workplace Diversity

Once you have a qualified staff of effective followers, you need to be a leader who can motivate and challenge each and every one of your workers. However, because of the cultural and generational diversity in the workplace, one management style will not be effective with all workers. For example, four distinct generations of workers exist in the current work force: the swing generation (born 1910–1929), the silent generation (born 1930–1945), the baby-boom generation (born 1946–1964), and the baby-bust generation (born 1965–1976). Each of these generations have different opinions of work and value different things.

The swing generation was involved in the rebuilding of America after World War II. While many of the workers in this generation have retired, the ones who remain in the work force often long for the "good old days" and may not be willing to accept change as quickly as the other generations. The silent generation has quietly gathered real estate, boats, and IRAs for their upcoming retirement. Members of this generation currently hold the majority of the power positions in business, and they view the world with a lack of true interest and no desire to make it better for those who come after. The baby-boom generation believes in the rights of the individual worker. This generation feels that no one should be dismissed without cause and that each employee should be rewarded on a merit basis, regardless of race, creed, color, or age. Over the next ten years, the baby boomers will begin to take on more roles of responsibility as the silent generation begins to retire. Finally, the baby-bust generation has no real sense of oneness. This generation believes that there is a true difference between the haves and the have-nots with respect to economic status and skills. As these workers begin to enter the work force, managers must be aware of the potential variation in the quality of the workers from this generation.[16]

Obviously, workers from each of these generations will not respond favorably to the same leadership techniques. Members of the silent generation are looking for security in their golden years; the baby boomers, who are looking for self-fulfillment, are realizing that it may not be found in the job, and the baby busters are looking for short-term gratification in the form of challenging jobs that take no more than 37.5 hours a week.[17] How does one manager make all these workers happy and productive? The key may be in the organization's culture. If top management can develop the goals for the organization and then find a way to incorporate the needs and rights of each generation into these goals, everyone will be a winner. Let's take a closer look at the blending of leadership and culture.

Leadership and Culture

What makes one company able to attract and retain quality leadership? One answer to this question is the overall organizational environment, or culture. Organizations that have better-than-average management also have been found to have the following qualities:

1. Strong human resource policies for compensation, promotion, development, and training
2. Clear communication of job possibilities in the firm
3. High-quality career planning
4. An overall quality work environment[18]

Fortune magazine asked experts to rate large American firms on their quality of management and their ability to attract, keep, and develop talented people. The twenty top firms are listed in Exhibit 11.6. Heading the list is IBM. IBM has been successful in recruiting and maintaining quality employees and managers for a number of reasons; one of the strongest is its organizational culture. Stories, myths, and rituals abound at IBM. Slogans such as "Once an IMBer, always an IBMer" clearly explain how workers feel about their company. IBM is quick to support this feeling with company sponsored activities that bring workers together on and off company grounds. The culture at IBM has allowed managers to provide a nurturing environment for employees—something that would not be allowed in other organizations.

EXHIBIT 11.6	**Top Twenty Firms with Respect to Quality of Management and Attracting and Retaining Quality Employees**	

RANK	ORGANIZATION	RATING
1	IBM	8.75
2	Dow Jones	8.40
3	Hewlett-Packard	8.40
4	Coca-Cola	8.35
5	Morgan Guaranty	8.30
6	Anheuser-Busch	8.30
7	3M	8.20
8	General Electric	8.15
9	Boeing	8.00
10	Citicorp	7.90
11	Standard Oil of Indiana	7.90
12	General Motors	7.80
13	DuPont	7.75
14	Merck	7.70
15	General Mills	7.65
16	Johnson & Johnson	7.60
17	Kodak	7.55
18	Abbott	7.55
19	Delta	7.55
20	First Boston	7.50

As discussed in Chapter 10, an organization's choice and use of culture is a strategic decision. Various types of cultures are available for organizations to use; however, the leadership style of the firm must closely mesh with the chosen culture. When an organization's culture is not in sync with the management or with the rapidly changing times, that organization may decide to change its image and develop a new corporate culture. One company to choose this route is Mobil Oil.

In the early 1980s, Mobil realized that the strong centralized controls that it used in the 1960s and 1970s were no longer appropriate and needed to be changed. In the past, Mobil could be described as a paternal, traditional organization who had a great deal of loyal, long-tenured employees. To change its culture, Mobil brought in outside consultants who looked at the current management style used and suggested changes to bring it in line with the 1980s style of management. The old management style included heavy layers of people checking up on other people, which interfered with performing effectively. To update its culture, Mobil changed the performance evaluations and compensation of the entire organization. Gone were the guaranteed raises every 12 or 15 months. Instead, a pay increase would come for "giving Mobil something extra." Managers were no longer "better than the rest." Instead, they were told to manage people and not try to be smarter than anyone else in the room. Mobil focused on a skills approach. Valued employees were ones who held the skills needed to perform the job effectively, and Mobil began to work closely with its people to ensure that they had the skills needed to succeed. One final change in the culture was an increase in communication. Even the CEO, Allen Murray, holds annual straight-talk meetings with a handful of employees to discuss the company's future.

HR CHALLENGES ●●

Ensuring Productivity at Mars

One company that has been able to implement a company-wide corporate culture that supports the organization's goals is Mars, Inc., best known for its candy bars. The best way to understand Mars' culture is to see it in action. All Mars subsidiaries worldwide look the same. There are no walls. Instead, the employees' desks are placed in concentric circles. The president and his or her staff are at the center of the circle and each ring after that is made up of the subordinate staffs. This makes all senior staffers totally accessible and information flows freely.

Quality is an obsession at Mars. The company refuses to allow "incremental degradation" (using lesser quality ingredients to lower costs) to occur. To avoid this, each and every employee is responsible for quality control. Line workers can ditch an entire run of candy bars if the chocolate covering is not perfect. Salespeople can discard entire showcases of products in stores if the expiration date is approaching.

One reason Mars' employees are so willing to take such risks is that they have a great deal of job security and are very well paid. Mars' pay schedule ranks in the 90th percentile when compared to other premier companies worldwide. While the pay is high, it is not diverse. The company has only six pay levels. All vice-presidents make approximately the same salary regardless of the function they lead. This allows Mars to transfer people from one business unit to another and one function to another without much difficulty. And transfer they do. It is rare to find a general manager who has not done at least two tours in different business units.

As is reflected in the organization's salary structure, the owners of Mars believe in treating everyone the same. This aspect of the culture has caused some problems for managers who disagree. For example, one vice-president who purchased fancy desks for himself and his immediate staff was dressed down by one of the owners for buying a desk more expensive than his immediate supervisor. While one might think that this type of public reprimand may have a negative effect on the workers and the firm, the opposite is true. The owners have an aura about them and their outbursts are quickly turned into stories and legends that are circulated around the company to reinforce the culture even more.

Obviously, not all companies can be like Mars and not everyone would want to work for Mars. However, this organization seems to have found a culture that fits its strategies, its goals, its leadership style, and its workers.

SOURCE: Adapted from Craig Cantoni, "Quality Control from Mars," *Wall Street Journal*, January 27, 1992, p. A12.

All of the changes made at Mobil did not come easy, and some did not work. However, Mobil made a strategic decision to alter its culture in order to be more in sync with the times, and it followed through on this decision. To be successful at changing a corporate culture, other companies who make this strategic decision should be aware of several things. First, corporate culture can never be imposed. You cannot force employees to change their values simply because it is in the best interests of the organization. However, you can change someone's behavior. By changing an employee's behavior, you can hope that his or her attitudes will change in the process. Management must be aware of this subtlety and attempt to help guide the change.

Another concern a corporation must keep in mind when developing or changing its culture is that certain cultures work best in specific environments. In order to determine what culture is right for a company, the goals, mission, and direction of the organization must be taken into consideration. The culture should be developed to support the organization's goal. By focusing on what the organization wants to accomplish, how to do this and what environment is needed become apparent. A culture that supports the organization's goals and environment can then be developed.

Organizational Restructuring

Many firms have tried to become more productive through organizational restructuring.[19] Since 1977, the Fortune 500 companies have slashed 2.8 million employees from their payrolls. Millions of other employees have taken pay cuts or surrendered their jobs. All of these changes were made in an effort to streamline and restructure corporations.[20] Organizational restructuring can take on a variety of forms: downsizing, mergers and acquisitions, joint ventures, and globalization. We will look at each of these in turn.

Downsizing

Companies who faced a decrease in sales, market share, or profits over the past ten years began to realize that their human resources were expensive and underutilized. In order to be more competitive, companies made a strategic decision to gradually lower their payroll numbers. The first step was to use attrition. By not replacing employees who retired or quit, substantial gains were made with respect to overall costs. Employees who were asked to take on the work done by others at first were disgruntled, but accepted the change after realizing that it was helping them to keep their jobs.

However, during the 1980s the economy continued to degrade. Older workers, who were required to retire under earlier laws, began to postpone retirement indefinitely once mandatory retirement was abolished. Some realized that the pension they would receive would not be enough to support them in the manner in which they were accustomed with the current economy, while others decided they were not ready to face the golf course on a daily basis. Similarly, voluntary turnover decreased as well. The poor job market, fueled by the weak economy, made any job better than the unemployment line. Attrition was no longer a suitable tool for downsizing the work force.

The next step was budget cutting. In this stage, managers were given mandates of decreasing their budgets anywhere from 5 to 50 percent. The easiest way to do this was to reduce the size of the work force. Often automation could be introduced to make a job that once took over a dozen people to complete manageable by only one or two. The other ten employees were dismissed. Another technique was to reduce the number of people all performing the same job by doubling the work load for half of them and dismissing the other half. Creative ways to cut staff was the focus of most managers during this time. The man with the ax became a very unfriendly sight, even after the cuts were completed. Morale dipped extremely low, even for the survivors. It was difficult for the manager who rearranged the workforce to lead it again after the dust settled.

Some companies fought to keep the morale of the firm up during even the worst times. Firms that communicated the changes early and provided the employees who were to be released with the opportunity to retrain or develop new skills before termination increased the morale for both the leavers and stayers. Additionally, the survivors who were asked to take on more responsibility and work were asked what they needed to make their jobs easier. Training, equipment, and more control were provided as a means of keeping the remaining workers satisfied. However, the quality of the product or service often takes a beating due to downsizing.

Downsizing and budget cutting are only reactions to the problem. They cannot even be considered strategies.[21] While these techniques may have helped to save several large companies, such as Caterpillar and Ford Motor Company, they do not provide a lasting solution to the problem. Some firms are finding that acquiring or merging with another company may be a more long term strategic approach to increase productivity.

Mergers and Acquisitions

During 1985, over 3,000 mergers and acquisitions were completed with a total value of over $18 billion.[22] While the financial value of these deals is easily calculated, what is not clear is the human value. Often in mergers and acquisitions the human resource division is completely left out of the picture. Likewise, the people who are being acquired are frequently given scant attention. In a recent survey, only 37 percent of the acquirers indicated that they audited the management and personnel prior to buying the firm. Further, the majority of these audits were to examine human resource policies that may limit the buyers freedom to act, not to examine the personnel themselves.[23]

As mergers and acquisitions become increasingly common, stages in which the process normally evolves have been established. One common set of stages is presented in Exhibit 11.7. It is important for human resource managers to become involved in the acquisition or merger process early on. To do this successfully, a few tips should be remembered.

1. Get to know the members of the acquisition/merger team. If they speak a different language, either literally or figuratively, learn it. They will be more open to your human resource concerns if you are more aware of theirs.
2. Bring something with you. Show them that you have training programs that could be beneficial to both sides of the merger. Explain how you can help to merge the two cultures. Show them that you are willing to help in any way.
3. Be realistic about what information they will provide you and how much interest they will have in your offers.
4. Be timely. Show them that you are willing to work under their time frame.
5. Maintain a balanced viewpoint. Try not to get bogged down in trivial issues, but continue to focus on the bigger picture.[24]

Other issues that human resource managers should be aware of during a merger or acquisition include the fact that personnel uncertainty will be extremely high. The only way to manage this is through accurate and frequent communication about the process. As employees try to manage the uncertainty in their lives, they will continually flip-flop between supporting the change and hating the change. Realizing that this behavior is common can help to avoid confusion for human resource managers. Employees will go through culture shock as the two cultures collide, and they will tend to pull out their support and patience if they anticipate more changes to the culture than they can handle. Communication, again, is one way to avoid this problem. Finally, it is important to note that not all mergers and acquisitions will be positive events. Research has shown that about 50 percent of the acquisitions examined were clear failures.[25] Many of these ventures failed because the acquirers did not realize the effectiveness of the current management and structure of the

| EXHIBIT 11.7 | Typical Stages of the Merger Process |

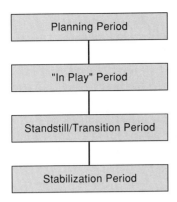

acquired firm and altered it upon arrival. Inevitably, the acquired staff were demoted or misplaced and eventually turned over. Ironically, the reason the acquirers wanted the acquired firm in the first place, the management team, may all have vanished.[26]

Joint Ventures

Joint ventures are another way in which organizations can become more productive. By using the strongest skills of each partner in the joint venture, the outcomes can be better than they would have been with each side working alone. One of the industries in which joint ventures frequently occur is in the automobile industry. There are so many, in fact, that one automobile trade journal gives subscribers a free wall chart that outlines the current joint ventures in the auto industry. One of the first was between General Motors and Toyota, who combined forces to build the Chevy Nova in Fremont, California. Their 50-50 joint venture, frequently called Nummi (New United Motor Manufacturing, Inc.), began producing Novas in 1984. The sales were slow, mainly due to the number of cars in the Chevy lineup that were so much like the Nova.[27]

Another car industry joint venture, the one between Mazda and Ford, produced what has been termed the first global car, the 1991 Ford Escort. The idea behind the global car is that it can be produced and sold in countries all over the world. The development of the Escort took over eight years. Its history is outlined in Exhibit 11.8. Throughout the planning process, Ford and Mazda had conflicts. One bone of contention was the fact that Mazda didn't feel that the U.S. supplier could provide quality materials and Ford didn't think it could keep up with the grueling pace of the Japanese manufacturing process. The successful, on-schedule prototypes made with over 50 percent U.S. parts in a Japanese plant helped to overcome those fears. Other debates ended in compromise. Engine noise, which Mazda wanted to reduce by retuning the engine and Ford wanted to quiet through other adjustments, was taken care of by retuning the engine, adding more insulation, and installing the motor on softer rubber mounts. While Ford doesn't expect to make money on the Escort, the company feels it has saved over $1 billion and has learned what it will take for Ford to be competitive in a world marketplace.[28]

· ·

EXHIBIT 11.8 The History of the Ford Escort

NOVEMBER 1981

Ford begins planning a 1991 replacement for its one-year-old Escort, its best-selling car. Initially, Ford plans to build a "world car" for the United States, Japanese, and European markets.

MAY 1983

Ford decides to scale back the program and cover only North America and Asia. Ford asks Mazda to take the lead development role and gives Mazda final say over the engineering decisions.

MARCH 1985

Ford belatedly decides that it will need the fuel-efficient Escort to help its domestic fleet meet U.S. fuel-economy regulations, but too many Japanese parts disqualify it from being classified as a domestic model. The decision is made to put a Ford engine in the new car.

LATE 1986

Due to the increasing value of the yen against the dollar, the project goes badly over budget. Ford decides it has to use more U.S. suppliers for the Escort.

OCTOBER 1987

The first prototypes of the Escort are built in a Mazda plant in Hiroshima, Japan. More than 50 percent of the car's parts are from Ford suppliers.

SEPTEMBER 1988

Ford and the United Auto Workers agree on a new labor pact covering the production of the Escort at Ford's Wayne, Michigan, stamping and body plant. The new agreement reduces the unskilled job classifications from 24 to 1.

FEBRUARY 1990

First production cars roll off the retooled Wayne assembly line.

APRIL 1990

Escorts go on sale in the United States.

· ·

Whenever two parties join forces, they both have a stake in the claim and what is good for one side may not necessarily be good for the other. GM faced that dilemma when Toyota asked if it could build Toyota trucks in the Nummi factory. There were large and certain payoffs for Toyota if GM said yes. If they could build truck in the United States, they could avoid the 25 percent tariff placed on imported trucks. The payoffs for GM were not so clear. Certainly the profits at the plant would increase and this would be good for GM. However, GM still competed with

FOCUS ON INTERNATIONAL ISSUES ·

Can American Managers Work for a Japanese Company?

In a global marketplace, American managers will be placed in foreign offices and asked to manage foreign workers. A global marketplace also means that foreign managers will be placed in U.S. companies and asked to manage American workers. While many say American managers are not ready for the challenge of an overseas assignment, just as many feel that the American workers, especially American managers, may not be ready for the challenge of working for a non-American manager.

Nationwide, more than 350,000 Americans work for Japanese companies. These workers, who hold positions from assembly line worker to executive, see many differences in working for a Japanese company rather than an American one. The line workers, now relabeled associates or team members, work in extremely clean, well-maintained, nonunion plants. They participate in morning exercises and wear company uniforms. They also participate in *kaizen*, a philosophy aimed at continually improving products and production. While these changes may seem drastic at first, they are understandable and acceptable, and workers are highly rewarded for doing so.

Managers who report to Japanese bosses face different changes. Striped of their decision-making authority and much of their individual responsibility, American managers now must embrace concepts such as *nemawashi* (consensus building) and *ringi* (shared decision making). Often these managers complain of a lack of feedback and of limited communication from their bosses. They also feel that they must fight to be heard by their Japanese colleagues. Some suggest that the problem is one of discrimination. Others suggest that it is simply an adjustment problem that will soon fade away. Whichever way the situation is viewed, American managers working for Japanese firms face some rough roads ahead.

SOURCE: Adapted from Thomas O'Boyle, "Under Japanese Bosses, Americans Find Work Both Better and Worse," *Wall Street Journal*, November 26, 1991, p. A1+.

Toyota in the marketplace, and allowing Toyota to have an even less expensive truck available to the U.S. consumers was not good business for GM.[29]

Japan is not the only country with which joint ventures have been popular. In 1989, there were 900 joint ventures deals with Hungary. This was up from 1 in 1981. Some of the biggest were with GE who paid $150 million for 50.1 percent of Tungsram, a Hungarian light bulb manufacturer, and Guardian Industries is spending $110 million in a joint venture to convert an obsolete glass plant. Hungary is selected frequently due to a lower wage base and availability of labor. For example, Schwinn Bicycle Company is making bikes in a joint venture with Csepel, a heavy-industry complex near Budapest. Schwinn-Csepel workers must wear badges that have both the U.S. and the Hungarian flags and follow different work procedures than the over ten thousand state workers all around them. The benefit to the worker is 25 percent more pay. It is difficult to even begin to imagine the problems human resource managers would face if the same production techniques were used on U.S. soil.[30]

Globalization

A global economy has been widely discussed since Europe unveiled its European Economic Community idea due to be a reality in 1992. When the remaining barriers between member states are removed, Europe will be a large and formidable marketplace competitor. To compete at this level, U.S. firms are looking to globalize.

The term *globalization* raises many questions in the minds of American businesspeople. What exactly is globalization? Does it mean that a certain percent of sales, say 25 percent, must take place overseas? Does it mean that top management must

....

| EXHIBIT 11.9 | Results of a CEO Survey on Globalization

WHY GO GLOBAL?

	UNITED STATES	EUROPE	JAPAN	PACIFIC RIM
Increase revenue	39%	52%	58%	46%
Increase profitability	27%	53%	53%	40%
Achieve technological leadership	20%	30%	44%	34%
Diversify into new business	23%	35%	53%	27%
Lower business costs	19%	39%	55%	34%
Improve product quality	19%	35%	34%	37%

HOW DO YOU PLAN TO DO IT?

	UNITED STATES	EUROPE	JAPAN	PACIFIC RIM
Open a new plant abroad	20%	36%	42%	25%
Launch new products abroad	49%	50%	42%	38%
Expand into new foreign markets	60%	60%	58%	65%
Roll out new technology abroad	28%	23%	37%	20%
Form new strategic alliances	44%	48%	60%	43%

HOW MUCH GLOBAL (WORLDLY) EXPERIENCE DO YOUR CEO'S HAVE?

	UNITED STATES	EUROPE	JAPAN	PACIFIC RIM
No foreign experience	14%	3.1%	1.1%	2.6%
Travel abroad only once or twice a year	23%	1.0%	15%	18%

....

have experience in a variety of countries? Or is it more of a global perspective, in which top officials scan the entire world before making decisions?[31] It is all of these, and more.

Globalization requires having global standards for quality, pricing, service, and design.[32] Ford's Escort was one of the first American products to be built on a global scale. But globalization takes more than just setting and adhering to standards, it also requires global leadership. This means that Americans will have to live and work overseas. Managers without international managing experience will not climb high in the ranks in a true global economy. However, in past years, an overseas stint meant a slow-down in a manager's career path, so many avoided it. For this reason, many U.S. firms may not be ready for a global economy.[33]

One company that is ready is General Electric. GE sold its consumer electronics business in Europe to Thompson SA of France and then bought Thompson's medical equipment business, Thompson CGR, in an effort to strengthen its own medical unit. CGR and GE Medical Systems Asia give GE a global organization that can

EXHIBIT 11.9 continued

Travel abroad more than twice a year	56%	80%	78%	75%
Studied abroad	16%	28%	13%	54%
Worked abroad	32%	47%	19%	46%
Managed a business abroad for current company	16%	37%	5.3%	21%
Firm has foreign directors	21%	34%	3.1%	41%

ON WHICH COUNTRY(IES) ARE YOU CONCENTRATING YOUR GLOBAL EFFORTS?

COUNTRY	TOTAL PERCENTAGE WHO MENTIONED IT
Spain	64
West Germany	62
France	60
Britain	59
Italy	55
Netherlands	42
Portugal	41
Belgium	38
Ireland	27
Non-EC Europe	27
Greece	21
Denmark	19
Luxembourg	19

effectively compete with Siemens, Phillips, and Toshiba in the world market for X-ray, CAT scan, magnetic resonance, and other medical equipment. Sales outside the United States for GE Medical Systems rose from just 13 percent in 1985 to over 45 percent in 1988. John Trani, the GE executive who runs the outfit is also using a global leadership style. He has developed a loose and flexible organization with no rigid chain of command. He also has formed leadership groups with managers from three continents to work toward shortening the product development cycle and other major global issues.[34]

Like GE, other firms have decided that globalization is the way to go. However, not all firms are so quick to follow. Some firms foresee a couple of hitches. First executives are not sure exactly how to go about the business of globalization, and second, they are not truly sure of the benefits of globalization. Exhibit 11.9 presents the results of a survey of 433 CEOs in the United States, Europe, Japan, and the Pacific Rim about their views on globalization. Among some of the more interesting findings, these figures indicate that Pacific Rim CEOs are the most worldly, having had many managers work and study abroad. Also of interest in these figures is the rather obvious closed nature of Japan with respect to foreign directors. Only 3.1 percent of those surveyed indicated that there were foreign directors of their firms. The United States, who placed second lowest, had 21 percent.

Globalization is definitely a strategic business decision, one that can and will be made by more and more companies as entry into other areas of the world becomes increasingly easier. What does it mean to the human resource department if an organization decides to go global? The ramifications seem endless. For one thing, training will be affected. Not only will it be important to train American employees who plan to go overseas in the language of the country into which they will be placed, but it will also be just as important to inform them of the ways of the culture of the country. Being literate in both word and deed will make the transition easier and more positive. What about training needs of overseas employees coming to America to work? The organizational culture and jargon must be taught to the new employees in a way that they will understand, but that is not demeaning. Further, socialization programs must be in place to ensure a smooth transition for these new employees.

Aside from training issues, human resource professionals will face many other problems. What about performance appraisals, reward programs, and compensation? Many of these functions have been so Americanized that they will not be effective with foreign workers. In Japan, telling one worker that she or he is doing better than the rest and rewarding that worker for doing so is not appropriate. Japanese workers want to fit in and be like the rest. They do not want to be recognized. Recognizing one worker in a group may cause work group problems and conflict resolution techniques may be needed. However, would it be wise to use the American models such as confronting one another and working out the problem? Probably not. This is not appropriate behavior in many foreign cultures. What about wages? Do you pay these new workers what their counterparts in the country from which they came would make, or do you pay them American wages? What if they are transferred back? Do they go back to their home country's pay base? The list of problems goes on and on. Suffice it to say, that globalization will have a significant impact on the human resource function of any organization that selects a globalization strategy.

Measuring Productivity

The techniques for measuring productivity are as varied as the industries in which the measurements are taking place. Traditional techniques were developed to measure assembly line productivity. These measures are based upon tracking output in units or dollars per inputs usually in the form of man-hours. These types of figures are still used in many production-oriented firms today. For example, the average number of man-hours required to produce one car in a European plant is 35.5 hours; in an American plant it is 24.9 hours; and in a Japanese plant it is 16.8 hours.[35] But what do these figures actually mean? Researchers at MIT suggest that each worker in these car plants can be viewed in terms of his or her "value added." In the car plants in Japan, it is difficult to find any worker than cannot be defined as adding value. However, in the European plants, these researchers found that you stumble over many people who not only have no added value, but their sole purpose for being there is to correct mistakes that should have never been made in the first place.[36]

EXHIBIT 11.10 Ways of Measuring Productivity

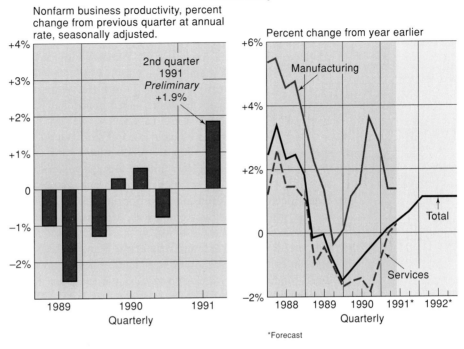

Productivity

Nonfarm business productivity, percent change from previous quarter at annual rate, seasonally adjusted.

2nd quarter 1991 *Preliminary* +1.9%

Percent change from year earlier

*Forecast

Exhibit 11.10 is a graphic representation of another traditional way to measure productivity—percent of change from a previous time period. As can be seen in these graphs, productivity is frequently measured quarterly.

In the service and professional areas, traditional productivity measures have fallen short. It is difficult, if not impossible, to measure some types of activities with respect to output per input. When the traditional measures are used in nonproduction areas, great productivity numbers may not result in good outcomes. One example of this was found at Motorola. Recruiters for Motorola were assigned the goal of spending less per hire each year as a measure of productivity. Each year productivity rose. Things should have been good, but they were not. The quality of the new hires began to decrease. Obviously, if you spend only a few dollars to select employees, the new hires selected may not be qualified or effective workers. By cutting costs in this way, the thoroughness of the screening process will deteriorate. To solve this problem, Motorola changed its policy. It now measures recruitment productivity by how well its recruits do at Motorola after being hired. For example, recruiters are measured on items such as how well qualified the person was for the job, and if the salary was determined correctly by whether or not the new hire leaves soon after employment for a higher paying job. Under the new productivity measures, price per recruit has risen, but so has the quality of the recruits.[37]

Other industries also have developed unique ways to measure productivity in nonproduction areas. Olsten, a temporary help agency and Avis, a car rental agency, routinely survey customers to help determine employee productivity. Results of the surveys can be used in a variety of ways. For example, one travel company uses the results to help show employees how to be more aware of customers' individual needs and desires. They have found that by treating each customer like an individual, return business (one measure of productivity) has improved. In the hotel business, similar techniques are used. It is almost impossible to stay overnight in a hotel and not see some type of customer response card asking for a rating of the hotel at some point in your stay. Many of the larger hotel chains will ask you upon checkout if you have completed a response card. Other chains leave them in your room, many personalized with the name of the person who cleaned the room for you that day. In addition to customer input, Quality Inns tracks the number of minutes it takes to clean a room, how many meals are served in an hour, and how frequently a booking agent can turn a call into a reservation.[38]

Whatever method is used, it is important that the results are used to do what they are intended to do—improve productivity. After realizing that other productivity measures, besides the recruitment area, were causing problems down the line, Motorola revamped its entire productivity measurement scheme. Motorola now defines productivity in terms of the opportunity to make mistakes. Most mistakes made are not made due to poor employees. Most mistakes are made because of the way people are told to do their job. Over the years, procedures and policies have become antiquated, complicated, and redundant. Managers at Motorola strive to locate poor procedures and replace them with more efficient ones. This new perspective has saved Motorola both time and money. For example, due to changes in the finance department, the company can now close its books at the end of a month in four days instead of eight. This provides a savings of 576,000 man-hours, worth about $20 million.[39]

Ways to Increase Productivity

Two major components influence whether or not an employee is productive: ability and attitude. Ability is simply whether or not the person is able to perform the job. Ability is influenced by whether or not the person has the training, education, skills, tools, or environment necessary to perform the job. Attitude, on the other hand, refers to whether or not the person *wants* to perform the job. Attitude is influenced by the level of motivation, satisfaction, and commitment the employee has about the job to be performed. Organizations have a great deal of control over both of these areas. Organizations who provide well-developed training and development programs, educational reimbursement plans, and state-of-the-art equipment can expect employees with extremely high ability. Likewise, organizations with strong personnel policies with respect to compensation, rewards, promotions, and career development will usually have employees with positive attitudes toward their job and the company. The following sections examine more closely the options organizations have with respect to increasing employees' abilities and attitudes.

Ability

In order to have employees who are able to perform their jobs effectively, organizations must provide them with the knowledge, skills, and abilities needed to perform the job. They must also be sure to provide a work environment that is conducive to performing well. This means that the tools and equipment that employees must have to succeed are provided. Furthermore, the organization's environment or culture also must be designed to promote high-quality performance. To achieve these goals, many organizations use a variety of techniques. Let's look first at training, development, and education of the work force.

The type of training and development required by lower- and higher-level employees differs. At the lower level, employees generally are provided with specific training that is designed to make them more productive on the job immediately. Higher-level employees receive this type of training, but they also receive more developmental types of training. Developmental training is designed to help the employee now, as well as in the future, by readying them for assignments with more and more responsibility. However, in recent years, it has become more and more obvious that firms who have a large number of lower-level employees, such as the hospitality and fast-food industries, may need to begin developing them as well as training them.

In the past, employees in the fast-food and hospitality industries were treated in the same manner as equipment was treated. They were replaceable. The jobs were designed to be "idiot-proof" so that they could be performed by any person who walked in off the street. However, due to the demographic changes in the marketplace, the increasing costs of turnover, and the ever increasing demand for quality service, this is no longer feasible. Organizations are quickly realizing that the management techniques used in the higher-levels may be applicable at the lower-levels as well.[40]

MMI Hotel Group, which owns Holiday Inns and Embassy Suites, has begun sending housekeepers and desk clerks to seminars around the country. Often, the employee will be exposed to his or her first airplane flight and hotel stay. This may also be the first time that the employee attends a large evening dinner party in which he or she is not serving. The company feels this type of training is essential for their employees because it is difficult for employees to understand quality service if they have never been on the receiving end.[41]

Vermont Heating and Ventilation, a winner of the Labor Department's LIFT (Labor Investing for Tomorrow) program, has embraced the idea of training and developing its people at all levels. The firm of only 250 people spends 10 percent of its gross revenue on training and educational programs. It is not unusual to see employees rise through the ranks at VHV. The vice-president of administration is one example. She began at the company as a journeyman sheetmetal worker and credits the educational focus of the organization with her ability to rise through the ranks.[42]

Not all training and educational programs need to be sponsored by the firm. Some innovative firms are finding ways to support education opportunities already available to the employees. For example, a Sonic drive-in manager in Tucson, Arizona, provides high-school-aged employees a retroactive bonus of 15 cents an hour if they maintain a 2.5 grade-point average for a semester. If the employee maintains a 3.0 grade-point average or better, the bonus is increased to 25 cents an hour.[43]

Training and development for managers is also on the rise. The American Society for Training and Development (ASTD) estimated that 60 percent of the nation's largest companies now offer leadership training. ASTD also noted that one-third of the companies include nonsupervisors in their programs. For example, Eastman Kodak trains shop-level workers to develop supportive and coaching skills, middle-level managers learn how to empower their workers, and high-level managers engage in "adventure learning," tasking on tough outdoor activities to explore how to perform under pressure or as part of a team.[44]

One specific type of outdoor adventure training was invented by the Japanese and recently exported to the United States—Hell Camp. Hell Camp is a 13-day program designed to develop management potential. Hell Camp is mandatory for any Japanese manager who wants to make it to the top. The two weeks include exercises such as singing solo in shopping malls, single-file, timed marches around the camp, and memorization of pages of nonsensical speeches. As one might expect, enrollment in the American version has been extremely low.[45]

To export this concept to the United States, the Japanese hired three Americans to go to Japan to be trained as instructors for the U.S. Hell Camp. However, the three quit soon after realizing that the concept would never catch on in the United States. Three new recruits were then hired to take their place. These three men wanted to change the program to be more in line with American values and expectations. The director of the camp refused and decreed that all American participants would memorize the same songs and speeches the Japanese participants did, regardless of how incomprehensible or inappropriate the English translations were. Some accommodations were made though. For example, all participants begin the two weeks with a shirt full of ribbons. As they successfully participate in the classes and exercises, the ribbons are removed. The Japanese participants' badges are called ribbons of shame, while the American participants wear ribbons of challenge. While the concept of Japanese Hell Camp may not ever be fully accepted by the American people, the participants do learn teamwork, one of the cornerstones of Japanese productivity.[46]

Organizations are also responsible for developing an environment that is conducive to high performance. Recent reports indicate that organizations may not be doing such a good job at this. Results from a two year study of over 250 organizations revealed that seven out of every ten employees are hesitant to speak up at work because they fear the repercussions. This means that a lot of good ideas are dying because of fear. This can only hurt a firm's productivity. While there is no easy solution to solving this problem, the researcher suggested that companies emphasize empowering the workforce by providing them with responsibility for tasks and giving them the authority to carry them out.[47]

Another aspect of the work environment is the job itself. Many of the elements of job design that were covered in Chapter 8 are crucial to developing a quality-based work environment. Offering flextime to employees who have obligations before or after work may help them to relax and concentrate on their work instead of having to worry about how they will meet their commitments. Sometimes it takes an act of nature to make organizations realize that flexible schedules are necessary. For example, after the 1989 earthquake in San Francisco, many firms *had* to go to a flextime schedule because the major commuting thoroughfares were closed. Some firms allowed employees to work at branch offices outside of San Francisco, while other firms allowed employees to work from computers in their homes.[48]

Working at home via computer, or telecommuting, is beginning to catch on as another way in which employers can provide a productivity-oriented work environment for employees. American Express recently ran a pilot test with a few of its travel agents. These agents, working at home, take client calls directly from the firm's Business Travel Center switchboard. They then book the necessary reservations for the client using their own computers, which are linked to modems at the office. Clients are unaware that the agent is working from home. There is one added twist to this electronic set-up. Back at the office, managers can monitor the agents by listening to their calls or by following their computer modems as the agents are speaking to clients. There are some rules that apply to the program. For example, parents with small children at home are not allowed to work from their homes. If they choose this option, they must make child-care arrangements in order to qualify.[49]

What American Express and other companies who are beginning to explore this technological opportunity are finding is that telecommuting workers who used to have long commutes are becoming much more productive employees. Commuting a long distance is an emotional and mental drain. A worker who has been sitting behind a steering wheel and fighting the traffic for over an hour simply cannot be in the same frame of mind as the person who only had to walk to the den. In the future, technological advances may provide other opportunities for organizations to provide a better working environment for their employees.

Attitude

Employee attitudes have a crucial effect on any firm's bottom line. An employee's attitude determines whether or not a defective part gets placed into a product, whether or not the customer continues to patronize the firm, and whether or not the firm is productive. Employees who are burned out, turned off, cynical, demoralized, or any combination of these will fail to buy into the spirit of the firm. And their bad attitudes are infectious.

Recent surveys have found that cynicism is running high in the American workplace. Cynical employees distrust their bosses. This distrust is reflected in their work. Cynical employees are less productive, less efficient, and less willing to accept change. The problem lies not only with the worker, however. Cynical bosses who treat employees without dignity are also to blame.[50]

Companies who have realized the impact cynicism and other negative attitudes held by employees have on the bottom line have taken steps to combat it. The most useful strategy is information. Anita Roddick, founder and managing director of The Body Shop, feels the best way to combat cynicism is with information. She bombards her staff with newsletters, videos, brochures, posters, and training programs. The goal is to teach employees that business does not have to be boring. She spends a lot of her time developing stories and articles for the newsletters, which are not just ordinary newsletters. Much of the newsletter is devoted to information about projects to save the environment or anthropological tidbits. Nor are the training programs ordinary. For example, clerks who sell the products participate in sessions that explain how to use the product, not how to sell it. The idea behind this type of training is that if the employees understand the products' benefits and are informed about them, they will be better salespeople.[51]

Other companies have decided to combat poor attitudes in workers with humor. Kodak recently established a humor task force that was charged with building a humor room at corporate headquarters when it was decided that the company needed to lighten up. It seems to be working. When Kodak's downsizing announcement coincided with the release of the movie "Honey I Shrunk the Kids," ingenious Kodak employees circulated a spoof memo entitled "Honey I Shrunk the Company." Humor can also be big business. Consulting firms that specialize in humor have been doing a brisk business by teaching firms to give up the old notion that humor is dependent upon putting someone else down. Instead, the focus is on teaching the firm to laugh at itself.[52] Exhibit 11.11 outlines some helpful hints for how one can go about having fun at work.

EXHIBIT 11.11 How to Start Having Fun at Work

1. Get to know your people. Then you'll understand what will be fun for them.
2. Acknowledge people's help. Write someone a personal letter of thanks for exceptional work performance. Then go by and shake his or her hand.
3. Think of someone you really respect, but who may not know it. Tell the person.
4. Make a joke about yourself. Tell someone one of the most embarrassing things that ever happened to you.
5. Pull a practical joke on someone who can take it.
6. Send someone a gift when he or she has done something exceptional for you or your organization.
7. Pick one or two people to "grow." Make them your special projects and help them in any way you can. (You do not need to tell them you are doing this.)
8. Create a social committee to organize events. Get actively involved in this committee.
9. Tell everyone coming to your next meeting to bring their best joke or work-related story with them to tell everyone at the meeting. (If you want, you could judge the best one and give that person a prize.)
10. Try this for a prize: When someone does a particularly great job of something, do his or her job for a day.
11. Throw a party for the people you work with, or throw a party for your customers and clients.
12. Get everyone involved in skits they make up about their strengths and their weaknesses at work.
13. Ask a customer, coworker, or supervisor to help you learn something new.
14. Make a list of three things you will do tomorrow to make your work more fun. Do them.
15. Start a new contest at work that is tied to people's performance. You could even create a contest just for yourself. If you are successful at meeting your goal, do something special for yourself.

Some employees find that laughter in the workplace is motivating. Monsanto researchers, who were taught to press a nickel to their foreheads and then drop it in a cup, reported a 50 percent surge in creativity after taking part in the exercise.[53] Other firms have found different ways to motivate employees. Jan Carlzon, president and CEO of Scandinavian Airlines, frequently tells his staff that there are two factors that motivate people: fear and love. He feels that managers who manage by fear will have employees who are unable to work up to their potential. However, managers who manage by love, trust, respect, and faith will manage people who will behave up to their capabilities.[54]

Carlzon is not alone in his feelings. Other managers in the service business also reported that management cannot provide quality customer service unless it first truly respects the employees.[55] The problem is that workers don't feel that managers are treating them with respect. Results from a survey that asked workers how well they were treated by their employers revealed that workers were not happy with the lack of respect they received from their supervisors. They felt that the communication they received from their boss was not honest and they felt as though the company was hiding things from them.[56] In a separate study, 95 percent of the workers polled reported that they could be more productive, but they were not pushed or rewarded to do so. Nearly two-thirds of the workers indicated that their employers failed to use their ideas at least half of the time they requested them.[57]

One company that is truly proving that respected employees can be productive and motivated, even when given little else, is Harbor Sweets. Harbor Sweets pays five dollars an hour, does not pay for medical or any other type of insurance, provides no pension plan, no 401(k) plan, and no sick days. It also lays off about 60 percent of the work force after the Christmas rush is over. How can a company with so little to offer find a qualified work force to support its business? The answer is to hire well-educated and responsible women who don't demand benefits because they are covered by their husbands' benefits packages, and who don't require supervision, because their work ethics take care of that, and who don't care if there is no work for months. It turns out that Harbor Sweets offers something that was more important to the workers than anything money could buy—it offered a substitute family for all of the women in the area whose real family had grown up and moved away. It offered a sense of purpose. Obviously, Harbor Sweets is in a unique position and has capitalized upon it.[58]

Providing rewards to employees is often used as a motivation technique. Some of the more commonly used methods include one time monetary rewards, pay raises, appreciation awards, stock options, or promotions. Because each person is different, what motivates one employee may not be an effective carrot to dangle in front of another. For example, pay is a strong motivating factor for some employees, especially when performance is tied to pay. Even Japanese firms who have traditionally tied pay to seniority and tenure have began tying to productivity in an effort to further increase employee performance. Their reasoning for the change was simple—problems arise when there is no difference in the raises and salaries for those people who work hard and those who don't.[59] American Airlines may agree with this philosophy, because they too announced a pay-for-performance policy. The interesting part of this announcement is that the Transport Workers Union agreed to it. The American ground crew, mechanics, and baggage handlers agreed to a contract in which they could earn pay increases for effective performance. This shatters the long time held union belief that pay is based on seniority, not performance.[60]

Recognition is also used as a motivational tool, it and can be very effective for some employees. For example, the Colgate-Palmolive Company sponsors a "You Can Make a Difference Award" where winning employees receive $3,500 in stock, a gold medal, an embroidered blazer, and an introduction at the annual meeting. One employee was rewarded for boosting toothpaste output by 50 percent, saving the company $160,000 on equipment. Similar programs are in effect at American Express where 43 employees, who are named "Great Performers," can receive up to $4,800 worth of travelers checks, a platinum pin, or other awards.[61]

The total cash outlay for firms who used monetary incentives are adding up. In 1988, it was estimated that firms spent over $2.1 billion on recognition programs. This is more than triple the figure reported in 1987.[62] Some firms are responsible for more than their share of these figures. For example, Union National Bank of Little Rock, Arkansas, paid employees $1 million in incentives in 1985. The payroll at that time was only $9 million. The incentives were used to increase productivity from 200 to 300 percent.[63]

Not all recognition awards have to be monetary. Harry Seifert, CEO of Winter Gardens Salad Company, uses a rubber stamp and makes notes in the margins of reports he receives from his employees to let them know that their work was appreciated. Since he has begun using the stamp he has noticed that the quality of the reports has increased.[64] Other nonmonetary incentives include refrigerators, projection television sets, beach headrests, steak knives, levitating globes, talking crystal

HR CHALLENGES •

Union Enforced Quality

On October 4, 1991, United Auto Workers in the Saturn plant in Spring Hill, Tennessee, donned black and orange arm bands and participated in a work slow down. While it may look like yet another labor problem, it really isn't. It is a management problem. What were the employees after? They wanted management to stop increasing output, because the speedup was causing quality to decrease. The union leader explained that the workers were not going to sacrifice quality to increase productivity, because the workers knew, and management temporarily forgot, that their future depended on making a high-quality product. Management conceded that the union was absolutely right. The workers concern for quality reinforced the urgency of getting the quality problems fixed, and fixed fast.

The reason management bumped up the total cars produced from 700 to 900 cars a day is simple: Consumers consider Saturns to be good cars and want to buy them. Saturns rank sixth in customer satisfaction—just below cars like Lincoln and Mercedes-Benz, which cost three times as much. Saturn owners recommend their cars to more people than any other owners of any other brand. However, it may be difficult to get a Saturn. In 1991, only 50,000 Saturns were built, one-third of the projected 240,000 cars.

However, as the workers realized, just turning up the speed is not the answer. The Saturn plant is so well tuned that problems in production will lead to a complete shut down in the assembly area in just six minutes. The faster the lines go, the greater chance of a problem. The greater chance of a problem, the less cars are actually produced. However with GM's car sales slumping and Saturn being one of the few bright spots on the horizon, the pressure is on the workers in Spring Hill, Tennessee.

SOURCE: David Woodruff, "At Saturn, What Workers Want Is . . . Fewer Defects," *Business Week*, December 2, 1991, pp. 117–118.

---

balls, chocolate bars with corporate logos, and relaxation tapes with sounds of birds and tropical rain forests. One of the most unique incentives a company can provide their employees is a "congratulator." A congratulator is a device that is placed on an employee's shoulder and when an attached string is pulled, a wooden hand pats him or her on the back. This way the employee can get recognition anytime he or she desires.[65] Some firms have even combined incentives with a corporate message by using T-shirts and mugs to advertise a new procedure the employees should follow. Drawing attention to the new policy through rewards and perks is less threatening to the employee than having the boss keep reminding the employees about it.[66]

Even though incentives seem to be a useful technique for motivating workers, they can sometimes backfire. As long as companies have prizes to give to workers, they will play along and be productive. However, when the prizes run out, so does the motivation. Some managers argue that incentive plans are short-ranged and even confusing to employees. For example, companies who want to place service first have a difficult time convincing employees of their goal when they reward employees for working faster and quicker. A California unit of GTE ran into this problem. After conducting a survey of service representatives, they found that employees thought speed came before service. To change this attitude, GTE sent all of the service representatives who wanted to attend to a weekend seminar. Employees who participated received overtime pay. The seminar was designed to show employees that when they pick up the phone, they "own the problem" and should do everything in their power to fix it, regardless of the time it takes to do so. However, when the workers returned to work, the message from the seminar got muddied. While they now realized that they owned the problem, they were confused by GTE's continual emphasis on speed, which included timing how long workers talk to each caller. Speed and "owning the problem" were incompatible.[67]

One final technique that some companies use to motivate employees is career path planning. This concept is becoming increasingly important as the available number of paths up the corporate management ladder begin to decrease due to downsizing and an abundance of middle-aged employees jockeying for one or two positions held by people very similar to themselves in age. National Semiconductor found an innovative way to address their decreasing number of management career paths. They designed career paths for individual contributors that are comparable to management paths and are just as rewarding in terms of such factors as decision making, influence, compensation, and responsibility. The design of these paths are good for both the employee and the company because they allow an individual to move from an individual contributor role to a management role, and back to an individual contributor role as the qualifications of the employee and needs of the firm change. Because the requirements for movement are clearly explained, employees take control over their own career development. As the individual needs of an employee change, he or she can decide to move into a new position in order to remain motivated and productive.[68]

Brooklyn Union Gas is another company that is finding creative ways to use career paths to keep its employees motivated. This company has found that many strong sales people would be content to stay in sales throughout their careers, but in order to advance they must move into management. To keep experienced salespeople in the sales area where they can be the most productive, Brooklyn Union Gas has developed account manager positions. In these positions, salespeople are placed in charge of up to 100 of the company's 2,000 largest clients. These clients, who before had to deal with several different sales representatives, now deal exclusively with the account manager. Besides having more prestige, the new positions allow the account managers to command a higher salary base and commissions, depending on how business expands with their clients.[69]

As previously mentioned, there is no one technique that can be used to improve employees' attitudes across the board. Instead, a combination of motivational tools should be used. Also, it is important to remember that the tools must be consistent with the corporation's culture in order for them to be effective. Exhibit 11.12 outlines a list of suggestions for human resource managers who are trying to find out what it takes to motivate employees to be productive.

INVOLVEMENT

Until recently, employee involvement (EI) was largely a Utopian ideal shared by only a few true believers. However, today it is a bona fide movement with an extremely large following. Strangely enough, EI has drawn unlikely bedfellows from camps that are usually diametrically opposed to one another's views: management and unions. EI has been openly welcomed by manufacturing and service industry employees and managers alike as a way to improve commitment, quality, and productivity in the workplace. Exhibit 11.13 shows a symbol that is now found in all Ford warranty packets in the glove compartments of new cars.

···

EXHIBIT 11.12 Motivation Tips for Human Resource Managers

1. Select the best. Motivation comes from within an individual. Therefore, if you hire only the people who have the potential to be motivated, half of the battle is won.
2. Use the Pygmalion effect. If you truly believe in your employees, they will believe in themselves. Take the time to psychologically invest in your employees.
3. Track success. Provide challenging goals with which employees agree and compare their performance regularly to these goals. Make sure to do this in a manner that is not critical or demeaning.
4. Recognize contributions. Provide public recognition for employees who have performed well. Be sure to be consistent about when the rewards are provided. For example, select an employee of the week and announce his or her name at a weekly meeting.
5. Provide incentives and rewards. Remember that the psychological reward of the incentive is often greater than the monetary reward. Also, incentives can be a useful motivator in the short term.
6. Empower employees. Make employees responsible for the company's product or service. Listen to what they have to say and use their ideas.
7. Enhance career development. Use training and development as a tool to ready employees for the next step in their career paths. Invest in your employees just as you would invest in new equipment.

···

What Is Employee Involvement?

Employee involvement is a series of strategies firms can adopt to allow workers more responsibility and accountability for preparing a product or offering a service. The term itself can refer to a wide range of practices, from simply soliciting employees' work-improvement ideas in small group meetings with front-line workers to forming self-managed work teams of workers who are given total control over their jobs and working environment. Also included in the concept of EI is the idea that unions or other worker-represented groups should have the power to participate in the plant- and company-level decision-making process.[70]

EI is based on two principles that managers have been familiar with for many years. The first is that people tend to support what they helped to create. For example, someone who is actively involved in developing a new procedure for handling the return procedures for a product is more likely to help ensure that the new procedure is carried out correctly, make sure that it really does work, and to sell it to their friends and coworkers. The second principle underlying EI is the idea that people who know most about the inner functioning of an operation are those who actually perform the work. Asking for information and participation of the people actually performing the job can provide insights not available from managers or consultants.[71]

Benefits of Employee Involvement

As more and more firms have begun to implement EI techniques, the benefits of doing so have began to surface. Below are a list of just some of the possible positive repercussions of using EI in an organization.

1. EI provides a greater understanding and acceptance of decisions by subordinates because the subordinates are involved in making those decisions.

EXHIBIT 11.13   Evidence of Employee Involvement at Ford

2. Similarly, employees who have a say in the decision are more committed to implementing it.
3. Involving employees in the decision making and planning practices of the organization provides a greater understanding of the organization's objectives and improves commitment to achieving these objectives.
4. EI provides greater fulfillment of psychological needs, and therefore it provides greater employee satisfaction.
5. EI can capitalize on the increased social pressure other members will place on fellow workers to comply with the decisions the group made as a whole.
6. EI provides a greater team and organizational identity, which is shown through greater cooperation and coordination among members at all levels.
7. When conflict does arise under EI situations, the people involved are better able to constructively deal with it.
8. EI produces better decisions.[72]

Communication and Involvement

One of the key components of successfully implementing EI is open and truthful communication among and between employees at all levels in the organization. Various techniques can be used to open the lines of communication in an organization. Some techniques are more appropriate for service firms, while others are more useful in manufacturing situations. Further, the usefulness of some techniques depends upon the level in the organization from which the employees are drawn.

For example, James Orr, CEO of UNUM Corporation, invites his 5,500 employees at corporate headquarters and any other offices in the United States or England who have terminals to "talk" with him via electronic mail. Every night he sits down and "reads" his mail. He has been known to respond to a letter with a personal phone call the following day. Some major changes have resulted from his communications with employees. For example, he has begun a company program to subsidize employee child-care expenses because he became aware of the needs of his employees espoused through the e-mail connection.[73]

Managers have tried other ways to reach employees and to be reached by them. One of the most easily installed, yet frequently beneficial ways to reach employees is through an open-door policy. Top managers, who normally have no time in a day to see the average worker schedule time specifically for conversations with employees. Some managers prefer to hold the meetings in their offices, while others select more neutral locations. Palmer Reynolds, CEO of Phoenix Textile Corporation, began hosting monthly "breakfasts with the president." She invites five different employees, one from each department, to join her each month at a local restaurant. She learned that her assumption that employees were communicating well was merely a perception. For example, at a recent breakfast, sales and production realized that they were both under quota systems. This realization, which came from a breakfast discussion, ended a long-time tug-of-war relationship and started a cooperative one.[74]

Advancements in technology have presented managers with a variety of communication tools from which to choose. Techniques such as voice mail and video-conferencing, which have only been available in recent years, have begun to revolutionize the business of communicating in the workplace.[75] Mike Walsh of Union Pacific uses both video tapes and video-conferencing to reach his employees. Important video-conferences are video-taped and edited copies of the five-and-a-half-hour meetings are sent directly to employees' homes.[76]

While CEOs suggest that video-conferencing is no substitute for face-to-face communication, they feel it has its benefits. Robert Horton, CEO of British Petroleum, noted that he will be old and gray before he reaches, in person, the number of people he can reach through video-conferencing. Other benefits he noted included the fact that video-conferencing is very efficient for business meetings. The travel costs it takes to get key players in one location for a meeting is completely cut. Video conferencing saves time, money, and executives' health because too much travel reduces one's stamina and lowers defenses, which frequently leads to illness.[77]

Less technical ways to communicate with employees exist as well. One frequently used method for getting a pulse on the workplace is simply by asking. Employees can be polled in several ways. Many firms use attitude surveys, which request employee opinions on topics such as benefits and compensation to menu suggestions for the cafeteria. Other ways to gather employee input is to interview them. Firms can either hire consultants to perform the interviews or use employees who have been trained in interviewing techniques to collect the information. While this is more formal, it has been found to be one way to generate a great deal of information in a limited amount of time.[78]

When managers are asked by their supervisors to communicate with lower-level employees, the response is generally, "But I *already* do that." The problem is that managers who think they may be talking and listening with their employees in reality are not. Managers who fall into this category are often referred to as "deaf, dumb, and blind." It's not that deaf managers cannot hear, it's that they don't take the time to listen. It's not that dumb managers cannot speak, it's that they have been taught to read from scripts and teleprompters and not to talk to employees. It's not that blind managers cannot see, it's just that they limit their reading to electronic mail and spreadsheets.

Many of these problems are due to the environment in which the managers work. For example, if a manager's schedule is planned for him or her and booked three weeks in advance, he or she literally doesn't have the time to talk with employees, unless it is scheduled into the calendar.[79] However, some managers have personalities that make them poor communicators. Several of these personalities are described in Exhibit 11.14. As you read them ask yourself if you fall into one of these categories or if you have ever worked for one of these managers.

Employees report that the message they receive from their managers is, "I want to hear what you have to say, but give it to me and let's get on with things." This rushed or hurried approach does not make employees feel that what they have to say is important. It makes them feel that they are simply being listened to because their supervisors were *told* to listen to them. The only way communication will be effective is if the employees feel that the managers care about what they have to say and if managers care about the employees as people and not just as employees.[80]

Techniques for Employee Involvement

Because communication is at the heart of all employee involvement efforts, managers can employ various ways to talk with and listen to their employees. Several different EI techniques, which are becoming increasingly popular in the American workplace, are described in the following sections.

Empowering

Whether the concept of empowering employees is real or rhetoric has been a hot topic for debate. People on one side of the argument suggest that many employers are simply talking about empowering their employees and doing very little to make it happen. People on the other side of the argument are actually taking steps to empower their employees. These steps generally include pushing decision making down to the lowest level in the organization to the most qualified people who can make the decision. Organizations who employ empowering techniques also try to applaud both the successful and unsuccessful risk-taking behavior of employees. These firms take on the attitude that each failure is a learning experience and more is learned by failing than by not doing anything at all. Also, managers in empowered organizations urge employees to find their own ways to boost productivity.[81] These managers ask employees to question silly rules and find better ways to do things, and then they allow the employee to use the new procedures.[82]

Essentially, empowerment means that management vests decision making or approval authority in employees instead of keeping it for themselves. Empowerment has become important for several reasons. First, globalization and competition have increased. This increased competition requires more and more innovation, which requires more freedom for the innovators. Finally, the increased competition has forced American businesses to be more productive than ever before.[83] However, before empowerment will work, several conditions, outlined in Exhibit 11.15 must be present. Without these, empowerment attempts will fail.

For the managers who have empowered employees, the payoffs have been great. For example, Federal Express, who recently was the first service category recipient of the Malcolm Baldridge Award for Quality, felt it owed the award to empowered employees. James Perkins, senior vice-president of personnel, said that empowering

EXHIBIT 11.14 The Profile of Poor Communication Managers

THE DEVELOPER

Developers are managers who seek to assist employees' personal development by becoming a teacher. As long as the employee accepts the role of student and views the developer's ideas as gospel, things work out fine. If the student begins to spout ideas of his or her own that are inconsistent with the developer, the developer will undermine the ideas and ultimately inhibit creativity.

INNOVATOR

Innovators are managers who are obsessed with innovation. They are constantly creating new and better approaches for doing things even if it means changing a system that works well in the first place. The work group is constantly in a state of flux and employees who question the group's status are viewed as not having the flexibility needed to survive in this manager's group.

INACTIVE LEADER

Managers who fall into the inactive leader category actively request information from subordinates, but then never use it. These managers may also forget to inform employees of important changes until they are actually implemented. This causes undue stress on the employees and makes them resistant to the change.

WORKAHOLIC

Workaholic managers are very supportive of employees who share their work ethic. Because workaholics spend the majority of their time at work, they view their workers as their surrogate family and treat them very paternalistically. Working for a workaholic manager can be very stressful for employees who do not share the workaholic's perspectives because it is difficult for them to relate to one another.

POLICITICAN

The politician as manager is known for trying to make everyone happy. The goal for this type of manager is to avoid conflict at all costs. This type of manager tends to tell employees what will make them happy, and not what is really happening. Workers feel that the politician is not being honest with them and begin to distrust him or her.

EXPERT

Because expert managers know everything about everything, they demand, not earn, respect from their employees. Experts usually do not request input from their employees because they feel that employees have nothing of interest to tell them. Since experts know everything, there is no need to ask others.

TERMINATOR

Managers who fall into the terminator category have high standards that they expect all employees to live up to. Because most terminators judge employees by unrealistic standards, the employees nearly always fall short. Hence, the communication between an employee and a terminator generally consists of the terminator reprimanding the employee.

....

| EXHIBIT 11.15 | Essential Conditions for Empowerment |

1. Employees must be properly trained.
2. There needs to be a shared vision between management and workers that their firm will provide the best customer service in the business.
3. There must be a shared set of values and beliefs about how things should be done.
4. The benefits from the empowerment must be shared.
5. Managers must have faith in the ability of their employees.
6. The organization's culture must support the risk-taking behavior that is needed to succeed.

....

employees was essential in the company's quest for 100 percent customer satisfaction.[84]

Jack Stack, CEO of Springfield Remanufacturing Corporation (SRC), used empowering techniques before the word was even coined. He called it "the great game of business." Stack found when people were put in charge of reaching a goal, they generally reached it. He decided that he would tell the lowest level workers *everything* about the business. By providing them information about where the company was and where it was headed, employees would realize that they were an important part of whether or not the company stayed in business. Stack explained to the workers the corporation's goals and mission and how he wanted to achieve these goals. Then, he asked his employees not to tell anyone. In other words, he trusted them. The trust he placed in his employees paid off well. He saw workers coming in after working hours crawling over the tractors to determine what parts were needed and when, and to make sure that enough parts, but only enough parts, were ready for use. The level of productivity in the plant increased greatly. As a team, the plant reached its goals. Stack feels that providing information is the key to productivity, and information is a key to empowering employees.[85]

Quality Circles

A quality circle is just one of the many concepts borrowed from Japanese management techniques. The main idea behind quality circles is that employees from various levels of an organization meet on a regular basis to make decisions about organizational concerns. The concerns can range from how to increase productivity to how to find a better supplier to stock the candy machine. By using quality circles, every employee in the organization has something to contribute. The quality circle provides an opportunity for them to contribute it.

Quality circles have been used in a variety of organizations. For example, the *Los Angeles Times* finds the concept of quality circles so valuable that it has three full-time people in charge of coordinating the organization's 40 quality circles composed of over 300 employees. Each quality circle consists of no more than 10 employees who meet weekly to solve a problem. The problem chosen to be discussed is determined by the consensus of the group. After the problem is selected, the group determines how it will proceed. For example, one group set its sights on cleaning up the chaotic data storage area near its work area. The team studied the legal requirements of data storage, lease agreements, and alternative storage methods. In the end, it recommended microfilming some documents, buying instead of leasing equipment, and purchasing a new filing system that revolved. The suggestions saved over $24,000 a year and led to a much more efficient and better-run storage room.[86]

Not all companies have found success in using quality circles. DuPont's Chamber Works in Deepwater, New Jersey, established a quality circle that brought both workers and management together in regular meetings to discuss any topic the group deemed important. But the local union felt that the circle encroached on its turf and filed a charge of unfair labor practices and won. The ruling was based on the fact that the quality circle, which was viewed as an employer-dominated labor organization, was in violation of the federal labor law. Rather than appeal the ruling, the quality circle was abandoned.[87] Currently, the National Labor Relations Board is considering whether quality circles and other employee involvement groups constitute labor organizations, and if so, what actions by employers would constitute illegal domination of such groups. The board's decision will have a dramatic effect on many companies.[88]

Work Teams

"Two heads are better than one" is the philosophy behind having employees work in teams. The work team concept has been catching on from assembly lines to high-level corporate office workers. About one in five American employers used self-managed work teams in 1992, up from about one in twenty in the early 1980s, and the percentage is expected to increase to nearly 50 percent by the year 2000.[89] It works because more information and more ideas are available to a team of workers than to one individual worker. Teams also have been found to help boost profits.[90]

The Adolph Coors Company has embraced the concept of work teams. Production workers are organized in teams of nine or ten employees. Each team is responsible for its own scheduling. An elected representative makes up the schedule each week. The system permits shift trading, as long as the team's work gets done. These production teams also participate in hiring decisions, manage budgets, and help improve efficiency. Have these teams improved things at Coors? Management seems to think so, statistics such as a turnover rate of less than 1 percent a year seem to prove it.[91]

The Wallace Company, Inc., another winner of the Malcolm Baldridge National Quality Award, has found teams a great way to do business. CEO John Wallace estimates that more than 80 percent of the company's day-to-day decisions are made through the team process. Wallace even uses the team approach to selling. Every major account has an outside selling agent, and inside selling agent, a sales assistant, and order filler, and an accounts receivable representative.[92]

Not every company will be able to successfully implement work teams. Some firms who have tried and failed have outlined several reasons why work teams did not work for them, some of which are listed below:

1. Uncooperative managers see work teams as an encroachment on their territory and an erosion of their own power to manage.
2. Workers who have always been given orders have difficulty giving orders to themselves.
3. Changes are sometimes made too fast for employees to accept.
4. One or more persons in the group may not be team-minded players and will have a difficult time working in a team environment.

5. Large teams that have been split into two smaller teams do not always work as a group.[93]

Another possible reason for the failure of teams may be using the wrong team for the wrong purpose. Teams can be categorized in three ways. First, there is the baseball team. Players on this type of team hold a fixed position and play on the team, not as a team. Next, there is a football team. While these players still have fixed position, they play as a team. Finally, there are the tennis doubles teams. Doubles players hold primary, not fixed positions and cover for one another. Each team has it advantages and disadvantages and each will work in a specific situation, but not in all situations. When managers try to use a baseball team when they really need a doubles team, problems can occur.[94]

Suggestion Boxes

The suggestion box was the forerunner of quality circles. The reasoning underlying each of these concepts is the same: employees who do the work should have good ideas of how to do it better. Unlike quality circles, which involve only a few people, suggestion boxes encourage all employees to participate. Frequently, the suggestor's identity is kept anonymous until the suggestion is implemented and an award is presented. This helps people feel more secure about participating.

Sometimes the suggestion-box format can be turned into a formal program. For example, Consolidated Edison Company of New York implemented a Front-Line Feedback program. The program requested that employees who work directly with the customer suggest ways in which service could be improved. Employees whose ideas were accepted earned $50 and their names and suggestions were written about in the company newsletter. Many of the recipients felt that the money was nice, but the recognition was better.[95]

The outcome of this program highlights one of the most beneficial reasons for implementing a suggestion box. The public recognition employees receive for submitting winning ideas boosts their self-esteem. Employees have an increased sense of their true abilities when their ideas are deemed good enough to be implemented by a firm. Every time a fellow worker uses the new method, the employee can say, "that's *my* idea."[96]

Japanese firms are strong believers in employee suggestions. A 1988 tally of suggestions made by employees in Japanese firms indicated that a total of 59.2 million suggestions were provided. The average number of suggestions made by a Japanese employee was 31.5. Some of these suggestions were really good ones too. One suggestion saved Canon Oita $123,000 while the combined benefit of the suggestions at Kawasaki Steel saved that company $370 million.[97]

One reason for the high levels of suggestions found in Japanese firms is that new employees are expected to submit four daily suggestions in the first few months on the job. Further, Japanese companies use more of the suggestions given by employees than American firms do, encouraging Japanese workers to continue making suggestions. On average, Japanese firms use four of every five suggestions made by their employees while American firms use only one of every four suggestions.[98] The main reason given for the different usage rate of Japanese and American firms is the quality of the suggestions. Quite simply, Japanese workers provide better suggestions than American workers do because Japanese workers have the luxury of lifetime job security. Lifetime commitment leads to a stronger bond with the firm, and more of a willingness to improve things for all. American workers who, in current times, are assured of a job only until the following pay period, are less willing to provide ideas that may help the company to eliminate their jobs.[99]

However, this may be changing. A report that surveyed 300 companies about their suggestion programs found that the firms saved $2.2 billion from employee suggestions in one year. Also, the number of suggestions provided was up by 60 percent from just three years earlier. This success may make some firms rethink their use of suggestions programs.[100]

Ownership

One piece of information a stock buyer can use when deciding which company to invest in is the degree of ownership the top management has in the firm. If top managers are paid a salary that is not dependent upon the success of the company, then the investor should pass on the stock. If, however, the management's salary is tied to the productivity of the firm—that is, a large portion of the their salary is in the form of stocks—then the investor should buy it. The investor will want someone who is running the firm to have the same interests the investor does—profitability. Managers who have a strong ownership in the organization will think in terms of profitability.[101]

The concept also can be pushed further down into the firm. Workers who have an ownership in the firm also will want the firm to be more productive. Armed with this philosophy, many firms are considering employee ownership. Exhibit 11.16 provides an example of this concept in action. A recent survey indicates that this idea has a great deal of support. Two-thirds of the personnel officers at 415 large companies indicated that they want more employees to own stock so that the employees will act like owners.[102] However, some firms have rejected proposals to allow more employee ownership. Some GM managers felt that one way to get the workers to be more productive would be to give them more of a stake in the company. However, not all of the voting membership agreed.[103]

Other ways to induce the feeling of ownership besides increasing stock purchases also have been tried. At Dominos, there are no employees, only team members, team leaders, and a coaching staff. DuPont also has no employees; it has people and team members. Replacing the term *employees* has proven beneficial for these firms. By eliminating the words *manager* and *employee*, they have also eliminated the "we-they" mindset. However, it takes more than just simple semantics to make this concept work. Not only does the vocabulary have to change, but the way in which employees turned teammates are treated also must be reflective of the feeling of ownership and importance the company wants to portray.[104]

Total Quality Management

One concept that seems to incorporate all or many of the topics discussed in these past few sections is Total Quality Management (TQM). TQM is an entirely new way of doing things. It asks employees to challenge old rules and find new and better ways to get things done. This can be accomplished in a group, individually, at the bottom of the organization, or at the top. The key is that everyone is involved.

TQM is a strategic, integrated management system for achieving customer satisfaction that involves all managers and employees and uses quantitative methods to continuously improve an organization's processes. TQM is designed to achieve cus-

EXHIBIT 11.16   Involvement through Ownership

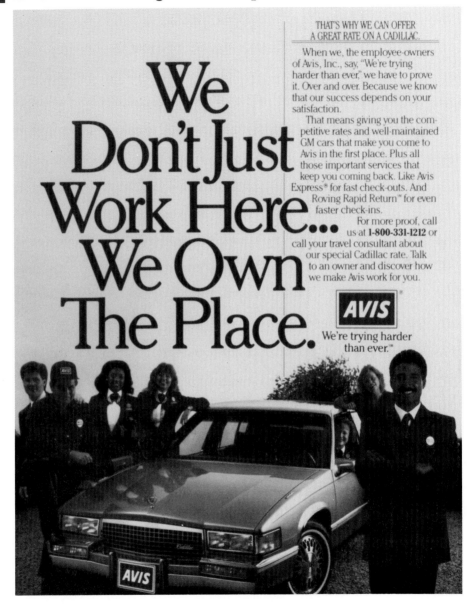

tomer satisfaction, make continuous improvements, and give responsibility to everyone. To achieve this goal, the organization must develop performance standards and valid ways of measuring these standards. It must strive to focus on the customer, on communication, and on employee involvement. Top management must support and direct the TQM effort by showing a commitment to training and by rewarding and recognizing quality work. Exhibit 11.17 illustrates a four-minute customer service course used by the service staff at Arthur Andersen's Training and Development Center.

....

EXHIBIT 11.17 Arthur Andersen's Four-Minute Customer Service Course

1. Smile.
2. Establish eye contact with the customer.
3. Use the person's name.
4. Mirror the individual's body language.
5. Try to match the individual's speech.
6. Show that you respect and accept the person.
7. Be calm and confident; be *the* expert.
8. Be well-groomed and look the part of a "service professional."

Remember, everything is based on perception and all it takes is four minutes for the customer to decide on just what level of service you are planning to provide.

....

The process of implementing TQM in an organization can be viewed in three phases. To begin, the firm must have an awareness of the need to change. This vision must be supported by the knowledge that workers will need to be trained and educated and that the tools they use to do their jobs may need to change. Once the organization recognizes these things, it then becomes committed to implementing TQM, which is the second phase. During this stage, the firm must develop support structures that include steering committees and TQM boards. These groups are responsible for determining the standards and capabilities of the firm. They also must be sure that the resources needed are provided and that the training required is available. Finally, performance improvement teams are established. At this point, the organization is ready to implement TQM. The performance teams begin to analyze the processes in the workplace with an eye toward improving them. During this analysis, seven basic quality tools can be used. They include

1. Process flow analysis—a step by step chart of the steps involved in the process under investigation;
2. Cause-effect diagram—an examination of the root cause for painful symptoms;
3. Run chart—an illustration of the trends and results over a specified period of time for a particular situation;
4. Control chart—indicates the variation from normal in the situation over time;
5. Scattergram—indicates whether or not a linear relationship exists between variables;
6. Histogram—depicts the distribution from the mean and how close to normal it is; and
7. Pareto chart—prioritizes categories from most to least important.[105]

These groups initiate changes and are recognized for their accomplishments. Once in place, TQM continues to provide the organization with a way of constantly pushing itself to be more and more productive.

Because TQM is completely different from the traditional way in which organizations have been run, it is frequently difficult to use in existing workplaces. Instead, TQM has been more successfully implemented in a new plant or branch of a company that is separate from the parent organization. For example, General Dy-

....

| EXHIBIT 11.18 | Guiding Principles of TQM at General Dynamics |

1. Quality comes first.
2. Our goal is never-ending improvement in customer satisfaction.
3. Teamwork is the way we make decisions.
4. Suppliers are part of our team.
5. Every activity and process is an integral part of the operation of our company.
6. Mistakes are not "someone's fault."
7. We manage our work by facts.
8. Decisions are made by the lowest appropriate organizational level.
9. We can never be satisfied with "good enough."
10. Employees have the right to as much information as possible about their jobs and the company.

....

namics is implementing a variety of TQM concepts that are only used in its Tallahassee plant. Responsibility and decision making is being pushed to the lower levels of the organization. Self-managed teams are relied upon to set their own production agendas, help to hire new employees, and certify members in the group before they are eligible for raises. Frequent meetings at General Dynamics provide the teams with access to the information they may need in order to manage themselves. Exhibit 11.18 is a list of the guiding principles of TQM at General Dynamics.[106]

Another company that decided to implement TQM at an off-site location was General Motors. GM used the ideas of TQM as the foundation for building its Saturn plant. To begin, the company set up a relocation policy task force composed of United Auto Workers; GM sales, service, marketing, human resources, engineering, and finance people; and representatives from Argonaut Realty, a relocation specialist. These members started with a blank sheet of paper and no rules or infrastructure. But they did have a common goal—world satisfaction.[107]

Throughout the entire development of the plant and the products offered by the plant, the team worked together. The United Auto Workers and GM engineers flew around the world together to investigate technologies and procedures that could be used by Saturn. The relocation team worked with every employee who was eventually relocated to Spring Hill, Tennessee. Even spouses who did not work for GM participated in workshops designed to help them understand the job possibilities and salary expectations in rural Tennessee. Saturn even worked closely with the people who would be maintaining and fixing the Saturn products. The company reasoned that it would not be wise to produce a top-quality product if the same level of quality service was not available for the vehicles. While the project seems to be a success, only time will tell. The 1993 car market will only be Saturn's fourth year out.

The pursuit of quality appears to be contagious, or at least it is at Hutchinson Technology Inc (HTI), a manufacturer of precision computer components. HTI hired consultants in 1983 to fix their problems. While HTI was skeptical at first, it implemented the programs in the manufacturing processes. HTI saw great improvements in as little as 18 months. By the end of the fifth year, HTI had saved over $30 million dollars. It was then that HTI decided to develop and implement a quality program in the nonmanufacturing parts of the firm as well. The process worked so well that HTI called their consultants back in and offered to show them how to implement quality programs. In this case it appears that the student can teach the teacher too.[108]

• • • • • • • • •

MANAGEMENT GUIDELINES

The productivity and involvement of employees should be major priorities for managers. However, no one set of steps can be followed to make all employees productive and involved. Also, not all companies will be more productive by simply involving their employees. With these two warnings in mind, let's review some suggestions for managers who want to build a more productive and involved work force.

1. Almost all of the concepts discussed in this chapter rest on one principle: management must trust its employees. For example, in order to provide employees with the knowledge necessary for them to set their own goals, they must understand what output is expected overall. In order for employees to know if the new technique they are suggesting is feasible, they have to know how much the old method costs. In order for employees to make the sound business decisions that they were empowered to make, they must have the information that they need. If management is not willing to trust its employees, it cannot have an involved organizaton. An unwillingness to trust employees may imply that quality employees were not selected in the first place and the company's hiring policies need to be reworked. However, if a company hires only competent, qualified employees, then trusting them with organizational information should not be a problem.

2. Productivity can also be stifled by inappropriate or out-of-date equipment. Managers must remain knowledgeable about current machines and techniques available in their field to help employees do their jobs. Investing in equipment to help increase productivity is one good way for firms that cannot use involvement techniques to increase productivity.

3. Before any steps can be made toward encouraging employees to become involved in the organization, a serious study of the overall corporate culture must be made. Will the current corporate culture allow management to initiate involvement programs? Which techniques, if any are appropriate for the organization? Implementing a new policy that runs counter to the culture will not be effective.

4. Start small. Once management decides to use involvement techniques, it should select one small project to begin with and see how it goes. Making too many changes all at once, even if they are all good ideas, may be too much for employees to handle.

5. Do not overlook the advantages of training employees. By providing training to employees, a manager can build a smarter, more loyal work force. The payoff from training is frequently increased productivity and lower turnover.

6. Remember that employee attitudes can be shaped. Monetary rewards coupled with strong promotional and career path planning can increase morale, productivity, and commitment to the organization's goals.

QUESTIONS FOR REVIEW

1. What is productivity? Discuss three ways in which productivity can be impacted.

2. How can training and development help to increase productivity?

3. How can managers influence employee attitudes? Why would they want to?

4. What is employee involvement? What are some of the benefits of involving employees in the organization?

5. Describe how communication can be used to help involve employees in their jobs.

6. Compare and contrast two of the techniques for increasing employee involvement.

7. How would you go about increasing involvement in a plant that assembled toys? In a plant that plucked and cut chickens? In a law firm? In a mail-order catalog organization?

CASE: Bruegger's Bagel Bakery [109]

It's the fourth quarter, your team is down by seven points, and the ball is at midfield with less than one minute left to play in the game. What strategy do you put into action to move your team down the field? Do you tighten up and get conservative or do you loosen up and call the unexpected play? Further, do you, as the coach, call the play, or do you let the quarterback call it? Mike Dressell, Nordahl Brue, ad Jim Briggs (who has since left the business), founders of Bruegger's Bagel Bakery, would probably opt for the latter. When the trio first considered the idea of opening a bagel bakery, they knew they had to develop a decentralized approach, that is, they knew they wanted to let the individual managers call the plays. Since each of them was busy in another occupation (Dressell has a construction company; Brue was an attorney, and Briggs was an accountant), they didn't have the time or knowledge to get involved in operating decisions.

Passing the Ball, Not the Buck

Basically, Dressell, Brue, and Briggs adopted the attitude that if you wanted something done right, you didn't necessarily have to do it yourself. Rather than getting involved directly in operating decisions, the founders made a strategic decision to hire local managers to run their bagel shops. Local managers were offered a partnership that gave them a 20 percent ownership of the individual shops they supervised. The managers were empowered with the responsibility and authority to make decisions that affected

their "cluster" of units. By offering the managers financial incentives beyond their salaries, the managers would have a higher stake in the survival of their shops and therefore more incentive to make things work.

Initially, the playing field was left wide open for local managers in terms of developing their own techniques for managing their shops, watching costs, and creating their own menu items. The principle partners took a sideline approach to overseeing each manager's game plan but would occasionally visit some of the units. Overall, they liked what they saw, as was evident in Brue's comment that "Managers took lots of initiative." Bruegger's created an environment that encouraged ingenuity and innovativeness. Each cluster manager was in the driver's seat; and all of them knew who buttered their bagels, so to speak—it was none other than themselves! Various clusters of stores offered different styles of bagels (some lighter, some darker) and different lines of beverages. Some had paper goods with the company logo, others didn't. Some offered creative bagel delights, such as pizza bagels, while others offered more traditional bagels. Again, the decisions were made by the individual managers of each cluster of stores thereby adding an element of uniqueness to each.

Smell of Victory

Since the principal partners first considered the idea of Bruegger's Bagel Bakery in 1983, the company has grown rapidly. The first market was in Albany, New York, and in less than three years, they added four other markets in Cedar Rapids, Iowa; Minneapolis; Boston; and Raleigh-Durham, North Carolina. Currently, Bruegger's is a $20-million company with eight cluster managers operating 32 stores. Obviously, Dressell and Brue's strategic business plan has worked well. Despite their success, however, the principal partners have not closed their eyes to the possibility that change is needed.

A Slight Shift in the Game Plan

As the company continued to grow, Bruegger reached a point where the decision to set some company-wide standards became evident. Although the partners wanted to continue giving managers the freedom to make decisions affecting their individual clusters, they believed there was a need to coordinate the activities of the various stores. For example, up until a few years ago the cluster managers have five different contracts with Coca Cola. The decision was made to combine forces and negotiate a single deal, which resulted in savings to each of the clusters. Such fine-tuning and coordination of activities needed to occur without restricting the responsibility and authority of the local managers.

Bruegger's strategic philosophy had always been in line with the idea of empowerment. The partners wanted their managers to have "bragging rights" for the success of their individual stores. After all, Breugger's success was reflective of the individual management techniques and decision making. Although the principal partners did not want to interfere with the managers' decisions to offer particular products, they did persuade the managers to rely on market research to ascertain the viability of keeping certain items on the menu. Cluster managers are still encouraged to develop new ideas, however, before the item gets adopted, it goes through extensive market testing.

Conclusion

Bruegger's Bagel Bakery has demonstrated that setting standards can be done without "robbing" managers of the motivation to run their shops the way they choose. By empowering people with responsibility and authority and by giving them a stake in their business, Bruegger's has the benefit of many minds working on the same problems and working to ensure the survival of the company.

QUESTIONS

1. The strategic philosophy behind Bruegger's Bagel Bakery is based upon at least one of the strategic choices mentioned at the beginning of the chapter. Explain how Bruegger's has been able to implement this strategic choice to develop a successful organization.

2. Various concepts discussed in this chapter have been implemented at Bruegger's. Identify two and discuss how they have been effectively utilized by Bruegger's.

3. What strategic choices described in this chapter has Bruegger's failed to take advantage of? What suggestions do you have for implementing these strategies?

4. If you were asked to measure Bruegger's productivity levels, how would you do it?

·················
ADDITIONAL READINGS

Bass, Bernard M., and Ralph M. Stodgill. *Bass & Stodgill's Handbook of Leadership.* New York: Free Press.

Bastien, David. "Common Patterns of Behavior and Communication in Corporate Mergers and Acquisitions." *Human Resource Management* 26. Spring 1987, pp. 17–33.

Beckhard, Richard, and Wendy Pritchard. *Changing the Essence: The Art of Leading Fundamental Change in Organizations.* San Francisco: Jossey-Bass, 1992.

Bell, Robert R., and John M. Burnham. *Managing Productivity and Change.* Cincinnati: South-Western, 1991.

Bennis, Warren. *Why Leaders Can't Lead?* San Francisco: Jossey-Bass, 1989.

Block, Peter. *The Empowered Manager.* San Francisco: Jossey-Bass, 1987.

Bolman, Lee, and Terrence Deal. *Reframing Organizations.* San Francisco: Jossey-Bass, 1991.

Boyett, Joseph H., and Harry P. Conn. *Workplace 2000: The Revolution Reshaping American Business.* New York: Dutton, 1991.

Brinkerhoff, Robert, and Dennis Dressler. *Productivity Measurement.* Newbury Park, CA: Sage, 1989.

Brown, Stephen, Evert Gummesson, Bo Edvardsson, and BengtOve Gustavsson. *Service Quality.* New York: Lexington Books, 1990.

Buono, Anthony, and James Bowditch. *The Human Side of Mergers and Acquisitions.* San Francisco: Jossey-Bass, 1989.

Campbell, John P., Richard J. Campbell, and Associates. *Productivity in Organizations.* San Francisco: Jossey-Bass, 1988.

Carkhuff, Robert. *Empowering—The Creative Leader in the Age of New Capitalism.* Amherst, MA: HRD Press, 1989.

Carnevale, Anthony Patrick. *America and the New Economy.* San Francisco: Jossey-Bass, 1991.

Casson, Mark. *Enterprise and Competitiveness.* New York: Oxford Press, 1990.

Crosby, Phil. *Let's Talk Quality.* New York: McGraw-Hill, 1989.

Deming, W. Edwards. *Out of Crisis.* Cambridge, MA: Cambridge University Press, 1986.

Denton, D. Keith. *Horizontal Management: Beyond Total Customer Satisfaction.* New York: Lexington Books, 1991.

Ernst and Young Quality Improvement Consulting Group. *Total Quality: An Executive Guide for the 1990's.* Homewood, IL.: Dow Jones-Irwin, 1990.

Gaddis, Paul. "Taken Over, Turned Out." *Harvard Business Review* (1987), pp. 8–22.

Gardner, John W. *On Leadership.* New York: Free Press, 1989.

Goldhaber, Gerald M. and George A. Barnett. *Handbook of Organizational Communication.* Norwood, NJ: Ablex, 1988.

Gomez-Meija, Luis R. *Compensation and Benefits.* Edison, NJ: Bureau of National Affairs, 1989.

Graham-Moore, Brian, and Timothy L. Ross. *Gainsharing for Improving Performance.* Washington, DC: BNA Books, 1990.

Hackman, J. Richard. *Groups That Work (and Those That Don't).* San Francisco: Jossey-Bass, 1989.

Helfgott, Roy B. *Computerized Manufacturing and Human Resources.* Lexington, MA: Lexington Books, 1988.

Hickman, Craig R., and Michael A. Silva. *Creating Excellence.* New York: Plume, 1984.

Holoviak, Stephen J., and Susan S. Sipkoff. *Managing Human Productivity: People Are Your Best Investment.* Westport, CT: Greenwood Press, Inc., 1987.

Hunt, James G., B. Rajaram Baliga, H. Peter Dachler, and Chester A. Schriesheim. *Emerging Leadership Vistas.* Lexington, MA: D.C. Heath, 1988.

Hunt, John. "Hidden Extras: How People Get Overlooked in Takeovers." *Personnel Management* 19 (July 1987), pp. 24–28.

Isen, Alice M. *Motivation and Emotion.* New York: Plenum Press, 1989.

Ivancevich, John, David Schweiger, and Frank Power. "Strategies for Managing Human Resources During Mergers and Acquisition." *Human Resource Planning* 10 (1988), pp. 19–35.

Jablin, Frederic M., Linda L. Putnam, Karlene H. Roberts, and Lyman W. Porter. *Handbook of Organizational Communication.* Newbury Park, CA: Sage, 1987.

Janis, Irving L. *Crucial Decisions: Leadership in Policymaking and Crisis Management.* New York: The Free Press, 1989.

Juran, J. M. *Juran on Quality by Design.* New York: Free Press, 1992.

Kanter, Donald L., and Philip H. Mirvis. *The Cynical American.* San Francisco: Jossey-Bass, 1989.

Ketchum, Lyman, and Eric Trist. *All Teams Are Not Created Equal.* Newbury Park, CA: Sage, 1992.

Kinlaw, Dennis. *Developing Superior Work Teams.* New York: Lexington Books, 1990.

Koestenbaum, Peter. *Leadership: The Inner Side of Greatness.* San Francisco: Jossey-Bass, 1991.

Kotter, John P. *The Leadership Factor.* New York: Free Press, 1988.

Kotter, John P. *Power and Influence.* New York: Free Press, 1985.

Kotter, John P., and James Heskett. *The Corporate Culture Connection.* New York: Free Press, 1992.

Kouzes, James M., and Barry Z. Posner. *The Leadership Challenge.* San Francisco: Jossey-Bass, 1987.

Larson, Carl, and Frank Lafasto. *Teamwork.* Newbury Park, CA: Sage, 1989.

Lawler, Edward E. *High Involvement Management.* San Francisco: Jossey-Bass, 1986.

Lawler, Edward E. "Pay for Performance: Making It Work." *Personnel.* October 1988, pp. 68–71.

Lax, David A., and James Sebenius. *The Manager As Negotiator.* New York: Free Press, 1986.

Lewis, Jordan D., *Partnerships for Profit.* New York: Free Press, 1990.

McIntosh, Stephen. "Buying Time by Delegating," *HRMagazine.* October 1991, p. 47.

McPhee, Robert D., and Phillip K. Tompkins. *Organizational Communication.* Newbury Park, CA: Sage, 1985.

Maidani, Ebrahaim. "Comparative Study of Herzberg's Two-Factor Theory of Job Satisfaction among Public and Private Sectors." *Public Personnel Management* 20 (1991), pp. 441–448.

Malick, Sidney, Solomon Hoberman, and Stephen J. Wall. *The Practice of Management Development.* Lexington, MA: Praeger Publishers, 1988.

Meyer, M. W., and L. G. Zucker. *Permanently Failing Organizations.* Newbury Park, CA: Sage, 1989.

Miller, Danny. *The Icarus Paradox: How Exceptional Companies Bring about Their Own Downfall.* Scarborough, Ontario: HarperCollins Canada, 1990.

Miller, Richard. *Participative Management Quality of Worklife and Job Enrichment.* Park Ridge, NJ: Noyes Data Corporation, 1977.

Morgan, Gareth. *Creative Organization Theory.* Newbury Park, CA: Sage, 1989.

Morgan, Gareth. *Images of Organizations.* Newbury Park, CA: Sage, 1990.

Nadler, Leonard, and Zeace Nadler. *Developing Human Resources.* San Francisco: Jossey-Bass, 1987.

Orsburn, Jack, Linda Moran, Ed Musselwhite, and John Zenger. *Self-directed Work Teams: The New American Challenge.* Homewood, IL: BusinessOne Irwin, 1990.

Pierce, Jon L., Jon W. Newstrom, Randall B. Dunham, and Alison E. Barber. *Alternative Work Schedules.* Needham Heights, MA: Allyn and Bacon, 1989.

Putnam, Linda L., and Michael E. Pacanowsky. *Communication and Organizations.* Newbury Park, CA: Sage, 1983.

Quinn, Robert. *Beyond Rational Management.* San Francisco: Jossey-Bass, 1991.

Robson, George. *Continuous Process Improvement: Simplifying Work Systems.* New York: Free Press, 1991.

Rosen, Corey M., Katherine J. Klein, and Karen M. Young. *Employee Ownership in America.* Lexington Books, 1988.

Rummler, Geary A., and Alan P. Brache. *Improving Performance.* San Francisco: Jossey-Bass, 1990.

Ryan, Kathleen D., and Daniel K. Oestreich. *Driving Fear Out of the Workplace: How to Overcome Barriers to Quality, Productivity and Innovation.* San Francisco: Jossey-Bass, 1991.

Sandy, William. *Forging the Productivity Partnership.* New York: McGraw-Hill, 1990.

Schein, Edgar. *Organizational Culture and Leadership.* San Francisco: Jossey-Bass, 1991.

Schoorman, F. David, and Benjamin Schneider. *Facilitating Work Effectiveness.* Lexington, MA: Lexington Books, 1988.

Shapero, Albert. *Managing Precessional People.* New York: Free Press, 1989.

Shetty, Y. K., and Vernon M. Buehler. *Productivity and Quality through Science and Technology.* Westport, CT: Greenwood Press, 1988.

Thibodeaux, Mary, and Dale Yeatts. "Leadership: The Perceptions of Leaders by Followers in Self Managed Work Teams." Paper presented at the 1991 International Conference on Self-Managed Work Teams. Dallas: 1991.

Thornburg, Linda. "The Push to Improve." *HRMagazine.* December 1990, pp. 36–39.

Tjosvold, Dean, and Mary, Tjosvold. *Leading the Team Organization.* New York: Lexington Books, 1992.

Tomer, John F. *Organizational Capital.* Westport, CT: Greenwood Press, 1987.

Varney, Glenn H. *Building Productive Teams.* San Francisco: Jossey-Bass, 1989.

Weisbord, Marvin. *Productive Workplaces.* San Francisco: Jossey-Bass, 1987.

Wellins, Richard, William Byham, and Jeanne Wilson. *Empowered Teams.* San Francisco: Jossey-Bass, 1991.

Womack, James, Daniel Jones, and Daniel Noos. *The Machine That Changed the World.* Boston: MIT, 1990.

Yeatts, Dale. "Self-Managed Work Teams: Innovation in Progress." *Business and Economic Quarterly.* Fall/Winter, 1990/1991, pp. 2–6.

Yasuda, Yuzo. *40 Years, 20 Million Ideas: The Toyota Suggestion System.* Cambridge, MA: Productivity Press, 1991.

Zeithaml, Valarie A. *Delivering Quality Service.* New York: Free Press, 1990.

···················
NOTES

1. L. Therrien, "The Rival Japan Respects," *Business Week*, November 13, 1989, pp. 108–118; and G. McManis and M. Liebman, "Management Development: A Lifetime Commitment," *Personnel Administrator*, September 1988, pp. 53–58.

2. G. Koretz, "The Surge in Factory Productivity Looks Like History Now," *Business Week*, October 8, 1990, p. 24.

3. William Baumol, "U.S. Industry's Lead Gets Bigger," *Wall Street Journal*, March 21, 1990, p. A14; Joseph Spiers, "Productivity Looks Promising," *Fortune*, March 9, 1992, pp. 21–22.

4. Bob Davis and Dana Milbank, "Job Blues," *Wall Street Journal*, February 7, 1992, p. A1+; Myron Magnet, "The Truth about the American Worker," *Fortune*, May 4, 1992, pp. 48–65; "Why Japan Must Change," *Fortune*, March 9, 1992, pp. 66–67.

5. R. Henkoff, "Make Your Office More Productive," *Fortune*, February 25, 1991, p. 72.

6. F. Feinstein, "Blame Bosses If Quality Is Poor," *Wall Street Journal*, July 10, 1990, p. A1; Jerry Bowles, "Is American Management Really Committed to Quality?" *Management Review*, April 1992, pp. 42–46.

7. S. Overman, "Leader Helps Improve Competitiveness," *HRMagazine*, May 1990, 58–60.

8. E. Carlson, "McDonald's Kroc Bloomed Late, but Brilliantly," *Wall Street Journal*, May 23, 1989, p. B2.

9. P. E. Steiger, "Ten for the Textbooks," *Wall Street Journal*, Centennial Edition, p. B1; and Von Johnston and Herff Moore, "Pride Drives Wal-Mart to Service Excellence," *HRMagazine*, October 1991, pp. 79–80.

10. R. E. Rustin, "How Grand Ambitions Proved the Undoing of Shearson's CEO," *Wall Street Journal*, January 31, 1990, p. A1+.

11. Walter Kiechel, "The Leader as Servant," *Fortune*, May 4, 1992, pp. 121–122.

12. Z. Schiller, "No More Mr. Nice Guy at P&G—Not by a Long Shot," *Business Week*, February 3, 1992, pp. 54–56.

13. Walter Kiechel, "When Management Regresses," *Fortune,* March 9, 1992, pp. 157–158.

14. R. E. Kelley, "In Praise of Followers," *Harvard Business Review,* November–December 1988, pp. 142–147.

15. Ibid.

16. "Managing Generational Diversity," *HRMagazine,* April 1991, pp. 91–92.

17. Ibid.

18. J. P. Kotter, "How Leaders Grow Leaders," *Across the Board* 25(3), March 1988, pp. 38–42.

19. Robert Tomasko, "Restructuring: Getting It Right," *Management Review,* April 1992, pp. 10–15.

20. J. McCormick, and B. Powell, "Management for the 1990s," *Newsweek,* April 25, 1988, pp. 47–48.

21. Ibid.

22. L. Baytos, "The Human Side of Acquisitions and Divestitures," *Human Resource Planning* 9(4), 1987, pp. 167–175.

23. J. Hunt, "Hidden Extras: How People Get Overlooked in Takeovers," *Personnel Management,* July 1987, pp. 24–28.

24. Baytos, "The Human Side of Acquisitions," p. 170.

25. D. T. Bastien, "Common Patterns of Behavior and Communication in Corporate Mergers and Acquisitions," *Human Resource Management,* 26(1), Spring 1987, p. 28.

26. P. O. Gaddis, "Taken Over, Turned Out," *Harvard Business Review,* July–August 1987, p. 9.

27. P. Ingrassia, and J. White, "GM Mulls Tough Call in Toyota Venture," *Wall Street Journal,* June 10, 1988, p. A2.

28. J. B. Treece, and A. Borrus, "How Ford and Mazda Shared the Driver's Seat," *Business Week,* March 26, 1990, pp. 94–95.

29. Ingrassia and White, "GM Mulls Tough Call," p. A2.

30. P. Revzin, "Ventures in Hungary Test Theory That West Can Uplift East Bloc," *Wall Street Journal,* April 5, 1990, p. A1+.

31. G. Anders, "Going Global: Vision vs. Reality," *Wall Street Journal,* September 22, 1989, pp. R20–21.

32. J. Main, "The Winning Organization," *Fortune,* September 26, 1988, pp. 50–60.

33. Ibid.

34. Ibid.

35. A. Taylor, "New Lessons from Japan's Carmakers," *Fortune,* October 22, 1990, p. 166.

36. Vic Heylin, "Europeans Keep Progress off Assembly Line," *Wall Street Journal,* June 3, 1991, p. A10.

37. Henkoff, "Make Your Office More Productive," p. 76.

38. A. Karr, "A Special News Report on People and Their Jobs in Offices, Fields, and Factories," *Wall Street Journal,* April 10, 1990, p. A1.

39. Henkoff, "Make Your Office More Productive," p. 76.

40. J. Solomon, "Managers Focus on Low-Wage Workers," *Wall Street Journal,* May 9, 1989, p. B1.

41. Ibid.

42. C. Trost, "Labor Department Announces Winners of Its Work-Force Quality Competition," *Wall Street Journal,* September 21, 1991, p. B8.

43. A. Karr, "A Special News Report on People and Their Jobs in Offices, Fields, and Factories," *Wall Street Journal,* July 25, 1989, p. A1.

44. C. Conte, "Leaders Are Born, But Many Companies Believe They Can Be Nurtured Too," *Wall Street Journal,* May 21, 1991, p. A1.

45. P. Waldman, "Japanese-Style Camp for Managers Is Lost in Translation in U.S." *Wall Street Journal,* March 1, 1988, pp. A1+.

46. Ibid.

47. B. Leonard, "Does Your Office Suffer from Workplacephobia?" *Society for Human Resources Management HRNews,* August 1991, p. 15.

48. C. Hymowitz, "Earthquake Prompts Greater Work Flexibility," *Wall Street Journal,* November 6, 1989, p. B1.

49. S. Overman, "American Express Tests Linking Home to Work," *Society for Human Resource Management HRNews,* August 1991, p. 3.

50. S. Feinstein, "Cynicism Runs High in the American Workplace, Two Researchers Conclude," *Wall Street Journal,* May 30, 1989, p. A1.

51. B. Burlingham, "This Woman Has Changed Business Forever," *Inc.,* June 1990, pp. 34–47.

52. D. Milbank, "In These Gloomy Times, Some Companies Provide Employees With Comic Relief," *Wall Street Journal,* February 19, 1991, pp. B1+.

53. Ibid.

54. A. Bennett, "SAS's Nice Guy Is Aiming to Finish First," *Wall Street Journal,* March 2, 1989, p. B12.

55. J. A. Oliver and E. J. Johnson, "People Motive Redefines Customer Service," *HRMagazine,* June 1990, pp. 119–121.

56. "Workers Want What You'd Expect, But Don't Often Think They Are Getting It," *Wall Street Journal,* June 6, 1989, p. A1.

57. C. Hymowitz, "Many Middle Managers Find Bosses Uninspiring," *Wall Street Journal,* November 6, 1989, p. B1.

58. M. E. Mangelsdorf, "Managing the New Workforce," *Inc.,* January 1990, pp. 78–83.

59. M. Kanabayashi, "Competence Ousts Seniority in Deciding Who Gets Paid What," *Wall Street Journal,* March 14, 1989, p. A1.

60. H. Collingswood, "Pay for Performance at American Airlines," *Business Week,* June 19, 1989, p. 41.

61. S. Feinstein, "We Love You: More Companies Reward Workers Who Go the Extra Mile," *Wall Street Journal,* May 2, 1989, p. A1.

62. Ibid.

63. R. Bunning, "Rewarding a Job Well Done," *Personnel Administrator,* January 1989, p. 61.

64. L. Brokaw, P. Brown, T. Lammers, M. Mangelsdorf, and B. Posner, "Stamp of Approval," *Inc.,* January 1990, p. 105.

65. G. Fuchsberg, and A. Bennett, "Need a Motivator for a Weary Worker? Try a 'Congratulator,' " *Wall Street Journal,* May 4, 1990, p. A1+.

66. C. Ronald Schwisow, "Tools for Your Motivational Campaign," *HRMagazine,* November 1991, pp. 63–64.

67. J. Rigdon, "More Firms Try to Reward Good Service, but Incentives May Backfire in Long Run," *Wall Street Journal,* December 5, 1990, p. B1+.

68. M. Hawkins, and M. Moravec, "Career Paths Discourage Innovation and Deflate Motivation," *Personnel Administrator,* October 1989, pp. 111–112.

69. T. Schellhardt, "Creating Career Ladders to Keep Stellar Sellers," *Wall Street Journal,* March 22, 1990, p. B1.

70. J. Hoerr, "The Strange Bedfellows Backing Workplace Reform," *Business Week,* April 30, 1990, p. 57.

71. S. Bicos, "Employee Participation without Pain," *HRMagazine,* April 1990, p. 89.

72. N. Margulies and S. Black, "Perspectives on the Implementation of Participative Approaches," *Human Resources Management* 26(3), Fall 1987, p. 386.

73. F. Rice, "Champions of Communication," *Fortune,* June 3, 1991, pp. 111–120.

74. Sunny Side Up," *Inc.,* January 1990, p. 104.

75. Susan Antilla, "What's on TV? Our 10 AM Meeting," *Working Woman,* February 1992, pp. 42–43.

76. Rice, "Champions of Communication," p. 120.

77. Ibid.

78. B. Shimko, "All Managers Are HR Managers," *HRMagazine,* January 1990, p. 67.

79. M. Falvey, "Deaf, Dumb, and Blind at the Helm," *Wall Street Journal,* April 10, 1989, p. A14.

80. P. Farish, "HR Update," *Personnel Administrator,* May 1989, p. 19.

81. A. Karr, "Empowering Workers: Is It Real or Overplayed?" *Wall Street Journal,* June 18, 1991, p. A1.

82. T. Peters, "Another Bright Idea Squashed by Congress," *Wall Street Journal*, November 22, 1989, p. A12.

83. Jeffrey Gandz, "The Employee Empowerment Era," *Business Quarterly*, Autumn 1990, pp. 74–79; and Peter Fleming, "Empowerment Strengthens the Rock," *Management Review*, December 1991, pp. 34–37.

84. B. Leonard, "Baldridge Award Winners Empower Workers," *Society for Human Resources Management HRNews*, November 1990, p. 13.

85. "Being the Boss," *Inc.*, October 1989, p. 50.

86. A. Halcrow, "Employee Participation Is a Sign of the Times in LA," *Personnel Journal*, January 1988, p. 10.

87. R. Koenig, "Quality Circles Are Vulnerable to Union Tests," *Wall Street Journal*, March 28, 1990, pp. B1+.

88. See Stephanie Overman, "NLRB Considers Whether EI Groups Violate Law," *HRNews*, October 1991, p. 6; and Christopher Conte, "Precedent Pending," *Wall Street Journal*, October 15, 1991, p. A1.

89. Joann Lubin, "Trying to Increase Worker Productivity, More Employers Alter Management Style," *Wall Street Journal*, February 13, 1992, p. B1+.

90. Jana Schilder, "Work Teams Boost Productivity," *Personnel Journal*, February 1992, pp. 67–71.

91. "Coors, AT&T Credit Find Building Teams Isn't Easy—But It's Worth It," *Tallahassee Democrat*, August 7, 1991, p. 7D.

92. S. Overman, "Teamwork Boosts Quality at Wallace," *HRMagazine*, May 1991, p. 32.

93. G. Odiorne, "The New Breed of Supervisor: Leaders in Self-Managed Work Teams," *Supervision*, August 1991, p. 16.

94. Peter Drucker, "There's More Than One Kind of Team," *Wall Street Journal*, February 11, 1992, p. A16.

95. "The Power of Suggestions at ConEd," *Personnel Journal*, January 1988, p. 11.

96. R. Meehan, "Programs that Foster Creativity and Innovation," *Personnel*, February 1986, p. 32.

97. "Suggestion Boxes Overflowing at Japanese Firms," *Productivity in Japan*, Autumn 1989, p. 3.

98. T. Schellhardt, "Power of Suggestion Stronger in Japan," *Wall Street Journal*, October 19, 1989, p. B1.

99. P. Ingrassia, "Wheel Deals: Who's in The Driver's Seat?" *Wall Street Journal*, November 23, 1990, p. A7.

100. Wendy Chamblee, "Suggestion Programs Empower Employee, Reap Profits," *HRNews*, December 1991, p. A9.

101. K. Fisher, "Ownership Counts," *Forbes*, November 14, 1988, p. 362.

102. A. Karr, "Labor Letter," *Wall Street Journal*, May 14, 1991, p. A1.

103. J. White, "GM Workers Float Plan to Lift Stock Prices, Including Boosting Employees' Holdings," *Wall Street Journal*, January 19, 1990, p. A3.

104. J. Solomon, "When Are Employees Not Employees? When They're Associates, Stakeholders . . . ," *Wall Street Journal*, November 9, 1989, p. B1.

105. Carla C. Cater, "Seven Basic Quality Tools," *HRMagazine*, January 1992, pp. 81–83.

106. F. Schneyer, "Team Management Takes Hold in Tallahassee," *Tallahassee Democrat*, August 7, 1991, pp. D1+.

107. L. Thornburg, "Teamwork, Early Start Key to GM Relocation," *HRNews*, June 1990, p. 11.

108. John Butman, "Quality Comes Full Circle," *Management Review*, February 1992, pp. 49–51.

109. Adapted from B. G. Posner, "Raising the Stakes," *Inc.*, March 1990, pp. 100–103.

12 *Strategic Compensation Systems*

Designing and implementing an effective compensation program is a critical human resource activity. While it may be difficult to say exactly how much a compensation system can influence an organization, the creative use of compensation plans can work to maximize human resource productivity and contribute significantly to the achievement of human resource and organizational objectives. A pay system can reinforce an overall corporate objective of increased profitability, focus on both individual and team effort, and emphasize both short-term and long-term strategies.

• • • • • • • • •
CHAPTER OBJECTIVES

After you have studied this chapter, you should be able to

1. Describe the various influences on the design and implementation of compensation systems.
2. Discuss the lead, match, and lag pay level policies available to organizations.
3. Explain the concept of pay for performance and the advantages and disadvantages associated with it.
4. Summarize the major issues in communicating salary information.
5. Understand the relationship between motivation and compensation.
6. Differentiate between salary, incentives, commissions, profit sharing, and gain-sharing plans for groups and individuals.
7. Be familiar with a variety of nonfinancial rewards that may be useful when designing compensation systems.

CASE: The Eleven-Million-Dollar Men[1]

While some retailers may find the going rough these days, Phillips-Van Heusen (PVH) is having its best year ever. PVH, a manufacturer of shirts, sweaters, and casual shoes, attributes its increased sales and earnings before interest and taxes to a deceptively simple incentive plan devised by its chair, Lawrence S. Phillips.

Each of the eleven senior executives, regardless of the size of their operations, will earn $1 million if earnings per share grow 35 percent during the four years ending in January 1992. The first $500,000 is earned in increments when EPS goals are met each year. The second $500,000 is the bonus for making the combined target in the fourth year. Even if they miss their target one year, they can make it up by the last year and still earn the full $1 million.

Alison Bisno, director of research for an investment bank, states, "The incentive compensation program has been critical to the success, evolution and expanding growth of Phillips-Van Heusen." In fact, the plan demonstrates that money motivates individual performance and it can be used to reinforce a team-oriented culture that focuses management's attention on achieving strategic goals.

Phillips had two goals in implementing this plan. The first goal was to aid refinancing after a successful, but costly battle against an unfriendly takeover. The second goal was to help PVH gain a measure of control over its destiny by eliminating "the cyclical swings of its notoriously fickle business."

As retailers have moved to limit the number of brands on their shelves or to push store brands, PVH found its merchandise being squeezed off the shelves of department stores and decided to fight back. In response, PVH expanded its wholesale business and created its own retail division, setting up a chain of specialty stores and factory outlets to sell its own products. The potential for competition between PVH's own wholesale and retail divisions had to be minimized. Thus, a major objective of the incentive plan was to foster camaraderie and cooperation between those units.

So far, the plan seems to be working. Soon after its introduction, the senior people, already close friends, jelled as a team. They began to meet more frequently, talk more openly about operations, and work harder to make each division more profitable. Cooperative efforts multiplied. Salespeople in the sweater and shirt divisions teamed up to sell color-coordinated combinations, boosting sales for both divisions. All groups contributed recommendations for a new chain to upscale mall stores targeted at shoppers who have "outgrown The Gap."

Plan participants easily met their goals for the first year. The second year, however, was tough on them. Even though the participants outlined and followed a detailed plan, the year was frought with unpredictable events that rendered the plan unsuccessful. For example, the revolt at Tiananmen Square hurt production of sweaters in China and Hurricane Hugo closed three suppliers in Puerto Rico for two weeks. Last, the Campeau retail empire's financial problems delayed payments for PVH merchandise. Soft sales in the retail division sealed the company's fate, and it failed to reach that year's target.

Management is optimistic and spirits are high, even though it may be difficult to reach an EPS of $3.48 in 1991. Mike Culang, sweater division chief, spoke for all eleven when he said, "It will be terribly difficult, but with our mind-set the way it is, if there is a way to make it, we will make it." Also, Phillips is truly satisfied with the results of his plan. "The [348] plan reinforced the religion and put everybody in his own confessional. Now each of these guys is terribly supportive of every other division of this company. You don't find that very often in corporate America."

● ● ● ● ● ● ● ●

STRATEGIC CHOICES

The design of an organization's compensation system may have a critical impact on the organization's ability to achieve its strategic goals. For this reason, the reward system's philosophy and objectives must reinforce and reflect the organization's culture, external environment, and business strategy.[2] Among other things, reward systems can influence (1) who is attracted to and who remains with an organization,[3] (2) an employees's motivation level,[4] and (3) the organization's operating costs.[5] Managers must face several strategic choices with respect to the organization's reward system.

1. Management must decide the *importance of external equity* in the organization's compensation system. This decision is manifest in the type of pay policy implemented by the firm. The firm must make the strategic choice as to how much to pay employees with respect to the competition. Is the firm going to pay the highest wages in the market in order to insure attracting the most qualified applicants, or is the firm going to match the market salary or even pay less? This strategic choice is one of the most important choices an organization must make. It frequently forms the basis upon which the rest of the compensation system is built.

   External equity occurs when an employer pays wage rates that correspond to those prevailing in the external labor markets. Factors that are potentially important to consider when defining the labor market include geography or the location of the organization, the education or technical background required, the industry type, licensing or certification requirements, and the experience required by the job.

Wage and salary surveys are designed to help the compensation analyst make informed decisions about wage rates that will maintain external equity. An organization can choose to run its own survey or use data collected by others. Creating an in-house survey will result in up-to-date comparisons; however, these surveys can be costly. When designing a wage and salary survey, managers must be concerned about (a) selecting which jobs should be examined, (b) defining relevant labor markets, (c) selecting firms to be surveyed, (d) determining information to be asked, and (e) determining data collection techniques.

Outside wage and salary surveys use data collected by others to determine external equity. Surveys are available from a variety of sources including the Bureau of Labor Statistics, trade groups, and professional compensation analysis (such as the Hay Group). Although less expensive than creating an in-house survey, using information collected by others may not be as relevant or timely.

2. An additional strategic choice a firm faces is *how closely the compensation plan will be linked to the organization's overall strategic plan.* It is important that the compensation plan rewards behavior that will lead to the accomplishment of the organization's overall goals. Rewarding managers for meeting short-term goals at the expense of long-term goals may indicate a reward system that is inconsistent with the organization's overall strategy.

3. With respect to raises, a firm must choose between *merit pay raises (paying for performance) or across-the-board raises.* Firms who elect to pay for performance face the challenge of setting standards of performance against which the employees can be compared. Firms who decide to provide equal raises across the board face the challenge of keeping highly productive workers motivated and committed to the organization.

4. Firms also must choose the *level of pay secrecy* the organization will enforce. Many firms have decided that how much an individual is paid is between the firm and that individual. Employees who violate this agreement may be terminated. Other firms have more open views on pay secrecy and publicly post the salaries of its employees.

5. An organization must also determine its stance on *internal equity* when designing compensation systems. Firms that strive to ensure identical pay for identical jobs have selected a strong internal equity stance. Other firms which determine pay based on the person in the job and not the job itself may have internal inequity with respect to compensation.

Internal equity is the objective of setting wage rates that conform to the job's internal worth to the employer. A job evaluation is a formal process by which management assigns wage rates to jobs according to some preestablished formula. Most job evaluation techniques employ compensable factors in assessing job worth. A compensable factor provides a basis for defining the internal worth of a job. The most commonly employed compensable factors are (a) skills required by the job, (b) responsibility for people and/or equipment, (c) effort required, and (d) working conditions. Four general types of job evaluations can be seen in Exhibit 12.1. Job evaluation techniques can be differentiated on the basis of (a) whether the job being evaluated is *compared to other jobs* directly or *against some standard* and (b)

···

EXHIBIT 12.1   Typology of Job Evaluation Methods

Review

	WHOLE JOB	SPECIFIC JOB FACTORS
JOB VS. JOB	RANKING METHOD	FACTOR COMPARISON METHOD
	Identify the job with the most "worth" to the company. Identify the next job with the most worth. Continue this until all jobs are in a hierarchical order.	Select compensable factors and describe the jobs in terms of these factors. Rank the jobs on each factor. Weight each factor in terms of its relative importance to the organization. Calculate the total points for each job.
JOB VS. STANDARD	CLASSIFICATION METHOD	POINT METHOD
	Decide how many grade levels the job value structure is to be broken into (usually varies from 5 to 15) and write generic definitions at each level. Compare the job descriptions with the description of the grade level. Assign each job to the grade level it most closely matches.	Select compensable factors and develop levels (with points attached) for each factor. Analyze the job in terms of the compensable factors and determine which point level best fits the job. Assign points for each factor for the total points for each job.

···

whether the comparison is based on the *job as a whole* or on *specific factors* in the job.

6. Finally, managers must decide how to *mix intrinsic (rewards that come from performing the job)* and *extrinsic (rewards that come from a person outside the job) rewards* when developing a compensation system. When monetary rewards are not available or applicable, firms must locate other means by which to reward employees. Managers can make the strategic choice to design jobs so that intrinsic rewards are available to workers.

···························

EXTERNAL ENVIRONMENTAL VARIABLES

When developing and designing a compensation system, organizations must take into consideration the external environment in which they do business. While many external environmental factors impact an organization, only a few have a direct effect on an organization's reward system. Three of these—the nature of the competition, the nature of the labor market, and governmental regulations—are discussed in the following sections.

Nature of the Competition

The level of competition a firm faces in the product market is an important consideration when designing a compensation system. When an organization has many product competitors, cost control assumes greater significance. Price pressures generally are downward, and salary increases cannot be passed on to customers without risking loss of market share. In this situation, noneconomic rewards (such as promotions, job enrichment, and training and development programs) may assume greater importance in the pay scheme. Few competitors, on the other hand, increases flexibility in the design of the compensation system because wage increases are absorbed into the cost of the product or service.

An example of an industry with few competitors is simulation training. Simulflite and FlightSafety International are the only two organizations (outside of individual airline companies) that provide pilots with flight simulation training. Because their services have a high level of demand and have no practical product substitutes, they are able to pass on any increase in costs to their customers.

Nature of the Labor Market

A discussion of the impact of the nature of the labor market on designing reward systems focuses on two issues: labor supply and demand, and what competitors are paying to their employees. When the supply of labor is greater than the demand, the competition among job applicants for a limited number of positions permits companies to pay lower salaries. When demand for labor is greater than the supply, competition for the scarce resource of labor increases, bidding up the cost of labor. Applicants can afford to "shop around" for a company that pays a higher salary when labor is in demand.

This is not the only way that wages paid by competitors in the labor market can influence a company's wages. Some industries or individual organizations pay higher salaries than others as a policy. Certainly, high-tech and research and development industries must attract highly qualified employees. One way to do this is to pay more than other employers in the area. The strategic choice of paying above the market rate is discussed in more detail later in the chapter.

Government Regulations

While specific employment legislation affecting compensation decisions is addressed in a separate chapter, it is included here again because of its significant organizational impact. Federal legislation affects almost every aspect of the compensation plan. It places a lower limit on wages that can be paid; it affects raise and incentive decisions; it proscribes wage discrimination; and it requires certain benefits be paid for all employees.

Recent changes in tax legislation have further complicated benefits decisions for many companies and made it very difficult to determine the employment tax status of an organization's workers. For federal employment tax purposes, one set of rules applies to employees, and a completely different set of rules applies to independent contractors. While the costs of misclassifying workers can be very costly, it is extremely difficult to categorize workers with accuracy. For example, an employee may be classified as a statutory employee, an employee whom the Internal Revenue Code specifically classifies as an employee for FICA and FUTA purposes, but as an

....

| EXHIBIT 12.2 | The History of Minimum Wage |

DATE	MINIMUM WAGE	DATE	MINIMUM WAGE
October 24, 1938	0.25	May 1, 1974	2.00
October 24, 1939	0.30	January 1, 1975	2.10
October 24, 1945	0.40	January 1, 1976	2.30
January 25, 1950	0.75	January 1, 1978	2.65
March 1, 1956	1.00	January 1, 1979	2.90
September 3, 1961	1.15	January 1, 1980	3.10
September 3, 1963	1.25	January 1, 1981	3.35
February 1, 1967	1.40	April 1, 1990	3.80
February 1, 1968	1.60	April 1, 1991	4.25

....

independent contractor for income tax withholding purposes. This crossover of status makes it important for an organization to categorize the employee for each specific tax purpose and not to simply categorize the employee and go on.[6]

A second recent governmental regulation change, the increase of the minimum wage, also has caused some companies problems with respect to compensation. Small businesses, who have had to increase pay rates in order to comply with the new wage law, have had to cut back on staff in order to stay in business. The owner of a small motel in Wisconsin noted that the increase in the minimum wage from $3.80 to $4.25 will cost her motel about $5,000 a year. Raising room rates to cover this cost would only decrease occupancy rates and thus reduce income even further. Also, if the hotel really had an extra $5,000 to spend, it would much rather invest in new carpet for the rooms than spend it on labor costs.[7]

The change in the minimum wage law, agreed to by Congress in late 1989, raised the minimum wage from $3.35 to $3.80 in April of 1990. A second increase from $3.80 to $4.25 took effect April of 1991. The law has a loophole that allows employers to pay a lower "training wage" to a new employees for up to six months while they are learning the job.[8] Originally, the minimum wage law was designed to hold the minimum wages paid to unskilled or part-time workers at one half of the average U.S. hourly wage. However, it has fallen behind its goal. Even with the recent increase, the current rate of $4.25 is only 43 percent of the average U.S. hourly wage.[9] The history of the minimum wage is depicted in Exhibit 12.2.

....

INTERNAL ENVIRONMENTAL VARIABLES

Not only are external environmental variables important to organizations when developing compensation systems, so are internal environmental variables. Four of the most salient internal variables—corporate strategy, management philosophy, the type of job, and productivity—are examined in the sections that follow.

Corporate Strategy

The overall corporate strategy provides the direction for the organization. Because its focus is primarily long term, the pay system should be designed to support this

EXHIBIT 12.3 Strategic Pay and the Organizational Life Cycle

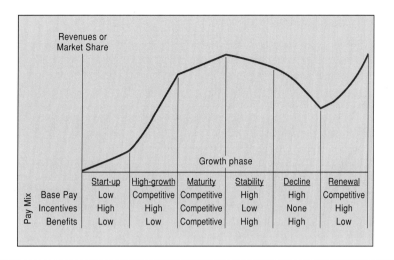

Pay Mix		Start-up	High-growth	Maturity	Stability	Decline	Renewal
	Base Pay	Low	Competitive	Competitive	High	High	Competitive
	Incentives	High	High	Competitive	Low	None	High
	Benefits	Low	Low	Competitive	High	High	Low

focus. One way to accomplish this goal is to tie the compensation system to the developmental stage of the company. Different combinations of pay are designed to fit with the strategic conditions faced by the firm. As shown in Exhibit 12.3, six organizational stages are possible, ranging from start-up through maturity, decline, and renewal. Each of these cycles requires a different combination of base pay, incentives, and benefits.

For example, a mature organization would have several product lines and strong earnings. The focus of its human resource department would be on cost cutting, consistency of program application, and efficiency. The most effective pay mix would offer a competitive base pay, incentives, and benefits. It is possible that a single organization could have more than one compensation strategy and system. Within an organization, the various subdivisions or units may be in different stages in their life cycle. This would require separate compensation plans for different divisions.

Management Philosophy

One component of management philosophy is the value it places on its human resources. This value is reflected in the relationship between management and line employees. Take, for example, this statement of company mission for Herman Miller, Inc., a manufacturer of office furniture. Central to the company's mission is that it attempts to share values, ideals, goals, and have respect for each person. To implement this mission, in 1950 Miller installed a plan that pays every employee a quarterly bonus based on attainment of production goals, employee cost-saving suggestions, customer satisfaction, and the company's return on assets. As you can see, an organization's culture is reflected in its pay system.

HR CHALLENGES •

The Culture at GM is Saturn Plant

The new Saturn plant in Spring Hill, Tennessee, provides an interesting example of how General Motors set out deliberately to create a new management philosophy and culture. GM wanted to implement a profound change in the way it treated its employees. At the center of this change is the relationship between labor and management, which now includes the United Auto Workers "in every aspect of the business." Power from top levels flows down to 165 work teams whose responsibilities include selecting team members, handling quality control problems, and deciding how to run their own areas.

The pay system echoes this trust. Workers receive an average yearly salary of $34,000, not an hourly wage. Part of that salary (20 percent, in fact) depends on a complex formula that measures car quality, productivity, and company profits. The inclusion of quality as a performance measure was critical because a major organizational strategy was to introduce this new product line as a "high-quality" American car with a level of excellence that was equal, or superior, to the quality found in Japanese cars. GM wanted to regain some of the market share lost to Japanese automobile manufacturers. Their new organization structure is radically different from the old GM, which was known for its bureaucratic structure, centralized decision making, and frequently combative employee relations.

SOURCE: Adapted from S. C. Gwynne, "The Right Stuff," *Time*, October 29, 1990, pp. 74–78, 81, 84.

The Type of Job

Jobs differ in many ways. These differences include the variety of tasks performed, the amount of physical or mental effort, the pleasantness of the working conditions, the degree of autonomy (control over how, when, and what to do), the responsibility for labor, materials, and equipment, and the amount of interaction with others.

Contrast the job of a coal miner with that of a computer analyst. A coal miner's job is mainly physical, involves a limited number of tasks, under working conditions that most of us would find unpleasant (working underground, in dangerous conditions, with the potential for health problems in the long run), with little or no control over how, when, or what to do on the job. A computer analyst, on the other hand, uses mainly mental skills, may have a wider variety of tasks (debugging programs, developing and writing computer programs and systems planning), a climate-controlled, generally pleasant environment, with some freedom as to program development and perhaps control over job priorities. It's possible that both of these jobs could exist within a large organization. How can a company develop a system that equitably compensates both employees? Their job tasks vary considerably; yet, each is a valuable employee to the organization.

Where the employee performs his or her job may also change the value and compensation associated with the position. For example, American managers who accept positions overseas often make more money than their stateside counterparts.[10] A manager who makes $100,000 in the United States earns three times that when transferred to London. That same manager would make close to a million dollars if transferred to Stockholm or Tokyo. Exhibit 12.4 provides an explanation for the increased costs. Due to these astronomical costs, opportunities for overseas positions have recently become harder to find. In 1989, 25 percent fewer Americans were assigned overseas positions. Instead, more firms were hiring locals who are paid a salary comparable to their American counterparts in the United States.[11]

··

| EXHIBIT 12.4 | The Price of an Expatriate in London |

ITEM	COST
Base salary	$100,000
Foreign service bonus	15,000
Good and service differential	21,000
Housing costs	39,000
Relocation allowance	5,000
Air fare to London	2,000
Moving household goods	25,000
Company car	15,000
Schooling costs (2 children)	20,000
Annual home leave for family (4 persons)	4,000
U.K. personal income tax	56,000
Additional costs:	20,000
Language/culture training	
Selling home/cars	
Miscellaneous	
Total	$322,000

··

Productivity

Productivity, as you have learned, is simply the ratio of outputs (product or service provided by the company) to inputs (for example, costs in terms of labor, capital, energy, materials, and machinery). Any increase in labor costs decreases productivity unless output increases or other costs decrease. In 1990, pay raises averaged 5.5 percent and a similar rise is expected in 1991. How to minimize the impact of these salary increases on productivity requires careful consideration.

Now that we've examined some of the major external and internal environmental variables that influence compensation decisions, let's turn our attention to a number of strategic options that must be considered. These options include the organization's pay level policy, the mix of extrinsic and intrinsic rewards, pay for performance systems, and pay secrecy versus openness.

STRATEGIC COMPENSATION OPTIONS

In developing a pay system, several policy decisions must be made. Three of the most critical are pay level policy, pay structure policy, and types of rewards offered.

Pay Level Policy

An organization's **pay level** is simply the average wage rate paid for a specific group of jobs.[12] Pay level is important because it influences both the organization's ability to attract and retain competent employees and its competitive position in the product market. **Pay level policy** refers to how an organization's pay level compares to its competitors' pay levels. The concept of **external equity**, how competitive the

....

| EXHIBIT 12.5 | Environmental Factors Affecting Pay Policy |

FACTORS IN THE EXTERNAL ENVIRONMENT	FACTORS IN THE INTERNAL ENVIRONMENT
Supply of Labor	Organization Size
Demand for Labor	Characteristics of the Work Force
Geographic Location of Company	Ability to Pay
Economic Conditions	Willingness to Pay
Product Competition	Unionization
Demand for Product	Desired Quality of Employee
Union Influence	Tradition
	Employer Prestige
	Ratio of Labor Costs to Total Costs
	Nature of the Job

Review

....

organization's wages are with its competitors' wages, is reflected in a firm's pay level policy.

Basically, three pay level policy options may be chosen: lead, lag, or match.[13] Employers with a lead policy pay higher wages than the average wage paid in the labor market. Employers who choose a lag policy pay lower than average wages, while employers with a match policy "match" the market wage rate.

Why does an organization choose one pay level policy over another? Many factors go into the decision and several are outlined in Exhibit 12.5. However, the basic answer to this question is that the organization chooses the pay level that (1) maximizes its ability to attract and keep qualified employees, (2) is within its ability to pay, and (3) allows it to remain competitive in its product market.

Most organizations use a "match" policy. This enables the organization to recruit and retain a competent (but not superior) work force, to pay their employees a wage that is perceived as fair, and to keep their labor costs in line with those of their competitors. Organizations who desire to attract the "cream of the crop" and therefore obtain higher product quality, lower turnover, less pay dissatisfaction and therefore fewer unionization attempts or labor disputes will select a lead policy. Firms that can offer some benefit (such as the ability to perform a job that is consistent with employees' beliefs and values) other than a high salary to employees or firms that always face an overabundance of qualified labor can choose a lag policy.

Some firms also may use one form of pay policy at one point, but be forced to switch to another at some future point. One example of this occurred at Public Service Company of New Mexico, a utility company. In the early 1980s, Public Service faced economic prosperity, a positive regulatory environment, high growth, and an increase in available workers. During this time Public Service prided itself on paying employees better than the going rate. In other words, it followed a lead pay policy. This policy served the company well, until the end of the 1980s. At this time a general downturn in the overall economy occurred. Further, deregulation and diversification entered the picture. Public Service was forced to cut 20 percent of its work force to remain competitive and now pays its remaining employees 8 percent below market rates.[14]

Pay Structure Policy

A company must also make a decision about **pay ranges**, the range of wages allowed by a specific wage classification and the amount of overlap between the ranges. While the government puts an absolute minimum on any pay range, in practice, an organization must decide on the maximum and minimum pay for any job or set of jobs in the pay structure. This maximum and minimum is based on external market wages and the internal job structure.

The results from a recent salary survey of 338 human resource professionals produced the following statistics with respect to pay range policies. First, 74 percent of the respondents reported that starting salaries for employees are generally in the first quartile of the pay range. Forty-three percent of the respondents indicated that a goal of the organization is to keep the salaries paid near the midpoint of the pay range. With respect to exceeding the pay range maximum, 52 percent reported that individuals were "seldom" paid more than the maximum allowed, while 31 percent reported that individuals were never paid above the maximum allowed in the pay range.[15]

A large spread between the minimum and maximum salary allowed in a pay range is termed a wide pay range. The wider the pay range, the longer the employee can stay in the same job and still receive pay increases. Wide pay ranges are common in organizations that have only a few **pay grades**. A pay grade is a group of jobs that have the same classification with respect to pay. Wide pay ranges are needed so that employees have room for movement in the pay range for a number of years before reaching a maximum. An organization with many pay grades, however, would have narrower pay ranges, and the maximum paid for any job could be reached more quickly. Companies using this type of pay structure would encourage their employees to receive pay raises through promotion and movement through pay grades instead of promotion and movement within the pay grade.

One form of pay grades that has fallen from favor is the two-tier pay system. Only a decade ago, two-tier wage scales were an extremely useful tool for dealing with escalating labor costs. However, today those that remain are a thorn in the side of both management and labor. Two-tier pay systems allowed existing workers to maintain their wage level while new employees were hired at a lesser wage rate. New employees, who worked side by side the longer-tenured workers, performed the same jobs, and received less pay, began to complain. As the size of the work force receiving the higher wages began to shrink due to retirement and attrition, and the size of the lower paid employees began to grow, the inequities between the two groups became too much. Only a few of the newly negotiated contracts now hold two-tier wage level clauses.[16] Interestingly, the opposite problem is even more prevalent—**wage compression,** This most often occurs when, due to inflation, new hires are brought in at about the same or higher salaries than the current employees. Organizations argue that in order to attract qualified employees, they must be willing to pay a premium. Unfortunately, organizations do not always adjust the salary levels of the current employees, which can lead to perceptions of inequity and dissatisfaction among employees.

Extrinsic versus Intrinsic Rewards

So far our discussion has centered around the financial reward system for the organization. However, financial returns are not the only alternatives the company has for compensating its employees. Recent economic downturns in the 1980s and early 1990s have led to increased cost consciousness for many companies. Companies have found it difficult to increase salaries, provide cash bonuses, or otherwise provide tangible rewards to its employees. In the absence of cash, some firms are looking for alternative ways to motivate employees.

Some nonmonetary motivators managers have reached for during lean times include intellectual challenges, a sense of purpose, more flexibility and responsibility, greater freedom and recognition, and increased input in decision making. To instill a sense of purpose, managers have doubled the praise bestowed upon their staff to let their employees know how much their work is appreciated. Other managers have tried to assign extremely challenging projects to employees to increase their mental stimulation. Assigning employees challenging projects can keep them from becoming bored and also can increase their intrinsic motivation for the job. Offering an employee a change in job title, which includes more prestige, also can be an effective nonmonetary reward. Finally, companies have found that flexibility is important in lean times. Sharper Image, who recently had to lay off 10 percent of its workers, relaxed its dress code at headquarters for employees who did not meet the public. Employees are now allowed to wear sweaters and slacks and can even wear jeans on Fridays.[17]

What kinds of benefits do individuals get from the nonmonetary rewards offered by managers? Some examples are a sense of pride and feeling of accomplishment when a job is done well, pleasure received from doing a task that is interesting and challenging, participation and involvement in decision-making, and an opportunity for personal and professional growth. The important point is that the design of the job itself, how it is performed, and what one wears while performing it all can be used to reward the individual. These types of rewards can have a powerful effect on motivation.

A STRATEGIC APPROACH TO COMPENSATION

An organization's compensation system should be consistent with the overall strategy of the organization. As discussed in Chapter 1, Miles and Snow observed that successful firms displayed a consistent strategy supported by complementary organizational structures, designs, and management processes. They identified three fundamental organizational strategies: the defender strategy (seeks narrow and relatively stable product-market domains), the prospector strategy (continually searches for product and market opportunities and experiments with response to environmental trends), and the analyzer strategy (operates in two types of product-market domains—one relatively stable and the other changing).[18]

In defender organizations, compensation systems are oriented toward an employee's position in the organizational hierarchy. The focus is on internal consistency and equity. Compensation is primarily driven by superior/subordinate differentials. Prospector organizations, on the other hand, are oriented toward employee performance (as opposed to hierarchical position) and focus on external performance (as opposed to hierarchical position) and focus on external competitiveness and equity. Total compensation packages are oriented toward incentives and driven by recruitment needs. Finally, analyzer organizations are primarily oriented toward hierarchical positions although performance is sometimes considered. Analyzers try to balance both internal consistency with external competitiveness.

PAY FOR PERFORMANCE

It used to be that hourly workers were paid by the hour, salaried workers were paid by the year, and only upper management received bonuses. Many companies now, however, have decided that this method does not work well enough and are experimenting with a variety of pay concepts to improve employee performance.

A report by the American Productivity and Quality Center found that 75 percent of U.S. employers claim to have nontraditional pay systems, with over 50 percent having performance-based compensation systems.[19] If a major goal of compensation is to motivate employees to work at their best level, then pay for performance is an intuitively appealing idea. After all, employees who are more productive are more valuable to the organization and should be rewarded for their superior performance.

The move toward paying employees for their contributions and not simply paying them for their time spent at work has been driven by the need for American firms to be more productive—to do more with less. The "less" normally extends into pay as pay-for-performance plans usually start with reduced base wages and salaries, but reward employees with handsome bonuses for hitting targets or meeting goals.[20]

The types of firms who have found ways to incorporate a pay-for-performance rewards system vary greatly. For example, American Airlines ground personnel, who are represented by the Transport Workers Union, ratified a contract that tied pay hikes to performance. Under this contract, baggage handlers could earn pay increases by getting luggage to passengers more quickly. This type of contract incentive provides a benefit to all involved, including travelers, the airline, and the baggage handlers.[21] Another place in which pay-for-performance systems have been introduced is on Wall Street. Shearson Lehman Hutton for example, introduced a plan called "BONUS." Each letter in BONUS stands for a specific way in which a stock can perform: buy, outperform, neutral, underperform, and sell. Analysts are expected to rate stocks in terms of these outcomes and their predictions are checked against what the stocks actually did using computers at the end of the year. Analysts' bonuses are related to how well they predicted over the year.[22]

The two pay-for-performance systems described above have one clear advantage over many other pay-for-performance systems: it is easy to measure performance. With respect to the baggage handlers, there is a specific time at which the plane's cargo doors can be opened. This time can be registered and compared to the time when the luggage from that flight begins to reach the luggage carousel. Similarly, Shearson can compare the actual data about the stocks and the ratings made by the analysts and develop an impossible-to-argue-with result.

Quantifying and defining performance standards is often a stumbling block when developing pay-for-performance systems. In order for pay-for-performance systems to work effectively, distinctions among employees' work must be made. However, because most managers are unwilling to make these distinctions, and because few companies force them to do so, most pay raises simply move in a lockstep fashion. Further, frequently it is a struggle to determine what workplace behavior is fair and meaningful to measure and reward. The measures frequently end up being global measures of safety and quality that, while they may be easier to quantify, may not be the workplace behavior that will actually increase productivity.[23]

The difficulty involved in determining and quantifying performance standards is not the only barrier to implementing a pay-for-performance system. Other problems rest in the traditional mindset of employers with respect to what employee compensation should include. For example, many firms believe that they have an obligation to keep employees pay even with inflation. This is normally accomplished by cost-of-living raises, which are equal across the board. While only 2.3 million workers are covered by a cost-of-living agreement, down from over 6 million in 1977, many more are enjoying the benefit of cost-of-living raises.[24] After providing employees with cost-of-living raises, frequently little money is left to reward outstanding performers. Similarly, if firms strive to maintain external equity and tie their pay scales to what the competition is paying, the majority of raise money may end up being spread across the board and not in the pockets of the most productive workers. Finally, companies can inhibit their ability to use a pay-for-performance system by striving to keep all workers at the midpoint of the salary range and by allowing managers to provide inflated performance appraisals, which increase expectations of large and deserved raises.[25]

How the pay-for-performance system is developed and implemented, who decides performance based raises, and who benefits from pay for performance systems also inhibit the successfulness of the programs. Pay-for-performance systems that were implemented via a "slam dunk" approach (someone from the top ordered someone below to implement a pay-for-performance system—pronto), frequently fail. The parameters of successful pay-for-performance systems must be negotiated and agreed to by all involved. Further, in some environments, pay-for-performance systems are not appropriate, and introducing a system in this type of environment will only result in failure.[26]

Once implemented, how the program is run also can result in problems. For example, in many firms, the immediate supervisor determines the merit increases subordinates will be paid, which allows them an extremely broad level of discretion and a good degree of control over the workers.[27] While the middle level managers may have the ability to determine the merit increases for their subordinates, they are all but forgotten in pay-for-performance reward systems. According to compensation consultants, barely 1 percent of the salary paid to middle-level executives earning from $20,000 to $50,000 will be paid through a pay-for-performance system.[28] Further, middle level managers are frequently evaluated to satisfy budgetary needs, not with respect to performance. If merit raises are provided, they are far too small and not as much, proportionally, as they should be with respect to lower performing colleagues.[29]

Recently, pay-for-performance reward systems have turned up in an unlikely location—Japan. Once noted for paying for time in grade and rewarding seniority, Japan has begun to take steps to link employee pay with performance. Much of the change can be traced to the changing demographics in the Japanese work force. The average age of a Japanese worker was 38.1 years in 1989 up from 33.9 in 1979. As the age of the work force increases, more and more employees expect to get promoted, as promotion after a certain time in grade was common in the past. However, with the top-heaviness being experienced by Japanese firms already, these traditions must change. The change has frequently been a push for pay and promotion for performance. Nissan is a good example of a Japanese company looking to change. After dropping the courtesy titles like *kacho* (section chief) that employees attached to their supervisors' names, Nissan told workers that it would base promotions on ability, rather than tenure. Ryobi, a die cast maker, took pay for performance one step further, and now bases middle managers' salaries on performance. This is quite a switch from the tenure-based salary structure that had been in place

EXHIBIT 12.6	Top Executive Perks Frequently Included in Compensation Packages

PERK	PERCENTAGE OF CEOS/PRESIDENTS WHO REPORTED HAVING THIS PERK
Company-owned or leased car for business use	70
Entertainment expense account	65
Telephone credit cards	58
Company car for personal use	55
Supplemental life insurance	50
Physical exams	40
Tax preparation assistance	30
Dining/social club memberships	25
Country club memberships	25
Car phone	22

since the company began. Ryobi hopes that the change in compensation will activate managers and spur initiative.[30]

Ryobi's desire to increase the activity and initiative of managers is but one of the positive outcomes that can stem from a well-designed pay-for-performance reward system. Other potential benefits include a movement toward focusing on the results rather than on the methods and focusing on the group or the whole instead of the individual.[31] Pay-for-performance systems also can be used to get employees to learn to think like shareholders. This is the main goal of the pay-for-performance system at General Dynamics. William Anders, chairman and CEO of General Dynamics, explains that if management can get employees to think and act like shareholders, then this partnering of interests will result in financial rewards for both. Further, these rewards will be tied to the long-term success of the organization.[32]

Executive Pay and Pay for Performance

Many aspects to the total compensation package are offered to top executives. Frequently, an executive's base salary is the lowest form of compensation received. Instead of a high base salary, executives receive a combination of perks that lead to a total compensation package that is well above the average pay of the workers or shareholders of the firm. The perks that are included in a compensation package differ with respect to the industry, the board of directors, and the firm. However, Exhibit 12.6 provides a list of some of the more common ones.

Some of the items that have been added to the list of executive compensation perks in the past few years have created some controversy. One such item is pension guarantees to protect executives from hostile takeovers and bankruptcies. Shareholders and employees argue that it is not fair that they risk losing their jobs and their investments when the firm is taken over or files for bankruptcy, while top executives stand to lose nothing. Companies defend the action, saying that it protects executives from losing the benefits that they have earned. Further, companies who normally offer such a plan are the ones that are in some trouble in the first place. It is difficult to retain qualified top executives in troubled firms without some type of guarantee.[33]

A second issue that concerns many stakeholders is the increased use of stock options in executive compensation plans. A stock option gives the holder the right to buy a certain number of shares at a set price some time in the future. Because the benefit of stock options depend upon the stock price, this option does not necessarily guarantee a large payoff. However, many stock option grants today are so large that even a small increase in the price of the stock could yield a sizeable payout.

Such guaranteed gains in executive compensation over the past few years has angered many stakeholders.[34] The tough economic times have made employees, who have been asked to tighten their belts and do more with less by top executives in their firms, ask the executives, "What about you?" For example, when the top management of United Press International (UPI) asked workers for a 90-day, 35 percent wage reduction, union officials said yes, but only if an equal cut for managers stays in place and no bonuses are awarded to executives.[35]

UPI is not alone in its demands; ITT shareholders are also rebelling. CEO, Rand Araskog, received a 103-percent raise, which upped his salary to $11.4 million making him one of America's highest paid executives in 1990, while profits for ITT rose just 4 percent. But it is not just this year's profit picture that has shareholders upset. Over the twelve-year tenure of Araskog, shareholder return has been in the bottom 30 percent of America's 406 largest companies while his compensation has grown from 87 times that of a blue-collar worker to more than 600 times as much. Shareholders are so angered by the ever increasing compensation for Araskog that they have threatened to vote out the company directors at the next annual meeting. While the shareholders may not succeed in changing the look of the top management at ITT this time around, top-level executives may want to take notice. It may no longer be possible to continue to increase their compensation at the expense of the firm and the shareholders.[36]

Shareholders and employees of other American firms like ITT are beginning to question exactly how a top-level executive's pay reflects the firm's performance. In an effort to answer this question, *Fortune* had a statistical model developed that, in effect, approximated the market rate for different CEOs. The model took into account, among other things, the company's performance, size, and the industry in which is competes.[37] Some of the results from this model are shown in Exhibit 12.7.

Another way in which top level executives pay for performance can be more evaluated is with respect to how much their firm gave to shareholders, or shareholder return. These calculations were performed by *Business Week* in their annual Executive Pay issue. The top five CEOs who gave their shareholders the most and the bottom five CEOs who gave their shareholders the least are presented in Exhibit 12.8. The exhibit also shows another set of interesting results from this report: the top and bottom five CEOs whose firms did the best and worst with respect to the CEO's individual pay.[38]

Finally, how top executives spend their pay also has been researched. Comparisons of how American, Japanese, German, and British executives spend their take-home pay is presented in Exhibit 12.9 (on page 417). It is interesting to note that these figures may indicate that American executives eat better away from home than they do at home, and have better cars and homes, but less of a wardrobe than their counterparts.[39]

While many people are in agreement that CEO compensation systems may need to be revamped, how this revamping should be accomplished is not as easily agreed

....

| EXHIBIT 12.7 | Computerized Comparison of CEO Pay with Firm Performance |

CEOS WHO MAKE MORE THAN THE MODEL PREDICTED

		COMPENSATION IN THOUSANDS OF DOLLARS	
CEO	FIRM	ACTUAL	PREDICTED
Steven J. Ross	Time Warner	39,060	2,670
Paul Fireman	Reebok International	20,770	1,960
Rand Araskog	ITT	11,460	2,860
Anthony O'Reilly	H.J. Heinz	10,650	2,660
Michael Eisner	Walt Disney	11,230	3,030
Howard M. Love	National Intergroup	4,380	1,340

CEOS WHO MAKE LESS THAN THE MODEL PREDICTED

		COMPENSATION IN THOUSANDS OF DOLLARS	
CEO	FIRM	ACTUAL	PREDICTED
Leon Hess	Amerada Hess	300	2,320
David Glass	Wal-Mart Stores	880	3,670
A. Dano Davis	Winn-Dixie Stores	600	2,490
John F. McDonnell	McDonnell Douglas	630	2,360
Harold B. Finch, Jr.	Nash Finch	400	1,440
Hugh L. McColl, Jr.	NCNB	750	2,660

....

upon. Some groups are suggesting reviving the fixed-ratio theory of executive pay.[40] This theory is based on the idea that the highest paid executives in the firm should make no more than X times the amount earned by the average worker in the firm (that is, a ratio of X to 1). Agreement with respect to what X should be is not clear. For example, Socrates, the Greek philosopher, suggested 5 to 1 as a solid ratio. However, more recently, Peter Drucker, the renowned management consultant, suggested a 20 to 1 ratio. One firm that has accepted and implemented Socrates' ratio is Ben and Jerry's Ice Cream.[41]

It is thought that firms who exhibit too great a differential between the CEO's pay and the average worker's pay are less effective. The higher differential leads to less trust, less teamwork, and overall, a less effective organization. In reality, however, this theory does not appear to be true. For example, Ben Cohen and Jerry Greenfield of Ben and Jerry's Ice Cream had a very difficult time finding a chief financial officer that would accept the position for $70,000 a year.[42] Michael Eisner, CEO of Walt Disney, makes approximately 238 times more than the average Walt Disney employee, assuming that the average pay at Disney is $40,000. But Walt Disney is known for its wonderful work environment and continued high overall corporate performance, and therefore, does not fit the theory. On the other hand, President George Bush makes a mere 10 times more than the average civil servant. However, his bureaucratic government is not reflective of teamwork, nor is the "senior management" of the United States often viewed as trustworthy by the majority

. . . .

EXHIBIT 12.8 CEO Pay for Performance Results

EXECUTIVES WHO GAVE SHAREHOLDERS THE MOST

CEO	FIRM	TOTAL PAY IN THOUSANDS	SHAREHOLDER RETURN
Albert Uetschi	Flight Safety International	$ 737	222%
George Lindemann	Metro Mobile CTS	1,113	266
Lawrence Ellison	Oracle Systems	3,809	801
Angelo Bruno	Bruno's	880	100
Robert Price	Price	708	46

EXECUTIVES WHO GAVE SHAREHOLDERS THE LEAST

CEO	FIRM	TOTAL PAY IN THOUSANDS	SHAREHOLDER RETURN
Lee Iacocca	Chrysler	$25,216	−10%
Paul Fireman	Reebok International	41,469	69
Michael Eisner	Walt Disney	56,413	162
W. Michael Blumenthal	Unisys	12,486	−34
William Stiritz	Ralston Purina	19,282	24

EXECUTIVES WHOSE COMPANIES DID THE BEST RELATIVE TO THEIR PAY

CEO	FIRM	TOTAL PAY IN THOUSANDS	RETURN ON EQUITY
I. MacAllister Booth	Polaroid	$1,997	28.2%
D. Euan Baird	Schlumberger	2,665	14.7
Morton Mandel	Premier Industrial	1,135	28.8
Albert Ueltschi	Flight Safety International	737	18.7
Robert Price	Price	708	20.0

EXECUTIVES WHOSE COMPANIES DID THE WORST RELATIVE TO THEIR PAY

CEO	FIRM	TOTAL PAY IN THOUSANDS	RETURN ON EQUITY
Edwin Lupberger	Entergy	$1,391	1.8%
Walter Shipley	Chemical Banking	3,447	−12.2
John McGillicuddy	Manufacturers Hanover	4,128	−18.1
William Catacosinos	Long Island Lighting	1,368	1.8
Charles Sanford, Jr.	Bankers Trust NY	6,583	− 9.2

. . . .

of the American public.[43] It appears that fixed ratio theory is not the answer to executive compensation problems.

An alternative plan that aims to make CEOs more accountable for their pay follows three basic steps:

1. Boards should require CEOs to hold substantial amounts of company stock. This makes them view what is good for the shareholders as good for themselves as well.

....

| EXHIBIT 12.9 | How Executives Spend Their Take-Home Pay |

	BRITAIN	GERMANY	JAPAN	UNITED STATES
Alcohol and tobacco	5.3%	1.7%	1.2%	1.8%
Cars and commuting	9.8%	8.6%	4.3%	10.0%
Clothing	7.3%	7.3%	8.1%	6.0%
Food at home	11.7%	10.3%	17.3%	8.0%
Food away from home	3.7%	4.2%	3.8%	5.5%
Furnishings and household operation	6.2%	8.6%	1.3%	6.3%
Housing	16.0%	13.2%	10.0%	17.2%
Medical care	0.6%	1.4%	2.3%	2.3%

....

2. Salary, bonuses, and stock options should be structured so as to provide big rewards for superior performance and big penalties for poor performance. This means that the pay-for-performance system has no guarantee base salary for CEOs. Instead, performance is tied to pay in both directions.
3. The threat of dismissal for poor performance should be made real. Not only is the CEO's compensation tied to firm performance, but the position of CEO should be too.[44]

Pay for Performance at Lower Levels

While often thought of as a method of payment for CEOs, the concept of pay-for-performance is being implemented at all levels in the organization in a variety of ways. The methods can be divided into three major types: individual, group, and a combination of the two. For individuals, pay-for-performance can take the form of merit pay, incentives, and bonuses. At the group level, profit-sharing, gainsharing, and stock ownership are the most prevalent.[45] Each of these options will be discussed in the sections that follow. This discussion begins by examining base pay and then introduces the various types of pay-for-performance plans most commonly used today.[46]

Base Pay

However a system is designed, most compensation programs use some form of **base pay**, which is the basic cash received for the work performed, adjusted for the individual's skill, education, experience, or some other attribute. The base pay may be either hourly (paid by the hour) or salaried (paid monthly or yearly). Base pay can be supplemented by incentives, lump sum bonus payments, or some other form of extra compensation.

Merit Pay

Perhaps the most familiar form of pay-for-performance plan is merit pay, which rewards work behaviors that have already occurred. Frequently, merit raises are based

··

EXHIBIT 12.10   Average Total Salary Increase Projections for 1991

COUNTRY	PERCENT FOR MANAGEMENT	PERCENT FOR NONMANAGEMENT	CONSUMER PRICE INDEX (%)
Australia	5.0–6.0	5.0–6.0	5.0
Canada	6.1	6.0	6.0–6.2
Germany	7.0	4.3	3.4–3.6
Hong Kong	12.8–15.0	12.8–15.0	10.5
Japan	5.0–6.5	5.7–6.0	2.8–3.1
Mexico	23.0–25.0	18.0–22.0	18.0–20.0
Singapore	8.0–9.0	8.0–9.0	4.3
United Kingdom	10.1	9.8	5.1–6.0
United States	5.3	5.0	6.7

··

on the level of the individual's performance in the past year relative to some standard of performance. Merit pay can be given either as an increase to the base salary or as a lump sum payment. To provide an idea of what constitutes an average merit pay increase, a list of the 1991 total salary increases for both management and nonmanagement positions in the United States and various other countries is presented in Exhibit 12.10.

A primary issue in merit pay-for-performance systems is whether pay truly is based on performance. Many researchers believe that the majority of merit pay systems simply do not work. Merit pay does not increase productivity because the difference in merit pay between the outstanding and poor performers is so small that the pay increase ends up being no incentive at all. For example, one survey of 459 companies found that top performers received, on average, a 7.7 percent increase while average performers received an average increase of 4.7 percent. While these figures appear to be significantly different, the difference in pay after taxes is approximately 20 dollars a week of a $40,000 employee. In these terms, the monetary increase is barely enough to cover lunch out for the week and can hardly be a motivating factor for high-quality workers.[47]

Another issue in merit pay for performance plans is whether employees perceive the relationship between pay and performance, if it does exist. Because it is often so unclear how a person got a higher or lower raise than another, it takes an enormous leap of faith for an employee to determine that pay and performance are really related. To make up for these problems, companies are getting rid of subjective appraisals and setting up bonus plans based on specific performance goals. These plans include a strong positive correlation with performance. If performance increases, so does pay. If, on the other hand, performance goes down, so does pay.[48]

When considering whether a performance-based pay system would work for your organization, the potential benefits and costs ought to be carefully weighed. Four major considerations are listed below.

1. If an organization employs predominately professionals, implementing a merit program is risky. Professional employees often have a marketable skill for which employers are always willing to pay. Thus, if the new merit compensation system is not in agreement with their perceptions of what their compensation should be, they will be likely and able to change jobs.

2. Employees who like what they are doing and who are enjoying a good deal of intrinsic motivation from their jobs may not like the extra pressure of external rewards placed upon their job when a merit system is implemented. In this case, it is better to simply let the employees enjoy their job without adding performance pressures.

3. If cooperation, teamwork, and work groups are valued above competition, individual initiative, and superstars, then a merit pay plan is not advisable. Merit plans tend to make individuals work to better themselves, perhaps even at the expense of others in the workplace.

4. In order for any merit pay system to be effective, management must enforce it. If managers are unable or refuse to take on the tough roles required by a merit pay system, such as providing accurate performance appraisals, the system will not work.[49]

Incentives

Like merit plans, incentive plans tie pay to some standard of performance. This standard can be defined as cost savings goals, quality standards, production levels or any number of goals. However, incentives differ from merit pay in that they are future-oriented; they are used to induce desired behavior. Their time orientation may be short-term, long-term, or a combination. They also may be tied to individual and/or group performance.

Most individual incentive plans are of two types: (1) the **straight piecework plan**, which pays a constant amount for each unit that is produced and (2) the **standard hour plan**, which ties pay to a standard amount of time that it takes to perform a service or complete a task. Under a straight piecework plan, an assembly line worker may receive 25 cents for each fishing tie that is completed. An example of the standard hour plan might be found in an appliance repair shop. Standard rates are determined for doing certain repairs, based on the average length of time it usually takes to do the job. If the standard time for a motor repair job is two hours, the repair person is paid for two hours. If the job is finished in less than two hours, the repair person is still paid the full amount. On the other hand, if the job takes longer than two hours, the repair person still earns the same amount.

Many companies have combined the basic incentive plan with a form of year-end bonus. Lincoln Electric in Cleveland is a shining example of a successful piecework plan instituted in 1934. Lincoln pays each factory worker for each acceptable piece that is produced. In addition, each employee receives a year-end bonus based on a yearly merit rating of the employee's dependability, ideas, quality, and output. For employees, the payoff has been bonuses averaging almost 98 percent of yearly wages. For Lincoln, the payoff has been 54 years without a losing quarter and 40 years without a layoff.

Group plans are similar to individual plans in that pay is tied to performance, but a major goal is to increase cooperative efforts and coordinate activities. Essentially, incentives are based on an increase in profits or a decrease in costs, relative to a "base year." The size of the group may range from work teams to the entire organization, with unitwide and organizationwide plans growing in popularity over the last 10 years.

The use of both individual and group incentive plans by all sizes of firms continues to grow. In 1989 it was estimated that nearly half of all companies offered some form of incentive to workers below the top executive level. One reason for the increase in use of incentives is that they seem to actually work. For example, introducing an incentive plan to workers has helped Domino's Pizza see an increase in sales, Ford Motor Company improve morale and quality of work, Avis to reduce customer complaints by 35 percent in one year, and Warner Lambert Company to witness an increase in the performance of its managers.[50]

There probably are as many incentive plans as their are firms using them. However, there is some agreement on the types of plans which work best. Two out of three companies who implemented incentive plans indicated that productivity increased when the plan offered to pay incentives to workers in discrete units for meeting specific targets.[51] One small company, headed by Hugh Aaron, that made color concentrates for the plastics industry capitalized on this formula and was able to increase productivity during even the leanest times.

After witnessing a flat profit line month after month after experiencing a period of intensive growth, Hugh Aaron decided that something had to be done. In order to increase sales he added to the salesforce, increased advertising, and purchased more equipment to enable him to produce more product. Profit continued to remain flat. While his strategy did allow him to win some new clients, he lost an equal number. He decided it was time to take a new approach, and he began focusing on the production line.

An incentive plan was introduced to reward plant workers whenever each production line produced more than the historical average of items per hour. Because the production line was run by a group of workers, teamwork improved and "slackers" received so much social pressure that most quit. When members of a team quit, the remaining team members requested that their positions not be filled. Because the bonus was split with the entire production line, fewer workers meant bigger rewards for the remaining workers. The new incentive system allowed production that used to take more than 100 employees to now be performed with less than 40 employees, and production increased more than 50 percent.

The incentive plan clearly produced a win–win situation. For every dollar in bonus the employees earned, the company earned two. Management met with the workers to express their appreciation for the level of performance they were receiving and were informed that even more could be produced, if only management would make one promise. The promise was that if the workers did increase productivity even further, the historical average production figures upon which the incentive program was based would not be changed. Management quickly agreed, in writing, and production levels increased to a point where the profits and productivity were higher than either side ever dreamed.[52]

Not all incentive programs result in a happy ending. Nearly one-third of the respondents to a survey of over 600 companies who were using incentive programs stated that their programs were ineffective or needed improvements. One reason why some of the programs did not work is because they were introduced primarily because the competition was doing the same thing. When the goals and conditions surrounding the plan are not clearly thought out and linked to overall firm performance goals, any incentive program is doomed to failure.[53]

A form of incentive-based pay that has received a great deal of attention in the past few years is **skill-based pay**. Under a skill-based pay plan, employees are paid for the skills they possess, not just the skills performed. Among the advantages of this type of pay system are a reduced competition among workers for higher supervisory ratings. Since an individual's pay is now determined by his or her ability and not the supervisor's rating, competition between workers is reduced. Similarly, supervisor costs decrease because the workers take on the responsibility for functions previously performed by supervisors as their skills increase. Finally, employees begin to have a greater understanding of how each position fits into the overall production process.

While the advantages of a skill-based pay plan seem impressive, there also are some problems associated with this type of incentive plan. First, the training costs are high. Frequently, the skills needed by workers are job or company specific and in order for the employees to gain these skills, in-house training must occur. The costs of setting up the programs and reduced production during the times employees are attending the training classes make a skill-based pay plan a costly proposal. An additional cost involved in this type of incentive program is the overall hourly wage costs. As employees complete the training programs, the overall hourly wage costs will increase. While highly trained employees allow the firm more flexibility, the wage costs must still be considered. Finally, even though employees see a skill-based pay plan as fair, compensation problems will still occur. Disagreements about the difficulty of the training, the time required, and how frequently the skills are required to be used will arise. Ways with which to deal with these problems must be developed.[54]

The increase in mergers, acquisitions, takeovers, and shutdowns in the past several years also has produced a new type of incentive: stay bonuses. **Stay bonuses** are a variety of cash bonuses and other inducements offered by firms to keep valued workers on the payroll during corporate reorganizations or closedowns. While frequently offered only to employees at higher levels in the organization, stay bonuses have begun to trickle down to even the lowest levels of the work force. For example, an office equipment company paid sales commissions even when there were no sales in order to maintain "business as usual" while it got ready to close. Often the most likely lower level employees to benefit from stay bonuses are workers who have skills that are difficult to replace. These skills may be job or company specific, or simply a skill that is currently in demand in the marketplace. Other employees who may be involved in stay bonuses are the experienced workers. For example, when Rouge Steel Company was acquired by Marico Acquisition Corporation, experienced workers were offered bonuses of up to $13,000 over three years if they would remain with the firm.[55]

Gain-Sharing Plans

Although gain sharing plans have been around for over 50 years, their recent increase in popularity has made them the fastest growing type of incentive. Exhibit 12.11 provides a brief look at the variety and prevalence of the types of gain-sharing plans used by both manufacturing and service firms. Gain-sharing plans involve a participative management approach and pay for gains in reduction of costs, whether or not the organization is profitable at year end. Gainsharing plans mold employees' perceptions about what they need to do to improve the organization's results overall and along the way.[56]

One widely-used cost saving plan that was developed in 1937 is the Scanlon plan. Scanlon plans focus on decreasing labor costs without decreasing output. The two major components of the plan are (1) the development of a productivity norm and (2) the use of a dual-committee system to encourage companywide participation in decision making. In developing a productivity norm, a base year is chosen that is neither a boom nor a bust year. Also, the base year must be fairly recent so that it

··

EXHIBIT 12.11	Number and Percent of Firms Using Various Types of Gain-Sharing Programs

TYPE OF PLAN	NUMBER USING	PERCENTAGE USING
Customized Plans	95	54.0
Improshare	47	27.0
Scanlon Plans	34	19.0
Rucker	1	00.006

··

represents current factors in the organizational environment. Worker committees are responsible for evaluating suggestions from employees about how to cut costs or improve productivity. Money is added to a bonus pool created each time that output exceeds the productivity norm. Monthly a portion of the fund is distributed to the employees and a portion is held aside for a reserve in case of a poor month. Whatever remains in the pool is paid out at the end of the year.[57]

Rucker plans, a second gain-sharing program, is also based on employee involvement but does not make as extensive use of employee committees as Scanlon plans. Instead, a suggestion box may be introduced in place of employee committees. Rucker plans also have a bonus formula that is based on value added. Rucker plans, because they are less radical than Scanlon plans, are frequently used by firms who are attempting to change their traditional management style by slowly adding employee involvement.[58] Unlike typical Scanlon plans, the Rucker value added formula allows workers to benefit from savings in production-related materials and supplies. Also, many of these plans have a reserve pool set aside for low productivity months. If the money in the reserve pool is not used during the year, it is paid out as an additional bonus to employees at the end of the year.[59] A more recent innovation in gain sharing is Improshare, developed in the 1970s by Mitchell Fein.

Successful gain-sharing plans can produce a number of important results for organizations as noted in the Improshare example. However, when deciding whether or not to implement a gain-sharing plan in order to achieve some of these benefits, several factors must be considered. First, it is important to clearly define the eligible employees of a group or unit to be included. Who is selected to be included and excluded may very well determine the successfulness of the plan. Second, a great deal of time should be spent specifying the measures and formula calculations that will be used to determine the rewards. The measures and calculations must be easy enough to implement and explain to those involved, but they must also be accurate and reward only the behavior that helps produce the wanted results. Finally, the proportion of total gains to be allocated to eligible employees and the frequency with which these gains will be paid must be clearly defined. The program should be designed to reward the behavior you want repeated as soon after it occurs as possible.[60]

More is involved in having a successful gain-sharing program than simply delineating the parameters of the plan. Management must also be involved and help to make the program work. Most of the items in the following list of common qualities found in over 300 successful gain-sharing programs fall directly on the shoulders of management.

HR CHALLENGES

Improshare

Programs based on Improshare stress quality and quantity goals derived from engineering standards. The bonus formula used in these types of plans is based on productivity standards that emphasize quality and quantity in relation to total labor hours expended. While Improshare plans need not include an employee involvement component, they have been used successfully in conjunction with quality circles and other types of work team situations.

Carrier, a subsidiary of United Technologies, introduced Improshare to its employees in 1988 and in its first year saw productivity increase 24 percent over its base year (1986) and rejects decreased dramatically.

Savings in labor costs are split fifty-fifty between the company and its employees, with each employee receiving the same percentage bonus. In 1988, 2,500 employees shared $3 million in bonus pay. Carrier claims its success is due to employee involvement. Plant productivity is posted daily on the bulletin board; quarterly meetings to discuss the budget, business conditions, and the economy are held with all employees in groups of 70 to 80; and employees are encouraged to talk to plant managers about their ideas.

SOURCE: Adapted from Edward Ost, "Gain Sharing's Potential," *Personnel Administrator*, July 1989, pp. 92–96.

1. Commitment—The most critical factor that has been found to make or break a gain-sharing program is the level of commitment to the program found in the management of the firm. Gain-sharing plans almost always succeed in organizations where the management staff works diligently to build a culture in which respect, cooperation, and communication are the norm.

2. Simplicity—The overall design of the plan, and specifically the formulas used, must be simple to use and to explain. When the plans are confusing to explain and interpret, mistrust increases and commitment decreases.

3. Involvement—Companies who have implemented successful gain-sharing programs have found ways to involve the workers and the management. Finding ways to get people to work together to achieve goals is one key to producing an accepted and successful gain-sharing program.

4. Communication—In order for employees to understand why the gain-sharing program is important to the company, information that is considered "for top level employees only" must be communicated to them. This information includes good (increased orders) and bad (loss of client) news and often the employees, once they understand the information, can provide feedback to their superiors about innovative ways to fix problems or capitalize on the firm's competitive advantage.[61]

Profit-Sharing Plans

Profit sharing ties employees bonus pay to the success of the company by focusing on profits. Profit-sharing plans generally reward employees only when a certain profit level is reached. These profits typically are distributed either in cash, deferred until a future time (retirement, severance, or disability), or paid in a combination of the two methods.

Profit sharing has several advantages. Generally, the incentive formula is simple and easy to communicate. Pay is variable because the plan only pays when the firm is profitable. Lastly, it promotes interest in the overall financial health of the company for both management and line employees.

Many companies have found success with profit-sharing plans. Hewlett-Packard believes profit sharing is a powerful tool for improving productivity.[62] Until recently, HP used deferred profit sharing only for upper management levels. Now, it pays cash bonuses to middle-management and white-collar staff each year that specific profit goals are met.

Another believer in profit sharing is Aluminum Company of America (Alcoa). After suffering from several years of downsizing and reorganization, Alcoa decided to use profit sharing as a way to share its hard-earned success with the employees who helped reach its goals. The plan begins once Alcoa's U.S. aluminum operating profits exceed 6 percent of the company's $5 billion in U.S. assets. In 1989, salaried employees received cash bonuses averaging 7 percent of each worker's salary. Alcoa believes that profit sharing, combined with a merit-raise system that replaced automatic yearly raises, gives them more flexibility in their compensation system.

Ford Motor Company launched a profit-sharing plan in 1983 by paying each employee an average of $400. The amount paid by the plan since its inception continued to grow until it reached a record high of an $3,700 in 1987. However, in 1988, the payout for Ford's employees dropped to an average of $2,800 and in 1989, Ford paid only an average of $1,025 to its workers. The drop in the payout reflected the drop in the firms earning. In 1989, Ford's yearly earning dropped 56 percent. Ford employees really have no reason to complain. Their profit-sharing checks have always been above those of their competitors. For example, in 1988, Chrysler's profit-sharing checks averaged only $720, while General Motors paid only $50 per employee, the amount required by the union contract. GM added salt to the employees' wounds by announcing that executives would divide a $224-million stock bonus pool for an average of $44,800 per executive at the same time it announced the $50 bonus for employees.[63]

Profit sharing does have its disadvantages. When payments are made annually, long-term goals may be ignored and short-term goals emphasized. Further, many times profits are beyond the control of company employees. As a result, employees who have made sacrifices or worked harder may feel cheated when their efforts do not pay off.

As you will see in the case at the end of the chapter, profit sharing is not always a success. Profits are influenced by a variety of variables, and many employees fail to see how their performance is tied to organizational performance. When payout is deferred for many years, the connection between performance and reward is further blurred.[64] However, some programs may succeed because they change the culture of the firm, leading employees to develop a broader view of the organization and its goals and inspiring greater commitment to those goals.[65]

In order for incentives to work, companies need a clear idea of their strategy and goals. Next, they must focus on jobs that can be measured and require peak performance levels. Companies must also allow individual business units to tailor their plans to their specific situations and provide conditions under which the program can be modified or even eliminated. Finally, incentives need to be separated from base pay so that employees can more readily see the link between rewards and performance. While these recommendations do not ensure success, they certainly increase the likelihood of successful implementation.

Commissions

Commission plans are typically developed for sales employees. They may be either straight commission plans, which pay the employee a percentage of sales that are made, or a combination of salary and commission (and/or bonus). The percentages vary with the industry, the product, and the nature of the sales job. For example, real estate commissions paid to the selling agency average around 3 percent, with up to 2 percent going directly to high performing agents. Plans also vary in the determination of how sales are calculated. Using the point of sale may encourage a very different set of sales behaviors than using the point of delivery.

Companies are working harder to make their commission plans more effective. Behlen Manufacturing in Columbus, Nebraska, ties its commissions partly to company profits. One-fourth of the commission on selling a preengineered building depends on the company's profit on the deal. A different plan is used by an Indianapolis product distributor, Seal Products, Inc. Seal pays up to four times as much when the sale is harder to make than when the customer walks in the front door and the sales person only has to show the product for the sale to happen. They believe their new plan helped boost sales by 25 percent in 1990.[66]

Another area, that has begun switching employees from salary to commission in an effort to boost sales is major department stores. The concept of an all commission salesforce in department stores is not new. Nordstrom's, a northwest service-oriented department store chain, has been using this type of compensation system successfully for quite some time. As lagging sales continue to close down operations and squeeze profit margins, retailers are looking to imitate Nordstrom's success.

The change in compensation plans has not been as smooth as some would have liked. For one thing, simply placing a salesperson on a commission-based compensation system does not create a customer-oriented salesperson. Customer service is a part of the culture and must be instilled and communicated throughout the organization. Similarly, some employees who had been working for the firm on a salary basis for many years had to be terminated because they were unable to effectively function on a commission-only basis. Also, new sales people were turning over as quickly as old. One firm saw its turnover rate jump from 4 percent before the introduction of commission based pay to over 18 percent after the introduction.

Some employees were thankful for the change in pay policies. These were the people who have been able to increase their pay under the new system. In theory, this should be an easy thing to do. For example, a clerk at Bloomingdale's in New York City was paid $7 an hour and 0.5 percent commission on sales of up to $500,000 under the old compensation system. The total compensation package for this employee would be $16,150 per year based on a 40-hour work week for 49 weeks out of the year ($7 × 1,950 hours + 0.5 percent of $500,000). Under the new plan, an employee who sells $500,000 worth of merchandise would earn $25,000 a year (5 percent of $500,000).[67]

Using commissions offers both advantages and disadvantages. Certainly commissions reward performance, are easy to communicate and administer, and allow fluctuation in pay. On the other hand, a straight commission plan may create a high variability in pay from one period to the next and generates lower organizational commitment. Further, the emphasis on volume of sales may cause employees to pay less attention to nonselling duties. Lastly, using commissions assumes that money is the primary motivator of employee behavior.[68]

For these reasons, the majority of organizations use a combination plan. A survey by the American Compensation Association in 1989 found that over 70 percent of sales compensation plans were of the salary plus commission or bonus type.[69] Aside from offering greater income security, it also motivates employees to perform even those duties that do not have an immediate sales-connected payoff. These advantages seem to outweigh the potential disadvantages of increased complexity and consequently higher administration costs.

Stock Ownership Plans

Stock ownership generally is a form of long-term incentive that traditionally has been available only for middle- to top-level management. In theory, managers who are partially paid with company stock have a higher interest in the long-term profitability of the company. Frequently, employees are required to remain with the firm for a specified time in order to qualify for ownership. Both the number of firms that require this and the length of employment required has risen in recent years.[70] Three major forms of stock ownership plans are stock options, stock purchase, and employee stock ownership plans (ESOP).

Stock Options

Two types of stock options are the **classic stock option** and the **restricted stock option**. A classic stock option gives the employee the right to buy the company's stock during a certain period of time (usually 10 years) for a set price. That price usually is the market value of the share on the day the option was offered. If the price rises above that level, the employee can exercise the option to buy the stock and immediately resell it for a "risk-free" gain. However, in order for the firm to gain the benefit of management thinking like a shareholder, it is hoped, but not always required, that managers hold on to their stock as long as they are with the company. In some companies there is no record-keeping procedure in place to check to see if managers sell or keep their stock. Further, the results from one survey of 774 publicly traded firms indicated that only 1 percent of the respondents required managers to own the company's stock.[71]

In a restricted stock option, the employee is given the shares with the restriction that they may not be resold for a specified period of time, generally five years. During that five years, the employee gets all dividends and voting rights. Even if stock prices fall, the sale of the stock still brings a certain sum of money to the employee.[72]

Stock Purchases

In the same way that stock options tie executives to the company's fate, organizations frequently allow employees to purchase stock shares either at regular market value or at a reduced value. Often the offer is for a limited time, commonly 30 days, or ongoing, in which the money needed to purchase the stock is withheld from the worker's paycheck. Workers then have a bigger stake in the success of the company and morale frequently is higher. For small organizations with participative management style, performance frequently improves and productivity increases. For large organizations, the effect is less pronounced unless all employees are allowed to participate in the plan.[73]

Employee Stock Ownership Plans (ESOP)

ESOPs work differently than stock purchase plans. Currently, about one-fourth, or about 10 million, of all corporate employees have enrolled in an ESOP. ESOPs, pioneered in the 1950s, allow employees to borrow against corporate assets to purchase stock. In some cases, however, employees accept wage concessions in return for stock. When companies do well, ESOP participants can amass significant nest eggs. A small construction firm in New York recently was purchased by its employees for $4.5 million. Since then, annual revenues jumped from $12 to $30, and shares are scheduled to be distributed to employees within 10 years.[74]

In general, the success of stock ownership depends on the situation and how it is used. In small organizations, stock ownership decreases the need for other forms of incentive plans; in larger organizations, stock ownership is more successful when used in conjunction with other pay-for-performance systems.[75]

In recent years, ESOPs have provided two additional benefits to firms. The first benefit is that ESOPs provide tax advantages to companies that give shares of stocks to their employees. Fifty percent of the interest on loans granted companies for use in ESOPs is tax-exempt. A second benefit is that ESOPs can be used as a defense against hostile takeovers. In 1989, Polaroid placed 14 percent of the company's stock in the hands of the employees in order to maneuver its way out of a hostile takeover situation. Since Polaroid's success, many other firms have rushed to place more of their company's stock into ESOPs.[76]

However, the success enjoyed by ESOPs may be short lived. As the economy continues to remain sluggish, the value of stocks of many firms have greatly decreased. In some cases, the stock has become worthless. Employees who may have had over $200,000 invested in the firm's stock may end up with nothing. The bankruptcy and law proceedings of Pan Am, for example, have reduced the value of the employees' ESOPs to nearly nothing. In Wall Street terms, individuals involved in ESOPs are holding an extremely undiversified portfolio. If the portfolio remains unprofitable, the holders will have nothing left with which to diversify.[77]

Many firms are attempting to develop a well rounded compensation system. To do this, they are using a variety of compensation options in developing their plans. Exhibit 12.12 provides one example of an overall compensation package that includes a variety of options. This package is one that is offered to managers at Toys 'R' Us. A second example, which describes an overall compensation package that has gone through some revisions lately, follows.

GM set up a new compensation system designed to push its salaried employees to work harder—and to help push those who don't out the door. The move, affecting 112,000 low-level managers, clerical workers, and other white-collar staffers, is part of a trend to tie compensation more closely to performance to make pay more variable from year to year. Two years earlier, GM had stopped giving annual cost-of-living raises. Temporarily suspended salary increases have been reinstated, but with a new philosophy: "A merit increase is something you have to earn," says Roy Roberts, vice-president for personnel. "To treat people fairly, you have to treat people differently." GM's new strategy involves base-pay merit raises, lump-sum payments, and profit sharing. The top 5,000 managers have also seen changes. Their 70-year old bonus plan was scrapped, decreasing annual pay for many executives by 50 percent. Instead of cash and stock right away, these managers are getting restricted stock grants that will take years to mature. All of this is to get people to work harder and encourage better cooperation.[78]

··

| EXHIBIT 12.12 | Management Compensation Benefits at Toys 'R' Us |

OPTION	DESCRIPTION
Stock Option	Management personnel receive stock options that are exercisable four years and nine months after they are granted at the original price. Options are issued each year, usually in November, at the then current price. The number of options granted is dependent upon your position at the time of the grant. (At this time, it is expected that a Manager's stock option in November 1989 will be 100 shares.)
Incentive Programs	In addition to regular compensation, a performance-oriented incentive award may be achieved annually. The following table summarizes the current award levels by classification.

Position	Incentive Range
Manager	0–15% of base salary
Assistant Director	0–22.5% of base salary
Store Director	0–30% of base salary

OPTION	DESCRIPTION
Profit-Sharing and Saving Plan	The company contributes a portion of its profits to the plan. You automatically qualify for the plan on your first anniversary date. Each year the company contributes an amount equal to approximately 8 percent of your W-2 earnings into your account. (This is over and above your actual pay.) A predetermined vesting schedule regulates the percentage of the total balance that you receive upon leaving the company. Currently, 100 percent vesting occurs after four years of service.
Performance	Upon completion of the training program, you will receive a raise. For the next year after promotion, you will be reviewed every six months and receive a raise based on your performance. At this point, you will become part of our annual review process, which occurs every April.
Stock Purchase	Eligibility: Age 18 years or older and completion of 90 days of continuous service. The Employee Stock Purchase Plan enables you to invest in company stock through automatic payroll deductions. The company will add 10 percent to your contribution and pay all commissions on purchases.

··

PAY SECRECY VERSUS OPENNESS

Organizations differ in the amount and type of information about pay that they readily communicate to their employees. To be sure, an organization that purports to use a pay-for-performance system increases employee trust and confidence in the system when it communicates to its employees how that system works, what level of raises will be received for different levels of performance, and pay increase schedules. Other information, such as pay maximums and minimums for various job classes or even specific individual salaries, also may be communicated.

Next, Inc., hangs a list of all employees' salaries in its company offices in Redwood City and Fremont, California. Phillip E. Wilson, vice-president of human resources, maintains that, "Anything less than openness doesn't establish the same level of trust."[79] Calfed, Inc., a bank in California, is more in the middle between pay secrecy and openness policies. Vanessa Jorgenson, a branch manager, believes that she is better able to handle pay problems and has a better chance of keeping people she has trained because of the bank's open pay policy. Calfed's performance guide, which she discusses with employees, includes data about how to compute a merit raise and salary brackets for every job.

In practice, however, the majority of companies prefer a policy of pay secrecy because they believe it gives them more freedom to make pay decisions and keeps employee pay dissatisfaction lower. Also, communicating information about a pay system that is not performance-related can reduce employee motivation. The results from a recent salary survey of 388 human resource professionals further documents the level of pay secrecy in the workplace. While 81 percent of the respondents reported that some information about pay ranges in the organization is made available to employees, 48 percent allowed employees to see only their own pay ranges and did not reveal pay structures for other positions, and approximately 20 percent indicated that no pay-scale information was provided to employees.[80]

Many employees also believe that pay secrecy is the best policy. For some, pay may be tied to the employee's ego. Others may simply be embarrassed about their pay or not want to know about others' pay for fear that it would just make them angry. At Electronic Data Systems, new hires are required to sign a form that acknowledges certain companywide policies. One of these states that while employees are permitted to reveal their salaries, they can be fired if such a disclosure leads to "disruptions."

All of our discussion so far assumes that money is a source of motivation to employees. In the following section, the relationship between motivation and compensation is discussed.

....

MOTIVATION THEORY

The general topic of motivation was discussed in an earlier chapter. In this section, the relationship of equity theory, expectancy theory, and reinforcement theory to compensation is more fully explained.

Equity Theory

A major goal of all compensation systems is fairness or perceived equity. Employees often determine their own individual perception of compensation equity by using the formula espoused in **equity theory**.[81] Equity theory proposes that employees examine the relationship between their outcomes from the job (such as pay, job satisfaction, recognition, and promotion) and their inputs (such as education, experience, skill, and effort). This ratio is then compared to the ratios of others (for example, other employees or the employees at a previous job). If the ratios are perceived as inequitable, dissatisfaction may result.

Dissatisfaction will probably not occur if positive inequity (the person feels overrewarded) is the result of the comparison. Research has shown that workers have been found to be happy when they feel they are paid more than they are worth. Further, this feeling of happiness also occurs when workers feel their colleagues are overrewarded.[82]

When negative inequity (the person is underrewarded) occurs, employees are generally dissatisfied. This dissatisfaction motivates the employee to reduce that inequity through increasing outcomes or decreasing inputs (either cognitively or physically) or changing the comparison in other ways so that the ratios are more equitable. Employees who want to increase their outcomes could ask for a raise or promotion, seek out greater recognition, or even change the perception of the level of satisfaction received from the job. Alternatively, the employee may choose to decrease inputs by using such mechanisms as cognitively downgrading the skill level or amount of experience or by not working as hard.

Research on equity theory has shown that individuals who believe they are paid too little relative to what others earn or what they think they *should* earn may become dissatisfied. This dissatisfaction may cause them to seek new employment, to become less productive, or to be absent more often. Thus, an individual's perception of equity is an important consideration in both the design and administration of the reward system.

One group of employees who often end up on the inequity side of the equity theory equation are women. For example, adult women with four years of high school on average earn about $17,800 a year. This figure is only two-thirds of what a man with a similar education level would earn. If that same woman earned a bachelor's degree, her salary would rise to an average of $27,300. Her new salary, however, would not change her feelings of inequity, because now she makes only $600 more than a man with a *high school degree.* A male with a college degree earns an average of $42,500 or $15,000 more than a female with a college degree.[83]

As women search for ways to rationalize the inequity they experience, several reasons surface. First, women may have shorter tenure than their male counterparts. For example, one study that found female lawyers made an average of $57,600 while male lawyers earned an average of $132,900 explained that the discrepancy was based on length of service differences. Females had been practicing law an average of 6.2 years, while males had practiced law for an average of 13.8 years. However, this logic failed when attempting to use it to explain the difference in wages between women and men lawyers who began practicing at the same time. Men reach the lucrative position of partner much sooner than women who graduated in the same year. Further, only 6 percent of the partners in law firms nationwide are women.[84]

A second reason used to explain why women earn less than men is based on the types of jobs they hold.[85] Women have traditionally held lower-paying positions such as teachers or nurses. When women begin to enter male-dominated jobs, the jobs change and the men leave. For example, when women began replacing men as cigarmakers in the late 1800s, the work was soon mechanized and wages fell. Before World War II, most of the positions of bank teller were held by men, and the pay was lucrative. Today, 95 percent of the positions are held by females and they make an average of $7.26 an hour. More recently, women have begun taking over other jobs that men, after the onset of computerization, decided were no longer attractive, such as typesetters and insurance adjusters. The wages in these positions also fell.[86]

If women really want to resolve their feelings of pay inequity, it may behoove them to move to Canada. In 1989, a law went into effect that covered all public or private firms in Canada that employed over 10 people. By law, employers were required to restructure pay rates so that females were compensated equally for comparable work. A firm must follow several steps in order to be in compliance with the law.

First, employers must define job classes or groups of jobs that have similar duties and qualification, are recruited in a similar fashion, and are paid along similar compensation schedules. If a class or group is dominated by women, it must be noted. A class is dominated by women if (1) more than 60 percent of the incumbents are female (2) less than 70 percent of the incumbents are male (3) historical precedent views the position as female or (4) popular perception views the job as female.

Next, the jobs are ranked with respect to skill, effort, responsibility, and working conditions. For each female-dominated class, the employer must locate a comparable male dominated class, and if the salaries, including benefits, are lower for females, the company must take action to raise them. If no comparable male class can be found at the same level, a male class at a lower level is used. Again, women's salaries, if they are lower, must be raised to meet that level of pay.

Finally, the employer must post a pay equity "plan" showing the job classifications for each job and how the pay will be adjusted. Male wages may not be cut to meet the wages paid females—only upward adjustments are allowed.[87] In the United States, at least 20 states have implemented similar programs in an effort to equalize salaries.

Expectancy Theory

In *Work and Motivation*, Victor Vroom's expectancy theory suggests that employee behavior is a function of the outcomes that are received for the work and the value of those outcomes to the individual.[88] Essentially, the theory has three key concepts: (1) performance-outcome expectancy, (2) value (or attractiveness), and (3) effort-performance expectancy.

The performance-outcome expectancy simply means that an individual believes that every behavior is connected to an outcome, and different levels of that behavior may be connected to different levels of that outcome. The attractiveness of that outcome differs from one individual to the next. For some, the outcome may be a highly valued reward; for another, the same outcome may be perceived as a punishment. For example, the individual who is afraid of the water or is terrified to get in front of a group will not be motivated to work hard enough to "win" an ocean cruise or receive recognition as "Employee of the Month" at an organizationwide meeting. These outcomes are not attractive to that employee.

Lastly, individuals evaluate the effort-performance expectancy relationship. In essence, the employee asks whether or not he or she is capable of performing successfully at certain levels and then translates those perceptions into probabilities of success. Individuals will then choose those behaviors that have the highest likelihood of success for obtaining valued outcomes.

When designing compensation systems, then, expectancy theory suggests that employers must follow several guidelines.

1. Make a clear connection between performance and outcome.
2. Develop flexible reward systems that provide a variety of potentially attractive outcomes.
3. Determine what rewards are valued by its employees.

....

EXHIBIT 12.13 Organizational Rewards

MATERIAL REWARDS, INCLUDING FRINGE BENEFITS		STATUS SYMBOLS	SOCIAL REWARDS	SELF REWARDS (FROM THE TASK)
Pay	Theater and sports tickets	Office size and location	Friendly greetings	Interesting work
Pay raise			Informal recognition	Sense of achievement
Stock options	Recreation facilities	Office with window		Job of more importance
Profit sharing	Reserved company parking		Praise	
Bonus plan	Work breaks	Carpeting	Smile	Job variety
Christmas bonus	Sabbatical leaves	Drapes	Evaluative feedback	Job-performance feedback
Provision and use of company facilities	Club memberships and privileges	Paintings	Compliments	Self-recognition
Deferred compensation, including other tax shelters	Discount purchase privileges	Watches	Nonverbal signals	Self-praise
		Rings	Pat on the back	Opportunities to schedule own work
Pay and time off for attending work-related training programs and seminars	Personal loans at favorable rates	Formal awards/ recognition	Invitations to coffee/lunch	Working hours
	Free legal advice	Wall plaque	After-hours social gatherings	Participation in new organizational ventures
Medical plan, including free physical examinations	Free personal financial planning advice			
	Free home protection-theft insurance			Choice of geographical location
Company auto	Burglar alarms and personal protection			Autonomy in job
Pension contributions	Moving expenses			
Product discount plans	Home purchase assistance			
Vacation trips				

....

4. Make sure that employees have the appropriate training and ability to perform the job successfully.

Reinforcement Theory

Reinforcement theories explain an individual's behavior as a response to a stimulus in the environment. Edward Thorndike's "Law of Effect" is the basis for many contemporary models of reinforcement and explains how a person's own actions in a situation interact with the environment to influence future reactions in that environment.[89] In essence, this "law" maintains that behavior that is positively reinforced (rewarded) tends to be repeated in that situation, while behavior that is punished tends to decrease in similar situations. Rewards, then, are positive reinforcers that strengthen the relationship between the situation and the behavior. They can be as subtle as a pat on the back or a smile or as obvious as a bonus or company car. Exhibit 12.13 gives a list of potential rewards provided by the organization and by the work itself.

The important point, again, is that rewards that are connected to a behavior will encourage that behavior to be repeated. As in expectancy theory, then, the manager must makes sure that rewards are applied in a timely fashion so that employees will (1) make the connection between behavior and outcome and (2) repeat the desired behavior in the future. Whether the behavior is short-term or long-term in focus, whether quality or quantity issues are relevant, management should understand the relationship between outcomes, their value to employees, and the impact that they have on employee behavior.

· · · · · · · · ·

MANAGEMENT GUIDELINES

1. Designing a reward system that reinforces the organization's business strategy can make the organization more competitive, increase its effectiveness, and help management focus on both short-term and long-term goals.

2. The goals of the compensation system can include
a. attraction and retention of employees
b. cost efficiency
c. legal compliance
d. equitable salaries for all employees
e. motivation of employee performance.

3. An organization's external environment interacts with its internal environment to influence the choice of compensation systems.

4. Effective reward systems include both intrinsic rewards (those that result from the job itself) and extrinsic rewards (those that are provided by others in the organization) to increase employee motivation.

5. Pay for performance plans are becoming increasingly popular because of their ability to tie pay to individual employee or group performance.

6. Three critical factors involved in pay for performance plans include
a. the ability to tie pay to performance
b. the ability to accurately measure performance
c. the ability to provide appropriate incentives.

7. Individual incentive plans tend to encourage competition among workers, while group plans are more likely to encourage cooperative efforts and teamwork.

8. Three motivation theories (equity, expectancy, and reinforcement theory) provide important insights into the role that rewards play in influencing employee behavior.

9. Internal and external equity, or perceived fairness, both in the design and implementation of the compensation system, increases employee acceptance of the system and lowers pay dissatisfaction.

10. All rewards are not relevant to all employees. Managers must identify what employees value and then try to match rewards with employees.

· · · · · · · · · · · · · · · ·
QUESTIONS FOR REVIEW

1. What are the important external and internal environmental variables affecting compensation plans? Which are most important? Why?

2. In what way does the competition in the labor market affect the wages a company has to pay?

3. What is one important objective for a compensation system? Why?

4. Define the term "pay-level policy" and discuss the three types of policies. Under what conditions might a company select each strategy?

5. Take a stand for or against the following statement and defend your answer:

> "Money is the most important tool that a manager has for motivating employees."

6. How does the expectancy theory relate to employee compensation?

7. Why have pay-for-performance plans increased in popularity recently? What are some problems associated with pay-for-performance programs?

8. What is the difference between gain sharing and profit sharing?

9. Why would a manager choose to use an individual incentive plan rather than a group plan?

10. If you were to design a pay system for sales employees at a large men's clothing store, how would you set it up and why?

 ## DuPont's Fiber Division Incentive Plan Unravels[90]

In January of 1988, DuPont Company's fiber division implemented an incentive pay plan tying pay for employees of every rank to profits. Unlike many profit-sharing programs, DuPont's plan didn't require a pay cut. Instead, at the end of a five-year phase-in-period, fiber workers would earn 6 percent less than their coworkers elsewhere in the company due to smaller raises. Fiber employees would collect the 6 percent difference if their group met its annual profit goal, but would collect nothing if profits fell below 80 percent of the goal. At the 80 percent level, they would receive a 3 percent bonus, and at 150% the bonus they received would boost them to 12 percent above the pay level of their peers in the other DuPont divisions.

The fiber division, the largest of the company's chemical businesses, employs 13,000 nonunion workers. Their

inclusion in the plan was mandatory. The division also employs 7,000 union workers at five plants who voted on their participation. Workers at four of those plants voted to participate and were included in the plan.

As a special inducement for union workers to join up, DuPont promised that all workers would immediately receive a payment as if raises had been put at risk throughout 1988, even though the plan didn't go into effect until 1989. In 1988, because the fibers segment was having a good year, employees received a total of $19,000 more than they would have received under a traditional plan. In 1989, the additional gain was $1 million. In 1990, profits were down 26 percent. By October, profits were only $397 million; to receive any bonus, profits needed to reach $580 million by year end. Employees in the fibers segment stood to lose 2 percent of their pay, which for most employees was about half of the raise they would have received under a traditional plan. Due to the anxiety felt by the workers, the incentive plan was canceled only two years into the three-year trial period.

What conditions contributed to the downfall of one of the most ambitious pay incentive plans in the country? At the beginning, the plan had a positive effect on employees who say they thought more about ways to cut costs. Employees hunted for cheaper air fares and took compensatory time off rather than overtime pay. One of the marketing specialists for DuPont likened it to "becoming a homeowner rather than a renter. You care more about keeping it up. I think more about what's best for the business." A manager in the floor-systems operation division, William Doan, believed that in the past they "did things because we had just been doing them. Now we're thinking: Do we really need to do them? Are they accomplishing what they were really intended to accomplish originally?" Other employees said they were more aware of the bigger picture, rather than concentrating on their own little job.

However, not all of the employees were that pleased with the idea. Some employees expressed concern over the plan and were distrustful of management. Since many higher level managers still participated in the companywide bonus plan, which is geared to the company's total profits, they worried that management didn't have as much at risk. "They have too many loopholes," is how one worker stated it. "What happens if a manager tries for the bonus one year at the expense of the next year's profits?"

Perhaps most importantly, many employees believed that they were powerless to influence profits. They also had a hard time devising more efficient work methods. Lastly, many employees believed that if a recession occurred, the resulting pay cut would be unfair because they had no control over the economy.

Certainly, in part, the DuPont program was a victim of the weakening economy. The fibers segment's business is tied closely to the housing and auto industries. However, some believe that the company simply didn't do enough at the beginning of the program to cultivate employee support. One union official stated that employees had no way of knowing for sure how the company calculated its profits nor could they analyze improvements in the program that could have been made. "We were completely frozen out," he said. James Kearns, the DuPont executive vice-president in the fibers division who spearheaded the pay-incentive plan, replied, "I'd have to say that's a management responsibility."

QUESTIONS

1. Officials at the company said that the plan represents a big part of DuPont's efforts to bring about changes in its corporate culture. How would you gauge the success of that change? What factors in the case lead you to believe that?

2. What factors in the organizational environment played the biggest part in the failure of the plan?

3. Using the four items found to be present in the implementation of every successful incentive program, redesign DuPont's program. What could the company have done to increase the probability of the plan's success?

••••••••••••••••• ADDITIONAL READINGS

Aaron, Hugh. "Making Incentives Pay During a Recession." *Wall Street Journal*, October 29, 1990, p. A14.

Balkin, David, and Luis Gomez-Mejia. "Matching Compensation and Organizational Strategies." *Strategic Management Journal* 11 (1990), pp. 153–169.

Belcher, David, W., and Thomas J. Atchison. *Compensation Administration*. Englewood Cliffs, NJ: Prentice-Hall, 1987.

Bergmann, Thomas, Harvey Gunderson, D. Weil, and B. Baliga. "Rewards Tied to Long-term Success." *HRMagazine*, May 1990, pp. 67–72.

Bunning, Richard. "Skill-based Pay." *Personnel Administrator*. June 1989, pp. 65–70.

Commerce Clearing House. *Executive Compensation*. Chicago, IL: Commerce Clearing House, Inc., 1989.

Drazin, Robert, and Ellen R. Auster. "Wage Differences between Men and Women: Performance Appraisal Ratings vs. Salary Allocation as Locus of Bias." *Human Resource Management* 26 (1987), pp. 157–168.

Ellig, B. "Pay Policies While Downsizing the Organization: A Systematic Approach," *Personnel* 60 (1983), pp. 26–35.

England, John. "Developing a Total Compensation Policy Statement." *Personnel*. May 1988, pp. 71–73.

Finkelstein, Sidney, and Donald Hambrick. "Chief Executive Compensation: A Synthesis and Reconciliation." *Strategic Management Journal* 9 (1988), pp. 543–558.

Foulkes, Fred. *Executive Compensation: A Strategic Guide for the 1990s*. Boston: Harvard Business School Press, 1990.

Gomez-Mejia, Luis. *Compensation and Benefits*. Washington, DC: BNA Books, 1989.

Gomez-Mejia, Luis, David Balkin, and George Milkovich. "Rethinking Rewards for Technical Employees." *Organizational Dynamics* 18 (1990), pp. 62–75.

Graham-Moore, Brian and Timothy Ross. *Gainsharing Plans for Improving Performance*. Washington, DC: BNA Books, 1990.

Hufnagel, Ellen. "Developing Strategic Compensation Plans." *Human Resource Management* 26 (1987), pp. 93–108.

Kerr, Steven. "On the Folly of Rewarding A, While Hoping for B." *Academy of Management Journal* 18, December 1975, pp. 769–783.

Kerr, Steven, and John Slocum. "Managing Corporate Culture through Reward Systems." *Academy of Management Executive* 1 (1987), pp. 99–108.

Kotlikoff, Laurence, and David Wise. *The Wage Carrot and the Pension Stick*. Kalamazoo, MI: W.E. Upjohn Institute, 1989.

Lawler, Edward. *Strategic Pay*. San Francisco: Jossey-Bass, 1990.

Leader, Laurie. *Wages and Hours: Law and Practice*. Albany, NY: Matthew Bender, 1990.

McCaffrey, Robert. *Employee Benefit Programs: A Total Compensation Perspective*. Boston: Kent Publishing, 1988.

Martin, James, and Thomas Heetderks. *Two-Tier Compensation Structures*. Kalamazoo, MI: W.E. Upjohn Institute, 1990.

Michael, Robert, Heidi Hartmann, and Brigid O'Farrell. *Pay Equity: Empirical Inquiries*. Washington DC: National Academic Press, 1989.

Ost, Edward. "Gain Sharing's Potential." *Personnel Administrator*. July 1989, pp. 92–96.

Patton, Thomas. *Fair Pay*. San Francisco: Jossey-Bass, 1988.

Rock, Milton, and Lance Berger. *The Compensation Handbook*. New York: McGraw-Hill, 1991.

Roth, William. *Work and Rewards: Redefining Our Work-Life Reality*. Westport, CT: Greenwood Press, 1989.

Schneier, G. "Implementing Performance Management and Recognition and Rewards (PMRR) Systems at the Strategic Level: A Line Management-Driven Effort." *Human Resource Planning* 12 (1989), pp. 205–220.

Tomasko, R. "Focusing Company Reward Systems to Help Achieve Business Objectives." *Management Review* 71 (1982), pp. 8–18.

VonGlinow, Mary Ann. 'Reward Strategies for Attracting, Evaluating, and Retraining Professionals." *Human Resource Management* 24 (1985), pp. 191–206.

Wallace, Marc, and Charles Fay. *Compensation Theory and Practice*. Boston: Kent Publishing, 1988.

••••••••••••••••• NOTES

1. Christopher Knowlton, "11 Men's Million-Dollar Motivator," *Fortune*, April 1990, pp. 65–67.

2. L. L. Cummings, "Compensation, Culture, and Motivation: A Systems Perspective," *Organizational Dynamics*, Winter 1984, pp. 33–34.

3. W. H. Mobley, *Employee Turnover: Causes, Consequences, and Control* (Reading, MA: Addison-Wesley, 1982).

4. Edward Lawler, *Pay and Organizational Development* (Reading, MA: Addison-Wesley, 1981).

5. Edward Lawler, "The Strategic Design of Reward Systems," in C. J. Fombrun, N. Tichy, and M. Devanna, eds., *Strategic Human Resource Management* (New York: Wiley, 1984), pp. 127–147.

6. Joel Walters, "Employment Tax Issues," *HRMagazine*, April 1990, pp. 72–76.

7. Jeffrey Tannenbaum, and Udayan Gupta, "Timing of New Basic Wage Hurts Firms," *Wall Street Journal*, April 9, 1991, p. B1.

8. Albert Karr, "Compromise on Minimum Wage Reached," *Wall Street Journal*, November 1, 1989, p. A3.

9. Gregory Spears, "Minimum-wage-increase Bill Is in Trouble As Some Say It Would Hurt More than Help," *Tallahassee Democrat*, May 6, 1988, p. 1A.

10. C. Conte, "U.S. Hard Hats and Managers Rank High in International Pay Comparisons," *Wall Street Journal*, March 3, 1992, p. A1.

11. Joann Lublin, "Grappling with the Expatriate Issue," *Wall Street Journal*, December 11, 1989, p. B1.

12. The group may include (1) all jobs in the company, (2) all jobs in a specific department(s), or whatever combination of jobs that the company wishes to analyze.

13. Much of this discussion relies on D. Belcher and T. Atchison, *Compensation Administration*, 2nd ed. (Englewood Cliffs, NJ: Prentice-Hall, 1987); and G. Milkovich and J. Newman, *Compensation* (Homewood, IL: BPI/Irwin, 1990).

14. Amanda Bennett, "When Money Is Tight, Bosses Scramble for Other Ways to Motivate the Troops," *Wall Street Journal*, October 31, 1990, p. B1.

15. "Most New Hires Start at Low End," *HRNews*, April 1991, p. 2.

16. Arthur Berkeley, "Companies Drop Tiered Pay Systems" *HRMagazine*, August 1990, p. 69.

17. Bennett, "When Money Is Tight."

18. R. Miles and C. Snow, "Designing Strategic Human Resources Systems," *Organizational Dynamics* 13, 1984, pp. 36–52.

19. Edward Baig, "Incentive Pay Plans," *Fortune*, December 19, 1988, pp. 51–52, 54, 58.

20. John Greenwald, "Workers: Risks and Rewards," *Time*, April 15, 1991, pp. 42–43.

21. Harris Collingwood, "Pay for Performance at American Airlines," *Business Week*, June 19, 1989, p. 41.

22. William Power, "Wall Street Firms Link Analysts' Pay to Performance," *Wall Street Journal*, September 9, 1989, p. B1.

23. Amanda Bennett, "Paying Workers to Meet Goals Spreads, but Gauging Performance Proves Tough," *Wall Street Journal*, September 10, 1991, pp. B1+.

24. Christopher Cont, "The Checkoff," *Wall Street Journal*, April 16, 1991, p. A1.

25. Selwyn Feinstein, "Pay for Performance Means Redefining What's Right," *Wall Street Journal*, February 20, 1991, p. A1.

26. Jerry McAdams, "Performance-based Reward Systems: Toward a Common-fate Environment," *Personnel Journal*, June 1988, pp. 103–113.

27. Selwyn Feinstein, "Pay for Performance Hangs Mostly on Boss's Subjective View," *Wall Street Journal*, October 24, 1989, p. A1.

28. Albert Karr, "Middle Managers Are Ignored in Accelerating Switch to Pay for Performance," *Wall Street Journal*, January 9, 1990, p. A1.

29. Selwyn Feinstein, "In Federal Government, Pay for Performance Doesn't Seem Very Effective" *Wall Street Journal*, December 12, 1989, p. A1.

30. Yumiko Ono, and Marcus Brauchli, "Japan Cuts the Middle-Management Fat," *Wall Street Journal*, August 8, 1989, p. B1.

31. Stephenie Overman, "Compensation Responds to New Marketplace," *HRNews*, June 1990, p. 7.

32. William Anders, "Hefty Bonuses for Hefty Gains, *Wall Street Journal*, May 20, 1991, p. A18.

33. Ron Suskind, "More Executives Get Pension Guarantees to Protect against Takeovers, Failures," *Wall Street Journal*, July 5, 1991, pp. B1+

34. Kevin Salwen, "Shareholder Proposals on Pay Must Be Aired, SEC to Tell 10 Firms," *Wall Street Journal*, February 13, 1992, p. A1.

35. Carol Hymowitz, "More Employees, Shareholders Demand That Sacrifices in Pay Begin at the Top," *Wall Street Journal*, November 8, 1990, pp. B1+.

36. John Greenwald, and David E. Thigpen, "Whose Company Is This?" *Time*, May 6, 1991, p. 48.

37. Graef Crystal, "How Much CEOs Really Make," *Fortune*, June 17, 1991, pp. 72–80.

38. John A. Byrne, Ronald Grover, and Robert Hof, "Pay Stubs of the Rich and Corporate," *Business Week*, May 7, 1990, pp. 56–108.

39. Joshua Mendes, and Cindy Mikami, "Where People Live," *Fortune*, March 11, 1991, pp. 44–54.

40. Jacqueline Mitchell, "Herman Miller Links Worker-CEO Pay," *Wall Street Journal*, May 7, 1992, p. B1.

41. Edward Giblin, Frank Sanfilippo, and Linda Ulrich, "Fixed Pat Ratio Is Bad Theory at Any Odds," *HRMagazine*, January 1991, p. 96.

42. A. Farnham, "The Trust Gap," *Fortune*, December 4, 1989, pp. 56–78.

43. Ibid.

44. Lindley Clark, "It's Not How Much You Pay CEOs—But How," *Wall Street Journal*, May 17, 1990, p. A18.

45. See Edward Lawler, "Pay for Performance: A Strategic Analysis," in Luis R. Gomez-Mejia, *Compensation and Benefits* (Washington, DC: BNA Books, 1989), for a thorough discussion of the strategic implications of individual and group pay-for-performance plans.

46. This section borrows from Milkovich and Newman, *Compensation*, and Gomez-Mejia, *Compensation and Benefits*.

47. Ira Kay, "Do Your Workers Really Merit a Raise?" *Wall Street Journal*, March 26, 1990, p. A8.

48. Ibid.

49. Barry Wisdom, "Before Implementing a Merit System . . . ," *Personnel Administrator*, October 1989, pp. 46–50.

50. Selwyn Feinstein, "Worker Incentives Proliferate," *Wall Street Journal*, December 12, 1989, p. A1.

51. Selwyn Feinstein, "Labor Letter," *Wall Street Journal*, December 5, 1989, p. A1.

52. Hugh Aaron, "Making Incentives Pay During a Recession," *Wall Street Journal*, October 29, 1990, p. A4.

53. Selwyn Feinstein, "Incentive Plans Keep Spreading Beyond Executive Suites. But Do They Work?" *Wall Street Journal*, November 6, 1990, p. A1.

54. Richard Bunning, "Skill-Based Pay," *Personnel Administrator*, June 1989, pp. 65–69.

55. Selwyn Feinstein, "Labor Letter," *Wall Street Journal*, December 5, 1989, p. A1; and "Labor Letter," *Wall Street Journal*, March 12, 1991, p. A1.

56. Judy Huret, "Paying for Team Results," *HRMagazine*, May 1991, pp. 39–41.

57. Gary Florkowski, "Analyzing Group Incentive Plans," *HRMagazine*, January 1990, pp. 36–39.

58. Edward Ost, "Gain Sharing's Potential," *Personnel Administrator*, July 1989, pp. 92–96.

59. Florkowski, "Analyzing Group Incentive Plans," p. 37.

60. John Dantico and Sandra Sipari, "Gainsharing: Consider a Plan for All Reasons," *HRNews*, February 1991, p. 12.

61. Kevin Paulsen, "Lessons Learned from Gainsharing," *HRMagazine*, April 1991, pp. 70–74.

62. Michael Shroeder, "Watching the Bottom Line Instead of the Clock," *Business Week*, November 7, 1988, p. 64.

63. Gregory Patterson, "Ford Motor Plans to Halve Payouts for Profit-Sharing," *Wall Street Journal*, February 21, 1990, p. C13; and "Ford Profit-Sharing Checks Will Average Over $2,800," *Wall Street Journal*, February 22, 1989, p. A9.

64. Pinhaus Schwinger, *Wage Incentive Systems* (New York: Halsted, 1975).

65. R. Bullock and E. Lawler, "Gainsharing: A Few Questions and Fewer Answers," *Human Resource Management* 23, 1984, pp. 23–40.

66. Roger Ricklefs, "Whither the Payoff on Sales Commissions," *Wall Street Journal*, March 6, 1990, p. B1.

67. "Now Salespeople Really Must Sell for Their Supper," *Business Week*, July 31, 1989, p. 50.

68. Several excellent articles and books provide details for designing sales compensation plans. For example, see Bruce Ellig, "Sales Compensation: A Systematic Approach," *Compensation Review*, 1982, pp. 21–45; and J. Barry and P. Henry, *Effective Sales Incentive Compensation* (New York: McGraw-Hill, 1981).

69. Luis Gomez-Mejia, *Compensation and Benefits* (Washington DC: Bureau of National Affairs, 1989).

70. Selwyn Feinstein, "Stay or No Pay," *Wall Street Journal*, February 27, 1990, p. A1.

71. Selwyn Feinstein, "A Special News Report on People and Their Jobs in Offices, Fields, and Factories," *Wall Street Journal*, April 24, 1990, p. A1.

72. Graef Crystal, "Incentive Pay That Doesn't Work," *Fortune*, August 28, 1989, pp. 101–104.

73. John McMillan, Ken Allen, and Robert Salwen, "Private Companies Offer Long-term Incentives," *HRMagazine*, June 1991, pp. 63–66; and John McMilliam, and Chris Young, "Sweetening the Compensation Package," *HRMagazine*, October 1990, pp. 36–39.

74. Frederick Ungenheur, "They Own the Place," *Time*, February 6, 1989, p. 51.

75. Gomez-Mejia, *Compensation and Benefits.*

76. Matthew Winkler, "IRS Approves Public ESOP Bond Sales," *Wall Street Journal*, June 2, 1989, p. C1.

77. James White, "As ESOPs Become Victims of '90s Bankruptcies, Workers Are Watching Their Nest Eggs Vanish," *Wall Street Journal*, January 25, 1991, p. C1.

78. Jacob Schlesinger, "GM's New Compensation Plan Reflects General Trend Tying Pay to Performance," *Wall Street Journal*, January 3, 1989, p. B1.

79. Julie Solomon, "Hush Money," *Wall Street Journal*, April 25, 1990, pp. R22–R24.

80. "Most New Hires Start at the Low End," *HRNews*, April 1991, p. 2.

81. For two classic articles regarding equity theory, see J. Stacey Adams, "Toward an Understanding of Inequity," *Journal of Abnormal and Social Psychology* 67, 1963, pp. 422–436; and George Homans, *Social Behavior: Its Elementary Forms* (New York: Harcourt Brace Jovanovich, 1961).

82. Selwyn Feinstein, "Pay Satisfaction Runs High, Especially at Companies That Street Teamwork," *Wall Street Journal*, October 9, 1990, p. A1.

83. "Women Aren't Getting Equal Pay for Equal Education," *Tallahassee Democrat*, November 14, 1991, pp. A1+.

84. "Women Still Earn Less Than Men as Lawyers," *Wall Street Journal*, April 21, 1989, p. B1.

85. "Youth, College Narrow Pay Gap a Bit for Women," *Wall Street Journal*, November 17, 1989, p. B1.

86. Aaron Bernstein, "So You Think You've Come a Long Way Baby?" *Business Week*, February 29, 1988, pp. 48–52.

87. Julie Solomon, "Pay Equity Gets a Tryout in Canada and U.S. Firms Are Watching Closely," *Wall Street Journal*, December 28, 1988, p. B1.

88. Victor Vroom, *Work and Motivation*, (New York: John Wiley & Sons, 1964).

89. Edward L. Thorndike, *Animal Intelligence*, New York: Macmillan, 1911, p. 244.

90. Material for this case was taken from Laurie Hays, "All Eyes on DuPont's Incentive-Pay Plan," *Wall Street Journal*, December 5, 1988, p. B1; and Richard Koenig, "DuPont Plan Linking Pay to Fibers Profit Unravels," *Wall Street Journal*, October 25, 1990, pp. B1, B4; and Richard Koenig, "DuPont Profit Fell 2.5% in Quarter Despite Oil Gains," *Wall Street Journal*, October 25, 1990, p. B4.

13 Strategies for Effective Performance Appraisal Systems

Performance appraisals are useful tools for not only evaluating the work of employees, but also for developing and motivating employees.[1] Unfortunately, performance appraisals also can be a tremendous source of anxiety and frustration for both the manager and the employee. This is often due to the uncertainties and ambiguities that surround many performance appraisal systems. In general, performance appraisals can be thought of as an interpretation of a performance measurement in terms of relative or absolute levels of effectiveness and/or the standards of performance met. The terms *performance appraisal* and *performance evaluation* are used interchangeably throughout this chapter. The purpose of this chapter is to examine the role of performance appraisals in human resource management and the relationship between performance appraisals and the strategy of the organization.

• • • • • • • • •
CHAPTER OBJECTIVES

After completing this chapter, you should be able to

1. Discuss some of the major strategic choices regarding the performance appraisals that are available to organizations.

2. Discuss the process of the performance appraisal.

3. Examine the requirements for an effective performance appraisal system.

4. Examine the various methods of performance appraisal, including appraisals based on a standard, personnel comparison systems, and results-oriented performance appraisals.

5. Identify a number of perceptual errors that can affect the objectivity and validity of the performance appraisal.

6. Discuss the relationship between the strategy of the organization and the performance appraisal process.

Participation at Westinghouse Electric Corporation[2]

Westinghouse Electric corporation created a new performance appraisal system to complement the new compensation program that had just been implemented for non-exempt employees. The system was designed by a task force that consisted of both management and non-exempt employees. "Our charter was to build a system that effectively linked pay with performance," said Jack Herrity, human resource manager for the headquarters site. "Creating it without giving the appraisers and appraisees the opportunity to contribute would have been a mistake. After all, these are the people who have to live with the system. They had a great deal at stake with this project." Mary Ann Belonus claimed that a participative approach to designing the system would help its ultimate success. "We wanted the people who will eventually be a part of the system to actually construct it and have ownership of it. We wanted the development of the system to be the ultimate people-input project because the credibility of the new system means everything. The participative approach was the only way to go."

The Task Force

The design group in charge of creating the equal appraisal system was divided into three separate committees: development, review, and performance standards. Each of these committees contained a mixture of both managers and non-exempt employees.

The performance standards committee was in charge of reviewing job descriptions and setting specific standards to match each description. The performance committee also looked for feedback on the current set of standards from other managers and non-exempt employees within Westinghouse. The development committee was partly involved in the creation of a new appraisal form that included both a job description and set performance standards for each position. The review group's purpose was to determine whether the appraisal system actually developed and evaluated employees. Further, this committee ascertained whether the appraisal system had established an effective link to the nonexempt compensation program. Finally, the review committee decided what should be done to improve the system.

Improving, Not Just Evaluating, Employee Performance

One interesting aspect of the new appraisal system was that at least three annual coaching/counseling sessions were to be required between the employee and his or her manager. A new form was created to help direct the manager through each of the sessions. The form was also to be used later as a reference in the completion of the employee's overall formal appraisal form at the end of the year.

Another feature of the appraisal system was the set of written performance standards that ultimately resulted in a more objective measurement of the employee's performance. A review of all the organization's position descriptions also was implemented to ensure that all the descriptions were up to date.

In order to increase the performance of certain employees, an improvement plan was created for employees who had received one or more below-standard ratings during the formal appraisal process. The manager would now be in charge of outlining a program designed to improve the employee's performance. In addition, the manager was expected to review the plan with the employee during the formal appraisal session to ensure that the employee understood what was expected from him or her and knew how to achieve the performance objectives.

• • • • • • • • •

Appraisal systems of the type described in this case are deemed fairer and more accurate by all those involved than the more traditional appraisal systems. Organizations can enjoy substantial benefits from appraisals, including the knowledge that the most deserving performers will be identified accurately and rewarded appropriately. Such employee knowledge contributes directly to productivity. Further, well-designed appraisal systems can alleviate some of the negative attitudes both managers and employees frequently hold. How this can be done successfully is the focus of this chapter.

STRATEGIC CHOICES

Managers have a number of strategic choices to make regarding the performance appraisal system. Some of the most important choices are outlined below.

1. Managers should decide on the *objectives and purpose for the performance appraisal.* Will the evaluations be for correcting problems, for determining rewards, or for other purposes?
2. Managers can choose between *formal and informal procedures* for the performance appraisal. Should the reviews be structured and occur at a specific point in time (formal), or should the manager and the subordinate discuss problems and ways to correct them as they occur (informal)?
3. Performance appraisal formats can emphasize more *objectivity versus subjectivity.* Should managers use their own judgments when evaluating subordi-

nates, or should more concrete factors such as number of units produced and absenteeism be used to judge an employee?

4. Managers must decide on the *frequency* of the performance appraisals. Most often yearly appraisals are performed. However, with new job procedures in which feedback about performance is given monthly, daily, and even hourly, perhaps less frequent reviews could be performed. On the other hand, if the job provides no specific feedback about performance, yearly intervals may be too long between appraisals.

5. Managers must decide *who conducts* the performance appraisal. While immediate supervisors are the frequent choice, as you will see in this chapter they are by no means the only choice.

PERFORMANCE APPRAISAL OBJECTIVES

A goal of any performance appraisal system is to effectively evaluate the performance of employees. However, performance appraisal systems also can be used to *improve* performance, motivate, and develop employees. One example of this is the systems-approach (versus the traditional individual approach) to performance appraisals.

An effective performance appraisal system will not only evaluate employees' abilities, but also opportunities—those elements in the work system that contribute to performance. According to some experts, opportunity factors are more important than individual variables in determining work performance.[3] Opportunity variables may include the physical environment, such as noise and lighting, available resources, such as human and computer assistance, and social processes, such as leadership. Thus, opportunity variables can influence performance indirectly by affecting individual variables, such as employee motivation.

Traditional performance appraisals often emphasize performance in terms of individual assessment and rewards or punishments. When using a systems framework for performance appraisals, the emphasis is on how the work system affects an individual's performance. In order to use a systems approach, managers must learn to appreciate the impact that the system-level factors have on individual performance and subordinates must adjust to the lack of competition between individuals. Thus, if a systems approach is going to be successful, employees must believe that by working toward common team goals, everyone will benefit.

Of course, the individual is still responsible for a large percentage of his or her work performance. Employees should not be encouraged to *seek* organizational reasons for their failure. The identification of system obstacles should be used to facilitate development and motivation, not to excuse poor performance. Exhibit 13.1 displays some of the differences between the more traditional performance appraisal approach and the systems-oriented approach.

Formal versus Informal Performance Appraisals

Formal performance appraisals usually occur at specified time periods once or twice a year. Formal appraisals are most often required by the organization for the purpose of employee evaluation. Informal performance appraisals can occur whenever the supervisor feels communication is needed. For example, if the employee has been consistently meeting or exceeding standards, an informal performance appraisal may be in order to simply recognize this fact. Discussions can take place in a variety of places in the organization ranging from the manager's office to the cafeteria. Of course, it is always wise to discuss employee performance in private.

···

| EXHIBIT 13.1 | Performance Appraisal Systems |

	TRADITIONAL	SYSTEMS
GUIDING VALUE	Attribution to individual	Attribution to system
PRIMARY GOALS	Control; documentation	Development; solving problems
LEADERSHIP PRACTICES	Directional; evaluative	Facilitative; coaching
APPRAISAL FREQUENCY	Occasional	Frequent
DEGREE OF FORMALITY	High	Low
REWARD PRACTICES	Individual orientation	Group orientation

···

Many organizations encourage a mixture of both formal and informal appraisals. The formal appraisal is most often used as the primary evaluation. However, the informal appraisal is very helpful for more frequent performance feedback. Informal appraisals should *not* take the place of a formal performance evaluation.

Objective versus Subjective Performance Appraisals

Organizations must choose the degree to which performance appraisals are to be objective (evaluating performance against specific standards) versus subjective (evaluating how "well" and employee performs in general). Although at first glance it may seem that objective measures would be the best strategic choice for an organization, subjective measures can be helpful when identifying desirable characteristics that are difficult to quantify. For example, objectively measuring communication skills or management potential is an extremely difficult task. However, the formal performance appraisal should not contain *only* subjective measures of performance.

Standards for performance appraisals should be based on an analysis of job requirements. Job requirements should be developed through the job descriptions, and should include documented standards based on a thorough job analysis. A detailed discussion of job descriptions and job analysis is provided in Chapter 7.

From a strategic view, it is often best for an organization to encourage objectivity in the formal appraisal process (that is, the employee should be rated on behavior rather than attitudes). Not only can this help to alleviate some of the ambiguities for employees and managers (such as determining what an "attitude" really is), but from a legal standpoint, objective measures are easier to defend. Unfortunately, the more objective performance appraisals, such as a behaviorally anchored rating scale discussed later, are often extremely time-consuming and expensive to develop. Thus, the organization must weigh the costs and benefits of developing such a format.

Frequency of Performance Appraisals

Traditionally, most organizations recommend that performance appraisals be conducted every six to twelve months for employees. Interestingly, many employees report that they are appraised much less frequently.[4] Infrequent performance appraisals are most often due to the manager's negative view of the process. For example, performance appraisals can be stressful for both the employee *and* the manager, especially when employee performance has been below expectations. Thus, the manager may want to avoid this situation. In addition, the manager may view the performance appraisal process as extra work and, thus, burdensome. Regardless of the reasons, managers should be encouraged (possibly through training) to view the performance appraisal process as opportunity to communicate with his or her employees and as a means of improving performance and developing employees.

Research has shown that many employees believe performance feedback should be given more frequently than once or twice a year.[5] In fact, over 80 percent of the employees asked rank feedback about their performance as one of their top five priorities, while only 45 percent feel they receive adequate feedback.[6] Interestingly, the employees desire not formal, but informal communication. Informal evaluations can reduce the anxiety stemming from the yearly formal appraisal session by minimizing the "surprises." Thus, one possible strategy for an organization might be to encourage frequent informal appraisal sessions between managers and employees while limiting the formal and more labor intensive sessions to one or two every year.

Who Conducts the Performance Appraisal?

KNOW

Performance evaluations can come from a variety of sources. Although most performance evaluations come from one source (such as the immediate supervisor), this is not necessarily the case. In matrix-type organizations, for example, employees most often have two immediate supervisors and receive ratings from both of them. Further, having more than one rater can increase the reliability of the performance evaluation. The following section describes a number of potential sources from which performance ratings can be derived:

Supervisor

The most common evaluator is the employee's immediate supervisor. It has been estimated that over 90 percent of all performance appraisals are completed *only* by the immediate supervisor.[7] In order for the supervisor to effectively rate the subordinate he or she should have frequent contact with the employee and be able to obtain the specific information regarding the employee's performance behavior. Although many would assume this degree of contact occurs regularly, many supervisors do not actually have much of an opportunity to observe their employees' behavior. For example, an employee who heads up a branch firm in a different city or even state from the "home office" may have little direct contact with his or her supervisor. Although the supervisor may be able to gather relevant information about this employee, the supervisor may benefit from obtaining information from some of the additional sources described below.

Coworkers

Another possible constituency from which to draw performance information is the employee's peer group or coworkers. Although coworkers may be somewhat uncomfortable and resistant to evaluating their peers, at least one study has shown that peer evaluations are more stable over time and may be the *most* accurate evaluations of employee performance.[8] An organization may choose to encourage peer evaluations, particularly if the contact between supervisor and employee is limited.

HR CHALLENGES •

Making Coworker Reviews Work

With an ever-increasing emphasis being placed on work teams and employee involvement, the use of coworker evaluations should begin to increase as well. Many firms have long overlooked this untapped resource. But who besides the person next to you day after day, frequently trained to perform the same job, knows your actual job performance better?

YSI, an instrumentation maker located in Yellow Springs, Ohio, agrees with this philosophy so much so that it has instituted a twice-a-year peer review in work centers throughout its production area. YSI employees realize that the feedback they receive from their peers is the most important information they will receive. While their leaders (formally supervisors) will also evaluate their performance, these leader ratings hold no more weight than the ratings received from coworkers.

The employees enjoy giving the feedback. For years they tried to tell management about the problems they encountered with other workers, but most of the criticism fell on deaf ears. But no more. Finally, what the workers say means something and changes usually occur.

While the process seems to be working, one drawback is the employee's disinclination to criticize a coworker one day and then work effectively with that person the next day. Some workers simply refuse to participate, and others find it impossible to take constructive criticism from fellow workers. However, as YSI found, minor adjustments and some transfers can overcome the majority of the resistance.

SOURCE: Adapted from "Measuring Performance," *Inc.*, October 1991, pp. 161–162.

Self-evaluation

Occasionally, employees are given the opportunity to assess their own performance. Although many are reluctant to engage in self-ratings, this information can be extremely valuable to the supervisor. Large discrepancies between the supervisor and employee ratings should be reason for concern. Discrepancies often occur due to a lack of communication and performance feedback by the supervisor. For example, if employees hear nothing from their supervisor for months, they might erroneously conclude that they are performing well (or poorly). However, when rating comparisons indicate a discrepancy, this information can be used to convince the manager to increase the amount of feedback the employee receives in the future.

Research has found that employees who are given the opportunity to evaluate themselves have a tendency to inflate their ratings.[9] One study reported that mean self-ratings for a group of workers were at least one standard deviation higher than were the mean supervisory ratings. Further, the range of ratings given by the employees for their performance was much smaller than those provided by their supervisors.[10]

Finally, self-evaluations have been found to be extremely helpful when used for employee development purposes.[11] Self-ratings can encourage discussions about the employee's strengths and weaknesses from both the employee's and supervisor's point of view. In addition, some companies are now encouraging employees to fill out "discussion forms" so that the supervisor is better able to help the employee's career development. If an organization's strategy is to hire more inexperienced workers at a lower salary ("make" versus "buy") or to simply promote from within, self-evaluations and discussion forms are an excellent way to motivate and develop employees.

Subordinates

Subordinates are valuable sources of information when examining managerial performance.[12] It is important to encourage subordinates to be candid if the information

HR CHALLENGES •

Employee Discussion Form

In order to encourage subordinates to talk about their self-evaluations, organizations have employed the use of discussion forms much like the example shown here.

HANDY-DANDY STORES

Please complete prior to performance appraisal interview.

Name:_____
Supervisor's Suggested Decision Date:_____
Discussion Date:_____
Present Job Title:_____

Please circle any of the following comments, questions, or ideas you want to talk about during your performance appraisal. For those areas you circle, I would like you to write down any specific thoughts you want to discuss.

1. MY JOB
   A. Responsibilities I'm unclear of:

   B. Things I'd like to do more of:

   C. Things I'd like to do less of:

2. OUR ORGANIZATION
   A. Things I'd like to know more about:

   B. Barriers that keep me from doing a better job.

3. ME
   A. Training and development I'd like to have:

   B. My future is this organization:

   C. Other areas I'm concerned about:

is to be at all useful. Candor, of course, is most likely to occur when subordinates are guaranteed anonymity and have no fear of reprisal.[13] Information from subordinates is not only helpful for determining how well a manager leads, communicates, plans, delegates, and organizes, but also for identifying general problem areas within a department. The use of subordinate input for managerial evaluations can be valuable if the information is gathered in an atmosphere of trust and candor.

Computers

Computer-aided management involves the use of computers to monitor, supervise, and evaluate employee performance electronically. It has been estimated that by the year 2000, as many as 30 million visual display terminal users might be evaluated and monitored by electronic methods.[14] Monitoring employees by computer is open to serious invasions-of-privacy issues. Some lawmakers are already attempting to introduce legislation that would limit the use of computer monitoring in organizations.[15] Despite the concerns, computerized appraisals could be a valuable aid to human resource managers. Computer monitoring must include benefits for both the employees and the employers if it is to be effective. Exhibit 13.2 outlines why using computers to monitor job performance can be useful for employers and employees.

Computers have an additional use in the appraisal process. By using artificial intelligence (making computers exhibit intelligent behavior), DuPont and the University of Minnesota built and are testing a multiple-rater appraisal system. The artificial intelligence component can evaluate ratings and determine whether or not they are reliable. Also, the system can pinpoint problems, such as a particular question that is being misinterpreted or a specific rater who is out of line when compared to all the other raters. The problems can be relayed back to the rater or the group

··

EXHIBIT 13.2 How and Why Computer Monitoring Can Work

1. **Response-Outcome Dependency:** Computer monitoring indicates to the worker which responses are correct. In turn, this can lead to an increase in the performance of desired behaviors. It also makes undesired behaviors salient.
2. **Effective Feedback Vehicle:** Summary reports from the computer can provide immediate feedback to employees so that they can choose to modify their behavior.
3. **Constructive Expectations:** Electronic performance monitoring sets specific standards accompanied by expectations that are incorporated into the daily work routines. Workers have a clear idea of what is expected of them.
4. **Reduced Unpredictability:** Computer monitoring allows the employee to track his or her performance throughout the year. Thus, the yearly performance evaluation will be less of a surprise.
5. **Direct Accountability:** Performance monitoring by computer is a direct measurement of that work, making it difficult for an employee to cover up errors or to blame others. Thus, those employees who are good performers would be the most likely to accept electronic monitoring.
6. **Better Training Programs:** Gathering summary information regarding the types of mistakes most commonly made could lead to training programs that precisely target the problems.
7. **Objective Documentation:** Electronic monitoring can identify good performers objectively because the computer generates a quantitative appraisal.
8. **Increased Flexibility:** Flexibility can occur because "fast" workers will have more control over scheduling of required work. "Slower" workers can be allowed some additional time to complete the tasks if the computer information shows that the worker output is adequate.

···

who developed the system for corrections. By using computers in this manner, the evaluation process can become more valid and reliable over time.[16]

Customers

In service organizations the customer is in a perfect position to provide performance feedback. For example, frequently guests checking out of a hotel are asked to complete a response card about their stay and indicate whether any one staff member enhanced the visit. Hampton Inn asks guests to "catch an employee in the act" of making their stay more enjoyable. Any employee who is singled out by a satisfied customer for a job well done has earned a Hampton Inn sticker, which the employee can prominently display on his or her name tag. This type of constant evaluation works as a reinforcing mechanism for Hampton Inn's motto: "100 percent satisfaction guaranteed."

The Job Itself

Finally, employees at all levels in the organization can receive feedback from the job they perform. For example, when a secretary mistakenly presses the wrong button on his or her word processor, a beep is heard. This negative feedback is a reminder that the last behavior was inappropriate. Similarly, workers who are linked by an interdependent work situation, that is one person cannot perform his or her job without input from someone else, are constantly aware of their level of performance as they watch others standing around waiting for them to supply the needed part or information. In order to use this type of performance feedback successfully, organizations must carefully design the jobs their workers perform.

Which and How Many Raters Should Be Used?

The organization's choice of which type and how many raters to use is not an easy task. The strategy of the firm, the culture within the firm, and purpose of the evaluation must all be taken into consideration. For example, if the culture and strategy of an organization emphasize efficiency and one-on-one supervisor-subordinate relationships, the most effective way to evaluate performance might be to have only the input from the immediate supervisor and/or input from computer monitoring. On the other hand, if the organization emphasizes development, training, and promotions from within, performance information might be solicited from a variety of sources including supervisors, coworkers, and self-assessments. Collecting information from a number of different sources can increase the reliability of the performance appraisal. However, this can also be a time-consuming endeavor.

PERFORMANCE APPRAISAL PROCESS

Developing and conducting performance appraisals should not be done in isolation. The performance appraisal is closely related to a number of human resource management activities that should be considered. Exhibit 13.3 illustrates some of these relationships.

Job Analysis

The performance appraisal should be based on a thorough job analysis. The results of a job analysis can be used to produce a **job description**, which describes the work to be performed, and **job specifications**, which outline the requirements necessary to accomplish the job. A discussion of job analysis is presented in Chapter 7.

Performance Standards

Performance standards should be derived from the job analysis information. Based on this information, levels of performance deemed to be acceptable versus unacceptable are developed. In essence, a standard against which to compare employee performance is determined. Performance standards focus on how well the job has been done. Each standard should be clearly stated and communicated so that the rater and the subject know what is expected and whether the standard has been met.

The Performance Appraisal System

In general, employees should be evaluated on a number of specific dimensions of job performance rather than on a single global or overall measure. Global measures are more prone to distortion on the part of the evaluator. For example, the Supreme Court ruling in 1975 regarding *Albemarle Paper Company* versus *Moody* was based on the fact that no specific job dimensions of performance were assessed.[17] Raters were asked to make evaluations of employees by comparing them to one another based on a single, global rating. The Court found significant racial differences on the criterion (the overall rating), with no "objective" information to back it.

EXHIBIT 13.3   Where the Performance Appraisal Process Fits with Respect to Other HR Functions

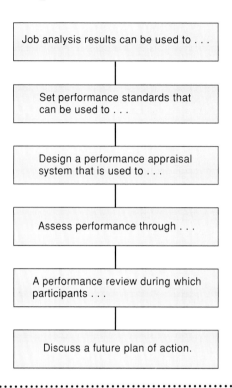

Job analysis results can be used to . . .

Set performance standards that can be used to . . .

Design a performance appraisal system that is used to . . .

Assess performance through . . .

A performance review during which participants . . .

Discuss a future plan of action.

Assessing Performance

The actual performance assessment is the determination of the employee's strengths *and* weaknesses. One purpose of a performance appraisal is to improve employee performance, thus performance weaknesses must be assessed. However, it is also important to reinforce existing behavior that is deemed to be strong.

If multiple raters are used, assessing performance also includes compiling all ratings into summary form. If the raters agree as to the employee's performance, high inter-rater reliability exists and summarizing the ratings is not problematic. However, if there is a substantial amount of disagreement as to the employees's performance, inter-rater reliability is low. The supervisor must use this information as more of a heuristic device or guide for the final evaluation.

Performance Review

The performance review is the actual discussion that transpires between the rater and the ratee regarding the ratee's performance. Research suggests that the performance review should be approximately 60 minutes long and be a mutual discussion.[18] However, employee responses to an employment survey indicated that most performance reviews are relatively short.[19] In fact, most employees reported that their last performance review session lasted less than 15 minutes!

Performance reviews should be considered an exchange of information—not simply a one-way communication from the rater to the subjects. Success in this area is

··

| EXHIBIT 13.4 | Tips for a Successful Performance Review |

1. Select a good time.
2. Minimize interruptions.
3. Reduce or eliminate physical "nonverbal" barriers.
4. Welcome; set at ease.
5. Start with something positive if at all possible.
6. Ask open-ended questions to encourage discussion.
7. Listen.
8. Manage eye contact and body language.
9. Be specific.
10. Rate behavior, not personality.
11. Lay out development plan.
12. Encourage subordinate participation.
13. Complete form.
14. Set mutually agreeable goals for improvement.
15. End in a positive encouraging note.
16. Set time for any follow-up meetings.

··

usually tied to the supervisor's ability to get the employee to express thoughts and ideas. However, many supervisors find it easier to talk than to listen. The result of not listening is not understanding the employee's point of view. If the goal of the supervisor is to encourage better performance, this can best be achieved from an open exchange of thoughts, which ultimately can be the key to motivating the employee to perform better. One approach to an exchange of information is to ask the employee to give a general assessment of his or her overall performance.

When beginning the performance review discussion, the employee should be told something about the review, such as its purpose and the goal. If the employee has done an outstanding job, it is a good practice to acknowledge this in the beginning. This will help set a positive tone for the meeting. When performance is less than satisfactory, it is often best to avoid a definite statement of the overall negative rating at the beginning. Instead, the rating will become self-evident as the accomplishments are reviewed with the employee. The overall rating can then be summarized at the end of the review. Exhibit 13.4 illustrates some tips for a successful performance review.

The format of the performance review is likely to undergo some significant changes in the future. As organizations move toward a more involved employee orientation, the supervisor-subordinate formal appraisal is no longer effective. Instead, a performance review discussion based upon the employees's evaluation of his or her own work for a specified period of time may be more useful. When this format is followed, the manager becomes a counselor instead of a judge. These types of review sessions appear to be more useful and enjoyable for both the rater and the employee.[20]

Future Plan of Action

By this point in the review, the employee should have an accurate idea of his or her performance evaluation. The employee should know where he or she "stands." Recapping key points and asking the employee to summarize the major issues discussed is usually a good way for the supervisor to assure joint understanding before ending the performance review.

Next, the supervisor and employee should focus on the future. Job performance objectives should be discussed in order to establish a future plan of action. This is often an appropriate time to explore the employee's career interest and developmental needs. The employee should be aware of plans listed and the supervisor's expectations in this area. In addition, the employee should be able to have some input into these plans.

Finally, the supervisor reviews the job performance and development plans, and then sets objectives for the next rating period. This will provide the employee with direction and guidance as to what is expected. The employee needs to understand areas *where* improvement is needed and *how* to strengthen job performance (such as additional training). In closing the discussion, the supervisor may wish to reassure the employee that the supervisor is interested in the employee's success and should indicate a willingness to talk further at a later date.

Given the importance of the performance evaluation, it is surprising that most supervisors do not receive any training in this area. It has been estimated that over 90 percent of raters receive no training at all in how to conduct a performance appraisal.[21] As the opening Westinghouse case illustrates, comprehensive training programs can help ensure the success of a new performance appraisal system. Performance appraisal training can also help the success of an existing performance appraisal system by fine tuning the evaluators' skills.

TYPES OF PERFORMANCE APPRAISAL METHODS

A number of different performance appraisal methods or formats are available from which to choose. Some methods focus more on employee behavior (for example, planning or organizing), while others are more results-oriented and emphasize the *results* of employee behavior (such as the extent to which an employee reaches goals and objectives). Within the behavioral methods, employees can be evaluated based on an organizational or departmental standard or they can be evaluated relative to others.

Behavioral Performance Appraisal Methods

Checklists

In its simplest form, the checklist is a list of descriptive statements and/or adjectives describing job-related behavior. If the rater perceives the employee as possessing a particular trait, the item is checked. If the rater does not perceive the employee as possessing this trait, the item is left blank. The number of "checks" represents the employee's rating.

Weighted Checklists

Similarly, the evaluator is given a list of job-related behaviors or characteristics and asked to check the items that apply to the employee. However, each item is not weighted equally. Those items that are deemed to be more predictive of success or that are more critical to organizational effectiveness are weighted more. The weights are unknown to the rater so she or he cannot slant the results. These item weights are then used in summing the ratings to determine overall performance.

Graphic Rating Scale

One of the most widely used performance evaluation formats is the graphic rating scale. Essentially, the evaluator is asked to rate employees on a number of job-related characteristics, such as quality of work or knowledge of the job. The ratings are made using a scale that ranges from one extreme to another, such as unsatisfactory to outstanding. The number of characteristics rated by using these scales can vary from a few to many. Exhibit 13.5 illustrates a graphic rating scale. The evaluator marks the appropriate category for each item and the total score is summed. Similar to weighted checklists, certain items on a graphic rating scale can be weighted differentially.[22]

Mixed-Standard Scales

One variation of the graphic rating scale is the mixed-standard scale. Instead of rating a behavior, such as attendance, the evaluator is given three conceptually compatible statements describing that behavior at high, medium, and low levels. To illustrate this type of scale, Exhibit 13.6 (on page 454) lists three statements describing different levels of attendance. The evaluator indicates whether an employee's performance is "better than," "as good as," or "worse than" the behavior described in each statement. The mixed-standard scale gives a wider range of scores than the simple graphic rating scale.

Forced-Choice

The forced-choice scale was designed to increase objectivity and decrease subjectivity in ratings.[23] A forced-choice scale is a checklist of statements that are grouped together according to certain statistical properties. The basic rationale is that the statements that are grouped appear to have equal importance or "social desirability." The evaluator is "forced" to select from each group of statements (usually four) a subset of those statements (usually two) that are "most descriptive" of each subject. The key is that the evaluator has no knowledge of the weights (which are based on how well the item discriminates between successful and unsuccessful performance) because all of the items appear to be of equal importance. Exhibit 13.7 (on page 455) illustrates an example of a forced-choice scale for a teacher. The two statements with the highest ability to discriminate are each worth one point. The other two items are worth zero points. Thus, the subject would receive two points if the rater chose items one and three and zero points if the rater chose items two and four. One problem with this procedure is the difficulty in developing items that are not related to performance, but that appear to be.[24]

Critical Incidents

When an employee is evaluated based on critical incidents, the evaluator collects reports of behavior that are considered to be "critical." Critical behavior is that which makes a difference in the success or failure of a particular work situation. Incidents are recorded for each employee as soon as possible after they occur. Critical incidents should contain (1) the circumstances that preceded the incident, (2) the setting in which the incident occurred, (3) precisely what the employee did that was effective or ineffective, (4) the consequences of the incident, and (5) the extent

···

EXHIBIT 13.5   Handy Dandy Stores Sales Associates Performance Appraisal

Employee Name_____ Store:_____

Store Manager (completing rating):_____ Date:_____

Type of Evaluation:_____

Rate the employee on each category, using the codes for descriptions listed below:

5 = Outstanding   Circle the 5 for "Outstanding" if the employee named does the desired behavior on almost every occasion.

4 = Above Average   Circle the 4 for "Above Average" if the employee named does the desired behavior most of the time.

3 = Satisfactory   Circle the 3 for "Satisfactory" if the employee is about average, does the behavior sometimes and does not other times.

2 = Minimum Standard   Circle the 2 for "Minimum Standard" if the employee frequently does not perform the behavior satisfactorily.

1 = Unsatisfactory   Circle the 1 for "Unsatisfactory" if the employee seldom, if ever, does the desired behavior.

0 = Not Applicable   Circle the 0 if the category does not apply to this employee.

I.   CUSTOMER SERVICE

5 4 3 2 1 0   A. Greets customers in friendly manner; smiles.
5 4 3 2 1 0   B. Serves customers promptly.
5 4 3 2 1 0   C. Utilizes suggestive selling.
5 4 3 2 1 0   D. Handles problems (loitering or disturbances).
5 4 3 2 1 0   E. Ensures store is open and operating according to policy.

II.   MERCHANDISING

5 4 3 2 1 0   A. Keeps all merchandise displayed.
5 4 3 2 1 0   B. Keeps merchandise fresh.
5 4 3 2 1 0   C. Maintains correct gas prices.

···

to which the consequences were within the employee's control. At the end of the evaluation period, these reports are used to appraise the employee's performance. Although recording employee behavior can help the evaluator remember the range of behavior that occurred during the evaluation period, it is very time consuming and difficult to quantify.

Behaviorally Anchored Rating Scales (BARS)

BARS is a sophisticated method of evaluating employee performance based on employee *behavior* rather than attitudes or assumptions about motivation or potential. BARS is a numerical scale that is anchored by specific narrative examples of behaviors that range from very negative to very positive descriptions of performance.[25]

BARS is a difficult and time-consuming scale to develop. Each job must be analyzed and a list of critical incidents developed by experts in the job. Once the critical incidents are developed, they are matched to a set of performance dimensions that are then scaled from effective to ineffective performance. Exhibit 13.8 (on page 456) illustrates one aspect of a BARS for a manager. The BARS technique

....

EXHIBIT 13.5 continued

5 4 3 2 1 0   D. Ensures that pumps are operating or that repairs are reported and completed.

5 4 3 2 1 0   E. Ensures that merchandise is priced correctly.

5 4 3 2 1 0   F. Makes price changes according to company procedures.

5 4 3 2 1 0   G. Orders adequate stock to ensure variety, quality, and quantity within inventory levels.

5 4 3 2 1 0   H. Marks down, writes off, or returns to vendor for credit all damaged, old, or unacceptable merchandise as instructed.

5 4 3 2 1 0   I. Displays advertising materials, banners, decorations, etc., as supplied and scheduled.

III. GENERAL

5 4 3 2 1 0   A. Attendance.

5 4 3 2 1 0   B. Dress code compliance.

5 4 3 2 1 0   C. Other_____

IV. STORE AND MERCHANDISE MAINTENANCE

5 4 3 2 1 0   A. Performs cleaning.

5 4 3 2 1 0   B. Gas island. (Cleans the gas island to standards.)

5 4 3 2 1 0   C. Performs maintenance duties.

5 4 3 2 1 0   D. Reports damage to building, fixtures, equipment or breakdown of equipment.

V. RECORDS AND ACCOUNTING

5 4 3 2 1 0   A. Money orders.

5 4 3 2 1 0   B. Gasoline.

5 4 3 2 1 0   C. Inventory.

5 4 3 2 1 0   D. Daily reports.

5 4 3 2 1 0   E. Personnel transactions.

5 4 3 2 1 0   F. Time cards.

....

offers a high degree of inter-rater reliability and objectivity because of its emphasis on behavior. Unfortunately, because of the complexity and expense of setting up the scale, managers should carefully consider the administrative investment before adopting BARS as their performance appraisal technique.

The performance appraisal methods just discussed base the employee's evaluation on some type of standard. The standard may be set at the department or the organizational level. The next three performance appraisal methods evaluate the employee's performance relative to that of others in the employee's department. These are called *personnel comparison systems*.

Personnel Comparison Systems

Ranking

This method requires the evaluator to rank employees from "best" to "worst." Some rank ordering methods allow for "ties" among employees. This most often occurs with those employees who score somewhere in the middle of the extremes. This method does not allow the evaluator to rate everyone high. Unfortunately, rank

....

EXHIBIT 13.6 Mixed-Standard Scale Example

ORGANIZATIONAL ATTENDANCE

RATING

_____   **High:** Always at work unless critical emergency.
_____ **Average:** Infrequently misses work (less than twice monthly).
_____   **Low:** Has many absences (more than twice monthly).

Indicate whether the employee's performance is

"Better than" the behavior described in the statement: __√ +__

"As good as" the behavior described in the statement: __√__

"Worse than" the behavior described in the statement: __√ −__

....

ordering produces ordinal data, thus, the *amount* of difference between employees is unknown. For example, it is impossible to determine if the second highest ranking is close to the highest performer or if there is a big gap between the top two employees.

Forced Distribution

This method requires the evaluator to place a certain percentage of employees into each of several categories based on overall performance. For example, 10 percent of the employees must be placed in the "unsatisfactory" category, 15 percent must be placed in the "fair" category, 50 percent must be placed in the "satisfactory or average" category, 15 percent in the "good" category, and 10 percent in the "outstanding" category. Similar to the ranking method, forced distribution forces the evaluator to discriminate between the employees; however, the absolute difference between them is not known.

Paired Comparisons

When the paired comparisons method is used, the evaluator compares all possible pairs of subordinates on their overall ability to do the job. From each possible pair of employees, the evaluator selects the employee with the higher overall ability to do the job. The number of comparisons required by the evaluator is based on a simple formula: number of pairs $= [N\,(N-1)]/2$ where N is the number of people who will be rated. Thus, 10 subordinates require 45 comparisons $(10\,(10-1))/2$.

Due to the subjectivity of evaluating "overall performance," some managers use a number of different job-related dimensions when comparing. If the rater compares all employees on more than one dimension (D), the number of pairs $= D\{[N\,(N-1)]/2\}$. Thus, ten employees compared on only five different job dimensions would result in 225 comparisons $(5[(10\,(10-1))/2])$. Obviously, this method can become very cumbersome if there are a lot of employees to evaluate or if the evaluation uses a variety of job dimensions.

EXHIBIT 13.7   Forced-Choice Rating Scale Example

Please check the two statements that *best* describe the employee:

STATEMENT	DISCRIMINABILITY INDEX	FAVORABLENESS INDEX
_____ 1. Shows patience with slow learners.	1.72	2.82
_____ 2. Lectures with confidence.	.51	2.75
_____ 3. Keeps interest in class.	1.80	2.78
_____ 4. Acquaints class with daily objectives.	.70	2.81

Unknown to Evaluator

Note that the statements are similar in their social desirability but differ in their ability to determine high from low performers (that is, discriminability).

Results-Oriented Performance Appraisal Methods

The following two performance appraisal formats are more results-oriented. Thus, the evaluator is rating the outcomes of the employee's behavior rather than the actual behavior itself.

Management by Objectives (MBO)

A frequently used performance appraisal method is management by objectives. Management by objectives (MBO) has been around for over thirty years and is usually credited to Peter Drucker. Drucker was trying to design a systematic approach to setting objectives and appraising by results that would lead to improved organizational productivity. Recent research findings indicate that MBOs do indeed increase productivity. In 68 of 70 studies, productivity gains were reported by organizations that have implemented MBO programs. However, this research also indicated that the degree of productivity increase enjoyed was directly linked to whether or not top management fully supported the MBO process. In organizations where top management did support MBO, the average productivity gain was 56 percent. However, in organizations where there was no or limited top level management support for the program, productivity gains only averaged 6 percent.[26]

Although there are a number of variations, MBO generally consists of the following steps: setting organizational objectives, setting individual objectives, and appraisal by results.

Since MBO takes a top-down approach, top management must decide the overall objectives of the organization and the departments. Objectives should always be stated so that they can be measured or quantified. Further, the objectives should include target dates for completion and action plans that discuss the process of achieving these objectives.

After the overall objectives have been set, individual objectives for employees at each level of the organization (for example, upper-level management, then middle-

··

EXHIBIT 13.8 Behaviorally Anchored Rating Scale Example

Position:_____

Job Dimension:_____

Plans work and organizes time carefully so as to maximize resources and meet commitments.	9	
	8	Even though this associate has a report due on another project, he or she would be well prepared for the assigned discussion on your project.
	7	This associate would keep a calendar or schedule on which deadlines and activities are carefully noted, and which would be consulted before making new commitments.
	6	As program chief, this associate would manage arrangements for enlisting resources for a special project reasonably well, but would probably omit one or two details that would have to be handled by improvisation.
Plans and organizes time and effort primarily for large segments of a task. Usually meets commitments, but may overlook what are considered secondary details.	5	This associate would meet a deadline in handing in a report, but the report might be below usual standard if other deadlines occur on the same day the report is due.
	4	This associate's evaluations are likely not to reflect abilities because of overcommitments in other activities.
	3	This associate would plan more by enthusiasm than by timetable and frequently have to work late the night before an assignment is due, although it would be completed on time.
Appears to do little planning. May perform effectively, despite what seems to be a disorganized approach, by concerted effort, although deadlines may be missed.	2	This associate would often be late for meetings, although others in similar circumstances do not seem to find it difficult to be on time.
	1	This associate never makes a deadline, even with sufficient notice.

··

level management, then lower-level management, and finally the employees with no supervisory responsibilities) are set. Employee objectives and the specified period of time for the accomplishment of these objectives are determined jointly by the supervisor and the employee. See Exhibit 13.9 for an illustration of an MBO performance worksheet. The objectives set should be specific, measurable, challenging, and accepted by both parties.

....

| EXHIBIT 13.9 | Handy Dandy Stores Performance Objectives Worksheet |

Directions: This sheet is to be completed at the <u>beginning</u> of the appraisal period.

Employee Name: Sam Swanson   Length of Time in Position: 4 years

Employee Number: 189   Date Prepared: 9/1/87, revised 4/1/91

Job Title: District Manager   Department/Region: Lakeland, Florida

STRATEGIC PLANNING GOALS	RESULTS EXPECTED	TIME FRAME (BY WHEN)
1. Reduce turnover 33%	Reduce turnover 33% in all stores	9/1/92
2. Improve store appearance	Paint outside of all stores	4/92
3. Improve store mgr. part.	Send store mgrs. to mgt. dev.	8/1/92
4. Improve communications	Send all mgrs. to comm. training	8/1/92
5. Increase sales	Increase sales by 10% per store	9/1/92
6. Reduce shrink	Reduce shrink losses by 45%	9/1/92

MAINTENANCE/ROUTINE GOALS	RESULTS EXPECTED	TIME FRAME (BY WHEN)
1. Monitor costs	Reduce costs by at least 8%	9/1/92
2. Reduce stock outs	Reduce stock out level by 20%	9/1/92
3.		
4.		

PERSONAL DEVELOPMENT GOALS	RESULTS EXPECTED	TIME FRAME (BY WHEN)
1. Improve communications	Attend communications workshop	9/1/92
2. Improve computer skills	Attend community college course on computers	9/1/91
3. Improve planning ability	Develop written plan for stores; attend	9/1/92
4.	planning workshop	

    Employee Signature   Supervisor Signature

....

These objectives play an important role in the feedback process and the final evaluation. Specifically, employees should be given periodic feedback on their progress toward their stated goals and objectives. In addition, the final performance appraisal should be based on how well the employee met the objectives set forth. Obviously, situations arise that might require the initial objectives to be modified throughout the year, such as a change in the competition or the economy. Changes in objectives can be made during periodic reviews or feedback sessions. The use of MBO as a performance appraisal technique is popular, partly because of the high level of employee involvement.

Work Planning

Work planning is similar to MBO except that its primary focus is the periodic feedback and review. Less emphasis is given to setting each objective in terms of being measurable. Thus, work planning allows the supervisor latitude for "judgment calls" regarding whether or not the employee met the objective.

Selecting a Performance Appraisal Method

In general, there is no one *best* performance appraisal method.[27] However, depending on the situation certain performance appraisal methods might be better than others. For example, if *objective* performance data are available, then MBO is a good strategy to use. If, however, employees are going to be compared for determining pay increases, promotions, and so on then some common denominator must be determined in order to make comparisons among many employees. This usually implies a numerical rating of performance, such as ranking or rating methods rather than MBO or work planning methods in which employee objectives can vary. Thus, the *purpose* of the performance appraisal is an important consideration when choosing a performance appraisal method.

An increasingly important factor in selecting a performance appraisal method is whether or not the technique is legally defensible. While there is no way to *guarantee* a completely "safe" performance appraisal, managers need to be aware of the outcomes of the court cases that made judgments about the performance appraisal process. In general, the important cases suggest, among other things, that the courts do not reject subjective reviews such as those made by the employee's immediate supervisor. Further, the use of objective measures, such as production figures, do not ensure favorable decisions for the organization. In each case, it is up to the court to determine if subjective or objective measures are appropriate for the job in question. It also has been found that techniques used to develop and refine the performance appraisal process, such as training raters and validating the process, have not helped win court cases. While these practices are useful to ensure a quality performance appraisal process, they do not carry much weight in the court's eyes except when these procedures are used to help ensure that the standards are being applied evenly to all employees.[28]

Another consideration to make when choosing an appraisal method is how well it will control the types of rater errors that will be most likely encountered. To better explain this factor, the following section defines and describes typical rater errors or biases that can occur in the performance appraisal process.

PERCEPTUAL ERRORS IN EVALUATION

Performance evaluations can be biased due to a variety of perceptual errors made by raters. Regardless of the performance criterion or the scientific nature of the appraisal method, perceptual error can occur. Typical errors include the halo effect, stereotypes, attributions, recency effects, leniency, strictness, and central tendency. Each of these errors are examined in the following sections.

Halo Effect

The halo effect occurs when the rater allows one trait or characteristic (either positive or negative) of the employee to override a realistic appraisal of other traits or characteristics. For example, if an employee is always on time to work, a supervisor might allow this positive characteristic to influence his or her evaluation of this

HR CHALLENGES ●

Tips for Developing a Legally Defensible Performance Appraisal

Based on outcomes of various court cases that centered on the performance appraisal, the following list suggests ways to create a legally defensible performance appraisal system. While reading this list, keep in mind that there is no such thing as a completely safe performance appraisal system.

1. Begin with a job analysis that determines the necessary characteristics for successful job performance.
2. From the job analysis results, determine performance standards.
3. These standards must be communicated and accepted by the employees who will be judged by them.
4. Using the standard as a guideline, develop a rating scheme. The scheme should measure clearly defined individual components of job performance rather than global or undefined measures. The standards and rating scheme should be distributed to all raters.
5. The type of scale you select is not all that important from a legal perspective. The courts have not indicted any problems with using simple graphic rating scales or trait ratings. However, when using these types of methods it is

helpful to avoid abstract trait names like loyalty and to anchor the scales with brief, logically consistent tags.
6. Train the raters to use the scale correctly. Focus on how to apply the standards when making decisions. It is important that the raters uniformly apply the standards because in six out of ten cases in which the organization lost the court case, the plaintiffs showed the standards were not uniformly applied.
7. Include a mechanism for appealing the rating. The appeal should be directed to upper-level management.
8. Document all appraisals. These are very useful in court cases.
9. Provide a way for poor performers to receive corrective guidance. When the organization made an attempt to help poor performers, the court ruled more favorably toward the organization.

SOURCE: Adapted from Gerald Barrett and Mary Kernan, "Performance Appraisal and Terminations: A Review of Court Decisions Since Brito v. Zia with Implications for Personnel Practices," *Personnel Psychology* 40, 1987, pp. 489–502; and Wayne Cascio and H. John Bernardin, "Implications of Performance Appraisal Litigation for Personnel Decisions," *Personnel Psychology* 34, 1981, pp. 211–226.

employee's performance on other dimensions. Thus, this employee might be judged as a good performer—not because of actual performance, but because of the halo effect. The halo effect has been examined extensively in the performance appraisal literature.[29] Some approaches used to control halo effects include using performance appraisal simulations prior to evaluations, and having raters listen to short lectures on the halo effect before rating employees.[30]

Of the different types of performance appraisal methods described in the previous section, several would be more susceptible to halo error than others. For example, any of the scales that request the evaluator to judge the individual on more than one factor, such as checklists and the graphic rating scale, could be subject to halo error. The best methods to use to avoid or reduce halo error might be the critical incident approach provided that the evaluator collected negative as well as positive incidents. Also, adding a weight, which is unknown by the evaluator, to the factors evaluated may help to alleviate this error. Finally, as with most of these errors, raters can be trained to recognize this bias and to work to overcome it.

Stereotypes

Stereotyping occurs when the rater places an employee into a class or category based on one or a few traits or characteristics. For example, an older worker may be stereotyped as being slower, more difficult to train, and unwilling to learn new approaches. Obviously, this perceptual error could negatively affect the overall performance evaluation. Of course, the older worker being evaluated may not fit this stereotype at all and may be quick to pick up new concepts and anxious to participate in new training programs. Some research has indicated that the composition of the group from which the stereotyped employee comes may influence whether or not the stereotype influences the rating. For example, women received lower ratings when the proportion of women in the group of employees was small; however, the stereotype did not lower ratings for blacks who came from a group that had more whites than blacks. These results suggest that some stereotypes may be stronger than others.[31] Similar to reducing the halo effect, stereotyping may be controlled by offering specialized training to raters and making the problem associated with stereotyping salient. Further, avoiding scales that are not tied to performance standards can help to reduce stereotyping errors.

Attributions

Another perceptual error that can affect the validity of the performance appraisal involves the attributions the rater makes about employee behavior. Making an attribution means to assign causation for another's behavior.[32] For example, if a supervisor attributes an employee's good performance to external causes, such as luck, holding an easy job, or receiving help from coworkers, then the performance evaluation will not be as positive as if the supervisor had attributed good performance to internal causes, such as effort or ability. Similarly, if the supervisor attributes poor performance to external causes rather than internal causes, the performance evaluation will not be as negative. Frequently, attribution errors can be avoided by using BARS, because this method requires the evaluator to rate the behavior, but not judge it.

Recency Effects

Recency errors occur when performance is evaluated based on performance information that occurred most recently. Essentially, supervisors rate the employee's most recent behavior. Recency errors are most likely to occur when there is a long period of time between performance evaluations (such as a year). Since recent employee behavior is the most salient to a supervisor, using a method that requires the rater to keep a log of employee performance throughout the year, such as the critical incidents approach, and forcing the rater to review the log before making a rating can help to alleviate this problem.

Leniency/Strictness Errors

Leniency and strictness errors occur when the rater tends to use one of the extremes of a rating scale. When leniency errors occur, most employees receive very favorable ratings, even though it is not warranted by their performance. Leniency errors can occur for a number of reasons. For example, a supervisor may be uncomfortable confronting particularly aggressive employees with less than favorable evaluations. In order to avoid conflict, the supervisor might choose to rate everyone high. It is also possible that the supervisor's own performance evaluation is based partially on the performance of his or her work group. Rating everyone favorably gives the impression that the entire work group is very effective.

Strictness errors, which are basically the opposite of leniency errors, occur when the rater erroneously evaluates most employees unfavorably. In this case, supervisors may simply want to appear "tough" or they may have unrealistic expectations of performance. Regardless, most employees are assigned ratings at the lower end of the performance scale.

Both of these errors can be eliminated by using any of the personnel comparison systems discussed previously. For example, the forced distribution method requires that the rater place a certain percentage of the people being evaluated in various categories, from outstanding to below average. By forcing the rater to use all of the categories, both leniency and strictness errors will disappear.

Central Tendency Errors

Central tendency errors occur when the rater avoids the extremes of the performance scale and evaluates most employees somewhere near the middle of the scale. This error results in most employees being rated as "average." Leniency, strictness, and central tendency errors limit the ability of the performance appraisal to discriminate between the performance of workers. Thus, employees are grouped together at the low, mid-point, or high end of the scale and it is virtually impossible to differentiate performance levels among the employees. As with the leniency and strictness errors described above, using a personnel comparison performance appraisal method can help to alleviate this problem.

STRATEGY AND THE PERFORMANCE APPRAISAL PROCESS

The performance appraisal system can be utilized to promote a variety of management goals and objectives. In addition to systematically encouraging high levels of performance, the appraisal system is useful in identifying employees with potential, rewarding performance equitably, and determining employees' needs for development. These are all activities that should support the organization's strategic orientation. Although these activities are clearly instrumental in achieving corporate plans and long-term growth, typical appraisal systems in most organizations have been focused on short-run goals.[33]

Organizational Strategy

Strengthening the linkage between the performance appraisal system and the organization's long-term strategic plans can improve organizational effectiveness. The following discussion is based on Miles and Snow's organizational strategy typology.[34] Specifically, the organizational strategies of defender, prospector, and analyzer will be examined as they relate to performance appraisal systems.

As discussed in previous chapters, defenders have a narrow and relatively stable product-market domain. As a result of this narrow focus, these types of organizations seldom need to make major adjustments in their technology, structure, or methods of operation. They devote primary attention to improving the efficiency of their existing operations. Because of the emphasis on skill building within the organization, successful defenders use the performance appraisal as a means for identifying training needs. The performance appraisal system is usually more behaviorally oriented as opposed to results oriented and the emphasis is on the *process* (such as

HR CHALLENGES •••

Effective Appraisal Systems Produce Effective Organizations

John Strazzanti, general manager and president of Com-Corp Industries, which produces light bulb shields for GM, knew it was time for a change. For years, the company had kept pay under raps and had rarely given employees raises. When his employees began to react emotionally to never being appraised or promoted, Strazzanti made his move.

He asked for volunteers for a salary committee, which he charged with setting wages in the organization based on salary surveys from the marketplace. He also gathered input about the criteria upon which the employees thought they should be evaluated.

As a result, a new performance appraisal system is administered three times a year. The employees are rated both quantitatively and qualitatively on technical proficiency and professional attitude. Workers are measured against their past performance, goals that they had set for themselves, and industry conditions and standards. If the review determines that a worker needs to improve, he or she can do so by participating in any of a number of ongoing instructional classes offered by Com-Corp.

Additionally, the new performance appraisal system allows the employees to review the firm. Each employee must submit a detailed review of the company's performance three times a year. They are encouraged to question the methods used and suggest ways to improve. Frequently, the suggestions are acted upon and new procedures are implemented.

The payback for all these changes can be seen in many ways. From a human resource perspective, turnover is low, averaging between 2 and 3 percent. Absenteeism and tardiness also are low at about 2.5 percent. With respect to profits, the company has earned money every year since the program was placed into effect. Finally, in terms of customer satisfaction, General Motors gave Com-Corp one of the highest ratings ever under its Targets for Excellence program for GM suppliers.

SOURCE: Adapted from "The Interactive Employee Review," *Inc.*, November 1991, pp. 73–75.

critical incidents). Finally, the focus is often on comparing individual or group performance with the previous year's performance.

Organizations with a prospector strategy continually search for different product and market opportunities. In addition, prospectors regularly experiment with potential responses to new and emerging environmental trends. These organizations are often the creators of change. Because of the emphasis on skill identification and acquisition of human resources *outside* of the organization as opposed to skill building within the organization, prospectors often use the performance appraisal as a means of identifying staffing needs. The emphasis is more results oriented (such as management by objectives) rather than process oriented. Finally, the focus is on division and corporate performance evaluations as they compare with other companies during the same evaluation period.

Organizations with an analyzer strategy operate in two types of product-market domains. One domain is stable while the other is changing. In their more innovative areas, managers watch their competitors closely and rapidly adapt to ideas that appear promising. In general, analyzers use cost-efficient technologies for stable products and project or matrix technologies for new products. Analyzers tend to emphasize both skill building and skill acquisition and employ extensive training programs. Thus, analyzers attempt to identify both training needs *and* staffing needs. The performance appraisal system most conducive to an analyzer strategy is one that is more behavioral and process oriented. Performance evaluations are considered at the individual, group, and division level. Finally, successful analyzers have a tendency to examine current performance with past performance within the organization; however, some cross-sectional comparisons (comparisons between companies) do occur.

EXHIBIT 13.10 Common Problems with Unsuccessful Performance
Appraisal Systems

1. A poorly defined appraisal system
2. A poorly communicated appraisal system
3. An inappropriate appraisal system
4. A poorly supported appraisal system
5. An unmonitored appraisal system

Identifying Successful versus Unsuccessful Appraisal Systems[35]

Performance appraisal systems can fail for a variety of reasons. Exhibit 13.10 illustrates some of the reasons why trouble may occur. The following discussion focuses on diagnosing the problems of an unsuccessful performance appraisal system.

Poorly Defined Systems

A poorly defined system means that something is wrong with the design. For example, the system might be lacking written documentation to use as a guide. Often poorly defined appraisal systems emerge out of "tradition." Another possibility is that the system is defined, but it is not defined well. The performance appraisal system must be tied directly to clearly stated organizational objectives and strategies. Managers should not have to guess as to the objectives of the organization, the purpose of the performance appraisal, and how these issues tie together.

Poorly Communicated Systems

Even a sophisticated appraisal system is doomed for failure if it is not communicated properly to everyone involved in the process. The evaluators and the employees should have similar expectations as to the purpose and the importance of the appraisal system. For example, the employee should know if the performance appraisal system will consist of periodic reviews of performance aimed at changing work behavior or if it is to be an annual evaluation to determine salary and promotion opportunities.

Inappropriate Systems

Some of the most common characteristics of inappropriate systems include measuring inappropriate types of performance (those that are not job-related), asking the wrong people to do the evaluating, conducting the performance appraisal discussions too infrequently, and using a rating system that is not suited to the performance being measured. Any of these problems could lead to an ineffective performance appraisal system.

Poorly Supported Systems

The performance appraisal system can fail if it is only supported by top management and not by the other levels of management or the employees. Even a good appraisal

···

| EXHIBIT 13.11 | Criteria for a Successful Performance Appraisal System

1. Built around clear objectives
2. Management and employee endorsement
3. Flexibility to adapt
4. Timing of appraisal should be predictable
5. Performance *dialogue*
6. Appropriate appraisal form
7. Periodic system checks

··

design can fail if the people using it are not committed to its success. Similarly, if the performance appraisal system is accepted and supported by employees, but not by top management, management may not choose to utilize the information gained from the appraisal. Essentially, a successful performance appraisal system should be accepted and supported by all who use it.

Unmonitored Systems

If problems with the performance appraisal system go unmonitored, these problems can become serious over time. For example, suppose that raters are consistently making leniency errors such that everyone receives high ratings. If this problem goes undetected, the performance appraisal becomes meaningless. Thus, a performance appraisal system, even a good one, can fail if problems are not monitored regularly.

Successful performance appraisal systems have a number of common characteristics. The following discussion focuses on the criteria for a successful performance appraisal system, which are listed in Exhibit 13.11.

Clear Objectives

A good performance appraisal should be built around unambiguous objectives. These objectives should cover all levels and areas of the organization and reflect the needs of each. The appraisal system should be clear as to its purpose. Participants should know whether it is being used to determine raises and promotions or to determine development needs. It is important to clearly delineate who should participate in the system. That is, will employees at all levels be involved or will some areas or layers in the organization be excluded? Finally, participants must be aware of what type of information will be collected, how often, and who will have access to this information.

Management and Employee Endorsement

To be effective, the appraisal system should be supported by the entire work force. This includes management support for possible expenses such as additional training, employee meetings, appraisal forms and other materials, and staff time. In addition, employees can benefit from involvement in the performance appraisal. For example, many companies encourage employees to do a self-appraisal as a means for discussion. The information solicited by self-appraisals should be consistent with both the organizational objectives and individual goals.

Flexibility

An organization must design its system with enough flexibility to adapt to any changes that might occur. For example, the appraisal system should be flexible enough to accommodate different management philosophies, employee subcultures, and geographical locations. Sometimes it is necessary to establish different sets of procedures for very different employee groups or locations.

Predictability

The timing of the performance appraisal(s) and any other feedback sessions should be predictable. For example, some organizations have an annual performance appraisal close to the hiring anniversary date of the employee. This enables the employee to prepare for the evaluation. Some organizations have two separate performance appraisals each year—one for salary considerations and one to assess employee development needs. Regardless of the number of evaluations, the employee should always have advance knowledge of what to expect in the performance review and when to expect it.

Performance Dialogue

Performance discussions between the rater and the employee are perhaps the most critical component of a successful performance appraisal system. Performance reviews should not emphasize a "tell-and-sell" approach, in which the rater tells the employees how good or bad their performance has been and attempts to convince the employee to accept this rating. Using a tell-and-sell approach can alienate the employee and destroy the possibility of open communication in the future.

Instead, the performance review should emphasize a dialogue between the evaluator and the employee. During the discussion, the employee should be given the opportunity to see all written appraisals of his or her performance, discuss them with the evaluator, and respond to them both verbally and in writing. Some organizations encourage employees to fill out a self-appraisal to facilitate these dialogues.

Appraisal Form

The importance of an appropriate appraisal form should not be overlooked. Many organizations simply adopt some "standard" form that may or may not be tailored to their goals and objectives. Failure to tailor the appraisal form to the objectives of the organization can lead to ratings based on irrelevant or unimportant issues. It is important that the form contain questions that directly relate to the employee's job in terms the employee can understand.

Periodic System Checks

Systematically evaluating the validity of the performance appraisal system should be a key feature. As previously mentioned, an unmonitored system can create havoc within an organization if problems go undetected. At a minimum, the performance appraisal system is consistent with the strategic objectives of the organization. Validity checks should occur more often if problems have been detected with the system.

• • • • • • • • •

MANAGEMENT GUIDELINES

This chapter has examined a number of issues regarding the process and requirements of an effective performance appraisal system. Various methods of performance appraisals have been presented as well as a number of perceptual and system errors that can hinder the success of an appraisal system. The following management guidelines on performance appraisals are offered as an aid to managerial decision making.

1. Performance appraisals should be based on a thorough job analysis that is current regarding both job descriptions and job specifications.

2. Performance standards should be developed from the job analysis as input into the performance appraisal.

3. Performance appraisals should evaluate a number of specific behaviors as opposed to evaluating "overall job performance" using one or a few global statements.

4. The performance review discussion should be a two-way communication between the rater and the employee.

5. The performance appraisal should be used not only as a means of evaluating performance, but also as a means of motivating and developing the employee.

6. The *purpose* of the performance appraisal and the *objectives* of the organization must be considered carefully before deciding on a performance appraisal method.

7. Training programs should be implemented to (a) help raters avoid common perceptual errors in evaluations and (b) help raters with their performance review/feedback skills.

8. The link between the performance appraisal system and the organization's long-term strategic plans should be clearly defined.

9. In general, a successful performance appraisal system should be built around clear objectives, have the support of both management and employees, be flexible enough to adapt to organizational changes, and foster open discussions between supervisors and employees.

10. The validity of the performance appraisal system should be examined at regular intervals.

QUESTIONS FOR REVIEW

1. What are some of the major strategic choices organizations should make prior to implementing a performance appraisal system?

2. Why is a job analysis important to the performance appraisal system design?

3. What are the differences between the behavioral methods and the personnel comparison methods of performance appraisal?

4. What is the purpose of a performance appraisal?

5. What is the relationship between the performance appraisal system and the strategy of the organization?

6. How does the halo effect differ from stereotyping?

7. What are some ways an evaluator can avoid recency effects?

8. How can evaluators avoid leniency, strictness, and central tendency errors in ratings?

9. What are some characteristics of an unsuccessful versus a successful performance appraisal system?

CASE: Xerox Revamps Performance Appraisal System[36]

In the mid-1980s Xerox corporation was faced with a problem—its performance appraisal system was not working. Rather than motivating the employees, their appraisal system was leaving them discouraged and disgruntled. Xerox recognized this problem and developed a new system in order to eliminate it.

The Old System

The original system used by Xerox encompassed seven main principles:

1. The appraisal occurred once a year.

2. It required employees to document their accomplishments.

3. The manager would assess these accomplishments in writing and assign numerical ratings.

4. The appraisal included a summary written appraisal and a rating from one (unsatisfactory) to five (exceptional).

5. The ratings were on a forced distribution, controlled at the three or below level.

6. Merit increases were tied to the summary rating level.

7. Merit increase information and performance appraisals occurred in one session.

This system resulted in inequitable ratings and was cited by employees as a major source of dissatisfaction. In fact, in 1983, the Reprographic Business Group (RBG), Xerox's main copier division, reported that 95 percent of its employees received either a three or four on their appraisal. Merit raises for people in these two groups only varied by one to two percent. Essentially, across-the-board raises were being given to all employees, regardless of performance.

The New System

Rather than attempting to fix the old appraisal system, Xerox formed a task force to create a new system from scratch. The task force itself was made up of senior personnel executives; however, members of the task force also consulted with councils of employees and a council of middle managers. Together they created a new system, which differed from the old one in many key respects:

1. The absence of a numerical rating system.

2. The presence of a half-year feedback session.

3. The provision for development planning.

4. Prohibition in the appraisal guidelines of the use of subjective assessments of performance.

The new system has three stages, as opposed to the one-step process of the old system. These stages are spread out over the course of the year.

The first stage occurs at the beginning of the year when the manager meets with each employee. Together, they work out a written agreement on the employee's goals, objectives, plans, and tasks for the year. Standards of satisfactory performance are explicitly spelled out in measurable, attainable, and specific terms.

The second stage is a mid-year, mandatory feedback and discussion session between the manager and the employee. Progress toward objectives and performance strengths and weaknesses are discussed, as well as possible means for improving performance in the latter half of the year. Both the manager and the employee sign an "objectives sheet" indicating that the meeting took place.

The third stage in the appraisal process is the formal performance review, which takes place at year's end. Both the manager and the employee prepare a written document, stating how well the employee met the pre-set performance targets. They then meet and discuss the performance of the employee, resolving any discrepancies between the perceptions of the manager and the employee. This meeting emphasizes feedback and improvement. Efforts are made to stress the positive aspects of the employees performance as well as the negative. This stage also includes a developmental planning session in which training, education or development experiences that can help the employee are discussed.

The merit increase discussion takes place in a separate meeting from the performance appraisal, usually a month or two later. The discussion usually centers on the specific reasons for the merit raise amount, such as performance, relationship with peers, position in salary range. This allows the employee to better see the reasons behind the salary increase amount, as opposed to the summary rank, which tells the employee very little.

A follow-up survey was conducted the year after the implementation of the new appraisal system. Results were as follows:

81 percent better understood work group objectives

84 percent considered the new appraisal fair

72 percent said they understood how their merit raise was determined

70 percent met their personal and work objectives

77 percent considered the system a step in the right direction.

In conclusion, it can be clearly seen that the new system is a vast improvement over the previous one. Despite the fact that some of the philosophies, such as the use of self-appraisals, run counter to conventional management practices, the results speak for themselves.

QUESTIONS

1. What "type" of performance appraisal is central to the new system at Xerox? Which, if any, of the criteria for a successful appraisal system does this new system have?

2. Given the emphasis on employee development, what implications does this have for hiring and promotions?

3. How do you think management feels about the new performance appraisal system? Why?

4. Are there any potential negative aspects of the new performance appraisal system?

ADDITIONAL READINGS

Becker, B. E., and R. L. Cardy. "Influence of Halo Error on Appraisal Effectiveness: A Conceptual and Empirical Reconsideration." *Journal of Applied Psychology* 71 (1986), pp. 662–671.

Borman, W. C., and G. L. Hallam. "Observation Accuracy for Assessors of Work-Sample Performance: Consistency Across Task and Individual-Differences Correlates." *Journal of Applied Psychology* 76 (1991), pp. 11–18.

Borman, W. C., Leonard A. White, E. D. Pulakos, and S. H. Oppler. "Models of Supervisory Job Performance Ratings." *Journal of Applied Psychology* 76 (1991), pp. 863–872.

Campbell, D. J., and C. Lee. "Self-Appraisal in Performance Evaluation: Development versus Education." *Academy of Management Review* 13 (1988), pp. 302–314.

Dorfman, P. W., W. G. Stephan, and J. Loveland. "Performance Appraisal Behaviors: Supervisor Perceptions and Subordinate Reactions." *Personnel Psychology* 39 (1986), pp. 579–597.

Giles, W. F., and K. W. Mossholder. "Employee Reactions to Contextual and Session Components of Performance Appraisal." *Journal of Applied Psychology* 75 (1990), pp. 371–377.

Glen, R. M. "Performance Appraisal: An Unnerving yet Useful Process." *Public Personnel Management* 19 (1990), pp. 1–10.

Greenhaus, J. H., S. Parasuraman, and W. M. Wormley. "Effects of Race on Organizational Experiences, Job Performance Evaluations, and Career Outcomes." *Academy of Management Journal* 33 (1990), pp. 64–86.

Hanges, P. J., E. P. Braverman, and J. R. Rentsch. "Changes in Raters' Perceptions of Subordinates: A Catastrophe Model." *Journal of Applied Psychology* 76 (1991), pp. 878–888.

Harris, M. M., and J. Schaubroeck. "A Meta-Analysis of Self-Supervisor, Self-Peer, and Peer-Supervisor Ratings." *Personnel Psychology* 41 (1988), pp. 43–62.

Hedge, J. W., and M. J. Kavanagh. "Improving the Accuracy of Performance Evaluations: Comparison of Three Methods of Performance Appraiser Training." *Journal of Applied Psychology* 73 (1988), pp. 68–73.

Kamouri, A. L., and W. K. Balzer. "The Effects of Performance Sampling Methods on Frequency Estimation, Probability Estimation, and Evaluation of Performance Information." *Organizational Behavior and Human Decision Processes* 45 (1990), pp. 285–316.

Klimoski, R., and L. Inks. "Accountability Forces in Performance Appraisal." *Organizational Behavior and Human Decision Processes* 45 (1990), pp. 194–208.

Larson, J. R., and C. Callahan. "Performance Monitoring: How It Affects Work Productivity." *Journal of Applied Psychology* 74 (1990), pp. 530–538.

Londao, M., and A. J. Wohlers. "Agreement between Subordinate and Self-Ratings in Upward Feedback." *Personnel Psychology* 43 (1991), pp. 375–390.

Longenecker, C. O., H. P. Sims, and D. A. Gioia. "Behind the Mask: The Politics of Employee Appraisal." *Academy of Management Executive* 1 (1987), pp. 183–193.

Ludeman, Kate. "Customized Skills Assessments." *HRMagazine.* July 1991, pp. 67–85.

Maurer, T. J., and R. A. Alexander. "Contrast Effects in Behavioral Measurement: An Investigation of Alternative Process Explanations." *Journal of Applied Psychology* 76 (1991), pp. 3–10.

McEvoy, F. M., and P. F. Buller. "User Acceptance of Peer Appraisals in an Industrial Setting." *Personnel Psychology* 40 (1987), pp. 785–797.

McEvoy, G. M. "Public Sector Managers' Reactions to Appraisals by Subordinates." *Public Personnel Management* 19 (1990), pp. 201–212.

Meyer, Herbert. "A Solution to the Performance Appraisal Feedback Enigma." *Academy of Management Executive* 5 (1991), pp. 68–76.

Mohrman, A. M., S. M. Resnick-West, and E. E. Lawler. *Designing Performance Appraisal Systems.* San Francisco: Jossey-Bass, 1989.

Nathan, B. R., A. Mohrman, and J. Milliman. "Interpersonal Relations as a Context for the Effects of Appraisal Interviews on Performance and Satisfaction." *Academy of Management Journal* 34 (1991), pp. 352–369.

Nathan, B. R. and N. Tippins. "The Consequences of Halo 'Error' in Performance Ratings: A Field Study of the Moderating Effect of Halo on Test Validation Results." *Journal of Applied Psychology* 75 (1990), pp. 290–296.

Pulakos, E. D., L. A. White, S. H. Oppler, and W. C. Borman. "Examination of Race and Sex Effects on Performance Ratings." *Journal of Applied Psychology* 74 (1989), pp. 770–780

Sackett, P. R., and C.L.Z. DuBois. "Rater-Ratee Effects on Performance Evaluation: Challenging Meta-Analytic Conclusions." *Journal of Applied Psychology* 76 (1991), pp. 873–877.

Solomon, R. J. "Developing Job Specific Appraisal Factors in Large Organizations." *Public Personnel Management* 19 (1990), pp. 11–24.

Waldman, D. A., and B. J. Avolio. "Race Effects in Performance Evaluations: Controlling for Ability, Education, and Experience." *Journal of Applied Psychology* 76 (1991), pp. 897–901.

Williams, K. J., T. P. Cafferty, and A. S. DeNisi. "The Effect of Performance Appraisal Salience on Recall and Ratings." *Organizational Behavior and Human Decision Processes* 46 (1990), pp. 217–239.

NOTES

1. D. Waldman, and R. Kenett, "Improve Performance by Appraisals," *HRMagazine*, July 1990, pp. 60–69.

2. D. Cowfer and J. Sujansky, "Appraisal Development at Westinghouse," *Training and Development Journal*, July 1987, p. 40; and Mark R. Edwards, "Implementation Strategies for Multiple Rater Systems," *Personnel Journal*, September 1990, p. 139.

3. D. Waldman and R. Kenett, "Improve Performance."

4. J. Laumeyer and T. Beebe, "Employees and Their Appraisal," *Personnel Administrator*, December 1988, pp. 76–80.

5. H. J. Bernardin, "A Performance Appraisal System," in R. A. Berk, ed., *Performance Assessment*, (Baltimore: Johns Hopkins University Press, pp. 277–304).

6. Kate Ludeman, "Customized Skills Assessments," *HRMagazine*, July 1991, pp. 67–85.

7. D. L. DeVries, A. M. Morrison, S. L. Shullman, and M. L. Gerlach, *Performance Appraisal on the Line* (New York: Wiley, 1981).

8. K. Wexley and R. Klimoski, "Performance Appraisal: An Update," in K. Rowland and G. Ferris, eds., *Research in Personnel and Human Resources Management* (Greenwich, CT: JAI Press, 1984), vol. 2, pp. 35–80.

9. See M. M. Harris and J. Schaubroeck, "A Meta-analysis of Self-supervisor, Self-peer, and Peer-supervisor ratings," *Personnel Psychology* 41, 1988, pp. 43–62; and G. C. Thornton, "Psychometric Properties of Self-Appraisals of Job Performance," *Personnel Psychology* 33, 1980, pp. 263–271.

10. C. C. Hoffman, B. R. Nathan and L. M. Holden, "A Comparison of Validation Criteria: Objective versus Subjective Performance Measures and Self-Versus Supervisor Ratings," *Personnel Psychology* 44, 1991, pp. 601–619.

11. D. Campbell and C. Lee, "Self-Appraisal in Performance Evaluation: Development versus Education," *Academy of Management Review* 13, 1988, pp. 302–314.

12. Albert Karr, "Rating the Boss," *Wall Street Journal*, July 11, 1991, p. A1.

13. J. Segal, "Ignorance Is No Defense," *HRMagazine*, April 1990, pp. 93–94.

14. N. Angel, "Evaluating Employees by Computer," *Personnel Administrator*, November 1989, pp. 67–72.

15. "Is Your Friendly Computer Rating You on the Job?" *U.S. News and World Report*, February 18, 1987, p. 66.

16. Mark Edwards, "Accurate Performance Measurement Tools," *HRMagazine*, June 1991, pp. 95–98.

17. *Albemarle Paper Company v. Moody*, 422 U.S. 405, 1975.

18. D. L. Kirkpatrick, "Performance Appraisals, Your Questions Answered," *Training and Development Journal*, 1986, pp. 68–71.

19. J. Laumeyer and T. Beebe, "Employees and Their Appraisal."

20. Herbert Meyer, "A Solution to the Performance Appraisal Feedback Enigma," *Academy of Management Executive* 5, 1991, pp. 68–76.

21. J. Laumeyer and T. Beebe, "Employees and Their Appraisal."

22. F. J. Landy and J. L. Farr, "Performance Rating," *Psychological Bulletin*, April 1980, pp. 72–107.

23. F. Blanz and E. E. Ghiselli, "The Mixed Standard Scale: A New Rating System," *Personnel Psychology* 25, 1972, pp. 185–199.

24. D. A. Bownas and H. J. Bernardin, "Suppressing Illusory Halo with Forced-Choice Items," *Journal of Applied Psychology* 76, 1991, pp. 592–594.

25. D. Gold and B. Unger, "Evaluating Employees through Rating Scales," *HRNews*, July 1990, p. 5.

26. R. Rodgers and J. E. Hunter, "Impact of Management by Objectives on Organizational Productivity," *Journal of Applied Psychology* 76, 1991, pp. 322–326.

27. H. J. Bernardin and R. W. Beatty, *Performance Appraisal: Assessing Human Behavior at Work,* (Boston: PWS Kent, 1984).

28. G. V. Barrett and M. C. Kernan, "Performance Appraisal and Terminations: A Review of Court Decisions Since Brito v. Zia with Implications for Personnel Practices," *Personnel Psychology* 40, 1987, pp. 489–503.

29. K. R. Murphy and W. K. Balzer, "Systematic Distortions in Memory-Based Behavior Ratings and Performance Evaluations: Consequences for Rating Accuracy," *Journal of Applied Psychology* 70, 1986, pp. 39–44.

30. See, for example, R. Smither, *The Psychology of Work and Human Performance* (New York: Harper & Row, 1988), p. 164.

31. P. R. Sackett, C. L. Z. DuBois and A. W. Noe, "Tokenism in Performance Evaluation: The Effects of Work Group Representation on Male-Female and White-Black Differences in Performance Ratings," *Journal of Applied Psychology* 76, 1991, pp. 263–267.

32. See, for example, J. H. Harvey and G. Weary, "Current Issues in Attribution Theory and Research," in M. R. Rosenzweig and L. W. Porter, eds., *Annual Review of Psychology* 35, 1984, pp. 427–459; and M. J. Martinko and W. L. Gardner, "The Leader/Member Attribution Process," *Academy of Management Review* 12, 1987, pp. 235–249.

33. C. Fombrun and R. Laud, "Strategic Issues in Performance Appraisal: 0

Theory and Practice." In K. Rowland and G. Ferris, *Current Issues in Personnel Management*, 3rd ed. (Boston: Allyn & Bacon, 1986).

34. R. Miles and C. Snow, "Designing Strategic Human Resources Systems," *Organizational Dynamics*, 1983, pp. 36–52.

35. The following discussion is based on C. Lee, "Smoothing Out Appraisal Systems," *HRMagazine*, March 1990, pp. 72–76.

36. Norman R. Deets and D. Tyler, "How Xerox Improved Its Performance Appraisals," *Personnel Journal*, April 1986, p. 50; Michael F. Wolff, "Appraising Performance at Xerox Corporate R & D," *Research Management*, July–August 1987, p. 8; and Mary Riley and Richard Noland, "Beyond Performance Reviews," *Management Solutions*, October 1987, p. 15.

PART

FOUR

Strategies for Maintaining Human Resources

14 Benefit Plans

Due to major changes in the benefit plans over the past years, many employees have difficulty understanding a firm's benefit program, let alone compare it to those of other firms.[1]

Yet virtually all employers believe that a benefits package is necessary to attract and keep employees.[2] However, the average cost of all benefits for an employee in 1986 was $10,283, a 31 percent increase over the same figure for 1984.[3] In 1991, employers paid an average of $4.13 an hour on top of the $10.84 an hour they paid in wages. The total benefits paid, including vacations, supplemental pay, insurance, retirement, and Social Security, came to 27.6 percent of the total compensation, which was up from 27.3 percent in 1989.[4] With so much being spent on benefits, it is important that a firm carefully plan its benefit strategy to ensure that it helps meet its overall human resource and corporate strategies.

• • • • • • • • •
CHAPTER OBJECTIVES

As a result of studying this chapter, you should be able to

1. Explain the strategic choices available to a firm in the area of benefits.

2. Explain how benefit plans tie into the overall human resource strategy.

3. List and define various forms of benefits.

4. Distinguish between traditional benefit plans and "cafeteria" or choice plans.

CASE: The Benefits of Xerox[5]

- We provide pay and benefits equal to progressive companies in the competitive environments in which we operate.
- We recognize and reward superior performers.
- We share the results of superior company performance with our employees.
- We protect our employees from unmanageable financial risks caused by disability or medical expenses.
- We provide our employees with flexibility in making benefits choices.
- We offer our employees incentives to save for their retirement.

So begins Xerox Corporation's philosophy on employee benefits. The company believes in tying benefits to the total compensation package as evidenced by the second and third statements above. The firm ties incentive compensation and profit sharing to its total benefit package. The firm also offers a comprehensive benefits package as is described below. Finally, the firm believes that it is important to design a benefit program that is equal to those of its competitors.

Benefits Plan Summary

Medical Plan. The Xerox medical plan is designed to help pay the costs of medical care for the employee and eligible dependents. The employee shares the cost of the covered medical expenses up to an annual limit after meeting a deductible. Xerox pays the other 80 percent of most expenses and covers the employee further by limiting annual out-of-pocket costs.

The plan pays benefits toward a wide range of medical expenses, such as hospital care, surgery, diagnostic services, doctor's visits, and prescription drugs. Health-related expenses not covered by this plan may be reimbursed by the Flexible Benefit Account or through salary redirection. Also, the Xerox Employee Assistance Program pays certain benefits for the treatment of emotional problems, as well as alcoholism and drug addiction.

Flexible Benefit Account. The Flexible Benefit Account (FBA) provides the employee with $400 a year to pay for most health-care expenses not fully covered under the Xerox Medical Plan, Dental Plan, and Employee Assistance Program.

Dental Plan. The Xerox dental plan pays benefits for a broad range of dental services and supplies, including X rays, fillings, crowns, bridges, dentures, extraction of teeth, oral surgery, and root canal therapy. It encourages a sound program of preventive care and early treatment. Dental expenses not covered by this plan may be reimbursed by the Flexible Benefit Account.

Life Insurance Plan. The Xerox life insurance plan provides financial protection for the employee's family during his or her working years and after retirement. Life insurance benefits are payable to the beneficiary in case of death from any cause, at any time or place. Under the travel accident insurance plan, benefits are payable to the beneficiary in case of accidental death during company travel, in addition to life insurance benefits.

Retirement Plan. The retirement plan is designed to help assure future financial security by providing a lifetime monthly income to the employee and spouse, if married, when retired from Xerox. The plan may also provide benefits if the employee leaves Xerox before retirement.

Savings Plan. The Xerox savings plan reflects the savings options of the Xerox profit sharing retirement and savings plan. The savings plan is designed to provide a way to save and invest for future financial security. Savings will be invested for future growth according to investment choice from the plan's three investment funds.

If the employee elects to save on a before-tax basis, the company will match savings by adding one dollar for every four dollars that are saved up to a maximum company contribution equaling one percent of pay.

Disability Income. The disability income plan is designed to provide a continuing income for illness or injury if the employee is unable to work. This plan is made of two types of coverage:

- Short-term disability benefits, which continue full pay starting the first day of absence and continuing for up to five months.
- Long-term disability benefits, which continue part of the employee's pay after disability for five months and are payable until the employee is no longer disabled, but in no event beyond the age 65.

Salary Reduction. Health-care and dependent care expenses can be paid with tax-free dollars. By signing up for payroll deduction, employees can "redirect" part of their salaries into special accounts from which health and/ or dependent care expenses will be reimbursed.

Xerox Employee Assistance Program. The Xerox Employee Assistance Program (XEAP) is designed to help the employee and dependents deal with personal problems in their early stages. Through this program, employees, retirees, and their dependents can obtain confidential counseling, referrals, and special diagnostic and treatment benefits for emotional and family difficulties as well as for alcohol and drug-related problems.

Holidays. Xerox employees are entitled to 12 paid holidays each year, including

- New Year's Day
- Memorial Day

- Independence Day
- Labor Day
- Thanksgiving Day
- Christmas Day
- plus 6 rolling holidays designated by the operating unit

Vacations. Paid vacation time is dependent upon the number of years the employee has worked for Xerox. The specific vacation policy is specified below:

YEARS	WEEKS
1 through 4	2 weeks
5 through 9	3 weeks
10 through 19	4 weeks
20 through 24	5 weeks
25 and beyond	6 weeks

Tuition Aid Plan. Xerox will reimburse employees for 100 percent of the tuition and laboratory fees for approved courses. Reimbursement will be made upon successful completion of each course of study.

The Xerox Credit Union. Employees are eligible to join the Credit Union on the first day of work.

Adoption Assistance Plan. The Xerox Adoption Assistance Plan provides reimbursement of up to $1,000 for covered expenses incurred in the adoption process.

The company is proud of the comprehensive nature of its benefits program and believes it offers a package competitive with any company in its industry. It also believes the package helps Xerox to attract and keep employees of superior ability and talent.

● ● ● ● ● ● ● ● ●

If you were interviewing with Xerox for a job, would its benefits package be a major factor in your deliberations? How would you know exactly how competitive the Xerox package is? Do you think a benefits program, such as Xerox's, actually helps the company keep good employees from leaving?

STRATEGIC CHOICES

You may have some difficulty answering the above questions. But so do human resource managers who must develop benefits packages for employees. When faced with a multitude of choices available, how does one decide which to offer?

Frequently the decisions boil down to three fundamental strategic choices managers must make. Each of these is outlined on the following page.

1. How much of the money that is used to cover employee benefits should be paid by the employer and how much of it should be covered by the employee? When making this decision, concepts such as corporate culture, corporate strategy, employee rights, and employer responsibilities must be kept in mind. If the firm wants to boast that it offers a comprehensive benefits package, then it must not require that the employee pay the majority of the costs. Likewise, if the firm is following a cost containment strategy, it will not want to pick up the total cost of the benefit package.

2. Second, managers must decide how comprehensive their plans should be. Some firms, like Xerox, pride themselves on covering any possible need the employee might have. Other firms may decide that only health insurance is important and offer only that to their employees. It may be difficult for some to believe that an employee would select to work for a firm that offers only health insurance, but many workers will. As we have seen in past chapters, not everyone is motivated by money or, in this case, benefits.

3. Finally, managers must make a fundamental choice as to how flexible the benefits program will be? The changes occurring in today's work force make some of the traditional benefit packages obsolete. For example, if both husband and wife work, it may be to their benefit to have one spouse cover dental and the other cover major medical because the plans are more comprehensive or less expensive. What they really do not need is for both of them to be covered under both plans. In order to allow these types of variations in benefit plans, flexibility is a must.

Let's look at each of these choices in more detail.

WHO PAYS FOR THE BENEFITS?

In the past, the employer has been responsible for paying most of the cost of a benefit program. This included premiums and deductibles for insurance as well as premium contributions. However, the trend is being reversed especially in health insurance.[6] The U.S. health-care system is the world's most expensive. It consisted of 11 percent of the gross national product in 1988 and is projected to consume 13 percent by 1992.[7] Employers paid an average of 92 cents an hour to cover workers in 1991. This amount was up 8.2 percent from 1990 and up nearly 28 percent from 1987.[8] In total, employers paid approximately $14,061 per employee or more than 40 percent of the payroll for employee benefits in 1991.[9]

But benefits are a labor cost, just as are wages and salaries. With the pressure to keep labor costs under control, caused in part by the increased competitiveness discussed in Chapter 2, in the 1990s employers will be forced to make a strategic decision regarding benefits: How much will we ask the employee to pay?

HOW COMPREHENSIVE A LIST OF BENEFITS SHALL BE OFFERED?

A second strategic choice faced by employers involves the breadth and depth of coverage. All employers must offer a certain range of benefits. These are called

....

EXHIBIT 14.1	Benefit Areas Projected for Major Growth by 1995

Flexible medical plan	84%
Long-term care coverage	82%
Elder care benefits	77%
Flexible work schedule	72%
Employer-sponsored day care	66%
Group universal life insurance	58%
Mail-order prescription drugs	54%

....

compulsory benefits, which are mandated by law such as workers' compensation and unemployment insurance.

But beyond these compulsory benefits, employers have a wide choice of benefit packages. As can be seen in the case at the beginning of the chapter, Xerox offers a comprehensive set of benefits. Most major employers do offer a comprehensive list of benefits and this list will likely continue to grow. Exhibit 14.1 shows the results of a survey completed in 1988 of directors from 100 major industrial companies on the benefit areas that would see "major growth by 1995."[10] Note that long-term care coverage and elder-care benefits are likely to see major growth, no doubt because of the aging baby boomers. Other benefits that employers have begun providing in the past few years include a month's worth of mass transit tokens, employer-assisted home mortgages, and college tuition for employees' children.[11] If other companies begin to offer these benefits, will most employers in the geographic area begin to offer them? The extent of benefit offering is a strategic question for each employer.

HOW FLEXIBLE SHALL THE BENEFIT OFFERING BE?

The third strategic choice involves the flexibility of benefit offerings. The employer needs to decide whether a standard list of benefits shall be offered to all employees or whether employees will be allowed to pick and choose among benefit offerings in a "cafeteria"-style plan. A 1987 survey by the Administrative Management Society showed that 20 percent of the 309 companies surveyed offered cafeteria plans. This was up from 17 percent in 1986 and just 12 companies in 1983.[12] An additional 12 percent were considering such plans for 1988. Thus, the trend seems to be toward cafeteria-style plans to allow increased flexibility to meet the needs of a varied work force. But each employer must decide how flexible a program is desired. Cafeteria plans are discussed in more depth later in the chapter.

THE QUESTION OF COMPETITIVENESS

As you no doubt have determined by now, one key underlining strategy that prevails in benefit offerings is *competitiveness.* Employers want to offer a benefit package that allows them to compete successfully in the labor market for employees but not one that is so costly that labor costs are raised above that of the competition. Exhibit 14.2 provides a list of the reasons given by employers for offering employee benefits. Essentially employers face the same dilemma with benefits costs as they do with wage

....

| EXHIBIT 14.2 | Reasons Given by Employers for Offering Employee Benefits |

	COMPANY SIZE IN NUMBER OF EMPLOYEES				
REASON	1–10	10–49	50–99	100–499	500+
Attract good employees					
Salaried	10%	38%	44%	57%	53%
Hourly	33%	48%	27%	46%	47%
Reduce turnover					
Salaried	30%	19%	32%	19%	11%
Hourly	33%	22%	42%	18%	18%
Motivate employees					
Salaried	10%	22%	4%	10%	32%
Hourly	11%	19%	8%	21%	12%
Tax-free benefits					
Salaried	40%	22%	12%	8%	6%
Hourly	22%	4%	0%	0%	0%
Keep out the union					
Salaried	0%	0%	4%	2%	0%
Hourly	0%	4%	12%	9%	18%
Meet union requirements					
Salaried	0%	0%	0%	0%	0%
Hourly	0%	4%	8%	5%	0%
Other					
Salaried	10%	0%	4%	4%	0%
Hourly	0%	0%	4%	2%	6%

....

costs: a high enough wage needs to be offered to attract and hold good employees but not one so high that labor costs exceed the labor costs of competitors. Of course, a higher wage rate can be offset by higher productivity, thus resulting in *lower unit labor costs* as we discussed in Chapter 12.

So the question becomes: Can benefits be used to achieve a competitive advantage? In "Using Employee Benefits," H. W. Hennessey argues that they cannot.[13] Citing various studies that show employees know little of their own benefit program, let alone those of competing firms, he argues that benefits cannot be used to achieve a competitive differential in hiring. Furthermore, the complexity of current benefit offerings with varying coverages and costs make it difficult for all but the most diligent employees to understand the package.

The implication is that if a firm wishes to achieve a differential advantage in its benefit offering it must know what is being offered by competitive employers in the labor market and then must design a program that is better. Next it must very clearly communicate this difference to all job applicants and present employees. Unless these two steps are taken, the benefit program will not be a way to gain competitive advantage.

Other employers, like Xerox at the beginning of this chapter, do not wish to gain a competitive advantage with their benefit program; rather they simply want to remain competitive. That is, they want to offer a package of benefits that compares to, even though it does not surpass, that of their competition. Of course, even with

HR CHALLENGES •••

Firms Ease Access to Benefits Information

Most employees cannot be bothered to read the company benefits handbook—even as benefit plans grow more complicated. Rather than creating an army of personnel staffers to field employee inquiries, many companies are turning to technology. "Kiosks are the 'in' thing," says Emmett O. Seaborn, a consultant with Towers Perrin, benefits consultants in New York.

At some companies, an employee at any facility can sit in privacy at a computer kiosk linked to a central data bank to enroll in a benefit program or make changes and inquiries. Or a diskette in an employee's PC can walk him through benefit choices and estimate tax consequences.

Convenience is the key. Especially in two-income families, "a lot of people do the financial work in the evenings and on weekends," says Nenette Kress, a senior consultant with Coopers & Lybrand, a New York consulting firm. So some employers are providing automated phone lines that can be used at any hour. Employees can use their pushbutton phones to get specific confidential information. Burroughs-Wellcome Co. installed such a system in June 1989 to handle inquiries on its 401(k) plan. So far, 30 percent of callers have used it in nonworking hours.

SOURCE: Adapted from Jolie Solomon, "Managing," *Wall Street Journal,* February 17, 1989, p. B1.

this approach clear communication of benefits to job applicants and present employees is essential.

COMPOSITION OF BENEFIT PLANS

While most companies today offer a standard list of benefits, a wide variety of additional benefits are also offered, especially by the larger companies. Some of the standard benefits are compulsory (required by law). Others have been offered for many years. In this section we explore the various types of benefits offered. Basically, we can classify benefits into six major categories as follows:

- Required or mandatory security
- Voluntary security
- Retirement-related
- Time-off related
- Health insurance
- Financial, social, and recreational service

Specific examples in each category are shown in Exhibit 14.3.

Required Security

Federal and state governments require that employers provide a certain minimum level of protection or a security floor for each employee. There are three primary areas of compulsory security: **workers' compensation, unemployment compensation, and Social Security benefits.**

Workers' Compensation

Workers' compensation protects the employee from costs due to injury on the job. The costs are paid entirely by the employer. Thus, industrial accidents are viewed as a cost of doing business, and like any other cost, the company is responsible for

....

EXHIBIT 14.3 A Typology of Benefits

MANDATORY SECURITY	VOLUNTARY SECURITY	RETIREMENT RELATED	TIME-OFF RELATED	HEALTH AND INSURANCE	FINANCIAL	SOCIAL AND RECREATIONAL
1. Workers' compensation 2. Unemployment compensation 3. Social Security (old age, survivors' and disability insurance) 4. Medicare hospital benefits	1. Severance pay 2. Supplemental unemployment benefits	1. Pension funds 2. Early retirement 3. Retirement annuity 4. Disability retirement benefits	1. Vacations 2. Holidays 3. Sick leave 4. Disability leave 5. Paid leaves of absence (sabbaticals) 6. Military reserve time 7. Pregnancy or parental leaves	1. Medical 2. Dental 3. Disability insurance 4. Life insurance 5. Group insurance rates 6. Survivors' benefits 7. Wellness and fitness programs 8. Employee Assistance Programs (EAP)	1. Profit sharing 2. Stock plans 3. Moving assistance 4. Tuition reimbursements 5. Legal services 6. Financial counseling 7. Company car 8. Credit union	1. Paid club membership 2. Recreational sports sponsorship (such as softball, bowling) 3. Professional and trade association dues and meeting costs 4. Child care 5. Cafeteria 6. Service awards (such as watches, jewelry) 7. Company sponsored social events (such as the Christmas party)

....

keeping the costs as low as possible by furnishing a safe workplace and safe work procedures.[14]

Workers' compensation started with the Federal Employee's Compensation Act of 1908 and the state laws of California, Washington, Wisconsin, and New Jersey passed in 1911. All states now have workers' compensation laws.

Prior to the passage of workers' compensation laws, if an employee was injured on the job, he or she had to take the employer to court and prove negligence. This was very difficult. Under the doctrine of **contributory negligence** even if the employee was only 1 percent negligent and the employer 99 percent negligent, the employee could not collect in the suit. Since most employers had no health insurance plans for employees at the time, the net effect was that employees injured on the job had to pay for their medical care entirely on their own. Of course, most workers simply did not have funds to do so.

Workers' compensation originally covered only physical injury. However, today it has been expanded to cover emotional consequences resulting from physical injury. In some cases, job stress and strain are covered if they lead to emotional illness. Furthermore, even an accident at a company-sponsored party may be covered if employees are expected to attend.

Employers pay premiums into a state-oriented or private insurance fund. Premiums are based on the company's experience with accident and job-related illness rates—the higher the accident rate the higher the premium. Thus employers have an incentive to provide a safe workplace and instruct in safe work habits. However, insurers often refuse to gear premium prices for small companies to their level of injury. The result is that some small firms who have had no accidents are placed in a pool with all other firms in their industry and end up paying a much higher premium than is warranted.[15]

Employees collect workers' compensation either in the form of cash paid directly to the employee or in the form of reimbursement for medical expenses, pain, and suffering. When work is missed, the employee is paid for lost work time. Although the amount varies from state to state, payment for lost work time due to illness or injury averages about two-thirds of the employee's regular earnings.

All but three states (Texas, New Jersey, and South Carolina) have compulsory workers' compensation plans. Every employer under these laws must comply with their provisions. Under the elective laws in the above three named states, employers have the option of accepting or rejecting the act. If the employer rejects the law, the employee must sue to initiate damage compensation.

In order to control rising costs of workers' compensation, several hospitals in Massachusetts have formed a self-insurance group and are paying a total of $2.5 million into a workers' compensation fund. The administrators of the fund have promised that a nurse will contact the injured employee within a day of when the claim was filed. This early involvement is intended to decrease the number of days missed from work, which will reduce the costs for the hospital.[16]

Criticism of Workers' Compensation

Since benefits and plans vary so much from state to state, organized labor and others have lobbied for more federal control and regulation. Of course, employers and business groups have strongly resisted this because they believe their costs will be raised. States also prefer to have their own plans, since those with low benefit levels use that fact as a strong inducement when attracting new industry. However, with the costs of workers' compensation rising rapidly, as shown in Exhibit 14.4, some changes are likely to occur.

The cost for workers' compensation was up to $60 billion, more than double the costs in 1982.[17] These rising costs have some managers worried about how they will pay the premiums. For example, Jean Stinson, a railroad contractor in Florida lost a great deal of business when her company's workers' compensation liability jumped 187 percent in one year. To cover the $250,000 costs, she raised her bids. However, her customers decided to put all but the necessary projects on hold. She faced a similar problem at the beginning of 1992 when Florida's rates again were increased by 25 percent.[18]

In order to deal with the higher costs, top management must become involved. Below are several steps recommended to help managers keep workers' compensation benefits in line.

1. Collect facts about the history of your firm's workers' compensation. Compare these figures to profits, sales, and salaries to see if they are out of proportion.
2. Be sure that you understand your current programs in safety and health. Are there areas in which you can improve?
3. Invite outside vendors, especially insurance carriers, who often have innovative plans that will help curb your rising costs.

EXHIBIT 14.4   Rising Costs of Workers' Compensation

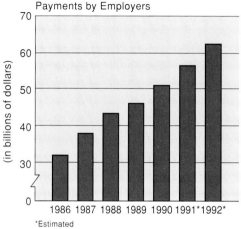

**Workers' Comp
Costs Balloon**

Payments by Employers

*Estimated

4. Become more involved in the workers' compensation reforms in the states where you do business. Your voice may help to change the process.

5. Communicate information about workers' compensation benefits to employees—it can keep them from taking an adversarial stance.

6. Show concern in an emergency. The use of in-house clinics that can provide immediate attention to injuries can reduce the need for outside care.

7. Penalize careless managers. Charge claims to the operating unit where the injury occurred.

8. Get employees back to work fast. The longer the employee stays away from work, the more attitudes toward him or herself and work change. The employee may never come back.

9. Find out what's causing injuries. Many injuries can result from common problems that are easily fixed.[19]

Unemployment Compensation

Unemployment compensation pays employees for work time missed due to layoff or termination. This is a state-administered plan, but it was established as part of the Social Security Act of 1935. The law was passed during the depths of the depression in order to provide income for the millions of people out work in order to revive the economy. Employers fund this program by paying up to 3.5 percent of an initial amount (often $7,000 of employee's salary).

Most employees are eligible for benefits unless fired for misconduct. They collect 50 to 80 percent of pay, depending on the state, for up to 26 weeks as long as they actively seek employment. During periods of high unemployment, Congress will extend the period for collecting benefits up to another 26 weeks. Unemployment compensation has been criticized for encouraging fraud and laziness. Yet it has provided a floor of income for people who leave their jobs usually through no fault of their own. Since the law requires that people actively seek work, people are officially encouraged to get off of unemployment compensation as soon as they can.

Some have suggested that the federal law should be changed in order to eliminate abuse, provide stronger requirements for work search behavior, and provide more funding for the plan, especially during recessions. Also, standardization among the states has been advocated.

Social Security

Virtually everyone who works today is covered by Social Security. Social Security provides benefits when an employee retires. It also covers old age, survivors, and disability insurance. Even such programs as Medicare and Medicaid fall under Social Security. In fact, several welfare programs, such as Aid to Families with Dependent Children (AFDC), the program which distributes food stamps, fall under the Social Security Act of 1935. However, our concerns are with those provisions of the program that deal with employment-related issues.

The Social Security program was established by the Social Security Act of 1935. This law was passed during the depths of the depression as part of Franklin D. Roosevelt's New Deal program. The rationale was that government needed to provide a mandatory social insurance program to provide a minimum income for those who retire or are disabled on the job and for their survivors. Although initially limited in coverage, virtually everyone who works today is covered by the law, even farmers who are not included in most programs.

Funding Benefits

Social Security is funded jointly by the employee and employer through a tax on a set amount of wages. Both the tax and the minimum wage covered have consistently increased throughout the years, as is shown in Exhibit 14.5. But Social Security benefits have also increased greatly and are now indexed to inflation.

The Social Security fund is not a strict insurance fund as found in a private insurance company. Rather, the contributions of current employees pay the benefits of current retirees and other eligible recipients. In fact, there is some concern that once the baby boomers begin to retire in the first decade of the next century, there will not be enough people working to cover the massive benefit payments needed to fund such a large number of retirees. That is one reason both the percentage and the wage base increased so drastically during the 1980s, as Exhibit 14.5 shows. In fact, the tax increased for both the employer and employee by over 1,200 percent from $300 per year to $3,604.80 per year from 1937 to 1989!

Social Security also provides disability payments to an individual who is disabled on the job for as long as the person lives. These payments are rather modest, however. Payments are also made to survivors (immediate family) if a person covered by Social Security dies while working or retired.

Finally, Medicaid benefits are funded under the Social Security Act that pays health benefits for the elderly covered under the Social Security Act.

In order to better fund the program, some changes were made in 1983 in an act passed to amend the basic law. Social Security begins to pay some benefits at age 62, but the normal retirement age is 65. By 2002, the retirement age will increased by 2-month increments to age 67 for all employees born in 1960 or later. The age

EXHIBIT 14.5 Changes in Rates and Minimum Salary Taxed for Social Security

YEAR	PERCENT*	WAGE BASE	TAX
1937	1	$ 3,000	$ 300.00
1951	1.5	3,600	540.00
1981	6.65	29,700	1,975.05
1988	7.51	45,000	3,379.50
1989	7.51	48,000	3,604.80
1990	7.65	51,300	3,924.45
1991	7.65	53,400	4,085.10
1992	7.65	55,500	4,245.75

*Employer and employee each pay this percent and amount of the wage base.

for coverage for widows and widowers will also increase from 62 to 65. Finally, people with higher incomes now pay a tax on their Social Security income.

Voluntary Security

Two of the major security benefit programs used by employers are voluntary: **severance pay** and **supplemental unemployment** benefits (SUB). Severance pay is pay given to the employee at termination. Its purpose is to provide funds to tie the employee over until he or she finds another job. The amount varies from a couple of weeks for hourly workers to several years worth of salary for executives. In fact, **"golden parachutes"** are paid to executives as a form of compensation in case they are terminated during a hostile takeover. Golden parachutes are a form of severance pay.

Executives who fear hostile takeovers often are able to obtain a golden parachute clause in their contract, which states that they will be paid a large amount—often several years worth of salary—if they are terminated. Since hostile takeovers usually result in termination of many executives in the acquired company, this serves as a protection to those executives and as a deterrent to hostile takeovers, since such a large amount of cash is needed to fund the golden parachutes.

The second form of voluntary security is *supplemental unemployment benefits (SUB)*. These are payments made by the employer to an employee who is temporarily laid off. They are made in addition to unemployment compensation received from the state. These payments were pioneered by the auto industry (economic recessions, model changeovers, and so on). In the auto industry, employers receive up to 95 percent of their normal wage through SUB and unemployment compensation.

Retirement

Fully 91 percent of full-time workers at companies with more than 100 employees are covered by retirement plans according to the Employee Benefits Research Institute. Yet only 43 percent of firms with fewer than 100 employees have pension coverage.[20] About 45 percent of all civilian workers work in firms of 100 or less employees, so a large percent of employees are not covered by pensions. In fact,

Congress is considering several bills to encourage more widespread use of premiums by employers; the incentives include reduced paperwork, portability, and tax credits.

Pension assets in private trusted funds stood at $1.25 trillion in the fall of 1988. Stock holdings were $514 billion during this time.[21] At the end of 1989, the pot had reached $2.5 trillion.[22] As you can see, pension funds are a major source of investment capital in the United States.

Pension plans are considered rewards for long service and are not incentives to work more efficiently or effectively unless the premium is tied to a stock option plan as is true of Sears. Pension plans are used primarily to retain a loyal work force.

Employment Retirement Income Security Act (ERISA) of 1974

This law was passed to correct many abuses in pension coverage and to set rules and regulations. It is the major law regulating pensions. It is complex, detailed and, at least for small firms, costly to adhere to. Hence many small firms have terminated their pension coverage to avoid the voluminous paperwork. Yet the law has provided increased security to ensure that employees actually receive their pensions when they retire.

The Internal Revenue Service (IRS) also developed guidelines to try to control discrimination in pensions. Specifically, rules were established so that higher paid employees would not benefit more than lower paid employees.[23] Higher paid employees in 1990 were defined by the IRS as any employee paid more than $85,485 a year or $56,990 if they were in the top 20 percent of a company's earners.[24]

Funding of Pensions

Funds for paying pension benefits are acquired in two basic ways. An **unfunded plan** pays pensions out of current income generated by the organization. A **funded plan** pays benefits out of money set aside and invested specifically to pay pension benefits. This is the more popular method since a specific fund is set aside to pay benefits. Current income of the firm, which can vary widely from year to year depending on economic conditions and other factors, is generally viewed as too variable and risky a way to fund pensions.

Insurance for Pensions

Insured pensions are administered through an insurance company that guarantees payment of the benefits. **Uninsured** plans are administered by the employer and are considered to be less stable and sound than insured pensions. However, some insured pensions are not all that safe. For example, Pacific Lumber's retirement payments to its workers were delayed and threatened to be cut completely when the state took over First Executive Corporation's largest insurance units in California and New York. These insurance units, who were responsible for Pacific Lumber's pension plan, invested heavily in junk bonds, and when the bottom fell out of that market, the insurance units had to be taken over. Workers like Bill Hunsaker, who worked for Pacific Lumber for 47 years, are devastated. Hunsaker's medical bills for his wife and himself are stacking up. Promises from the company do little to ease his pain.[25]

EXHIBIT 14.6   Retirement Plans by Type

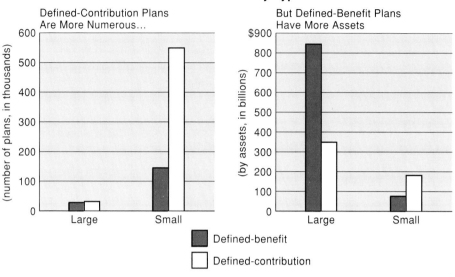

Contributions

A **non-contributory** pension is one in which all of the funds for the pensions are paid by the employer. In a **contributory fund,** both the employee and the employer fund the pension.

Pension Benefits

Retirement plans come in two main types: defined-contributions and defined-benefit plans. Exhibit 14.6 illustrates the number of employees involved in both and the assets associated with each. A **defined contribution plan** is one in which the **contribution rate** paid by the employee is *fixed* and retirement benefits *vary.* Profit sharing, employee stock ownership plans (ESOPs), and thrift plans are defined contribution plans. In a **defined benefit plan,** the benefits paid to employees are *set* and the method used to determine the benefits are *set.* This allows the use of statistics to determine the employer contribution. Because a defined benefit plan provides a greater assurance of benefits and predictability of benefits available at retirement, older employees generally prefer this type of plan.[26]

Defined benefit plans have become more costly to administer because of new tax and accounting rules. Consequently, more firms have adopted defined-contribution plans, in which salary and service determine annual payments to an employer's account. Merrill Lynch changed from a defined benefit plan to defined contribution plan in 1988 and generated a surplus of $220 million. However, this move penalized employees in the 50s and up age group who earned higher salaries than younger employees and expected higher benefits at retirement under a defined benefit plan.[27] For this reason, younger workers generally prefer this type of plan.[28]

Portability

In a **portable pension plan,** employees can move their pension benefits from one employer to another without losing benefits. Portability has become an increasingly important aspect of pensions because the average worker changes jobs every two to three years before age 30 and four to seven years thereafter. To deal with these demographic changes, in 1978, the Internal Revenue Service addressed the demand for portable pensions by creating 401(k) plans and reducing the number of years needed for vesting, and in 1991 the Department of Labor proposed the Pension Opportunities for Workers Expanded Retirement (POWER) to simplify and increase the flexibility of pension systems. As the baby boom generation continues to age, there will be even more demand for portability and security for retirement.[29] If an employee is not in a portable pension, then a lump sum benefit must be taken at termination, provided the employee is vested.

Vesting Rights

Vesting is the right to receive benefits from a retirement plan. A person becomes vested after working and contributing for a period of time. Five- and ten-year vesting periods are common. If the employee leaves prior to the vesting requirement, the only funds the employee receives when employment is terminated are the funds the employee has contributed. Once vested, however, pension rights are retained and both employee and employer funds are received.

Retirement Equity Act of 1984

This law liberalized pension regulations that affect women, guaranteed access to benefits, lowered the vesting age, and prohibited employers from discriminating against people who take leaves of absence (such as pregnancy leave). Other provisions of the act lowered the age at which workers can receive pension credits and the age at which they can enroll.

Individual Retirement Accounts (IRAs)

A popular retirement fund is the individual retirement account. Although IRAs are funded entirely by the employee, they are popular because the salary money contributed, up to $2,000 per year, is not subject to taxes under certain total income limitations. Also, the interest earned on the amount set aside is not taxed regardless of total income.

Money can be set aside until age 70½ and money can be withdrawn without penalty beginning at age 59½. Funds drawn prior to that date are subject to income tax plus a 10 percent penalty. The major advantages of an IRA are that the employee can decide where to invest the extra retirement income, and a tax shelter is created since income tax is deferred until retirement when presumably total income is lower and hence is taxed at a lower rate.

401(k) Plans

Named for the section of the IRS code that set them up, these plans work much like an IRA in that they serve as a tax shelter for a portion of income until

HR CHALLENGES ●●●

Using 401(k) Plans at Coors

During 1990, Coors Brewing Company increased 401(k) participation by 16.5 percent and hiked pension benefits by an average of 7.1 percent for all employees. Employees have become involved in their retirement plans. More than one third of Coors employees have requested a computer program to project their retirement benefits. What sparked this dramatic increase? Coors says it's simply communication.

Coors implemented a campaign called the Tax Effective Retirement Account (TERA). This plan was designed to increase employee participation in the company's 401(k) plan. When Coors realized that employees failed to see their retirement income should come from 3 sources: pensions, Social Security, and personal savings, they decided to do something about it. The TERA promotion focused on helping employees understand the importance of making steady contributions to a retirement savings account in order to maintain a style of living after retirement to which they have grown accustomed.

One key to the program's success was the TERA turtle, which served as the mascot for the program. The

turtle, inspired by the Aesop's fable of the tortoise and the hare, represented that steady dependable savings is the way to win the retirement race. All employees who enrolled in the 401(k) plan received a turtle lapel pin, and all nonparticipants who requested a personalized computer projection received a pin too. If the nonparticipants joined, they also received a turtle coffee mug as did those who increased their deferral percentage. To maintain interest in the program, Coors sponsored a weekly drawing for $100. However, the name pulled as the winner could only collect if they were wearing their turtle pin.

All of these efforts paid off for Coors. In just 10 months, participation in TERA jumped from 73 percent to 84 percent of the work force. More than 2,200 employees increased their deferral percentage and more than 1,200 employees signed up for first-time participation. Coors feels that its efforts will help to ensure that its employees will be able to retire in style.

SOURCE: Adapted from Shari Caudron, "Boosting Retirement Benefits," *HRMagazine,* December 1991, pp. 76–79.

retirement. The difference is that the employer deducts the salary and the money can be invested only in a limited set of employer-approved funds. Also a larger amount can be set aside in these plans—$7,000 per year or up to $9,000 for educators. These plans are popular with higher paid managers and executives, but cannot be limited only to these employees. These types of plans have been used to encourage executives to remain with the company.[30]

Keogh Plans

Keogh plans, or self-employment plans (SEPs) are self-directed retirement plans that self-employed individuals can use for retirement. These act much like an IRA in that a $2,000 limit is observed and the individual directs the plan. Of course, the income and interest is sheltered from taxation until withdrawn.

Early Retirement

Most companies offer early retirement whereby a person can retire at a lower age with fewer benefits. This is attractive, especially if a person can supplement company retirement with 401(k), IRA, or Keogh retirement plans. Many companies will "encourage" early retirement when attempting to pair down the number of employees by offering an extra one-time bonus for those to take early retirement. However, they cannot force people to retire against their will. Because of a 1986 amendment to the Age Discrimination in Employment Act, most employees can no longer be forced to retire before age 70.[31]

Forcing older workers out the door has not been a problem. Actually in some cases, the reverse has occurred. For example, a petroleum firm that offered early retirement to its workers was forced to temporarily shut down a refinery because nearly every worker at the power plant that supplied the power for the refinery took early retirement. West Virginia's early retirement plan is costing the state $11 million more than it saved. DuPont was forced to hire back some of the employees it lost through an early retirement offer as consultants because almost twice as many people accepted the offer as the company had anticipated.[32]

Statistics indicate that the number of employees who opt for early retirement offers may continue to increase. For example, in 1955, 65 percent of the men over age 55 were working, but this figure had dropped to only 46 percent by 1980. For the men in the age group of 65 to 69, 57 percent were employed in 1955 as compared to only 29 percent by 1980. While the figures are not so dramatic for women, there has been an increase in their retirement percentages as well.[33] One thing that may make potential retirees think twice about early retirement is a lower standard of living after retirement. In order for a retiree to who earned $40,000 in 1988 to maintain that standard of living, the retiree would need an income of about 68 percent of that amount plus Social Security. By 1992 the amount had risen to 77 percent of that amount. Two of the major culprits for the increase are higher medical costs and lower savings.[34]

Time-Off Related Benefits

Most companies offer time-off related benefits in the form of holiday pay, vacation pay, and leaves of absence.

Holiday Pay

Most employers provide pay for all established holidays such as New Year's Day, Memorial Day, Fourth of July, Thanksgiving, and Christmas. Other firms also provide holiday pay for Christmas Eve, the day after Thanksgiving, and the employee's birthday. Federal employees also receive President's Day, Veteran's Day, Martin Luther King's Birthday, and Columbus Day. The average number of holidays given are ten per year and many employers offer floating holidays, such as the employee's birthday.[35] Unionized companies negotiate holidays as part of the labor agreement.

Vacations

Most employers offer paid vacations that range from one to six weeks per year depending on length of time (seniority) with the company. In a 1988 poll, employees rated paid vacations and holidays as the third most important benefit behind medical insurance and pensions.[36]

Leaves of Absence

Leaves are given for military service, jury duty, election, disability, funerals (bereavement), sickness, and maternity/paternity. Longer leaves called **sabbaticals** are also given for renewal or special service. For example, IBM and several other large firms offer four-to-six month service leaves that allow managers and executives to do special service with organizations. Several IBM executives have taught at Florida

A&M University in Tallahassee over the past several years while on leave from IBM. Most leaves are paid, but some leaves are only partially paid or unpaid. For example, Florida State University offers a number of fully paid one-semester leaves to qualified faculty members after seven-year periods of service. The number is limited and faculty members are selected on a competitive basis. However, many more full academic year leaves are available to faculty, but at only one-half pay.

The 1978 Pregnancy Discrimination Act requires that **maternity leave** be treated in the same manner as any other medical disability or condition that involves a leave. So if an employer has certain guarantees for employees on leave as to rights to certain jobs and pay on return, these must be made available to those on maternity leave also. Companies are finding that with the increase in the number of women in the work force, an up-to-date maternity leave policy is extremely important. Firms that do not have such a policy may find themselves loosing valuable employees.[37]

Several bills are being considered at the national level to require employers to provide maternity leave as well as paternity leave, family leave, adoption leave, and leave to care for an ill parent, and four states have adopted parental-leave laws: Oregon, Minnesota, Wisconsin, and Rhode Island. In a 1990 survey of the major employers in these states, there were no major reports of increased costs or difficulty administering the policy.[38] Dade County Florida was the nation's first locality to require family and medical leave from employers.[39]

Both the Equal Employment Opportunity Commission (EEOC) and a federal court ruled that fathers must be offered the same child-care leave as mothers. These so-called gender-blind leaves are mandated by 14 states.[40] However, not many fathers are taking them. While more dads may be changing diapers and helping with child rearing, few can afford to take off work, for both financial and career reasons. Normally, after childbirth, the mother cannot work so the father's paycheck becomes more important. However, fear of negative career consequences keep most men at their desks. Even with the guarantee that they will return to the same job, men fear taking the leave. Some critics say that the men have watched women who have been "guaranteed" the same position after returning from maternity leave end up in a less than equal role and do not want to face the same outcome.[41]

Finally, **disability** leaves are offered by employers for employees hurt or who become ill on the job. These leaves are above and beyond those provided under Social Security and Workers' Compensation and are usually funded under an insurance program of some sort. However, since they involve absence from the job they are discussed in this section.

A 1988 survey was conducted by the American Society of Personnel Administrators (ASPA). Of 366 companies responding, 90 percent said they offer long-term benefits, and three-quarters provide short-term disability plans that offer coverage for up to 26 weeks, although the range was from one to 52 weeks. Companies with fewer than 100 employees tended to offer fewer weeks of coverage.

Some organizations are actively seeking ways to minimize disability costs by trying to find ways to keep the employee on the payroll. For example, when an assistant professor at the University of Pittsburgh became disabled with chronic fatigue syndrome, she, her rehabilitation specialist, and her university developed a way in which she could continue her teaching. She videotaped her lectures and held telephone office hours. This unique arrangement not only saved the university $63,000 in disability benefits, but it kept the position filled with an employee who loves her job.[42]

HR CHALLENGES ••

Just Whom Should Be Covered?

As the traditional American life-style continues to change, some employees are asking that some not so traditional dependents be included on their insurance. For example, some employees want their retired parents to be included on their policies. Older workers are sometimes dropped from their own employer's insurance policies after they retire and it is much too costly to purchase insurance for older citizens, especially if they are in poor health. On the other end of the spectrum, some children get married, have children, and then, for various reasons, move back home. Some employees are requesting insurance help for the children of their dependent children. Also, unmarried live-in domestic partners and their children are frequently asked to be included on the insurance policies employees hold. Sometimes allowing this to happen stirs up quite a controversy.

In September of 1991, Lotus Development Company became the nation's first well-known company to offer health insurance to partners of its gay and lesbian employees. In order to qualify, gay and lesbian couples must sign an affidavit stating that they are each other's "sole spousal equivalent and intend to remain so indefinitely." They must also state that they live together and that they are responsible for each other's welfare. The announcement was expected to raise protests from within and from outside the organization, but not the kind of ruckus that ensued, especially from within.

Lotus employees sent so many internal mail messages using the company's electronic mail system that it crashed. Some employees showed up for meetings scheduled by the human resource department to discuss the issues, while others simply discussed it in the halls, elevators, and lunch.

Why all the commotion? Some employees feel that if other companies don't follow Lotus' lead that the company will become a magnet for gay employees. Others argue that the provision is unfair because single heterosexual employees are being discriminated against. All of the arguments can be traced back to strong opposition to a homosexual life-style in the business community.

But organizations must face the fact that the definition of family has changed. Currently, only 25 percent of the households would fall under the 1950s Ozzie and Harriet model in which the husband works and the wife stays home to raise their two children. Some firms, such as Digital Equipment, is rewriting its statement on the definition of family and is requiring each employee to define for himself or herself what his or her "family" includes.

SOURCE: Adapted from William Bulkeley, "Lotus Creates Controversy by Extending Benefits to Partners of Gay Employees," *Wall Street Journal*, October 25, 1991, pp. B1+; and Ceel Pasternak, "Health-Care Coverage for Nontraditional Dependents," *HRMagazine*, November 1990, p. 21.

Health and Insurance-Related Benefits

Health and insurance benefits are a major benefit expense for most firms. Employers offer various types of insurance coverage, including medical, disability, dental, life, legal, and auto insurance.[43] These health costs and related insurance have increased dramatically in recent years. Maintaining adequate coverage while keeping costs within bounds is a challenge for organizations.

Health Benefits

The U.S. health-care system is one of the world's most expensive. It consumed 11 percent of the gross national product in 1988 and is projected to consume 13 percent by 1992. Canada spends 8.5 percent of its GNP on health care, while Britain spends 6 percent.[44] About 85 percent of the U.S. population has either private or government-sponsored insurance.[45] Yet in 1988, 35 million people were uninsured; of these, 23 million were employed and 12 million were unemployed.

Rising health-care costs have driven up premiums for health insurance. A 1988 survey indicated that premiums for many employers increased 10 to 30 percent over the previous year.[46] In 1991, corporate health costs rose 12 percent and accounted

| EXHIBIT 14.7 | GM's Annual Health-Care Costs (in billions of dollars) |

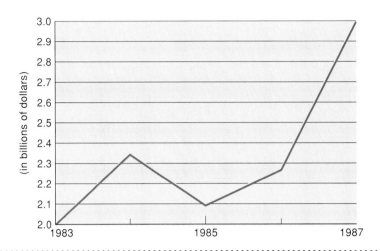

for 46 percent of profits.[47] Many firms have had a similar experience to that of General Motors Corporation. In 1985 GM, whose medical plan covers 1 percent of the U.S. population, actually cut its costs by 10 percent or $200 million in 1985, as is shown in Exhibit 14.7. But due to health-care inflation, GM's costs rose by more than 30 percent in 1987 to 2.9 billion.

Corporate medical bills soared 21.6 percent in 1990 after rising 20.4 percent in 1989.[48] Reasons for cost increases in health insurance are summarized in Exhibit 14.8. In addition to these reasons cited by the *Wall Street Journal,* costs of health care for retirees and costs due to high malpractice insurance awards are also often cited as contributory to increasing health-care costs.[49]

Attempts to cut retiree health-care costs have been met by aggressive resistance by retirees.[50] Yet the courts have ruled that retiree medical is no longer a "sacred cow" and that employers have the right to change or terminate health benefits for retirees.[51] And change they will. By 1995, 62 percent of the firms surveyed indicated that they will or will definitely consider raising insurance premium contributions for retirees[52] and one in 20 say they will cancel the plan altogether.[53] The Government Accounting Office estimates that annual health-plan costs for retirees will climb to $22 billion in 2008 from about $9 billion in 1988.[54]

In addition to the above mentioned reasons for rising health-care costs, requirements mandated by the Consolidated Omnibus Budget Reconciliation Act (COBRA) passed in 1986 have also increased health-care costs.[55] Under the law, employers with 20 or more employees (except the federal government and churches) must provide extended health-care coverage to the following groups, *even when not employed* by the company:

1. Employees who quit, but not those terminated for "gross misconduct."
2. Widowed or divorced spouses and dependent children of former or current employees.
3. Retirees and their spouses whose health-care coverage ends.

EXHIBIT 14.8   Major Reasons That Health Insurance Premiums Continue to Rise

OUTPATIENT SERVICES. While employers have been able to reduce hospital expenditures, cost of outpatient treatment has risen significantly.

HEALTH MAINTENANCE ORGANIZATIONS (HMOs). HMOs are raising prices in order to survive a highly competitive situation. Originally developed to reduce health costs, they are now thought to raise costs since they often siphon off a company's youngest, healthiest workers.

COST SHIFTING. Some hospitals and doctors are submitting inflated bills to traditional corporate health plans to offset cutbacks in payments from Medicare and managed-care plans.

TECHNOLOGY. Technological advances, such as CAT scans, as well as advanced medical procedures associated with these are expensive.

STATE-MANDATED BENEFITS. More and more benefits are being mandated by various states. Forty states required insurers to include coverage for alcohol treatment in their health plans in 1988.

Its various requirements on notification, coverage period, and so on have caused COBRA to be a somewhat burdensome and costly law requiring more paperwork for most employers.

Cost-Containment Methods

Typically, large employers were very generous with health-care coverage during the 1960s, 1970s, and 1980s. Coverages included many services, very few if any employees paid deductibles, and all of the premium was paid by the employer. In addition, the family of the employee shared in these coverages. In 1989, approximately 45 percent of employees helped pay for their medical coverage. In 1990, this figure had risen to around 57 percent.[56] By 1991, 9 percent of employees paid all of it.[57] Some firms even pay bonuses to employees who will volunteer to be covered under a spouse's plan.[58] However, over 60 percent of the 1,000 employees surveyed indicated that they would gladly pay more of their premiums in return for better benefits.[59] Surprisingly, smaller firms are more likely to continue to pay all of an employee's medical coverage (53 percent) than are larger Fortune 500 firms (44 percent).[60]

However, because of the rapid increases in health-care costs, employers are trying a variety of methods and arrangements to cut costs. These are shown in Exhibit 14.9. Let's look at each of these methods.

Health Maintenance Organizations (HMOs) Although originally established to cut health-care costs, a survey of 163 companies indicated that less than 25 percent said their HMOs actually did cut costs.[61] In fact, in Exhibit 14.8 HMOs are cited as a reason health-care costs have *increased* due to their tendency to siphon off younger and healthier workers leaving the remainder to be covered by other plans offered by the employer.

In theory, HMOs make a lot of sense. Health care is prepaid. Prevention is

....

EXHIBIT 14.9 Ways That Employers Try to Cut Health-Care Costs

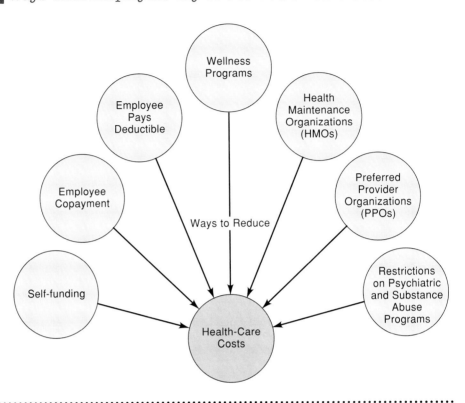

....

emphasized. Employers contract with an HMO, which has doctors on its staff. (Hospitalization is usually not covered.) For a fixed fee per enrolled employee, employers can visit the physician as often as necessary for a very small per unit charge. Thus minor ailments and preventive medicine can be practiced before sickness and illness escalate. Employees are required to work through their primary physician who refers them to other care or hospitalization. This practice also helps to keep costs down because the primary physician can do screening.

HMOs are widespread and there is much competition. In 1989, 14 percent of all Americans had enrolled in an HMO, switching from traditional indemnity insurance plans.[62] There is likely to be a major shakeout as those less efficient HMOs cease operations. During 1987, several major HMOs in South Florida ceased operations. The prevalence of HMOs is partly caused by federal law that requires employers with at least 25 employees to offer an HMO or an option to regular health insurance if an HMO exists in the area.

Preferred Provider Organizations (PPO) Another form of contract health service is the Preferred Provider Organization (PPO). This is a group usually organized by a hospital or a group of physicians. It operates much like an HMO, but a larger group of physicians are usually involved and a "looser" organization is provided in that the physicians are still independently operating under the umbrella of an HMO. A PPO allows employees more choice than an HMO. Costs can still be kept low through prenegotiated fees, rapid claims payment, cost controls, and claims review procedures.

Employee Copayment   Some organizations are requiring employees to pay a part of the annual monthly premium. For example, Florida pays about three-fourths of individual health care premiums and one-half of family coverage premiums. The employee picks up the rest.

Employee Payment of Deductible   Also called comprehensive coverage, the deductible system requires that the employee pay an initial fee for each office or hospital procedure. In some cases, the employee pays 20 percent of each visit for an 80 to 20 cost-sharing ratio. In other cases, the employee must pay a certain amount per year before insurance coverage pays. For example, the state of Florida government family coverage under Blue Cross in the mid-1980s required that two members of a family each meet a $200 annual deductible—a total of $400 before insurance benefits were paid to any member of the family.

In effect, requiring employees to pay a deductible helps to reduce costs and claims for minor illnesses. Of course, it *discourages* employees from obtaining preventative treatment for early illness, since the deductible must first be established.

Self-funded   Self-funded plans are funded by the employer—not an insurance company.[63] In this instance, the employer sets aside a certain amount of money to pay claims during the year (for example, $1 million). In addition, a contract often is written with a health insurance company such as Blue Cross/Blue Shield or Aetna for coverage of claims over the amount set aside and to administer the claims payment process.

Self-funded insurance can cut costs in several ways. First, the employer earns interest on the money set aside for claims, provided it is invested. Secondly, by paying such a huge deductible (for example, $1 million) the actual policy with the insurance carrier can be very low. Thirdly, the middleman (the carrier) is eliminated on the bulk of the claims.

Self-insurance has become very popular as a cost-cutting strategy. For it to work, an employer should have at least 100 or more employees over which to spread the costs.

Wellness/Fitness Programs   Many companies are becoming more aggressive in preventive actions in order to cut health-care costs. For example, IBM has fitness rooms and jogging tracks in many of its facilities. Many companies have a no-smoking policy and encourage employees through contests and awards to give up smoking. Others sponsor weight-loss programs.[64] Some employ health and fitness experts to advise executives and managers. Others, such as Xerox, sponsor employee teams to run in major races like the Boston Marathon. Finally, although done primarily for social reasons, many firms sponsor employee athletic teams and tournaments in bowling, softball, golf, and basketball.

Some firms are even paying employees to get healthy. Bank of Delaware employees receive $6 a month if they agree to wear a seat belt and promise to attend a couple of health seminars. If they agree to take a fitness evaluation and adhere to the prescribed exercise plan, they can earn $9 a month. If they participate in both, they earn $12 a month.[65] U-Haul is taking the reverse approach by fining employees who do not have a healthy lifestyle. Any employee who is overweight, underweight, or who smokes is required to pay up to $10 a paycheck.[66] These companies are not alone. International Paper Corporation, who was hit with seven claims that topped $200,000 in 1989, moved to limit exposure caused by life-style excesses. The company now charges extra insurance or increases the deductibles for workers who smoke, are overweight, do not wear seatbelts, or who drive while intoxicated.[67]

Restrictions on Psychiatric and Substance Abuse Programs   Finally, one area of the rapidly escalating costs falls under the provision of counseling, psychiatric, and substance-abuse treatment. From 1986 to 1988, hospital admissions for such treatments jumped 30 percent nationwide.[68] Small companies are finding that offering employee counseling is extremely expensive.[69] Attempts are being made to limit hospital admissions and use more outpatient care as a way to cut these costs. However some critics argue that cuts in these programs are beginning to hurt the patients and their families by pushing people out of treatment too soon.[70] In order to keep employee assistance programs (EAPs), some firms are requiring that human resource professionals measure the cost effectiveness of the program.[71]

Other Techniques   One much debated technique that companies have been using to reduce health-care costs is called managed-care.[72] Essentially, managed-care programs direct employees to a specific doctor, hospital, or treatment center that will offer the employer a negotiated lower rate. Additional data such as quality monitoring and dependability are also factored into the equation used to determine where to send the employees. Employees who become patients also can be used to help reduce the cost of health care. By thoroughly informing patients about their medical problems by providing videotapes and other forms of information, patients can make informed decisions about treatment possibilities. Such programs have greatly reduced the number of unnecessary surgeries. For example, in Seattle, surgery rates fell by 60 percent.[73] Managed-care policies also stress second opinions.[74] While many companies have reported that a managed-care program has reduced their costs, others complain that they have had little or no effect.[75]

In order to reduce the cost of prescription drugs, companies are looking at new ways to deal with pharmacies. Some options include joining discount mail-order drug plans,[76] requiring that all prescriptions be filled using generic drugs, and negotiating with local pharmacies to win lower prices on drugs. Some firms are even toying with the idea of an in-company pharmacy. While the employer would gain control over prescription costs, the overall price tag may not make it worthwhile.[77] Another in-company trend is employers providing medical care for workers at job locations or in company-run clinics to lower health-care costs and reduce employee downtime due to doctor's office visits.[78]

School unions in California have developed trusts to manage the health care costs and to reduce the friction between union and management. The trust is a board of about 16 members who meet regularly to find ways to cut costs through wellness programs and negotiating new contracts with doctors and pharmacies.[79] Some firms have limited costs by tailoring the insurance programs to their specific needs and by not paying for services not used by their employees.[80] Others have reduced their costs by focusing on the "at-risk" portion of their work force: those who have terminal diseases such as cancer, heart, and respiratory diseases, childbirth costs, and mental health.[81] Recent studies have shown that infant health and child-birth related problems cost businesses over $5 billion a year.[82]

Even cities and states are getting into the action. When Clevelanders found out that they could load their sick employees on a plane and fly them 750 miles to the Mayo Clinic for treatment and still pay less than they would have if their employees checked into the nearby Cleveland hospitals, they knew it was time to do something. They enlisted the help of hospital administrators in order to obtain costs for hospital procedures and used a computer program to determine what facilities will offer the most effective and efficient services. Employees are then directed to the "winning" facility.[83] Approaches like this are being used by other areas as well in an attempt to set up a market approach to health care where only the most efficient and effective survive.[84]

One alternative to the market approach being used by several cities is a "pay-or-play" proposal.[85] Basically, this approach requires employers to provide medical coverage to all employees (play) or contribute to a government-financed health plan through a new tax (pay).[86] Some firms, such as Chrysler, have announced that they would drop their corporate insurance and pay into the public pool instead if the tax costs were less than the nearly 17 percent of the payroll that now goes toward health insurance.[87]

Finally, some firms that have cut their portion of the payment for employees insurance costs have established "flexible spending accounts" (FSA) to ease the burden on employees. A FSA is an account funded by an employee's pretaxed income that can be used to pay for specified health-care bills, such as deductibles, day care, or medical bills. There are several benefits to this type of account. For example, the money is not taxed. Also, it reduces the employee's taxable income. However, if the employee does not spend the money by the end of the year, it is lost.[88]

Additional Issues in Health Insurance

Several additional issues are having a profound effect on the health insurance and medical industries and will, consequently, affect employers.

An Aging Population   The U.S. Census Bureau indicates that the United States will become a gerontocracy as the baby boomers age and the birth rate remains low. By the year 2010, 33.8 percent of the nation will be over age 50.[89] Older people consume vast amounts of health care and this will likely get worse as medical advances keep older people alive for longer periods of time. How will the nation adequately fund the care of its elderly in the next millennium?

AIDS   Acquired Immune Deficiency Syndrome (AIDS) is a deadly disease for which, at the time of this writing, there is no cure. At the beginning of 1989, 87,188 people were diagnosed with AIDS, producing 49,976 deaths.[90] Once thought to be a disease of male homosexuals, now male heterosexuals, women, and children have the disease. Costs of finding a cure and treating the disease are likely to place a heavy burden on our medical system. Employers should be aware that placing an exclusion or ceiling for AIDS on insurance benefits may be illegal. As the number of legal remedies available to AIDS patients rises, the risk of employer liability climbs.[91]

Drug Testing   The use of illegal drugs in society has caused many employers to adopt a drug testing policy. This policy might involve testing at the time of hire or unannounced tests during work. There are legal guidelines and prohibitions to follow in order to have valid tests (chain of custody, invasion of privacy issues, and so on).

Drug use on the job and its prevention is a critical health issue with which many employers will continue to be concerned.

Expansion of Coverage Many firms are beginning to offer coverage for dental, chiropractic, and optometric work in addition to mental health coverages. Often these coverages are offered on copayment and fee-share basis. In addition, states are requiring employers to add coverage for such medical services as care by lay midwives, ambulance transport, and breast reconstruction.[92]

Other Insurance Benefits

Besides health-related insurance, employers also provide other forms of insurance. For example, many employers provide life insurance policies based on a group rate. A typical level is 150 percent of an employee's annual salary, but executives often receive much more than this as part of an executive compensation package. *Long-term* disability coverage is also provided by many employers, which provides a continuation of income in the event of a long-term injury or illness.

Legal insurance is provided by some firms, often in the form of prepaid or negotiated fees between the employer and a group of attorneys. The employee often shares in the premium for this insurance and/or in the fee payment at the time of the service.

Some firms also offer group insurance rates for automobile insurance. These rates are often lower than individual rates.

Financial, Social, and Recreational Benefits

Many companies offer a variety of financial benefits to managers and employees. These are usually not taxed as income to employees and are very popular. These benefits include **perks** (perquisites), which are special types of additional or added noncash compensation in the form of benefits or special privileges. Let's examine these additional benefits.

Nonfinancial

The use of a company car, company expense accounts, club memberships, help in buying and selling a home, and the use of company-owned resort condominiums are all examples of perks that are available to managers, executives, and some employees. Also, financial planning and counseling, including tax preparation advice, are often offered to managers and executives.

Additionally, most medium and larger companies offer *credit unions* to employees for lending and saving services. Some firms offer purchase discounts to employees in the form of buying clubs or employee discounts on company merchandise.

Thrift/Stock

Employee **thrift, saving, or stock purchase investment plans** are also popular. For example, in a stock option plan, an employee is often guaranteed the right to buy shares of company stock at a discount or at a certain price. Alternatively, the company may purchase the stock for the employee. (This is taxable compensation unless it is in the form of a defined stock plan; then the tax is not levied until the stock is actually taken by the employee.)

EXHIBIT 14.10   Firms Controlled by ESOPs

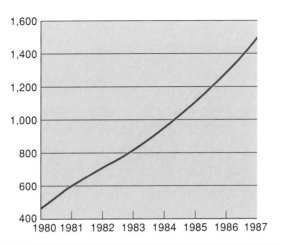

ESOP When stock is provided as a part of a profit-sharing plan, an Employee Stock Ownership Plan (ESOP) is developed. (ESOPs are also discussed in Chapter 12.) ESOPs receive favorable income tax treatment and have become very popular. They give employees a sense of ownership in the company and allow them to share in the company's success and profits.

ESOPs also have been used in leveraged buyouts (LBOs) of firms by employees.[93] As shown in Exhibit 14.10, from 1980 to 1987 the number of employee buyouts of firms went from 500 to 1500, a 300 percent increase. However, in 1989 and 1990, things began to slow down. In 1989, 830 new ESOP plans were established and in 1990, only 480 ESOPs were formed. The main reason suggested for the slowdown was that tighter credit restrictions limited borrowing.[94]

In the early 1980s, workers used ESOPs to buy relatively small companies or to become buyers of last resort for large troubled companies. However, by the 1980s, because of favorable tax treatment and as a tactic to thwart hostile takeovers, healthy companies, such as Avis, were purchased by employees through LBOs financed through ESOPs.

As the economy began to worsen in the late 1980s and early 1990s, some ESOPs lost favor with employees. Falling stock prices and rising corporate bankruptcies are rendering the ESOPs null and void. At Thomson McKinnon, where brokers and other employees owned as much as 77 percent of the firm's shares, ESOP employees saw their plan devalued from $140 million to nothing. In 1989, employees received a letter indicating that it was possible that their ESOP would have no value whatsoever.[95]

Educational Benefits

Many firms offer a tuition reimbursement plan for employees who attend school, college, or university. Usually the firm requires that the employee take a course related to work, although this is often broadly defined, and that a passing grade be earned in the course.

···

EXHIBIT 14.11 Percentage of Companies Offering Child-Care Programs by Region

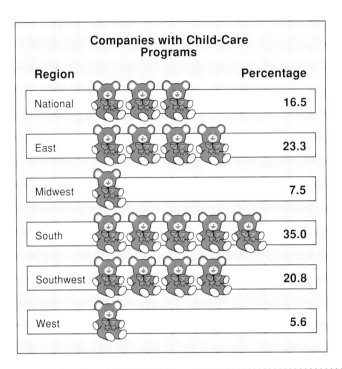

···

Child-Care Benefits

Working women with small children have become very common in our society as we have previously explained. Although only 6 percent of surveyed employees offered employer-sponsored child care in 1987, one study showed that 66 percent of surveyed benefit directors saw child care as a "major growth" area by 1995.[96] Exhibit 14.11 shows how each region of the country stacks up with respect to corporate sponsored child care.

Costs of day care and the inconvenience of taking and picking up children are stumbling blocks for many working parents. Home care either from relatives or neighbors is often unavailable or simply too expensive. The quality of care is also an issue. All of these factors are increasing the pressure on employers to provide affordable, quality, and convenient child care for employees who desire it as part of the insurance package. Some firms are responding to this need.[97]

St. Joseph's Hospital in Marshfield, Wisconsin, is a 524-bed hospital in a town of 20,000. The hospital employs 2,200 employees, many of whom require child care. Because demand was so great, the hospital opened up an on-site day-care center in 1981. In 1989 it expanded its facilities so that it could take care of twice as many children—130. It also extended the hours to midnight and allowed up to 50 children to be there during the evening. Because the center has a waiting list, the hospital can no longer use it as a recruiting tool. However, it can use the benefits offered by the hospital, which are much better than other local facilities, as a recruiting tool for day-care workers.[98]

Some critics argue that child care is being used as a tool to discriminate against employees. For example, Merck & Company opened a day care facility 10 years ago in Rahway, New Jersey, after one of its top female scientists threatened to resign. However, the monthly cost of using the facility is $680. While professionals can easily afford this service, secretaries cannot. While Merck now has plans to open two other facilities, it is also considering subsidizing the costs for lower-paid employees. The company is anxious not to look like it is favoring one type of employee over another.[99]

Child care may be one area in which the Japanese can learn something from Americans. Tokyo parents are flocking to the first corporate child-care center, which opened as a result of a joint venture between Bright Horizons Children's Center in Cambridge and Temporary Center Corporation, Tokyo's largest temporary-placement agency. The center opened January 6, 1992, with all 44 slots taken and a waiting list. Every person who visited the center during its developmental phase enrolled his or her child. With demand so high, two additional facilities have been planned.[100]

Elder Care

A study of benefit directors in 1988 indicated that 77 percent of them believed elder care—plans to provide for care of the elderly—will be a major growth benefit in 1995.[101] As the number of elderly citizens increases greatly into the 1990s, and as the baby boomers age, demands will be placed on employees to provide benefit plans to assist with the care of aged parents—and aged employees.

One study uses the "dependency ratio" to explain this issue.[102] This ratio compares the number of current workers to the number of dependents. Dependents are defined as those below age 18 and above age 64. Between 1950 and 1982, the ratio of youthful dependents fell from 51.0 per 100 workers to 44.1 and is expected to drop to 36.2 by the year 2080. At the other end, the elderly dependency ratio climbed from 13.3 to 18.8 in the same period, and is expected to soar to 41.9 by the year 2080. Thus the number of retirees will continue to grow at a much faster pace relative to the number of current workers.

With more and more retirees living longer, a greater number of employees will be supporting their retired parents in addition to their own children. Hence, strong demand will be placed on employers to help with this burden.

Cafeteria Plans

Because of the variety of options in the benefit area, many employers have shifted to or are considering "cafeteria plans." Cafeteria plans allow employees to pick and choose from a variety of benefit options much as a person chooses food at a cafeteria. This allows a person to tailor a benefit program that meets his or her needs. Employees generally purchase benefits with flex credits allocated through their employers or through a salary reduction agreement.[103]

For example, a young, single-parent mother may place greater value on child care, health care, and similar benefits than a 55-year-old male who may be more interested in retirement benefits, long-term health care, and life insurance. Other employees may want to buy extra vacation days, while others would like to trade the ones they have in for cash.[104] Cafeteria plans allow for such switches.

Twenty percent of surveyed companies in 1987 offered cafeteria plans and an additional 12 percent were either considering or implementing such a plan.[105] By

1989, 23 percent of employers offered flexible benefits and by 1990 the figure had risen to 27 percent. Half of the companies with such programs say they have been able to demonstrate cost savings as a result. Frequently the cost savings comes in the form of higher employee contributions.[106] Accurate prediction of employee selections also can help control costs.[107]

Nine out of ten flexible benefit plans surveyed offered major medical and hospitalization coverage. More than half the plans included life insurance, long-term disability, and dependent care. While flexible plans were most popular in the western part of the country, in medium-sized and large companies, and in the education/government/nonprofit sector, one recent survey indicted that 90 percent of the 1,000 employees surveyed would prefer a job which offered flexible benefits over one that did not.[108]

FUTURE BENEFIT CHANGES

While no one can accurately predict the future state of benefits with a high degree of certainty, one analysis suggests the following trends:[109]

1. *More Paid Leave.* Leave will be provided to employees with newborn children as well as elderly parents. Leave will also be provided for longer term "refresher" sabbaticals and for social service pursuits.
2. *Education and Training.* Rapidly changing job skill requirements and a shortage of new entrants into the labor force will compel employers to regularly offer education and training programs, leaves, and reimbursement for a wide variety of employees.
3. *Career Planning.* Many employers will offer formal career counseling programs to help employees plan careers that adjust to their changing lives.
4. *Housing.* Moving assistance and mortgage aid will become even more common.
5. *Late Retirement.* As baby boomers age and shortages of workers and skills increase, companies will be bending over backwards to help their older employees. TRW's Pat Choate calls these "Platinum Handcuffs"—consisting of company-paid vacation trips, shorter hours, and bonus plans that reward employees for staying on past a certain age or period of service.
6. *Flextime.* Flexible work schedules and job sharing (allowing two or more people to share one 40-hour-a-week job) will become more common as employers adjust to alternative life-styles and schedules of the elderly and single parents with children in order to keep enough skilled employees. Many companies have instituted flextime, including DuPont, IBM, Aetna, GE, and Volvo (Saab and Scandia). Flextime has proven to be a form of cost cutting that keeps the best people.[110]
7. *Vacations.* Employees will be able to "buy" extra vacation time if they deserve it by trading it for other available benefits such as sick leave or even a portion of hospital care.

STRATEGIC MANAGEMENT OF BENEFITS

As you can see, benefits have become a costly and complicated area in human resource management. As a reaction more firms are taking an aggressive strategic approach to benefits—instead of simply "administering" a benefit program many firms attempt to strategically manage it in order to obtain the greatest results at the least cost.

Competitive Advantage and Benefit Costs

Many employers develop a benefit program that meets, but does not necessarily exceed, that of competitors. As we pointed out earlier in the chapter, it is unlikely that employers can use a benefit program to achieve a competitive advantage unless they can offer similar benefits at a reduced cost. In fact, Hennessey concludes, "competitive advantage will be most easily enhanced by controlling benefit costs to the maximum extent possible within constraints improved by competition."[111] He also concludes that benefit programs do little to attract, motivate, or retain employees.

Yet many employers believe that benefits do, in fact, help to attract and retain, if not motivate employees and are attempting to verify this through careful study. While such studies are often difficult to conduct and are fraught with measurement problems, the next section summarizes some key actions of employers to measure the cost-effectiveness of benefits.

CORPORATE EFFORT TO MEASURE BENEFIT EFFECTIVENESS

Ideally, to determine the cost-effectiveness of a benefits program, controlled experiments comparing the advantages and costs of one type of benefit with the advantages and costs of an alternative benefit need to be conducted. For example, AT&T is conducting a study with AT&T's insurers comparing the medical claim data of 1,600 participants in a wellness program with a control group of 1,800 nonparticipants.[112] They expect that wellness program participants will have a lower use of hospitals and doctors, thereby saving medical costs overall.

Some companies attempt to measure problems that would occur if benefits were *not* provided. These costs usually include such negative consequences as turnover, absenteeism, and tardiness. For example, Corning Glass Works decided to measure out-of-pocket expenses associated with turnover, such as interview costs and hiring bonuses. Costs were estimated at $16 million to $18 million annually. This led to a look at the causes of turnover and to the adoption of new policies in flexible work hours and career development in order to cut turnover.[113]

Some companies are even attempting to measure more complicated linkages. One company that has attempted to quantify productivity figures and flexible scheduling is Merck & Company. It interviewed and surveyed a large number of managers and developed a list of 30 cost variables attached to turnover. After developing several methods of cost determination, they determined that, depending on the job, turnover costs Merck 1.5 to 2.5 times the annual salary paid for the job.[114] As a result of this study, the company is attempting to enhance the benefit programs it believes reduce turnover.

In a study of day care at Union Bank in California, using before-day-care and after-day-care cost data on absenteeism, turnover, and maternity leave time for both a control group and an experimental group, Union concluded that the day-care center saves the bank $138,000 to $232,000 a year.

Measurement Issues

Quantifying the benefits of any one program is more difficult than estimating its costs. Estimating the costs of not having a program in the firm of higher absenteeism, turnover, and lost productivity is also very difficult. Yet employers will increasingly devote more time and attention to doing this as benefit options proliferate and as their costs increase.

Human resource managers in all areas are being asked to demonstrate how their programs and actions contribute to the bottom line. Nowhere is this more evident than in the management of benefits. With adequate cost and effectiveness data for various benefit options, human resource managers will be in a better position to make strategic decisions as to which benefit programs an organization should have.

• • • • • • • • •

MANAGEMENT GUIDELINES

Several key guidelines in the benefits area need to be recognized from a strategic viewpoint:

1. Benefits should be strategically managed and not jut "administered."

2. Benefit costs and options are increasing dramatically. Many choices are available, and many ways to reduce costs have been found. Human resource managers need to be aware of the possibilities in order to provide the best advice to their organizations.

3. The cost-effectiveness of benefits and benefit contributions to the bottom line is and will continue to be emphasized.

4. Benefits can best be used to gain competitive advantage by maintaining or increasing benefit levels while decreasing benefit costs.

5. A changing heterogeneous work force will require a flexible or cafeteria-style program.

6. Management of benefits must comply with a host of federal and state regulations and requirements.

7. Since present and prospective employees are often unaware of the value of benefits provided them, benefit packages should be clearly and succinctly communicated to employees on a regular basis.

8. Health care and insurance costs as well as retirement costs for the elderly will likely increase dramatically as baby boomers age and life-spans are increased, thereby placing pressure on employee benefit plans.

. . . .
QUESTIONS FOR REVIEW

1. Why is it that so many potential and present employees are unfamiliar with the benefit plan offered by an organization?

2. What strategic choices does an employer face in managing a benefit program? What factors affect the decision on each choice?

3. Why are health-care costs rising so much? What can organizations do to reduce them?

4. Who should pay the cost of health care: the employee, the employer, or the government? Explain your answer.

5. What are cafeteria-style benefits? Why are they becoming so popular?

6. Critique the Xerox benefits plan presented at the beginning of the chapter. What are its strengths and weaknesses? Would it be a factor to you in deciding to take a job with Xerox?

7. How should benefit plans tie into an overall human resource strategy?

8. How will the structure of benefits likely change as our population ages?

9. Assume you were asked to determine the value or worth of a wellness-fitness program for a company. How would you go about this?

10. Although managers believe that benefits aid in attracting, motivating, and retaining employees, studies show little support for this belief. Why do you think that benefits may not be helping to attract, motivate, and retain employees?

 Milwaukee Firms Look for $2-Million Savings [115]

In 1985, a Blue Cross/Blue Shield user group and other employers, a total of 34 members, formed the Milwaukee Chapter of the Midwest Business Group on Health. The group's goal was to represent the business community in purchasing health care, act as a major purchaser of health-care services, and improve the cost-effectiveness of high-quality health care.

Health Task Force

At the same time as the Milwaukee Chapter was developing local purchasing plan specifications, Milwaukee area community leaders created a health care task force. The groups shared a goal: the development of methods to curtail rising medical plan costs. So they joined forces and became the Greater Milwaukee Health Care Purchasing Plan, Inc.

The Milwaukee Purchasing Plan enlisted a health-care purchasing consultant, CCN, Inc., of San Diego. A model purchasing plan, the group determined, should include price and quality control principles and change the health-care marketplace. Under such a plan, employers and employees become "buyers" of health care.

Richard Salzetti, the corporate benefits supervisor for Miller Brewing Company, explained some of the major features of the Purchasing Plan:

- A board of directors composed of employee benefit managers from major local employers.
- Its own purchasing agent to manage the day-to-day operation and contract with providers.
- Identification of the good quality providers and the poor quality providers.
- A network of 13 local hospitals and, effective March 1, 1988, 450 physicians, including primary care physicians.
- A Physician Advisory Committee (PAC), which aids the board in physician evaluation and selection through established criteria.
- Quality assessment components developed by the purchasing agent and the PAC.
- Predetermined payments for services. Participating providers agree to accept the scheduled fees. Per diem rates are negotiated with the hospitals, and physician rates are based on the California Relative Value Scale adjusted for Milwaukee area rates.
- Each employer maintains its own medical plan, whether comprehensive or basic and major medical. Claims generally are submitted first to the employer's claim administrator for verification of eligibility. The administrator then forwards network claims to the Health Care Network for pricing and claims are then returned to the administrator for payment.
- Employees and dependents are encouraged, through incentives, to use selected providers.
- Each hospital in the network is responsible for its own preadmission review. All participating providers assume the financial risk for unnecessary care.

Utilization review is a basic element of the program and includes a preadmission review, concurrent hospital review, second opinion, discharge planning, and individual case management. Reviews occur at the provider and plan levels. Each provider's performance is measured using non-acute profiles and other quantitative criteria.

The next step for the program is data collection and management. To this end, the Purchasing Plan intends to hire a database manager to develop a database, including specific inpatient/outpatient hospital and physician data. Once the data is in place, Salzetti observed, the local data may be compared to national and specific illness standards. In addition, the physician data may aid in measuring the quality of care and to monitor use. The source of data will be the provider's bills, which are sent to a central pool.

Employees are primarily concerned that the purchasing plan maintain the existing level of benefits, provide a high level of financial protection, and offer an advisor hotline. Employers, on the other hand, are concerned with encouraging employees to use the purchasing plan providers either through rewards with higher benefits or "punishment" with lower benefits. Communications are important in this process, perhaps through use of identification cards and explanation of benefit statements.

Other employer concerns are whether the administration of the program (the insurer and third-party administrator) is cost-effective, whether to continue using the present administrator, and how to negotiate and deal with union representatives.

The Purchasing Plan aims to expand its contracted provider network to include dental, vision, and chiropractic care, prescription drugs, nursing services, and medical supplies.

Other goals are to identify the best providers, increase the number of plan participants, and use cost and quality data to ease negotiations.

Thus far, the Purchasing Plan has contracts with 13 employers, all self-insured, covering 30,000 employees. Negotiations are proceeding with an insurer to include its entire book of business in the Milwaukee area in the network.

The Purchasing Plan's cost savings ratio overall is 1 to 3.8 and it is expected to save more than $2 million the first year, Salzetti said. Other positive outcomes are that the plan allows the "buyer" to obtain more control in health services, and the continuous review of providers will improve quality, monitor charging patterns, and allow the development of data for evaluations.

How much did it cost to put the program together? Initially, 12 employers in the Milwaukee Purchasing Plan contributed $10,000 each, Salzetti said. Currently, each member employer contributes $1.50 annually per employee and a percentage of the savings realized.

QUESTIONS

1. What is the goal of a health-care purchasing program such as the Milwaukee Purchasing Plan? How does such a plan work?

2. What is required to make such a plan successful?

3. Would a plan like the Milwaukee plan work in your geographic area? Why or why not?

·············· ADDITIONAL READINGS

Brockhart, James, and Robert Reilly. "Employee Stock Ownership Plans after the 1989 Tax Law: Valuation Issues." *Compensation and Benefits Review.* 1990.

Callan, Mary, and David Yeager. *Containing the Health Care Cost Spiral.* New York: McGraw-Hill, 1990.

Cave, Douglas, and Larry Tucker. "10 Facts about Point-of Service Plans." *HRMagazine.* September 1991, pp. 41–46.

Crawford, Lou Ellen. *Dependent Care and the Employee Benefits Package.* Westport, CT: Quorum Books, 1990.

Denenberg, Tia S., and R. V. Denenberg. *Alcohol and Drugs: Issues in the Workplace.* Washington, DC: BNA Books, 1983.

Driver, R. An investigation of the relative efficacy of various techniques for communicating benefits to employees: A quasi-experiment in a field setting. *Dissertation Abstracts International* 40, 344A. (University Microfilms No. 7915483), 1979.

Flexible Benefits: Will They Work for You? Chicago: Commerce Clearing House, 1991.

Haar, Jerry, and Sharon Kossack. "Employee Benefit Packages: How Understandable Are They?" *Journal of Business Communication.* 1990, pp. 185–200.

Harrington, Harry, and Nancy Richardson. "Retiree Wellness Plans Cut Health Costs." *Personnel Journal* 69 (1990), pp. 60–62.

Hay/Huggins Benefits Comparison. Philadelphia: The Hay Group, 1987.

Hayes, Cheryl, John Palmer, and Martha Zaslow. *Who Cares for America's Children.* Washington, DC: National Academic Press, 1990.

Huseman, R., J. Hatfield, and R. Robinson. "The MBA and Fringe Benefits." *Personnel Administrator* 23(7) (1978), pp. 57–60.

Iseri, Betty, and Robert Cangemi. "Flexible Benefits: A Growing Option," *Personnel.* 1990, pp. 30–32.

Koenig, R. "Comparison Shopping: Companies Seek New Data on Health-care Costs to Gain Leverage in Bargaining for Services." *Wall Street Journal,* April 22, 1988 pp. 19R–20R.

Konrad, W., and G. DeGeorge. "U.S. Companies Go for the Gray." *Business Week.* April 3, 1989 p. 66.

Lee, Alice, and Fred Lee. *A Field Guide to Retirement: 14 Lifestyle Opportunities and Options for Successful Retirement.* Doubleday, 1991.

Lock, E., K. Shaw, L. Saari, and G. Latham. "Goal Setting and Task Performance 1969–1980." *Psychological Bulletin* 90 (1981), pp. 125–152.

McGregor, Eugene *Strategic Management of Human Knowledge, Skills, and Abilities: Workforce Decision Making in the Post-Industrial Era.* San Francisco: Jossey-Bass, 1991.

Masterson, Joe. "Benefit Plans That Cut Costs and Increase Satisfaction." *Management Review,* April 1990.

Meadows, Anne. *Caring for America's Children.* Washington DC: National Academy Press, 1991.

Mitchell, O. "Fringe Benefits and Labor Mobility." *The Journal of Human Resources* 17(2) (1982), pp. 286–298.

Mitchell, O. "Fringe Benefits and the Cost of Changing Jobs." *Industrial and Labor Relations Review* 37(1) (1983), pp. 70–78.

Mobely, W., R. Griffeth, H. Hand, and B. Meglino. "Review and Conceptual Analysis of the Employee Turnover Process." *Psychological Bulletin* 86 (1979), pp. 493–522.

Mowday, R., L. Porter, and R. Steers. *Employee Organization Linkages: The Psychology of Commitment, Absenteeism, and Turnover.* New York: Academic Press, 1982.

1987 Employee Benefits. Washington, DC: Chamber of Commerce of the United States, 1987.

Phillips, Mary Ellen, Carol Brown, and Norma Nielson. "An Expanding Employee Benefit: Personal Financial Planning with Expert Systems," *Management Accounting.* September 1990, pp. 29–33.

Pillsbury, Dennis. "Nipping Workers' Comp in the Bud." *Risk and Insurance,* October 1991.

Porter, M. *Competitive Advantage: Creating and Sustaining Superior Performance.* New York: Free Press, 1985.

Porter, M. *Competitive Strategy: Techniques for Analyzing Industries and Competitors.* New York: Free Press, 1980.

Roberts, Karen, and Sandra Gleason. "What Employees Want from Worker's Comp." *HRMagazine.* December 1991, pp. 49–54.

Rosenbloom, Jerry S., and G. Victor Hollman. *Employee Benefit Planning.* 2nd ed. Englewood Cliffs, NJ: Prentice-Hall, 1986.

Salancik, G., and J. Pfeffer. "An Examination of Need-Satisfaction Models of Job Attitudes." *Administrative Science Quarterly* 22(3) (1977), pp. 427–456.

Salancik, G., and J. Pfeffer. "A Social Information Processing Approach to Job Attitudes and Task Design." *Administrative Science Quarterly* 23(2) (1978), pp. 224–253.

Shanklin, Catherine. "Unemployment Insurance: Survive the System" *Personnel Journal*, March 1990.

Schiller, B., and R. Weiss. "The Impact of Private Pensions on Firm Attachment." *The Review of Economics and Statistics* 62(4) (1979), pp. 369–380.

Schiller, B., and R. Weiss. "Pension and Wages: A Test for Equalizing Differences." *The Review of Economics and Statistics* 62(4) (1980), pp. 529–538.

Smith, Doyle. *Kin Care and the American Corporation: Solving the Work/Family Dilemma*. Business One Irwin, Homewood, IL: 1991.

Spirig, John. "Human Resources Information Systems Can Help Employers Plan and Implement Flexible Benefits Programs." *Employment Relations Today* 16 (1989), pp. 9–17.

Stepina, L., H. Hennessey, and B. Weschler, eds. *Florida's Compensation System: A Comprehensive Study of Career Service Pay and Benefits.* (Final Report, Contract #1986-068). (Available from State of Florida, Department of Administration, Carlton Bldg., Tallahassee, FL), 1987.

Sutton, N. "Are Employers Meeting Their Benefit Objectives?" *Benefits Quarterly* 2(3) (1986), pp. 14–20.

Sutton, N. "Do Employee Benefits Reduce Labor Turnover?" *Benefits Quarterly* 1(2) (1986), pp. 16–22.

Taulbee, Pamela. "What's Ahead for Retiree Health?" *Business & Health*, 9, December 1990, pp. 25–36.

Wilson, M., G. Northcraft, and M. Neale. "The Perceived Value of Fringe Benefits." *Personnel Psychology* 38(2) (1985), pp. 309–320.

· · · · · · · · · · · · · · · ·
NOTES

1. M. Wilson, G. Northcroft, and M. Neale, "The Perceived Value of Fringe Benefits," *Personal Psychology* 38, no. 2, 1985, pp. 309–320.

2. Nancy Sutton, "Are Employers Meeting Their Benefit Objectives?" *Benefits Quarterly* 2, no. 3, 1986, pp. 14–20.

3. R. Koenig, "Comparison Shopping: Companies Seek New Data on Health-Care Costs to Gain Leverage in Bargaining for Services," *Wall Street Journal*, April 22, 1988, pp. 19R–20R.

4. Selwyn Feinstein, "Employee-Benefits Costs Rose 5.9% in Past Year, Paced with Health Insurance," *Wall Street Journal*, July 31, 1991, p. A1.

5. *You and Xerox: 1987–1988: Benefits for Salaried Employees* (Stamford, CT: Xerox Corporation, n.d.).

6. Glen Ruffenach, "Health Insurance Premiums to Soar in '89: Workers Likely to Take on More of Costs," *Wall Street Journal*, October 25, 1988, p. B1.

7. Lee Smith, "The Battle Over Health Insurance," *Fortune*, September 26, 1988, p. 145.

8. Feinstein, "Employee Benefits Costs," p. A1.

9. Ceel Pasternak, "The Cost of Benefits," *HRMagazine*, November 1991, p. 27.

10. Jolie Solomon, "The Future of Employee Benefits," *Wall Street Journal*, September 7, 1988, p. 29.

11. Rita Dommermuth, "Mass Transit: A New Employee Benefit," *HRMagazine*, March 1991, p. 64; Gilbert Fuchsberg, "RJR Benefit Makes the Grade for Collegians," *Wall Street Journal*, March 2, 1992, pp. B1 +; and "Housing Assistance Gains as an Employees Benefit," *Wall Street Journal*, September 24, 1991, p. A1.

12. "Cafeteria Plans, Wellness Programs Gaining in Popularity," *Employee Benefit Plan Review*, July 1987, p. 91; and Michael Waldholz, "Cafeteria Benefit Plans Let Employees Fill Their Plates, Then Pay with Tax Free Dollars," *Wall Street Journal*, May 9, 1983. p. 58.

13. H. W. Hennessey, Jr., "Using Employee Benefits to Gain Competitive Advantage," *Benefits Quarterly*, Winter 1989, pp. 51–57.

14. James Swanke, "Ways to Tame Workers' Comp Premiums," *HRMagazine*, February 1992, pp. 39–41.

15. Barbara Marsh, "Rising Worker's Compensation Costs Worry Small Firms," *Wall Street Journal*, December 31, 1991, p. B2.

16. Ron Winslow, "Hospitals Team Up to Trim Workers' Comp," *Wall Street Journal*, December 8, 1989, p. B1.

17. Michael Pritula, "Worker's Comp: Tranquilizing a Benefit Gone Mad," *Wall Street Journal*, January 13, 1992, p. A14.

18. Marsh, "Rising Worker's Compensation Costs," p. B2.

19. Pritula, "Workers' Comp," p. A14 and Mark D. Fefer, "What to Do about Workers' Comp," *Fortune*, June 29, 1992, pp. 80–82.

20. "Labor Letter," *Wall Street Journal*, September 13, 1988, p. 1.

21. Albert Karr, "Labor Letter," *Wall Street Journal*, December 6, 1988, p. 1.

22. Selwyn Feinstein, "Pension Funds," *Wall Street Journal*, May 15, 1991, p. A1.

23. Linda Thornburg, "The Pension Headache," *HRMagazine*, January 1992, pp. 39–46; Wallace Campblee, Jr., "Plans That Upgrade Pensions," *HRMagazine*, November 1991, pp. 71–73; and Selwyn Feinstein, "IRS Regulations on Pension Plans Promise Headaches for Major Employers," *Wall Street Journal*, May 22, 1990, p. A1.

24. Selwyn Feinstein, "Rules Change for Pensions: Who Gets What," *Wall Street Journal*, July 3, 1990, pp. B1 +.

25. Pauline Yoshihashi, "Junking of Pensions Angers Mill Workers," *Wall Street Journal*, April 18, 1991, p. A5.

26. Allen Steinberg, "Best Bets for Retirement," *HRMagazine*, January 1992, pp. 47–50.

27. Scott R. Schmedel, "Tax Report," *Wall Street Journal*, October 19, 1988, p. 1.

28. Steinberg, "Best Bets for Retirement," p. 47.

29. Ellen Schultz, "Changing Jobs Means Having to Find a New Home for Cash in Retirement Plan," *Wall Street Journal*, March 9, 1992, pp. C1 +; "Pension Portability," *HRMagazine*, February 1992, pp. 99–100.

30. James Herlihy and Jamie Owens, "Methods of Implementing a Nonqualified 401(k) Plan," *HRMagazine*, January 1992, pp. 52–56.

31. Richard Hill and Patricia Dwyer, "Grooming Workers for Early Retirement," *HRMagazine*, September 1990, pp. 59–63.

32. Joann Lubin, "Bosses Alter Early-Retirement Windows to be Less Coercive—and Less Generous," *Wall Street Journal*, pp. B1 +.

33. Catherine Fyock, "Crafting Secure Retirements," *HRMagazine*, July 1990, pp. 30–33.

34. Christopher Conte, "Falling Behind," *Wall Street Journal*, March 3, 1992, p. A1.

35. *Paid Holidays and/or Vacation Policies*, Personnel Policies Forum no. 130 (Washington, DC: Bureau of National Affairs, November 1980), p. 1.

36. Jolie Solomon, "The Future Look of Employee Benefits," *Wall Street Journal*, September 7, 1988, p. 29.

37. Gene DeLoux, "Is Your Maternity Policy Ready for the '90s?" *HRMagazine*, November 1990, pp. 57–59.

38. Cathy Trost, "Survey Fortifies Parental-Leave Backers," *Wall Street Journal*, August 9, 1990, p. B1.

39. "Florida Update," *Employment Relations Bulletin*, February 10, p. 1.

40. Albert Karr, "The Daddy Track," *Wall Street Journal*, April 30, 1991, p. A1.

41. Suzanne Alexander, "Fears for Career Curb Paternity Leave," *Wall Street Journal*, August 24, 1990, pp. B1 +; and Albert Karr, "Maternity Leave," *Wall Street Journal*, April 28, 1992, p. A1.

42. Jim Mishizen, "In the Eye of the Health-Care Storm," *HRMagazine*, September 1991, pp. 47–50.

43. "Most Employers Offer Disability Leaves," *American Society for Personnel Administration/Resources*, December 1988, p. 4.

44. Lee Smith, "The Battle Over Health Insurance," *Fortune*, September 26, 1988, pp. 145–146.

45. Ibid., p. 146.

46. Glenn Ruffenach, "Health Insurance Premiums Soar in 1989," *Wall Street Journal*, October 25, 1988, p. B1.

47. Ron Winslow, "Firms Restrain Rate of Growth of Health Care," *Wall Street Journal*, January 28, 1992, p. B1.

48. Ron Winslow, "Costs of Medical Care Continue to Soar, Defying Corporate Efforts to Find Cures," *Wall Street Journal*, January 29, 1991, pp. B1+.

49. Armondo Bennett, "Firms Stunned by Retiree Health Costs," *Wall Street Journal*, May 24, 1988, p. 41.

50. Richard Schmidt, "Retirees Fight Cuts in Health Benefits," *Wall Street Journal*, December 8, 1988, p. B1.

51. Gary Laugharn, "Caught in the FASB Crossfire," *HRMagazine* July 1990, pp. 38–42.

52. Ceel Pasternak, "HRM Update," *HRMagazine*, August 1991, p. 19.

53. Timothy Schellhardt, "Retirees Benefit Cuts Won't End Soon," *Wall Street Journal*, September 19, 1990, p. B1.

54. Albert Karr, "Labor Letter," *Wall Street Journal*, February 7, 1989, p. 1.

55. Gary Kushner and Gina Williams, "COBRA: Answers to the Most-Asked Questions," *Legal Report* (Alexandria, VA: HR Society for Human Resource Management).

56. Albert Karr, "More Burden Shifting," *Wall Street Journal*, April 30, 1991, p. A1.

57. Ceel Pasternak, "HRM Update," *HRMagazine*, September 1990, p. 26.

58. Selwyn Feinstein, "Heal Thyself," *Wall Street Journal*, July 10, 1990, p. A1.

59. Albert Karr, "Tough Trade-off," *Wall Street Journal*, December 17, 1991, p. A1.

60. Michael Selz, "Small Firms Score Well on Health Insurance," *Wall Street Journal*, August 15, 1991, p. B1.

61. Ruffenbach, "Health Insurance Premiums," p. B1.

62. Albert Karr, "Health Maintenance," *Wall Street Journal*, May 8, 1990, p. A1.

63. Karen Munson and David Israel: "Self-Insurance Checkup," *HRMagazine*, February 1992, pp. 83–87.

64. Ceel Pasternak, "Incentives for Wellness," *HRMagazine*, August 1991, p. 19.

65. Hilary Stout, "Paying Workers for Good Health," *Wall Street Journal*, November 26, 1991, pp. B1+

66. Aaron Bernstein, "Health Care Costs: Trying to Cool the Fever," *Business Week*, May 21, 1990, pp. 46–47.

67. Selwyn Feinstein, "Companies Target Catastrophic Illnesses in Bid to Curb Soaring Health Cost," *Wall Street Journal*, July 30, 1990, p. A1.

68. Glenn Ruffenach, "Firms Tighten Benefits in Counseling Programs," *Wall Street Journal*, January 12, 1989, p. B1.

69. Eugene Carlson, "Firms Get State Help on Employee Counseling," *Wall Street Journal*, April 30, 1991, p. B1.

70. Glenn Ruffenach, "Slashes in Mental-Health Benefits Start to Hurt Patients, Medical Officials Say," *Wall Street Journal*, March 19, 1991, pp. B1+.

71. Eileen Settineri, "Effectively Measuring the Costs of EAPs," *HRMagazine*, April 1991, pp. 53–56.

72. Ron Winslow, "Managed-Care Artworks Show Promise,'" *Wall Street Journal*, March 24, 1992, p. B1.

73. Ron Winslow, "Videos, Questionnaires Aim to Expand Role of Patients in Treatment Decisions," *Wall Street Journal*, February 25, 1992, pp. B1+.

74. Edward Felsenthal, "Managed Care Helps Curb Costs, Study Says," *Wall Street Journal*, August 12, 1991, p. B1; Glenn Ruffenach, "Managed-Care Networks Help Rein in Costs," *Wall Street Journal*, March 27, 1991;

Ron Winslow, "Some Companies Try 'Managed Care' in Bid to Curb Health Costs," *Wall Street Journal*, February 1, 1991, pp. A1+; and Ron Winslow, "Firms Perform Own Bypass Operations, Purchasing Health Care from the Source," *Wall Street Journal*, August 19, 1991, pp. B1+.

75. Ceel Pasternak, "It Doesn't Work," *HRMagazine*, September 1991, p. 24; and Richard Anderson, "Handling Health-care Costs in the '90s," *HRMagazine*, June 1990, pp. 89–94.

76. Ceel Pasternak, "Dealing in Drugs," *HRMagazine*, March 1992, p. 26.

77. Ceel Pasternak, "In-Company Pharmacy?" *HRMagazine*, September 1991, p. 23.

78. Albert Karr, "Make Workplace Calls?" *Wall Street Journal*, May 7, 1991, p. A1.

79. Glen Ruffenach, "California School Unions Use Trusts to Cut Costs," *Wall Street Journal*, March 3, 1992, p. B1.

80. John Sturges, "Examining Your Insurance Carrier," *HRMagazine*, February 1992, pp. 43–46; and William Wymer, George Faulkner, and Joseph Parente, "Achieving Benefit Program Objectives," *HRMagazine*, March 1992, pp. 55–62.

81. Stephenie Overman and Linda Thornburg, "Beating the Odds," *HRMagazine*, March 1992, pp. 42–47.

82. Ron Winslow, "Infant Health Problems Cost Business Billions," *Wall Street Journal*, May 1, 1992, p. B1+.

83. John Morley, "The Cleveland Health-Care Experiment," *Wall Street Journal*, February 10, 1992, p. A16; and Walt Bogdanich, "Clevelanders Bet Top Health Care Will Be Cheaper," *Wall Street Journal*, February 2, 1992, pp. B1+.

84. Ron Winslow, "How Local Businesses Got Together to Cut Memphis Health Costs," *Wall Street Journal*, February 4, 1992, pp. A1+; Alain Enthoven, "How Employers Boost Health Costs," *Wall Street Journal*, January 24, 1992, p. A14; and David Wessel and Walt Bogdanich, "Laws of Economics Often Don't Apply in Health-Care Field," *Wall Street Journal*, January 22, 1992, pp. A1+.

85. Edmund Faltermayer, "Let's Really Cure the Health System," *Fortune*, March 23, 1992, pp. 46–58.

86. Stuart Butler, " 'Pay or Play' Health-Care Is Bound to Be a Loser," *Wall Street Journal*, January 3, 1992, p. A6; Hilary Stout, "Health Care Choices: A Bigger Federal Role of a Market Approach?" *Wall Street Journal*, January 15, 1992, pp. A1+; Linda Thornburg, "U.S. Health Care Called a System in Crisis . . ." *HRNews*, January 1992, p. A14; Christine Keen, "National Health-care Reform: Politics vs. Policy," *HRNews*, February 1992, p. A5; and Linda Thornburg, "Medical Community Proposes National Health-care Reforms," *HRNews*, February 1992, p. A11.

87. "Pay or Play," *Wall Street Journal*, January 21, 1992, p. A1.

88. Jill Fraser, "Flexible Spending," *Inc.*, October 1990, pp. 164–167; and Georgette Jason, "Medical Reimbursement Accounts Are a Good Deal for Many Workers," *Wall Street Journal*, July 26, 1991, p. C1.

89. Walecia Konrad and Gail DeGeorge, "U.S. Companies Go for the Gray," *Business Week*, April 3, 1989, p. 66.

90. Marilyn Chase, "Science Edges Closer to Designing Drugs to Defeat AIDS Virus," *Wall Street Journal*, March 3, 1989, p. A1.

91. David Israel and Debra Scott, "AIDS-Related Insurance Ceilings Are Risky," *HRMagazine*, November 1990, pp. 85–86.

92. David Stipp, "Laws on Health Benefits Raise Firms' Ire," *Wall Street Journal*, December 28, 1988, p. B1.

93. James P. Miller, "Some Workers Set Up LBOs of Their Own and Benefit Greatly," *Wall Street Journal*, December 12, 1988, pp. 1, A6.

94. "Employee Stock Ownership Plans Spread More Slowly in 1990," *Wall Street Journal*, March 12, 1991, p. A1.

95. James White, "As ESOPs Become Victims of '90s Bankruptcies, Workers Are Watching their Nest Eggs Vanish," *Wall Street Journal*, January 25, 1991, pp. C1+.

96. "Cafeteria Plans, Wellness Programs Gaining Popularity," *Employee Benefit Plan Review*, July 1987, p. 92; and Jolie Solomon, "The Future Look of Employee Benefits," *Wall Street Journal*, September 7, 1988, p. 29.

97. Stephenie Overman, "3M Arranges Summer Child Care," *HRMagazine*, March 1991, pp. 46–47.

98. Linda Thornburg, "On-site Child Care Works for Health-Care Industry," *HRMagazine,* August 1990, pp. 39–40.

99. Janet Guyon, "Inequality in Granting Child-Care Benefits Makes Workers Seethe," *Wall Street Journal,* October 23, 1991, pp. A1+.

100. Sue Schellenburger, "U.S.-Style Child-Care Wins Fans in Japan," *Wall Street Journal,* February 12, 1992, p. B1.

101. Solomon, "The Future Look of Employee Benefits," p. 29.

102. *America in Transition: Benefits for the Future* (Baltimore Employee Benefits Research Institution, 1988).

103. Richard Gisonny, "Benefits and Taxes," *HRMagazine,* February 1991, pp. 37–42.

104. Albert Karr, "Vacations for Sale," *Wall Street Journal,* September 17, 1991, p. A1.

105. "Cafeteria Plans, Wellness Programs Gaining Popularity," p. 91.

106. Glenn Ruffenach, "Odds and Ends," *Wall Street Journal,* March 27, 1991, p. B1.

107. Melissa Barringer, George Milkovich, and Olivia Mitchell, "Predicting Employee Health Insurance Selections in a Flexible Benefits Environment," *On Center,* no. 1, 1992, p. 7.

108. Albert Karr, "Favoring Options," *Wall Street Journal,* April 30, 1991, p. A1.

109. Solomon, "The Future Look," p. 29.

110. Carol Hymowitz, "As Aetna Adds Flextime, Bosses Learn to Cope," *Wall Street Journal,* June 18, 1990, pp. B1+; Albert Karr, "IBM Expands Its Flexible-Hours Policy," *Wall Street Journal,* June 18, 1991, p. A1; Sue Schellenburger, "GE Unit Sees Advantage in More Family Benefits," *Wall Street Journal,* February 12, 1992, pp. B1; and Cathy Trost, "To Cut Costs and Keep the Best People, More Concerns Offer Flexible Work Plans," *Wall Street Journal,* February 18, 1992, pp. B1+.

111. Hennessey, "Using Employee Benefits," p. 57.

112. Jolie Solomon, "Companies Try Measuring Cost Savings from New Types of Corporate Benefits," *Wall Street Journal,* December 29, 1988, p. B1.

113. Ibid.

114. Ibid.

115. Adapted from "Milwaukee Firms Look for $2-Million Savings," *Employee Benefit Plan Review* 42, no. 11, May 1988, pp. 10–12.

15 Managing Health, Safety, and Stress

Employee safety and health is an area that is undergoing continual change. Materials that were not considered hazardous in the past are later found to be extremely dangerous as the long-term effects of exposure become known. New ailments caused by acts performed or equipment used on the job are coming to the public's attention more and more frequently.[1] Pressure on employees from both home and work can cause both emotional and physical problems, increased health-care costs, and decreased productivity at work.[2] Because of all of the flux in this area, it is imperative that organizations remain informed and aware of the changes taking place.

● ● ● ● ● ● ● ● ●
CHAPTER OBJECTIVES

After studying this chapter, you should be able to

1. Outline the strategic choices available to managers with respect to employee safety, health, and stress management.

2. Discuss the Occupational Safety and Health Administration (OSHA) and explain its purpose, scope, and procedures.

3. Examine some of the current safety and health problem facing employees, such as repetitive motion problems and AIDS, of which managers need to be aware.

4. Present information regarding fetal protection available in the workplace.

5. Identify types and consequences of workplace stress and present ways to reduce it.

6. Discuss possible organizational strategies available to help improve and maintain the health and safety of workers.

CASE: Health and Safety at General Electric[3]

Although problems associated with health and safety problems cost organizations in excess of $33 billion annually in terms of lost wages, medical costs, and indirect costs, few organizations proactively seek out opportunities to reduce these losses. One exception is General Electric (GE), who has significantly reduced bottom-line costs by establishing programs aimed at employee health and safety.

Healthy Employees are Productive Employees

In 1987, GE developed the General Electric Fitness Center, which consisted of a running track, weight training facilities, and other fitness-related equipment. In addition, the center is staffed by full-time program directors who provide guidance and assistance aimed at nutrition and stress management. Also, the General Electric Employee Activity Association (GEEAA) was developed to offer employees additional recreational activities, such as bowling, tennis, and golf, in addition to a host of educational and cultural programs.

When compared to employees who chose to take part in the fitness and recreation programs, it was determined that employees not enrolled in the fitness program were absent twice as frequently. In addition, members not enrolled in these programs reported lower levels of job satisfaction and motivation. These findings are similar to those found by Coors Brewery and Johnson & Johnson who also saw that programs of this nature reduced employee absences while increasing worker motivation.

In terms of bottom-line economic figures, these two programs were shown to save the organization nearly $3 million in terms of absence costs in the first year alone not to mention the benefits of increased productivity and lower medical claims.

Safe Working Conditions Facilitate Productivity and Commitment

General Electric's commitment to the work force did not end with employee health concerns. The organization has made great strides toward reducing accidents at work. General Electric's self-directed work teams have taken an active role in developing and implementing safety programs and rules recognized across all divisions of the plant. The organization contends that the responsibility for developing safety programs rests with those individuals who are most affected by an unsafe work environment—the firm's employees. Hence, all important programs regarding health and safety are initiated at the worker level with a maximum amount of feedback from workers employed at lower levels of the plant. The participative safety management program not only reduces accidents and the accident costs absorbed by the firm, but employees participating in the program feel a sense of ownership as their promotion of a safer work environment leads to increased morale and commitment. In addition to the typical pep talks exclaiming the virtues of a safe work site, pocket size cards are given to each employee to be passed on to a fellow employee if an unsafe act is perceived. The employee keeps the card until he or she sees another employee working dangerously. Also, each unit of the plant is responsible for developing a safety work team whose mission is to eliminate work site accidents at its unit. A special unit, Make Accidents Stop Happening (MASH), was developed to focus on the financial implications of having an unsafe work environment. Employees involved in MASH call other GE plants to encourage them to become involved in similar safety programs.

GE has seen great financial savings affecting the participating plant's bottom line. When it was determined that a small GE plant could save $120,000 annually in medical costs alone, management took notice. In addition, a plant in Columbia, Missouri, saved $1.5 million in worker's compensation claims in the first three years alone following the development of the participative safety management system. Finally, visits to the medical department at the plant were significantly reduced following the inception of the program.

A Commitment to Health and Safety

By developing the fitness/activity and participative safety programs, upper management is sending a clear message to its employees: "The organization cares about *your* health and safety while an employee at GE." Not only do programs of this nature instill a feeling of commitment among its participants, organizational bottom-line objectives are frequently realized. In an era of labor shortages at key positions (positions that make up a large portion of GE's work force), GE's active role in the health and safety of its work force will assure employees of the company's good will and allow General Electric to continue to be one of America's most profitable and respected companies.

• • • • • • • • •

STRATEGIC CHOICES

The decisions managers make regarding the health and safety of their workers becomes increasingly more important as time passes due to ever increasing penalties, some aimed directly at the top management,[4] for willfully endangering the lives of employees. Many of the decisions made are based on strategic choices available to the organization. Some of these strategic choices are outlined below:

1. Managers must determine the *level of protection* the organization will provide for employees. Some firms, for financial or liability reasons, perfer a minimum level of protection while other organizations prefer a maximum level of protection.

2. Managers can decide whether *safety regulations will be formal or informal.* Formal regulations are written and carefully monitored while informal regulations are enforced through peer pressure or good training.

3. Managers also can be *proactive or reactive in terms of developing procedures or plans* with respect to employee safety and health. Proactive managers seek to improve the safety and health of their employees prior to a need to do so while reactive managers fix safety and health problems after they occur.

4. Managers can decide to use the *safety and health of workers as a marketing tool* for the organization. This type of strategy would involve advertising that Company X is a great place to work because of how much it cares about the worker. "Safety before production" would be this company's motto. Other firms take the opposite strategy and stress output over safety.[5]

OCCUPATIONAL SAFETY AND HEALTH ADMINISTRATION[6]
Occupational Health and Safety Act of 1970

Due to the overwhelming number of workers killed on the job (more than 14,000 in 1970 alone), the estimated 300,000 new cases of occupational diseases discovered each year, and the emotional and economic impact these problems caused, Congress passed the Occupational Health and Safety Act of 1970. This act was designed to offer, as far as possible, every working man or woman a safe and healthy working environment.

In order to include as many employers and employees as possible, Congress passed the Occupational Safety and Health Act under the Commerce Clause of the United States Constitution. By defining the act under this clause, all employers and employees of businesses affecting interstate commerce are included. The few exceptions to this act include federal and state government employees, the self-employed, and domestic servants.

The Birth of the Occupational Safety and Health Administration (OSHA)

The Occupational Safety and Health Administration (OSHA) was created as the primary administrative agency for the Occupational Safety and Health Act of 1970. OSHA is within the Department of Labor and has the authority to set safety and health standards, conduct inspections to ensure compliance with the standards, and seek enforcement actions for noncompliance. This authority is supervised by the Secretary of Defense.

The act also created two other agencies: the National Institute of Occupational Safety and Health (NIOSH) and the Occupational Safety and Health Review Commission (OSHRC). NIOSH is a research center for occupational safety and health. As such, it studies various health and safety problems occurring in the workplace and provides technical advice and standards recommendations based upon its findings. OSHRC is the enforcement arm. While OSHA may recommend a penalty for a discovered violation to OSHRC, only OSHRC may actually assess the penalty.

How OSHA Works

The act provides the secretary of labor with the authority to establish three different types of health and safety standards: interim, permanent, and temporary emergency standards. Interim standards were those established from the date of the act and up to two years later that were usually generated from preexisting national consensus standards. Permanent standards are either newly created or revised from interim standards. They often stem from suggestions taken from interested parties (such as unions, employers, or NIOSH) or from an appointed advisory committee. Permanent standards must be published in the Federal Register to provide the public time to respond. If publishing the standard results in a requested public hearing, OSHA must schedule and publicize one. OSHA has 60 days after the close of public comment in which to publish the standard, its effective date, and reasons for its adoption. If the secretary of labor feels that workers are in grave danger from a newly found hazard, he has the authority to bypass the permanent standard formalities and establish temporary emergency standards. Once the temporary standard is published it becomes effective immediately, but for only six months. At the time of publishing, the secretary must also begin the normal procedure for establishing a permanent standard in order to keep it effective after the temporary emergency status has expired.

Employer Responsibility

The Occupational Safety and Health Act charges employers with three major responsibilities: to furnish and maintain a healthful work environment, to keep records of occupational injuries and illnesses, and to comply with OSHA standards. With respect to the first responsibility, the act specifically states that employers must provide a workplace that is free from recognized hazards that are likely to cause death or other serious physical harm. In order to prove a violation of this general requirement, the secretary of labor must show that the employer failed to produce a hazard-free environment, the hazard was recognized by either the employer or the industry, the hazard did or may cause death or serious harm, and there was a means by which the employer could have eliminated or reduced the hazard. If all four elements are not proven, the secretary's case has not been met.

The act also requires that organizations with eight or more employees keep records of any occupational injury or illness if it results in death, loss of consciousness, transfer to another job, medical treatment other than first aid, or one or more lost work days. An occupational injury is defined as any injury that results from a work-related accident, while an occupational illness is any condition resulting from exposure to environmental factors at the workplace. The information must be recorded on specific OSHA forms. The organization is required to post this information once a year so employees are aware of the records and the organization must present these records if requested to do so by an OSHA compliance officer.

Inspections

To enforce its standards, OSHA conducts workplace inspections in all establishments covered by the act. Obviously, this is a monumental job. With the current budget, OSHA can only visit 2% of the 6 million workplaces every year.[7] In order to concentrate its efforts on the areas most in need of inspections, a four-tier priority system has been established by OSHA. Top priority is given to cases in which death or serious injury have occurred, followed by cases of valid employee complaints, high-hazard industries, and, finally, general random inspections.

An inspection is unannounced, except for conditions of imminent danger where advance notice is given to allow the employer the opportunity to correct the situation as quickly as possible. The inspector must present proper identification and a warrant in order to conduct the inspection. A warrant is not needed if the employer consents to the inspection, if the site is open to public view, or if there is an emergency situation in which imminent danger to employees would not allow the time needed to obtain a warrant.

The compliance officer may be escorted on a tour by a representative of the employer or the employees. On this tour, the inspector may question workers and employers in private, take samples, make readings, observe, take photographs, and inspect records. At the end of the inspection tour, the compliance officer holds a closing conference with the employer to review the findings and report any possible violations found. The inspector then reports to the area director who has six months to decide whether or not to issue a citation and impose a penalty.

While organizations feared OSHA during the Carter administration, severe budget cuts took the bite out of OSHA during the Reagan administration.[8] However, a new OSHA chief, Gerald Scannell, has been appointed who has pledged to make OSHA a zealous regulator once again. Scannell has the background to hold true to his pledge. Before becoming the director of OSHA, Scannell was Safety Chief at Johnson & Johnson where, from 1979 to 1989, he reduced the number of work days lost due to injuries by 92 percent by making managers responsible for their units' safety records. Special attention will be paid to the required use of safety belts for employees who drive as part of the job and the levying of large fines on companies for alleged violations of OSHA standards.[9]

Violations, Citations, and Penalties

The Occupational Safety and Health Act delineates the types of violations possible. Exhibit 15.1 provides an overview of these as well as the penalties associated with each violation. The area director, after reviewing the compliance officer's report, sends a certified letter outlining the citations and the proposed penalties. Normally, 30 days are provided as the abatement period during which time the employer must correct the violation, or the penalty is imposed. The act allows civil sanctions for each day in which the violation has not been corrected after the abatement period.

Willful violations are the only type that include a prison sentence as well as a fine. Additionally, three states (Illinois, New York, and Michigan) have ruled that the Occupational Health and Safety Act does not preempt states from taking criminal actions against company officials for endangering the safety and health of their employees.[10] While relatively few employers have been criminally prosecuted for workplace hazards,[11] this seems to be changing. In Illinois five senior executives of Chicago Magnet Wire Company were charged with allowing workers to become ill

EXHIBIT 15.1 Violations of the Occupational Safety and Health Act

VIOLATION	DEFINITION	PENALTY
Willful	Conscious, intentional, or deliberate decision or a careless disregard for the OSHA standards or indifference to employee safety	Criminal: Up to $10,000 fine or up to 6 months in prison Civil: Up to $10,000 fine
Repeated violations	Prior violation of the same standard	Up to $10,000 fine
Serious	Substantial likelihood that death or serious physical harm could result	Up to $1,000 fine
Nonserious	Causes an unsafe work environment, but probably would not cause death or serious physical harm	Up to $1,000 fine, but only if ten or more nonserious violations are cited
De Minimus	Violation has no immediate relationship to job safety	Notice issued

from exposure to hazardous chemicals and three senior officials of Film Recovery Systems, Inc., were prosecuted on murder and reckless conduct charges after a worker died from inhaling cyanide fumes.[12] In New York, William and Edward Pymm, the former operators of Pymm Thermometer Corporation, were charged with recklessly endangering the lives of several employees by exposing them to mercury during work in an unventilated cellar. They face up to 15 years in prison.[13]

Even without the state's help, OSHA can cause top officials to rue the day they were less than diligent in enforcing OSHA regulations. In one case, Howard Elliott, president of Elliott Plumbing & Heating, was sentenced to six months in jail, of which 45 days must be served, for willfully failing to comply with OSHA trenching standards. Failing to abide by the standards resulted in the death of two of Elliott's company's workers. Elliott will also be on probation for three years and was also fined $21,452 in a lump sum payment or $544 per month for three years to cover restitution for funeral expenses and lost earnings.[14] In a more severe case, Phillips Petroleum Company was fined $5.7 million for willful safety violations in connection with a chemical plant explosion near Houston that resulted in 23 deaths and more than 130 injuries.[15]

Recently, a new OSHA bill was proposed in both the House and the Senate which, if passed, would significantly modify the Occupational Safety and Health Act by creating new standards.[16] Specifically, the new law would require employers to provide immediate notification of all work-related fatalities and 24-hour notification of all accidents requiring hospitalization of two or more workers. Employers would also be required to formulate written health and safety plans, form workplace safety and health committees, and designate a safety and health officer.[17] Finally, the law would require broader training requirements and the establishment of standards for monitoring exposure to toxic or harmful materials.[18]

This bill was backed by labor unions, and for good reason. Research has shown that unionized workers are more likely to complain about unsafe work conditions than are nonunion employees, and union workers dramatically increase the enforcement of existing OSHA standards.[19] Further, this same study found that union-

HR CHALLENGES ●

Beware of Salt and Candles!

One unfortunate outgrowth of the recent "right to know" legislation is a distorted sense of proportion and common sense on the part of the makers of caution labels. The purpose of "right to know" legislation is to guarantee the workers' rights to be informed about the hazardous substances they may come into contact with at work.

The following warning appears on a certain laboratory chemical: "WARNING: CAUSES IRRITATION. Avoid contact with eyes, skin or clothing. Avoid breathing dust. Wash thoroughly after handling." The chemical in question is sodium chloride, better known as table salt. A similar warning appears as an advisory against another "hazardous" chemical—paraffin wax, found in ordinary candles.

The problem becomes apparent when one compares the warnings for sodium chloride and paraffin wax to a truly hazardous chemical, such as tetrodotoxin. Tetrodotoxin is thought to be the magic behind Haitian voodoo practices intended to paralyze victims, and is found in certain species of fish. The warning for tetrodotoxin, although more stringent than that of salt and paraffin wax, is similar enough in impact to cause some to speak out against "crying wolf" over trivial risks. The result of such warnings may be to lower workers' vigilance for real risks, because the intensity of warnings may blur true distinctions between high- and low-risk chemicals.

SOURCE: Adapted from Michael M. Segal, M.D., "Spilled Some Salt? Call OSHA," *Wall Street Journal*, July 9, 1991, p. A16.

ized workplaces face greater scrutiny during a compliance inspection than do nonunion workplaces, and unionized firms are more likely to pay higher fines for violations than their nonunion counterparts.

Other changes may also be in store for the enforcement of OSHA standards. During a House Education and Labor Committee meeting investigating a fire in an Imperial Foods plant in North Carolina where 25 people were killed because they were trapped inside by locked doors, representatives threatened to strip authority from the 21 states who have the responsibility for enforcing federal OSHA laws.[20] If successful, enforcing OSHA standards would become the responsibility of the federal government.

"Right to Know" Legislation

In recent years, many states have passed legislation that guarantees individual workers the right to know if there are hazardous substances in the workplace, requires employers to provide the chemical composition of workplace substances to employees' physicians, and provides local officials and residents the right to be notified if local employees are working with hazardous substances. While the laws vary from state to state, it is not uncommon for the law to require training programs for employees who work with hazardous materials to inform them about the properties of the material, safe handling procedures, and emergency treatments for overexposure. Also, several states have enacted legislation that requires labels for containers of toxic substances. However, as the box entitled "Beware of Salt and Candles" indicates, efforts to protect employees can sometimes appear to be overdone.

CURRENT SAFETY AND HEALTH PROBLEMS FOR EMPLOYEES

While the sweatshop work environment has all but disappeared, employers are still concerned about productivity.[21] One way in which increased productivity can be achieved is through automation. Sometimes, however, the introduction of new technology can be responsible for adding safety and health problems. One example is cumulative trauma disorders (CTD) caused by repeated motions of the same muscles hundreds or thousands of times each day.[22] Between 1983 and 1987, reported cases of job-related CTD have more than tripled to 73,000 cases, making it the fastest growing occupational injury in the 1980s.[23] By 1989, CTD accounted for 51.8 percent of all occupational illnesses.[24] CTD injuries have been reported by grocery cashiers, mail sorters, assembly-line workers, violinists, and jackhammer operators, but the most prevalent reports of this disorder come from employees in both the computer and meat-packing industries.[25] By the year 2000, OSHA and National Safety Council experts predict that 50 percent of all workers' compensation cases will be related to CTDs.[26]

Computers and CTD

The personal computer has changed the American office. Its introduction into the workplace has enabled typists to move 40 percent faster than when using a typewriter because no manual margin adjustments or paper changes are required with word processors.[27] However, this change in the variety of hand motions required to type has caused an increase in the reported cases of CTD in all jobs associated with keyboarding.

The experience of Deborah Tager is a good example of how CTD can debilitate a worker. She was a features editor at the *Monitor* in Concord, New Hampshire. One of the requirements of this job was to edit stories on her personal computer 8 to 12 hours a day. At first, Tager just assumed it was fatigue. However when the tingling and burning in her hands and arms woke her at night, she knew she had a problem. After being diagnosed with CTD, she was no longer able to use her computer. In December of 1988, Tager was fired.[28]

Meat Packing and CTD

The meat industry has faced some hard times since early 1970. Americans have given up eating red meat at least once a day in favor of a more healthy diet consisting of more fish and poultry.[29] This change in American diet forced the meat firms to trim back on staff and run the production lines faster to continue to reach production quotas. This procedural change has caused the meat-packing industry to be dubbed "America's No. 1 disaster area."[30] One extreme example of this was found at Morrell's Sioux Falls plant.

OSHA proposed a record fine of $4.33 million against John Morrell & Company for failure to prevent CTD at the company's Sioux Falls meat-packing plant. OSHA reported that between May 1977 and April 1988, 880 of the 2,000 employees at the Sioux Falls plant sustained injuries, such as tendinitis, elbow and shoulder injuries, and carpal tunnel syndrome, classifed under the CTD heading. All of the injuries were traced to the repetitive hand, wrist, and arm motions required for meat packing.[31] Beverly Whaley was one of the Morrell employees stricken with CTD. Her job involved ripping the kidneys from hog carcasses using only her right hand. Before long the pain in her hand would wake her at night and she would have to run cold water on her hand in order to get it to open in the morning. Even after two operations, she has not regained full use of her hand and complains that it is difficult to even pick up a coffee cup.[32]

Fighting CTD

Some companies have made a strategic decision to fight CTD in the workplace. Chrysler and the United Auto Workers recently agreed to begin a program at five assembly plants to control carpal tunnel syndrome and other production-line repetitive motion disorders.[33] IBP, a major meat-packing firm, also introduced a safety program aimed at reducing repetitive motion injuries. This agreement between the union and management has been called a historic agreement that may lead to a redesign of all meat-packing plants in America.[34] Other corrective measures management can take include introducing an appropriate ergonomics program that focuses on fitting the job to the worker, not the worker to the job, and training workers to be aware of the possible symptoms of CTD and ways to curtail this disease.[35] A properly positioned terminal and keyboard punctuated with frequent breaks can go a long way in reducing or eliminating CTD.

Chemicals

Some health problems, such as CTD, are consider new threats to workers while others, such as chemical poisoning and lung disease, have always plagued workers. While chemical poisoning is an old problem, several new chemical health risks, such as indoor air pollution and passive smoking, have gained prominence in recent years. Another reason chemicals in the workplace have received increased attention was OSHA's issuing of new standards for hazardous materials in May of 1988 under the name Hazard Communication Standard. This standard, which once only applied to manufacturers, now requires *every* workplace in the country to identify hazardous substances on the premises, list them, and train employees in their use.[36] To comply, employers must observe the following procedures:

1. Identify and list hazardous chemicals in the workplace.
2. Obtain and retain a material safety data sheet (MSDS) for each chemical and make these sheets available to employees.
3. Create and maintain a written chemical communication program.
4. Identify workers who should be trained and provide training that includes instructions in each substance's dangers, safe handling techniques, how to read the MSDS and warning labels, and what to do in case of an emergency.[37]

Due to the complexities of the regulations and the severity of the penalties for noncompliance, OSHA designed and distributed a "Hazard Compliance Kit."[38] It contains looseleaf materials designed to provide employers with simple instructions regarding compliance with OSHA's hazard communication standard. Purchasers of the kit, which sells for $18, will also have amendments and updates sent to them over the next several years.[39]

Indoor Air Pollution

The 1976 American Legion convention in Philadelphia will be remembered for many years to come. It was at this convention that 29 people died from Legionnaire's disease contracted from a bacteria in the hotel's cooling tower that spread through the ventilation system.[40] This was one of the first and most publicized cases of sick-building syndrome.

Sick-building syndrome is an outgrowth of the energy crisis of the 1970s. Buildings were being designed with sealed windows and heavy insulation resulting in inadequate fresh air and poor ventilation systems. The buildup of chemicals from photocopying machines, cleaning liquids, and solvents have caused workers to complain of headaches, dizziness, and bleeding.[41] Four women with such symptoms, who were fired because they refused to work in the building, sued their employer, its parent company, the building's designer, and the contractor.

While only a handful of lawsuits have been filed on the grounds of indoor air pollution, the Environmental Protection Agency estimates that the economic costs of indoor air pollution totals tens of billions of dollars in such forms as lost productivity, medical care, lost earning, and sick days. With the increase in both litigation and indirect costs, architects have begun redesigning buildings so that fresh air is available and engineers are improving air circulation systems for office buildings.[42]

Smoking in the Workplace

The 1990s will likely be referred to as the decade of the smoke-free workplace. The movement toward eliminating smoking in the workplace is being fueled by reports that the 50 largest industrial companies are working to eliminate workplace smoking. Reports indicate that 85 percent of American companies restrict smoking in the workplace, up from 54 percent in 1987. Reasons given for these actions include concern for employee health, worker complaints, the classification of environmental tobacco smoke (ETS) as a human carcinogen by the Environmental Protection Agency (EPA), and the increase in state and local laws.[43]

While not cited, employers may want to see their employees quit smoking for a variety of other reasons. Smokers are 50% more likely to be hospitalized than nonsmoking employees. Smokers lose 80 million work days a year due to their habit and their absenteeism rates are 50 percent higher than their nonsmoking counterparts. Employers pay an average of $300 more in insurance claims for smokers than for nonsmokers. Smokers have twice as many job-related accidents as nonsmokers, in part due to loss of attention, hand occupation, eye irritation, and coughing.[44] Smokers also have been found to have more car accidents.[45]

Some companies have made a strategic decision to promote a smoke-free workplace and have gained some notoriety for doing so. Mereck & Co., a pharmaceutical corporation based in Rahway, New Jersey, has severely restricted smoking in all of its 24 sites in the United States. Further, it also has banned smoking at Mereck-sponsored off-site events. To help their employees kick the habit, Mereck uses the following techniques:

1. Reimburses employees and their dependents for successful completion of approved smoking-cessation programs.
2. Encourages smokers to quit through a year-long communications program.
3. Helps fund a smoking clinic at a local hospital.
4. Donates money to the American Cancer Society and the American Lung Association to support public education and no-smoking programs.
5. Produces an antismoking commercial that aired repeatedly on 14 commercial radio stations serving communities surrounding Mereck sites nationwide.[46]

It is not always easy to get your employees to quit smoking. Research has found that only about one-fifth of those attending organized programs were smoke-free a year later. However, smokers using less than a pack of cigarettes a day were more than twice as likely to quit as heavy smokers.[47] Further, the type of employee you have may also increase their chances of smoking and quitting. Reports indicate that married employees are less likely to smoke than are divorced employees, and working women are less likely to smoke than are homemakers or unemployed women.[48]

Asbestos[49]

Asbestos is a fiber that was used extensively in insulation for over a century, until it was linked to cancer. Workers who were exposed to asbestos contracted a form of cancer called asbestosis, which slowly suffocates its victims. The first lawsuit filed by a worker exposed to asbestos was in the 1950s. The lawsuits continued for the next 40 years, with plaintiffs winning big beginning in the 1980s when juries learned that companies knew the risks associated with asbestos, but did nothing to protect the workers. Some of the judgments were so high that companies were forced to file Chapter 11 bankruptcy to protect themselves.

As the rewards and the number of suits continued to grow, the asbestos manufacturers' insurance companies grew tired of paying and began to reread the contracts for loopholes. Many filed suit against the asbestos manufacturers and these cases also ended up in court.

The only people who were sure to win in an asbestos suit were the lawyers. Asbestos suits were becoming so common that lawyers specialized in asbestos cases. It is estimated that over 1,100 law firms around the country were involved in defending asbestos manufacturers, insurance firms, or victims. Something had to be done to stop the escalation of lawsuits.

The solution came in the form of the Asbestos Claims Facility. It was conceived of as a one-stop settlement shop for asbestos claims. The designers saw it as a faster, less costly, and more orderly way of resolving claims. Fifty companies, who included the largest asbestos manufacturers and insurance companies, joined the facility. These companies provided funding for the facility, which was to be used to settle claims quickly and without the use of the courts.

Soon after its inception, the flood of claims turned into a deluge. New claims poured in at a rate of 1,300 a month, more than triple the rate from a few years before. With over 60,000 claims pending, the Asbestos Claims Facility folded. Seven of the biggest participants withdrew their financial support, which accounted for over 60 percent of the funding available. Now companies and plaintiffs alike are forced to return to the overcrowded courts in order to reach an agreement.

Accidents and Death on the Job

Another lingering health and safety problem in organizations is occupational accidents. While accidents on the job seriously injure or kill one out of every eleven U.S. workers,[50] some occupations have been found to be more dangerous than others. Exhibit 15.2 lists the top 25 occupations most likely to result in death for both white- and blue-collar workers.

As you read the list in Exhibit 15.2, you may notice a job you or a family member hold or have held. Research has found that when a hazardous job is held by the father, the son is more likely to follow in his footsteps.[51] Sons appear to feel they can control the dangers associated with the job. Another contributing factor is the rate of pay. The higher the income associated with the job, the higher the

EXHIBIT 15.2	Top 25 Occupations Most Likely to Result in Death

WHITE COLLAR			BLUE COLLAR		
RANK	JOB	DEATH RATE PER 100,000	RANK	JOB	DEATH RATE PER 100,000
1	Airplane pilots	97.0	1	Timber cutting and logging workers	129.0
2	Messengers and office help	14.5	2	Asbestos and insulation workers	78.7
3	Sales managers and department heads in retail trade	12.3	3	Structural metal workers	72.0
4	Geologists	9.5	4	Electric power line and cable installers and repairers	50.7
5	Agricultural scientists	9.0	5	Fire fighters	48.8
6	Vehicle dispatchers and starters	8.3	6	Garbage collectors	40.0
7	Physicists and astronomers	7.6	7	Truck drivers	39.6
8	Public administration and construction inspectors	7.6	8	Bulldozer operators	39.3
9	Meter readers and office machine operators	7.4	9	Earth drillers	38.8
10	Engineers	7.3	10	Specified craft apprentices	37.5
11	Public administrators and officials	7.2	11	Mine operatives	37.5
12	Weighers	7.1	12	Boilermakers	35.0
13	Engineering and science technicians except health	6.7	13	Taxicab drivers and chauffeurs	34.0

....

chance of the son choosing a hazardous career. However, education level has been found to decrease the rate of occupational following as does race. Research has found that the higher the level of education attained by the son, the less likely he is to perform his father's job. Also, white males are more likely to pursue their fathers' careers than are black males.

One occupation that did not make the list reported in Exhibit 15.2 was farming, even though the reported accidental death-rate was 48 per 100,000, a rate as high as the top 5 ranked occupations for job-related deaths. About 1,500 farmers and farmhands are killed each year.[52] Causes for these deaths range from the number one killer, tractor accidents, to angry farm animals and suffocation under tons of grain. Even though farming has proven to be a hazardous occupation, it is not covered by OSHA standards, and farmers fiercely resist any attempts to change this.

Congress has forbidden OSHA to enforce federal safety standards on 97 percent of the nation's farms, those with 10 or fewer employees.[53] Family workers, who are not paid, are not considered employees, nor are neighboring farmers who pitch in

EXHIBIT 15.2 continued

	WHITE COLLAR			BLUE COLLAR	
RANK	JOB	DEATH RATE PER 100,000	RANK	JOB	DEATH RATE PER 100,000
14	Coaches and physical education teachers	6.6	14	Construction laborers and carpenter helpers	33.5
15	Managers and administrators	6.6	15	Millers: grain, flour, and feed	33.3
16	Real estate agents and brokers	6.6	16	Surveyor helpers	33.3
17	Pharmacists	6.5	17	Sheriffs and bailiffs	32.4
18	Athletes and kindred workers	6.5	18	Roofers and slaters	31.9
19	Surveyors	6.1	19	Metal molders	26.6
20	Building managers and superintendents	5.8	20	Flight attendants	23.0
21	Veterinarians	5.2	21	Oilers and greaser, except auto	22.5
22	Assessors, controllers, and treasurers in local public administration	5.2	22	Excavating, grading, and road machine operators	20.9
23	Restaurant, bar, and cafeteria managers	5.1	23	Crane, derrick, and hoist operators	19.3
24	Engineering computer specialists	5.0	24	Police and detectives	17.5
25	Insurance adjusters, examiners, and investigators	4.9	25	Bakers	16.9
			26	Engravers	16.9

to help each other when needed. Farmers feel that farming is one of the last free things a person can do, and they do not want government changing that. Instead, they have decided to change things themselves. The American Farm Bureau Federation (AFBF) has introduced educational programs and redesigned farm implements to improve safety. The AFBF continues to argue that it is doing a good job, even though 341 people died in tractor rollovers in 1987.[54]

Not only does the type of job one holds influence the accident rate, so does the type of person holding the job. Research has found that left-handed men are one-third more likely to have accidents on the job than right-handers due to the bias of right-handed equipment.[55] Furthermore, while it was always assumed that blacks, who tend to work in more dangerous occupations, had a higher accident rate than whites, recent reports contradict this assumption. A study by the National Center for Health Statistics reported that whites have slightly higher rates of work-related accidents than blacks, especially in the growing service sector.[56]

Management also has been accused of causing job-related accidents, especially

··

| EXHIBIT 15.3 | Worker Fatality Rates Compared by Country |

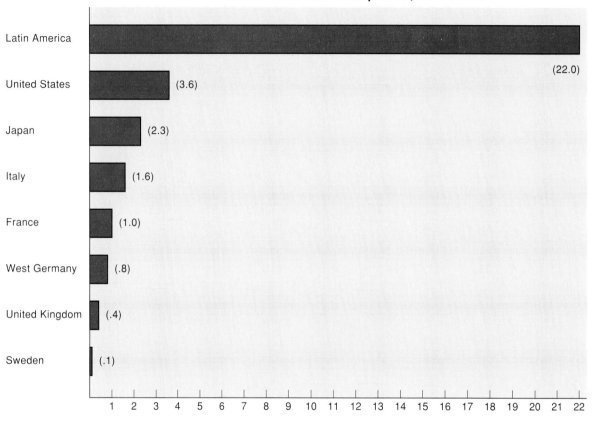

Industrial Accident Death Rates per 100,000 Workers

Latin America (22.0)
United States (3.6)
Japan (2.3)
Italy (1.6)
France (1.0)
West Germany (.8)
United Kingdom (.4)
Sweden (.1)

1 2 3 4 5 6 7 8 9 10 11 12 13 14 15 16 17 18 19 20 21 22

··

because of the current trend of downsizing and doing more with less. Job-related disabilities jumped 16 percent in 1987, up by 10,000, and labor officials are tieing this increase to the effects of mergers and competition. They argue that work crews are becoming smaller but the work load is not. The use of overtime and increased speeds on the assembly lines cause fatigued workers to make mistakes that may even cost them their lives.[57]

Such an incident occurred at Bastian Plating Company in Auburn, Indiana. The company had decided to install a speedier chemical process to increase production, but the change over was running behind schedule. In order to speed up the change over, untrained workers at the end of their 12-hour shift were asked to clean the chemical tanks that had been drained. One worker climbed in and was soon overcome by the hydrogen cyanide gases in the tank. Four workers who saw him fall face first into the muddy vat tried to rescue him. Three died in the vat with their colleague while the fourth died later in the hospital. The firm was fined $41,700 for numerous violations, which included the lack of adequate respirators, air monitoring systems, and training for employees.[58]

American firms are not the only ones plagued with the problem of job-related accidents. Exhibit 15.3, compares the fatality rates for workers in various countries, including the United States. As shown in Exhibit 15.3 Latin America heads the list. The total number of job-related accidents for Latin America was an alarming 30,000. However this figure does not represent the whole picture. The accidents that occurred in rural areas and in small operations are not included in this number. However, accidents that occur on the way to work, which have increased by 150 percent over the past 12 years, are reflected in these numbers. The Latin American Center for Occupational Safety and Health has begun to reverse these numbers through an effort that involves information, prevention, and legislation.[59]

An ever increasing cause of accidents and death on the job is violence in the workplace. A review of litigated cases shows various types of workplace violence. A youth, who was struck by an usher carrying a flashlight, sued the theater operator for damages. A fast-food restaurant employee sued her employer for fraud and bad faith after being injured in a robbery. She charged that the employer promised police protection and other security measures, but reneged on his promises. A woman, who was raped and sexually abused by an individual employed by a corporation to prepare bids for construction jobs, sued the employer for negligent retention of the employee and vicarious liability for the employee's violent actions.[60]

While the causes of workplace violence are varied, in most cases, the employers can be held responsible because they are obligated by law to provide a safe working environment for their employees and a safe place for nonemployees to conduct business. To protect themselves, employers should make a strategic decision to implement policies and practices designed to limit the risk of employing unfit, dangerous, or incompetent employees.

Acquired Immune Deficiency Syndrome (AIDS)

AIDS, which was known only to a small group of medical personnel a decade ago, has quickly become a serious health threat to Americans. AIDS also has caused significant confusion and disruption in the work force. Individuals who have AIDS are protected by federal, state, and local legislation. This protection is guaranteed under the Federal Rehabilitation Act of 1973 because AIDS is considered a handicap. This protection generally comes in the form of protection against discrimination and is based on the fact that the virus cannot be spread by casual contact.[61]

The Centers for Disease Control (CDC) has concluded that the kind of nonsexual, person-to-person contact that generally occurs among workers and clients or consumers in the workplace does not pose a risk for transmission of HIV, the virus that causes AIDS. Similarly, the United States Surgeon General has indicated that there is no known risk of nonsexual infection in most situations we encounter in our daily lives.[62] However, even with these reassurances, some employees fear working with coworkers who are infected with AIDS. The fear may stem from the fact that employees know so little about AIDS, and what they do know is extremely frightening.

What most people do know is that there is no cure for AIDS. The majority of people who are HIV infected will die as nonlife threatening diseases attack their bodies that no longer have the ability to fight back. People know there are no vaccines to prevent AIDS and few drugs available to the general public that help fight the disease once it is contracted. Finally, people know that they do not want to contract AIDS.

This final fact has sometimes caused irrational behavior in some employees. When employees realize that they are working with an infected coworker, they sometimes issue an ultimatum: "Either he goes or we go and if we go, we'll go public." To some employers, this can be an extremely effective scare tactic. Few employers want to be faced with the empty tables, beds, or desks that may appear after the public learns that a chef, chambermaid, or engineer has AIDS.[63] What choice does the employer have? If the employee with AIDS is discharged, the law has been violated. If the other employees leave and make the situation public, the business could suffer irreparable damage.

The only choice available to employers is to prevent employees from acting irrationally, by educating employees about AIDS. Several guidelines must be followed if the educational program is going to be effective:

1. One goal of the program is to be certain that employees understand *how* AIDS is contracted. If they understand that the activities required to contract AIDS do not occur in their workplace, the irrational behavior should disappear.
2. Because the message presented is going to include sexual references, the presentation should be informed and professional so that the workers do not feel that management is "butting in where it does not belong." To achieve this goal, it may be necessary to hire an external expert to present the educational program.
3. Finally, it is imperative that *all* employees attend the sessions.[64]

If these guidelines are followed, employers may not be faced with ultimatums.

Fetal Protection in the Workplace

In 1982, Johnson Controls, a manufacturer of automobile batteries established an employment policy forbidding women between the ages of 18 and 70 from holding jobs in any of their sixteen battery producing plants nationwide.[65] The policy was enacted to protect unborn children from the lead that was found to be present at all battery manufacturing sites. The only way for a woman to gain employment in these units was to provide written medical evidence of infertility.[66]

In 1989, the United Auto Workers brought suit against Johnson Controls claiming that the fetal protection policy was discriminatory toward women seeking employment in this high-paying unit of the organization. In the court case, called by Judge Frank Easterbrook "the most important sex discrimination case in any court," the courts upheld the employer's decision barring fertile women employment in this division.[67] The courts found that fetal exposure to high levels of lead resulted in a variety of birth defects including retardation. In addition, the courts concluded that the fetal-protection policy met the requirements of a bona fide occupational qualification (BFOQ) by stating that ". . . Johnson Controls has demonstrated that its fetal protection policy is reasonably necessary to industrial safety."[68] In addition, the court rejected the claim that the harmful environment would have any impact on the reproductive abilities of males, even though medical reports show that wives of men employed in certain industries have unusually high rates of stillbirths, premature deliveries, underweight pregnancies, and children born with birth defects.[69]

The initial decision was appealed at various sites across the United States. In the Ninth Circuit Court in Chicago, the original decision was upheld, while the Seventh Circuit Court in California found that lead has an impact on both men and women.[70] Because of the confusion as to the legality of the organizational-based fetal protection policies, the Supreme Court of the United States was asked to provide the final interpretation.

In 1991, the Supreme Court ruled that employers may *not* bar women of child-bearing age due to possible fetal dangers.[71] The decision, by a vote of six to three, concluded that this policy represents a sex bias that has been outlawed by previous civil right laws. According to the court, women as capable of doing their jobs as male counterparts should not be forced to decide between having a job and having a child. The decision is currently under appeal.

To many, the controversy over this issue seems misplaced. Lead has been found to cause disease in *all* humans. Those who work with lead, regardless of sex, face a health and safety problem. Companies should focus on this problem and fix it, not the worker. As civil liberties lawyers argue, "If something made your spleen become infected at work, you wouldn't say, 'We'll only take workers who don't have spleens.' "[72]

WORKPLACE STRESS

What Is Stress?

Stress has been defined as the interaction between the individual and the environment characterized by physiological and psychological changes that cause a deviation from normal performance.[73] This deviation from normal may have a positive or negative outcome. A moderate amount of stress can help to stimulate employees to work longer, harder, and better. However, an extremely low level of stress can leave employees unstimulated resulting in low productivity while an extremely high level of stress can lead to poor performance due to increased energy being diverted away from production and on to dealing with the stress itself.

Stress has both an internal and an external factor. Internal factors are primarily a person's attitudes and expectations. Difficulty living up to these values may cause self-induced stress. External factors can be divided into two categories: physical and psychological factors. Physical stressors can include poor ventilation or lighting or physically demanding tasks. Examples of psychological stressors include demands of the job or demands from home.[74]

An increase in a person's stress level can result in several physical changes. These changes, often referred to as a stress response, include increased blood pressure, heart rate and respiration, an increased output of mental activity and gastric juices, and changes in the blood flow patterns. These changes can result in employee responses such as fatigue or anxiety.[75]

Causes of Stress

It is difficult to categorize stressors as high level or low level or to even list them because a situation which creates a high level of stress for one person may not cause any stress for another. Further, a person who views a situation as stressful one day may not view the same situation as stressful on another day. However, it is safe to say that every aspect of a person's life is a potential source of stress. Specifically, stress can come from pressures at work, at home, or because of personality traits.

....

| EXHIBIT 15.4 | Categorizations of Occupations |

Active jobs:	These jobs have a heavy pressure to perform, but provide leeway in problem solving. Hours may be long, but are partly at the worker's discretion. There are chances to advance and to learn new skills. Initiative is a big part of the job. Examples: farmers, doctors, engineers, executives, and other professionals.
Low-strain jobs:	These are the self-paced occupations. There are low demands from others and a high degree of decision freedom. What is done, in what order, and often at what pace is determined by the incumbent. Examples: tenured professors, carpenters, repairmen, or artists.
Passive jobs:	These jobs require a low degree of skills and mental-processing ability and have little leeway for learning or for making decisions. This type of job offers almost no latitude for innovation. Some jobs may actually cause workers' skills to decline. Examples: janitors, billing clerks, night watchmen, or data-entry operators.
High-strain jobs:	These jobs have a heavy pressure to perform, but provide no leeway in decision making. Hours and procedures are rigid and the threat of lay-offs is present. The jobs provide no opportunities to learn new skills. It is extremely difficult to take an unscheduled break or to take time off for personal reasons. Examples: assembly-line workers, telephone operators, or waiters/waitresses.

....

Work Pressures

The type of job you hold has a significant impact on the degree of stress you face at work. Some occupations have a great deal of stress associated with them while others are less stressful. Exhibit 15.4 lists a four-part categorization of occupations based upon the tasks associated with the job. Surprisingly, the high-strain jobs listed in Exhibit 15.4 are the jobs in which the highest levels of stress and stress-related diseases are reported. It appears that the bossed, not the bosses, are the ones who suffer the most from the effects of stress. It is these individuals who have little control, but high accountability. Employees who hold active jobs report the lowest levels of stress-related diseases, while the passive and low-strain employees fall in between. To determine how healthful your job is, take the quiz in Exhibit 15.5.

Another way in which the workplace can cause an employee stress is by living and working with the constant fear of being replaced. With the downturn in the economy in the late 1980s, companies began looking for ways to increase productivity and cut costs. Frequently this meant consolidating jobs and laying off employees. Even IBM, who was famous for its policy of lifetime employment, found itself in a position in which it had to lay off workers. Another type of consolidation that has been on the rise since the late 1980s is mergers and acquisitions. These types of activities also led to a reduction in the work force as the newly merged company found itself with two identical accounting or human resource departments. Yet another fear of workers is automation. Workers and managers alike know that one machine can do the jobs of many men, and never requires a coffee break.

The stress from the fear of being replaced or actually being replaced can cause severe reactions. In one Citibank unit in which 2,000 jobs were eliminated, two

....

EXHIBIT 15.5	How Healthful Is Your Job?

Place the number that best agrees with your feelings about each of the following statements with respect to your job in the blank before each statement. Total scores below 14 indicate a job that encourages good health, while total scores over 30 indicate a stress-inducing job.

Strongly Agree		Neither Agree Nor Disagree		Strongly Disagree
1	2	3	4	5

_____ My job requires me to make maximum use of my skills and offers me a chance to increase them.

_____ I am free from worker-as-child disciplines. I control the machines on which I work, I can participate in long-term planning, and I have flexible work hours.

_____ The demands placed on me are mixed. The changes made are challenging, but predictable. I have some input with respect to the magnitude of changes made.

_____ Collaboration on my job is encouraged.

_____ My workplace believes in the democratic process. I have an avenue to air and settle grievances.

_____ I know what it is I produce and why it is necessary. Customers provide me feedback so that I know how well I am performing.

_____ My job allows me time and energy for activities other than work.

....

employees killed themselves and the number of traffic accidents increased significantly.[76] In 1987, after Westinghouse Electric announced a restructuring and downsizing plan, employees were surveyed. Researchers found a higher than average prevalence of depression among white-collar workers induced by the stress of the impending changes.[77]

The ramifications of downsizing have begun to reach the employers as well. Studies have found that cutting jobs to save money actually increases costs. These costs come in the form of adding stress to the survivors. When the degree of stress felt by an employee reaches a point where he or she feels it has become debilitating, a lawsuit may be filed. Over the last ten years, stress disability cases have doubled and each case has cost the employer an average of $73,270.[78]

Home Stressors

Americans have seen some dramatic changes in the family structure over the last ten years. Single-parent families, which include fathers raising children, and dual-career couples, are becoming commonplace. These changes have made the conflict between parent-as-parent and parent-as-paid-employee an extremely deep source of stress and anxiety in the American family member today.[79]

Mothers frequently report stress induced by the guilt of not being a good parent when work pressures are high and not being a good employee when home pressures take priority. In a recent survey, 16 percent of the 3,000 working mothers surveyed reported they felt intense guilt about spending too little time with their children and spouses or not spending enough time on themselves. These were the mothers who reported little support at home and few work rewards.[80]

Fathers, too, have begun to wrestle with the pressures from both career and family. One survey of over 1,600 employees at a large public utility company indicated that almost as many men as women (36 percent versus 37 percent) reported feeling "a lot of stress" in balancing their work and family lives.[81] A separate survey of over 1,200 employees at a Minneapolis company found that more than 70 percent of the fathers under the age of 35 had serious concerns about problems they were having managing work and family conflicts with their spouses. Over 60 percent of the male respondents reported that family concerns were affecting their work goals and plans. Many indicated that they were not seeking promotions or transfers because they needed to spend more time with their families.[82]

Research also suggests that women may be better able to handle the stress of both family and career. Researchers, who had 166 couples in Detroit keep diaries of when they felt extreme pressure from both work and home or when they had arguments, found that men, not women, reported more incidents. Evidence also showed that men were more likely to have work problems spill over into family time and vice versa than women. Researchers suggested that differences in upbringing and role expectations have made women better able to handle family/work stress.[83]

Personality

Individuals who have what has been referred to as a "Type A personality," hard-driving workaholics, have long been thought to be prime candidates for heart problems.[84] The reason behind this is that Type As have a strong bodily reaction to stressful situations. Their heart rate and blood pressure rise, causing increased blood flow to their muscles. This change in their systems, when repeated over and over throughout their lives, can place severe strain on their heart and eventually cause damage.

Other personality characteristics can lead to increased stress as well. Researchers have found that certain personal characteristics draw certain individuals to specific jobs. These jobs, in turn, tend to cause stress in the people they attract. For example, clergy, who often have a distorted view of "selflessness," tend to have extremely high levels of stress that may eventually lead to burnout because they ignore their own needs and give too much of themselves to others.[85] Other examples of jobs and the people who are attracted to them are presented in Exhibit 15.6. As you read through the lists, see if your personality has drawn you to a specific career.

Consequences and Expense of Job Stress

Stress can cause physical and emotional problems for people who suffer from excess stress. The most frequent disorders range from chronic fatigue to depression brought on by insomnia, anxiety, migraine, emotional upsets, stomach ulcers, allergies, skin disorders, lumbago and rheumatic attacks, high blood pressure, tobacco and alcohol abuse, overeating, family abuse, cynicism, distrust, and even colds. In severe cases, the end results can even be death from heart attacks, accidents, or suicide.[86]

All of the medical complications associated with stress are an ever increasing burden on the medical costs for companies. Some experts have estimated the overall cost for many large corporations at over $200 million a year for employee medical benefits. This figure rises to over $150 billion a year when the costs to the overall

....

EXHIBIT 15.6 Jobs to Which Certain Personalities Are Drawn

JOB TITLE	PERSONALITY TRAITS	OUTCOME
Police	Courage, penchant for action	Stress from never admitting fear causes strain
Lawyers	Love to give advice	Stress from fear of giving poor advice
Teachers	Need to have rules and procedures to follow	Fear confronting authority and may place themselves in jeopardy for following some imposed rules
Dentists	Exacting personalities	Patients and staff who are not as exact frustrate them and cause stress
Government workers	Simply, people who don't like to cause problems or draw attention to themselves	Having their passive behavior rewarded tends to turn them into lethargic, automated individuals
Computer programmers	Love to play with machines	Find people difficult to control and predict causing them stress when having to deal with people
Managers	Seek stability	As companies begin to downsize even the once stable ranks of management, instability is causing stress
Actors	Low self-esteem	After becoming successful, actors, who had hoped for an increase in self-esteem find themselves asking, "Is this all?"
Politicians	Lack of reality	Some begin to believe the commercials made about them and are stressed when they realize they are not that image
Physicians	Need to help others and save the world	When doctors lose patients, they face a great deal of stress
Therapists	Want to know what makes people tick	Difficult to stop analyzing people puts a strain on their interpersonal relations
Air traffic controllers	Quick thinkers	Ambiguity in human relationships does not allow them to analyze situations and make quick decisions

....

economy, caused by repercussions of stress, such as reduced production due to ill, absent, or non-motivated employees, are factored in.[87]

Additional costs in the form of court-awarded settlements also are beginning to grow. Americans filed a record number of stress-related workers' compensation claims in 1987 accounting for 14 percent of all occupational-disease claims. This is an increase of 9 percent since 1980. The cases recorded range from a female deputy sheriff who sued because her personality was not suited for police work and having to perform such work caused her to have a chronic psychiatric disability to a furniture rental manager who claimed her stress was induced by a hostile supervisor who

FOCUS ON INTERNATIONAL ISSUES •

High-Tech Stress Therapy

The Japanese are known for their ability to excel at innovative product development and for the long hours they spend at work, well above our 40-hour standard. It should come as no surprise that the latest solution to the stress created in everyday Japanese life is a high-technology Brain Mind Gym.

Here, Japanese workers go for a mental massage that helps them relax. Comfortable chairs, soothing music, herbal tea, and pastoral scenes shown on television monitors all combine to set the mood for relaxation. Special goggles shoot light patterns through the client's closed eyelids. The environment is thought to allow complete relaxation, something very rare and valued by the hard-working Japanese who often suffer from high levels of stress and fatigue. In fact, a recent

newspaper survey in Japan found that almost 90 percent of the surveyed workers said they feel chronic fatigue, and most took no more than half of their allowed vacation time.

The Brain Mind Gym boasts 800 members and has only been in business for three years. Most clients are men between the ages of 25 and 35, seeking relief from everyday stress. Although more traditional methods of relaxation are still popular in Japan (such as yoga, health clubs, and drinking with friends), this high-technology answer to the stress of a demanding lifestyle is gaining in popularity.

SOURCE: Adapted from "Japanese Are Hard at Work Finding Ways to Relieve Stress," *Tallahassee Democrat*, September 9, 1991, p. 6A.

blamed her for everything from a dead cricket on the floor to another store's long-distance phone bill.[88]

Stress Reduction Techniques

In an effort to reduce their costs, companies have begun implementing stress reduction or control programs for their employees. These programs come in a variety of forms, depending upon the needs of the employees. Commonly found programs include discussion groups, stress education classes, relaxation techniques, time management programs, physical fitness programs, weight-loss clinics, drug and alcohol rehabilitation clinics, family counseling, hobbies, sports, and goal-setting classes.

Some firms have taken an even more innovative approach. H. J. Heinz Company in Pittsburgh is one of these companies. Overworked and stressed-out employees at H. J. Heinz can look forward to a fifteen minute massage in the director's lounge. With the lights dimmed and jazz piano music playing softly in the background, Sabina Vidunas, the masseuse gently kneads the tightly knotted necks and shoulders of fully-dressed employees sitting in a massage chair. A massage chair, a padded easel-looking apparatus, is used so that customers can lean forward and rest their chest and face on padding, taking the pressure off of their neck and shoulders.[89] The Japanese have taken the idea of a massage one step further and developed the Brain Mind Gym where over-stressed Japanese workers can go for a high-tech mental massage. See the box titled "High-Tech Stress Therapy" for a description of this technological innovation.

Other companies have invested in programs directed at reducing problems caused by workers who are overstressed. For example, fear of quality control slips by overworked or overstressed employees made Boeing step up its training. Before placing its employees on the assembly line, workers at the Everett, Washington, plant take blueprint reading classes and practice riveting and drilling techniques. Boeing also conducts preemployment training for serious job candidates at local vocational and technical schools.[90]

Stress in one's life is virtually unavoidable. For those who are not lucky enough to have a stress reduction program available to them, or for those who are between programs, a few techniques are available to help oneself.

1. List items that cause you stress. Isolate the ones you can fix and concentrate your time and effort on these. Avoid the ones that you can do nothing about.
2. We all need to take pride in our accomplishments and receive praise from others. If your job does not provide for these needs, find an activity that does.
3. Experiment with different forms of relaxation, such as exercise, sports, or meditation, until you find one that relieves your anxiety.
4. Remember that a sense of control and a reason to live leads to a healthy and productive life.[91]

STRATEGIES FOR IMPROVING HEALTH AND SAFETY

Managers have the extremely important role of providing a safe and healthful environment for their employees. The opportunities available for doing this have become more and more varied over time. Two of the most important health programs currently are fitness plans and drug testing and rehabilitation.

Fitness Programs

The number of health and fitness programs sponsored by corporations has increased over the past few years and continues to climb. A 1986 survey of the 1,500 largest firms in the United States found that more than 32 percent had established health-promotion policies and objectives. Over 40 percent offered or paid for programs to help workers quit smoking, nearly 40 percent sponsored stress management courses, 27 percent provided back-care programs, and more than 28 percent provided physical fitness centers either on or off the premises.[92]

Perhaps one reason for these increases is that fact that health promotion has proven to be a cost-effective organizational strategy. Each dollar invested in workplace health education can yield $1.42 over two years in lower absentee costs. Some companies have reported absences from illness dropping by as much as 15 percent.[93] Other studies have found that the difference in the productivity of participants and nonparticipants in organization-sponsored health programs was valued at over $1 million.[94]

The key to building an effective organizational fitness program is to follow some basic rules. First, remember that employees must see something in it for them or their family. If employees see it as just another cost-cutting ploy, they will not be responsive to it. To make it appeal to employees, offer incentives and rewards. Second, it must appeal to all employees, so make sure the program is varied and fun. If in doubt about what the employees want, ask them. Finally, do not have a workplace environment that contradicts your goals. Some examples include banning smoking in the workplace, providing nutritional meal alternatives in the cafeteria, and sponsoring fun runs and not bake sales.[95]

Companies that have followed these guidelines have reported great success. One of the most impressive was introduced by Mesa Limited Partnership, a holding company in Amarillo, Texas, headed by T. Boone Pickens. The first phase of the program is a computerized health-risk appraisal. All participants are eligible to receive up to $240 annually for participating. They must complete a written test, and submit to a glucose, cholesterol, and blood pressure screening. Results from these tests are used in phase 2: goal setting for weight loss or weight control, strength improvement, and general health maintenance. In order to get employees to participate in phase 2, more monetary incentives are provided. Employees can receive up to $916 a year for participating. For example, an employee may receive $36 for exercising three times a week. An additional $216 can be earned if a spouse participates. In total, Mesa has paid $115,000 in bonuses to employees, but has more than earned it back in lower health-care costs. Mesa estimates that the health-care costs for employees who did not participate averaged $434 per person as compared to only $173 for participants. The differences in these figures equates to about a $200,000 a year savings companywide.[96]

Drug Testing and Rehabilitation

One area of employee safety and health that continues to evolve is drug testing. In 1988, President Reagan issued Executive Order 12564 in order to establish a drug-free workplace in the federal government. This order established a drug testing program for federal workers. Also in 1988, Congress passed the Drug Free Workplace Act to abolish drug use among employees within an organization that works directly with the federal government.[97]

The Drug Free Workplace Act states that employers must notify their employees of drug-free workplace requirements, outline actions that will be taken against employees who violate the requirements, and establish awareness programs that include supervisory staff training in identifying drug abuse.[98] However, as organizations begin to implement these requirements, they must be mindful of not violating the rights guaranteed their employees under the Fourth Amendment, specifically, the right to be free of illegal search and seizures.

Although only contractors who are awarded government contracts over $25,000 are required to comply with the act, many other businesses have begun implementing drug testing programs. Exhibit 15.7 outlines the industries in which drug testing is prevalent. A recent survey by the American Management Association found that 63 percent of the firms surveyed use drug testing. This figure represents an increase from 51.5 percent reported in a survey the previous year. While only one-third of the companies surveyed say they fire workers who test positive, 96 percent indicated that they refuse to hire applicants who test positive.[99]

While one would expect employees to hold a negative view concerning drug testing in the workplace, at least one survey has found the opposite to be true. An attitude survey of the Anchorage Telephone Utility indicated that employees actually held a more favorable view than expected. Employees indicated that although they felt drug testing was an invasion of their privacy, they did not feel that it was unreasonable. However, they also indicated that all levels in the organization should be required to participate if a drug testing program is enforced.[100]

Other people hold a less favorable view of drug testing, especially if it is used as a deterrent for use. Ray Richardson, who held a $3-million contract with the New Jersey Nets, was informed that he would be banished from the National Basketball Association if he tested positive for drugs once more. In 1986, Richardson tested positive once more, and was expelled from the NBA. His agent at the time, who

| EXHIBIT 15.7 | Industries in Which Drug Testing Is Used |

INDUSTRY	TOTAL TESTED IN THOUSANDS	PERCENT WHO TESTED POSITIVE
Mining	72.0	12.7
Construction	326.6	11.9
Durable goods manufacturing	767.6	11.2
Nondurable goods manufacturing	1106.5	12.7
Transportation	451.8	9.9
Communications, utilities	143.5	5.5
Wholesale trade	260.5	17.4
Retail trade	169.7	24.4
Finance, insurance, and real estate	308.4	6.7
Other services	306.2	9.9
Total	3913.7	11.9

went on to become the director of the NBA, indicated that he began to doubt the deterrent power of drug testing in the NBA if a person can say yes to drugs and no to $3 million dollars.[101]

One positive outcome of the drug testing issue is the continued development of Employee Assistance Programs (EAPs) to help employees who are found to be using drugs. One of the requirements of the Drug Free Workplace Act is that employees who are convicted of drug usage must be required to satisfactorily complete a rehabilitation program. Many organizations are taking it upon themselves to pay for or offer these programs to their employees because they are finding that EAPs may be more helpful in curbing drug abuse that drug testing.[102]

EAPs are company-sponsored programs designed to help employees whose personal problems have an adverse impact on their job performance. These programs may be administered in-house or through outside organizations. EAPs can be designed to help employees with a variety of personal problems, ranging from alcohol and drug abuse to marital problems, financial concerns, and stress.[103] EAPs have been found to save employers $17 for every $1 spent on the program.[104]

While these programs are generally designed to help employees, the employers reap advantages as well. Early intervention in chemical dependency can save the organization a great deal. Medical care utilization by a drug using employee can be cut by up to 69 percent, sick days can be reduced by 47 percent, and reduced accident benefits can be reduced by as much as 48 percent if the drug abuse is caught early enough. Alcohol rehabilitation has a better success rate than drug abuse. If one defines success as not having a drink one year after treatment, 40 to 50 percent of those who complete the program would be deemed successful. One way to help the employee ensure a successful recovery is to require follow-up treatment after the initial rehabilitation. IBM requires employees who have completed a drug rehabilitation program to participate in medical monitoring for a minimum of one year as a way to increase their chances of remaining drug free. If they relapse, IBM may

---

EXHIBIT 15.8 Tips for Implementing a Safety Program That Works

1. Avoid asking workers to "Do as I say, not as I do." Managers and supervisors must serve as role models for the safety program. If workers see their supervisors performing jobs in an unsafe manner, they feel they have every right to do so too. It is the manager's responsibility to perform the job exactly as outlined by the safety program.

2. Avoid having a "participatory facade." Asking for employee suggestions for improving workplace safety will only be effective if the suggestions are implemented in a timely fashion. If the ideas provided by workers are ignored or implementation is postponed, when they are eventually implemented, the workers will not be motivated to support them.

3. Avoid the problem of workers feeling that "If I'm not in on it, I'm not up on it," by allowing workers at all levels to participate in the development of the safety program. If workers or managers feel that the program is being pushed down their throats without concern for their feelings, they will not be motivated to abide by the rules.

4. Workers will want to know "what's in it for me." While the company is sure to benefit from increased safety through reduced medical and insurance costs, workers may not see a personal advantage to abiding by the new safety plan. Including an incentive for workers often reverses this trend and increases compliance. However, be sure that the incentive is awarded frequently and as soon after good compliant behavior occurs in order to tie the reward to the behavior you want to see repeated.

---

terminate them or, if they appear to have a sincere interest in seeking immediate help, they may be retained.[105]

On the surface, EAPs appear to be a win–win solution to a severe problem. They are a cost-effective way for organizations to provide help for employees who really need it. However, are EAPs really effective in helping employees overcome their problems? With respect to the effectiveness of EAPs as a drug intervention program, the answer to this question would be "fairly effective." Research has found that 26.1 percent of the programs rated were only fairly effective, 37 percent were rated as having limited effectiveness, 10.7 percent were rated not very effective, the effectiveness of 17.7 percent was uncertain, and only 8.4 percent were rated as very effective.[106]

Whether or not a program is deemed effective depends upon your definition of success. Overall, drug rehabilitation success has not been high. Some firms feel they are very successful if they can keep 20 to 30 percent of their members off drugs.

Safety Programs That Work

In order for a safety program to be effective, it must be followed. All too often a program is implemented and ignored. There are various reasons why some programs work and others do not. Exhibit 15.8 provides tips for implementing safety programs that work. One of the most important items in this list is that workers must be aware that it is to their advantage, not just for the company's benefit, if they adhere to the safety plan. This has been referred to the "What's in it for me?" problem.

Luitink Manufacturing Company of Menomonee Falls, Wisconsin, implemented a safety program that overcame this problem: a lottery. Workers who have not had accidents in one month receive a ticket. The ticket holders are then eligible for a jackpot, which is awarded every three months. The jackpot starts at $250 and is reduced by $50 for every accident. By the end of the year, employees may be eligible to win jackpots ranging from $1,000 to $250 depending upon the total number of accidents companywide. If more than 12 accidents occurred during the year, no awards are provided. The program cut the rate of accidents from 20 in 1987 to 4 in 1988. Company officials indicated that if the accident rate continues at the new lower level, the company will save about $40,000 in insurance premiums over a three-year period.[107]

A second successful safety program was introduced by the Coca-Cola Company. Entitled "Back to Work," the program is aimed at the employees who are required to load and lift the company's products. Before starting the program, employees' backs were examined for strength and overall condition. Employees were then required to attend workshops designed to show how to prevent injury and how to develop a safe exercise routine. Because exercise is one of the best deterrents to back injury, the program incorporated exercise into their daily work routine. The first few minutes of each morning are spent doing exercises that prepare them to perform their jobs. Since the start of the program, the company has reduced back injuries by an average of 32 percent and slashed the number of lost work days by 78 percent.[108]

It is apparent that more and more successful safety programs will emerge as companies realize that good safety is good business. Companies such as DuPont, who abandoned safety for productivity and quality a few years ago, are now back to emphasizing both safety and productivity after realizing that the two concepts are actually Siamese twins. Kodak also found that safety fit nicely with its overall theme of quality leadership because safety programs boosted morale and output and strengthened public relations.[109] These hidden benefits of a safe working environment will guide the development of safer workplaces for all.

The Cost of Insurance for Small Companies

Health-care insurance has become a nightmare for thousands of small businesses due to soaring premiums. One manager of a welding firm with eight employees was forced to drop the insurance plan for employees when the insurance company raised their premium by 214 percent. Other small businesses are faced with the same problem. One manager was required to pay $105 a month to insure a worker who was paid $5 an hour. The $105 coverage did not include maternity coverage or office visits and required a $500 deductible. Prices like these have caused the number of uninsured workers in companies of less than 25 employees to increase from 23 percent to 24.4 percent in just one year. While the percentage increase may seem small, the actual number of employees who lost their insurance coverage may be as high as 1 million.[110]

While there is no immediate remedy for this problem in sight, small businesses can take several steps to reduce their insurance costs. First, companies can become involved in insurance pools designed specifically for small businesses. Some states (for example, Connecticut, Maine, Florida, and New Jersey) are creating insurance pools for small companies. This will provide for lower premiums for participating firms because the monetary foundation is larger and the risk of an expensive claim is reduced. Some larger insurance companies are also providing small-group risk pools designed to cover small business insurance needs. However, in order to qualify, there must be four low-risk employees for every one high-risk employee enrolled.[111]

Another alternative is called partnering, or direct contracting with health-care providers. The major building blocks of partnering include long-term exclusive contracts between employers and health-care providers, promoting a healthy workplace through maintenance and wellness programs, risks and rewards shared among the providers, employers, and employees, and communication among all of the participants. This alternative is available to small businesses who ban together to form coalitions.[112]

A final alternative, which may not be available in the immediate future, is government help. The national health insurance issue, which would require all employers to offer minimum coverage through a private insurance plan, is virtually dead due to the strong opposition from small companies. However, with the ever increasing costs of insurance coverage small businesses face, the resistance to government intervention has begun to wear down. In a 1989 survey, over 49 percent of the small business surveyed wanted national health care. This was up from only 39 percent a year before. It is hoped that a compromise can be developed by Congress that will be acceptable to both large and small businesses.[113]

• • • • • • • • •

MANAGEMENT GUIDELINES

The following guidelines represent many of the important elements that organizations need to include as part of an effective safety program. Management must give employee safety and well-being serious consideration and ensure that these issues never be neglected or ignored. An effective safety program can help ensure that the strategic plan, goals, and objectives of the company are realized.

1. Employee safety and health programs should be a major priority for management because they save lives, increase productivity, and reduce costs. These health and safety programs should stress employee involvement, continued monitoring, and an overall wellness component.

2. Jobs employees currently perform should be examined in an effort to locate the ones that may present a potential health or safety problem for employees. Steps should be taken to eliminate these problems.

3. It is important to be aware of the health risks that production may cause workers. All sources of workplace chemicals or other health concerns should be recorded and all employees be made aware of these records.

4. Safe-handling procedures for harmful substances should be developed and employees should be trained in these procedures.

5. Employee Assistance Programs should be developed to help employees deal with emotional, physical, or other problems caused by their employment.

6. Jobs should be analyzed for potential sources of stress and redesigned to eliminate these pressures.

7. Employers should strive to meet and surpass the health and safety guidelines imposed by OSHA. Frequent and continual updating of procedures may be necessary in order to remain in compliance.

8. If you decide to offer a fitness or wellness program to your employees be sure that it is something they will want to use and make it easy for them to participate. Offering incentives to participate may also be useful.

9. AIDS informational campaigns in your organization should focus on reducing the fear of workers about AIDS through education about the disease.

10. As court decisions continue to change and redefine the rules in the workplace, it is imperative that human resource managers are up-to-date with respect to the rules and regulations governing their industry. Providing educational incentives for these managers will help them achieve this goal.

QUESTIONS FOR REVIEW

1. When and why was the Occupational Safety and Health Act passed? Describe some of the provisions of this act.

2. What are two of the current safety and health problems facing American businesses today?

3. If asked to design an employee health and safety program that would help to eliminate accidents in the workplace, what would your plan include?

4. What is the relationship between job stress and productivity?

5. How can employers reduce job stress?

6. What are some techniques that employers can use to ensure that employees participate in fitness or wellness programs?

7. Why is it important for organizations to provide informational programs about AIDS?

8. Fetal protection policies have almost always been directed at female workers. Why is this? Why is it not important to protect potential fathers from chemicals that may harm their potential children?

9. What are some of the tips managers should be aware of when developing safety programs that work?

10. If an organization makes a strategic decision to stress employee health and well-being, what are some of the potential advantages of adopting this strategy?

CASE: Safety in the Workplace—Whose Responsibility Is It?[114]

"On this site, 146 workers lost their lives in the Triangle Shirtwaist Co. fire on March 26, 1911. Out of their martyrdom came new concepts of social responsibility and labor legislation that have helped make American working conditions the finest in the world."

The above quotation appears on a plaque commemorating the 146 people who died in the fires at Triangle Shirtwaist Company. The majority of those who died were low-paid young women who were trapped inside the building. Management at Triangle routinely kept doors locked to prevent employees from stealing. Although Triangle had four major fires in the nine years prior to the 1911 blaze, they failed to prepare their workers for such a crisis (for example, no fire drills were conducted).

The Triangle fire was a landmark incident that led to legislation requiring companies to install sprinkler systems, have wider exits, unlock doors, and conduct regular fire drills. This incident, along with other workplace accidents, focused attention on the need for employers to provide a safe and healthful work environment for their workers and eventually led to the creation of the Occupational Safety and Health Administration (OSHA).

However, a recent accident has called into question the effectiveness of health and safety regulations in the workplace. Despite efforts to improve working conditions, has significant improvement been made over the last 80 years?

Fire at Imperial Food Products Plant

September 3, 1991, started out as a typical work day for workers at the Imperial Foods Products plant in Hamlet, North Carolina. Workers arrived to work on Tuesday morning and began preparing for the day. No one had any reason to suspect that this day would be any different from any other. At 8:30 A.M., however, an event took place that would change the lives of each and every worker at Imperial; a fryer at Imperial's chicken processing plant caught fire leaving 25 workers dead, over 40 injured, and countless grieving. Although workers were heard banging on doors screaming "Let me out!" witnesses outside were unable to open the locked doors. Just as at Triangle, management at the Imperial plant also routinely kept doors locked to prevent employees from stealing. In addition to locked doors, one of the exits was blocked by a delivery truck, and workers had to wait for it to be moved.

Safety in the Workplace

With the exception of those who work under extremely hazardous conditions, most of us rarely think about safety in the workplace. We assume that the company will provide a safe working environment and that officials at OSHA will ensure that the company is not in violation of safety regulations. Unfortunate and tragic accidents at the workplace, however, remind us that the idealistic situation presented above is not always in accord with the realistic situation.

In 1970, OSHA began requiring employers to keep exit doors clear so they can serve as escape hatches. Why then, was Imperial placing its employees at risk by keeping exits locked on a continual basis in an environment where fires have posed a threat in the past? Similar to Triangle, Imperial had three fires in the last eleven years, and they also did nothing to prepare their workers for such a crisis, such as conduct fire drills. Federal laws allow states to set up their own regulatory agencies, and although OSHA is responsible for monitoring these state programs, they rarely ever enforce safety regulations in the 23 states that currently have their own programs.

State Programs

North Carolina is one of the 23 states responsible for performing their own inspections and fining those in violation. Imperial Foods, however, had never been inspected in its eleven years of operations, which is not surprising considering North Carolina's state legislature has cut the safety budget by 40 percent over the last decade. North Carolina has only 27 inspectors and trainees to patrol over 180,000 employers.

Whereas not every state program is so lax in enforcement, many are less than rigorous in their effort to protect workers on the job. It is often the business community itself who pushes for state-run programs in an effort to "keep the monkey off their backs" and to reduce costly fines that may be imposed on them by the federal government. North Carolina, for example, fined Perdue Farms, another poultry processing plant, $39,000 for exposing workers to repetitive motion injuries in two plants; whereas, Cargill, Inc., was fined by OSHA to the tune of $1 million for similar violations at plants in Georgia and Missouri. This is an indication of why companies may prefer to be out from under OSHA's thumb and why they may prefer to keep the control at the state level.

What Now?

The incident in North Carolina has prompted renewed interest in health and safety in the workplace. Should states be allowed to run their own safety and health programs? Should OSHA take a more active role in monitoring state programs? Should employees have more say in the safety of the working conditions? Although any new legislation will not make restitution for those who lost their lives in the fires at both Triangle and Imperial, it may serve to prevent similar accidents from occurring in the future.

An important footnote to this case came on Monday, March 9, 1992, when three management officials of the Imperial Foods plant were indicted on charges of involuntary manslaughter. Families of those killed in the fire filed criminal charges against the managers who allowed the safety violations to occur. This development raises the costs of willfully violating safety standards to a new level.

QUESTIONS

1. How true is the opening quotation in this case today, given all of the workplace hazards presented in this chapter? What can be done at any and all levels to make this quotation true?

2. Would a state inspection of the Imperial Foods plant have prevented this accident? Why or why not? What could have been done to prevent it?

3. The case mentions fines imposed by OSHA and the state for exposing workers to CTD. Do you think the differences in the size of the fines caused the companies to react differently to them? Why or why not?

4. How appropriate do you think it is for states to have control over the safety of the workplace? Devise a state plan that would allow for effective policing of workplace safety. Why hasn't your plan been implemented?

· · · · · · · · · · · · · · · ·
ADDITIONAL READINGS

Backer, T. E. *Strategic Planning for Workplace Drug-abuse Programs.* Rockville, MD: National Institute on Drug Abuse, 1987.

Baker, T. L. "Preventing Drug Abuse at Work." *Personnel Administrator.* July 1989, pp. 56–59.

Cooper, C. L., and R. Payne. *Causes, Coping and Consequences of Stress at Work.* Somerset, NJ: John Wiley & Sons, 1988.

Cooper, C. L. and M. Smith. *Job Stress and Blue Collar Work.* Somerset, NJ: John Wiley & Sons, 1986.

Cox, W. N. *Employee Relations, Occupational Safety and Health, and Product Liability: A Handbook for Business.* Holland, MI: CR & Associates, 1988.

DeCarlo, D. T., and D. H. Gruenfeld. *Stress in the American Workplace—Alternatives for the Working Wounded.* Washington, PA: LRP Publications, 1989.

DeCresce, R. P., M. S. Lifshitz, A. C. Mazura, and J. E. Tilson. *Drug Testing in the Workplace.* Chicago, IL: ASCAP Press, 1989.

Denenberg, T. S., and R. V. Denenberg. *Alcohol and Drugs: Issues in the Workplace.* Washington, DC: BNA, 1983.

Fassel, D. *Working Ourselves to Death: The High Cost of Workaholism and the Rewards of Recovery.* San Francisco: Harper, 1990.

Frances, R. J., and J. E. Franklin. *Concise Guide to Treatment of Alcoholism and Addictions.* American Psychiatric Press, Inc., 1989.

Garrett, J., L. Cralley and L. Cralley. *Industrial Hygiene Management.* Somerset, NJ: John Wiley & Sons, 1988.

Golembiewski, R. T., and R. F. Munzenrider. *Phases of Burnout: Developments in the Concepts and Applications.* New York: Praeger Press, 1988.

Hartstein, B. A. "Drug Testing in the Workplace: A Primer for Employers." *Employee Relations Law Journal.* Spring 1987.

Klarreich, S. H. *Health and Fitness in the Workplace: Health Education in Business Organizations.* New York: Praeger Press, 1987.

Kupfer, A. "Is Drug Testing Good or Bad?" *Fortune.* December 1988, pp. 133–140.

Miletich, J. J. *Work and Alcohol Abuse: An Annotated Bibliography.* Westport, CT: Greenwood Press, 1987.

Mintz, B. M. *OSHA: History, Law, and Policy.* Washington, DC: BNA, 1984.

Murphy, L. R., and T. F. Schoenborn. *Stress Management in Work Settings.* New York: Praeger Publishers, 1989.

Nogay, B. *The New Drug-free Workplace Act: The Complete Guide for Federal Contractors and Grantees.* Washington, DC: BNA, 1989.

Pritchard, R. E., and G. C. Potter. *Fitness Inc: A Guide to Corporate Health and Wellness Programs.* Homewood, IL: Dow Jones-Irwin Books, 1990.

Quick, J. C., R. S. Bhagat, J. E. Dalton, and J. D. Quick. *Work Stress: Health Care Systems in the Workplace.* New York: Praeger Publishers, 1987.

Riley, A. W., and S. J. Zaccaro. *Occupational Stress and Organizational Effectiveness.* New York: Praeger Press, 1987.

Rumpel, D. A. "Motivating Alcoholic Workers to Seek Help." *Management Review.* July 1989, pp. 37–39.

Salvendy, G. *Handbook of Human Factors.* Somerset, NJ: John Wiley & Sons, 1987.

Segal, J. A. "How Reasonable Is Your Suspicion?" *Personnel Administrator.* December 1989, pp. 103–104.

Sethi, A. S., D. Caro, and R. S. Schuler. *Strategic Management of Technostress in an Information Society.* Lewiston, NY: Hogrefe & Huber Publishers, 1987.

Sloan, R. P., J. C. Gruman, and J. P. Allegrante. *Investing in Employee Health: A Guide to Effective Health Promotion in the Workplace.* San Francisco: Jossey-Bass, 1987.

Slothe, L. *Handbook of Occupational Safety and Health.* Somerset, NJ: John Wiley & Sons.

Smith, C. C. *Recovery at Work: A Clean and Sober Career Guide.* San Francisco: Harper Collins Publishers, 1990.

Smits, S. J., L. D. Pace, and W. J. Perryman. "EAPS Are Big Business," *Personnel Journal.* June 1989, pp. 96–106.

Speller, J. L. *Executives in Crisis: Recognizing and Managing the Alcoholic Drug-Addicted, or Mentally Ill Executive.* San Francisco: Jossey-Bass, 1989.

Timmins, W. M., and C. B. Timmins. *Smoking in the Workplace: Issues and Answers for Human Resource Professional.* Westport, CT: Greenwood Press, 1989.

Wadden, R. A., and P. A. Scheff. *Indoor Air Pollution: Characterization, Prediction, and Control.* Somerset, NJ: John Wiley & Sons, 1982.

Withers, J. *Major Industrial Hazards: Their Appraisal and Control.* Somerset, NJ: John Wiley & Sons, 1988.

···················
NOTES

1. Stanley Kalin, "The Ubiquitous Nip Point: The Booby Trap of Industry," *Experts-at-Law,* September–October 1990, pp. 39–42.

2. S. A. Joure et al., "Stress: The Pressure Cooker of Work," *Personnel Administrator,* March 1989, pp. 92–95.

3. "Labor Letter," *Wall Street Journal,* April 14, 1987, p. 1; K. Shinew and J. Crossly, "A Comparison of Employee Recreation and Fitness Program Benefits," *Employee Benefit Journal* 4, 1988, pp. 20–23; T. Callahan, "Adolph Coors Company," *Company Fitness and Recreation* 5(4), 1986, pp. 11–12; J. Hoffman and C. Hobson, "Physical Fitness and Employee Effectiveness," *Personnel Administrator* 29(4), 1986, pp. 101–114; and J. Jenkins, "Self-directed Work Force Promote Safety," *HRMagazine* 2, 1990, pp. 54–56.

4. "Contractor Sentenced under OSHA after Two Die," *American Society for Personnel Administration/Resource,* February 1989, p. 15.

5. C. Ansberry, "Nucor Steel's Sheen Is Marred by Deaths of Workers at Plants," *Wall Street Journal,* May 10, 1991, pp. A1 +.

6. The following dicussion is based on D. P. Twomey, *A Concise Guide to Employment Law EEO & OSHA* (Cincinnati: South-Western, 1986), pp. 109–134.

7. S. B. Garland, "A New Chief Has OSHA Growling Again," *Business Week,* August 20, 1990, p. 57.

8. Ibid.

9. Ibid.

10. A. D. Marcus, "Employers Can Face Charges for Endangering Workers," *Wall Street Journal,* October 17, 1990, p. B5.

11. S. Wermiel, "Justices Let States Prosecute Executives for Work Site Hazards Covered by OSHA," *Wall Street Journal,* October 3, 1989, p. A5.

12. S. B. Garland, "This Safety Ruling Could Be Hazardous to Employers' Health," *Business Week,* February 20, 1989, p. 34.

13. Marcus, "Employers Can Face Charges for Endangering Workers."

14. "Contractor Sentenced Under OSHA after Two Die," *American Society for Personnel Administration/Resource,* February 1989, p. 20.

15. A. R. Karr, D. D. Medina, and C. Solomon, "OSHA Seeks to Fine Phillips Petroleum $5.7 Million for 'Willful' Safety Breaches," *Wall Street Journal,* April 20, 1990, p. A4.

16. L. Thornburg, "Proposed OSHA Bills Set New Standards, Mandates." *Society for Human Resource Management/HRNews,* September 1991, A8.

17. Ibid.

18. Ibid.

19. "Study Finds Unions Affect OSHA Enforcement," *Society for Human Resource Management/HRNEWS/Legal Report,* March 1991, p. A11.

20. "Congress Hears Tale of Horror," *Tallahassee Democrat,* September 13, 1991, p. 4A.

21. S. Cohen, "Pain with the Paycheck," *Tallahassee Democrat,* November 12, 1989, pp. 1D +.

22. R. F. Bettendorf, "Curing the New Ills of Technology," *HRMagazine,* March 1990, p. 35.

23. M. Mallory, "An Invisible Workplace Hazard Gets Harder to Ignore," *Business Week,* January 30, 1989, pp. 92–93.

24. "Safety Measures for Users of Computers," *HRMagaizne,* July 1991, pp. 77–78.

25. D. Huntly, "Key Injuries Hurt Companies," *HRMagazine,* June 1990, pp. 72–75.

26. S. Overman and L. Thornburg, "Hidden Health Care Costs," *HRMagazine,* March 1992, pp. 48–53.

27. A. Gabor, "On-the-job Straining," *U.S. News & World Report,* May 21, 1990, pp. 51–53.

28. Mallory, "An Invisible Workplace Hazard."

29. J. S. Hirsch, "U.S. Diet Mixes Idulgence, Health, *Wall Street Journal,* December 6, 1989, p. B1.

30. Gabor, "On-the-job Straining," p. 51.

31. "OSHA hit John Morrell & Co. with Record $4.33 Million Fine," *American Society for Personnel Administration/Resource/Legal Report,* December 1988, p. 16.

32. Gabor, "On-the-job Straining," p. 51.

33. A. R. Karr, "Chrysler, UAW Agree to Fight Motion Injuries," *Wall Street Journal,* November 3, 1989, p. A4.

34. "Meatpacker Launches Model Safety Program," *The Miami Herald,* November 24, 1988, p. 22A.

35. Bettendorf, "Curing the New Ills of Technology," p. 36.

36. S. L. Jacob, "Small Business Slowly Wakes to OSHA Hazard Rule," *Wall Street Journal,* November 22, 1988, p. B2.

37. Ibid.

38. "OSHA Issues Hazard Compliance Kit," *American Society for Personnel Administration/Resource/Legal Report,* February 1989, p. 20.

39. Ibid.

40. A. D. Marcus, "In Some Workplaces, Ill Winds Blow," *Wall Street Journal,* October 9, 1989, p. B1.

41. Ibid.

42. Ibid.

43. "Smoking in the Workplace," *Society for Human Resource Management's HRNews,* September 1991, p. A8a.

44. "Smoking Employees Pose Cost Risks," *Communications,* September–October 1990, p. 1.

45. C. Pasternak, "High-cost Habit," *HRMagazine,* October 1990, p. 23.

46. C. Pasternak, "Totally Smoke-free," *HRMagazine,* February 1990, p. 21.

47. "It Doesn't Matter Much How You Quit Smoking," *Wall Street Journal,* November 28, 1989, p. B1.

48. D. Feinstein, "Labor Letter," *Wall Street Journal,* September, 26, 1989, p. A1.

49. The following discussion is based on C. F. Mitchell, and P. M. Barrett, "Trial and Error: Novel Effort to Settle Asbestos Claims Fails as Lawsuits Multiply," *Wall Street Journal,* June 7, 1988, p. A1 + .

50. S. Cohen, "Pain with the Paycheck," *Tallahassee Democrat,* November 12, 1989, p. D1.

51. Feinstein, "Labor Letter."

52. B. Ingersoll, "Perilous Profession: Farming Is Dangerous, but Fatalistic Farmers Oppose Safety Laws," *Wall Street Journal,* July 20, 1989, pp. A1 + .

53. Ibid.

54. Ibid.

55. G. Feinstein, "Labor Letter," *Wall Street Journal,* August 8, 1989, p. A1.

56. A. L. Otten, "People Patterns," *Wall Street Journal,* April 6, 1989, p. B1.

57. C. Ansberry, "Risky Business: Workplace Injuries Proliferate as Concerns Push People to Produce," *Wall Street Journal,* June 6, 1989, pp. A1 + .

58. Ibid.

59. "LA Takes on Safety and Health Challenge," *ILO Information,* October 1989, p. 2.

60. R. P. Hunter, "Workplace Violence: A Growing Trend," *Legal Report for the Society for Human Resource Management,* Summer 1990, p. 1.

61. T. J. Dilauro, "Relieving the Fear of Contagion," *Personnel Administrator,* February 1989, p. 52.

62. W. F. McHugh, "AIDS in the Workplace: Policy, Practice, and Procedure," *AIDS in the Workplace: Florida and Federal Legal Guidelines 1989,* December 1988, p. 39.

63. J. A. Segal, "AIDS Education Is a Necessary High-risk Activity," *HRMagazine,* February 1991, p. 82; and V. Alliton, "Financial Realities of AIDS in the Workplace," *HRMagazine,* February 1992, pp. 78–81.

64. Ibid.

65. "Fetal Protection Policies," *HRMagazine,* January 1991, pp. 81–82.

66. H. Simon, "Fetal Protection Policies after Johnson Controls: No Easy Answer," *Employee Relations Law Journal* 15, 1990, pp. 491–511.

67. C. Trost, "Businesses and Women Anxiously Watch Suit on 'Fetal Protection,' " *Wall Street Journal,* October 8, 1990, pp. A1 + .

68. R. Sand, "Current Developments in Health and Safety," *Employee Relations Law Journal* 16, 1990, pp. 99–106.

69. "Fetal Protection Policies," p. 82.

70. Simon, "Fetal Protection Policies after Johnson Controls," p. 493.

71. "Justices Bar 'Fetal Protection' Policy," *Wall Street Journal,* March 21, 1991, pp. A1 + .

72. "Fetal Protection Policies," p. 81.

73. J. D. Brodzinski, R. F Scherer, and K. A. Goyer, "Workplace Stress," *Personnel Administrator,* July 1989, pp. 76–80.

74. Ibid.

75. Ibid.

76. T. F. O'Boyle, "Fear and Stress in the Office Take Toll," *Wall Street Journal,* November 6, 1990, p. B1.

77. R. Winslow, "Workplace Turmoil Is Reflected in Depression Among Employees," *Wall Street Journal,* December 13, 1989, p. B1.

78. "Wrapup," *Washington Report* 13, June 1991, p. 4.

79. "Workplace Stress," *HRMagazine,* August 1991, pp. 75–76.

80. A. R. Karr, "Guilty or Innocent?" *Wall Street Journal,* May 14, 1991, p. A1.

81. C. Trost, "Men Too, Wrestle with Career-Family Stress," *Wall Street Journal,* November 1, 1988, p. B1.

82. Ibid.

83. A. L. Otter, "How Work, Home Stress Affects Working Couples," *Wall Street Journal,* February 22, 1991, p. B1.

84. S. A. Joure, et al., "Stress: The Pressure Cooker of Work," *Personnel Administrator,* March 1989, p. 92.

85. R. Sandroff, "Is Your Job Driving You Crazy?" *Psychology Today,* July–August 1989, pp. 41–45.

86. A. Bennett, "Is Your Job Making You Sick?" *The Wall Street Journal Reports,* April 22, 1988, p. 1; "Coming to Terms with Stress," *ILO Information,* February 1991, p. 1; M. Snider, "Stress May Be Something to Sneeze About," *USA Today,* August 29, 1991, p. 1A; and R. Winslow, "Study Uncovers New Evidence Linking Strain on the Job and High Blood Pressure," *Wall Street Journal,* April 11, 1990, p. B4.

87. A. Miller et al., "Stress on the Job," *Newsweek,* April 25, 1988, pp. 40–45.

88. Ibid.

89. J. S. Hirsch, "Doesn't Everyone Need to Be Kneaded Once in a While?" *Wall Street Journal,* October 17, 1989, p. A23.

90. M. Shao et al., "Trying Times at Boeing," *Business Week,* March 13, 1989, pp. 34–36.

91. D. Robinson, "Stressbusters," *Parade Magazine,* July 22, 1990, pp. 12 + .

92. P. N. Keaton, and M. J. Semb, "Shaping up the Bottom Line," *HRMagazine,* September 1990, pp. 81–86.

93. S. Feinstein, "Health Promotion Brings Dollar-and-cents Return, a Study Shows," *Wall Street Journal,* September 18, 1990, p. A1.

94. Keaton and Semb, "Shaping up the Bottom Line."

95. C. Garzona, "How to Get Employees behind Your Programs," *Personnel Administrator,* October 1989, pp. 60–62.

96. Keaton and Semb, "Shaping up the Bottom Line," p. 81.

97. S. Mazaroff, and J. P. Ayres, "Controlling Drug Abuse in the Workplace: The Legal Groundrules," *Human Resources Management Legal Report,* Spring 1989, p. 1.

98. Deming, J. "Drug-free Workplace Is Good Business," *HRMagazine,* April 1990, pp. 61–62.

99. "Drug Testing," *Wall Street Journal*, March 19, 1991, p. A1.

100. D. McGlothin, and T. Stimson, "Employees Hold Favorable View of Drug Testing," *Society for Human Resource Management/HRNews*, August 1991, p. 14.

101. D. Wessel, "Evidence Is Skimpy That Drug Testing Works, but Employers Embrace Practice," *Wall Street Journal*, September 7, 1989, p. B1.

102. A. Karr, "Labor Letter," *Wall Street Journal*, August 21, 1990, p. A1.

103. D. Gold and B. Unger, "Better Pregnancy Benefit Not Discriminating," *Society for Human Resource Management/HRNews*, January 1990, p. 7.

104. Deming, "Drug-free Workplace Is Good Business," p. 62.

105. S. Bergsman, "Help Employees Who Help Themselves," *HRMagazine*, April 1990, p. 48; J. Castelli, "Employer-provided Programs Pay Off," *HRMagazine*, April 1990, p. 57.

106. C. Pesternak, "HRM Update," *HRMagazine*, August 1990, p. 24.

107. "Safety First," *Inc.*, September 1989, p. 114.

108. M. N. Martinez, "Reduce Health Costs with Back-care Programs," *Society for Human Resource Management/HRNews*, September 1991, p. A12.

109. Labor Letter," *Wall Street Journal*, January 29, 1991, p. A1.

110. A. Bernstein, "Small Companies Are in Big Pain Over Health Care," *Business Week*, November 26, 1990, pp. 187–190.

111. Ibid.

112. C. F. Hendricks and G. L. McManis, "Partnering for Employee Health Care," *Personnel Administrator*, November 1989, pp. 32–37.

113. Bernstein, "Small Companies Are in Big Pain Over Health Care," p. 190.

114. Bill Bishop, "Those Who Died in the Plant Fire Are Waiting for Justice," *Tallahassee Democrat*, September 15, 1991, p. 3B; *Wall Street Journal*, September 4, 1991, p. A7; S. B. Garland, "What a Way to Watch Out for Workers," *Business Week*, September 23, 1991, p. 42; and "Three Indicted in Plant Fire," *Tallahassee Democrat*, March 10, 1992, p. 3A.

16 Ethics, Employee Rights, and Employer Responsibilities

Ethical behavior, employee rights, and employer responsibilities are all dynamic segments of the human resource management field. Important issues are always developing, and new issues emerge with a startling frequency. Organizations that do not pay attention to the latest developments in the ethics-rights-responsibility field are likely to face large lawsuits and many forms of hostile actions, from both employees and the government. We examine these and a number of other issues in this chapter, including discrimination, employment at will, privacy, and due process, to name only a few.

● ● ● ● ● ● ● ● ●
CHAPTER OBJECTIVES

After studying this chapter, you should be able to

1. Describe the strategic choices managers face with respect to ethical considerations, employee rights, and employer responsibilities.

2. Be familiar with the laws pertaining to employee rights.

3. Understand the ethical and legal responsibilities employers have to both their employees and the community at large.

4. Discuss how to manage a problem employee.

5. Delineate the characteristics of a good disciplinary climate.

CASE: I Believe in the Second Coming of Christ and Other Test Questions[1]

How would you feel if you were asked the following true/false questions as part of a job application test?

- I am very strongly attracted to members of my own sex.
- I believe in the second coming of Christ.
- I have no difficulty starting or holding my urine.

These questions are part of an ongoing battle over employee rights and the employer's need to know. They are just some of the over 700 questions that are part of a test routinely used by many organizations in the hiring process. The test helps evaluate an individual's personality characteristics, including honesty, motivation, and ambition. Sibi Soroka had to answer these questions as a candidate for a job as security guard with Minneapolis-based Target Stores. Soroka got the job, but felt these questions were too intrusive of his private life and did not reflect his qualifications as a security guard. Target has countered that the test is necessary to screen applicants for sensitive positions that may involve theft from the company. Soroka has challenged Target's right to use this test. It is now up to a federal court to decide the answer.

The controversy is part of a larger battle emerging over an employer's right to test its current and its potential employees. Testing can take many forms. These include personality tests, polygraph tests, drug tests, and even genetic tests. On a broader scale, the issue includes the employer's ability to obtain and use other kinds of supposedly confidential employee information such as medical records and credit histories. At stake is the very question of employee's privacy and an employer's need to know about its employees.

In recent years, organizations have come under increasing pressure to hire employees with escalating amounts of scrutiny. Organizations that hire carelessly, or those exhibiting negligent hiring practices, are often the targets of massive lawsuits when these employees make errors or commit crimes. Examples include the possibility that Federal Express might be judged liable for an employee who stole merchandise from a client's store if it cannot prove that it was not negligent in the hiring process and the wave of lawsuits filed against Northwest Airlines after two of its pilots were found guilty of flying drunk. In order to avoid these legal problems, many organizations have begun to test extensively both current and potential employees. But which tests are legal and which are not?

Polygraph Tests

Polygraph machines were once one of the most commonly used devices for determining employee honestly and truthfulness regarding specific events. It is estimated that approximately 2,000,000 such tests were given in 1987. Of these, 1.3 million were given to job applicants while another 500,000 were given to current employees. Experts guess that 30 percent of America's Fortune 500 firms used polygraph testing.

In general, polygraph tests measure changes in a subject's physiological reactions (through a series of electrodes) as the subject answers a set of questions. Certain kinds of changes indicate that the subject was experiencing stress, and possibly lying. Despite its widespread use, it was generally believed to be unreliable in determining whether the subject was telling the truth or a lie. Subjects' individual physiological characteristics and testing conducted by improperly trained examiners all complicated the test's reliability. In addition, many organizations tended to place too much emphasis in the test results without taking into account other circumstances or evidence. All of these factors proved to be insurmountable. Congress and President Reagan outlawed the use of polygraph tests by organizations by passing and signing the Employee Polygraph Protection Act of 1988.

Personality Tests

Personality tests also have long been used by organizations and are being more widely used since polygraphs have been outlawed. Popular tests include the Minnesota Multiphasic Personality Inventory (MMPI), the California Personality Inventory (CPI), and the Inwald Personality Inventory (IPI). In addition to some of the issues related above, personality tests can also be used to determine whether a person is introverted or extroverted, self-driven or other-directed and a host of other personality traits.

Many components of these tests are widely accepted. For example, it is generally agreed that an organization has the right to know whether an applicant for a sales position is introverted or extroverted. The problems arising with these tests stem from some of their predictive components and their probing into what many contend are private areas that are not job-related, such as requests for information like that encountered by Sibi Soroka.

Many of these tests were designed for specific purposes, yet are administered in a wide variety of situations. Also, like the problems with polygraph testing, the tests often are administered by untrained professionals. As Sibi Soroka's case illustrates, a long line of court cases and government legislation is likely to occur before the hows, whens, and whys of personality testing are resolved.

Financial Data and Medical History or Testing

Another problem is caused by the increasing use of personal credit and medical histories in the hiring process. This issue includes the right of organizations to demand that potential employees undergo various medical tests, such as the AIDS test, as a condition of employment. Although this information is supposedly confidential, technology has given organizations the ability to gather much of this information and current law provides little restrictions concerning accessing it. Two large issues are emerging here. The first is strictly a question of access. Does your future boss have the right to know that your mother had leukemia or that your aunt has a history of chronic depression? Does he or she have the right to demand that you undergo genetic testing? Or how about knowing that you missed a Visa payment in March 1988?

Organizations assert that this information is vital for several reasons. First, they argue that the skyrocketing cost of medical coverage makes it necessary for them to know an employee's complete medical history before that person is hired. In many instances, organizations are requiring applicants to undergo certain kinds of medical exams, such as AIDS tests. This can help them plan their medical expenses, employee absenteeism, and turnover, among other things. In addition, there is an increasing trend for insurance companies not to cover illnesses or diseases for individuals who have those genetic predispositions. Many argue against these practices, however, because they assert that they are essentially clever methods by organizations to practice discrimination against perceived undesirables.

Second, organizations argue that this information, especially financial information, can help determine employee reliability. They argue that employees who cannot manage their own finances are viewed as being unlikely to be able to manage a department's budget. Organizations have also used the negligent hiring doctrine as a basis for obtaining employee medical and financial data.

Drug Tests

Perhaps some of the most talked about and controversial tests today are drug tests. The most common of these tests are urinalysis and hair sampling. Drug testing is a particularly sensitive issue for several reasons. First, many people feel that drug tests, especially urinalysis, are particularly intrusive of their privacy. Second, organizations that do not screen for drug users are most open to lawsuits concerning the negligent hiring doctrine. A third emerging issue is that of the conflict between the individual's right to privacy and the public's right to safety. While the issues are by no means settled, several trends are emerging.

The first of these trends concerns the issue of public safety. The right to perform drug tests on employees who are directly responsible for public safety, such as military personnel, police officers, airline pilots, and bus drivers, is being increasingly supported by both court precedent and public legislation. Another trend is the increasing frequency of employees winning in court against organizations that conduct poorly planned and poorly implemented drug-testing programs. This includes nonrandom testing or testing without justifiable cause, improper test administration, or other forms of discriminatory actions. Like the other testing issues discussed above, the future of drug testing employees is uncertain. While it is safe to say that drug testing is a permanent part of organization life, it is unwise to predict exactly what form drug testing will be allowed to take in the future.

● ● ● ● ● ● ● ● ●

The above issues relating to employee testing represent only one portion of the ethical behavior, employee rights, and employer responsibility segment of human resource management. Many of these issues are emotion packed, and virtually everyone has an opinion or strong feeling about them. While managers have laws, precedents, and corporate policies to guide their behavior, sometimes these may not be enough. Decisions managers make concerning these issues are difficult and often extremely important to the organization.

STRATEGIC CHOICES

Many factors influence the choices managers make about how they will carry out their responsibilities in recognizing and respecting employee rights. Several of the choices they must make are listed below.

1. How can the organization ensure that the managers are treating employees with the respect they deserve?
2. What type of ethical standards should the organization set for their managers? How shall these standards be disseminated to the managers?
3. Is there ever a time when a manager has the right to violate an employee's right to privacy?
4. How does an organization keep all of its managers up to date with respect to the legal ramifications of their treatment of employees?

STRATEGIC FACTORS

The main factors that directly influence managers' decisions about how they will treat employees include (1) management philosophy, (2) the tightness of the labor market, (3) the law, (4) union and employee power, and (5) organizational culture as it relates to discipline and control.

....

| EXHIBIT 16.1 | Statement of Core Values of a Hospital |

1. We will treat each employee with respect.
2. We will observe the Golden Rule when dealing with all employees regardless of rank or job title.
3. We will make every effort to communicate with each employee and will listen to each.
4. We will respect the individual rights of each employee as a human being.
5. We will make every effort to involve each employee fully in his or her work.

....

Management Philosophy

The main question under the topic of management philosophy is, to what extent do top management and other managers throughout the organization believe in protecting employee rights? If top managers strongly believe in protecting employee rights, they will more likely ensure that company policy and action respect these rights. They will more likely treat their subordinates with respect and will expect them to do likewise with theirs. Furthermore, they will develop and communicate a set of core values that manifest these beliefs.

If, on the other hand, top management holds little regard for the rights of individual employees, very little, if anything, will be communicated on protecting these rights. Employees will more likely be treated as common factors of production without explicit consideration or respect for individual human dignity. In her study of General Motors, Maryann Keller shows how this basic orientation among top management permeated the organization and was a major cause for the decline of GM competitiveness in the labor market.[2] By creating a stifling bureaucracy that provided little respect or allowance for individual differences, managers were not encouraged to explicitly recognize individual rights. She quotes an employee's letter which points out management's failure to recognize him as a human being. She indicates that mutual respect for the rights of each party, management and workers, is the way for GM to finally pull out of its tailspin.

Sometimes an organization will formulate a set of core values that act as a basic guide for the treatment of employees. For example, Exhibit 16.1 shows a set of core values for a large hospital in the southeastern United States. These core values appeared in the employee manual, the firm's strategic plan, and were posted in the lobby of the hospital. In addition, they were printed on wallet-sized cards that all managers and employees were encouraged to carry with them. While it is certainly possible for an organization to develop such statements of core values for public relations purposes, the fact that this statement was developed by the CEO and other members of the top management team and was circulated so widely gave the statement real meaning. One of your authors worked with this organization for several months and it was apparent that management attempted to live by these values.

Tightness of the Labor Market

The second variable that affects the extent to which a firm respects the rights of employees is the tightness of the labor market. If labor is plentiful and readily available at prevailing or below prevailing wage rates, firms are less likely to respect individual rights than if labor markets are tight, everything else being equal. This occurs because management knows that disgruntled and unhappy employees who quit or are fired can easily be replaced when there is an abundant supply of labor.

The United States experienced this most dramatically during both the great immigration waves of the early twentieth century and the Great Depression of the 1930s. During both of these periods, employee rights were frequently abused because of the abundance of labor relative to the demand. Child labor, long hours, unsafe and unhealthy working conditions, low wages, and arbitrary and discriminatory treatment were all too common during these periods. In fact, because of these abuses, both industrial unions were formed and legislation was passed in an attempt to protect the rights of employees. These two factors are discussed below.

Legislation

To the extent that legislation exists and to the extent that this legislation is vigorously enforced, employee rights will be protected. If laws and court cases clearly define employee rights and if agencies exist specifically to uphold these laws, then employers will more likely respect employee rights out of respect for the law and fear of sanctions. Initially, much of the law protecting employee rights was passed at the state level. For example, early in this century Wisconsin had laws regulating child labor and working conditions for women. These laws varied greatly from state to state and many states had no legislation. It was not until federal legislation was passed that comprehensive coverage and enforcement practices occurred.

Unions and Employee Power

The greater the power of employees to protect their rights, especially through collective action (unions), the more likely employers will respect employee rights, all other things being equal. If employers know that employees can take concerted action to enforce rights, the power of employees is heightened. To a large extent, respect for rights depends on a power relationship: those that have power tend to get their way. Their rights are protected because they have the power to enforce their protection.

Unions have played a very strong role in defining and protecting employee rights. By uniting, employees have greatly increased their power in relation to employers. Unions have acted as advocates for employees both in collective bargaining with employers and in lobbying Congress for legislation to protect employee rights. Chapters 17 and 18 further explain the important role that unions play in the management of human resources.

Culture

The final variable we consider is culture. Both the external culture and the organization's internal culture are key variables in terms of how the employer defines employee rights. For example, historically communist countries, such as the Soviet Union, guaranteed employees jobs, resulting in a very low reported unemployment rate. Western countries traditionally have not actually made this guarantee, although most have a national economic policy of full employment to be achieved through monetary and fiscal policy (government spending, taxation, and central bank

---

EXHIBIT 16.2 Corporate Values of Apple and Hewlett Packard toward Their Employees

APPLE'S STATEMENT OF VALUES

Individual Performance—We expect individual commitment and performance above the standard for our industry. Only thus will we make profits that permit us to seek our other corporate objectives. Each employee can and must make a difference in the final analysis. *Individuals* determine the character and strength of Apple.

Individual Reward—We recognize each person's contribution to Apple's success, and we share the financial rewards that flow from high performance. We recognize also that rewards must be psychological as well as financial, and strive for an atmosphere where each individual can share the adventure and excitement of working at Apple.

HEWLETT PACKARD'S STATEMENT OF VALUES

Our People
To help HP people share in the company's success, which they make possible; to provide employment security based on their performance; to ensure them a safe and pleasant work environment; to recognize their individual achievements; and to help them gain a sense of satisfaction and accomplishment from their work.

---

actions). Communist countries experimenting with free enterprise will likely allow some unemployment to exist in the future.

Secondly, internal culture—organizational culture—also determines employee rights. A culture that places great value on employees and the worth of the individual will likely define and protect more employee rights than a culture that does not value employees as individuals. For example, Exhibit 16.2 shows the corporate values of Apple Computer and Hewlett Packard in relation to their employees. Apple and Hewlett Packard have reputations as two of the most innovative and highest performing firms in the computer industry. Yet, as Exhibit 16.2 shows, their approaches to their employees are completely different. Hewlett Packard is known as a company that historically fosters and nurtures its employees. Its pay scale is average for the computer industry, but it is committed to a no-layoff policy.[3] Apple in contrast, is often viewed as a high-stress organization with high levels of employee turnover. In turn, Apple places a great emphasis on financially rewarding high performance. Apple does not even have a formal retirement policy, because, as one Apple executive states, "We don't expect people to last that long." Another Apple executive asserts, "Someone who worries about a retirement plan isn't an Apple type of person."[4] It is obvious that these two organizations take different attitudes toward employee rights. Much of this difference is due to their corporate cultures.

The key factors that affect the strategic choices employers have in defining employee rights and management responsibilities are as follows: management philosophy, the tightness of the labor market, the law, union and employee power, and the outside as well as the organizational culture. These variables are interrelated and work together. Therefore, it is important to try to understand their cumulative effect in order to understand how rights and responsibilities are played in individual organizations.

Since so many rights have been codified either in legislation or case law, we now examine one key aspect of employee rights—the law. We do not intend to cover each and every aspect of the law—much of this has been done in other chapters of the book. Rather our intent is to highlight those aspects of the law that deal with rights and responsibilities.

THE LAW AND EMPLOYEE RIGHTS

We review three key areas of the law: discrimination, employment at will, and privacy. The basic legislation and case law in each area is summarized.

Discrimination

As we saw in Chapter 5, employees have the right to employment free from discrimination based on race, color, creed, religious belief, country of national origin, age, sex, or physical or mental handicap. This protection covers all aspects of employment—from hiring to placement, training, promotion, pay, discipline, or termination. The primary law which protects this right is Title VII of the 1964 Civil Rights Act as amended and as interpreted by case law. Employees are also protected against sexual harassment since this has been defined as a type of sexual discrimination.

The law on discrimination is quite complex, but basically it says that employment decisions should be made strictly on factors relevant to the job. This means that the decisions should be based on skill, job knowledge, and abilities—factors that relate to a person's ability to do the job. Even such factors as experience and educational level could be ruled as discriminatory if these factors are not relevant to the job at hand. In fact, they could serve as institutional forms of covert (hidden) discrimination if white people consistently have higher levels of education than minority groups and if this educational level is irrelevant to the job at hand. What is desired from an employment standpoint is the skills and knowledge that education and experience represent. In other words, just because a person has a certain formal education level or years of experience does not necessarily mean that the person has the required skill or knowledge to do the job. Employers use education and experience to represent skill and knowledge because it is an easy to use screening device and because so few sophisticated tests exist to test job knowledge and skill. Also, these tests are relatively expensive to administer—it is much easier to require a certain education level and use this prerequisite to screen out the mass of applicants.

So discrimination can be overt or covert. The law has pretty much eliminated overt discrimination, but covert discrimination is more difficult to eliminate. The major controversial aspects of discrimination, particularly affirmative action, which was adopted as national policy even before the passage of Title VII, as a way to eliminate discrimination, as was discussed in Chapter 5.

Employment at Will

In many states the doctrine of "employment at will" exists. This doctrine means that an employer or an employee is free to break the employment relationship "at will" unless there is a written or implied employment contract. Examples of employment-at-will statements are provided in Exhibit 16.3. The rationale behind this concept is the belief that an employee ought to be free to quit to seek employment

....

EXHIBIT 16.3	**Employment-at-Will Clause Examples**

Strong Form

I understand that if I am employed by _____ Company that my employment and compensation can be terminated with or without cause and with or without notice at any time, at the option of either the company or myself. I also understand that neither this application for employment nor any present or future employee handbook or personnel policy manual is an employment agreement, either expressed or implied, and that no employee or manager of _____ Company, except the vice-president of human resources, has any authority to enter into any agreement for employment for any specified period of time, or make any agreement contrary to the foregoing.

Moderately Strong Form

In the event of employment, I understand that my employment is not for any definite period or succession of periods and is considered an "at-will" arrangement. This means that I am free to terminate my employment at any time for any reason, as is the company, so long as there is no violation of applicable federal or state law.

Soft Form

I understand that no representative of the company is authorized to state or imply that a contract for permanent employment shall exist between the company and me..

....

elsewhere and that an employer ought to be able to terminate an employee in order to hire another one.

Four primary factors temper the employment at will concept: (1) an employment contract, (2) civil service protection, (3) discrimination law, and (4) unions.[5]

Employment Contract

In an individual employment contract, a clause specifying reasons for terminations will usually be spelled out. This protects the employee from termination for other reasons. Below is an example of such a clause:

> This Agreement shall, at the employer's sole option and without further notice, be terminated upon the occurrence of any one or more of the following events:
> (a) the conviction of the employee of a felony;
> (b) the conviction of the employee of a misdemeanor involving moral turpitude;
> (c) gross negligence by the employee in the performance of his duties;
> (d) the willful and intentional commission of any act which act or failure to act the employee knew, or should have known, would result in substantial and material harm to employer's business or goodwill.

These are vague terms and would need to be specifically defined by a court or arbitrator if contested by the employee. Yet, if this were in an employment contract, these would be the only reasons an employee could be terminated.

In the absence of a written contract, a court will often infer a contract of employment. For example, if in the employee handbook a statement is made that a new employee moves from probationary to permanent status after a period of time, such as ninety days, courts have held that the word "permanent" implies a

FOCUS ON ETHICS AND SOCIAL RESPONSIBILITY •••••••••••••••

Relocation Can Lead to an Implied Contract

Getting employees to transfer to a new location seems to be getting more and more difficult. Issues such as dual careers, children having to change schools, especially high school, and extreme differences in the cost of living or quality of life sometimes make it hard to sell an employee on a transfer.

All too frequently, while managers are trying to convince an employee to make a move, seemingly harmless sentences used to persuade the employee can become the grounds for an implied contract lawsuit. For example, mentioning that the move will "be worth the employee's while over the long haul" or that this move is "simply one more step in the employee's career ladder" may be interpreted in a court as an implied contract.

A case recently decided on this issue illustrates this problem. After 25 years of service as an accountant at Dresser Industries, Thomas Krause had worked his way up to the highest accounting position in southern Louisiana. During a general cutback, he was demoted and was told that he would have to move to Oklahoma

City to keep his job. After being assured by his supervisor that if he moved his job would be safe because future job cuts would be determined by seniority, he decided to move to Oklahoma City. When he arrived there he found that the only other accountant was the 27-year-old son of a senior vice-president. Soon the ax fell and he was fired. When the VP's son found a new position in Dresser and Krause didn't, he sued for both age discrimination (he was 52 at the time of the firing) and for wrongful discharge under the implied contract theory. He won on both accounts—$168,000 for the age discrimination claim and an additional $166,000 for the wrongful discharge suit.

As can be seen from this one example, relocation is a gray area. Managers must be made aware that the what they say may be used against them later if the transferred employee is terminated.

SOURCE: Adapted from Jack Raisner, "Relocate without Making False Moves," *HRMagazine*, February 1991, pp. 46–50.

contractual relationship. For this reason, employers should use the word "regular" instead of permanent in employee manuals, other publications, and policy statements unless they wish to imply permanent status.

An implied contract can also be inferred from oral statements made by superiors in the organization.[6] For example, organizations should be careful about saying things like the following at the time of hire: "We plan to keep you here for your entire career" or "we view our relationship as a long-term, permanent one." Statements similar to these have been ruled in cases as an implied contract of lifetime employment in the supreme courts of New Jersey, New Mexico, and Michigan.[7]

The costs an organization incurs to protect itself from wrongful termination lawsuits are being passed on to the employees in the form of fewer jobs. To offset the costs involved, some firms are simply hiring less. However, it appears that the actual court costs are minimal; it is the actions organizations are taking to prevent litigation that are so costly. Many firms are spending more per employee to avoid litigation than they are spending for litigation itself.[8]

To minimize your chances of being sued over an implied contract, the following steps can be taken:

1. Establish a written at-will statement and place it on all applications. Make potential employees sign the form.
2. Stipulate the standards for conduct for your employees and the kinds of conduct that will lead to termination.
3. Indicate that even though you use progressive discipline, it is by no means a guarantee of employment and the progression can be suspended at any time.

4. Reserve the right to dismiss the employee without following disciplinary procedures.
5. Do not establish a probationary period for new hires. They may expect that if they pass they are guaranteed employment.[9]

Civil Service Protection

Employees working for government agencies are protected from discharge without justifiable cause through civil service rules and regulations. These not only specify dischargeable offenses, they also spell out the procedure to be used. Exhibit 16.4 shows such an example of a civil service clause and procedure.

Discrimination Law

People cannot legally be dismissed from a job if it occurs because of their race, creed, color, religious belief, county of national origin, sex, age, physical or mental handicap as provided by the law.

Unions

The final factor that modifies the employment-at-will doctrine is the presence of a union. As we will see in Chapters 17 and 18, unions, through the collective bargaining process, negotiate and enforce a collective bargaining agreement called a contract, which specifies causes and procedures for discharge. These items, as well as other aspects of unions and collective bargaining are discussed in the next two chapters.

....

TYPES OF RIGHTS

Any listing of employee rights is likely to be incomplete. No one source lists employee rights just as no one source lists the rights we have as citizens of our country. However, both legislation and case law, as well as in certain key documents such as the Constitution, provide us with a framework that we can use to construct a list of employee rights. For our purposes, we will look at the seven rights that follow.[10]

1. Privacy.
2. Fair treatment.
3. Safe and healthful workplace, including freedom from a hostile environment regarding sexual harassment.
4. Collective bargaining.
5. Communication and involvement in the organization.
6. Notice of plant closings and of disciplinary action.
7. Due process.

Privacy

The right to privacy is grounded in the U.S. Constitution. The Fourth Amendment prevents unreasonable search and seizure. Most state constitutions provide for some form of protection similar to the Fourth Amendment. Ten states even have specific

....

EXHIBIT 16.4 Florida's Career Service Discharge Statute

110.227 SUSPENSIONS, DISMISSALS, REDUCTIONS IN PAY, DEMOTIONS, LAYOFFS, AND TRANSFERS.

(1) Any employee who has permanent status in the career service may only be suspended or dismissed for cause. Cause shall include, but not be limited to, negligence, inefficiency or inability to perform assigned duties, willful violation of the provisions of law or agency rules, conduct unbecoming a public employee, misconduct, habitual drug abuse, or conviction of any crime involving moral turpitude. Each agency head shall ensure that all employees of the agency are completely familiar with the agency's established procedures on disciplinary actions and grievances.

(2) The department [Florida Department of Administration] shall establish rules and procedures for the suspension, reduction in pay, transfer, layoff, demotion, and dismissal of employees in the career service. Such rules shall be approved by the Administration Commission prior to their adoption by the department.

(3)(a) When a layoff becomes necessary, such layoff shall be conducted within the competitive area identified by the agency head and approved by the Department of Administration. Such competitive area shall be established taking into consideration the similarity of work; the organizational unit, which may be any agency, department, division, bureau, or other organizational unit; and the commuting area for the work affected.

(b) Layoff procedures shall be developed to establish the relative merit and fitness of employees and shall include a formula for uniform application among all employees in the competitive area, taking into consideration the type of employment, the length of service, and the quality of performance.

(4) Any permanent career service employee subject to reduction in pay, transfer, layoff, or demotion shall be notified in writing by the agency prior to its taking such action. Such notice shall be sent by certified mail with return receipt requested. Such actions shall be appealable to the Public Employees Relations Commission, pursuant to s. 447.208 [Florida Statutes] and rules adopted by the commission.

....

privacy guarantees in their constitution. Beyond this, the law is complex and unclear. Most of the privacy concept has evolved as the result of hundreds of past and current court cases. The right to privacy is an ever-changing and evolving concept.

Basically, however, the right to privacy means that employees are free to work without undue interference from their employer and that employee records are protected from examination unless a legitimate interest exists.

Monitoring employee behavior without invading an employee's right to privacy can raise some sensitive issues.[11] For example, does an employer have the right to search an employee's desk? How can drug tests be conducted without violating the right to privacy? How can employers monitor the conversations held by telephone operators without violating privacy rights? Employee monitoring has become one of the most controversial issues in human resource management today. According to corporate lawyer Eric Joss it will be "the hottest employment law topic of the 1990s."[12] These issues will be explored more fully in the case at the end of the chapter.

EXHIBIT 16.4 continued

(5)(a)   Any permanent career service employee who is subject to suspension or dismissal shall receive written notice of such action at least 10 days prior to the date such action is to be taken. Subsequent to such notice, and prior to the date the action is to be taken, the affected employee shall be given an opportunity to appear before the agency or official taking the action to answer orally and in writing the charges against him. The notice to the employee required by this paragraph shall be sent by certified mail with return receipt requested. An employee who is suspended or dismissed shall be entitled to a hearing before the Public Employees Relations Commission or its designated agent pursuant to s. 447.208 and rules adopted by the commission.

(b)   In extraordinary situations, such as when the retention of a permanent career service employee would result in damage to state property, would be detrimental to the interests of the state, or would result in injury to the employee, a fellow employee, or some other person, such employee may be suspended or dismissed without 10 days prior notice provided that written or oral notice of such action, evidence of the reasons therefor, and an opportunity to rebut the charges are furnished to the employee prior to such dismissal or suspension. Such notice may be delivered to the employee personally or may be sent by certified mail with return receipt requested. Agency compliance with the foregoing procedure requiring notice, evidence, and an opportunity for rebuttal must be substantiated. Any employee who is suspended or dismissed pursuant to the provisions of this paragraph shall be entitled to a hearing before the Public Employees Relations Commission or its designated agent pursuant to s. 447.208, except that such hearing shall be held no more than 20 days after the filing of the notice of appeal by the employee.

110.233 POLITICAL ACTIVITIES AND UNLAWFUL ACTS PROHIBITED

(1)   No person shall be appointed to, demoted, or dismissed from any position in the career service, or in any way favored or discriminated against with respect to employment in the career service, because of race, color, national origin, sex, handicap, religious creed, or political opinion or affiliation.

Fair Treatment

The second right we examine is the right to fair treatment by employers. By fair treatment we mean freedom from arbitrary and capricious behavior on the part of the employer. It means that individual employees will not be singled out for discipline when others also deserve it. It means that overt favoritism on the part of the employer will be minimized. It also means that in the absence of mitigating circumstances, precedence will be followed by the employer. In a recent survey, this issue was cited as the most serious ethical problem human resource managers must deal with.[13]

For example, the fair treatment issue applied to Florida Governor Bob Martinez's firing of Florida Department of Corrections classification officer Phillip Adams. Adams recommended, against inmate classification guidelines, that convicted murderer Donald Dillbeck be reclassified from medium security to minimum security. Governor Martinez fired Adams after Dillbeck walked away from a work detail and murdered a woman in a mall parking lot. A hearing officer ruled Adams had been treated

How Far Can the Employer's Arm Reach?

As a manager, do you have the right to know whether or not an employee has been accused of a crime while in your employ? Is it legal to terminate an employee due to his or her violation of the law, even it the employee is extremely productive and has never missed a day's work? Does the severity of the crime matter? What if the employee was convicted of child molestation, or drunk driving, or armed robbery? Managers who must answer these tough questions are being guided by an ever-increasing body of laws.

In general, the case laws suggest that misconduct outside of the workplace may not be a lawful justification for employee discipline, in some cases. As a defense, an employee could argue that what he or she does outside of work is none of the company's business as long as the employee is still productive. This defense is being taken more and more seriously as privacy issues become a significant area for judicial examination.

The employer's best defense is to link the crime to some aspect of the job. For example, Pepsi-Cola was able to terminate a vending-machine serviceman who was convicted of child molestation because he worked unsupervised in areas where children frequented. Also, an employer could argue that the employee's presence in the workplace is disruptive. In one case, the workers were so repulsed by an employee who was accused of sexual misconduct that the peer pressure they exerted upon him made him quit. However, the firm would have chosen to terminate him if he did not quit on his own on the grounds that the employee's misconduct had a disruptive impact on the workplace.

These issues are very controversial. While some states, such as Hawaii, have laws that specifically preclude employers from basing disciplinary actions on the fact that the employee has been arrested for a crime, other states do not have such laws. Further, businesses also enjoy special protection in this areas by some laws. Regardless of the laws protecting either side, the employer is frequently placed in a difficult situation that must be handled with extreme care.

SOURCE: Adapted from Steve Bergsman, "Employee Conduct Outside the Workplace," *HRMagazine*, March 1991, pp. 62–64.

differently than other officers who were not fired after violating the same decision-making guidelines and recommended that he be reinstated.[14]

Safe and Healthful Workplace Free from Sexual Harassment

The Occupational Safety and Health Act of 1970, as amended, gives employees the right to a safe and healthful workplace. The major provisions of the law are in Exhibit 16.5. The law set up the Occupational Safety and Health Administration (OSHA) to enforce the law. It also gave OSHA the power to conduct inspections, levy fines, and, in severe cases, shut down operations. Finally, the law gives employees the right to complain to OSHA about safety violations without fear of retribution from employers.

Hostile Environment

In the landmark case of *Meritor Savings Bank, FSB* v. *Vinson*, the U.S. Supreme Court ruled that Vinson had been subjected to sexual harassment on the job by her employer, Meritor Savings Bank, because the employer had created a **hostile environment** with regard to sexual harassment. A series of activities took place involving off-color jokes, fondling, and even sexual intercourse. The plaintiff, Vinson, did not complain until she was terminated for excessive sick leave, even though the company had a complaint procedure in place. She claimed that she was afraid to complain for fear of losing her job. The court ruled in her favor and stated that the employer had created a hostile environment that prevented Vinson from voicing her

....

████ EXHIBIT 16.5 ████ Basic Provisions of the Occupational Safety and Health Act of 1970

The act empowers the Occupational Safety and Health Administration (OSHA) to establish specific standards and working environment regulations the employers are required to meet.

The act's "general duty" clause states that employers have a general duty to provide safe and healthy working conditions in areas where no standards have been adopted. Employers are required to post OSHA regulations in prominent places and enforce OSHA regulations concerning the use of protective equipment. Furthermore, employees who report safety violations to OSHA cannot be punished or fired by their employees.

Information about hazardous substances must be made available by the employers to employees, unions, and health professionals.

In certain instances, employees may refuse to work when the work is unsafe. These instances are as follows:

- When the employee's fear is objectively reasonable;
- When the employee tried to get the dangerous situation corrected; and
- When using normal procedures to solve the problem have not worked.

The act empowers OSHA to require a standard system of employer recordkeeping and reporting relating to job-related injuries, accidents, and fatalities.

The act empowers OSHA agents to conduct on-the-spot inspections. Generally, agents are allowed to conduct "no knock," or without warning, inspections. Agents are required to obtain search warrants for employers who refuse inspections.

The act also empowers OSHA to issue various levels of citation and violation notices to employers who are not in compliance with OSHA regulations. OSHA also has the power to impose penalties and fines.

....

complaint.[15] The EEOC guidelines define a hostile environment as one in which sexual harassment interferes with the employee's work behavior or creates an offensive work environment.[16]

Collective Bargaining

Employees have the right to form unions or to join unions to bargain collectively with their employers with regard to wages, hours, and other terms and conditions of employment. This right is protected by federal law. By bargaining collectively, employees increase their power relative to their employer. This increased power enables them to secure those aspects desired in an employment relationship, such as higher wages, better hours, better working conditions, and better terms and conditions of employment. Chapters 17 and 18 examine this right in more depth.

Communication and Involvement in the Organization

Employees have the right to be communicated with about aspects of their jobs and their employment. They also have the right to be fully involved in their employing organization. In some countries, this right is commonly adhered to by employers who communicate with and involve their employees through quality circles,

EXHIBIT 16.6	A Comparison of Advance Notice on Plant Closing Laws in the United States and Other Nations

NATION	ADVANCE NOTICE REQUIREMENT
United States	60 days
Canada	1–16 weeks, depending on case
West Germany	30 days after notifying government
Great Britain	60–90 days, depending on case
France	2–14 weeks, depending on case
Sweden	60 days to 6 months, depending on case
Belgium	60 days
Japan	"Sufficient" advance notice

suggestion programs, and consensus decision making. However, U.S. employers have not always believed in this right, although more employers such as Ford, GM, 3M, Motorola, and Florida Power Corp., are embracing this right today.

No doubt, some would argue that while this communication and involvement might be good management practice, it does not constitute an employee right. However, we take the position that for an employee to properly do his or her job, he or she must be kept informed as to what is expected of him or her. Furthermore, as an employee, an individual is entitled to full membership privileges in the employing organization. This includes participation in the benefit programs offered and access to information on organizational operations, at least in so far as they relate to the individual's job duties and responsibilities. Some would argue that this right also includes the right to knowledge of organizational missions, goals, and objectives.[17] Finally, an employee has the right to know how he or she will be evaluated. This includes the criteria and the process used. This right is part and parcel of the right to be communicated with on aspects related to job duties and expectations.

Notice of Plant Closings and Disciplinary Action

Federal law requires that employers provide notice to employees of planned plant or facilities closings. The Worker Adjustment and Retraining Notification Act of 1988 (WARN) was passed by Congress after nearly 15 years of legislative battling. WARN basically requires that all firms employing more than 100 full-time workers give at least 60 days advance notice of any plans to close plants or lay off workers. Firms are required to notify their employees under the law if a plant closing results in the loss of more than 50 jobs at one location. Notice is required in mass-layoff situations if the firm lays off more than 500 people for more than six months or if it lays off 50 workers that constitute more than 33 percent of its work force. Firms that employ less than 100 people are exempt from the law. It is estimated that only 2 percent of the companies in the United States are large enough to be affected by the law, but these companies employ approximately 50 percent of the work force.[18] Exhibit 16.6 compares WARN to similar laws in other nations.

In addition, it is well established in arbitration hearings that an employer must give notice to employees on new rules or regulations or when it intends to enforce a previously existing but unenforced rule or regulation. Employees cannot be expected to adhere to rules and regulations that have not been made public or otherwise communicated to them. Even an existing rule or regulation that the organization has not been enforcing is unenforceable unless the organization first puts employees on notice stating that the rule will be enforced from this day forward.

For example, one of your authors is familiar with a nosmoking rule that existed in a warehouse of a large consumer products manufacturer. This rule had been communicated to employees; in fact no-smoking signs were clearly posted on walls in the warehouse. The rule was clearly stated in the employee handbook. The penalty for violating the rule was also clearly stated—an immediate three-day suspension without pay on the first offense and termination on the second offense.

However, this rule was not enforced by the supervisors in the warehouse nor by the warehouse superintendent. When the old superintendent retired and a new one was appointed, he decided to enforce the rule. The morning of his first day on the job he suspended an employee caught smoking. The employee filed a grievance through the union, which went to third party arbitration. The arbitrator ruled that the suspension was improper because past practice showed that the rule existed on paper only, since the company did not enforce it. He ruled that the employer should have first put all employees on notice that the rule would now be enforced, even though it had not been in the past. This ruling is well established in arbitration cases—the arbitrator looks to past practice prior to making a ruling.

Due Process

The final right we examine here is the right to due process. Due process means the right to a fair hearing or adjudication if charged with a rule violation. In most cases, this means the right to file a grievance and have it heard. In a unionized organization, this right is protected by the labor agreement and the grievance process is usually spelled out in the contract. However, even in a nonunion organization a grievance process is often spelled out. A typical grievance starts with the immediate supervisor and ends with arbitration, which is a binding ruling by an outside neutral third party. This process allows both the employee and the employer to state their cases—to have "their day in court," so to speak.

Of course, if arbitration is not present in a grievance process, an employee can sue an employer for damages and take the employer to court. This too allows for due process, but it is usually more time consuming and costly than a grievance and arbitration. Grievances and the arbitration process are discussed in Chapter 18.

EMPLOYER RESPONSIBILITIES

Up to now we have been discussing the rights of employees. Employers have responsibilities with respect to these rights. This responsibility is not the reverse side of the same coin, although employee rights do suggest corresponding employer responsibilities. Rather, employers have other responsibilities to the community at large. While this is not a book on the social responsibilities of business, some concepts from this field are helpful.

For example, actions of employers often have impact beyond the immediate boundary of the organization. This was the key issue in the U.S. government's loan guarantee to Chrysler in late 1977. It was reasoned that it would be better for the federal government to guarantee the loans to Chrysler in hopes of saving the

FOCUS ON ETHICS AND SOCIAL RESPONSIBILITY • • • • • • • • • • • • • •

A Company with a Conscience

Working Assets is a tiny, eight-year-old consumers services firm located in San Francisco. A part of its profits is donated to socially responsible causes. Laura Scher, a 1985 Harvard graduate who placed in the top 5 percent of her business school class, is the CEO. Why would a woman who could have gone to work for virtually any other company select to work for Working Assets? Because the company has a conscience.

For example, one of Scher's most recent projects was Working Assets Long Distance. It's a phone company that targets people who want to speak out on political and environmental issues. Along with the usual services offered by a long-distance carrier, WA's long distance program offers Free Speech Days, during which time customers can call Congress for free. She signed up 20,000 customers in three months. She has also developed a WA Visa card. Every time a customer uses the card, WA donates a nickel to a pool that supports 36 nonprofit groups. The 120,000 cardholders have charged enough items to create a pool of almost $1.5 million.

As Scher's work indicates, plenty of socially conscious consumers are out there. The trick is appealing to them. These customers are leery of three-color mail-out pamphlets and are suspicious of advertisers' motives. What these people want is simply to support causes they believe in. The top four causes include economic justice, the environment, peace, and human rights.

How does Scher please her audience? She follows three principles in running her business. First, she identifies an opportunity within an existing industry, like credit cards and long-distance calling, then she finds ways to piggyback her services onto these everyday needs. Second, because she knows that her customers are big readers, she explains everything about the program in brochures and advertisements. Finally, she doesn't try to be all things to all people. She is sure to be outspoken only in areas that she really cares about. Obviously her rules are working for Working Assets.

SOURCE: Adapted from "Making Money While Making a Difference," *Working Woman*, February 1992, pp. 31–34.

company than to let the company go bankrupt and thereby throw thousands of people out of work. The potential costs in unemployment insurance, food stamps, and other welfare programs was thought to far exceed the costs of guaranteeing the loan. In retrospect, the decision appears to have been the correct one since the company recovered nicely and even paid off the loans ahead of schedule.

Therefore, firms have responsibilities not only to their employees and stockholders, but also to other groups and to the community at large. Making charitable donations, supporting the United Way, backing arts groups, supporting colleges and universities, working to reduce or eliminate drugs and crime—these are but some examples of the steps firms take to improve the quality of life in the communities where they operate. While firms may have selfish motives for doing these things—they want good schools and safe streets for their employees—the community as a whole benefits.

Stakeholder Concept

One way to view these responsibilities of companies is to take a **stakeholder** approach. This approach holds that organizations serve multiple constituencies and each group has a set of expectations or a vested interest in what the organization does. Consequently, the organization has a responsibility to each of these groups. Exhibit 16.7 shows some of the stakeholder groups for a large corporation. Notice that the corporation has a responsibility to try to fulfill the expectations of each of the stakeholder groups. For example, owners want a return on their investment so the organization strives to earn a profit. Employees want good wages, security, and fair treatment. Customers want a product or service at desired quality, quantity,

....

| EXHIBIT 16.7 | Examples of Organization Stakeholders |

INTERNAL STAKEHOLDERS	EXTERNAL STAKEHOLDERS
Employees	Suppliers
Management	Distributors
Board of Directors (internally-chosen)	Board of Directors (externally-chosen)
Owner (sole proprietorship)	Customers
	Government Agencies
	Public Interest Groups
	Shareholders

....

place, time, and price. Government agencies want taxes and want the organization to obey appropriate laws.

In fulfilling these obligations to these various groups, organizations often face conflicting expectations. For example, employees make a claim to profit in the form of higher wages or other incentive pay, such as profit sharing. They compete with owners who want a share of profit in the form of dividends. The organization must balance these competing interests. Requests for financial support for college and university programs come from many institutions of higher learning, the corporation must decide which ones it will support and which ones it will not. This requires that the organization practice the art of compromise and that it properly assess the power of each stakeholder and the consequences of not fulfilling the expectations of each.

Ethics

Often the decision that balances what managers do is based on what is ethically correct. For example, when managers must decide how to dispose of toxic waste, various options are available. While the most inexpensive option may be the one that the owners and shareholders would like the firm to use because it would mean a larger return on their investment, this option might not be in accordance with state or local laws regarding the disposal of toxic waste. Therefore, managers must put aside cost issues and select a legal option that is ethically correct.

In recent years, courses on business ethics have been added to the curriculum of many major universities. In-house ethics training classes at large corporations have been developed. Orientation programs have begun to include sections on the ethical stance of the organization. Below is a list of several reasons why ethics has become such a hot topic.

1. There appears to be a widespread breakdown in ethical conduct among senior managers. As the double standard, usually employed to allow top managers to take advantage of the system, gradually gets revealed to the American public (such as via the savings and loan scandal, or the Wall Street problems), people are growing concerned and are beginning to ask for changes.

EXHIBIT 16.8	The Ten Most Serious Ethical Situations Reported by Human Resource Professionals

1. Hiring, training, or promoting based on favoritism.
2. Allowing differences in pay, discipline, promotion, and so on due to friendships with top management.
3. Sexual harassment.
4. Sex discrimination in promotion.
5. Using discipline for managerial and nonmanagerial personnel inconsistently.
6. Not maintaining confidentiality.
7. Sex discrimination in compensation.
8. Nonperformance factors used in appraisals.
9. Arrangements with vendors or consulting agencies leading to personal gain.
10. Sex discrimination in recruitment or hiring.

---

2. Time and productivity can be stolen more easily than goods and services. Workers who are treated as professionals may take advantage of the freedoms they enjoy. Experts estimate that payroll could be cut by 20 percent without any change in productivity.
3. The family, where the ethical values were conveyed, has all but disappeared. The "family meal," during which family members discuss their problems and learn the "correct" way to solve them, no longer exists.
4. Organizational loyalty is declining sharply as employees adopt a "what's in it for me" attitude. This attitude shift often has been a reaction to selfish acts of management, such as greenmail, leveraged buyouts, and golden parachutes, witnessed by workers.[19]

In a recent survey, human resource professionals were asked to report their feelings and observations about the ethical conduct in their organization. Exhibit 16.8 lists the top 10 most serious ethical problems reported in this survey. As one might expect, most of the issues raised were human resource–related problems. This is because one of the main functions of the human resource staff is to monitor compliance with ethical guidelines established either by laws or by the organization itself.

In the next section, we briefly discuss employer responsibilities as they pertain primarily to employees. However, it is important to recognize that these responsibilities are tempered by other responsibilities to other stakeholder groups.

Know the Law

"Ignorance of the law is no excuse" is an old saying that is especially pertinent to employee rights. The law is so complex and changes so rapidly that it is vital that both human resource managers and other managers not only try to stay abreast of the law as best they can, but also seek legal assistance on a regular basis. Actively staying current on legal matters is an important responsibility of human resource managers today. Communicating to line managers legal requirements is a very important part of every human resource manager's job. Human resource managers must read extensively, attend workshops on legal matters, and communicate frequently with counsel in order to properly keep line managers educated and informed as to what they legally can and cannot do.

Communicate with Employees

Human resource managers should communicate effectively with employees and should serve as a catalyst to ensure that line managers also communicate effectively with employees. This responsibility is related to the employee right to notice described previously. The right to notice cannot be fulfilled if the employer does not adequately communicate with employees.

Today, companies use many forms of communication. In addition to the standard ways of face-to-face communication through one-on-one encounters and meetings, letters, memoranda, postings, telephoning, and reports, organizations use the fax machine, videos, and electronic communication (E-mail). For example, IBM, among other organizations, regularly uses video in the communication process, not only from central headquarters, but also within regions. A multimedia approach seems to be more effective in reaching employees than using just one communication medium and adding visual images enhances the communication process.

Treat with Human Dignity

A third employer responsibility is to treat employees with human dignity. People are not just another factor of production as is a machine, desk, or factory. They deserve respect and consideration. This is sometimes difficult to achieve, as we saw during the massive restructuring effort in the 1980s when thousands abruptly lost their jobs. Yet ethical values and our system of morals based on the Judeo-Christian ethic as well as our political system gives people certain rights to be treated with dignity and respect. The movie *Roger and Me* demonstrated the conflict that can result when a large corporation (GM) takes action to close a plant that the citizens of the town wish to keep open. In situations such as this, individual rights and dignity are sometimes lost in the process and the question becomes who can exercise the most power in order to best assert their rights as they interpret them. Certainly, GM has the right to close a plant, but those involved have the right to be treated with individual dignity.

Bargain Collectively

The law requires that employers bargain collectively with employees if a union has been certified as the bargaining agent. The employer has no choice as to whether to bargain in good faith or not. However, the employer does have a choice in trying to keep a union from forming. As we will see in Chapter 17, an employer can legally take action to keep a union from forming, although strict guidelines as to what can and cannot be done must be followed.

Provide Due Process

The right to a fair treatment and a fair hearing on the part of the employee requires that the employer accept the responsibility to provide due process. Due process means that the employee has the right to tell his or her side of the story and to have all the facts weighed in a fair and impartial manner.

When a union is present, this is often done through the grievance process. Governmental organizations usually provide some sort of civil service hearing procedure. Nonunionized employers often have impartial panels of employees and managers to hear an employee complaint or grievance. Many Japanese companies do this. For example, Toyota uses a series of committees made up of elected worker representatives and appointed managers to hear disciplinary cases involving workers. At Northrop Corporation in Los Angeles, a management appeals committee is used to hear complaints from employees who believe they have been treated unfairly.[20] We discuss the right to due process in more depth in Chapters 17 and 18.

In the next section we look at a particularly difficult situation which is all to common in organizations today—the problem employee. Employee rights and employer responsibilities come to a head in the problem employee situation. Because this is so difficult a situation and involves rights and legal responsibilities, we devote the remainder of the chapter to discussing the issues involved.

MANAGING THE PROBLEM EMPLOYEE

Suppose you find yourself in this position: one of your employees comes in to work acting very strangely. He seems to be in a fog and unable to concentrate. You do not smell alcohol on the employee's breath. Furthermore, you have noticed this employee acting in this manner several times over the past six weeks. You have talked with the employee twice in the past about this "spacey" behavior only to be told that everything was all right and that the employee was simply tired and under a lot of stress because of an impending divorce. Yet, you suspect drug use and are concerned that the employee's judgment and coordination is severely impaired. What do you do? If you order a drug test, will you violate the employee's right to privacy? If you take no action, will you be held liable for any accident or injury caused by the employee?

This example shows just how difficult it is to handle problem employee situations. The employer must find a way to deal effectively with the problem employee situation, while protecting the employee's rights. In the above example, the employer would be much better off if a policy on drug testing had been developed, checked with legal counsel, and circulated to all employees prior to the incident. The employer would also be better able to handle a situation such as the one above if an employee assistance program (EAP) existed (see Chapter 15). Absent a drug policy and an EAP, the employer can still take effective action. That action is the subject of the remainder of this chapter.

Problem Employee versus the Employee with Problems

All employees have problems from time to time. Usually these are transitory and clear up with little if any help from the employer. However, a problem employee is characterized by the following factors:

- The problem is a major one.
- The problem is chronic; it will not go away or keeps coming back.
- The costs of resolving the problem are high.
- The costs of not resolving the problem are also high.

From a strategic standpoint, the organization must decide how much action it can afford to take in resolving the problem: that is, how much can it afford to spend to salvage an employee? The answer to this question is usually not easy to determine and depends on a number of factors as follows:

- What the law says
- How good the employee is
- How easy it is to replace the employee
- The returns that will come to the organization by saving the employee
- The organization's human resource philosophy

Of course these factors are not always easy to determine, especially the costs and potential benefits involved in the process. This issue is discussed below.

Taking Action versus Not Taking Action

At first, managers typically ignore problem employees. They do this for several reasons. They hope the problem is not serious. They believe the problem will go away on its own. They are unsure about what to do. They have other things on their minds that divert their attention from the problem employee situation. Of course, in many cases the problem does clear up with little, if any, managerial action. This reinforces the inactivity on the manager's part. But if it does not resolve itself, then the manager is in a difficult situation because he or she has let the problem go on for some length of time.

From a strategic standpoint, this becomes dangerous because the costs associated with clearing up the problem at this point can become quite high. In addition, if the organization is tolerant of a problem employee's behavior, it will be noticed by other employees and a bad precedent could be set throughout the organization. Should tolerance for this type of behavior become established in the organization's culture, it will be very difficult and costly to correct.

Consequently, it is recommended that managers take immediate action when a problem employee is initially encountered. To wait can exacerbate the situation and make it very difficult and expensive to rectify later. Of course, to assist managers in this process, good policy guidance is needed from human resource professionals to help line managers take action that is both effective and legal.

Cost Issues

The costs involved in resolving a problem employee situation are difficult to predict. At the onset, managers do not know how much it will cost them to resolve the situation. It is difficult to predict just what will work, what will be covered by insurance, and what the costs are of lost production due to the problem employee's behavior. Furthermore, there are opportunity costs associated with trying to correct problem employee behavior: the manager could be doing something else with his or her time and effort besides trying to deal with the problem employee.

Because of these costs, many managers become frustrated and simply attempt to terminate the employee. While termination is sometimes an effective solution, it is considered the "capital punishment" in the employment relationship and generally should not be the first action taken. In addition, all sorts of liability issues are associated with termination such as wrongful discharge, discharge that could be interpreted to violate a union contract or civil service protection in government, or discharge which might be judged to be a discriminatory act based on race, sex, age, creed, and so on. For these reasons, termination should be carefully thought out and substantiated with documentation that will stand up in a hearing or court of law. We discuss termination further in Chapter 19 of the book, which deals with restructuring.

HR CHALLENGES ••

Model Employment Termination Act (META)

The current state of wrongful discharge litigation is more like a lottery than a legal process. Some complaintants become rich with awards for damages, while others with similar complaints receive nothing. Neither the employers nor the employees benefit from such actions. To correct this problem, the Model Employment Termination Act (META) was introduced.

One reason for the random outcomes in the courts for wrongful discharge cases is due to the ever increasing common-law exceptions being developed on a case-by-case basis as states decided wrongful discharge cases brought on by terminations in employment-at-will situations. The main provision of META would be arbitration instead of court litigation for discharges. The arbitrator will be severely limited in the amount of damages that can be awarded, usually to back pay and up to four years of future pay.

META would also provide a universal definition of just and unjust dismissals that could be used by all states. Just discharges would be those based upon performance problems, economic problems, company relocations and the like.

Currently META favors the employers for several reasons. First, the threat of large settlements are gone, only back and front pay can be offered. Second, because just cause is clearly defined, there is no fear of a poor interpretation of the situation. Finally, an arbitrator, not the court system decides the case. This is less costly and frequently quicker.

The employee also receives some benefits. First, all employees must be made aware of the process when terminated. In the past, many suffered in silence because they did not know they had any other options. Also, because the termination policy is standardized across states, employees have a clearer idea of why and how the termination process works. While not a law yet, META is sure to attract a lot of attention as the debate continues.

SOURCE: Jeremy Fox and Hugh Hindman, "State to Address Model Termination Law," *HRNews*, January 1992, pp. 1+.

One final note on the termination of problem employees. In many states, alcohol and drug abuse are considered to be treatable illnesses. If termination is carried out without first trying to rehabilitate the employee, a court or hearing officer may order reinstatement based on the fact that the employee was dismissed on the basis of a handicap—a reasonable accommodation was not first attempted (in this case a rehabilitation program). Other actions that an employer can take other than termination are discussed below.

The Counseling Process

Managers should counsel problem employees to the extent they can and should readily refer employees to professional counseling as necessary. This is why having an EAP program is so beneficial in dealing with problem employees. We are not suggesting here that managers attempt a full-blown counseling program with the employee; rather we are suggesting that management constructively confront the employee about the problem and attempt to find out more information about what is going on and how the behavior can be changed.

In this book, we do not get into the details of counseling; however, we do suggest a few guidelines below:

- Talk with the employee to specifically define the problem in terms of the behavior that needs to be changed.
- Focus on behavior that the employee can change—behavior that is within control of the employee.
- Enlist the employee's assistance in coming up with specific suggestions for changing the behavior in order to create a sense of ownership on the part of the employee for the solution to the problem.

- Jointly establish a means of monitoring and follow up with the employee to verify compliance.
- Emphasize the consequences of not fulfilling the "behavior contract"—specifically deal with the question of what will happen to the employee. Schedule follow up meetings with a timetable.
- Offer encouragement and indicate that you support the employee and that you want him or her to do better.

Avoid getting involved in personal off-the-job problems with the employee, and certainly avoid telling the employee specific steps he or she should take in his or her personal life.[21] For example, do not ever tell an employee that he or she should divorce his or her spouse. If the problem rests here, suggest marriage counseling.

Types of Problem Employees

Managers can encounter a variety of problem employees. We do not list every type here, nor do we go into extensive detail as to how to handle each type. Rather, our purpose is simply to identify each type and to point out some strategic considerations that must be kept in mind from a rights and responsibilities standpoint.

Alcohol/Drug Abuser

Unfortunately this problem is becoming more common in organizations. An estimated 12 percent of the nation's work force suffers from some form of substance abuse today, and the figures are not improving.[22] The primary consideration here is to give the employee the opportunity to rehabilitate without risking injury to self or others and without doing damage to the organization's operations. As indicated earlier in the chapter, it is essential for the organization to have a policy on drug use, drug testing, and alcohol use and to thoroughly communicate and enforce it. Exhibit 16.9 shows sample guidelines that organizations should follow when adopting a drug/alcohol policy. It is also important to have or have access to an EAP.

Approaching alcohol and drug abuse as treatable medical problems is legally safer and usually better protects employee rights by giving the employee the opportunity to correct behavior prior to disciplinary action or termination.

Marginal/Low Performer

This employee is one who is just meeting minimum standards of job accomplishment. The employee is not neglecting job duties to the extent that termination is warranted. Since the employee is actually meeting job standards, termination can bring legal challenges. From a strategic standpoint, it is better for the organization to create a culture of involvement and leadership so as to prevent these problems from occurring, and to use peer pressure to resolve them once they do occur. Also a reward system that provides financial and nonfinancial incentives for top performance can work to prevent and alleviate problems of this type.

Tardy/Absent Employee

A person can be absent or tardy for many reasons, but the fact is that if a person is gone, regardless of the reason, the work is not getting done. In order to avoid being

| EXHIBIT 16.9 | General Alcohol/Drug Policy Development Guidelines |

- Address the problem of alcohol and drug abuse squarely
- Conduct proper investigations of suspected violations
- Follow appropriate disciplinary guidelines
- Train supervisors and educate employees
- Develop a policy on rehabilitation or employee assistance
- Be sensitive to employees' privacy rights
- Take reasonable steps to protect employees and others from harm caused by substance abusers
- Know the applicable statutes and regulations
- Practice good employee relations

In addition:

- Define the problem in workplace terms while avoiding legal, moral, and medical definitions
- Safeguard privacy, due process, and confidentiality
- Avoid conflict with applicable federal, state, and local statutes and regulations
- Apply substance-abuse policies equitably throughout the organization

placed in the position of ruling on the appropriateness of the reason for absence or tardiness, many organizations have adopted one or more of the following policies:

- Flexible working hours (flextime)
- Call-in rules if one is absent that, if violated, may result in loss of the job
- The accumulation of leave time that can be taken for either vacation or illness
- Bonuses at the end of the year or at retirement for unused sick leave
- Wellness programs that encourage employees to develop good health and fitness habits, thereby reducing illness
- Day care for employees with small children

Whatever policy the organization comes up with, it should be clearly communicated to all employees and consistently enforced. With the advent of newer work arrangements, such as telecommuting (working at home via computer link to office), the tardiness and absence problem that sometimes plagues organizations may subside as an issue.

Saboteur/Thief

Our system believes that an individual is innocent until proven guilty. Yet continuing the employment of a person suspected of a criminal act against the organization can be disastrous. How can the organization protect itself from criminal actions while protecting the rights of a suspected employee?

One common action taken by employers is to suspend suspected employees with or without pay until a hearing can be held to determine whether the evidence indicates a possibility of guilt. Assuming a speedy and fair hearing is held, the organization can either reinstate the employee or take other disciplinary action up to and including termination and prosecution through the courts.[23]

Caustic/Sarcastic/Negative Attitude

This employee can be the rotten apple that spoils the barrel in that the adverse attitude can become contagious. This situation must be dealt with by focusing on the behavior that results from the negative attitude. For example, if this attitude causes the employee to lose his or her temper when working with customers or other employees, it is appropriate for management to point out that such behavior will not be tolerated in the future. Or if the attitude results in the spreading of vicious lies, gossip, or character assassinations, the employee must be confronted with such remarks and told such statements must cease.

Changing an attitude is very difficult because it is not directly observable and is open to much debate. For example, just what exactly is a "bad attitude"? Behavior also is not easy to change in many cases, but at least it is observable and verifiable.

The final section of this chapter addresses the issue of discipline and relates it to the protection of employee rights and the handling of problem employees. Creating the proper disciplinary climate is important for preventing and resolving disciplinary issues while protecting the rights of employees.

BUILDING A GOOD DISCIPLINARY CLIMATE

From a strategic standpoint, management has a responsibility to create the proper disciplinary climate rather than just allow any climate to evolve. This means that management and human resource managers must have in mind a set of desirable criteria. A good disciplinary climate is usually characterized by the following:

- Emphasizes self-discipline over externally imposed discipline
- Is positive and future oriented
- Emphasizes prevention as well as correction
- Is progressive in nature
- Is properly communicated—people are put on notice
- Is fairly and impartially administered

We will briefly look at each of these characteristics.

Self-discipline

The best discipline is discipline that employees impose upon themselves. They do the right thing because they know it is expected and they want to do it. This is a difficult goal to reach in many organizations. Instead, many external control measures are imposed to ensure that people do the right thing. While some level of external control is always necessary, the emphasis should be shifted to creating a culture that fosters and rewards self-control and self-discipline. For example, Thomas J. Peters and Robert H. Waterman, in their book *In Search of Excellence*, report on the astounding success of IBM. They attribute this success to IBM's focus on its people:

> Treat people as adults. Treat them as partners; treat them with dignity; treat them with respect. . . . Thomas J. Watson, Jr. [former CEO of IBM], puts it well: "IBM's philosophy is largely contained in three simple beliefs. I want to begin with what I think is the most important: *our respect for the individual.* This is a simple concept, but in IBM it

occupies a major portion of management time. We devote more effort to it than anything else."[24]

Peters and Waterman report on dozens of companies who succeed by enabling their employees to control themselves. The advantage of self-control is that the bureaucratic red tape and cumbersome reporting and check-up procedures are greatly reduced. Instead, managers *manage by exception.* People are assumed to be doing the right thing unless they demonstrate otherwise. Managers need only monitor in a general sense and only become involved when performance gets out of line and is not quickly self-corrected. This approach reflects Theory Y assumptions about people as described earlier. People want to work and want to do a good job and the manager's role is to create conditions that allow this to happen.

Positive and Future Oriented

Discipline should focus on positive actions expected in the future rather than on negative ones experienced in the past. This means that the climate should focus on explaining what behaviors are expected and how employees can achieve these behaviors rather than on punishing behaviors of the past.

Preventative and Corrective

A good disciplinary climate prevents as well as corrects undesirable behavior. Of course from a strategic standpoint, it is better to prevent undesirable behavior from occurring in the first place than it is to correct it after the fact. In other words, there must be incentives to do the right thing and anticipated negative sanctions for doing the wrong thing. These negative sanctions can serve as a deterrent provided they are

- known ahead of time,
- administered in a timely fashion, and
- equally applied to everyone (the "hot stove" rule: the consequence is immediately applied to everyone who touches the hot stove).

Corrective actions should focus just on that: correcting the behavior. This means managers and human resource managers must clearly spell out in very specific terms what the employee must do and must instruct the employee on how to do it. Incentives for compliance as well as negative sanctions for noncompliance should also be clearly indicated.

Progressive

Progressive discipline means that the severity of the sanction increases with the severity and repeated nature of the offense. Some actions might warrant immediate dismissal, such as theft. But others trigger a series of steps. For example Exhibit 16.10 shows the progressive discipline schedule used by a restaurant chain for a series of relatively minor offenses. These minor offenses can range from showing up late for one's shift to failing to clean up one's work station at the end of the shift. Notice that the disciplinary action proceeds from a relatively light sanction of oral warning to a serious one of termination. Of course, this schedule is clearly spelled out to the employees ahead of time so they know what to expect.

EXHIBIT 16.10   An Example of Progressive Discipline

DISCIPLINARY PROBLEM: FAILURE TO REPORT TO SHIFT ON TIME

First offense: Oral warning
Second offense: Written warning
Third offense: Loss of one shift's pay
Fourth offense: Three days off without pay
Fifth offense: Dismissal

Properly Communicated

As indicated above, proper communication with employees is essential for good discipline. Employees must be absolutely clear as to expectations. They must also know what is required to achieve these expectations and what happens to them if they do not. Further, they need to be properly put on notice if a previously unenforced rule is now going to be enforced or else they will claim in a hearing that past practice ruled over the written rule and they will win their case.

To ensure good communication, a variety of methods should be used to clearly communicate expectations and desired behavior: face-to-face meetings, written handouts, bulletin board postings, and videos. Sunshine Junior Stores, Inc., a convenience store chain in the southeastern United States, makes extensive use of videos in new employee orientation where expectations, policies, procedures, and rules are clearly covered. The advantage of video is that the desired and undesired behavior can be very clearly demonstrated visually.

Fairly and Impartially Administered

Finally, the disciplinary process should be fairly and impartially administered. This means that individual rights should be protected and that favoritism should largely be absent from the process. People are treated alike no matter what their relationship to key people, wealth, or other factors. In practice, of course, this is difficult to achieve. But the system must be perceived as fair if it is to be respected and voluntarily adhered to. In a union situation, the concepts of fairness and equity are often spelled out in the labor agreement. Since the employees have had some say on discipline through their union in collective bargaining negotiations, the system might have higher perceptions of equity than in a nonunion situation.

The Right of Appeal

Perceptions of fairness and equity also involve the right of appeal. That is a dissatisfied employee should have the right to appeal a disciplinary decision to a person or board. As we see in the next two chapters, this right is clearly spelled out in union agreements. In nonunion situations the right might involve simply appealing the decision to the next higher level of supervision.

These rights and responsibilities are further discussed in Chapters 17 and 18, which deal with unions. Unions present a special strategic challenge to organizations since they provide employees with an organized way to make their wishes known and to seek redress for grievances. The unions of the 1990s are far different from unions of the 1930s, 1940s, and 1950s. The next two chapters explore these differences and explore these challenges for organizations.

• • • • • • • • •

MANAGEMENT GUIDELINES

Based on the issues addressed in this chapter, the following management guidelines can be presented.

1. Five basic factors influence management's approach to its responsibilities and employee rights: management philosophy, the tightness of the labor market, the law, union and employee power, and organizational culture. Managers must consider the balance these factors create when developing their approach to rights and responsibilities.

2. The law has a large influence on employee rights. Legislation on discrimination, employment at will, and privacy all play major roles in management's creation of employee rights policies.

3. Employee rights policies must deal with seven basic areas to be complete. These areas are privacy, fair treatment, workplace health and safety, organization communication and employee involvement, notice of plant closings and disciplinary action, and due process. Management failure to adequately deal with any of these areas is likely to result in severe organizational problems.

4. Managers must seek to reduce the conflict between its responsibilities to its internal and external stakeholders without unduly harming any one group, such as employees. This can usually be accomplished by making ethically correct decisions.

5. Management responsibilities are closely related to employee rights, but do not represent two sides of the same coin. These responsibilities include knowing the law, providing open communication, treating all employees with dignity, bargaining collectively, and providing due process.

6. Managers must recognize the differences between problem employees and employees with problems. Managers must treat these as different situations and deal with each according to its own rules and methods.

7. Employee discipline is essential to organizational success. In general, the best policies are those that emphasize employee self-discipline. Good discipline policies are positive and future oriented, emphasize prevention and correction, are progressive and properly communicated, and are fairly and impartially communicated. Poor policies are likely to produce organizational turmoil and severely hamper company performance.

QUESTIONS FOR REVIEW

1. What arguments can an employer use to justify having a drug or AIDS testing policy? Why might an applicant or employees be concerned about such a test?

2. Give three examples of how the culture of a society can influence how employers treat their employees.

3. Many firms who thought they were operating under an employment-at-will doctrine later ended up in court defending themselves. Describe two precautions that managers can take to ensure that their organization does not get sued for a wrongful discharge.

4. This chapter lists and describes seven basic employee rights. Identify two and explain them.

5. What is the stakeholders concept with respect to employer responsibilities? What are some of the problems with this approach?

6. What is organizational ethics? How are ethical standards instilled in people? What, if anything, can an organization do to increase or alter the ethical standards of its employees?

7. What is the difference between a problem employee and an employee with a problem? What can be done to help either or both of these types of employees?

8. List four different types of problem employees. Compare and contrast how a manager should deal with each type.

9. Describe how one can go about developing a good disciplinary climate.

10. At your yearly performance evaluation interview, you are informed by your boss that she has been spying on you periodically throughout the year in order to gather accurate information to be used in your appraisal. You received high marks and a large raise. How do you feel about the fact that you boss has been spying on you? What if you received a poor evaluation and no raise? Would it change your opinion about the boss' spying?

 CASE: The Clash between Employee Rights and Employer Monitoring[25]

Imagine you were at work and you needed to use the phone. How would you feel if you knew that your employer might be listening in on your conversation? Is your employer justified in listening to you in an effort to save expenses and monitor your job performance? Or is this an all-out invasion of your right to privacy? The technology exists today for employers to electronically monitor employees' phone calls, watch what they type at their computer terminals, read their electronic mail, and watch them talk to their coworkers.

The advent of the modern electronics age has made the privacy issue one of the decade's hottest topics in employee rights. Consider the following situations:

- General Electric uses fisheye lenses mounted in wall and ceiling pinholes to watch employees suspected of crimes.
- DuPont uses long-distance cameras to watch employees on its loading docks.

- Delta Airlines monitors booking agent productivity through its computer system.
- Management Recruiters, Inc., monitors computer-based employee schedules to see who interviews the most candidates.
- Holy Cross Hospital in Silver Spring, Maryland, mounted a surveillance camera in the women nurses' locker room to investigate missing narcotics.
- Safeway Stores uses electronic systems in its trucks to monitor employee driving habits.
- Until recently, police departments in Connecticut, Rhode Island, West Virginia, and Utah routinely tapped all incoming and outgoing phone calls to the barracks—including privileged defendant-attorney conversations.

Which of these actions are fair and which ones represent an invasion of employee privacy? Almost all forms of electronic monitoring have been challenged in court (see for example, *James* v. *Newspaper Agency Corporation* for phone monitoring or *United States* v. *McIntyre* for bugging), but federal, state, and local legislation and court decisions still do not make clear what is acceptable and what is not.

From the employer's perspective most of the above monitoring situations can be attributed to one of two basic causes: (1) the need to increase employee performance and (2) attempts to reduce employee theft. Many firms argue that lost revenues due to theft and poor productivity are hampering their ability to compete. Estimates of losses due to employee theft in U.S. companies range between $15 and $25 billion per year. Productivity losses are assumed to be much higher. Employers are turning to electronic monitoring techniques more frequently to combat these problems. A recent survey indicates that 15 percent of the nation's firms use employee phone monitoring. One estimate calculates that 14,000 firms monitored 1.5 million workers' phone calls in 1987—all without worker knowledge. All told, approximately 15 million people work in industries where some form of electronic monitoring is used.

Most challenges to electronic monitoring are based on the "reasonable expectation of privacy" doctrine. This doctrine generally holds that there are situations where a person can reasonably expect to be free of any form of monitoring or surveillance. Any invasion of this reasonable expectation of privacy should not be allowed. Unfortunately, the problem is, what constitutes a reasonable expectation of privacy? In "Protecting Private Employees," Terry Dworkin suggests that in areas where employees have high expectations of privacy, such as private offices, changing areas, and bathrooms, use of electronic monitoring equipment could lead to successful employee suits against the employer unless the employer can show a great need for the surveillance. However, she adds that there are even exceptions to this rule. A recent federal court case, *Postal Workers Union* v. *United States Postal Service*, held that "relative lack of scrutiny" in these areas did not necessarily create a reasonable expectation of privacy.

Furthermore, violations of privacy rights generally are a combination of civil and criminal offenses. Often, victims must sue in civil courts to obtain damages and must prove that the employer's monitoring was done without sufficient cause to do so. In criminal cases, courts have generally held that people give up a great deal of privacy expectations when they become employees of an organization. Even when privacy rights are generally established, organizations can often monitor their employees by informing workers that monitoring is a general policy or by making workers sign privacy waivers as a condition of employment.

Another problem is that it is believed that the use of monitoring techniques generally harms employee morale, strains labor-management relations, and often produces increased stress in employees under surveillance. Managers are strongly cautioned to consider these side effects when developing a monitoring policy.

All of these problems with employee monitoring are likely to make it one of the most controversial—and litigated and legislated—human resource issues of the 1990s.

QUESTIONS

1. What other ways, besides electronic monitoring, are available to managers to determine how productive employees are?

2. One aspect of the human resource function is to hire employees whom the organization can trust. If managers feel compelled to spy on employees to reduce employee theft, is human resource failing at its job?

3. Telephone operators who are aware that their manager may be listening or watching them have reported higher incidents of headaches, back pain, fatigue, shoulder soreness, anxiety, and sore wrists. Obviously, these problems could reduce an employee's effectiveness. Do you think these managers are hurting productivity by monitoring their employees?

4. Several software packages are on the market that can be used by managers to spy on their employees by tapping into the employees' computers and viewing what is on their screen. Often these programs can be run without the knowledge of the employee. Should it be illegal for software companies to market this type of product? Why or why not?

ADDITIONAL READINGS

Barrar, Peter, and Cary Cooper. *Managing Organizations in 1992.* New York: Routledge, 1992.

Barrett, Paul. "High Court Upholds Workers' Comp Law in Setback to Employer-Rights Advocates," *Wall Street Journal.* March 10, 1992, p. A3.

Bellingham, Richard, and Barry Cohen. *Ethical Leadership: A Competitive Edge.* Amherst, MA: HRD Press, 1991.

Bible, Jon. "When Employers Look for Things Other than Drugs: The Legality of AIDS, Genetic, Intelligence, and Honesty Testing in the Workplace." *Labor Law Journal.* April 1990, pp. 195–213.

Brown, Darrel, and George Gray. "A Positive Alternative to Employment at Will" *Advanced Management Journal.* Summer 1988, pp. 13–16.

Carrell, Michael, and Christina Heavrin. "Before You Drug Test." *HRMagazine.* June 1990, pp. 64–68.

Center for Employment Relations and Law, College of Law, Florida State University. "Wrongful Discharge." *Employment Relations Bulletin.* January 1990.

Cross, Jeffrey. "The Employee Polygraph Protection Act of 1988: Background and Implications." *Labor Law Journal.* October 1989, pp. 663–671.

Daniels, Robert. "Storm Is Brewing between Employers, Employees Over the Right to Privacy." *Wall Street Journal.* August 10, 1990, p. B6A.

Dworkin, Terry. "Protecting Private Employees from Enhanced Monitoring: Legislative Approaches." *American Business Law Journal* 28 (1990), pp. 59–85.

Etziono, Amitai. *The Responsive Society.* San Francisco: Jossey-Bass, 1991.

Florida Statutes 1989, Chapter 110.227 and Chapter 447.208.

Goff, J. Larry. "Corporate Responsibilities to the Addicted Employee: A Look at Practical, Legal, and Ethical Issues." *Labor Law Journal.* April 1990, pp. 214–221.

Goldblatt, Michael. "Preserving the Right to Fire." *Small Business Report.* December 1986, p. 87.

Hawkins, Robert. "Diversity and Municipal Openness." *Public Management.* January 1992, pp. 33–35.

Hayes, Arthur. "Layoffs Take Careful Planning to Avoid Losing the Suits that Are Apt to Follow." *Wall Street Journal.* November 2, 1990, p. B1.

Henry, Sandra. "Can You Recognize the Wrongful Discharge?" *Labor Law Journal.* March 1989, pp. 168–176.

Henshaw, Georgeanne, and Kenwood Youmans. "Employee Privacy in the Workplace and an Employer's Right to Conduct Workplace Searches and Surveillance." *Society for Human Resource Management Legal Report.* Spring 1990, pp. 1–5.

Israel, David, Pamela Sweeny, and Michael Mitchell. "Workplace Surveillance Risky Business for Employers." *HRNews/Society for Human Resource Management.* January 1990, p. 15.

Kelly, Kevin, and Michael Oneal. "This Turnaround Will Be Tougher Than Al Cheechi Thought." *Business Week.* December 24, 1990, pp. 28–30.

Marcus, Amy. "Courts Uphold Oral Pledges of Lifetime Employment." *Wallstreet Journal.* December 12, 1989, p. B1.

Mathis, Robert, and John Jackson. *Personnel/Human Resource Management.* 5th ed. New York: West, 1988.

Miceli, Marcia, and Janet Near. *Blowing the Whistle.* New York: Free Press, 1992.

Oliver, Bill. "Do You Drug Test Your Employees?" *HRMagazine.* October 1990, p. 57.

Pace, Larry, and Stanley Smits. "Workplace Substance Abuse: A Proactive Approach." *Personnel Journal.* April 1989, pp. 84–88.

Peters, Thomas, and Robert Waterman. *In Search of Excellence: Lessons from America's Best-Run Companies.* New York: Warner Books, 1982.

Rosen, Benson, and Catherine Schwoerer. "Balanced Protection Policies." *HRMagazine.* February 1990, pp. 59–64.

Rothfeder, Jeffrey, et al. "Is Nothing Private?" *Business Week.* September 4, 1989, pp. 74–82.

Rothfeder, Jeffrey, Michelle Galen and Lisa Driscoll. "Is Your

Boss Spying on You?" *Business Week.* January 15, 1990. pp. 74–75.

Salaman, Graeme. *Human Resource Strategies.* Newbury Park, CA; Sage, 1992.

Segal, Jonathan. "Follow the Yellow Brick Road." *HRMagazine.* February 1990, pp. 83–86.

Segal, Jonathan. "Test Suspected Users Only." *HRMagazine.* November 1990, p. 79.

Sheppard, Blair, Roy Lewicki, and John Minton. *Organizational Justice.* New York: Free Press, 1992.

Smits, Stanley, and Larry Pace. "Workplace Substance Abuse: Establish Policies." *Personnel Journal.* May 1989, pp. 88–93.

Staudohar, Paul. "New Plant Closing Law Aids Works in Transition." *Personnel Journal.* January 1989, pp. 87–90.

Tompkins, Jonathan. "Legislating the Employment Relationship: Montana's Wrongful-Discharge Law." *Employee Relations Law Journal.* Winter 1988/1989, pp. 387–398.

Willard, Richard. "Drug Test All Employees Randomly." *HRMagazine.* November 1990, p. 78.

Zachary, G. Pascal. "Bruised Apple." *Wall Street Journal.* February 15, 1990, p. A1.

·················
NOTES

1. Jon Bible, "When Employers Look for Things Other Than Drugs: The Legality of AIDS, Genetic, Intelligence, and Honesty Testing in the Workplace," *Labor Law Journal*, April 1990, pp. 195–213; Michael Carrell and Christina Heavrin, "Before You Drug Test," *HRMagazine*, June 1990, pp. 64–68; Robert Daniels, "Storm Is Brewing between Employers, Employees over the Right to Privacy," *Wall Street Journal*, August 10, 1990, p. B6A; Terry Dworkin, "Protecting Private Employees from Enhanced Monitoring: Legislative Approaches," *American Business Law Journal* 28, 1990, pp. 59–85; Georgeanne Henshaw and Kenwood Youmans, "Employee Privacy in the Workplace and an Employer's Right to Conduct Workplace Searches and Surveillance," *Society for Human Resource Management Legal Report*, Spring 1990, pp. 1–5; David Israel, Pamela Sweeny, and Michael Mitchell, "Workplace Surveillance Risky Business for Employers," *HR News/Society for Human Resource Management*, January 1990, p. 15; Benson Rosen and Catherine Schwoerer, "Balanced Protection Policies," *HRMagazine*, February 1990, pp. 59–64; Jeffrey Rothfeder, Michelle Galen, and Lisa Driscoll, "Is Your Boss Spying on You?" *Business Week*, January 15, 1990, pp. 74–75; Kevin Kelly and Michael Oneal, "This Turnaround Will Be Tougher Than Al Checchi Thought," *Business Week*, December 24, 1990, pp. 28–30; Jeffrey L. Cross, "The Employee Polygraph Protection Act of 1988: Background and Implications," *Labor Law Journal*, October 1989, p. 663; Jeffrey Rothfeder et al., "Is Nothing Private?" *Business Week*, September 4, 1989, pp. 74–82; "Division of Workers' Compensation Proposes Changes to Drug Testing Rules," *Florida Employment Lawletter*, October 1991, pp. 1–2; and David Gold and Beth Unger, "Weigh Legalities in Formulating AIDS Policy," *HRNews*, August 1991, p. 5.

2. Maryann Keller, *Rude Awakening: The Rise, Fall, and Struggle for Recovery of General Motors* (New York: William Morrow, 1989).

3. Thomas Peters and Robert Waterman, *In Search of Excellence: Lessons from America's Best-Run Companies* (New York: Warner Books, 1982), pp. 244–245.

4. G. Pascal Zachary, "Bruised Apple," *Wall Street Journal*, February 15, 1990, p. A1.

5. To date, 40 states have enacted some form of legislation that modifies the employment-at-will concept. For more information on employment-at-will legislation, see Michael Goldblatt, "Preserving the Right to Fire," *Small Business Report*, December 1986, p. 87; and Darrel Brown and George Gray, "A Positive Alternative to Employment at Will," *Advanced Management Journal*, Summer 1988, pp. 13–16. In 1987 Montana became the first state to pass a wrongful discharge law, which essentially allows workers to challenge the employment-at-will doctrine in court under several conditions. For more information on the Montana law, see Jonathan Tompkins, "Legislating the Employment Relationship: Montana's Wrongful-Discharge Law," *Employee Relations Law Journal*, Winter 1988/1989, pp. 387–398.

6. "Distribution of Employee Manual Does Not Give Rise to Contract," *Employment Law Report*, November 1991, p. 1.

7. See, for example, Amy Dockser Marcus, "Courts Uphold Oral Pledges of Lifetime Employment," *Wall Street Journal*, December 12, 1989, p. B1.

8. Milo Greyelin and Jonathan Moses, "Rulings on Wrongful Firing Curb Hiring," *Wall Street Journal*, April 9, 1992, p. B3.

9. Debbie Keary, "Minimize the Risk of Wrongful Discharge, Urges Brown," *HRNews*, June 1990, p. 7.

10. We recognize that this list is somewhat arbitrary and that other authors might have a different list. However, our list generally conforms to accepted listings. See James Hunt, *The Law of the Workplace: Rights of Employers and Employees* (Edison, NJ: BNA, 1988).

11. Jonathan Segal, "A Need Not to Know," *HRMagazine*, October 1991, pp. 85–90.

12. Jeffrey Rothfeder, Michele Galen, and Lisa Driscoll, "Is Your Boss Spying on You?" *Business Week*, January 15, 1991, p. 74.

13. "Most Serious Ethical Problems Involve Differences in the Way People Are Treated Based on Favoritism or Relationship to Top Management," *1991 SHRM/CCH Survey*, June 1991, p. 3.

14. Center for Employment Relations and Law, College of Law, Florida State University, "Wrongful Discharge," *Employment Relations Bulletin*, January 1990, p. 3.

15. See Kenneth L. Sovereign, *Personnel Law*, 2nd ed., (Englewood Cliffs NJ: Prentice-Hall, 1989), pp. 87–93.

16. 29 CFR 16.011 (A).

17. See, for example, Thomas Peters and Robert Waterman, *In Search of Excellence: Lessons from America's Best-Run Companies* (New York: Warner Books, 1982).

18. Paul Staudohar, "New Plant Closing Law Aids Workers in Transition," *Personnel Journal*, January 1989, p. 90.

19. Alan Weiss, "Seven Reasons to Examine Workplace Ethics," *HRMagazine*, March 1991, pp. 69–74.

20. David W. Ewing, "Corporate Due Process Lowers Legal Costs", *Wall Street Journal*, October 23, 1989, p. A14.

21. "Employees' Rights, after Hours," *Manager's Legal Bulletin*, Alexander Hamilton Institute Incorporated.

22. Larry Pace and Stanley Smits, "Workplace Substance Abuse: A Proactive Approach," *Personnel Journal*, April 1989, pp. 84–88.

22. Michael Allen, "Security Experts Advise Firms to Avoid Panic, Excess Zeal in Probing Data Leaks," *Wall Street Journal*, September 20, 1991, pp. B1+.

24. Thomas J. Peters and Robert H. Waterman, *In Search of Excellence: Lessons from America's Best Run Companies* (New York: Warner Books, 1982), p. 238.

25. Terry Morehead Dworkin, "Protecting Private Employees from Enhanced Monitoring: Legislative Approaches," *American Business Law Journal* 28, pp. 59–85; David Israel, Pamela Sweeny, and Michael Mitchell, "Workplace Surveillance Risky Business for Employers," *HRNews/Society for Human Resource Management*, January 1990, p. 15; Robert Daniels, "Storm Is Brewing between Employers, Employees Over the Right to Privacy," *Wall Street Journal*, August 10, 1990, p. B6A.; Jeffrey Rothfeder, Michele Galen, and Lisa Driscoll, "Is Your Boss Spying on You?" *Business Week*, January 15, 1990. pp. 74–75; Georgeanne Henshaw and Kenwood Youmans, "Employee Privacy in the Workplace and an Employer's Right to Conduct Workplace Searches and Surveillance," *Society for Human Resource Management Legal Report*, Spring 1990, pp. 1–5; Gene Bylinsky, "How Companies Spy on Employees," *Fortune*, November 4, 1991, pp. 13–140; and Michael Allen, "Legislation Could Restrict Bosses from Snooping on Their Workers," *Wall Street Journal*, September 24, 1991, pp. B1+.

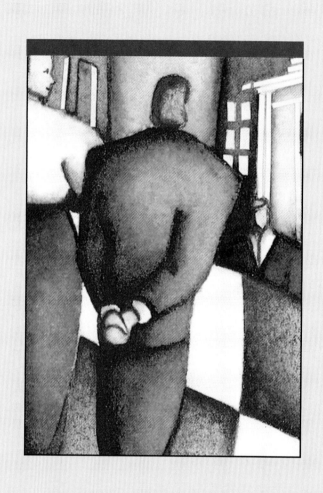

PART FIVE

Strategies for Dealing with Unions

17

The Role of Unions

One of the most significant issues facing managers in the 1990s is the changing role that unions are playing in the economy. Important economic shifts have impacted not only companies and unions but also the very essence of their relationship. Worldwide markets, changing demographics, and attitude changes make it necessary for managers, and particularly human resource managers, to understand the strategic role of unions.

This chapter examines how and why unions came into existence in this country, the legal basis for unions, some of the driving forces that are causing the shift in roles, the current state of union-employer relationships, innovative solutions to some old labor-management problems, and the outlook for labor relations in the 1990s.

• • • • • • • • •
CHAPTER OBJECTIVES

As a result of studying this chapter, you should be able to

1. Identify strategic issues that affect labor unions today.
2. Identify strategic choices made by management and unions.
3. Discuss the historical development of unions in the United States.
4. Describe the current state of union growth, decline, and development.
5. Discuss the role and desires of unions in society today.
6. Explain the law that regulates relations between union and management.

Eastern Airlines: Up, Up and into Bankruptcy[1]

As late as August of 1989, organized labor was proclaiming that it still had what it took to score a labor victory at Eastern Airlines. The fact that the Airline Pilots Association (ALPA), in March of 1989, had joined the machinists in their long and bitter strike was initially read as proof that, indeed, organized labor still had the muscle and could use it. One only had to walk through the Atlanta International Airport, a major Eastern hub, in the summer of 1989 to feel the effect. Dozens of Eastern jets were parked with their engines covered for protection for a long and protracted battle. The victory was short-lived however, and the hopes faded when in late November 1989 the ALPA announced that it was calling off its 264-day strike and was prepared to go back to work.

Flying at a New Low

The once high-flying Eastern Airlines that had dominated the east coast corridor had hit a new low. What had brought about this decline and deterioration in a few short years? While there were many potential explanations, the turbulence created by deregulation and the accompanying labor-management disputes played a major role in the decline. Exhibit 17.1 demonstrates the slide in terms of overall market share, profitability, and employee levels.

It is not unusual for labor and management to blame each other when a company or an industry starts to suffer declines. But in this case the dispute was particularly bitter.

Dramatic Changes in the Airline Industry

As long as the airline industry was a stable, regulated industry, with high barriers to entry and almost guaranteed fares, the unions and management could work out a liveable arrangement. But in the mid to late 1970s and on through the 1980s several economic environmental changes occurred. First, fuel prices rose drastically. Then the 1981–1982 recession hit airlines particularly hard. The final and perhaps most significant change transpired with the deregulation of the airlines. New nonunionized upstart airlines like People Express forced down air fares. No longer could an airline deliver what it deemed acceptable at an artificially supported price. But the

---

EXHIBIT 17.1 Eastern's Troubled Outlook

Mounting Losses...

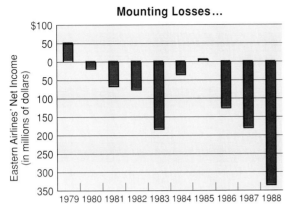

Reduced Workforce...

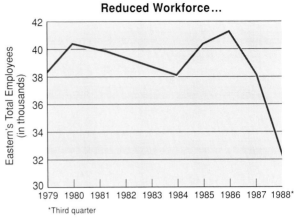

*Third quarter

And a Shrinking Share...

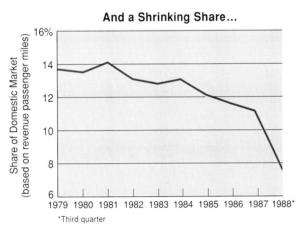

*Third quarter

Of a Competitive Market

Largest U.S. airlines ranked by market share based on revenue passenger miles		
Airline January	1989	1988
American Airlines	16.6%	15.2%
United Airlines	16.2%	16.4%
Texas Air	15.9%	19.3%
Delta Airlines	13.3%	12.0%
Northwest Airlines	9.6%	8.9%
Continental Airlines*	9.3%	10.5%
Trans World Airlines	7.2%	7.4%
USAir Group	7.2%	7.2%
Eastern Airlines*	6.6%	8.7%
Pan American Airlines	5.9%	7.1%

*Part of Texas Air

---

management and the unions, who had grown comfortable in the previous environment, seemed to have difficulty aligning with the new market conditions.

Frank Borman, the former astronaut, was brought in as CEO at Eastern to make change. Ultimately Borman reached an impasse with the strong and militant International Machinists Union. Borman and the Eastern Board threatened to sell off Eastern Airlines if concessions were not made. In fact, the sale did take place in 1986 to Texas Air. That's when the real trouble started.

Lorenzo—Brilliant Strategist or Greedy Opportunist?

Frank Lorenzo, who made his reputation by breaking the unions of Continental Airlines, was now the formidable foe. Lorenzo was in a fighting mood from the very beginning after the Eastern Airlines acquisition. He had sought a showdown with Eastern's 8,500 machinists. But it was clear that the unions also were ready for a fight. They wanted to humble Lorenzo—even if they did not win the battle—because he had, in their eyes, smashed the machinists and pilots at Continental in 1983.

A series of important events occurred from March through July 1989. The sequence ran as follows:

- March 4—The pilots and airline attendants voted not to cross the picket line. (This apparently caught Lorenzo off guard.)
- March 9—Eastern Airlines filed for Chapter 11 bankruptcy.
- April 6—Eastern announced its sale to Peter Uberroth's investment group, subject to agreements with the unions.
- April 12—The sale collapsed because Lorenzo and Uberroth could not agree on who would control the airline before the sale was consummated. Lorenzo would not relinquish control until he had been paid.
- April 12—Judge ruled that the pilots' strike was legal.
- April 17—Texas Air took Eastern off the block.
- April 24—Eastern told creditors that it will sell $1.8 billion of assets and shrink to 60 percent of its current size.
- Mid-May—Two separate bids came to bankruptcy examiner Shapiro and he rejected both.
- June 1—Eastern began negotiating a reorganization.
- July 2—Eastern resumed service with 30 percent of its reduced flight schedule.
- October 1989—Eastern sold its lucrative Eastern Air Shuttle to businessperson Donald Trump for $365 million.

By July of 1989 the tide had turned toward management and away from the Eastern unions. Lorenzo was determined to change Eastern. "Eastern has to change and is going to change," he boldly stated. Even before the strike, Eastern had a recent reputation of limited reliability and spotty service. Stranded passengers were left holding $125 million in worthless tickets. Eastern became the airline of the oldest planes and the newest pilots.

Early Union Optimism Turns to Pessimism

The unions had always been militant, but they were not unified. The machinists had been unwilling to take any cuts while the other unions had taken about a 28-percent cutback. This set the different unions into a somewhat adversarial relationship. The unions had high hopes because Lorenzo's actions tended to cause unions to coalesce into a solidarity unknown in the modern labor movement. Strikebreaking pilots formed the cornerstone at Continental but this did not work at Eastern. Initially, labor groups hailed this as a new era, but their optimism was to be cut short.

The pilots had taken a rather bold move in supporting the machinists union but the strike produced devastating effects for both the unions and the airline. By mid-march Eastern laid off 2,500 nonunion employees, 9,500 union employees, and reduced its schedule to just 4 percent of its prestrike flight levels. The unions had gambled and lost. Labor lost much of its momentum when Lorenzo sought protection under bankruptcy, which is tedious and favors management. "Of all the options, ours is the only one left on the plate," Phil Bakes, president of Eastern, stated confidently.

A Small Eastern Returns to the Sky

By November of 1989 Eastern was back up to 800 flights a day (75 percent of the prestrike level) and had a staff of 20,000 employees (about two-thirds the level prior to the strike). Eastern officials maintained that they would survive and prosper. Many analysts believed that the Eastern Airline-union dispute was very different from the traditional economic labor-management dispute. It was really more of an issue of who was going to control the airline.

In the final analysis, the market settled the dispute. Many travelers and travel agents who were burned during the strike steered away from Eastern. Year-end figures for 1990 showed Eastern flying only 800 daily flights to 70 cities. Losses for 1990 were $1.1 billion. By the end of 1990 there was serious doubt if Eastern could survive, as it was losing $2.5 million a day. Fueled by travel agents—who were reluctant to book their customers on Eastern for fear of a repeat of the fiasco of March 1989 or because of Eastern's poor service record—Eastern Airlines went out of business January 18, 1991. At the time of its death, Eastern was the ninth largest airline employing approximately 18,000 employees.

• • • • • • • • •

The Eastern case shows that organized labor is not as powerful as it once was in our society. Management is taking more strategic actions to deal with labor than it had in the 1950s, 1960s, and 1970s. This chapter explores these strategies and provides a basis for understanding the union-management relationship.

STRATEGIC CHOICES

Managers have a number of strategic choices to make regarding the role of unions in the organization. Some of the most important choices are outlined below:

1. Managers who work for organizations that are unionized must decide what type of union-management relationship they want. Once determined, they must take appropriate steps to make this type of relationship a reality. Many additional strategic choices will arise as these steps are determined and taken.

2. Managers who work for organizations without a union must decide how important it is to keep the union out of the company. If it is deemed important to remain nonunion, then management must determine the necessary steps to keep unions out.

3. Management must also choose the type of bargaining tactics to use during contract negotiations with unions.

THE HISTORICAL DEVELOPMENT OF UNIONS

To fully understand today's trends in the labor movement, managers should appreciate the historical basis and development of unions over the last 150 years. Much of the current policy debate and future direction of the labor movement is rooted in the uniquely American experience with unions, which has developed within the context of democratic institutions.

Early History of the Labor Movement

Early attempts at organization go back to around the time of the American Revolution. The earliest movements involved mostly craft organizations and were local in nature.[2] These unions had a common bond of common skill. They sought to protect their chosen occupation through entrance requirements, apprenticeship training, and a form of certification using the "journeyman" and "master" designations. This practice assured employers that they could depend on the quality of work provided by a union member. These same concepts of controlled entrance, apprenticeship training, and quality assurance serve as the basis of craft unions even today. In fact, craft unions often operate a *union hiring hall* that maintains a list of qualified individuals for work. This actually helps employers with the recruiting, screening, hiring, and training functions. The American Federation of Labor (AFL) eventually grew as the group or federation of allied craft unions.

Industrial Unions

Prior to the 1930s, organizing industrial (factory, mining, and so on) workers met with little success. In the 1930s, however, industrial unions began to grow in both numbers and power. Some would argue that the powerful emergence of the unions in the 1930s was a result of excesses and the unchecked power of large emerging corporate entities.[3]

The AFL was against industrial unions because it viewed the workers as unskilled. The unwillingness of the AFL to pursue industrial unionism eventually resulted in the formation of the Congress of Industrial Organization (CIO) which served as the federation for the developing industrial unions. During the 1950s, the AFL and the CIO merged and now most, but not all (the most notable nonmembers include the West Coast Longshoremen and until 1987 the Teamsters) are members of the AFL-CIO union federation in the United States.

Because members of industrial unions typically are not highly skilled, industrial unions do not perform the same screening, training, and placement functions performed by craft unions. Rather their strength lies in numbers; they seek to get as many employees into the union as possible.

Legal Framework

As unions began to grow, many bloody, violent battles erupted between unions and management. The courts and the federal government played a role in trying to stem this violence and to provide a "web of rules" to govern unionization and collective bargaining, or the process of contract negotiation between union and management representatives about issues such as wages, hours, and working conditions. Each of these rules is described and summarized in Exhibit 17.2.

UNIONS TODAY

Growth/Decline and Power

Approximately 18 million workers belong to unions of some type. However, the number, while it remains moderately stable, has to be viewed in light of the growth in the overall labor market. Some sectors, as noted earlier, have declined severely while growth in the public sector and education has countered the decline somewhat. Over 40 percent of public sector employees were unionized in 1989.

However, the overall percentage of unionized workers has declined significantly.[4] From 1970 to 1987 the unions' share of nonfarm labor force declined from 27.3 percent to about 17 percent. Perhaps even more disconcerting to the membership was the fall of average annual wage rate increases during the recession of the early 1980s from a hefty 7.9 percent in 1981 down to only 2.8% in 1983.[5] In 1985 it was only 2.6% compared to 4.6% for nonunion workers.[6] An AFL-CIO study on the wages is controversial but provides a more optimistic view. The report claims that as of June 1987 the average union employee was paid $18.51 in salary and benefits as compared to $13.30 for nonunion workers. The report concedes that the nonunion employees rate gains had been faster in the three preceding years but that it would take more than twenty years for nonunion workers to catch up.[7]

With respect to wage and membership figures, 1991 seemed to be a very good year for unions. Union wages rose and almost caught up with nonunion pay increases in 1991.[8] Further, after three decades of decline, unions' share of total employment leveled at 16.1 percent. While this looks like good news for unions, it is too early to tell. Even though the percentage held, union membership declined by over 170,000 in 1991. The main reason for the optimistic percentage is that the total number of people employed dropped and more of the newly unemployed were not union members.[9] The decline in the total number of employed may be good news for unions. The majority of the people laid off in 1991 had never personally experienced a layoff before. Their feelings of helplessness make them a good target for organizing.[10] These new workers may only help keep the union membership constant, and not increase it because there are many current union members who are willing to cross a picket line in order to not lose their job to replacement workers.[11]

The growth of unions in the future is uncertain. However, the following sectors are among those likely to be explored:

service sector

professional associations (such as the teachers association)

sunbelt workers

smaller businesses

| EXHIBIT 17.2 | **Major Labor Decisions and Laws**

GENERAL COURT INJUNCTION

A court order is used to control the actions of another part. These were used by employers to stop strikes, boycotts, picketing, and organizing activity, but are rarely used today.

SHERMAN ACT (1914)

Originally passed to break up monopolies and trusts, it was used against unions because they were viewed as monopolies in restraint of trade.

CLAYTON ACT (1914)

Sought to exclude unions from provisions of the Sherman Act.

DUPLEX CASE (1921)

Supreme Court affirmed earlier right to prosecute unions under antitrust legislation.

RAILWAY-LABOR ACT (1926)

First favorable legislation for unions. Gave railway workers the right to organize and bargain collectively.

NORRIS-LAGUARDIA ACT (1935)

Made it much more difficult for employers to obtain a court injunction and eliminated yellow-dog contracts under which an employee had to sign a pledge never to join a union to gain employment.

WAGNER ACT (1935)

Guaranteed the right of employees to form, join, assist, and bargain collectively. Formulated procedures for establishing a union and limited employers' actions. Created the National Labor Relations Board (NLRB).

JONES AND LAUGHLIN STEEL CASE (1937)

Supreme Court upheld the Wagner Act as a valid regulation of interstate commerce.

TAFT-HARTLEY (1947)

Prohibited unions from refusing to bargain in good faith, using secondary boycotts, and featherbedding (paying for time not worked), among other things. Set the stage for "right to work laws."

LANDRUM-GRIFFIN ACT (1959)

Regulated the internal working of unions and set standards for union treatment of members.

One factor that may interfere with the unions' expansion plans is the loss of a recent court case. The case revolved around whether or not union organizers should be allowed on company property to communicate with potential union members. Specifically, Lechmere, a variety retail establishment, did not allow union organizers to gather in a parking lot that was generally open to the public. The organizers sued and the case wound up in the Supreme Court. The Court's ruling was in favor of Lechmere. Basically the Court felt that only when employees are so inaccessible that reasonable attempts to reach them through normally used channels do not work, can organizers enter company property.[12]

The Role of Unions Today

The success of unions in the next 10 to 15 years clearly will be based on how well they match their objectives and strategies with the opportunities and threats for unions in the environment. Unions must establish a strategic fit just as must other organizations. This means unions must re-evaluate their role in society given the major changes in the workplace over the last twenty years. The 1985 AFL-CIO report recognized that change was needed. Let's look at some of these potential roles, positions, or fits and discuss how they are changing or might change. To aid our understanding, let's review those roles from both the union and managerial perspectives.

From the Members' Perspective

Unions can provide the following roles: negotiator of wages and benefits, job security advocate, social affiliator, training and development advocate, and political advocate. Larry Reynolds, in "Labor's Leaders Changing to Meet the Times," states that union leaders are no longer billing themselves just as the guardians of organized labor, but also as employee rights advocacy groups. They seek cooperation over confrontation and participation in both decision making and profits.[13]

Wages and Benefits

A prime role that unions play, and perhaps most important for the rank and file, is that of a collective bargaining agent on behalf of employees with a company. As noted above, in recent years the success of these negotiations has been somewhat limited. Union leaders contend, however, that in an age of givebacks and concessions, unions prevented deeper erosion and unfair singling out of workers for cuts. Increasingly, unions have turned their attention to issues like job security in exchange for lower raises or, perhaps, actual reduced wage rates. As unions seek to diversify their membership, the need to look at additional issues will be increasing. Issues such as health benefits for part-time employees, child care, and flexible hours will be important.[14]

Provision of job security continues to be an important issue for union members. In the era of the Go-Go 1960s, jobs were plentiful and employment was steady. Employees stayed with employers for many years. In those days, the job security issue was often one of providing protection against what the union considered unfair retribution and arbitrariness on part of management or protection against cyclical layoffs, such as those that occurred in the steel and auto industries. Elaborate grievance procedures were set up for employees who felt they had been treated unfairly. Work rules and rigid job classifications also were developed to keep a certain number of jobs intact. When the company had considerable financial resources and slack, having extra positions was not a problem. Unions, such as the United Automobile Workers (UAW), negotiated contracts with pay clauses to cover layoffs (supplemental unemployment benefits) and other clauses, such as the "thirty and out provision" whereby a worker could "retire" after thirty years of service, regardless of age with a very attractive financial package. Today, in the age of cutbacks, buyouts, and global competition, unions have difficulty maintaining these clauses.

Health-care benefits have become a major issue of contention between labor and management. With an aging work force at one end, and young families, or single parent families at the other end, basic health care becomes a high priority. The problem is that the premiums that employers have to pay have risen far more sharply than the general inflation rate, as we saw in Chapter 14. Many workers have come to expect the employer to pay a full 100 percent of the premium. But, as we saw in Chapter 14, employers caught in the squeeze are seeking to share the costs, reduce benefits, and raise deductibles. The bitter Pittston-United Mine Workers strike that went on for over nine months in 1989–1990 was over the health-care issue—not wages.[15]

Job Security

Due to the economic turbulence of the 1970s, 1980s and into the 1990s, long-term employment is no longer assumed. When the slack disappeared, layoffs and givebacks became pervasive. Akio Morita, chairman of Sony, espouses the Japanese philosophy of life time employment. He severely criticized the layoff practice of American businesses when he said, "American management treats workers as just a tool to make money. You know, when the economy is booming, they hire more workers, and (when) the recession comes, they layoff the workers. But, you know, recession is not caused by the workers."[16] Some large U.S. companies have no-layoff policies, but several of them have discontinued this policy under increasing financial pressures; these companies include Bank of America, Eastman Kodak, Morgan Guaranty, R.J. Reynolds Tobacco, and IBM.

Several Japanese companies doing business in the United States have tried to avoid layoffs whenever possible. It may be that as more Japanese companies do business here, pressure will increase for U.S. companies to modify their long-standing philosophy of "lay-em' off."[17] Traditional union seniority systems provided protection to those members with the most tenure. However, many times the seniority systems came under fire because they were seen as very discriminatory against the young, women, and minorities.

Union leadership has increasingly turned to the issue of guaranteed job security in exchange for reduced wages, two-tiered wage systems (where new workers are paid a lower wage scale than existing employees), and so forth. Companies, such as Maxwell House, are making the distinction between job security and employment security. Employees with at least five years seniority may be guaranteed no layoffs (except in the event of extreme economic conditions), but they are not necessarily guaranteed their present job duties.

A relatively new approach to the job security issue has been for unions to become more actively involved in mergers and buyouts through union-sponsored ESOPs, which was discussed in Chapter 14. Some labor leaders believe workers can bring a different investment perspective to the company. Whereas public stockholders want the highest rate of return, union members-owners may be more interested in good wages or job saving capital investment programs.

Union ownership poses interesting questions. What will happen if the union is forced to impose wage cuts on their members? The process of ownership, some argue, will change the union's very outlook and operation.[18] Recent employee ownership attempts at United Airlines, WFI Industries, and Northwestern Steel & Wire indicate that this will be another important trend for the 1990s. Just how this will change the role of the human resource function is a serious unresolved question at this time.

Social Affiliation

Unions offer an important social affiliation role for their members. This can provide a sense of community and help to avoid alienation from the work routine. Unions may provide day-care facilities, sponsor social events, and involve themselves in the community. During hard economic times the union can help ease the problems associated with shutdowns and reduction in income by providing a sense of social, psychological support.

Training and Development

Many unions are instrumental in the training of their membership. As we discussed earlier, this is particularly true of craft unions. They often provide apprenticeship programs to develop highly skilled workers. As plant closedowns continue, industrial unions will need to be more involved with the company in helping their members to be retrained for new jobs requiring new skills. When International Harvester was preparing to shut down its Rock Island, Illinois, plant permanently, the union and management negotiated significant dollars for retraining and basic job search programs in cooperation with state and local officials.

Political Advocacy

Unions often support political issues or causes. This can be a double-edged sword. A great deal of legislation protecting workers (union and nonunion as well) has been passed as a result of direct lobbying or through support of certain unions. One of the difficulties with political action is that union members may hold a wide diversity of views. When the union leaders take an official position or support a certain candidate, they risk the estrangement of rank-and-file members.

In recent years, labor has advocated more "mandated benefits," such as guaranteed medical insurance, higher minimum wages, and time off for the fathers and mothers of newborns. It is certainly more efficient to do this on a national scale than to resort to local unions, state legislatures, or even industry-wide efforts. With organized labor's shrinking percentage of the work force, these national efforts allow labor to build coalitions with other political and social advocacy groups who may share some or all of their views on certain issues. These coalitions may be one way to maintain past union political clout.

From Management's Perspective

As a general rule, management has resisted unionization and has viewed unionization as a severe limitation of its power and discretion. Management resistance can be classified into two types of strategies: (1) union suppression and (2) union substitution. **Union suppression** includes a variety of active legal or perhaps illegal opposition tactics during the organizing campaign. **Union substitution** entails progressive and proactive human resource policies designed to reduce the desire for a union. Such tactics may include high wages, complaint systems, and participation plans.[19] In *Labor Relations*, Sloane and Whitney have defined the following five different management philosophies toward labor:

1. Conflict involves open hostility and direct action opposing the objectives of labor. It was widespread before World War II and led to bitter strikes, union militancy, and even sometimes physical violence. Today open conflict is rare because of laws protecting the rights of both employers and employees.

2. An armed truce philosophy consists of a letter-of-the-law approach. The company believes that the interests of the union and the company are far apart. The company will stay inside of the law but be very rigid in bargaining and then insist on strict adherence by the union of even the smallest details of the contract.

3. A power bargaining approach recognizes the reality of a union but focuses on maximizing the power and posture of the company at the bargaining table.

4. The accommodation philosophy is not full cooperation but does recognize the rights of union members. The company adjusts to the reality of the union and tries to minimize conflict and disputes. There still is, however, a clear distinction between management and union roles.

5. A cooperative approach means accepting the union as an active partner in the decision-making process.[20]

In "Toward the Study of Human Resources Policy," George Strauss believes that a "high commitment" labor policy is a viable alternative to the traditional practices of the past. According to Strauss, high commitment policies are those designed to develop broadly trained, highly motivated employees—ones who are prepared to exercise high orders of discretion. The organization commits itself to provide job security and a career, not just a job. Specific policies may include the following:

1. Broad job classifications, team oriented decision making, quality of work life programs.

2. Lifetime employment or efforts to at least moderate dislocation during economic downturns.

3. Training in both skills and attitudes along with orientation programs that stress corporate values.

4. New compensation plans, including profit sharing and pay-for-knowledge.[21]

A variety of attitudes exist today in the employer-union area. Many companies and unions are experimenting with a more cooperative role or the high commitment policies.[22] On the other hand, labor disputes like the Eastern and Greyhound conflicts seem to be moving in the opposite direction. Regardless of the philosophy of the company, unions can play several key roles that can actually be helpful. These include providing common wage scales, reducing the number of individual negotiations, easier communications, and workplace standards. Each of these is discussed below and shown in Exhibit 17.3.

···

| EXHIBIT 17.3 | Roles of Unions Today—Membership and Management Perspectives |

FROM THE UNION MEMBER'S PERSPECTIVE

Negotiation of wage and benefits

Job security protection

Social affiliation

Training and development opportunities

Social/political advocate

FROM THE PERSPECTIVE OF COMPANY MANAGEMENT

Common wage scale

Reduced number of negotiations transactions

More efficient communication

Predictable standards

···

Common Wage Scales

Once a contract is negotiated with the union, the managers need not worry about being approached by individual workers for raises or special benefit considerations. The manager merely needs to refer to the contract. From a planning perspective, this provides greater certainty in forecasting costs. With multiple year contracts, wage contracts can greatly reduce the time that must be spent on the compensation issue. Of course the preparation for the negotiations and the actual sessions do put a peak load on managers and particularly the human resource managers once every contract cycle.

If there is a dispute over wage and benefit issues, the company will deal with the representative of the union and not with the individual worker. While union representatives may be more skillful in negotiations than individual workers, at least the process is more predictable and procedures are usually outlined in the contract. The next chapter will outline in detail how this might work.

Reduced Number of Negotiations

What is true about wages and benefits can also be applied to work rules, disagreements, and grievances. The contract may tie the hands of management to a degree, but it also can clearly define the prerogatives of management. If an individual worker disagrees with an action taken by his or her supervisor, and yet the supervisor is acting within the rules agreed to by the union, it is not a problem between the supervisor and the employee, but rather is an issue that the union steward must work out with the worker. This may reduce the information processing load on the supervisors and the human resource department. Dr. Richard Lyles contends that for financial reasons, companies may prefer keeping a union intact. Lyles uses the example of a company not giving an employee a wage increase. If the employee is represented by a union the dispute goes through a grievance process. If the company can not resolve the issue and has to go to arbitration it may spend $2,500. On the

HR CHALLENGES ●

Using the Union Is the Answer

Shawmut Design & Construction is located in Boston. The company wanted to get involved in the downtown Boston building boom, but basically the downtown area was tied up by the unions. So the company decided to hire union workers. Many questioned why it would be willing to deal with union rules, union pay scales, and the risks of work stoppages. However, even though Shawmut's wage and benefit rate increased from about $17 an hour to approximately $25 an hour, it has actually become more profitable. When asked why, Jim Anasara, the company president, maintained that he gets a higher quality, more productive worker. For example, instead of 25-year-old novice carpenters, he now gets experienced carpenters 35 to 45 years of age with lots of know how. Anasara sums up his experience:

I was sick of dealing with personnel problems with people in the field. Early on, I had personal relationships with

all the people, but it became impractical. Meantime, we had a company with no rules or policies. People were happy to work here, but there was too much energy expended on solving problems. Someone was mad at someone else; young people weren't used to showing up with their tools at 7 a.m. . . . I saw the union as a way to solve these problems quickly. Everybody would follow the rules. There would be no arguing over who gets more money than someone else, and everybody gets big money so we can attract good people. We were struggling on so many fronts that personnel problems were just draining energy away.

SOURCE: Adapted from Tom Richman, "Why Jim Anasara Unionized His Own Company," *Inc.*, March 1987, pp. 60–66.

---

other hand, without a union the dispute may end up in court and the same complaint may cost the company $250,000.[23]

Communication and Standards

Communication can be facilitated by a union contract. In many cases the company will communicate with the union and the union in turn with its members. Because the contract often spells out in some detail the various procedures, work rules, and ways of handling disputes, the total number of channels may be reduced as compared with a union-free environment. This may eventually be a benefit to management as well. If participative management is introduced into a plant, the communication channels that already exist can be used to help disseminate the required information.[24]

Unions can be the source of highly qualified, well-trained, and disciplined workers, which can help to maintain productivity and high standards. This is especially true when it comes to craft unions, such as carpenters, electricians, steamfitters, millwrights, tool and die makers, and the like. They may have long apprentice programs, certification examinations, and high levels of craft pride. Building contractors often hire from union halls, rather than maintain their own employee rolls. One advantage to the employer is the ability to hire only for the duration of the project. The company, while being assured of adequately trained employees, does not have to permanently employ workers in slack demand phases.

To summarize this section, Exhibit 17.3 illustrates the roles that unions play from both the perspective of the members and the management of the company. Unionization holds advantages and disadvantages for *both* members and management. While members may see their unions as providing substantial benefits, they also are aware that they must pay a price in terms of dues, reduced opportunity for individual action, and adherence to union rules and discipline. Historically managers have been opposed to unionization and to a large degree still are. It can be argued, however, that management can reap certain benefits from a carefully and skillfully managed union relationship. Of course management also pays a price for these benefits. In "Avoiding Labor Management Conflict," Alexander Trowbridge has identified several new approaches that unions and companies are exploring. These include the following:

1. Gainsharing, that is, paying workers exceeding base productivity levels
2. Employee participation in decision making
3. Employment security and productivity agreements
4. Corporate acceptance of the union in a partnership role[25]

The point here is that, once a company has been unionized, managers need to make the best of the situation and exploit potential new areas of productive relationships.

UNION GOVERNANCE

Unions are democratic institutions. Workers initially elect to have a union, and once selected, vote on officers of the unions. They also vote on accepting or rejecting a labor agreement once it is negotiated by the leaders of the union. This process is called *ratification*. The governance structure of unions is by no means simple and easy to understand. A quick overview is important, though, for human resource and other managers. There are three levels of concern: (1) the local union (2) the national union, and (3) the federation—the AFL-CIO. Each level of the union will generally have officers, rules, and procedures. In addition, state and regional offices may interface with the local and national unions.

Most of today's approximately 65,000 local unions are affiliated with one of the approximate 170 national or international unions. Over 90 of the national unions belong to the AFL-CIO. However, several large unions, such as the United Mine Workers, remain independent.[26] Most unions are organized along a craft or industrial line, while several contain both types of workers.

The Local Union

For the rank and file, the local union is the most visible and important level. Generally, a union comes into existence through a certification vote. Then the new local applies for membership in the national union. In exchange for the services and support of the national union, the local union subjects itself to the rules and procedures of the national union. Once the local is established, the membership elects officers, including a president, vice-president, secretary-treasurer, and other necessary positions as specified in the charter. Typically, these positions are unpaid at the local level unless the local is quite large.[27] Some locals will hire a professional business manager to run the day-to-day operations of the union if the membership is large enough to pay the fees. These local officials usually are working alongside their membership and are consequentially well versed with issues of concern.

While a great deal of variation exists regarding the responsibilities of the local union's governing body, some elements are characteristic. The unions are charged with the negotiation of contracts or, in the case of a company-wide agreement such as with the auto makers, with working out local issues. In addition, they set up a structure to deal with contract disputes and grievances. A high percentage of the union's time is devoted to the grievance issue.[28] Unions also are charged with the discipline of members who have violated the union-contract provisions and local and national bylaws.

Financial management of dues and benefit payments in the event of a strike are also a primary concern. Local officials may be requested or required to provide local support for the national unions political or social agenda. In addition, the local representatives may be charged with supporting local civic and community projects. Finally, the local officials will be responsible for maintaining communications with appropriate state, regional, and national offices.

The National or International Union

The most powerful tier in the union movement is at the national level. Most locals are chartered by a national union and to a large degree are controlled by the national bylaws and procedures. National unions, like locals, have elected officials. The nationals meet every two to five years in national conventions to elect officers and take care of other business. Because of their size and resources, national unions have a paid professional staff to assist in their operations. This staff might include financial managers, lawyers, accountants, public relations personnel, and professional lobbyists, among others.

National unions exercise a great deal of control over their member unions. They set standards of conduct and operating procedures. Rank-and-file members do not hold membership in the national union, the local unions do. The national unions are supported by assessments of the local unions based on the size of the membership. A national union typically provides a range of resources and services to its local member unions including organizing support, aid in negotiations, education and research services, lobbying efforts, the publication of a union newsletter or newspaper, the allocation of strike funds, and the provision of legal services.

The ability to negotiate national contracts is a powerful leverage tool. For instance, the UAW chooses one of the big three automakers every contract period and negotiates a general national agreement. If Ford was the target, then the UAW and Ford would hammer out a general agreement that would apply to all U.S. Ford plants. After the pattern is set, then the general provisions are usually accepted at the remaining two companies. In a way, this is an advantage for the companies as well. They put forth their best negotiation efforts at one point in time and consequently do not have to "reinvent the wheel" at each facility. Of course, the local management usually will have to work out a few local issues at each facility, but the general provisions provide the baseline.

One drawback for the local union is that "wildcat" strikes—that is strikes at a local level without the national union's approval—are usually severely sanctioned. From the management's viewpoint, the negative side of national agreements is that they may not give enough latitude in negotiating local issues and concerns. As is apparent from several previous examples, many work groups turn down attempts at organizing. One of the reasons may be that they are not willing to yield control to a national union that is far away from the their work facility. For example, in the case of a Nissan plant in Tennessee, the workers indicated they would rather negotiate at the local level. There is the tradeoff, then, from the manager's viewpoint. A national union may reduce the amount of negotiations that are necessary at each facility but also limit the discretion of both the workers and the employer.

The AFL-CIO

The American Federation of Labor–Congress of Industrial Organization (AFL-CIO) is the highest organizational level of the labor movement. The two independent organizations joined forces in 1955. The AFL-CIO is a "federation" of national unions that allows national member unions to cooperate in order to achieve broad national goals. The AFL-CIO does not engage in collective bargaining activities—that is the sole domain of the national unions. The national federation can be compared to the United Nations. National unions are not required to join and may withdraw at will.[29] If a national does join, it agrees to certain rules and guidelines. One of the major benefits and/or limitations of membership is that national members agree not to raid another union's work force for members.

The AFL-CIO has the power to expel members if the union does not abide by the rules. For example, after repeated warnings regarding corruption, the AFL-CIO expelled the Teamsters Union in 1957. Not until October of 1987 did the Federation and Teamsters reunite. In some quarters there is considerable concern about the effect the Teamsters rejoining will have on the AFL-CIO's attempts to improve its image.[30] Not all national labor unions belong to the Federation. Because of past histories, style, and objectives, some unions remain outside of the umbrella. A notable development has been the recent decision of the large and powerful United Auto Workers to rejoin the Federation.

The Federation does provide a number of benefits to affiliate national unions including the following:

1. Protection from "raiding"
2. National lobbying efforts
3. Political education through the Committee on Political Education (COPE)
4. National campaigns to improve labor's image
5. Enforcement of procedures and standards and resolution of disputes among member unions

The Federation, headquartered in Washington, D.C., also operates state offices in all 50 states and Puerto Rico. In addition, they have several hundred offices in cities through the nation to provide services and information at the local level. Exhibit 17.4 displays the rather complex structure of the AFL-CIO.

The 1985 AFL-CIO report made a number of suggestions on how to improve and strengthen the union movement in this country. A $13 million national radio and television campaign was launched in 1988 to try to improve labor's image. Directed at the 20 to 40-year-old age group, the "Union Yes" campaign has been a bold attempt to get away from the cigar-smoking, smoked filled room image that labor has often had. The jury is still out on the results of the labor movement to change itself. Managers will need to closely follow, not only the local and national unions, but the direction and changes being attempted by the AFL-CIO.

THE ROLE OF LABOR UNIONS IN SOCIETY TODAY

As was made clear by the Eastern Airline case, the role, power, and relative influence of unions changed dramatically in the 1980s. Human resource managers need to be well versed in these changes. Several strategic variables must be considered to

EXHIBIT 17.4   AFL-CIO Governance Structure

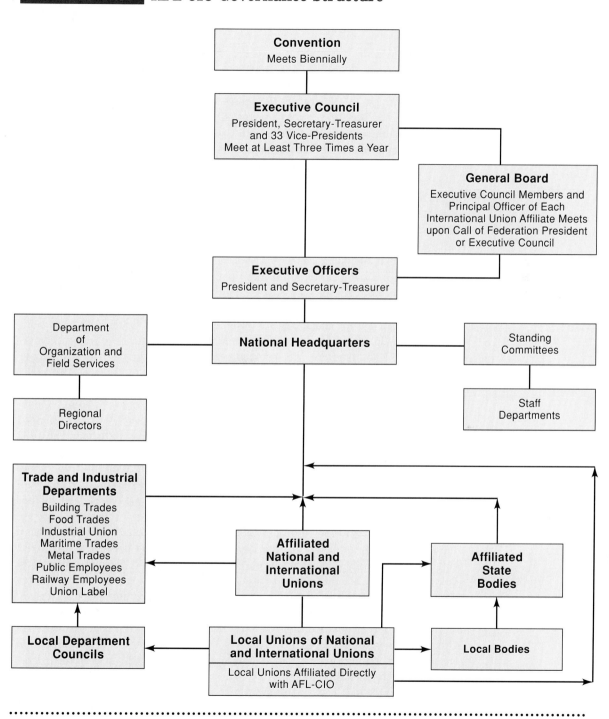

understand the current situation we face in the 1990s. Let us consider them one at a time.

Strategic Variables

Competition

Both foreign and domestic competition poses a threat to the unions' base of power and influence. Up until the mid to late 1960s there was little foreign competition in many major industrial sectors such as autos, steel, and electronics. American manufacturers dominated the U.S. domestic markets and exported a considerable amount of products as well. ("Made in Japan" in the 1960s was not considered a complimentary product feature.) Labor unions dominated many of these core industries and had the ability to negotiate top benefits and wage rates from prosperous American companies. When high-quality, price-competitive foreign products started making inroads in the 1970s and 1980s many previously insulated U.S. corporations had to compete with the manufacturing facilities of countries such as Japan, China, Poland, and Mexico that had significantly lower wage rates. Often higher quality products could be sold at a significantly lower rate than products made in the United States.

Fluctuating currency exchange rates, along with what many economists and politicians considered unfair trade barriers for our products, made a once strong export industry decline. During the 1980s, for example, the United States went from being the largest creditor nation to that of the largest debtor nation. This foreign competition limits the ability of the U.S. companies to simply pass along higher labor costs in the form of increased prices.

The trend of foreign competition seems to be increasing. The growth of sophistication among third world nations such as Korea, Malaysia, and the Peoples Republic of China promises to keep pressure on from below. On the other hand, planned and emerging changes in Europe represent another major area of change. The 1992 common market agreements will turn Western Europe into a super economic power. Political and economic changes in Eastern Europe and the dissolution of the Soviet Union promise additional sources of competition as well as opportunity. To summarize, the industrial corporations that have been the stronghold of labor unions must now truly compete in a worldwide market.

At home, domestic competition by nonunion workers can radically affect a labor union's ability to negotiate. Take the long and bitter dispute between Local P-9 of the United Food and Commercial Workers and the George A. Hormel Company in Minnesota. For years, the company and union prospered together and there was relative labor peace. Then, the Iowa Beef Processors (IBP) became more aggressive. IBP set out to be a low-cost, price-leading firm by holding labor cost to a minimum. Riding the antiunion sentiment of the late 1970s and early 1980s, IBP was successful in setting up nonunion shops. In the process it created significant price competition for established union firms such as Oscar Mayer, Wilson Foods, and Hormel. Hormel, in order to remain competitive, sought major concessions from its unionized work force. The result was a long and bitter strike. An interesting feature of this labor dispute was that the national union was opposed to it and ordered the strike ended, but the P-9 defied the national union and continued the walkout.[31] This nonunion type of competition has become a major concern for the large national unions. In many cases, the choice is between a crippling strike, wage, and benefit concessions, and forcing the company into bankruptcy. The Eastern case at the

....

EXHIBIT 17.5 Societal Events and Factors Leading to Antiunion Sentiment

Perception of inflationary wages caused by unions

Personal inconvenience of public from strike or slowdown

Political rhetoric of Reagan administration

"Me" generation unwilling to join communal group

Strikes by professionals such as teachers viewed as "unprofessional"

Poor quality workmanship perceived by customers of domestic products, e.g., autos

View that unions have narrow parochial interest, antithetical to the common good

Professional sports strikes, such as professional football players in 1987 or baseball players in 1990

Violence associated with strikes, such as the 1990 greyhound bus drivers' strike

....

beginning of the chapter illustrates the increasing difficulty of maintaining union solidarity.

Union Sentiment

Clearly, the 1980s saw a dramatic shift in the sentiment toward unions. According to a Gallup poll, labor's approval rating dropped from 76 percent in 1957 to about 55 percent by 1987–1988.[32] A number of factors contributed to that change, including well-publicized union corruption cases, such as that of Jackie Presser the Teamsters president;[33] the disruption of the public conveniences via airline, train, or bus strikes, such as the Greyhound Bus Drivers Strike in 1990; a public perception that the high union wage settlements led to inflationary cycles; and a generation more dedicated to personal goals than to group action. Also, strikes by public employees, such as teachers, had very mixed reactions. Many Americans believed that the unions epitomized parochial greed over the public good.

The Reagan firing of the air traffic controllers in 1981 may have served as a watershed that demonstrated the change in the public's attitude toward labor. Even though such "illegal" strikes by public employees happened on occasion, it was unthinkable in the past that the employees would actually be fired. While there may have been some protests over the firings there certainly was not a mass public outcry. In fact, the action was perceived by many as a bold, courageous step by the president. Exhibit 17.5 illustrates several factors that may lead to antiunion sentiment.

Dispersion of Labor

Much of the successful labor organizing activity earlier in the century was based in the Northeast or Midwest where there were large concentrations of industrial installations. For example, the auto industry was concentrated in states like Michigan and Ohio, the farm implement industry in Iowa and Illinois, steel making in Pennsylvania, and apparel in the Northeast. Since the factories were large and geographically concentrated, it was easier to organize and to control the labor supply in these areas.

FOCUS ON ETHICS AND SOCIAL RESPONSIBILITY • • • • • • • • • • • • • •

Is Ravenswood Acting Like Reagan?

Dan Stidham, president of the local United Steelworkers union, which represents the unionized workers at Ravenswood Aluminum Corp. in rural Ohio, is hopping mad. While federal law prohibits management to fire workers who are on strike, it does not prohibit management from permanently replacing them. Stidham argues that it's the same thing: The workers lose their jobs.

Management argues that in order to keep their businesses functioning, they frequently have to offer permanent replacement status. The unions argue that it is simply another management ploy to break the union.

Congress is currently considering a bill to help the workers. If passed, the bill would forbid management from offering permanent replacement status to workers during a strike. This bill would reverse the 1983 Supreme Court decision that legalized permanent replacement workers.

Stidham argues that management wanted a strike so that it could replace the union workers. As he describes the many steps taken by Ravenswood in preparation for the negotiations, one would have to agree. For example, Ravenswood informed all of its security guards that they had to become salaried employees or be transferred to production jobs. It installed steel plates to protect the plant's electrical equipment from bullets. It hauled in truckloads of food and supplies so managers could reside inside the plant. Before negotiations even began, Ravenswood advertised in Ohio for replacement workers, boarded up its front office windows, and encircled the plant with a barbed-wire fence.

Negotiations began September 25, and an impasse was called by the company on October 31. The replacement workers began November 1. The union argues that Ravenswood made the replacement workers permanent even though labor withdrew over 20 demands and were within 80 percent of the cost gap during negotiations.

In desperation, the union is looking to the National Labor Relations Board, who is investigating unfair labor practices. If the board finds that Ravenswood bargained in bad faith, the union workers could get their jobs back. Now, they sit and wait.

SOURCE: Adapted from Dana Milbank, "Row Escalates Over Striker Replacements," *Wall Street Journal*, July 3, 1991, pp. B1+.

Several important changes have occurred over the last 10 to 20 years. More factories and facilities are moving into smaller, rural communities, often in the Sunbelt states. One reason for the shift is the "right-to-work" legislation that is more common in the Sunbelt region. In addition, many new specialized companies are smaller. James Medoff, a Harvard economist, maintains that unions can not survive unless they learn to represent workers in smaller units. He estimates that about one-half of all nonunion workers are employed in companies that hire less than 100 workers.[34] Large corporations may prefer to set up a more decentralized system with smaller plants. Service organizations, because of their need to be near the customer, also result in smaller units. The change in economy away from the "smokestack" industries toward a service-information based economy, may have profound effects on the ability of labor organizers who try and use traditional approaches to implement collective bargaining agreements. Unions are now winning less than 50 percent of representation elections compared to about 80 percent in the 1940s.[35]

Economic Conditions and Employment

From 1982 to the early 1990s, the U.S. economy experienced the longest sustained economic expansion in history. Overall job growth was occurring, despite the de-

EXHIBIT 17.6   Declining Percentage of Union Victories in National Labor Relations Board

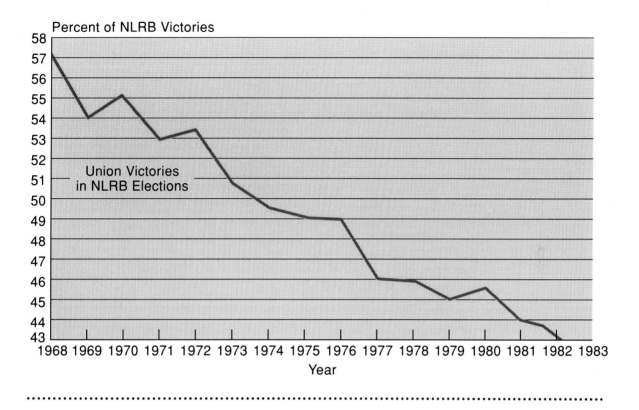

Percent of NLRB Victories

Union Victories in NLRB Elections

Year

cline of employment in industries such as steel and autos. During relatively prosperous times it is hard to organize new unions around the issue of unemployment and poor wage and working conditions. In *Megatrends 2000*, Naisbitt and Aburdeen forecast an ever increasing shortage of skilled labor in the 1990s.[36] When jobs are plentiful and wages are rising it is difficult for unions to get a hearing from potential members. As Exhibit 17.6 shows, the percentage of successful union elections is decreasing. Even though the number of jobs in manufacturing rose by more than 335,000 jobs in 1988, labor's traditional stronghold, union membership fell by 113,000. As of 1988 only 24.9 percent of the nation's manufacturing jobs were held by union members.[37] According to a Hudson Institute study sponsored by the Department of Labor, the manufacturing sector will generate almost no new jobs by the year 2000 and will shrink to only 17 percent of the gross national product contribution.[38] Many of the remaining manufacturing jobs will be seriously impacted by computer-integrated manufacturing, robotics, and JIT (just in time—see Chapter 4) systems.

If the economy turns sour and unemployment rises dramatically, as was seen in the early 1990s, the situation could reverse itself. Unemployed or under employed workers might again turn to labor unions for help in difficult times. Human resource managers need to study the trends in their business to be able to predict the likely effect of such economic changes on the company's labor relations environment.

Law

As we saw in Chapter 16, more and more employee rights have been codified into the law through court decisions and the legislative process. This trend has the potential to "forge revolutionary changes in the workplace and the way companies manage people."[39] Broad legislative action has been written to protect employee privacy, severance pay, plant shutdowns, and discrimination based on age, sex, and race. Health and safety issues have been addressed at both the state and federal levels. It is clear that many times large labor groups like the AFL-CIO lead these actions. For instance, in the late 1980s, unions urged Congress to undertake legislation that would provide some controls against corporate buyouts, takeovers, and mergers. Mergers and acquisitions have often eliminated whole divisions or plants. Not infrequently are entire communities decimated. The AFL-CIO is advocating legislation that would do the following:

Force raiders to honor all pre-existing contracts

Protect existing pension trusts from being used in leverage buyouts

Restrict and limit profits from corporate executives and raiders who engage in hostile takeovers

Force raiders to disclose their future plans for the company[40]

These advances in legislation may be a mixed blessing for the unions, however. These issues in the past have provided the unions a platform on which to attract new members. When the issues that were formerly won through the collective bargaining process are thrust into the legislative and legal systems, it takes away some of the power, prestige, and ability of the labor unions to deliver "benefits."[41] Organized labor has increasingly emphasized "mandated" benefits, particularly through its work with the Democratic party in Congress.

Legal solutions also usually apply to a much broader segment of the labor force than do those gained in collective bargaining, therefore the differential advantage of belonging to a union may narrow. Given the other costs associated with belonging to a union, such as dues, limitation of individual action, and the requirement to participate in strikes, it may be unattractive to potential members. In "Unions' Future Is Bleak," Audrey Freedman argues that labor dropped the ball on several potential issues that were then made legislative priorities. She argues that unions might have moved directly toward a strong equal-opportunity agenda at the end of World War II, but they did not. Instead, unions fought to preserve privilege, seniority, and preference of the past. Often the public has suspected that unions are basically special interest groups representing a privileged elite. This became a campaign issue in the 1984 election.[42]

The trend toward legally based employee rights protection is likely to increase in spite of the overall decline in union strength. Nonunionized members can bring potential pressure to bear that may, over time, result in significantly more benefits than what organized labor can produce. The human resource manager must carefully monitor the legislative and court actions at the national, state, and local levels.

Enlightened Management

Through a combination of factors including the above cited legislation, education, and cultural changes, it is often argued that the management of many companies has taken a more progressive view toward the human resources of the organization. Unions have long maintained that they would have little reason to exist if it were not for poor and self-serving management. Whether for humane reasons or economic self-interest, many companies have begun to understand that either avoiding unionization altogether or working in harmony with its union makes sense. After six years of trying to organize workers at the Nissan plant in Smyrna, Tennessee, the United Auto Workers acknowledge defeat. The results in this 1989 election were convincing—1,622 workers voted against the union while 711 were in favor of it. Bucky Kahl, the director of human resources at the plant stated, "We pride ourselves in being a company that functions in a participatory way. The vote was a statement of support for the strongly participatory management."[43]

Management can take an openly hard-line or a more subtle-hidden approach toward union avoidance. In *The Transformation of American Industrial Relations*, Kochan, Katz, and McKersie argued that during the late 1950s and early 1960s managers in nonunion plants started introducing "innovative, new systems of human resource management" into their shops.[44] A number of companies, such as Motorola, General Motors, Ford, Honeywell, Mead, Xerox, and GTE among others, have publicly committed to changes in the way they manage their employees.[45] An important question for both the unions and management in the 1990s is if management gets better, will unions have a reason to exist in their present form and with their present objectives?

Changing Demographics

The changing demographics of America's labor force can have a significant effect on the union movement. The "graying" of the work force can potentially pit one segment against the other. For instance, older workers may be much more interested in pension and retirement benefits while younger workers may desire current higher wages.

The entry into the work force of more minorities and women may make union growth more unlikely. The demographic shifts will be dramatic. Today's work force is approximately 47 percent native white males. Many of the current core workers are middle-aged and will be retiring from the work force in the next few years. By the year 2000, the percentage of white males in the work force will drop to about 15 percent. The Hudson Institute study forecasts that five-sixths of the new workers entering the labor force between 1988–2000 are likely to be minorities and women.[46] Unions that protect the old seniority system often find it difficult to support the demands of the new type of worker. Not only will the economic issues be different, but there will be many cultural and sociological differences as well. As Freeman points out, the unions have been lukewarm toward legislation to correct past discriminatory practices. In many cases they have led the fight against such reforms.[47] Exhibit 17.7 summarizes these critical variables.

....

EXHIBIT 17.7   Strategic Variables Concerning Unions

COMPETITION

Foreign and domestic competition poses a threat the the unions' power base.

UNION SENTIMENT

The 1980s saw a growing suspicion and disfavor toward unions.

DISPERSION OF LABOR

Many companies are relocating or building new plants in the South and/or rural areas to escape the stronghold area of unions—particularly unions in the Northeast and Midwest.

ECONOMIC CONDITIONS AND EMPLOYMENT

Strong growth in jobs and nonunion wages have dampened the incentive to join organized labor.

LAW

Many basic employee rights are now legislated or decreed by court decisions, thereby removing many issues from bargaining and negotiation.

ENLIGHTENED MANAGEMENT

Management tends to be better trained and more effective in dealing with human relation issues without being forced to by contracts.

CHANGING DEMOGRAPHICS

More older workers, part-time employees, women, and minorities are entering the work force. Unions have been the stronghold of white male workers for the past 50 years or so.

....

....

STRATEGIC CHOICES MADE BY UNIONS

Unions face several strategic choices as they fight for their survival and power in society. Each of these is discussed below and is summarized in Exhibit 17.8.

Bread and Butter versus Political Objectives

Unions differ, of course, as to their particular objectives and goals, but generally two broad classes of goals can be identified that unions in the United States have stood for. As can be seen in Exhibit 17.8, "bread and butter" issues include economic issues for the members, such as wage rates, life and health insurance, paid vacations, and job security. Historically, unions have emphasized the money issues. When Samuel Gompers was asked what unions wanted he boldly declared, "More!" The late Jimmy

....

| EXHIBIT 17.8 | **Examples of the Economic and Political Objectives of Unions** |

ECONOMIC ISSUES—BREAD AND BUTTER

CATEGORY	EXAMPLE
Wages	United Auto Workers bargaining with Ford for a 6 percent annual increase for 3 years
Benefits	Teamsters asking for full family health coverage to be paid by employer
Seniority	Steelworkers negotiating with USX to give priority to longer tenured employees in awarding overtime hours
Working Conditions	Airline Pilots Association working out an agreement with United Airlines on maximum number of nights away from home
Security	UAW agreeing to two-tiered wage structure in return for non-layoff clauses

POLITICAL ISSUES

CATEGORY	EXAMPLE
Political Endorsements	AFL-CIO endorsement of Michael Dukakis in the 1988 presidential election
Political Action Committees (PACS)	Contribution of campaign funds to local, state, and national elections
Endorsement or Opposition to Government Policies	During the Vietnam War era certain unions supported while others opposed the war
Endorsement of Certain Political Stances	The American Federation of Teachers encouraging defense cuts and more money for education

....

Hoffa said the success of the unions depended on their ability to deliver "the highest buck."[48]

Unions sometimes engage in political issues as well. For example, unions can provide support for or opposition to the country's foreign policy objectives or allocation of government spending programs, such as increasing spending for education. It should be noted that when compared to countries, such as Great Britain where there is an established Labor party, the political influence of American unions is usually more indirect. Consider the trade movement union solidarity led by Lech Walesa in Poland. Its prime objective has been broader political and national economic change.

Generally, American unions have done best with the economic issues, although as the environment has changed the economic paradigm may be increasingly outdated.[49] Frequently when unions have gotten involved in political issues they have stirred up hostility not only among the general population but among their members as well. For example, even though the AFL-CIO endorsed Jimmy Carter in 1980 and Walter Mondale in 1984, there was a mass defection among the rank and file who voted for Ronald Reagan in both elections.

Adversarial versus Cooperative Role

It should be emphasized that over the past century or so the union-employer relationship has basically been adversarial in nature. Unions have seen their role as one of challenging management rather than cooperating with management. Unions saw this as the best way to advocate their members' interests and believed it was a philosophy consistent with our pluralistic political and economic system. However, many union members and company managers are now questioning whether the adversarial relationship has to be generally hostile or if perhaps closer cooperation is essential in this era of global competition.

Secretary of Labor Lynn Martin feels that overall the relationship between the Department of Labor and organized labor, particularly in terms of opening up other countries for trade, has been very good. This she attributes to the fact that additional trade outlets help everyone. However, or a disagreement that has arisen is over free trade with Mexico. Unions oppose it fearing that it will lead to U.S. job losses. Martin argues for free trade to help establish an economically healthy Mexico and to help reduce immigration.[50]

In the mid-1980s the United Auto Workers and the Big Three automakers put together a "jointness effort." The new attitude was designed to reduce conflict in the name of cooperation. The alliance was one of convenience that was devised to deal with higher quality, more dependable and lower priced imports threatening the U.S. auto industry. Union members gave up work rules in return for more job security. They also got more involved in participatory management programs and received a portion of profits.[51] The idea was to get across to the union and to the rank and file that the welfare of the company is synonymous with their welfare. The message is getting through. Blyth, a 12-year veteran at Ford's Kansas City assembly plant says, "If Ford doesn't make . . . money, then I don't have a job."[52] There are, however, dissenting views inside the UAW. The opponents who have formed themselves into a New Directions alliance, believe that the Union members have sacrificed too much. The issue is critical for the UAW. As demonstrated in Exhibit 17.9, the UAW has contracted significantly during the 1980s.

Other examples of cooperative efforts include Xerox and the Amalgamated Clothing and Textile Workers Union (see the case at end of the chapter) and United Steel Workers of America and National Steel Corporation. Frequently the driving force behind these efforts is to threaten the very existence of a local plant or facility or at least a major cutback of the labor force.

Unions have responded to, talked about, or actually implemented workplace innovations, such as jointness programs, in a variety of ways. Some have simply said "No." Blocking and destroying the plan as early as possible is their only goal. Some sit tight and wait to see if the program will self-destruct itself without their help. Others have pledged their protective involvement. As long as the contract is upheld and not weakened, they go along. Some unions have offered their wholehearted cooperation and collaboration with the innovations. Many unions who follow this path feel that the current situation is hurting their members and a change may help

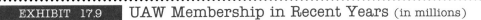

EXHIBIT 17.9 **UAW Membership in Recent Years** (in millions)

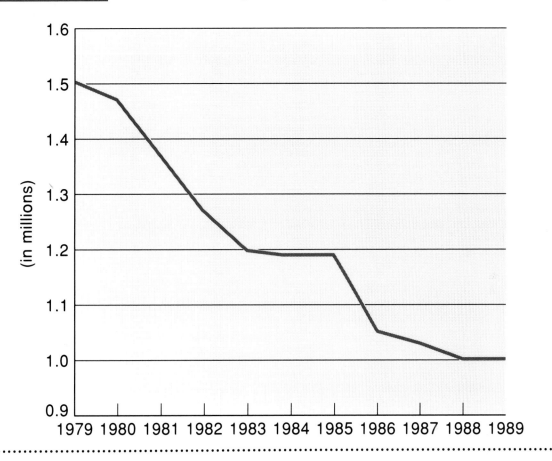

everyone involved. Finally, unions can use the innovations to assert their own interests. For example, the innovations may improve the quality of worklife for their members and the bargaining unit will be sure to include it in the next negotiated contract.[53]

From a strategic human resource management perspective, these partnership experiments are important. If more cooperative partnerships are to yield beneficial results, the human resource professionals and line managers must rethink their positions just as the labor movement is doing. It may be just as difficult for the managers of the company to reorient their stance toward cooperation as it is for the union leadership to put aside a long history of confrontation. Substantial training efforts can facilitate these changes. In "Union-Management Cooperation," Cohen-Rosenthal and Burton indicate that any joint union-management training effort needs to include the following:

- An explanation of what the program is and how it will work
- The basic principles, process, and procedures of the program

FOCUS ON INTERNATIONAL ISSUES •

HR Can Help Initiate Changes in Union-Management Relationships

If the United States is to maintain its competitive edge and succeed in the global market, the American work force must operate at full capacity. To do this, some changes must be made in the workplace. Managers must use their human resources to their fullest potential. This means that concepts like participative management, training programs, and teamwork must be implemented, even in union organizations.

Simply purchasing the latest technology and investing in new production techniques is not enough to compete globally. In order to succeed, managers must change the adversarial role they have with the unions and the workers and begin to treat them with respect. They must listen to their ideas and allow them to help solve problems. However, first the workers must know

what the problems are. This means that management must communicate with their workers.

While management might find this surprising, workers are in favor of changes in the workplace. They generally welcome the introduction of work teams who control the work pace and flow. They also are supportive of eliminating work rules and strict job classifications in favor of more job variety. While these changes will require management to train and retrain employees, to trust and value their abilities, and to include them in the decision making process, it is a small price to pay in order to remain competitive.

SOURCE: Adapted from Shane Premeaux, R. Wayne Mondy, Art Bethke, and Ray Comish, "Managing Tomorrow's Unionized Workers," *Personnel*, July 1989, pp. 61–64.

- Skills training in the specific areas necessary to meet the goals and objectives of the program
- A component on commitment and motivation[54]

Domain Considerations

Exhibit 17.10 illustrates several of the environmental factors that will affect the unions' strategic choices. Earlier we mentioned the changes in the economy that have affected the traditional strength of the unions, for example, the decline of smokestack industries, growth of service sector jobs, movement of jobs to the Sunbelt, a more global economy with worldwide competition now a reality, and growth of jobs in small companies.

Several additional factors also need to be considered. High-technology jobs are often filled by well-trained, often college-educated individuals. This presents a new type of worker that has to be communicated with differently. Professionals such as accountants, nurses, doctors, and market researchers may consider themselves more closely aligned with management than the unions. Yet the growth of professional positions has been significant and unions must consider such groups for inclusion as the number of unskilled or semi-skilled jobs decline in other sectors. In 1988, the Service Employees' International Union (SEIU) agreed to fight on behalf of health care workers at the Los Angeles Midway Hospital. The SEIU was successful in reversing give-backs. In exchange the workers agreed to join the union. Health-care workers may represent one of the bright spots for union organizers. From 1980 to 1988 the percentage of America's 6.9 million health-care employees belonging to unions rose from 14 percent to 20 percent.[55]

The entry of more women into the labor force implies some needed changes in how unions organize. Women now hold over 53 million jobs, which represent about 45 percent of the labor force. They only earn, however, about 64 cents for each

EXHIBIT 17.10   Factors Affecting Strategic Choices of Unions

dollar earned by men. Yet with relatively low wage levels, only 15 percent belong to unions. One reason for that is that 30 percent of women are in low-paid clerical positions, which have been difficult to organize.[56] Unions that have been dominated by male leadership need to understand the possibility of different objectives. Women, of course, will be concerned about the traditional issues of wages, fair treatment, benefits, and so on. In addition, however, issues such as child care may need to be addressed. In "Profiles of Local Union Officers," Chaison and Andiappan have found that women are not represented in union leadership positions to the degree that they should be based on their numbers in the work force.[57]

One of the most significant trends in the labor movement in the last twenty-five years or so has been the growth in public sector unionization. Employees at the federal, state and local levels have participated in this phenomenon. John F. Kennedy's 1960 campaign promise and his 1962 Executive Order 10988 was regarded by the postal workers and federal workers as their "magna carta."[58] This order provided postal workers the ability to bargain collectively in all aspects of their job, except wages. However, later legislation (Postal Reorganization Act of 1970) granted them

HR CHALLENGES ●

Union Membership Has Its Privileges

The AFL-CIO has begun offering the Union Privilege program. The program is designed to help union members off the job. Eventually, the AFL-CIO hopes to offer over 60 different programs to their members. John Ross, the communications director for the program, states that he wants the membership to begin turning to the union for any need.

The goal is to attract associate union members who are not part of any collective bargaining unit. Offering associates program benefits will keep them tied to the union and in step with the union movement. Over 325,000 associates have signed up for the program. Because the associate members are not part of a union, the AFL-CIO links them geographically to a union.

Several benefits are currently offered by the program:

- A credit card with no annual fee and a variable rate of only 5 percent above the prime rate. The credit card has no cash advance fees or check fees.

- Money market deposit accounts available that paid an average of 6.26 percent in 1990.
- Mortgages with rates at or below the national average and low down payments and closing costs with special deals for first-time home buyers.
- Life insurance plans that Union Privilege says are up to 25 percent lower than comparable plans.
- Prescription discounts for union members and their families. The mail service prescription plan allows members to save up to 30 percent on most brand name medications and more on generic drugs.
- Legal services including a free 30 minute consultation and a 30 percent discount on services.

SOURCE: Adapted from Stephanie Overman, "The Union Pitch Has Changed," *HRMagazine*, December 1991, pp. 44–46.

the right to bargain for wages too. The continued growth in public sector employment and the relatively high percentage of union membership is changing the balance of the private/public influence in the overall labor movement.

The union movement must make strategic choices in the last decade of the century regarding where it will position itself. Should it double its effort at organizing what is left of the basic manufacturing industries? Should it change its approach and try and organize more white- and pink-collar workers? Should it change its outlook toward women and minorities and move more of them into union leadership positions?

These are more than minor considerations; rather they determine whether the labor movement will remain a viable force in society. In 1985 the AFL-CIO issued a landmark report on "The Changing Situation of Workers and Their Unions." It recognized these questions and the shifting environment and suggested more cooperative and productive relationships with management.

Traditional Labor Issues versus New Services

Unions have undertaken several new services in an attempt to enhance their viability as organizations. Some of these services are discussed below.

Affinity Marketing

One relatively new development is the concept of the union as a service provider called an affinity group. An affinity group is a collection of people whose membership is used as a marketing, purchasing, or service acquisition medium. For example, a union may go out and negotiate a special deal for its membership in the provision of credit card services. The union could get the annual fee waived for its members and the credit card company may agree to rebate a portion of each purchase back to the union when its members purchase goods and services utilizing the credit card.[59] Runners, alumni groups, and other organizations have done this extensively. This is called "affinity marketing." Other examples include purchasing a group membership to large discount houses such as SAM's or PACE, special vacation packages, discounts on automobile purchases, or additional life insurance coverage at a special discount rate. "Affinity" services such as these have a twofold purpose. First, they provide services to the union's membership. Second, and often more importantly, they provide an additional source of operating funds for the union.

Associate Memberships

Recently, large unions, in an attempt to prevent their base from eroding, have started a new classification of membership. These are called associate members.[60] Associate members are not designed to be bargaining units but to participate in affinity services. Credit card availability, group health and life insurance, and lobbying efforts are the main benefits provided these members. Unions hope, though, that associate members may decide to become full union members at a later date. This concept has received mixed reviews. Some analysts see it as an indication that unions are changing with the times.[61] Some critics, however, view it as a desperate attempt to stave off the inevitable decline of union power and prestige.

• • • • • • • • •

MANAGEMENT GUIDELINES

Some of the managerial implications from this chapter include the following:

1. It is important for managers to understand that the nature of union activity has changed dramatically in the last twenty years due to a variety of circumstances encompassing economic shifts within the United States and global economy, demographic changes, and political and social attitudes. As a percentage of the work force, union representation has declined significantly. Managers of facilities both with and without unions need to be aware of these changes.

2. Unions must determine the degree to which they should concentrate on "bread-and-butter" issues, working conditions, job security, or affinity services. Human resource managers need to understand what their unions want and what they are willing to give in return.

3. While the 1970s and 1980s became a time of conflict, concession bargaining, and some notable bitter struggles, the 1990s offer hopeful signs of new cooperative efforts. Managers must try to explore and develop these areas.

4. The historical development of the labor movement in this country is important for the manager to understand today because it helps in analyzing current trends and issues.

5. A variety of laws, including the Sherman-Clayton, Taft-Hartley, Wagner Act, and the Landrum-Griffin Act, clearly spell out the legal rights and responsibilities of labor and management. In addition, a plethora of court decisions impact the general legal framework. Managers need the advice of legal experts when dealing with unions.

QUESTIONS FOR REVIEW

1. What, if anything, could the management and labor unions have done at Eastern to avoid the long bitter struggle that ultimately destroyed the airline?

2. How will the changing demographics of the work force affect union attempts at organizing?

3. In your opinion, should management resist the formation of a union? Why or why not? What are the advantages for the company? Are there any disadvantages to having a union?

4. Suppose you were attempting to organize a union in a large restaurant of 150 employees. How would you convince fellow employees they should vote for a union? Now reverse the role and think about how you as a manager would respond.

5. What are the most important roles that unions play today? Are they the same as they were twenty years ago? Why or why not?

6. In your opinion, what are the two most important labor laws that have influenced labor management-relations in the last 70 years? Explain your choice.

7. What is meant by jointness efforts? Provide an example of where it is being tried.

8. What is the governance structure of unions in this country?

9. Have unions outlived their usefulness? Make a case for and against this issue.

10. Forecast the shape of union-management relations for the year 2000.

CASE: Xerox—Can Its Experience Be Copied by Others?[62]

Xerox Corporation has been recognized as one of the most successful American technological companies created in this century. Chester Carlson, the inventor of xerography, changed the way business operates. This Rochester, New York, company once had a near monopoly in the photocopying business. In recent years, however, increasing competition, especially from the Japanese, has eroded market share and put increasing pressure on management and the unions alike.

The labor-company relationship has been a mixed one. Like many U.S. companies, in profitable times Xerox could negotiate from a strong position; but in many cases, the company found it easier to make concessions than to risk excessive labor trouble. At other times the "us versus them" attitude prevailed. For example, in the 1970s workers surrounded the gate at the Webster facility (a suburb of Rochester) with baseball bats. Xerox's managers called in the state police. During one labor disagreement, workers sabotaged the plant's conveyor belts.

In 1983, Xerox was faced with the closing of its Webster, New York, plant. To become more competitive with its toner products, Xerox started investigating the replacement of its Webster plant operation with a whole new facility. The favorite among the possible new cites was Oklahoma City. The Oklahoma cite was superior because of lower electricity rates, tax structure, and wage rates, and it fit into existing operations.

Rather than have the move create a major labor problem, the Amalgamated Clothing and Textile Workers Union (ACTWU) and the management approached each other about not moving the plant and keeping the work at Webster. Teams of union and salaried workers were able to negotiate a 35 percent reduction in utility rates from the local utility company. The team convinced the city of Webster to grant property tax concessions. The cooperative team also was involved in the design and implementation of the new facility. Ground-breaking for the new Webster facility took place in August 1984 and was on-line by April 1987. One hundred and eighty jobs were saved and productivity went way up. Both sides were enthusiastic about the arrangement. "We had the union involved in every step of the process," noted Peter Miller, a quality control manager. Said Ralph Garner, the facility manager, "When I found we had problems, it was because we didn't follow the damn employee involvement process." Tony Costanza, who is international vice-president of the ACTWU and represents about 6,000 workers, joined in by saying, "I still feel Xerox is far ahead of anybody else in the country in employee involvement."

Cost Cutting

The idea of involvement at Xerox had emerged both from above and below. The grass roots efforts of cooperation and employee involvement was seen as a remedy for Xerox's competitive decline. The company's market share had slid from the monopoly position in the 1970s to below 50 percent in the early 1980s. Xerox cut approximately 3,500 workers in the Rochester area, and 15,600 worldwide. Yet, the attitude became "we're all in this together." Xerox began to share information on costs and quality with the union. Costanza, the union leader, remarked, "We said to the company, give us a chance to compete." The employment at the Rochester area stabilized at 12,000 in 1988.

The other employee involvement effort was top down. David Kearns, Xerox CEO, led a new program—"Leadership through Quality." The program combined employee involvement with techniques such as benchmarking, where each unit measures itself against the best competitor in the industry, in terms of problem solving, statistical control, and quality improvement. Every one of Xerox's 110,000 employees have gone through a minimum of 32 hours of training.

One reason the "Leadership through Quality" process works is that it has a high level of endorsement and championing on both sides. Kearns, the CEO, and Costanza, the union leader, are committed to keeping it working. There has been a payoff for both as well. Costanza has saved about 600 jobs for his workers and Xerox has become more competitive.

Wiring Harness

A much touted example of benefits is the wiring harness project. The harness serves as the nerve system for copiers. In 1980, Xerox was making plans to lay off 180 workers to save an estimated $3.2 million by using outside vendors. The union set up problem solving teams and came up with a plan to save $3.7 million. Xerox in turn kept the project in-house and avoided the layoffs. Now, as a rule, before work is awarded to outside groups the inside members have an opportunity to review it and suggest ways to lower costs.

This sort of cooperation has changed the overall tone of the management-union relationship. Contract negotiations are quicker and more efficient. Gainsharing is becoming an issue for future discussion. Efficiency and quality are up. Is it perfect? Costanza does see some potential problems. He thinks there might be a collision between the top down "Leadership through Quality" and the joint union-management "Quality of Work-Life" (QWL) programs. The management top-down approach tends to emphasize issues such as productivity, headcount, quality, cost, and delivery. The QWL approach tends to emphasize more human needs. Time will tell if the newfound cooperation can grow and flourish.

QUESTIONS

1. Do you think good economic times will extend the cooperative relationship or in some way hurt it?

2. As a human resource manager, how would your role be different than it would be in a more traditional labor-management arrangement?

3. What sort of rewards and sanctions are necessary in the Xerox type of situation in order to make cooperation work?

4. Can this sort of arrangement be copied by other companies? Why or why not?

ADDITIONAL READINGS

Aaron, Benjamin, Joyce M. Najita, and James L. Stern, eds. *Public Sector Bargaining.* 2nd ed. Washington, D.C.: The Bureau of National Affairs, Inc., 1988.

Adams, Roy. "Industrial Relations Systems: Canada in Comparative Perspective." In John C. Anderson, Morley Gunderson, and Allen Ponak, eds., *Union-Management Relations in Canada,* 2nd ed. Ontario: Addison-Wesley, 1989.

Chelius, James, and James Dworkin, eds. *Reflections on the Transformation of Industrial Relations.* Metuchen, NJ: IMLR Press/ Rutgers University, 1990.

Cimini, Michael. "Union Members in 1989." *News: United States Department of Labor.* Washington, DC: Bureau of Labor Statistics, February 7, 1990.

Clark, Paul F. *The Miners' Fight for Democracy: Arnold Miller and the Reform of the United Mine Workers.* Ithaca, NY: IRL Press, 1986.

Coleman, Charles J. *Managing Labor Relations in the Public Sector.* San Francisco: Jossey-Bass, 1990.

Cooke, W. N. *Union Organizing and Public Policy.* Kalamazoo, MI: Upjohn Institute, 1985.

Dunlop, John T. *Industrial Relations Systems.* New York: Henry Holt, 1958.

Dunlop, John T. *The Management of Labor Unions.* New York: Lexington Books, 1989.

Evans, Martin G., and Daniel A. Ondrack. "The Role of Job Outcomes and Values in Understanding the Union's Impact of Job Satisfaction: A Replication." *Human Relations.* May 1990.

Freeman, Richard, and James Medoff. *What Do Unions Do?* New York: Basic Books, 1984.

Fulmer, William E., and Ann C. Casey. "Employment at Will: Options for Managers." *Academy of Management Executive* 4, no. 2 (1990), pp. 102–107.

Gilbert, Beth. "The Impact of Union Involvement on the Design and Introduction of Quality of Work Life." *Human Relations.* December 1989.

Gold, Charlotte. *Labor-Management Committees: Confrontation, Cooptation, or Cooperation.* Ithaca, NY: IRL Press, 1981.

Heckscher, Charles C. *The New Unionism.* New York; Basic Books, 1988.

Herrick, Neal Q. *Joint Management and Employee Participation— Labor and Management at the Crossroads.* San Francisco: Jossey-Bass, 1990.

Huang, Wei-Chiao, ed. *Organized Labor at the Crossroads.* Kalamazoo, MI: Upjohn Institute, 1989.

Hurd, Richard W. "Big Labor Regains Its Muscle." *Business & Society Review,* issue 68, Winter 1989, pp. 4–8.

Hutchens, Robert M., and David B. Lipsky. *Strikers and Subsidies— The Influence of Government Transfer Programs on Strike Activity.* Ithaca, NY: ILR Press, 1989.

Ichniowski, Casey, and Jeffrey Zax. "Today's Associations, To-morrow's Unions." *Industrial and Labor Relations Review* 43 (1990), pp. 191–208.

Kalish, Doug. "The New-Collar Workers and Unions' Changing Roles." *Personnel Journal* 55, no. 12. December 1986, pp. 16–21.

Kressel, Kenneth, and Dean G. Pruitt, and Associates. *Mediation Research—The Process and Effectiveness of Third-Party Intervention.* San Francisco: Jossey Bass, 1989.

Kerr, Clark, and Paul D. Staudor, eds. *Industrial Relations in a New Age.* San Francisco: Jossey-Bass, 1986.

Kochan, Thomas A., and Harry C. Katz. *Collective Bargaining and Industrial Relations.* 2nd ed. New York: McGraw-Hill, 1988.

Kochan, Thomas A., Harry C. Katz, and Nancy R. Mower. *Worker Participation and American Unions—Threat or Opportunity?* Kalamazoo, MI: Upjohn Institute, 1984.

Kochan, Thomas A., Harry C. Katz, and Robert B. McKersie. *The Transformation of American Industrial Relations.* New York: Basic Books, 1986.

Martin, James E. *Two-Tier Compensation Structures—Their Impact on Unions, Employers, and Employees.* Kalamazoo, MI: Upjohn Institute, 1990.

Meier, Gretl S. *Job Sharing—A New Pattern for Qualtiy of Work and Life.* Kalamazoo, MI: Upjohn Institute, 1979.

Mills, Daniel Quinn. *Labor Management Relations.* 4th ed. New York: McGraw-Hill, 1989.

Moore, Christopher W. *The Mediation Process—Practical Strategies for Resolving Conflict.* San Francisco: Jossey Bass, 1986.

Schuster, M. H. *Union-Management Cooperation.* Kalamazoo, MI: Upjohn Institute, 1985.

Siegel, Irving H., and Edgar Weinburg. *Labor-Management Cooperation—The American Experience.* Kalamazoo, MI: Upjohn Institute, 1982.

Slichter, Sumner, James Healy and E. Robert Livernash. *The Impact of Collective Bargaining on Management.* Washington, DC: The Brookings Institute, 1960.

Stern, Robert N., K. H. Wood and Tove H. Hammer. *Employee Ownership in Plant Shutdowns—Prospects for Employment Stability.* Kalamazoo, MI: Upjohn Institute, 1979.

Strauss, George, David Gallagher and Jack Fiorito, eds. *The State of the Unions.* Madison, WI: Industrial Relations Research Association, 1991.

Uly, William L., Jeanne M. Brett, and Stephen B. Goldberg. *Getting Disputes Resolved—Designing Systems to Cut the Costs of Conflict.* San Francisco: Jossey Bass, 1988.

Wendling, Wayne R. *The Plant Closure Policy Dilemma—Labor, Law, and Bargaining.* Kalamazoo, MI: Upjohn Institute 1984.

Whyte, William F., et al. *Worker Participation and Ownership: Cooperative Strategies for Strengthening Local Economies.* Ithaca, NY: ILR Press, 1983.

·················
NOTES

1. Bridget O'Brian, "Eastern Pilots, Attendants End 264-Day Strike," *Wall Street Journal,* November 24, 1989, p. A3; Bridget O'Brian, "Bankruptcy Strategy for Eastern Airlines Could Fail Lorenzo," *Wall Street Journal,* March 10, 1989, pp. A1, A10–A11; Pete Engardio, Gail DeGeorge, Aaron Bernstein, and Todd Vogel, "Lorenzo Is Running Out of Choices—and Time," *Business Week,* March 20, 1989, p. 37; Bridget O'Brian, "Up to the Gate: Eastern Seems Poised to Begin Its Comeback," *Wall Street Journal,* July 3, 1989, pp. A1, A8; Aaron Bernstein et. al., "Back to You, Frank," *Business Week,* April 24, 1989, pp. 24–26; James T. McKenna, "Trump Pays $365 Million for Eastern Air-Shuttle," *Aviation Week & Space Technology,* October 17, 1989, pp. 110–111; and Jonathan Dahl, "Eastern Hits

Turbulence on the Ground As Travel Agents Steer Fliers Elsewhere," *Wall Street Journal,* February 20, 1990, p. A1.

2. *Brief History of the American Labor Movement* (Washington, DC: U.S. Department of Labor Statistics, 1970), Bulletin 1000, p. 1.

3. Arthur A. Sloane and Fred Whitney, *Labor Relations* 4th ed. (Englewood Cliffs, NJ, Prentice Hall, 1981), pp. 69–76.

4. Gary Chaison and Dileep Dhavale, "A Note on the Severity of the Decline in Union Organizing Activity," *Industrial and Labor Relations Review* 43, April 1990, pp. 366–373.

5. Leo Troy and Neil Sheflin, *Union Sourcebook* (West Orange, NJ: U.S. Department of Labor, National Labor Relations, 1984).

6. *New York Times,* January 29, 1986, p. D1.

7. Larry Reynolds, "Labor's Leaders—Changing to Meet the Times," *Management Review,* February 1988, pp. 57–62.

8. Albert Karr, "Union Wages Rise," *Wall Street Journal,* April 14, 1992, p. A1.

9. Christopher Conte, "End of the Tunnel?" *Wall Street Journal,* March 3, 1992, p. A1.

10. Marcus Marry, "New Hope for Old Unions?" *Newsweek,* February 24, 1992, p. 39.

11. Dana Milbank, "Unions' Woes Suggest How the Labor Force in U.S. Is Shifting," *Wall Street Journal,* May 5, 1992, pp. A1+.

12. Paul Barrett, "Employers Win Supreme Court Ruling I Fight with Unions Over Recruiting," *Wall Street Journal,* January 28, 1992, p. A5.

13. Larry Reynolds, "Labor's Leaders Changing to Meet the Times," *Management Review,* February 1988, pp. 57–58.

14. Peggy Connerton, "Union's Future Is Bright," *Personnel Administrator,* December 1989, pp. 99–100.

15. Stephanie Overman, "Commission to Tackle Pittston Strike Issues," *HRM News,* February 1990, pp. A1, A4.

16. John Hoerr and Wendy Zellner, "A Japanese Import That's Not Selling," *Business Week,* February 26, 1990, pp. 86–87.

17. Ibid., pp. 86–87.

18. Aaron Bernstein, "Move Over Boone, Carl and Irv—Here Comes Labor," *Business Week,* December 14, 1987, pp. 124–125.

19. Cheryl L. Maranto, "Corporate Characteristics and Union Organizing," *Industrial Relations* 27, no. 3, Fall 1988, pp. 352–370.

20. Sloane and Whitney, *Labor Relations,* pp. 69–76.

21. George Strauss, "Toward the Study of Human Resources Policy," in *Reflections on the Transformation of Industrial Relations,* James Chelius and James Dworkin, eds. (Metuchen, NJ: IMLR Press–Rutgers University, 1990), pp. 73–106.

22. Dana Milbank, "National Steel Claims Strength in Its Labor-Management Alloy," *Wall Street Journal,* April 30, 1992, pp. B1+.

23. Don Nichols, "The Management Revolution and Loss of Union Clout" (An interview with Dr. Richard I. Lyles), *Management Review,* February 1988, pp. 25–26.

24. Ben Fisher, "Union Busting or Empowerment?" *Across the Board,* April 1990, pp. 11–12.

25. Alexander B. Trowbridge, "Avoiding Labor-Management Conflict," *Management Review,* February 1988, pp. 47–49.

26. Sloane and Whitney, *Labor Relations,* p. 140.

27. Ibid., p. 169.

28. Ibid., p. 170.

29. Ibid., p. 141.

30. Larry Reynolds, "Labor's Leader," p. 62.

31. Jeremy Main, "The Labor Rebel Leading the Hormel Strike," *Fortune,* June 9, 1986, pp. 105–110.

32. Rod Willis, "Can American Unions Transform Themselves?" *Management Review,* February 1988, pp. 14–21.

33. James Neff, *Mobbed Up: Jackie Presser's High-Wire Life in the Teamsters, the Mafia, and the FBI* (New York: Atlantic Monthly Press, 1989).

34. Rod Willis, "Can American Unions Transform Themselves?" pp. 14–21.

35. Donald E. Cullen, "Where Have All the Unions Gone?" *Survey of Business* 21, no. 4, Summer 1986, pp. 12–21.

36. John Naisbitt and Patricia Aburdeen, *Megatrends 2000—Ten New Directions for the 1990's* (New York: Morrow, 1990), p. 42.

37. John Deckert, "More Factory Workers—But Fewer with Union Cards," *Business Week*, June 12, 1989, p. 18.

38. Rod Willis, "Can American Unions Transform Themselves?" p. 15.

39. John Hoerr et al., "Beyond Unions," *Business Week*, July 8, 1985, p. 72.

40. "Labor's M/A/D List," *Personnel Administrator*, November 1989, p. 32.

41. Peter Drucker, "Reinventing Unions," *Across the Board*, September 1989, pp. 12–13.

42. Audrey Freedman, "Unions' Future Is Bleak," *Personnel Administrator*, December 1989, p. 98.

43. Stephie Overman, "Nissan Sees Union's Loss As Management Style's Win," *Resource*, September 1989, p. 1.

44. Thomas A. Kochan, Harry C. Katz, and Robert B. McKersie, *The Transformation of American Industrial Relations* (New York: Basic Books, 1986).

45. Edward E. Lawler and Susan A. Mohrman, "Unions and the New Management," *Academy of Management Executive*, 1, no. 3, 1987.

46. Rod Willis, "Can American Unions Transform Themselves?" p. 16.

47. Audrey Freeman, "Unions' Future Is Bleak," p. 98.

48. Edward E. Lawler III and Susan A. Mohrman, "Unions and the New Management," *Academy of Management Executive* 1, no. 3, 1987.

49. Alan I. Murray and Yonatan Reshef, "American Manufacturing Unions' Stasis: A Paradigmatic Perspective," *Academy of Management Review* 13, no. 4, 1988, pp. 639–652.

50. Stephanie Overman, "Moving Labor into the 21st Century," *HRMagazine*, December 1991, pp. 36–39.

51. Gregory A. Patterson, "UAW Hotly Debates Whether It Is Too Cozy with Car Companies," *Wall Street Journal*, June 15, 1989, pp. A1, A8.

52. Ibid., p. A8.

53. Adrienne Eaton and Paula Voos, "The Ability of Unions to Adapt to Innovative Workplace Arrangements," *AEA Papers and Proceedings*, vol. 79, May 1989, pp. 172–176.

54. Edward Cohen-Rosenthal and Cynthia Burton, "Union-Management Cooperation," *Training and Development Journal*, May 1986, pp. 96–98.

55. Kevin Kelly and Hazel Bradford, "Labor May Have Found an Rx for Growth," *Business Week*, February 22, 1988, pp. 162–166.

56. Constance Gustke, "Unions Move to Recruit Women," *Management Review*, February 1988, p. 52.

57. Gary N. Chaison and P. Andiappan, "Profiles of Local Union Officers: Females v. Males," *Industrial Relations* 26, no. 3, 1987, pp. 281–283.

58. Benjamin Aaron, Joyce M. Najita, and James L. Stern, eds. *Public-Sector Bargaining*, 2nd ed. (Washington, D.C.: The Bureau of National Affairs, 1988).

59. Paul Jarley and Jack Fiorito, "Associate Memberships: Unionism or Consumerism?" *Industrial and Labor Relations Review* 43, January 1990, pp. 209–224.

60. Marcus Marry, "New Hope for Old Unions?" *Newsweek*, February 24, 1992, p. 39.

61. Jerome Roscow, "Positive, Gradual Change," *Management Review*, February 1988, pp. 16–17.

62. Gary Jacobson, "Employee Relations at Xerox—A Model Worth Copying," *Management Review*, February 1988, pp. 22–27.

18 Strategic Collective Bargaining

Changing demographics, international competition, attitudes toward unions, deregulation of various industries, and legislative solutions have dramatically shifted the influence and role of labor unions in the United States and Canada. How these and other concerns impact the collective bargaining process is the focus of this chapter.

• • • • • • • • •
CHAPTER OBJECTIVES

Upon completion of this chapter, you should be able to

1. Identify strategic variables and choices regarding the collective bargaining process.
2. Understand the difference between an adversarial versus a cooperative relationship.
3. Distinguish between power bargaining and mutual problem-solving approaches.
4. Debate the pros, cons, and legalities of "union-busting" tactics and union avoidance techniques.
5. Characterize how enlightened management sometimes make unions unnecessary.
6. Identify possible negative consequences of a failure to reach an agreement including violence and sabotage, and describe techniques that will lessen the probability of such occurences.
7. Outline the formal bargaining process including preparation, negotiations, compromise, settlement, mediation, and arbitration.
8. Portray effective administrative processes to carry out the contract.
9. Describe the grievance process.

CASE:	Re-engineering the Collective Bargaining Process[1]

General Motors workers face a quagmire. They are uneasy because after a lifetime of seeing the company in an adversarial role they are now being asked to cooperate. Having witnessed what management has done to thousands of their fellow workers, they are finding it hard to believe that a new cooperative arrangement can really be in their best interest. They are fearful that they will be the next to lose their jobs.

Something Has Changed!

A modern day Rip Van Winkle that went to sleep in the late 1960s might not recognize the 1990 United Automobile Workers (UAW)–Big Three automakers bargaining process. It does not even remotely resemble the old style threat and counter threat bargaining game he was used to. Clearly, the process and results have changed. The recent relatively smooth, non-acrimonious bargaining between the auto workers and the car companies illustrates how things have changed. Chapter 17 outlined a number of reasons why this is happening. However, not everyone is prepared to declare that we have entered into a utopian period of collective bargaining. There is a certain uneasiness over the changes and uncertainty among union leaders, rank and file, and company managers as to what this apparent change really means.

The Best of Times—The Worst of Times

The 1990 negotiations between the UAW and the Big Three automakers were seen as potentially explosive. The auto industry had been hit hard by foreign competition and a relatively lackluster couple of years in 1989 and 1990. Large incentives to move inventory had become the rule rather than the exception. Through a series of cost-cutting measures and new approaches, the automakers did manage to turn profits, although the results were mixed. Ford continued to prosper with a reputation for quality and innovative designs. General Motors (GM), whose U.S. market share had slid from a whopping 41 percent in 1986 to 35 percent in 1989, had more than 30,200 workers on layoff. Chrysler had special problems, including slumping demand, high labor costs and more competition for its mini-van line. Because they were overstocked in inventory, the automakers were in position, many analysts felt, to take a tough stance and even be willing to accept a strike. In 1990 the UAW chose GM for the target company in their traditional pattern bargaining approach, even though Ford was in the strongest financial position. The strategy of the UAW was to negotiate a deal that GM, which employs the largest number of UAW workers, could live with and then get Ford to go along with it. Chrysler, however, presented a special problem.

The UAW found itself in difficult straits as well. Membership had shrunk from 1.5 million members in 1979 to a little less than 1 million members in 1990. In 1987 the UAW had negotiated a ban on plant closings other than those related to sales downturns. In spite of this ban, however, GM had "indefinitely idled" four plants and laid off 30,200 workers. Members felt betrayed and unwilling to trust the company. This anger and mistrust sometimes carried over to animosity against union leaders who appeared to be too willing to make concessions.

Along with normal negotiation issues, the UAW was particularly irritated by the growing practice of outside contracting or "outsourcing." Outsourcing occurs when a company hires other companies, usually smaller companies, to produce parts or services. In most cases these smaller companies are not covered by UAW contracts. The auto companies argue that this is one of the only ways it can remain competitive in light of worldwide competition. The unions see it as a way to sidestep paying "fair" rates, and when taken to the extreme, a form of union busting.

The Strike That Never Happened

Even though the potential was there for a strike, the negotiators for the UAW and GM worked out a pact that was overwhelmingly ratified by the union's bargaining committee of 400 and the general membership. Why did things work out as smoothly as they did and what did each party give and receive in the collective bargaining process?

It is apparent that business in the 1980s was a sobering experience for both the carmakers and the union. An ever increasing share of the market was going to the Japanese car manufacturers. In the last half of the decade, a number of Japanese companies entered the United States and constructed plants in this country, such as Nissan, Honda, and Toyota. Exhibit 18.1 lists these plants. The practice, while it saved some U.S. jobs, still hurt both the domestic producers and the unions.

Many of the new plants were nonunionized and will probably remain that way. While the UAW has been successful in organizing the three U.S. assembly plants where Japanese automakers are teamed with U.S. automakers, the same success was not found in wholly owned Japanese auto plants. When the UAW tried to unionize the Honda plant in Marysville, Ohio, it suffered an embarrassing defeat, as it did in the Nissan election in Smyrna, Tennessee. At this plant, the workers voted 1,622 to 711 against UAW representation.

The domestic producers had a vast over-capacity and too many workers. Consequently, the union leadership, over time, had to shift much of its

EXHIBIT 18.1   Japanese Auto Plants in the United States and Canada

FIRMS	LOCATION	PRODUCTION STARTED	YEARLY CAPACITY	EMPLOYMENT
Honda	Marysville and East Liberty, Ohio	11/82	510,000	8,000
Nissan	Smyrna, Tennessee	6/83	440,000	5,100
Toyota/General Motors	Fremont, California	12/84	300,000	3,400
Honda	Alliston, Ontario	11/86	80,000	850
Toyota	Georgetown, Kentucky	7/88	200,000	3,500
Mazda	Flat Rock, Michigan	9/88	240,000	3,400
Mitsubishi/Chrysler	Normal, Illinois	9/88	240,000	2,900
Toyota	Cambridge, Ontario	11/88	50,000	1,000
Suzuki/General Motors	Ingersoll, Ontario	4/89	200,000	2,000
Fuji (Subaru)/Isuzu	Lafayette, Indiana	9/89	120,000	1,700
TOTAL			2,380,000	31,850

collective bargaining agenda to job security issues. Companies shifted their negotiations strategy to reduce cumbersome work rules and job classifications and also increasingly emphasized costs control and quality issues. By 1990 the new realities of the marketplace had left an impression on the autoworkers as well as the manufacturers.

Negotiations started in late summer 1990 and the usual sort of posturing, proposals, and counter-proposals occurred up until the eleventh hour. When it became apparent that the deal could not be cut by the deadline, the 1987 contract was extended. This demonstrated that the union and company were close to an agreement and that neither party felt that a strike would be of any benefit in negotiations. While the negotiations were tough, they were businesslike and avoided the bitter tone of some past sessions.

Not only was the settlement signed by General Motors, but comparable pacts were agreed to by Ford and Chrysler as well without any major disruption. Whether this signals a new era for collective bargaining and union-management cooperation will not be known for several years. The ultimate success will depend on many factors, including the ability of company managers, union officers, and the rank and file to redefine their roles somewhat to be able to survive and prosper within the turbulent environment of worldwide auto competition.

• • • • • • • •

This case demonstrates a potentially significant shift in the labor-management bargaining relationship in the 1990s. Both labor and management are having to face the new realities of a global marketplace. Both parties may find it to their benefit to develop a smoother collective bargaining process that still protects their unique interests as is illustrated by the GM-UAW contract negotiations of 1990. Many of these shifts are examined in this chapter.

STRATEGIC CHOICES

When faced with a collective bargaining situation, managers must make many strategic choices. Some of the more important ones are listed below.

1. Managers must decide when to open the negotiations. Sometimes it is advisable to try to open the talks long before the contract expires if a strike will cripple the business. At other times, it may be advantageous to wait until closer to the contract expiration date in order to force the union's hand. It is up to the managers involved to interpret the situation and make the decision.

2. Managers must examine the possibility of a strike and decide what actions to take if the chances for a strike are good. For example, managers must decide how important it will be for them to build up their inventory and make sure their distributors have an abundance of stock, which may involve overtime pay and large inventory costs.

3. It is also important for managers to understand which issues to raise first and which to wait on. If management knows that a particular issue will cause a problem, perhaps it would be best to leave it undiscussed until progress is being made in the negotiation process.

4. Managers must decide who they will use to represent their side in the negotiation process. The importance of the contract should help determine who should be involved.

5. Managers need to decide how closely they will follow the contract, once it is agreed to. Management may want to take some issues through the grievance process in order to get a ruling that is the opposite of what the contract stipulates. In these cases, it is imperative that management have a strong support network for the grievance procedures.

STRATEGIC VARIABLES

Managers many times are faced with the reality of working with a union. The union may be a long standing fixture that was organized in response to problems and abuses of past decades, or the union may be relatively new in response to current management or economic conditions. Regardless of how and why the company became unionized, the managers face several key strategic variables in the collective bargaining process. Exhibit 18.2 displays five variables that managers should be concerned about. Each one is described below.

Harmony

Probably the biggest change to occur during the 1980s from a strategic standpoint was a reduction in the confrontational approach between union and management and an increase in the more collaborative approach. Most managers recognize the value of harmony in creating a work climate that can lead to high productivity. Harmony is working together on common goals without conflict or discord. At the

EXHIBIT 18.2   Key Strategic Variables in the Collective Bargaining Process

same time, experienced managers would also agree that harmony may be a necessary but not sufficient condition for productivity. For example, harmony could almost always be achieved in the short run by simply agreeing to every union demand. However, in most cases short-term harmony would result in financial bankruptcy and business failure.

Not only does disharmony disturb the ability of a company to produce goods and services, but in this age of aggressive news media investigation and reporting, unfavorable coverage can inflict long-term damage. Frequently, the discord spills over and directly affects the customer, such as the 1990 Greyhound bus drivers dispute which threatened the lives of passengers as well as replacement drivers.

Managers must examine their history with the union and keep in touch with the current attitudes of supervisors and union members in order to increase the commitment to harmony whenever possible. With the fast-changing environment, managers and union officials may find that past bitter disputes color the present attitudes, which may be highly detrimental to *the current* interest of both sides.

Power

Much of the relationship between unions and companies is of a political nature. Paradoxically, two extreme conditions can lead to the perception that union power is fading. Unions exist to deliver benefits to their members. Many union members candidly admit that if managers managed more effectively, perhaps unions would not be necessary.[2] Union members, and particularly the union leaders, may become worried if things go too smoothly, especially if the history has been one of winning bitter fights with management. As illustrated in the opening case, less rancor and fighting may be interpreted as a weakness rather than as effective union-management cooperation.

The other extreme that may lead to the perception of union powerlessness is the results of give-backs or concession bargaining. Exhibit 18.3 demonstrates several conditions that can lead to this appearance of loss of power for the union. At the one extreme, the rank and file may start to question whether the union leadership

| EXHIBIT 18.3 | Conditions That Can Lead to the Perception of Union Power Loss |

- More enlightened management that is committed to working out issues rather than disputing them
- Recent cooperative efforts by union officials that contrast sharply with a past aggressive confrontation approach
- Necessary give-backs demanded by the company
- Reduction in overall level of employees and union membership
- Reduction in union campaigns, strike benefits, etc. caused by falling union budgets
- Reduction in union supported candidates being elected to political office

is too cozy with the managers. Collusion may even be suspected. Therefore, union officials may feel the necessity of occasionally provoking a dispute to reassert their power or at least create the perception of a power play. It has been suggested that company managers sometimes let the union win these relative nonissues so as to avoid more serious problems.

The power issue cuts both ways. Managers, based on their personalities, education, previous work experience with unions, and corporate policy, may feel compelled to demonstrate that management is in charge. Many tradition-bound managers may see attempts at cooperation as giving away management rights and responsibilities that should be retained. The management of the company should be clear as to what its objectives are and make sure that the strategic exercise of power is used to achieve those ends and not to fulfill the ego needs of managers, which could lead to unnecessary conflict and destructive results.

A company may believe it is beneficial to use its power to gain advantage. Use of power is nothing new and has a long-standing historical precedent. Today the collective bargaining process still involves bluffing, and proposals and counterproposals. Generally the process, however, employs a more rational approach and issues are discussed and settled more or less based on facts.[3] Still, power tactics are often employed, but in a more subtle way. From the management's perspective, power bargaining may be used to intimidate the union into concessions that would not otherwise be obtainable. The management may imply that a plant will be closed or cut back if concessions are not made. A union might threaten a strike at an inopportune time over long-standing disagreements. For example, a company may be in a high demand situation and making substantial profit margins. But if a strike is called, products simply would not be available and consequently opportunities for profits would go to competitors.

With the relative balance of power shifting in the last few years, unions have accused management of deliberately resorting to power and making totally unreasonable demands that will force strikes and allow the company to hire permanent replacement workers. The unions contend this is just disguised union busting. During the fall of 1990, a collection of labor lobbyists worked on a "Striker Replacement Bill" that would force companies to rehire striking workers and fire replacement workers if necessary to reinstate the union members. *Wall Street* journalist Robert Thompson argues that "The simple, underlying motivation of the Striker Replacement legislation is power—union power."[4] He goes on to say that often the only defense a company has is to let the union strike rather than yield to the unreason-

FOCUS ON ETHICS AND SOCIAL RESPONSIBILITY • • • • • • • • • • • • • • •

Power Bargaining or Boulwarism

Based on issues such as their past history and the state of competition in the industry, the union and the company may seek to demonstrate their relative power by making unreasonable or even showy demands. One form of power bargaining that is generally considered illegal is known as Boulwarism named after Lemuel Boulware, General Electric's former vice-president of Public and Employee Relations.

For many years the management of GE observed that the old conventional way of bargaining, which included exaggerated opening demands, proposals, counterproposals, bluffing, and no genuine agreement until the last possible minute, was inefficient and wasted the time and money of both the union and the company. GE believed a better system was possible and under the leadership of Boulware developed a four-phased procedure to make the process smoother. From the 1940s to the 1970s, GE executed these tactics. The phases were as follows:

1. The management assembled what it called "the steady accumulation of all facts available on matters likely to be discussed."
2. It would modify these findings only on the basis of new facts or different facts.
3. It offered the facts suggested early in the negotiations.
4. The company made it a policy to change the initial offerings based *only* on new facts.

In a nutshell, the company believed it was voluntarily doing what was right. If the union did not agree to what the company perceived as being right, then a ruthless game of take-it or leave-it was played. GE played a sophisticated public relations game in conjunction with the approach. It communicated directly not only with the workers but also the community that was dependent on the GE installation for the large payroll. Often GE was the central economic entity in a community. The company tried to convey to the community that it was more than fair in dealing with the union and that if a strike occurred, the economic disaster could not be blamed on GE. The company was highly successful in the use of these policies. Almost without exception it transferred its original offers into the final labor contracts.

Whether the company was actually sincere and fair in its approach was challenged by the unions. They believed that the approach was an attempt to undermine the credibility of the unions and it was furthermore a refusal to bargain in good faith. After the 1960 negotiations, International Union of Electrical Workers (IUE) took its charges to the National Labor Relations Board, which found the company guilty of bad faith negotiating. This ruling was upheld by the New York Court of Appeals and sustained when the United States Supreme Court refused to undue the decision. Gradually during the 1960s and early 1970s, GE migrated back toward the old pattern of proposals, counterproposals, and compromise.

Many of the GE managers believed that totally abandoning the approach was a mistake. Certainly the Boulwarism approach influenced negotiations at other companies in the late 1970s and 1980s. While the term Boulwarism is not often referred to today, many of the tactics employed in recent labor disputes, such as the conflicts between the Reagan administration and the air traffic controllers, Frank Lorenzo and Eastern Airlines, and the management and drivers at Greyhound, may be rooted in the take-it or leave-it philosophy. Many union leaders argue though that in these latter type of cases the company does not attempt to do what is right but rather seeks a provocation with a take-it or leave-it approach.

SOURCE: Adapted from Arthur Sloane and Fred Whitney, *Labor Relations*, 4th ed., Englewood Cliffs, NJ: Prentice-Hall, 1981, pp. 205–207.

able demands. If the union had no risks of permanent replacement the number of strikes would mount significantly.

It should be clear that power bargaining can have unintended and destructive consequences. Many companies and unions are now trying to explore more of a mutual problem-solving approach in their bargaining. But many of the old sentiments remain, and union members frequently are suspicious of any such efforts. In July 1990, Chrysler offered union employees stock in the company in exchange for help in slashing costs. The union dismissed the proposal immediately. The company has been faced with slumping demand and sliding earnings. When compared to other domestic auto producers, Chrysler has the highest cost for labor (wage and benefits) at $33 per hour versus $31 for Ford and $30 for GM, and this figure is a full $10 per hour more than that expended by Japanese owned-plants.[5]

Corporate Strategy

A company's overall strategy must be considered in relationship to the collective bargaining process. The company's grand strategy drives its strategy toward the union. For example, if a company is pursuing a low-cost price strategy, it may have to take a very tough stance in negotiating any significant increases in wages and benefit costs that would negate its competitive advantage. It may be more agreeable to quality of work life issues or sharing in decision making as long as the costs are not forced up as a result. On the other hand, another company may choose to pursue a product differentiation strategy that relies on a special, highly trained labor force. If the company can more easily pass along these costs, it may yield on wages but seek concessions that require a reduction in the number of labor classifications, which will allow more flexibility in scheduling skilled craftspeople for a variety of tasks.

Mergers and acquisitions present special strategic problems for managers. Mergers frequently do not live up to their expectations or often are outright failures. One salient problem is bringing together two differing cultures.[6] When unions are involved, the political problems may even be intensified. Entirely different unions, with different goals and expectations, may be inherited or different locals of the same international union may have to be dealt with. USAir's merger with Piedmont, generally hailed as a model of success, caused significant headaches in the combining of existing contracts with various unions. Journalist James Fraze, referring to the merger, argued "The thorniest problem for company officials has been the merger of existing contracts among the various employee unions." Particularly difficult was the issue of pilot seniority, which is critical because it means who will sit in which seat and the pay difference between the pilot and copilot is significant. USAir decided to let a committee of pilots work out the differences and then try to accept any reasonable agreement that was advanced.[7] Exhibit 18.4 demonstrates several examples of how a given strategy might affect collective bargaining.

In "Strategic Human Resources Management," Legnick-Hall and Legnick-Hall advocate the need to tie together human resource planning and strategy.[8] This proactive stance provides an organization with the proper mix of personnel for its present as well as future needs. A significant change in strategic direction may very well require different human skills than companies currently possesses. In the collective bargaining process, constraints and opportunities need to be carefully examined in terms of current and future strategic thrusts and whether the contract allows enough flexibility for training, relocating, promoting, hiring, or laying off personnel as needed.

Management Philosophy

Managers hold different views toward unions. Some are opposed to unions at any cost and are even willing to engage in intimidation to avoid or get rid of an existing union. While this extreme position is usually rare today, the 1980s gave rise to an increasing hostility or at least a high level of opposition toward the unions. Managers may feel that the 1980s provided an opportunity to correct the imbalance they perceived toward labor in the 1940s, 1950s, 1960s, and 1970s. Many feel that the

··

| EXHIBIT 18.4 | Corporate Strategy and Collective Bargaining Impact |

STRATEGY	COLLECTIVE BARGAINING IMPACT
Low-cost producer High-quality/high priced goods	Tough negotiations over wages More flexibility in work rules in order to utilize skilled workers
Lower costs by cutting expenses	Seek wage concessions Reduce benefits
Downsizing—reducing overcapacity and inefficient plants	Layoffs clauses, earlier retirements, seniority revisions, improve productivity
Merger, acquisitions	Common contract provisions Change in pension language

··

firing of the air traffic controllers (PATCO) by President Reagan set the stage for the decline of the unions during the decade.

Regardless of the shift, the collective bargaining process is often the vehicle used to express the growth of power vis-à-vis organized labor. In the late 1980s unions leaders sometimes accused management of deliberately provoking labor problems by negotiating in bad faith. Clear guidelines have been set by the NLRB regarding good faith negotiations, but labor would argue that the NLRB has not enforced these provisions as closely as it may once have.

Another aspect of management philosophy may be the belief that management has improved and that unions may actually inhibit the company from doing what is in the best interest of the workers. If management can not remove the union, it may at least seek a more cooperative atmosphere with the union and workers.

Some managers may even have a philosophy of open support for the union because they would rather deal with one union that, in turn, has an obligation to "manage" its members, than to deal with the problems and concerns of dozens or hundreds of individuals.

Cost/Benefit of Unions

It is important that managers have closely analyzed the cost and benefits of having a union. It is almost unheard of for a management team to do an analysis and then conclude that they should actively seek a union. More typically management must negotiate with a union that is already in place. The positive benefits of having a union are offset by increased costs in terms of higher wages, benefits, and so on. Once management understands this relationship, it is in a better position to negotiate and seek more effective contract provisions or even concessions if necessary. Exhibit 18.5 lists several potential benefits and costs that managers would be well served to study and analyze before negotiations begin. Whenever possible these costs and benefits should be quantified.

In the collective bargaining process, management needs to minimize the costs and maximize the benefits associated with the union. For example, management, in exchange for supporting the seniority system, might seek to offset higher health premiums by negotiating higher deductibles and higher copayments.

....

| EXHIBIT 18.5 | Possible Benefits and Costs of Unions

COSTS ASSOCIATED WITH UNIONS

- Higher wages and benefits
- More time spent in negotiations
- More grievances to adjudicate
- Lower productivity growth rate in some industries
- Potentially higher compensation of older workers associated with seniority system
- More staff devoted to labor issues
- Losses associated with slow down, strike
- Potential boycotts if union does not achieve its objectives

BENEFITS ASSOCIATED WITH UNIONS

- May be more skilled, mature work force
- Reduces the amount of time needed to manage individual workers—can deal with employees as a group
- Unions provide training/apprenticeship programs for members
- Potentially higher level of pride and craftsmanship associated with union membership
- Potential partnership for excellence and productivity may be easier to implement if a union is supporting it
- Stable, predictable labor costs once contract is settled
- Clear enforceable, discipline is possible

....

UNION REMOVAL/DECERTIFICATION VERSUS UNION BUSTING

During the 1980s, attempts were made to remove unions from companies. From the perspective of the unions, this "union-busting" activity is perceived as a sinister attempt to undo the rights that workers have gained through hard-fought battles with companies for over a century. Many times managers argue that unions have gotten excessively powerful, are out of touch with the needs of their members, and are unwilling to recognize that U.S. companies are engaged in worldwide competition. These managers see the removal of the union or the reduction of its power as beneficial to everyone concerned, except perhaps the union leadership.

A union *can* be removed through the formal process of decertification. Up until the Taft-Hartley Law of 1947 it was generally assumed that once a union was certified, it was forever.[9] Decertification is more or less the reversal of the certification process. The management of a company cannot initiate the action. It must be initiated by the union members themselves. The timing of the filing is important. The petition must be signed by at least 30 percent of the bargaining unit members and must be filed between sixty and ninety days. If all procedures are followed, the NLRB will schedule an election. A majority of votes to decertify is required. While unions have won about 50 percent of certifying elections in recent years, they have lost approximately 75 percent of decertification elections.[10] Over 600 bargaining units per year have decertified their unions over the past several years.[11] While management can not initiate decertification, it can legally support the decertification *after* the petition is filed. The company can use the following strategies to show support:

1. Meet with the union members to discuss the merits of becoming a union-free shop.
2. Provide legal assistance in preparing for decertification.
3. Change the corporate culture and atmosphere so that workers feel they no longer need a union as an intermediary.

An alternative to a formal decertification election process has been used in recent years. Employees can oust the union by collecting 50 percent or more signatures of the bargaining unit's employees and then demanding that the management stop any further bargaining with the union's representatives.[12]

If a company desires to remove a union, it must remember the following:

1. It has to be very careful in following the rules laid down by the NLRB or else the decertification election will likely be voided. At the same time, it cannot be timid in voicing its position within the legal guidelines.
2. It must be prepared to change the company to the extent that employees believe that a union is no longer needed.
3. The human resource function must be prepared to change its emphasis after a union is removed from that of grievance handling and contract negotiation to creating an atmosphere in which productive cooperative arrangements can be facilitated.

UNION AVOIDANCE

Moving to Another Region of the Country

In an expanding market a company may leave its union facilities intact and seek to open new facilities in a union-free environment. What has been more typical, however, has been the closing of labor union dominated old facilities in the North and building new plants elsewhere without a union. This strategy has been especially offensive to unions and is seen as one of the many antiunion and union busting strategies that labor considers unfair and even immoral. While it is illegal to close or move a plant solely to avoid a union, a firm can often make a case that the move is based on cost savings brought about by lower taxes, a newer plant, or lower wages. As a result of this type of action, unions are seeking to bring more security issues to the bargaining table. Not only have unions gotten involved in this process, but the communities that stand to lose a major tax base are supporting the unions.

During the 1970s and 1980s, a number of communities, states, and localities provided a variety of subsidies in forms of training dollars, wage subsidies, and tax abatements to either lure new business into a community, provide funds for an expansion, or at least avoid major shutdowns. In return for those incentives, cities have often joined union lawsuits when deals went sour or the company decided it wanted to move to a more attractive location.[13] While companies may argue persuasively that economic conditions do not allow them to compete effectively using high-priced labor, and in some cases outdated equipment, the argument falls on unsympathetic ears. Community leaders counter that companies lose a measure of that freedom if they accept public money. Dan Boroff, city manager of Clarksburg, West Virginia, states that companies "have the freedom to come and go . . ." but that they should not "accept taxpayer dollars to subsidize these moves."[14] The implication is that the strategic flexibility of a company may be greatly impaired by these agreements.

Beyond local and state legal action to prohibit or restrict plant closings, the 1988 Worker Adjustment and Retraining Notification Act was passed by Congress. This law, which took affect February 4, 1989, requires companies (who hire over 100 workers) to notify their employees at least 60 days in advance of a plant closing.[15] This allows workers and communities to better cushion the impending closure. This legislation was heavily supported and lobbied for by organized labor in an attempt to slow down its eroding power base.

Managers need to carefully evaluate the long-term consequences of incentives that a community gives its firms as well as the hidden costs sometimes associated with collective bargaining concessions made by the unions. The company may strive to be a good corporate citizen, but it must not, for short-term peace, ignore the reality of world economic trends nor its own domestic competitiveness. Companies like General Motors and Chrysler, after negotiating worker and community concessions, are often hard pressed to keep the promises they make at the bargaining table.

Moving Offshore

Another manifestation of this attempt to escape unionization involves going offshore, that is, producing goods in countries that are predominantly nonunion. These are often third-world or developing countries that desire and welcome industrial jobs. While the workers may be paid anywhere from one-half to less than one-tenth of what their U.S. counterparts would receive for the same hour of labor, in many countries this wage puts the worker in a much higher economic class than most other workers in that country. When the wages are low enough, and productivity rates are similar to those in the United States, increased shipping costs and other costs associated with doing business in a foreign land are not serious limitations to competitiveness.

Offshore production in such countries such as Mexico, Taiwan, and Korea can reduce labor costs, but potential problems can partially reduce what appears to be overwhelming reasons for doing it. Many critics, and particularly organized labor, are quick to point out these limitations, which include the following factors:

1. Lower productivity per worker due to lack of adequate education, training and benefits.
2. Lower quality of goods because of less able workers.
3. Many goods may have less than 10 percent of their total cost as labor and, consequently, the cost of cheaper labor does not offset the other higher costs of doing business in a foreign country.
4. Going offshore demonstrates a lack of "loyalty" to America and can cause a backlash by the American public.

Other analysts maintain that these criticisms are basically the self-serving propaganda of the unions and believe that American companies cannot compete in world markets unless they produce for markets in a variety of countries, which can range from technologically advanced to third-world countries depending on a variety of factors such as labor costs and closeness to the markets.

These issues are not going to be resolved soon but will affect more companies in the next few years and will directly affect the collective bargaining process. Whether a given company is selling in global markets today or not will not insulate the company or its unions from this issue. Very likely, more and more domestic and foreign competitors in almost all industries will consider using a mixed U.S. and foreign labor force as a competitive strategic weapon. Union officials and company management need to be concerned because this type of international work force will likely become more of a bargaining issue.

Outsourcing

A relatively recent trend that has become a major point of contention in contract bargaining is the issue of outsourcing. Outsourcing occurs when a company subcontracts to other companies work that it was doing in-house before. Say for example, that a machined component for a large truck transmission costs $150 for materials and uses six hours of labor. At a labor rate of $33 per hour (including benefits) the total costs of the part would be $348. The company may go out and find a small job shop that has a nonunion work force and an average wage rate of $21 per hour. If the outsourcing subcontractor takes a $32-per-piece margin, the total costs comes to $314. The company may decide to reduce its union labor force and buy externally.

The company can accrue other benefits, such as a provision that it will pay for only "perfect" parts, thereby eliminating scrap. If demand falls, the company can eliminate its contract and not be saddled with long-term unemployment compensation liabilities. Of course, this trend has some liabilities as well, but outsourcing has led unions to accuse companies of using this procedure as just one more union busting tactic. It is likely that outsourcing will become more of a collective bargaining issue in the 1990s.

Managers and union leaders do need to recognize, however, that outsourcing can work to the benefit of both parties in certain situations. It provides more flexibility for the company in adjusting to varying demands and can provide a more stable core of unionized workers. When a downturn occurs, these external contracts can be eliminated before well-trained, experienced union members are laid off. Generally, though, union members see this trend as threatening to their current jobs and an effective counter to increasing their membership, since additional work will not be done by new union workers but rather by subcontractors, many of whom are nonunion.

MAKING A UNION UNNECESSARY

Many companies have never had a union or the union has been decertified. If the company wants to remain a union-free shop, it must take care to develop and maintain policies that will balance the needs of the company to make a fair profit with the legitimate needs of the workers. Managers need to remember that economic issues are not the only issues that concern workers. Exhibit 18.6 illustrates a variety of issues that need to be addressed.

It is not uncommon for companies to clearly state their commitment to remain union free and try and persuade the employees that the company has their best interests at heart. A formal policy statement is frequently made indicating that the success of the company is based on the skill and efforts of the employees and that in the opinion of the management, unionization would interfere with the respect that the company feels for its employees. The statement might go on to say that a union-free environment is in the best interest of the employees, the customers, and the company itself.[16] Such a statement may be included in an employee handbook and emphasized during new employee orientation sessions.

The company should be very careful in its policy considerations to ask what effect a given policy will have on the company's union-free environment. In some

EXHIBIT 18.6 Some Factors of Concern to Workers That Must Be Addressed in Order to Maintain Good Industrial Relations

ECONOMICS-RELATED ISSUES

- Wages and benefits
- Secure pension and retirement benefits
- Assignment of hours, overtime
- Layoff provisions and protection
- Profit sharing
- Promotions
- Subcontracting limitations

QUALITY OF WORK-LIFE ISSUES

- Clean, safe working environment
- Recreational facilities
- Daycare subsidies and/or on-site daycare
- Work team involvement, such as quality teams
- Grievance procedures
- Recognition for work
- Training and development programs that can lead to advancements
- Internal hiring policies whenever possible

situations a company may have paid a substantial price to maintain its nonunion status. For example, a company fearing a union may be very generous in granting wage increases in an attempt to discourage union organizers. But the company may find that the cost increases can not be fully supported by the market price of its product. That will, in turn, decrease the company's bottom line. Having made such sacrifices in order to remain union free, the company must not risk its union-free status over some minor disagreement with the work force. These issues can not be left to chance but need to be a part of a comprehensive human resource management strategy that is linked with corporate and strategic business unit master strategies.

VIOLENCE AND SABOTAGE AS A RESULT OF NEGOTIATION BREAKDOWNS

While sabotage and violence is not common today, it still happens. Managers need to develop contingency plans to deal with outbreaks of violence should they occur. But first and foremost, careful planning and negotiations should prevent this from ever happening. Today, most union officials and company managers realize that the tough bargaining disagreements should stay at the bargaining table and not spill into the streets or into the workplace. Not only is there a very real danger to lives and property, but the public's tolerance and sympathy does not extend to violence, no matter how deep the disagreements run. In the Pittston strike, one Sunday afternoon in the early fall of 1989, 99 men in camouflaged fatigues took over a Pittston Company plant. Even though the men were unarmed, the security guards retreated into the safety of an office building.[17] Fortunately, no serious violence took place, but the event was a grim reminder that preparations need to be made to counter any attempts at unlawful and destructive behavior where everyone loses.

HR CHALLENGES •

Management Can Deunionize a Work Force

Using only the most positive tactics available, Kenneth Barr, president of Cyprus Mineral Company, set out to convince his workers that they no longer needed a union to protect themselves. This was a tough job, considering the mine's history.

Cypress is a copper mine located in Miami, Arizona. The mine has been a part of the Teamster and United Steelworkers Union for nearly 50 years. Even though the workers were loyal union members and stood by the union in strikes and hard times, Barr was able to convince them to decertify the union, and he did so by a convincing margin of 2 to 1.

To orchestrate this turnaround, Barr used a psychological—not physical—game plan. He provided "charm school" seminars, called "I'm OK, You're OK" to get the workers and managers talking about the 50-year chasm that stood between them. Barr instituted changes in the workplace too. He provided raises, changed work rules, started cross-training, and pushed for a safer workplace. All of these tactics helped to convince most of the workers that there was a better way than "us versus them."

Without the union contract to guide their behavior, managers have decided to make even more changes. They have started giving extra days off when they feel it is justified, allowing truck drivers to get out and walk around when they feel tired without fear of being yelled at by a foreman, and most of all, they are listening when their workers tell them something is or is not working.

As with every change, there are some people who do not like it. Older workers point to the new policies that favor youth over seniority as favoritism. Some workers complain about having to learn new tasks. Some family members have found themselves supporting opposite sides of the union decertification process. However, many workers felt that in the end, the union was more interested in self-preservation than in helping the workers, and that is why they chose to decertify it.

SOURCE: Adapted from Marj Charlier, "How a Mine in Arizona Wooed Workers Away from Union Loyalties," *Wall Street Journal*, August 8, 1989, pp. A1+.

In summary, the management of the company should seek an ironclad commitment from its union counterparts to avoid, prevent, and denounce the use and advocacy of violence and/or sabotage. In especially bitter disputes, management should have a plan in place that will protect the lives and property of those involved.

PATTERNS OF BARGAINING

Structure of Bargaining Relationships

While the law mandates that the employer bargain with the union that is the legal representative of its unionized members, it does not require a particular structure. The structure employed has a significant effect on negotiating strategy and specific tactics. The most common structure is a single employer negotiating with a single union or union affiliate. This is the most straightforward approach. Usually management is represented by a top management team member: the CEO (especially in small operations) or designated representative (more typical in middle to large size organizations), the human resource manager, selected managers, and perhaps a corporate labor specialist and/or labor lawyer. The union is likely to be represented by the local union president, local union officers, a group of rank-and-file members, and the union's international representative or business agent.[18]

The following structures are also utilized:

1. *Multiemployer or industry-wide bargaining.* A group of employers in an area or industry join in an association and agree to negotiate a contract with the union that represents all of the association's members.

The Look of Bargaining in 1992

Even though the economy is in a recession, union workers are looking forward to negotiations in 1992. Surveys have found that over 85 percent of the employers who will bargain with their unions in 1992 expect to offer raises that equal or surpass the inflation rate. Some of the companies whose union contracts are due to expire in 1992 include the Aerospace Industry, affecting 61,000 workers in April; AT&T, affecting 100,000 workers in May; and the Bell Companies, affecting over 300,000 workers in August.

Why are the unions receiving such good news during such bad economic times? The answer is simple. Organizations are facing low inflation and increased productivity. These two forces combine to provide a near zero increase in the cost per unit of output, even when employees receive raises. This is good news for the union members who have not done as well with respect to raises as their nonunion counterparts since 1983.

However, all is not rosy. One sticky spot for the 1992 negotiations will be health care. Managers indicated that they are being forced to ask for more input in this area from the workers simply to offer the same coverage as they had in the last contract. Additionally, some unions are going to ask for more than they will probably get. For example, the Screen Actors Guild (SAG), whose contract expires in June, will want a wage increase in its $448 a day minimum. However, with record low numbers at the box office, and lackluster video and cable sales, the producers will not be in a giving mood.

SOURCE: Adapted from Aaron Bernstein and Ronald Grover, "Union Workers Will Get Some Breaks in '92," *Business Week*, February 3, 1992, p. 50.

2. *Multiunit bargaining.* In this case, employers do not belong to a formal association but in order to save time and other resources agree to bargain in one set of negotiations. Each employer does reserve the right to make alterations in the general agreement and each employer signs a contract with its particular union.

3. *National-local bargaining.* The national union and the corporate representative negotiate a master agreement on the economic issues. Local facilities and local unions agree to abide by the provisions but reserve the right to negotiate local issues.

As various forces cause the economy to shift, sometimes a previously useful structure can cause significant problems. Take the case of the bitter 1989–1990 strike between the United Mine Workers (UMW) and the Pittson Coal Company in southwest Virginia that was discussed earlier. Over 400 charges of unfair labor practices have been brought against the company and union by the NLRB. The problems began in 1987 when Pittston decided to pull out of the Bituminous Coal Operators Association (BCOA). Since 1950 BCOA had negotiated industrywide agreements with the UMW. The company alleged that industrywide bargaining was no longer appropriate because they ship about 75 percent of their high-quality metallurgical coal overseas and thus the company had to compete with foreign competitors that receive subsidies from their governments. UMW estimated that the concessions Pittston was asking for would undercut domestic producers by $4 to $6 an hour. One sought-after major concession that really riled the UMW membership was Pittston's goal to stop contributing to the industrywide pension and health benefits fund. One such fund, called the 1950 benefit, covered pre-1974 retirees and their employees and required companies to pump $2.17 per hour into the virtually bankrupt fund.[19]

This example illustrates three important points, which appear on the following page:

1. Environmental changes not only affect the individual companies and the union, but the very structure of collective bargaining in an industry. In this case, when the long standing BCOA no longer serves the interests of one of its most influential members, that company quickly seeks to abandon the 29-year-old established way of doing business.

2. International economics are driving domestic negotiations. As John Naisbitt points out in *Megatrends 2000*,[20] the global economy will have an ever increasing impact on all sectors of the economy, including labor.

3. Retirees are living longer and demanding higher benefits. The costs of funding these plans are likely to grow astronomically. Who will pay for these liabilities? This major issue will be contested not only in the legislative chambers and the judicial system, but also at the bargaining table.

Mandatory, Permissive, and Prohibited Bargaining Issues

It is important in designing a strategic negotiating approach that managers understand that they have to bargain on certain issues while on other issues they are prohibited from doing so. Exhibit 18.7 summarizes some of the major items in each category.

The 1947 Taft-Hartley law defines three types of issues:

1. *Mandatory issues* include such items as wages, hours, benefits, and other terms and conditions of employment. These have the most direct impact on the worker's day-to-day functioning. Refusal to bargain on these issues can result in charges of unfair labor practices and an NLRB investigation. It should be pointed out that these issues are mandatory for both sides not just the employer.

2. *Permissive issues* may be discussed if both parties agree to it. It is not mandatory that these issues be put on the table. Permissive issues often include items that are of mutual interest. Specific examples might include a company's pricing policy, the pensions and benefits of retired workers, or safety rules. Neither the union nor the employer can refuse to sign a contract based on failure to reach agreement on a permissive issue.

3. *Prohibited or illegal issues* are strictly forbidden by law. They cannot be subject to negotiation even if both parties want to negotiate them. Included in the prohibited list are closed-shop agreements, discrimination against protected classes of individuals, featherbedding, and hot-cargo agreements.

In most contracts, a special section called a managerial prerogative clause reserves certain rights for management that are not specifically enumerated in the contract. It might read like this:

It is herewith recognized that all management functions shall be retained by the company. These functions include, but are not limited to, the full, complete, and exclusive control of direction of the work force, scheduling of production, operation of the plant, acquisition of materials, production of products, the location of such production, and the methods of sale and distribution of its products; the right to change or establish job classifications and descriptions; the right to introduce new or improved procedures; the right to abolish any job or department; the right to make and enforce reasonable shop rules; and the right to hire, fire, suspend, train, discipline, discharge, advance, transfer, lay off, and recall employees. These rights shall all be the function of management unless expressly stated otherwise within this agreement.[21]

....

EXHIBIT 18.7 Mandatory, Permissive, and Prohibited Bargaining Issues

MANDATORY ISSUES	PERMISSIVE ISSUES
Wages	Pricing policy of firm
Benefits, including insurance, vacation, holidays	Pensions and benefit level and rights of retired personnel
Overtime rules and compensation	Supervisory compensation
Subcontracting work out	Supervisory discipline
Vacant job posting procedures	
Layoff plan	**PROHIBITED ISSUES**
Shift differentials	
Safety	Featherbedding
Promotions	Hot-cargo agreements
Layoffs	Discrimination against protected classes
Stock purchase plans	Closed-shop agreements
Seniority	Union or agency shop clauses in right-to-work states
Management rights clause	Secondary boycott agreements
Retirement age	

....

Basically these provisions allow management a great deal of discretion in the day-to-day and strategic management of the company. Traditionally, unions have taken the attitude that management can make its decisions and the union will be there to challenge those decisions that it perceives to be unfair. Management has sought maximum flexibility and has been reluctant to give up any more control than absolutely necessary. These past attitudes, however, may be changing on both sides. For a variety of reasons, more cooperative-collaborative relationships may be in the offing.

In exchange for concessions, the union may ask for a bigger role in decision making. With increased foreign competition, the union and management may come together and decide to jointly work on increasing productivity. These shifting attitudes will have a definite and profound effect on the collective bargaining process in two ways. First, the issues that come to the table may change from a primary focus on economic issues to an increasing interest in quality of work, decision control, and jointly determined investment decisions. Secondly, these changes can take both management and union members into unchartered waters. Roles may not be as clear as before. Human resource managers need to think through the implications of these changes *before* they get to the bargaining table. Many benefits are to be gained from cooperative efforts, but there is a price to be paid in terms of control on the part of management and increased responsibility and accountability on the part of unions.

....

THE COLLECTIVE BARGAINING PROCESS

The bargaining process consist of five stages: (1) preparations, (2) negotiations, (3) compromise, (4) settlement, and (5) mediation and arbitration. Each is illustrated in Exhibit 18.8 and described in the following sections.

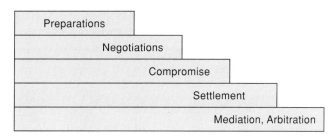

| EXHIBIT 18.8 | The Collective Bargaining Process |

Preparations
Negotiations
Compromise
Settlement
Mediation, Arbitration

Preparations

Preparations for the negotiation process can be divided into components that include clearly understanding the strategic thrust of the company, analyzing the strengths and weakness of both the company and union, analyzing the environment, analyzing the history of the labor-management relationship, analyzing relevant stakeholders, anticipating the union's likely demands and prioritizing them, clearly stating the company's demands and desires along with a prioritized list, and selecting the team for negotiations.

The Strategic Position of the Company

We have emphasized the strategic nature of the collective bargaining process. Implicit in this process is a high level of planning and research. In a strategic model the overall corporate mission will drive the SBU business strategy which, in turn, will drive policies toward finance, marketing, accounting, manufacturing, and human resource issues. Thus, those responsible for labor negotiations need to be well aware of the total strategic thrust of the company. Certain issues may be "nonnegotiable," while other issues may be mandatory given the strategic direction of the company.

Financial Strengths and Weaknesses of Company and Union

A careful review of financial statements, inventory levels, sales forecasts, and market share is important. For instance a company may find that a large inventory and slow sales provide a cushion against a potential strike. In many cases, companies with relatively strong sales and a low inventory crank up production several months in advance just in case the negotiations go poorly. This can be an expensive defense though because overtime often is paid and inventory holding costs rise dramatically. The financial strength and vulnerabilities need to be assessed carefully and the negotiation posture adjusted accordingly.

Also, a careful assessment of the union's position should be carried out. A union that is cash rich in strike funds is very likely to negotiate differently than a union that has had a recent history of costly strikes. Both the union and the company are likely to investigate the others' position. Not only is accurate, reliable data necessary, but also a careful judgement of possible scenarios based on this information should be thought through. Often the best estimate of what will happen in the future is a clear understanding of past negotiation behavior. Careful evaluation of the union-company history is an indispensable part of the analysis. From this historical base, managerial judgement can intertwine current trends and issues to produce a set of realistic scenarios.

Human Resource Attributes of Company and Union

A precise assessment of the human resource base is important. Are the workers so highly skilled that the company would have to shut down in the event of a work stoppage or can management keep the company running? Are operations automated to the extent that a certain level of service can be maintained? For example, in recent labor disputes in the telephone industry involving NYNEX, managerial personnel were able to keep the system up and running with a minimum of disturbance. While this is not a long-term solution, the movement toward automated systems can change the complexion of the negotiations to reduce the power of a threatened strike.

Another aspect of the human resource concern is the age and educational level of the management and employees who will do the negotiations. Usually the negotiation team for the union will be less well educated and younger than that representing the management level. This is not to say, however, that the union members are naive and poor negotiators; they are often more "street smart" than their management counterparts.

Within the limits of propriety, it is highly recommended that each side analyze and try to predict how the various personalities are going to behave in the collective bargaining session. We have already mentioned that much of the process involves bluffing, window dressing, and other emotional and psychological tactics. While the substantive issues should never be forgotten, the emotional and psychological aspects of the process should be evaluated and prepared for. Participants can prepare for negotiations by considering the following questions:

1. Who is the most influential person on both sides?
2. What sort of emotional tactics are team members likely to employ?
3. Can some negotiators be "read" easier than others?
4. Based on past negotiations, what are the tactics that each side should be prepared for, and how can one react to these tactics to gain an advantage?

Negotiations and Compromise

The primary objective of the negotiation process is to reach an agreement both parties can live with. A written contract, signed by both parties, that will govern the employment relationship should be the objective of both sides. This does not mean that management needs to "give away the store" nor that the union must sell out to management. But it does mean that both parties must be willing to compromise on issues until a reasonable accommodation is reached.

Bargaining and Negotiations Defined

Bargaining between the union and management is the give-and-take process that goes on between the two parties. Each party tries to maximize its position relative

HR CHALLENGES ●

Negotiation Rules to Follow to Reach an Agreement

Robert J. Harding, a veteran labor negotiator, offers the following seven rules for negotiations that enhance the chances of reaching agreement.

1. Use the preliminary meetings to set the ground rules for future sessions. For example, the negotiators might agree up front that negotiations will take place during normal business hours and not in all-night marathon sessions.
2. Document carefully all meetings. Include who was there, what was said, what the intent was behind contract language, and what proposals and counterproposals were made. At the end of each day's session the note taker can dictate the outlines of the sessions and have typewritten documents prepared for review. Missing information or disagreement can be filled in. This documentation will not only help in the negotiation process, but it can also help in interpreting the contract once it is signed.
3. If the company CEO is well regarded by the employees, consider using him or her in certain negotiating sessions, particularly the early ones. This helps the CEO understand the position of the union.
4. Within the bounds of what is legal, establish a comprehensive file on the in-plant union negotiating committee. This can be a basis for bet-

ter participation and drawing out the union members who are perhaps the most qualified to speak on a given issue. For instance, if a worker has been with the company 20 years and a management representative believes that the current proposal might not benefit him, the representative might post a question like, "Ken, are you aware that the current proposal will give workers with 20 years seniority only about half the benefits as those who have been with the company from 5 to 10 years?"

5. Never underestimate the union negotiators abilities. Accept them as equal peers. A condescending attitude can hurt the process and may result in management winning an ego battle and losing the contract war. Many of the union people are street smart and savvy when it comes to negotiations.
6. Sustain strong communication links with managers and first-line supervisors after the contract is settled. They are the ones who actually administer the contract on a day-to-day basis.
7. If an impasse is reached consider federal mediation. This demonstrates good faith and a commitment to avoid a bitter labor dispute.

SOURCE: Adapted from Robert J. Harding, "Seven Tips for Successful Collective Bargaining," pp. 220–221.

to the other party. Technically, the bargaining process goes on daily as the two parties live under the contract. The *contract negotiations process is the actual bargaining* that goes on between the two parties to reach agreement on a contract. It is a more specific aspect of the entire collective bargaining process. The total bargaining process sets the tone for contract negotiations. For example, if during a three-year contract, there have been continuous disagreements on the contract in force and numerous grievances have been filed, this atmosphere of confrontation is almost sure to carry over to the negotiations for the next contract.

Not only will a confrontational atmosphere affect the negotiations, but less than satisfactory negotiations will, in turn, fuel difficulties in contract administration. What one party is not able to win during the contract negotiations they may try to win during grievance bargaining when the actual contract is being interpreted in specific instances. Suppose for example, the contract stipulates that a person is paid for at least four hours whenever called in to work by his or her department head on a weekend or other shift when he or she is not normally scheduled. Now suppose that a worker is called in by a foreman, works two hours, and is only paid for two hours, not four hours. The company might justify this action by saying the foreman called the worker in, not the department head as is stipulated in the agreement. The union obviously would support the employee stating it does not matter who called the employee in; the fact is that the employee came in and worked two hours and should be paid for four. Such a case would likely go to arbitration, especially if the company is trying to find a means to do away with this call-in provision and has not been able to eliminate it in actual contract negotiations. The company is attempting to win something through arbitration that it could not win at the bargaining table.

It is not uncommon for companies to try and circumvent a strict "letter-of-the-law" interpretation of the contract. Managers will argue that during a three-year contract, economic and competitive conditions can change so radically that they need some flexibility. Depending on the union's strength and/or goals, it may agree to this flexibility or may hold the management's feet to the fire and demand absolute compliance by initiating a host of grievances and charges of unfair labor practices. It is very possible that both parties may benefit from some flexibility. If this is so, it should be built into the contract negotiation process rather than relying on the grievance and arbitration process, which can be extremely costly and disruptive.

Stages in the Bargaining Relationship

The bargaining relationship between union and management has four stages, although each relationship may not necessarily progress from one stage to the next nor start out at stage one. In recent times we have seen many cases in which the relationship has actually declined rather than moved forward. These stages, depicted in Exhibit 18.9, exist on a continuum, and there are an infinite number of points along this scale.

Hostility   The management and union may be very hostile toward each other based on a bitter organizing campaign or, for a more established relationship, a history of strife and dissention. Often a great deal of both overt and covert conflict exists between the two parties. They have little trust in each other and can point to specific examples of the other party's "flagrant" violations of fairness. In the case of a newly organized union, management may feel it has lost the war and now has to deal with a third force. Union members may feel a new sense of power but also realize that items they may have come to expect are now only guaranteed through bargaining. Both sides are feeling their way and are trying to get a reading on one another.

Grudging Acceptance   Some bargaining relationships move from hostility to the next stage. In this stage, management realizes that it has no other choice, at least for the time being, but to accept the union and work with it. The acceptance is not altruistic or voluntary, but rather a matter of federal law that is guaranteed by the NLRB. In this situation, small amounts of trust between the parties usually exist. Conflict is somewhat reduced. The union feels a bit more secure now and does not feel that management is trying to "do it in." At this point, the union's creditability is usually higher with both management and the employees it represents.

Tolerance and Mutual Accommodation   Many union-management relationships never get beyond stage two, but a significant number move to stage three. At this level, the bargaining relationship has matured considerably. There is significant trust between the two parties. Conflict is more constructive than destructive. It is healthy, controlled, and channeled. The two parties have generally accepted each other and try to accommodate one another through bargaining. Essentially, a bal-

....

EXHIBIT 18.9   Stages in the Bargaining Relationship

Hostility	Grudging Acceptance	Tolerance with Some Mutual Accommodation	Integrative Bargaining

....

ance of power exists between the two. This state of affairs was perhaps more common 15 to 20 years ago, when the economic environment was less turbulent, than it is today. With the advent of international competition and fast changing technology, the union-management relationship has often been pushed back down the continuum toward more bitter confrontation.

Integrative Bargaining   This is also referred to as mutual problem solving or cooperative bargaining. In this stage, the two parties almost fully accept one another. The acceptance may be a function of a long process of building working relationships or, more importantly today, the recognition that the very survival of both the company and the union membership's jobs are at stake. The parties view themselves as cooperating to solve mutual problems and become partners in the employment relationship. They try to maintain more of a cooperative rather than an adversarial relationship. They have a high degree of trust for one another and depend on each other. Conflict is of the healthy, positive type and centers on ideas rather than personalities. It should be recognized that the extreme end of this continuum is probably utopian and can never be achieved. But the GM-UAW case at the beginning of this chapter is an example of a relationship that is moving toward the integrative bargaining model.

Stages and Negotiation Strategy

The actual negotiation process—its strategies and steps—will vary greatly depending upon in which of the four bargaining stages the two parties find themselves. If they are in the hostility stage, there may very well be shouting matches and stomping off as one party leaves the table in a huff. The strike threat is also likely to be used as a weapon. Bargaining is likely to go on and on with little real progress being made.

On the other hand, in the integrative or problem-solving stage, strikes will be virtually nonexistent and actual bargaining will be more productive per hour spent at the table. Tactics will still be used, but they are likely to be less confrontational and more constructive in nature.

A Bargaining Model

Bargaining and negotiations depend on the relative *power* of each party. Power is the ability to get another party to do some act it would normally not do or to refrain from doing something it would normally do. For instance, in September 1990 the management of the *New York Post* presented an ultimatum to the International Typographers Union—either take a 20 percent cut in wages or the paper will close down permanently. The union members grudgingly gave in to this large concession because they were powerless to anything about it.

··

EXHIBIT 18.10 A Simplified Model of the Bargaining Process

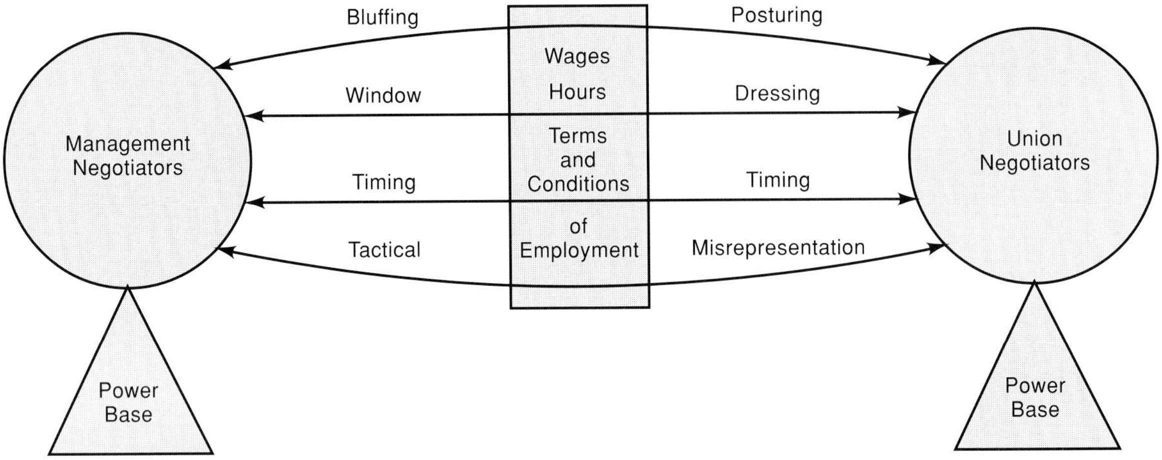

For one party to have power over another party in the bargaining relationship, the party must have something the other party wants. If you've ever tried to sell a car to someone else, you're aware of how this comes into play. It is much easier to sell a car at the price you want if the other person *really* wants the car. In the employment relationship, the union wants higher pay, better hours, and, in the case of the auto workers, job security. The employer has these things. But the employer needs a stable, skilled work force that it can employ in a flexible manner so as to produce a sufficient quantity of quality goods and services at a competitive price to allow growth and a reasonable level of profitability. The union controls the labor factor of production. The two parties then bargain with each other over what each one can give up relative to what the other wants. Thus, bargaining involves a trade-off, as is shown in Exhibit 18.10.

A trade-off means that there is compromise and some conflict. It also means that various **tactics** are used. For example, **bluffing and posturing** are used in bargaining. Each party tries to create false positions that it can then trade away. **Window dressing** involves listing extraneous, unimportant demands that can easily be traded away. **Timing** is another tactic used in presenting demands. For example, some bargainers save their more important demands until later in the actual contract negotiation process. **Tactical misrepresentation** involves misrepresenting your side to the other. It borders on lying, perhaps, and involves using fabricated data, withholding data, or actually stating a position the party does not believe. Careful preparations for the negotiations should ameliorate the vulnerability of each side to these tactics. Background research on what the other side is likely to propose is an important element in the preparation stage.

Expanded Bargaining Model

Exhibit 18.10 is an oversimplification of the bargaining process. Exhibit 18.11 is a bit more realistic, even though it still simplifies the highly complex process of collective bargaining. As can be seen in Exhibit 18.11, not only do the two parties bargain with each other, but they also bargain among themselves and to please their constituencies who do not always agree on what their position as a group should be.

EXHIBIT 18.11   The Bargaining Process

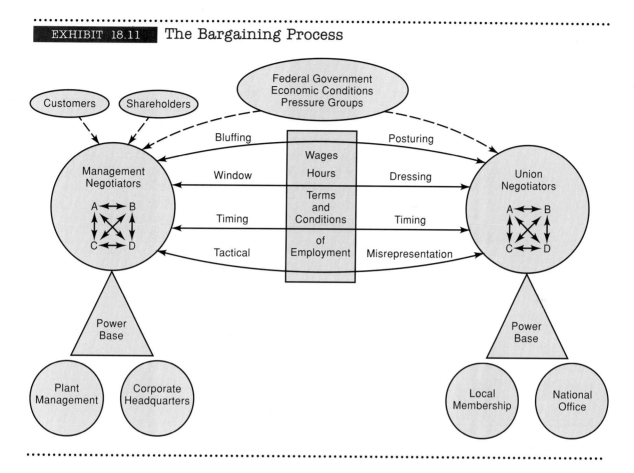

Settlement

In large organizations the final settlement is the result of a complex procedure over an extended period of time. Settlements in smaller companies, on the other hand, are frequently straightforward and the logical end of the process.

In large organizations the immediate union bargaining team will typically have to submit the agreement to a larger representative council. In the case of the GM-UAW negotiations, the tentative agreement was submitted to the Council of 400 for its scrutiny before it was sent to the rank and file. Finally, the rank and file will have the opportunity to vote on the agreement. This is called the **ratification process.** If the rank and file does not accept the agreement, it's back to the table. Rarely will the rank and file reject the recommendation of the negotiation team, but it is not unheard of. In recent years, approximately 10 percent of negotiated contracts were not ratified on the first vote. If the union leadership is in close contact with the desires and needs of its membership, this should not happen.

Assuming that ratification does take place, then the following implementation steps are suggested:

1. The contract provisions should be submitted to lawyers on both sides to make sure that the agreed upon provisions get transferred into appropriate language that is both understandable and enforceable.

2. Depending on the nature of the negotiations, appropriate news releases and a joint union-company news conference may be appropriate. Whether the outcome is good news or bad news it is better that the parties involved explain the facts rather than let rumor and innuendo permeate the media. For example, if the contract calls for the shutdown of a production line in Muncie, Indiana, but at the same time gives workers the chance to be retrained, retire, or relocate, it is important that both the union and company manage this information output.

3. Internal publications from the union and company should be used to communicate the most important aspects of the agreement.

4. If major changes in work rules, compensation packages, or benefit allowances are forthcoming, it will be wise for human resource managers to propose appropriate training and development programs for managers and workers. For example, if a new quality improvement program and related compensation rules are included in a new contract, management cannot just assume that everyone will know what to do. Specific technical training may be called for. If there has been a particularly bitter struggle with the union in the past, it may be important for the first-line supervisory staff to attend to appropriate human relations topics.

5. Both the union leadership and the management of the company need to clearly state their commitment to make the agreement work, recognizing that whether the process was smooth or rough, all the parties must now work together to accomplish the organization's objectives.

Mediation and Arbitration

In some cases, the negotiation process breaks down and a settlement cannot be reached through normal channels. Rather than resort to a strike on the part of the union and a lockout or hiring replacement workers by the company, the two parties may seek the outside intervention of a third party. Mediation involves a neutral third party who tries to break a bargaining impasse. Mediators may be called upon to get the parties to start negotiating again, clarify points that have been misunderstood, suggest alternative compromises that have not occurred to the bargaining parties, and improve trust and communication. While mediators have no power to enforce a settlement, they may bring a fresh viewpoint into the process that can get things moving again.

The Federal Mediation and Conciliation Service (FMCS) was created as an independent agency by the 1947 Taft-Hartley Act. Labor, management or both can seek the assistance of FMCS or they can seek some other third party. Since these mediators have no power to force a settlement, they must have a reputation of being impartial, fair, well informed, and patient. Caterpillar and the United Auto Workers (UAW) agreed to mediation after a long and ugly five-month strike. To reach this point, management threatened to hire replacement workers if the UAW did not send its people back to work. Only about 300 of the 12,600 striking workers crossed the picket line on the deadline day set by Caterpillar.[22]

Arbitration, on the other hand, involves a neutral third party listening to both sides, evaluating the evidence, and making a binding recommendation. Arbitration is of two basic types: contract rights arbitration and interest arbitration. **Contract rights arbitration** consists of settling impasses in the actual administration of the contract and is usually the outcome of a grievance procedure that cannot be settled by the parties. **Interest arbitration** involves the terms of the contract itself. While interest arbitration is used in the public sector where strikes are illegal, it is rarely used in the private sector.[23] Normally, neither of the bargaining parties are willing to give up control of such basic issues as wages, benefits, working conditions, and so forth. They generally would rather rely on the negotiation process and the threat of economic pressure. In *The Labor Relations Process*, Holley and Jennings point out that relying on interest arbitration has some additional drawbacks: delays and extra costs may occur; the arbitration may put a damper on the working environment; arbitrators may be inconsistent from case to case; arbitrators may end up splitting the difference, causing the parties to take extreme positions; and reliance on the arbitration process may lead to over reliance on arbitration rather than working out differences through negotiations.[24]

Contract arbitrators generally come from two sources: either the FMCS or American Arbitration Association (AAA). The AAA is a nonprofit organization that acts as a clearinghouse for qualified arbitrators. To be considered for the list, the potential arbitrators must be able to demonstrate his or her credentials and must be recommended by a representative of labor, management, and a neutral third party. While not always true, a fairly large number of arbitrators and mediators tend to be members of the legal profession and may specialize in labor law.

Sometimes the parties cannot conclude a workable agreement. They may have not sought mediation or the mediation efforts were not successful. With binding arbitration, both parties must agree to accept the outcome. If either party or both parties refuse to agree to arbitration, then a labor stoppage is almost assured. Surprisingly, in the 1980s, strikes and lockouts were relatively infrequent. The total percentage of work time lost due to stoppage for facilities employing 1,000 workers or more has decreased from .10 percent in 1965 and .09 percent in 1975 to .03 percent in 1985.[25]

The FMCS requires unions to file a 30-day notice of all contract expirations. It estimates that about 2 to 3 percent of these expirations involve a strike. Cynthia Gramm however, asserts that this may be misleading because of the amount of smaller companies in the FMCS sample. Her research indicates that between 1971 and 1980 companies with over a 1,000 employees had a strike rate of 13.8 percent.[26]

Last Resort Options for the Unions

A Strike

A union frequently takes a strike authorization vote to give the labor negotiation team a bargaining lever. A strike is a refusal by labor to work. It is not casually used. The union has to measure carefully the cost/benefit factor in considering a strike. Timing of a strike is crucial. For instance, if the demand for the company's product is high and in a growth phase, the company may not want to bear the opportunity cost of lost sales or alienated customers. On the other hand, if demand is slack and inventory is high, labor's threat of a strike may ring hollow. Companies sometimes even start working overtime to build up inventories in anticipation of tough bargaining and a potential strike; this is common in both the steel and auto industries among others.

A strike may force the company to give in on key union demands, but a strike is a high risk strategy for the union. A 1989 Supreme Court ruling determined that if a company hires replacement workers during a labor walkout, it does not have to fire its replacement workers once the strike is over (*TWA* v. *Independent Federation of Flight Attendants)*. This can effectively eliminate or greatly reduce the size of the

....

EXHIBIT 18.12 Illustration of What a Strike Could Cost Union Members*

WEEKS OF STRIKE	HOURS LOST	WAGES LOST	UNION BENEFITS	NET LOSS	HOURS TO MAKE UP	WEEKS TO MAKE UP
1	40	$340	$150	$190	447.1	11.2
2	80	$680	$300	$380	894.1	22.4
3	120	$1,020	$450	$570	1341.2	33.5
4	160	$1,360	$600	$760	1788.2	44.7
5	200	$1,700	$750	$950	2235.3	55.9
10	400	$3,400	$1,500	$1,900	4470.6	111.8
15	600	$5,100	$2,250	$2,850	6705.9	167.6
20	800	$6,800	$3,000	$3,800	8941.2	223.5

*Example assumes a company offer of $8.50 per hour (3% over previous rate) vs. a union demand of $8.925 per hour (8%).

Table illustrates the point that even if the company finally meets the union's 8% demand, it will take a long time for the union members to make up their losses due to the strike.

....

union. Even if replacement workers are not hired, it can take a significant amount of time to make up for losses incurred in a strike situation.

For example, imagine the workers of a canning factory striking over a dispute of a 3 percent company-offered raise versus an 8 percent union-demanded raise. If the average worker would make $8.50 under the company's offer, Exhibit 18.12 demonstrates how long it would take to make up the lost wages under different strike lengths, assuming that the company finally gives in. Of course, there is the risk that the company may (1) hire replacement workers, (2) only agree to the previous 3 percent raise, or (3) maybe lower the raise to 1 percent or even ask for a decrease. This example presumes that the worker receives a $150 a week strike benefit package from the union fund and/or unemployment. Some unions members might receive more or some might receive less. Even with a relatively short strike, the union members may take up to two-thirds of a year to make up for the losses. In the case of a prolonged 20-week strike, it could take several years to make up for the losses. The company correspondingly has to weigh the long-term cost of increasing pay and benefits against the potential of lost revenue and profits.

Both the company and the union have to evaluate carefully not only the possibility of lost profits and wages but also intangibles like reputation, competitiveness, discord, and various other social and psychological factors. Human resource managers and union leaders have come to realize that other avenues are generally more attractive to settle even wide differences. Yet unions will sometimes strike on even a small wage difference as a matter of principle, although this is not as common today as it was during the 1960s and 1970s. In fact, work stoppages fell to a near record low in 1991. There were only 40 work stoppages affecting 392,000 workers in 1991. This averages to workers being idle two of every 10,000 available work days.[27]

Boycotts

A boycott can be defined as an agreement of union members not to buy or use the company's goods or services. Secondary boycotts, in which the union openly encourages suppliers and customers to not purchase from the targeted company, were made illegal by the Taft-Hartley Act. Boycotts are difficult to use effectively because in most cases the share of a company's sales made to union members and their families are a small proportion of the total sales volume.

A local business that operates in a strong pro-union community may be the most vulnerable. An example would be a grocery store that has a union contract with its checkout clerks. In the event of a labor dispute, the worker's families and friends may stop shopping at that grocer. While that may not be enough of a economic lever, other union members from nonrelated industries as well as other community members may join in the boycott in sympathy. According to the law, the union that is in dispute with the chain could not openly solicit a secondary boycott. However, it may happen through word of mouth and/or media attention to the issue. Even these quasi-secondary boycotts rarely meet the objectives of the unions. The boycott against California lettuce, led by labor leader Cesar Chavez during the 1980s, was eventually dropped without forcing the growers to concede to Chavez's demands.

Last Resort Options for the Company

Lockouts

A management tactic somewhat akin to a strike is a lockout. Management may prohibit union members from entering the facility and instead run the company with management employees and temporary replacement workers. As industries become more automated and less reliant on highly skilled employees, lockouts are more feasible. The communications business is becoming much more automated. Telephone companies, for instance, are increasingly dependent on computer hardware and software that minimizes the need for human intervention. Think about what happens when you make a long distance call with a credit card. By using a touchtone phone you can complete the call without any direct human intervention. Such technology made it possible for NYNEX managers during a labor dispute in 1989 to keep the company up and running all basic services with management employees.

Other industries that are becoming increasingly automated are banking, continuous process operations like oil refining and chemical manufacturing, and even retailing with an increased emphasis on self-service and phone based orders.

Hiring Replacement Workers

While the lockout tactic often utilizes temporary workers, it is usually designed to get the union back to the bargaining table and move toward a settlement that will allow resumption of normal operations. During the mid-to late 1980s, a somewhat different emphasis was placed on hiring replacement workers, not to just temporarily fill the gap, but to permanently replace the striking union members. The 1981 firing of the air traffic controllers (*Professional Air Traffic Controllers* or PATCO union members) by the Reagan administration and subsequent hiring of replacement controllers actually paved the way for a more widespread use of this tactic. As mentioned earlier, a controversial 1989 Supreme Court decision confirmed the employers' right to keep the replacement workers after a strike was over. From the union's perspective this is a powerful counter to a strike, and it can result in the effective end of a union's influence in a company. Union leaders have accused management of deliberately provoking strikes so as to allow management the opportunity to hire replacement workers who will decertify the union.

National labor leaders have been pressing Congress to pass a restrictive law that would prohibit the hiring of permanent workers. National labor policy has tended to recognize two parallel but competing rights. Unions have been given the clear right to strike, but businesses have been given an equal right to stay open.[28] During the 1990s these competing rights will certainly be at the center of attention in legislative and court decisions.[29]

Administering the Contract

Once the contract is ratified the day-to-day implementation is critical. If a contract is well written and clearly specifies the responsibilities of both sides, then administering the contract becomes much easier. The tone of the negotiations can affect the contract administration process. If the contract is settled without a strike or lockout, the agreement is less likely to lead to grievances. If the negotiations were tough and resulted in a prolonged walkout, the day-to-day administration may develop into a version of the cold war.

It should be obvious that the negotiations process cannot be taken lightly nor can the consequences of the signed contract be ignored. From a strategic viewpoint, long-term implementation should always be kept in mind during the negotiation process. Frequently, the management team involved in the bargaining process will not be as involved in the day-to-day administration as will the first-line supervisors. Therefore, the management team should carefully review the feasibility of the provisions, anticipate potential areas of conflict, and try to preempt as many of these situations as possible. Management should establish an effective channel of communication between these supervisors to make sure that ongoing problem areas are properly dealt with in subsequent negotiations.

Grievance Causes

Even when a satisfactory agreement is negotiated, inevitable disagreements occur regarding contract language. Management has the primary responsibility of administering the contract. The union watches carefully to make sure that the contract language is observed. In most contracts, a specific procedure is spelled out about how complaints and concerns over contract administration will be handled. Grievances have several causes.

Misunderstanding or Misinterpretation

While a contract may vary from a few pages to over 50 pages, every eventuality cannot be anticipated, so the language is written in general terms. The worker and foreman might interpret the language differently. For a variety of legal reasons, the contract may be full of judicial terms. The average supervisor or worker may interpret these provisions in his or her own particular way. Long-term employees may think they understand the agreement and not bother to read the actual contract assuming that the new contract is just about the same as the old one. This can lead to a contract violation due to neglect.

Premeditated Contract Violation

Occasionally, one side or the other will intentionally violate a contract provision in order to draw attention to an issue that could not be resolved in the negotiations process. For instance, a union might be unhappy about a work rule that allows a supervisor to change a worker's assignment to a different machining operation more than three times in a shift. The union worker may complain and deliberately slow down after being transferred the third time to test management's intent to enforce the contract. Management may choose to ignore the worker's behavior and in the future only assign a worker to a maximum of two machines, leading to a *de facto* drop of the provision. Or the management may discipline the worker, the worker subsequently files a grievance, and the union may force the grievance to binding arbitration where it hopes to get a change in the contract provision.

The management, likewise, sometimes forces an issue for economic reasons. Changes in economic conditions might make a work rule too restrictive to allow the company to remain competitive, thus the management may disregard the rule. Here the union may ignore the violation if it thinks the violation will serve its interest or it may immediately file a grievance. The outcome of these willful violations is often a function of the relative power of the management and the union, which could change dramatically during the course of a contract. Some provisions in contracts that run from 2 to 5 years are usually open to negotiation every year.

"Smokescreen" Violations

It is possible that a grievance may be filed for a less than obvious reason. If the union leadership seems to be losing control, or if the members are starting to wonder whether the union officials are too cozy in their relationship with the company, a grievance may be provoked by the union to prove to the membership that it is in control and is serving the needs of the members after all.

Management as well may provoke a problem in an attempt to embarrass the union or test its power. If the management of the company is working to move to a union-free environment, a series of violations may also serve as a means to divide the union into factions.

Smoke-screen violations can be very risky and dangerous because the other party may misinterpret the intent and take retaliatory action. It is recommended that disagreements either be dealt with during the contract negotiations or through a formal grievance process rather than by covert political moves. We will now explain the grievance process in more detail.

THE GRIEVANCE PROCESS

When employees believe that they have been wronged or have concerns about how the contract provisions are being applied, they may choose to file a grievance. It is important that neither party panic when a grievance is filed. The grievance process is a bit like an internal court set up specifically to resolve disagreements to the mutual satisfaction of both parties. Most grievance systems also try to settle the matter at the lowest level possible. A typical system could involve four levels, as Exhibit 18.13 illustrates.

··

EXHIBIT 18.13 Typical Grievance Process

LEVEL	GROUP/REPRESENTATIVE INVOLVED	
4	AAA or FMCS Arbitrator	
3	Company president or vice-president —industrial relations	International representative president
2	HRM manager/plant manager	Union grievance committee
1	Foreman/supervisor	Union steward
	Union/Employee	

··

Level 1

If a worker believes his or her rights have been violated under the contract he or she will usually take it up with the supervisor directly or may report the alleged violation to the union steward who will approach the supervisor along with the worker. A high percentage of the grievances are settled at this level, and the company and the union need to encourage this because it is cheaper and more efficient. It is important that the company properly train foremen and supervisors to deal with complaints in a cool, rational fashion and use confrontation, whenever possible, to assert concern for *both* the interests of the company and its employees. Frequently the dispute will be over an inadvertent violation of the contract or it may be that the employee does not understand the provision properly. The organizational climate as well as past union-employer practice will determine whether the contract is administered strictly according to the letter-of-the-law or in a somewhat looser fashion.

If the grievance cannot be settled to the satisfaction of the employee, the grievance will be taken to the next level. Reasons for **nonresolution** may include the following:

1. The supervisor and employee are unable to agree on what the contract language actually means in day-to-day application.
2. Either the union or employer is using this as a smokescreen to advance a hidden agenda.
3. The dispute involves a personal disagreement between the supervisor and the employee.
4. The supervisor has repeated an act previously settled at the first level. By appealing, the union hopes to have more clout to force the supervisor from continuing to carry out the action.

Level 2

Here the grievance is put into a written format. The document usually includes a detailed account of what happened, who was involved, and what contract provision has allegedly been violated. Furthermore, the union will suggest what it will take to rectify the situation. The document is signed and dated by the employee and union steward. A meeting is set up between the higher level managers, including the human resource manager and possibly the plant manager, the union business agent, and union grievance committee. The company will typically respond with a written

··

Advantages and Disadvantages of Grievance Arbitration

ARBITRATION ADVANTAGES

+ Usually less expensive for the union and company than a strike or work stoppage.
+ Provides a procedural way to handle severe disagreements.
+ Since it is binding in nature it can finally resolve a difficult and ongoing problem.
+ Gives both sides a chance for an impartial hearing and impartial decision.
+ Can provide a basis for the next negotiation cycle to correct any widespread difficulties in the contract.
+ Once the award is decided parties are more likely to work in a cooperative spirit than if the issue is settled through a strike.

ARBITRATION DISADVANTAGES

− Costs for the arbitrator can be high, especially if hearing is detailed and dragged out.
− Ties up productive time of company managers and union officials.
− May encourage failure to resolve issues at lower level earlier in the process.
− High-quality arbitrators are in short supply and this may delay the resolution of the grievance.
− An arbitrator's award might be used as a precedent for the next contract cycle, thereby expanding a very localized problem to a more global environment.

··

decision and implementation plan. For example, the company may agree that the employee's claim is legitimate and issue a directive for correcting the situation and trying to avoid it in the future. On the other hand, the company might find that an employee deserved a disciplinary action and stand by the action of the supervisor. The union can either accept the decision or take it to the next level.

Level 3

Few disagreements make it this far. If they do, they are generally quite serious and will demand the attention of the top industrial relations officer and maybe the president of the company. On the union side, a high-level team that includes representatives of the international union headquarters staff will be convened. The designated company official, often the president, will issue a written decision within a specified time limit. If the union is still not satisfied and further negotiations cannot resolve the issue, either party can request that an arbitrator be brought in.

Level 4

Arbitration, while rarely used in contract negotiations, is utilized from time to time in the settlement of major contract administration disagreements. Both parties submit their cases regarding the disputed provision. The arbitrators are usually limited to interpreting the contract and are prohibited from altering the contract language.

Arbitration is customarily run like an informal court proceeding in the sense that both parties call witnesses, provide testimony, and can cross-examine the other side's witnesses. The arbitrator may ask each side to submit all or part of their evidence in writing so he or she can review it upon completion of the actual hearings. In large companies, labor lawyers are customarily used to represent the interests of the parties involved. In smaller organizations, the human resource staff and union official may represent their interests without attorneys.

After the arbitrator hears the case, he or she generally issues a written finding along with an award. The award will give a summation of the evidence, provide the rationale of the arbitrator's award, and lay out the action that needs to be taken. Contracts provide that once the grievance has reached this stage, both parties will abide by the binding decision. Of course, if either party feels that the arbitrator has erred in the agreed upon procedure, that party may seek relief in the courts. Courts, however are very reluctant to set aside arbitration awards unless it can be shown that the arbitrator's decision was unreasonable and did not address the issues that were presented, or that the award violated a federal or state law, or that the arbitrator exceeded his or her proper authority. The advantages and disadvantages of arbitration are outlined in Exhibit 18.14 (on page 649).

• • • • • • • •

MANAGEMENT GUIDELINES

Collective bargaining is one of the primary tasks of the human resource staff and management in general. It is challenging and not for the weak kneed. As this chapter has explained, the collective bargaining process is not something that just happens once every 2 to 3 years but is an ongoing process that must be monitored and proactively pursued. Collective bargaining can have a major impact on the strategic position of a company. A fair and equitable labor contract can facilitate the company's attempt to reach its long-term goals and objectives. Ineffective negotiations can put the very survival of the organization into jeopardy. As we have learned in this chapter, a wide variety of negotiating structures and situations are utilized in the business environment. Nevertheless, we can offer several important guidelines for managers who confront a union environment.

1. Management needs to be clear about just what its strategic goals are and then align its labor policy with those goals. For example, if a company wants to serve a high-quality–high-price niche, it may be more flexible in negotiating wages but more stringent on flexible work assignments that will allow it to take advantage of highly skilled craftspeople without cumbersome job classifications.

2. The negotiating team must be very well prepared before it goes into the bargaining sessions. Preparations should include
a. a thorough review of past contracts;
b. a listing of disagreements, disputes, and grievances since the last contract;
c. an analysis of what the union will ask for and a careful assessment of the personalities and issues for both sides; and
d. a list of objectives that they want to obtain.

3. Once an agreement is worked out, the manager should make sure that foremen and supervisors understand the provisions of the contract with particular focus on how it is different from the last contract. The human resource department should make sure the contract is distributed to all management personnel. It is also wise to hold workshops or briefing sessions to make sure that everyone understands the precise language. New management personnel who join the company between contract cycles need to be thoroughly and completely briefed.

QUESTIONS FOR REVIEW

1. What are the most important reasons why some unions and managers now believe that a more collaborative relationship is in their best interest?

2. How does the relative power of the company and union affect the collective bargaining process?

3. What connection is there between a company's strategy and its approach to collective bargaining? How would the issues differ for a low-cost producer strategy versus a company that produces high-quality, high-priced luxury items focused on a special market niche?

4. What are some ways in which companies that currently have unions try to eliminate to them? What are some ways that companies without unions try and remain union free? What are the legal and ethical issues involved in each case?

5. Regarding the collective bargaining process, what is the difference between mandatory, permissible, and prohibited issues? Give an example of each.

6. Who are the key management players that are usually involved in the collective bargaining negotiations? Who are the key players for the union?

7. Why is it so important to be prepared before the negotiations start? What can managers do to adequately prepare for the negotiations?

8. When negotiations break down, what are some tactics employed by unions to try to force a settlement? What tactics might a company use?

9. How would you define a grievance? How are grievances settled? What is the role of arbitration in the settlement of grievances?

10. "The next ten years are likely to be a period of increasing labor/management strife based on the resurgence of militant union power." Do you agree or disagree with this statement? Explain your answer.

CASE: Greyhound Racing for Its Life[30]

While the GM/UAW case at the beginning of the chapter illustrates new, more cooperative approaches to negotiations and collective bargaining, the Greyhound bus drivers strike and the subsequent hiring of replacement drivers provides an example of what can go wrong in the process.

A New Start

When Fred G. Currey bought the Greyhound Lines from the parent Greyhound Corporation in 1987, he faced a formidable challenge in trying to revive the ailing transportation company. Greyhound had at one time served a broad diversity of passengers, including students, servicemen, retired senior citizens, and working and middle-class families. The glory days of the buslines were undercut by cut-rate airfares, the wider availability of cars, a deteriorating network of bus depots, aging equipment, reduced routes, and labor troubles. This combination of negative factors caused Greyhound's traffic to nosedive 55 percent from 1980 to 1986.

Currey, who paid $375 million for Greyhound, embarked on an ambitious strategy to revive the line. His actions included

establishing a computer reservations system to increase traffic;

spending over $110 million to overhaul old depots and open new ones;

increasing the advertising budget by 50 percent to $27 million; and

pursuing more package delivery innovations.

In addition, Currey sought and won a $25-million wage concession from drivers and mechanics in 1987. At first the workers were supportive.

Currey considered himself a model employer. He actively solicited the views of drivers and ticket agents on how he might restructure the company. He sponsored banquets to honor exemplary workers. Emloyees felt he was a good boss and wanted to believe his promises of better times ahead. The 1989 results seemed promising. Net income was $727,000 on sales of $1 billion, up from a loss of $17 million in 1988. Passenger miles rose significantly by 10 percent, up to a total 7.4 billion.

The Hound Shows Its Teeth

But the era of good feelings did not last long and by early 1990 workers were comparing Currey to Frank Lorenzo of Texas Air. Union members from the Amalgamated Transportation Union started voicing their discontent and impatience. Some union members believed that pushing Greyhound into bankruptcy would be better than relying on Currey's promises. Adding fuel to the fire, Currey proposed sweeping route changes and consolidations that would eliminate more than 2,000 jobs. By late February 1990, 9,000 employees walked out. Following the lead of other companies, Greyhound's management almost immediately hired 700 replacement drivers and claimed its ridership was back up to 38 percent of normal levels.

While Currey expected that as many as 3,000 drivers would cross the picket line and return to work, only 500 had by April. The results were disastrous for the bottom line. First quarter 1990 results showed $55.8 million in losses and put the company on the verge of bankruptcy.

Violence and Bitterness Prevails

Not only were drivers unwilling to cross the picket lines, but there were reports of snipers firing on buses in nine states. In Florida, seven passengers were injured by flying shrapnel caused by a bullet piercing a bus. An unfortunate accident in Redding, California, added to the tension. A striking driver with 30 years of service with the company was crushed to death by a bus driven by a replacement driver. While union leaders generally dissociate themselves with these sort of tactics, the effects can be devastating on the public's confidence in the safety of the bus line. Fred Currey was adamant in his determination to prevail and held the union responsible. He accused them of "violence, terrorism and intimidation."

Is the collective bargaining employed in the GM-UAW conflict an example what can be expected of labor negotiations in the future or is the Greyhound dispute, full of bitterness, discord, and even violence, a forecast of things to come? Management cannot play a passive role in determining the answer to this question but most proactively and strategically assume responsibility for the labor-management relationship.

QUESTIONS

1. Where do you think Currey went wrong? What happened to change the healthy relationship into one of "us versus them"?

2. As management, you may be asked to take over the jobs left empty by the strike. How would you feel about this? Would you do it, or would you hire replacement workers? Why?

3. Currey faced larger problems than the union struggle, such as inexpensive airline travel and a car in virtually every garage. What strategy would you have selected to turn around Greyhound?

4. Put yourself in Currey's position. You are about to sit down to the table and bargain with the union. You need concessions and labor needs the work. How would you prepare for the negotiation talks?

....
ADDITIONAL READINGS

Arthur, Jeffrey, and James Dworkin. "Current Topics in Industrial and Labor Relations Research and Practice." *Journal of Management* 17 (1991), pp. 515–551.

Ballott, Michael. *Labor-Management Relations in a Changing Environment.* New York: Wiley, 1992.

Barbush, Jack. "Do We Really Want Labor on the Ropes? We're Entering a New Era of Industrial Relations and That's Cause for Concern." *Harvard Business Review* 63. July–August 1985, pp. 10–16.

Barling, Julian, E. Kevin Kelloway, Eric Bremermann. "Preemployment Predictors of Union Attitudes: The Role of Family Socialization and Work Beliefs." *Journal of Applied Psychology* 76 (1991), pp. 725–731.

Barney, Jay B., and William G. Ouchi. *Organizational Economics: toward a New Paradigm for Understanding and Studying Organizations.* San Francisco: Jossey-Bass, 1986.

Blake, Robert R., and Jane S. Mouton. *Solving Costly Organizational Conflicts.* San Francisco: Jossey-Bass, 1984.

Doherty, Robert E. *Labor Relations Premier: An Introduction to Collective Bargaining through Documents.* ILR Bulletin, No. 54. Ithaca, NY: ILR Press, 1984.

Dunlop, John. *The Management of Labor Unions.* Lexington, MA: Lexington Books, 1989.

Freeman, Richard B., and James L. Medoff. *What Do Unions Do?* NY: Basic Books, 1984.

Gerhart, Paul F. *Saving Plants and Jobs: Union-management Negotiations in the Context of Threatened Plant Closing.* Kalamazoo, MI: Upjohn Institute, 1987.

Gold, Charlotte. *Labor-Management Committees: Confrontation, Cooptation, or Cooperation?* Ithaca, New York: ILR Press, 1986.

Helfgott, Roy. *Computerized Manufacturing and Human Resources.* Lexington, MA: Lexington Books, 1986.

Herrick, Neal. *Joint Management and Employee Participation.* San Francisco: Jossey-Bass, 1990.

Hill, Marvin, Jr., and Anthony Sinicropi. *Management Rights:* Washington, D.C.: Bureau of National Affairs, 1986.

Ichniowski, Casey, and Anne E. Preston. *The Competitive Edge: Managing Human Resources in Non-Union and Union Firms.* Glenview, IL: Scott-Foresman, 1988.

Kerr, Clark, and Paul Straudor, eds. *Industrial Relations in a New Age.* San Francisco: Jossey-Bass, 1986.

Kleiner, Morris M., Robert A. McLean, and George F. Dreher. *Labor Markets and Human Resource Management.* Glenview, IL: Scott-Foresman, 1988.

Kochan, Thomas A., Harry C. Katz, and Robert B. McKersie. *The Transformation of American Industrial Relations.* New York: Basic Books, 1986.

Lareau, N. Peter. *Drafting the Union Contract.* Albany, NY: Matthew Bender, 1988.

Lawler, John J. *Unionization and Deunionization: Strategy, Tactics, and Outcomes.* Columbia, SC: University of South Carolina Press, 1990.

Lewin, David, Peter Fruille, Thomas Kochan, and John Delaney. *Public Sector Labor Relations.* Lexington, MA: Lexington Books, 1988.

Lipset, Seymour M. *Unions in Transition: Entering the Second Century.* San Francisco: ICS Press, 1986.

Lipsky, David, and Clifford Donn. *Collective Bargaining in America Industry.* Lexington, MA: Lexington Books, 1981.

Moore, Christopher W. *The Mediation Process.* San Francisco: Jossey-Bass, 1986.

Quaglieri, Philip. *America's Labor Leaders.* Lexington, MA: Lexington Books, 1989.

Rosenbloom, David H., and Jay M. Shafritz. *Essentials of Labor Relations*. Reston, VA: Reston Publishing Company, 1985.

Rosow, Jerome M., ed. *Teamwork: Joint Labor-Management Programs in America*. Elmsford, NY: Work in America Institute, Inc., 1986.

Rothstein, Lawrence E. *Plant Closings: Power, Politics, and Workers*. Dover, MA: Auburn House Press, 1986.

Taylor, Benjamin J. *Cases in Labor Relations Law, 1987*. Englewood Cliffs, NJ: Prentice-Hall, 1987.

Uly, William L., Jeanne M. Brett, and Stephen B. Goldberg. *Getting Disputes Resolved: Designing Systems to Cut Costs of Conflict*. San Francisco: Jossey-Bass, 1988.

Zack, Arnold M. *Grievance Arbitration*. New York: American Arbitration Association, 1989.

NOTES

1. David Woodruff, "The UAW May Be Chasing an Impossible Dream," *Business Week*, October 8, 1990, p. 40; Gregory A. Patterson, "Chrysler Offers Union Workers a Share in Ownership, Bonuses for Productivity," *Wall Street Journal*, July 23, 1990, p. A4; Gregory A. Patterson and Joseph B. White, "GM-UAW Pact Allows Company to Cut Payroll in Return for Worker Buy-Outs," *Wall Street Journal*, September 19, 1990, p. A3; Gregory A. Patterson and Joseph B. White, "GM to Spend Up to $4 Billion on UAW Pact," *Wall Street Journal*, September 18, 1990, pp. A3, A14; "Chrysler, Mitsubishi Venture Has Reached Accord with UAW," *Wall Street Journal*, August 16, 1989, p. A3; Gregory Patterson, "Nissan Workers Reject UAW Bid to Organize Plant in Tennessee," *Wall Street Journal*, July 28, 1989, p. A3; and Gregory Patterson, "The UAW's Chances at Japanese Plants Hinge on Nissan Vote," *Wall Street Journal*, July 25, 1989, pp. A1+.

2. Alexander B. Trowbridge, "A Management Look at Labor Relations," *Unions in Transition* (San Francisco: ICS Press, 1988), p. 415.

3. Arthur Sloane and Fred Whitney, *Labor Relations*, 4th ed. (Englewood Cliffs, NJ: Prentice-Hall, 1981), p. 185.

4. Robert T. Thompson, "An Anti-Worker Labor Bill," *Wall Street Journal*, August 31, 1990, p. A10.

5. David Woodruff and Aaron Bernstein, "Chrysler Headache No. 2: The UAW," *Business Week*, October 8, 1990, p. 8.

6. Robert Blake and Jane S. Mouton, "How to Achieve the Integration on the Human Side of the Merger," *Organizational Dynamics* 13, no. 3, 1985, pp. 41–56.

7. James Fraze, "After Model Merger Taking Two Years, USAir Growing, Pilot Seniority Issue Unresolved," *Resource-Society for Human Resource Management*, September 1989, p. 11.

8. Cynthia A. Lengnick-Hall and Mark L. Lengnick-Hall, "Strategic Human Resources Management: A Review of the Literature and a Proposed Typology," *Academy of Management Review* 13, no. 3, 1982, pp. 454–470.

9. Daily Congressional Record 3954 (23 April 1947).

10. Francis T. Coleman, "Once a Union Not Always a Union," *Personnel Journal*, March 1985, pp. 42–45.

11. R. Wayne Mondy and Robert M. Noe III, *Human Resource Management*, 4th ed. (Boston: Allyn & Bacon, 1990), p. 650.

12. Marc Singer, *Human Resource Management* (Boston: PWS-Kent, 1990), p. 414.

13. Joseph B. White, "Worker's Revenge: Factory Towns Start to Fight Back Angrily When Firms Pull Out," *Wall Street Journal*, March 8, 1988, pp. A1, A26.

14. Ibid., p. A1.

15. Paul D. Staudohar, "New Plant Closing Law Aids Workers in Transition," *Personnel Journal*, January 1989, pp. 87–90.

16. James F. Rand, "Preventive-Maintenance Techniques for Staying Union-Free," *Personal Journal* 59, June 1980, p. 497.

17. John Hoerr, Michael Schroeder, and Todd Vogel, "The Mine Workers Must Win This Fight to Survive," *Business Week*, October 9, 1989, pp. 144–148.

18. Vida Scarpello and James Ledvinka, *Personnel/Human Resource Management*, Boston: PWS-Kent, 1988, p 607.

19. Hoerr et al., "The Mine Workers Must Win," pp. 144–148.

20. John Naisbitt and Patricia Aburdeen, *Megatrends 2000* (New York: Morrow, 1990).

21. Singer, *Human Resource Management*, p. 437.

22. Stephenie Overman, "Caterpillar and UAW Agree to Mediation," *HRNews*, May 1992, pp. A1+; Gregory Patterson and Robert Rose, "Labor Makes a Stand in Fight for Its Future at Caterpillar Inc.," *Wall Street Journal*, April 7, 1992, pp. A1+.

23. Richard Johnson, "Interest Arbitration Examined," *Personnel Administrator*, January 1983, pp. 53–57.

24. William H. Holley and Kenneth M. Jennings, *The Labor Relations Process*, 3rd ed. (Chicago: The Dryden Press, 1988), p. 246.

25. Thomas A. Kochan and Harry C. Katz, *Collective Bargaining and Industrial Relations*, 2nd ed. (Homewood, IL: Irwin, 1988), p. 243.

26. Cynthia T. Gramm, "The Determinants of Strike Incidence and Severity: A Micro-Level Study," *Industrial and Labor Relations Review* 39, April 1986, pp. 361–376.

27. Christopher Conte, "Work Stoppages," *Wall Street Journal*, March 3, 1992, p. A1.

28. Robert T. Thompson, "An Anti-Worker Labor Bill," *Wall Street Journal*, August 31, 1990, p. A10.

29. Andrew Kupfis, "Caterpillar's Union Fallout," *Fortune*, May 18, 1992, p. 16.

30. Eric Shrine, "Greyhound Is Bringing Travelers Down to Earth Again," *Business Week*, June 19, 1989, pp. 52–53; "Even So the Concorde Isn't Worried," *Fortune*, January 1, 1990. p. 65; Kevin Kelly, "Greyhound May Be Coming to the End of the Line," *Business Week*, May 21, 1990, p. 45; and Janice Castro, "Labor Draws an Empty Gun," *Time*, pp. 56–59.

PART

SIX

Strategic Separation of Human Resources

CHAPTER 19

Strategic Restructuring

19

Strategic Restructuring[a]

Restructuring has had a profound effect on many organizations during the 1980s and will likely continue into the 1990s. It has become a fact of life for many firms. One survey estimated that more than half of the U.S. companies in the Fortune 1000 have undergone significant restructuring since 1980.[1] Other surveys show that this figure may be high as 80 percent.[2] From October 1991 to December 1991 corporations have announced cutbacks in staff at a rate of 2,600 a day.[3] Companies that have restructured include AT&T, Mellon Bank, Xerox,[4] General Motors, CBS, DuPont, Kodak, Exxon, General Electric, Atari, Polaroid, Chevron, and Union Carbide,[5] most of whom have been discussed throughout this book.

A major issue in most restructuring decisions is how to deal with the organization's human resources. The possibilities range from nontermination, such as reassignment and retraining, to temporary layoffs, to permanent terminations. Restructuring affects workers on the shop and office floors as well as the highest-ranking executives. It almost always involves a reduction in the size of an organization's work force. As a result, deciding how to handle the human resources part of a restructuring is among the most difficult decisions that an organization's managers will ever face. Issues and alternatives are rarely clear, and each path has its own problems. A poorly planned or carried out restructuring may cause hostility and fear, and it may destroy trust for both those separated and those who remain in the organization.[6] The unique role of the human resource manager as the link between employees and management becomes even more crucial during restructuring.

CASE:

IBM—If at First You Don't Succeed . . .[7]

In 1986 and 1987 the computer industry was hit by its first real slump. Many newer and smaller organizations had a tough time weathering the recession, but most expected International Business Machines to lead the industry back to record levels in 1988. Instead, IBM, the world's largest and most profitable computer company, and a dominant player in almost every segment of the industry, continued to slump even when the rest of the industry set new performance records in 1988. Its sales grew at a meager 8 percent compared to the 20 percent plus performance of most of its competitors. To many observers, this was the first sign that IBM was not the invincible firm that it was perceived to be. Many placed the blame for IBM's poor performance on its highly centralized management system, its bloated headquarters bureaucracy, and its sheer size of almost 400,000 workers worldwide.

IBM responded to the situation by announcing that it was restructuring its operations and cutting back on the size of its work force. This was the second reorganization that the company was undertaking since the beginning of the 1980s. The first reorganization took place in 1981 and 1982 under the direction of IBM CEO John Opel. Opel is credited with putting IBM back into contact with its customers. He created two marketing and sales divisions, National Accounts (NA) and National Marketing (NM), to respond to the unique needs of various types of customers. He also initiated Independent Business Units (IBUs) and Special Business Units (SBUs) in an attempt to expand product lines and foster innovation and technical excellence. One result of this approach was the creation of the IBM Personal

Computer, or PC, which legitimized the young subindustry and provided a standard for other PC makers to match.

Despite these changes, IBM's infamous bureaucracy and size soon caught back up with it again. John Ackers took over as CEO in 1985 and the company was back to its old ways. The goals of the 1988 restructuring were twofold. First, Ackers wanted IBM to really recommit to the customer's wants and needs, instead of following the product-driven strategy that had guided the company for the better part of a decade. Second, IBM had to make its structure more responsive and more cost-effective.

Redeployment of Human Resources

Both of these goals involved extensive redeployment of IBM's human resources. IBM has practiced a "no-layoff policy" since the early 1940s when Thomas Watson, Sr., the company's founder, decreed that one of the main beliefs of IBM was to maintain loyal and happy employees. One method of achieving this restructuring was to increase IBM's sales and marketing force from 55,000 to 71,000 people by the end of 1988. Another area that IBM sought to emphasize was the newly emerging software market. Consequently, IBM also experienced a tremendous need for computer programmers. These needs for new salespeople and programmers, coupled with the need to reduce the over-inflated corporate bureaucracy by approximately 16,000 people, all had to be dealt with within the no-layoff framework. Ackers used several approaches to achieve this goal including the development of an early retirement program, a normal attrition rate of three percent, and the elimination of overtime and temporary employees. In order to redirect personnel to expanded operations, such as programming and sales, IBM retrained thousands of its employees, with some retraining courses lasting as long as eighteen months.

The cost of the restructuring was not cheap, however. Over 6,000 employees took advantage of the early retirement program in 1988 at a cost of $870 million. Many employees were also faced with the bleak decision of having to take IBM's generous severance package or relocate their families to other IBM facilities, which were often hundreds or thousands of miles away. Structurally, IBM reorganized itself into seven basic business segments and appears to have reduced its bureaucracy. Critics have suggested that IBM's decision making has become more nimble under Ackers' leadership. Its new internal slogan, "Just Say Yes," showed its renewed dedication to the customer. Its goal of offering a price quote or a leasing deal in a matter of hours was a vast improvement over the days or weeks it used to take.

IBM's restructuring was not without its critics, however. One observer pointed out that one marketing division had its reporting responsibility transferred four times since 1981 from the Data Processing Division (DFD) to the Information Systems Group (ISG) to the National Accounts Division (NAD) to the National Marketing Division (NMD) to the North

Central Marketing Division (NCMD). This constant change not only confused the customer about who he or she needed to talk to, but also diverted the employees' attention away from the main focus—namely the customer.

Success?

Were these two restructurings successful? In spite of some extremely competitive new products and a more responsive bureaucracy, IBM's earnings have continued to lag. This is due in part to extensive price cutting by competitors and new slowdowns in some of IBM's traditional strongholds, such as mainframe systems. On December 5, 1989, IBM announced that it was beginning its second restructuring in two years and its third restructuring in the 1980s. Once again IBM was seeking to cut 10,000 jobs from its work force using no-layoff methods. This included a third early retirement program in as many years, and this time IBM was making the offer to nearly 23,000 employees. If IBM reaches its goal of cutting another 10,000 employees, it will have reduced its work force by 37,000 people since 1985—all without a single termination or layoff.

However, this third restructuring of the 1980s appears not to have been enough to pull IBM out of its sluggish state. In late 1991, Akers announced that IBM will again need to cut its work force. This time the total number of jobs to be eliminated is 20,000 by 1992. Akers also indicated that he will reevaluate the situation in mid-1992. If IBM's results have not improved at that point, he said he may even consider layoffs, breaking the company's no-layoff tradition.

Another uncharacteristic move by IBM was its announcement of a joint venture with Apple, it former arch rival. This may be yet another step in IBM's plan to revive itself. The joint venture was designed to create a new operating system that makes computers inherently easier to use, allows users on different machines to link up to one another and swap information, and that taps the underused potential of the latest microprocessors.[8]

Once again, the programs will not be cheap. IBM has announced that it expects to spend $2.3 billion restructuring this time around. The severance portion of the package is expected to cost $500 million alone. The restructuring is expected to cut IBM's costs by $1 billion per year. Many analysts are still skeptical about the potential impact of IBM's third restructuring. Consultant Dave Hanna believes that IBM really needs to cut another 20,000 to 30,000 employees from its work force if it is to get itself back on track.

Can IBM really restructure itself this time around? Or will it need a fifth or sixth time to really succeed? Some have called IBM an elephant that needs to learn how to dance. It certainly has taken a number of lessons over the past few years and now appears capable of doing a basic two-step. However, only time will tell if the two-step solves the problem or whether IBM needs something more exotic and difficult—like the lambada.

• • • • • • • • •

Probably no other event of the 1980s has had as much effect on a firm's management of its human resources as has restructuring. Certainly this is true for IBM. The human resource department at IBM has been an integral part of each restructuring program the company has undertaken. It has been responsible for retraining, for monitoring the early retirement programs, and for coordinating the transfers. The expertise and professionalism in this area has helped IBM successfully manage the changes it has faced over the past ten years.

STRATEGIC CHOICES

As in the case of IBM, the human resource unit plays a strategic role in periods of restructuring for several reasons. Human resources are used to increase efficiency, achieve a competitive position, and contribute to the company's survival. To achieve these goals, human resource managers must make strategic decisions that are frequently difficult to make. Some examples of these choices are listed below.

1. Managers must decide how to downsize. The choices seem endless. Should the firm follow IBM's lead and retrain workers, or is permanently severing ties a better way to go? Perhaps asking employees to work part-time may be enough to weather the recession? These and many other alternatives need to be weighed to determine the appropriate approach.
2. Management must decide when the downsizing should take place. While it is not nice to lay off employees just before Christmas, it may not be feasible to keep them on if sales do not pick up. Balancing what is good for the company and the employee is another strategic choice managers face.
3. Often managers must decide which employees will be laid off. If the company is not unionized and restricted by a contract, the decisions about whom to let go fall in management's lap. The criteria by which these decisions will be made must be developed.
4. Managers must also decide when to stop downsizing. At some point, laying off one more worker will not help the bottom line and it may begin to hurt the firm's reputation. This point must be determined and managers must be able to recognize it before it passes.

RESTRUCTURING OPTIONS

Broadly defined, **restructuring** is any major change in the way an organization operates. Exhibit 19.1 provides some of the most common restructuring situations. The goal of restructuring is to have fewer employees serving the same function at the same level of efficiency.[9] Restructuring usually involves cutbacks, downsizing, and consolidation. **Cutbacks** are attempts by organizations to react to temporary changes in the marketplace by reducing spending and controlling costs. Cutbacks are the most general type of restructuring. Downsizing is typically more long term in its focus. **Downsizing** is the process by which a firm seeks to reduce its overall size and scope permanently, usually the result of changes in the organization's strategy or in the marketplace. **Consolidations** are actions to cut functions or activities that may be redundant within an organization. Consolidations are frequently the result of mergers and acquisitions of firms, but they may also occur independently of these activities. Of course, cutbacks, downsizing, and consolidations are not mutually ex-

EXHIBIT 19.1 Most Common Restructuring Situations

CAUSE/TYPE	PERCENT OF TOTAL
Acquisition	36.8
Retrenchment/Downsizing	31.5
Merger	7.5
Leveraged Buyout	5.0
Facilities Relocation	4.1
Divestiture	3.2
Plant Closure	3.0
Bankruptcy	2.1
Other	6.8
Total	100.0

clusive activities. One, two, or all three of these activities may occur simultaneously depending on the scope of the restructuring.

In particularly difficult circumstances, the only restructuring choice for a firm may be bankruptcy. Under a Chapter 11 filing, the firm may be able to reorganize as a smaller operation. Under a Chapter 7 filing, however, the firm will cease operations. Drexel Burnham Lambert's recent bankruptcy is an example of a Chapter 7 filing. The Campeau acquisition discussed later in the chapter is an example of a Chapter 11 filing.

STRATEGIC VARIABLES

An organization's decision to restructure results from an examination of several different strategic variables. The strategic variables involved in the restructuring decision include (1) the organization's competitive strategy, (2) management's philosophy toward employees and technology, (3) the business cycle effects, and (4) the goals and types of cost restructuring of the organization, or a combination of the above factors. All of these variables affect the choices that the organization's management must make about the type of restructuring that it will undertake. Exhibit 19.2 briefly summarizes these variables and each is explored below.

Competitive Strategy

Often, an organization will restructure as a result of a change in its **competitive strategy**. In *Competitive Strategy*, Michael Porter defines an organization's competitive strategy as "a combination of the ends (goals) for which the firm is striving and the means (policies) by which it is seeking to get there."[10] Porter identifies three generic types of strategies that an organization may pursue. A firm may choose to pursue an overall cost leadership, a differentiation, or a focus strategy in relation to its competitors.[11]

Firms pursuing an **overall cost leadership** strategy seek to sell products that are less expensive in price than their competitors' products. This strategy involves vigorous pursuit of organizational efficiency. Managers emphasize efficient and large-scale assembly line and manufacturing techniques and strict control of operating and overhead costs. In addition, they reduce spending on perceived nonessential areas

. . . .

EXHIBIT 19.2 An Organization's Strategic Restructuring Variables

VARIABLE	ASPECTS
The Organization's Competitive Strategy	Overall cost leadership Differentiation Focus Stuck in the middle
Management Philosophy Concerning Employees and Technology	Attitudes about employees Attitudes about skills/training Attitudes about automation and flexibility
Business Cycle Effects	Prosperity Recession Depression Recovery
Type of Cost Restructuring of the Organization	Goals of restructuring Cause of restructuring

such as research and development, maintenance, and sales. When an organization adopts a cost leadership strategy it will often seek to reduce what it views as nonessential workers by cutting levels of bureaucracy, reducing redundant functions within the organization, and trimming staffing in nonessential departments. It will also try to reduce the number of workers on the assembly line by investing heavily in automation, robotics, and other related techniques.

Firms pursing a **differentiation** strategy seek to create a product or service that is unique within the industry, and thus gain a competitive advantage. Firms using this strategy try to build a brand loyalty in their customers. Increased brand loyalty will reduce the customer's sensitivity to price and substitute products. Product design, quality, customer service, dealer networks, technology, features, or a combination of these factors all serve to increase brand loyalty. While a differentiation strategy does not allow firms to ignore costs, many of its parts are costly. Organizations that adopt a differentiation strategy must build some form of strength. This strength may be in marketing, research and development, manufacturing skill, or other related capabilities. This strategy requires personnel that are highly skilled, creative, and talented. Critical areas include R&D labs, marketing departments, and product design/engineering shops. Quality people in these areas are always in high demand. As a result, getting the necessary skills to be a strong competitor using the differentiation strategy is time consuming and expensive. This strategy is often costlier to adopt than other strategies because success is more difficult to measure. The basis of employee performance ratings are subjective, and not quantitative, because their output is difficult to measure.

A third option is the **focus** strategy. Firms adopting a focus strategy seek to "get back to the basics." Instead of trying to compete in many markets with a wide range of products, they concentrate on a narrow segment that matches their skills.[12] Firms cut nonessential functions and personnel not directly serving the direct aim of the organization's focus. Many focused firms are smaller than those using a low-cost or differentiation strategy. Management often organizes focused firms functionally to

....

EXHIBIT 19.3	Common Organizational Requirements of Porter's Three Generic Strategies

GENERIC STRATEGY	COMMON ORGANIZATIONAL REQUIREMENTS
Overall Cost Leadership	Tight cost control
	Frequent, detailed control reports
	Structured organization and responsibilities
	Incentives based on meeting strict quantitative targets
Differentiation	Strong coordination among functions in R&D, product development and marketing
	Subjective measurement and incentives instead of quantitative measures
	Amenities to attract highly skilled labor, scientists, or creative people
Focus	Combination of the above policies directed at the particular strategic target

....

avoid waste and duplication. It puts its resources into doing one or two jobs well. Segmentation may occur by focusing on certain buyers, products, or geographic locations. A firm with a focus orientation may be the low-cost producer or have high differentiation in the market segment it serves.

An example of a firm that is pursuing a focus strategy is Hayes Microcomputer Products. Hayes is a leading manufacturer of modems and related equipment for microcomputers. The company has experienced problems in recent years as it has tried to branch into other areas. Its revenues have stagnated at the $120-million rate that they reached in 1985. From 1986 through 1990 Hayes has came under attack by several competitors who have offered clone products at significantly lower prices. In May 1990, Hayes announced that it was cutting the size of its work force by 25 percent. Hayes now intends to refocus its efforts on its most profitable products and abandon its forays into other areas. Hayes expects that its refocusing will enable it to maintain its leadership position in the modem market.[13]

A final strategy is essentially a lack of strategy. Porter calls this the **stuck in the middle** strategy. Firms stuck in the middle are unable to adopt successfully a generic strategy due to a lack of capital, market share, products, or managerial skill. They wander from one strategy to another and do poorly in each. This results in declining profits and market share. Decisive action may be the only solution to this problem if the firm wishes to remain a real competitor. This action almost always includes some form of restructuring. Exhibit 19.3 summarizes the common organizational requirements necessary for each of Porter's three generic strategies.

Management Philosophy Concerning Employees and Technology

The philosophy of the firm's managers concerning its employees and technology may also influence restructuring. Some firms, such as Japanese automobile producers, commit

....

| EXHIBIT 19.4 | Easy- and Hard-to-Fill Jobs

HARD-TO-FILL JOBS: TRY TO AVOID LAYING OFF WORKERS IN THESE AREAS

Physical Therapists	Registered Nurses
Veterinarians	Electrical Engineers
Computer Systems Analysts	Computer Scientists
Physicians	Dietitians
Pharmacists	Chemical Engineers
Biological Scientists	Dentists
Vocational Counselors	Legal Assistants
College Professors	

EASY-TO-FILL JOBS: LAYOFFS IN THIS AREA SHOULD
NOT RESULT IN PROBLEMS

Telephone Operators	Butchers/Meat Cutters
Rail Transport Workers	Telephone Installers
Machine Operators	Typists
Water Transport Workers	Statistical Clerks
Barbers	Data Processors
Photographers	Stenographers
Metalworkers	Firefighters
Plumbers	

....

themselves to no-layoff policies. Honda in Marysville, Ohio, employs 10,200 workers and is the region's largest employer. To date, it has not laid off one worker.[14] Other organizations view personnel as easily replaced assets. Many organizations that require skilled people, such as those in the electronics industry, believe that it is cheaper to keep employees than to let them go during a restructuring and then have to rehire and train new people later.

Firms in some industries can easily replace employees due to the low level of skills needed to perform many of the jobs. This is particularly true of service industries, such as fast-food restaurants. Many firms in these industries have relatively low training costs for new employees. If not, they are willing to pay for the increased training costs due to high employee turnover because alternatives are less appealing. These alternatives may include automation or increased salaries for employees. Exhibit 19.4 highlights some of the jobs that are easy and not so easy to refill.

Management philosophy toward automation may also affect a firm's restructuring decision. Some firms believe that high levels of automation are necessary to compete effectively in the market. As a result, employees in these organizations become more expendable during times of restructuring. Other firms place an emphasis on the flexibility of humans over robots. In these cases, capital investment may suffer during times of restructuring compared to employment levels. In any situation, management's philosophy toward its employees and its technology will play a significant role in determining the form of the restructuring.

Business Cycles

Business cycle stages may also influence a firm's restructuring decision. Each stage of the business cycle—prosperity, recession, depression, and recovery—has a unique effect on an organization. Weak economic conditions often force restructuring decisions upon firms. In other instances, restructuring can arise from the opportunities to make changes in times of prosperity. Restructuring during these times is often less painful to carry out than during slowdowns.

Characteristics of **prosperity** and **recovering** economic times are strong and increasing sales. Organizations have extra resources and capital as a result of the prosperous times and restructuring often causes little disruption to the organization. Firms will typically add extra employees to meet the strong demand from the market. Other firms may choose to restructure by putting a freeze on hiring or only filling critical positions, thus limiting the size of the organization. Other firms may restructure by reassigning personnel from noncritical to critical positions. This enables organizations to emphasize those areas that are essential to their success. Many firms will transfer employees out of corporate headquarters or support roles into sales and marketing positions.

Digital Equipment Corporation (DEC), the world's second largest computer company, is trying this transfer strategy after falling victim to its own success. After experiencing phenomenal sales and organization growth in the mid-1980s, the firm discovered in 1989 that it had vastly exceeded organization hiring goals. DEC realized this at about the same time it discovered that several of its new computer lines confused both its old and new customers about its future product direction. The net result was an unexpected slump in sales for an organization that had experienced well over 20 percent average annual sales growth during the 1980s. Digital's solution was to move employees out of its least critical areas, namely manufacturing and corporate support staff. DEC has placed these people in field sales positions so that it could explain to customers exactly what its slew of new products means. Most analysts believe that this is exactly what Digital needs to put itself back on the fast track for the 1990s.[15]

Restructuring often occurs during times of recession or depression. **Recessions** are periods of general economic slowdowns. Rising unemployment, lack of market demand for goods and services, and excess productive capacity all characterize recessions. **Depressions** are severe forms of recessions. Unemployment may reach 25 percent of the total work force and firm bankruptcies reach extremely high levels. Fortunately, business cycles do not always pass through all four stages. The last general depression in the United States coincided with the start of World War II.

In addition, not all segments of the economy are all at the same stage of the business cycle. Thus, the electronics industry may be in a period of prosperity while the steel industry is in a recession. Recessions and depressions often force firms to restructure to survive. Restructuring during these times is often more radical as a result. While in times of prosperity the question may be, "What is the optimal number of employees we need to succeed?," during recessions and depressions the question becomes, "How many employees can we cut and still function?" However, recessions and depressions allow organizations to make changes that they would not have been able to make during prosperous times.

Many union contracts forbid layoffs or worker reassignments during strong economic periods, but allow them during downturns. Resistance to restructuring may

FOCUS ON ETHICS AND SOCIAL RESPONSIBILITY • • • • • • • • • • • • • •

Honesty Is the Best Cost-Cutting Strategy

Against the better judgment of everyone he knew, Hugh Aaron, CEO of a small plastics firm, decided that the best way to make his workers understand why he had to make major cost-cutting changes was to let them see the books. He decided that his hourly workers should be made privy to the profit and loss statement. By showing them the facts and figures, they would surely agree with his plans.

So one day Aaron closed the plant for an hour and a half, and with the use of a chalkboard he explained the financial picture of the firm to all of his workers. As he began to explain the situation, he was asked many questions. Some, such as "What is gross profit?" made him realize that just explaining the situation would not be enough. He would first have to educate the workers about the business of being in business.

One of his managers volunteered to hold daily work sessions with the employees to explain business concepts to them. He was also given the task of explaining the profit and loss statement to the workers at the next organization wide meeting.

At that meeting the workers began to accuse the management of having two sets of books. The ones it was sharing with the workers to show how bad things were and garner wage cuts, and the real set the accountants and lawyers used.

To combat these fears, the lawyers and accountants were present at the next meeting to reassure the workers that the figures they saw were the figures that the firm actually reported. Once the workers began to believe that the numbers were accurate, things started to change.

Some of the changes were small, others were not so small. For example, the workers noticed that there was a $4,000 entry on the books for renting and laundering uniforms. They suggested that the firm purchase an industrial washing machine to use at the end of the shift to save the laundering costs. This one change saved the firm $12,000 a year, approximately the same amount of money as one worker's yearly salary.

The only workers who did not seem to enjoy the new open information format were the managers. They seemed to thrive under the old traditional style of closed shops, which is exactly where Aaron asked them to go.

SOURCE: Adapted from Hugh Aaron, "In Troubled Times, Run an Open Company," *Wall Street Journal*, December 10, 1990, p. A10.

be high during periods of prosperity since it is difficult to justify cutbacks when the latest quarter just produced record profits. Resistance is often much lower if the organization's members are convinced that a restructuring is necessary to ensure the organization's continued existence. As a result, restructuring is often easier to accomplish during periods of recession or depression, and greater changes are possible than in stable economic times.[16] However, once workers are laid off during poor economic times, they may not be rehired when the economy turns around. More and more companies are deciding to remain lean and keep the jobs cuts permanent.[17]

Cost Restructure

The 1980s saw great changes in U.S. business practices. Many organizations underwent radical changes in their operating methods. These changes were largely due to the increase in international competition. Many U.S. firms discovered that their decades-old methods of operating were unsuitable to match the increase in foreign competition. Many foreign firms began to sell products that were both less expensive and higher in quality than those produced by their American counterparts. Peter Reid, in the book *Well Made in America*, described the reaction of a group of Harley-Davidson managers and employees who toured the Honda motorcycle plant in Marysville, Ohio, in 1982. He remembers that Honda's total overhead staff at Marysville

....

EXHIBIT 19.5	Companies That Have Eliminated Jobs to Cut Costs

COMPANY	NUMBER OF JOBS ELIMINATED
BankAmerica/Security Pacific	10,000
Pan Am	5,000
Eastman Kodak	3,000
DuPont	1,550
America West Airlines	1,500
Atlantic Richfield	1,500
Total	22,550

....

(president, secretaries, personnel department, accounting, material planning, and so on) numbered 30 out of 500 employees. Harley's managers were surprised that they could find no squadrons of engineers and planners stashed in the back room. Further, Harley managers couldn't even conceive of how to do such a thing. This episode was a sobering lesson in the basic difference between Honda's costs and Harley's: overhead staff.[18]

Harley-Davidson's reaction to this problem was typical of many American firms facing the similar situations in the 1980s. It began a process of **cost restructuring.** A cost restructuring is a process in which a firm seeks to change certain costs within the organization, usually with the goal of reducing them to a lesser level. Cost restructuring is usually a common goal of any organization restructuring strategy. A 1989 joint survey of 1,837 firms undertaken by the American Society for Personnel Administration and the Commerce Clearing House shows that the main goal of almost 50 percent of all restructuring efforts is labor cost reduction. The survey also found that over two-third of the firms that had restructured experienced a decrease in the size of their work force.[19] Exhibit 19.5 provides a sample of some of the firms who have eliminated jobs as a means of cutting costs.

In Harley-Davidson's case, one of its main cost restructuring goals was to reduce its overhead costs. Other common cost restructuring goals include reducing production costs, inventory costs, and capital spending costs. Firms such as Oryx, a Texas oil and gas producer, have achieved significant cost restructuring by cutting or reducing bureaucratic red tape. This red tape may include rules, procedures, reviews, reports, and approval processes.[20] Kodak has restructured four times since 1982. Each effort was suppose to make it more efficient and allow it to post better earnings. Kodak also wanted the restructuring to put them on the growth track again. But in 1991, Kodak had a 5.7 percent drop in profit after adjusting for inflation. Even Kodak conceded that some of the restructuring attempts have not achieved their goals.[21]

Another major cause of cost restructuring in the 1980s has been the widespread use of the **leveraged buyout** (LBO). An LBO is the takeover of a company, usually using borrowed funds, either in the form of bank loans or low-rated "junk bonds." Collateral for the buyout is usually the target company's own assets. The acquirer generally pledges to repay the loans out of the cash flow of the acquired company.[22]

··

EXHIBIT 19.6 Some of the Best and Worst LBOs of the 1980s

THE BEST

COMPANY/YEAR	PRICE	RESULT
Allegheny Ludlam (1980)	$223 million	Went public in 1987; stock market star
Cain Chemical (1987)	$1 billion	Company resold to Occidental Petroleum for $2.1 billion nine months later
Gibson Greetings (1982)	$80 million	Company worth more than many times its current selling price
Metromedia (1984)	$1.1 billion	Some parts of organization sold off for $3.3 billion
Wilson Sporting Goods (1985)	$132 million	Dramatic increase in sales; sold to Amer Group in 1989 for $200 million cash

THE WORST

COMPANY/YEAR	PRICE	RESULTS
Dart Drug Stores (1984)	$160 million	Filed for Chapter 11
Fruehauf (1986)	$1.5 billion	Sold off in pieces as a result of industry slump
Hillsborough Holdings (1987)	$2.4 billion	Filed for Chapter 11
Revco (1986)	$1.3 billion	Filed for Chapter 11
SCI Television (1987)	$1.2 billion	Debt payments exceed cash flow

··

The number of LBOs rose from 11 in 1980 to 275 in 1989, with a peak of 377 in 1988. Overall, there were about 2,800 LBOs in the 1980s with a total value of $235 billion dollars.[23] LBOs represented the opportunity of a lifetime for many organizations, but have been disastrous for many others. Exhibit 19.6 highlights some of the good and bad LBOs. As LBO mania peaked in the middle to late 1980s, financing methods often became poorly thought out or unsound. **Junk bonds,** which are high-yielding, low-grade bonds, formed the basis of many LBOs financing plans. In short, junk-bond buyers were paid high rates of interest to offset the inherent riskiness.

Many LBOs gave firms the unique opportunity to restructure their costs. This is true because LBOs often involve the arrival of a new management team not tied to the old ways. As a result, the new management team may sell off operations that are not part of the organization's core business, thereby shifting the organization's emphasis from one business to another and achieving a cost restructuring in the process. Other LBOs are successful because they often force firms to be conscious about their cost structures. This may be because there are strict rules about the organization's cost structure in the debt covenant. Management may also seek to control costs that would cause the organization to default on its debt payments. Payment defaults often result in the firm being forced into bankruptcy.

The main problem with less successful LBOs is the inability to meet the debt payments. Many organizations are unable to reduce costs enough to generate the extra cash necessary to make the debt payments. These payments are often large since the interest rate on the debt is usually high. Other organizations run into problems when economic conditions change. Both of these situations occurred during Robert Campeau's $6.5 billion acquisition of Federated Department Stores in April 1988.

This acquisition, coupled with Campeau's $3.6 billion purchase of Allied Stores in October 1986, helped to create a giant retailing chain. Campeau's empire included Bloomingdale's, Maas Brothers, Jordan Marsh, Bonwit Teller, and Stern's, to name just a few. Campeau's acquisitions left him with almost $8 billion in debt at an approximate annual interest rate of over 16 percent. Interest payments alone approached $900 million annually. These payments were huge compared to the firm's pretax, preinterest profits of about $680 million. Campeau planned to make up the difference between profits and debt payments through the firm's new economies of scale and by cutting payrolls through a consolidation of activities. This would have produced an additional $300 million in savings and provided enough cash to meet the debt payments. Unfortunately, Campeau based his estimates on two assumptions. These assumptions were strong sales for the organization and the ability to cut costs through consolidation.

The cost-cutting program proceded mostly as planned. The 1989 Christmas season started weaker than expected, however. The Campeau stores reacted by cutting prices to stimulate sales and generate the necessary cash flow to meet the massive debt payments. Other competitors matched the move in the price-conscious and competitive retailing industry. This resulted in severe cash flow problems for the Campeau stores. When Campeau did not pay suppliers for the old merchandise, additional new merchandise shipments stopped. This further hurt sales and cut into the cash flows even more.

In January 1990, less than two years after acquiring Federated, Campeau filed for bankruptcy. The bankruptcy has caused an uncertain future for over 100,000 Campeau employees. In addition, Campeau's 300,000 suppliers are still waiting for payment for their merchandise. It will take years before the bankruptcy courts fully resolve the situation. The whole series of events prompted *Fortune* magazine to call the Campeau LBO "The Biggest Looniest Deal Ever."[24]

Another problem LBOs have been accused of causing is a decrease in R&D expenditures. Some have suggested that an acquisition can be used as a substitute for innovation and that managers absorbed in LBOs will lose sight of the importance of R&D. To avoid this pitfall, several suggestions have been made.

1. LBOs should be focused to complement the firm's R&D.
2. R&D should be woven into the organization's new mission after the LBO.
3. Top management should keep interest in R&D high.
4. R&D projects should be linked directly to key executives.[25]

Finally, LBOs can lead to failures on the part of recently placed executives. With LBOs come new management teams who are not familiar with current procedures and cultures. While the entrance of new management can be advantageous to the firm from a cost cutting perspective, it can be detrimental to the manager's career. LBOs often do not provide sufficient time for managers to become familiar with key players and understand what is expected of them before they must make major decisions—decisions that can cause the LBO to succeed or to fail.[26]

THE IMPACT OF RESTRUCTURING ON HUMAN RESOURCES

Once an organization decides to restructure, its managers must make several broad choices to determine the type of human resource restructuring it will use. These choices are based on the answers to four basic questions:

- Should the firm use a no-layoff strategy?
- If the firm does not use a no-layoff strategy, should it use wage cuts?
- If the firm uses layoffs, should they be temporary layoffs or permanent plant closings?
- Should the organization cushion its terminations or use "harsh" terminations?

These issues represent the increasing severity of the impact of restructuring on employees. No-layoff strategies usually represent the least severe impact to employees as a whole in the organization. They are, however, often the most difficult for the firm to control and implement. Terminations, at the other end, are often the easiest form of restructuring for the organization to control and implement. Terminations hurt because they usually have the greatest negative impact on the employees. The time frame of each type of strategy also creates problems. No-layoff strategies usually take the longest to implement, but often have the greatest long-term benefits to the organization if they are successful. Layoff and termination strategies, on the other hand, can take effect almost immediately after management has chosen them as courses of action.

Layoffs may have unintended long-term side effects that are difficult to control, however. These side effects include losing valuable employees and long-term employee morale problems. Of course, a firm that is facing imminent bankruptcy may need the immediate benefits of massive layoffs to survive. For other firms, the shock of large-scale layoffs may be the solution for revitalizing a lethargic and unresponsive organization.[27] Each strategy has its own unique characteristics and advantages and disadvantages. These issues will be discussed in the remainder of this chapter.

No-Layoff Strategies

Many firms view their employees as their most valuable assets. Many employees have unique skills gained over years of service to the organization. Other employees have skills that are rare in the marketplace, thus increasing their value to the firm. In other cases, groups of employees have unique combinations of skills that make them valuable to the organization. Organizations often face a problem in these situations. They need to reduce the number of active employees on the payroll, but they also need the employees' special skills. If the organization terminates employees, they

· ·

EXHIBIT 19.7   A Comparison of Changes in No-Layoff Policies

WHERE NO-LAYOFF PRACTICES HAVE VANISHED		AND WHERE THEY HAVE NOT VANISHED	
COMPANY	TOTAL U.S. EMPLOYEES	COMPANY	TOTAL U.S. EMPLOYEES
Advanced Micro Devices	7,200	Delta Airlines	60,000
Bank of America	47,000	Digital Equipment	74,000
Chase Manhattan Bank*	41,570	Federal Express	69,000
Eastman Kodak	82,900	IBM	216,000
Hewlett-Packard	60,000	S.C. Johnson	3,450
Manufacturers Hanover*	23,550	Lincoln Electric	2,630
Morgan Guaranty*	14,207	Mazda Motor*	3,555
R.J. Reynolds Tobacco	12,500	Motorola**	60,000
		National Steel*	10,675
*Worldwide employment		New United Motor*	2,800
		Nissan Motor	3,430
		Nucor	5,500
		Xerox*	55,700

*Labor contract prohibits layoffs
**Applies only to employees with 10 years service

· ·

may never return, or the unique combination of skills that made particular work teams valuable may be lost forever. On the other hand, if the organization does not reduce the size of its work force, then its operating costs may be too high. Many firms in this position choose to use a **no-layoff** policy of restructuring.

No-layoff strategies are organization actions that seek to reduce the size of its work force without having to lay off or terminate anyone. No-layoff policies usually involve some combination of three alternatives: (1) firms can reduce the work force through attrition, (2) they can provide for worker reassigment/retraining, or (3) they can loan out their employees to other firms. Exhibit 19.7 provides a list of some firms that follow a no-layoff policy and also gives a list of companies that have dropped no-layoff policies in recent years.

Work Force Reduction through Attrition

Perhaps the most common method of no-layoff restructuring is reducing the work force through attrition. Firms that use this method try to stop the growth in the total number of employees. They also seek to reduce the total number of people employed by the firm without laying off anyone. This is a popular method in government organizations. There are three basic types of attrition: hiring freezes in new and planned jobs, nonreplacement of current job vacancies, and nonreplacement of fired workers. While all three methods are different from one another, they share some similarities. Most firms will use all three to some extent when carrying out a work force attrition strategy.

Perhaps the most common method that firms use for work force attrition is the **hiring freeze.** Firms operating under hiring freezes forego all new planned hirings. In many instances hiring freezes are organizationwide. In other instances firms will selectively implement hiring freezes. In these situations firms will stop hiring in most departments while continuing to hire in areas critical to the success of the organization. While both methods appear in practice, the remainder of this discussion will concentrate on total, or organizationwide hiring freezes.

Hiring freezes have several advantages and disadvantages. One advantage is that firms can immediately control and predict their wage and benefit expenses. Since no new employees are being hired, the firm can easily calculate how much it is spending and decide how to control these costs in the future. Another advantage lies in controlling costs related to recruitment and training of new employees. These costs include advertising funds, the time and money spent by managers interviewing potential employees, the internal costs related to new hires such as placement on payroll, the assignment of office supplies and equipment, and the funds allocated to train and orient new employees. Other costs saved include state and federal taxes paid on employees and wages and benefits. For example, if a firm chooses not to fill a $30,000-a-year position in the engineering department, the actual savings may look like this:

Salary saved:	$30,000
Benefits saved (such as insurance and vacation):	10,000
Taxes saved:	7,000
Training costs saved (such as orientation, familiarization with rules and procedures, and job education)	2,000
Office supplies and equipment (desk, chair, computer, supplies)	5,000
Hiring costs saved (such as entering in payroll, establishing employee file, and insurance policy paperwork)	1,000
Recruitment costs saved (such as campus interviews, advertising, manager's interviewing time, and committee decision time)	5,000
Total Savings	$60,000

The above example shows that the actual savings from not hiring new employees is much greater than just an employee's salary. These costs may be higher or lower depending on the nature of the job and the company, but either way, the savings can be large.

Using such a strategy has several possible disadvantages, however. First, not hiring new employees may overburden current employees. This may result in decreased productivity and lower morale. Hiring freezes may also have additional effects on employees who are seeking promotion within the organization. Many hiring freezes either explicitly or accidentally result in promotion freezes as well since current workers become more needed in the positions that they now hold. As a result, many employees who are in line for promotions may become frustrated at a perceived lack of advancement potential. This, coupled with the additional work load that accompanies hiring freezes, may cause these employees to seek other employment opportunities.

In addition, firms that compete in technology-based industries may find themselves falling behind the competition as they fail to hire employees with new and valuable skills. For example, let's return to the example of the above firm that did not hire the new engineer. If the firm needed a civil engineer, it probably would not experience too many competitive problems in the future as a result of not hiring the engineer since the supply of civil engineers is relatively good compared to the demand. If the position was for a computer engineer, however, the firm may soon experience severe problems since the average computer technology lasts for less than three years before it becomes obsolete, and well-trained computer engineers are, therefore, relatively scarce. Firms that choose to use selective hiring freezes can often escape this problem, as mentioned earlier.

In summary, hiring freezes have two main advantages and disadvantages. They can help a firm immediately control costs and can save other related costs in hiring new employees. On the other hand, hiring freezes can have a negative impact on current employees and can result in the loss of competitive advantage from failing to gain new and valuable skills.

Another attrition method that firms use is *not to replace those people who "naturally" leave the organization.* Unlike hiring freezes, which try to stop growth by halting the creation of new jobs, this method seeks to reduce total employment by not filling current positions as they become vacant. People who quit, retire, die, or leave at the end of a contract are considered to have "naturally" left the organization. Organizations often offer some form of incentive to employees to accelerate this process. These incentives include **cash bonuses** to people who leave during a specified period, **accelerated or early retirement benefits,** and **free outplacement services** (discussed in more depth later in the chapter).[28] This method has several advantages. First, organizations can save a lot of money in the recruitment, hiring, and training of new employees. This is the same type of advantage gained by organizations that use the no-new-hire strategy discussed earlier.

Another advantage of attrition is the ability to cut positions that have become unneeded or inefficient within the organization. A position that was important to an organization in the past may become obsolete as the organization changes. Positions created to fit certain needs during periods of success with little forethought or planning may have outlived their benefits. These positions may become redundant or unnecessary during periods of retrenchment.

When a firm decides to downsize, it may be difficult to cut positions due to several factors. These factors include the building of an "empire" by the individuals holding the positions. **Empire building** occurs when individuals entrench themselves in positions through a combination of politics, length of time in the job, and the ability to project a perceived value to the firm. Management may also be reluctant to fire or lay off an individual who is close to retirement. Finally, struggles by individual managers to protect the size of their departments may affect downsizing. These struggles often serve as a surrogate measure of the individual power and prestige of each manager. Firms that choose not to replace people who naturally leave the organization are often able to avoid most of these problems.

A main disadvantage of using a strategy of not replacing people who naturally leave is that the organization is unable to control exactly who leaves and who stays. The organization may seek to reduce its overhead positions, but it may also lose a significant number of people in marketing and research and development in the process. Another disadvantage is that this method may take a long time to carry out. Unlike other strategies, such as worker layoffs, which take only days or weeks, a nonreplacement strategy may take months or even years to reach its full potential. Since the organization is not forcing employees to leave, it must wait for individuals to decide to leave. The incentives mentioned earlier can help to speed up the process, but even they do not guarantee that the firm will reach its goals in the time desired. Finally, the nonreplacement of workers who naturally leave can be problematic in the short term. Many of the incentives designed to encourage workers to leave require the organization to spend large sums of money up front. This is often contrary to the immediate goals of a restructuring.

Another major type of no-layoff restructuring is **worker reassignment or retraining.** Firms that use this strategy often do not want to reduce the size of their work force. Instead, worker reassignments involve moving workers out of one job and into another that may be more important to the organization. For example, a common reassignment involves transferring workers to sales and manufacturing jobs and out of support and overhead positions. This is typical because sales and manufacturing jobs often create "real value" for the organization because they both directly generate revenues. A larger sales force can generate more sales for the company while a larger manufacturing force can produce more items and become more specialized. Since support and overhead positions such as clerical staff, maintenance workers, and corporate headquarters staff do not directly produce real value for the organization, they get treated as a "necessary evil."

In addition, worker productivity is more easily measured in sales and manufacturing jobs. Sales employees' productivity measures are based on sales volume. The productivity of manufacturing employees is based on the number of units produced and the percentage of defective units produced. The productivity of support and overhead positions are not as easily measured. Output in these positions is not as quantifiable as it is in sales and manufacturing. For example, how can the value of a raw materials price forecast prepared by a corporate analyst be determined? Is one good forecast equivalent to three average forecasts produced by another analyst? Could the money spent by the organization in preparing the forecast (employee salaries, purchasing or development of economic information, use of computer resources, and so on) be better used in other areas, such as purchasing a more efficient milling machine for the assembly line? How can one tell today if the forecast for the future is good or poor? How would the organization's performance be affected if the forecast was not produced? Clearly, it is difficult to determine how helpful these positions are to the organization. Many of these questions can be answered, but often only after a long time has passed and at a great expense. Thus many firms are willing to move workers into sales and manufacturing because it is much easier to measure their contribution in terms of how well the organization is operating.

Organizations will often use worker reassignments as a prelude to or with other types of restructuring. The transfer of workers into sales and manufacturing, in addition to directly impacting the firm's performance, enables the organization to begin the process of cutting workers. The productivity measures in sales and manufacturing jobs make it easier to determine which employees are worthwhile to the organization and which are not. Hence, it is easier to document and release poor performers in these areas. In addition, these transfers can either be voluntary programs or mandated by the organization. If the transfers are voluntary, the organization is often able to keep good employees who may have been getting stale in their previous positions. In these situations the transfers often result in improved employee morale and performance.

Voluntary transfers present problems to organizations which are looking to lay off workers, however. Many poorer performing employees will choose to stay in their current jobs out of a fear of failing in a new job. Again, it may be difficult to lay off or replace these workers since productivity measures are difficult to arrive at in these positions. Employees who are valuable in these support and overhead positions may also transfer into manufacturing and sales. This can hurt the organization since they may be more valuable in their original positions. For example, a purchasing agent may have spent years learning the dynamics of the firm's industry and may have built up strong relationships with many suppliers. The loss of these intangible benefits to the organization may be far greater than the immediate additional revenues generated by the purchasing agent who transferred to sales. The chance also exists that a good performer in one position may transfer into a new position and become a poor performer because individual skills, interest, and abilities may not be transferrable.

Mandatory transfers also have specific advantages and disadvantages. Unlike voluntary transfers, the results of mandatory transfers are more certain. Firms using mandatory transfers can target areas it considers to be less important and reduce them while emphasizing other areas with a virtual certainty of achieving its goals. Mandatory transfer programs often permit firms to target specific employees for transfer. This can produce a better match of job skills, or essentially force unwanted employees to leave the organization. This method is not without its problems, however. Mandatory transfers can hurt employee morale as the organization moves people into positions they do not want. They can also disrupt synergies that have developed in various work groups over the years.

Union contracts often prohibit organizations from implementing these programs and they may meet fierce resistance from unions where the practice is not prohibited. Several recent union contracts have begun to accept the need of firms to transfer employees to remain competitive. In recognizing this need in contracts, unions are, in turn, getting more of a voice in determining the nature of these transfers. Members of nonunion firms may also fight the transfers. Their fights may range from subtle resistance to open hostility or even to legal challenges. Finally, mandatory transfers may also result in valued employees leaving the organization.

Another complementary method to worker reassignment is organizational incentives to employees to undergo **retraining,** or career development. While worker reassignment often involves some form of skills retraining, retraining here refers to an upgrading or improvement of jobs skills, not the learning of new and unrelated skills. Organization incentives to retrain include unpaid sabbaticals, financing of education, a partial release from duties, and possible future promotions to name just a few.

The advantages of such a policy are many. First, the strategy can help to reduce employee anxiety caused by the restructuring. With the organization sponsoring or encouraging retraining, employees often feel more secure about their futures with the organization. If retraining programs are offered on a large scale, the resistance to the restructuring may decrease dramatically or at least help the employees accept what is happening.[29] Another advantage is that retraining programs during restructuring are often complimentary to the new work systems and new directions that the organization seeks to achieve with the restructuring. Finally, the organization is often able to reduce the immediate direct and indirect labor costs that would result if the employee were working full-time during the restructuring.

Of course, some disadvantages do exist. Some employees who may benefit the most from retraining may be the employees who are most needed to help the organization successfully complete the restructuring. Furthermore, without a specific contract binding the employee to the company after the retraining period is over, the employee may take his or her additional skills to a new job. Despite these potential disadvantages, the case for further training during restructuring is strong. It is important that firms understand that career development training should still be enacted under these conditions, but designing it within such an environment may be challenging.

A final no-layoff restructuring strategy that has emerged within the past few years is the **worker loan-out program.** Although this strategy is somewhat rare, it might become more common during the 1990s. Worker loan-out programs involve the lending of workers by one organization to another for a specified period, such as firms lending their employees to government or charitable organizations. For example, IBM and Polaroid support programs that allow their employees to work as teachers in public schools and universities for up to two years while still drawing a salary from their companies.[30] Motorola has begun training workers to pass on their knowledge to students through an advisement program and Sears has assigned officials to work with schools to build stronger curriculums.[31]

Another recent example of the loan-out strategy is the loan-out of employees by Lockheed to Boeing. Lockheed's aircraft division derives most of its business from military orders. Recent cutbacks in U.S. military budgets have resulted in a work slowdown for Lockheed. In contrast, Boeing is the world's leading manufacturer of commercial aircraft. Some of its planes have order backlogs as long as ten years. Rather than having to lay off, and possibly lose highly skilled employees, Lockheed has agreed to lend 670 of its workers to Boeing, which due to its recent success, needs more employees than it can recruit. Boeing agreed to use Lockheed's workers and pay their salaries for the loan-out period.[32] Hewlett Packard used an internal employee loan program, among other plans, to deal with more than 400 employees who were displaced when HP made a strategic decision to exit the fabrication business. Employees were loaned to other divisions where short-term hiring needs existed. Some of the loans were for as short a duration as one day while others lasted up to a year. HP provided housing and transportation costs if the loan crossed regional boundaries.[33]

There are several advantages to both organizations involved in these situations. The organization that is loaning out its employees can keep them as members of the organization, often without having to incur the expenses of paying their salaries or laying them off, during the loan-out period. Consequently, the organization can gain many of the advantages of a layoff and restructuring without incurring all of the related expenses, such as severance pay, outplacement services, and the recruitment and training costs of new employees in the future. These programs also enable the loaning companies to keep their employees' skills up to date, or learn new skills, without incurring the retraining expenses. Another advantage for the loaning organization is that its employees often return to the organization with new ideas and new outlooks as a result of their experiences. This may result in significant improvements in how the organization operates. These programs often generate large amounts of goodwill within the organization's home community, especially if the organization that is receiving the employees is a local government agency or charity. This goodwill can result in positive press and publicity and favorable attitudes toward the organization by the receiving organization.

These programs also can generate goodwill with the organization's employees, who may interpret the move in several different ways. These ways range from perceptions that the organization is willing to let the employees get involved in activities that are personally important without hurting their careers in the organization to increased loyalty to an organization that is not willing to let its employees join the unemployment line.

The organization that gets the loaned-out employees also receives some advantages. One advantage is the training expenses saved by borrowing workers that are already skilled. Another advantage is the saving of recruiting costs. Since the length of the worker loan-out is usually fixed, the receiving firm also saves money by having workers for only as long as they are needed. The receiving firm also does not have to incur layoff and separation expenses. Receiving organizations can also gain the same type of benefit from the fresh outlook of the loaned-out employees. Finally, charities and government organizations can get employees and skills that they would not be able to afford under normal circumstances.

Of course, this type of strategy has some disadvantages. If there is a sudden change in the circumstances of the loan-out, for example, the loaning company's business suddenly picks up, the workers cannot return until the end of the agreed loan-out period. Hence a firm may be unable to recover workers that it needs, or it may not be able to get rid of workers that it does not need. There is also the chance that the loaning firm may permanently lose its employees—possibly even to competitors. Some loan-out agreements may specifically forbid a receiving firm from hiring loaned-out employees after the expiration of the loan-out period, but nothing prevents individuals from deciding not to return to their first organization. Finally, an organization may inadvertently give up some of its skills or secrets in loaning out its employees.

Layoff Strategies

Layoffs are among the most common strategies used in restructuring. Layoffs usually involve some form of temporary reduction in the organization's work force and are particularly common in cyclical industries. Under this strategy, the organization releases employees from work for a specific time. They remain employees of the organization and continue to receive benefits. Under an **indefinite layoff**, the organization may release the employees from the company after a fixed period, such as six months or a year. An indefinite layoff strategy is typical in situations in which the work force is highly skilled and the costs of recruiting and training new employees may be high. Thus, the organization tries to keep its employees as long as possible without having to terminate them. Layoffs primarily seek to allow firms to reduce labor costs temporarily without losing valuable employees. Layoffs are commonly found in industries where union contracts may prohibit the firing of employees due to changes in business conditions. Industries where layoffs are common include automobile manufacturing, agriculture, steel, and tourism.

Several layoff methods are available. One popular method within the automobile and steel industries is the use of **supplemental unemployment benefits**, or SUBs. SUBs provide a fixed percentage (up to 95 percent in some instances) of a laid-off employee's wages through a combination of state and federal unemployment benefits and additional organization payments for periods up to one year. SUBs are common in these industries because they are cyclical or they involve periods of major plant shutdowns for renovations.

For example, most American automobile plants will shut down for a period each summer to allow the company to change or "gear up" assembly lines for the new automobile model year that begins in October. Steel plants will often close for routine maintenance or major upgrades in equipment. A major advantage of SUBs is that they allow firms to lay off their skilled employees for up to one year with little risk of losing them to other firms. Critics of SUBs, however, point out that the high level of benefits often discourages employees from seeking other jobs. This may wind up hurting the laid-off workers more than it helped when the benefits expire at the end of the year and the firm chooses not to bring the employees back to work. Another disadvantage of SUBs is their high cost to the firm, but these costs must be weighed against the costs of hiring and training new employees.

Another common lay-off strategy is the use of the **reduced work week** for employees. The reduced work week allows organizations to reduce their payroll costs while still holding on to and providing work for employees. The size of the reduction will vary from firm to firm, but most reduced work weeks are between 20 and 30 hours long for full-time employees.[34] Like SUBs, the reduced work week enables firms to keep their valuable employees, but it also enables employees to keep their skills up-to-date. Many firms will also try to lessen the impact of the reduced work week by scheduling special work that would not be done during normal company operations. Examples of this work include repair and maintenance of plant and equipment to reorganizing plants and warehouses or taking special inventories. Some states will even make up the difference in the workers' pay if the firm will keep them on at least part-time. The money spent by the state is less than the firms would spend for unemployment benefits, and the workers have the chance to go back full time if the company's business picks up.[35]

Reduced work weeks have several disadvantages. A main disadvantage is the problem of predicting the number of hours that employees are needed each week. Reduced work weeks may also require that many staff members must continue to work full-time to support those employees working reduced weeks. This is because it is difficult to cut back support functions only partially. An example of this would include the need to keep a fully staffed payroll department, where the volume of work does not depend on the number of hours worked by line employees. Finally, reduced work weeks may prevent employees from seeking other jobs. This is because they cannot predict when they will be available for work due to the unpredictable hours of the first job.

A third lay-off strategy includes the use of **reduced shifts**. Reduced shifts involve cutting back the total number of hours that the organization operates. Reduced shift layoffs can take one of two forms. One type of reduced shift cuts back on the total number of employees per shift. For example, a firm may usually operate three eight-hour shifts per day during normal conditions with 300 employees per shift. The first type of reduced shift strategy may be to reduce the total number of employees to 200 per shift. This approach affects all shifts equally. Another form of reduced shifts is the elimination of one or more shifts from the schedule entirely. In the above example, the firm may choose to cut the midnight to 8:00 A.M. shift entirely while still maintaining the other two shifts at full capacity.

Organizations may, of course, take a middle ground between these two extremes. They may decide to drop one shift and partially cut back on other shifts or use some other combination of cutbacks. Several factors usually determine the type of reduced shift approach used. The first factor is the nature of the work being done on each shift and the skills of the employees. If each shift performs essentially the same job, then many organizations will consider cutting entire shifts, especially the late-evening/early morning shifts that have some form of salary differential. If a job takes several shifts to complete, with each shift performing a specialized function, the organization may consider laying off some employees on each shift, but maintaining all shifts to some extent.

Other factors may also affect the choice of reduced shifts. A major factor in many decisions is the type of production process that the organization uses. If the organization's equipment is geared toward long continuous runs that would be expensive to interrupt, such as would be the case in the glass, steel, or papermaking industries, then it may choose to reduce the number of employees per shift. This is typical of the papermaking industry where it is expensive to start up and shut down machinery and the process of papermaking is a round-the-clock effort.[36]

If the organization employs a batch production process, with each shift capable of producing a complete job, then the decision may be to close down an entire shift instead of reducing all shifts. This is typical of clothing manufacturers.[37] A similar situation exists in the automobile industry, where the production process is a machine-paced line flow. Since the production process is standardized over each shift and the cost of shutting down and starting up machinery is not prohibitively expensive, reduced shift layoffs are often an entire shift approach.

Another common layoff strategy is the use of **plant or office closings**. Unlike reduced shifts, which affect only a portion of the employees of the work unit, plant and office closings affect all employees of the unit. Plant and office closings are the temporary or permanent shutdown of independent work units as part of an organization's restructuring. Plants may be entire production facilities, such as when General Motors closed seven car plants in the first half of 1990.[38] An example of an office closings may be the closing of a district sales office by a national organization. Of course, other closings also qualify under this definition, even though they are not offices or plants. Burger King's plans to close some of its older stores and Ames' plans to close many of its retail stores as part of its bankruptcy reorganization are also examples of this type of strategy.

Closings may occur for a variety of reasons. They may be part of a focus strategy discussed earlier in the chapter. The closings may be the result of a downsizing due to bankruptcy, as is the case with Ames. Or, as is the case with GM, they may result from the modernization of facilities or the conversion of facilities to meet a change in strategic orientation.[39] Closings are often the only practical means of conversion or modernization since an attempt to undertake such an operation while still operating may be prohibitively expensive and time consuming.

Plant and office closings have several human resource side effects that management must consider. First, closings affect all employees of the unit. Unlike other layoff strategies, closings affect everyone from the plant's part-time personnel to its upper level management. Thus, a firm may inadvertently lose some of its best people if it does not plan the closing carefully. This also means that the organization will lose its thirty-year veterans as well as its recent hires. The advantage of this strategy, however, is that the firm may be able to keep its best employees by offering to move them to other parts of the organization. Of course, the organization may find itself in the position of having nowhere to send its skilled individuals, even though it does not want to lose them. Plant closings may be expensive since they often involve some form of lay-off pay, such as the supplemental unemployment benefits used by the automobile and steel industries mentioned earlier.

Plant closings can often have serious effects on morale in other parts of the organization. This is particularly true if the organization is undertaking a large restructuring and is not completely communicating its plans to its employees, that is, closings are not announced and explained beforehand. In situations such as these, employees begin to wonder if their plant or office will be the next one closed. In addition to damaging morale organizationwide, plant closings will often affect worker productivity and may result in higher employee turnover in other parts of the organization as employees begin to seek what they perceive to be safer employment.

Recent federal legislation, the Federal Worker Adjustment and Restraining Notification Act (WARN), has made it mandatory that organizations with more than 100 employees announce the decision to close plants or engage in massive layoffs at least sixty days in advance of the action.[40] Critics argue that it is unnecessary because it will hurt productivity in the plant as employees seek new jobs and take time off to do so. They also argue that early announcements of plant closings hurt the competitiveness of American firms since they are, in effect, forced to reveal prematurely valuable information about their strategies in a tough marketplace. Finally, critics of the legislation assert that since many decisions to close plants are made less than sixty days before an actual closing, the law puts management in a bind of having to make crucial decisions earlier than they would normally have been made. Supporters of the law argue that productivity losses are minimal. They also assert that management has an obligation to inform its employees of decisions affecting their future employment as soon as they are made. Finally, supporters argue that management should plan ahead in situations that have as broad an impact on employees as plant and office closings. Both arguments contain valid points, but it is still too early to tell what the effects of the new law will be.

A final issue in using a layoff strategy is how organizations determine who gets laid off and who gets to keep their jobs. In plant closings the issue is rather clear—everyone gets laid off. In other situations, such as reduced shifts, the task is not so easy. Two of the most common methods for determining layoffs are the use of **employee seniority** and the use of **employee ability** criteria. Firms that use employee seniority criteria lay off workers according to the length of time that each employee has worked with the firm. This is common in unionized firms. Most systems based on this method give greater protection to the employees with the most tenure or seniority, all other things being equal. If a firm has to lay off one of two welders, with each performing the same job, then the welder who has been with the organization the longest will be kept.

Organizations that use an ability criteria take a different approach. These firms lay off workers according to the skill level and productivity of each employee. Using the example of the two welders, the firm would keep the better of the two welders and lay off the other one. An example of the use of ability criteria in cutbacks is the United States Army and Air Force. Both services are cutting back their total troop levels by as much as 25 percent as a result of budget cuts in the Department of Defense. Both are trying to use attrition methods, but are prepared to make cutbacks if necessary. The Air Force is using a standard proficiency test as a measure of ability to determine which pilots and aircraft mechanics to rehire and which ones to let go.[41]

Each layoff approach has a number of advantages and disadvantages. Perhaps the greatest advantage of using a seniority-based layoff strategy is the objective manner in which it can be applied. Since layoffs using this type of strategy are based on length of service to the organization, workers will know what their position is in a layoff program. It is also very hard to accuse management of "playing favorites" with employees using a seniority-based system since the layoff order is well known in advance. Any deviation from this system is likely to be noticed immediately by the work force. The appearance of fairness and the ease of checking deviations from policy have made seniority-based layoff systems particularly popular in unionized organizations.

A main rationale behind a seniority-based layoff strategy is that employees who have been with the organization a long time have earned the right to be insulated from temporary changes in the firm's environment. Another belief behind a seniority-based layoff system is that it is easier for younger employees to find work and adapt their lives to layoffs than it is for older workers.

There are two common objections to a seniority-based system. The first is that a seniority-based system ignores worker talent and effort. Critics of the system argue that adherence to these types of rules are arbitrary and without merit. The long-standing ethic of "reward good work" often loses its value in organizations that adhere to seniority-based layoff systems. If workers know in advance that layoffs will be based on seniority, then the incentive for them to operate at their peak levels is reduced. Instead they may do only the minimal work necessary to ensure that they keep their jobs. In short, critics argue that this system shifts the focus from rewarding good work to job survival. If this is the case, then the organization should experience higher labor costs, lower productivity, and lower work quality compared to its competitors who use other types of layoff strategies. Critics also argue that this system may keep the organization's payroll bloated because more experienced workers tend to earn higher wages. Hence, a seniority-based layoff system will tend to cut back on the lower paid employees while keeping the higher paid ones. Of course, the counter argument is that more experienced employees have a greater familiarity with the organization and how it operates. Ideally, this should make them more valuable to the organization since the organization has already sunk a great deal of money into training and developing the employee over the years. Either way, this can be a particularly problematic decision when the main goal is often some form of cost restructuring.

Ability-based layoff systems seek to address some of the problems of seniority-based systems. Perhaps the greatest advantage of ability-based systems is that they keep the best workers during layoffs often enabling the firm to maintain or increase productivity and quality levels during a restructuring. Firms using ability-based layoff systems should also realize a greater cost savings than firms using seniority-based layoffs. Further, ability-based systems appeal to the ethics of rewarding good work and should give workers incentives to seek to improve their performance. This approach may run into problems in reality, however. The greatest problem of such a system is defining ability. In many instances this is not a problem, especially where the work is standardized. For example, in the textile industry, where productivity is based on the volume of material produced, determining the best workers is usually a straightforward process. The problem becomes more complex in other situations, especially in white-collar and skilled craft positions. As we discussed earlier, how does one place a quality figure on a raw materials price forecast prepared by a corporate analyst? The situation can even be complex in assembly-line situations where one worker's productivity depends on the output of another worker. Management must devise a system for determining how much one employee's work affects another. This is often a complicated and expensive process. Even when a fair system is in place, it is often difficult to communicate all of its aspects to employees in a clear and understandable manner.

In addition, ability-based systems encourage political behavior by workers. These systems sometimes generate the impression that it is the manager's favorite workers, not the best workers, who are kept during layoffs. Many workers will oppose such a system as a result of the difficulty in understanding the rules of the system and the perception of managerial favoritism. Consequently, ability-based systems are more likely to generate hostility with unions and possibly lead to lawsuits against the organization than are seniority-based systems.[42]

Termination Strategies

Finally, organizations may choose to use **employee terminations** as part of a restructuring strategy. Terminations are actions initiated by the organization to permanently separate employees from the organization, and they may come in many forms. Terminations may be the end result of an indefinite layoff or plant closing. They may also be the first action taken by a firm in a restructuring. Unlike firings, where employees are released from the organization for causes like poor performance or high absenteeism, terminations are initiated with the purpose of reducing the size of the work force.

Termination Issues

Organizations that pursue termination strategies must consider a number of issues. For example, all termination decisions must consider the organization's employee **protection and compensation** plans. Protection and compensation plans are organizational policies relating to the handling of employees during termination situations. Many organizations have clearly defined plans for their employees. Others have no formal policies in place. Either way, the organization must deal with these issues. These issues typically include tenure, golden parachutes, severance pay, outplacement services, and career counseling.

Tenure relates to the length of time that an employee has worked in an organization and the rights that the person accrues as a result. It is similar to seniority. In many instances employees with greater tenure, or length of service (seniority), have greater rights and benefits than less or nontenured employees. These rights may include added benefits such as increased vacation time, sick leave, and insurance benefits, office and parking space privileges, stock options, and company cars. Many organizations also offer greater job protection to tenured employees. In universities and colleges tenure for professors means guaranteed employment for life, as long as the professor continues to do his or her job. Even if the professor becomes incompetent or fails to do his or her job, tenure results in a long and formal termination process.

Consequently, organizations that use terminations as part of a restructuring must examine their tenure policies. Many of these tenure benefits are given as rewards for service, and many represent a long-term commitment by the organization to the employee. For example, an organization may guarantee stock options worth 20 percent of an executive's pay over 10 years as part of his or her promotion to upper management. Suppose, however, the organization decides to close the executive's division and terminate all employees in the division (including the manager) three years after the manager has taken over the division. The organization must consider how to handle the stock options. The manager has been guaranteed the options due to performance, but a change in the organization's strategy—a variable beyond the manager's control—eliminates the firm's need for the manager's services. This issue is complicated further by the fact that the manager is not being released for incompetence, but rather as a change in organization strategy.

Scenarios like this are becoming more and more frequent as the rate of terminations at the white-collar level continue to climb. From January 1990 to May of 1991, managerial unemployment rose by over 60 percent. Many of the managers terminated were well-known figure such as John Sununu, President Bush's chief of staff; William Powe, head of Westinghouse's credit union; and George Conrades, senior vice-president at IBM.[43] Further, many of the unemployed managers were terminated from more than one job within a year. As the length of time they are out of work increases, it becomes harder and harder for them to find jobs. They become paralyzed by depression and numbed by the economic pain they are inflicting on their families.[44]

In previous years, U.S. law has given precedence to the **employment-at-will** doctrine. The employment-at-will doctrine states that workers are employed at the will of the organization and that the organization is free to end this employment at any time it chooses and for any reason it chooses. This doctrine also applies in reverse—employees are free to choose the organizations that they work for and can leave the organization at any time they wished for whatever reason they wished. As we saw in Chapter 16, this concept has come under a great deal of challenge in recent years and its validity is no longer guaranteed, especially when applied to employees who may have built up tenure within an organization. Courts have been increasingly sensitive to instances that are deemed wrongful or abusive discharges on the part of the employer.[45] Wrongful or abusive discharge situations involve firing without cause, discrimination of almost any kind, failure to properly document the cause of the firing, or situations where the procedure for firing is not standardized. Even if the organization is sure that it is in a situation in which the employment-at-will doctrine is valid, tenure-related issues often assure that terminated employees may bring legal action against the organization to recover or be compensated for lost benefits and privileges.[46] The average jury verdict in wrongful discharge cases is over $500,000. To avoid this outcome companies are retaining poor performers, using overtime or temporary workers, offering generous severance payments, and adopting elaborate screening and performance review processes.[47]

Many organizations are responding to these problems by offering **golden parachutes** to their employees, especially top managers. Golden parachutes are guarantees by organizations to the employees detailing the type of benefits they will receive in termination situations. Golden parachutes are offered as enticements to convince managers to take on the responsibility of joining a struggling firm for the purpose of turning it around. Golden parachutes are popular in organizations that are targets of

LBOs or hostile takeovers. As we mentioned earlier, many LBOs end with the replacement of the old management team by a new one. In these situations the board of directors may vote golden parachutes to key managers as a reward for their performance with the organization and because it makes it prohibitively expensive for a new management to replace the old management. Finally, golden parachutes are also popular since they represent a contractual agreement between the firm and the employee. Hence, if a situation does arise in the future where the employee is terminated, then there is less of a chance of a legal challenge by the employee.

A main problem with golden parachutes is that they tend to be rather expensive to the organization. It is not uncommon to find golden parachutes containing provisions that range from one to two years salary and other substantial cash payments. As a result, golden parachutes are mainly used for key managers. They are rarely offered to rank-and-file organization employees. Golden parachutes, if their existence is made known to the organization, may cause a great deal of hostility among other organization members that are not protected in a similar manner. For example, in the recent bankruptcy of Drexel Burnham Lambert, top managers of the organization received $260 million in bonuses just weeks before the firm was forced into bankruptcy. When the organization filed for bankuptcy, all of its employees were terminated without any form of compensation, even though the organization owed them approximately $40 million in severance payments—which it looks like the employees will never receive. Many employees are upset that these bonuses were paid because the nature of their timing resembled that of a golden parachute to upper management. Even though the bonuses were, in reality, regularly scheduled payments to management, their perceived appearance as golden parachutes alienated many former organization members.[48]

Even with their negative connotations, golden parachutes can serve broader organizational purposes. Eastman Kodak has added a unique twist to golden parachutes to protect itself from the threat of a hostile takeover. Kodak's plan, nicknamed "tin-parachutes," guarantees all 80,000 of its employees severance pay, health and life insurance benefits, and outplacement assistance if they lose their jobs in the wake of a takeover. Such a plan means that any organization that took over Kodak (which has a stock value of approximately $25 billion) could also face another $12 billion in debt if it started releasing Kodak employees.[49] Of course, the main advantages of golden parachutes is that they can convince key individuals to join or remain in particularly risky situations for the organization, and they reduce the chances of legal action against the organization by terminated employees. Kodak's case illustrates that parachutes, whether they are made of gold or tin, can also be highly effective weapons against unwanted takeover attempts.

A related and more common approach to terminations than golden parachutes is the use of **severance pay.** Severance pay is a payment to terminated workers based on their years of service to the organization and their salary. A typical severance pay might be four weeks of full pay for each year the employee has worked for the organization. So an employee who has worked for an organization for seven years and earned $400 per week would receive 7 years × 4 weeks per year = 28 weeks × $400 per week = $11,200 in severance pay. Severance packages may also include other payments such as accrued vacation and sick leave, and possibly some medical expenses. How the pay is provided can vary by organization. Some firms offer a lump-sum payment. Others offer the money over a specified period of time, like a weekly paycheck. Other firms use a combination of these tactics or let the employee

HR CHALLENGES ●

Developing a Strong Outplacement Program

Traditionally, outplacement programs were established by organizations to minimize the negative experiences associated with the loss of a job and to fend off any possibility of litigation by dismissed employees. However, companies are now realizing that it is important that employees who are joining or leaving the organization have a positive experience. Developing an effective and cost-efficient outplacement program is one way to assure departing employees a positive experience.

Developing an effective outplacement program should be done as soon as possible. If brought in early, an outplacement company can help managers to more effectively handle the termination interview. Often if the interview is inappropriately handled, employees do not understand why they have been terminated and spend a great deal of time pondering why. This takes away from the time they could be preparing for a new job.

Be sure to introduce the employee to the outplacement program early in the week so that they can begin immediately to prepare themselves for the job market.

By focusing the terminated employee's attention on the outplacement process rather than on the termination, more positive outcomes will occur. Further, by introducing the employee to the outplacement program immediately after termination, the outplacement company can be ready to offer crisis interventions if necessary.

Finally, be prepared to pay for a good outplacement program. In general, the base cost for a full-service outplacement program is 15 percent of the outplaced worker's W-2 earnings for the previous year plus an administrative fee that averages about $1,000. Some firms set a minimum fee of between $6,000 and $7,000 per program. Group programs can also be arranged. Costs for these services include a per diem of between $1,000 and $1,500 plus an additional charge for each participant of $40 to $50. Be sure to check prices. Programs that are significantly lower than these ranges may not be of a high quality.

SOURCE: Adapted from Virginia Gibson, "The Ins and Outs of Outplacement," *Management Review*, October 1991, pp. 59–61.

decide how they want the money.[50] Like golden parachutes, a clearly defined severance pay policy may reduce the chances of legal action against the organization if widespread terminations occur. But, where golden parachutes are designed as incentives and rewards to top management, severance pay is usually a hardship compensation to all employees.

A main advantage of a severance package is that it immediately clears most of the organization's obligations to its former employees. Severance packages are also used by organizations to help them improve employee relations. Many organizations will use the existence of the severance programs as a recruiting tool for new employees. Firms that terminate employees with the possible intention of rehiring them at a later date face a much better chance of getting them back if there is some form of severance pay involved in the termination.

The main disadvantage of severance pay is that it requires the organization to spend large sums of money almost immediately. This may be particularly difficult for the organization, especially if the terminations are a result of a restructuring or bankruptcy. In LBOs or consolidations, severance pay may be an ideal solution. Since both LBOs and consolidations often involve the acquisition of one organization by another, severance pay is a convenient way to accelerate the transition process. This is because many restructuring costs are tax deductible and the organization may write-off the severance expense and realize a tax savings or reduction as a result.

The cost of firing a manager differs by country. In the United States it costs about $19,000 to fire a $50,000 manager. Only Ireland has a lower termination cost,

$13,000. Italy and Spain spend more than $100,000 when terminating the same $50,000 manager, while Greece falls somewhere in between at $67,000.[51]

Another issue that an organization must consider before it begins terminating employees is its **outplacement policy**. Outplacement programs are corporate programs whose purpose is to help terminated employees adjust to their terminations and to assist them in finding other jobs.[52] Most outplacement programs assist terminated employees in three areas: **financial support, psychological support**, and **job search support**. Financial support functions typically include wage/salary continuation, health insurance, unemployment compensation, and credit management. Psychological support functions usually include self-esteem counseling, stress management, spouse and family counseling, and counseling for retained employees. Job search support includes secretarial services, office space, telephones, self assessment, job search skills, resume writing, interviewing, follow-up and evaluation, and other forms of career counseling.[53]

Well-run outplacement programs can greatly ease the former employee's transition into a new job or career while also maintaining the organization's image both internally and within its community.[54] On the other hand, outplacement programs can quickly become expensive if they are not managed properly. Most organizations cannot afford to offer all of the above outplacement services and consequently they are placed in the position of having to decide the level of outplacement services they will offer. Since an outplacement program can have such a large impact on the outcome of a termination strategy, its design should be carefully tailored to meet the most critical needs of the organization's overall termination strategy.

Types of Terminations

An organization may pursue three basic types of termination strategies. The first is a **leave 'em naked** termination strategy. Firms that pursue this strategy essentially release employees from the organization without providing any protection or compensation benefits or outplacement services. Such a strategy has two main advantages. First, it involves relatively little up-front cash investment on the part of the organization since it provides no severance pay, outplacement, or counseling benefits. Second, the firm can decide exactly who it wishes to release from the organization and who it wishes to keep. These advantages can also be its main liabilities, however, since it often exposes the organization to lawsuits by terminated employees who are likely to attack the organization with wrongful or abusive discharge claims. Other disadvantages include the likely adverse reactions from the remaining employees, the terminated employees, and the community at large. This is due to the fact that leave 'em naked strategies can easily be perceived as the result of a firm acting with only its own concerns in mind. Even with these disadvantages, many firms will still choose to pursue this type of strategy—especially if immediate cash-flow problems are the main concern of the organization.

Two other common strategies are **forced resignation** and the use of **early retirement** incentives before proceeding with terminations. Early retirement strategies usually provide some form of inducements for employees to retire from the organization before they reach the normal retirement age. Typical inducements are called "5-5-4" packages. These packages add five years of service to the employees' record with the company and five years to the employee's age when calculating early retirement benefits. The "4" part of the package is typically the number of weeks of full pay

....

EXHIBIT 19.8	Comparison of Two Methods of Downsizing and Their Impact upon Critical Organizational Variables

METHOD OF DOWNSIZING

VARIABLE	EARLY RETIREMENT	FORCED RESIGNATIONS
Cash outlays	Relatively high	Relatively low
Legal issues	Relatively low risk of litigation	Relatively higher risk of litigation
Risk of losing valued employees	Relatively high risk	Relatively low risk
Impact on organization climate and culture	Minimal impact	Relatively high likelihood of negative impact
Impact upon public image	Relatively low negative impact	Relatively high risk of negative impact

....

that the employee will receive for each year he or she has worked for the organization. Other common packages include "3-3-2" or "2-2-1" plans.

Telecommunications giant AT&T is one of several firms that operates with a 5-5-4 early retirement plan as a part of its restructuring strategy. In late 1989, the firm expanded the scope of its program. Approximately 34,000 AT&T managers qualified for the program and the company expected as many as one-third of all eligible managers to take advantage of it in 1990. The total savings from the program are expected to reach $450 million in 1990.[55] AT&T is also considering extending a similar program to at least some of its 173,500 nonmanagement workers. If this second plan is adopted, AT&T's total savings could reach $1 billion annually.[56] There are added benefits in the form of lower health-care costs when firms select to implement an early retirement plan. As health-care costs soar, companies have responded by cutting the number of the most expensive employees to cover: older workers.[57]

Forced resignations are much more direct in nature. Where early retirements are usually offered as inducements, forced resignations are usually offered as alternatives to outright terminations. Each of these strategies has its own unique comparative restructuring advantages and disadvantages. The two types of strategies differ in cash outlays, legal issues, risks of losing valued employees, the impact on organization climate and culture, and the impact upon the organization's public image. Exhibit 19.8 compares these two methods of downsizing and we will now discuss their impact on critical organization variables.[58]

First, the organization must consider the cash outlays involved in deciding whether to use an early retirement or a forced resignation termination strategy. Organizations must make early retirement financially attractive to employees if they are going to accept the program. Consequently, organizations that choose to use early retirement programs should be prepared to spend large sums of money early on to induce employees to retire. In addition, the costs of the program may increase rapidly as the

HR CHALLENGES •

Disgruntled Customers—A Big Disadvantage of Downsizing

The story of former AT&T customer Gary Russell, telecommunications chief at KeyCorp in Albany, New York, is not all that uncommon. Russell complained that AT&T circuits were constantly out of service. Whenever he called for help, he received no response. Finally, he offered his business to a competitor of AT&T's. The competition gladly accepted the challenge and things have run smoothly ever since. Russell feels that AT&T is continuing to treat its customers as if it were the only game in town when that is no longer true.

In actuality, AT&T is having trouble managing its downsizing. For example, Al Caron, who had been a technician for AT&T for over seven years, recently quit. He said the pressure of trying to keep his family intact after three moves in one year was more than he could take. It appears that the determination of AT&T to become efficient and flexible through restructuring, may come at the expense of its reputation for reliability, which is central to its success.

Losing qualified employees such as Caron has forced AT&T to subcontract work. One angry AT&T customer who is paying a great deal of money for an AT&T maintenance contract feels cheated when a non-AT&T employee shows up to work on the system,

especially when the subcontractor has been shown how to get into the system and how it works. More significant problems have also been traced to AT&T. In September of 1991, a voice communications outage in the Northeast crippled Wall Street and closed down the air traffic control system on the East Coast.

Major problems such as these can create a positive outcome—for competitors. For example, in the long distance market, AT&T's market share fell from 80 percent in 1989 to 61 percent in 1991, and it is predicted to fall to 55 percent by 1993. Competitors like MCI and U.S. Sprint are eagerly picking up disgruntled AT&T customers.

It appears that AT&T realizes that its reputation is on the line. One of its recent advertising campaigns simply asks for old AT&T customers to come back. The company is offering to waive the switchover fee for its returning customers and to pay to switch the customers back if they are not satisfied with the service they receive. AT&T hopes that the service will be better than that offered to Russell.

SOURCE: Adapted from John Keller, "Some AT&T Clients Gripe That Cost Cuts Are Hurting Service," *Wall Street Journal*, January 24, 1992, pp. A1+.

---

size of the program grows. In contrast, forced resignation programs require relatively little up-front cash investment on the part of the organization. Usually, forced resignations offer little to employees. At best, a forced resignation program will offer a small severance package.

The organization must also consider the legal aspects of each type of program. Since early retirement programs are strictly voluntary on the part of the employees, there is relatively little chance of legal action against organizations using such a program. Forced resignations, on the other hand, incur a great risk of legal action, especially when issues such as tenure are involved or wrongful discharge can be proven.

The type of strategy that the organization undertakes will also determine whether or not it looses valuable employees. Since voluntary retirements must generally be offered to all eligible employees, organizations run the risk of losing valuable employees as well as less valuable ones. In addition, valuable employees usually have skills that enable them to continue working with another organization. By taking early retirement from one organization and going to work for another, they are often able to increase their incomes dramatically as they receive funds from both organizations. As a result, the organization may wind up losing its most valuable employees

HR CHALLENGES ●

Suggestions for Easing Termination Shock

Handling the termination process effectively can go a long way in easing tensions and reducing the chances of employee retaliation. The following suggestions may help managers to be better prepared for terminating employees.

1. Plan the termination for early in the week so that the employee does not get the weekend to mull over the termination.
2. Do not let the termination interview last longer than 15 minutes. Long meetings allow time for debate. Simply state your case and move on.
3. Go to the worker's office so that he or she does not have to leave the meeting and explain it to other workers he or she may run into on the way back to his or her office. Make sure that the location is private.
4. Do not plan the meeting on important dates such as birthdays or holidays or when the employee has just returned from a vacation.
5. Don't leave room for confusion. Tell the employee in the first sentence that he or she is terminated. Make it clear that the decision is final.
6. Clearly communicate all aspects of the severance package offered to the employee.
7. It is natural for a terminated employee to be emotional and hostile so be prepared for an outburst.
8. Outline the remaining steps in the termination process, such as the last day, key return policies, and so on.
9. Provide the employee with the name of an individual at the outplacement service if one is being offered. If possible, personally introduce the employee to the counselor.
10. Discuss the transfer of the employee's responsibilities and work to other employees.
11. Wish the employee luck and express confidence in his or her ability to find a new job.

SOURCES: Adapted from Phyllis Macklin and Lester Minsuk, "10 Ways to Ease Dismissal Dread," *HRMagazine*, November 1991, pp. 104–105; and Susan Alexander, "Firms Get Plenty of Practice at Layoffs, but They Often Bungle the Firing Process," *Wall Street Journal*, October 14, 1991, p. B1.

to competitors during voluntary retirement programs. Forced resignations generally do not suffer from these problems. Again, the organization essentially decides who is going to resign and who is going to be kept, and it is natural to assume that the organization is not going to ask its key members to resign.

Finally, the organization must consider the impact of each strategy on its culture and climate and on its public image. Since forced resignations are involuntary in nature, they tend to have a large negative impact both internally and externally. The public is likely to interpret such actions as cold and uncaring on the part of the organization, especially if the program affects members with long tenure in the organization and the organization does not fully explain the rationale behind the actions. Internally, forced resignations are likely to foster hostility and resentment against upper management by the employees. Even generous severance packages, which are usually rare in these situations, generally cannot overcome the resentment generated by making employees leave the organization. While the level of resentment felt may differ by employee, research has found that women executives cope better with forced resignations than do men. It appears that men take the firing personally. They view it as age discrimination or a conflict in personalities. Women, on the other hand, more readily accept the fact that the change is due to downsizing or economic conditions rather than a problem with them.[59] Early retirement programs, on the other hand, do not suffer from such a stigma. Many organizations make employee retirement an occasion for celebration, and the community is likely to react positively to an organization that offers generous incentives to those employees who wish to retire early.[60]

Whatever method of termination is selected, human resource managers generally offer an exit interview so that terminated employees can have the opportunity to candidly discuss their work experience. Topics covered during this interview include the worker's impressions of the supervisor's performance, the adequacy of the training and development received, company policies, advancement opportunities, and overall job satisfaction. Managers can learn a lot about how employees feel during these interviews and should endeavor to hold one whenever an employee leaves.[61]

Organizations that consider a termination strategy as part of a restructuring plan have many issues with which to contend. Each strategy has its own advantages and shortcomings. In many instances termination strategies can help the organization achieve its restructuring in a faster manner than either layoff and no-layoff strategies. The risks and costs may be greater, however, depending on the type of strategy used. About the only absolute in determining what type of strategy to use is that management should carefully consider all alternatives and the likely impact of each one. Often the best solution is not a single restructuring approach, but rather a combination of methods, and rarely can one organization's experiences be directly applied to another organization.

● ● ● ● ● ● ● ● ●

MANAGEMENT GUIDELINES

Based on the information presented in this chapter, several guidelines for managers who face an organizational restructuring can be offered.

1. Any organization restructuring involves a trade-off between the impact on the employees and the immediate benefits to the organization. It is the manager's responsibility to balance the impact against the benefits.

2. Each type of restructuring strategy has its own time horizon for implementation. The manager must match the strategy to the time frame needed for the restructuring.

3. Each type of restructuring strategy has a different basic cost structure. The manager must consider the costs involved in each type of restructuring and the organization's ability to pay for it.

4. A critical determinant of a successful reorganization is the amount of managerial communication about the reasons for and goals of the restructuring. Poor communication between managers and employees may ruin the best planned restructuring.[62]

5. There are several laws and doctrines concerning organization restructuring. Managers should make sure that they are in compliance with these laws and doctrines before they begin a restructuring.

6. All types of restructuring involve organizational trauma. In order to reduce trauma and ensure a successful restructuring, managers should attempt to plan out the elements of a restructuring before they begin the restructuring.

7. The strategic variables and choices facing an organization are often strong determinants of the type of restructuring that the organization undertakes. Managers should carefully examine these variables and choices before embarking on a restructuring.

8. The three types of restructuring strategies are not mutually exclusive. Managers should always consider using elements of all three types of restructuring strategies before making a final decision on how to organize the restructuring.

QUESTIONS FOR REVIEW

1. What is organization restructuring? What does it usually involve?

2. Identify and briefly discuss the three general types of restructuring. How are they alike? How do they differ?

3. What is the role of the human resource professional in a restructuring?

4. Briefly identify and discuss the strategic variables involved in a restructuring decision. Describe the elements of each variable.

5. What is an LBO? How is it usually related to a restructuring decision?

6. Identify the four broad strategic choices that an organization must make in deciding to restructure. Discuss the general impact on both the employees and the organization in each type of restructuring decision.

7. What are no-layoff strategies? Briefly compare and contrast the different types of no-layoff strategies.

8. What are layoff strategies? List the various types of layoff strategies and discuss the advantages and disadvantages of each.

9. What are termination strategies? How do they differ from other restructuring strategies?

10. What roles do tenure and protection and compensation plans have in a termination strategy?

11. What is the employment-at-will doctrine? How does it relate to termination strategies?

12. Briefly describe the role of golden parachutes in termination strategies.

13. How is severance pay used in a termination strategy? What are its main advantages and disadvantages?

14. Discuss an organization's outplacement policy in relation to termination strategies. What are the three elements of a typical outplacement policy?

15. Identify and discuss the three basic types of termination strategies that an organization may pursue. How are they alike? How do they differ?

 The Safeway LBO— Need or Greed?[63]

James White had worked for Safeway supermarkets as a trucker for nearly 30 years. One year after Safeway had taken itself private in a 1986 leveraged buyout (LBO) worth $5.65 billion, White was laid off in a massive restructuring. In 1988 White marked the one year anniversary of his layoff by locking himself in his bathroom and killing himself with his .22 caliber hunting rifle.

White was one of the 63,000 people who have lost their jobs with the world's largest supermarket chain since the LBO, and he was not the only one to have died from the experience. Patricia Vasquez, a 14-year Safeway veteran and recipient of numerous company awards, was found dead on her bathroom floor from a heart attack the day after she was laid off. Richard Quigley, a transportation manager, lost his wife less than a week after he was laid off. He claims that the trauma of his layoff caused her to have a diabetic relapse for the first time in several years. Phil Anich died of a heart attack a week after filing for unemployment. Friends attribute his heart attack to the stress created by his layoff.

Other former employees have also paid the price. Mikhail Vaynberg, a refrigeration engineer who has saved Safeway $1.6 million per year with an improvement to its cooling systems, has been unable to find work since he has been laid off. Bill Mayfield, Jr., a 15-year Safeway mechanic, slashed his wrists and shot himself in the stomach after he was laid off. He survived. In spite of claims to the contrary by upper management, the LBO has crippled employee morale in a company that was once noted for its loyal and hardworking employees. All of this happened in a company whose pre-LBO employee motto was "Safeway Offers Security."

Greed or Struggle

Is the Safeway LBO another example of greed run wild or a company's struggle to survive in an ever-increasingly competitive world? It all depends on who you talk to. Critics of the LBO point out that the company had earned a record $231.1 million in profits on $19.6 billion in sales in 1985, the last year before the buyout. These results represented a doubling of earnings in less than four years. During that time, Safeway's stock price had tripled in value and dividends had just posted their fourth straight yearly increase. The buyout netted $25 million for the company's management. Shareholders saw the value of their stock increase 82 percent as a result of the buyout. The Hafts, father and son Wall Street takeover specialists, made $100 million on the deal. Kolberg Kravis Roberts, the LBO specialists, charged $60 million just to arrange the deal. Lawyers, accountants, and investment banks associated with the buyout made another $90 million.

In 1989, the company's profit was a meager $2.5 million on sales of $14.3 billion. This was down from $31 million in 1988. The company recently had to settle for a $11.25 per share initial stock offering instead of its anticipated $20 per share due to a lack of market confidence in the success of the LBO. One prime reason was the fact that Safeway lacks the ability to generate the approximate $3.2 billion in capital it needs to renovate and open new stores over the next five years.

The company has sold off 1,100 of its 2,325 stores and has closed numerous other operations. In 1987 Safeway closed its entire Dallas-area division. Over 9,000 employees, with an average tenure of 17 years, were laid off. The action had a ripple effect in the already-depressed Dallas economy. Numerous food and beverage suppliers, construction firms, and even the local food bank have fallen on even harder times as a result of the closings. More than 300 people were laid off in corporate headquarters almost immediately after the takeover was completed.

The company has not been particularly generous to its former employees. Many of the layoffs have come without warning, and employees claim that they had to sign waivers agreeing not to sue the company later to get their severance package—one-half to one week's worth of pay for every year with the company up to a maximum of eight weeks of pay. The unions representing the former Safeway employees have even had to go to arbitration to get these benefits. There are complaints that some employees had to wait up to eight months to receive their severance pay and as long as a year and a half for their accrued vacation time. Many former Safeway employees have attempted to get jobs with the organizations that have bought the old Safeway stores, but so far their luck has been minimal. Even those who have gotten their old jobs back have had to take substantial cuts in salary.

Low Morale

The 110,000 employees who still work with Safeway are not much happier. Worker morale is at an all-time low, and many employees complain of being overworked—even to the point of being dangerous. Many Safeway truckers report having to work 16-hour days, and one company joke advises "if you see a Safeway truck, get out of the way," since the drivers may be asleep at the wheel from overwork. Many accuse the company of trying to lower costs by forcing out older workers or using arcane job classifications with lower pay scales to bring in newer workers. Employees say it is not untypical for store managers to cut employee pay, or in the case of older workers, drop them from full-time status to part-time. This drop in hours not only reduces salaries (needed hours are made up by other new, lower paid part-time employees), it also results in employees losing medical and other benefits.

Another aspect of the restructuring that is strongly opposed by workers is Safeway's new Return on Market Value (ROMV) productivity quota system. Many store managers complain that if they do not meet weekly quotas determined by the ROMV system, they are penalized by actions like being forced to work a seven-day week and twelve-hour days. Many managers report that they have worked entire months without a day off. Managers also complain that in some areas less than 10 percent of the managers have ever actually qualified to receive incentive pay as a result of having met the quotas. Safeway executives claim the figure is more like 50 percent.

Rank-and-file employees complain that the incentive system does not trickle down to them, but they must make sacrifices to make it work. Reportedly, the incentive plan is linked to the number of employee grievances and work-related medical claims. Charles Mercer, president of the Denver local of the United Food and Commercial workers union, reports that many of his employees have been actively discouraged from filing workman's compensation claims because it will hurt the store's bonus.

Productivity Up

Supporters of the Safeway LBO paint another picture of the situation. Peter Magowan, son of the founders of Safeway and the current CEO, points out that worker productivity is up since the restructuring began and that Safeway is now number one or number two in every market in which it competes. He argues that the wage reductions were necessary to compete with other firms that have a less expensive salary structure. He defends the closings and the selling off of units as necessary actions to trim organization fat. One sale of the company's 132 stores in Britain netted Safeway $929 million, or 40 percent more than had initially been predicted. In addition, the operating profit per employee has risen more than 62 percent since 1985, the last year before the buyout.

Since the buyout, Safeway has also been able to install in some of its stores "boutique style" departments to cater to the yuppie crowd. Even though the company has turned in disappointing operating profits over the past few years, it has been able to significantly increase its cash flows, which are now about twice the level needed to cover the interest payments on its debt. The company has even begun to pay off some of its debt earlier than expected.

Magowan strongly disagrees with the supposed employee morale problems, too. He agrees that there have been problems in the past, but he states, "I am convinced that today's typical Safeway employee feels better about the company than he or she has at any point since the buyout." He even refers to a recent survey sponsored by the company that finds 80 percent of Safeway's employees feel that the organization offers advancement opportunity and other advantages.

So far, the jury is out on the results of the Safeway LBO. Was it really needed? Were the actions of top management justified and are the employees just reacting to changes that were necessary to keep the chain competitive in the market? Or, is Safeway's experience typical of the LBO binge of the 1980s in which management prospers at the expense of its employees?

QUESTIONS

1. What advantages and disadvantages were there for each of the constituencies involved in Safeway's LBO? Who stands to gain the most? Who stands to lose the most?

2. Do you think that any of the horrible consequences, such as death and attempted suicide of released workers, were preventable? If so, how?

3. As a human resource manager for Safeway, what are some of the challenges you would face before, during, and after the LBO?

4. What, if anything, does Safeway owe to the employees whose jobs were lost or changed due to the LBO?

5. If you were asked to fix the morale problems reported in this case, what would you do?

ADDITIONAL READINGS

Beer, Michael, Russell Eisenstat, and Bert Spector. *The Critical Path*. Boston: Harvard Business School Press, 1991.

Bolman, Lee, and Terrence Deal. *Reframing Organizations*. San Francisco, CA: Jossey-Bass, 1991.

Boyette, Joseph, and Henry Conn. *Workplace 2000: The Revolution Reshaping American Business*. New York: Dutton, 1991.

Bridges, William. *Managing Transitions*. Reading, MA: Addison Wesley, 1991.

Cameron, Kim, Sarah Freeman, and Aneil Mishra. "Best Practices in White-collar Downsizing: Managing Contradictions." *Academy of Management Executive* 5 (1991), pp. 57–73.

Carrier, Leana, and Daniel Feldman. "Layoffs: How Employees and Companies Cope." *Personnel Journal*. September 1988, p. 31.

Carroll, Paul. "Hurt by a Pricing War, IBM Plans a Writeoff and Cut of 10,000 Jobs." *Wall Street Journal*. December 6, 1989, p. A6.

Carroll, Paul. "IBM Launches Retirement Plan to Cut Outlays." *Wall Street Journal*. October 2, 1989, p. A4.

Cohen, Laurie. "AT&T Expands Early-Retirement Plan; Earnings Climbed 19% in Third Period." *Wall Street Journal*. October 20, 1989, p. A4.

"Corporate Restructuring." *1989 ASPA/CCH Survey*. June 27, 1989.

Coulson, Robert. *Empowered at Forty: How to Negotiate the Best Time and Terms of Your Retirement*. New York: Harper-Business, 1992.

Dorn, Phillip. "Change and Change Again at IBM." *Computer World*. October 31, 1988, p. 19.

Downes, John, and Jordan Goodman. *Dictionary of Finance and Investment Terms*. 2nd ed. New York: Barron's, 1987.

Faludi, Susan. "The Reckoning: Safeway LBO Yields Vast Profits but Exacts a Heavy Human Toll." *Wall Street Journal*. May 16, 1990, pp. A1; 6.

Farrell, Christopher. "LBOs: The Stars, the Strugglers, the Flops." *Business Week*. January 15, 1990, pp. 58–62.

Ford, Robert, and Pamela Perrewe. "After the Layoff: Closing the Barn Door before All the Horses Are Gone." 1992, paper under review at *Academy of Management Executive*.

Fox, Isaac, and Alfred Marcus. "The Causes and Consequences of Leveraged Buyouts." *Academy of Management Journal* 17, (1992), pp. 62–85.

Hartley, Jean, Dan Jacobson, Bert Klandermans, and Tinka Van Vuuren. *Job Insecurity*. Newbury Park, CA: Sage, 1991.

Heery, William. "Outplacement through Specialization." *Personnel Administrator*. June 1989, p. 151.

Henkoff, Ronald. "Cost Cutting: How to Do It Right." *Fortune*. April 9, 1990, p. 41.

Hogan, Mike. "Hayes Reduces." *PC World*. June 1990, p. 11.

Hymowitz, Carol. "Kodak Passes Out 'Tin Parachutes' to All Its Employees." *Wall Street Journal*. January 12, 1990, p. B1.

IBM. *1988 Annual Report*, p. 40.

Karr, Albert. "As the Army Shrinks, the Civilian Market Will Tighten for Job Seekers." *Wall Street Journal*. June 19, 1990, p. A1.

Keller, John. "AT&T Weighs Early Retirement Plan that May Slash Non-Management Staff." *Wall Street Journal*. March 15, 1990, p. A3.

Kissler, Gary. *Change Riders*. Reading, MA: Addison-Wesley, 1991.

Kuhn, Susan. "How Business Helps Schools." *Fortune*. Education 1990 Issue, pp. 91–106.

Kuzmits, Frank, and Lyle Sussman. "Early Retirement or Forced Resignation: Policy Issues for Downsizing Human Resources." *SAM Advanced Management Journal*. Winter 1988, p. 28.

Leana, Carrie, and Daniel Feldman. "Layoffs: How Employees and Companies Cope." *Personnel Journal*. September 1988, p. 31.

Loomis, Carol. "The Biggest Looniest Deal Ever." *Fortune*. June 18, 1990, pp. 48–72.

Mainiero, Lisa, and Paul Upham. "Beating a Stacked Deck—

Restructuring vs. Career Development." *Personnel Journal.* June 1987, p. 126.

Messmer, Max. "Right-Sizing Reshapes Staffing Strategies." *HRMagazine.* October 1991, pp. 60–62.

Meyer, Alan. "Adapting to Environmental Jolts." *Administrative Science Quarterly,* 27. December 1982, pp. 515–537.

Milkovich, George, and John Boudreau. *Personnel/Human Resource Management: A Diagnostic Approach.* Plano, TX: Business Publications, 1988.

Petras, Kathryn, and Ross Petras. *The Only Retirement Guide You'll Ever Need.* New York: Poseidon, 1992.

"Plant-Closing Law Affects Casino." *HRM News/Society for Human Resource Management.* February 1990, p. A11.

Porter, Michael. *Competitive Strategy.* New York: Free Press, 1980.

Reid, Peter. *Well Made in America: Lessons from Harley-Davidson on Being the Best.* New York: McGraw-Hill, 1990.

Schmenner, Roger. *Production/Operations Management.* 3rd ed. Chicago: SRA, 1988.

Shao, Maria. "Boeing: A Backlog Strains Its Assembly Line." *Business Week.* May 8, 1989, pp. 35–36.

Siconolfi, Michael. "Drexel Owes Its Former Employees About $40 Million in Severance Fees." *Wall Street Journal.* February 26, 1990, pp. A4; 1.

Siehl, C., and D. Smith. "Avoiding the Loss of a Gain: Retaining Top Managers in an Acquisition." *Human Resource Management* 29 (1991), pp. 167–185.

Soukup, William, Miriam Rothman, and Dennis Brisco. "Outplacement Services: A Vital Component of Personnel Policy." *SAM Advanced Management Journal.* Autumn 1987, pp. 19–23.

Starbuck, William, and Bo Hedberg. "Saving an Organization from a Stagnating Environment," in H. Thorelli, ed. *Strategy + Structure = Performance.* Bloomington: Indiana University Press, 1977, pp. 249–258.

Sweet, Donald. *A Manager's Guide to Conducting Terminations.* Lexington, MA: Lexington Books, 1990.

Walsh, J., and J. Ellwood. "Mergers, Acquisitions, and the Pruning of Managerial Deadwood." *Strategic Management Journal* 12 (1991), pp. 210–217.

White, Joseph. "GM's Plant Closings Help It Win Wall Street Applause." *Wall Street Journal.* May 25, 1990, p. C1.

Wilke, John. "At Digital Equipment, Slowdown Reflects Industry's Big Changes." *Wall Street Journal.* September 15, 1989, p. A1.

∙∙∙∙∙∙∙∙∙∙∙∙∙∙∙∙∙∙
NOTES

a. The bulk of the research and writing of this chapter was conducted by Charles Fornaciari of Florida State University.

1. Carrie Leana and Daniel Feldman, "Layoffs: How Employees and Companies Cope," *Personnel Journal,* September 1988, p. 31.

2. "Corporate Restructuring," 1989 ASPA/CCH Survey, June 27, 1989, p. 2.

3. Alan Murray and David Wessel. "Torrent of Job Cuts Shows Human Toll of Recession Goes On," *Wall Street Journal,* December 12, 1991, pp. A1+.

4. Brian Dumaine, "The Bureaucracy Busters," *Fortune,* June 17, 1991, pp. 36–50.

5. Ibid.; and Frank Kuzmits and Lyle Sussman, "Early Retirement or Forced Resignation: Policy Issues for Downsizing Human Resources," *SAM Advanced Management Journal,* Winter 1988, p. 28.

6. Carrie Leana and Daniel Feldman, "Layoffs: How Employees and Companies Cope," *Personnel Journal,* September 1988, p. 31.

7. William Anthony and B. J. Hodge, "IBM: The Elephant Learns to Dance," in *Organization Theory* (Boston: Allyn and Bacon, 1991); IBM *1988 Annual Report,* p. 40; Paul Carroll, "Hurt by a Pricing War, IBM Plans a Writeoff and Cut of 10,000 Jobs," *Wall Street Journal,* December 6, 1989, p. A6; Phillip Dorn, "Change and Change Again at IBM," *ComputerWorld,* October 31, 1988, p. 19; Paul Carroll, "IBM Launches Retirement Plan to Cut Outlays," *Wall Street Journal,* October 2, 1989, p. A4; Lawrence Hooper, "IBM Announces Big Write-Off, Restructuring," *Wall Street Journal,* December 6, 1989, p. A3; and Alan Murray and David Wessel, "Torrent of Job Cuts Shows Human Toll of Recession Goes On," *Wall Street Journal,* December 12, 1991, pp. A1+.

8. Andrew Kupfer, "Apple's Plan to Survive and Grow," *Fortune,* May 4, 1992, pp. 68–72; and Paul Zachary and Laurence Hooper, "IBM and Apple Open New Front in PC Wars with Strategic Alliance," *Wall Street Journal,* July 5, 1991, pp. A1+.

9. Dean Tjosvold. "Foolproof Your Restructuring Plan," *HRMagazine,* November 1991, pp. 79–84.

10. Michael Porter, *Competitive Strategy* (New York: Free Press, 1980), p. xvi.

11. Ibid., pp. 34–46.

12. Harold Weinstein and Michael Liebman, "Corporate Scale Down, What Comes Next?" *HRMagazine,* April 1991, pp. 33–36.

13. Mike Hogan, "Hayes Reduces," *PC World,* June 1990, p. 11.

14. Zachary Schiller and Robert Neff, "The Backlash Isn't Just Against Japan," *Business Week,* February 10, 1992, p. 30; and Krystal Miller, "Honda, Seeking to Avert Output Cuts, Stores 2,000 Cars at Ohio Parking Lot," *Wall Street Journal,* March 5, 1991, p. A5.

15. John Wilke, "At Digital Equipment, Slowdown Reflects Industry's Big Changes, *Wall Street Journal,* September 15, 1989, pp. A1; 6.

16. Alan Meyer, "Adapting to Environmental Jolts," *Administrative Science Quarterly,* 1982, pp. 515–537.

17. Albert Karr, "Staying Lean," *Wall Street Journal,* July 16, 1991, p. A1.

18. Peter C. Reid, *Well Made in America: Lessons from Harley-Davidson on Being the Best* (New York: McGraw-Hill, 1990), p. 14.

19. 1989 ASPA/CCH Survey, pp. 2–3.

20. Ronald Henkoff, "Cost Cutting: How to Do It Right," *Fortune,* April 9, 1990, p. 41.

21. Joan Rigdon, "Kodak's Changes Produce Plenty of Heat, Little Light," *Wall Street Journal,* April 8, 1992, p. B4.

22. John Downes and Jordan Goodman, *Dictionary of Finance and Investment Terms,* 2nd ed. (New York: Barron's, 1987), p. 209.

23. Christopher Farrell, "LBOs: The Stars, the Strugglers, the Flops," *Business Week,* January 15, 1990, pp. 58–62.

24. Carol J. Loomis, "The Biggest Looniest Deal Ever," *Fortune,* June 18, 1990, pp. 48–72.

25. Shaker Zahra and Michael Fescina, "Will Leverage Buyouts Kill U.S. Corporate Research & Development?" *Academy of Management Executive* 5, 1991, pp. 7–21; and Michael Hitt, Robert Hoskisson, Duane Ireland, and Jeffrey Harrison, "Are Acquisitions a Poison for Innovation?" *Academy of Management Executive* 5, 1991, pp. 23–34.

26. Halya Duda, "The Honeymoon Is over for Corporate American," *HRMagazine,* February 1992, pp. 66–70.

27. William Starbuck and Bo Hedberg, "Saving an Organization from a Stagnating Environment," in H. Thorelli, ed., *Strategy + Structure = Performance* (Bloomington: Indiana University Press, 1977), pp. 249–258.

28. Stephanie Overman, "The Layoff Legacy," *HRMagazine,* August 1991, pp. 29–32.

29. Lisa Mainiero and Paul Upham, "Beating a Stacked Deck—Restructuring vs. Career Development," *Personnel Journal,* June 1987, p. 126.

30. Susan Kuhn, "How Business Helps Schools," *Fortune,* Education 1990 Issue, pp. 91–106.

31. "Job-based Learning: Some Firms Build Closer Ties between School and Work," *Wall Street Journal,* September 10, 1991, p. A1.

32. Maria Shao, "Boeing: A Backlog Strains Its Assembly Line," *Business Week,* May 8, 1989, p. 36.

33. James Francis, John Mohr, and Kelly Anderson, "HR Balancing: Alternative Downsizing," *Personnel Journal*, January 1992, pp. 71–78.

34. "The Axeman Cometh," *The Economist*, December 1990, pp. 15–16.

35. Udayan Gupta, "Cutting Payrolls without Axing Any Employees," *Wall Street Journal*, March 26, 1991, pp. B1 + .

36. For more information, see Roger W. Schmenner, *Production/Operations Management*, 3rd ed. (Chicago: SRA, 1987), pp. 5–23.

37. Ibid., pp. 52–85.

38. Joseph White, "GM's Plant Closings Help It Win Wall Street Applause," *Wall Street Journal*, May 25, 1990, p. C1.

39. White, p. C1.

40. "Plant-Closing Law Affects Casino," *HRM News/Society for Human Resource Management*, February 1990, p. A11.

41. Albert Karr, "As the Army Shrinks, the Civilian Market Will Tighten for Job Seekers," *Wall Street Journal*, June 19, 1990, p. A1:5.

42. Kim Cameron, "Downsizing Can Be Hazardous to your Future," *HRMagazine*, July 1991, pp. 96 + .

43. Gabriella Stren, Paul Carroll, and Michel McQueen, "In a Weak Economy, Some Top-Level Aides Are Bound to Topple," *Wall Street Journal*, December 13, 1991, pp. A1 + .

44. Joann Lublin, "Executives Find Unemployment Takes a Heavier Toll the Second Time Around," *Wall Street Journal*, July 9, 1991, pp. B1 + .

45. "Wrongful Discharge: Legal Experts Propose a New Approach," *Wall Street Journal*, September 10, 1991, p. A1.

46. George Milkovich and John Boudreau, *Personnel/Human Resource Management: A Diagnostic Approach*, Plano, TX: Business Publications, 1988, pp. 465–467.

47. Christopher Conte, "Litigation Losses," *Wall Street Journal*, May 12, 1992, p. A1.

48. Michael Siconolfi, "Drexel Owes Its Former Employees About $40 Million in Severance Fees," *Wall Street Journal*, February 26, 1990, p. A4; 1.

49. Carol Hymowitz, "Kodak Passes Out 'Tin Parachutes' to All Its Employees," *Wall Street Journal*, January 12, 1990, p. B1; 3.

50. "Severance: The Corporate Response," *The Right Research Report* (Fort Lauderdale: Right Associates).

51. "Goodbyes Can Cost Plenty in Europe," *Fortune*, April 6, 1992, p. 16; and Christopher Conte, "Terminating Workers," *Wall Street Journal*, May 12, 1992, p. A1.

52. William Heery, "Outplacement through Specialization," *Personnel Administrator*, June 1989, p. 151.

53. William Soukup, Miriam Rothman, and Dennis Brisco, "Outplacement Services: A Vital Component of Personnel Policy," *SAM Advanced Management Journal*, Autumn 1987, pp. 19–23.

54. A. B. Karr, "There Is Life after Outplacement, but Career Views Change," *Wall Street Journal*, December 24, 1991, p. A1.

55. Laurie P. Cohen, "AT&T Expands Early-Retirement Plan; Earnings Climbed 19% in Third Period," *Wall Street Journal*, October 20, 1989, p. A4; 2.

56. John Keller, "AT&T Weighs Early Retirement Plan That May Slash Non-Management Staff," *Wall Street Journal*, March 15, 1990, p. A3; 2.

57. Lenore Schiff, "Is Health Care a Job Killer?" *Fortune*, April 6, 1992, p. 30.

58. The following discussion is based on the article "Early Retirement or Forced Resignation: Policy Issues for Downsizing Human Resources," by Frank E. Kuzmits and Lyle Sussman in *SAM Advanced Management Journal*, Winter 1988, pp. 28–32.

59. J. E. Rigdon, "Women Appear to Take Firings Less Personally," *Wall Street Journal*, December 6, 1991, p. B1.

60. Gregory Patterson, "More Employers Offer Early Retirement to Help Shrink Blue-Collar Work Force," *Wall Street Journal*, August 30, 1991, p. B1.

61. Robert Wolfe, "Most Employers Offer Exit Interviews," *HRNews*, June 1991, p. A2.

62. David Gold and Beth Unger, "Communication Boosts Morale after Downsizing," *HRNews*, February 1992, p. A7.

63. Susan Faludi, "The Reckoning: Safeway LBO Yields Vast Profits but Exacts a Heavy Human Toll," *Wall Street Journal*, May 16, 1990, pp. A1 + .

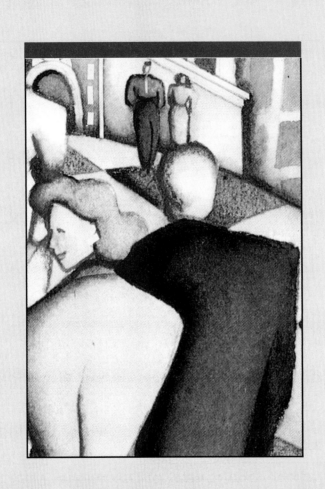

PART SEVEN

Cases

CASE 1

Federal Express Corporation

Federal Express became a leader in the air transport industry in only a few years.[1] The company founded the small-package/document express market in 1973, and it constantly adds products and services and extends its service areas. Its main air freight forwarding competitors, most notably United Parcel Service (UPS) and Emery Air Freight, have been around for twenty-five years, and were content with the market positions they occupied. Federal Express "changed the rules of the game" and took the market by storm.[2]

INDUSTRY

Firms involved in cargo movement include all-cargo air carriers, traditional freight forwarders, passenger airlines, ground transportation companies, and air couriers. Competitors directly involved in the small-package/document express market include Federal Express, Purolator, UPS, and the United States Postal Service.

Regulation for this industry falls under the Federal Aviation Act of 1958 and is enforced by the Federal Aviation Administration (FAA). The FAA's regulatory authority relates primarily to the safety aspects of air transportation, which includes aircraft standard and maintenance. Federal Express operations are also subject to regulation by the Federal Communications Act of 1934 because of the use of radio and communication equipment in ground and air units. In addition, the Department of Transportation exercises regulatory authority over the company.

COMPANY BACKGROUND

Frederick W. Smith, founder of Federal Express, earned his pilot's license before entering college. His experience as an aviator and his observation of material shipments out of airports while a student majoring in political science and economics at Yale University in the 1960s were the impetus for developing his firm in 1973. His initial conceptualization of Federal Express was that of an air cargo firm that specialized in overnight package delivery on a door-to-door basis using its own planes.

The idea for Federal Express was first laid out in an overdue economics paper. To cut cost and time, packages from all over the country would be flown to a central point, or hub, late at night when the traffic lanes were comparatively empty. At the hub the packages would be sorted, redistributed, and flown out again to their ultimate locations. Airports in sizable cities would be used, and trucks would carry the packages to their final destinations. The destinations served would include the airport locations and smaller communities in the vicinity. The goal was to deliver

This case was prepared by Mark Dawkins.

equipment and documents shipped from any location in the United States to any other location within the United States the next day.[3]

Federal Express received its name because of Smith's ambition to serve the Federal Reserve and to create a name with a broad geographic connotation. He wanted to assist the Federal Reserve in its float management efforts by selling them a delivery system that would cut down on float time (the period between receipt of a check and collection of funds). Unfortunately, Fred Smith's contract bid was turned down by the Federal Reserve.

After college, Smith served two tours of duty in Vietnam. He decided to give his air express idea a try after returning home. A study showed that Memphis, Tennessee, was near the center of business shipping in the continental United States. Its airport offered long runways, a large abandoned ramp, and a pair of inexpensive hangars from World War II, and it was closed only an average of ten hours per year due to adverse weather conditions.[4] Thus, Smith chose Memphis as a home base and started his firm with $4 million he had inherited.

FINANCING

Since $4 million was not enough for an entire fleet of planes, Smith went to New York and Chicago in search of additional funds. With his impressive knowledge of the air freight industry and his ability to impress investors, Smith raised $72 million in loans and equity investment within one year.

With fresh capital, Federal Express expanded its focus from operating a charter service to its present business. It began transporting packages weighing less than 70 pounds from thirteen airports in April 1973. Volume increased rapidly, resulting in extended service. Federal Express appeared to be an overnight success. The success, however, did not last long as the Organization of Petroleum Exporting Countries' inflation of fuel prices increased expenses faster than revenues were growing. By mid-1974 the company was losing more than $1 million per month.[5]

Bankruptcy became a real possibility, forcing Smith to return to his disappointed investors for more money to keep the company growing until revenues could catch up with expenses. He raised $11 million in additional funds. Having lost $27 million during its first two years, Federal Express posted profits of $3.6 million in 1976 on revenues of $75 million. Profits increased annually throughout 1986.

MANAGEMENT/PERSONNEL

Fred Smith's charisma enabled him to motivate investors and employees to share his vision for Federal Express. A man of great integrity, Smith attributed his drive to scars from his military service tours. He stated that he would not have the same perspective if not for his Vietnam experiences.[6]

Despite many challenges, Smith never relinquished his entrepreneurial vision. He courted investors for more money when the Arab oil embargo resulted in skyrocketing fuel costs. He went to Washington and lobbied for airline deregulation when the Civil Aeronautics Board (CAB) regulations made it impossible for Federal Express to use the larger aircraft it needed. He jumped at the opportunity to deliver overnight letter service when the postal service relaxed its regulations against private delivery of extremely urgent mail.[7]

Smith's colleagues had the same entrepreneurial attitude toward Federal Express. All were former pilots and entrepreneurs. Although most thought his idea very strange, the comradery and loyalty exhibited by employees of Federal Express was strong from day one. This comradery and loyalty strengthened Federal Express. By the late 1970s, however, Federal Express had grown too large for the entrepreneurial approach to management used by Smith and his colleagues.

Company president Art Bass, one of the initial team members, decided to leave in 1979. He took five vice-presidents with him, all but one of whom had been with Federal Express from the start. Bass and his colleagues felt that Federal Express had matured, and that they lacked the ability to adapt their entrepreneurial perspectives to managing this mature operation. Smith replaced his former colleagues with managers who were comfortable with the traditional corporate organization, including several key executives in 1990:[8]

Frederick W. Smith, chairman, president, and CEO

James L. Barksdale, executive vice-president and COO

David C. Anderson, senior vice-president and CFO

Kenneth R. Masterson, senior vice-president and general counsel

T. Allan McArtor, senior vice-president of air operations.

Thomas R. Oliver, senior vice-president of international operation

James A. Perkins, senior vice-president and chief personnel officer

Ron J. Ponder, senior vice-president and chief information officer

Carole A. Presley, senior vice-president of marketing/customer ssrvice

Jeffrey R. Rodek, senior vice-president of central support services

Theodore L. Weise, senior vice-president of the United States and Canada divisions

W. Jack Roberts, vice-president and controller

Robert L. Cox, secretary

Federal Express' backbone from the beginning has been its employees. The dedication of its more than 75,000 employees to professional, faultless service has kept Federal Express at the forefront of the air cargo industry. Its policies and commitment to provide an array of training programs for employees helps maintain its image of professionalism and stability. These policies include paying the tuition in full for college students working at the Memphis hub.

Each employee hired is viewed as a long-term investment. Part-time employees are scheduled to permit operations to expand or contract according to traffic levels, thereby avoiding the need to furlough full-time employees.[9] In addition, by employing part-time college students who come and go as they complete their education, Federal Express has created a buffer between its operations and the entrance of unions to the hub.[10] This has allowed Federal Express to keep its labor costs lower than any other company in the industry.[11]

....

OPERATIONS

Federal Express provides overnight express delivery service for high-priority packages and documents on a door-to-door basis. Services are available Monday through Saturday in 127 countries—the majority of the industrial world.[12] These services are provided through Federal Express' hub-and-spoke system, an intricate ground/air network.

Federal Express' central sorting facility in Memphis made its service operation unique in the field. Every package and letter handled by Federal Express passes through the center in Memphis to be sorted and dispatched to its delivery destination. Federal Express now has five U.S. sorting facilities, or hubs: Indianapolis, Memphis, Newark, Oakland, and Anchorage. Regional metroplexes in Chicago and Los Angeles support these five facilities as additional sites for sorting and distribution.[13]

Hub operations are fine tuned for maximum efficiency. Packages are collected in sorting facilities and offices during the day in hundreds of cities. Packages are then transported to the local airport and flown to the nearest hub. The planes are unloaded, and the packages are then sorted and loaded back into the planes headed for their intended destinations. Couriers then transport the packages from sorting facilities at local airports to local offices, where they are routed to the receiver.

Contact with couriers is maintained through the use of digitally assisted dispatch units (DADs). Dispatch information can be left in couriers' vans, even when unoccupied.[14] Federal Express also uses a computer network for dispatch entry and tracking. The satellite and telephone network, called COSMOS, uses a satellite and telephone network to locate a package as it passes through numerous electronic gates during transit. Each parcel is bar-coded for monitoring and recording each step of the journey.[15]

As of year-end 1990, Federal Express operated 384 aircraft and over 31,000 delivery vehicles. Other vehicles owned by the company include ground support equipment, cargo loaders, transports, and aircraft tugs.

PRODUCT LINES [16]

On a domestic level, Federal Express offers six basic services: priority overnight service (POS), standard overnight service (SOS), international priority service (IPS), economy two-day service (ES), heavyweight service (HS), and deferred heavyweight service (DHS). Products are grouped into three weight classifications: documents and light parcels, boxes, and air freight.

Documents and light parcels are items shipped primarily in FedEx packaging. Boxes are unlimited weight shipments, provided no single piece weighs more than 150 pounds. Air freight shipments have no size or weight limitations. The products offered by weight class are identified below:

Documents and light parcels—POS, SOS, and IPS

Boxes—POS, and ES

Air freight—HS, and DHS

POS guarantees delivery by 10:30 A.M. the next business morning. SOS guarantees delivery by 3:00 P.M. the next business day. IPS guarantees door-to-door delivery, including customs clearance, within 1 to 3 business days. ES guarantees delivery on the second business afternoon by 4:30 P.M. HS guarantees delivery the second business morning by 10:30 A.M. DHS guarantees delivery the second business afternoon by 4:30 P.M.

On an international level, Federal Express offers three basic services: international priority service (IPS), international distribution service (IDS), and airport-to-airport service (AAS). Products are grouped into the three weight classifications identified earlier. The products offered by weight class are identified below:

Documents and light parcels—IPS

Boxes—IPS, IDS, and AAS

Air freight—IDS, and AAS

IPS guarantees door-to-door delivery, including customs clearance, within 1 to 3 business days. IDS guarantees 1 to 3 day airport-to-airport service, excluding customs clearance. AAS is a committed or space-available, international, airport-to-airport service, and delivery is guaranteed within 2 to 4 days excluding customs clearance.

MARKETING/ADVERTISING

Federal Express was an innovator. Having founded the small-package/document express market, Federal Express hoped to dominate it. Fred Smith stated that Federal Express was selling time, thereby allowing people to be more effective in their day-to-day activities.[17] Smith went all out to get the message across. Initial emphasis was on building the public's trust by convincing customers that Federal Express would do what it claimed to do—"get it there overnight." Price was and is seen as a distant factor, becoming important to customers after they are assured that the package will be delivered on time.

ACQUISITIONS

In 1987, Federal Express purchased the assets of the Island Courier Companies and acquired Cansica, Inc. In 1989, the company acquired Tiger International for $895,000,000, a major strategic acquisition. In 1989, it also acquired East-West Couriers, Ltd., Yuill Courier Services, Ltd., and Bluejay Courier Services in Canada; Winchmore Developments, Ltd., and Home Delivery Services, Ltd., in the United Kingdom; Transport Group Alvarcht in Holland; Elbe-Klaus in Germany; Saimex in Italy; Rainer's in Australia; the Daisei Companies in Japan; and the Binghalib Express in the United Arab Emirates. In 1990, the company acquired Transports Transvendeens Chronoservice in France and Aeroenvios in Mexico.[18]

COMPETITION

In 1990, Federal Express' major competitors were United Parcel Service, the United States Postal Service, and Emery Air Freight Corporation.

United Parcel Service provides transportation services, primarily through the delivery of small packages. The company is the giant in package delivery and occupies a strong position in the transportation industry. Only the Postal Service can rival its package volume. Service is offered throughout the United States, Western

Europe, and Canada. Service is also provided to many locations in the Soviet Union, Eastern Europe, Asia, the Middle East, Africa, and Central and South America.

UPS has long enjoyed a reputation of dependability, productivity, and efficiency. As of late 1989, the company owned and operated a fleet of more than 112,000 vehicles, utilized 347 aircraft (101 owned and the remainder leased), and employed a work force of over 230,000.[19] The company entered the overnight package delivery market late in 1982 with their rate substantially lower than those charged by Federal Express.[20] Reported revenue was $12.3 billion in 1989, $11.0 billion in 1988, and $9.7 billion in 1987. Net income was $693 million in 1989, $759 million in 1988, and $784 million in 1987.[21]

The U.S. Postal Service competes in the overnight package delivery business with its Express Mail next-day service, which guarantees delivery to the addressee the following day by 3:00 P.M. The addressee, at his or her option, can pick up the package as early as 10:00 A.M. on the delivery day. Customers can obtain full refunds for shipments not arriving on time. Postal Service statistics show that 95 percent of all shipments do arrive on time.[22] Regularly scheduled package pickup is also available for a flat charge, regardless of the number of packages.

The U.S. Postal Service employed over 760,000 people as of late 1988.[23] Service areas include most major metropolitan areas in the United States, with international service to major cities in the United Kingdom, Australia, Brazil, Japan, Belgium, France, Hong Kong, and the Netherlands.[24] Reported revenue was $35.6 billion in 1988 and $32.2 billion in 1987. Net losses of $597.0 million and $22.7 million were reported in 1988 and 1987, respectively.[25]

Emery is also a major competitor in the domestic and international markets. The company provides worldwide air courier/air cargo service through an integrated courier/cargo system. Overnight door-to-door delivery service for packages of any size and weight, and 24- to 72-hour door-to-door service to cities throughout the world are provided. Emery's overnight delivery services include Same Day (A.M. or P.M.), Day 2, and the Emery Urgent Letter.[26] Emery also has several subsidiaries engaged in closely related activities.

During the 1980s, the company made major capital investments in state-of-the-art technology, as well as expanded and modernized existing facilities and aircraft for purposes of fostering future business growth. Emery also purchased Purolator Courier Corporation in 1987.[27] The company employed approximately 16,600 employees as of late 1988. Reported revenue was $1.22 billion in 1988 and $1.17 billion in 1987. Net losses of $50.3 million and $47.7 million were reported in 1988 and 1987, respectively.[28]

....

FINANCIAL

Federal Express was not an immediate financial success. It took four years, $70 million in venture capital, and several perches on the edge of bankruptcy before the company reported its first profitable period in late 1975. The initial offering in 1974–1975 raised only $32 million, and new capital for 1975 was $10 million. The company constantly asked banks, other corporations, and venture capitalists for additional loans and equity participation arrangements. The company survived because a dozen or more equity groups participated in three rounds of critical financing. During this difficult period Smith gave up virtually all his equity in Federal Express, but earned true loyalty from his employees for his determination and steadfast belief

| EXHIBIT 1 | Consolidated Statement of Income (as of May 31) |

	1990	1989	1988
Revenues	$7,015,069	$5,166,967	$3,882,817
Operating expenses:			
Salaries	3,045,250	2,308,969	1,799,584
Equipment	717,443	467,221	332,435
Fuel	521,256	269,803	176,938
Depreciation	479,188	387,318	289,578
Maintenance	424,923	279,121	187,542
Other	1,413,430	1,030,100	717,288
Total	6,601,490	4,742,532	3,503,365
Operating income	413,579	424,435	379,452
Other income (expense):			
Interest, net	(188,109)	(115,260)	(67,108)
Gain on equipment	13,791	4,709	457
Other, net	(20,838)	(15,552)	(10,473)
Total	(195,156)	(126,103)	(77,124)
Income before taxes	218,423	298,332	302,328
Provision for taxes	102,659	131,881	114,612
SFAS 96 adjustment	0	18,100	0
Net income	$ 115,764	$ 184,551	$ 187,716
Earnings per share	$2.18	$3.53	$3.56
Average shares outstanding	53,161	52,272	52,670

Note: Figures in thousands of dollars, except per share amounts.

in the company. (Smith recaptured a substantial portion of his equity in later refinancings.)

Exhibits 1, 2, and 3 contain selected financial information about Federal Express and its operations. In addition to the financial and operating data, Federal Express' commitment to geographic growth and expansion of service is evidenced by its capital outlay expenditures. These expenditures totaled $1.2 billion in 1990, $749 in 1989, and $694 million in 1988.[29] The bulk of these outlays were for aircraft and to expand and improve sorting facilities. These expenditures have been necessitated by domestic volume growth and the company's efforts to reduce costs through the continued automation of package handling and routing systems. Federal Express expects significant capital expenditures to continue into the future.[30]

HUMAN RESOURCE POLICIES AND PROGRAMS

Federal Express management believes that the company's most important component is the human one: employees whose commitment and dedication results in continuing prosperity.[31] The company is equally committed to its employees. Over the past decade, the company has routinely been cited for its no-layoff policy, its minority recruitment efforts, and its guaranteed fair treatment policy. Several human resource policies and programs are discussed below.

....

| EXHIBIT 2 | Consolidated Balance Sheet (as of May 31) |

	1990	1989	1988
Current assets:			
Cash	$ 98,499	$ 157,308	$ 54,945
Receivables, net	997,808	767,278	491,324
Spare parts, fuel	110,573	83,563	48,798
Prepaid expenses	108,523	91,931	34,938
Total current assets	1,315,403	1,100,080	630,005
Property and equipment:			
Flight equipment	2,310,764	2,313,082	1,301,978
Package handling	1,130,131	934,426	755,585
Electronic equipment	671,207	553,204	438,527
Other	1,356,724	1,100,657	853,019
	5,468,826	4,901,369	3,349,109
Less acc. depr.	1,902,505	1,469,555	1,117,234
Net property/equipment	3,566,321	3,431,814	2,231,875
Other assets:			
Goodwill	588,874	593,938	22,377
Other	204,475	167,590	124,292
	793,349	761,528	146,669
Total assets	$5,675,073	$5,293,422	$3,008,549
Current liabilities:			
Current long-term debt	$ 70,082	$ 69,249	$ 69,138
Accounts payable	454,445	398,502	199,328
Accrued expenses	715,687	621,345	303,586
Total current liabilities	1,240,214	1,089,096	572,052
Long-term debt	2,148,142	2,138,940	838,730
Deferred taxes	637,530	571,862	267,088
Owners equity:			
Common stock (par)	5,315	5,286	5,286
Additional capital	639,676	625,828	623,057
Retained earnings	1,010,090	901,429	726,036
	1,655,081	1,532,543	1,354,379
Less treasury stock	21	26,619	0
Less deferred comp.	5,873	12,400	23,700
Total owners equity	1,649,187	1,493,524	1,330,679
Total liabilities and owners' equity	$5,675,073	$5,293,422	$3,008,549

....

In preparing for global expansion, the company began a round-the-clock meteorology service with a satellite-based forecasting system. The system, which is named McIDAS, performs "nowcasting," a weather assessment at a particular moment and briefly into the future. The most up-to-date and specific weather data are important because it allows Federal Express to make contingency plans for its chief function: safe delivery of packages on time.[32] Estimates for the cost of this system are as high as $2.5 million, further evidence of the company's commitment to providing a safe and enjoyable environment for its employees.

| EXHIBIT 3 | Selected Financial and Operating Data |

	1990	1989	1988
Operating results:			
Revenues	$ 7,015,069	$ 5,166,967	$ 3,882,817
Expenses	6,601,490	4,742,532	3,503,365
Operating income	413,579	424,435	379,452
Other income (expense)	(195,156)	(126,103)	(77,124)
Income before taxes	218,423	298,332	302,328
Income taxes	102,659	131,881	114,612
Net income	115,764	184,551	187,716
Earnings per share	2.18	3.53	3.56
Average shares o/s	53,161	52,272	52,670
Stock price range	42.88–57.88	41.25–56.13	35.63–75.38
Average number of employees	75,102	58,136	48,556
Financial position:			
Current assets	$ 1,315,403	$ 1,100,080	$ 630,005
Property equipment, net	3,566,321	3,431,814	2,231,875
Total assets	5,675,073	5,293,422	3,008,549
Current liabilities	1,240,214	1,089,096	572,052
Long-term debt	2,148,142	2,138,940	838,730
Owners' equity	1,649,187	1,493,524	1,330, 679
Working capital	75,189	10,984	57,953
Other operating data:			
Express package:			
Average daily volume	1,246,311	1,059,882	877,543
Average pounds/package	5.3	5.4	5.3
Average revenue/pound	$ 3.12	$ 3.04	$ 3.10
Average revenue/package	$ 16.50	$ 16.28	$ 16.32
Heavyweight package:			
Average daily pounds	3,310	4,019	—
Average revenue/pound	$ 1.12	$ 1.06	—
Aircraft fleet:			
Boeing 747s	19	21	—
Douglas DC-10s	26	24	21
Douglas DC-8s	6	6	—
Boeing 727s	130	106	68
Cessna 208s	184	147	109
Fokker F-27s	19	7	5
Total aircraft	384	311	203
Vehicle fleet	31,000	28,900	21,000

Note: Dollar amount are in thousands, except per share and other operating data.

In early 1988 the company started *FedEx Overnight*, a regular morning newscast that has developed a loyal employee viewing audience.[33] *FedEx Overnight* is a daily staple of Federal Express Television (FXTV), the broadcast network established by the company to keep employees better informed. The program includes basis statistics (package volume, stock price, and weather forecast) and operational information (new services or billing system changes). The program is broadcast to over 700 receiving stations daily, where it is automatically recorded for viewing throughout the day as employees report to work.

The remaining time on FXTV is used for management communication and development, sales communication, and ad hoc events. The company notes three distinct advantages to the system: (1) timeliness, (2) the interaction the format affords (important issues and concerns can be addressed with employees through live feeds), and (3) the consistency and immediacy of message content (message content is not diluted because the system eliminates the need for messages to be relayed through the ranks). This direct communication system provides further support of Federal Express' commitment to its employees.[34]

The company has been committed to the goal of developing the leadership potential of its employees since its founding in 1973. One method that has proved highly successful is the executive retreat, or "wilderness experience."[35] This intensive program of outdoor activities helps people gain self-confidence in their ability to make quick decisions in a stressful environment. In 1986, the company implemented a leadership development program that combines elements of the wilderness experience concept with some classroom approaches to leadership training. This program, called "Exploring Leadership," focuses on four qualities the company believes a good leader must have: the ability to (1) understand others, (2) learn from the feedback of others, (3) understand one's self, and (4) calculate and take risks.[36] A fundamental philosophy practiced by the program's staff is that a person never fails when he or she tries, and that failure is guaranteed when he or she does not try. Participants have given the programs high marks.

Since treating employees properly is good for business and contributes to company profits, Federal Express developed a system in 1985 that will display, for each company unit, the correlations among profit margin, service levels, and human factor indices.[37] It is called the "Early Warning System" and is a combination of financial data, human resource records, and service information. Data available include such items as attitude surveys, involuntary termination rates, safety and security levels, effectiveness in administering performance and merit reviews, and success rates at providing required training and meeting regulatory prescriptions. Managers can get a monthly report indicating how the group compares with other units on the same level. Statistically significant differences can be investigated further to identify causes of the difference.

James Perkins, the company's chief personnel officer, views his position as one for boosting employee morale and making sure that the company achieves corporate excellence in its extremely competitive market.[38] He has been quite successful, as the company has been cited by numerous books and magazines as one of the best companies to work for. This holds particularly true for minorities and working mothers.

....

PRISM

Perkins keeps track of Federal Express employees on a $1-million employee tracking system he developed in 1982 called PRISM.[39] The database allows managers to access the pertinent information on in-house candidates for promotions. The system has been touted by many human resource experts as the best in the country, and other corporate entities such as Exxon, the FAA, and the U.S. Postal Service have been trying to adopt it.

Perkins instituted the company guaranteed fair treatment procedure in 1983.[40] This five-step employee complaint and grievance process is used to protest alleged unfair treatment on the job. Typical complaints pertain to salary levels, lack of opportunities to advance, or unfair disciplinary action. This procedure has also been hailed as one of the best systems in the country for employee complaint resolution. The objectivity and fairness of this procedure has been instrumental in keeping the company nonunion. Perkins feels Federal Express has created an environment where unions are unnecessary.[41]

The organization's corporate culture encourages and accepts employee honesty and recognizes and rewards a job well done. One such program called Star/Superstar was started in 1987.[42] Carriers and handlers can receive lump sum payments of up to 2 percent of their annual salary if they receive top rankings in their performance evaluations. Around 1980, the company also implemented the Survey Feedback Action Program, a series of employee surveys that seek to determine whether employees believe they are being adequately compensated and treated fairly by superiors.[43]

With innovative and successful programs and policies such as those discussed above, it is no wonder that Federal Express' employees are committed and extremely loyal to the company. Obviously, this commitment and loyalty works both ways.

· · · · · · · · · · · · · · · · ·
NOTES

1. Standard & Poors *Industry Surveys,* December 6, 1984, p. A36.

2. Geoffrey Colvin, "Federal Express Dives into Air Mail," *Fortune,* June 15, 1981, pp. 106–108.

3. Henry Altman, "A Business Visionary Who Really Delivered," *Nation's Business,* November, 1981, p. 50.

4. Geoffrey Colvin, "Federal Express Dives," p. 107.

5. Altman, "Business," p. 54.

6. "Creativity with Bill Moyers: Fred Smith and the Federal Express," *PBS Video,* 1981.

7. "The Memphis Connection," *Marketing and Media Decisions,* May 1982, p. 62.

8. Federal Express 1990 Annual Report, pp. 20,21.

9. Federal Express 1982 Annual Report, p. 14.

10. Colvin, "Federal Express Dives," p. 107.

11. Ibid., p. 108.

12. Federal Express 1990 Annual Report, p. 6.

13. Ibid., p. 6.

14. Colvin, "Federal Express Dives," pp. 6,7.

15. Ibid., p. 9.

16. Information in this section contained in the Federal Express 1990 Annual Report, pp. 17,18.

17. Sean Milmo, "British Air Couriers Welcome U.S. Entrant," *Business Marketing,* April 1984, p. 9.

18. Moody's *Transportation Manual,* 1990, p. 1173.

19. Ibid., 1990, pp. 1216,1217.

20. "Behind the UPS Mystique: Puritanism and Productivity," *Business Week,* June 6, 1983, p. 66.

21. Moody's *Transportation Manual,* 1990, pp. 1216,1217.

22. "Express Mail Next Day Service," *U.S. Postal Service Pamphlet Notice # 43,* July 1977, p. 2.

23. Moody's *Municipal & Government Manual,* 1990, p. 41.

24. "Express Mail Next Day Service," *U.S. Postal Service Pamphlet Notice # 43,* July 1977, p. 6.

25. Moody's *Municipal & Government Manual,* 1990, p. 41.

26. Emery Air Freight 1983 Annual Report, Introduction.

27. Moody's *Transportation Manual,* 1990, p. 1171.

28. Ibid., p. 1171.

29. Federal Express 1990 Annual Report, p. 27.

30. Ibid., p. 27.

31. Ibid., p. 16.

32. *Aviation Week & Space Technology,* February 2, 1987, p. 38.

33. *Personnel Journal,* October 1988, p. 18.

34. Ibid., p. 18.

35. *Personnel,* July 1986, p. 4.

36. *Personnel,* July 1986, p. 4.

37. *Personnel Administrator,* October 1985, p. 14.

38. *Black Enterprise,* June 1988, p. 308.

39. Ibid., p. 310.

40. Ibid., p. 312.

41. Ibid., p. 312.

42. Ibid., p. 312.

43. Ibid., p. 312.

CASE 2 Delta Air Lines, Inc.

Delta Air Lines is a certified trunk air carrier providing scheduled air transportation for passengers, freight, and mail over a network of routes throughout the United States and abroad.[1] These routes connect the Northeast and Midwest with the southern states; the Southeast to the Midwest, West, Northwest, and California; and the East Coast to Florida.[2] The company also operates flights to Canada, Bermuda, the Bahamas, France, Ireland, Japan, South Korea, Mexico, Taiwan, Puerto Rico, England, the Netherlands, Thailand, and West Germany.[3] As of June 30, 1990, the company provided air transportation to 148 domestic cities in 48 states, Washington, D.C., and Puerto Rico, and to 26 cities in 13 foreign countries.[4]

In these challenging times for the airline industry, Delta's strategic plan places a high priority on steady and cost effective growth.[5] This strategy is designed to maintain Delta's financial strength and flexibility, while keeping service to its passengers as its number one objective.[6] The following is an overview of Delta Air Lines from a strategic human resource perspective, since the key to Delta's success is the dedication of its more than 60,000 employees. These employees are committed to the highest standards of excellence in every area of Delta's operations.

HISTORY[7]

Delta Air Lines is one of the most successful air carriers in the United States. With the exception of 1983, the company has not lost money since 1947. The company was originally founded as a crop dusting service in 1924. This start resulted from a conversation between Collet Everman Woolman, an associate, and some Louisiana farmers concerned about the threat to their crops from boll weevils.

Woolman, an agricultural scientist and pilot, knew that calcium arsenate would kill boll weevils. The problem he faced was devising a way to apply the chemical effectively to crops. Woolman wanted to drop the chemical from an airplane and engineered a "hooper" for the chemical. After perfecting the system he began selling his services to farmers throughout the region, thus forming the world's first crop-dusting service.

Woolman left the agricultural extension service in 1925 to take charge of the duster's entomological work. The crop-dusting operation was separated from its parent company in 1928 to form a new company named Delta Air Service. Woolman expanded his crop-dusting business into Mexico, South America, and throughout the South. The company also diversified by securing air mail contracts. Passenger service was inaugurated in 1929, with initial service to Jackson, Dallas, Atlanta, and Charleston.

This case was prepared by Mark Dawkins.

Delta Air Service began its climb to prominence when it received a U.S. government airmail contract in 1930. The company, now called Delta Air Corporation, received three more airmail contracts by 1941. During World War II, the company, under contract to the War Department, devoted itself to the allied war effort by transporting troops and supplies. Delta returned to civilian service in 1945, entering an age of growth and competition never seen before in the airline industry.

Delta prospered as a major regional trunk carrier through the 1950s and 1960s. Several mergers were consummated during these two decades. On May 1, 1953, Delta merged with Chicago and Southern Airlines. In June of 1967, Delta merged with Delaware Airlines and officially adopted the name of Delta Air Lines.

Delta's exposure to the Northeast increased with the acquisition of Northeast Airlines on August 1, 1972. Delta also purchased Storer Leasing in July of 1976, a move that added several jets to the existing fleet of about 200. Delta formed two computerized marketing subsidiaries in the early 1980s to coordinate and sell more passenger seats on all Delta flights. These subsidiaries are named Epsilon Trading Corporation and Datas Incorporated.

Delta's consistent growth can be partially attributed to its successful transition of leadership. In the early days of commercial air transport, airlines were run by individual men who would be better described as aviation pioneers first and as businessmen second. For example, Woolman led Delta until his death in 1966, a period covering forty years. His influence at Delta is similar to the influence of his counterparts at Delta's three major competitors: Eddie Rickenbacker at Eastern, Juan Trippe at Pan Am, and Howard Hughes at TWA.

At Eastern, Pan Am, TWA, and Delta, these pioneers established almost dictatorial operations. They retained their posts as long as they possibly could. Many of these men were majority stockholders who refused to share their power or prepare a successor to operate the company after they died. As a result, many airline companies faced a difficult period of adjustment to new management after the chairman died.

Woolman's departure at Delta was not surrounded by difficulties. After suffering a heart attack, he was forced to relinquish some of his duties to other Delta board members. The board members gradually assumed more of his duties as his health deteriorated. Woolman died at the age of 76, and the airline was able to make a smooth transition to a more modern, corporate style of collective management.

Delta has adhered to the principles of its founder, C. E. Woolman, by placing a high value on people, both its customers and its personnel. Woolman used to ride on flights and mingle with passengers in an effort to gauge the public opinion concerning his airline. He was once quoted as saying, "We have a responsibility over and above the price of a ticket, let's put ourselves on the other side of the counter."

MANAGEMENT

Delta is recognized for having one of the best planning and management teams in the airline industry. Specifically, Delta's management is agile and responsive to problems that arise. Delta's sound financial policy allows greater flexibility in decision making, even at the highest levels. Also, its consensus-style of management affords Delta cohesiveness and enduring stability.

Delta's productivity in the "trunk," or domestic, airline business is the highest among major carriers. The company's employees are nonunionized, with the exception of pilots and dispatchers. The machinist union, for example, reports that it is difficult to organize Delta employees because the company maintains pay and benefits above its unionized competition. Clearly, workers have little incentive to unionize as long as the company outperforms union contracts.

Overall, management-employee relations are generally on very good terms. In the absence of union rules and constraints, employees regularly move to other positions in order to fill temporary labor shortages. The employees' willingness to adjust to the needs of the company gives Delta the unique ability to weather hardships in the airline industry and is a major reason why the company remains competitive.

The company's willingness to adjust to the needs of the employees has also not gone unnoticed. Delta is known for treating all of its employees as "family," and has gone a long way to avoid layoffs. For example, the airline refused to release workers during the 1973 oil crisis and the 1981 PATCO strike. Company profitability suffered as a result. However, employee commitment and loyalty is high as a result of Delta's willingness to support its work force in difficult times.

OPERATIONS

Delta was the first airline to employ the "hub-and-spoke" system. Under this system, a number of flights are scheduled to land at a hub airport within a 30-minute time-span. Passengers can then make connections for final destinations conveniently and quickly, thus avoiding long layovers. This process is known as the "big push," and is regarded by management as an effective marketing tool. The process, however, is not immune to problems caused by inclement weather or maintenance delays. Delta has hub operations in Atlanta, Dallas/Fort Worth, Boston, Memphis, and Cincinnati.

Delta's jetliner fleet is the most modern fleet in domestic service. The company's policy is to not purchase new models until they have been proven, often in a costly way, at other airlines. This "wait-and-see" policy has saved the company large amounts of money. It is typical of Delta that a 15-year strategy for flight equipment and support facility planning is used. Former vice-chairman and chief financial officer Robert Oppenlander once said that "success is based on the long-term maintenance of a technical edge, which is cost efficiency."

Delta is currently replacing its fleet of Boeing 727s with the 757, 767, and MD-88. During 1990, the company accepted delivery of 36 new aircraft: 3 international range B-767-300ERs, 10 B-757-200s, and 23 MD-88s.[8] These planes are technologically advanced and fuel efficient, and should serve the company for the next 20 years or longer. The company also completed an agreement with Boeing to purchase up to 113 B-737-300 airplanes. Negotiations are underway with McDonnell Douglas to contract and acquire up to 160 MD-90 airplanes and 2 additional MD-11 airplanes.[9] These purchase arrangements give Delta substantial flexibility in implementing its long-term growth plans.

Delta made large investments in 1990 to improve its competitive position and implement its strategic plan. Major investments included $1.42 billion in flight equipment, $265 million in ground property and equipment, $267 million to acquire equity interests in two international carriers, and $48 million to purchase an additional interest in a new computer reservation system partnership called WORLD-

SPAN.[10] This partnership (with Northwest Airlines and TWA) offers computerized reservations system (CRS) services to travel agents around the world, and it has begun to form links with other international CRS organizations.

To support its continued growth and to provide a separate data center for WORLDSPAN, Delta announced plans in 1990 to construct a new reservations office and a second computer center near its general office complex in Atlanta.[11] Renovations to other buildings are also planned. The company also purchased 23 acres of land adjacent to its general office complex for future growth. Construction of a hangar in which three airplanes at a time can be stripped and painted within a controlled environment began at the Technical Operations Center in Atlanta during 1990.[12] Other construction projects at this site include a wide-body hangar bay, a ground support equipment maintenance building, and expansion and renovation of certain shops and support facilities.

INDUSTRY EXPANSION

Delta has taken on a more aggressive corporate personality in recent years. The company's commitment to internal growth has been threatened by the general trend in the industry toward external growth. As a result, Delta is becoming relatively smaller as companies such as TWA, Texas Air, and Northwest expand through mergers.

Mergers and acquisitions are not foreign to Delta, however. David Garrett, Delta's retired chairman of the board and chief executive officer, once explained that "for a merger to be worthwhile, two plus two has to equal seven." A case in point is the 1986 purchase of Western Air Lines, another air carrier based in Los Angeles, for $680 million. This purchase added Western's hubs in Los Angeles and Salt Lake City to Delta's existing network.

International service is increasingly important to Delta's growth and development. Revenues from international operations increased significantly in 1990, reflecting Delta's growing presence in Asia, Europe, and Mexico.[13] That same year the company enplaned over one million passengers on its transatlantic flights for the first time in its history.[14] In an attempt to broaden its international base, Delta filed applications to serve West Berlin, Germany; Milan and Rome, Italy; Leningrad, Moscow and Tbilisi in the Soviet Union; Barcelona and Madrid, Spain; Manchester, England; and Hong Kong.[15] In addition, Delta hopes to commence service to Tokyo, Japan, soon.

In an effort to improve its ability to serve international travelers and shippers, Delta completed equity cross purchases with Swissair and Singapore Airlines.[16] These airlines are as committed to providing outstanding customer service as is Delta. Cooperative programs have been initiated to facilitate operational integration and reduce costs. These cooperative programs include promotions, code sharing, and employee cross training.[17] Future cooperative efforts include joint maintenance, technical development, and ground handling.

MARKETING

Delta continued to implement aggressive marketing programs in 1990. The company's major initiatives included strengthening its route system, solidifying its relationship with Swissair and Singapore Airlines via a cross-purchase arrangement, and enhancing its position in the computer reservations system market via WORLD-SPAN.[18]

Cooperative marketing programs planned with Swissair and Singapore Airlines include code sharing, schedule coordination, possible joint services on certain routes, around-the-world-fares, joint advertising and promotional activities, and Frequent Flyer programs.[19] Delta's Frequent Flyer program currently has over 6.8 million members.[20]

Advertising and promotional programs for the year supported Delta's marketing efforts for business and leisure travel, military and government travel, and package tours. Delta's Fantastic Flyer program for children, a natural tie-in with the company's official airline relationships with Walt Disney World in Florida and Disneyland in California, continues to be successful.[21] Other continuing official airline relationships include those with the Atlanta Braves, the Los Angeles Dodgers, The Professional Golf Association of America (PGA) and the PGA Tour, the Kentucky Derby, the Breeders Cup, the Portland Rose Festival, and the Tournament of Roses.[22]

Delta's cargo marketing efforts resulted in its being the second largest passenger/cargo combination carrier in terms of U.S. domestic mail ton miles (a measure of cargo volume).[23] Delta also led U.S. airlines in market share for both domestic and overseas military traffic.[24]

Delta added 138 flights and 15 new nonstop markets to its route system in 1990, bringing the company's average number of daily flights to 2,446.[25] The Delta Connection airlines—Atlantic Southeast Airlines, Business Express, Comair, and Sky West—continued to expand their services and connecting traffic at the company's major hubs. These carriers provided over 1,800 daily departures to 188 cities and delivered over 1.4 million connecting passengers to Delta flights.[26]

FINANCIAL CONDITION

Delta is known for having the most conservative balance sheet in the industry. The company's debt-to-equity ratio is consistently below one to one, enabling the company to do most of its financing internally. Selected financial results for Delta Air Lines are presented in Exhibits 4 through 11. As previously indicated, the company has not lost money since 1947, with the exception of 1983.

HUMAN RESOURCE ISSUES

As previously stated, Delta is largely nonunion. Despite being nonunion, however, the company does not exploit its workers. In fact, Delta's employees are some of the highest paid among the major carriers. They earn approximately 21 percent more than the industry average.[27] This favorable pay rate and absence of restrictive union rules results in good employee morale, which leads to high productivity and good service.[28] The good service rendered by employees has resulted in Delta having the fewest number of consumer complaints of any major carrier for the past 16 years.[29]

As Russell Heil, Delta's executive vice-president of operations and personnel, puts it, "Passenger airlines are a tough industry, because you have to provide the best possible service or you lose your customers. And it's the individual employee who is the key in that process. The company expects performance from employees,

| EXHIBIT 4 | Summary Operating and Nonoperating Results |

	1990	1989	1988	1987
Operating revenue	$8,582,231	$8,089,484	$6,915,377	$5,318,172
Operating expenses	8,162,719	7,411,159	6,418,293	4,913,647
Operating income	419,512	678,325	497,084	404,525
Net income	302,783	460,918	306,826	263,729
Income per share	5.28	9.37	6.30	5.90
Total dividends paid	84,550	59,054	58,456	44,397
Dividends per share	1.20	1.20	1.20	1.00
S/E per share	56.32	53.17	44.99	39.84
Average shares outstanding	46,086,110	49,265,884	48,706,851	44,712,993
Debt-to-equity	34%/66%	22%/78%	25%/75%	35%/65%
Flyers enplaned	67,240,233	64,242,212	58,564,507	48,172,626
Flyer miles (000)	58,986,912	55,903,857	49,009,094	38,415,117
Available miles (000)	96,463,052	90,741,541	85,833,959	69,013,669
Flyer mile yield	13.63	13.56	13.15	12.81
Flyer load factor	61.15%	61.61%	57.10%	55.66%
B/E load factor	57.96%	56.09%	52.69%	51.09%
Cargo ton miles (000)	790,697	744,474	652,833	480,969
Cargo yield/ton mile	52.63	52.88	53.58	58.27
Fuel gallons (000)	1,965,602	1,862,770	1,753,538	1,435,801
Price per gallon	62.71	53.08	56.09	46.80
Flyer miles/gallon	30.0	30.0	27.9	26.8
Available miles/gallon	49.1	48.7	49.0	48.1
Available seats/mile	168.9	169.4	169.0	169.2
Cost per seat mile	8.46	8.17	7.48	7.12
Average flyer trip (miles)	877	870	837	797
Average flight (miles)	665	657	640	617
Plane utilization (Hours per day)	8.82	8.75	8.62	8.37

Note: Dollar amounts are in thousands, except per share figures.

and in turn Delta provides the best possible work situation and compensation for its employees."[30]

Delta also has the unique distinction of never having laid off an employee.[31] States Heil, "We have a strict no-furlough policy. Delta has never had to furlough any employees and that really means a lot to the employees and its a great boost to morale."[32] This human resource practice translates into contented workers, who repay the company's loyalty to them with loyalty of their own.[33] The company gets increased productivity from its employees by having them perform multiple jobs (such as ticket agent and baggage handler). This is only possible because the company is free from the restrictive rules associated with unions. As Chairman and Chief Executive Ronald Allen says, "This is a people business. You're serving customers. We want to do it in a courteous way. If you want to do that, you must have a loyal, dedicated crew."[34]

··

| EXHIBIT 5 | Earnings and Dividends |

	1990	1989	1988	1987
Operation income	$419,512	$678,325	$497,084	$404,525
Other income (expense):				
Interest expense	(83,937)	(70,647)	(97,533)	(94,000)
Less: Interest capital	57,226	31,778	32,329	32,092
	(26,711)	(38,869)	(65,204)	(61,908)
Gain (loss) on flight equipment	17,906	16,562	(1,016)	96,270
Miscellaneous income (net)	57,205	55,200	24,992	8,312
	48,400	32,893	(41,228)	42,674
Income before taxes	467,912	711,218	455,856	447,199
Income taxes	(186,722)	(279,214)	(180,851)	(219,715)
Amortization of ITCs	21,593	28,914	31,821	36,245
Net income	302,783	460,918	306,826	263,729
Preferred dividends (net)	(18,144)	0	0	0
Net income, common	284,639	460,918	306,826	263,729
Net income per share	$5.28	$9.37	$6.30	$5.90
Average shares outstanding	46,086,110	49,265,884	48,706,851	44,712,993

Note: In thousands of dollars, except per share amounts.

··

Heil takes great pride in the people of Delta Airlines. He believes that the company's employees have made the airline one of the most successful in the history of aviation.[35] His experience with Delta during the early 1970s oil embargo, during which pilots and flight attendants had to be reassigned but no jobs were lost, helped him realize how much Delta cared about its staff. "I learned then that when people know you really care and are willing to do everything to save their jobs, they are willing to work that much harder for you."[36]

Heil landed his first job with Delta as an aircraft performance engineer after an eight-month tour of duty in Vietnam.[37] After completing his MBA he became an administrative assistant at Delta. He was asked to help with the personnel function on a temporary basis after the company merged with Northeast Airlines in 1972.[38] The arrangement was so satisfactory to both parties that the job became permanent. Heil became senior vice-president of personnel for Delta after the then senior vice-president of personnel, Ron Allen, was named president and chief operating officer for Delta.[39] Allen later became chairman and chief executive officer for Delta.

"Ron Allen's appointment as president and then chairman of the board proves Delta's commitment to human resources," says Heil. "It is very rare in any industry, especially airlines, that the chief executive officer comes from the personnel function."[40] In fact, two of the company's last three chief executive officers came from the airline's personnel function. Heil attributes this fact to the company's philosophy and personnel policy, the essence of which is that airlines are basically alike and people make them different.[41] Delta strives to ensure that it has the best people on the job.

| EXHIBIT 6 | Operating Revenues and Statistics | | | |

(In thousands)	1990	1989	1988	1987
Passenger	$8,042,496	$7,579,716	$6,443,111	$4,921,852
Freight	300,969	273,930	225,382	178,407
Mail	115,199	119,732	124,393	101,864
Other, net	123,567	116,106	122,491	116,049
Total	$8,582,231	$8,089,484	$6,915,377	$5,318,172
Flyer miles	58,986,912	55,903,857	49,009,094	38,415,117
Flyers enplaned	67,240,233	64,242,212	58,564,507	48,172,626
Flyer load factor	61.15%	61.61%	57.10%	55.66%
Flyer mile yield	13.63	13.56	13.15	12.81
Freight ton miles	546,739	507,861	427,483	313,457
Mail ton miles	243,958	236,613	225,350	167,512
Freight yield/mile	55.05	53.94	52.72	56.92
Mail yield/mile	47.22	50.60	55.20	60.81

Note: Miles in thousands.

Heil demonstrates a genuine concern for Delta's employees. According to Maurice Worth, Delta's vice-president of personnel, "Russ is extremely sensitive to the concerns of our people and I think most of our employees here realize and appreciate that. . . . You can't be around him and not feel good about Delta and the way the airline handles its employees."[42] Worth adds that Heil is "always willing to go that extra mile for the employees. He wouldn't ask his staff to do anything that he wouldn't do himself."[43] This trait, combined with his excellent communication skills makes Heil an effective leader. "He will always let you know what's happening and why it's happening," Worth said.[44]

Heil feels that communication is the most important part of his job because he serves as the fundamental link between Delta's employees and upper management.[45] Heil says that the most important lesson he has learned while working at Delta is that communication is essential.[46] ". . . Most of the problems between management and employees are just a lack of communication. . . . If you can identify the problems and communicate why certain decisions were made, you can avoid bigger and more costly problems later . . . It is most important we continue communicating with our employees."[47]

Heil has also helped develop several programs and policies at Delta. These include an open-door policy through which an employee can speak with anyone in management concerning questions or problems.[48] Delta also holds personnel/employee meetings about every six weeks. These meetings, which are run by department heads, update employees on the company's financial picture and other topics of interest, such as new equipment and aircraft.[49] A question-and-answer period is conducted after each meeting. Questions that cannot be answered during the meeting are directed to the appropriate department and the response is relayed to the employees as quickly as possible.[50]

> >

EXHIBIT 7   Operating Expenses and Statistics

	1990	1989	1988	
Salaries	$3,425,865	$3,122,279	$2,703,462	$2,228,814
Aircraft fuel	1,232,561	988,734	983,590	672,004
Maintenance	241,024	224,500	208,483	127,856
Aircraft rent	325,781	329,763	256,656	150,653
Facility rent	219,761	206,429	178,639	145,473
Landing fees	137,278	119,850	109,724	89,519
Flyer services	367,504	341,296	290,575	219,834
Flyer commissions	768,140	747,269	616,629	432,066
Depreciation/amortization	459,162	393,095	354,087	277,975
Other	985,643	937,944	716,448	569,453
Total	$8,162,719	$7,411,159	$6,418,293	$4,913,647
Plane miles	571,265	535,619	507,811	407,773
Available miles	96,463,052	90,741,541	85,833,959	69,013,669
Available ton miles	12,499,745	11,724,797	11,249,578	8,999,668
Fuel gallons	1,965,602	1,862,770	1,753,538	1,435,801
Price per gallon	62.71	53.08	56.09	46.80
Flyer load factor	61.15%	61.61%	57.10%	55.66%
B/E load factor	57.96%	56.09%	52.69%	51.09%
Cost per seat mile	8.46	8.17	7.48	7.12

Note: Miles and gallons in thousands.

> >

NOTES

1. Moody's Transportation Manual, 1990.

2. Standard and Poor's Corporate Record.

3. Ibid.

4. Moody's Transportation Manual, 1990.

5. 1990 Annual Report, p. 3.

6. Ibid.

7. The history section is principally a reproduction of Delta's corporate history as compiled by the *International Directory of Company Histories,* 1988, Vol. 1, pp. 99–100.

8. 1990 Annual Report, p. 2.

9. Ibid.

10. Ibid.

11. Ibid., p. 16.

12. Ibid.

13. Ibid., p. 2.

14. Ibid., p. 13.

15. Ibid., p. 2.

16. Ibid., p. 3.

17. Ibid.

18. Ibid., p. 13.

19. Ibid., p. 14.

20. Ibid.

21. Ibid.

22. Ibid.

23. Ibid.

24. Ibid.

25. Ibid., p. 13.

26. Ibid., p. 14.

27. Seth Lubove, "Full Speed Ahead—but Cautiously," *Forbes,* October 29, 1990, pp. 36–38.

28. Ibid.

29. Ibid.

30. Bill Leonard, "Making the Message Clear," *Personnel Administrator,* November 1989, pp. 47–49.

31. Ibid.

32. Ibid.

33. *Forbes,* October 29, 1990, p. 37.

34. Ibid.

35. *Personnel Administrator,* November 1989, p. 47.

36. Ibid., p. 48.

37. Ibid., p. 47.

38. Ibid., p. 48.

39. Ibid.

40. Ibid.

EXHIBIT 8   Flight Equipment and Purchase Commitments
(as of June 30, 1990)

TYPE	SEATS	OWNED	LEASED	TOTAL
B-727-200	148	106	23	129
B-737-200	107	1	58	59
B-737-300	128	—	13	13
B-757-200	187	35	25	60
B-767-200	204	15	—	15
B-767-300	254	—	15	15
B-767-300ER	218	3	—	3
DC-9-32	98	31	5	36
L-1011-1	302	22	—	22
L-1011-100/200	300	1	—	1
L-1011-250	260/295	6	—	6
L-1011-500	213/233/237	11	—	11
MD-88	142	30	33	63
Total		261	172	433

| | | | | ORDERS | | |
DELIVERY IN YEAR ENDING JUNE 30:	BOEING B-737-300	BOEING B-757-200	BOEING B-767-300	BOEING B-767-300ER	MCDON DOUG. MD-88	MCDON DOUG. MD-11
1991	—	9	6	6	20	—
1992	—	9	3	—	8	6
1993	3	—	—	—	—	3
1994	10	—	—	—	—	—
1995	9	—	—	—	—	—
After 1995	35	—	—	—	—	—
Total	57	18	9	6	28	9

| | | | | OPTIONS | | |
DELIVERY IN YEAR ENDING JUNE 30:	BOEING B-737-300	BOEING B-757-200	BOEING B-767-300	BOEING B-767-300ER	MCDON DOUG. MD-88	MCDON DOUG. MD-11
1991	—	—	—	—	—	—
1992	—	—	—	—	14	—
1993	—	6	3	2	15	—
1994	—	8	—	3	15	2
1995	—	7	—	3	15	2
After 1995	56	31	—	8	60	27
Total	56	52	3	16	119	31

41. Ibid.
42. Ibid.
43. Ibid., p. 49.
44. Ibid.
45. Ibid.

46. Ibid.
47. Ibid.
48. Ibid.
49. Ibid.
50. Ibid.

··

EXHIBIT 9 Consolidated Balance Sheet

	1990	1989	1988	1987
Current assets:				
Cash	$ 68,457	$ 529,657	$ 822,791	$ 379,928
Accounts receivable (net)	726,105	752,154	644,527	626,139
Supplies	68,344	57,024	52,413	42,337
Prepaid expenses	155,127	135,937	131,507	131,170
Total current assets	1,018,033	1,474,772	1,651,238	1,179,574
Property and equipment:				
Flight equipment	6,399,117	5,402,865	4,624,630	4,485,898
Less: Accounts depreciation	2,568,655	2,298,172	2,125,879	1,951,494
	3,830,462	3,104,693	2,498,751	2,534,404
Leased flight equipment	173,284	173,284	221,811	221,811
Less: Accounts amortization	71,356	51,014	54,461	16,307
	101,928	122,270	167,350	205,504
Ground property	1,617,786	1,469,870	1,222,314	1,078,185
Less: Accounts depreciation	707,242	634,783	548,499	451,643
	910,544	835,087	673,815	626,542
Equal prepayments	556,006	415,823	226,319	307,461
Total property and equipment	5,398,940	4,477,873	3,566,235	3,673,911
Other assets:				
Market securities	244,092	0	0	0
Investment in companies	167,402	66,651	63,017	55,427
Goodwill (net)	309,358	317,853	326,348	371,756
Prepaid pension costs	0	72,247	83,680	0
Other	89,177	74,590	57,837	61,715
Total other assets	810,029	531,341	530,882	488,898
Total assets	$7,227,002	$6,483,986	$5,748,355	$5,342,383

Note: In thousands.

··

| EXHIBIT 10 | Liabilities and Stockholders' Equity |

	1990	1989	1988	1987
Current liabilities:				
Current long-term debt	$ 27,593	$ 5,516	$ 5,491	$ 8,406
Current leases	12,495	11,343	14,793	12,921
Short-term borrowings	65,351	0	16,163	25,836
Accounts payable	717,065	711,042	558,619	455,686
Air traffic liability	738,477	746,111	504,083	506,669
Accrued vacation	145,209	132,472	118,344	110,835
Transportation tax payment	78,668	83,083	67,396	60,705
Accrued income tax	47,783	73,242	107,041	0
Total current liabilities	1,832,641	1,762,809	1,391,930	1,181,058
Noncurrent liabilities:				
Long-term debt	1,180,909	556,770	563,129	837,201
Capital leases	134,290	146,244	166,364	181,216
Other	208,784	160,037	72,937	80,320
	1,523,983	863,051	802,430	1,098,737
Deferred credits:				
Income taxes	505,972	519,052	539,908	590,876
Unamortization ITCs	26,572	48,323	79,257	98,525
Manufacturing credits	119,681	121,921	151,976	137,611
Sale/leaseback gain	596,653	545,270	569,279	297,050
Other	3,298	3,853	4,752	614
	1,252,176	1,238,419	1,345,172	1,124,676
Commitments and contingencies:				
ESOP Preferred stock	500,000	0	0	0
Less: Unearned	477,367	0	0	0
	22,633	0	0	0
Common stockholders' equity:				
Common stock (par)	163,040	147,798	147,304	145,918
APIC	879,660	514,079	505,553	484,398
Retained earnings	2,157,919	1,957,830	1,555,966	1,307,596
Less: Loss on MES	13,896	0	0	0
Treasury stock	591,154	0	0	0
	2,595,569	2,619,707	2,208,823	1,937,912
Total liabilities and stockholders' equity	$7,227,002	$6,483,986	$5,748,355	$5,342,383

Note: In thousands.

EXHIBIT 11

Consolidated Statements of Income

	1990	1989	1988	1987
Operating revenues:				
Passenger	$8,042,496	$7,579,716	$6,443,111	$4,921,852
Freight	300,969	273,930	225,382	178,407
Mail	115,199	119,732	124,393	101,864
Other, net	123,567	116,106	122,491	116,049
Total	8,582,231	8,089,484	6,915,377	5,318,172
Operating expenses:				
Salaries	3,425,865	3,122,279	2,703,462	2,228,814
Aircraft fuel	1,232,561	988,734	983,590	672,004
Maintenance	241,024	224,500	208,483	127,856
Aircraft rent	325,781	329,763	256,656	150,653
Facility rent	219,761	206,429	178,639	145,473
Landing fees	137,278	119,850	109,724	89,519
Flyer services	367,504	341,296	290,575	219,834
Flyer commissions	768,140	747,269	616,629	432,066
Depreciation/amortization	459,162	393,095	354,087	277,975
Other	985,643	937,944	716,448	569,453
Total	8,162,719	7,411,159	6,418,293	4,913,647
Operating income	419,512	678,325	497,084	404,525
Other income (expenses):				
Interest expenses	(83,937)	(70,647)	(97,533)	(94,000)
Less: Interest capital	57,226	31,778	32,329	32,092
	(26,711)	(38,869)	(65,204)	(61,908)
Gain (loss) on flight equipment	17,906	16,562	(1,016)	96,270
Miscellaneous income (net)	57,205	55,200	24,992	8,312
	48,400	32,893	(41,228)	42,674
Income before taxes	467,912	711,218	455,856	447,199
Income taxes	(186,722)	(279,214)	(180,851)	(219,715)
Amortization of ITCs	21,593	28,914	31,821	36,245
Net income	302,783	460,918	306,826	263,729
Preferred dividends (net)	(18,144)	0	0	0
Net income/common	284,639	460,918	306,826	263,729
Net income per share	$5.28	$9.37	$6.30	$5.90

Note: In thousands, except per share amounts.

CASE 3 McDonald's Corporation

....

INTRODUCTION

History

McDonald's is the largest fast-food chain in the world. It has become a leading institution and symbol of American culture since it burst onto the scene in the mid-1950s. Its computerized, standardized operations and premeasured servings have been labeled "quintessentially American,"[1] and its restaurants have been hailed as "monuments to our culture!"[2] The company philosophy of Q.S.C.&V. (Quality food; fast, friendly service; restaurant cleanliness; and a menu that provides value) and its family-oriented image are the product of a Mr. Ray Kroc.

The first McDonald's was a drive-in restaurant started in San Bernardino, California, by two brothers, Dick and Mac McDonald, in 1948. Ray Kroc, the man who made McDonald's the household name it is today, became a franchising agent for the McDonald brothers in 1954 and opened his first McDonald's in Illinois in 1955. The McDonald brothers sold the company to Ray Kroc in 1961 for $2.7 million. In 1990 alone McDonald's generated over $6.5 billion in total revenues.[3] The company menu, which originally consisted of only hamburgers, cheeseburgers, french fries, sodas, milkshakes, milk, and coffee, has grown considerably since.

A more technical definition of McDonald's would be "an organization that develops, operates, franchises, and services a worldwide system of restaurants that prepare, assemble, package, and sell a limited menu of quickly prepared, moderately priced foods. These restaurants are operated by the company, or, under the terms of franchise arrangements, by franchisees who are independent third parties, or by affiliates operating under joint venture agreements between the company and local business people. The company has uniform standards for quality, service, cleanliness, and value."[4]

Financial Information

Most aspects of McDonald's consolidated balance sheet (see Exhibit 12) and consolidated statement of income (see Exhibit 13) reflect the company's growth. Current assets in 1990 increased 11 percent over the previous year, with total revenues increasing 9.4 percent and net income increasing 10 percent.

Average sales at restaurants open at least one year were $1,649,000 for 1990, a $28,000 increase over 1989. However, the majority of McDonald's growth was due

This case was prepared by Alexandra Orsin, Mike Martin, Ken Nielson, and Robert Graves.

EXHIBIT 12	Assets, Liabilities, and Shareholders' Equity		

BALANCE SHEET (IN MILLIONS OF DOLLARS)	DEC 31, 1990	DEC 31, 1989
Assets		
Current assets		
Cash equivalents	142.8	136.9
Accounts receivable	222.1	207.2
Notes receivable	32.9	27.2
Inventories, at cost, not in excess of market	42.9	46.1
Prepaid expenses and other current assets	108.3	77.3
Total current assets	549.0	494.7
Other assets and deferred charges		
Notes receivable due after one year	102.2	75.8
Investments in and advances to affiliates	335.2	290.5
Miscellaneous	250.0	229.6
Total other assets and deferred charges	687.4	595.9
Property and equipment		
Property and equipment, at cost	11,535.5	9,873.9
Accumulated depreciation and amortization	(2,488.4)	(2,115.6)
Net property and equipment	9,047.1	7,758.3
Intangible assets, net	384.0	326.1
Total assets	10,667.5	9,175.0
Liabilities and shareholders' equity		
Current liabilities		
Notes payable	299.0	75.8
Accounts payable	355.7	386.1
Income Taxes	82.6	70.7

to higher sales on the international market. The company intends to add about 600 restaurants per year, including further acceleration outside of the United States.[5]

Company-operated margins decreased slightly as a percentage of sales. However, the consistency of margins over the years illustrates McDonald's ability to compensate for escalating costs by generating greater customer traffic, improving operating efficiencies, and adjusting menu prices. Labor costs have been influenced by unemployment levels and minimum-wage legislation, though the impact of such legislation is not expected to be significant.[6] McDonald's labor cost as a percentage of sales in 1980 was 22.5 percent (Burger King's was 25 percent) and in 1990 was 22.3 percent (Burger King's was 28 percent).[7]

Historical Growth

McDonald's strategy for growth focuses on three key elements: adding restaurants, maximizing sales and profits at existing restaurants, and improving international profitability.

EXHIBIT 12 continued

BALANCE SHEET (IN MILLIONS OF DOLLARS)	DEC 31, 1990	DEC 31, 1989
Other taxes	68.6	66.7
Accrued interest	133.2	134.8
Other accrued liabilities	194.9	173.5
Current maturities of long-term debt	64.7	58.6
Total current liabilities	1,198.7	966.2
Long-term debt	4,428.7	3,902.0
Security deposits by franchisees and other long-term liabilities	162.7	143.3
Deferred income taxes	695.1	613.1
Shareholders' equity		
Preferred stock, no par value; authorized 165 million shares; issued 6.9 and 7 million	199.7	200.0
Guarantee of ESOP Notes	(196.5)	(199.2)
Common stock, no par value; authorized 1.25 billion shares; issued 415.2 million	46.2	46.2
Additional paid-in capital	173.7	158.9
Retained earnings	5,214.5	4,545.5
Equity adjustment from foreign currency translation	46.7	(29.0)
	5,484.3	4,722.4
Common stock in treasury, at cost; 56.1 and 53.3 million shares	(1,302.0)	(1,172.0)
Total shareholders' equity	4,182.3	3,550.4
Total liabilities and shareholders' equity	10,667.5	9,175.0

Adding restaurants can be achieved with our people and capital resources. Maximizing sales and profits at existing restaurants can be accomplished through better operations, reinvestment, product development, effective marketing, and lower development costs. Improving international profitability can be realized as economies of scale are achieved in individual markets.[8]

In 1967 McDonald's moved into Canada and Puerto Rico, the first countries outside of the United States to have a McDonald's franchise. McDonald's operated 8,576 restaurants in the United States in 1990, a growth of 18 percent in the past five years. In the same time frame, restaurants in the international market increased 50 percent to number 3,227 (see Exhibit 14).

Franchise

The unprecedented growth of the McDonald's Corporation is due largely to its successful use of franchisee entrepreneurs to promote the McDonald's product. McDonald's is highly selective in choosing its franchisees—it sends 20,000 brochures

EXHIBIT 13 Revenues and Income

BALANCE SHEET (IN MILLIONS OF DOLLARS)	DEC 31, 1990	DEC 31, 1989	
STATEMENT OF INCOME (IN MILLIONS OF DOLLARS)	DEC 31, 1990	DEC 31, 1989	DEC 31, 1988
Revenues			
Sales by company-operated restaurants	5,018.9	4,600.9	4,196.1
Revenues from franchised restaurants	1,620.7	1,464.7	1,324.7
Total revenues	6,639.6	6,065.6	5,520.8
Operating costs and expenses			
Company-operated restaurants			
Food and packaging	1,683.4	1,560.3	1,441.7
Payroll and other employee benefits	1,291.0	1,174.4	1,074.1
Occupancy and other operating expenses	1,161.2	1,043.1	936.7
	4,135.6	3,777.8	3,452.5
Franchised restaurants-occupancy expenses	279.2	240.6	217.5
General, administrative and selling expenses	724.2	656.0	606.3
Other operating (income) expense—net	(95.3)	(46.5)	(43.1)
Total operating costs and expenses	5,043.7	4,627.9	4,233.2
Operating income	1,595.9	1,437.7	1,287.6
Interest expense-net of capitalized interest of $36.0, $29.8, and $29.6	381.2	301.9	237.3
Other nonoperating income (expense)—net	31.6	21.4	(3.8)
Income before provision for income taxes	1,246.3	1,157.2	1,046.5
Provision for income taxes	444.0	430.5	400.6
Net income	802.3	726.7	645.9
Net income per common share	2.2	2.0	1.7
Dividends per common share	0.3	0.3	0.3

each year to interested parties and receives 5,000 applications for 100 new placements. Before franchisees open their restaurant, they generally spend more than two years in training and work about 2,000 uncompensated hours in a McDonald's restaurant.

A franchise arrangement is generally for a term of 20 years and requires an investment of approximately $610,000, 60 percent of which may be financed. In addition, a business facilities lease arrangement enables individuals who do not have sufficient capital, but who meet all other criteria, to become franchisees. Candidates for this program generally must have liquid assets of approximately $66,000.

With limited exceptions, McDonald's does not supply food, paper, or equipment to any of its restaurants, but approves suppliers from which franchised and company-operated restaurants can purchase these items. Franchisees are required to pay related occupancy costs, which include property taxes, insurance, maintenance, and a refundable, noninterest-bearing security deposit.[9]

Revenues from franchised restaurants are based on fees paid as a percent of sales, with specified minimum payments. Expenses associated with these restaurants are rent and depreciation, which are relatively fixed. Accordingly, the franchise margins are positively impacted by increases in sales, yet protected from rises in operating costs. Fees from franchisees to McDonald's typically include rent and service fees, often totaling at least 11.5 percent of sales.

Product

McDonald's restaurants offer a substantially uniform menu consisting of hamburgers and cheeseburgers. Menu items include the Big Mac, Quarter Pounder, and McLean Deluxe sandwiches, the Filet-O-Fish and McChicken sandwiches, french fries, Chicken McNuggets, salads, lowfat milk shakes, sundaes and cones, pies, cookies, and a limited number of soft drinks and other beverages. McDonald's restaurants in the United States, and some overseas, offer a full breakfast menu that includes the Egg Mc-Muffin, hotcakes, sausage, eggs, cereal, and apple-bran muffins. The company tests new products on an ongoing basis.[10]

Competition

McDonald's competes with international, national, and regional restaurants and carry-out operations and with locally owned businesses, drive-ins, and other such establishments.[11] In the United States, about 376,000 restaurants generate about $180 billion in annual sales. Competitors include, but are not limited to, Kentucky Fried Chicken, Burger King, Wendy's, Hardees, and Taco Bell.

Employees

Employees of eating and drinking establishments are paid considerably less than are employees of any other nonagricultural industry. Most of the employees are students and other young people working for the first time with an average work week of less than 26 hours.[12] Wages in the fast food industry in the United States are largely unaffected by collective bargaining or the threat of unionization with the exception of one Burger King in Detroit.[13]

The typical McDonald's restaurant has sixty employees and a $350,000 payroll with $1.6 million in sales. In 1989, when minimum wage was $3.35 an hour, McDonald's average hourly wage was $4.60 an hour.[14]

Managers in company-owned stores in 1989 average $28,000 a year. A profit-sharing plan contributed an additional 14 to 14.5 percent to the managers' compensation. Managers were also entitled to stock options in some cases.[15]

McDonald's employee strategy hinges on its ability to infuse every store with its gung-ho culture and standardized procedures. Every job is broken down into the smallest of steps, and the whole process is automated. So rule bound is McDonald's, that one sociologist recently claimed jobs in its restaurants are unfit for young people. "These are breeding grounds for robots working for yesterday's assembly lines, not tomorrow's high-tech posts," contends Professor Anitai Ezioni of George Washington University.[16]

··

| EXHIBIT 14 | (a) Number of Restaurants in the United States |
| (b) Number of Restaurants in Foreign Markets |

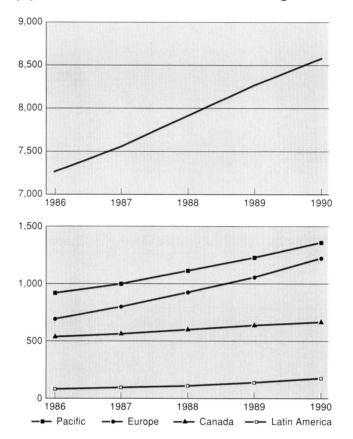

-■- Pacific -●- Europe -▲- Canada -□- Latin America

··

Agency Costs

One relevant market parameter that can make agency costs high is the physical dispersion of operations. Franchising avoids the monitoring costs of specialization because the local manager is now an investor whose wealth is strongly dependent on the performance of her or his local unit, thus making franchising more common with physically dispersed operations, as in rural areas. Also, for a given level of output, monitoring costs will rise with an increasing labor/output ratio. Using local managers who make heavy site-specific investments and post a large bond in the form of a franchise fee makes quality debasing less likely, because a franchisee has much more to lose upon termination than a local employee-manager.[17]

Turnover

McDonald's finds a strong link between the quality of its labor force at the store level and the sales of a given restaurant. Michael Quinlan, chief executive officer

EXHIBIT 14 continued   (c) Domestic and International Change in Number of Restaurants

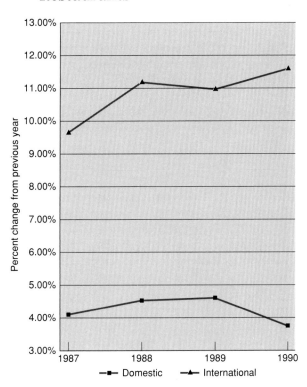

Percent change from previous year

—■— Domestic   —▲— International

for McDonald's, has indicated that reducing turnover is a key priority for the chain. In 1989, turnover was 130 percent, down from 180 percent five years prior.

OVERALL CORPORATE STRATEGY

McDonald's is the largest food service organization in the world with nearly 12,000 stores. Its goal has been to provide the highest quality products, friendly service, in clean restaurants, at good values (Q.S.C.&V.). To meet this goal, McDonald's current strategies have focused on the following.

Customer Satisfaction

McDonald's was founded on the principle of uniformity. An operations manual of 600 pages ensured the consistency and quality of products served by McDonald's. While this strategy worked well in the past, customers are now demanding more than consistency. In response to the changing market, McDonald's has taken a "do whatever it takes to make a customer happy"[18] strategy and has given its employees, managers, and stores the flexibility to carry out this new strategy.

Healthier Foods

Customers are demanding that restaurants provide healthier foods. McDonald's has heard their cry, and it has changed the way foods are prepared: hamburgers are made with lean ground beef and enriched sandwich buns, french fries and hash browns are fried in 100 percent vegetable oil, milk shakes are made with 1% lowfat milk, and the amount of sodium used has been decreased. It has also added more nutritious foods to the menu: whole-grain breakfast cereals, apple bran muffins, fresh fruit and vegetables, and lowfat frozen yogurt. As one advertisement states, "McDonald's is committed to making sure that when you've got an appetite for healthy food, [McDonald's will] always have the choices to satisfy you."[19]

Larger Menus

In addition to healthy foods, customers want more choices. In response, McDonald's added a breakfast menu that included eggs, sausage, biscuits, Canadian ham, rolls, pancakes, and cereals. Other items, such as chicken fajitas, Chicken McNuggets and McRibs, have also been added. In fact, "McDonald's kitchens are developing more than 150 new menu items,"[20] which include pizza, lasagna, egg rolls, and corn on the cob.

Restaurant Diversity

When Ray Kroc was CEO of McDonald's, each restaurant looked the same and served the same food. He wanted products to look and taste the same no matter where the customer was. In the 1990s, the customer wants more than fast food. Michael Quinlan, the current CEO, has recognized these changes and is allowing individual stores to experiment with their formats. The new store formats that are being tested include self-service stores, drive-thru only stores, cafes, and customized outlets. Flexibility also exists in selecting menu items. Stores no longer have to carry a standard menu. Franchisees can experiment with new items and alter the menu to conform to regional and ethnic tastes.

Diversification

According to projections, the U.S. population in the 5- to 14-year old age group is expected to grow at over 14 percent through the year 2000 (see Exhibit 15). Since children help make 36.6 percent of the family dining decisions,[21] McDonald's has targeted them with nonfood-related products. It has installed playlands at its stores, marketed McDonald's clothes and toys, and started a new venture called Leaps and Bounds that allows parents and children to play together. McDonald's hopes that this strategy of diversification will make children think of McDonald's when it is time to eat.

Untapped Markets

The dinner and international markets have remained virtually untapped by McDonald's and new strategies are focusing on penetrating these markets.

| EXHIBIT 15 | United States Population Projections |

	1990		1995		2000	
AGE GROUP	NUMBER (THOUSANDS)	% CHANGE TOTAL	NUMBER (THOUSANDS)	% CHANGE TOTAL	NUMBER (THOUSANDS)	% CHANGE TOTAL
Under 5	19,198	7.7	18,615	7.2	17,626	6.6
15 to 19	16,968	6.8	16,968	6.5	18,943	7.1
20 to 24	18,580	7.4	17,142	6.6	17,145	6.4
25 to 29	21,522	8.6	18,822	7.3	17,396	6.5
30 to 34	22,007	8.8	21,698	8.4	19,019	7.1
35 to 39	20,001	8.0	22,052	8.5	21,753	8.1
40 to 44	17,846	7.1	19,945	7.7	21,990	8.2
45 to 49	13,980	5.6	17,678	6.8	19,763	7.4
50 to 54	11,422	4.6	13,719	5.3	17,356	6.6
55 to 64	21,051	8.4	20,923	8.1	23,767	8.9
65 and over	31,697	12.7	33,888	13.1	34,921	13.0
All ages	249,656	99.9	259,559	100.2	267,956	100.2

Dinner

Currently, McDonald's dinner sales are only 20 percent of daily sales.[22] In order to boost this figure, McDonald's has plans to offer a separate dinner menu that will include roast chicken and spaghetti with meatballs. More than a dinner menu is needed, however. The proper atmosphere needs to be created. "People's expectations at dinner are totally different than at lunch."[23] "Evidence suggests that diners often want full course meals with table service, and maybe even a cocktail or two."[24] Dinner at McDonald's is an eventual reality, even though the specifics are still unknown.

International

The domestic operations have not fared well in recent years. Operating income has been declining,[25] market share is being eroded by heavy competition (see Exhibit 16), and the growth rate of domestic systemwide sales is slipping (see Exhibit 17).

The international operations are a completely different story. In 1990, international systemwide sales posted a 22 percent gain,[26] and operating income increased to $610 million (see Exhibit 18). This growth should continue since McDonald's, which currently operates in 53 countries, plans to penetrate new markets around the world. This, in turn, will increase the international contribution even more in years to come. In fact, one analyst predicts that profits from international sales will surpass domestic sales by 1995.[27]

Social Responsibility

McDonald's annual report states that "being a good corporate citizen means treating people with fairness and integrity, and sharing success with the communities in which

··

EXHIBIT 16   Fast-Food Market Share, 1985 and 1990

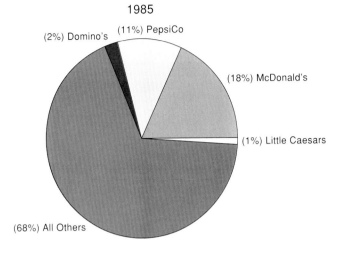

1985

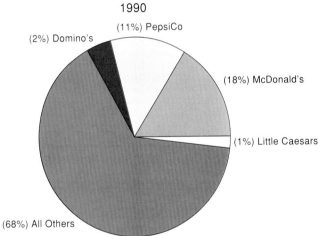

1990

··

we do business."[28] Because of this, McDonald's overall corporate strategy includes social responsibility.

Education

Supporting and providing education is one way McDonald's helps society. In addition to sponsoring events that encourage and recognize achievement, it has created four programs designed to further education. Two of the programs, "When I Grow Up" and "Stay in School," focus on the importance of education, while the "It's Our Business" program teaches economic principles to students in grades 7 through 10 and the "Hispanic American Commitment to Education Resources" program provides college scholarships.

EXHIBIT 17   Domestic Systemwide Sales

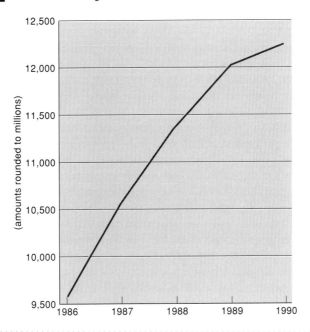

Equal Opportunity

Equal opportunity is also an ideal supported by McDonald's. McJobs, McMasters, and affirmative action programs are aimed at ensuring full and equal participation by all members in society.[29]

Children's Charities

McDonald's is "dedicated to helping children achieve their fullest potential."[30] The Ronald McDonald Charities provide grants to programs that support education, drug awareness, health care, medical research, and rehabilitation.

To help families of seriously ill children, the Ronald McDonald House program provides a place for the families to stay while their child is hospitalized.

Environment

Environmental issues have taken a prominent place in today's society and McDonald's is doing what it can to make the world a better place to live. It is reducing packaging, using recycled materials, promoting conservation, and trying to protect the tropical rain forests. In summary, the strategies developed by McDonald's focus on satisfying the customer, penetrating new markets, and being socially responsible.

....

HUMAN RESOURCE STRATEGY

Managing Diversity/Labor Shortage

According to the Bureau of Labor Statistics, annual work force growth in the United States will slow dramatically, from 2 percent a year in 1988 to 1.2 percent until the year 2000. Another prediction is that 73 percent of the new entrants to the work force will be minorities, elderly, and women. The buzz word for recruiting, training, and retaining this new rainbow coalition of human resources is "managing diversity." In recognition of the changing demographics and the shrinking labor force, McDonald's has created programs to deal with employee diversity.

In addition to billions of hamburgers every year, McDonald's is serving up employment opportunities to two growing segments of the work force: the disabled and the elderly. The McDonald's corporate identification is strategically named in these employment programs, which are known as McJobs and McMasters.

At sites across the country, more than 9,000 mentally and physically disabled people have graduated from the McJobs program and have begun work at McDonald's restaurants. Specially trained and selected managers serve as job coaches, who work closely with local vocational rehabilitation agencies to monitor each candidate's progress. Job coaches work one-on-one with four or five candidates at a time. Each receives standard McDonald's training—classroom instruction, demonstration, and supervised practice at various job stations.[31]

McMasters is a nationwide program that identifies, recruits, trains, and retains workers who are 55 years of age and older. It also features job coaches, who function in much the same capacity as the coaches in McJobs, as well as a referral program that works through a vast network of agencies that alert older workers to the opportunities at McDonald's. Workers hired through McDonald's referral program are immediately teamed up with a "partner"—an experienced worker who helps the team member through the initial training.

The corporation offers its managers solid diversity training, including a workshop designed to help managers deal with older workers, minorities, and the mentally and physically handicapped. "We believe that management must understand what diversity is, and how it works to the company's and the individual's advantage," said Monica Boyles, past director of McDonald's Changing Workforce program. She adds,

> Not only do we want a representative work force, but we want to clearly empower cultural differences so that we have full advantage of what everybody brings; we want to ensure that people at all levels of McDonald's are free to be themselves and to bring their energy and creativity into the work environment.[32]

In addition, McDonald's offers career-development programs designed for various minority groups and training for managers that identifies diversity from a value-added perspective. As a result of their programs, 56 percent of the top managers at restaurants owned by McDonald's are women and minorities.[33]

Training

Each year, more than 3,000 franchisers and McDonald's managers graduate with a degree in hamburgerology from Hamburger University, Oak Brook, Illinois.[34] Hamburger U. is an 80-acre campus that all the company's managers and franchise hold-

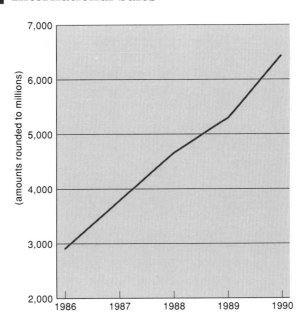

EXHIBIT 18   International Sales

(amounts rounded to millions)

ers must attend. Formal classroom sessions are provided in which participants learn management skills, market evaluation, financial budgets, and the reinforcement of Ray Kroc's philosophy of Q.S.C.&V.

Training for employees begins with in-store videotapes and one-on-one instruction "even before the crew member cooks their first french fry."[35] "The book" at McDonald's—the company's policies and procedures manual—spells out the precise details at each station in the restaurant. "Cooks must turn, never flip, hamburgers one, never two, at a time." Or, "If they haven't been purchased, Big Macs must be discarded ten minutes after being cooked and french fries in seven."

Training programs are always being refined and updated to provide the crew with the tools needed to handle the challenges of operating a McDonald's restaurant.[36] Recently, McDonald's has added a class to its career-development program designed to build leadership and communication skills.

Careers: The Golden Opportunity under the Arches

McDonald's is not only the biggest fast-food restaurant in America, it's also the nation's largest youth employer. About half of the more than 500,000 employees are under the age of 20. "Its impact on the U.S. work force greatly exceeds its current employment, because it trains so many high school students for their first jobs."[37]

Every new employee begins as a trainee on the easiest of jobs—cooking french fries. Once that station is perfected, an employee moves to the next designated station and so on. McDonald's functions as a de facto job-training program by teaching youth discipline and the basics of how to work.[38] For workers who show initiative, McDonald's offers opportunities for quick advancement. An employee can work his or her way up to "crew chief" where he or she can manage an entire operation and its crew.

The youth will continue to work as crew chief—given that the annual turnover rate is more than 100 percent—until promotion to a manager. McDonald's has a long tradition of promoting from within on the basis of skill and hustle, not academic credentials.[39] More than half of its corporate executives never graduated from college. This fits right into the philosophy of Ray Kroc on what education should be:

> Career education, that's what this country needs. Many young people emerge from college unprepared to hold down a steady job or to cook or do housework and it makes them depressed. No wonder! They should train for a career, learn how to support themselves and how to enjoy work first. Then if they have a thirst for advanced learning, they can to go night school.[40]

The possibilities for advancing to corporate headquarters are also attainable. More than half of McDonald's top corporate management started out as crew members. However, the organizational chart is "flat" for being one of the nation's biggest employers. As Kroc states, "I believe that *less is more* in the case of corporate management; for its size, McDonald's is the most unstructured corporation I know and I don't think you could find a happier, more secure, harder working group of executives anywhere."[41]

Benefits

Profit Sharing

The company's program for U.S. employees includes profit sharing, 401(k) (Mc-DESOP—McDonald's Employee Stock Ownership Plan), and leveraged employee stock ownership features.[42] McDESOP allows employees to invest in McDonald's common stock by making contributions that are partially matched by the company. Certain foreign subsidiaries also offer profit sharing, stock purchase, or other similar benefit plans. The company does not provide any other postretirement benefits.

Preferred Provider Organization (PPO)[43]

PPO applies to all full-time staff and store management selecting McDonald's medical coverage. PPO is a network of hospitals across the United States that provides quality care and a discount to McDonald's employees who use these facilities for either inpatient or outpatient services.

Educational Assistance Program[44]

McDonald's supports the educational objectives of its employees and offers a job-related Education Assistance Program (EAP). Eligible employees (store management and their assistants with at least 6 months of service) will be reimbursed for 75 percent of their course fees to a maximum of $400 per course (two courses per semester). Home office approval is required.

Sabbaticals[45]

McDonald's believes that sabbaticals are the best way to replenish their employees' energy. After 10 years of service, you are eligible for a sabbatical leave program acknowledging "the need to nurture individuals within a corporate culture dedicated, in part, to mass-producing an identical, high-quality product and service."[46]

Child Care[47]

McDonald's makes available to all employees, through Kinder Care and La Petite Academy, a tuition discount for child care.

....

ACCOMPLISHMENTS

Domination of the Industry

McDonald's Corporation operates, licenses, and services the world's largest chain of fast-food restaurants and competes with virtually all restaurants (as well as with food stores on certain items). McDonald's Corporation has broadened its menu over the years to compete, to some extent, in virtually all areas. While McDonald's sales of food service or fast-food restaurants in the United States totaled 20 percent in 1990, its market share of all restaurants, including convenience stores, cafeterias, and caterers, was 7 percent of the $180-billion market. Hence, it appears that the company has room to grow from its current base.[48]

Growth

In recent years, domestic growth has slowed down as a result of market saturation, the recession (and its impact on consumer spending), and most recently the Persian Gulf War. According to McDonald's senior executive vice-president and chief finance officer, Jack Greenberg, transactions and sales "are best described as flat year over year," and even though they have improved between July and August, they have "not improved enough to signal a turnaround." As it is shown in Exhibit 19, this slowdown in domestic sales has impacted overall growth. The growth in sales over the years went down from about 17 percent between 1986 and 1987 to about 14 percent between 1987 and 1988 to only 9.5 percent between 1989 and 1990. As a result, overall profit has grown at a slower rate from about 18 percent between 1987 and 1988 to about 13 percent the next year to about 10 percent between 1989 and 1990. From a qualitative point of view, the company's domestic profit mix is becoming more and more tied to franchise fee income. Oppenheimer & Co., Inc., estimates that in 1991, earnings from co-owned stores will represent about 10 percent of total operating income, down from 25 percent five years ago, and McDonald's Corporation appears to be restructuring its domestic operations somewhat to receive more profits from franchise fees and less from store operations.

Contrary to domestic profit, profits from international operations are growing at an increased rate. Over the last five years, they grew at a 25 percent compounded rate, and Oppenheimer and Co., Inc., estimates that they are likely to grow 20 to 25 percent annually and could account for 45 percent of the company's profits this year, up from 38 percent in 1990 and 32 percent in 1989.

··

EXHIBIT   19   Sales, Profits, and Assets

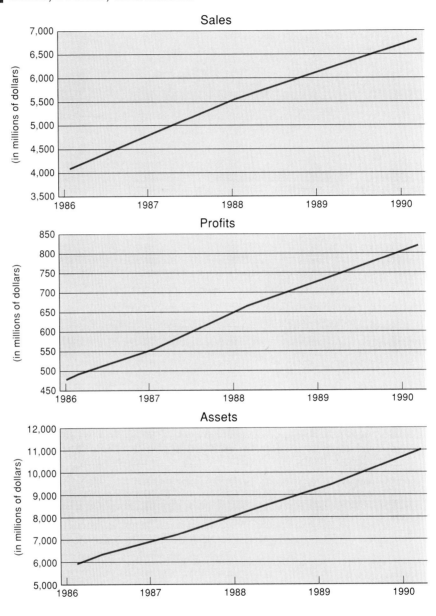

International Sector

Since the first international restaurant opened in Canada in 1967, McDonald's restaurants have expanded throughout the globe. Between 1985 and 1990, the number of McDonald's international restaurants has almost doubled. By December 31, 1990, there were 8,576 units in the United States and 3,227 units in foreign countries, mostly in Japan, Canada, Germany, the United Kingdom, and Australia.[49] Contrary to domestic operations, international operations remain very strong with a 22 percent increase in operating earnings as of July 24, 1991. Sales per store are expanding at a 5 percent to 10 percent rate. Those improvements were achieved despite the effects of the Persian Gulf War and the weak economies in several countries (including Canada and the United Kingdom where McDonald's has a large percentage of its restaurants).

Because it presents the most growth potential, the international market is being emphasized to address the sluggish sales problem. In September, Greenberg said he expected to open 400 to 450 new restaurants annually in international markets in the coming years (as opposed to 250 to 300 per year in the domestic market) on the base of 3,227. McDonald's Corporation just opened two restaurants in Lisbon, Portugal, a new market, and they are doing well. In other international markets, McDonald's continues to work on opening a second restaurant in the Soviet Union (the first one was opened in 1990) and is seeking more sites in Eastern Europe. Also the U.K. unit of McDonald's Corporation said earlier this summer that it will open its first two restaurants in Belfast, Northern Ireland, by the end of the year and is seeking five more sites in Northern Ireland so that it may open more restaurants in the next few years. McDonald's has considerable profit growth potential in the international area because, although it has units in only 53 countries, 84 percent of foreign profit is derived from only six countries: Canada, the United Kingdom, Germany, Japan, Australia, and France.[50]

REFERENCES

"Big Mac Attacks with Pizza." *Fortune*. February 26, 1990, pp. 87–89.

Bowie, Norman. "New Directions in Corporate Responsibility." *Business Horizons*. July–August 1991, pp. 56–65.

Brown, Miriam. "Burger, Fries, Coke and a Career: Tallahassee's Fast-Food Managers Feel Good about Their Job Choice but Admit That Sometimes the Going Can Get Tough." *Tallahassee Democrat*. October 13, 1991, p. E1.

"Company Profile, McDonald's Corporation." *Fortune Business Reports*. October 9, 1991.

Curtis, James R. "McDonald's Abroad: Outpost of American Culture." *Journal of Geography*, January–February 1982, pp. 14–19.

Deveny, Kathleen. "McWorld?" *Business Week*. October 13, 1986, pp. 78–86.

"The Economics of the Golden Arches: A Case Study of McDonald's." *American Economist* 34. Fall 1990, pp. 60–64.

Emerson, Robert L. *The New Economics of Fast Food*. New York: Van Nostrand Reinhold, 1990, pp. 98–104.

Gerber, Beverly. "The Disabled: Ready, Willing and Able." *Training*. December 1990, pp. 29–36.

"Getting In on the Ground Floor." *Fortune*. Fall 1990, pp. 61–67.

Gibson, Richard. "Discount Menu Is Coming to McDonald's." *Wall Street Journal*. November 30, 1990, p. B1.

Hassell, Greg. "Making Change." *Houston Chronicle*. January 6, 1991.

Hesselberg, George. "McDonald's in Moscow: A New Culture." *Wall Street Journal*. February 25, 1990, p. G1.

Keeler, Bill. "Of Famous Arches, Beeg Meks and Rubles." *New York Times*. January 28, 1990, pp. 1, 7.

King, Margaret J. "McDonald's and the New American Landscape." *USA Today*. January 1980, p. 46.

Krueger, Alan B. "Ownership, Agency, and Wages: An Examination of Franchising in the Fast Food Industry." *Quarterly Journal of Economics*. February 1991, pp. 75–101.

Laabs, Jennifer J. "The Golden Arches Provide Golden Opportunities." *Personnel Journal*. July 1991, pp. 52–57.

Love, John F. *McDonald's: Behind the Arches*, Toronto, New York: Bantam Books, 1986.

Mabry, Marcus. "Inside the Golden Arches." *Newsweek*. December 18, 1989, pp. 46–47.

McDonalds 1990 Company Report.

"McDonald's Corporation." Securities and Exchange Commission Form 10-K for Year Ended December 31, 1990.

"McD's Sizzles with New Ideas." *Advertising Age* 61. September 3, 1990, pp. 1, 53.

"The McDonald's Mystique." *Fortune*. July 4, 1988, pp. 112–116.

Melloan, George. "Global View." *Wall Street Journal*. February 5, 1991, p. A15.

Noren, D. L. "The Economics of the Golden Arches." *American Economist*. Fall 1990, pp. 60–64.

Norton, Seth. "An Empirical Look at Franchising as an Organizational Form." *Journal of Business* 61, no. 2 (1988), pp. 197–214.

"Nostalgia's Free at Golden Arch: New McDonald's Restaurant Concept." *Advertising Age* 61. September 10, 1990, p. 28.

Raiter, Gregory. "Inside Intelligence on Soviet Ventures." *HRMagazine*. January 1991, pp. 46–49.

"Reduced-fat Burgers and an Environmental Sense Help McDonald's Change Its Image." *Tallahassee Democrat*. June 12, 1991, p. D5.

"Slow Food: McDonald's in Moscow." *The Economist*. February 3, 1990, p. 25.

"Strategy." *Business Month* 136. October 1, 1990, pp. 38–42.

Therrien, Lois. "McRisky." *BusinessWeek*. October 21, 1991, pp. 114–122.

Therrien, Lois. "Michael Quilan." *Business Week 1000,* (1991), p. 62.

Therrien, Lois. "Restaurants: Doing Well by Being Big." *Business Week.* January 14, 1991, p. 92.

Upchurch, Jenny. "Burger, Fries, Coke, and a Career: Managers of Fast-Food Restaurants Are Finding Plenty of Opportunities." *Tallahassee Democrat.* October 13, 1991, p. E1.

" 'Value' Trend Nibbles at Fast-Food Profits." *Advertising Age 62.* May 6, 1991, p. 20.

Waldrop, Judith. "Meet the New Boss." *American Demographics.* June 1991, pp. 26–38.

"Wanna Make a Deal in Moscow?" *Fortune.* October 22, 1990, pp. 113–115.

Wilcox, John. "A Campus Tour of Corporate Colleges." *Training & Development Journal.* May 1987, pp. 51–56.

Wildavsky, Ben. "McJobs." *Reader's Digest.* January 1990, pp. 126–130.

Willis, Clint. "Starting Out Right." *Money.* June 1991, pp. 85–96.

· · · · · · · · · · · · · · · · ·
NOTES

1. "The Burger That Conquered the Country," *Time,* September 17, 1983, p. 84.

2. Margaret J. King, "McDonald's and the New American Landscape," *USA Today,* January 1980, p. 46.

3. McDonald's 1990 Annual Report, p. 32.

4. McDonald's Securities and Exchange Commission Form 10-K for year ended December 31, 1990, p. 1.

5. McDonald's 1990 Annual Report, p. 6.

6. Ibid., p. 8.

7. Robert L. Emerson, *The New Economics of Fast Food,* (New York: Van Nostrand Reinhold, 1990), p. 102.

8. McDonald's 1990 Annual Report.

9. Ibid.

10. McDonald's Form 10-K, p. 1.

11. McDonald's 1990 Annual Report, p. 17.

12. Emerson, *The New Economics of Fast Food,* p. 99.

13. Alan B. Krueger, "Ownership, Agency, and Wages: An Examination of Franchising in the Fast Food Industry," *Quarterly Journal of Economics,* February 1991, p. 81.

14. Ibid.

15. Ibid.

16. Kathleen Deveney, "McWorld?" *Business Week,* October 13, 1986, pp. 78–86.

17. Seth W. Norton, "Empirical Look at Franchising As an Organization Form," *Journal of Business 61,* April, 1988, pp. 197–218.

18. Lois Therrien, "McRISKY," *Business Week,* October 19, 1991, p. 117.

19. *Time,* September 9, 1991, pp. 38–39.

20. Therrien, "McRISKY," p. 120.

21. Denise Brennan, "The Name of the Games: Kidding Around," *Restaurant Business,* June 10, 1991, pp. 98–106.

22. Sales after 4:00 P.M. are considered dinner sales.

23. Therrien, "McRISKY," p. 120.

24. Ibid.

25. Ibid., p. 116.

26. McDonald's 1990 Annual Report, p. 1.

27. Therrien, "McRISKY," p. 116.

28. McDonald's 1990 Annual Report.

29. These programs are discussed in further detail in the Human Resources section.

30. McDonald's 1990 Annual Report, p. 18.

31. Jennifer J. Laabs, "The Golden Arches Provide Golden Opportunities," *Personnel Journal,* July 1991, pp. 52–57.

32. Telephone interview with Monica Boyles, past director of McDonald's Changing World Force Program.

33. Laabs, "The Golden Arches Provide Golden Opportunities," pp. 52–57.

34. John Wilcox, "A Campus Tour of Corporate Colleges," *Training & Development Journal,* May 1987, pp. 51–56.

35. McDonald's 1990 Annual Report.

36. Ray Kroc, *Grinding It Out: The Making of McDonald's* (Chicago: Contemporary Books, 1977).

37. John F. Love, *McDonald's Behind the Arches,* (Toronto: Bantam Books, 1986).

38. Marcus Mabry, "Inside the Golden Arches," *Newsweek,* December 18, 1989, pp. 46–47.

39. Ibid.

40. Ray Kroc, *Grinding it Out: The Making of McDonald's.*

41. Ibid.

42. McDonald's 1990 Annual Report.

43. McDonald's Brochure on Benefits and Compensation, January 1991.

44. Ibid.

45. Ibid.

46. Ray Kroc, *Grinding it Out: The Making of McDonald's.*

47. Ibid.

48. J. C. Frazzano, "McDonald's Corporation—Company Report," Oppenheimer & Co., Inc., 1991, Thomson Financial Network Inc., May 2, 1991.

49. Company Profile, McDonald's Corporation," *Fortune Reports.*

50. Frazzano, "McDonald Corporation-Company Report."

CASE 4   The Walt Disney Company

....

INTRODUCTION

Overview of the Company

The Walt Disney Company is the purveyor of a Magic Kingdom that includes theme parks, resort hotels, movies, consumer goods, and some of the most memorable cartoon characters ever created. From Mickey Mouse to Roger Rabbit, animation is the original product of the Disney Company and brings in over $1 billion in film revenues. Warren Beatty, Robin Williams, Madonna, and Kim Basinger now head the list of Disney live-action film stars via Touchstone Pictures, and Steve Martin is scheduled to join soon. Consumer products bring in over $400 million, the result of strong alliances with licensees, manufacturers, and retail outlets. A TV station, the Queen Mary, and Howard Hughes' Spruce Goose have been added to the ever diversifying fold. In 1990, Mickey Mouse finally opened up his own restaurant called Mickey's Kitchen.[1] All this from the talent of one man, Walter E. Disney, and the public's love affair with a mouse.

Company History

Since Walt Disney's personality, dreams, and attitudes still influence the company, a look at both his and his company's history until his death offers insights into the Disney of today. His successes and battles with distributors, strikers, merchandisers, and even friends left an indelible mark on the man and the realization of his dream.

The Beginning

Walter Elias Disney was born in 1901 in Chicago, but his family moved to a farm near Marcilene, Missouri, in 1906. It was this place that proved to be the inspiration for things to come and also the place where four-year-old Walter first learned to draw. The story goes that Walt and his sister Ruth discovered a barrel of tar on the farm and proceeded to draw on the newly whitewashed fence with sticks dipped in the black liquid. Since his father Elias was rather a strict disciplinarian, Walt and Ruth were appropriately punished. Despite this, Walt's Aunt Margaret encouraged him by bringing paper and crayons from Kansas City, where she lived.[2]

    Walt was an avid reader, but in grammar school his first love remained drawing. His unusual style sometimes got him in trouble, though. Once, when he was asked

This case was prepared by Kathleen Peterson, Jennifer Bowers, Troy Smith, and Warren Saunders.

to draw a pot of flowers, he added faces to the blooms and arms instead of leaves. He attended children's art classes at the Kansas City Art Institute and persuaded his father to pay for a correspondence course in art, which he did. As Walt grew older, it seemed that he was either in school (McKinley High), washing bottles at his father's jelly factory, or drawing.[3]

Walt was eager to play his part in the war effort, and in 1918 enlisted in the American Ambulance Corps. He convinced his mother to sign his passport application, which showed Walt to be of age, and he was sent to France. He kept up his drawing, and when he returned to the United States he applied for jobs as a cartoonist at several papers. He failed to find an opening, but soon signed on at the Pesmin-Rubin Commercial Art Studio for the sum of $50 per week.[4]

Walt's Early Efforts

Walt didn't realize that he was taken on to meet a seasonal increase in work, and he was laid off after the Christmas rush. He and a friend, Ub Iwerks, created a company called Iwerks-Disney Commercial Artists, which quickly failed. This trend continued at a slightly less disastrous company called Laugh-O-Grams, which Walt and other investors formed in 1920. Following his brother Roy's advice to "get out of there," Walt traveled to Hollywood in 1923, after the firm went bankrupt.[5]

Hollywood met all of Walt's expectations, and he set up shop in a small office and got some stationary printed that boldly said "Walt Disney—Cartoonist." He contacted a distributor in New York that he had sent information to while with Laugh-O-Gram, and explained an idea for a cartoon/live action series called "Alice Comedies." He prevailed upon the creditors of Laugh-O-Gram to allow him to release the only existing cartoon to the distributor. With a few changes, a deal was struck, and Walt hired a lot on Hollywood Boulevard for live-action filming. He rented a shop adjoining the premises, called the signwriters in, and emblazoned the words "Disney Bros. Studio," with his brother Roy as partner.[6]

Temporary Success

Roy had more of a talent for managing the money than for animation, and Walt had quite a talent for spending what little money they had. This was characteristic of the quest for quality that obsessed Walt, and the early days were a preamble of what was to come. Walt and Roy begged loans from anyone they could, and the company was in a perilous situation in 1924. Walt had no choice but continue on with the relationship.[7]

About this time, Universal Pictures was looking for a new cartoon series featuring a rabbit, and it was suggested that Walt be given the project, with the Alice Series' company as the distributor. Walt gladly accepted, and created "Oswald, the lucky rabbit." The series was a critical and financial success, and all seemed to be going well for the studios. The frequent checks were now being delivered by Walt's distributors.[8]

During this time, Walt married Lillian Bounds, who was employed as an ink-and-paint girl at the studios. She and Walt took a trip to New York to negotiate a deal for the next series of Oswald cartoons with his distributor. Walt had intended to ask the distributor for an increase in the fee per picture, but they offered Walt a reduced price. Walt angrily refused and was informed that if he chose to refuse the offer, the distributor would take his whole firm away from him (they had signed up all his animators). A quick phone call to Roy revealed that what the distributor said was true, and Walt started to look frantically for an alternative distributor. However, Walt's distributor informed him that even if he did find another distributor, Universal held all the rights to the character he had created. Walt and Lillian took the train back to Hollywood, and Walt vowed never to lose control over his interests again.[9]

The Mouse

"DON'T WORRY EVERYTHING OK GIVE DETAILS WHEN I ARRIVE." This was the cable that Walt sent Roy before leaving for home from New York, and it is definitely an example of the incredible optimism that so characterized Walt Disney. The truth was, however, that things were not okay, but Walt viewed the situation as an opportunity to create a character that could be even more successful than Oswald, the not-so-lucky rabbit.

No one really knows how the idea of the character came about. So much of the tale is shrouded in myth, to the delight of Walt Disney, that we may never know exactly what happened. What we do know is that out of the turmoil of that visit to New York came a character that would become perhaps the best-known icon of our time and the key to the success of Disney Studios. As Walt would later remark to his employees, "I hope we never lose sight of one fact . . . that this was all started by a mouse. . . ."[10]

When he arrived back in Hollywood, Walt had to break the news about the loss to his brother Roy and the only other loyal animator, Ub Iwerks. He was able to temper it with news about the new cartoon series he had envisioned. The mouse, originally to be named Mortimer, would be called Mickey (at the insistence of Lillian). The defecting animators would not be leaving for another three months, so Walt and Ub had to labor in secret and very quickly to boot. The cartoon, called *Plane Crazy*, was churned out in only two weeks, with Ub averaging an amazing seven hundred drawings per day—one per minute! The plot revolved around a rickety plane built by Mickey and his barnyard friends after Mickey reads about Charles Lindbergh. Mickey then sets off with his girlfriend Minnie, and the two characters became symbols of youth, optimism and adventure.[11]

The cartoon was received warmly, but no distributor could be found. It seemed that the mouse was likable enough, but he didn't have a unique hook to set him apart from other cartoon characters. After *The Jazz Singer*, the first movie with synchronized sound, was released, Walt decided that this would be what made Mickey different—sound. He authorized Roy to hock everything, including his car. With the company teetering on the edge of bankruptcy, Walt made the first cartoon to incorporate sound, *Steamboat Willie*.[12]

The film was held over two weeks at the Roxy Theater and was no less than a triumph. The next three Mickey Mouse cartoons had sound added, and "the mouse" was soon so popular that more animators had to be added to the staff. More films came, including the *Silly Symphony* series, and soon Mickey and Minnie were as popular as any flesh-and-blood movie actors. In 1929, Walt was approached by a man offering him $300 to put the image of Mickey and Minnie on children's notebooks. As usual, the money was needed, and Walt agreed. Within a year, hundreds of manufacturers were producing officially licensed products, and the fortunes of the company seemed safe at last.[13]

The Company Takes Off

Mickey's place among the public was secure, and the offshots of the cartoons were bringing in substantial revenues. Consumer products, such as the Mickey Mouse watch, sold like hotcakes, and the Mickey Mouse Clubs that cinema owners across the country put together boasted a million members. In 1930, one of the most well-regarded promoters in the country, Herman Kamen, offered to manage the licensing of Disney characters, and the brothers jumped at the opportunity.[14]

The cartoons were the core business of the studios, after all, and they were turned out one after another. In addition to the *Silly Symphonies* and Mickey Mouse cartoons, the studios put out *The Ugly Duckling, Three Blind Mouseketeers,* and *The Three Little Pigs.* In the 1930s, Mickey got such sidekicks as Clara Cluck, Pluto, Goofy, and the irrepressible Donald Duck. These characters were successful, but Walt had a more ambitious project in mind—a full length animated film.

Snow White—A New Era

No one else had dared to make a full-length animated feature previously. The task was daunting, and the amount of drawings alone would be enormous. But Walt was positive that not only could it be done, but that it would be successful. He began preparation for this full-length cartoon as a general would prepare for battle. By the time it was over, the *Snow White* team would include eighty-five animators, story and gag writers, inkers, painters, and several departments of technicians. Not only did *Snow White* have to be produced, but the regular quota of short films had to be continued. Both tasks were accomplished, but the financial and personal pressures were great. Production took five years.[15]

What had been called "Disney's folly" was an absolute success, both nationally and internationally with its release on February 4, 1938. The studio's place in history had been assured, and the genius of Disney and his artists was without question. Adding to the success of the film were the revenues from various consumer products, including seeds, shampoos, and even diapers.[16]

"The Golden Years"

It was clear to Walt that the current studio was not adequate to meet the needs of an ambitious schedule as the company grew, so a suitable site was located in Burbank and construction began. During this time, Walt also felt it necessary to reorganize the company. In 1938, a huge document detailing organizational structure and job descriptions was drawn up, a far cry from the ad hoc type of arrangement that had been operating for years.

Disney Goes Public

Germany invaded Poland on September 1, 1939. As the war consumed more and more of Europe, the 45 percent in revenues that Disney enjoyed from that part of the world quickly dried up. As income diminished, costs escalated, particularly on the production of *Fantasia.* Disney had over 1,000 people working for him, and despite *Pinocchio*'s critical success, the film did not do well at the box office. The new studios were just being completed and payment was due. Roy Disney confronted his brother in the spring of 1940 with the news—the company was $4.5 million in debt.[17]

Walt's first response was to laugh, because he remembered a time in the not-so-distant past when the studio could not borrow a thousand dollars, much less a million. But the situation was serious, so the Disney brothers opted for an issue of stock on the public market. In April of 1940, the company offered 155,000 shares of 6 percent cumulative convertible preferred stock at $25 par value and 600,000 shares of common stock at $5 per share. The offering raised $3,500,000 in much-needed capital.[18]

An ominous threat was brewing, however, and it would prove to be more trying to Walt than merely funding the company.

The Strike

It seemed that ever since the move from the old studios, the atmosphere of camaraderie and creativity had been on the wane. The artists felt cut off from the creative process and, worst of all, from Walt himself. Rumors about the staff and management began to circulate, ranging from the cost of the number of waitresses in the cafeteria to a fictitious "inner ring" of Walt's employees who enjoyed privileges that others did not. The legalistic job descriptions and organizational charts did nothing to help, and it wasn't long before there was unrest in the Disney organization.

The disharmony was evident, and when the price of Disney stock began to fall, many employees chose to cash in. Walt demonstrated his belief in the company by buying the shares of anyone who wanted to sell. The stage was set for some type of union organization, and the Disney animators became the prime target for activists.

Disney had always operated a closed shop with various other trades, but the animators were not organized. Two separate unions canvassed the animators: the independent Federation of Screen Cartoonists and the Screen Cartoonists Guild, led by Herbert Sorrell and affiliated with the Brotherhood of Painters, Paperhangers, and Decorators of America. Many animators, being a bit naive, joined both unions, and some joined neither. Sorrell tried to get Walt Disney to join his union, claiming that a majority of his animators already had. Walt told Sorrell that he wanted the matter put to a ballot organized by the National Labor Relations Board, but Sorrell refused.[19]

Walt tried to calm the rumors and increase communication with his staff by issuing a recorded speech addressing the concerns of the animators. He stressed that he had never been interested in a personal gain or profit, and said that instead of complaining, the employees of the company should count their blessings. Despite this plea, the tensions came to a head when Goofy's chief animator, Art Babbit, was dismissed. He had long been a supporter of the Guild and Herb Sorrell maintained that the dismissal was in reprisal for union activities. The long threatened strike was called in May of 1941. Walt said "to me, the entire situation is a catastrophe."[20]

The strike was settled in October of 1941, with Sorrell claiming victory for the unions. Walt said that the strike was settled in the simplest way—"the negotiators gave Sorrell everything he wanted."[21] The animosities and confrontations were not easily forgotten, and within two years many of the strikers had left the company, including Art Babbit. A noticeable change came over Walt, and, wary of further trouble, he insisted that every employee join the proper union, down to the gardeners. He became more cautious and remote in his relationships.

....

THE YEARS 1940–1966

A New Outlook on Costs

The financial problems that had always plagued the company did not vanish, however, and Walt announced a new policy regarding costs. Staff were urged to adopt "a constructive attitude toward every dollar that went into developing, producing, and selling the scheduled pictures."[22] From now on, there would be a production schedule that would be adhered to, movies would come in within budgets, stories would be more thoroughly prepared to eliminate costly changes, and all departments would be policed in order to prevent unnecessary expenses. Selling and exploiting the pictures to the fullest would also be of utmost importance.

Under the new rules, the studio continued to produce hits. *Cinderella* was released in 1950, followed by *Alice in Wonderland* in 1951. *Peter Pan* arrived in 1953, along with the Disney signature fairy, Tinkerbell. The greatest production of all, however, was just beginning to brew in the mind of its creator.

Disneyland

The original concept for Disneyland came to Walt's mind in early 1939, but the details were not thought out until 1951. Walt formed WED Enterprises so that stockholders would not object to the new venture, and attempted to persuade investors to fund the project. This proved difficult, so Walt backed his idea with his own money. A site was selected in 1953—160 acres in Anaheim, California, just 25 miles from Los Angeles. As Walt put it:

> There's nothing like it in the whole world—I know, because I've looked. That's why it can be great; because it will be unique. A new concept in entertainment, and I think—I *know*—it can be a success.[23]

Disneyland opened on July 17, 1955. That morning traffic was jammed for over seven miles on the roads leading to the park, and by midday over 30,000 people had passed through the turnstiles. It was the beginning of what Walt was later to term "Black Sunday." The staff had been hired from agencies and treated the guests with the same belligerence they used for dealing with crowds at racetracks and ballparks. Several rides broke down, with others were dangerously overcrowded. The food and drinks ran out, water fountains were inadequate, and the park became littered with trash.

To make the changes necessary, Walt built an apartment over the Main Street Fire Station and spent 24 hours a day at the park for two weeks. An army of young men was employed to clean up the litter, standards for staff courtesy and efficiency were established, and ways of speeding up the waiting times for rides were found. It was a headache, but this experience afforded an opportunity not found in the movies—a chance for continual improvement. Disneyland, as it turned out, was a turning point in the fortunes of the company. After 16 months, net profits were the highest in the company's history.[24]

From Disneyland until Walt's Death

For the World's Fair in 1964, Walt approached a number of corporations and asked to design their attractions. It was a decision that would have far-reaching consequences. The Ford Motor Company bought Walt's design for a car ride through history from caveman to spaceman, and Pepsi helped develop the idea that would eventually become the boat ride known as "It's a Small World." The president of the World's Fair commissioned what would become one of the fair's major attractions, a three-dimensional, talking and moving Abraham Lincoln. Audiences experienced a sensation of being in the crowd listening to a Lincoln speech. The Disney designed exhibits drew over forty-six million visitors.

During this time, Walt also began to acquire land for "Disneyland East," another theme park to be located in Orlando, Florida. The idea of a prototype community, later to be known as EPCOT, was also taking shape, and Walt began sharing his dream with the world—after the land was purchased, however. The cost of the two projects was estimated at $500 million.[25]

Unbeknownst to anyone but his closest aides, Walt Disney was very ill. He was admitted to the hospital on November 2, 1966, and X rays showed a spot on his left lung. It was found to be cancerous and was removed, and Walt seemed to be recovering. He went back to work, but soon fell ill again. After two more weeks in the hospital, he rallied somewhat, and even spoke with his brother Roy about details of the Disneyworld project on December 14. The next morning, Walt Disney died of acute circulatory collapse. As Richard Zanuck said, "No eulogy will be read or monument built to equal the memorial Walt Disney has left in the hearts and minds and imaginations of the world's peoples."[26]

LIFE AFTER WALT

The years after Walt Disney's death were marked by feuds between "Roy men," the financial types, and "Walt men," the creative types. Nearly everything, including film making, was undertaken only after a discussion over what Walt would have done. This philosophy worked for a while but eventually led to the deterioration of the film segment of the company. This was marked by Disney's refusal to produce *Raiders of the Lost Ark* and *E.T.*, simply because of the creator's desire to have a share of the profits. The dismal decisions led to a devaluation of Disney's stock and a takeover effort in 1984 by Roy Disney, Jr., among others.[27]

Sid Bass and Stanley Gold were the "white knights" that helped stave off the raiders. On the inside, they insisted upon a shakeup in management. This resulted in the hiring of Michael Eisner, Frank Wells, and Jeffry Katzenberg, who are still with the company. These individuals engineered a remarkable turnaround in the film division as well as other divisions within the company, and Disney has shown record earnings and growth for the past few years. It was a choice that Walt would have approved.

What Disney Sells?

Disney's "sells" family entertainment through its theme parks, resorts, filmed entertainment, and consumer products. These entertainment products can be found throughout the world. Disney products, along with the music of Michael Jackson and Madonna have allowed pop culture to account for America's second largest export.[28]

Due to the growing affection for Mickey Mouse and friends, Disney theme parks are scattered across the globe. Park attractions now include Walt Disney World and

Disney-MGM Studios in Orlando, Florida; Disneyland in Anaheim, California; Tokyo Disneyland in Japan; EuroDisney in Marne-La-Vallie, France. Disney has used the public's growing affection to venture into different markets.

Acquisitions and Developments

Disney has begun to sell its products outside of the normal settings of its theme parks. Currently, Disney products can be found in department stores on clothing, in grocery stores on food products, and in toy stores. Also, the Disney name can now be found on Mattel products, since the two companies joined forces in the toy industry. From this alliance will come "Mattel-sponsored attractions at Disney theme parks, the development of park-related toys, and the expansion of Disney's lucrative toy-licensing pacts with Mattel."

However, EuroDisney is the most popular development at Disney these days. EuroDisney has promised to be the "boost" that Disney needs right now to pull out of its current economic slump. This 4,500 acre theme park located 20 miles east of Paris opened in April 1992. Disney will retain management control and 49 percent of EuroDisneyland's shares with the remaining 51 percent being distributed by share offers in London, Paris, and Brussels.[29] The French government intends to make the park the nucleus of an entire new town. The first phase of the project, scheduled to be totally complete by 1997, will include a theme park, 5,200 hotel rooms, and a golf course. The second phase, which is scheduled to be completed by 2017, is supposed to include another theme park, 12,800 hotel rooms, a shopping mall, and an office park. The American markets are looking to EuroDisney for indications of where Disney is headed. If EuroDisney is successful, the outlook for Disney in the stock markets is sure to improve. Disney officials are expecting 11 million visitors in the first year. Disney expects revenues from the park and the "themed" hotels to reach 5.5 billion francs in the first year and triple to 16 billion francs by 1996.[30] Earnings are expected to start at 132 million francs and soar to over 1 billion francs after 5 years.[31] Robert Fitzpatrick, president of EuroDisney, said "the park aims to be not the best choice, but the only choice: by the quality of the show, the cleanliness of the facility and the friendliness of the staff."[32]

Globalization

EuroDisney may just be the beginning of Disney's efforts to expand its theme parks globally. The global expansion of Disney theme parks into other cold-weather climates lies on the shoulders of EuroDisney. Disney does have plans to open other theme parks abroad and possibly more in the United States.

Disney films have been in the global market for quite some time. Disney blockbusters have also been very popular overseas. For example, *Dead Poets Society* did 25 percent more business in foreign countries than in the United States.[33] Disney home videos and consumer products are faring well in foreign lands. Even though only seven of Disney's twenty-two animated movies have been released overseas, the response for this market has been overwhelming.

Theme Parks and Resorts

Theme parks and resorts are the largest segment of Disney, accounting for over 60 percent of Disney profits.[34] However, with the gloomy economic picture, park admissions have been declining. Park attendance this year is expected to decrease by 10 to 12 percent. "Everything went wrong; you had a recession, a war—and very tough comparisons with last year because of the tremendous success of the studio tour in Orlando, which opened in May of 1989," states Goldman Sach's Richard Simon.[35] Again, the opening of EuroDisney in 1992 is expected to improve the outlook of theme parks and resorts for the rest of this decade.

Filmed Entertainment

The Disney popularity has carried over from the theme parks into its other product lines. For example, Disney movies have always been known as major players in the field of family entertainment. Disney Studios have produced such blockbusters as *Pretty Woman, 101 Dalmations, Snow White,* and *Dick Tracy*. These movies, along with others from Disney's Touchstone and Hollywood Pictures, have lead to Disney's continued success in film entertainment.

Currently, Disney films are suffering setbacks because of the release of some major flops. For example, *Three Men and a Little Lady* did not yield the box office profits Disney expected. Further, *Run, Scenes from a Mall,* and *The Marrying Man,* did not produce the big dollars needed to brighten Disney's film outlook. However, Disney officials appear to be optimistic about the Disney film industry. Jeffrey Katzenburg, Disney Studio chairman, states "the movies are only a small part of [Walt Disney studios]."[36] Further, Walt Disney Studios only accounts for a little more than 20 percent of the net income for Disney.

Consumer Products

In 1987, the people who brought us everything from Mickey Mouse to *Pretty Woman* decided to open their first retail store outside of their theme parks. The first store was opened in the Glendale Galleria, near Disney company headquarters in Anaheim, California. By 1991, The Disney Store had become one of the most sought-after chains in the shopping center industry.[37] Disney consumer products are doing well in both the domestic and foreign markets. These products range from watches and clothing to toys and food products. Disney consumer product lines are carried in Disney theme parks, department stores, specialty stores and supermarkets. As of May 1991, there were 78 Disney Stores and one Mickey's Kitchen Restaurant. Disney planned to add 25 to 40 stores in 1991, two of which would be located in England: Shuffield and Thurrock.[38] Sales volume for the chain has doubled almost every year since its inception in 1987, with sales in 1991 expected to reach $200 million.[39] This segment of Disney is growing rapidly and depends on the success of other Disney products, such as the theme parks and movie characters. The stores expertly combine retailing and entertainment, while promoting Disney's films and theme parks at the same time. Disney has several joint ventures or alliances with companies in related businesses. For example, Disney has a 10-year contract with Nestle that allows Nestle to produce food products using Disney characters. These ventures and others will help Disney to make a strong stand in the consumer products market.

Human Resources

Walt Disney once said, "You can dream, create, design, and build the most wonderful place in the world, but it requires people to make that dream a reality" ("The

Disney Approach to People Management"). The success of the entire Disney empire is built on the excellent customer service that Disney provides for its guests. Disney calls this customer service "Disney Courtesy." The key for getting all 39,000-plus Disney cast members to live, eat, breathe, and sleep Disney courtesy is the Disney Orientation process, part of Disney's well-organized, structured approach to human relations.

Orientation

Disney's orientation process is ongoing for all Disney cast members beginning from the recruitment stage. It continuously reinforces the values, philosophies, and guest service standards that Disney has prided itself on for so many years. Exhibit 20 shows Disney's comprehensive approach to employee relations. It is reinforced with activities, management style, and language. Employees at Disney are called "cast members" and they do not work at a job, they are "cast in a role for the show." Disney uses this terminology to immerse its employees in an environment that constantly reinforces the image Disney wants to project to the public. Also, cast members work either on-stage or back-stage, and they wear costumes instead of uniforms. Since they could interact with guests at any time, all Disney employees, whether they are on-stage cast members or back-stage cast members, are required to learn and use Disney courtesy at all times. (See Exhibit 21.)

Recruitment

Disney has a clean-cut image and conservative reputation that helps potential employees self-select; thus, Disney usually attracts the type of applicants it wants. The Disney "casting" department (known as the human resource department in most businesses), is responsible for hiring qualified applicants that will be cast for a role in Disney's show. This department hires for general employment and college, international, and professional staffing. Hiring for general employment can come from both internal and external sources. Approximately 85 percent of Disney's middle- and executive-level management are hired from within; therefore, the majority of new general employment applicants come from internal sources.

All new-to-Disney applicants go through the same recruitment process. First, there is an eight-to-ten minute preliminary interview that contains a great number of applicants. The main emphasis of this initial interview is to give a realistic view of employment at Disney, to eliminate those who are not interested or are not qualified, and to reschedule a full interview for those applicants that are still interested in becoming a Disney cast member. Would-be cast members need to understand that a job at Disney is not all glamour and that it takes a lot of hard work. For example, Disney theme parks, resorts, and hotels are open 365 days a year and cast members work early mornings, days, evenings, weekends, holidays, and vacations. Additionally, all cast members must adhere to strict grooming standards. All would-be employees are shown a film that details the discipline, grooming, and dress codes that Disney expects all cast members to adhere to at all times. People with extreme styles will know at this point of the interview process if they will be able to adapt in order to be a part of Disney's show. The next step, the full interview, is conducted with three prospective candidates for forty-five minutes. These peer interviews allow the interviewer to get a closer look at the applicant by observing how each interacts with one another. One Disney manager stated, "This is a good indi-

....

| EXHIBIT 20 | Employee Relations Philosophy

We believe in

1. Being fair and impartial in our relations with all employees without regard to race, religion, color, national origin, age, sex, marital status, and handicaps.
2. Providing an opportunity for all employees to reach their personal goals while accomplishing the goals of the organization.
3. Providing a safe and meaningful working environment that contributes to a feeling of worth and individual dignity for each member of our "family."
4. Providing opportunities for growth and development on the job through comprehensive training programs.
5. Providing competitive pay and benefits which recognize employee loyalty, dedication, and individual contribution.
6. Promoting from within our organization when and where feasible.
7. An informal, friendly management style, encouraging open lines of communications at all levels.
8. Teamwork—each of us working together toward common, understood goals.

....

cation of how they'll work with fellow cast members and guests. We're looking for human relations and communications skills. We can train them in the technical skills."[40]

Disney University

Disney University is the corporate structure that teaches "Disney courtesy," translates company policy, and trains employees.[41] In other words, it is the framework that keeps all those things together. The concept of the Disney University started in Disneyland in 1955, along with Walt Disney's vision of an amusement park unlike any other. Disney dreamed of a family park that would be safe and friendly, and where people would return. Thus, he decided that Disneyland (the only theme park at that time) needed a training facility to introduce new employees to the business of entertainment as he imagined it. Sharon Haywood, manager of the Disney Studio Disney University stated, "I doubt that (Walt Disney) called it the 'Disney Culture' but he had his finger on the pulse of what was necessary. He knew that you need to treat employees in the same way you want them to treat the guests."[42] What started as a one-hour program called "You Create Happiness" grew as Disneyland grew. In the 1960s, the Disney University was officially established.

Today, since each Disney facility has unique challenges and varying employee needs, each Disney facility has its own Disney University. Each university is responsible for training and development, employee activities, employee communications (such as on-going written and audiovisual communications), researching and analyzing the organization's people needs, proposing plans to meet those needs, and, lastly, continually researching the effectiveness of the orientation and training programs.

Traditions I & II at Disney University

All new cast members at any Disney facility begin their Disney careers with a two-day orientation seminar called "Traditions" that is conducted at the Disney Univer-

━━

EXHIBIT 21 The Disney Product: Guest Service

In providing the Disney brand of GUEST SERVICE, our cast members are . . .

I. COURTEOUS

- Tone of Voice
- Smile
- Considerate
- Hospitable

II. IMAGE-CONSCIOUS

- Appearance
- Demeanor
- Attitude
- Eye Contact

III. HIGH PERFORMERS

- Knowledgeable
- Accurate
- Thorough
- Helpful
- Creative

━━

sity. (See Exhibit 22.) The role of the Disney University and the Traditions seminar is to provide cast members with a sound understanding of Disney's corporate tradition and values, provide skills essential to job performance, and provide accredited continuing professional growth and development for all cast members. (See Exhibit 23.) The Traditions two-day seminar is carefully scripted and conducted in a comfortable, specially designed training room. The first day of orientation, Traditions I, cast members learn the history, traditions, and milestones of the worldwide Disney team, Walt Disney's philosophy and the standards of guest service, where they fit into the corporate structure (their role in the show), and they receive a tour of the Disney property where they will work. Cast members are also introduced to the intangible product, happiness, and their role in creating it. The second day of orientation, Traditions II, is devoted to the Disney policies and practices cast members must know to perform their jobs, an overview of what the company provides the cast members in terms of social, recreational, and personal services, and a four-hour orientation of their specific work area that includes meeting with their supervisors, learning what costumes they will wear, and reviewing general policies and procedures.

When the two-day Traditions orientation is completed, cast members begin a series of learning experiences at on-site practice sessions and classes at the university. This training may run from 8 to 16 hours before cast members are allowed to go to their specific work area after closing and practice.

The next step, paired training, allows exceptional cast members to act as role models. The benefits of paired training include (1) the new cast member rehearses with a respected member of the troupes and (2) the veteran cast member is recognized by management, as well as their peers, and held in esteem. These new cast

| EXHIBIT 22 | Orientation and Development Process |

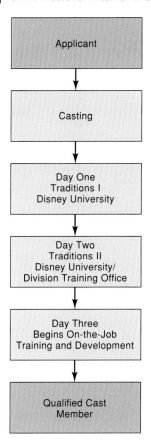

members are required to have between 16 to 48 hours of paired training and are not allowed to interact solo with guests until they have successfully completed paired training and have successfully answered questions on the training checklist.

Reinforcement Keeps Cast Members Committed to Disney Principles

Many of Disney's hourly jobs can be routine and repetitive, but Disney still expects "energy, enthusiasm, commitment and pride" from its cast members at all times. Recognition, communications, and social relations programs are especially important at Disney. Disney's goal is to constantly look for a variety of ways to tell workers how much they are valued. Cast member appreciation from Disney management comes in the form of service recognition awards, peer recognition programs, attendance awards, informal recognition parties, and milestone banquets for 10, 15, and 20 years of service.

Each year the centralized Disney University gives special recognition to several outstanding cast members who are called University Leaders. Four to six hourly, costumed cast members are interviewed and selected for a year-long assignment at the Disney University. The entire Disney University orientation is conducted by

··

| EXHIBIT 23 | Why Extensive Orientation? |

Disney Provides Extensive Orientation:

- to establish the corporate culture and overall company knowledge
- to strengthen the self-image of cast members
- to communicate employee benefits, activities, and services
- to communicate the why and wherefore of company policies and procedures
- to transmit to cast members the people skills and attitudes prerequisite to the job skills needed to perform their roles in the show
- to create a team spirit among new members of the Disney cast
- to answer the initial questions of new cast members
- to review safety procedures, right-to-know regulations, and other required regulations

··

these University Leaders. These cast members help bring the philosophical Disney ideals to reality by a person who is currently fulfilling that role. This program allows Disney to recognize outstanding cast members while better utilizing their talents.

Another expression of gratitude and appreciation from Disney management comes during the Christmas holidays. All Disney theme parks reopen one evening for cast members and their families. The management team says "Happy Holidays" by dressing in costume and operating the parks.[43]

Development: An Ongoing Process

Training does not stop when cast members learn their roles. Hourly cast members are offered career development, goal setting, and interviewing technique classes. Clerical staff are offered courtesy and clerical stress management classes. Disney's Leaders (hourly workers who have been given a leadership role for their job classification) and trainers receive special development including performance appraisals and how to train and lead development, all of which strengthen their human resource skills. Salaried cast members can attend classes such as counseling and listening, understanding people as individuals, Disney's courtesy, stress and time management, and an array of specific skill-related programs.

Since Disney promotes 85 percent of its middle- and executive-level management from within, Disney has developed the Disney Intern Program to meet these needs. Cast members from different divisions of the company who have management potential go through six months of on-the-job training. Halfway through the program, these students are given an assignment to develop an idea or modification to implement at Disney. Small groups work together to develop a presentation for top management. The six-month program ends with an exam and graduation. Unfortunately, completion of the internship is no guarantee of a job, but at least, cast members know this going into the program. Rather than promote and then train them for the job, Disney trains them in advance. Division managers project how many salaried people they think they will need and the company tries to make sure that there will be enough interns to meet those needs.

NOTES

1. Ron Grover, *The Disney Touch,* Homewood, Il: Business One Irwin, 1991.

2. Richard Holliss and Brian Sibley, *The Disney Studio Story,* London: Octopus Books Ltd., 1988.

3. Ibid.

4. Adrian Bailey, *Walt Disney's World of Fantasy,* Secaucus, NJ: Chartwell Books, 1982.

5. Hollis and Sibley, *The Disney Studio Story.*

6. Ibid.

7. Ibid.

8. Ibid.

9. Ibid.

10. Bailey, *Walt Disney's World of Fantasy.*

11. Hollis and Sibley, *The Disney Studio Story.*

12. Ibid.

13. Ibid.

14. Ibid.

15. Bailey, *Walt Disney's World of Fantasy.*

16. Hollis and Sibley, *The Disney Studio Story.*

17. Ibid.

18. Ibid.

19. Ibid.

20. Ibid.

21. Ibid.

22. Ibid.

23. Ibid.

24. Ibid.

25. Ibid.

26. Ibid.

27. Grover, *The Disney Touch.*

28. John Huey, "America's Hottest Export: Pop Culture," *Fortune,* December 31, 1990, pp. 50–60.

29. Sarah Grey, "Not a Mickey Mouse Organization," *Accountancy* (UK), November 1989, pp. 16–17.

30. Jane Sasseen, "Mickey Mania," *International Management,* November 1989, pp. 32–34.

31. Ibid.

32. Anne Ferguson, "Maximizing the Mouse," *Management Today* (UK), September 1989, pp. 56–62.

33. Maggie Mahar, "No Mickey Mouse Company: Wall Street's Losing Sight of Disney's Bright Prospects," *Barron's.* June 24, 1991, pp. 8–25.

34. Ibid.

35. Ibid.

36. Ibid.

37. "Mice, Magic, and Malls," *Shopping Centers Today,* May 1991, pp. 27–43.

38. Cyndee Miller, "Disney Plans Global Expansion of Its Stores," *Marketing News,* May 13, 1991, pp. 1, 22.

39. Penny Gill, "The Disney Store Blends Retailing & Entertainment," *Stores,* June 1991. pp. 20–24.

40. Charlene Marmer Solomon, "How Does Disney Do It?" *Personnel Journal,* December 1989, pp. 50–57.

41. Ibid.

42. Ibid.

43. Ibid.

Wal-Mart Stores, Inc.

When J.C. Penney let Samuel Moore Walton slip away from its management trainee program in 1942, the company had no warning of the resounding impact that resignation would have on its industry in the coming decades. After three years in the army, Sam Walton opened the first Walton's Ben Franklin store in Newport, Arkansas, in September 1945. By 1990, Sam Walton's retail venture had grown to be the largest retailer in the nation with sales of over $32 billion annually.[1] Profits reached over $1 billion annually by 1989, and the "dime store" no longer dealt in pocket change.

In 1950, Mr. Sam (as he was known to his associates) relocated to Bentonville, Arkansas, after losing the lease on his Newport store. During the 1950s, Mr. Sam increased the number of Walton-owned Ben Franklin stores to nine; in 1962, Mr. Sam and his brother, Bud, opened the first Wal-Mart Discount City in Rogers, Arkansas. Growth was anything but exponential during that period; the second Wal-Mart store didn't open for two more years. David Glass, now president and CEO, attended that grand opening in Harrison:

> It was the worst retail store I had ever seen. Sam had brought a couple of trucks of watermelons in and stacked them on the sidewalk. He had donkey rides out in the parking lot. It was 115 degrees, and the watermelons began to pop, and the donkeys began to do what donkeys do, and it all mixed together and ran all over the parking lot. And when you went inside the store, the mess just continued. He was a nice fellow, but I wrote him off. It was just terrible.[2]

From that dubious beginning, Wal-Mart Corporation has surprised Wall Street as well as its competitors by becoming America's leading retailer in 1990.[3] Late in 1969, the company was incorporated; 12 months later, its stock was publicly traded over the counter. In another two years the stock was approved and listed on the New York Stock Exchange. Sales for 1970 were $44 million. By 1979, sales had reached $1.248 billion (a 39.7 percent annualized growth rate). Sales growth through the 1980s was comparable; Wal-Mart has averaged a 34 percent growth in revenue during the past 11 years. Earnings have grown at a commensurate rate of 39 percent, compounded annually over the past 11 years.[4]

Wal-Mart became America's leading retailer while targeting what Mr. Sam recognized as an untapped market: rural communities with an average population of 15,000.[5] He believed that if Wal-Mart offered prices as good or better than the prices in stores that were several hours away by car, people would shop at home. This was operationalized into "backward expansion." First, a cluster of 30 to 40 Discount City stores were built in a targeted rural area within a 600-mile radius of a distribution center. Some of these stores would be located in selected towns around a more populous city. Then, Wal-Mart would locate one or more stores in the met-

This case was prepared by Steve R. Avera, Elizabeth D. Ellis, Don W. Reinhard, Andrea M. Thomas, and Lanny Wilkerson.

ropolitan area and begin major market advertising. When market saturation was approached, the backwards expansion effort moved to adjoining market areas.

Although the store location strategy was innovative, several other factors have played a strong role in vaulting Wal-Mart to the top of the discount retail mountain. For instance, Mr. Sam's management practices were even more trendsetting than his store location strategy. A strong advocate of participatory management practices, Wal-Mart has been a prototype in employee relations. Employees are not employees; they are "associates," a term coined by Mr. Sam at the very first Wal-Mart. A well-defined corporate strategy, rigorous cost control, and technological advantage are other factors that have contributed to Wal-Mart's success, as are an efficient distribution network and a strong corporate culture.

OVERALL CORPORATE STRATEGY

The core concept of Wal-Mart discount stores is maintaining its position as the low-cost leader in rural towns, the typical market area. However, market expansion has become the byword of the 1990s. The nucleus of the company's overall strategy is to sell name-brand, quality merchandise at low prices. Rather than special promotions and feature items, the company emphasizes everyday discount prices. The goal of each store is to saturate the market territory and become the dominant retailer in most of the communities it serves.[6] A unique feature in this type of retailing is that it is virtually recession-proof. In times of economic downturn, consumers flock to discount retailers. During the recession of 1974–1975, sales expanded 42 percent, and during the 1981–1982 recession, sales grew 44 percent annually.[7] As such, Wal-Mart is not materially affected by economic downturn like other retailers are.

Wal-Mart has obtained a distinct competitive advantage by targeting small, rural communities: lower operating costs. These result from lower rents, moderate wages, and the absence of unionization. Real estate is significantly cheaper. Smaller communities also typically have a more loyal customer base and productive work force.

EFFICIENT OPERATIONS

Wal-Mart is proud of its efficient operations, which have been a decisive factor in Wal-Mart's ascension to become America's top discount store. With its stated goal to be the low-cost leader,[8] Wal-Mart has built a network of store/offices that serve two important functions: they avoid the cost of building separate administrative offices, and they create a close feeling between store management and customers while promoting a better working bond between coworkers. This design allows managers to interact with the customers during business hours. It also has the added feature of allowing managers close contact with associates.

Operating efficiency can be analyzed through operating ratios. For instance, Wal-Mart's gross margin (sales minus cost of goods sold, divided by sales) is almost 24 percent, versus 27 percent for K mart.[9] Although K mart has a clear advantage in gross margin, it is offset by Wal-Mart's higher sales per square foot ($250 for Wal-Mart; $150 for K mart). Coupled, these two factors mean that Wal-Mart's expenses are nearly six percentage points *lower* than K mart's (22.5 percent versus 17 percent as a percentage of sales). Consequently, Wal-Mart's operating profit margin for its discount retail stores is 7.9 percent, while K mart's is 5.2 percent. While this 2.7

percent differential in operating margin may seem minor, when translated to real dollars, Wal-Mart cleared $2 billion (pretax), while K mart cleared $1 billion on essentially the same amount of total sales.[10] Another interesting side note is that Wal-Mart achieved these sales in 1,573 stores, while K mart operated 2,205.[11] It is estimated that Wal-Mart will operate the same number of discount stores in the United States as K mart by 1995, so Wal-Mart plans to extend its advantage in this area.[12]

Another measure of efficiency of which Wal-Mart is particularly proud is inventory shrinkage. Shrinkage occurs as a result of shoplifting, inventory shortages, and employee theft. While the discount retail industry's average shrinkage per store is 2 percent, Wal-Mart employees pride themselves on a per-store shrinkage that is around 1 percent.[13] With this low shrinkage rate comes clear rewards: stores that achieve target shrinkage rates earn bonuses of several hundred dollars each.

Clearly, operating efficiencies have played a critical role in the success of Wal-Mart. These operating efficiencies have allowed Wal-Mart to offer services that customers notice, such as keeping extra checkout lines open and posting a "greeter" at the entrance to each Wal-Mart store. This results in what Stephen F. Mandel, Jr., an analyst with Tiger Management Corporation, calls the "productivity loop," in which Wal-Mart's ability to offer lower prices and better service will inevitably attract more shoppers. This prompts more sales, making the company more efficient and able to lower prices even more.

Operating efficiencies have been translated into what many have termed the wave of the future in discounting, the wholesale club warehouse. Wal-Mart entered this market in 1983 with the founding of Sam's Wholesale Club.[14] Since then, sales have grown significantly, to approximately $7 billion annually in 1991. This makes Sam's Clubs the fourth largest discount store in America by volume, behind Wal-Mart, K mart, and Minneapolis-based Target. Sales in 1991 for the 148 warehouses averaged almost $47.3 million per store. Although K mart entered the wholesale warehouse arena before Wal-Mart with its PACE Membership Warehouses, K mart's 78 stores generated only an average of $29.4 million per store in 1991. David Glass asserts that wholesale clubs are the biggest sustainable advantage in retailing since the emergence of discounters in the early 1960s. Although gross margins run between 9 and 10 percent (less than half that of a discount store), they produce equal or better returns.[15] With the largest network of these wholesale membership clubs in the United States and the complementary distribution network to support it, Wal-Mart is clearly in the driver's seat of this opportunity for the 1990s.

DISTRIBUTION NETWORK

Wal-Mart's distribution system is another key component of Wal-Mart's strategy. Its 19 distribution centers strategically blanket Wal-Mart's market areas. Most Wal-Mart stores are located within one day's drive of a distribution center. Deliveries are made daily to each Wal-Mart store.

Between 70 and 80 percent of all purchasing is done centrally, taking advantage of Wal-Mart's state-of-the-art satellite network (see the discussion of computer technology that follows). Similarly, 77 percent of the purchases made by Wal-Mart stores were shipped from the distribution centers in 1991. The remaining 23 percent were shipped directly to the stores from suppliers.[16] All but one of the distribution centers are automated, utilizing a complex conveyor system which involves up to 11 *miles* of belts. Laser scanners route the goods (up to 190,000 cases per day), which are also strategically tied to the satellite network core in Bentonville.

A recent addition to Wal-Mart's distribution network occurred in December 1990, when Wal-Mart acquired McLane Company, a specialty distributor of more than 12,500 grocery and nongrocery, convenience-related products. McLane's distribution network touches approximately 26,000 stores throughout the United States. The company supplies about 50 percent of Wal-Mart's stores. Prior to the merger, Wal-Mart accounted for 20 percent of McLane's business.[17]

COMPUTER TECHNOLOGY

Wal-Mart boasts the world's largest private, fully integrated satellite network.[18] This satellite network connects the Wal-Mart management information system (MIS) to every Wal-Mart store and distribution center in 26 states. By using audio, video, and data signals via more than 1,400 earth stations, it maintains constant communication between the organization's communications center and all of its operations and suppliers. As a result, every store is connected in real time to the corporate information center in Bentonville so that each and every transaction is made on-line. The network not only monitors inventory and orders replacement stock, it also electronically approves credit transactions. Authorization is sent back to the remote store in less than six seconds.

The operational goal of this network is to provide better customer service and improve business efficiency. For instance, if a credit authorization transaction can be completed in 25 percent less time, one checker can handle four customers in the time it took to handle three using the manual system. Hence, a checker can process more customers in the same amount of time. Customers spend less time in the checkout line and leave with positive feelings toward the store.

Other business efficiencies that result from the network include the monitoring of inventory and movement, the ability to track trends by item, and the assurance of a smooth product flow from supplier to distribution center to retail stores to consumers. Products that are in demand flow into the stores at the desired rate. This rapid response time has allowed Wal-Mart to maintain an enviable in-stock rate, a high asset utilization rate, and industry leadership in holding waste and costs down while keeping productivity and profits high.[19]

BUY AMERICAN PROGRAM

As a result of Mr. Sam's concern for the economy's high balance of trade deficits and the subsequent loss of jobs (and American dollars flowing out of the country), in 1985, Mr. Sam sent a message to his merchandise managers: "Find products that American manufacturers have stopped producing because they couldn't compete with foreign imports." This was the foundation for the "Buy American Program," begun that year. It was not an anti-import campaign or an effort to organize grassroots support of trade regulation legislation, tariffs, or other controls on import items. It was not a mandate by the company to buy domestic goods that are inferior just because they are domestic. The program, as defined by Mr. Sam, "is a cooperative effort between retailers and domestic manufacturers to re-establish a competitive position in price and quality of American made goods to the market place."

The cooperative nature of the program requires that both Wal-Mart and its suppliers employ flexibility and creativity in the production of their products. American producers are forced to be more "market driven," and Wal-Mart extends many of the terms and cooperation formerly given only foreign suppliers. Payment for products is made on a more timely basis, allowing the producers to decrease their cost of financing inventories. Wal-Mart suppliers have a commitment to improve facilities where necessary, remain financially conservative, and work with Wal-Mart to meet the needs of their customers. The key to the program is improving employee efficiency, which reduces costs and allows the supplier to be more competitive with the foreign competition.

One example of this cooperative is Farris Fashions, which in 1984 was a struggling shirt manufacturer in eastern Arkansas. After Van Heusen, the men's shirt and clothing manufacturer, pulled its contract to manufacture shirts, 90 employees faced permanent layoff. Mr. Sam and David Glass contacted President Farris Burroughs. A few weeks later, Farris Fashions had a contract to make 240,000 flannel shirts, a product that Wal-Mart had been buying in the Far East. By 1988, Wal-Mart's order from Farris Fashions had leaped to 1.5 million garments, and employment has exploded to 325 workers. The company has invested over $1 million in new production equipment, which has increased productivity and further lowered costs. Another cost-lowering mechanism is Wal-Mart's cooperation with Farris Fashions' suppliers. Wal-Mart buys the material for the shirts and gives Farris the benefit of the lower prices it can command.

OPERATING SEGMENTS

Wal-Mart Stores, Inc., has made a conscious strategic decision to focus on retailing; therefore, it has focused its resources on businesses that help it achieve its stated retail strategies. Expansion into other areas has been through market penetration: Sam's Clubs cater to small businesses; SuperCenters incorporate both food and general merchandise in a simple, massive store; and Hypermart USA is a European experimental retail concept. A variation on the SuperCenters, the Hypermart USA, offers a combination discount store and supermarket, as well as 15 to 20 free-standing, fast-food and specialized service providers, such as photo finishing, dry cleaners, optical shops, shoe repair, and hair salons. The SuperCenter and the Hypermart USA formats have been refined somewhat by Wal-Mart; this new hybrid retail format will be called Supercenters.[20]

Sam's Clubs has become the front-runner among the discount wholesale clubs that emerged during the 1980s. These large, no-frills warehouses handle a limited number of fast-selling products (approximately 3,000 stock keeping units [SKUs], compared to Wal-Mart's typical 65,000 SKUs). Inventory turnover and minimal operating costs are the keys to profitability. An established Sam's Club will turn over its inventory about every 20 to 22 days, more than three times faster than the typical Wal-Mart store. With vendor terms of net/30 days, inventory is sold before the company must pay for it. Cannibalization (losing business at one company owned store to another company owned store) between Sam's Clubs and Wal-Mart stores is minimal due to limited merchandise overlap, which is less than several hundred SKUs.[21] With 212 Sam's Clubs and the addition of 38 new Clubs in 1992, Wal-Mart has strategically positioned itself with Sam's Clubs.

Competition is intensifying. K mart is increasing the number of its PACE Warehouse Stores, and some industry shakeout is anticipated during the 1990s. However, Wal-Mart's efficient operating network, including its satellite information system and its distribution network, should allow Sam's Clubs to remain the dominant retailer in this industry. Sales for 1991 totaled $9.9 billion. Sales growth for 1992 is expected to be 30 percent.

The refinement of the Supercenter retailer will provide the convenience-minded consumer with "one-stop shopping": both food items and general merchandise can be found under one roof, both at discount prices. Like Wal-Mart Stores and Sam's Clubs, this retail concept is anticipated to be recession-proof. There are currently four Hypermart USAs and six Supercenters. The company anticipates 12 new Supercenters will be opened during 1992.[22]

With the acquisition of McLane Distribution on December 10, 1990, Wal-Mart strengthened its ability to distribute merchandise at reduced costs. McLane services 26,000 customers through 13 distribution centers in 11 states. Most of its customers are convenience stores such as 7-Eleven and Circle K. Wal-Mart had enjoyed a business relationship with McLane prior to the acquisition ($500 million annually); however, since the acquisition, Wal-Mart has funnelled approximately $1 billion (annualized) to McLane for distribution services.[23] Wal-Mart will realize immediate benefits from McLane's distribution of cigarettes, candy, music products, sporting goods, and value-added foods sold through Wal-Mart's in-store snack bars.

HUMAN RESOURCES

Corporate Culture/General Philosophy

Our philosophy is that management's role is simply to get the right people in the right places to do a job and then encourage them to use their own inventiveness to accomplish the task at hand.[24]

Sam Walton

We have no superstars at Wal-Mart; we have average people operating in an environment that encourages everyone to perform way above average.[25]

David Glass

Most of us wear a button that says, "Our People Make the Difference." That is not a slogan at Wal-Mart, it is a way of life. Our people really do make a difference.[26]

David Glass

In the late 1960s when Sam and his brother, Bud, owned about 20 Wal-Marts, a union tried to organize two stores in Missouri, and Sam hired labor lawyer John Tate, now an executive vice-president of Wal-Mart, to help. Tate told Walton, "You can approach this one of two ways. Hold people down, and pay me or some other lawyer to make it work. Or devote time and attention to proving to people that you care." Sam chose the latter and subsequently held his first management seminar, entitled "We care."

Sam insisted upon calling all employees "associates," since it implies a partnership. Department managers see figures that many companies never show general managers. Profit goals are set for each store, and if exceeded, hourly associates share part of additional profit. This "partnership" goes past monetary participation to open-door policies and an atmosphere that says, "Hey, if you've got a problem, talk to somebody. Don't talk about it in the lounge or the parking lot; come to management." This is ingrained in Wal-Mart's culture.

Wal-Mart's culture is its most fearsome weapon. The company gospel is "Be an agent for consumers, find out what they want, and sell it to them for the lowest possible price."[27] One source described Wal-Mart as follows:

> The key to Wal-Mart's success is the quality of their management, its style and its recognition of the importance of the individual player in the overall team effort. Other companies are striving to achieve the same cultural level, but no other retail company is close. Wal-Mart people work harder than most, probably because they have more fun. They are constantly being challenged by one another and forced to laugh at themselves. They take pride in working for perhaps the finest company in the world and their individual contributions are recognized.[28]

It is Wal-Mart's familylike environment that emphasizes teamwork and encourages employee ideas and participation. The work atmosphere is a down-home "concern for the individual." Individual contributions to the team effort are welcomed and rewarded. Participatory management from top to bottom is stressed, and listening is an important part of a manager's job.

According to Mr. Sam, "99 percent of the best ideas we ever had came from our employees."[29] His explanation was simplistic but to the point: "If people believe in themselves, it's truly amazing what they can accomplish."[30]

Sam Walton "managed by walking around," and expected the same from his managers. Glass, along with other top executives, spends several days a week visiting the stores. To heighten associates' sense of mission, they are given plenty of responsibility. Managers for each of the 34 departments within a typical Wal-Mart are expected to run their operations as if they were running their own businesses.[31] According to one manager, 90 percent of his day is spent walking around stores communicating with associates—he praises them for well-done jobs, discusses how improvements could be made, and listens to comments and solicits suggestions. This management style also encourages the steady stream of ideas that Wal-Mart receives from its associates.

Low threshold of change (LTC) is a highly valued concept at Wal-Mart. The planning process begins with store management asking each associate what he or she could do individually or how store operations could improve. Associates are encouraged to challenge and change any policies perceived to detract from operations.

Store Meetings

Every morning before stores open and every evening after stores close, associates and managers meet for ten minutes to discuss overall operations, expectations, how things went, and so on. Every Friday morning, each store has a general store meeting during which associates at every level can ask questions and expect to get straightforward answers from management. These meetings communicate to associates information on new company initiatives and policy change announcements. Video training films are also shown from time to time. As part of these meetings, corporate management, via satellite, emphasizes the company's five most important priorities, which gives employees goals and keeps them focused.[32]

Each week department and store figures are posted on the back wall of each store so associates can see how they rank. If the figures are better than average, associates are praised. Associates in departments that regularly outperform averages can expect annual bonuses and raises. Performances lower than average are discussed so solutions can be found.[33]

Saturday Morning Meetings at Headquarters

Since 1961, every Saturday morning in Bentonville, Arkansas, at 7:30 A.M., Wal-Mart conducts a very informal and relaxed meeting. Employees dress casually, some in hunting or tennis clothes for after-meeting fun. Employees attending include top officers, merchandising staff, regional managers who oversee store districts, and the Bentonville headquarters staff (over 100 people). They meet to discuss Wal-Mart issues, such as the week's sales, payroll percentages, special promotional items, unusual problems, and reports on transportation, loss prevention, and information systems.[34]

People Division

Instead of a personnel department, Wal-Mart has a people division. According to Von Johnston, director of the people division, "We deal with people; people are our job. One of our board members last year suggested that we change our name to reflect our job and we did."[35]

This division is divided into five functions: store operations, warehouse personnel, training and development, general office personnel staff, and the Walton Life Fitness Center staff. A primary focus of this division has been the recruitment of new associates.

"The Wal-Mart Way"

"The Wal-Mart Way" summarizes the company's unconventional approach to business and the determination of the associates. This commitment to "total quality" is essential to the company's future success; it proliferates the very best things the company does, while incorporating the new ideas of company employees.[36] "Quality the Wal-Mart Way" is an ongoing focus, with the emphasis on doing everything right the first time, since that is the most efficient way. Key elements are productivity, teamwork, the "elimination of dumb things," innovation that calls for "breaking the frame," and an effort to continuously improve. This mindset has also been adopted by Sam's Clubs, which has adopted HEATKTE—"high expectations are the key to everything"—as its strategic rallying cry.[37]

Wal-Mart's senior management is able to keep on top of all that is happening because management believes in delegating authority, sharing decisions, and trusting the people charged with specific responsibilities. "The esprit de corps and the desire of the individuals to excel are so engendered as to assure that the best possible job is performed in practically every sector of Wal-Mart."[38] Wal-Mart's people are focused, responsive, willing to change, and willing to execute their jobs in a superior fashion. The company has grown tremendously without losing sight of the basic principles that made it great in the first place. Wal-Mart's corporate culture is very much ingrained in all of its associates since they have had the benefit of working in such a positive environment over nearly 30 years.

....
STAFFING

Wal-Mart has been the number one creator of new jobs in the United States since 1984.[39] As of January 31, 1991, Wal-Mart employed 328,000 full- and part-time employees, which was an increase of approximately 57,000 employees for the year.[40]

Employees at Wal-Mart consist of two categories: managers (salaried) and associates (hourly). Every retail outlet is managed by a store manager and one or more assistants. Managers are hired in one of three ways:

1. Hourly associates move up through the ranks from sales to department manager of check lanes to store management training.
2. People from other retail companies with outstanding merchandising skills are recruited.
3. College graduates are hired.

Approximately 50 percent of all managers began in hourly positions, 35 percent are recent college graduates, and 15 percent are from other retailers. Wal-Mart hires over 1,500 management people per year, just to maintain management staffing levels in its stores and corporate headquarters.

Each time a new store opens, corporate headquarters selects a store manager, who is brought to company headquarters for a one-week orientation, during which one day is devoted to hiring practices. Store managers are either transferred from another store or are assistant managers who have been promoted. Assistant managers transferred from stores in the community or at least the same state are also selected by corporate headquarters. The store manager and the assistant manager(s) are totally responsible for hiring all of the store's associates.

Wal-Mart's recruitment process is highly structured, yet decentralized. Established stores have a rotating employee screening committee responsible for hiring new associates. This committee consists of five associates. Before being hired, candidates are interviewed by the committee a minimum of two times.

Wal-Mart views drug screening, initiated in 1987, as an important part of its hiring process. According to Von Johnston, director of the people division, "If you don't have plans for drug screening, then you will be hiring our rejects." Drug screening is done subsequent to a candidate passing the second interview.[41]

Wal-Mart does not try to hire a large ratio of part-time employees to avoid paying benefits. In 1985, the ratio of full-time to part-time employees was approximately 5 to 1.[42] Part-time employees are primarily sales personnel.

Wal-Mart has created a unique atmosphere by positioning associates with whom shoppers interact at various points in the store. For example, greeters placed at the front door add warmth to the customers' shopping experience. "The addition of more people to the stores comes at a time when other retailers are trying to reduce their expense ratios and are firmly limiting the number of payroll hours budgeted for the stores."[43] Wal-Mart's financial strength has allowed it the opportunity to offer value-added services such as this, which has changed the "rules of the game."

....
TRAINING AND DEVELOPMENT

Wal-Mart considers people development its number one priority. Developing people allows the company to push decision making down to lower levels. Extensive training is provided to managers at the corporate level; managers, in turn, are expected to train hourly associates.

Management Training

In order to assure well-trained future store managers, Wal-Mart is committed to an ongoing training program for store managers, assistant managers, and department managers. All managers complete a structured management training program which consists of on-the-job training and book work.[44] Areas studied include management topics, such as internal/external theft, scheduling, store staffing, retail math, merchandise replenishment, and the Wal-Mart "keys to supervision" series dealing with interpersonal skills and personnel responsibilities. After completing the training program, trainees are made responsible for an area in a store. The length of time they are in this position varies according to how the trainee progresses. Subsequent to this training, the trainee is promoted to assistant manager.

As an assistant manager, training continues with the one-week Retail Management Training Seminar.[45] According to Suzanne Allford, vice-president of the people division,

> We believe our store and club managers are our best teachers and instructors; corporately, it's our job to provide them with the very best tools and facilities; our belief that this can only be done using practical hands-on methods led us to move our retail management seminars from our home office out to ten of our distribution centers, near to the store and clubs, to expose our management team to the heart of our distribution network.

In 1985, Wal-Mart created the Walton Institute of Retailing, which was opened in affiliation with the University of Arkansas. Currently, every Wal-Mart corporate and store manager is expected to participate in the Institute's special programs to strengthen and develop the company's managerial capabilities.[46]

Wal-Mart believes that good people need new challenges. Therefore, with respect to senior management, Wal-Mart offers cross training to enable them to master new areas.

Associate Training

"If you are not looking at those people who are at the bottom of the line and looking to train and develop them, you're going to continue having employment problems," according to Von Johnston.[47]

Upon hiring, employees are immediately placed in positions for on-the-job training (OJT). No formal training is provided from Wal-Mart headquarters for hourly associates. OJT is Wal-Mart's philosophy regarding associate training. Store managers and department managers train and supervise employees. The use of video films is a popular training technique, shown from time to time in the Friday morning meetings.[48]

....

PERFORMANCE EVALUATIONS AND REWARD SYSTEMS/BENEFITS

Preformance Evaluations

Wal-Mart calls the process of performance appraisals "evaluations."[49] All managers and associates are evaluated annually.

Associates are hired at higher than minimum wage ($5 per hour in Tallahasee), and can expect a raise within the first year at two of the three performance evaluations. New associates receive three evaluations during their first year—the first at 90 days, the second at six months, and the third upon their anniversary date. Assuming performance is satisfactory, the employee receives raises at the 90-day evaluation and at the annual evaluation. Employees who are performing at outstanding levels may receive merit raises any time during the year. After successfully completing the first year, associates receive annual evaluations. Exceptions to this include promotions or ratings other than "marginal progress."[50]

Reward Systems

As previously indicated, management positions are salaried. Store managers receive additional compensation based on their store's profits. Assistant store managers receive additional compensation based on the company's profitability. All other personnel are compensated on an hourly basis with the opportunity of receiving additional incentive bonuses based upon the company's productivity and profitability.[51]

Relatively speaking, Wal-Mart's people are highly motivated, well trained, and very productive. Ideas for productivity and efficiency are quickly disseminated. For example, each week, an average of about 1,200 stores submit approximately 5,000 suggestions. The best of these ideas are adopted, leading to substantial sales gains, cost reductions, and improved productivity. Successful ideas receive companywide recognition, such as a mention in Saturday morning meetings at headquarters, or even the personal praise of the chairperson. This reward system motivates employees to think of ways to improve operations, such as how to decrease shoplifting or improve merchandising.

Shrinkage bonuses were implemented in 1980 to control losses from theft and damage. If a store holds shrinkage below the corporate goal, every associate in that store receives up to $300.[52] In the second quarter of 1991, Wal-Mart paid $6.3 million in bonuses to stores for improving their shrinkage problem.[53]

A very successful incentive program is its Volume Producing Item contests, whereby departments within a store do special promotions and pricing on items they want to feature. This program helped boost sales and sell slow-moving items. It also encouraged employees to be innovative.

Profit Sharing and Stock Options Plans

Wal-Mart believes that each of its associates is a partner in the company and encourages stock ownership. Profit sharing is available to every associate. Eighty percent of Wal-Mart's full time associates own stock, and 203,000 shareholders work for the company.[54]

The company maintains a profit sharing plan under which most full and many part-time employees become participants. They are eligible to participate in the plan one month following one year of employment with the company. Annual contributions, based on the profitability of the company, are made at the sole discretion of the company. Participants are fully vested after seven years of service. For fiscal years ended January 31, 1987, through January 31, 1991, the following contributions were made:[55]

1987	$51,772,000
1988	$59,466,000
1989	$77,067,000
1990	$90,447,000
1991	$98,327,000

Wal-Mart's stock purchase plan allows eligible associates a means of purchasing shares of common stock at market prices through regular payroll deductions of no more than $75 per biweekly pay period, or $1,800 per year. The company will contribute 15 percent of each participant's contribution under the stock plan. As of April 9, 1991, 26 percent of its 328,000 employees were participating in the plan.[56]

NOTES

1. "Facts About Wal-Mart Stores, Inc." Wal-Mart Stores, Inc., 1991.

2. John Huey, "America's Most Successful Merchant," *Fortune,* September 23, 1991, pp. 46–59.

3. Subrata N. Chakravarty, "A Tale of Two Companies," *Forbes,* May 27, 1991, pp. 86–96.

4. Ibid.

5. Kem A. King, "Wal-Mart Stores, Inc," *Strategic Management,* Homewood, IL: Richard D. Irwin, 1985.

6. D. T. Spindel, "Wal-Mart Stores, Inc.—Company Report," A. G. Edwards & Sons, Inc., July 9, 1991.

7. Gene G. Marcial, "Why Wal-Mart Is Recession-Proof," *Business Week,* February 22, 1988, p. 146.

8. Wal-Mart Stores, Inc. *1991 Annual Report,* Wal-Mart Stores, Inc., 1991.

9. D. A. Poneman, 'Discount Department Stores—Industry Report," Sanford C. Bernstein & Co., Inc., May 3, 1991.

10. Bill Saporito, "Is Wal-Mart Unstoppable?" *Fortune,* May 6, 1991, pp. 50–59.

11. Cathy Dybdahl, "The Discount Department Store Industry: The New 'Big 3,' " *Chain Store Age Executive* (Section 2), vol. 67, no. 8. August 1991, pp. 19A–20A.

12. Bernard Sosnick and Dorothy Lakner, "Wal-Mart Stores Bigger and Better," Oppenheimer & Co., Inc., May 31, 1991.

13. Huey, "America's Most Successful Merchant."

14. Sam M. Walton, David D. Glass, Donald G. Soderquist, Dean L. Sanders, Al Jones, and Lee Stuckey. "Wal-Mart: A Focus on Retailing with Sam Walton," Live satellite broadcast from Bentonville, Arkansas, October 3, 1991.

15. Saporito, "Is Wal-Mart Unstoppable?"

16. Wal-Mart Stores, Inc. *1991 Form 10-K,* Securities and Exchange Commission, 1991.

17. Spindel, "Wal-Mart Stores, Inc.—Company Report."

18. Jamal Munshi, *MIS: Cases in Action,* New York: McGraw-Hill, 1990.

19. Ibid.

20. Spindel, "Wal-Mart Stores, Inc.—Company Report."

21. Ibid.

22. Ibid.

23. Sosnick and Lakner, "Wal-Mart Stores Bigger and Better."

24. King, "Wal-Mart Stores, Inc."

25. "Quality of Management," *Fortune,* January 29, 1990.

26. King, "Wal-Mart Stores, Inc."

27. Saporito, "Is Wal-Mart Unstoppable?"

28. First Boston. *Wal-Mart Stores, Inc., Equity Research Report.* Number RT2697. December 3, 1990.

29. Saporito, "Is Wal-Mart Unstoppable?"

30. John Huey, "Wal-Mart: Will It Take Over the World?" *Fortune,* January 30, 1989, pp. 52–61.

31. "Quality of Management."

32. Joan Bergmann, "Saga of Sam Walton," *Stores,* January 1988, pp. 129–142.

33. King, "Wal-Mart Stores, Inc."

34. Ibid.

35. Allan Halcrow, "Voices of HR Experience—Part II," *Personnel Journal* 68, no. 5. May 1989, pp. 38–53.

36. Wal-Mart Stores, Inc., *1991 Annual Report.*

37. Ibid.

38. First Boston, *Wal-Mart Stores, Inc., Equity Research Report.*

39. Halcrow, "Voices of HR Experience—Part II."

40. Wal-Mart Stores, Inc., *1991 Form 10-K.*

41. Halcrow, Voices of HR Experience—Part II."

42. King, "Wal-Mart Stores, Inc."

43. Oppenheimer & Co., Inc., "Wal-Mart Stores Bigger and Better," Report Number 91-698, May 31, 1991.

44. Sandy Brummett, Personal Interview with Public Relations Assistant of Wal-Mart Stores, Inc., Bentonville, Arkansas. Interview conducted by telephone on November 19, 1991.

45. Ibid.

46. Ibid.

47. Halcrow, "Voices of HR Experience—Part II."

48. George Wilkins, Personal Interview with Assistant Manager of Wal-Mart Store (Capital Circle Southeast, Tallahassee, Florida). Interview conducted by telephone on November 18, 1991.

49. Halcrow, "Voices of HR Experience—Part II."

50. Wilkins, personal interview.

51. Wal-Mart Stores, Inc., *1991 Form 10-K.*

52. Wilkins, personal interview.

53. M. A. Gilliam, "Wal-Mart Stores, Inc.—Company Report," The First Boston Corp. July 8, 1991.

54. Ibid.

55. Wal-Mart Stores, Inc., *1991 Form 10-K.*

56. Ibid.

GLOSSARY
·········

Abilities The physical and mental capacities needed to perform tasks not requiring the use of tools, equipment, or machinery. (Ch. 7)

Ability Requirements Scales A method of job analysis that focuses on worker characteristics and yields standardized information. (Ch. 7)

Acquisition A method of implementing a growth strategy wherein one company buys another but maintains its own name. (Ch. 3)

Acculturation The process of acquiring the culture of an organization or society. (Ch. 10)

Administrative Decision Making Day-to-day decisions. (Ch. 1)

Analyzers A strategy wherein the organization has a product in a stable market as well as a product in a changing market. (Ch. 2)

Anticipatory Decision Making See **Proactive Approach.** (Ch. 1)

Artificial Intelligence The use of computers to simulate the knowledge and thinking patterns of experts. (Ch. 2)

Attribution Theory The process whereby people assign meaning based on the specific attributions or associations they make. (Ch. 4)

Base Pay The basic cash received for the work performed, adjusted for the individual's skill, education, experience, or some other attribute. (Ch. 12)

Bluffing (also referred to as posturing) A tactic used in bargaining wherein each party tries to create false positions that it can then trade away. (Ch. 18)

Boundary Spanning The process of scanning the environment in an effort to link the organization to its environment. (Ch. 2)

Captive A defensive strategy wherein an organization allows another organization to manage it in return for promising to buy a certain amount of the captive's products or services. (Ch. 3)

Change Agent An internal or external consultant who facilitates the change effort aimed at improving the organization. (Ch. 10)

Cognitive Dissonance A psychological phenomenon that occurs when a decision maker, after reflecting back on the decision, begins to question whether or not he or she made the right decision. (Ch. 4)

Competitive Advantage A combination of the ends (goals) for which the firm is striving and the means (policies) by which it is seeking to get there. (Ch. 19)

Compressed Work Week A work week in which employees put in their 40 hours in less than five working days. (Ch. 8)

Compulsory Benefits A range of benefits that all employers must offer, as mandated by law. (Ch. 14)

Concentration Growth Strategy The organization's plans to focus its growth on a single product or on a group of closely related products. (Ch. 3)

Concentric Diversification A type of diversification that occurs when related but clearly differentiated products or services are developed or obtained. (Ch. 3)

Conglomerate Diversification A type of diversification wherein the organization diversifies into an area totally unrelated to its current products or services. (Ch. 3)

Consolidations Actions to cut functions or activities that may be redundant within an organization. (Ch. 19)

Constituent See **Stakeholder.** (Ch. 3)

Contract Rights Arbitration A type of arbitration that consists of settling impasses in the actual administration of the contract and is usually the outcome of a grievance procedure that cannot be settled by the parties. (Ch. 18)

Contributory Fund A type of pension that is funded by both the employer and the employee. (Ch. 14)

Contributory Negligence A workers' compensation doctrine wherein if an employee was even slightly (e.g., 1%) at fault in an accident on the job, he or she would be unable to collect in a suit against the employer. (Ch. 14)

Critical Incident Technique A method of job analysis which focuses on the things a worker does that distinguish the person as an effective or ineffective employee. (Ch. 7)

Cutbacks Attempts by an organization to react to temporary changes in the marketplace by reducing spending and controlling costs. (Ch. 19)

Defenders A strategy wherein the focus is on a narrow line of products and the organization strongly defends its position in the market. (Ch. 2)

Defined Benefit Plan A retirement plan in which the benefits paid to employees are set and the method used to determine the benefits is set. (Ch. 14)

Defined Contribution Plan A retirement plan in which the contribution rate paid by the employee is fixed and retirement benefits vary (e.g., profit sharing). (Ch. 14)

Depressions Severe forms of recessions. (Ch. 19)

Differentiation A strategy wherein an organization seeks to create a product or service that is unique within the industry, and thus gain a competitive advantage. (Ch. 19)

Disability A leave of absence offered by employers for employees hurt or who become ill on the job. (Ch. 14)

Disparate Treatment A situation that occurs when a manager intentionally treats an applicant or employee differently because of race, color, religion, national origin, sex, or age. (Ch. 5)

Diversification A growth strategy wherein an organization moves into products or services that are clearly different from its current businesses. (Ch. 3)

Divestiture A defensive strategy wherein an organization sells or divests itself of a business or part of a business. (Ch. 3)

Domain Consensus Individuals who have a vested interest in the organization agree to its domain. (Ch. 2)

Dominant Coalition Group of individuals in the organization who make strategic decisions. (Ch. 4)

Downsizing The process by which a firm seeks to reduce its overall size and scope permanently, usually the result of changes in the organization's strategy or changes in the marketplace. (Ch. 19)

Early Retirement A type of termination strategy wherein some form of inducement for employees to retire from the organization before they reach the normal retirement age is provided. (Ch. 19)

Empire Building A strategy of individuals who entrench themselves in positions through a combination of politics, length of time in the job, and the ability to project a perceived value to the firm. (Ch. 19)

Equity Theory The belief that employees examine the relationship between their outcomes from the job and their inputs to the job. This ratio is then compared to the ratios of relevant others. (Ch. 12)

Employee Ability A method for determining layoffs wherein the criteria used to lay off workers is the skill level and productivity of each employee. (Ch. 19)

Employee Seniority A method for determining layoffs wherein the criteria used to lay off workers is the length of time that each employee has worked with the firm. (Ch. 19)

Employee Terminations Actions initiated by the organization to separate employees from the organization permanently. (Ch. 19)

Employment-at-Will Doctrine A doctrine stating that workers are employed at the will of the organization and

that the organization is free to end this employment at any time it chooses and for any reason it chooses. (Ch. 19)

Environmental Scanning The process of examining the external environment to determine trends and projections of factors that will affect the organization. (Ch. 2)

External Equity The degree to which the organization's wages are competitive with its competitors' wages. (Ch. 12)

Fiberoptics The transmission of data, voice, pictures, or other types of information along a light beam (laser). (Ch. 2)

Forced Resignation A type of termination strategy wherein employees are usually offered the opportunity to resign as an alternative to an outright termination. (Ch. 19)

Functional Job Analysis A method in which the functions of a job can be examined in relation to three classifications: data, people, and things. (Ch. 7)

Funded Plan A method of funding pension benefits that pays benefits out of money set aside and invested specifically to pay pension benefits. (Ch. 14)

Generic Strategies A core set of basic strategies that an organization may choose to follow. (Ch. 3)

Genetic Engineering Artificially changing the DNA molecule in genes to change biological characteristics. (Ch. 2)

Golden Parachutes Guarantees by organizations to the employees detailing the type of benefits they will receive in termination situations. (Ch. 19)

Halo Effect The notion that one characteristic or behavior of the job applicant (positive or negative) overrides all or most other characteristics. (Ch. 9)

Harvest Strategy A stability strategy that attempts to maintain the status quo. The idea behind this particular strategy is to retrieve the value of earlier investments because the firm intends to sell its assets and get out of the business. (Ch. 3)

Hiring Freeze A common method used for workforce attrition wherein organizations forego all new planned hirings. (Ch. 19)

Historical Costs Actual expenses for recruiting, training, development, etc. (Ch. 4)

Indefinite Layoff The organization may decide to release the employees from the company after a fixed period, such as six months or a year. (Ch. 19)

Insured Pensions Payment of pension benefits that is guaranteed through an insurance company. (Ch. 14)

Intended Strategy The strategy formulated during the planning period. (Ch. 1)

Interest Arbitration A type of arbitration that involves the terms of the contract itself. (Ch. 18)

Internal Growth Method A method of implementing a growth strategy that occurs when current market share with current products is expanded. (Ch. 3)

Job Analysis The process of collecting information about jobs, which typically becomes the basis for the job description and job specification. (Ch. 7)

Job Description A description of the duties, responsibilities, working conditions, and activities of a particular job. (Ch. 7)

Job-Element Method A method of job analysis that yields worker-oriented information. An individual familiar with the job identifies various job elements (e.g., knowledge, skills, abilities, and personal traits) needed to perform the job. (Ch. 7)

Job Sharing An employee shares his or her job with another employee. (Ch. 8)

Job Specifications A description of employee qualifications, such as experience, knowledge, skills, or abilities, that are required to perform the job. (Ch. 7)

Job-Oriented Job Analysis Methods A job analysis method which yields information about the actual tasks that comprise the job. (Ch. 7)

Joint Venture A method of implementing a growth strategy that occurs when two or more companies work together for a specific project. (Ch. 3)

Knowledge The degree to which a job holder is required to know specific technical material. (Ch. 7)

Leave 'em Naked Strategy A termination strategy wherein the firm essentially releases employees without providing any protection or compensation benefits or outplacement services. (Ch. 19)

Leveraged Buyout A takeover of a company, usually using borrowed funds, either in the form of bank loans or low-rated "junk bonds." (Ch. 19)

Liquidation A defensive strategy that occurs when the organization is either sold or dissolved. (Ch. 3)

Logical Incrementalism Measured change or reaction to a particular event. (Ch. 1)

Management Development The training and development programs specifically designed for supervisors and managers. (Ch. 10)

Mental Imagery A process used to project decision outcomes by allowing decision makers to use projective imagery to role-play a decision mentally. (Ch. 4)

Mentor An individual within the organization who is responsible for coaching or guiding various subordinates. (Ch. 10)

Merger A method of implementing a growth strategy wherein two companies join to form a new company and adopt a new name. (Ch. 3)

Neutral Strategies A stability strategy that attempts to maintain the status quo. This particular approach is a "do-nothing" approach wherein the organization continues doing what it has always done without a growth goal in mind. (Ch. 3)

Non-Contributory A pension in which all the funds for the pensions are paid by the employer. (Ch. 14)

Opportunity Cost The foregone productivity because a job was not filled or because it was filled with a new, less well-trained employee. (Ch. 4)

Organizational Development A change-oriented process wherein the emphasis is on an organization's overall improvement (e.g., structure, policies, procedures, or objectives). (Ch. 10)

Orientation The process of welcoming new employees, bringing them into the organization, and familiarizing them with organization operations and culture. The **formal** orientation is conduced by the organization. The **informal** orientation occurs through daily interactions with fellow employees. (Ch. 10)

Outplacement Policy Corporate programs intended to help terminated employees adjust to their terminations and to assist them in finding other jobs. These programs often provide assistance to employees in three areas: financial support, psychological support, and job search support. (Ch. 19)

Overall Cost Leadership A strategy wherein an organization seeks to sell products that are less expensive in price than their competitors' products. (Ch. 19)

Participation The level of involvement in the decision-making process among managers and employees. (Ch. 4)

Pay Grades A group of jobs that have the same classification with respect to pay. (Ch. 12)

Pay Level The average wage rate paid for a specific group of jobs. (Ch. 12)

Pay Level Policy The degree to which an organization's pay level compares to its competitors' pay levels. (Ch. 12)

Pay Ranges The range of wages allowed by a specific wage classification and the amount of overlap between the ranges. (Ch. 12)

Personnel Audit A procedure used to collect data to help the organization determine how well its human resource functions are performing. (Ch. 4)

Personnel Research The evaluation of the human resource department's effectiveness in serving the organization's personnel needs. (Ch. 4)

Planning Horizon The length of time over which the objectives and the plan for accomplishing them will occur. (Ch. 6)

Plant Closings A layoff strategy that affects all employees of the unit; the temporary or permanent shutdown of independent work units as part of an organization's restructuring. (Ch. 19)

Portable Pension Plan A pension plan in which employees can move their pension benefits from one employer to another without losing benefits. (Ch. 14)

Position-Specific Methods A job analysis method that yields information specific to a job/position within a particular organization. (Ch. 7)

Proactive Approach An approach to strategy formulation or decision making wherein strategies are formed in anticipation of problems. (Ch. 1)

Problem-Solving Action/behavior that emphasizes what the organization should do and why in resolving a problem. (Ch. 1)

Prospectors A strategy wherein the organization looks for new market opportunities and aggressively seeks to develop both new products and new markets. (Ch. 2)

Protection and Compensation Plans Organizational policies relating to the handling of employees during termination situations. (Ch. 19)

Quality Circles Groups of employees who meet to recommend ways to improve production and quality. (Ch. 4)

Ratification Process The process wherein a tentative union agreement is submitted by a union bargaining team to a larger representative council for review before being sent to the rank and file to be voted on. (Ch. 18)

Reactive Approach An approach to strategy formulation or decision making wherein an organization reacts to threats "after the fact." (Ch. 1)

Reactors Organizations who see major changes in their environment but have difficulty changing quickly enough to meet these changes. (Ch. 2)

Realized Strategy The "actual" strategy the organization follows. (Ch. 1)

Recession Periods of general economic slowdowns. (Ch. 19)

Reduced Shifts A layoff strategy that entails cutting back the total number of hours that the organization operates. (Ch. 19)

Reduced Work Week A common layoff strategy that allows organizations to reduce their payroll costs while still holding on to and providing work for employees. (Ch. 19)

Restructuring Any major change in the way an organization operates. (Ch. 19)

Retrenchment Strategy A corporate-level strategy that involves actions taken to reverse a negative situation or overcome a crisis or problem. (Ch. 3)

Robotics The use of computer assisted machines to weld, cut, etc. (Ch. 6)

Sabbatical A leave of absence that is longer in duration than other types of leaves (e.g., jury duty, maternity, etc.). (Ch. 14)

Scanning The gathering of information about environmental issues on a regular basis and interpreting them in light of the organization's business. (Ch. 1)

Severance Pay A voluntary security benefit program wherein pay is given to an employee at termination. Severance pay refers to payment to terminated workers based on their years of service to the organization and their salary. (Chs. 14 and 19)

Skill Adequate performance on tasks requiring the use of tools, equipment, and machinery. (Ch. 7)

Skill-Based Pay A form of incentive-based pay wherein employees are paid for the skills they possess, not just the skills performed. (Ch. 12)

Skills Bank A complete, current listing of all occupational categories in the organization with explanatory job descriptions that specify the duties. (Ch. 6)

Stakeholders Those individuals who have a vested interest or claim on the operations or output of the organization. (Ch. 2)

Standard Hour Plan A type of individual incentive plan that ties pay to a standard amount of time that it takes to perform a service or complete a task. (Ch. 12)

Standardized Job Analysis Methods The extent to which a method yields data/information in the form of norms so that jobs analyzed in different settings can be compared. (Ch. 7)

Stay Bonuses A variety of cash bonuses and other inducements offered by firms to keep valued workers on the payroll during corporate reorganizations or closedowns. (Ch. 12)

Straight Piecework Plan A type of individual incentive plan that pays a constant amount for each unit that is produced. (Ch. 12)

Strategic Control Ensuring that what actually happens is what the company wants to happen. (Ch. 1)

Strategic Planning The systematic determination of strategic goals and the strategies to obtain them. (Ch. 1)

Strategic Planning Retreats Off-site meetings of key executives where plans are made and strategies are formulated. (Ch. 2)

Strategy The formulation of organizational missions, goals, and objectives, as well as action plans for achievement, that explicitly recognize the competition and the impact of outside environmental forces. (Ch. 1)

Stuck in the Middle A so-called type of strategy that is essentially a *lack* of strategy. (Ch. 19)

Superconductivity Transmitting electricity at almost zero resistance. (Ch. 2)

Supplemental Unemployment A voluntary security benefit program wherein payments are made by the employer to an employee who is temporarily laid off. (Ch. 14)

Supplemental Unemployment Benefits (SUBs) A layoff method wherein the laid-off employee is provided with a fixed percentage of his or her wages through a combination of state and federal unemployment benefits and additional organization payments for periods up to one year. (Ch. 19)

Sustainable Competitive Advantage A differential advantage a particular organization can achieve over its competition. (Ch. 1 and 3)

System A set of activities that takes inputs, transforms them into useful items, and then outputs the new items to where they can be used. (Ch. 4)

Tactical Misrepresentation A tactic used in bargaining that involves misrepresenting your side to the other side. (Ch. 18)

Task Inventory—CODAP A structured job analysis questionnaire consisting of a list of tasks relevant to a particular occupational area. (Ch. 7)

Telecommuting Employees working from their home or another location of their choice and communicating through the use of computers, express mail, facsimiles, and improved telephone networks. (Ch. 8)

Tenure The length of time that an employee has worked in an organization and the rights that the person accrues as a result. (Ch. 19)

Threshold Traits Analysis A job analysis method designed to provide normative data on the worker attributes required for successful job performance across all types of jobs. (Ch. 7)

Timing A tactic used in bargaining wherein more important demands are often presented later in the negotiation process. (Ch. 18)

Training The instruction provided to an employee for his or her current job that will benefit the organization rather quickly. (Ch. 10)

Turnaround A strategy designed to reverse a negative trend, such as falling profits or increasing costs. (Ch. 3)

Unfunded Plan A method of funding pension benefits which pays pensions out of current income generated by the organization. (Ch. 14)

Uninsured Pension Plan A pension plan that is administered by the employer and is considered to be less stable and sound than insured pensions. (Ch. 14)

Union Substitution A type of strategy used by management to resist unionization that entails progressive and proactive human resource policies designed to reduce the desire for a union. (Ch. 17)

Union Suppression A type of strategy used by management to resist unionization that includes a variety of active legal or perhaps illegal opposition tactics during the organizing campaign. (Ch. 17)

Utility Theory Selecting the decision alternative that provides the maximum payment. Utility theory provides a framework for making decisions that requires decision makers to state goals clearly, specify outcomes of the decision options, and attach differing values or utilities to each outcome. (Ch. 14)

Vertical Integration A growth strategy wherein the organization acquires its suppliers (backward integration) or acquires its distributors (forward integration). (Ch. 3)

Wage Compression New hires are brought in at about the same or higher salaries than the current employees. (Ch. 12)

Window Dressing A tactic used in bargaining that involves listing extraneous, unimportant demands that can easily be traded away. (Ch. 18)

Worker Loan-Out Program A non-layoff restructuring strategy that involves the lending of workers by one organization to another for a specified period, such as firms lending their employees to government or charitable organizations. (Ch. 19)

Worker-Oriented Job Analysis Methods A job analysis method that yields information regarding workers' activities on the job. These methods identify actual worker behaviors necessary to perform the job. (Ch. 7)

Worker Reassignments A non-layoff restructuring strategy that involves moving workers out of one job and into another that may be more important to the organization. (Ch. 19)

EXHIBIT SOURCES AND CREDITS

• • • • • • • •

Chapter 1 **1.12:** Reprinted from October 15, 1990 issue of *Business Week* by special permission, copyright © 90 by McGraw-Hill, Inc.

Chapter 2 **2.3, 2.4, 2.5:** *Economic Indicators.* Washington, D.C.: United States Government Printing Office, October 1991. **2.6:** Reprinted by permission of *The Wall Street Journal,* © 1992 Dow Jones & Company, Inc. All Rights Reserved Worldwide; *Economic Indicators.* Washington, D.C.: United States Government Printing Office, October 1991. **2.7, 2.8, 2.9, 2.10:** United States Department of Labor, Bureau of Labor Statistics. **2.14:** Reprinted with permission © *American Demographics,* December 1990. **2.15:** Adapted from Michael E. Porter, "How Competitive Forces Shape Strategy," *Harvard Business Review* Vol. 57, No. 2 (March–April, 1979), p. 141. **2.16, 2.17:** Reprinted by permission of *The Wall Street Journal,* © 1991 Dow Jones & Company, Inc. All Rights Reserved Worldwide.

Chapter 3 **3.4:** Adapted from A. S. Tsui, "A Multiple-Constituency Model of Effectiveness: An Empirical Examination at the Human Resource Subunit Level," *Administrative Science Quarterly* 35 (1990), pp. 458–483. **3.5, 3.6:** Reprinted by permission from pp. 205 and 254 of *Organization Theory,* third edition, by B. J. Hodge and William P. Anthony; copyright © 1988 by Allyn & Bacon, Inc. All Rights Reserved. **3.8:** Reprinted by permission from Cynthia A. Lengneck-Hall and Mark L. Lengneck-Hall, "Strategic Human Resources Management: A Review of the Literature and a Proposed Typology," *Academy of Management Review,* Vol. 13, No. 3 (July 1988), p. 467. **3.11:** Reprinted by permission of The Wall Street Journal, © 1989 Dow Jones & Company, Inc. All Rights Reserved Worldwide.

Chapter 4 **4.9:** Reprinted through the courtesy of Deluxe Corporation. **4.10:** Reprinted by permission from *Personnel/Human Resource Management,* fifth edition, by Robert L. Mathis and John H. Jackson; copyright © 1988 by West Publishing Company. All Rights Reserved.

Chapter 5 **5.7:** Adapted from L. Z. Lorber, "Legal Report: The Civil Rights Act of 1991," *Society for Human Resource Management,* Spring, 1992; M. Kobata, "The Civil Rights Act of 1991," *Personnel Journal,* March 1992, p. 48. **5.8:** *Fortune,* September 23, 1991, p. 9.

Chapter 6 **6.1:** Reprinted by permission of *The Wall Street Journal,* © 1991 Dow Jones & Company, Inc. All Rights Reserved Worldwide.

Chapter 7 **7.2:** From "Job Analysis: National Survey Findings," by Jean L. Jones Jr. and Thomas A. Decoths, copyright May 1974. Reprinted with the permission of *Personnel Journal,* Costa Mesa, California; all rights reserved. **7.3:** Adapted from J.

McCormick, "Job and Task Analysis," in *Handbook of Industrial and Organizational Psychology* (Chicago: Rand McNally College Publishing Company, 1976), pp. 652–653. **7.7:** Adapted from P. Wright and K. Wexley, "How to Choose the Kind of Job Analysis You Really Need," in *Personnel* (1985), pp. 51–55. **7.9:** Reprinted by permission from Ernest J. McCormick, *Job Analysis: Methods and Applications,* copyright © 1979 AMACOM. All Rights Reserved. **7.10:** Adapted from W. W. Tornow and P. R. Pinto, "The Development of a Managerial Job Taxonomy: A System for Describing, Classifying and Evaluating Executive Positions," in *Journal of Applied Psychology* (1976), pp. 61, 410–418. **7.11, 7.12:** United States Department of Labor, *Dictionary of Occupational Titles,* fourth edition (Washington, D.C.: United States Government Printing Office, 1977), pp. xviii, 98. **7.13:** From F. M. Lopez, G. A. Kesselman, and F. E. Lopez, "An Empirical Test of a Trait-Oriented Job Analysis Technique," in *Personnel Psychology* (1981), pp. 479–502.

Chapter 8 **8.2:** Adapted from J. R. Hackman and G. R. Oldham, "Motivation Through the Design of Work: Test of a Theory," *Organizational Behavior and Human Performance,* 16 (1976), pp. 250–279. **8.3:** Adapted from J. R. Hackman, G. R. Oldham, R. Janson, and K. A. Purdy, "A New Strategy for Job Enrichment," *California Management Review* (Summer 1975), pp. 57–71. **8.4:** Reprinted by permission of *The Wall Street Journal,* © 1990 Dow Jones and Company, Inc. All Rights Reserved Worldwide. **8.5:** Adapted from R. W. Griffin, *Task Design: An Integrative Approach* (Glenview, IL: Scott, Foresman, 1982) p. 208.

Chapter 9 **9.2:** Adapted from B. Leonard, "Right Questions on Applications Avoid Trouble," *HRNews,* February 1990, pp. B9, B15. **9.5:** Adapted from E. Gottschalk, "New Test Quantifies the Way We Work," *The Wall Street Journal,* February 7, 1990, p. B1. **9.6:** Adapted from G. Dreher and P. Sackett, *Perspectives on Employee Staffing and Selection: Readings and Commentary.* Homewood, IL: Irwin, 1983.

Chapter 10 **10.6:** Adapted from R. Federico, "Six Ways to Solve the Orientation Blues," *HRMagazine,* May 1991, pp. 69–70. **10.7:** Reprinted by permission from Quaker Sales Careers: Leadership Through Innovation; copyright © Quaker Oats Company. All Rights Reserved. **10.9:** Reprinted by permission from "Banker Development Program for Management Associates" in Barnett: Extra Effort Does Make the Difference; copyright 1988 © Barnett Banks, Inc. All Rights Reserved. **10.15:** Adapted from C. Lee, "Where Training Dollars Go," *Training,* p. 60.

Chapter 11 **11.1:** Reprinted by permission of *The Wall Street Journal,* © 1992 Dow Jones & Company, Inc. All Rights Reserved Worldwide; and reprinted from October 8, 1991 issue of *Business Week* by special permission, copyright © 91 by McGraw-Hill,

Inc. **11.2:** From W. Edwards Deming, *Out of Crisis.* Cambridge, MA: Cambridge University Press, 1986. **11.4:** Adapted from P. Nulty," America's Toughest Bosses," *Fortune,* February 27, 1989, pp. 40–54. **11.5:** Adapted from R. E. Kelly, "In Praise of Followers," *Harvard Business Review,* November/December 1989, pp. 143–147. **11.6:** Adapted from J. P. Kotter, "How Leaders Grow Leaders," *Across the Board,* March 1988, Vol. 25, p. 40. **11.7:** Adapted from J. M. Ivancevich, D. M. Schweiger, and F. R. Power, "Strategies for Managing Human Resources During Mergers and Acquisitions," *Human Resource Planning,* 1987, Vol. 10 (1), p. 24. **11.8:** Adapted from J. B. Treece and A. Borrus, "How Ford and Mazda Shared the Driver's Seat," *Business Week,* March 26, 1990, pp. 94–95. **11.9:** Reprinted by permission of *The Wall Street Journal,* © 1989 Dow Jones & Company, Inc. All Rights Reserved Worldwide. **11.10:** United States Department of Labor; Todd May, "Inflation Is Not Dead Yet," *Fortune,* September 9, 1991, p. 28, © 1991 The Time Inc. Magazine Company. All Rights Reserved. **11.11:** From D. Abramis, "Fun at Work," *Personnel Administrator,* November 1989, p. 63. **11.12:** Adapted from K. Dawson and S. Dawson, "How to Motivate Your Employees," *HRMagazine,* April 1990, pp. 78–80. **11.13:** From Mercury Sable 1990 *Owner's Manual.* **11.14:** Adapted from M. Barton, "The End-of-the-Story Manager," *Personnel Administrator,* February 1989, pp. 78–80. **11.15:** From J. Gandz, "The Employee Empowerment Era," *Business Quarterly,* Autumn 1990, pp. 74–79. **11.16:** Courtesy of Avis, Inc. **11.18:** Adapted from F. Schneyer, "Team Management Takes Hold in Tallahassee," *Tallahassee Democrat,* August 7, 1991, pp. B1 + .

Chapter 12 **12.3:** George Milkovich and Jerry Newman. Compensation, second edition. Homewood, IL: BPI/Irwin, 1987, p. 16. **12.4:** Adapted from J. Lublin, "Grappling With the Expatriate Issue," *The Wall Street Journal,* December 11, 1989, p. B1. **12.6:** Adapted from T. J. Bergmann, H. Gunderson, W. Weil, and B. R. Baliga, "Rewards Tied to Long-term Success," *HRMagazine,* May 1990, p. 68. **12.7:** Graef Crystal, "How Much CEOs Really Make," *Fortune,* June 17, 1991, p. 72, © 1991 The Time Inc. Magazine Company. All Rights Reserved. **12.8:** Reprinted from May 7, 1990 issue of *Business Week* by special permission, copyright © 90 by McGraw-Hill, Inc. **12.9:** Joshua Mendes and Cindy Mikami, "Where People Live," *Fortune,* March 11, 1991, p. 46, © 1991 The Time Inc. Magazine Company. All Rights Reserved. **12.10:** Adapted from C. Pasternak, "HRM Update," *HRMagazine,* June 1991, p. 22. **12.11:** Adapted from E. Ost, "Gain Sharing's Potential," *Personnel Administrator,* July 1989, p. 93. **12.12:** © 1992 Toys "R" Us, Inc. **12.13:** Reprinted by permission from page 179 of "Managing Behavior Through Learning and Reinforcement" by H. P. Sims, Jr. in Organizational Behavior, second edition, by D. Hellriegel and J. W. Slocum, Jr.; copyright © 1979 by West Publishing Company. All Rights Reserved.

Chapter 13 **13.1:** Adapted from D. A. Waldman and R. S. Kenett, "Improve Performance by Appraisal," *HRMagazine,* July 1990, p. 67. **13.2:** Adapted from N. F. Angel, "Evaluating Employees by Computer," *Personnel Administrator,* November 1989, pp. 67–72. **13.10, 13.11:** Adapted from C. Lee, "Smoothing Our Appraisal Systems," *HRMagazine,* March 1990, pp. 72–76.

Chapter 14 **14.1** Adapted from J. Solomon, "The Future of Employee Benefits," *The Wall Street Journal,* September 7, 1988, p. 29. **14.2:** Adapted from N. Sutton-Bell, "Employee Benefits," September 10, 1990, p. 4. **14.3:** Reprinted by permission from p. 389 of *Personnel/Human Resource Management* by Robert L. Mathis and John H. Jackson; copyright © 1988 by West Publishing

Company. All Rights Reserved. **14.4:** Reprinted from February 3, 1992 issue of *Business Week* by special permission, copyright © 92 by McGraw-Hill, Inc. **14.6, 14.8, 14.10:** Reprinted by permission of *The Wall Street Journal,* © 1991, 1988 Dow Jones & Company, Inc. All Rights Reserved Worldwide. **14.11:** Adapted from C. Pasternak, "HRM Update," *HRMagazine,* December 1990, p. 21.

Chapter 15 **15.2:** J. P. Leigh, "Estimates of the Probability of Job-related Death in 347 Occupations," *Journal of Occupational Medicine,* June 1987, pp. 512–515. **15.3:** S. Cohen, "Pain with the Paycheck," *Tallahassee Democrat,* November 12, 1989, p. D1 and "LA Takes on Safety and Health Challenge," *ILO Information,* October 1989, p. 2. **15.4, 15.5:** Adapted from R. Karasek and T. Theorell, *Healthy Work.* New York: Basic Books, 1991. **15.6:** Adapted from R. Sandroff, "Is Your Job Driving You Crazy?", *Psychology Today,* July/August 1989, pp. 41–45. **15.7:** Reprinted by permission of *The Wall Street Journal,* © 1989 Dow Jones & Company, Inc. All Rights Reserved Worldwide. **15.8:** Adapted from R. A. Reber, J. A. Walling, and D. L. Dubon, "Safety Programs that Work," *Personnel Administrator,* September 1989, pp. 66–69.

Chapter 16 **16.2:** Apple Computer and Hewlett Packard. **16.3:** Adapted from R. Hilgert, "Employers Protected by At-Will Statements," *HRMagazine,* March 1991, pp. 57–60. **16.4:** Section 110.227, Florida Statutes 1989. **16.5:** Adapted from Robert Mathis and John Jackson, *Personnel/Human Resource Management,* fifth edition. New York: West Publishing Company, 1988, pp. 445–452. **16.6:** Adapted from the article "New Plant Closing Law Aids Workers in Transition," by Paul Staudohar, copyright January 1989. Reprinted with the permission of *Personnel Journal,* Costa Mesa, California; all rights reserved. **16.8:** Adapted from "HR Professionals Agree: Workplace Ethics Require People to be Judged Solely on Job Performance," *1991 SHRM/CCH Survey,* June 1991, p. 1. **16.9:** Adapted from S. J. Smits and L. Pace, "Workplace Substance Abuse: Establish Policies," *Personnel Journal,* May 1989, p. 88.

Chapter 17 **17.1:** Reprinted by permission of *The Wall Street Journal,* © 1989 Dow Jones & Company, Inc. All Rights Reserved Worldwide. **17.4:** Bureau of Labor Statistics, *Director of National Unions and Employee Associations,* 1980. **17.6:** National Labor Relations Board. **17.9:** Reprinted by permission of *The Wall Street Journal,* © 1989 Dow Jones & Company, Inc. All Rights Reserved Worldwide.

Chapter 18 **18.1:** Reprinted by permission of *The Wall Street Journal,* © 1989 Dow Jones & Company, Inc. All Rights Reserved Worldwide. **18.5:** Adapted from L. Reynolds, "Labor's Leaders—Changing to Meet the Times," *Management Review,* February 1988, pp. 57–62; S. M. Jacoby and D. J. B. Mitchell, "Measurement of Compensation: Union and Nonunion," *Industrial Relations* 27(2), Spring 1988, pp. 215–231; and S. G. Allen, "Productivity Levels & Productivity Change Under Unions," *Industrial Relations* 27(1), Winter 1988, pp. 94–113.

Chapter 19 **19.1:** "Corporate Restructuring," *1989 ASPA/CCH Survey,* June 27, 1989, p. 2. **19.3:** Michael Porter, *Competitive Strategy.* New York: The Free Press, 1980, pp. 40–41. **19.4:** Adapted from G. Fuchsberg, "Despite Layoffs, Firms Find Some Jobs Hard to Fill," *The Wall Street Journal,* January 22, 1991, p. B1. **19.5:** Adapted from "Vanishing Jobs," *Fortune,* September 9, 1991, p. 11. **19.6:** Reprinted from January 15, 1990 issue of *Business Week* by special permission, copyright © 90 by McGraw-

Hill, Inc.   **19.7:** Reprinted from February 26, 1990 issue of *Business Week* by special permission, copyright © 90 by McGraw-Hill, Inc.   **19.8:** From Frank E. Kuzmits and Lyle Sussman, "Early Retirement or Forced Resignation: Policy Issues for Downsizing Human Resources," in SAM *Advanced Management Journal,* Winter 1988, p. 32.

Cases   **C-1–C-14:** McDonald's 1990 Annual Report.   **C-15:** United States Department of Commerce, Population Series P-25.   **C-16:** Reprinted from October 21, 1991 issue of *Business Week* by special permission, copyright © 91 by McGraw-Hill, Inc.   **C-17, C-18:** McDonald's 1990 Annual Report.   **C-19:** Fortune Business Reports.   **C-20:** McDonald's 1990 Annual Report.

NAME INDEX

•••••••

SUBJECT INDEX

•••••••••